MILLER'S
Antiques
PRICE GUIDE

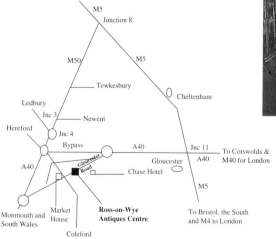

MILLER'S
Antiques
PRICE GUIDE

Consultant
Judith Miller

General Editor
Elizabeth Norfolk

1999
Volume XX

Created and designed by
Miller's
The Cellars, High Street,
Tenterden, Kent, TN30 6BN
Tel: 01580 766411

Consultant: Judith Miller

General Editor: Elizabeth Norfolk
Editorial and Production Co-ordinator: Sue Boyd
Editorial Assistants: Jo Wood, Christine Cooper
Production Assistants: Gillian Charles, Nancy Charles, Caroline Bugeja
Advertising Executive: Elizabeth Smith
Advertising Assistants: Melinda Williams, Jill Jackson
Design: Kari Reeves, Shirley Reeves
Advert Design: Simon Cook
Index compiled by Hilary Bird
Additional photography: Ian Booth, Roy Farthing, David Merewether,
Dennis O'Reilly, Robin Saker

First published in Great Britain in 1998
by Miller's, a division of Mitchell Beazley,
imprints of Octopus Publishing Group Ltd,
2–4 Heron Quays, London, E14 4JP

Reprinted in 1999

A CIP catalogue record for this book is
available from the British Library

ISBN 1 84000 085 6

Film output by Perfect Image, Hurst Green, E. Sussex
Illustrations and bromide output by CK Litho, Whitstable, Kent
Colour origination by Pica, Singapore
Printed and bound in Italy by
Rotolito Lombarda S.p.A.

Front cover illustrations:
top left: *A black slate mantel clock, c1880, 18in (46cm) high.* **£100–200** *CSK*
top right: *A Nantgarw porcelain plate, c1820.* **£600–700** *P*
bottom: *A George II burr and figured walnut kneehole desk, 32in (81cm) wide.* **£8,000–9,000** *C*

F. G. BRUSCHWEILER (Antiques) LTD.

41-67 LOWER LAMBRICKS, RAYLEIGH

ESSEX SS6 7EN

(Only 35 minutes from London, 1 hour from Gatwick and Heathrow airports)

35,000 square feet of antiques
over 10,000 items in stock at all times
always over 20 bars in stock

large oak counter bār above 12′ long

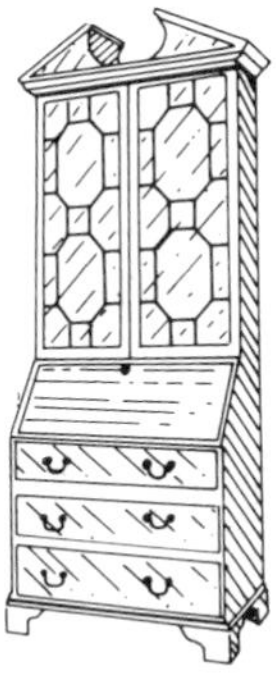

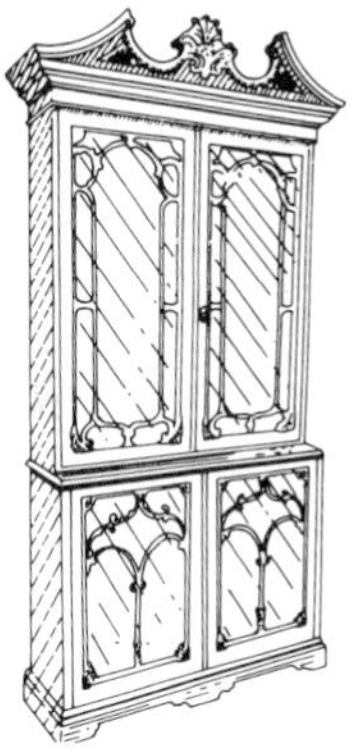

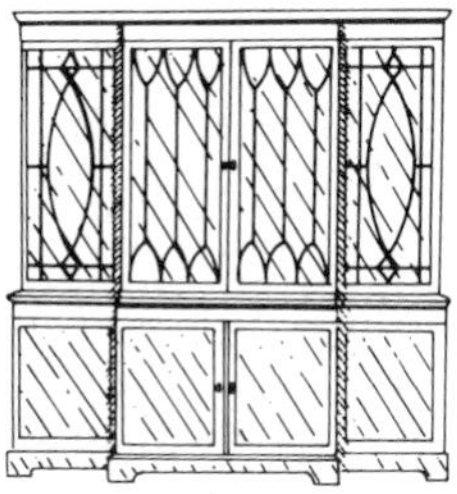

oak corner bar above 6′ x 6′ x 7′6″ high

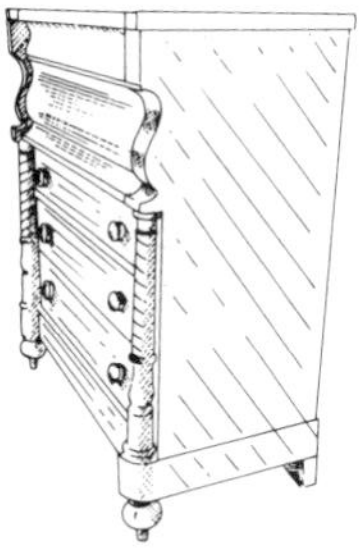

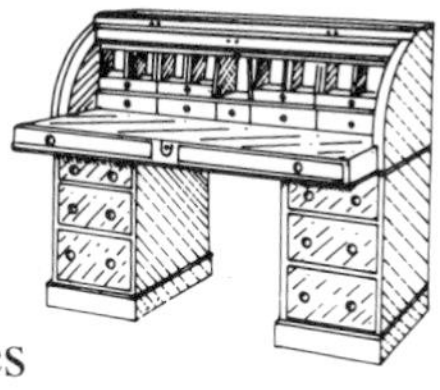

We have a varied stock of quality antiques
to suit all markets, USA, Japan, Australia,
Italy, Spain, Portugal, Belgium, etc.

Send for our brochure

ESTABLISHED
SINCE
1963

Tel (01268) 773 761
(01268) 773 932
Fax (01268) 773 318

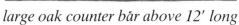

MEMBER OF
LAPADA

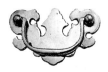

Phillipe Coste *...the man to see in Brittany, France*

Extensive stocks of French furniture

Competitive prices, containers arranged.

All your needs catered for.

Export Bedroom/Dining Suites, Henri II, Breton, Louis-Phillipe.

Rustic Form Tables, Amoires, etc., in Chestnut, Cherry, Oak.

Antiques Commodes, Salon Sets, Conooles, etc.

Decorative Mirrors, Clocks, Statues, etc.

Antiquites du Roy (TRADE ONLY)

Z.A. de Bellevue, 35235 Thorigné Fouillard

(2 miles to Rennes, 40 miles St. Malo)

Tel 00 33 2 99 04 59 81. Fax 00 33 2 99 04 59 47

Mobile 00 33 6 07 37 01 00

Fior-fhiodh na Alba

TRADITIONAL AND ANTIQUE FURNITURE

20,000 square feet of quality European, Georgian, Edwardian and Victorian furniture and antiques. We also have a fine selection of pre-war furniture.

You will be spoilt for choice with our wide range of quality pre-war British and North European shipping furniture. Particularly suitable for the Japanese, American and Australian markets. Here in Bonny Scotland there are no big City overheads so no big City prices. You can afford to let us have your requirements and we will source and supply to your specifications.

Try mixing business with pleasure. Yes it is possible, here is how:

- Pick up the telephone and make an appointment to visit us. Tours by appointment only, you will have **our undivided attention.**
- We will send you a **welcome pack**, giving lists of top quality local hotels, restaurants and events. Also enclosed, you will find a range of **special offers** and discounts on room rates, negotiated by us on your behalf.
- Before you set off we will arrange for our **courtesy car** to meet you upon your arrival in this country. This service is available from Glasgow or Edinburgh airports and train stations.
- Containers are packed free of charge, so all you have to do is make your purchases and then relax. Better still go out and avail yourself of the special offers in local shops and restaurants.

Call us now on +44 (0)1383 739101 or +44 (0)411 242241

CONTENTS

MILLER'S 1999

KEY TO ILLUSTRATIONS

Each illustration and descriptive caption is accompanied by a letter code. By referring to the following list of Auctioneers (denoted by *) and Dealers (•) the source of any item may be immediately determined. Inclusion in this edition in no way constitutes or implies a contract or binding offer on the part of any of our contributors to supply or sell the goods illustrated, or similar articles, at the prices stated. Advertisers in this year's directory are denoted by †.

If you require a valuation for an item, it is advisable to check whether the dealer or specialist will carry out this service and if there is a charge. Please mention Miller's when making an enquiry. Having found a specialist who will carry out your valuation it is best to send a photograph and description of the item to the specialist together with a stamped addressed envelope for the reply. A valuation by telephone is not possible. Most dealers are only too happy to help you with your enquiry; however, they are very busy people and consideration of the above points would be appreciated.

A&A • Antiques & Art, 116 State Street, Portsmouth, NH 03802 USA Tel: 603 431 3931
AAC • Arundel Antiques Centre, 51 High Street, Arundel, Sussex BN18 9AJ Tel: 01903 882749
AAN • Appledore Antiques Tel: 01233 758272
AAV * † Academy Auctioneers & Valuers, Northcote House, Northcote Avenue, Ealing, London W5 3UR Tel: 0181 579 7466
ADE • † Art Deco Etc, 73 Upper Gloucester Road, Brighton, Sussex BN1 3LQ Tel: 01273 329268
AEF • A & E Foster, Little Heysham, Naphill, Bucks HP14 4SU Tel: 01494 562024
AG * Anderson & Garland (Auctioneers), Marlborough House, Marlborough Crescent, Newcastle-upon-Tyne, Tyne & Wear NE1 4EE Tel: 0191 232 6278
AH * † Andrew Hartley, Victoria Hall Salerooms, Little Lane, Ilkley, Yorkshire LS29 8EA Tel: 01943 816363
AHO • Amanda House, The Barns, Twigworth Court, Twigworth, Glos GL2 9PG Tel: 01452 731296
AIL • Antique Irish Linen, Dublin, S. Ireland Tel: 00 353 1 451 2775
AL • † Ann Lingard, Ropewalk Antiques, Ropewalk, Rye, Sussex TN31 7NA Tel: 01797 223486
ALB • Albany Antiques, 8-10 London Road, Hindhead, Surrey GU26 6AF Tel: 01428 605528
ALD * Aldridges, 130-132 Walcot Street, Bath, Somerset BA1 5BG Tel: 01225 462830
ALS • † Allan Smith Clocks, Amity Cottage, 162 Beechcroft Road, Upper Stratton, Swindon, Wiltshire SN2 6QE Tel: 01793 822977
AMH • Amherst Antiques, 23 London Road, Riverhead, Sevenoaks, Kent TN13 2BU Tel: 01732 455047
ANG • † Ancient & Gothic, PO Box 356, Christchurch, Dorset BH23 1XQ Tel: 01202 478592
ANO • † Art Nouveau Originals, Stamford Antiques Centre, Exchange Hall, Broad Street, Stamford, Lincolnshire PE9 1PX Tel: 01780 762605
ANT • † Anthemion, Bridge Street, Cartmel, Grange-over-Sands, Cumbria LA11 7SH Tel: 015395 36295
ANV • † Anvil Antiques, Cartmel, Grange-over-Sands, Cumbria LA11 6QA Tel: 015395 36362
AP * † Andrew Pickford, Hertford Saleroom, 42 St Andrew Street, Hertford, Hertfordshire SG14 1JA Tel: 01992 583508
ARE • Arenski, 185 Westbourne Grove, London W11 2SB Tel: 0171 727 8599
ART • † Artemis Decorative Arts Ltd, 36 Kensington Church Street, London W8 4BX Tel: 0171 376 0377/0171 937 9900
ASA • † A. S. Antiques, 26 Broad Street, Pendleton, Salford, Greater Manchester M6 5BY Tel: 0161 737 5938
ASB • † Andrew Spencer Bottomley, The Coach House, Thongs Bridge, Holmfirth, Yorkshire HD7 2TT Tel: 01484 685234
ASe • Alan Sedgwick E-mail: Alan.Sedgwick@BTInternet.com Tel: 01452 521337
ASG • Asahi Gallery, 44A Kensington Church Street, London W8 4DB
ASM • Art Smith, Antiques at Wells Union, Route 1, 1755 Post Road, Wells, ME 04090 USA Tel: 207 646 6996
ATQ • Antiquarius Antiques, 131/141 King's Road, Chelsea, London SW3 5ST Tel: 0171 351 5353
AW • † Alan Walker, Halfway Manor, Halfway, Nr Newbury, Berkshire RG20 8NR Tel: 01488 657670
AWH • A. W. Hone & Son, Oriental Carpets, 1486 Stratford Road (Robin Hood Island), Hall Green, Birmingham, West Midlands B28 9ET Tel: 0121 744 1001
AWT • Antique Associates at West Townsend, 473 Main Street, PO Box 129W, West Townsend, MA 01474 USA Tel: 508-597-8084
B * Boardman Fine Art Auctioneers, Station Road Corner, Haverhill, Suffolk CB9 0EY Tel: 01440 730414
B&B * Butterfield & Butterfield, 220 San Bruno Avenue, San Francisco, CA 94103 USA Tel: 415 861 7500
BAL • A. H. Baldwin & Sons Ltd, Numismatists, 11 Adelphi Terrace, London WC2N 6BJ Tel: 0171 930 6879
BaN • Barbara Ann Newman, London House Antiques, 4 Market Square, Westerham, Kent TN16 1AW Tel: 01959 564479 Mobile 0850 016729
BAS • Brighton Architectural Salvage, 33 Gloucester Road, Brighton, Sussex BN1 4AQ Tel: 01273 681656
BBA * Bloomsbury Book Auctions, 3/4 Hardwick Street, off Rosebery Avenue, London EC1R 4RY Tel: 0171 833 2636
BBR * BBR, Elsecar Heritage Centre, Wath Road, Elsecar, Barnsley, Yorkshire S74 8HJ Tel: 01226 745156
BCO • British Collectables, 1st Floor, 9 Georgian Village, Camden Passage, Islington, London N1 8EG Tel: 0171 359 4560
Bea(E)* Bearnes, St Edmund's Court, Okehampton St, Exeter, Devon EX4 1DU Tel: 01392 422800
BED • Johann Bedingfeld, 1 West Street, Dorking, Surrey RH4 1BL Tel: 01306 880022
BEE • † Jonathan Beech, Westport, Co. Mayo, S. Ireland Tel: 00 353 98 28688
BEL • Bell Antiques, 68A Harold Street, Grimsby, Humberside DN35 0HH Tel: 01472 695110
Ber • Berry Antiques, Berry House, 11-13 Stone Street, Cranbrook, Kent TN17 3HF Tel: 01580 712345
BERA • † Berry Antiques, 3 High Street, Moreton-in-Marsh, Glos GL56 0AH Tel: 01608 652929
BEX • Daniel Bexfield, Bond Street Antiques Centre, 124 New Bond Street, London W1Y 9AE Tel: 0171 491 1720
BHa • † Judy & Brian Harden Antiques, Glos Tel: 01451 810684
BIG * Bigwood Auctioneers Ltd, The Old School, Tiddington, Stratford-upon-Avon, Warwickshire CV37 7AW Tel: 01789 269415
BKK • † Bona Art Deco Store, The Hart Shopping Centre, Fleet, Hampshire GU13 8AZ Tel: 01252 616666
BKS * Brooks Auctioneers Ltd, 81 Westside, London SW4 9AY Tel: 0171 228 8000
BLH * † Black Horse Agencies Ambrose, 149 High Road, Loughton, Essex IG10 4LZ Tel: 0181 502 3951
Bon * † Bonhams, Montpelier Street, Knightsbridge, London SW7 1HH Tel: 0171 393 3994
Bon(C)* Bonhams, 65-69 Lots Road, Chelsea, London SW10 0RN Tel: 0171 393 3900
Bon(M)/ Bon(N)* Bonhams, 57 Mansfield Road, Nottingham, Notts NG1 3PL Tel: 0115 947 4414
BOR • Bed of Roses, 12 Prestbury Road, Cheltenham, Glos GL52 2PW Tel: 01242 231918
BOS * Bosley's, 42 West Street, Marlow, Bucks SL7 2NB Tel: 01628 488188
BR * † Bracketts, Auction Hall, Pantiles, Tunbridge Wells, Kent TN1 1UU Tel: 01892 544500
Bri * † Bristol Auction Rooms, St John's Place, Apsley Road, Clifton, Bristol, Glos BS8 2ST Tel: 0117 973 7201
BRT • Britannia, Grays Antique Market, Stand 101, 58 Davies Street, London W1Y 1AR Tel: 0171 629 6772
BRU • Brunel Antiques, Bartlett Street Antiques Centre, Bath, Somerset BA1 2QZ Tel: 01225 310457/446322
BrW • Brian Watson Antique Glass, The Grange, Norwich Road, Wroxham, Norwich, Norfolk NR12 8RX Tel: 01603 784177
BSA • Bartlett Street Antiques, 5/10 Bartlett St, Bath, Somerset BA1 2QZ Tel: 01225 446322/310457
BTC • Beatcity, PO Box 229, Chatham, Kent ME5 0PW Tel: 01634 305383/0370 650890
BUSH • † Bushwood Antiques, Stags End Equestrian Centre, Gaddesden Lane, Hemel Hempstead, Hertfordshire HP2 6HN Tel: 01582 794700

BWA • Bow-Well Antiques, 103 West Bow, Edinburgh, Scotland EH1 2JP Tel: 0131 225 3335
BWC • British Watch & Clock Collectors Association, 5 Cathedral Lane, Truro, Cornwall TR1 2QS Tel: 01872 241953
BWe * † Biddle & Webb Ltd, Ladywood Middleway, Birmingham, West Midlands B16 0PP Tel: 0121 455 8042
ByI • † Bygones of Ireland, Westport Antiques Centre, Lodge Road, Westport, County Mayo, S. Ireland Tel: 00 353 98 26132
C * Christie, Manson & Wood Ltd, 8 King Street, St James's, London SW1Y 6QT Tel: 0171 839 9060
CaC * † Cato Crane & Co, Liverpool Auction Rooms, 6 Stanhope St, Liverpool, Merseyside L8 5RF Tel: 0151 709 5559
CAG * † The Canterbury Auction Galleries, 40 Station Road West, Canterbury, Kent CT2 8AN Tel: 01227 763337
CaH • The Camera House, Oakworth Hall, Colne Road, Oakworth, Keighley, Yorkshire BD22 7HZ Tel: 01535 642333
CAT • Lennox Cato, 1 The Square, Edenbridge, Kent TN8 5BD Tel: 01732 865988/Mobile 0836 233473
CATH • Cathac Books, 10 Duke Street, Dublin 2, S. Ireland Tel: 00 353 1 6718676
CB • † Christine Bridge, 78 Castelnau, London SW13 9EX Tel: 07000 445277
CBC • † Cheshire Billiards Co, Springwood Lodge, Ermine Street, Appleby, Lincolnshire DN15 0DD Tel: 01724 852359/848775
CBP * † Comic Book Postal Auctions Ltd, 40-42 Osnaburgh Street, London NW1 3ND Tel: 0171 424 0007
CCO • Collectable Costume, Fountain Antique Centre, 3 Fountain Buildings, Lansdowne Road, Bath, Somerset BA1 5DU Tel: 01225 428731
CCP • Campden Country Pine, High Street, Chipping Campden, Glos GL55 6HN Tel: 01386 840315
CDC * Capes Dunn & Co, The Auction Galleries, 38 Charles Street, Off Princess Street, Gt. Manchester M1 7DB Tel: 0161 273 6060/1911
CEX • Corn Exchange Antiques Centre, 64 The Pantiles, Tunbridge Wells, Kent TN2 5TN Tel: 01892 539652
CGC * Cheffins Grain & Comins, 2 Clifton Road, Cambridge, Cambs CB2 4BW Tel: 01223 358721/213343
CHA • † Chislehurst Antiques, 7 Royal Parade, Chislehurst, Kent BR7 6NR Tel: 0181 467 1530
CHe • † Chelsea Clocks & Antiques, Stand H3-4, Antiquarius, 135 Kings Road, London SW3 4PW Tel: 0171 352 8646
ChS • † The Chair Set, 82-84 Hill Rise, Richmond, Surrey TW10 6UB Tel: 0181 332 6454/ Mobile 0411 625477
CIR • † Circa 1900, 11-13 Holts Arcade, India Buildings, Water Street, Liverpool, Merseyside L2 0RR Tel: 0151 236 1282
CMF • Childhood Memories, The Farnham Antique Centre, 27 South Street, Farnham, Surrey GU9 7QU Tel: 01252 724475
CoA • † Country Antiques (Wales), Castle Mill, Kidwelly, Carms, Wales SA17 4UU Tel: 01554 890534
CoH * † Cooper Hirst Auctions, The Granary Saleroom, Victoria Road, Chelmsford, Essex CM2 6LH Tel: 01245 260535
CoHA • † Corner House Antiques, High Street, Letchlade, Glos GL7 3AE Tel: 01367 252007
COM • Combe Cottage Antiques, Castle Combe, Chippenham, Wiltshire SN14 7HU Tel: 01249 782250
COP • Stephen Copsey Antique Centre, George Street, Huntingdon, Cambs PE18 6AW Tel: 01480 435100
CORO • † Coromandel, PO Box 9772, London SW19 3ZG Tel: 0181 543 9115
CPA • Cottage Pine Antiques, 19 Broad Street, Brinklow, Nr Rugby, Warwickshire CV23 0LS Tel: 01788 832673
CPS • Country Pine Shop, Northampton Road, West Haddon, Northants NN6 7AS Tel: 01788 510430
CRI * Criterion Salerooms, 53 Essex Road, Islington, London N1 2BN Tel: 0171 359 5707
CRV • Cremona Violins, Dublin, S. Ireland Tel: 00 3531 2833381
CS • † Christopher Sykes, The Old Parsonage, Woburn, Milton Keynes, Bucks MK17 9QM Tel: 01525 290259
CSA • Church Street Antiques, 10 Church Street, Godalming, Surrey GU7 1EH Tel: 01483 860894
CSK * Christie's South Kensington Ltd, 85 Old Brompton Road, London SW7 3LD Tel: 0171 581 7611
CTO • † Collector's Corner, PO Box 8, Congleton, Cheshire CW12 4GD Tel: 01260 270429
DA * † Dee, Atkinson & Harrison, The Exchange Saleroom, Driffield, Yorkshire YO25 7LJ Tel: 01377 253151
DaH • Dale House Antiques, High Street, Moreton-in-Marsh, Glos GL56 0AD Tel: 01608 650763
DAN • Andrew Dando, 4 Wood Street, Queen Square, Bath, Somerset BA1 2JQ Tel: 01225 422702
DBA • † Douglas Bryan Antiques, The Old Bakery, St Davids Bridge, Cranbrook, Kent TN17 3HN Tel: 01580 713103
DD * † David Duggleby, The Vine St Salerooms, Scarborough, Yorkshire YO11 1XN Tel: 01723 507111
DDM * Dickinson Davy & Markham, Wrawby Street, Brigg, Humberside DN20 8JJ Tel: 01652 653666
DeA • † Delphi Antiques, Powerscourt Townhouse Centre, South William Street, Dublin 2, S. Ireland Tel: 00 353 1 679 0331
DFA • † Delvin Farm Galleries, Gormonston, Co Meath, S. Ireland Tel: 00 353 841 2285
DHo • Derek Howard, Bourbon Hanby Antiques Centre, 151 Sydney Street, Chelsea, London SW3 6NT Tel: 0171 352 4113 Mobile 0973 507145
DIA • Mark Diamond Associates, Essex Tel: 0181 508 4479
DIC • D & B Dickinson, The Antique Shop, 22 & 22a New Bond St, Bath, Somerset BA1 1BA Tel: 01225 466502
DKH • David K. Hakeney, 400 Wincolmlee, Hull, Humberside HU2 0QL Tel: 01482 228190
DMA • David Masters Antiques, Elm Tree Farm, High Halden, Ashford, Kent TN26 3BP Tel: 01233 850551
DMC * Diamond Mills & Co, 117 Hamilton Road, Felixstowe, Suffolk IP11 7BL Tel: 01394 282281
DN * † Dreweatt Neate, Donnington Priory, Donnington, Newbury, Berkshire RG13 2JE Tel: 01635 31234
DN(H) * Dreweatt Neate Holloways, 49 Parsons Street, Banbury, Oxfordshire OX16 8PF Tel: 01295 253197
DNW * Dix-Noonan-Webb, 1 Old Bond Street, London W1X 3TD Tel: 0171 499 5022
Doc/DOC * Dockrees, Cheadle Hulme Business Centre, Clemence House, Mellor Road, Cheadle Hulme, Cheshire SK7 1BD Tel: 0161 485 1258
DOL • Dollectable, 53 Lower Bridge Street, Chester, Cheshire CH1 1RS Tel: 01244 344888/679195
DOR • † Dorset Reclamation, Cow Drove, Bere Regis, Wareham, Dorset BH20 7JZ Tel: 01929 472200
DORO/DURO * Dorotheum, Palais Dorotheum, A-1010 Wien, Dorotheergasse 17, Austria Tel: 0043 1 515 600
DRA • † Derek Roberts, 24-25 Shipbourne Road, Tonbridge, Kent TN10 3DN Tel: 01732 358986
DRU • † Drummonds of Bramley, Birtley Farm, Horsham Road, Bramley, Guildford, Surrey GU5 0LA Tel: 01483 898766
DSG • † Delf Stream Gallery, 14 New Street, Sandwich, Kent CT13 9AB Tel: 01304 617684
DSP • David & Sarah Pullen, PO Box 24, Bexhill-on-Sea, Sussex TN39 4ZN Tel: 01424 848035
DUB • Dubey's Art & Antiques, 807 N. Howard Street, Baltimore, MD 21201 USA Tel: 001 410 383 2881
DW * † Dominic Winter Book Auctions, The Old School, Maxwell Street, Swindon, Wiltshire SN1 5DR Tel: 01793 611340
E * † Ewbank, Burnt Common Auction Room, London Road, Send, Woking, Surrey GU23 7LN Tel: 01483 223101
Ech • Echoes, 650a Halifax Road, Eastwood, Todmorden, Yorkshire OL14 6DW Tel: 01706 817505
EH * Edgar Horn, Fine Art Auctioneers, 46-50 South Street, Eastbourne, Sussex BN21 4XB Tel: 01323 410419
EKK • Ekkehart, USA Tel: 001 415 571 9070
ELI • Eli Antiques, Stand Q5 Antiquarius, 135 King's Road, London SW3 4PW Tel: 0171 351 7038
EMC • Sue Emerson & Bill Chapman, Bourbon Hanby Antiques Centre, Shop No 18, 151 Sydney Street, Chelsea, London SW3 6NT Tel: 0171 351 1807
EON • Eugene O'Neill Antique Gallery, Echo Bridge Mall, 381 Elliot Street, Newtown Upper Falls, MA 02164 USA Tel: (617) 965 5965

EP * † Evans & Partridge, Agriculture House, High Street, Stockbridge, Hampshire SO20 6HF Tel: 01264 810702
ET • † Early Technology, 84 West Bow, Edinburgh, Scotland EH1 2HH Tel: 0131 226 1132
EW • Elaine Whobrey, Glos Tel: 01451 821670
FAG • Fagins Antiques, The Old Whiteways Cider Factory, Hele, Exeter, Devon EX5 4PW Tel: 01392 882062
FB • Francis Bowers Chess Suppliers, 34 Middle Road, Whaplode Spalding, Lincolnshire PE12 6TW Tel: 01406 370166
FD • Frank Dux Antiques, 33 Belvedere, Bath, Somerset BA1 5HR Tel: 01225 312367
FHF * Frank H. Fellows & Sons, Augusta House, 19 Augusta Street, Hockley, Birmingham, West Midlands B18 6JA Tel: 0121 212 2131
FOX • Foxhole Antiques, Swan & Foxhole, Albert House, Stone Street, Cranbrook, Kent TN17 3HF Tel: 01580 712720
FW&C * Finan, Watkins & Co, The Square, Mere, Wiltshire BA12 6DJ Tel: 01747 861411
G&CC • † Goss & Crested China Ltd, 62 Murray Road, Horndean, Hampshire PO8 9JL Tel: 01705 597440
GAK * † G A Key, Aylsham Salerooms, 8 Market Place, Aylsham, Norfolk NR11 6EH Tel: 01263 733195
Gam * Clarke Gammon, The Guildford Auction Rooms, Bedford Road, Guildford, Surrey GU1 4SJ Tel: 01483 566458
GAZE * † Thomas Wm Gaze & Son, Diss Auction Rooms, Roydon Road, Diss, Norfolk IP22 3LN Tel: 01379 650306
GBr • Geoffrey Breeze Antiques, 6 George Street, Bath, Somerset BA1 2EH Tel: 01225 466499
GD • † Gilbert & Dale, The Old Chapel, Church Street, Ilchester, Nr Yeovil, Somerset BA22 8ZA Tel: 01935 840464
GeC • † Gerard Campbell, Maple House, Market Place, Lechlade, Glos GL7 3AB Tel: 01367 252267
GEM • † Gem Antiques, 28 London Road, Sevenoaks, Kent TN13 1AP Tel: 01732 743540
GeM • † Gerald Mathias, R5/6 Antiquarius, 135 King's Road, Chelsea, London SW3 4PW Tel: 0171 351 0484
GeW • † Geoffrey Waters Ltd, F1 to F6 Antiquarius Antiques Centre, 135-141 King's Road, London SW3 4PW Tel: 0171 376 5467
GH * Gardiner Houlgate, The Old Malthouse, Comfortable Place, Upper Bristol Road, Bath, Somerset BA1 3AJ Tel: 01225 447933
GIN • The Ginnell Gallery Antique Centre, 18-22 Lloyd Street, Gt. Manchester M2 5WA Tel: 0161 833 9037
GIO • Giovanna Antiques, Bourbon & Hanby Antiques Centre, Shop 16, 151 Sydney Street, London SW3 6NT Tel: 0171 565 0004
GKe • Gerald Kenyon, 10 Lower Ormond Quay, 10 Great Strand Street, Dublin 1, S. Ireland Tel: 00 353 1 873 0625/873 0488
Gle * Glendinings & Co, 101 New Bond Street, London W1Y 9LG Tel: 0171 493 2445
GN • † Gillian Neale Antiques, PO Box 247, Aylesbury, Bucks HP20 1JZ Tel: 01296 423754
GOR * Gorringes Auction Galleries, 15 North Street, Lewes, Sussex BN7 2PD Tel: 01273 472503
GOR(B) * † Gorringes Auction Galleries, Terminus Road, Bexhill-on-Sea, Sussex TN39 3LR Tel: 01424 212994
GRP • † Grayshott Pine, Crossways Road, Grayshott, Hindhead, Surrey GU26 6HF Tel: 01428 607478
GS • Ged Selby Antique Glass, Yorkshire Tel: 01756 799673 by appointment
GSP * Graves, Son & Pilcher, Hove Auction Rooms Hove Street, Hove, Sussex BN3 2GL Tel: 01273 735266
GV • † Garth Vincent, The Old Manor House, Allington, Nr Grantham, Lincolnshire NG32 2DH Tel: 01400 281358
HAC • † French Depot, Halifax Antiques Centre, Queens Road/Gibbet Street, Halifax, Yorkshire HX1 4LR Tel: 01422 366657
Hal/ HAL * † Halls Fine Art Auctions, Welsh Bridge, Shrewsbury, Shropshire SY3 8LA Tel: 01743 231212
HALL • Hall's Nostalgia, 21 Mystic Street, Arlington, MA 02474 USA Tel: 001 781 646 7757
HAM * † Hamptons Antique & Fine Art Auctioneers, Baverstock House 93 High Street, Godalming, Surrey GU7 1AL Tel: 01483 423567
Har/ HarC • Hardy's Collectables/Hardy's Clobber, 862 & 874 Christchurch Road, Boscombe, Bournemouth, Dorset BH7 6DQ Tel: 01202 422407/303030
HCC * † H C Chapman & Son, The Auction Mart, North Street, Scarborough, Yorkshire YO11 1DL Tel: 01723 372424
HEG • † Stuart Heggie, 14 The Borough, Northgate, Canterbury, Kent CT1 2DR Tel: 01227 470422
HEI • † Heirlooms Antiques, 68 High Street, Tenterden, Kent TN30 6AU Tel: 01580 765535
HEM • † Hemswell Antique Centre, Caenby Corner Estate, Hemswell Cliff, Gainsborough, Lincolnshire DN21 5TJ Tel: 01427 668389
HIG • Highcroft Antiques, Red Lion, 165 Portobello Road, London W11 2DY
HOA • † Bob Hoare Antiques, Unit Q, Phoenix Place, North Street, Lewes, Sussex BN7 2DQ Tel: 01273 480557
HOB • Hobday Toys, 44 High Street, Northwood, Middlesex HA6 2XY Tel: 01923 820115
HofB • Howards of Broadway, 27A High Street, Broadway, Worcestershire WR12 7DP Tel: 01386 858924
HOLL * Dreweatt Neate Holloways, 49 Parsons Street, Banbury, Oxfordshire OX16 8PF Tel: 01295 253197
HON • Honans Antiques, Crowe Street, Gort, County Galway, S. Ireland Tel: 00 353 91 631407
HRQ • † Harlequin Antiques, 79-81 Mansfield Road, Daybrook, Nottingham, Notts NG5 6BH Tel: 0115 967 4590
HSS/ P(HSS) * Phillips, 20 The Square, Retford, Notts DN22 6XE Tel: 01777 708633
HUB • † Hubbard Antiques, 16 St Margaret's Green, Ipswich, Suffolk IP4 2BS Tel: 01473 233034
HUR • Hurst Gallery, 53 Mt. Auburn Street, Cambridge, MA 02138 USA Tel: 617 491 6888 Internet: www.hurstgallery.com
HYD * H Y Duke & Son, Dorchester Fine Art Salerooms, Dorchester, Dorset DT1 1QS Tel: 01305 265080
IM * † Ibbett Mosely, 125 High Street, Sevenoaks, Kent TN13 1UT Tel: 01732 452246
IW • † Watkins, Islwyn, 1 High Street, Knighton, Powys, Wales LD7 1AT Tel: 01547 520145
JAA * Jackson's Auctioneers & Appraisers, 2229 Lincoln Street, Cedar Falls, IA 50613 USA Tel: 319 277 2256
JAd * † James Adam & Sons, 26 St Stephen's Green, Dublin 2, S. Ireland Tel: 00 353 1 676 0261
JAK • Clive & Lynne Jackson, Glos Tel: 01242 254375 Mobile: 0589 715275
JAS • Jasmin Cameron, Antiquarius J6, 131-141 King's Road, London SW3 5ST Tel: 0171 351 4154
JBB • Jessie's Button Box, Great Western Antique Centre, Bartlett Street, Bath, Somerset BA1 2QZ Tel: 01225 310388
JES • John Jesse, 160 Kensington Church Street, London W8 4BN Tel: 0171 229 0312
JFG • Jafar Gallery, London Tel: 0181 300 2727
JH * † Jacobs & Hunt, 26 Lavant Street, Petersfield, Hampshire GU32 3EF Tel: 01730 233933
JHa • Jeanette Hayhurst, Fine Glass, 32a Kensington Church Street, London W8 4HA Tel: 0171 938 1539
JHo • † Jonathan Horne, 66B&C Kensington Church Street, London W8 4BY Tel: 0171 221 5658
JIL • † Jillings Antiques, London Tel: 0171 235 8600
JM * † John Maxwell of Wilmslow, 133A Woodford Road, Woodford, Cheshire SK7 1QD Tel: 0161 439 5182
JMC • J & M Collectables, Kent Tel: 01580 891657
JNic * John Nicholson, The Auction Rooms, Longfield, Midhurst Road, Fernhurst, Surrey GU27 3HA Tel: 01428 653727
JO • † Jacqueline Oosthuizen, 23 Cale Street, Chelsea, London SW3 3QR Tel: 0171 352 6071
JP • † Janice Paull, 16A High Street, Kenilworth, Warwickshire CV8 1LZ Tel: 01926 851311/0831 691254
JRe • John Read, 29 Lark Rise, Martlesham Heath, Ipswich, Suffolk IP5 7SA Tel: 01473 624897
JUN • Junktion, The Old Railway Station, New Bolingbroke, Boston, Lincolnshire PE22 7LB Tel: 01205 480068
JVa • † Jenny Vander, 20-22 Market Arcade, George Street, Dublin 2, S. Ireland Tel: 00 353 1 677 0406
JWA • † J.W.A. (UK) Limited, P.O. Box 6, Peterborough, Cambs PE1 5AH Tel: 01733 348344
KES • Keystones, PO Box 387, Stafford, Staffordshire ST16 3FG Tel: 01785 256648
KEY • Key Antiques, 11 Horsefair, Chipping Norton, Oxfordshire OX7 5AL Tel: 01608 643777
L * Lawrence Fine Art Auctioneers, South Street, Crewkerne, Somerset TA18 8AB Tel: 01460 73041

L&E * † Locke & England, Black Horse Agencies, 18 Guy Street, Leamington Spa, Warwickshire CV32 4RT Tel: 01926 889100
LAY * David Lay ASVA, Auction House, Alverton, Penzance, Cornwall TR18 4RE Tel: 01736 361414
LB • Lace Basket, 116 High Street, Tenterden, Kent TN30 6HT Tel: 01580 763923/763664
LCA • La Chaise Antiques, 30 London St, Faringdon, Oxfordshire SN7 7AA Tel: 01367 240427
LCC • The London Cigarette Card Co Ltd, Sutton Road, Somerton, Somerset TA11 6QP Tel: 01458 273452
LEW * † Lewes Auction Rooms (Julian Dawson), 56 High Street, Lewes, Sussex BN7 1XE Tel: 01273 478221
LF * † Lambert & Foster, 77 Commercial Road, Paddock Wood, Kent TN12 6DR Tel: 01892 832325
LHAr • Artifacts, USA Tel/Fax: 001 415 381 2084
LHB • Gallery Les Hommes Bleus, Bartlett Street Antique Centre, 5/10 Bartlett Street, Bath, Somerset BA1 2QZ Tel: 01225 316606
LIB • Libra Antiques, 81 London Road, Hurst Green, Etchingham, Sussex TN19 7PN Tel: 01580 860569
LIN • Peter Linden, Georges Avenue, Blackrock, Dublin, S. Ireland Tel: 00 353 1 288 5875
LPA • † L.P. Furniture, (The Old Brewery), Short Acre Street, Walsall, West Midlands WS2 8HW Tel: 01922 746764
LRG * Lots Road Galleries, 71-73 Lots Road Chelsea, London SW10 0RN Tel: 0171 351 7771
LT * † Louis Taylor Auctioneers & Valuers, Britannia House, 10 Town Road, Hanley, Stoke on Trent, Staffordshire ST1 2QG Tel: 01782 214111
LUC • R. K. Lucas & Son, The Tithe Exchange, 9 Victoria Place, Haverfordwest, Wales SA16 2JX Tel: 01437 762538
M * Morphets of Harrogate, 6 Albert Street, Harrogate, Yorkshire HG1 1JL Tel: 01423 530030
M&K * Mellors & Kirk, The Auction House, Gregory Street, Lenton Lane, Nottingham, Notts NG7 2NL Tel: 0115 979 0000
MAC • Mall Antique Centre, The, 400 Wincolmlee, Hull, Humberside HU2 0QL Tel: 01482 327858
MAT * Christopher Matthews, 23 Mount Street, Harrogate, Yorkshire HG2 8DQ Tel: 01423 871756
MAV • May Avenue, Antiquarius V13, 131-141 Kings Road Chelsea, London SW3 4PW Tel: 0171 351 5757
MCA * † Mervyn Carey, Twysden Cottage, Benenden, Cranbrook, Kent TN17 4LD Tel: 01580 240283
MCN • MCN Antiques, 183 Westbourne Grove, London W11 2SB Tel: 0171 727 3796
MEA * † Mealy's, Chatsworth Street, Castle Comer, Co Kilkenny, S. Ireland Tel: 00 353 56 41229
MEG • Megarry's & Forever Summer, Jericho Cottage, The Green, Blackmore, Essex CM4 0RR Tel: 01277 821031 and 01277 822170
MiA • Old Mill Antiques Centre, Mill Street, Low Down, Bridgnorth, Shropshire Tel: 01746 768778
MIC • Trevor Micklem, Combesbury Antiques, Combesbury Farm, Buckland St Mary, Chard, Somerset TA20 3ST Tel: 01460 234323
MIL Milverton Antiques, Fore Street, Milverton, Taunton, Somerset TA4 1JU Tel: 01823 400592
Mit * Mitchells, Fairfield House, Station Road, Cockermouth, Cumbria CA13 9PY Tel: 01900 827800
MJa • † Mark Jarrold, The Grey House, Tetbury Street, Minchinhampton, Glos GL6 9JH Tel: 01453 887074
MJW • Mark J West, Cobb Antiques Ltd, 39a High Street, Wimbledon Village, London SW19 5YX Tel: 0181 946 2811
MLa • † Marion Langham, London Tel: 0171 730 1002
MLL • † Miller's Antiques Ltd, Netherbrook House, 86 Christchurch Road, Ringwood, Hampshire BH24 1DR Tel: 01425 472062
MON • Monty Lo, Stand 369, Grays Antique Market, 58 Davies Street, London W1Y 1AR Tel: 0171 493 9457
MRT • Mark Rees Tools, Somerset Tel: 01225 837031
MRW • Malcolm Russ-Welch, PO Box 1122, Rugby, Warwickshire CV23 9YD Tel: 01788 810 616
MSB • Marilynn and Sheila Brass, PO Box 380503, Cambridge, MA 02238 0503 USA Tel: 617 491 6064
MSW * † Marilyn Swain Auctions, The Old Barracks, Sandon Road, Grantham, Lincs NG31 9AS Tel: 01476 568861
MTa • Maggie Tallentire, Cousy 82160 Caylus, Tarn et Garonne, France Tel: 00 33 05 63 24 05 27
MTay • † Martin Taylor Antiques, 140B Tettenhall Road, Wolverhampton, West Midlands WV6 0BQ Tel: 01902 751166
MUL • Mullock & Madeley, The Old Shippon, Wall-under-Heywood, Church Stretton, Shropshire SY6 7DS Tel: 01694 771771
NC • The Nautical Centre, Harbour Passage, Hope Square, Weymouth, Dorset DT4 8TR Tel: Day 01305 777838
NCA • New Century, 69 Kensington Church Street, London W8 4BG Tel: 0171 376 2810
NEW • New Ashgate Gallery, Waggon Yard, Farnham, Surrey GU9 7PS Tel: 01252 713208
NOA * New Orleans Auction Galleries Inc, 801 Magazine Street, AT 510 Julia, New Orleans, Louisiana 70130, USA Tel: (504) 566 1849
Nor • Sue Norman, L4 Antiquarius, 135 King's Road, London SW3 5ST Tel: 0171 352 7217
NOST • † Nostalgia, 61 Shaw Heath, Stockport, Cheshire SK3 8BH Tel: 0161 477 7706
NP • Neville Pundole, 8A & 9 The Friars, Canterbury, Kent CT1 2AS Tel: 01227 453471
NTM • Nostalgia Toy Museum, High Street, Godshill, Isle of Wight PO38 3HZ Tel: 01938 526254
NWE • † North Wilts Exporters, Farm Hill House, Brinkworth, Wiltshire SN15 5AJ Tel: 01666 510876/824133
NWi • Neil Wilcox, 113 Strawberry Vale, Twickenham, Middlesex TW1 4SJ Tel: 0181 892 5858
OCH • Gillian Shepherd, Old Corner House Antiques, 6 Poplar Road, Wittersham, Tenterden, Kent TN30 7PG Tel: 01797 270236
OCP • † Old Court Pine (Alain & Alicia Chawner), Old Court, Collon, Co Louth, S. Ireland Tel: 00 353 41 26270 Mobile 00 353 86 2310084
OD • Offa's Dyke Antique Centre, 4 High Street, Knighton, Powys, Wales LD7 1AT Tel: 01547 528635/528940
Odi * † Odiham Auction Sales, The Eagle Works, Rear of Hartley Wintney Garages, High Street, Hartley Wintney, Hampshire RG27 8PU Tel: 01252 844410
Oli * † Oliver's, Oliver's Rooms, Burkitts Lane, Sudbury, Suffolk CO10 6HB Tel: 01787 880305
OLM • † The Old Mill, High Street, Lamberhurst, Kent TN3 8EQ Tel: 01892 891196
ONS * † Onslow's, The Depot, 2 Michael Road, London SW6 2AD Tel: 0171 371 0505 Mobile: 0831 473 400
OO/PO • † Pieter Oosthuizen, 1st Floor Georgian Village, Camden Passage, London N1 8EF Tel: 0171 359 3322
OPH • Old Pine House, 16 Warwick Street, Royal Leamington Spa, Warwickshire CV32 5LL Tel: 01926 470477
ORE * † O'Regans of Cork, 21 Lavitts Quay, Cork, S. Ireland Tel: 00 353 21 271550
ORI • Oriental Gallery Tel: 01451 830944 appointment only
OT • Old Timers, Box 392, Camp Hill, PA 17001-0392, USA Tel: 001 717 761 1908
OTA • On The Air, 42 Bridge Street Row, Chester, Cheshire CH1 1NN Tel: 01244 348468
OTB • † Old Tackle Box, PO Box 55, Cranbrook, Kent TN17 3ZU Tel: & Fax 01580 713979
P * † Phillips, 101 New Bond Street, London W1Y 0AS Tel: 0171 629 6602
P(B) * Phillips, 1 Old King Street, Bath, Somerset BA1 2JT Tel: 01225 310609
P(Ba) * Phillips Bayswater, 10 Salem Road, London W2 4DL Tel: 0171 229 9090
P(C) * Phillips Cardiff, 9-10 Westgate Street, Cardiff, Wales CF1 1DA Tel: 01222 396453
P(E) * Phillips, Alphin Brook Road, Alphington, Exeter, Devon EX2 8TH Tel: 01392 439025
P(EA) * Phillips, 32 Boss Hall Road, Ipswich, Suffolk IP1 59J Tel: 01473 740494
P(F) * Phillips Folkestone, 11 Bayle Parade, Folkestone, Kent CT20 1SG Tel: 01303 245555
P(G) * Phillips Fine Art Auctioneers, Millmead, Guildford, Surrey GU2 5BE Tel: 01483 504030
P(M) * Phillips, 158 Queen Street, Woollahra, Melbourne, NSW 2025 Australia Tel: (612) 9326 1588
P(NE) * Phillips North East, St Mary's, Oakwellgate, Gateshead, Tyne & Wear NE8 2AX Tel: 0191 477 6688
P(NW) * Phillips North West, New House, 150 Christleton Road, Chester, Cheshire CH3 5TD Tel: 01244 313936
P(NY) * Phillips New York, 406 East 79th Street, New York, NY10021 USA Tel: 00 1 212 570 4830

P(O) * Phillips, 39 Park End Street, Oxford, Oxfordshire OX1 1JD Tel: 01865 723524
P(R) * Phillips Fine Art Auctioneers, 54 Southampton Road, Ringwood, Hampshire BH24 1JD Tel: 01425 473333
P(S) * Phillips Fine Art Auctioneers, 49 London Road, Sevenoaks, Kent TN13 1AR Tel: 01732 740310
P(Sc) * Phillips Scotland, 65 George Street, Edinburgh, Scotland EH2 2JL Tel: 0131 225 2266
P(Sc) * Phillips Scotland, 207 Bath Street, Glasgow, Scotland G2 4HD Tel: 0141 221 8377
P(W) * Phillips of Winchester, The Red House, Hyde Street, Winchester, Hampshire SO23 7DX Tel: 01962 862515
P(WM)* Phillips, The Old House, Station Road, Knowle, Solihull, West Midlands B93 0HT Tel: 01564 776151
P(Z) * Phillips, 27 Ramistrasse, 8001 Zurich, Switzerland Tel: 411 25 26962
PAD * Padworth Auctions, 30 The Broadway, Thatcham, Berkshire RG19 3HX Tel: 01734 713772
PAO • † P. A. Oxley, The Old Rectory, Cherhill, Nr Calne, Wiltshire SN11 8UX Tel: 01249 816227
PEN • Pennard House Antiques, 3-4 Piccadilly, London Road, Bath, Somerset BA1 6PL Tel: 01225 313791/ 01749 860260
PEx • † Piano-Export, Bridge Road, Kingswood, Bristol, Glos BS15 4PW Tel: 0117 956 8300
PF * † Peter Francis, The Curiosity Saleroom, 19 King Street, Carmarthen, South Wales SA31 1BH Tel: 01267 233456
PFK * † Penrith Farmers' & Kidd's plc, Skirsgill Salerooms, Penrith, Cumbria CA11 0DN Tel: 01768 890781
PGH • Paris, 42A High Street, Tenterden, Kent TN30 6AR Tel: 01580 765328
PHA • † Paul Hopwell, 30 High Street, West Haddon, Northants NN6 7AP Tel: 01788 510636
PKT • Glitter & Dazzle, Pat & Ken Thompson Tel: 01329 288678
POSH • Posh Tubs, Moriati's Workshop, High Halden, Ashford, Kent TN26 3LZ Tel: 01233 850155
POT • † Pot Board, 30 King Street, Carmarthen, Wales SA31 1BS Tel: 01834 842699/01267 236623
POW • Sylvia Powell Decorative Arts, 28 The Mall, Camden Passage, London N1 0PD Tel: 0171 354 2977/0181 458 4543
PrB • Pretty Bizaar, 170 High Street, Deal, Kent Tel: 0973 794537
PSA •† Pantiles Spa Antiques, 4, 5, 6 Union House, The Pantiles, Tunbridge Wells, Kent TN4 8HE Tel: 01892 541377
PSG • Patrick & Susan Gould, Stand L17 Gray's Mews Antique Market, Davies Mews, Davies Street, London W1Y 1AR Tel: 0171 408 0129
PT • † Pieces of Time, 26 South Molton Lane, London W1Y 2LP Tel: 0171 629 2422
RA • Roberts Antiques, Lancashire Tel: 01253 827798
RAC • Rochester Antiques Centre, 93 High Street, Rochester, Kent ME1 1LX Tel: 01634 846144
RAR * † Romsey Auction Rooms, 86 The Hundred, Romsey, Hampshire SO51 8BX Tel: 01794 513331
RAW • † John Rawlinson, 22 Elliot Road, Love Lane Estate, Cirencester, Glos GL7 1YS Tel: 01285 653532
RBA • Roger Bradbury Antiques, Church Street, Coltishall, Norfolk NR12 7DJ Tel: 01603 737444
RBB * † Russell, Baldwin & Bright, Ryelands Road, Leominster, Herefordshire HR6 8NZ Tel: 01568 611122
RCh • Rayner & Chamberlain, London Tel: 0181 293 9439
RdeR • † Rogers de Rin, 76 Royal Hospital Road, London SW3 4HN Tel: 0171 352 9007
RDG • Richard Dennis Gallery, 144 Kensington Church Street, London W8 4BN Tel: 0171 727 2061
RECL • Reclamation Services Ltd, Catbrain Quarry, Painswick Beacon, Above Paradise, Painswick, Glos GL6 6SU Tel: 01452 814064
REF • † The Refectory, 38 West Street, Dorking, Surrey RH4 1BU Tel: 01306 742111
Riv/RIV • Riverbank Antiques, Wells Union, Route 1, PO Box 3009, Wells, ME 04090 USA Tel: 207 646 6314
RKa • Richardson & Kailas, London Tel: 0171 371 0491 By appointment
RMC • Romsey Medals, 5 Bell Street, Romsey, Hampshire SO51 8GY Tel: 01794 512069
RPh • † Phelps Ltd, 133-135 St Margaret's Road, East Twickenham, Middlesex TW1 1RG Tel: 0181 892 1778/7129
RRA • Rambling Rose Antiques, Marcy & Bob Schmidt, Frederick, MD USA Tel: 301 473 7010
RTh • † The Reel Thing, 17 Royal Opera Arcade, Pall Mall, London SW1Y 4UY Tel: 0171 976 1830
RTo * † Rupert Toovey & Co Ltd, Star Road, Partridge Green, Sussex RH13 8RJ Tel: 01403 711744
RTw • † Richard Twort, Somerset Tel: 01934 641900
RUM • † Rumours Decorative Arts, 10 The Mall, Upper Street, Camden Passage, Islington, London N1 0PD Tel: 01582 873561/0836 277274/0831 103748
RWB • Roy W. Bunn Antiques, 34/36 Church Street, Barnoldswick, Colne, Lancashire BB8 5UT Tel: 01282 813703
RYA •† Robert Young Antiques, 68 Battersea Bridge Road, London SW11 3AG Tel: 0171 228 7847
S * Sotheby's, 34-35 New Bond Street, London W1A 2AA Tel: 0171 293 5000
S(Am) * Sotheby's Amsterdam, Rokin 102, Amsterdam, 1012 KZ Netherlands Tel: 31 (20) 550 2200
S(Cg) * Sotheby's, 215 West Ohio Street, Chicago, Illinois 60610 USA Tel: (312) 670 0010
S(G) * Sotheby's, 13 Quai du Mont Blanc, Geneva, CH-1201 Switzerland Tel: 41 (22) 732 8585
S(HK) * Sotheby's, Li Po Chun Chambers 18th Floor 189 Des Vouex Road, Hong Kong, China Tel: 852 524 8121
S(LA) * Sotheby's, 9665 Wilshire B'd, Beverly Hills, California, 90212 USA Tel: (310) 274 0340
S(NY) * Sotheby's, 1334 York Avenue, New York, NY 10021 USA Tel: 212 606 7000
S(S) * Sotheby's Sussex, Summers Place, Billingshurst, Sussex RH14 9AD Tel: 01403 833500
S(T) * Sotheby's Taipei, 1st Floor, No 79 Secl, An Ho Road, Taipei, Taiwan R.O.C. Tel: 00 886 2 755 2906
S(Z) * Sotheby's Zurich, Bleicherweg 20, Zurich, CH-8022 Switzerland Tel: 41 (1) 202 0011
SA • Somerville Antiques & Country Furniture Ltd, Moysdale, Killanley, Ballina, Co Mayo, S. Ireland Tel: 00 353 963 6275
SAnt • Seaby Antiques, 14 Old Bond Street, London W1X 4JL Tel: 0171 495 2590
SAS * † Special Auction Services, The Coach House, Midgham Park, Reading, Berkshire RG7 5UG Tel: 0118 971 2949
SAU • Mary Sauter, Churchill Antiques Centre, 6 Station Street, Lewes, Sussex BN7 2DA Tel: 01273 474842
SCO • Peter Scott, Stand 39, Bartlett Street Antiques Centre, Bath, Somerset BA1 2QZ Tel: 01225 310457 or 0117 986 8468
SeH • † Seventh Heaven, Chirk Mill, Chirk, Wrexham, County Borough, Wales LL14 5BU Tel: 01691 777622/773563
SER • † Serendipity, 168 High Street, Deal, Kent CT14 6BQ Tel: 01304 369165
SFL • † The Silver Fund Ltd, 40 Bury Street, St James's, London W1Y 6AU Tel: 0171 839 7664
SHA • Shambles, 22 North Street, Ashburton, Devon TQ13 7QD Tel: 01364 653848
SHa • † Shapiro & Co, Stand 380, Gray's Antique Market, 58 Davies Street, London W1Y 1LB Tel: 0171 491 2710
SI • † Sound Instruments, Worth Farm, Little Horsted, Nr Uckfield, Sussex TN22 5TT Tel: 01825 750567
SIL • The Silver Shop, Powerscourt Townhouse Centre, St Williams Street, Dublin 2, S. Ireland Tel: 00 3531 6794147
SK * Skinner Inc, The Heritage On The Garden, 63 Park Plaza, Boston, MA 02116 USA Tel: 001 617 350 5400
SK(B) * Skinner Inc, 357 Main Street, Bolton, MA 01740 USA Tel: 0101 508 779 6241
SLL • Sylvann Llewelyn, Bourbon-Hanby Antiques Centre, 151 Sydney Street, Chelsea, London SW3 6NT Tel: 0171 351 4981

SLM * Sloan's Auctioneers & Appraisers, Miami Gallery, 8861 NW 18th Terrace, Suite 100, Miami, Florida 33172 USA Tel: (305) 592-2575 (800) 660-4524
SLN * Sloan's, C. G. Sloan & Company Inc, 4920 Wyaconda Road, North Bethesda, MD 20852 USA Tel: 001 301 468 4911/669 5066
SMI •† Janie Smithson, Lincolnshire Tel & Fax: 01754 810265/Mobile: 0831 399180
SnA • Snape Maltings Antique & Collectors Centre, Saxmundham, Suffolk IP17 1SR Tel: 01728 688038
SO •† Sam Orr Antique Clocks, 36 High Street, Hurstpierpoint, Nr Brighton, Sussex BN6 9RG Tel: 01273 832081
Som •† Somervale Antiques, 6 Radstock Road, Midsomer Norton, Bath, Somerset BA3 2AJ Tel: 01761 412686
SPa •† Sparks Antiques, 4 Manor Row, High Street, Tenterden, Kent TN30 6HP Tel: 01580 766696
SPU •† Spurrier-Smith Antiques, 28, 30, 39 & 41 Church Street, Ashbourne, Derbyshire DE6 1AJ Tel: 01335 343669/342198
SSW • Spencer Swaffer, 30 High Street, Arundel, Sussex BN18 9AB Tel: 01903 882132
STA •† Michelina & George Stacpoole, Main St, Adare, Co Limerick, S. Ireland Tel: 00 353 61 396 409
STE • Stevenson Brothers, The Workshop, Ashford Road, Bethersden, Ashford, Kent TN26 3AP Tel: 01233 820363
STG • Stone Gallery, 93 The High Street, Burford, Oxfordshire OX18 4QA Tel/Fax: 01993 823302
STK • Stockbridge Antiques, 8 Deanhaugh Street, Edinburgh, Scotland EH4 1LY Tel: 0131 332 1366
SUC • Succession, 18 Richmond Hill, Richmond, Surrey TW10 6QX Tel: 0181 940 6774
SUS • Susannah, 142/144 Walcot Street, Bath, Somerset BA1 5BL Tel: 01225 445069
SWA •† S.W. Antiques, Abbey Showrooms, Newlands, Pershore, Worcestershire WR10 1BP Tel: 01386 555580
SWB •† Sweetbriar Gallery, Robin Hood Lane, Helsby, Cheshire WA6 9NH Tel: 01928 723851
SWN • Swan Antiques, Stone Street, Cranbrook, Kent TN17 3HF Tel: 01580 712720
SWO *† G E Sworder & Sons, 14 Cambridge Road, Stansted Mountfitchet, Essex CM24 8BZ Tel: 01279 817778
TaB • Tartan Bow, Suffolk Tel: 01379 783057 (open Fridays 10-5pm, other days by appt)
TAC Tenterden Antiques Centre, 66-66A High Street, Tenterden, Kent TN30 6AU Tel: 01580 765655/765885
TAN • Tanglewood Antiques, Tanglewood Mill, Coke Street, Derby, Derbyshire DE1 1NE Tel: 01332 346005
TAY * Taylors, Honiton Galleries, 205 High Street, Honiton, Devon EX14 8LF Tel: 01404 42404
TC • Timothy Coward, Devon Tel: 01271 890466
TCF • 20th Century Frocks, 65 Steep Hill, Lincoln, Lincolnshire N1 1YN Tel: 01522 545916
TED •† Teddy Bears of Witney, 99 High Street, Witney, Oxfordshire OX8 6LY Tel: 01993 702616/706616
Tem • Great Western Antiques, Torre Station, Newton Road, Torquay, Devon TQ2 5DD Tel: 01803 200551
TEN *† Tennants, The Auction Centre, Harmby Road, Leyburn, Yorkshire DL8 5SG Tel: 01969 623780
TH • Tony Horsley, Sussex Tel: 01273 732163
THOM • S. & A. Thompson, Stand V12 Antiquarius 131/141 Kings Rd, London SW3 5ST Tel: 0171 352 8680
TIH • Time In Our Hands, The Platt, Wadebridge, Cornwall PL27 7AD Tel: 01208 815210
TIM • Timepiece Antiques, 58 Patrick Street, Dublin 8, S. Ireland Tel: 00 353 1 4540774
TMA *† Brown & Merry, Tring Market Auctions, Brook Street, Tring, Hertfordshire HP23 5EF Tel: 01442 826446
TMe • Thomas Mercer (Chronometers) Ltd, 32 Bury Street, St James's, London SW1Y 6AU Tel: 0171 930 9300
TOM •† Charles Tomlinson, Chester Tel/Fax: 01244 318395
TPA • Times Past Antiques, 59 High Street, Eton, Windsor, Berkshire SL4 6BL Tel: 01753 857018
TPC •† Pine Cellars, 39 Jewry Street, Winchester, Hampshire SO23 8RY Tel: 01962 777546
TT • Treasures in Textiles, 53 Russian Drive, Liverpool, Merseyside L13 7BS Tel: 0151 281 6025
TUR • W.F. Turk, London Tel: 0181 543 3231 (appointment only)
TVM • Teresa Vanneck-Murray, Vanneck House, 22 Richmond Hill, Richmond-upon-Thames, Surrey TW10 6QX Tel: 0181 940 2035
UTP • Utility Plus, 5 Watts Lane, Eastbourne, Sussex Tel: 01323 739928
VCL • Vintage Cameras Ltd, 254 & 256 Kirkdale, Sydenham, London SE26 4NL Tel: 0181 778 5416/5841
VH • Valerie Howard, 2 Campden Street, London W8 7EP Tel: 0171 792 9702
VS *† T. Vennett-Smith, 11 Nottingham Road, Gotham, Notts NG11 0HE Tel: 0115 983 0541
VSP * Van Sabben Poster Auctions, Oosteinde 30, 1678 HS Oostwoud, Holland Tel: 31 (0) 229 202589
VSt • Vera Strange, 811 Christchurch Road, Boscombe, Dorset BH21 1TZ Tel: 01202 429111
W&S • Pat Woodward and Alma Shaw, Unit G43, Ground Floor, Gloucester Antiques Centre, In The Historic Docks, Severn Road, Gloucester, Glos GL1 2LE
WAB • Warboys Antiques, Old Church School, High Street, Warboys, Cambridge, Cambs PE17 2SX Tel: 01487 823686
WAC • Worcester Antiques Centre, Reindeer Court, Mealcheapen Street, Worcester, WR1 4DF Tel: 01905 610680
WaH • The Warehouse, 29-30 Queens Gardens, Worthington Street, Dover, Kent CT17 9AH Tel: 01304 242006
Wai • Peter Wain, Glynde Cottage, Longford, Market Drayton, Shropshire TF9 3PW Tel: 01630 639613
WAL *† Wallis & Wallis, West Street Auction Galleries, Lewes, Sussex BN7 2NJ Tel: 01273 480208
WaR • Wot a Racket, 250 Shepherds Lane, Dartford, Kent DA1 2PN Tel: 01322 220619
WBB •† William Bentley Billiards, Standen Manor Farm, Hungerford, Berkshire RG17 0RB Tel: 0181 940 1152/01488 681711/01672 871214
WBH *† Walker, Barnett & Hill, Waterloo Road Salerooms, Clarence Street, Wolverhampton, West Midlands WV1 4JE Tel: 01902 773531
WCa • Wendy Carmichael, S126-129, Alfies Antique Market, 13-25 Church St, London NW8 8DT Tel: 0171 723 6066
WEE • Weedon Bec Antiques, 66 High Street, Weedon, Northants NN7 4QD Tel: 01327 349910
WeH • Westerham House Antiques, The Green, Westerham, Kent TN16 1AY Tel: 01959 561622/562200
WELD •† J. W. Weldon, 55 Clarendon Street, Dublin 2, S. Ireland Tel: 00 3531 677 1638
WELL •† Anthony Welling, Broadway Barn, High Street, Ripley, Woking, Surrey GU23 6AQ Tel: 01483 225384
WL *† Wintertons Ltd, Lichfield Auction Centre, Wood End Lane, Fradley, Lichfield, Staffordshire WS13 8NF Tel: 01543 263256
WRe • Walcot Reclamations, 108 Walcot Street, Bath, Somerset BA1 5BG Tel: 01225 444404
WSA •† West Street Antiques, 63 West Street, Dorking, Surrey RH4 1BS Tel: 01306 883487
WW * Woolley & Wallis, Salisbury Salerooms, 51-61 Castle Street, Salisbury, Wiltshire SP1 3SU Tel: 01722 424500
WWY • When We Were Young, The Old Forge, High Street, Harmondsworth Village, Middlesex UB7 0AQ Tel: 0181 897 3583
YAG • The York Antiques Gallery, Route 1, PO Box 303, York, ME 03909 USA Tel: 207-363-5002
YAN • Yanni's Antiques, 538 San Anselmo Avenue, San Anselmo, CA 94960 USA Tel: 001 415 459 2996
YC • Yesterday Child, Angel Arcade, 118 Islington High Street, London N1 8EG Tel: 0171 354 1601
ZEI • Zeitgeist, 58 Kensington Church Street, London W8 4DB Tel & Fax: 0171 938 4817

ACKNOWLEDGEMENTS

The publishers would like to acknowledge the great assistance given by our consultants:

FURNITURE:	**Leslie Gillham,** Gorringes Auction Galleries, 15 North Street, Lewes, East Sussex BN7 2PD
OAK & COUNTRY FURNITURE :	**Anthony Rogers,** Sotheby's Sussex, Summers Place, Billingshurst, West Sussex RH14 9AD
FRENCH PROVINCIAL FURNITURE:	**Pierre Farouz,** L. P. Furniture, The Old Brewery, Short Acre Street, Walsall, West Midlands, WS2 8HW
POTTERY & PORCELAIN:	**Mark Law,** Dreweatt Neate, Donnington Priory, Newbury, Berks RG13 2JE
POTTERY, PORCELAIN & MAJOLICA:	**John Sandon,** Phillips, 101 New Bond Street, London W1Y OAS
STAFFORDSHIRE FIGURES:	**Jacqueline Oosthuizen,** 23 Cale Street, Chelsea, London SW3 3QR
POT LIDS:	**Andrew Hilton,** Special Auction Services, The Coach House, Midgham Park, Reading, Berkshire RG7 5UG
ORIENTAL CERAMICS & WORKS OF ART:	**Peter Wain,** Glynde Cottage, Longford, Market Drayton, Shropshire TF9 3PW
	Lita Solis-Cohen, USA. Tel: 001 215 884 3510
GLASS:	**Jeanette Hayhurst,** 32a Kensington Church Street, London W8 4HA
SILVER:	**Alastair Crawford,** The Silver Fund Ltd, 40 Bury Street, St James's, London SW1Y 6AU
CLOCKS & WATCHES:	**Oliver Saunders,** Bonhams, Montpelier Street, Knightsbridge, London SW7 1HH
BAROMETERS:	**Alan Walker,** Halfway Manor, Halfway, Nr Newbury, Berks RG20 8NR
DECORATIVE ARTS:	**Keith Baker,** Phillips, 101 New Bond Street, London W1Y OAS
POOLE POTTERY:	**Lucy Lafferty,** Poole Pottery, The Quay, Poole, Dorset, BH15 1RF
TWENTIETH CENTURY DESIGN:	**Paul Rennie,** 13 Rugby Street, London W1X 1RF
RUGS & CARPETS:	**Andrew Middleton,** Bonhams, Montpelier Street, Knightsbridge, London SW7 1HH
ISLAMIC WORKS OF ART:	**Deborah Freeman,** Christie's, 8 King Street, St James's, London SW1Y 6QT
ANTIQUITIES:	**Peter A Clayton FSA,** Seaby Antiquities, 14 Old Bond Street, London W1X 4JL
TRIBAL ART:	**Siobhan Quin,** Phillips, 101 New Bond Street, London W1Y OAS
BOOKS & BOOK ILLUSTRATIONS:	**Catherine Porter,** Sotheby's, 34–35 New Bond Street, London W1A 2AA
CAROUSEL ANIMALS:	**Grierson Gower,** The Old Chapel, Long Street, Tetbury, Gloucestershire GL8 8AA
SCIENTIFIC INSTRUMENTS & MARINE:	**Mark Jarrold,** The Grey House, Tetbury Street, Minchinhampton, Gloucestershire GL6 9JH
IRISH ANTIQUES:	**Mark Kenyon,** Gerald Kenyon Antiques, 10 Lower Ormond Quay, Dublin 1, Ireland

We would like to extend our thanks to all auction houses, their press offices, dealers and collectors who have assisted us in the production of this book.

HOW TO USE THIS BOOK

It is our aim to make the Guide easy to use. In order to find a particular item, consult the contents list on page 19 to find the main heading, for example, Clocks. Having located your area of interest, you will find that larger sections have been sub-divided. If you are looking for a particular factory, designer or craftsman, consult the index which starts on page 796.

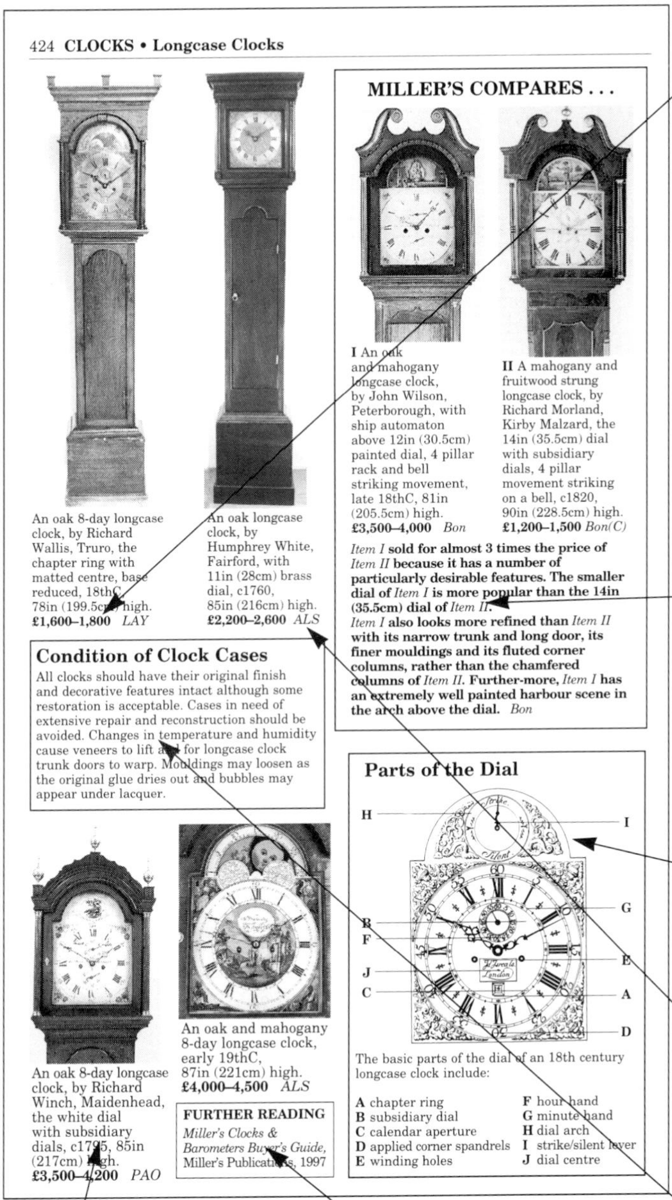

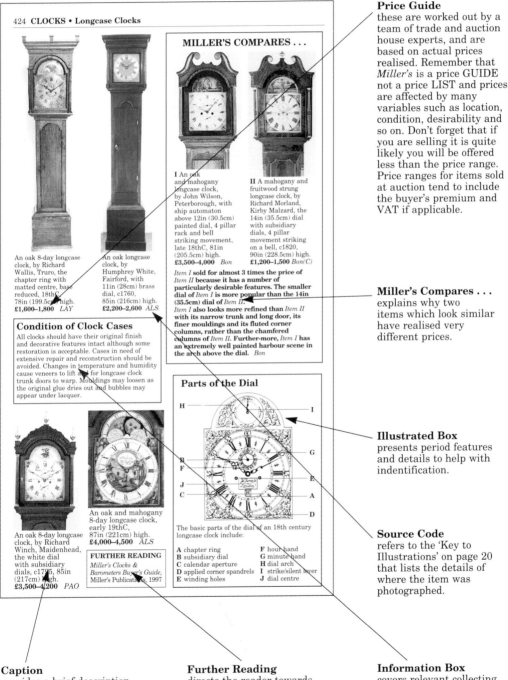

424 **CLOCKS • Longcase Clocks**

An oak 8-day longcase clock, by Richard Wallis, Truro, the chapter ring with matted centre, base reduced, 18thC, 78in (199.5cm) high.
£1,600–1,800 *LAY*

An oak longcase clock, by Humphrey White, Fairford, with 11in (28cm) brass dial, c1760, 85in (216cm) high.
£2,200–2,600 *ALS*

MILLER'S COMPARES . . .

I An oak and mahogany longcase clock, by John Wilson, Peterborough, with ship automaton above 12in (30.5cm) painted dial, 4 pillar rack and bell striking movement, late 18thC, 81in (205.5cm) high.
£3,500–4,000 *Bon*

II A mahogany and fruitwood strung longcase clock, by Richard Morland, Kirby Malzard, the 14in (35.5cm) dial with subsidiary dials, 4 pillar movement striking on a bell, c1820, 90in (228.5cm) high.
£1,200–1,500 *Bon(C)*

***Item I* sold for almost 3 times the price of *Item II* because it has a number of particularly desirable features. The smaller dial of *Item I* is more popular than the 14in (35.5cm) dial of *Item II*.**
***Item I* also looks more refined than *Item II* with its narrow trunk and long door, its finer mouldings and its fluted corner columns, rather than the chamfered columns of *Item II*. Further-more, *Item I* has an extremely well painted harbour scene in the arch above the dial.** *Bon*

Condition of Clock Cases
All clocks should have their original finish and decorative features intact although some restoration is acceptable. Cases in need of extensive repair and reconstruction should be avoided. Changes in temperature and humidity cause veneers to lift and for longcase clock trunk doors to warp. Mouldings may loosen as the original glue dries out and bubbles may appear under lacquer.

Parts of the Dial

The basic parts of the dial of an 18th century longcase clock include:

A chapter ring
B subsidiary dial
C calendar aperture
D applied corner spandrels
E winding holes
F hour hand
G minute hand
H dial arch
I strike/silent lever
J dial centre

An oak 8-day longcase clock, by Richard Winch, Maidenhead, the white dial with subsidiary dials, c1795, 85in (217cm) high.
£3,500–4,200 *PAO*

An oak and mahogany 8-day longcase clock, early 19thC, 87in (221cm) high.
£4,000–4,500 *ALS*

FURTHER READING
Miller's Clocks & Barometers Buyer's Guide, Miller's Publications, 1997

Price Guide
these are worked out by a team of trade and auction house experts, and are based on actual prices realised. Remember that *Miller's* is a price GUIDE not a price LIST and prices are affected by many variables such as location, condition, desirability and so on. Don't forget that if you are selling it is quite likely you will be offered less than the price range. Price ranges for items sold at auction tend to include the buyer's premium and VAT if applicable.

Miller's Compares . . .
explains why two items which look similar have realised very different prices.

Illustrated Box
presents period features and details to help with indentification.

Source Code
refers to the 'Key to Illustrations' on page 20 that lists the details of where the item was photographed.

Caption
provides a brief description of the item including the maker's name, medium, year it was made and in some cases condition.

Further Reading
directs the reader towards additional sources of information.

Information Box
covers relevant collecting information on factories, makers, care and restoration, fakes and alterations.

INTRODUCTION

If you are wondering what 1960s chairs in acrylic, fibreglass and plywood are doing in *Miller's Antiques Price Guide*, you will be even more astonished at the values, for some are worth the same as a George II and George III mahogany chests of drawers. Doulton figurines can have the same value as ancient Chinese tomb statues or Chelsea figures, while in his silver introduction Alastair Crawford notes how Georg Jensen silver costs far more than Georgian counterparts. It all begs the question of when does an antique become a work of fine art? This year we feature the modern pottery of Dame Lucie Rie and moulded furniture by Charles Eames, expensive commodities that are likely to be bought by public collections, for any museum worth its salt these days must boast a gallery devoted to 20th century design. Christopher Dresser teapots of the 1870s and Clarice Cliff vases from the 1930s are marketed as design icons with appropriately high prices being realised. Nobody sits on an Alvar Aalto chair any more – they admire its design instead.

This is all in such contrast to the world of traditional antiques. Several of our contributors recommend using antiques for their original purpose. Jeanette Hayhurst reminds us how pleasant it is to drink from 18th and 19th century glasses, while Anthony Rogers tells us how everyday use enhances early oak furniture. Furniture is, of course, the most usable of all antiques, and in this regard Leslie Gillham's summary of recent market changes makes interesting reading. He tells of a growing number of private buyers who choose restored pieces that can be delivered from the antique shop or auctioneers straight into their living rooms looking polished and smart. Many dealers still prefer to buy objects in their original, unrestored condition, but it is worth remembering that antique collectors rarely want to look at damaged porcelain or clocks that do not work. Oliver Saunders reminds us that restoration to clocks can be quite expensive, and a good china restorer can take a long time. I never used to recommend that anyone should get a piece restored before placing it in an auction, but attitudes have changed. Today a slightly damaged piece of Majolica that has been well restored is likely to sell for the same price as a perfect example, a situation unheard of a decade ago.

In the present buoyant market a great deal hinges on how well an antique looks in a photograph, as our auctioneers' catalogues are becoming ever more glossy brochures. Instead of traditional mixed sales of antiques, New York auctioneers now offer 'English Country House' sales presented as prestigious events, where some of the prices recently paid by private American buyers have left English furniture dealers stunned. In Britain, Phillips have pioneered 'Fine Sales in Fine Places', taking antiques out of the saleroom and into period room settings hired for the purpose. Meanwhile many dealers' traditional selling exhibitions have become erudite presentations with catalogues that resemble interiors magazines. Traditional rivalry has given way to co-operation as dealers and auctioneers co-ordinate their programmes. Lita Solis-Cohen discusses the success of the Asian Fair in New York and there is no doubt that the present shift in the Oriental art market from Hong Kong to New York is due in part to this joint strategy by auctioneers and dealers playing to the strength of the American collectors market.

Several contributors to this year's *Miller's Antiques Price Guide* have noted that the market in their specialist field has become more global. With computer search facilities now available to collectors, there is no need to travel to keep up to date with the international auction market. These are exciting times as technology spirals ahead. As Sotheby's Duke and Duchess of Windsor auction took place in New York, telephone bidders from every continent joined in the action. Meanwhile I sat in a TV studio in London discussing live with millions of viewers the lots actually being sold at that moment on the other side of the Atlantic. Viewers in Britain could not yet join in the bidding from their armchairs, but it will only be a matter of time before fully televised auctions are a regular feature of our cable or satellite schedules alongside the latest antiques gameshows.

The internet has truely turned antique hunting into a worldwide market as it allows many dealers and auction houses to be in touch with new foreign customers. I know of specialist dealers who have given up costly stands at antiques fairs, preferring instead to offer all their latest stock for sale on their web pages. A good photograph scanned on to the Super-Highway is all it takes as more and more buyers choose to collect antiques in this way. Goods are bought unseen, and so it is very important to study an image closely and ask vital questions. In this regard the 'Miller's Compares' features throughout *Miller's Antiques Price Guide* are of particular significance: our expert consultants explain the difference between two apparently similar objects from which vital lessons can be learned. However, touching, handling and inspecting the real thing is still the most reliable way to both learn about and buy antiques.

We are always eager to make this guide better. If we have omitted what you collect or if you have any other comments please let us know – we value your opinion.

John Sandon

Dates	British Monarch	British Period	French Period
1558–1603	Elizabeth I	Elizabethan	Renaissance
1603–1625	James I	Jacobean	
1625–1649	Charles I	Carolean	Louis XIII (1610–1643)
1649–1660	Commonwealth	Cromwellian	Louis XIV (1643–1715)
1660–1685	Charles II	Restoration	
1685–1689	James II	Restoration	
1689–1694	William & Mary	William & Mary	
1694–1702	William III	William III	
1702–1714	Anne	Queen Anne	
1714–1727	George I	Early Georgian	Régence (1715–1723)
1727–1760	George II	Early Georgian	Louis XV (1723–1774)
1760–1811	George III	Late Georgian	Louis XVI (1774–1793) Directoire (1793–1799) Empire (1799–1815)
1812–1820	George III	Regency	Restauration Charles X (1815–1830)
1820–1830	George IV	Regency	
1830–1837	William IV	William IV	Louis Philippe (1830–1848) 2nd Empire Napoleon III (1848–1870) 3rd Republic (1871–1940)
1837–1901	Victoria	Victorian	
1901–1910	Edward VII	Edwardian	

German Period	U.S. Period	Style	Woods
Renaissance	Early Colonial	Gothic	Oak Period (to c1670)
Renaissance/ Baroque (c1650–1700)		Baroque (c1620–1700)	Walnut period (c1670–1735)
	William & Mary		
	Dutch Colonial	Rococo (c1695–1760)	
Baroque (c1700–1730)	Queen Anne		
Rococo (c1730–1760)	Chippendale (from 1750)		Early mahogany period (c1735–1770)
Neo–classicism (c1760–1800)	Early Federal (1790–1810)	Neo–classical (c1755–1805)	Late mahogany period (c1770–1810)
Empire (c1800–1815)	American Directoire (1798–1804) American Empire (1804–1815)	Empire (c1799–1815)	
Biedermeier (c1815–1848)	Late Federal (1810–1830)	Regency (c1812–1830)	
Revivale (c1830–1880)	Victorian	Eclectic (c1830–1880)	
Jugendstil (c1880–1920)		Arts & Crafts (c1880–1900)	
	Art Nouveau (c1900–1920)	Art Nouveau (c1900–1920)	

FURNITURE

A comparison of the trends in the furniture market over the last twelve months with those of the previous year closely resembles the dosage instructions on nanny's medicine bottle: 'The same, only more of it.'

Certainly, English brown furniture continues on its course as the shooting star of the middle-range firmament. For the uninitiated, 'brown furniture' is the rather sniffy sobriquet given to the more utilitarian pieces of 18th and 19th century mahogany which possess neither the style nor the pedigree to make them items for serious collectors. This, of course, does not prevent them from frequently being both elegant and practical pieces of furniture, and it is undoubtedly these virtues that are continuing to drive up prices.

Although a recent report in *The Times* by a leading estate agent informed us that their clients no longer require well-appointed dining rooms in their town houses, as yet there has been no obvious easing off on prices for good sideboards, tables and large sets of chairs. One thing that has changed is that the Americans are back in the British market, although it could be argued that when it came to the very top end of the market they were never away. Just recently they were again making a big splash in a London sale of oak and country furniture, where a West Coast dealer accounted for the £17,000 top lot – an oak double-dome bureau bookcase – while an American private buyer carried off a mid-18th century Windsor chair for £13,000. This was no ordinary Windsor chair since it bore the paper label of its maker, John Pitt, and is the earliest English Windsor chair attributable to a particular maker. While this illustrates that American collectors have always been interested in the best, their return to the less rarefied atmosphere of the middle-range market, from which they have been absent for some time, is bound to drive up prices.

Another minor phenomenon is the great patina revolution. In the past, the appearance of a freshly restored and repolished piece of furniture in an auction would be shunned as 'trade goods', and it would be ignominiously 'bought in' by the auctioneer as he hurried on to the next, more profitable, lot. This is no longer the case, and the reason would seem to be the growing influx of non-trade buyers to auctions.

What the private purchaser wants is a piece which can be transported straight from the saleroom to the home without expensive detours via the restorer's workshop. As a result, furniture which has been repaired, repolished, rebuilt or even somewhat reinvented, is currently finding a ready market where one formerly barely existed. As always there is a proviso: the price has to be right. These new buyers are no mugs and they have very clear views on what they will and will not pay.

This new trend has not been mirrored by any slow down in demand for unrestored items. The trade is desperate for good, untouched pieces of furniture which can then be restored to the standard required by an individual dealer's clientele. In no area is this demand more marked than that of early 18th century English walnut, where auction prices have been spiralling upwards all year. The George I bureau bookcase illustrated on page 38 is a good example, although its £15,000–18,000 price tag begins to look quite reasonable when stood alongside some recent results. A George III walnut bachelor's chest made £26,400 in Salisbury despite having a warped top and the wrong handles; a near-derelict George I chest-on-chest which, among other faults, had lost its cornice, its handles and a considerable amount of moulding, been converted into two separate bits of furniture and, most bizarre of all, had been partially re-veneered in rosewood, still sold in Sussex for £7,260; while a Queen Anne walnut bureau made £29,700 in the north of England.

Although the current rush into walnut furniture is probably partly attributable to the much-hyped and highly successful sale of the Parry collection (a husband and wife team who amassed a large collection) of oak and walnut in London last year, there are deeper underlying causes for what amounts to a price explosion. The main one would seem to be that the market supply of really important early 19th century furniture has all but dried up. This has brought about a revaluation of the next level down in quality, and the present record figures are the result.

So far, so good: English brown furniture is still on the up, and owners of honest, unrestored early 18th century walnut are laughing all the way to the bank. But what about late 19th century furniture? Does anybody want that? Well, the answer would seem to be a very definite 'yes'! Not only do buyers want late Victorian and Edwardian pieces, they are prepared to pay more for some examples than they are for the 18th century equivalent. The corner cupboards shown on page 46 illustrate this trend: a slightly plain George III example is listed at £3,200–3,800, while a more decorative piece dating from 1910 comes in at £4,800–5,300.

Finally, another niche market is Victorian soft furnishings. Look out for easy chairs and sofas that still have their original coverings like the Liberty & Co Turkeywork examples shown on page 61.

Leslie Gillham

FURNITURE
Beds

A carved mahogany tester bed, the canopy with painted arcaded frieze and ribbon-tied floral sprays, with plain back posts, late 18thC, 60in (152.5cm) wide.
£11,000–13,000 *WW*

A Federal figured mahogany four-poster bed, with arched and spurred headboard, on square tapering legs ending in spade feet, Philadelphia, c1800, 80in (203cm) long.
£1,400–1,600 *S(NY)*

A late Federal turned and figured maple bedstead, with panelled pine headboard and acorn finials, on turned tapering legs ending in caps, American, c1830, 55in (140cm) wide.
£3,500–4,000 *S(NY)*

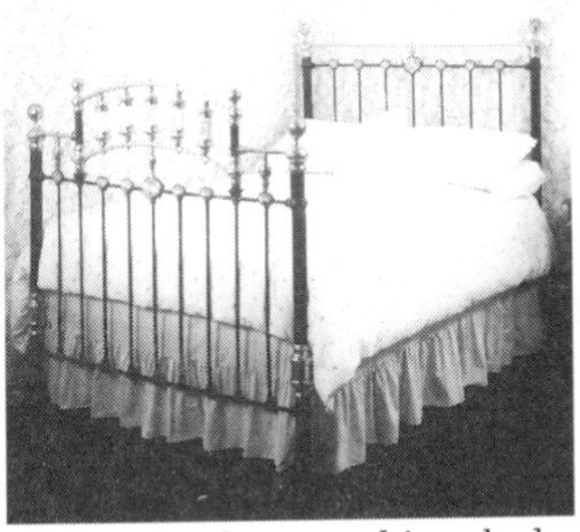

A Victorian brass and iron bed, with porcelain decoration, 75in (190.5cm) long.
£1,000–1,200 *SWA*

A French walnut *lit en bateau*, c1870, 72in (183cm) long.
£1,200–1,450 *SeH*

A Louis XVI style mahogany bed, with ormolu-mounted quarter-veneered panels and tapering fluted posts, 19thC, 63in (160cm) wide.
£2,000–2,250 *SeH*

A Victorian brass bedstead, by Hoskins & Sewell of Birmingham, c1885, 54in (137cm) wide.
£1,300–1,500 *SeH*

A Victorian cast iron and brass bedstead, with ring and spindle decoration, West Midlands, c1885, 54in (137cm) wide.
£900–1,000 *SeH*

A cast iron bedstead, with decoratively cast plaques and mouldings, Birmingham, c1875, 48in (120cm) wide.
£750–900 *SeH*

A Victorian 'crown and canopy' four-poster bedstead, with engraved posts and decorative post fittings, produced for the export market, c1875, 60in (152.5cm) wide.
£6,000–7,000 *SeH*

An elm bedstead, with carved head and footboard, original side rails, c1890, 54in (137cm) wide.
£1,100–1,300 *SWA*

A Louis XV style carved giltwood bed, the tailboard decorated with a panel depicting Venus and Cupid, on scroll feet, late 19thC, 57in (145cm) wide.
£1,500–1,800 *P*

r. A Portuguese mahogany bedstead, with spindle and 'peacock' headboard, c1900, 54in (137cm) wide.
£1,650–1,850 *SeH*

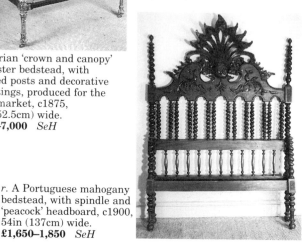

l. A French Louis XV style carved rosewood bed, with cabriole legs, 19thC, 60in (152.5cm) wide.
£1,000–1,200 *HAC*

A walnut bed, with carved head and footboard and turned supports with finials, c1900, 54in (137cm) wide.
£1,100–1,300 *SWA*

Bonheurs du Jour

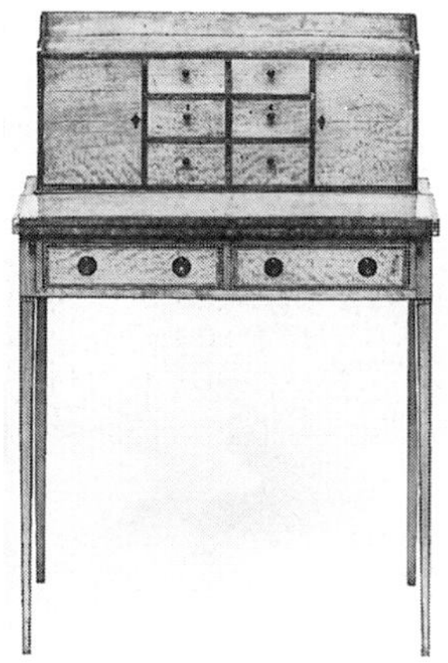

A George III Sheraton satinwood and tulipwood crossbanded bonheur du jour, with hinged writing flap, raised on square tapered legs, 28in (71cm) wide.
£3,200–3,500 *P(O)*

A Victorian carved, figured and burr walnut bonheur du jour, the upper section with arched pediment, 2 satinwood-lined side cupboards and central open shelf, with applied carved decoration in the classical manner, the base with 3 frieze drawers, on carved, turned, tapering, fluted legs, 42in (106.5cm) wide.
£4,000–4,500 *JM*

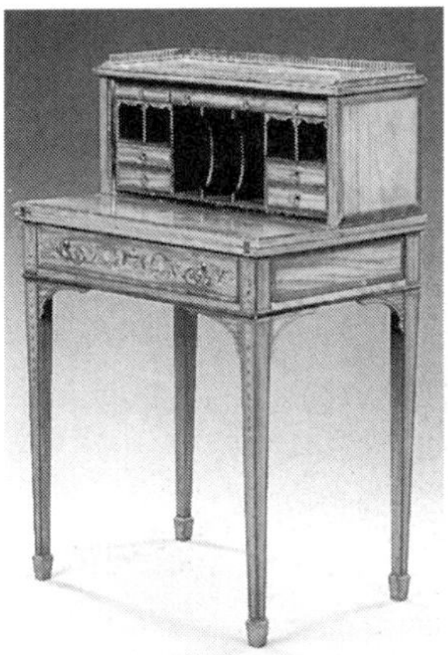

A Napoleon III rosewood and marquetry bonheur du jour, in the Louis XV manner, with gilt-bronze mounts and inlaid with foliage, the superstructure with marble top, the frieze drawer fitted with a writing slide, on cabriole legs, 35½in (90cm) wide.
£2,500–2,750 *AH*

Inlays

This is the process of letting other woods, usually of contrasting colours, into the surface of a piece of furniture. The practice is commonly associated with veneered furniture, but early solid pieces are also occasionally inlaid. Inlaying was popular on English and Continental furniture of the 17th, 18th and 19thC. In America its appeal was more limited before the 19thC. The 3 main types of inlay are line inlay, marquetry and parquetry.

An Edwardian boxwood-bound bonheur du jour, the upper section with 2 side cabinets enclosed by doors with oval satinwood panels, the base with fold-out writing surface with large oval panel inlay, on square tapering legs, 30½in (77.5cm) wide.
£1,100–1,200 *JM*

l. An Edwardian satinwood bonheur du jour, inlaid with musical trophies and arabesques, the fold-over top with a tooled-leather inset, the raised back with drawers and pigeonholes, on square tapered legs with bell-flowers and surmounted by urn motifs and spade feet, c1910, 40in (101.5cm) wide.
£3,500–4,000 *S(S)*

A Regency rosewood and gilt-metal-mounted bonheur du jour, by Wilkinson, the frieze fitted with a secretaire drawer enclosing a maple-veneered interior, on an inverted and stepped breakfront plinth with brass ball feet, inlaid throughout with satinwood bandings, c1810, 39½in (101cm) wide.
£3,000–3,500 *S*

The firm of Wilkinson was established c1790 by William Wilkinson, working in partnership with a relation, Thomas Wilkinson. By 1814 William had established a business of his own at 14 Ludgate Hill and built up a flourishing trade. Wilkinson worked in a variety of styles, producing furniture in the Egyptian, rococo, and Grecian manner.

Bookcases

Glazing

Until the mid-18thC cabinets and bookcases were glazed with small rectangular panes, retained by fairly solid glazing bars, or astragals. The more intricate patterns used from the mid-18thC resulted in lighter glazing bars. Some bookcases from the 19thC were designed without astragals and just had plain glass set into a shaped panel.

A Georgian mahogany bookcase, with a broken arch pediment centred by a scallop shell cornice, a pair of astragal glazed doors below enclosing adjustable shelves and a pair of panelled doors under, on blind fret carved bracket feet, 54in (137cm) high.
£2,200–2,500 *AG*

A George III mahogany bookcase, the fretwork pediment with inlaid paterae roundels, fitted interior shelves in sliding niches, enclosed by 2 astragal glazed panelled doors, lower section fitted with provision for trays, enclosed by doors, crossbanded with ebony and box stringing, on ogee bracket feet, late 18thC, 48½in (123cm) high.
£5,500–6,000 *L&E*

A George III mahogany crossbanded bookcase, the glazed ribbed doors enclosing adjustable shelves, the lower section with 2 short frieze drawers inlaid with oval figured panels above 2 doors with oval inlay, damage and restorations, c1795, 48in (122cm) wide.
£3,500–4,000 *Hal*

A late Georgian satinwood and marquetry bookcase, with a moulded cornice and frieze with oval medallion inlay, enclosed by a pair of astragal glazed doors, and a shaped apron, on bracket feet, 38in (97cm) wide.
£3,700–4,000 *P*

l. A Regency mahogany bookcase, with moulded, arched and tracery astragals, on later secretaire base, with panelled doors between blind-fret carved sides, 49in (124.5cm) wide.
£900–1,000 *CoH*

A Victorian figured-walnut and inlaid bookcase, with gilt-metal mounts, the glass panel doors enclosing a velvet-lined interior and shelves, a pair of panel doors with a conforming interior below, c1850, 54in (137cm) wide.
£3,000–3,500 *S(S)*

A George IV mahogany bookcase, the upper part with a pair of glazed doors, the lower part enclosed by a pair of panelled doors, 39in (99cm) wide.
£3,000–3,500 *L*

A mid-Victorian mahogany bookcase, the moulded cornice above arched glazed doors, the lower section with a moulded frieze drawer, above a pair of arched panelled doors flanked by foliate carving, 44in (112cm) wide.
£2,200–2,500 *Bon*

A mahogany library bookcase, with 2 glass doors, 2 drawers, 2 lower doors and internal drawer, c1860, 52in (132cm) wide.
£2,000–2,400 *GBr*

r. A Continental walnut bookcase, in 3 sections, the central section with 2 glazed panel doors, a scroll decorated panelled fall with 3 long drawers below, flanked by side sections, each with glazed panel doors, mid-19thC, 104in (264cm) wide.
£2,500–3,000 *P*

A mid-Victorian mahogany bookcase, the glazed doors flanked by rectangular pillars, the lower section with rectangular top above a pair of panelled doors, 42in (107cm) wide.
£1,800–2,000 *Bon*

A Victorian mahogany bookcase, in 2 sections, the top half with a pair of glazed panelled doors, enclosing a series of adjustable shelves flanked on either side with applied pillars above the base, with a pair of panelled cupboard doors also flanked by applied mouldings and enclosing shelves, 48in (122cm) wide.
£1,600–1,800 *Mit*

A Victorian mahogany bookcase, the glazed panel doors with a mirror-lined interior with shelves, the serpentine base with a frieze drawer above 2 panelled doors, the sides with carved corbels, 45in (114cm) wide.
£1,800–2,000 *S(S)*

A Victorian mahogany bookcase, in 2 sections, the top half with a central fixed glazed panel flanked on either side by a pair of cupboard doors with applied mouldings to outer edge, the base fitted with 2 drawers above a central panel with applied shield moulding flanked on either side by similiar panelled cupboard doors and mouldings, 60in (152.5cm) wide.
£1,400–1,600 *Mit*

l. An Edwardian mahogany and blind fret carved bookcase on stand, by Edwards & Roberts, the astragal glazed doors enclosing adjustable shelves, the stand with 2 drawers, the square legs with a galleried undertier, on block feet, mouldings partially lacking, 41in (104cm) wide.
£1,700–2,000 *S(S)*

A Victorian mahogany bookcase, the pair of glazed panelled doors enclosing adjustable shelves, with 3 short drawers above 3 panelled cupboards doors, each with brass drop handles and flanked by applied mouldings, 53in (134.5cm) wide.
£1,200–1,500 *Mit*

A Victorian carved oak floor standing bookcase, the upper part fitted with 2 arched glazed doors, and 2 similar doors to the base, the whole with lion mask foliate and figural carving, on bun feet, 44in (111cm) wide.
£1,000–1,200 *WL*

A Victorian mahogany and ebony line inlaid bookcase, by James Shoolbred, Tottenham Court Road, with 4 astragal glazed doors enclosing shelves, 4 panelled doors under enclosing cupboards, 2 of the cupboards with internal cupboard doors, 96in (244cm) high.
£6,000–7,000 *E*

A Victorian mahogany breakfront bookcase, with 4 arched glazed doors enclosing adjustable shelving and divided by panelled pilasters headed by scrolled and flower-carved brackets, the base with arched panel doors and similar pilasters, 97in (246.5cm) wide.
£7,000–8,000 *AH*

A late Victorian mahogany bookcase, the glazed doors flanked by 2 leaf-capped columns, the lower section with frieze drawer and 2 panelled cupboard doors flanked by ring-turned leaf-capped columns, 60½in (154cm) wide.
£1,500–1,800 *P(C)*

An American walnut walnut bookcase, with glazed cupboard doors, flanked by reeded columns, the lower section with panelled cupboard doors, on ogee bracket feet, late 19thC, 46½in (118cm) wide.
£1,700–2,000 *SLN*

Bureau Bookcases

A George I walnut bureau bookcase, the top section with mirrored panel doors enclosing shelves and 6 small drawers, with candle slides below, the fall-flap with crossbanded and herringbone inlaid decoration enclosing a fitted interior with well, over 2 short and 2 long graduated drawers with herringbone inlay, replacement oval handles, on bracket feet, 40½in (103cm) wide.
£18,000–20,000 *P(G)*

This bookcase was considered by the auctioneers to be completely original, so it could be restored to the buyer's own taste.

A George II mahogany bureau bookcase, the associated top with crossbanded glazed doors, the lower section with sloping fall opening to reveal a fitted interior of pigeonholes and drawers, above 4 long drawers, on bracket feet, parts later, 44½in (113cm) wide.
£1,400–1,600 *P(C)*

A George III mahogany bureau bookcase, the astragal doors enclosing adjustable shelves, the crossbanded and strung fall revealing stationery compartments, 2 short and 3 long graduated drawers below, on ogee bracket feet, 56in (142cm) wide.
£5,000–5,500 *S*

A George III mahogany bureau bookcase, the dentil-moulded broken pediment cornice above a pair of astragal glazed doors, the lower section with hinged fall enclosing a fitted interior, above 4 long graduated drawers, raised on bracket feet, 43½in (111cm) wide.
£2,800–3,200 *Bon*

A George III mahogany bureau bookcase, with later fret-carved swan neck pediment, 2 astragal glazed doors, sloping flap enclosing a cupboard, drawers and pigeonholes, 4 graduated long drawers below, on shaped bracket feet, 43in (110cm) wide.
£4,000–4,500 *Bea(E)*

A George III mahogany bureau bookcase, with moulded and drop bead decorated cornice, a pair of astragal glazed doors enclosing adjustable sliding shelves, above fall-front enclosing shell-inlaid fitted interior, 4 long graduated drawers on bracket feet, 41in (104cm) wide.
£6,000–6,500 *HOLL*

A George III mahogany kneehole bureau bookcase, the upper part with a swan neck pediment with pierced fret and flowerhead ornament, enclosed by a pair of glazed astragal doors, the sloping fall enclosing a fitted interior with one long and 6 short drawers about a central recessed cupboard with fielded panel door, on bracket feet, some parts later, 46½in (118cm) wide.
£4,500–5,000 *P*

A George III mahogany bureau bookcase, crossbanded with string inlay, 2 astragal glazed doors enclosing shelving, the associated base with fall-front revealing fitted interior, over 4 long drawers with brass oval handles, on bracket feet, 48in (122cm) wide.
£3,000–3,500 *AH*

r. An oak bureau bookcase, by Globe Wernicke of London, the fall revealing a fitted interior above a drawer, a pair of cabriole supports below and a recessed glazed bookcase above a moulded apron drawer, early 20thC, 34in (87cm) wide.
£520–600 *S(S)*

Globe Wernicke

Globe Wernicke was a London-based manufacturer of specialist office and library furniture between WWI and WWII. The company is probably best known for its highly distinctive interlocking sectional bookcases, comprising individual shelf units each enclosed by a glazed up-and-over door.

Low Bookcases

A George III mahogany bookcase, the top with central shell inlay and thick boxwood stringing to the edge, above a shallow frieze boxwood strung and with inlay, above a pair of glazed doors with ebony, mahogany and boxwood feather-veneered astragals in a Sheraton design, 48in (122cm) wide.
£1,200–1,500 *Mit*

A Victorian figured-walnut bookcase, inlaid with banding, the pair of glazed doors flanked by moulded terminals, the velvet-lined interior with shelves, c1900, 48in (122cm) wide.
£700–850 *S(S)*

Three oak library bookcases, each in 4 sections, by Globe Wernicke, all with elongated diamond pattern leaded light doors, one base section with fielded panelled door, 1920s, 34in (86.5cm) wide.
£1,800–2,000 *EH*

Open Bookcases

A Regency rosewood-veneered and brass-inlaid low bookcase, the fixed shelves with brass inlaid fronts, 85in (216cm) wide.
£1,300–1,500 *LAY*

A George III mahogany open bookcase, the graduated tiers above a drawer, on splayed bracket feet, c1800, 21in (53cm) wide.
£1,800–2,000 *S(S)*

A Regency *faux* rosewood and decorated open dwarf bookcase, with arched floral cornucopiae gallery, a *verre eglomisé* panel door with classical figures within beaded ornament, on square tapered legs, brass cappings and casters, 21in (54cm) wide.
£2,700–3,000 *P*

A Regency mahogany bookcase, the graduated upper stage with open shelves above a boxwood strung door enclosing a shelf, the base with a deep drawer and gilt brass ring handles, on square tapering feet with casters, 23½in (60cm) wide.
£950–1,100 *DN*

Revolving Bookcases

An Edwardian mahogany satinwood-banded and boxwood and ebonised strung revolving bookcase, inlaid with neo-classical marquetry style floral motif, the 2 tiers each fitted with 8 sections, raised on short cabriole legs with pad feet, 18in (46cm) wide.
£750–850 *GAK*

An Edwardian mahogany and crossbanded revolving bookcase, the top with central fan inlaid decoration, slatted sides, on platform base and casters, 20in (50cm) wide.
£500–550 *HOLL*

Cross Reference
Colour Review

An Edwardian mahogany and crossbanded revolving two-tier bookcase, with string and chequer inlay, slatted sides incorporating 3 small drawers with brass drop handles and a small cupboard, on casters, 21in (53.5cm) wide.
£2,100–2,300 *AH*

An Edwardian mahogany and satinwood crossbanded revolving bookcase, on cabriole legs with serpentine platform, some damage, 18in (46cm) wide.
£600–650 *EH*

Secretaire Bookcases

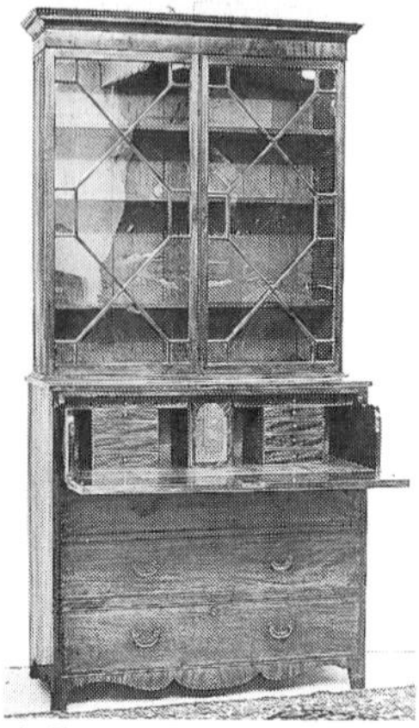

A George III mahogany secretaire bookcase, the upper part with astragal glazed doors enclosing adjustable shelves, the lower projecting part with deep cockbeaded secretaire drawer, the front with string inlay, the interior fitted with small drawers and pigeonholes with 3 long graduated cockbeaded drawers beneath, shaped apron, on splay feet, 45in (114.5cm) wide.
£3,800–4,200 *PF*

A George III mahogany bookcase, the base with a line inlaid and crossbanded frieze drawer fitted with a hinged baize-lined writing surface revealing 2 drawers, over 2 cupboards, each line inlaid and crossbanded with a moulding, on ogee bracket feet, 52½in (133.5cm) wide.
£2,800–3,200 *P(WM)*

Veneers

A veneer is a thin layer of attractively grained, fine wood which has been applied to the surface of furniture made of a coarser wood. The technique was imported to England by Dutch craftsmen in the late 17thC. Early veneers were cut in a saw pit and vary in thickness, while modern veneers are machine-cut and much thinner. Decorative effects can be achieved in a variety of ways – for instance, if the veneer is cut lengthways from the tree, the grain will be longitudinal, or it can be cut across the roots to create a burr effect. A particularly popular form of decoration is quarter-veneering, in which 4 sheets are sliced in succession from one block, and then each pair laid in juxtaposition to create a mirror image pattern.

A late Regency mahogany secretaire bookcase, the upper part with astragal glazed doors enclosing adjustable shelves, the secretaire drawer enclosing pigeonholes and satinwood faced drawers, 2 figured and panelled doors below flanked by turned pillars, with Bramah locks, on turned feet, 35½in (90cm) wide.
£2,000–2,200 *P(S)*

An oak, ebonised and gilded secretaire bookcase, the doors decorated in pokerwork, the upper part enclosed by painted panel doors, with secretaire drawer, 19thC, 41in (104cm) wide.
£7,500–8,500 *MAT*

This most unusual piece, profusely decorated in pokerwork, exceeded the auctioneer's expectations when sold at auction.

A George III mahogany secretaire bookcase, the upper part with a dentil and fluted cornice, enclosed by a pair of geometrically glazed doors, the projecting lower part with a fitted secretaire drawer above 3 graduated long drawers, on bracket feet, 41½in (105cm) wide.
£5,000–5,500 *L*

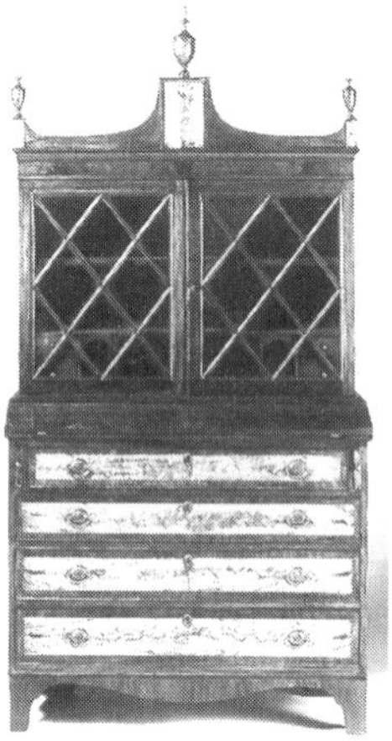

A Federal flame birch-wood veneered and mahogany secretaire bookcase, repairs to veneer and right finial, American, c1800, 40½in (103cm) wide.
£2,800–3,200 *S(NY)*

r. A Victorian mahogany secretaire bookcase, with glazed panelled doors enclosing adjustable shelves, the fielded secretaire drawer with fitted interior, a pair of panelled doors under, 48in (122cm) wide.
£1,500–1,800 *AG*

Bramah Locks

Bramah locks were invented by Joseph Bramah and patented in 1784. They are set in a characteristic circular escutcheon and have small cylindrical keys.

l. An Edwardian mahogany secretaire bookcase, crossbanded in satinwood and strung with ebony and box, the upper section with broken swan neck pediment, green cloth shelves enclosed by a pair of glazed doors, the projecting base with long secretaire drawer to the frieze, cupboards below, 49in (125cm) wide.
£2,300–2,600 *HSS/P*

Buckets

A mahogany brass-bound peat bucket, with brass handle, c1760, 15in (38cm) high.
£500–550 *Odi*

A mahogany and brass-bound bucket, with original liner, late 18thC, 14in (35cm) high.
£2,000–2,200 *S*

A George III oval mahogany and brass-bound peat bucket, with brass handle and liner, 12½in (32cm) high.
£1,100–1,200 *P*

A George III mahogany and brass-bound bucket, with brass handle, 16½in (42cm) high.
£1,200–1,400 *S*

Buffets

A Dutch mahogany and floral marquetry buffet, with hinged top enclosing folding shelves, 2 swivel frieze drawers and 2 simulated tambour panel doors, on square tapered legs and bar ball feet, late 18thC, 36½in (93cm) wide.
£1,700–1,850 *P*

A William IV mahogany plate buffet, on turned supports, on turned legs and brass casters, c1835, 55in (139cm) wide.
£2,700–3,000 *S*

An early Victorian two-tier buffet, 45in (114cm) wide.
£850–950 *DN(H)*

r. A French oak dessert buffet, carved with fruit, flowers and vine leaves, 19thC, 36in (91.5cm) wide.
£700–850 *HAC*

A Victorian four-tier mahogany dumb waiter, with moulded shelves and turned corner columns, on brass casters, 48in (122cm) wide.
£900–1,000 *CoH*

From the 19thC the terms 'buffet' and 'dumb waiter' were interchangeable.

An American Victorian walnut server, the shelves with block, ring and baluster-turned supports ending in knop finials, on porcelain casters, 19thC, 36in (91.5cm) wide.
£1,000–1,200 *S(Cg)*

Bureaux

A William and Mary walnut bureau, the rising slope crossbanded and with a bookrest, revealing enclosed interior of drawers and pigeonholes, on 6 turned and tapered walnut legs with veneered stretchers at the base, on turned feet, 36in (91.5cm) wide.
£15,000–18,000 *B*

This bureau is of particular interest because it represents a transitional stage between early bureaux which had a flat, lift-up top, and Georgian examples with a slope and a bank of drawers underneath. Although not in the finest condition, this did not count against it as pieces that have never been touched by restorers are often very popular.

A burr yew-veneered bureau, with boxwood line inlay, the sloping flap enclosing a cupboard, drawers and pigeonholes with 2 drawers below, the later stand with shaped apron, on cabriole legs with pad feet, early 18thC, 38½in (98cm) wide.
£950–1,150 *Bea(E)*

A George I walnut bureau, the feather banded fall enclosing a fitted interior of drawers and pigeonholes, above 2 short and 3 long drawers, on bracket feet, 31½in (80cm) wide.
£6,500–7,200 *Bon*

A German rococo red lacquer chinoiserie bureau, with leather-lined fall-front revealing stepped drawers to interior, on cabriole legs, possibly Ansbach, c1760, 37in (94cm) wide.
£3,000–3,500 *S(Z)*

A George III mahogany bureau, the fall-front revealing an arrangement of 9 drawers and 7 pigeonholes and a later baize insert, above 4 long graduated cockbeaded drawers with later brass swing handles, raised on later bracket feet, some re-veneering, 42in (107cm) wide.
£750–900 *Hal*

Cockbeading is a bead moulding applied to the edges of drawers.

A George II figured-ash bureau, the feather and crossbanded moulded fall-front enclosing a shaped interior of drawers and pigeonholes around a cupboard flanked by opening pilasters, above a frieze drawer with 2 short and 2 long drawers below, on bracket feet, c1730, 37in (94cm) wide.
£3,500–4,200 *S*

l. A George III mahogany bureau, the fall-front opening to reveal a fitted interior of drawers, cupboards and pigeonholes above 2 short and 3 long graduated cockbeaded drawers with brass drop handles, on bracket feet, 46in (117cm) wide.
£700–800 *Mit*

Handle Styles

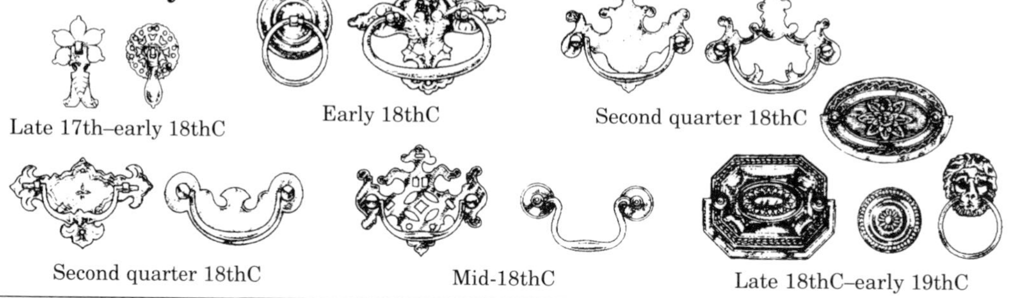

A Dutch walnut and marquetry inlaid bureau, the sloping fall opening to reveal a fitted interior, the blocked front fitted with lopers, 2 short drawers and 3 long graduated drawers, on bracket feet, late 18thC, 38in (96.5cm) wide.
£3,600–4,000 *P(Sc)*

A George IV mahogany cylinder bureau, with kingwood cross-banding, boxwood stringing and Bramah locks throughout, the superstructure with 3 drawers, with fitted interior, 2 short and 3 graduated long drawers below, on bracket feet, 45in (114cm) wide.
£1,400–1,600 *Bea(E)*

A Louis XV style kingwood parquetry *bureau de dame*, with gilt-metal mounts, the shaped quarter-veneered fall enclosing fitted interior, above 2 short, one simulated and one long drawer, on cabriole legs with gilt-metal sabots, mid-19thC, 30in (76cm) wide.
£2,500–3,000 *P*

A Swedish walnut bombé bureau, the top with a sloping fall crossbanded in bands with a fruitwood edge, enclosing a fitted and graduated interior with steel pull-out lopers, on splayed legs with pierced sabots, 18thC, 36in (91.5cm) wide.
£3,700–4,000 *P*

A late Victorian inlaid mahogany cylinder bureau, with pierced brass gallery, 4 drawers with brass handles, barrel roll-top movement revealing pigeonholes and drawers, the base fitted with central drawer flanked by 2 box drawers with drop handles, shaped apron, raised on square tapering supports, 41in (104cm) wide.
£2,000–2,200 *BIG*

A burr-walnut, kingwood and marquetry bombé *bureau de dame*, in the Louis XV style, with gilt-bronze mounts, the foliate and butterfly inlaid shaped fall enclosing 3 serpentine drawers and 2 sliding wells, on cabriole legs with gilt metal sabots, 19thC, 33½in (85cm) wide.
£7,000–8,000 *P*

Decoration

Many 18thC pieces of furniture have decorative veneers known as banding, used around the edges of drawer fronts, panels and on table tops to complement the principal veneer. There are 3 main types of banding:

- crossbanding
- straight banding
- feather or herringbone banding

Crossbanding

This is laid in short sections at right angles to the veneered surface.

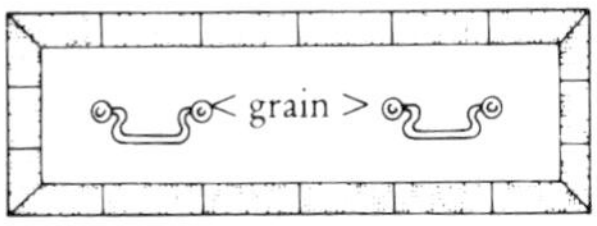

Straight banding

Straight banding is applied in one long strip along, for example, a drawer front and is simpler to apply than crossbanding as it follows the grain of the main veneer.

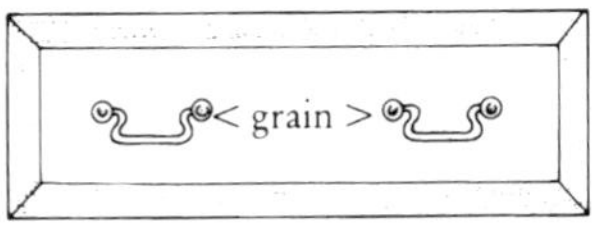

Feather/herringbone banding

This consists of 2 narrow strips of diagonally banded veneers placed together to give a feather-like appearance. It was popular during the early 18thC, especially on bureaux and bureau bookcases, when it was usually placed in widths of approximately ¼in (0.5cm) between the crossbanding and the main veneer.

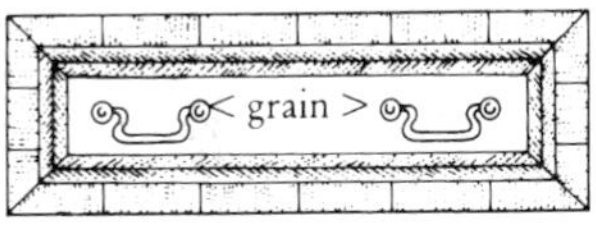

The dimensions, grain and angle of any decorative veneers should correspond on both parts.

An Edwardian Sheraton design mahogany and satinwood crossbanded cylinder bureau, with scrolled three-quarter gallery over 3 drawers, a tambour shutter enclosing fitted interior above 2 further drawers, on square tapered legs and spade feet, 36in (91.5cm) wide.
£2,500–3,000 *EH*

Cabinets

A walnut-veneered cabinet-on-chest, with feather banding throughout, the 2 crossbanded doors enclosing a cupboard and small drawers, the base with 4 graduated long drawers, on bracket feet, some alteration and restoration, early 18thC, 40in (101cm) wide.
£3,500–4,000 *Bea(E)*

A German or Austrian mahogany and giltwood cylindrical cabinet, with marble top and small glazed door to front, on lion's paw feet, c1810, 19in (48cm) diam.
£3,000–3,500 *S(Z)*

l. A mahogany cylindrical pedestal cabinet, with marble top, door to front, c1850, 21in (53.5cm) diam.
£600–700 *GBr*

r. A late Victorian oak pedestal cupboard, with frieze drawer and single cupboard door, 17in (43cm) wide.
£180–200 *TAC*

A Transitional style oval parquetry cabinet, the marble top with pierced gilt-metal gallery above a cupboard door faced as 3 drawers above 3 further drawers, on cabriole legs, c1890, 24in (61cm) wide.
£1,000–1,200 *Bon*

Bedside Cabinets

A George III mahogany night table, in Gillows style, the galleried top above a recess flanked by moulded downswept arm facings, the base and panelled sides with a hinged top, on moulded and chamfered square legs, c1780, 23½in (60cm) wide.
£2,800–3,200 *S*

A George III mahogany pot cupboard, on square tapering legs, c1800, 14in (35.5cm) square.
£720–800 *ANT*

A George III satinwood night cupboard, with marble top within broad rosewood crossbanding, the front enclosed by 2 panel doors, on turned feet, distressed, 26in (66cm) wide.
£550–600 *L*

A mahogany bedside cabinet, c1860, 16in (40.5cm) wide.
£225–275 *GBr*

r. An Edwardian Sheraton revival satinwood bowfronted bedside cabinet, quarter-veneered with ebony stringing, the ledged back with moulded crest and inlaid with ribbon-tied swags, the frieze drawer with brass drop handle and cupboard door with batwing patera, on square tapering supports, 15½in (39.5cm) wide.
£500–550 *AH*

l. An Edwardian inlaid mahogany pot cupboard, with serpentine gallery back, above veneered top and one short drawer above bowfronted boxwood strung and oval satinwood crossbanded panelled door, with boxwood and ebony line inlay, 18in (45.5cm) wide.
£620–680 *Mit*

Bureau Cabinets

A mahogany bureau cabinet, the shaped bevelled mirrored doors enclosing shelves and 2 candle slides below, the fall enclosing a fitted interior of drawers and pigeonholes, above an arrangement of 6 drawers, on ogee-moulded bracket feet, part 18thC, 45½in (115.5cm) wide.
£3,500–4,200 *Bon*

Cross Reference
Colour Review

A George I walnut bureau cabinet, with herringbone banding, the upper part with 2 doors with chamfered cross-banding, enclosing shelves, small drawers and pigeonholes, and with 2 candleslides below, the base with a conforming interior above an arrangement of 2 short and 3 long drawers, with a crossgrain moulding, later bracket feet, and engraved brass handles, the door panels probably replacing mirror plates, 43in (109cm) wide.
£9,000–10,000 *DN*

A Dutch burr-walnut and marquetry bureau cabinet, with boxwood and ebony chequer bands and marquetry flowers, urns, figures, birds and putti, the upper part with a double dome pediment above 2 arched panelled doors enclosing shelves and 3 drawers, the base with a stepped interior and a well, above 3 short and 2 long breakfront drawers, on bracket feet, 18thC, 46in (117cm) wide.
£7,000–8,500 *DN*

A George II mahogany bureau cabinet, the shaped mirrored doors enclosing a central cupboard flanked by an arrangement of drawers and pigeonholes beneath shelves, the fall enclosing a central cupboard with secret drawers, flanked by fluted pilasters and an arrangement of drawers and pigeonholes, above 4 long graduated drawers, on later bracket feet, restored, 42in (107cm) wide.
£3,500–4,200 *Bon(N)*

A Biedermeier mahogany cylinder bureau cabinet, with arched pediment enclosed by a panel door with drawer below flanked by bowed enclosed cupboards, the fall enclosing fitted interior, over 3 long drawers, on bracket feet, 1830s, 43½in (111cm) wide.
£4,500–5,500 *P*

FURTHER READING
Miller's Late Georgian to Edwardian Furniture Buyer's Guide,
Miller's Publications, 1998

An early Victorian mahogany cylinder bureau bookcase, the upper part with 3 adjustable shelves, enclosed by a pair of glazed, scroll and floral moulded panel doors, the lower part with cylinder revealing a sliding writing surface and fitted interior, above a pair of panelled doors, flanked by scrolled pilasters, on a plinth base, 43½in (110.5cm) wide.
£3,500–4,000 *P(F)*

Corner Cabinets

A walnut-veneered hanging corner cupboard, with broken arched pediment, canted corners and central door with later mahogany fielded panel, early 18thC, 29½in (75cm) wide.
£900–1,100 *Bea(E)*

A George III mahogany standing corner cupboard, the 2 pairs of fielded panelled cupboard doors enclosing a painted interior with shaped shelves, flanked by panelled canted corners, on ogee bracket feet, c1780, 41in (104cm) wide.
£3,200–3,800 *Bon*

r. A Sheraton revival mahogany and marquetry standing corner cupboard, crossbanded in satinwood and decorated with urns, ribbons, leaves, birds and garrya, the upper part with a pierced fret and dentil scroll pediment, above 2 glazed astragal doors enclosing shaped shelves, the base with a drawer and 2 false drawers above 2 panelled doors, on bracket feet, c1910, 40in (101.5cm) wide.
£4,800–5,300 *DN*

A garrya is a catkin-bearing evergreen shrub.

A George III mahogany bowfronted corner cupboard, with boxwood stringing to the cornice, c1800, 29in (73.5cm) wide.
£1,200–1,400 *ANT*

A pair of Biedermeir fruitwood corner cabinets, each with moulded cornice above a single door with 2 glass panels enclosing interior shelves, raised on bracket feet, 19thC, 34in (86.5cm) wide.
£3,500–4,200 *S(Cg)*

A George III mahogany corner cupboard, with moulded and dentil breakfront cornice, 2 arched panelled doors enclosing shaped shelving and spice drawers, canted corners, and ogee bracket feet, 38½in (98cm) wide.
£1,500–1,800 *AH*

A late George III mahogany bowfronted corner cupboard, with original hinges and finish to the interior, lock replaced, c1800, 36in (91.5cm) wide.
£2,000–2,400 *BERA*

A mahogany corner cupboard, c1920, 13½in (34.5cm) high.
£35–40 *WEE*

Display Cabinets

A Dutch walnut and floral marquetry vitrine, the glazed astragal panel doors between chamfered ends, the lower part with 2 long drawers, on scroll legs ending in later bun feet, c1800, 55in (139.5cm) wide.
£2,700–3,200 *P(EA)*

A late Victorian mahogany cross and chequer-banded display cabinet, the oval glazed top with re-entrant corners enclosing bowed glazed end panels, hinged glazed door, on tapered legs and brass casters, 27in (69cm) wide.
£1,100–1,200 *HOLL*

A late Victorian satinwood and marquetry serpentine display cabinet, in 2 parts, in Sheraton style, the swan neck and ebonised pediment above a pair of glazed doors and sides enclosing 2 shelves, the lower section with a moulded top above a paterae, swag and anthemion inlaid frieze and a pair of glazed doors enclosing a shelf flanked by ribbon-tied marquetry garlands, on short cabriole legs, 51in (129.5cm) wide.
£7,000–8,000 *P*

l. A pair of Louis XVI style satinwood and inlaid display cabinets, each with rectangular top and canted corners, the rosewood frieze with harewood inlay, above a glazed full length door enclosing lined shelves between canted angles and glazed side panels, raised on square tapering legs, c1900, 29in (73.5cm) wide.
£2,500–3,000 *Hal*

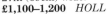

r. A mahogany and glazed display cabinet, enclosed by one serpentine glazed and panelled door flanked by conforming panels, on square tapering legs, late 19thC, 55in (139.5cm) wide.
£1,500–1,800 *DN*

l. A late Victorian inlaid satinwood display cabinet-on-stand, with broken swan neck pediment above a frieze inlaid with intertwined ribbon and flowerheads, the astragal glazed door inlaid with floral swags and urns, the stand inlaid with laurel swags and paterae, on outswept square tapered legs, tied by a shaped platform stretcher inlaid with an oval patera and foliate scroll, c1900, 29½in (75cm) wide.
£4,200–4,700 *Bon*

An 18thC style green painted and silvered display cabinet, decorated with acanthus and stringing, on shaped bracket feet, early 20thC, 48in (122cm) wide.
£1,500–1,800 *S(S)*

A Chippendale style serpentine-front mahogany display cabinet, with moulded cornice, scroll-carved blind frieze, the glazed upper cabinet enclosed by a single door, the base with gadrooned rim and blind fret decoration, with 3 central drawers and 2 side cabinets on square tapering legs and moulded feet, early 20thC, 55in (139.5cm) wide.
£3,500–4,000 *JM*

An Edwardian painted satinwood display cabinet, the central glazed doors with Gothic tracery glazing bars flanked by serpentine glazed doors, enclosing fabric-covered shelves, the lower part with a pair of central doors, flanked by serpentine doors decorated with grapes and putti after Angelica Kauffman, raised on square tapered legs and spade feet, Waring & Gillow, Oxford St, London, 57in (145cm) wide.
£11,000–12,000 *PF*

This piece is of the finest quality and in excellent original condition. It was made of satinwood, a particularly desirable wood, rather than mahogany as is usual for Edwardian display cabinets.

An Edwardian inlaid mahogany display cabinet, with satinwood stringing, on square tapering legs and spade feet, with undertray, 36in (91.5cm) wide.
£1,500–1,800 *RBB*

An Edwardian mahogany display cabinet, with raised back and bowfronted central panel door enclosing lined shelves, with astragal panels on either side centred by painted floral motifs, garlands and ribbons below, raised on square tapering legs with spade feet, 48in (122cm) wide.
£900–1,000 *AG*

An Edwardian satinwood display cabinet, with string inlay and painted with foliage and flowers, panelled fascia with 2 brass trimmed central doors, enclosing interior shelf, on square tapering legs with spade feet, 48in (122cm) wide.
£2,000–2,500 *AH*

l. An Edwardian satinwood, rosewood-banded and boxwood and ebony line-inlaid display cabinet, 48in (122cm) wide.
£2,200–2,500 *E*

r. An Edwardian mahogany inlaid display cabinet, the 2 central astragal glazed doors with ribbon tied decoration and rectangular urn tablets, flanked by a pair of bowed glazed doors, on tapered square legs ending in spade feet, c1910, 75in (190.5cm) wide.
£2,700–3,000 *S(S)*

Music Cabinets

A Victorian burr walnut and tulipwood-banded music cabinet, with gilt-metal mounts, the fall-front with fitted interior, by Holland & Sons, London, c1860, 19½in (50cm) wide.
£3,300–3,700 *S(S)*

A Victorian inlaid burr walnut music cabinet, the upper tier with a pierced gilt-metal gallery and turned column supports, above a pair of glazed cupboard doors, on turned bun feet, c1865, 26½in (67.5cm) wide.
£1,000–1,200 *Bon*

A Victorian burr walnut-veneered music cabinet, with inlay and burr yew banding, the mirror back with a shelf, 27in (68.5cm) wide.
£1,100–1,200 *WW*

A Victorian figured walnut music cabinet, with amboyna bandings and brass gallery, 24½in (63cm) wide.
£650–700 *P(G)*

A late Victorian inlaid mahogany music cabinet, with glazed cupboard above 2 drawers and a further cupboard, c1890, 23in (58cm) wide.
£1,500–1,700 *GBr*

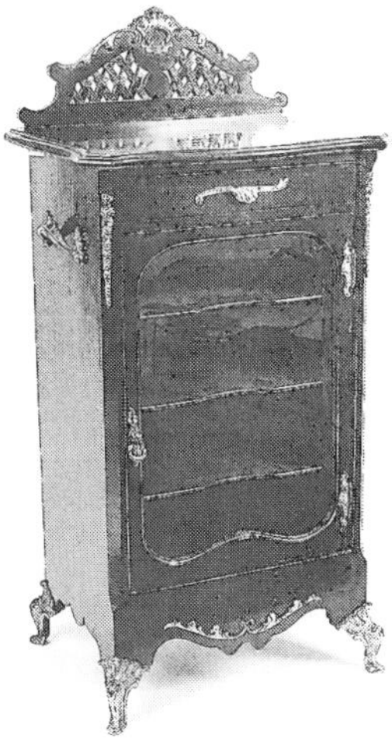

An Edwardian stained mahogany music cabinet, with rococo style brass mounts, the glazed door enclosing shelves, on scrolling feet, stamped 'S. Hall', 24in (61cm) wide.
£550–600 *P(Sc)*

Secretaire Cabinets

A George III mahogany secretaire cabinet-on-stand, the warped fall front with twin lozenge motifs, the satinwood-veneered interior with small drawers, pigeonholes, a door and concealed compartments and with a green baize-lined writing surface, over a drawer with conforming lozenge inlay, the tapered square legs ending in brass cappings and casters, 21in (53cm) wide.
£2,000–2,200 *S(S)*

An Italian walnut, rosewood and marquetry secretaire cabinet, with a long drawer above a fall front and inlaid panel depicting a mythological scene, the interior of the fall inlaid with an oval panel depicting a rural scene, the interior with pigeonholes, shelves and 8 small inlaid drawers and enclosing a shelf, on tapered square legs, faults and restored, c1800, 39½in (100cm) wide.
£5,750–6,250 *S(S)*

A French Empire mahogany *secrétaire à abattant*, the grey marble top above a frieze drawer, the fall front revealing a fitted interior, 3 long drawers below and with shaped plinth base, splits to sides, c1810, 37½in (95cm) wide.
£1,200–1,500 *S(S)*

A Scandinavian Biedermeier inlaid satin birch secretaire cabinet, with 3 cupboard doors flanked by turned columns above fall enclosing an arrangement of drawers and pigeonholes centred by a mirrored recess, above 2 long drawers on square section tapered feet, early 19thC, 44½in (113cm) wide.
£4,000–4,500 *Bon*

Biedermeier

Biedermeier furniture was made principally in the 1820s and '30s in Austria, Germany and parts of Scandinavia and named after a fictional character who symbolised the German bourgeoisie of the early 19thC. Designed for a relatively mass market, it was constructed mainly of blond woods such as ash, maple, cherry and other fruitwoods. In Austria and Germany mahogany was also used, and these designs tended to be more sophisticated and elaborate, whereas Scandinavian forms were simple and relatively austere. Ornamentation was mainly restricted to columns and palmettes, and these were often applied in ebony to contrast with the pale colour of the carcass.

A German Biedermeier cherrywood and ebonised secretaire cabinet, the upper part with a door flanked by ebonised stiles, above a frieze drawer and a hinged flap enclosing a fitted interior, above 2 drawers and one further drawer with an arched shaped panel, on turned feet, restored, 39in (99cm) wide.
£3,000–3,500 *S(Am)*

A George IV mahogany free-standing secretaire, the crossbanded top with a three-quarter gallery above a calamander banded frieze and a double-fronted fall-front drawer with brass ring handles, the interior with a leather inset, sliding trays, pigeonholes and small drawers, above 2 panelled doors enclosing 3 trays, on splayed bracket feet, the conforming back with false drawers and doors, 42½in (108cm) wide.
£1,400–1,600 *DN*

A south German cherrywood, ebonised and giltwood secretaire, with feather banded fall-front revealing drawers and pigeonholes, kneehole with 3 cupboards and drawer above, flanked by columns surmounted by small drawers and sphinxes, c1815, 60in (152cm) wide.
£3,500–4,200 *S(Z)*

A French parquetry and gilt-bronze *secrétaire à abattant*, with inset marble top, the parquetry flap above 3 similar drawers flanked by fluted, gilt-bronze mounted columns, on toupie feet, c1910, 31in (79cm) wide.
£5,000–5,500 *S*

l. A kingwood and rosewood parquetry secretaire *semanier*, in Louis XV/XVI Transitional style, applied with gilt-metal mounts, the serpentine marble top above 3 simulated drawers enclosing a maple-lined interior of a shelf and 2 short drawers, 4 long drawers below, on outswept feet with sabots, marble top damaged, late 19thC, 26½in (68cm) wide.
£1,500–1,800 *P*

Side Cabinets

A fruitwood marquetry and parquetry side cabinet, the 2 doors inlaid with ornamental vases and birds, on slightly splayed legs, c1775, 42½in (108cm) wide.
£5,750–6,250 *S(Z)*

A George IV faded rosewood-veneered chiffonier, the panelled raised back with a shelf, the front frieze with florets, flanked by open scrolls, 44in (112cm) wide.
£2,600–3,000 *WW*

A Regency mahogany side cabinet, the crossbanded top with brass stringing, a pair of latticed brass grille doors between spiral reeded pilasters, on brass paw feet, 52in (132cm) wide.
£2,000–2,200 *Oli*

A Regency mahogany bowfronted side cabinet, with a frieze drawer over a pair of panel doors, on turned tapered feet, 37in (94cm) wide.
£2,000–2,200 *P*

An early Victorian walnut and marquetry inlaid breakfront credenza, with gilt-metal mounts, central cupboard door flanked on either side by a glazed door, 68in (172.5cm) wide.
£1,200–1,500 *LF*

A Regency rosewood chiffonier, the moulded frieze above a brass grille door enclosing 2 rosewood-faced shelves between reeded split pillars with acanthus and lotus-carved bases, on lobed bun feet, damaged, 32in (81.5cm) wide.
£1,500–1,800 *EH*

A Victorian walnut and inlaid pier cabinet, the shaped panel door with floral marquetry on an ebonised ground, the interior with adjustable shelves, the terminals with gilt-metal mounts, on a plinth base, 39in (99cm) wide.
£2,000–2,200 *S(S)*

A Victorian burr walnut pier cabinet, the frieze inset with floral painted porcelain plaques within gilt-metal guilloche and a glazed cupboard door flanked by fluted pilasters, on a plinth base with turned feet, c1860, 34in (87cm) wide.
£2,400–2,800 *Bon*

A French walnut credenza, carved with scenes from the life of Alexander The Great, c1850, 60in (152.5cm) wide.
£7,500–8,000 *HAC*

An American carved mahogany cabinet, the cupboard door inset with an oval mirror, flanked by mirrored back with 4 shaped shelves, over conforming case with 3 short drawers and cupboard with shaped mirrored inset, flanked by 2 cupboard doors with floral moulding raised on carved scroll feet, c1850, 57in (145cm) wide.
£1,000–1,200 *SLN*

A mid-Victorian mahogany chiffonier, the shaped and scrolled-edged back with carved leaf and flower surmount and shaped display shelf on wrythen supports, serpentine front with frieze drawer, 2 arched panelled doors and conforming plinth, 50in (127cm) wide.
£750–850 *AH*

Line Inlay

This is the letting in of narrow lines of one or more woods, usually at the edge of a surface or slightly inset. It is also known as stringing. Line inlay was especially popular from the late 18thC onwards.

r. A French ebonised and ormolu-mounted side cabinet, decorated with painted panels of flowers and scrolls, c1860, 34in (86.5cm) wide.
£750–850 *MAT*

A Victorian marquetry and ebony single door cabinet, with ebony and ivory mouldings and marble top, c1860, 33in (84cm) wide.
£2,200–2,400 *SPa*

A Victorian ebonised and gilt-metal-mounted credenza, the brass-strung top above a central door inset with Sèvres style porcelain plaques, flanked by a pair of bowfronted glazed doors and Corinthian capped fluted columns, raised on toupie feet, 67in (171cm) wide.
£1,200–1,500 *CGC*

A Victorian walnut breakfront credenza, decorated with inlaid stringing and honeysuckle motifs, with applied gilt-metal bands and foliate scrolls, the central panel door flanked by a pair of convex glazed doors enclosing lined shelves, raised on a plinth base, 59in (150cm) wide.
£2,250–2,500 *AG*

A Victorian carved rosewood low breakfront side cabinet, the top with a projecting foliate edge, the central cupboard fitted with 2 short drawers and shelf enclosed by glazed panel doors in carved foliate scroll and rocaille cartouche surround, the cupboards to either side enclosed by a domed panel door decorated with scrolling foliage and banding, 76in (193cm) wide.
£2,200–2,500 *P(E)*

A French cabinet, with marble top, the single door painted with a scene depicting a courting couple, the concave sides painted with landscape panels, the whole with ormolu mounts, on short fluted ormolu-mounted feet, late 19thC, 39in (99cm) wide.
£1,400–1,600 *WL*

A French ebonised parquetry side cabinet, the front all-over inlaid with central flowerhead-like motifs and raised oval cushion in ormolu surround, the canted front corners with ormolu female figure mounts, original marble top missing, late 19thC, 33in (84cm) wide.
£750–900 *DA*

A Victorian breakfront walnut side cabinet, with floral inlay, the central panel door flanked by 2 mirrored doors, all enclosing 2 shelves, with later metal mounts, on shaped plinth base, 70in (178cm) wide.
£2,000–2,200 *Bri*

A French figured-walnut credenza, the frieze inlaid with stylised foliage motifs and ormolu style gilt rope work, the bowed glass canted cabinets revealing 2 cloth covered shelves, the slight breakfront with a central panelled oblong cupboard with oval Sèvres design porcelain plaque, c1870, 54in (137cm) wide.
£1,750–2,000 *HCC*

A Continental ebonised and ivory-inlaid pedestal side cabinet, the lower centre section with turned ivory balustrade over 2 glazed doors, flanked on either side by a tall cupboard with fielded parquetry panels inlaid with ivory in the Mannerist style, fluted pilasters, moulded base and turned feet, 19thC, 94in (239cm) wide.
£1,400–1,600 *AH*

r. A French breakfront side cabinet, the marble top with a pierced gilt-brass gallery above a frieze, inlaid trellis panels with brass mounts and a drawer over a shelf enclosed by a glazed door and bowed side panels, brass stop-fluted pilasters, a chased gadroon and leaf moulding to the plinth, on square tapered legs, c1900, 38in (96.5cm) wide.
£2,500–2,750 *WW*

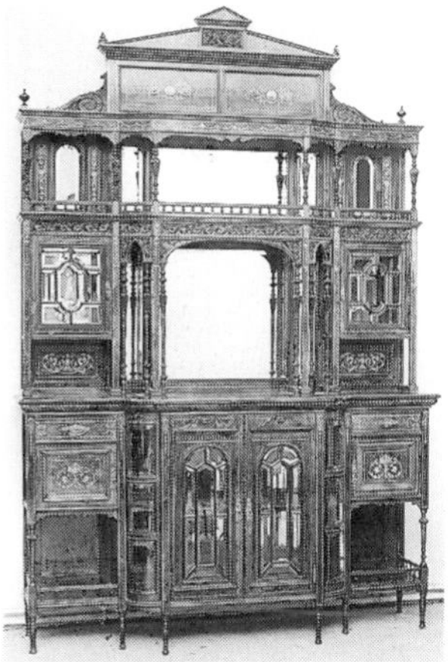

A marquetry inlaid rosewood side cabinet, the superstructure with architectural pediment above a canopied galleried shelf, a pair of bevel-glazed cabinets and an arrangement of 4 bevelled mirror plates, the lower part with a pair of central bevel glazed doors, flanked by a pair of drawers above cupboard doors with open galleried shelves beneath, raised on turned legs, late 19thC, 71in (180.5cm) wide.
£4,700–5,200 *PF*

An Edwardian satinwood and painted dwarf cabinet, painted in the Sheraton manner with ovals of classical females in landscapes within leaf and floral scrolls, the single bowed door inlaid with rosewood bandings, on square tapered and splayed legs, 36in (91.5cm) wide.
£1,850–2,000 *CAG*

Cabinets-on-Stands

A Flemish rosewood, ebony and *pietra paesina* cabinet-on-stand, the upper part with a moulded cornice, fitted with 2 long and 6 short drawers about a central cupboard fitted with 6 drawers with foliate scroll inlay, the base containing a drawer, on column legs united by an undertier, 17thC, later parts, 31in (78.5cm) wide.
£2,500–3,000 *P*

An Anglo-Indian padouk cabinet-on-stand, the sides carved with concentric bands of flowerheads and with carrying handles, the glazed doors enclosing an arrangement of sandalwood drawers carved with scrolls and foliage with silvered ring handles, on a stand with C-scroll brackets, ebonised borders and stepped block feet, early 19thC, 35in (89cm) wide.
£1,250–1,500 *DN*

Insurance Values

Always insure your valuable antiques for what it would cost to replace with a similar item, regardless of the original price paid. Both dealers and auctioneers will provide a valuation service for a fee.

A Flemish ebony and tortoiseshell veneered cabinet-on-stand, the hinged top revealing 3 mirrors and a lined well, the doors with mirrors to the reverse, the interior with tortoiseshell-veneered small drawers surrounding a cupboard with a classical maiden mount, the architectural interior with mirror panels, pilasters and chequered floor, shallow apron drawer below, late 17thC, later stand, 26in (66cm) wide.
£2,700–3,000 *S(S)*

A Colonial mahogany specimen cabinet-on-stand, the upper section with 2 cupboard doors opening to reveal multiple drawers, the lower section with 3 dummy drawers, on cabriole legs, American, 18thC, 23in (59cm) wide.
£1,700–2,000 *SLN*

A Flemish ebonised and tortoiseshell cabinet-on-stand, the moulded hinged top above a pair of doors revealing a tortoiseshell-veneered interior of small drawers surrounding a sliding architectural recess with mirror sides and parquetry floor, c1700, stand later, 29in (74cm) wide.
£3,200–3,500 *S(S)*

An Italian rosewood, ebonised and ivory inlaid cabinet-on-stand, the frieze inlaid with various Classical figures above a pair of panelled cupboard doors inlaid with scenes of soldiers on prancing horses within an arched platform, flanked by ebonised turned columns inlaid and carved with grotesque masks, the base with a conforming single frieze drawer on columnar supports tied by a shelf stretcher, on bun feet, c1860, 42in (107cm) wide.
£3,000–3,500 *Bon*

l. A Chinese export black lacquer and gilt cabinet-on-stand, decorated with Oriental landscapes, buildings and figures, the panelled doors enclosing an arrangement of pigeonholes, drawers and a pair of cupboard doors, the front with a hinged section, with brass carrying handles, the divided top revealing a divided interior with small trays and covers, a writing drawer below, on cabriole legs with hairy paw-and-ball feet, c1840, 26in (66cm) wide.
£1,700–2,000 *S(S)*

Table Cabinets

A William III walnut and seaweed marquetry spice cupboard, the top and door centred by a lobed arabesque medallion within a stylised berried leaf border, the interior revealing an arrangement of 8 drawers further inlaid with panels of marquetry, on later bun feet, inlaid throughout with stringing, c1700, 14½in (37cm) wide.
£2,700–3,000 *S*

An Italian bone-inlaid walnut table cabinet, the arched top with an ebonised moulded cornice above an arched central cupboard door, flanked by an arrangement of 15 drawers, all inlaid in bone and green stained bone with figures, cherubs and animals, c1700, 25½in (65cm) wide.
£4,600–5,000 *Bon(M)*

A Venetian part-silvered and *lacca povera* table cabinet, the fall-front decorated with figures on horseback within a carved rococo cartouche, the sides similarly decorated with equestrian figures within shell-carved surrounds, the interior revealing 10 various drawers with gilt mouldings, bone handle pulls and some with mirrored roundels, the central cabinet with 3 drawers, 18thC, 31in (78.5cm) wide.
£4,600–5,000 *P*

A George III mahogany table cabinet, crossbanded in rosewood, on bracket feet, early 19thC, 19in (48.5cm) wide.
£900–1,000 *ANT*

l. A north German mahogany and gilt-metal-mounted cylinder table writing cabinet, fitted with a frieze drawer, the fall enclosing an architectural mirrored compartment with parquetry floor with marble columns and penwork ornament, the slide with hinged compartment and drawers, c1800, 25in (63.5cm) wide.
£750–850 *P*

A coromandel brass-bound smoker's cabinet, with carrying handles, c1890, 13in (33cm) wide.
£600–700 *CORO*

A Victorian burr walnut letter cabinet, with brass handle and an ivory inset plaque inscribed 'Bills and Letters', above 2 doors enclosing 6 pigeonholes with conforming ivory plaques, 12in (32cm) wide.
£650–750 *DN*

l. A table top display cabinet, veneered in tulipwood and with brass mounts and feather banding, with a coffered top and one glazed fall-front door, shaped sides with leaf chased scroll mounts, 19thC, 31in (79cm) wide.
£1,700–2,000 *DN*

Canterburies

A George III mahogany canterbury, with cut-out centre handle, one long drawer to the base, on turned supports with brass casters, 20in (51cm) wide.
£1,350–1,500 *AG*

Canterburies

In 1803 the furniture designer, Thomas Sheraton, coined the name 'canterbury' to describe these popular music stands, because the first person to order one from him was the Archbishop of Canterbury. Canterburies were originally intended to hold books or sheet music, but in modern life they make useful magazine racks.

A William IV rosewood canterbury, the X-shaped divisions with laurel wreath motifs, the apron drawer above turned feet, on brass cappings and casters, c1830, 20in (51cm) wide.
£1,700–2,000 *S(S)*

A French rosewood canterbury, on carved cabriole legs, with original wooden casters, c1860, 17in (43cm) wide.
£1,400–1,600 *CHA*

A George III mahogany canterbury, with latticework sides above a drawer, on turned and tapered legs with brass casters, 24in (61cm) wide.
£3,500–4,000 *S*

A George IV mahogany canterbury, with ring-turned supports and ball finials above a drawer, on turned legs and brass casters, 16in (40cm) wide.
£2,000–2,400 *S*

A Victorian burr walnut canterbury, initialled 'V.R.', on turned feet with porcelain casters, 22in (56cm) wide.
£1,400–1,600 *LEW*

A Victorian burr walnut canterbury, with spindle-turned supports, on turned feet with ceramic casters, 22½in (57cm) wide.
£1,800–2,000 *S(S)*

A Regency mahogany four-division canterbury, with slatted sides, containing a drawer, on ring-turned tapering legs, brass cappings and casters, 20in (51cm) wide.
£2,000–2,200 *P*

A Victorian walnut music canterbury, with figured veneered pierced fretwork gallery, on scroll end supports with spiral-twist vertical stretchers, the base with divisions on turned supports, pierced fretwork panels, spiral-twist corner supports, a front swept frieze drawer above turned feet on casters, 22in (56cm) wide.
£1,350–1,500 *WW*

A Victorian burr walnut canterbury/whatnot, the inlaid top on turned supports above the canterbury with drawer under, terminating in brass cup casters, 24in (60cm) wide.
£1,100–1,200 *Bri*

Open Armchairs

A George II mahogany armchair, upholstered in red damask, with mahogany scrolling arms and reeded terminals, S-scroll reeded supports, the front cabriole legs carved at the knees with pendant harebells and foliage, terminating in claw-and-ball feet, on brass angled casters.
£3,200–3,500 *B*

A George III mahogany open armchair, with interlaced splat back with scroll carving, shaped arms with scroll terminals, stuffed seat, on square moulded tapering legs with block feet and brass casters.
£2,300–2,500 *E*

MILLER'S COMPARES . . .

I A giltwood open armchair, the moulded frame with a floral cresting and leaf-capped arm terminals, upholstered in close-nailed blue and ivory striped damask, on turned legs, regilded and restored, late 18thC.
£900–1,000 *P*

II A late George III giltwood open armchair, with moulded and fluted frame, upholstered in close-nailed pale green and ivory damask, the outswept arms with leaf-capped terminals and downswept reeded supports, on turned fluted legs and later blocks.
£1,500–1,800 *P*

When these 2 chairs were sold *item I* **proved less popular because it had been regilded and restored. In addition,** *item II* **has a number of features which enhance its appeal, such as the fluting on the seat rail. It is generally of a more pleasing shape, with reeded outswept arms, and the pale coloured upholstery makes it easier to sell. If the bright colours of** *item I* **do not fit in with an existing colour scheme, the purchaser will have the added expense of reupholstering the chair.** *P*

A Federal mahogany open armchair, the serpentine crest flanked by shaped arms on moulded downswept supports centering an upholstered bowed seat, on square tapering moulded legs joined by stretchers, some repairs, American, c1790.
£2,800–3,200 *S(NY)*

l. A Regency mahogany elbow chair, in Thomas Hope style, with shaped scrolling bar-back decorated with a pair of lion's masks, on reeded uprights united by a similarly shaped splat, the part reeded arm supports with padded elbow rests, stuff-over seat, raised on reeded tapering front legs terminating in claw feet.
£2,000–2,200 *P(E)*

An American rosewood armchair, with foliate carved and arched crest rail, oval padded back, moulded arms and upholstered seat, the serpentine seat rail, centered with foliate carving on moulded cabriole legs, c1850.
£1,500–1,800 *SLN*

Cross Reference
Colour Review

Legs & Feet Styles

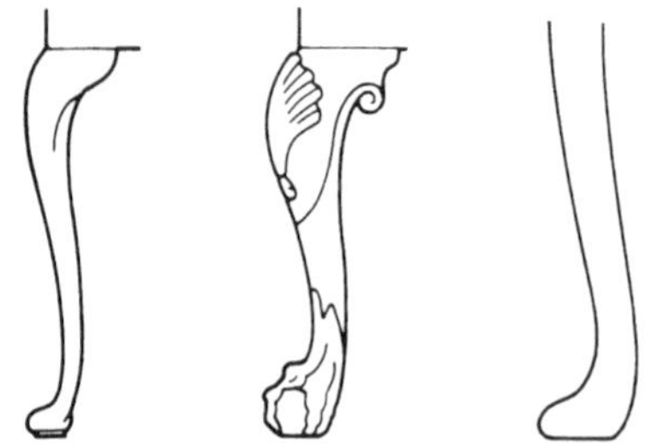

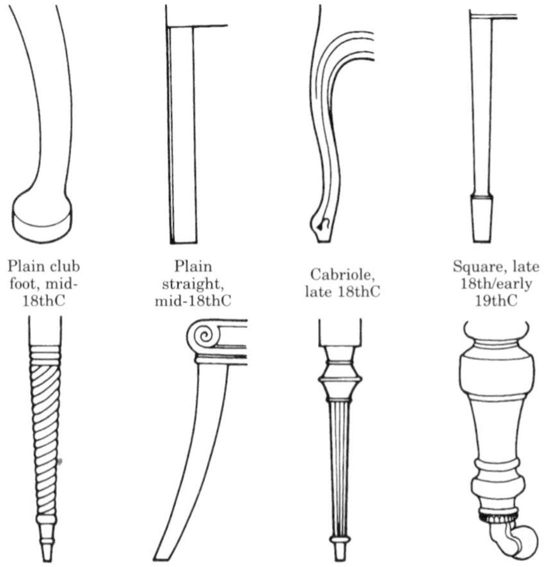

The variety of legs and feet found on chairs can help to date them, although many styles were also revived and produced in later periods.

Having casters that are original to a piece is always desirable, especially if they are attached to decoratively carved feet.

A Regency mahogany carver chair, with rope-twist back and downswept arms and turned legs.
£900–1,000 *ANT*

A pair of early Victorian walnut upholstered armchairs, with shaped and carved backs, on cabriole legs with casters, in need of restoration, c1860.
£4,500–5,000 *BERA*

A Victorian walnut armchair, with upholstered button back and overstuffed seat, on carved cabriole legs.
£550–650 *RTo*

A mid-Victorian mahogany gentleman's armchair, with Rexine upholstery, the scroll-over back between moulded and carved stiles, with padded arms, on baluster-turned supports, above moulded and bowfronted seat rail, on turned and knopped front legs with rosette enriched corner blocks and casters.
£320–380 *P(Sc)*

A Victorian walnut X-frame ladder-back armchair, the back with waved horizontal bars.
£280–320 *L*

A Victorian walnut open armchair, with carved scrolling serpentine back above the padded arms and circular shaped seat covered in tapestry, on scrolling legs and ceramic casters.
£1,100–1,200 *AG*

A pair of Victorian mahogany library armchairs, in early 19thC style, with rail backs, open reeded arms and hide upholstered seats, on turned and reeded legs, bearing original paper label 'Marsh, Jones, Cribb & Co of Leeds', Workman's name 'Connell' and 'J. Davis' on the 2 chairs, indicating that they were made by different craftsmen, faults, c1880.
£4,000–4,500 *S(S)*

A Victorian walnut armchair, with moulded frame and raised on turned supports.
£500–550 *Ber*

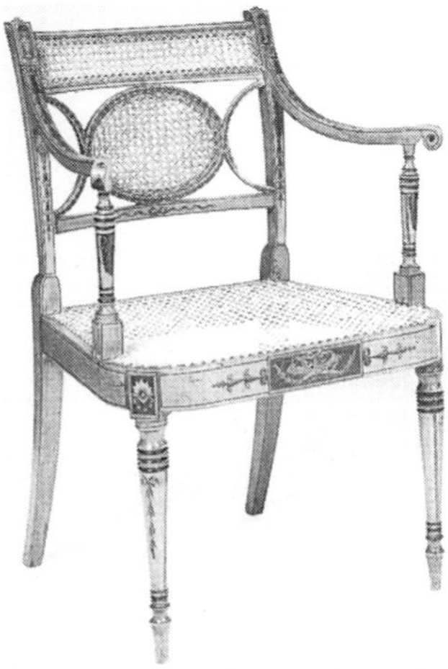

A pair of Edwardian satinwood and painted elbow chairs, decorated with husk, urn and leaf ornament, cane top-rail and similar cane oval splat and seat, the squab cushion between outswept scrolling arm supports, on turned tapered legs.
£2,500–2,750 *P(G)*

A Hepplewhite style mahogany armchair, with shield-back, carved with swags and husks, c1880.
£1,250–1,500 *ANT*

A pair of Continental mahogany open armchairs, with high backs and seats covered in striped tapestry, the scrolling reeded arms decorated with carved acanthus leaves, raised on scrolling legs and understretchers, 19thC.
£1,100–1,200 *AG*

An Edwardian Sheraton style rosewood elbow chair, with inlaid floral arabesques, griffins and scrolls, upholstered in floral needlework, on square tapering legs and brown china casters.
£320–350 *AP*

A pair of Regency style mahogany armchairs, 19thC.
£750–850 *GAK*

A pair of giltwood open armchairs with scrolling backs, padded arms and seats, the arms supported by carved giltwood owls, the frieze decorated with applied paterae, on moulded sabre legs, 19thC.
£16,000–18,000 *AG*

Catalogued as French, and estimated at £1,000–1,500, these chairs attracted considerable interest before the sale. Requests for a small area to be viewed underneath the upholstery where there was no gilding alerted the auctioneers to the fact that they could be earlier than stated in the catalogue. It was also thought that they were probably English, perhaps in the manner of Thomas Hope. Most of the bidders dropped out at around £8,000, but a New York dealer had to bid double that amount to secure them.

An Edwardian walnut chair, with woven rush seat, on square supports.
£30–35 *CaC*

Upholstered Armchairs

A Charles II walnut upholstered wing chair, with matching stool, c1670.
£3,500–4,000 *WELL*

A Queen Anne walnut wing armchair, upholstered in gold damask, the bowfront seat with matching cushion, on carved cabriole legs and pad feet, restored, c1710.
£3,500–4,000 *S(S)*

A wing armchair, with floral woolwork upholstery, on cabriole legs with pad feet, 18thC.
£5,500–6,000 *P(B)*

This chair was given a conservative estimate at auction because it was thought that the tapestry upholstery was not original. It became clear on the day of the sale that a number of people were not of that opinion. This chair in untouched condition sold for nearly 7 times its top estimate.

A Chippendale mahogany wing chair, with serpentine crest, outscrolled arms, a loose-fitted cushion and over-upholstered seat, on square moulded legs joined by stretchers, c1780.
£4,500–5,000 *S(NY)*

A Regency rosewood and brass-mounted armchair, the padded back and scrolled arms with shaped supports, on turned tapered legs with casters, c1820.
£4,500–5,000 *S*

A George IV upholstered mahogany chair, with turned reeded front legs, c1830.
£1,000–1,100 *ANV*

A William IV armchair, upholstered in buttoned green leather, the moulded show frame carved with leaf scrolls, on turned legs with casters.
£1,100–1,300 *DN*

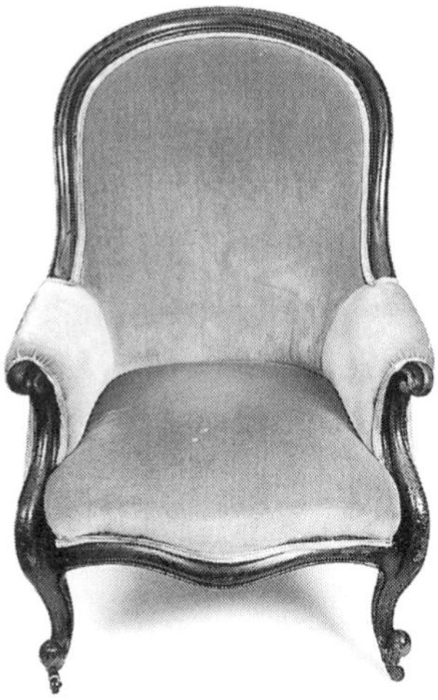

A Victorian mahogany lady's chair, with shaped and moulded back, carved supports ending in cabriole legs and casters, c1870.
£300–350 *CaC*

A mid-Victorian wing back armchair, with turned mahogany legs and original brass and porcelain casters.
£1,000–1,200 *LCA*

A hoop-back upholstered mahogany armchair, on straight moulded legs with plain stretcher, 19thC.
£1,350–1,500 *DaH*

A late Victorian oak-framed wing-back armchair, by Howard & Sons, on leaf-carved cabriole legs with ball-and-claw feet.
£1,300–1,500 *HOLL*

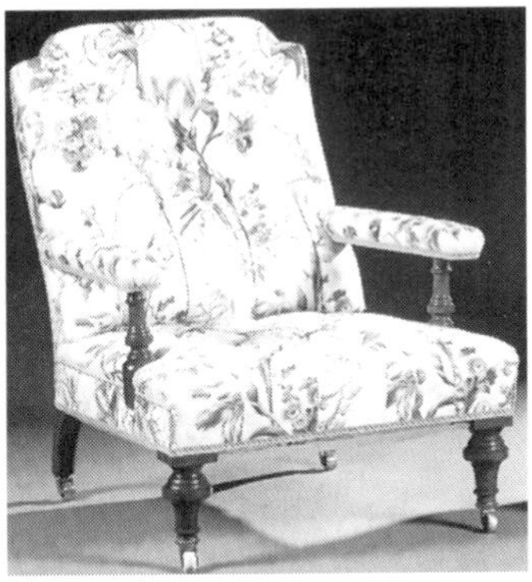

A Victorian walnut easy chair, by James Shoolbred, with shaped button-back and arms with turned supports, on turned tapered legs with brass casters, c1880.
£1,400–1,700 *S*

First established in 1822 as a firm of linen drapers in Tottenham Court Road, Shoolbred later expanded to become one of London's earliest and most important department stores. They specialised from the 1870s onwards in furniture and decorations.

l. A fully-sprung club armchair, with sprung headrest, on original walnut turned front legs with brass and brown porcelain casters, 1870s.
£1,000–1,200 *LCA*

An Edwardian easy chair, on turned legs with casters, c1910.
£700–800 *RPh*

A set of 3 Victorian upholstered easy chairs, after a design by Liberty & Co, the backs, arms and seat upholstered in 'Turkeywork' pattern velvet with deep fringes, on turned legs and casters, late 19thC.
£4,800–5,200 *S*

l. A pair of George II style walnut and upholstered wing armchairs, upholstered in nailed hide, on leaf-carved cabriole legs with turned stretchers, c1910.
£3,700–4,000 *S(S)*

Bergère Chairs

A mahogany and cane-panelled bergère chair, with reeded rectangular back and downswept arms on turned supports, loose back and seat squabs, on ring-turned legs with brass casters, early 19thC.
£1,000–1,200 *Bea(E)*

A George III mahogany library bergère, the moulded square back with leather-covered cushion, the moulded arms with turned and tapered supports, the caned seat on turned tapered legs with brass casters, c1810.
£5,750–6,250 *S*

A mahogany library bergère, with caned back and sides, shaped arms, leather-covered cushion back and seat, on square tapered legs and brass casters, early 19thC.
£3,700–4,000 *S*

A Regency rosewood library bergère, the crest and seat rail incised with a rosette and bell-flowers, the tub-shaped caned back and seat flanked by arms decorated with leaf and paterae, on sabre legs ending in brass casters, c1815.
£2,750–3,250 *S*

A George IV mahogany library bergère, the tub-shaped caned back and sides above a caned seat, on reeded turned legs headed by disc mouldings and on brass casters, c1820.
£4,000–4,500 *S*

A George IV mahogany library bergère, the reeded caned back above a caned seat flanked by caned sides with padded and reeded arms, the reed-moulded seat-rail on ring-turned tapering legs with brass casters, c1820.
£2,800–3,200 *S*

A William IV mahogany bergère, with carved scroll arms, on turned legs ending in casters.
£2,000–2,200 *LRG*

A George IV mahogany library bergère, the shaped and curved buttoned-leather back with cane-filled leather padded arms and turned supports, the cushioned seat on turned and tapered legs headed by turned paterae and on brass casters, c1825.
£4,500–5,000 *S*

A pair of French Louis XVI style bergères, the giltwood frames carved with flowers, ribbons, laurel and flutes, 19thC.
£1,800–2,000 *P(G)*

Children's Chairs

A child's polychrome decorated chair, the back, uprights, arms and legs formed of dentil carved scrolls, the former joined by a cartouche-shaped splat, with leaf side panels and cherub's head legs, on scrolled feet, southern Italy or Austria/Hungary, early 18thC.
£3,500–3,800 *P(Z)*

A Victorian child's ash highchair, with scroll-over back, turned arm rests, legs and stretchers.
£260–300 *WL*

An early Victorian child's walnut prie-dieu chair, on turned legs with casters, c1850.
£320–350 *SSW*

A Louis XV style carved beechwood bergère, the arched rectangular back with downswept arms, serpentine-fronted seat with shaped rails, caned back, seat and arm panels, on cabriole legs, late 19thC.
£350–400 *SLM*

r. A Victorian child's simulated rosewood chair, with bobbin-turned back-rails and uprights, rush seat, on bobbin-turned front legs and stretcher.
£240–280 *TAC*

A Victorian child's beech chair, with caned seat, c1880.
£240–280 *MLL*

A child's oak chair, with drop-in seat, c1920.
£90–110 *AAN*

Corner Chairs

An early George III mahogany corner armchair, with solid fret vase splats and columns, slip-in seat, on cabriole front leg with shell-carved knee, claw-and-ball foot and 3 rounded tapered legs united by X-stretchers.
£1,800–2,000 *P*

A Queen Anne style walnut and maple corner chair, with shaped crest on turned flaring columnar supports, centering pierced vase splats, removable rush seat, raised on a front angular cabriole leg and joined by cross stretchers, New England, 1740–60.
£1,100–1,200 *S(NY)*

For American furniture 'Queen Anne' refers to the style rather than the period.

A George III mahogany corner armchair, with solid fret vase splats and fluted column uprights, slip-in seat, on cabriole front leg with claw-and-ball foot and 3 rounded straight legs.
£650–700 *P*

A George III mahogany corner chair, with drop-in seat, on square tapered legs, late 18thC.
£1,100–1,200 *S(Cg)*

Dining Chairs

A set of 6 Carolean walnut high-back dining chairs, with arched scroll crestings and cane panel backs with column uprights, cane panel seats, on turned baluster legs united by H-stretchers and arched front stretcher, with gouged splayed scroll feet.
£3,500–4,000 *P*

An early George III elm dining chair, the arched top rail with rocaille cresting and paper scroll terminals, the solid wedge splat carved in relief with interlocking 'g' circles, drop-in seat, on square chamfered legs.
£320–350 *L*

A matched set of 8 George III mahogany shield-back dining chairs, including an armchair, with pierced and partially carved splats, the stuffed seats covered in nailed green hide, on square tapered legs, some damage and restoration, c1780.
£3,800–4,200 *S(S)*

A set of 4 George III mahogany dining chairs, each with a bowed cresting rail set on reeded stiles with interlacing centre supports, drop-in seat, on reeded square tapered legs united by stretchers.
£600–700 *Mit*

A pair of George III mahogany dining chairs, with serpentine top-rail, pierced splat back, drop-in seat, on square moulded legs joined by an H-stretcher.
£350–400 *LF*

A set of 5 George III mahogany dining chairs, including an armchair, with carved rail backs, gros point floral tapestry seats, on square tapered legs.
£1,250–1,500 *AP*

A set of 7 George III mahogany dining chairs, including an elbow chair, the backs with shaped top-rails and pierced splats above drop-in seats, on square legs and stretchers, several stamped with maker's name 'I. Ashley' on corner blocks.
£1,350–1,500 *P(B)*

A pair of George III Chippendale style mahogany dining chairs, with pierced slatted backs, drop-in seats, on square legs joined by stretchers.
£700–800 *BERA*

A set of 6 French walnut dining chairs, the shaped backs with shell-carved crests and seat rails, C-scroll upright rails, padded serpentine seats, on cabriole legs with scroll toes and X-stretchers, 18thC.
£700–800 *DN*

l. A set of 7 George III carved mahogany dining chairs, the top rails and splats headed with husk ornament, with slip-in seats, on square moulded chamfered legs.
£2,500–3,000 *P(EA)*

A Sheraton rosewood and satinwood bonheur du jour, with tulipwood crossbanding, c1780, 30½in (77.5cm) wide.
£6,000–7,000 *SPa*

A Regency rosewood and gilt-brass-mounted bonheur du jour, with secretaire drawer, on brass ball feet, c1815, 30in (77cm) wide.
£4,500–5,000 *S*

A George IV bonheur du jour, the superstructure centred by a pair of cupboards flanked by a bank of drawers, on turned and tapered legs ending in brass casters, c1820, 48½in (123cm) wide.
£13,500–15,000 *S*

A Victorian thuya wood bonheur du jour, the top with a mirror, flanked by panelled cupboard doors with Sèvres style porcelain plaques, the base with a central frieze drawer flanked by a pair of drawers, with a mirrored back, on bun feet, c1870, 53in (135cm) wide.
£3,000–3,500 *Bon*

A Queen Anne walnut bureau, the slope with book ledge, above 3 graduated drawers, 23in (58cm) wide.
£9,000–10,000 *P*

A George III harewood bonheur du jour, by Gillows of Lancaster, the superstructure with an open shelf and a drawer flanked by cupboards, above a writing drawer, c1795, 32in (82cm) wide.
£9,500–11,000 *S*

A north Italian walnut and tulipwood-inlaid serpentine bureau, the concave-moulded edge incorporating a pair of hidden drawers to the sides, with 3 long drawers flanked by canted moulded corners, on scrolled cabriole legs, c1740, 42in (107cm) wide.
£14,000–16,000 *Bon*

A Biedermeier mahogany roll-top bureau, the fitted interior over a shaped drawer and cupboard, c1830, 42in (106.5cm) wide.
£5,500–6,000 *BERA*

A Louis XVI style mahogany *secrétaire à cylindre*, in the manner of Henri Dasson, inlaid with marquetry and parquetry, with applied gilt-metal mounts, on square tapering legs, 19thC, 45in (115cm) wide.
£4,500–5,000 *P*

l. A painted satinwood bureau, veneered and decorated, with fully fitted interior, mid-19thC, carcass 18thC, 39½in (100.5cm) wide.
£12,000–14,000 *BERA*

A George III mahogany tester bed, with a moulded cornice, c1770, 70in (177cm) wide.
£20,000–22,000 *S(S)*

A French walnut double bed, in Henri II style, 19thC, 54in (137cm) wide.
£650–800 *HAC*

A Louis XV style bed, with later parquetry and carved panels, 19thC, 60in (152.5cm) wide.
£1,400–1,500 *SWA*

An Empire ormolu-mounted mahogany bed, the panelled headboard and footboard with circular top rail, 81in (206cm) long.
£4,500–5,000 *S(NY)*

A Louis XVI style bedstead, with ormolu decoration, tapered and fluted posts, c1895, 55¼in (140cm) wide.
£1,850–2,000 *SeH*

A Spanish mahogany bed, with gilt decoration, early 20thC, 60in (152.5cm) wide.
£950–1,100 *SWA*

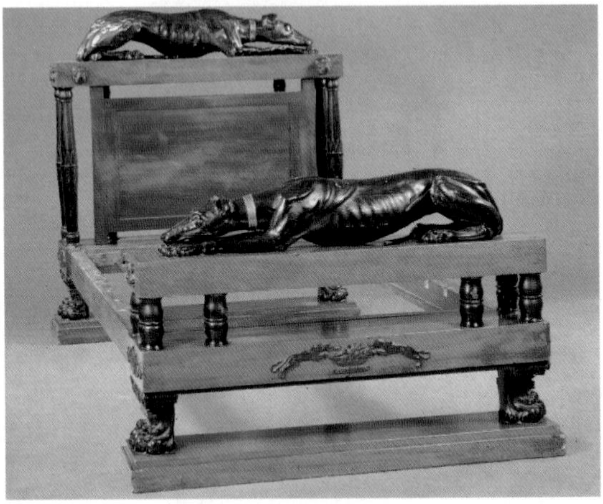

A Regency mahogany, bronze-mounted and ebonised bed, in the manner of Thomas Hope, the ends with recumbent hounds wearing gilt collars, the friezes applied with leopards' heads, 48¾in (124cm) wide.
£50,000–55,000 *P*

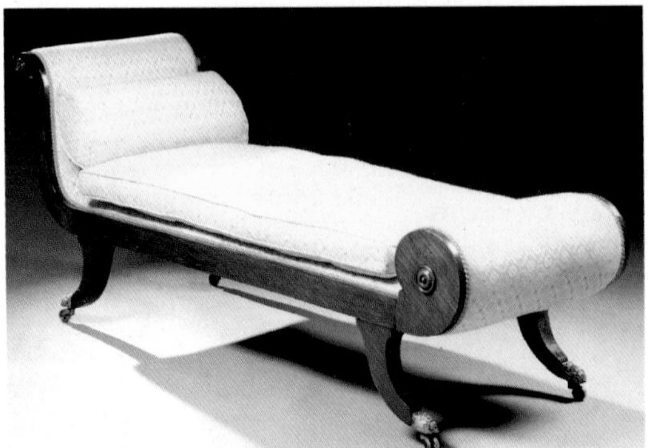

A Regency simulated rosewood chaise longue, the padded seat with squab cushions and scrolled ends, one side carved and moulded, 72in (183cm) long.
£4,500–5,000 *S*

A William IV mahogany chaise longue, upholstered in green and cream fabric, on turned tapering feet, 84in (213.5cm) long.
£1,200–1,300 *SWA*

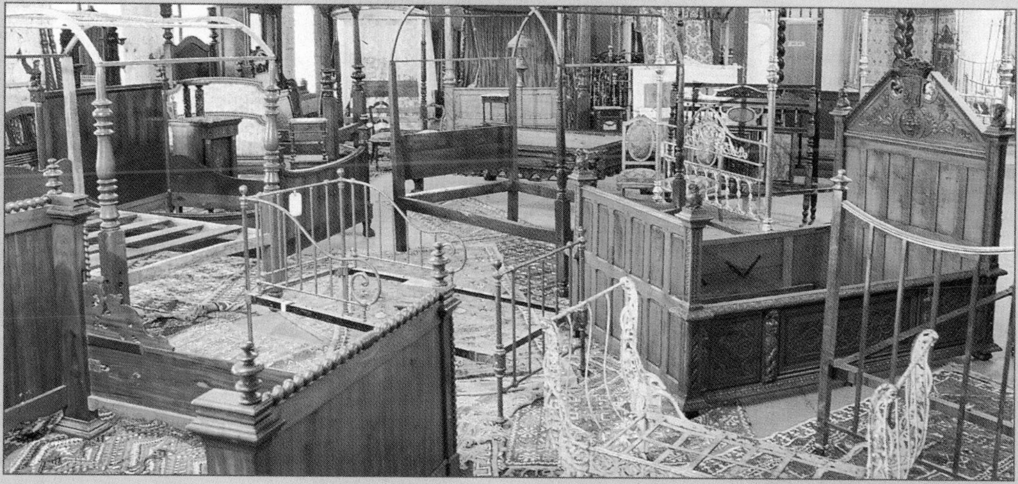

One of our showrooms.

For further details see page 33

A Regency mahogany and boxwood-lined bookcase, with writing slide, 48in (122cm) wide.
£4,500–5,000 *Mit*

A Victorian carved oak library bookcase, with 3 glazed doors and frieze drawers over 3 panelled doors, 82in (208.5cm) wide.
£2,500–3,000 *AH*

A George III mahogany and line-inlaid secretaire bookcase, on bracket feet, 47in (119.5cm) wide.
£2,200–2,500 *CAG*

r. A Victorian mahogany and marquetry breakfront bookcase, with secretaire drawer enclosing a fitted interior, 109½in (278cm) wide.
£20,000–24,000 *S*

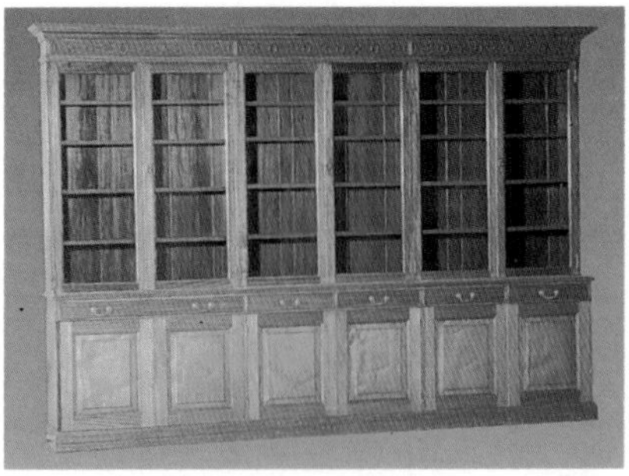

An Edwardian mahogany library bookcase, the dentilled cornice and blind fret frieze above 6 glass doors, 3 pairs of panelled doors below, 130in (330cm) wide.
£3,200–4,000 *S(S)*

A George IV mahogany breakfront library bookcase, with 4 glazed doors above panelled cupboard doors, c1825, 112in (284.5cm) wide.
£21,000–24,000 *S*

A Victorian burr walnut library bookcase, with inlaid upper and lower friezes, ebonised moulding throughout, c1860, 110in (280cm) wide.
£13,000–14,000 *S*

A Regency mahogany, ebony-moulded and inlaid lady's bookcase, in the manner of Richard Brown and George Bullock, with brass grille panels, 7 drawers to one side, 28in (71cm) wide.
£8,000–10,000 *P*

A mahogany and satinwood-inlaid bureau-bookcase, with blind fret carving and astragal glazed doors, 18thC, 36in (91.5cm) wide.
£4,500–5,000 *BUSH*

A Sheraton style inlaid mahogany secretaire bookcase, late 18thC, 35in (89cm) wide.
£5,000–6,000 *GH*

A Regency rosewood and brass-inlaid breakfront low bookcase, with pierced brass gallery, on bracket feet, c1815, 67in (170cm) wide.
£3,000–3,500 *Bon*

A Regency goncalo alves breakfront low bookcase, on reeded bun feet, c1820, 72in (183cm) wide.
£9,000–10,000 *Bon*

A pair of William IV mahogany open bookcases, slate marble tops replaced, c1830, 72½in (184cm) wide.
£10,500–12,000 *S*

A George IV mahogany free-standing open bookcase, c1820, 30in (77cm) wide.
£7,000–8,000 *S*

A Regency mahogany and ebonised revolving circular bookcase, 48½in (123cm) high.
£30,000–35,000 *P*

A George III mahogany night table, with galleried top, commode section converted, c1770, 19in (48cm) wide.
£2,300–2,800 *S*

An amboyna and ebony-inlaid bedside cabinet, early 19thC, 22in (57cm) wide.
£2,000–2,500 *S*

A walnut dwarf breakfront bookcase, with ring and paterae-carved stiles, late 19thC, 39in (99cm) wide.
£450–500 *DN(H)*

A mahogany cabinet, c1870, 17in (43cm) wide.
£400–450 *GBr*

A Victorian inlaid rosewood standing corner cupboard, 26in (66cm) wide.
£380–420 *CaC*

An Edwardian inlaid rosewood standing corner cupboard, c1900, 26in (66cm) wide.
£700–800 *E*

A George IV satin birch canterbury, with 3 divisions and frieze drawer, on turned legs and brass casters, c1820, 18½in (47cm) wide.
£2,750–3,000 *S*

A George IV rosewood canterbury, with 3 divisions, on turned legs with casters, c1820, 21in (53.5cm) wide.
£2,200–2,500 *ANT*

A William and Mary walnut and marquetry inlaid cabinet-on-stand, the cupboard doors enclosing a fitted interior, on later twist-turned and tapered legs, c1690, 43in (109cm) wide.
£7,500–9,000 *S*

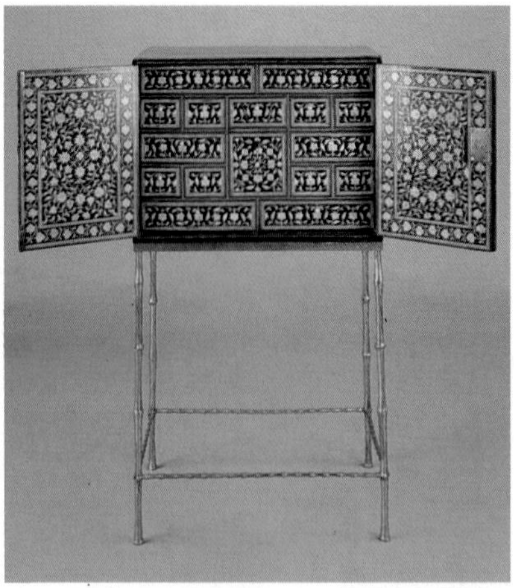

An Indian ivory-inlaid padouk cabinet-on-stand, the pair of cupboard doors enclosing an arrangement of 15 drawers, on a later *faux* bamboo brass stand, c1900, 26in (66cm) wide.
£5,000–5,500 *Bon*

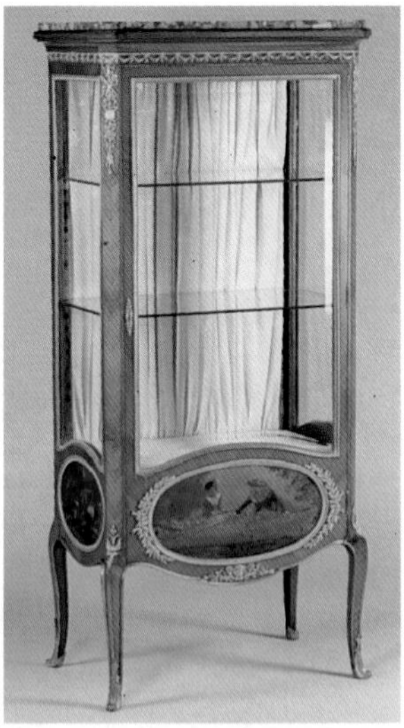

A French kingwood and ormolu vitrine, with Vernis Martin style panels, marble top, late 19thC, 26in (66cm) wide.
£3,000–3,500 *MAT*

A William and Mary burr walnut and feather-strung cabinet-on-chest, one drawer stamped 'Wilson, 68 Great Queen St, London', 42½in (108cm) wide.
£4,500–5,500 *P*

An Edwardian Sheraton revival painted satinwood display cabinet, with astragal glazed and mirror-backed cupboards, 53½in (136cm) wide.
£5,250–6,000 *AH*

A William and Mary walnut and herringbone-inlaid escritoire, with yew-wood interior, 44in (111cm) wide.
£4,500–5,500 *P(WM)*

A George IV mahogany and gilt-brass-mounted secretaire cabinet, by Wilkinson of Ludgate Hill, the fall-front enclosing pigeonholes labelled with painted letters of the alphabet, c1820, 48in (122cm) wide.
£8,500–10,000 *S*

A Louis XV/XVI tulipwood and fruitwood marquetry serpentine *secrétaire à abbatant*, with marble top, signed 'Denizot', c1760, 27in (68.5cm) wide.
£15,000–16,500 *S(NY)*

A mahogany secretaire cabinet, the altered interior with a recess and 4 small drawers, a pair of doors below with floral porcelain panels, on tapered square feet, 19thC, 38in (97cm) wide.
£13,500–15,000 *S(S)*

A Victorian thuya wood and purple heart-veneered side cabinet, with marquetry inlay, 81in (206cm) wide.
£10,500–12,000 *Bea(E)*

A Regency mahogany side cabinet, with veined marble top, the doors with brass mesh panels, 48in (122cm) wide.
£4,500–5,000 *RBB*

A Regency rosewood chiffonier, with mirrored back and reeded bun feet, c1825, 34in (86.5cm) wide.
£4,500–5,000 *BERA*

A fruitwood parquetry demi-lune commode, German or Alsatian, late 18thC, 32in (81.5cm) wide.
£3,500–4,000 *S(Z)*

A Victorian gilt-metal mounted walnut side cabinet, the panelled cupboard door inlaid with an eagle, c1870, 62in (157.5cm) wide.
£4,000–5,000 *Bon*

A Victorian marquetry-inlaid burr walnut serpentine side cabinet, the central cupboard flanked by glazed doors, c1865, 65in (165.5cm) wide.
£3,500–4,000 *Bon*

A Dutch mahogany and marquetry-inlaid chiffonier, with a frieze drawer above a pair of cupboard doors, 19thC, 45in (114.5cm) wide.
£1,000–1,200 *CAG*

A Louis XV style kingwood and tulipwood marquetry-inlaid side cabinet, with marble top above an open shelf and tambour doors, on cabriole legs, late 19thC, 49in (125cm) wide.
£2,000–2,200 *P*

A Regency rosewood chiffonier, with brass gallery, the 2 arched panelled doors with brass grilles, 25½in (65cm) wide.
£2,500–2,800 *AH*

A burr walnut side cabinet, with ebony banding and mirrored back shelf over 2 glazed doors, on a moulded base, by Marsh, Jones & Cribb, 19thC, 70in (178cm) wide.
£2,200–2,500 *AH*

A Napoleon III kingwood and marquetry *meuble d'appui,* with gilt-metal mounts, c1860, 51½in (131cm) wide.
£12,000–14,000 *S(S)*

A George III style painted satinwood commode, early 20thC, 39in (99cm) wide.
£5,000–5,500 *S*

A pair of George III mahogany library armchairs.
£11,000–12,000 *S*

A George IV mahogany, rosewood and cut-brass inlaid library armchair.
£2,300–2,800 *S*

A George IV mahogany library armchair, rear legs replaced, c1825.
£2,200–2,500 *S*

A set of 6 mahogany side chairs, c1840.
£3,500–4,000 *CHA*

A pair of French painted side chairs, on reeded legs, late 19thC.
£270–300 *SPa*

A Victorian walnut scroll-carved side chair, on cabriole legs.
£220–250 *MiA*

A Louis XVI style walnut occasional chair, 19thC.
£150–180 *CaC*

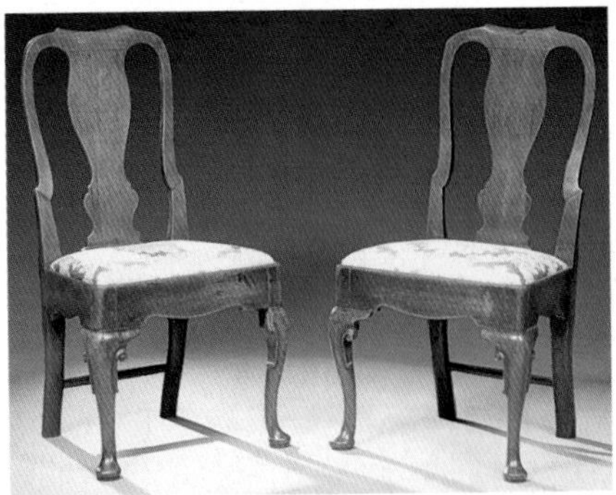

A set of 6 George II red walnut dining chairs, the shaped top-rails above solid splats within curved uprights, on scroll-carved cabriole legs with pad feet, c1730.
£7,000–8,000 *S*

A set of 7 George III mahogany dining chairs, including a pair of open armchairs, in Sheraton style, with stuffover seats, c1780.
£3,500–4,000 *P*

A pair of James II high-back ebonised beechwood chairs, with cane panels, c1685.
£1,600–1,800 *MIC*

A set of 8 George III mahogany dining chairs, including 2 open armchairs, with pierced splat backs and drop-in seats.
£2,600–3,000 *E*

A set of 6 George III mahogany dining chairs, with carved top-rails and splats, on cabriole legs, restored, c1760.
£11,500–13,000 *S*

A set of 6 mahogany chairs, designed by I. Lawrence, for Gillows of Lancaster, c1795.
£16,500–18,500 *ANT*

A set of 4 George IV rosewood and brass-inlaid dining chairs.
£1,400–1,600 *ChS*

A set of 6 Victorian rosewood balloon-back dining chairs, c1850.
£3,300–3,750 *BERA*

A set of 4 George III mahogany chairs, with reeded and turned backs, c1790.
£1,800–2,000 *ANT*

A set of 6 George IV mahogany dining chairs, c1820.
£3,500–4,000 *S*

A set of 6 George III mahogany dining chairs, including 2 carvers, with pierced splats, on square tapering legs, c1790.
£7,000–7,500 *ANT*

A set of 6 Regency mahogany dining chairs, with rope-carved top-rails and carved back bar, c1810.
£5,000–5,500 *BERA*

A set of 6 mahogany dining chairs, inlaid with satinwood and ebony, the curved crest-rails between reeded uprights, early 19thC.
£1,500–1,800 *AH*

A set of 4 Louis XV painted *fauteuils*, with cartouche-shaped backs and on cabriole legs.
£6,500–7,500 *P*

A George III mahogany 'cockpen' armchair, in Chinese style, c1750.
£2,000–2,500 *SPa*

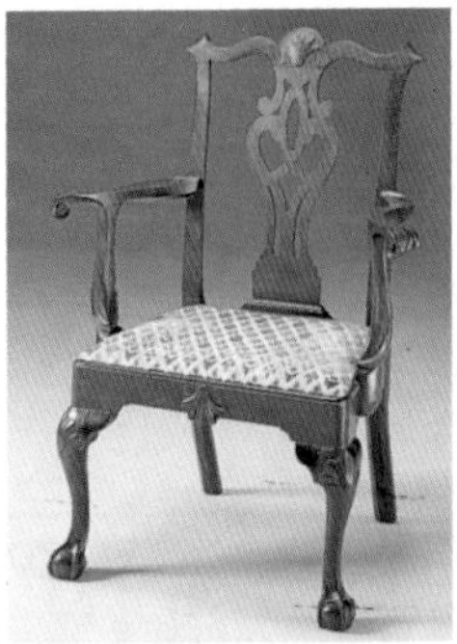

A figured walnut open armchair, with shell-carved crest, on cabriole legs, Pennsylvania, c1780.
£13,000–15,000 *S(NY)*

A metamorphic library chair, by B. Harmer, after a design by Morgan & Sanders, with fluted scrolled arms and cane seat, on sabre legs, c1815.
£15,000–18,000 *S*

A pair of mahogany armchairs, with bead and leaf-carved moulded stick splats with flowerhead paterae, upholstered seats, on moulded tapered legs, c1775.
£4,000–4,500 *S*

A pair of carved oak X-framed armchairs, the back supports with turned finials, c1880.
£3,200–3,500 *S(S)*

Four giltwood *fauteuils*, the carved rail with floral cresting, with Aubusson tapestry, c1880.
£6,700–7,500 *S*

A pair of mahogany open armchairs, with brass line inlay, c1830.
£2,000–2,250 *ANT*

A mahogany Chippendale style open armchair, with paw feet, c1890.
£800–900 *BERA*

A pair of Louis XVI style giltwood *fauteuils*, with wrythen-fluted turned legs, mid-19thC.
£1,500–1,650 *GH*

A set of 4 French painted *fauteuils*, the back and seat rail with floral cresting, padded arms, 19thC.
£3,500–4,000 *DaH*

A set of 10 carved limed walnut 17thC Venetian style upholstered armchairs, c1890.
£5,500–6,000 *S(S)*

A painted satinwood bergère, with turned supports, on tapered legs with casters, c1910.
£2,000–2,200 *S*

A William and Mary walnut and marquetry-inlaid chest of drawers, with moulded top, 2 short and 3 long drawers, on bun feet, c1690, 38in (96.5cm) wide.
£13,000–15,000 *S*

A William and Mary burr walnut crossbanded chest of drawers, with moulded edge, on turned bun feet, c1695, 38in (96.5cm) wide.
£9,000–10,000 *S*

A Dutch walnut serpentine and bombé chest, with gilt-metal handles, on splayed feet, 18thC, 34in (87cm) wide.
£4,700–5,200 *P(EA)*

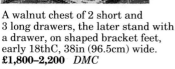

A walnut chest of 2 short and 3 long drawers, the later stand with a drawer, on shaped bracket feet, early 18thC, 38in (96.5cm) wide.
£1,800–2,200 *DMC*

A French Louis XV walnut commode, with shaped apron, c1720, 50in (127cm) wide.
£7,000–8,000 *DaH*

A William and Mary walnut secretaire chest, with fitted interior above 4 short and 2 long drawers, on bun feet, c1695, 38in (96.5cm) wide.
£11,500–13,000 *S*

A Scottish burr walnut chest of drawers, the 3 long drawers feather banded, with brass handles and oval escutcheons, on bun feet, early 18thC, 32½in (82.5cm) wide.
£3,500–4,000 *WW*

A Dutch oak chest of drawers, walnut veneered and inlaid with marquetry, gilt-bronze escutcheons, c1820, 35in (89cm) wide.
£5,300–5,800 *BERA*

A George II mahogany bachelor's chest, with moulded top and brushing slide, 4 long drawers, on shaped bracket feet, c1750, 30in (76cm) wide.
£7,000–8,000 *S*

A mahogany serpentine chest of drawers, in the manner of Gillows of Lancaster, with 2 short and 3 long graduated drawers, c1780, 43½in (110.5cm) wide.
£13,500–15,000 *ANT*

A walnut chest of drawers, with crossbanded and quarter-veneered top, 2 short and 3 long drawers with brass drop handles, early 18thC, 37in (94cm) wide.
£2,800–3,200 *AH*

A George III mahogany chest of drawers, the 2 short and 3 long drawers with brass swan neck drop handles, flanked by reeded columns, 41in (104cm) wide.
£1,750–2,000 *Mit*

A Queen Anne walnut chest-on-chest, crossbanded and featherstrung, the lower part with brushing slide, on bracket feet, 41½in (105cm) wide.
£8,000–9,000 *P*

A George II walnut chest-on-chest, with cavetto-moulded cornice, the drawers flanked by fluted pilasters, on shaped bracket feet, c1730, 44½in (113cm) wide.
£11,500–13,000 *S*

A George I walnut chest-on-chest, with brushing slide, 41in (104cm) wide.
£13,000–15,000 *JNic*

An early George III mahogany chest-on-chest, with 2 short and 6 long drawers, 41in (104cm) wide.
£800–1,200 *Bea(E)*

A walnut and oyster laburnum chest-on-stand, boxwood crossbanded, the top with segmented veneers, stand altered and with a drawer, now on shaped bracket feet, c1700, 37in (94cm) wide.
£6,500–7,500 *S(S)*

A William and Mary oyster-veneered chest-on-stand, crossbanded in holly, the later base with arcaded frieze and bulbous supports, on bun feet, 34in (86.5cm) wide.
£3,500–4,000 *Bon*

A George III mahogany chest-on-chest, the top and base with fluted canted corners, on bracket feet, c1770, 42in (106.5cm) wide.
£4,500–5,000 *ANT*

A Queen Anne walnut chest-on-chest, the top quarter-veneered and crossbanded, the lower part with arched apron and one long and 2 short drawers, on later bun feet, 42in (106.5cm) wide.
£4,700–5,200 *P*

A Queen Anne walnut and crossbanded chest-on-stand, the stand with arched apron and 3 drawers, the cabriole legs with shell-carved knees and fluted pad feet, c1710, 41in (104cm) wide.
£4,500–5,000 *S(S)*

An American walnut and tiger maple highboy, the lower section with shaped apron, the tapering legs ending in slipper feet, probably Newport, Rhode Island, c1730, 38½in (98cm) wide.
£10,000–11,000 *S(Cg)*

A rosewood davenport, with fretwork gallery, c1850, 36in (91.5cm) wide.
£2,500–2,750 *BERA*

A Victorian walnut davenport, with concave front, 24in (61cm) wide.
£2,000–2,200 *BIG*

A burr walnut davenport, c1870, 20in (51cm) wide.
£1,500–1,800 *TAY*

A walnut and marquetry kneehole desk, early 18thC, 31½in (80cm) wide.
£4,500–5,500 *P*

A George II burr walnut kneehole desk, top later, interior missing, 41½in (105.5cm) wide.
£21,000–25,000 *P*

A George III mahogany partners' desk, the top with a moulded edge and later tooled red leather insert, above 6 frieze drawers, on pedetals with 6 graduated drawers and plinth bases, c1780, 73½in (186.5cm) wide.
£7,500–9,000 *Bon*

A late George III mahogany three-tier dumb waiter, on wrythen-turned and channelled support, carved tripod base, 48½in (123cm) high.
£1,800–2,200 *DN(H)*

A George IV mahogany dumb waiter, attributed to Gillows, with reeded baluster-turned supports, c1830, 39in (99cm) high.
£3,700–4,000 *S*

A mahogany étagère, by James Shoolbred, with glass tray top, inlaid and crossbanded, on tapered flared legs, c1890, 35in (89cm) wide.
£2,700–3,000 *BERA*

A George I walnut, oak and crossbanded lowboy, with quarter-veneered top, 2 short and one long drawer, on oak cabriole legs with pointed pad feet, 28in (71cm) wide.
£5,000–5,500 *P*

A George III walnut lowboy, repaired and altered, c1790, 27½in (70cm) high.
£800–1,000 *MEG*

A chestnut and marquetry-inlaid jardinière, with brass liner, on tapering legs, 10½in (27cm) wide.
£2,400–2,800 *S(Z)*

A George III red walnut lowboy, with 3 drawers above a shaped apron, c1770, 32in (81.5cm) wide.
£2,400–2,700 *ANT*

A George III mahogany dressing-table mirror, the frame and base crossbanded and chequer-strung, c1780, 18in (46cm) wide.
£2,000–2,200 *S*

A mahogany dressing-table mirror, inlaid with satinwood, the drawer with brass knobs, c1825, 14in (35.5cm) wide.
£200–230 *A&A*

A French mahogany cheval mirror, the columns with brass finials and collars, joined by a turned support, on in-swept legs, early 19thC, 38½in (98cm) wide.
£1,000–1,200 *S(Z)*

A walnut high-back open arm settee, late 17thC, 48½in (123cm) wide.
£2,700–3,000 *P(O)*

A George III mahogany double chair-back settee, 45in (114.5cm) wide.
£2,400–2,700 *ChS*

A Louis XVI painted canapé, on circular tapering legs, late 18thC, 51½in (131cm) wide.
£6,500–7,000 *S(NY)*

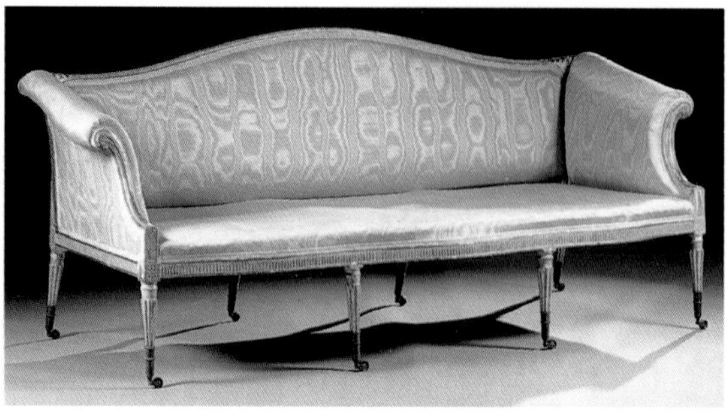

A George III carved giltwood settee, with turned fluted legs, on brass casters, c1775, 84in (221cm) wide.
£8,500–9,500 *S*

A George III mahogany upholstered sofa, with moulded tapering legs, c1800, 76in (193cm) wide.
£3,000–3,300 *ANT*

A Regency rosewood scroll-end settee, with sabre legs, 84in (213.5cm) wide.
£6,000–7,000 *SWO*

A George IV oak and parcel-gilt sofa, after a design by J. Taylor, the arm facings carved with gadroons, Vitruvian scrolls and shells, 84½in (214.5cm) wide.
£5,750–6,500 *S*

A William IV carved rosewood sofa, after a design by George Smith, c1830, 86½in (220cm) wide.
£10,000–11,000 *S*

A Victorian double-ended serpentine settee, with plain seat and deep button back, on 2 front carved cabriole legs, 68in (172.5cm) long.
£2,000–2,400 *LCA*

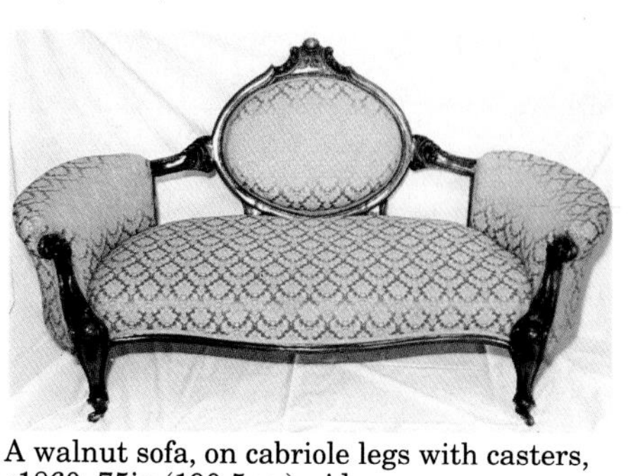

A walnut sofa, on cabriole legs with casters, c1860, 75in (190.5cm) wide.
£1,400–1,600 *GBr*

A William IV carved mahogany settee, on lion paw and scroll-carved feet, c1835, 91½in (232.5cm) wide.
£4,000–4,500 *S*

A mahogany crossbanded and string-inlaid serpentine sideboard, possibly Scottish, late 18thC, 90in (228.5cm) wide.
£8,500–10,000 *BIG*

A George III mahogany sideboard, possibly by Gillows of Lancaster, c1810, 44in (112cm) wide.
£3,500–4,000 *ANT*

A mahogany pedestal sideboard, with inverted breakfront, 3 panelled drawers above a moulded cupboard, flanked by tapered panelled cupboards with gadroon-carved moulding, c1835, 49in (124.5cm) wide.
£2,750–3,250 *S*

A burr oak buffet, by Pratt & Prince, Bradford, with turned supports, above 3 drawers with moulded fronts, on a plinth base, c1850, 66in (167.5cm) wide.
£3,000–3,500 *GBr*

A pair of mid-Victorian mahogany jardinière stands, on turned columns and moulded round bases, 30in (77cm) high.
£900–1,000 *DN(H)*

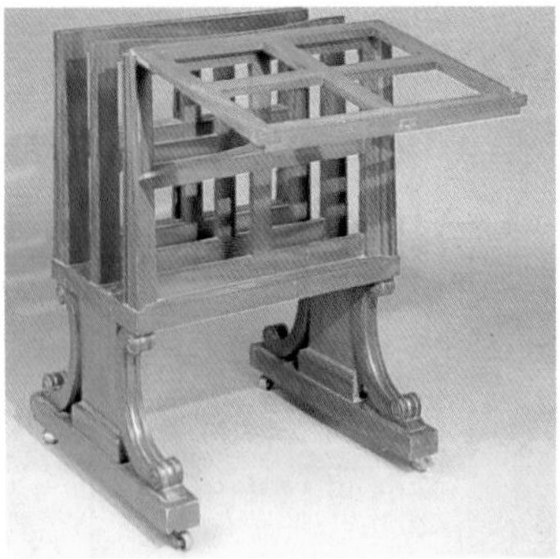

A George IV mahogany folio stand, after a design by Gillows, on sleigh bases with casters, 27½in (70cm) wide.
£2,300–2,800 *P*

A set of George IV mahogany bedsteps, with hinged cupboard, c1825, 20in (51cm) wide.
£2,000–2,400 *S*

A Victorian walnut torchère, with turned column, 48in (122cm) high.
£300–400 *MEG*

A Queen Anne walnut stool, with original needlework upholstery, c1705, 19in (48.5cm) wide.
£2,200–2,500 *MIC*

A George III carved giltwood and gesso stool, the cabriole legs carved at the knees, c1760, 24½in (62cm) wide.
£3,500–3,800 *S*

A William IV mahogany butler's tray on stand, with 3 pierced handles, 30½in (77.5cm) wide.
£3,300–3,800 *S*

A Regency mahogany gout stool, 15in (38cm) wide.
£1,800–2,000 *P*

A Victorian papier mâché tray, decorated with flowers, foliage and insects, c1850, on modern stand, 31½in (80cm) wide.
£3,000–3,300 *S*

A burr walnut and inlaid whatnot, with turned column supports, c1870, 47½in (120.5cm) high.
£2,000–2,350 *BERA*

A Victorian rosewood whatnot, with turned spindles, c1840, 42½in (108cm) high.
£340–380 *TMA*

A late Victorian satinwood, tulipwood, rosewood and parquetry three-tier étagère, 21in (53.5cm) wide.
£5,000–5,500 *P*

A mahogany wine cooler and stand, with brass bands and carrying handles, c1800, 20in (51cm) diam.
£3,500–3,850 *ANT*

A Regency mahogany cellaret, stamped 'Thomas Willson', on paw feet with brass casters, 28½in (72.5cm) wide.
£4,500–5,500 *S*

A rosewood and brass-bound wine cooler, with lead-lined interior, early 19thC, 18½in (47cm) wide.
£5,000–6,000 *S*

A George III Sheraton style mahogany breakfast table, the snap-top crossbanded in rosewood and satinwood, on a baluster turned shaft, 60in (152.5cm) wide.
£7,200–8,000 *P*

A Regency Gothic style five-sided oak table, with an ebonised moulded top, over a shaped moulded frieze with panels, the five-sided legs joined by a stretcher, c1820, 57in (145cm) wide.
£7,500–9,000 *S*

A satinwood centre table, painted with a portrait of a lady, c1900, 24in (61cm) diam.
£1,300–1,450 *ANT*

A Sheraton revival rosewood octagonal centre table, stamped 'Shoolbred & Co', c1900, 30in (76cm) diam.
£820–900 *SWO*

A carved and figured walnut drop-leaf dining table, the shaped skirt continuing to cabriole legs, on ball-and-claw feet and casters, Philadelphia, c1770, 59½in (146cm) wide.
£12,500–14,000 *S(NY)*

A Regency mahogany concertina action extending dining table, the rounded reeded top with 5 additional leaves, on ring-turned legs with brass cappings and casters, 189½in (481cm) long.
£14,000–16,000 *P*

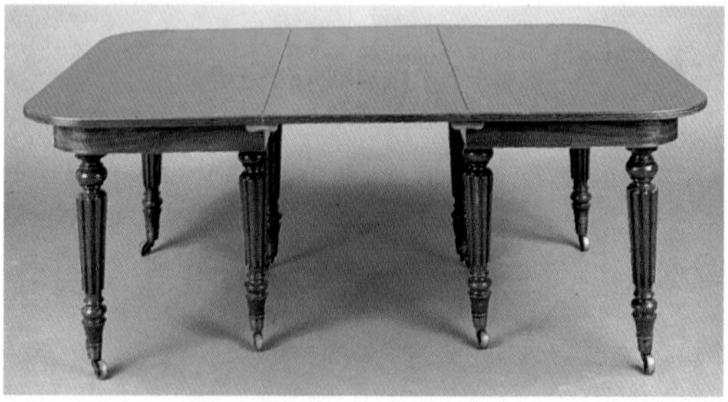

A Regency mahogany extending dining table, by Gillows of Lancaster, with 2 extra leaves, the reeded edge above a band frieze, on 8 turned reeded legs, c1820, 94in (239cm) extended.
£5,000–5,500 *Bon*

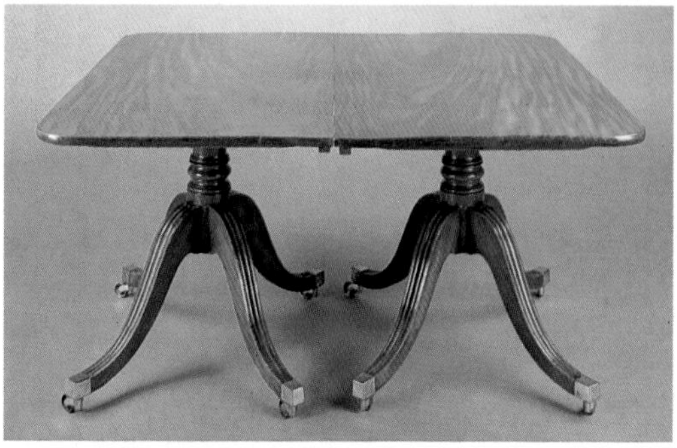

A Regency mahogany twin-pillar dining table, the rounded top above ring-turned supports and channelled outswept legs, including one extra leaf, alterations, 84in (213.5cm) wide.
£5,000–6,000 *Bon*

A William IV mahogany dining table, the circular top with moulded edge veneered in satinwood and rosewood, with 6 extra leaves, 61in (154.5cm) diam.
£10,000–11,000 *P*

A George III mahogany and ebony-strung library table, the crossbanded top inset with tooled leather, with 3 frieze drawers, on tapered legs, 60in (153cm) wide.
£7,000–8,000 *P*

A Regency satinwood and marquetry library table, in the manner of George Bullock, 52in (132cm) diam.
£58,000–65,000 *P*

A Regency rosewood and brass-inlaid library table, inlaid with fleur-de-lys, with square tapered stem and concave-sided platform, on splayed legs and leaf-cast brass casters, c1815, 50in (127cm) diam.
£3,700–4,500 *S*

A George IV rosewood library table, the frieze with bead-and-reel moulding, on shaped platforms with carved paw feet and casters, c1820, 60in (152.5cm) wide.
£8,500–9,500 *S*

A pair of Edwardian satin burr walnut bedside tables, each with 2 drawers, 14in (35.5cm) wide.
£230–260 *MiA*

A Victorian specimen marble and polished slate pedestal table, 25½in (64.5cm) diam.
£3,800–4,200 *Bea(E)*

An ebonised, giltwood and penwork X-frame occasional table, the top finely painted with chinoiserie figures, 19thC, 31in (78.5cm) wide.
£1,250–1,500 *P*

A French mahogany and gilt-bronze *guéridon*, c1890, 23½in (60cm) diam.
£5,000–5,500 *S*

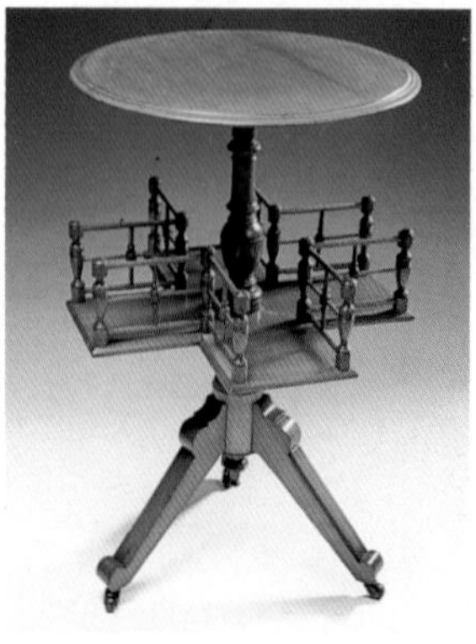

A Victorian walnut book table, with spindled under tier, 18in (45.5cm) wide.
£360–400 *TMA*

A pair of George III mahogany Pembroke tables, each with an ebonised cockbeaded drawer, 32in (81.5cm) extended.
£5,500–6,000 *P*

A pair of mahogany occasional tables, with tripod bases, late 19thC, 20in (51cm) diam.
£1,800–2,200 *SPa*

A George III satinwood-veneered and marquetry-inlaid Pembroke table, 20in (51cm) wide.
£15,500–17,000 *WW*

A Continental neo-classical mahogany and satinwood tilt-top tripod table, the top with leather insert, c1800, 30½in (77cm) diam.
£4,500–5,000 *S(NY)*

A kingwood and porcelain-mounted side table, c1870, 34in (86.5cm) wide.
£3,700–4,000 *S(S)*

A George III oval satinwood work table, with pleated silk work bag, 17in (43cm) wide.
£3,000–3,500 *S*

A burr walnut work table, with fitted interior, c1870, 25in (63.5cm) wide.
£1,500–1,650 *CHA*

A matched set of 9 Federal carved mahogany shield-back dining chairs, including an armchair, the shield backs inset with shaped leaf and reed-carved supports with leaf-carved base, on square tapering legs ending in spade feet, restored, New York, c1800.
£7,000–8,500 *S(NY)*

A set of 6 George III mahogany dining chairs, including 2 carver armchairs, with shaped stiles between bowed top and mid-rails, the scroll arms with scrolling supports, stuff-over seats, on tapered square section legs.
£1,800–2,000 *Mit*

A set of 6 George III mahogany dining chairs, with reeded back supports, horizontal curved splats, on square tapered legs, c1800.
£2,500–2,800 *ChS*

A set of 6 north Italian bone-inlaid walnut dining chairs, the scooped backs inlaid with flower-filled baskets, a cartouche and foliate scrolls above padded seats, on sabre legs, repairs to legs, early 19thC.
£2,500–2,750 *Bon*

A set of 8 Regency mahogany rail-back dining chairs, including an armchair, with ebonised banding and key pattern, with upholstered Trafalgar seats, on sabre legs, c1810.
£9,500–10,500 *S(S)*

Trafalgar seats are removable seats which are held in position by a small peg in the top centre of the front rail of the chair, which fits into a corresponding hole in the underside of the front seat frame.

r. A set of 6 Regency mahogany dining chairs, the backs with curved bar top-rails and horizontal scroll splats above stuff-over seats, on turned and tapered legs.
£750–825 *P(B)*

l. A set of 6 Regency mahogany dining chairs, including a carver chair, with scroll arms on ball supports, the backs with horizontal splats and centred roundel with flutes within serpentine rails, over padded seats, on sabre legs.
£1,500–1,800 *WW*

A set of 8 Regency dining chairs, including a carver, with reeded horizontal splats and brass scroll-inlaid curved top rails, drop-in seats, on sabre legs.
£5,500–6,000 *P(O)*

A set of 5 Regency brass-inlaid simulated rosewood dining chairs, the uprights and knees applied with pressed brass rosettes, the top-rails and crossbars centred by cut-brass foliage, drop-in seats, on sabre legs, repairs and restoration.
£750–850 *Bea(E)*

A set of 8 Regency mahogany dining chairs, the reeded rectangular backs with bowed top-rails and shaped stick splats, drop-in seats, on reeded tapering square legs with stretchers, 2 chairs now fitted with later arms, some restoration.
£2,200–2,700 *Bea(E)*

A set of 6 Regency brass-inlaid simulated rosewood dining chairs, the curved cresting rails moulded and carved with stylised foliage, the centre rails of scrolled and panelled form inlaid with a brass foliate and bell motif, cane seats with drop-in squabs, on sabre legs.
£1,400–1,600 *P(S)*

A set of 8 George IV mahogany and brass-strung rail-back dining chairs, with ball clad mid-rails, with stuffed seats, on sabre legs, c1825.
£2,300–2,500 *S(S)*

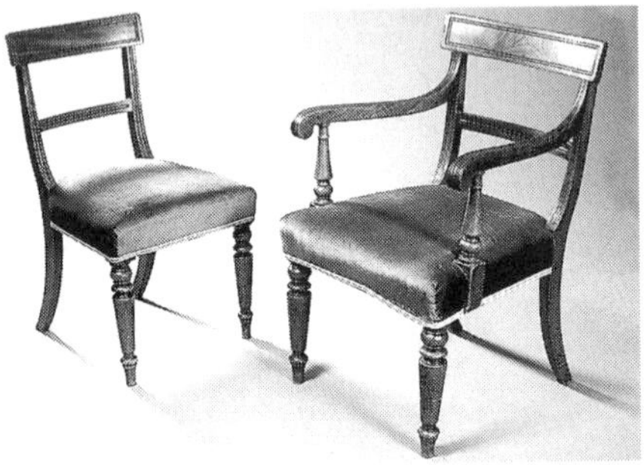

A set of 6 George IV mahogany bar-back dining chairs, including 2 armchairs, with moulded top-rail and back rest, green upholstered stuff-over seats, on turned front legs and sabre back legs.
£2,000–2,200 *DN(H)*

A set of 6 Regency simulated rosewood and beechwood dining chairs, with curved bar top-rails, gadrooned crestings with pierced foliate scroll splats and roundel ornament, slip-in seats, on sabre legs.
£1,400–1,600 *P*

r. A set of 4 William IV mahogany dining chairs, with acanthus-carved top-rails, upholstered back and lotus-clad turned legs, c1830.
£1,600–1,800 *BERA*

A set of 6 William IV mahogany dining chairs, including 2 carvers, each with wide bowed top-rails set on shaped stiles, bowed mid-rail and downswept scrolling arms with short supports, drop-in seats, on tapered octagonal legs.
£1,400–1,700 *Mit*

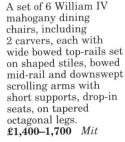

A set of 4 George IV mahogany dining chairs, each with foliate carved top-rail, pierced and carved horizontal splat, on turned reeded legs, c1830.
£1,250–1,400 *ChS*

A set of 8 George IV mahogany rail-back dining chairs, including 2 armchairs, the stuffed seats covered in striped brocade, on turned and reeded tapering legs, c1825.
£4,600–5,000 *S(S)*

l. A set of 4 William IV mahogany dining chairs, with curved moulded crest-rails, horizontal splats and uprights, with stuff-over seats, on turned and fluted front legs.
£550–600 *LF*

A set of 6 William IV rosewood rail-back dining chairs, with clasp shaped mid bars and Trafalgar seats, on lotus-clad turned legs, c1835.
£1,750–2,000 *S(S)*

A set of 8 Hepplewhite style mahogany dining chairs, with pierced shield-backs, with bow and wheat ear crests, shaped open arms, on leaf-carved tapering supports, upholstered shaped seats, with turned and carved tapering front legs on rounded feet, rear sabre legs, in need of restoration, 19thC.
£1,450–1,600 *TMA*

A set of 10 Victorian mahogany dining chairs, the rounded open backs with scroll and rosette centre rails, padded serpentine seats, on turned legs.
£2,300–2,500 *DN*

A set of 8 William IV rosewood dining chairs, the beech rail-backs with spiral turned supports, padded seats, on reeded tapering legs, the crest-rails previously painted to simulate rosewood.
£850–950 *DN*

A set of 6 Chippendale style mahogany dining chairs, each with an interlaced top-rail and carved scrolling splat, downswept stiles and drop-in seats, on cabriole legs terminating in claw-and-ball feet, 19thC.
£2,000–2,500 *Mit*

A set of 6 Victorian mahogany open-back dining chairs, the central splats carved with scrolling foliage, loose seats, on turned legs.
£1,500–1,800 *E*

A set of 4 William IV mahogany dining chairs, the bar backs above lotus-moulded uprights and foliate carved horizontal splats, curved drop-in seats, on reeded ring-turned tapering legs, with 2 similar chairs.
£520–570 *Bri*

A set of 8 mahogany dining chairs, including 2 carvers, with undulating top-rails and pierced waisted splats, stuff-over leather seats, on square chamfered legs joined by stretchers, 19thC.
£3,000–3,500 *P(EA)*

A set of 6 Victorian mahogany dining chairs, the moulded balloon backs with C-scrolls and cabochon carved splats, above serpentine stuff-over seats, on tapered reeded legs.
£1,450–1,600 *P(B)*

A set of 7 Victorian mahogany dining chairs, with shaped balloon backs, lotus carved middle rail, fluted baluster front legs and Trafalgar seats, on turned tapering front legs and curved back legs.
£1,400–1,600 *AP*

A matched set of 10 mahogany dining chairs, including a carver, with pierced ladder-backs, serpentine shaped rails, brass-nailed padded seats, on straight legs, mid-19thC and later.
£2,600–3,000 *DN*

A set of 6 Victorian mahogany dining chairs, on turned legs, seats upholstered in striped floral damask, the horizontal splats with carved rosettes.
£1,000–1,100 *LEW*

A set of 8 Victorian mahogany open-back dining chairs, with scroll and foliage carved rails, drop-in seats, on turned reeded legs.
£2,200–2,500 *E*

A set of 6 Victorian walnut balloon-back dining chairs, with leaf-carved cresting, on turned fluted legs, some damage.
£900–1,000 *AP*

A set of 4 Victorian walnut dining chairs, the marquetry inlaid spindle backs with arched crest, over-stuffed seats and turned tapering front supports.
£525–625 *AH*

A set of 8 mahogany dining chairs, including 2 carvers, each with a scroll-carved top-rail and pierced vase-shaped splat carved with foliate motifs, between waisted uprights above drop-in serpentine front seats, on acanthus-carved cabriole legs and claw-and-ball feet, c1900.
£5,000–5,500 *Hal*

A set of 6 Sheraton revival mahogany dining chairs, with carved and pierced vase-shaped splats, with fan corners, padded seats, on square tapering legs with spade feet, late 19thC.
£900–1,100 *DN*

A set of 14 Queen Anne style mahogany dining chairs, including 2 armchairs, with slip-in seats, vase-shaped splats, on cabriole legs with pad feet, c1910.
£2,300–2,500 *S(S)*

l. A set of mahogany dining chairs, with pierced ring backs and shaped cresting rails, slip-in seats, on cabriole front legs with carved shoulders and claw-and-ball feet, early 20thC.
£600–700 *GAK*

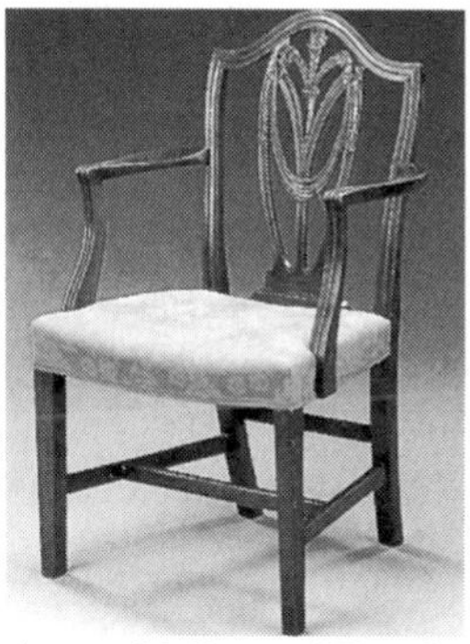

A set of 8 George III style mahogany dining chairs, including 2 armchairs, the moulded arched backs with pierced central splats, on tapered square legs joined by stretchers, c1950.
£3,500–4,000 *S(S)*

A set of 10 George III style carved mahogany chairs, including 2 armchairs, the oval backs with drapery and bellflower surmounts above pierced vase-shaped splats, on moulded tapered square legs ending in spade feet, c1920.
£4,800–5,200 *S(S)*

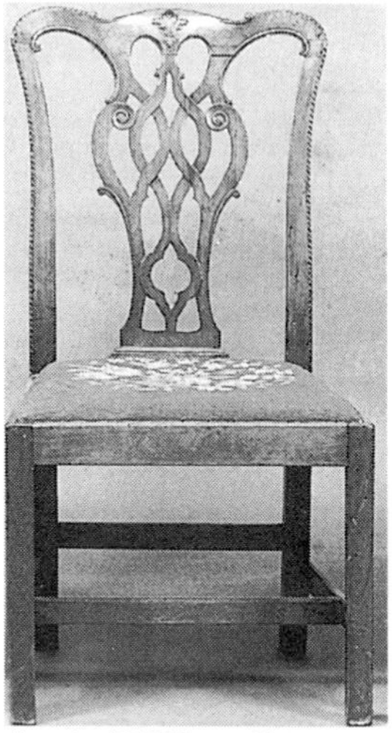

A set of 7 Edwardian Chippendale style mahogany dining chairs, including 2 elbow chairs, the carved interlaced splats with rope-edge uprights, on block legs joined by rail stretchers.
£1,500–1,800 *P(WM)*

A set of 6 Edwardian satinwood and inlaid dining chairs, the shield-shaped backs with vertical bell-flower and ebony-inlaid splats, above serpentine shaped overstuffed seats, on square section tapering legs with spade feet.
£1,700–2,000 *Bon*

A set of 10 Chippendale revival style mahogany dining chairs, each with an undulating top-rail with foliate terminals, above a pierced foliate vase-shaped splat, overstuffed leather seats, on acanthus carved tapering cabriole legs and reeded pad feet, early 20thC.
£8,000–8,500 *Hal*

Hall Chairs

A pair of Regency mahogany hall chairs, the backs with scrolls and double eagle's head ring-turned top-rails, crescent shaped panels, on foliate shaped upright splats, with balloon-shaped solid seats and moulded seat rails, on sabre legs.
£2,500–2,800 *P*

A Swiss carved walnut musical hall chair, the back carved and with central etched panel of stag and doe, carved on the back with the Zurich coat-of-arms, the shaped seat with a central etched panel of 2 deer with hinged seat and back rising to reveal a Swiss music box with a key-wind movement and 7in cylinder, on carved cabriole legs and cloven feet, dated '1882'.
£750–850 *TMA*

A pair of William IV mahogany hall chairs, in the style of Gillows, the cartouche-shaped backs with vacant shields and leaf spray crests, petal sides, tapering seats, on front turned legs.
£1,100–1,200 *WW*

A pair of Victorian mahogany hall chairs, with shaped carved backs, curved front supports and turned front legs.
£1,000–1,200 *DRU*

Library Chairs

A set of 4 Regency rosewood library chairs, with scroll carved terminals, above drop-in seats, on tapered stylised lotus-carved turned legs with brass caps and casters.
£6,500–7,000 *P(W)*

A George III mahogany desk chair, the tub-shaped back with shaped moulded supports and cushioned serpentine seat, on square tapered moulded legs and brass casters, c1790.
£4,600–5,000 *S*

A George II walnut library armchair, the upholstered back, padded arms and seat flanked by acanthus-carved downswept supports, the cabriole legs with stylised shell and leaf-carved knees, on hairy paw feet, c1750.
£8,500–9,500 *S*

MILLER'S COMPARES . . .

I A mahogany library armchair, the button back, sides and bowed seat upholstered in hide, on reeded turned tapering legs with brass casters, c1820.
£5,500–6,000 *S*

II A beechwood library armchair, upholstered in hide, the moulded and scrolled lyre-shaped arm facings carved with palms, on reeded turned legs with brass casters, c1820.
£3,500–4,000 *S*

The reason *Item I* fetched more than *Item II* at auction is because it has a more unusual and elegant shape, with all four legs reeded and turned. The button-back is an attractive feature of this chair, and its small size makes it easier to accommodate in today's houses. *Item II* is a larger, more common design, and more 'Victorian' in shape. *S*

r. An oak reading or library chair, with close-nailed red leather upholstery, adjustable reading slope, turned legs and stretchers, c1870.
£1,500–2,000 *SPa*

A George IV mahogany and upholstered library armchair, on turned and tapered legs ending in brass casters, c1820.
£4,000–4,500 *S*

Nursing Chairs

A Victorian mahogany balloon-back nursing chair, with upholstered button-back and overstuffed seat, on carved cabriole legs.
£450–500 *RTo*

A rosewood-framed nursing chair, with carved and arched back, on leaf-carved cabriole legs with scroll toes and brass casters, mid-19thC.
£320–350 *P(Sc)*

A Victorian mahogany spoon-back nursing chair, moulded in the centre with foliate scrolls, on short cabriole front legs with hoof feet and casters, mid-19thC.
£600–650 *GAK*

Side Chairs

A pair of William and Mary walnut high back side chairs, with pierced and scroll-carved top rails, slender padded back panels enclosed by turned stiles, stuff-over seat on scroll and shaped carved legs united by carved and turned stretchers, originally with caned seat and back.
£450–550 *HOLL*

A pair of George III mahogany side chairs, with upholstered seats, c1780.
£1,200–1,500 *CHA*

A pair of Louis XV painted, carved and moulded beech side chairs, with shaped aprons, on cabriole legs, c1760.
£1,400–1,700 *S(Z)*

A pair of George III mahogany side chairs, carved with anthemia, c1780.
£1,800–2,000 *ANT*

A pair of Victorian walnut chairs, with stuff-over seats, on turned front legs.
£120–150 *LF*

l. A set of 4 George IV brass-mounted rosewood side chairs, each with a reeded bowed top rail, with stuff-over seats, on bulbous gilt-brass knop-headed tapered fluted legs, some restoration.
£1,300–1,500 *P(NW)*

A Queen Anne style walnut side chair, the yoke-form crest above a vasiform splat flanked by chamfered stiles, the slip-in seat within a shaped apron, on cabriole legs joined by block-and-vase turned stretchers, ending in pad feet, repairs and replacements, Boston, Massachusetts, 1740–60.
£2,300–2,500 *S(NY)*

A George III painted beech side chair, the back with a shaped crest and pierced splat decorated with ribbons, leaves and drapery, with borders of beads and pendant leaves, on square tapering legs.
£250–300 *DN*

A pair of George III mahogany side chairs, with carved interwoven splats, c1780.
£1,250–1,500 *ANT*

A pair of walnut chairs, with carved splat backs, cabriole front legs on claw-and-ball feet, 19thC.
£850–950 *DaH*

A set of 4 walnut salon chairs, with shaped backs, floral carved decoration and button upholstery, on cabriole legs, c1860.
£1,000–1,200 *HUB*

l. A Victorian papier mâché chair, inlaid with mother-of-pearl, on cabriole legs.
£170–200 *HOLL*

A Victorian rosewood salon or side chair, the spoon-back with floral needlework covering in a pierced and carved scrolling foliate surround, padded bowfronted seat, on leaf-carved cabriole front legs and lion paw feet.
£700–800 *AH*

A Victorian walnut spoon-back upholstered occasional chair, with arched moulded frame to the back, on cabriole front legs, damaged.
£400–450 *LF*

A set of 4 German giltwood ballroom chairs, with carved top-rail over turned uprights, on sabre legs, c1850.
£1,500–1,800 *S(Z)*

A pair of American laminated rosewood side chairs, by John Henry Belter, with foliate and fruit carved crest rail, padded backs, the upholstered seats over serpentine seat rails, centered with floral carving, on cabriole legs with foliate carved knees, ending in casters, mid-19thC.
£1,400–1,600 *SLN*

John Henry Belter (1804–63)

Born in Germany, John Henry Belter emigrated to the United States in 1833 and developed a range of sumptuously carved and heavily proportioned furniture which was intended to grace the urban and suburban houses of the country's nouveau riche. Belter's furniture was rarely exported and is hardly ever found outside the United States. It was particularly fashionable in places such as New Orleans, New York City and Baltimore, which were populated by wealthy Parisian exiles after the 1848 Revolution in France. Belter's furniture is seldom marked, although some examples are inscribed 'J. H. Belter & Co'. In 1863 the company was taken over by Belter's brother-in-law and became known as Springfield Bros. It ceased trading in 1867.

An ebonised wood upholstered chair, with casters, 19thC.
£340–375 *SPa*

r. A French painted and upholstered chair, late 19thC.
£270–300 *SPa*

A set of 12 Louis XVI style cream-painted salon or side chairs, the oval guilloche carved padded backs and serpentine seats upholstered in close-nailed green leather, above fluted and paterae-moulded friezes, on acanthus fluted tapering legs and spool feet, 19thC.
£5,000–6,000 *P*

A set of 4 Louis XVI style painted side chairs, including 2 armchairs, covered with later needlepoint panels, on fluted tapering legs, 19thC.
£1,100–1,250 *HAC*

l. A pair of Louis XVI style giltwood side chairs, the back rests with pierced lyre-form splats between twist-turned columns with urn finials, gadrooned crest rails and panelled cross-bars, on tapered and stop-fluted legs headed with paterae, 19thC.
£600–700 *SLM*

An Edwardian mahogany inlaid bedroom chair, with padded seat.
£30–40 *CaC*

Chaises Longues & Daybeds

A Louis XV beechwood and walnut *duchesse brisée*, the chair with arched upholstered back, floral cresting and scroll arm supports, with carved seat rail, on cabriole legs, parts renewed, mid-18thC.
£2,400–2,700 *P*

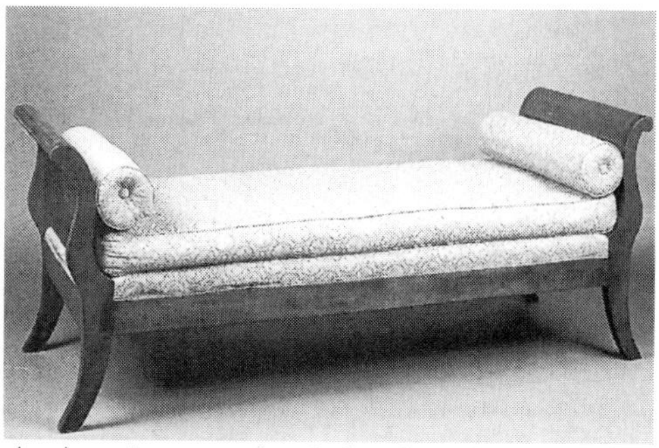

An American neo-classical style walnut daybed, with a pair of scrolled arms over a rectangular loose cushion and plain apron, raised on sabre legs, early 19thC, 69in (175.5cm) long.
£700–800 *S(Cg)*

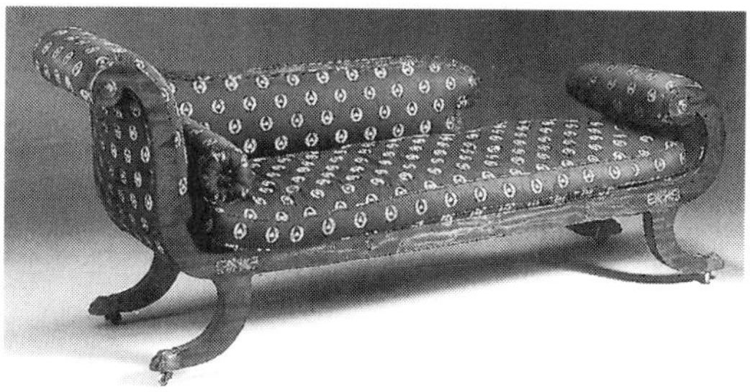

An American figured mahogany daybed, with a reverse-scrolling headrest and shaped, padded backrest centering a loose fitted cushion and ormolu-mounted seat rail, the footrest similarly scrolling, on downswept legs ending in brass paw caps and casters, c1820, 92in (234cm) long.
£2,000–2,500 *S(NY)*

A French rosewood chaise longue, with scroll-padded back, arms and seat covered in floral fabric, the frame inlaid with floral sprays, on bracket feet, c1830, 54in (137cm) long.
£1,600–1,800 *S(S)*

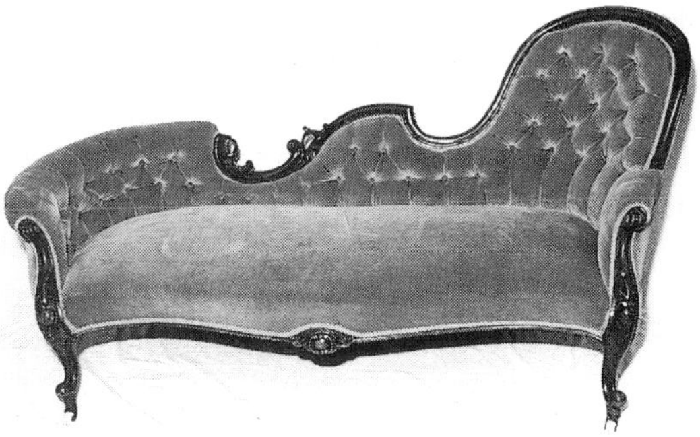

A carved mahogany chaise longue, with deep buttoned upholstery, on carved cabriole legs with original brass and white porcelain casters, c1850, 68in (172.5cm) long.
£2,000–2,400 *LCA*

A Victorian satinwood daybed, with bowed top rails continuing to scrolled channelled downswept padded arms, the shaped seat with a loose padded cushion, on lobed turned channelled legs and brass cap casters, c1880, 71in (180.5cm) long.
£1,600–1,800 *Bon*

A Swedish neo-classical birch daybed, with an undulating upholstered backrest and outscrolled side, raised on scrolled splayed legs, mid-19thC, 67in (170cm) wide.
£2,500–3,000 *S(NY)*

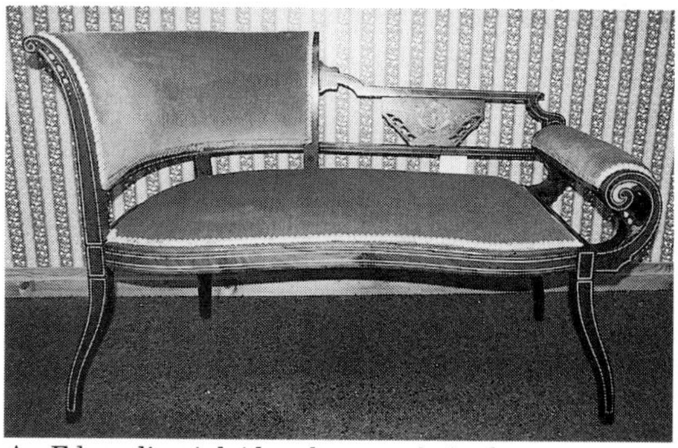

An Edwardian inlaid mahogany chaise longue, 56in (142cm) long.
£600–700 *SWA*

Chests of Drawers & Commodes

An Italian rosewood serpentine commode, the shaped cross-banded top with moulded edge above 4 short off-centre drawers and a shaped apron with applied gilt-metal acanthus mount, on cabriole legs and sabots, c1750, 38in (96.5cm) wide.
£4,000–4,800 *Bon*

A walnut and burr walnut-veneered chest of 2 short and 3 graduated long drawers, with feather banding throughout, crossbanded top, ovolo carcass mouldings and on later short cabriole feet, some restoration, early 18thC, 41in (104cm) wide.
£2,000–2,200 *Bea(E)*

A George II mahogany chest, the moulded edge top above 2 short and 3 long drawers with oak linings, the engraved decorative brass swan neck handles with rococo plates and escutcheons, the ogee bracket feet on lignum vitae casters, 37in (94cm) wide.
£3,700–4,200 *WW*

An oyster-veneered walnut and floral marquetry inlaid chest of 2 short and 3 long graduated drawers, with later cast-brass lion mask ring handles, 17thC, 38½in (198cm) wide.
£10,500–11,500 *DA*

Oyster Veneering

To make oyster veneer, the smaller branches (2–3in (5–8cm) diameter) of certain trees were cut transversely into veneers and pieced together as parquetry, or mosaic. Oyster-pieces were generally cut from walnut and laburnum saplings, but other woods such as lignum vitae, kingwood and olive were also used.

An Anglo-Dutch walnut chest, with a moulded edge, the 3 long drawers between concave angles, on bracket feet, early 18thC, 35½in (90cm) wide.
£5,000–6,000 *P*

A George III mahogany chest of drawers, with a brushing slide, 4 long cockbeaded graduated drawers, brass swan neck drop handles, oak-lined drawers, pine triple plank back panelling and bracket supports, 33in (84cm) wide.
£2,000–2,200 *HCC*

A William III oyster-veneered chest of 2 short and 3 long graduated drawers, cross-banded and inlaid with strung roundels and lines, on bun feet, 39in (100cm) wide.
£8,000–9,000 *P(O)*

A German Baroque walnut-veneered commode, with 5 drawers locking at the side, on bun feet, early 18thC, 40½in (103cm) wide.
£5,500–6,000 *S(Z)*

A George II walnut chest, by Giles Grendey, with herringbone and crossbanding, the quartered top with moulded borders, fitted with a slide above 4 long drawers with original brass handles, on bracket feet with concealed wooden rollers, restored, 30in (76cm) wide.
£28,000–32,000 *DN*

Giles Grendey, 1693–1780, was elected to the Livery of the Joiners Company in 1729 and became Master in 1766. His most important commission was that for the Duke of Infantado in northern Spain for at least 77 pieces of scarlet japanned furniture. He also carried out commissions at Longford Castle, Stourhead and Keddleston Hall. A number of labelled pieces by him are still in existence.

A George III mahogany serpentine chest, with 4 long graduated drawers, the top with moulded edge and canted corners, supported on shaped bracket feet, 48½in (123cm) wide.
£4,000–4,500 *TMA*

A late George III mahogany bowfronted chest of drawers, 48in (122cm) wide.
£650–750 *Ber*

A George III yew chest of drawers, with brass swan neck handles, on shaped bracket feet, 36in (91.5cm) wide.
£1,700–2,000 *HOLL*

A George III mahogany Lancashire chest, with quarter-turned and reeded side columns, the 6 short and one long drawer with brass swan neck handles and ogee bracket feet, 63in (160cm) wide.
£1,200–1,400 *JM*

A George III mahogany chest, with inlaid boxwood stringing to the top, 4 graduated long drawers with a slide above, brass rectangular plates and handles, with shaped apron, on splayed bracket feet, 36in (91.5cm) wide.
£1,600–2,000 *Gam*

A George III mahogany Lancashire chest, with a rising top, reeded canted corners, plain frieze with 5 false drawers and 4 drawers below, with brass handles, supported on ogee bracket feet, 66in (167cm) wide.
£2,300–2,800 *L&E*

A Milanese rosewood commode, the frieze and upper drawer with marquetry flower and oak leaf swags, baskets and ribbons, the lower 2 drawers and the ends with oval panels of classical figures, crossbanded in tulipwood and walnut with leaf borders and pilasters with urns, baskets, leaves and dolphins, on square tapering legs, late 18thC, marble top later, 46in (117cm) wide.
£4,800–5,800 *DN*

An American Chippendale style maple chest of drawers, the moulded rectangular top, over 4 long graduated drawers, on shaped bracket feet, 33in (84cm) wide.
£1,350–1,500 *SLN*

MILLER'S COMPARES . . .

I A George III satinwood bowfront chest of drawers, with 3 long graduated drawers and shaped apron, on splayed bracket feet, splits to top and sides, c1800, 39in (99cm) wide.
£4,000–4,500 *S(S)*

II A George III mahogany bowfront chest of 3 long drawers, later shallow rear gallery, with a shaped slide, above an apron, on splayed bracket feet, c1780, 37in (94cm) wide.
£1,600–1,750 *S(S)*

Whilst these 2 chests of drawers appear very similar in a black and white illustration, it is the use of exotic golden satinwood that adds dramatically to the value of *Item I.* *Item II*, **although an attractive piece, is made of the more common mahogany, and the later addition of a rear gallery detracted somewhat from the value.** *S(S)*

A George III satinwood, mahogany and tulipwood-banded bowfront chest of drawers, the quarter-veneered top centred with a harewood oval, cross-banded and inlaid with boxwood and ebonised lines on splayed legs, c1800, 36in (91.5cm) wide.
£5,750–6,250 *P*

A Regency mahogany bowfront chest of 3 long graduated drawers, between leaf-headed reeded column uprights, on turned front feet and rear bracket feet, 38in (96.5cm) wide.
£1,100–1,200 *TMA*

A Regency mahogany chest of drawers, with 4 crossbanded drawers flanked by reeded pilasters, on dwarf sabre legs, 47in (119.5cm) wide.
£1,100–1,200 *RBB*

A mahogany bowfront chest of drawers, with crossbanded drawer fronts, c1920, 39in (99cm) wide.
£600–700 *SWA*

An American Chippendale style tiger maple tall chest of drawers, one long top drawer with 3 false fronts over 2 short drawers and 5 long graduated drawers raised on shaped bracket feet, 19thC, 39in (99cm) wide.
£4,000–4,500 *SLN*

A late Federal mahogany chest of drawers, the 4 graduated cockbeaded drawers with bird's-eye maple fronts, flanked by ring-turned and fluted columns, shaped apron with central pendant, on peg feet, New England, c1830, 43in (109cm) wide.
£2,500–3,000 *S(Cg)*

A Victorian mahogany chest of drawers, with 5 long graduated drawers each with bevelled edge and turned wooden handles, 30in (76cm) wide.
£850–900 *BWe*

A Dutch walnut marquetry chest of 6 drawers, decorated with floral and diamond marquetry, with marble top, square tapering front legs and rear carved bracket feet, early 19thC, 38in (96.5cm) wide.
£1,500–1,800 *TMA*

A Victorian mahogany bowfronted chest of drawers, the 2 short and 3 long flame-figured drawers with wooden knob handles, between semi-circular section pilasters, on turned legs, 43in (109cm) wide.
£400–480 *EH*

An Adam revival style green painted and parcel-gilt commode, the top decorated with a tableau of cherubs and foliate motifs, with a floral border, the breakfront central section with 3 mahogany-lined drawers decorated with floral swags, the sides with bowed cupboard doors decorated with oval panels depicting 18thC scenes, on turned tapered fluted legs, c1910, 61½in (155.5cm) wide.
£3,700–4,500 *S(S)*

Chests-on-Chests

A walnut secretaire chest-on-chest, with moulded pediment, fitted with 3 short drawers over 3 long graduated drawers, the fall-front enclosing a fitted interior, 2 further long graduated drawers below, 18thC, 42½in (108cm) wide.
£20,000–22,000 *GAK*

This chest-on-chest was bought from the same auctioneer some 8 years ago for £12,000 and proved equally popular when it came to be sold recently.

A George III mahogany tallboy, with dentil cornice, the frieze and canted corners carved with repeating X-motifs, 2 short and 6 graduated long drawers, on shaped bracket feet, 45½in (115.5cm) wide.
£1,200–1,400 *Bea(E)*

A George III mahogany chest-on-chest, the top with moulded cornice, 2 short and 3 long drawers, flanked by satinwood banded and ebony strung canted corners, the base with 3 long drawers with brass handles, on bracket feet, 43in (109cm) wide.
£2,500–3,000 *DN*

A George III mahogany chest-on-chest, the dentil cornice above 3 short and 3 long drawers with original brass swan-neck handles, the base with 3 long drawers and shaped apron, on splayed bracket supports, minor restorations, 47½in (120.5cm) wide.
£1,000–1,100 *Bri*

A walnut, oak and chevron-banded chest-on-chest, the moulded cornice above 2 short and 6 long graduated drawers, on bracket feet, 18thC, 43in (109cm) wide.
£5,000–5,500 *P(Ba)*

A Georgian mahogany inlaid chest-on-chest, with satinwood and ebony-banded cornice, 2 short and 4 long graduated cockbeaded drawers over 3 long drawers, brass drop handles with sphinx mask embossed lozenge-shaped backplates, on bracket feet, 42in (106.5cm) wide.
£1,500–1,800 *AP*

r. A Regency mahogany bowfront chest-on-chest, the curved crossbanded cornice inlaid with a central lozenge motif, above 2 short and 6 long graduated cockbeaded drawers, on a shaped apron and splay bracket feet, moulding losses, some handles replaced, c1805, 44in (112cm) wide.
£1,500–2,000 *Hal*

MILLER'S COMPARES . . .

I A George II walnut-veneered tallboy, the cavetto cornice above 2 short and 3 long drawers, the base with 3 long oak-lined drawers, the fronts with herringbone line inlay, shaped brass plate handles and escutcheons, on bracket feet, 40in (101.5cm) wide.
£15,000–18,000 *WW*

II A George II Virginian walnut and mahogany tallboy, the cavetto cornice above 2 short and 3 long drawers, between fluted angled corners, the base with a brushing slide and 3 long oak-lined drawers, brass open plate handles and escutcheons, on bracket feet, 42½in (108cm) wide.
£3,000–3,500 *WW*

Both tallboys pictured above have desirable features such as original handles and escutcheons. The herringbone inlay, crossbanding and cockbeading on *item I*, **and the fluted canted corners and brushing slide on** *item II* **are all decorative additions which help to lift the value. Factors which enhanced the value of** *item I* **compared to** *item II* **were its earlier date – about 20 years – its good proportions, the subtle moulding to the corners and the book-match veneers.** *Item I* **also had the attractive honey colour of period walnut, whereas** *item II* **was made of Virginian walnut which has the darker appearance of mahogany.** *WW*

Chests-on-Stands

A William and Mary walnut chest-on-stand, the upper part with a cushion frieze drawer, 2 short and 3 long drawers below, the stand with ogee arched apron, on cup and turned legs united by stretchers, 38in (96.5cm) wide.
£2,500–3,000 *P*

A Queen Anne walnut and crossbanded chest-on-stand, with 2 short and 3 long drawers, the stand with 3 drawers and ogee arched apron, on oak cabriole legs and hoof feet, restored, 41in (104cm) wide.
£3,000–3,500 *S(S)*

A Queen Anne walnut, mulberry and herringbone-strung chest, containing 2 short and 3 long graduated drawers, on later stand with cabriole legs and pad feet, 38½in (98cm) wide.
£2,800–3,200 *P(EA)*

A walnut and feather-banded chest-on-stand, on later cabriole legs and pad feet, early 18thC, 40½in (103cm) wide.
£3,600–4,000 *P(O)*

A walnut-veneered chest-on-stand, with 3 short and 3 long crossbanded drawers, the later stand with a shaped apron and 3 drawers, on cabriole legs and club feet, early 18thC, 41in (104cm) wide.
£2,800–3,200 *P(S)*

A walnut and chevron-banded chest-on-stand, the upper part with 2 short and 3 long drawers, the lower part with 3 frieze drawers and shaped arched apron, on cabriole legs and pad feet, early 18thC, 40in (101.5cm) wide.
£2,800–3,200 *P*

l. A George I walnut chest-on-stand, the ogee moulded cornice above 2 short and 2 long drawers with fretted brass swan neck handles, the base with single deep drawer, on 4 carved cabriole supports, stand later, 42½in (108cm) wide.
£1,000–1,200 *Bri*

r. An American cherrywood chest-on-stand, the upper section with 3 short and 3 long drawers between canted and fluted stiles, the outset, moulded, lower section with a frieze drawer over an arrangement of 3 short drawers, handles later, Pennsylvania, c1760, 43in (109cm) wide.
£2,000–2,500 *SLM*

Secretaire Chests

A George III mahogany crossbanded secretaire chest, with satinwood line inlay, the fall-front revealing a writing surface, fitted interior, and flanked by 2 short and one deep drawer over base with 3 long graduated drawers, on carved bracket feet, 48in (122cm) wide.
£1,000–1,200 *TMA*

A George III mahogany secretaire chest, the writing drawer with oval segmented veneers, the fitted interior with an inset, 3 long drawers below, now with turned handles, on splayed bracket feet, c1800, 47in (119cm) wide.
£1,100–1,200 *S(S)*

A Regency mahogany secretaire chest, the central secretaire drawer flanked by a short drawer and a false drawer enclosing slides, above 3 further brass-inlaid long drawers, raised on bracket feet, 47½in (121cm) wide.
£1,000–1,200 *Bon*

Miller's is a price GUIDE not a price LIST

A George III yew-wood secretaire chest, the top drawer simulating 2 long drawers and enclosing a fitted interior, above 3 long drawers, on bracket feet, in 2 parts, 40in (101.5cm) wide.
£3,000–3,500 *L*

A mahogany secretaire campaign chest, in 2 sections, the secretaire drawer fitted with drawers and pigeonholes, 3 long drawers below, with Bramah locks, brass recessed handles and corner mounts, on bun feet, early 19thC, 39½in (100.5cm) wide.
£1,800–2,000 *Bea(E)*

A mahogany secretaire military chest, in 2 sections, the fall concealed by 2 dummy drawer fronts enclosing a satinwood interior of short drawers above arched pigeonholes, 3 long graduated drawers below, with brass carrying handles to the sides, on bracket feet, 19thC, 33in (84cm) wide.
£1,000–1,200 *P*

A George III mahogany secretaire chest, with moulded edge, the top inlaid with floral marquetry, the similarly inlaid fall-front enclosing a fitted interior of drawers and pigeonholes, 3 long graduated drawers below, on bracket feet, late 18thC, inlay possibly later, 44½in (113cm) wide.
£1,100–1,200 *GAK*

A camphor wood and ebony-strung secretaire military chest, the top with fitted drawer and fall-front concealing a fitted interior, 2 short and 2 long drawers below with campaign handles, raised on scrolling bracket feet, early 19thC, 37½in (95.5cm) wide.
£2,000–2,500 *P(G)*

FURTHER READING
Miller's Late Georgian to Edwardian Furniture Buyer's Guide, Miller's Publications, 1998

A mahogany and crossbanded chest of 2 short and 2 long drawers, with boxwood and ebony line inlay, the top right secretaire drawer with fall-front enclosing a fitted interior of drawers and pigeonholes, on splay bracket feet, 19thC, 33½in (85cm) wide.
£600–700 *P(NW)*

Wellington Chests

A Regency bird's-eye maple Wellington chest, with 8 long drawers over a plinth base, early 19thC, 21½in (54.5cm) wide.
£2,000–2,500 *SLN*

Bird's-eye maple is a yellow-brown wood with dark spots like birds' eyes, linked by wavy lines.

A Victorian mahogany Wellington chest, with 7 graduated drawers and locking bar, c1860, 22in (56cm) wide.
£2,500–2,850 *BERA*

A Victorian oak Wellington chest, with locking pilasters, 24in (61cm) wide.
£1,100–1,200 *DN*

A Victorian walnut Wellington chest, with 5 graduated drawers and double drawer-fronted cupboard beneath, rectangular side standards with applied scrolls to the top, mid-19thC, 24in (61cm) wide.
£1,200–1,400 *GAK*

A Victorian walnut secretaire Wellington chest, with locking bars and carved corbels, c1860, 22in (56cm) wide.
£4,250–4,750 *BERA*

A Victorian mahogany Wellington secretaire chest, with hinged top over 8 graduated drawers, 2 fitted as a secretaire, 24½in (62cm) wide.
£2,600–3,000 *P(G)*

A mahogany Wellington chest, the top with moulded edge above 7 drawers, raised on a plinth base, mid-19thC, 29in (74cm) wide.
£1,600–2,000 *Bon*

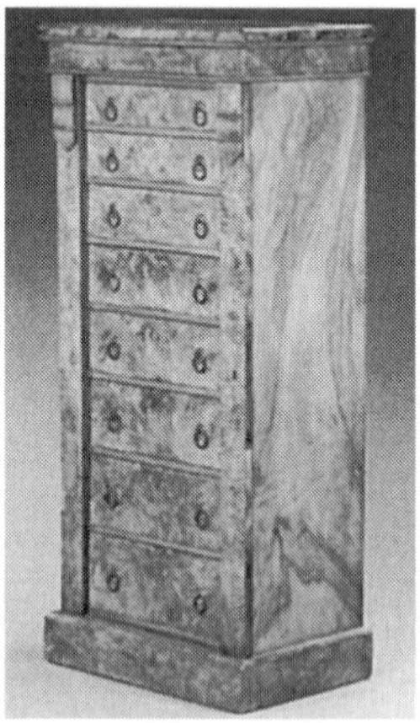

A Victorian walnut Wellington chest, the 8 drawers with hinged pilaster terminals and carved scroll corbels, on a plinth base, split to top, c1860, 27in (68.5cm) wide.
£2,000–2,200 *S(S)*

A late Victorian walnut Wellington chest, the top with dentil moulded frieze above 6 graduated drawers, flanked by a locking pilaster and raised on a plinth base, stamped 'J. A. Shoolbred & Co', 23in (58cm) wide.
£1,100–1,200 *Bon(C)*

A Victorian burr walnut secretaire Wellington chest, the locking side flap enclosing 2 short fitted drawers, double dummy drawer fall-front enclosing a fitted interior, 3 further graduated drawers below, mid-19thC, 24½in (62cm) wide.
£1,850–2,000 *GAK*

A Victorian burr walnut Wellington chest, with 8 graduated drawers and moulded corbels to the terminals, on a plinth base, c1860, 22in (56cm) wide.
£3,000–3,200 *S(S)*

A mahogany secretaire Wellington chest, by Flashman, c1890, 23in (58.5cm) wide.
£2,200–2,500 *GBr*

Cupboards

A Queen Anne walnut and feather-banded cabinet, the upper part fitted with adjustable shelves, the lower part with a moulded overhanging edge fitted with a baize-lined slide and long drawer, 40½in (103cm) high.
£3,700–4,000 *P*

A Regency mahogany linen press, the flame mahogany panelled doors enclosing a slide, the base with 2 short and 2 long drawers, on shaped apron with outswept splayed feet, handles replaced, 47in (119.5cm) wide.
£1,200–1,400 *Bri*

A late George III mahogany linen press, the upper part adapted for hanging and enclosed by a pair of panelled doors, 2 short and 2 long drawers below with brass bail handles, on bracket feet, 43in (109cm) wide.
£1,300–1,500 *MCA*

A Victorian mahogany bowfronted cupboard-on-chest, with arched surmount on moulded cornice, 2 panelled doors enclosing shelving, the protruding base with 3 small frieze drawers over 2 short and 3 long drawers with turned handles, turned corner columns and feet, 51½in (131cm) wide.
£750–900 *AH*

l. A Continental mahogany and burr walnut cupboard, the top with stylised carved spread eagles over 2 glazed doors and 2 drawers, flanked by barley twist columns, above 2 panelled cupboards on a moulded stepped base and block feet, probably Dutch, c1870, 60in (152.5cm) wide.
£600–700 *AAV*

r. A George III style mahogany gentleman's clothes press, c1900, 38½in (98cm) wide.
£1,200–1,400 *Doc*

A flame mahogany linen press, with oval panels and tulipwood cross-banding, 2 short and 2 long drawers to base, c1800, 49in (124.5cm) wide.
£2,300–2,600 *SPa*

A Victorian flame-veneered mahogany linen press, with 2 short and 2 long drawers, on a plinth base and compressed bun feet, 48in (122cm) wide.
£1,100–1,200 *CoH*

Davenports

A rosewood davenport, with sliding top, slope with leather inset and three-quarter brass gallery to the rear, slide and 4 graduated drawers to the right side, dummy drawers to the left, raised on squat circular fluted feet, c1800, 20in (51cm) wide.
£1,800–2,000 *GAK*

A mahogany davenport, with fitted interior, flanked by 3 drawers, c1830, 25in (63.5cm) wide.
£1,100–1,400 *BUSH*

A Victorian walnut davenport, the leather inset top enclosing maple interior, with 4 true and 4 false drawers, on turned supports with casters, 21in (53cm) wide.
£450–500 *Bri*

r. A Victorian walnut davenport, with pierced brass gallery and secret stationery compartment, hinged writing surface with pierced scroll and leaf-carved supports opening to reveal 4 dummy drawers, side door enclosing 4 drawers, on turned feet, with porcelain casters, 22in (56cm) wide.
£2,000–2,500 *AH*

A George IV rosewood davenport, with carved fan corners and gadrooned borders, the sliding top with pen tray and inkwells, the interior with secret drawers, 4 drawers under, flanked by spiral-turned columns on each side, on square gadrooned bun feet, 19½in (49.5cm) wide.
£1,600–1,750 *E*

A William IV mahogany and burr walnut-veneered davenport, the sliding top with a balustraded gallery, the slope inset with green tooled-leather, revealing 2 drawers and 2 dummy drawers, hinged pen and ink drawer to the side, above 4 graduated drawers, the other side with a slide above dummy drawers, outline panelled front and back, the moulded edge base on melon fluted feet with brass casters, 23½in (59.5cm) wide.
£2,600–3,000 *WW*

A Regency mahogany davenport, the top with a leather inset and rear brass gallery, the side with a swivel pen drawer above 4 long drawers, on reeded bun feet and concealed casters, damaged, c1810, 19in (48cm) wide.
£2,750–3,000 *S(S)*

A burr walnut-veneered davenport, decorated with boxwood lining, the hinged superstructure enclosing stationery rack, the top with hinged lid and pull-out writing surface with compartments, the base with bowed doors to the sides enclosing drawers and shelves, on sledge base with scroll-carved brackets, mid-19thC, 24½in (62cm) wide.
£2,300–2,500 *P(Sc)*

A Victorian figured walnut piano-top davenport, with rising top, sliding front with writing surface on ratchet, panelled door to the sides enclosing 4 drawers, with curving front legs carved with flowers, 21in (53.5cm) wide.
£2,800–3,200 *JNic*

A George IV mahogany davenport, with a pierced gallery above the sloping front, inset with a tooled-leather writing surface lifting to reveal a fitted interior, the top sliding, flanked to the right by 4 graduated drawers with wooden knob handles and to the left by dummy drawers, on short turned feet, 22in (56cm) wide.
£2,800–3,200 *Mit*

A Victorian walnut davenport, the raised back with pierced brass gallery, hinged to reveal fitted stationery compartment, the slope on wrythen-turned and block supports, and enclosing 4 small drawers, 4 side drawers with turned wood handles, on turned feet and casters, 21in (53.5cm) wide.
£2,400–2,700 *AH*

A Victorian walnut and boxwood-strung davenport, with domed pen box above leather inset fall-front, 4 real and 4 dummy drawers to each side, with turned, scroll-carved front supports on platform base and casters, 21in (53cm) wide.
£1,000–1,200 *HOLL*

Desks

A walnut and feather banded kneehole desk, the top cross-banded and quarter-veneered, with one long and 6 short drawers, arched apron with a recessed enclosed cupboard below, on later bracket feet, early 18thC, 34in (86.5cm) wide.
£2,000–2,200 *P*

A George III mahogany, satinwood crossbanded and inlaid tambour roll top desk, the fall enclosing a fitted interior with a hinged fall compartment between drawers and pigeonholes and a tooled leather surface, the fluted frieze containing 2 drawers and dummy drawers to the side and reverse, on square tapered legs, brass cappings and casters, 36in (91.5cm) wide.
£5,500–6,000 *P*

A George II red walnut kneehole desk, the frieze drawer with original brass swan neck handles, the central cupboard flanked by 2 sets of 3 graduated drawers, on shaped bracket feet, moulding and veneer losses, 32½in (82.5cm) wide.
£1,850–2,200 *Bri*

l. A Federal birch and satinwood inlaid mahogany lady's desk, with 3 cockbeaded cupboard doors enclosing a fitted interior, over projecting base opening to reveal baize-lined writing surface, over 3 long cockbeaded drawers, on square tapering inlaid legs, American, c1800, 41½in (105.5cm) wide.
£3,500–4,000 *SLN*

A George IV mahogany kneehole pedestal desk, the top with tooled green leather inset, above one long frieze drawer and 3 graduating drawers to the kneehole, with false drawers on the opposing side, raised on bracket feet, 43½in (110.5cm) wide.
£3,500–4,000 *Bon*

A mahogany double-sided twin pedestal desk, one side with an arrangement of 9 drawers, the other with 2 doors beneath 3 drawers, brass carrying handles with shaped backplates, casters concealed within the plinth bases, cast brass furniture incomplete, 18thC, 60in (162.5cm) wide.
£15,000–18,000 *LAY*

This desk was discovered by the auctioneers in the back of a local chemist's shop. Its potential was recognised despite its peeling veneer, missing beading and cracked top, and bids were attracted from as far afield as America and Germany. It finally sold for over 7 times its top estimate. This is an indication of the very high prices currently being paid for some unrestored items which are new to the market.

l. A north Italian olivewood and walnut-veneered small writing desk, with one long drawer over kneehole flanked by 4 short drawers, on cabriole legs with bronze sabots, c1800, 48½in (123cm) wide.
£2,750–3,000 *S(Z)*

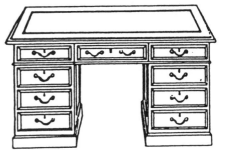

A Victorian oak writing table, with inset leather top, the gadroon-edged border with carved leaf corners, one central drawer above kneehole with carved brackets flanked by 2 deeper drawers to front and back, on turned, fluted and leaf-capped legs with casters, 71in (180.5cm) wide.
£1,300–1,500 *CAG*

A Victorian mahogany partners' desk, the leather inset top above 3 frieze drawers on either side, and raised on pedestals each with 3 drawers to either side, 60in (153cm) wide.
£2,400–2,800 *B*

A French carved oak desk, with 5 drawers around an open recess in the superstructure, c1880, 48in (122cm) wide.
£1,000–1,250 *HAC*

A Victorian mahogany desk, with leather inset top, a central drawer flanked by 4 bowfronted drawers on each side, turned wood handles, on plinth base, 48in (122cm) wide.
£1,200–1,300 *E*

A mahogany partners' desk, with oak lined drawers, c1880, 62in (157.5cm) wide.
£3,800–4,250 *GBr*

A late Victorian neo-classical style rosewood and bone-inlaid writing desk, by Gillows, the shelved superstructure containing a pair of concave hinged compartments inlaid with oval paterae, scrolling acanthus and swags above small drawers, the tooled red leather shaped and moulded top above a frieze drawer flanked by 4 small bowed drawers, on square tapering legs and spade feet, 48½in (123cm) wide.
£3,500–4,000 *P*

An oak pedestal desk, with brass handles and ash-lined drawers, c1880, 48in (122cm) wide.
£1,000–1,250 *GBr*

An oak desk, the roll-top opening to reveal drawers and pigeonholes, c1900, 54in (137cm) wide.
£1,700–2,000 *GBr*

A Louis XVI style mahogany parquetry and gilt-metal mounted desk, by F. Linke, the kingwood parquetry top veneered with an interlocking cube design within beaded gilt-metal borders, above a long frieze drawer applied with a foliate gilt-metal scroll tablet with foliate ring handles, opposed by a similar design with false drawer handles, each side applied with a Bacchanalian mask, raised on florally mounted and acanthus lappeted fluted cylindrical legs and turned toupie feet, slight damage, c1900, 43in (109cm) wide.
£6,000–7,000 *Hal*

François Linke (Austrian 1855–1946), established himself at the Paris Exposition Universelle of 1900, and was known for fine quality furniture in the Louis XV and XVI styles. He later became disillusioned with copying 18thC pieces and worked with the sculptor Message creating a completely new style which was a pastiche of Louis XVI and Art Nouveau.

l. An American Renaissance revival style walnut partners' desk, the frieze with 2 drawers with foliate-carved pulls flanking an arched centre, the sides with brass handles, the double pedestal with 3 cupboard doors and a bank of 3 drawers with carved pull handles, late 19thC, 65½in (166.5cm) wide.
£2,200–2,500 *S(Cg)*

An Edwardian mahogany kneehole writing desk, by Maple & Co, with leather writing surface, c1905, 39in (99cm) wide.
£1,200–1,400 *RPh*

An Edwardian Sheraton revival writing desk, by Maple & Co, with concave central drawer between 2 further drawers, on square tapered legs, 42in (106.5cm) wide.
£2,000–2,300 *EH*

An Edwardian oak roll-top desk, with S-shaped tambour and fielded panels all-round with 4 drawers to each pedestal, on plinth bases, 55in (139.5cm) wide.
£1,250–1,400 *Mit*

An Edwardian inlaid mahogany writing desk, fitted with stationery compartments, inset leather-lined writing surface below, 2 short drawers with brass handles, raised on square tapering legs and spade feet, 42in (106.5cm) wide.
£700–800 *AG*

An Edwardian mahogany and inlaid kneehole desk, the top with a gilt tooled green leather inset and walnut banding, with an arrangement of 9 drawers, on plinth bases, restored, c1910, 47in (120cm) wide.
£1,600–1,800 *S(S)*

An oak roll-top single pedestal desk, c1920, 36in (91.5cm) wide.
£1,200–1,300 *GBr*

An Edwardian mahogany partners' desk, with 3 frieze drawers, each pedestal with 3 drawers with brass handles, 51in (129cm) wide.
£1,750–2,250 *BUSH*

A Chippendale revival style mahogany desk, with tooled-leather inserts, the acanthus-carved bevelled edge above 2 cockbeaded frieze drawers, with foliate brass swing handles, the lockplates stamped 'Maple & Co', on acanthus-carved tapering cabriole legs and claw-and-ball feet, c1920, 48in (122cm) wide.
£2,000–2,200 *Hal*

Dumb Waiters

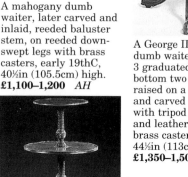

A George III mahogany folding top two-tier dumb waiter, the graduated swivel tiers on urn knopped column and inswept tripod legs with brass casters, 38in (96.5cm) high.
£2,800–3,500 *P*

A George III mahogany three-tier dumb waiter, the tiers with raised moulded borders, on turned columns and 3 splayed legs with casters, 45in (114.5cm) high.
£1,200–1,300 *DN*

A mahogany dumb waiter, later carved and inlaid, reeded baluster stem, on reeded downswept legs with brass casters, early 19thC, 40½in (105.5cm) high.
£1,100–1,200 *AH*

A George III mahogany dumb waiter, with 3 graduated tiers, the bottom two revolving, raised on a turned and carved column with tripod supports and leather-covered brass casters, 44½in (113cm) high.
£1,350–1,500 *AG*

l. A George III mahogany dumb waiter, the 3 dish-moulded and graduated tiers with spiral fluted supports above a turned pillar, on tripod cabriole legs with pad feet and casters, c1760, 42in (112cm) high.
£2,750–3,000 *S*

Etagères

A Louis XV style amboyna and marquetry three-tier étagère, the pierced gilt three-quarter gallery with a geometric inlaid top above a frieze drawer, the similarly inlaid tiers joined by shaped ebonised supports and outswept feet, damaged, late 19thC, 16in (40.5cm) wide.
£275–300 *P*

A Napoleon III three-tier étagère, the upper tier with a pierced gilt-metal gallery and turned finials, each tier inlaid with a floral spray on an embossed ground, on slender scrolled ebonised legs, c1860, 14½in (37cm) wide.
£300–350 *Bon*

l. A Louis XV style mahogany étagère, the *brêche violette* marble top with a bronze gallery, the conforming freeze with a drawer, 3 concave fluted supports, the lower parquetry shelf with bronze gallery, raised on 3 canted square tapering cabriole legs ending in foliate cast bronze sabots, late 19thC, 14in (35.5cm) wide.
£400–450 *SLM*

A Victorian satin birch and painted three-tier étagère, decorated with flowering branches and birds, the shaped shelves with pierced brass galleries, on gilt turned supports, 24in (61cm) wide.
£650–750 *S(S)*

A French Louis XV style ebonised and amboyna three-tier étagère, applied with gilt-metal mounts, on cabriole legs, late 19thC, 17in (43cm) wide.
£650–750 *P*

Marquetry

Marquetry is an elaborate form of inlay which involves cutting shapes in a veneer, usually floral patterns and other decorative motifs such as birds, urns, shells and scrollwork. These shapes are then inlaid with wood, ivory, bone or mother-of-pearl. The technique first became popular in England in the late 17thC, with the influx of Dutch craftsmen following the coronation of William of Orange as King of England in 1688.

Frames

An Augsburg silver and enamelled frame, the wood core with brass borders mounted with silver and tortoiseshell heightened with enamelling, c1720, 8½ x 7in (21.5 x 17.5cm).
£1,500–1,650 *S*

Miller's is a price GUIDE not a price LIST

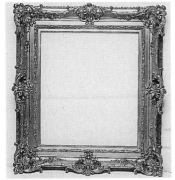

A Continental giltwood frame, with pierced foliate carved centres and corners, late 19thC, 29 x 26in (73.5 x 66cm).
£400–450 *SLN*

A French gilded composition Empire style frame, with stepped sight, pin and ribbon-twist, fluted hollow with acanthus corners and bound berry and laurel leaf D-section top edge, early 19thC, 21 x 16½in (53.5 x 41.5cm).
£350–400 *Bon(C)*

A carved and pierced gilded frame, with stepped sight, centred gadrooned motif, acanthus hollow between C-scroll quarters and leaf cartouche centres and corners, 19thC, 47 x 34in (119.5 x 86.5cm).
£1,800–2,000 *Bon*

A gilded composition frame, with cavetto sight, the arched slip with flowers to the spandrels, fluted hollow with pronounced foliate cabochon centres and corners, 19thC, 49 x 39in (124.5 x 99cm).
£550–650 *Bon(C)*

A Continental pierced and gilded composition frame, with wedge sight, stylised leaf, plain frieze, and plain hollow between foliate cartouche centres and corners joined by bound cluster-reeded top-rail, late 19thC, 31½in x 25in (90 x 63.5cm).
£450–500 *Bon(C)*

Jardinières

A Victorian gilt-metal mounted walnut jardinière, the detachable lid enclosing a tin liner above a shaped frieze, on cabriole legs with foliate sabots, the whole decorated with gilt-metal foliate mounts, c1870, 26in (66cm) wide.
£1,600–1,750 *Bon*

A Louis XVI style giltwood and composition jardinière, the circular caned basket applied with swags, on outswept tripod legs headed by rams' heads and joined by a circular caned undertier, on hoof feet, late 19thC, 43½in (110.5cm) high.
£1,000–1,200 *P*

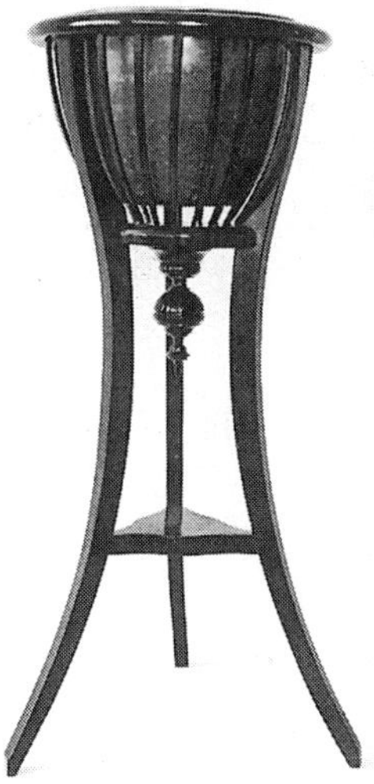

An Edwardian mahogany jardinière, with open slatted sides, anodised brass container, splayed trefoiled supports with turned finial under, triangular undertier, 35½in (90cm) high.
£300–350 *HCC*

Lowboys

A Queen Anne walnut lowboy, inlaid with banding, the crossbanded top with cusped corners, with 3 drawers and an arched apron, the sides in pine, on cabriole legs ending in pad feet, restored, 33in (84cm) wide.
£1,500–1,800 *S(S)*

A Queen Anne style inlaid sycamore and maple lowboy, the top inlaid with 6 diamonds centring a heart, 6 short thumb-moulded drawers, the shaped apron below with applied beaded edge and pendant finials, on cabriole legs ending in pad feet, New England, c1740, 29½in (75cm) wide.
£3,500–4,200 *S(NY)*

A George II fruitwood lowboy, the top with moulded edge and re-entrant corners, with one drawer, on cabriole legs with volute feet, restored, 32in (81cm) wide.
£700–800 *DN*

A George II mahogany lowboy, 30½in (77.5cm) wide.
£1,350–1,500 *TMA*

A burr elm lowboy, the moulded edge top containing 3 drawers around an arched apron, on cabriole legs and pad feet, mid-18thC, 27½in (70cm) wide.
£5,200–5,800 *P*

A Queen Anne style carved and figured cherrywood lowboy, the top above one long drawer and 3 short drawers, the centre drawer blocked and fan-carved, the shaped apron below with pendant acorns, on cabriole legs ending in pad feet, American, mid-18thC, top later, 35in (89cm) wide.
£5,000–5,500 *S(NY)*

Miniature Furniture

A Charles II walnut miniature chest-on-stand, the quarter-veneered top above 2 short and 3 long graduated drawers, the base with a single frieze drawer and double arched apron centred by a drop finial, on bulbous turned legs and bun feet, tied by a waved X-stretcher, c1680, 25½in (65cm) wide.
£12,000–15,000 *Bon*

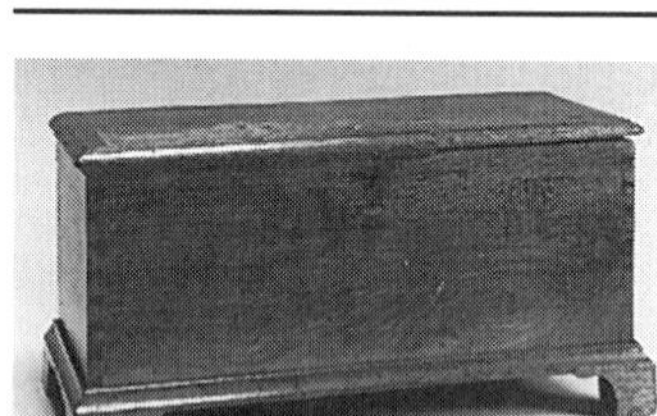

A walnut miniature blanket chest, the hinged lid opening to a well and a till, on bracket feet, American, mid-18thC, 25in (63.5cm) wide.
£1,400–1,600 *S(NY)*

A Federal inlaid and figured-mahogany miniature bowfront chest, shaped apron below on splayed bracket feet, American, c1800, 17½in (44.5cm) wide.
£630–700 *S(NY)*

A Federal inlaid and figured mahogany dressing chest and mirror, the shaped scrolling crest above a miniature plate, 4 graduated drawers above a shaped apron and straight bracket feet, American, c1790, 13½in (34.5cm) wide.
£1,750–2,000 *S(NY)*

A German walnut and fruitwood crossbanded bowfront miniature chest, with chequer-strung top and 3 long drawers between ebonised column corners, on bun feet, early 19thC, 14½in (37cm) wide.
£800–1,000 *P*

A Victorian mahogany miniature sideboard, the low mirror panelled back with arched pediment, 3 frieze drawers above recessed centre, fitted cupboards enclosed by 2 pairs of doors with raised centre panels with scroll carving, 12in (30.5cm) wide.
£600–700 *CAG*

An inlaid mahogany miniature chest, with 3 drawers, c1880, 14in (35.5cm) high.
£900–1,000 *GeM*

A Dutch neo-classical gilt-metal mounted tulipwood and fruitwood miniature chest of drawers, with 2 drawers of slightly breakfront outline, raised on hipped cabriole legs, 19thC, 14in (35.5cm) wide.
£2,300–2,600 *S(NY)*

A Biedermeier walnut and ash root miniature chest of drawers, with a hinged top opening to a fitted interior, above a simulated frieze drawer and 2 long drawers flanked by ebonised pilasters, raised on block feet, early 19thC, 16in (40.5cm) wide.
£1,200–1,500 *S(NY)*

A mahogany miniature chest of drawers, the rosewood cross-banded top above 3 graduated drawers flanked by ebony inlay, on turned tapered feet, 19thC, 17½in (44.5cm) wide.
£2,400–2,700 *S*

A south German rococo style walnut and fruitwood parquetry miniature commode, with serpentine-fronted top above 3 long drawers, raised on splayed legs, late 19thC, 17in (43cm) wide.
£1,750–2,000 *S(NY)*

A Victorian camphor wood and brass-bound miniature campaign chest, in 2 parts, with 2 short and 3 long drawers, with countersunk handles, on block feet, c1850, 17in (43cm) wide.
£4,000–4,500 *S*

A George III style mahogany miniature chest-on-chest, the 2 short and 3 long graduated drawers with canted chequer-strung corners above 3 further long graduated drawers, inlaid throughout with chequered stringing, on ogee bracket feet, 19thC, 12in (30.5cm) wide.
£4,500–5,000 *S*

A mahogany miniature chest of drawers, late 19thC, 10in (25.5cm) wide.
£80–100 *Ber*

l. A late Victorian mahogany miniature half-tester bed, 20in (51cm) long.
£600–650 *DaH*

Cheval Mirrors

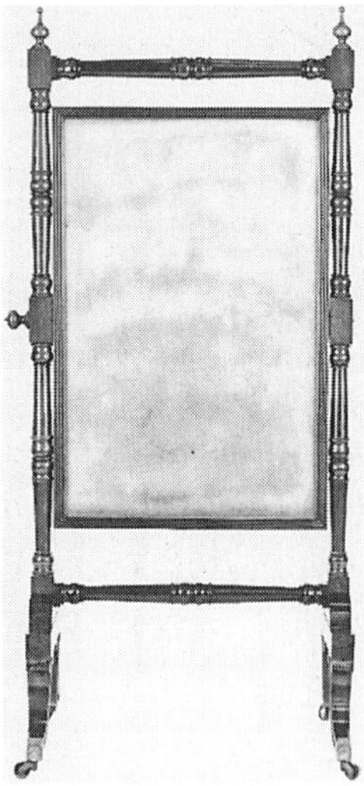

A Regency mahogany cheval mirror, the mirror plate within a reeded frame with baluster-turned and block carved outer frame, on sabre end standards, terminating in shell brass caps and casters, 68in (172cm) high.
£1,500–1,700 *HSS/P*

A Regency mahogany cheval mirror, possibly by Gillows, the rectangular mirror frame with a carved scrolling mount above the arched mirror with foliate carving and set between turned supports, with cast brass handles, turned stretchers and down-swept legs terminating in brass caps and casters with supports, 36in (91.5cm) wide.
£1,800–2,000 *Mit*

A Regency mahogany and ebony-strung cheval dressing mirror, the arched pediment with oval stringing, the rectangular plate flanked by adjustable candle sconces and branches, on dual splayed standard end supports, brass cappings and casters, 65½in (166cm) high.
£1,800–2,000 *P*

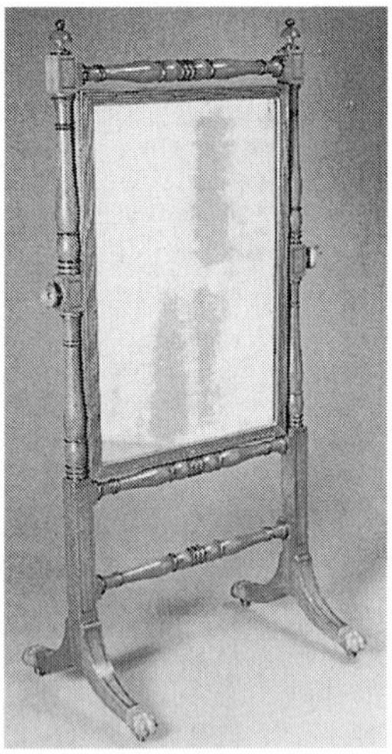

A late George IV mahogany and ebony inlaid cheval mirror, the rectangular plate with reeded edge frame, enclosed by ring-turned supports on splay legs, brass paw caps and casters, 66in (167cm) high.
£900–1,000 *HOLL*

A George III mahogany cheval mirror, the telescopic plate with brass carrying handle, on arched supports with brass cappings and casters, c1790, 58in (147cm) high.
£2,200–2,500 *S*

A George III satinwood cheval mirror, the mirror plate with telescopic action flanked by purple heart-inlaid and boxwood-strung uprights, articulated brass candle arms, on arched supports with brass casters, c1790, 71in (180cm) high.
£4,000–4,500 *S*

A Regency mahogany cheval mirror, supported by ring-turned uprights with finial surmounts and inlaid with brass and rosewood panels, on splay supports with applied half-round bead moulding, on turned feet with brass casters, 63½in (161cm) high.
£1,500–1,800 *MSW*

A William IV mahogany cheval mirror, on moulded square tapering supports with scrolled ends, twin pole stretchers and bun feet with casters, 64½in (164cm) high.
£1,000–1,200 *AH*

l. A Victorian mahogany cheval mirror, with arched top, on cabriole supports, 62in (157.5cm) high.
£700–750 *DN*

r. A Victorian satin birch cheval dressing mirror, the turned and fluted supports with a conforming stretcher, the block feet on concealed casters, c1870, 30in (76cm) wide.
£1,000–1,200 *S(S)*

The Tenterden Galleries

FLOWER HOUSE ANTIQUES

Flower House Antiques

FINE ENGLISH & CONTINENTAL FURNITURE, COLLECTABLES, VALUATIONS, RESTORATION, ITEMS PURCHASED

90 High Street, Tenterden,
Kent TN30 6JB

Telephone: 01580 763764

We buy and sell quality furniture, collectables, jewellery, porcelain, silver. A wide range of antique and interesting items always available.

Open 7 days a week.

Full or part house clearances undertaken, sound advice given.

Ask for Jan Byhurst (Proprietor)

Heirloom Antiques
68 High Street, Tenterden, Kent
01580 765535

GABY GUNST

ANTIQUE CLOCKS
& BAROMETERS

140 High Street, Tenterden, Kent
Tel: 01580 765818

3 showrooms of antique Longcase, Grandmother, Skeleton, Bracket & Wallclocks all restored in our own workshop.

Trading for 25 years. Closed Sundays

Sparks Antiques

English & Continental furniture, objects & collectors' items.

4 Manor Row,
Tenterden, Kent TN30 6HP

Tel: 01580 766696

Dressing Table Mirrors

A Queen Anne walnut and crossbanded toilet mirror, the plate within a moulded frame and tapering uprights with brass finials, 3 frieze drawers in the base, on bracket feet, 17in (43cm) wide.
£1,500–1,700 *P*

A walnut-veneered dressing table mirror, with 3 concave-fronted drawers to the box base and on ogee bracket feet, early 18thC, 17½in (44.5cm) wide.
£300–350 *Bea(E)*

A George IV mahogany dressing table mirror, the moulded mirror frame within turned and tapered uprights and turned finials, the rectangular plinth on turned bun feet, c1825, 16½in (42cm) wide.
£650–700 *S*

A Queen Anne walnut toilet mirror, the plate within a moulded border, the bureau style plinth inlaid with feather banding, the fall-front revealing 3 small drawers, one side with a later adjustable brass candle branch and sconce, on ogee bracket feet, restored, 18in (46cm) wide.
£1,200–1,400 *S(S)*

A late George III mahogany and tulipwood crossbanded toilet mirror, on a serpentine box base fitted with 3 drawers, on ogee bracket feet, 18½in (47cm) wide.
£500–550 *P(O)*

A pair of William IV mahogany dressing table mirrors, each with scroll surmount and leaf-carved scrolling supports above a bowfront base with single frieze drawer, on scroll feet, 38½in (98cm) wide.
£1,100–1,200 *P(G)*

A George I walnut toilet mirror, the bevelled plate within a moulded frame, the burr veneered and crossbanded plinth with narrow feather-banding, the moulded drawer above shaped bracket feet, restored, 18in (46cm) wide.
£600–700 *S(S)*

A George III mahogany dressing table mirror, the rectangular plate surmounted by 3 ivory finials and a central partridge-wood cresting, the bowfront plinth with a narrow rosewood crossbanding, above 3 drawers, inlaid throughout with stringing, on turned ivory ball feet, 21in (53cm) wide.
£1,000–1,200 *S*

A Victorian mahogany toilet mirror, 29in (73.5cm) wide.
£180–200 *MiA*

Wall Mirrors

A Spanish tortoiseshell, bone and mother-of-pearl framed wall mirror, the chamfered margin with segmented geometric veneers and inlaid scroll, late 17thC, 22in (55.5cm) high.
£1,500–1,800 *S(S)*

An Italian giltwood mirror, carved with C-scroll borders, shells and acanthus leaves, mid-18thC, 50in (127cm) high.
£2,000–2,200 *DN*

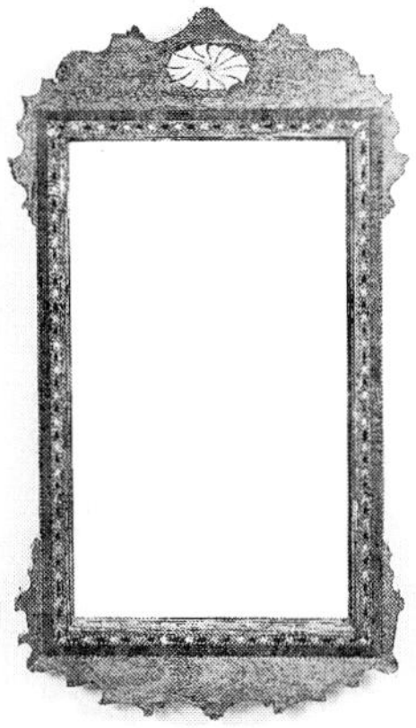

A George III mahogany chevron-strung and crossbanded wall mirror, the bevelled edge plate within a fret-carved frame surmounted by a fan inlaid crest, 17½in (44.5cm) high.
£350–400 *P*

A Queen Anne carved giltwood and gesso wall sconce, the arched plume cresting above a shaped and bevelled plate with an incised border, the shaped foliate surround flanked by bellflower pendants and with a conforming shaped apron surmounted by a single silver metal candle arm, 28in (71cm) high.
£3,700–4,000 *S*

A carved giltwood rectangular wall mirror, with applied corner rosettes and original shallow bevelled mirror plate, 18thC, 43½in (110.5cm) high.
£1,000–1,200 *RBB*

A walnut cushion frame wall mirror, decorated with panels of scrolling foliage, inset with a later rectangular plate within moulded surround, 17thC, 32½in (82.5cm) wide.
£3,500–4,000 *P(EA)*

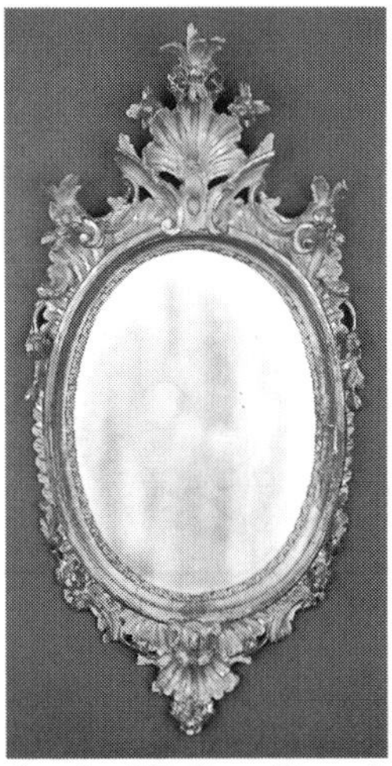

A pair of Italian giltwood mirrors, the plate with a concave moulded edge surmounted by a floral carved crest centred by a shell flanked by C-scrolls and flowers, the apron with further flower and shell carving, mid-18thC, 38in (96.5cm) high.
£4,000–4,500 *Bon*

A George II giltwood wall mirror, the frame carved and pierced with flowers, leaves and C-scrolls, 48in (122cm) high.
£2,000–2,500 *P(W)*

A George II giltwood mirror, within a frame carved with foliate scrolls and flowerheads and with a pierced arched cresting, 23in (56.5cm) wide.
£1,100–1,300 *Bea(E)*

r. A late George III giltwood oval wall mirror, with hawk, sparrow and leaf-moulded crest, husk and moulded sides, and 3 candle branches to the base supported by a putti, 47in (120cm) high.
£900–1,000 *HOLL*

Care of Mirrors

If the silver backing of an antique mirror has badly deteriorated, repair should not be attempted as any restoration will always substantially devalue the piece.

To clean a mirror wipe the glass with a lint-free linen cloth moistened with either paraffin or methylated spirit, or alternatively use a lint-free linen cloth wrung out in lukewarm water to which a few drops of ammonia have been added. It is essential to avoid any moisture getting behind the glass, as this will cause further deterioration of the silvering.

A Federal giltwood and églomisé wall mirror, the églomisé panel decorated with shells, coral and floral paterae on a diaperwork field, the mirror plate below flanked by reeded columns with leafy capitals, on a beaded base, some losses to gilding, églomisé panel refreshed, c1815, American, 41½in (105.5cm) high.
£500–600 *S(NY)*

A Regency overmantel mirror, with 3 bevelled plates in a gilt-moulded frame flanked by reeded pilasters with Corinthian capitals, the classical frieze with spherical moulded inverted breakfront cornice, 35½in (90cm) wide.
£900–1,000 *Gam*

A George IV giltwood-framed convex wall mirror, with eagle surmount and foliate scrollwork, c1830, 37½in (95cm) high.
£600–700 *S(S)*

An Italian crescent-shaped mirror, in limewood frame carved with amorini and a dragon, c1870, 33in (84cm) high.
£850–950 *GBr*

A late Victorian Aesthetic Movement ebonised looking glass, the bevelled chamfered plate set in a flat cushion panelled frame, mounted with white plaques, depicting the Seasons, a bird and dolphin inhabited foliate scrolls, 42in (107cm) high.
£2,300–2,500 *L*

A Regency style gilt gesso convex mirror, with eagle surmount, convex plate and rope-twist surround, the foliate apron issuing 3 scrolling candle arms, 19thC, 43in (109cm) high.
£1,200–1,300 *LRG*

A Transitional style gilt and composition framed mirror, the bevelled plate with beaded slip tied to a rosette, on tongue moulded frame by C-scrolled and rocaille cartouche, mid-19thC, 52in (132cm) high.
£650–750 *Bon(C)*

A Venetian glass wall mirror, with etched foliate decoration, the oval bevelled edge plate and marginals within a moulded, spiral-twist and flowerhead decorated frame, late 19thC, 49½in (125.5cm) high.
£700–800 *P*

A Dieppe bone and ivory wall mirror, with oval bevelled plate surrounded by foliage, cherubs and coats-of-arms, the base with a basket of flowers and 2 cherubs holding wreaths, 19thC, 33in (84cm) high.
£2,200–2,500 *E*

Dieppe was one of the most important centres for the production of carved ivory smallwork and figures, as well as larger pieces like this.

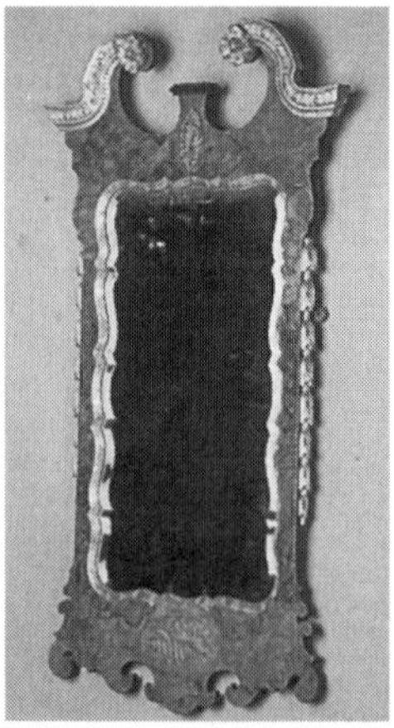

l. An Edwardian walnut and parcel-gilt mirror, in George I style, with scroll cresting above an inlaid shell medallion and shaped bevelled mirror plate flanked by graduated tassels, the fretwork apron with an oval conch shell inlaid medallion, c1910, 46in (117cm) high.
£620–680 *S(S)*

A Dutch mirror, the central bevelled plate with flared bevelled side plates between die-stamped gilt-brass foliage and crimple mouldings, with gilt-brass foliage dividers, 19thC, 49in (124.5cm) high.
£1,700–2,000 *WW*

Screens

An Italian rococo polychrome painted leather-covered six-panel screen, with flowering foliage and birds centring a large cartouche for a reserve decorated with mythological scenes, mid-18thC, each panel 24in (61.5cm) wide.
£2,250–2,500 *S(LA)*

Ex-Marlene Dietrich collection.

A mahogany four-fold screen, each framed panel with a claret fabric inset, early 19thC, each panel 31½in (80cm) wide.
£1,000–1,200 *S(S)*

A Louis XV style three-leaf leather screen, painted with a Watteauesque scene, surrounded by floral and foliate scroll borders, raised on scroll-carved walnut cabriole legs, late 19thC, 54in (137cm) wide.
£850–1,000 *SLM*

A four-fold screen, composed of Spanish polychrome and gilt stamped leather panels, with cartouche sprays of foliage and flowers, within giltwood frames, 18thC, each panel 22½in (57cm) wide.
£3,500–4,000 *P*

An Empire painted paper four-panel screen, the panels *en grisaille* depicting figures in period costume in a landscape setting with a fox hunt in the foreground, now in a later *grisaille* border, early 19thC, each panel 21in (53.5cm) wide.
£4,000–4,500 *S(NY)*

A Louis XVI style giltwood three-fold screen, the central panel with an upper glazed section fitted with foliate-scrolls and a floral-filled basket above an Aubusson tapestry panel, flanked by floral Aubusson panels, late 19thC, 81in (207cm) wide.
£5,500–6,500 *S(NY)*

A Chinese export black and gilt lacquer six-fold screen, decorated on both sides with pavilions amid trees and water, with figures and boats, within a broad border of entwined dragons, late 18thC, each panel 21½in (54.5cm) wide.
£3,700–4,000 *P(WM)*

A four-fold gilt leather screen, the panels painted with exotic foliage and birds, 19thC, each panel 22½in (57cm) wide.
£500–600 *P(Sc)*

Miller's is a price GUIDE not a price LIST

An Edwardian satinwood and marquetry three-panel screen, the crest of each panel with fan inlay surmounting a clear glass panel, with a carved draped ribbon and bellflower garland above a pair of elaborate carved S-scrolls flanking a long-stem tulip issuing carved scrolls, the frame string-inlaid, the lower sections with fabric panels, late 19thC, each panel 21½in (54.5cm) wide.
£1,500–1,800 *S(Cg)*

Fire Screens

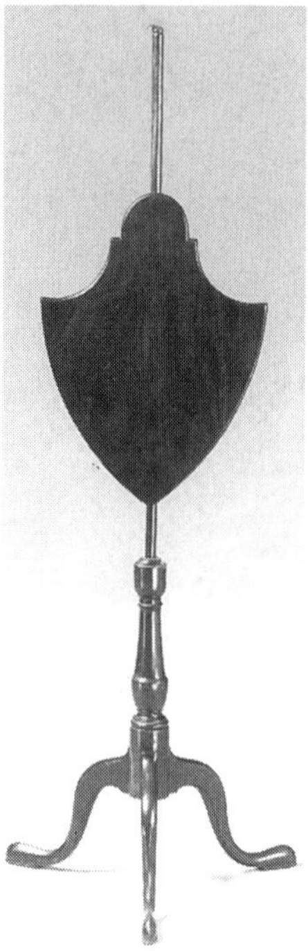

A Federal mahogany fire screen, with an adjustable shield-shaped screen, repaired, American, c1800, 54in (137cm) high.
£900–1,000 *S(NY)*

A Regency mahogany framed fire screen, with 3 adjustable rectangular panels, on sabre legs with brass caps and casters, 39½in (100.5cm) high.
£400–450 *CGC*

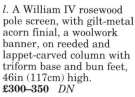

l. A William IV rosewood pole screen, with gilt-metal acorn finial, a woolwork banner, on reeded and lappet-carved column with triform base and bun feet, 46in (117cm) high.
£300–350 *DN*

A mid-Victorian walnut and thuya wood inlaid pole screen, the needlework screen with foliate crest and base, raised on a machined brass pole and foliate-carved tripod base, 56in (142cm) high.
£300–350 *Bon*

A Victorian rosewood pole screen, the stand with lobed baluster base and moulded cabriole legs with scrolled toes, the woolwork banner worked with a hawk, 20in (51cm) high.
£300–350 *L*

A Victorian mahogany pole screen, with woolwork panel depicting a lady dismounting from a camel at a desert camp, within a rectangular foliate and C-scroll frame, on a barley-twist column with tripod base on scrolled feet, 25in (63.5cm) high.
£500–550 *M*

A Victorian mahogany pole screen, the foliate scroll-carved panel inset with needlework coat-of-arms, the stem on three-sided base carved with leaves, on reeded scroll legs with block feet, 66in (168cm) high.
£400–450 *Oli*

l. A Louis XV style giltwood fire screen, incorporating an associated 17thC tapestry fragment, within a moulded frame and open carved border, the arched cresting with leafy scrolls, on acanthus-carved cabriole legs, 19thC, 28½in (72.5cm) wide.
£500–550 *P(Z)*

A Brazilian rosewood pole screen, the brass pole with chased end finial, the screen with floral damask to a ribbon-tied moulded frame, with a fluted column, on leaf-carved scroll legs, 19thC, 50in (127cm) high.
£220–250 *WW*

Settees & Sofas

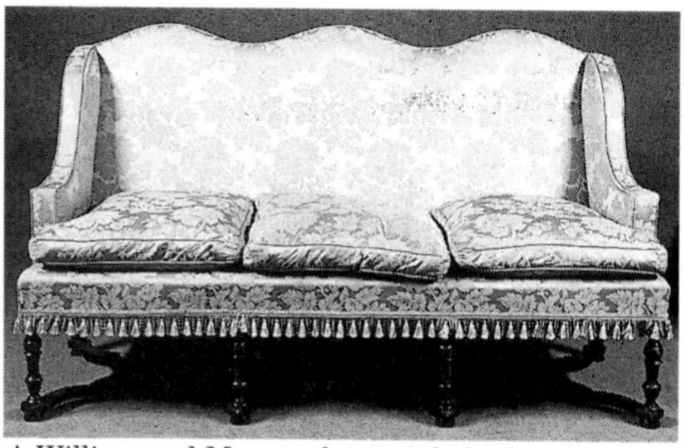

A William and Mary walnut triple-back settee, with shaped arms, turned front legs united by double curving X-stretchers, each with turned upright finials at the centres, 75in (190.5cm) wide.
£5,200–5,800 *B*

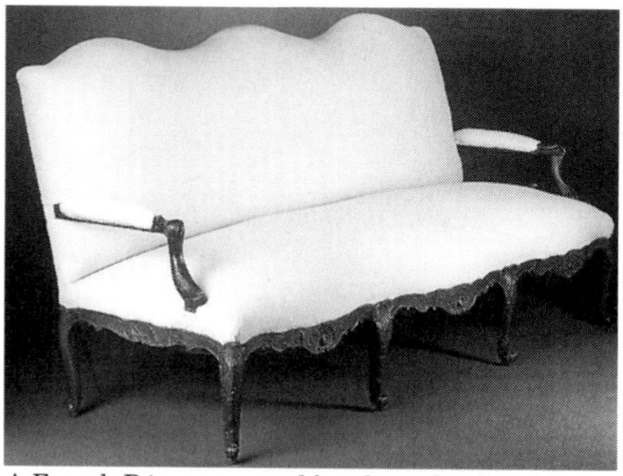

A French Régence carved beechwood sofa, with carved apron, on cabriole legs with scrolled feet, early 18thC, 85in (216cm) wide.
£3,000–3,500 *S(Z)*

A George III painted chairback settee, decorated throughout with flowers, ribbon-tied swags and an urn on a green ground, the triple rail-back with pierced X-shaped splats above a caned seat, with open arms, on turned tapering legs with brass casters, painted decoration later, c1790, 58½in (148.5cm) wide.
£2,000–2,500 *S*

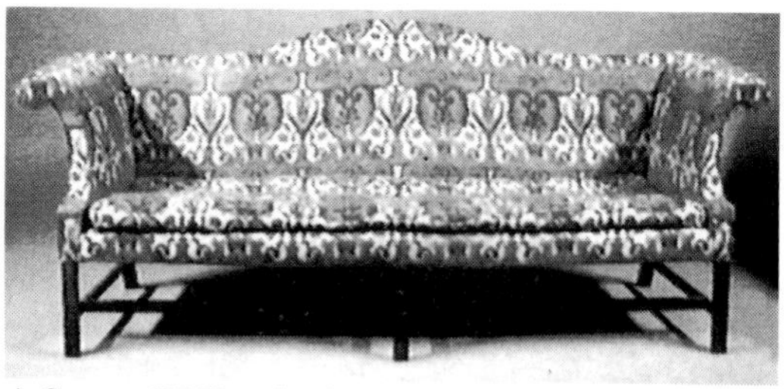

A George III Hepplewhite mahogany humpback settee, with scrolling ends and separate cushion, square chamfered front legs united by stretchers, 88in (223.5cm) wide.
£2,300–2,500 *B*

A Swedish Gustav III blue and gold painted sofa, the moulded top-rail and padded back continuing to downswept channelled padded arms, the padded seat on turned tapered fluted legs headed by paterae, attributed to Eric Holm, maker's guild paper label, c1780, 75in (190.5cm) wide.
£1,700–1,850 *Bon*

In 1765 the Guild of Chair Makers decreed that all master chair makers were to apply the guild's paper label to all their works. The labels can be found on seat furniture up to the early 19thC.

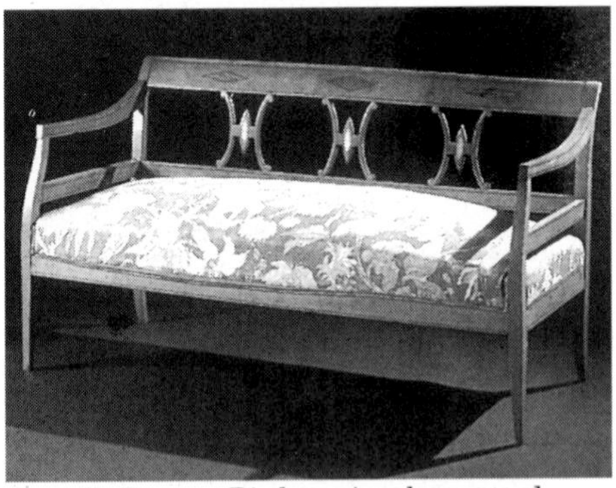

A south German Biedermeier cherrywood settee, the top rail inlaid with lozenges, the open back set with C-scrolled splats, on square tapering legs, upholstered with floral fabric, c1825, 59in (150cm) long.
£1,700–2,000 *S(Am)*

A William IV rosewood settee, upholstered in tapestry style material, the upright pillars with stiff-carved leaves, moulded frame, floral carved bosses, raised on turned and leaf-carved legs with brass casters, 80in (203cm) long.
£2,400–2,800 *DMC*

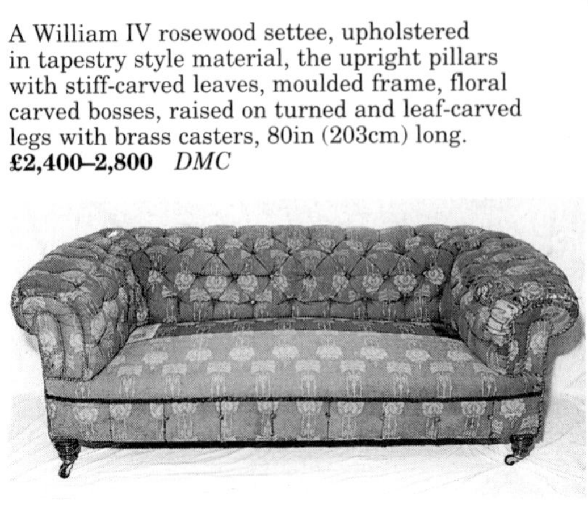

l. A Victorian chesterfield three-seater settee, with walnut turned front legs and original brass and brown porcelain casters, 82in (208.5cm) wide.
£900–1,000 *LCA*

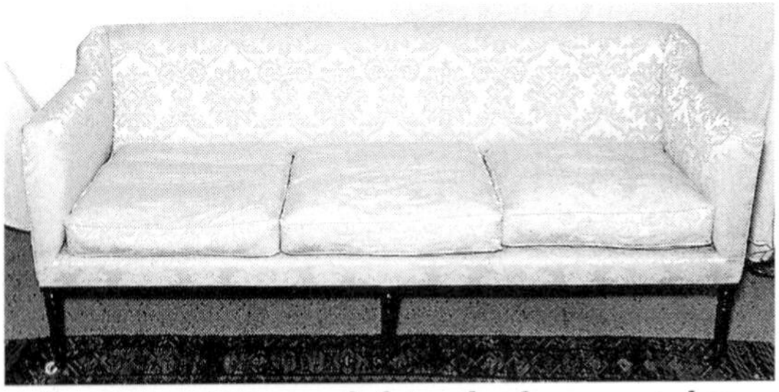

A Regency mahogany upholstered sofa, supported on turned legs, terminating in brass casters, c1820, 82in (208.5cm) long.
£2,700–3,000 *ANT*

A Regency ebonised and gilt-framed sofa, with padded back and sides, turned arm supports painted with leaves and foliate motifs, loose seat squab, on tapering ring-turned legs, some repainting, 76in (193cm) wide.
£900–1,100 *Bea(E)*

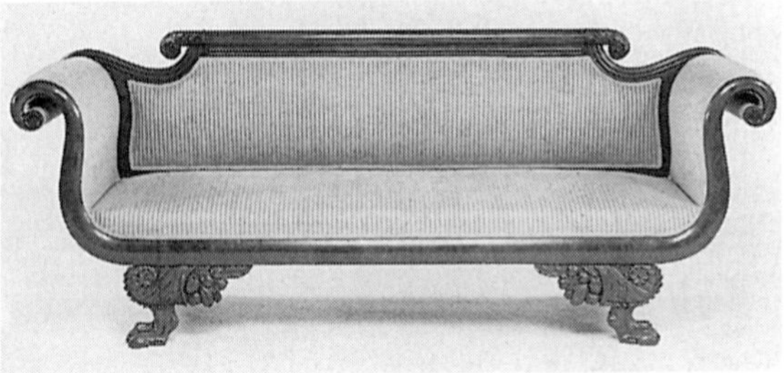

An early Empire mahogany sofa, the turned crest-rail terminating in foliate carving, over padded back, the outscrolled arms and upholstered seat over moulded seat rail, raised on cornucopia carved legs, ending in carved hairy paw feet, American, c1825, 83in (211cm) wide.
£1,000–1,200 *SLN*

An early Victorian sofa, the back with a plain mahogany-veneered arch rail, each arm with fruit and cornucopia shaped and carved front support, 82in (208.5cm) wide.
£500–600 *LAY*

A Victorian mahogany settee, the arched back with foliate carved crest over rounded arms, with carved and scrolled front supports, 87in (221cm) long.
£950–1,100 *SWO*

Inside a Sprung Sofa

From 1830 most sofas were upholstered with coiled metal springs covered with padding and webbing, which made them more comfortable.

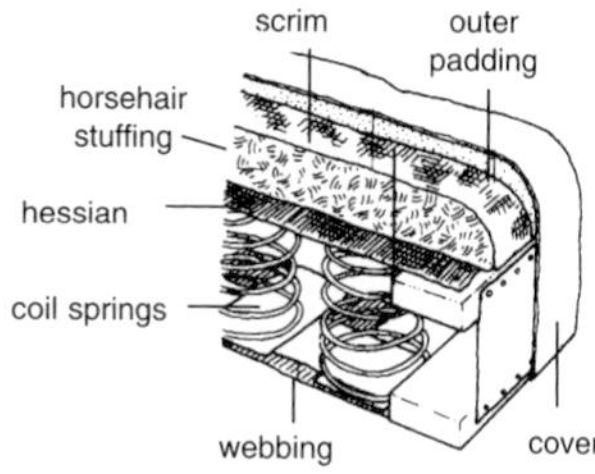

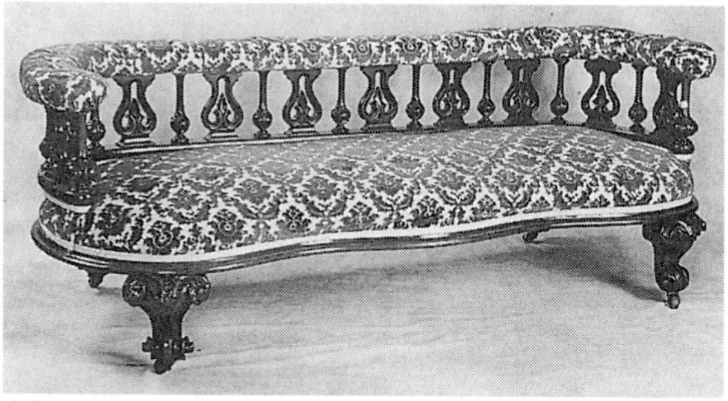

A Victorian mahogany sofa, with cream ground red velvet patterned floral upholstery, serpentine seat, on scrolled legs, 75in (190.5cm) wide.
£400–500 *EH*

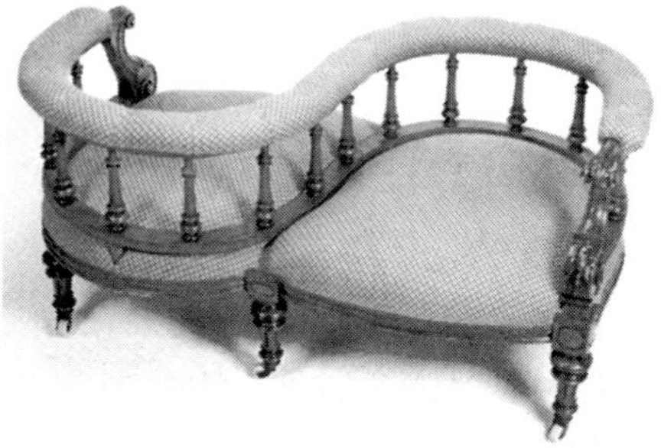

A Victorian carved and turned mahogany conversation seat, with padded and upholstered continuous back and arm support and sprung double seat, raised on turned and fluted supports and casters, 64in (162.5cm) wide.
£1,300–1,500 *BIG*

A French carved oak sofa, the back with a central lion mask, lion heads on the arms, on barley-twist legs and stretchers, c1900, 58in (147cm) wide.
£1,200–1,300 *HAC*

An Edwardian mahogany sofa, with hooped back and slightly splayed arms, boxwood-strung uprights, joined by serpentined apron, splayed feet, 50in (127cm) wide.
£420–480 *GAK*

An Edwardian two-seater sofa, banded throughout in boxwood and satinwood with ebonised stringing, the padded back with a central pierced splat, inlaid with a rosette, the slightly splayed arm rests raised on shaped uprights, on tapering square supports, 45½in (115.5cm) wide.
£420–480 *GAK*

A William and Mary style oak and upholstered knole settee, upholstered in burgundy damask, with hinged sides, the turned and moulded legs joined by scroll and foliate-carved stretchers, early 20thC, 79in (200.5cm) long.
£1,100–1,200 *S(S)*

Shelves

A set of George III mahogany hanging shelves, c1800, 36in (92.5cm) wide.
£1,400–1,600 *ANT*

A set of mahogany hanging shelves, mid-19thC, 16in (40.5cm) wide.
£340–375 *ANT*

A set of walnut shelves, c1890, 25in (63.5cm) wide.
£200–225 *MLL*

For more furniture refer to our special Focus On Ireland section.

Sideboards

A George III mahogany inverted bowfront sideboard, probably by Gillows, with blind gallery above the inverted bowfront, the single drawer with brass drop handles and pierced circular back plates, an arched recess flanked by 2 short drawers with cockbeading, on turned tapered legs ending in brass-capped casters, 44in (112cm) wide.
£2,800–3,200 *Mit*

A Georgian mahogany sideboard with satinwood crossbanding, with foliate and ribbon-tied swags, the raised plinth of inverted serpentine form and with a pair of cupboards flanking 2 frieze drawers, lion mask and ring handles, on square tapering legs and spade feet, 78in (198cm) wide.
£4,200–4,700 *LRG*

A George III mahogany and boxwood-strung serpentine sideboard, the shaped top with broadly crossbanded edge above a central frieze drawer, flanked on each side by a cellaret drawer, on square section tapering legs, 54in (137cm) wide.
£2,500–3,000 *Bon*

r. A George III mahogany and inlaid bowfront sideboard, the frieze drawer flanked to the right by a cellaret drawer formed as 2 dummy drawers and to the left by 2 drawers, on square tapered legs with spade feet, c1790, 55in (140cm) wide.
£3,700–4,500 *S*

A mahogany serpentine sideboard, with inlaid stringing and tulipwood banding, on square tapering legs and socket feet, replaced brass handles, alterations, late 18thC, 72in (183cm) wide.
£3,200–3,600 *WW*

A George III mahogany and crossbanded bowfront sideboard, the central drawer with oval stamped brass handles, flanked by side cupboards/cellaret drawers, on 6 square tapering block legs, 72in (183cm) wide.
£3,000–3,500 *WL*

A George III mahogany sideboard, with tulipwood crossbanding and boxwood stringing, with original handles, c1790, 66in (167.5cm) long.
£7,750–8,500 *ANT*

A Federal inlaid mahogany sideboard, the top with inlaid edge, fitted with a central frieze drawer with hinged front, opening to a writing surface and an arrangement of 7 short drawers and 6 valanced pigeonholes, with reeded cupboard doors below, flanked by 4 drawers, on square tapering legs ending in spade feet, American, some damage, c1800, 71in (180.5cm) wide.
£3,200–3,500 *S(NY)*

A late George III mahogany serpentine sideboard, crossbanded and boxwood strung, with one frieze drawer, flanked by one deep drawer and one door, with later lion mask handles, on square tapering legs with later brass casters, some restoration, 78in (198cm) wide.
£4,000–4,500 *DN*

A Dutch inlaid mahogany sideboard, the hinged top with canted corners and a dentil moulded frieze, concealing hinged flaps and folding shelves, above 3 frieze drawers and a pair of shell-inlaid cupboard doors, flanked by fluted canted corners on square tapered feet, c1800, 46½in (118cm) wide.
£1,800–2,000 *Bon*

An Empire tiger maple and walnut sideboard, the shaped backboard above walnut top over 2 drawers flanked by inset walnut panels, the inset lower case flanked by free-standing faceted flared columns, raised on block, ring and baluster-turned feet, American, 1804–15, 43in (109cm) wide.
£1,100–1,200 *S(Cg)*

A mahogany serpentine-fronted sideboard, the drawer and cupboard fronts with boxwood and chevron stringing and inlaid fan spandrels, the top with medallions and crossbanded rim above frieze drawer and shaped apron, flanked by quadrant-fronted drawer and cupboard, on ring-turned and tapering legs, early 19thC, 74½in (189cm) wide.
£3,000–3,500 *P(Sc)*

r. A Regency mahogany break-front sideboard, with boxwood stringing, the central frieze drawer and arched underframe flanked on each side by a cellaret drawer and on tapering reeded legs, 52in (132cm) wide.
£4,500–5,000 *Bea(E)*

A Regency mahogany and inlaid bowfront sideboard, with a central and a recessed arched apron drawer, flanked by enclosed cupboards, pot cupboard to one side, on reeded tapered legs and spool feet, 70½in (179cm) wide.
£5,500–6,000 *P*

A Regency mahogany sideboard, the crossbanded and ebony-strung top above a central long drawer and cutlery compartment below, flanked by a pair of bowfronted cupboard doors, on ring-turned tapering legs, 75in (190.5cm) wide.
£3,000–3,500 *CGC*

A Regency mahogany pedestal sideboard, with later marquetry inlay, the raised back inlaid with stringing flanked by drawers, above tapering cupboards, the panelled doors inlaid with urns, on front carved tassel and ribbed splay feet, 82in (208.5cm) wide.
£2,600–3,000 *WW*

A Regency walnut bowfront sideboard, with central short drawer, flanked on either side by 4 further drawers, on ring-turned tapering cylindrical supports with peg feet, 54in (137cm) wide.
£3,000–3,500 *GAK*

A George IV mahogany sideboard, the shaped serpentine front fitted with a long drawer above a recessed bowfront napkin drawer, flanked each side by deep crossbanded drawers, outset spiral twist and turned lobed tapering legs, 85in (216cm) wide.
£2,200–2,500 *L*

A Victorian mahogany pedestal sideboard, the mirrored-back with straight moulded crest and carved scrolled brackets, the inverted breakfront base with moulded edged top, 3 frieze drawers, arched cupboard door to each pedestal flanked by scrolled brackets, 82in (208.5cm) wide.
£1,500–1,800 *AH*

A solid oak carved sideboard, c1890, 73in (185.5cm) wide.
£800–900 *MiA*

A Federal style inlaid mahogany sideboard, the backsplash over serpentine-fronted top, over one long drawer flanked by 2 short drawers, over 2 cupboard doors, flanked by 2 cupboard doors, raised on square tapering legs, American, late 19thC, 72in (183cm) wide.
£1,000–1,200 *SLN*

A Victorian carved and figured mahogany pedestal mirror-back sideboard, the arched plate with moulded and carved fruit frame, the frieze with a central serpentine-fronted drawer flanked by a pair of doors with cartouche-shaped panels enclosing shelves, drawer and cellaret drawer, c1850, 80in (203cm) wide.
£2,000–2,200 *S(S)*

A Victorian pollard oak mirror-back sideboard, by Lamb, Manchester, the bevelled shelf with brass balustraded gallery, above a long mirror flanked by louvered and roundel moulded brackets, above an inverted breakfront top with a central panelled recess flanked by boss centred moulded panelled cupboard doors, one enclosing a cellaret drawer, c1880, 82½in (209.5cm) wide.
£1,400–1,700 *Hal*

A Sheraton revival mahogany satinwood banded and ebonised strung sideboard, the central frieze drawer inlaid with central shell motif, flanked on either side by drawer and cupboard, on tapering square legs, late 19thC, 60in (152.5cm) wide.
£450–500 *GAK*

l. An Edwardian mahogany bowfront sideboard, the galleried top above 2 frieze drawers flanked by cupboard doors, on square section tapering legs with spade feet, 78in (193cm) wide.
£1,500–1,700 *Bon*

A mid-Victorian oak sideboard, the upper stage fitted with an arched bevelled glass mirror flanked by foliate carved and panelled cupboard doors, the lower stage fitted with an arrangement of drawers and cupboards, 84in (213.5cm) wide.
£2,000–2,200 *WL*

A mahogany inverted breakfront pedestal sideboard, the raised back with scroll and foliage carving, 3 drawers above 2 panelled doors enclosing on one side sliding trays and on the other a single drawer, 19thC, 72in (183cm) wide.
£750–900 *E*

A mahogany sideboard, by Maple & Co, the shallow gallery back with applied moulding and brass stringing, above a chevron-banded top and centre drawer with brass drop handles, flanked on either side by a shallow bowfronted drawer, a cellaret cupboard and a further cupboard, on tapered reeded legs, late 19thC, 66in (167.5cm) wide.
£1,700–2,000 *Mit*

Stands

A Regency mahogany butler's stand or plate canterbury, with central carrying handle flanked by 2 lidded compartments, a semi-circular galleried section to one side, on turned tapering legs with brass casters, 22in (56cm) wide.
£720–850 *Bea(E)*

A Sheraton mahogany and boxwood strung urn stand, c1790, 14in (35.5cm) high.
£1,650–1,850 *ANT*

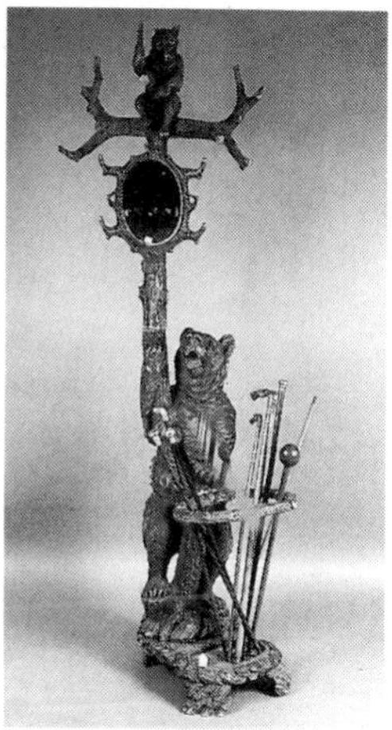

r. A Black Forest carved wood hall stand, c1870, 84in (213.5cm) high.
£3,000–3,300 *SWO*

A Victorian mahogany shaving stand, 54½in (137cm) high.
£500–550 *DOC*

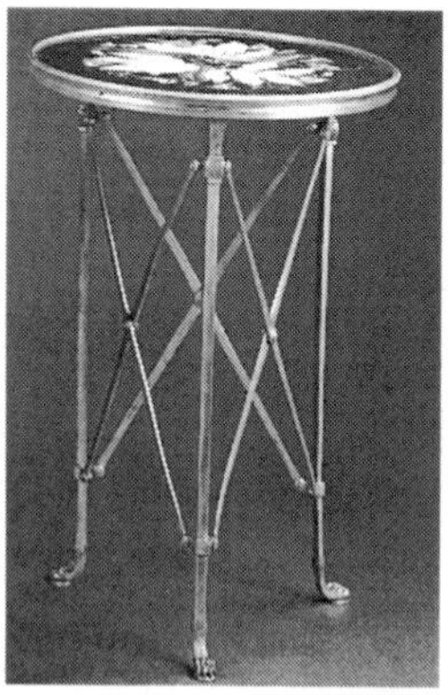

r. A pair of Transitional style scagliola and gilt-metal *guéridons,* the tops decorated with magnolia and convolvulous, on square tapering supports with claw feet and tied by X-stretchers, c1900, 18in (46cm) diam.
£5,200–5,800 *Bon*

Scagliola is a type of imitation marble.

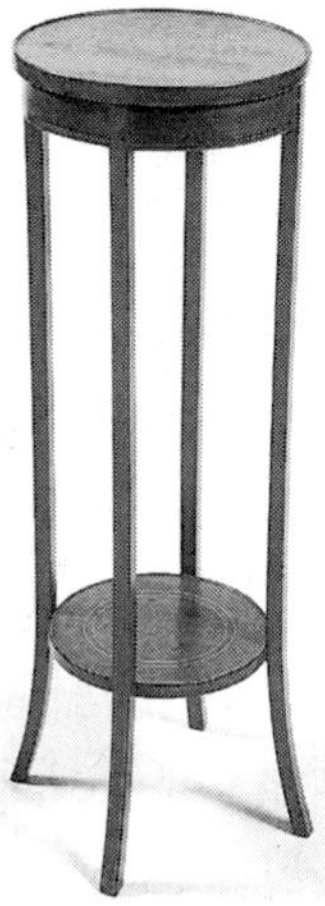

r. An Edwardian inlaid mahogany two-tier plant stand, c1910, 13in (33cm) diam.
£150–200 *BUSH*

Folio & Reading Stands

A George III mahogany and brass-inlaid adjustable reading stand, the reeded top fitted with a moulded book rest, on a turned and reeded adjustable stem with brass collar and on a downswept tripod base, c1800, 28½in (72.5cm) high.
£4,500–5,000 *S*

A George III mahogany book stand, the top with applied brace opening to an adjustable stand, on a baluster and ring-turned pedestal ending in a square support, raised on 3 downswept legs with casters, early 19thC, 29in (73.5cm) high.
£1,400–1,600 *S(Cg)*

A Regency mahogany duet stand, on triform plinth, 19¼in (49cm) wide.
£700–750 *P(G)*

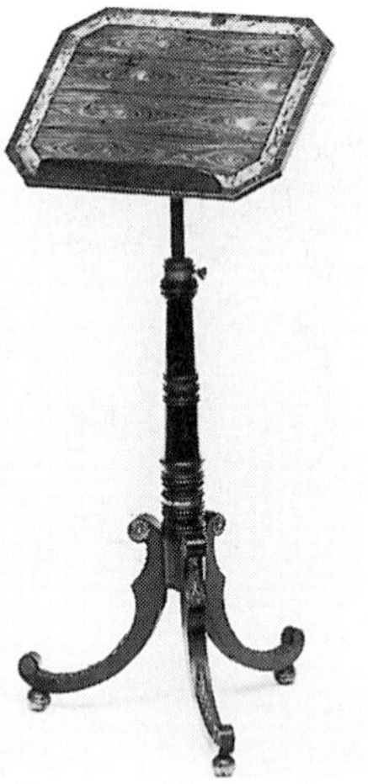

A Regency kingwood, maple-banded, ebonised and gilt-brass mounted adjustable reading stand, the top with canted angles and lift-off book rest, raised on a ring-turned column with swept scroll legs, 29½in (75cm) high.
£3,000–3,300 *P(O)*

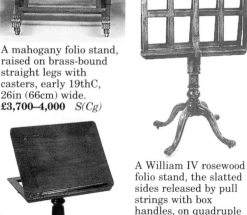

Holland & Sons

The firm of Holland & Sons was founded c1803 as Taprell, Stephen & Holland, which became Taprell, Holland & Sons in 1835, continuing to trade under this name until 1843 when it became Holland & Sons. The firm was amongst London's most distinguished cabinet-makers, producing high quality furniture throughout the Victorian period. They worked extensively for the Royal family, notably at Osborne House, Balmoral and Sandringham, and undertook over 300 commissions for the government, including the Palace of Westminster. The firm employed some of the leading designers of this period and produced furniture in a variety of styles including Gothic, Jacobean, Grecian and French, and played a prominent part in the 1851, 1862 and 1878 International Exhibitions.

A mahogany folio stand, raised on brass-bound straight legs with casters, early 19thC, 26in (66cm) wide.
£3,700–4,000 *S(Cg)*

A William IV rosewood folio stand, the slatted sides released by pull strings with box handles, on quadruple stand with lappet feet, 27½in (70cm) wide.
£1,500–1,700 *P(G)*

r. A William IV rosewood folio stand, the pierced trelliswork sides with adjustable rachet supports, the tapered square ends on moulded splayed turned stretchers and on brass cappings and casters, stamped 'Holland & Sons', c1830, 34in (86.5cm) wide.
£9,000–10,000 *S*

l. A William IV adjustable reading stand, with fluted column and acanthus carved legs, c1835, 20in (51cm) wide.
£1,000–1,200 *HUB*

Steps

l. A set of George III mahogany library steps, with leather-covered side rail, early 19thC, 21in (53.5cm) wide.
£1,100–1,200 *S(Cg)*

r. A set of mahogany library steps, each side with 7 treads and chamfered supports, on casters, early 19thC, 65½in (166cm) high.
£4,500–5,000 *S*

A set of mahogany library steps, 19thC, 23in (58.5cm) wide.
£1,450–1,600 *P(O)*

Stools

A mahogany stool, with moulded frame and drop-in seat, on square beaded legs joined by a central stretcher, c1780, 24in (61cm) wide.
£900–1,000 *S(NY)*

A William Kent style carved hardwood stool, the upholstered seat on imbricated and scrolled X-frame supports centred by scallop shells and acanthus foliage, on paw feet, joined by a turned stretcher, 18thC, 25in (63.5cm) wide.
£3,500–3,800 *S*

A Regency rosewood dressing stool, the opposing C-scroll frame united by a centre simulated rosewood stretcher, the stuff-over seat upholstered in contemporary material, 42in (106.5cm) long.
£750–850 *Mit*

A pair of Regency Tatham style mahogany stools, the panelled and banded tops with scroll ends and rounded terminals, on simulated fluted tapered legs and waisted spade feet, 24in (61cm) wide.
£17,000–18,500 *P(EA)*

These stools attracted enormous interest because they were in pristine condition, from a very good private source, and had not appeared on the market for a long time.

A William IV mahogany stool, with woolwork seat, c1835, 18in (45.5cm) square.
£270–300 *SPa*

An early Victorian walnut footstool, with cabriole legs, 15in (38cm) square.
£525–575 *BERA*

A mahogany stool, with embroidered top, c1850, 25in (63.5cm) diam.
£500–600 *GBr*

A mother-of-pearl and ivory-inlaid figural stool, the upholstered oval seat with a bird-form frame, inlaid overall with geometric motifs, early 20thC, 22in (56cm) wide.
£4,200–4,700 *S(NY)*

Music Stools

r. A Regency mahogany music stool, with adjustable revolving top, crossbanded with ebony stringing, on 4 outswept ring-turned legs, supported by a ring turned base, reupholstered, 12in (30.5cm) diam.
£550–600 *LCA*

l. A mahogany piano stool, with lyre-shaped design to the back, c1810, 32½in (82.5cm) high.
£1,650–2,000 *CAT*

An Edwardian mahogany cross-frame music stool, inlaid with urns and swags, 28in (71cm) wide.
£370–400 *RTo*

Bedroom Suites

An Edwardian inlaid harewood bedroom suite, bordered with boxwood lines, each piece raised on foliate carved and reeded tapered legs, comprising: a wardrobe, 2 kidney-shaped kneehole dressing tables, a pair of single beds with panelled headboards and bowfronted footboards, a bow-fronted bedside cabinet, a pair of occasional chairs, a kidney-shaped stool and a folding towel rail, wardrobe 83½in (212cm) wide.
£2,600–2,850 *P(E)*

An Edwardian satinwood composite bedroom suite, by James Shoolbred & Co, inlaid with foliate lozenge motifs in coloured woods, crossbanded in rosewood and with chequered boxwood and ebony stringing, comprising: a washstand, a triple wardrobe, a break bowfront dressing table with oval bevelled mirror plate, a pair of chests each with 2 short and 3 long graduated drawers, and a shoe cupboard, wardrobe 84in (213.5cm) wide.
£4,500–5,000 *HSS/P*

James Shoolbred & Co was a retailer of high quality furniture in Tottenham Court Road, London, in the late 19th and early 20thC.

A Spanish brass-mounted bedroom suite, comprising: a dressing table, a pair of pot cupboards, and a single bed with an arched glazed headboard, the whole decorated with foliate scrolls and flowerheads, early 20thC, bed 54½in (138.5cm) wide.
£3,300–4,000 *Bon*

A Victorian salon suite, comprising: a chesterfield settee with walnut turned legs and original porcelain and brass casters, and 2 armchairs with square tapered front legs and original brass casters, settee 60in (152.5cm) wide.
£5,000–5,600 *LCA*

Salon Suites

r. A south German Biedermeier cherrywood salon suite, comprising: a settee and 4 chairs, with shaped and pierced splats, on square tapering legs, restored, c1825, settee 50in (127cm) long.
£2,400–2,700 *S(Am)*

A Victorian carved walnut salon suite, comprising: a set of 6 salon chairs, an occasional chair, a bergère armchair, and a chaise longue, c1850, chaise longue 70in (178cm) long.
£3,500–4,000 *S(S)*

A Victorian carved walnut drawing room suite, comprising: a settee, a lady's and gentleman's chair, and 6 balloon back side chairs, the crestings carved with bellflowers and leaves, on cabriole legs and scroll feet, together with a pair of matching oval footstools with turned feet, settee 80in (203cm) long.
£3,200–3,500 *P*

l. A Victorian carved walnut salon suite, comprising: a set of 6 chairs, an occasional chair and matching armchair, with carved cresting rails, and a serpentine-fronted settee, c1855, settee 75in (190.5cm) long.
£5,000–5,500 *S(S)*

A Victorian walnut part salon suite, comprising: a settee and an open armchair, each with foliate-carved shaped arched cresting rail to the oval upholstered medallion back, with outward curving buttoned arms and overstuffed seat, foliate carved fluted seat rail, acanthus carved arm terminals extending to cabochon carved cabriole front supports terminating in knurl feet and ceramic casters, together with a pair of later similar foot stools, settee 76in (193cm) long.
£2,600–3,000 *HSS/P*

A Victorian walnut and boxwood inlaid drawing room suite, comprising: a chaise longue, lady's chair, gentleman's chair and 6 single chairs, each inlaid with floral motifs in boxwood, on turned legs ending in ceramic casters, chaise longue 76in (193cm) long.
£2,300–2,600 *Mit*

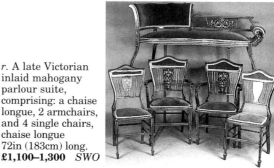

r. A late Victorian inlaid mahogany parlour suite, comprising: a chaise longue, 2 armchairs, and 4 single chairs, chaise longue 72in (183cm) long.
£1,100–1,300 *SWO*

A late Victorian mahogany salon suite, comprising: a two-seater settee on cabriole legs, with scroll arms and buttoned back, carved and pierced scroll and leaf decoration, a pair of armchairs, 4 standard chairs and 2 nursing chairs, settee 50in (127cm) wide.
£1,100–1,300 *Gam*

A Louis XVI style walnut salon suite, comprising: a three-seater sofa with arched top-rail and leaf-carved moulded edge, the acanthus carved scrolled arms on turned fluted tapered supports headed by paterae, with 4 large and 4 small *fauteuils,* all upholstered in an Aubusson tapestry, c1900, sofa 72in (183cm) wide.
£4,200–5,000 *Bon*

A walnut three-piece bergère suite, the moulded and scrolled backs with carved shell to centre, leaf-capped scroll arm terminals, on cabriole front legs with hoof feet, c1920, sofa 52in (132cm) wide.
£1,800–2,000 *CAG*

r. A Louis XVI style giltwood salon suite, comprising: a two-seater canapé, 4 chairs and one *fauteuil*, the gadrooned top-rails with acorn finials above padded backs flanked by reeded columns and paterae, on reeded tapering legs and spool feet, 19thC, and one similar *fauteuil* of an earlier date, canapé 50in (127cm) wide.
£3,000–3,300 *P*

Breakfast Tables

A George III mahogany and satinwood-banded breakfast table, with boxwood and ebony-strung top and hinged rounded drop flaps, one end of concave outline fitted with a drawer opposing a dummy drawer and a cupboard below enclosed by a pair of sunk panel doors, on tapered square legs with brass caps and casters, restored, 30in (76cm) wide.
£850–1,000 *P(W)*

A George III mahogany and boxwood-strung breakfast table, the tilt-top with rosewood banding, on a ring-turned baluster support with quadruple splayed legs ending in brass cappings and casters, c1810, 57in (145cm) wide.
£5,500–6,000 *S*

An American Empire marquetry inlaid rosewood breakfast table, with a bulbous columnar standard, raised on downswept legs ending in scroll feet, mid-19thC, 41in (104cm) diam.
£850–950 *SLN*

r. A Victorian satinwood breakfast table, by Holland & Sons, the moulded edged top over a crossgrained frieze, on fluted tapering pedestal and 4 swept moulded legs with carved panels and floral carved toes, 47½in (121cm) wide.
£1,600–1,800 *P(WM)*

A George III 'plum pudding' mahogany octagonal tilt-top breakfast table, the top with stringing and satinwood crossbanding, the tripod base with sabre legs ending in brass cappings and casters, c1790, 37½in (95cm) wide.
£1,800–2,200 *S(S)*

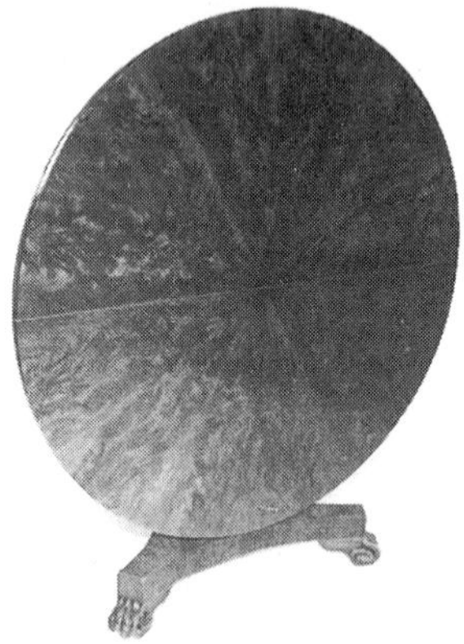

A figured mahogany segmented veneered tilt-top breakfast table, supported on a tapering turned column on a tricorn base with scrolled feet, early 19thC, 54in (137cm) diam.
£1,200–1,400 *GAK*

A William IV mahogany breakfast table, the tilt-top with a gadrooned border and reel-moulded frieze, the concave-sided tapered pillar support on a moulded platform base with carved paw feet and casters, c1835, 49½in (126cm) diam.
£3,700–4,000 *S*

A satinwood and rosewood crossbanded breakfast table, the tilt-top centred by a marquetry panel depicting musical instruments and foliage, on a hexagonal column and tripod hipped outswept legs with brass cappings and casters, early 19thC, 54in (137cm) diam.
£2,300–2,800 *P*

A Regency coromandel breakfast table, with crossbanding and stringing, raised on a turned bulbous column with quatreform base, the 4 splay legs terminating in brass paw feet and casters, 49in (124.5cm) wide.
£1,500–1,800 *AG*

A Victorian walnut breakfast table, the quarter-veneered top with moulded undulating outline, on turned carved column, moulded quadripartite base with carved knees and scroll feet, 58½in (148cm) wide.
£1,000–1,200 *HOLL*

A Thomas Hope style burr elm and rosewood-banded breakfast table, the octagonal top with ebony and satinwood inlaid border, above a square section tapering column inlaid with anthemia and bell flowers, and raised on a stepped plinth base, further inlaid with anthemia and with gilded scroll feet, early 20thC, 59in (150cm) wide.
£3,000–3,500 *Bon*

Card Tables

A George III satinwood demi-lune card table, the crossbanded top inlaid with ribbon-tied branches and a batwing lunette, the frieze inlaid with blind fluting, a concealed drawer to the rear, 36in (91.5cm) wide.
£4,500–5,000 *AH*

A George III serpentine satinwood card table, with tapered legs, 18thC, 28in (96.5cm) long.
£1,500–1,800 *HUB*

A George III mahogany D-shaped fold-over card table, the top crossbanded and inlaid in satinwood, on turned legs, 36in (91.5cm) wide.
£1,300–1,500 *MAT*

A William IV rosewood veneered card table, the shaped frieze with acanthus carving over a circular column, on claw feet, c1835, 36in (91.5cm) wide.
£3,200–3,500 *BERA*

A George IV mahogany card table, with wide rosewood crossbanding and inlaid with brass stringings, the panelled apron with carved scroll paterae and bead mouldings, the base with quadruple moulded and leaf-capped splayed supports, heavy brass paw toes and casters, 36in (91.5cm) wide.
£1,650–2,000 *CAG*

A Regency rosewood and brass-inlaid card table, the swivel fold-over top revealing baize-lined interior, with gadrooned edge, on an octagonal tapering column, circular platform, 4 reeded splay feet terminating in brass casters, 36in (91.5cm) wide.
£2,000–2,200 *L&E*

A rosewood serpentine card table, the top supported by an oak-lined pull-out drawer, with shaped and carved skirt, on cabriole legs, c1850, 36in (91.5cm) wide.
£900–1,000 *LCA*

A walnut serpentine fold-over card table, the top veneered in 2 sections, with moulded edge above a baize-lined interior, supported on a heavily turned centre column, the down-swept scrolling legs with carving at the knees terminating in casters, 19thC, 37in (94cm) wide.
£1,100–1,300 *Mit*

A late Victorian ebonised and amboyna card table, the canted rectangular top on 4 gilt-metal mounted column supports and outswept legs with block feet and casters, c1890, 38in (96.5cm) wide.
£800–1,000 *Bon*

An Edwardian walnut envelope top card table, with single frieze drawer, on foliate carved cabriole legs terminating and casters, 23½in (59.5cm) square.
£400–450 *WL*

A Louis Philippe style figured walnut serpentine card table, crossbanded in burr walnut with satinwood stringing and moulded rim, the swivel fold-over top lined in maroon baize bordered in gilt-tooled leather, on cabriole legs mounted with ormolu classical female busts within a C-scroll cartouche, acanthus leaf foliate trails and sabots, mid-19thC, 36½in (92.5cm) wide.
£3,000–3,300 *M*

A walnut and gilt-mounted serpentine folding card table, the top inlaid with flowers within a border of scrolling foliage, on tapering cabriole legs, 19thC, 38in (96.5cm) wide.
£1,500–1,800 *E*

A Victorian rosewood envelope card table, with string inlay, the moulded edge top opening to reveal counter wells, the frieze drawer with brass drop handle, on square tapering supports with brass toes and casters, c1900, 22in (56cm) wide.
£750–900 *AH*

r. An Edwardian Adam style satinwood crossbanded and gilt bowfront card table, the quarter-veneered hinged top with rounded projecting corners, above a guilloche and fluted frieze with applied paterae and swags opposed by a drawer, on reeded tapering legs headed by leafy capitals on spool feet, 36in (91.5cm) wide.
£2,750–3,000 *P*

A Victorian burr walnut card table, with D-shaped top, the frieze applied with foliate carving, on a fluted baluster column and moulded and foliate carved cabriole legs, 36in (91.5cm) wide.
£1,150–1,250 *L*

A walnut fold-over card table, with banded and quartered top, on fluted columns with carved cabriole trestle supports and brass casters, 19thC, 35in (89cm) wide.
£750–850 *BIG*

A Sheraton revival mahogany card table, banded in satinwood, the 2 fold-over leaves with marquetry flowers, above one drawer, on square tapering legs, c1900, 18½in (47cm) wide.
£1,100–1,200 *DN*

Centre Tables

An Italian rosewood and ivory centre table, on later ebonised legs, the top with a radiating sunburst cartouche panel framed by symmetrical panels with stylised foliate inlay, above a cavetto frieze, on angular cabriole legs with pointed pad feet, 18thC, 59½in (151cm) high.
£1,800–2,200 *P*

An American mahogany centre table, the shaped marble top over a conforming moulded apron, raised on carved cabriole legs, joined by scrolled stretcher centred with an urn finial, c1860, 44in (112cm) wide.
£520–580 *SLN*

An American Renaissance style gilt-bronze mounted walnut centre table, the shaped top inset with a marble and floral marquetry panel within gilt-bronze borders, the frieze inset on all sides with a floral marquetry roundel, raised on scrolled legs headed by female warrior busts, late 19thC, 51in (129.5cm) wide.
£4,200–4,700 *S(NY)*

l. A Victorian rosewood and marquetry octagonal centre table, inlaid with stringing and satinwood banding, the moulded top centred by a floral medallion with urns and flowers, the shaped supports headed by urns and conjoined by a square undertier with a floral medallion, the splayed legs ending in brass cappings and ceramic casters, c1890, 36in (91.5cm) wide.
£900–1,000 *S(S)*

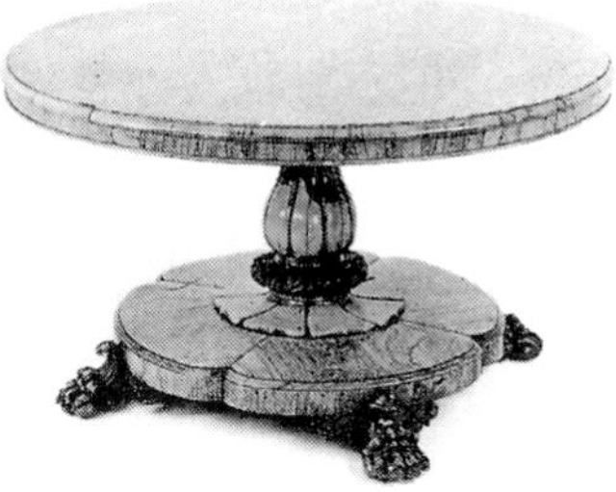

A Regency rosewood centre table, the fluted baluster column with carved acanthus leaf platform, the waved edge base with projecting lion claw feet, 55in (139.5cm) diam.
£2,500–2,800 *L&E*

A Louis XV style gilt-metal mounted satinwood centre table, the top with rounded outset corners inlaid with strapwork and foliate scrolls, on cabriole legs with gilt-metal female mask mounts and foliate sabots, c1860, 42in (107cm) wide.
£3,000–3,500 *Bon*

A French style inlaid centre table, the serpentine top with marquetry vine and convolvulus border framing the central parquetry panel of inter-connecting and starburst designs, with an ormolu rim, the marquetry apron with one drawer, the cabriole supports with floral and acanthus ormolu mounts, mid-19thC, 50in (127cm) wide.
£4,750–5,250 *BIG*

A Victorian rosewood oval centre table, the moulded tilt-top above a jewelled baluster pillar and triple moulded downswept legs ending in scroll feet with brass casters, c1850, 55½in (141cm) wide.
£1,000–1,100 *S(S)*

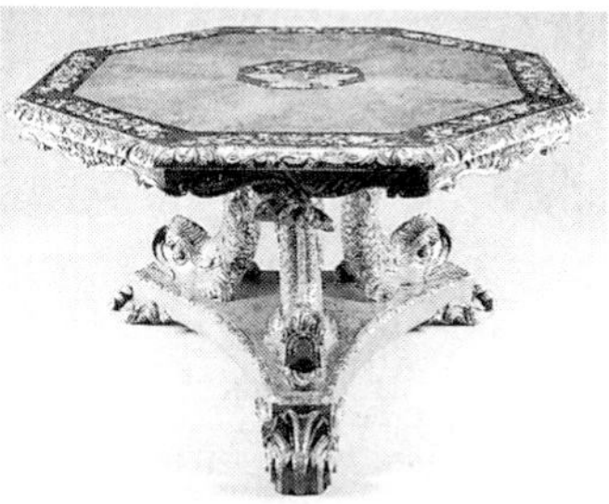

A Victorian mahogany centre table, the octagonal top centred with an ebony panel with a marquetry winged dragon crest amidst flowers and fruits, with radiating veneers and a broad band of flowers and anthemion on an ebony ground within a bird and foliate carved border, and a scroll and foliate carved apron, supported by 3 carved dolphins, on a triform base with shell scroll feet, 54in (137cm) diam.
£4,500–5,000 *DN*

Parquetry

Parquetry is a decorative form of inlay often confused with marquetry. It is the process of building up a design of small pieces of veneer of contrasting colours, in a geometric design. It was popular in England during the second half of the 17th century, and there was a brief resurgence of interest during the early 19th century on smaller items. It enjoyed a longer period of popularity in Continental Europe.

A French rosewood centre table, the top with deep carved frieze, the base with baluster stem and leaf-carved legs, c1900, 42in (106.5cm) diam.
£1,200–1,500 *HAC*

Console & Pier Tables

A giltwood rococo console table, with grey variegated marble top, the pierced trellis frieze with central rocaille cartouche with foliate flowerheads, on C-scroll cabriole legs and stretcher, with scroll feet, mid-18thC, 40½in (103cm) wide.
£3,000–3,500 *P*

A console table, with marble top, pierced and decorated frieze of classical motifs and united at the base by a four-way stretcher with pierced shell motifs and scrolls, on 4 scrolling legs, split to marble top, 18thC, 79in (200.5cm) wide.
£4,500–5,000 *B*

An Italian carved giltwood console table, with granite top, above a shaped frieze drawer panelled with beading and lion mask handle, the corners carved with acanthus leaves, on fluted tapering legs joined by an X-form stretcher, centred by a pineapple finial, on leaf-carved toupie feet, c1780, 43in (109cm) wide.
£11,500–12,500 *S*

A south German rococo carved giltwood console table, with marble top and carved floral apron, on cabriole legs joined by carved floral motif, c1760, 23½in (60cm) wide.
£3,000–3,500 *S(Z)*

A pair of French painted pier tables, with *faux* marble tops, c1800, 24in (61cm) wide.
£4,000–4,500 *SPa*

An American Empire mahogany console table, with marble top over one long drawer with ormolu mount, shaped scroll supports ending in concave platform base, on paw feet, c1840, 42in (106.5cm) wide.
£800–900 *SLN*

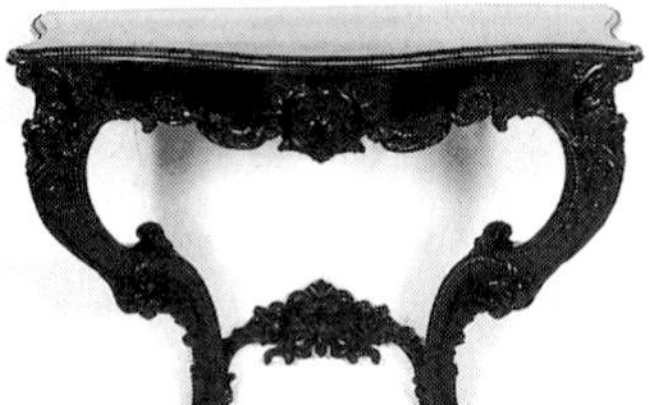

A rosewood serpentine console table, the carved rococo frame with leaf and shell decoration, brass bead decoration to edge, c1860, 44in (112cm) wide.
£1,500–1,850 *HUB*

A pair of Louis XV style gilt decorated serpentine console tables, each green veined marble top above a pierced shell-carved frieze, on scaley cabriole and scrolling leaf-carved legs joined by shell-carved stretchers, with hoof feet, 19thC, 31in (78.5cm) wide.
£2,700–3,000 *P*

r. A George III style painted pier table, decorated with floral garlands and medallions, the shaped top with a semi-elliptical painted landscape, the ring-turned and splayed legs with ornate pierced stretchers and rails, together with bevelled plate glass tops, c1910, 33in (78.5cm) wide.
£2,500–2,750 *S(S)*

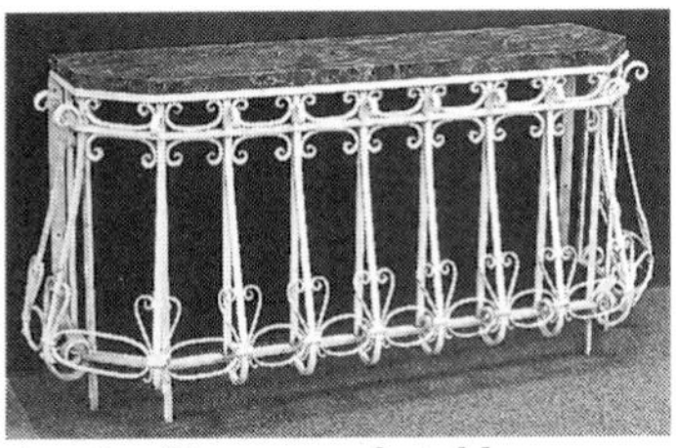

A pair of iron console tables, the marble tops above openwork C-scroll friezes, and square vertical and scrolling uprights, late 19thC, 65in (165cm) wide.
£1,500–1,800 *SLM*

Dining Tables

A red walnut gateleg table, with a pair of opposing frieze drawers above baluster-turned legs joined by stretchers, on Braganza feet, feet partly lacking, early 18thC, 54in (136.5cm) extended.
£2,300–2,700 *S(S)*

A Regency mahogany extending dining table, the top with reeded edge and rounded corners and 4 leaf insertions, the concertina action with 2 central legs, the 6 ring-turned legs ending in brass cappings and casters, c1810, 131in (333cm) extended.
£3,500–4,500 *S(S)*

A George III mahogany D-end dining table, the satinwood-banded top above a conforming frieze and raised on boxwood strung square tapering legs with satinwood collars, 109in (277cm) extended.
£2,000–2,200 *Bon*

A mahogany dining table, with 2 pull-out leaves, 2 opposing drawers to the apron with boxwood stringing and brass swing handles, on square tapered legs with brass caps and casters, 18thC, 61in (155cm) wide.
£950–1,200 *M*

This design is similar to Sheraton's 'Universal Table'.

A George III mahogany and inlaid D-end dining table in 3 parts, bordered with boxwood lines, with a drop-flap centre section, the frieze with ebonised banding, raised on square tapered legs terminating in spade feet, 121in (307.5cm) extended.
£4,500–5,000 *P(E)*

An Austrian Biedermeier fruitwood extending dining table, the chequer-inlaid top above a conforming frieze, on 4 sabre legs, including 3 extra leaves, early 19thC, 73½in (183cm) extended.
£3,200–3,500 *Bon*

A Regency mahogany extending dining table, comprising 2 ends, a centre section, with double gateleg action, and 2 leaf insertions, on turned and reeded legs, 164in (418cm) extended.
£10,500–12,000 *P(NE)*

A Regency mahogany dining table, the 2 D-ends with reeded edge and telescopic action, 12 turned and reeded legs with brass toes and casters, with 4 inset leaves, 179in (455cm) wide.
£13,000–15,000 *B*

This table is desirable because of its large size and the fact that it is Regency rather than Victorian.

l. A George IV mahogany drop-leaf extending dining table, the top with telescopic action, on reeded turned tapering legs with brass casters, c1825, 96in (253cm) extended.
£8,000–9,000 *S*

A George IV mahogany extending dining table, with 2 drop leaves and one loose leaf, on turned tapering legs with brass terminals and casters, 93in (236cm) wide.
£1,500–1,800 *DN*

A George IV mahogany extending dining table, with reeded top, on slender turned and fluted tapering supports, brass toe caps and casters, one original leaf and 2 later leaves, 96in (244cm) extended.
£5,000–5,500 *RBB*

A George IV mahogany extending drop-leaf dining table, the reeded top with a concertina action, 2 leaf insertions, on 8 ring-turned legs ending in brass cappings and casters, c1825, 92in (234.5cm) extended.
£3,200–3,500 *S(S)*

A George IV mahogany extending dining table, the top with reeded edge, raised on 6 lobed tapering legs with cup casters, together with 3 leaves, 157in (389cm) extended.
£3,000–3,500 *Bon*

A William IV mahogany extending dining table, raised on turned and lobed legs with casters, together with 4 leaves, centre leg associated, 150in (381cm) extended.
£3,800–4,500 *Bon*

A Victorian mahogany extending dining table, the top with 2 leaf insertions and with telescopic action, the moulded frieze above turned and reeded legs, on casters, possibly associated, c1850, 106in (269cm) extended.
£1,750–2,000 *S(S)*

An oak extending dining table, with 5 leaves, on gadrooned and fluted legs and brass casters, mid-19thC, 88in (224cm) extended.
£2,200–2,500 *L&E*

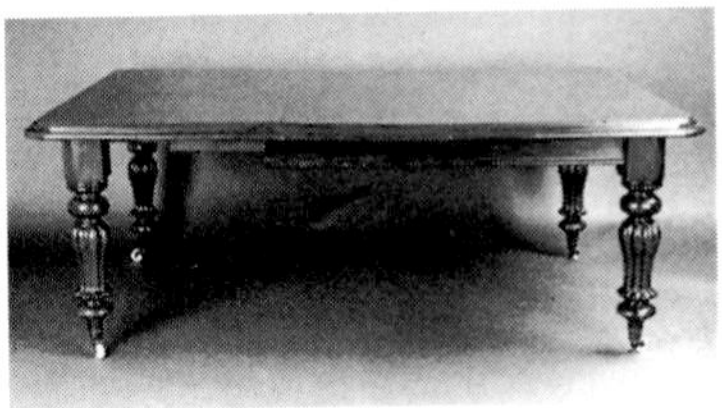

An early Victorian mahogany extending dining table, the top with double moulded edge above a conforming frieze, on 4 lobed tapering legs, with 2 leaves, restorations, 59in (150cm) long.
£2,200–2,500 *Bon*

r. A walnut extending dining table, with 3 leaves, on reeded cylindrical tapering legs ending in casters, mid-19thC, 90in (228.5cm) extended.
£700–800 *SLN*

A mid-Victorian oak extending pedestal dining table, the top with moulded edge above a conforming oak leaf and acorn carved frieze, raised on a central baluster turned shaft with an egg-and-dart carved knop and lion carved outswept legs, with 2 leaves, 83in (211cm) wide.
£2,000–2,200 *Bon*

A Victorian mahogany drop-leaf dining table, the large top with moulded edge, raised on 6 cabriole legs with claw-and-ball feet, stamped 'Edwards & Roberts', 75in (191cm) wide.
£3,500–4,000 *Bon*

It is rare for English furniture to be signed or stamped with the makers name. Although many 18th century makers applied trade labels (which have long since been lost), Gillows were one of the few to actually mark their furniture. By the end of the 19th century certain makers and retailers were stamping or fixing trade plates to their pieces as a matter of course. Included among these were J. Shoolbred & Co, Liberty & Co, Heal & Son, Edwards & Roberts, W. Walker & Sons and Williamson & Co.

A Victorian mahogany extending dining table, the top with a telescopic action, 2 leaf insertions and a winding handle, on turned tapering legs ending in brass cappings and ceramic casters, c1880, 99½in (252.5cm) extended.
£3,000–3,300 *S(S)*

A Victorian mahogany extending dining table, on turned reeded and fluted legs with casters, c1880, 73½in (186.5cm) extended.
£1,750–2,000 *E*

A Victorian mahogany extending dining table, with turned and reeded legs ending in brass cappings, 93in (236cm) extended.
£3,000–3,500 *S(S)*

A French Empire style satinwood and ormolu-mounted D-end extending dining table, with 3 leaf insertions and telescopic action, early 20thC, restored, 152in (380cm) extended.
£6,700–7,300 *S(S)*

A Victorian mahogany D-end extending dining table, with 3 leaf insertions and a winder, the turned and reeded legs with reeded terminal surmounts, on ceramic casters, c1870, 95in (241cm) extended.
£2,700–3,000 *S(S)*

A late Victorian mahogany extending dining table, with 2 leaves, the top with gadrooned edge, raised on cabriole legs carved with acanthus, 94in (239cm) extended.
£2,200–2,500 *P(G)*

r. An Edwardian mahogany extending dining table, with 3 leaves, with a stop-fluted frieze, raised on square section tapering legs with bellflower carved panels and headed by paterae, 56in (142cm) long.
£2,700–3,000 *Bon*

A Victorian mahogany extending dining table, including one leaf insertion, on baluster turned and reeded legs ending in brass cappings and ceramic casters, winding handle broken, c1870, 67½in (171.5cm) extended.
£650–750 *S(S)*

A Continental walnut extending dining table, including 3 leaf insertions, on quadruple baluster turned supports joined by an X-form stretcher with an urn finial, the ends each with twin turned legs, on casters, c1900, 120½in (306cm) extended.
£2,000–2,500 *S(S)*

Display Tables

A mahogany display table, with floral marquetry inlay and gilt-metal mounts, hinged serpentine edge top with bevelled glass, glazed sides, shaped frieze, on slender cabriole legs with splayed feet and sabots, 19thC, 23½in (59.5cm) wide.
£1,300–1,500 *AH*

A Louis XV style kingwood and tulipwood marquetry serpentine bijouterie table, applied with gilt-metal mounts, the hinged, glazed and brass-bound top enclosing a velvet-lined interior above a shaped frieze, on cabriole legs with sabots, late 19thC, 39½in (100.5cm) wide.
£2,000–2,200 *P*

A French rosewood and ormolu-mounted bijouterie table, c1870, 21in (53.5cm) wide.
£1,550–1,650 *CHA*

An Edwardian mahogany bijouterie table, by Edwards & Roberts, with serpentine sides, crossbanded and inlaid with satinwood swags and scrolls, the top with rising glass panel with velvet interior, the base forming a free-standing bookcase with 3 open shelves on all 4 sides, supported on tapering legs with brass casters, 24in (61cm) square.
£4,500–5,000 *JNic*

A Victorian mahogany table cabinet, with glazed top and sides, the rear with 2 hinged wooden access panels, on turned and faceted tapering legs, c1880, 72in (182.5cm) wide.
£1,750–2,000 *S(S)*

An Edwardian Sheraton style inlaid satinwood display table, 32in (81.5cm) wide.
£770–850 *TMA*

An Edwardian mahogany and satinwood bijouterie display table, c1910, 24in (61cm) wide.
£550–650 *BUSH*

Dressing Tables

A George III dressing table, veneered in satinwood, the banded twin-flap top with a fitted mahogany interior with a mirror on an easel ratchet, divisions and lidded compartments, the front inlaid with stringing, the dummy drawer with brass knob handles, on square tapering legs and concave galleried undertier, brass casters, c1790, 26in (66cm) wide.
£3,500–4,000 *WW*

A George III mahogany and rosewood crossbanded dressing table, the fold-over top with segmented veneers and inlaid paterae, on rear gate supports, fitted interior, the sides with dummy drawers, the chamfered square legs with an undertier, on block feet and casters, c1780, 27in (69cm) wide.
£2,200–2,500 *S(S)*

A George III mahogany breakfront dressing table, by Gillows of Lancaster, the central bowed frieze drawer above an arched apron flanked by an arrangement of 2 short drawers, one deep drawer with a divided interior, on tapered square legs, c1795, 48in (122cm) wide.
£4,000–4,500 *S*

A Federal inlaid mahogany dressing table, the hinged top opening to a tripartite interior fitted with wells centring a hinged adjustable inlaid mirror plate, one false and one real long drawer, on square tapering line-inlaid legs ending in crossbanded cuffs, New York, c1800, 27½in (70.5cm) wide.
£2,800–3,200 *S(NY)*

Gillows

Founded in 1695 in Lancaster by Robert Gillow, a joiner, the firm of Gillows (later Waring & Gillow) grew and prospered in the 19thC, opening a London branch in what is now Oxford Street in 1761. The company's records, which go back as far as 1731, are now preserved in the Victoria & Albert Museum.

A William IV mahogany dressing table, attributed to Gillows, the top with a three-quarter gallery above 3 frieze drawers, the reeded turned tapering legs headed by bead-moulded panels and on brass casters, c1835, 41½in (105.5cm) wide.
£3,000–3,500 *S*

A George III mahogany gentleman's dressing table, the hinged top revealing a fitted interior with a ratchet adjustable mirror, divisions, lidded compartments and removable trays, above a green baize-lined ratchet adjustable slope, 3 drawers simulating 2 drawers, ring-turned legs ending in brass cappings and casters, c1800, 28in (71cm) wide.
£1,100–1,300 *S(S)*

A Victorian figured walnut dressing table, with adjustable mirror above an arrangement of drawers, on carved scrolled supports linked by shaped platform base, 45in (114.5cm) wide.
£700–800 *CRI*

An Edwardian mahogany boxwood and chequer-strung dressing table, with 2 drawers, on square tapering legs, 34in (86.5cm) wide.
£1,000–1,100 *HOLL*

l. A French kingwood and marquetry *poudreuse*, with ormolu mounts and fitted interior, c1870, 24in (61cm) wide.
£2,300–2,600 *CHA*

An Italian scarlet lacquer and gilt dressing table, decorated with chinoiserie scenes within floral borders, the hinged top with a peacock and sun motif between hinged compartments, with a central short and 2 deep drawers in the arched apron, on fluted tapered legs with spool feet, probably Venetian, 18thC, 35in (89cm) wide.
£3,800–4,500 *P*

A Victorian mahogany pedestal dressing table, the superstructure with an adjustable mirror flanked by 4 drawers, above an arrangement of 9 drawers around an open kneehole compartment, c1870, 54in (137cm) wide.
£1,000–1,250 *GBr*

A Dutch marquetry dressing table, of undulating outline, the superstructure with a swing frame mirror flanked by 4 short drawers, the top decorated with birds and baskets of flowers, a frieze drawer and shaped apron between 8 graduated drawers, on claw-and-ball feet, 19thC, 48in (122cm) wide.
£2,500–3,000 *P*

Drop-Leaf Tables

An American Queen Anne style tiger maple drop-leaf table, the hinged oval top over shaped apron, on cylindrical tapering legs ending in pad feet, early 18thC, 43½in (110.5cm) wide.
£2,500–3,000 *SLN*

A Chippendale style carved and figured walnut drop-leaf table, the two-board top flanked by rectangular leaves with shaped corners, shaped frieze below, on cabriole legs ending in claw-and-ball feet, Philadelphia, c1765, 49in (124cm) wide.
£2,800–3,200 *S(NY)*

r. An American Queen Anne style walnut drop-leaf table, the hinged top with 2 drop leaves over a shaped apron, raised on cabriole legs ending in pad feet, south Jersey or Philadelphia, mid-19thC, 59½in (150cm) wide.
£1,300–1,500 *SLN*

An American Queen Anne style carved and figured walnut drop-leaf dining table, the top flanked by notched leaves, centring a shaped apron, on cabriole legs ending in trifid feet, Pennsylvania, c1730, 54½in (138cm) wide.
£2,300–2,500 *S(NY)*

A mahogany drop-leaf dining table, the hinged top with rounded corners, raised on shell-headed cabriole legs, with claw-and-ball feet, 18thC, 57½in (146cm) diam.
£2,400–2,800 *P(G)*

An American Queen Anne mahogany drop-leaf dining table, the top with bowed ends, flanked by D-shaped leaves on cabriole legs ending in pad feet, New England, probably Massachusetts, repaired, 1750–70, 52in (132cm) wide.
£3,000–3,500 *S(NY)*

A George III mahogany drop-leaf table, the square top on a turned stretchered spider-leg frame with turned feet, 30in (76cm) wide.
£1,700–1,850 *WW*

Miller's is a price GUIDE not a price LIST

A George III mahogany rectangular drop-leaf table, on 6 chamfered square legs, c1760, 68½in (174cm) long extended.
£650–700 *S(S)*

Drum Tables

A mahogany drum-top table, the oilskin top above 4 true and 4 false drawers, on a turned pedestal column with tripartite base and scrolled foliate feet, early 19thC, 42in (107cm) diam.
£1,700–2,000 *Bon*

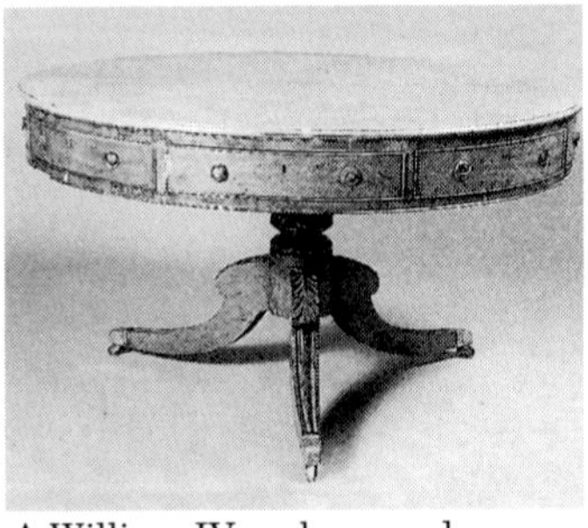

A William IV mahogany drum-top table, with 5 frieze drawers and 3 simulated drawers, on a lotus leaf turned shaft and hipped outswept reeded legs, with brass caps and casters, 50½in (128.5cm) diam.
£4,000–4,500 *P*

An early Victorian mahogany drum table, the top with a black and gilt tooled-leather inset above 4 frieze drawers and 4 false drawers, on an octagonal baluster column with a stylised lotus leaf base, on a concave tripartite base ending in bun feet, 42½in (133.5cm) diam.
£3,300–3,800 *P(Sc)*

Games Tables

An American Federal inlaid and figured mahogany games table, the bowed front above a frieze with an inlaid oval reserve, on turned tapering reeded legs ending in bottle-form feet, Massachusetts, c1810, 36½in (92.5cm) wide.
£1,400–1,600 *S(NY)*

A late Regency rosewood games/ centre table, the top with pull-out slide, alternating dummy and frieze drawers, on dual trestle legs and brass claw-and-ball feet, 39in (99cm) wide.
£3,500–4,000 *P(C)*

A Regency ebonised and penwork games table, the chessboard within a band of fruit and foliage, on a bobbin-turned stem and tripod base, 17½in (44.5cm) square.
£700–800 *Bea(E)*

An early Victorian rosewood games and work table, with partly fitted drawer, on twin lyre-shaped legs terminating in flat bases and scroll feet, 22½in (57cm) wide.
£900–1,100 *P(G)*

An early Victorian burr walnut veneered and marquetry-inlaid games table, the interior with designs of cards to the corner wells, 36in (91.5cm) wide.
£3,200–3,500 *LRG*

An ebony and box games board, with draughts set, on later stand, mid-19thC, 15in (38cm) square.
£1,000–1,150 *ANT*

An early Victorian rosewood table, with draughts board inlaid to top, fitted with 4 drawers to the frieze, on tapered octagonal column and in-swept triangular platform base, on bun feet, 25in (63.5cm) diam.
£350–400 *LF*

A Victorian walnut games/work table, with string and marquetry inlay and amboyna banding, the frieze drawer over sliding work box, on baluster-turned twin end supports, turned stretcher with finials, scroll feet and casters, 28in (71cm) wide.
£2,400–2,800 *AH*

l. A Victorian burr walnut games/work table, with a sliding needlework box, raised on ring-turned tulip baluster uprights, joined by similar stretchers, on moulded splayed legs, mid-19thC, 20½in (52cm) wide.
£850–950 *GAK*

Library Tables

A George III mahogany library writing table, with boxwood stringing and inlay, inset leather panel, 3 frieze drawers and 2 to the reverse, each centred by a flowerhead panel, on square tapered legs, with brass cappings and casters, 47in (119cm) wide.
£5,500–6,000 *P(EA)*

A William IV rosewood library table, the top above a pair of real and opposing dummy frieze drawers, the scroll-carved end supports with stylised leaf capitals and a turned stretcher, on a pair of moulded plinths with lotus-carved scroll feet and concealed casters, c1830, 48in (123cm) wide.
£2,500–3,000 *S*

A William IV rosewood veneered library table, supported by inverted columns at either end with scrolled mouldings below, on short scrolled feet, 55in (139.5cm) wide.
£1,400–1,600 *Mit*

A Victorian mahogany library table, with inset leather top, 2 real and 2 dummy drawers, a decorative turned rail to each end, on twin square section end supports, united by 2 turned stretchers, on shaped platform feet and casters, 50in (127cm) wide.
£3,200–3,800 *HOLL*

A George IV mahogany library table, the top veneered with flame-cut segments, on a tapered triangular stem with moulded and scroll-carved corners, the tricorn plinth with leaf and scroll-carved lion paw feet, 51½in (131cm) diam.
£8,000–9,000 *S*

A William IV mahogany library table, in George Smith style, the pair of frieze drawers flanked by scroll angle brackets, the twin end supports joined by a turned and acanthus-carved pole stretcher, on gadrooned bun feet with concealed casters, c1830, 54in (137cm) wide.
£2,500–3,000 *S(S)*

A Victorian thuya wood and ebonised library table, with gilt-metal mounts, turned end supports and splayed feet, on ceramic casters, 43in (109cm) wide.
£2,200–2,500 *S(S)*

A Renaissance revival mahogany library table, the moulded top over carved trestle base with 6 turned stiles, raised on conforming base with dog carvings, late 19thC, 68½in (174cm) wide.
£1,300–1,500 *SLN*

A George IV mahogany partners' library table, with a tooled green leather top, 4 drawers, on reeded tapered legs, brass cappings and casters, 48in (122cm) wide.
£5,000–6,000 *P*

A William IV mahogany library table, with inset leather top and 2 frieze drawers to each side, on turned tapering legs, brass cappings and casters, 48in (122cm) wide.
£1,800–2,000 *P*

A Victorian figured walnut library table, the top with 2 frieze drawers, on turned and fluted end supports with a conforming stretcher, the splayed scroll feet with ceramic casters, 45½in (116cm) wide.
£2,800–3,200 *S(S)*

A Victorian mahogany library table, with inset leather top, the panelled frieze fitted with 2 short drawers to either side, on turned reeded and fluted end columns, united by a ring-turned stretcher, terminating in bar-shaped supports with scroll decoration, paw feet and casters, the drawer stamped 'T. Willson, 68 Great Queen Street, London', 64½in (164cm) wide.
£4,500–5,000 *P(E)*

Nests of Tables

A nest of Regency rosewood quartetto tables, each with beaded top on square end supports to trestle bases, with turned feet, 19½in (49.5cm) wide.
£3,000–3,500 *Bea(E)*

A nest of 4 Chinese export decorated black lacquer and gilt quartetto tables, on ring-turned legs and splayed feet with carved claw feet, mid-19thC, 19½in (49.5cm) wide.
£1,000–1,200 *S(S)*

A nest of George IV specimen veneered quartetto tables, in the style of Gillows, including rosewood, maple and amboyna, the smallest table with chessboard inlay and platform undertier, on turned rosewood legs joined by stretchers, slight damage, 23½in (59.5cm) wide.
£5,000–5,500 *S(S)*

A nest of 3 Edwardian mahogany tables, 20in (51cm) wide.
£320–350 *Ber*

A nest of mahogany quartetto tables, the tops with central oval figured veneers outlined with stringing and within outer ebonised beadings and crossbanding, the slender ring-turned supports joined by concave stretchers and on splayed feet inlaid with ebonised stringing, 19thC, 19in (48.5cm) wide.
£5,000–5,500 *S*

A nest of 4 Regency mahogany tables, each raised on slender bulbous ring-turned legs on a trestle base, with bowed stretcher at the base, 19thC, 29in (73.5cm) wide.
£2,700–3,000 *S(Cg)*

r. A nest of 3 Edwardian mahogany occasional tables, with chequered stringing and oval satinwood motifs, on slender turned legs and splayed feet, 21in (53.5cm) wide.
£1,000–1,200 *S(S)*

Occasional Tables

A Regency 'plum' mahogany occasional table, with reeded edge, over a turned column on a solid mahogany quadriform base and gilt-brass scroll feet, c1800, 24in (61cm) wide.
£2,500–3,000 *BERA*

An Indian bone-inlaid table, with octagonal top, early 19thC, 30in (76cm) wide.
£650–750 *SPa*

r. A George IV pollard oak table, the frieze fitted with a drawer, on an octagonal baluster stem and incurved platform base with scroll feet, c1830, 21in (54cm) wide.
£1,500–1,800 *S*

A mahogany occasional table, in Gillows style, with reeded support, c1820, 19in (48.5cm) wide.
£1,000–1,200 *ANT*

A William IV mahogany snap-top occasional table, the turned support on a quadriform base, on paw feet terminating in casters, 30in (76cm) wide.
£800–900 *Mit*

An early Victorian rosewood occasional table, with serpentine-shaped top, turned and carved columns and cabriole legs, on original casters, c1845, 35in (89cm) wide.
£1,700–2,000 *BERA*

An early Victorian coromandel and parcel-gilt occasional table, the octagonal top, shaft and base marquetry-inlaid with anthemia, scrolls and various flowers, on bun feet, 17½in (44.5cm) diam.
£2,700–3,000 *P*

A mahogany wine table, the spiral-turned central support on trefoil base, c1850, 19in (48.5cm) diam.
£350–400 *GBr*

A walnut cricket table, on turned legs, c1890, 20½in (52cm) diam.
£160–180 *SPU*

l. A late Victorian rosewood occasional table, with string and marquetry inlay, the triform top with moulded shaped flaps, on shaped square supports with down-curved legs joined by a galleried undershelf, on casters, 23in (58.5cm) wide.
£700–800 *AH*

A Victorian amboyna and ebonised occasional table, the octagonal top with incised banding, on fluted baluster turned supports, the quadripartite base with porcelain casters, 30in (76cm) wide.
£900–1,000 *AH*

A late Victorian rosewood occasional table, with boxwood and marquetry inlay, with single frieze drawer, on square tapered legs united by secondary tier with fret-cut gallery, red pottery casters, 36in (91.5cm) extended.
£900–1,000 *EH*

An Edwardian mahogany drop-leaf occasional table, banded in tulipwood, with frieze drawer, raised on tapered supports and shaped X-stretcher, 33in (94cm) wide.
£700–800 *TMA*

l. A Portuguese rosewood occasional table, with gadrooned edge, drawer and dummy drawer to frieze, raised on spiral-twist and square legs joined by stretchers, 19thC, 25½in (65cm) wide.
£650–700 *AG*

r. An Edwardian satinwood and marquetry-inlaid occasional table, the crossbanded top inlaid with a central sunburst, ribbon-tied swags and paterae, on inlaid square tapering legs with brass caps and casters, 27in (68.5cm) wide.
£500–550 *P*

Pembroke Tables

A George III mahogany Pembroke table, with 2 drop flaps and one oak-lined drawer, on 4 square tapered legs, the whole marquetry-inlaid with leaves, urns, lines and floral sprays, 28in (71cm) long.
£900–1,100 *P(G)*

A George III 'plum pudding' mahogany and satinwood Pembroke table, the butterfly top inlaid at each corner with a boxwood and ebony stellar motif within chequer-strung borders, above 2 crossbanded and chequer-strung end drawers, raised on inlaid square tapering legs and spade feet, 40in (101.5cm) extended.
£4,500–5,000 *Hal*

'Plum pudding' or 'plum' mahogany has a curled knotty grain which resembles the blotchy appearance of a plum pudding.

A Federal mahogany Pembroke table, with one short drawer, on ring-turned cylindrical tapering legs ending in ball feet, American, early 19thC, 33½in (85cm) long.
£350–400 *SLN*

A George III mahogany Pembroke table, satinwood-banded and string-inlaid, the frieze drawer with brass knobs, on ring-turned tapering legs with brass caps and casters, 32in (81.5cm) long.
£1,200–1,300 *AH*

A mahogany Pembroke table, with frieze drawer, on square tapering legs with brass caps and casters, c1790, 33in (84cm) long.
£2,500–2,750 *ANT*

A Regency mahogany Pembroke table, the frieze with a drawer and dummy drawer, raised on central ring-turned support, quadripatite base with brass caps and casters, early 19thC, 36in (91.5cm) long.
£650–700 *GAK*

A George III satinwood veneered Pembroke table, the top with panels of burr yew, string-inlaid and bordered in tulipwood, with oak-lined frieze drawer and dummy drawer to the other end, replaced gilt-brass plate handles, flanked by inlaid panels of purple heart, the square tapering legs with replaced brass casters, 27½in (70cm) long.
£4,000–4,500 *WW*

A satinwood and rosewood banded Pembroke table, later painted with trailing briars, the top above a frieze drawer and false drawer, on tapering square legs with brass casters, early 19thC, 37½in (95.5cm) long.
£1,450–1,600 *Bea(E)*

A Regency mahogany Pembroke table, with frieze drawer to one end, on a central column, c1820, 40in (101.5cm) wide.
£2,000–2,200 *ANT*

l. An Edwardian satinwood and crossbanded Pembroke table, in George III style, inlaid with marquetry and ebonised lines, the quarter-veneered top above a frieze drawer flanked by oval paterae, on fluted tapering legs and spool feet, 42in (106.5cm) wide.
£3,500–4,000 *P*

Reading Tables

A Regency reading table, with lift-up top, on bobbin-turned legs and casters, c1810, 18in (45.5cm) wide.
£1,000–1,200 *HUB*

A Regency rosewood reading and writing table, the divided ratcheted top containing 3 frieze drawers, on a lotus-carved turned column, quatrefoil platform, paw feet and casters, 36in (91.5cm) wide.
£1,800–2,200 *P*

A Victorian mahogany reading table, with divided adjustable ratcheted top, raised on octagonal column and quadripartite base, c1850, 36in (91.5cm) wide.
£600–700 *GBr*

Serving Tables

A George III mahogany bowfront serving table, with 3 frieze drawers, brass three-quarter spindle gallery, inlaid with stringing, on square tapering legs, restored, 67in (170.5cm) wide.
£3,000–3,500 *S(S)*

A mahogany veneered bowfront serving table, with 3 frieze drawers, on square tapering legs, late 18thC, 45½in (115.5cm) wide.
£2,000–2,500 *WW*

A George III mahogany serving table, with concave front, the top inlaid with stringing, fitted with a long frieze drawer flanked by 2 short drawers, on square tapering legs, 48in (122cm) wide.
£850–950 *L*

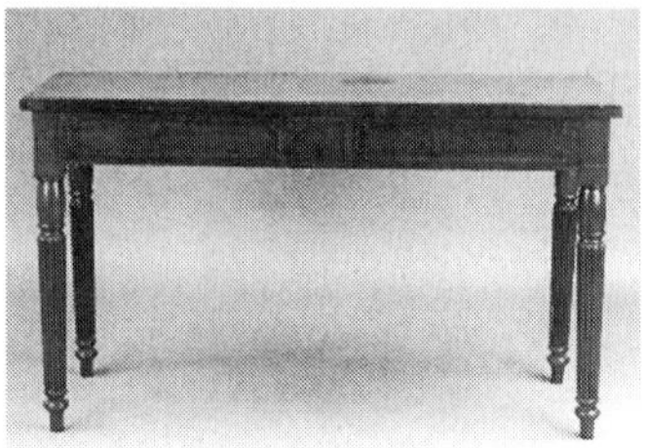

A Regency mahogany serving table, the top with reeded edge above a pair of frieze drawers with reeded panels, raised on turned lobed supports, 57in (145cm) wide.
£1,400–1,600 *Bon*

A George IV mahogany serving table, the panelled frieze centred by a roundel and containing 3 drawers, the tapered square legs with leaf-carved capitals and collared spade feet, c1820, 43½in (217cm) wide.
£6,500–7,000 *S*

A William IV mahogany serving table, in Gillows style, with rear gallery, the associated top above 2 frieze drawers, the turned and reeded legs ending in brass cappings and casters, top restored, c1835, 30in (152cm) wide.
£1,400–1,800 *S(S)*

A Victorian yew-wood serving table, the parquetry top above 2 drawers, with panelled and 'jewelled' tapered square legs, faults, c1870, 59½in (151cm) wide.
£800–1,000 *S(S)*

A George III style mahogany serving table, the fluted frieze with 2 drawers, on fluted tapered square legs surmounted by anthemia motifs, on block feet, c1890, 30in (153cm) wide.
£3,200–3,500 *S(S)*

A Victorian oak serving table, with moulded edge top and one frieze drawer supported by 2 carved griffin-type figures, on flat shelf base, associated carved scroll backboard, 64½in (164cm) wide.
£3,700–4,000 *P(G)*

Side Tables

A William and Mary oyster laburnum and walnut side table, the top with segmented veneers and boxwood stringing, the frieze drawer above spiral-twist legs joined by an X-shaped stretcher, on bun feet, c1690, 36in (92cm) wide.
£4,000–4,500 *S(S)*

A George III mahogany side table, the single drawer with original handles, c1790, 29½in (75cm) wide.
£1,300–1,450 *ANT*

A William IV rosewood side table, with veneered top over turned column supports and reeded shaped feet, c1830, 22in (56cm) wide.
£800–1,000 *BERA*

A George III mahogany side table, with one long and 2 short frieze drawers surrounding a shaped apron centred by an ogee arch, on square tapered legs, c1780, 31in (79cm) wide.
£2,200–2,500 *S*

A Dutch mahogany side table, the shaped edge top marquetry-inlaid with a vase of flowers, scrolling foliage and birds, above a breakfront drawer inlaid with foliage, stepped apron, on square tapering fluted legs, c1800, 31in (78.5cm) wide.
£1,000–1,100 *S(Am)*

Painted Furniture

The practice of painting furniture goes back to medieval times when much oak furniture was painted. Paint was used again on furniture during the late 18thC. Satinwood in particular was highlighted with delicate paintwork in the neo-classical style, and this technique enjoyed a big revival in Edwardian times when much previously plain 18thC furniture was decorated. Edwardian painting can be distinguished from neo-classical painting by its relative lack of restraint and its sentimental subject matter. Some late 18thC and Regency furniture is painted all over.

r. A painted satinwood side table, c1900, 21in (53.5cm) wide.
£1,500–1,750 *DKH*

l. A pair of mahogany side tables, each with serpentine top and carved scrolling freize, raised on moulded scrolling legs and understretchers, 19thC, 56½in (143.5cm) wide.
£1,600–1,800 *AG*

A George III French style serpentine mahogany side table, with moulded shaped frieze centred by a spray of flowers, on slender moulded cabriole legs with scroll feet, 45in (114.5cm) wide.
£4,500–5,000 *P*

A George III mahogany side table, with frieze drawer and ebony inlay, c1810, 36in (91.5cm) wide.
£1,000–1,200 *ANT*

A fruitwood and ebonised side table, with later white marble galleried top, probably Italian, c1830, 18½in (47cm) wide.
£4,500–5,000 *S*

Sofa Tables

A Regency rosewood and brass marquetry sofa table, the hinged top above a frieze drawer with opposing drawer, on a square shaft and quadripartite platform base, with brass paw caps and casters, 58½in (148.5cm) wide.
£2,500–3,000 *P*

A Regency rosewood veneered sofa table, with 2 drawers, supported on columns with a turned stretcher, spiral and fleur-de-lys style brass inlays to top and knees, the swept legs terminated by brass caps and casters, 40in (101.5cm) wide.
£2,000–2,200 *TAY*

A Regency rosewood sofa table, with boxwood stringing and 2 frieze drawers, the ring-turned end supports above splayed feet with brass cappings and casters, c1810, 41in (104cm) wide.
£5,500–6,000 *S(S)*

A George IV rosewood sofa table, with 2 frieze drawers, with turned and reeded supports joined by a turned stretcher, on hipped reeded legs with leaf-cast brass casters, stamped 'James Winter', c1825, 31in (155cm) extended.
£5,000–5,500 *S*

A Regency rosewood veneered sofa table, with brass marquetry inlay and stringing, 2 frieze drawers with brass knob handles, the reverse with dummy drawers, on hipped sabre legs with chased brass sabots on casters, 39in (99cm) wide.
£3,500–4,500 *WW*

A Regency mahogany sofa table, with crossbanded top, 2 frieze drawers, the lyre end supports joined by a pole stretcher and on moulded splayed legs with brass lion paw caps and casters, some damage, 60½in (153.5cm) wide.
£2,500–3,000 *Bea(E)*

A Regency rosewood sofa table, with satinwood and calamander crossbanded top, square section end supports and downswept legs tied by a scrolled stretcher, 37½in (95cm) wide.
£5,000–5,500 *Bon*

A George IV mahogany sofa table, with 2 frieze drawers, the end supports joined by an arched stretcher, on outswept legs with brass caps and casters, 39in (99cm) wide.
£1,400–1,800 *P*

A Regency mahogany sofa table, with 2 frieze drawers, on solid vase-shaped standard end columns and dual reeded splayed legs united by a ring-turned stretcher, terminating in brass paw cappings and casters, 52in (132cm) extended.
£3,200–3,500 *P*

A George III mahogany sofa table, with turned baluster twin end supports joined by turned and ringed understretchers, on splayed legs with brass terminals and casters, 57½in (146cm) extended.
£1,700–2,000 *HCC*

A Regency mahogany and boxwood strung sofa table, the frieze with 2 boxwood strung drawers, 2 false drawers to the reverse, on end supports with reeded downswept legs with brass terminals and casters, 68in (172.5cm) wide.
£2,300–2,800 *DN*

A rosewood and brass-mounted sofa table, with 2 frieze drawers, on scroll end supports with flowerhead ornament united by a turned stretcher, reconstructed, 19thC, 54in (137cm) wide.
£1,700–2,000 *P*

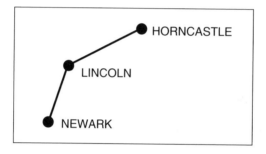

Sutherland Tables

A rosewood Sutherland table, with barley-twist supports and stretcher, on scrolled feet, original brass casters, c1840, 43in (109cm) extended.
£700–800 *LCA*

A Victorian walnut Sutherland table, on turned end supports linked by a turned stretcher, c1860, 47in (119.5cm) wide.
£1,500–1,700 *GBr*

An Edwardian mahogany Sutherland table, banded in tulipwood, the flaps with canted angles, on tapered underframe, 37in (94cm) wide.
£450–500 *Ber*

Tea Tables

A George II mahogany tea table, the fold-over top above a diaper trellis and paterae-carved frieze with gadrooned apron moulding, on cabriole legs with acanthus carved knees and claw-and-ball feet, c1755, 30in (76cm) wide.
£6,000–6,500 *S*

An Anglo-Indian tea table, with rising side shelves and galleried lower shelf, constructed from a variety of solid exotic woods, c1850, 40in (101.5cm) extended.
£1,500–1,800 *CORO*

r. A mahogany tea table, the hinged top with reeded edge above a plain frieze, raised on square tapering supports, 19thC, 35in (89cm) wide.
£350–420 *Bon(C)*

A George III figured mahogany demi-lune fold-over tea table, crossbanded in rosewood with boxwood stringing, with deep apron, on moulded square tapered legs, 35in (89cm) wide.
£1,100–1,200 *M*

A Victorian rosewood tea table, the hinged swivel top and plain frieze raised on an octagonal bulbous column, the quatreform base decorated with applied scrolling motifs and on bun feet, 38in (96.5cm) wide.
£800–900 *AG*

A George III mahogany demi-lune fold-over tea table, inlaid with boxwood and ebony chevron lines, on square tapering legs, c1790, 36in (91.5cm) wide.
£4,000–4,500 *GH*

A late Victorian mahogany and boxwood-strung tea table, the top with removable glass-bottomed tray and inlaid with central fan, urn and scrolling dragon heads and mask decoration, the sides with 4 similarly inlaid retractable panels falling to form plate stands, on square tapering legs and casters united by an undertier, 21in (54cm) wide.
£900–1,000 *DN(H)*

Tripod Tables

A George II mahogany tripod table, the associated top on a turned and fluted stem, c1755, 15in (38cm) diam.
£4,200–4,800 *S*

A Regency mahogany tripod table, the reeded legs terminating in turned feet, c1810, 25in (63.5cm) diam.
£1,100–1,250 *ANT*

A mahogany wine table, with turned column and tripod base, mid-19thC, 14in (35.5cm) diam.
£750–850 *ANT*

A George III mahogany tripod table, the dish-moulded tilt-top above a birdcage support, on a vase-shaped turned stem and cabriole legs with pad feet, 25½in (65cm) diam.
£2,500–2,800 *S*

r. A William IV satinwood and rosewood tripod table, with pietra dura inset marble top, on a turned column and scroll carved legs, 21in (54cm) diam.
£1,400–1,600 *P*

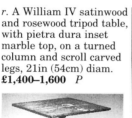

A Shaker maple candlestand, with turned flaring standard on 3 downswept legs, American, c1830, 15in (38cm) wide.
£650–750 *S(NY)*

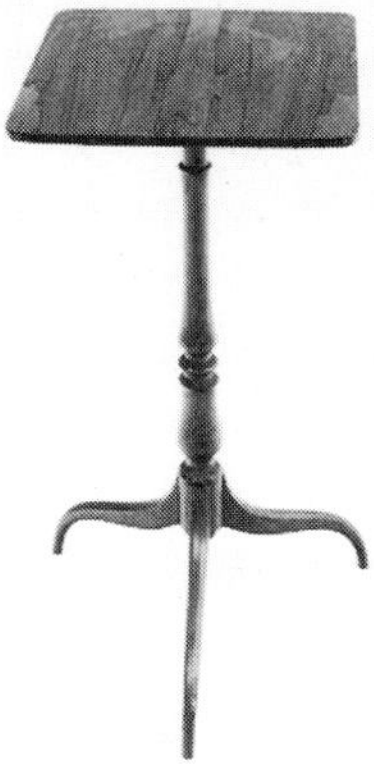

A rosewood tripod table, the turned stem with tulip base, on splayed down-turned legs, mid-19thC, 15in (38cm) wide.
£1,500–1,650 *Bea(E)*

l. A Victorian walnut and marquetry tripod table, on a wreathed and carved shaft and cabriole legs with scroll feet, 26½in (67cm) wide.
£630–700 *P*

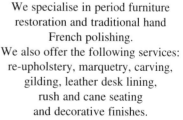

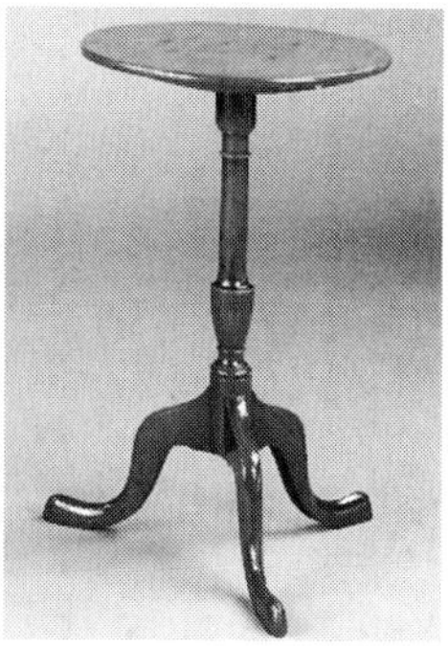

A George III mahogany tripod table, the tilt-top above a slender vase-shaped turned column and outswept legs with pad feet, c1770, 17in (43cm) diam.
£900–1,000 *Bon*

A George III mahogany tripod table, the tilt-top on turned column and splayed legs, repaired, 31in (79cm) diam.
£500–600 *DN*

A George IV rosewood tripod table, with a turned and shaped column, on sabre legs, c1825, 25in (63.5cm) diam.
£1,200–1,400 *BERA*

Two-Tier Tables

A William IV rosewood two-tier table, with graduated spindled galleries, turned column and trefoil base with bun feet, 18in (45.5cm) diam.
£1,000–1,100 *P*

A late Regency rosewood two-tier table, with marble top and gadrooned friezes, on triple scroll uprights and splayed legs united by a marble undertier, terminating in brass cappings and casters, 16in (41cm) diam.
£1,500–1,650 *P*

A painted mahogany two-tier table, with pierced gilt-metal galleries, on down-scrolled legs, c1890, 28in (71cm) diam.
£1,000–1,200 *Bon*

An Edwardian mahogany two-tier table, the tray top with glass bottom and brass handles, raised on slender arched tapering supports, 35in (89cm) wide.
£700–800 *BIG*

Work Tables

A George III mahogany drop-leaf work table, with 2 drawers and 2 dummy drawers, on square tapered supports carved with leaf scroll and bellflower ornament and spade toes, 27in (68.5cm) wide.
£1,000–1,200 *CAG*

A Regency mahogany pedestal work table, with drop-leaf top, 2 drawers, baluster stem and 4 moulded splayed supports with turned feet, 31in (78.5cm) wide.
£1,100–1,300 *Bea(E)*

A Regency mahogany sewing table, in the manner of Gillows, the rounded drop-leaf top above a frieze drawer with a fitted interior, on reeded turned legs and brass casters, c1820, 22in (56cm) wide.
£2,500–2,800 *ANT*

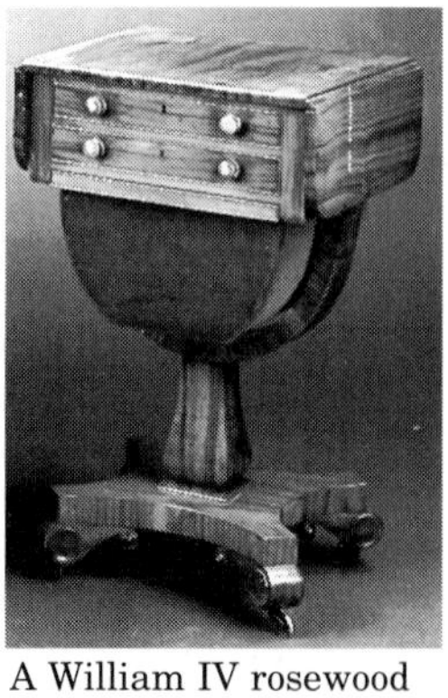

A William IV rosewood work table, the hinged top above a pair of drawers, the sliding work basket covered in red velvet on a U-shaped stretcher and lobed column, the quadripartite base on scrolled feet, c1835, 29in (73.5cm) wide.
£1,000–1,200 *Bon*

A George III satinwood work table, the chamfered hinged top with cavetto moulding, enclosing interior compartments, pleated fabric work bag below, the scrolled and leaf-carved supports on ring-turned legs joined by conforming stretchers, and with brass casters, 17in (44cm) wide.
£2,300–2,600 *S*

A carved mahogany work table, stencil-decorated and parcel-gilt, the hinged top rotating and opening to reveal a paper-lined well, the case below with a short drawer and a simulated short drawer above a long drawer, with cast-brass lions' head pulls, the acanthus-carved standard on scrolling animal paw feet, on casters, New York, c1820, 25in (63.5cm) wide.
£1,200–1,500 *S(NY)*

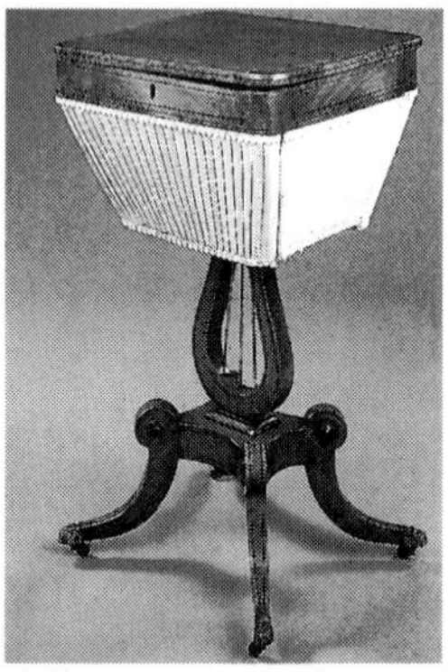

A Regency mahogany work table, inlaid with ebonised stringing, the crossbanded top revealing compartments and a well, the lyre support with quadruple splayed legs ending in brass paw caps and casters, top warped, c1810, 18in (46cm) wide.
£2,000–2,200 *S(S)*

Don't Forget!
If in doubt please refer to the 'How to Use' section at the beginning of this book.

A William IV mahogany work table, the shaped casket top with hinged lid, the waisted tapering column with leaf collar, on a concave platform with lions' paw feet, 20½in (52cm) wide.
£600–750 *AH*

An early Victorian burr walnut work table, with rising top and fitted drawer, on baluster turned central column, 4 leaf-capped S-scroll supporting brackets and quadruple scroll legs, 21in (53.5cm) wide.
£1,400–1,600 *LF*

An early Victorian rosewood sewing table, the top inlaid to the underside and enclosing a satinwood fitted interior, with basket below, on scroll-carved legs united by a pole stretcher, 22in (56cm) wide.
£1,300–1,500 *P(C)*

A Victorian rosewood work table, the frieze drawer above a pleated workbag, on pierced flat baluster trestle legs joined by a turned stretcher, on scrolled toes, 21in (53cm) wide.
£1,000–1,100 *L*

A Victorian figured walnut sewing table, the top opening to reveal a fitted interior of decoratively pierced lidded compartments, with a string-inlaid walnut storage compartment, on a turned trestle frame with turned stretcher and carved supports on casters, 23½in (59.5cm) wide.
£1,000–1,200 *BIG*

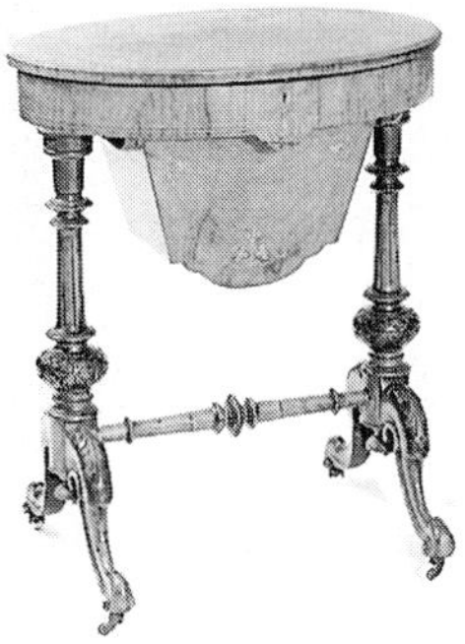

A mid-Victorian burr walnut work table, the boxwood inlaid top enclosing a fitted interior and central work bag, raised on turned and carved end supports, on downswept scroll legs joined by a turned stretcher, 24in (61cm) wide.
£1,200–1,400 *P(NW)*

A Victorian black papier mâché work table, with mother-of-pearl inlay and gilt decoration, the domed hinged cover revealing a brocade-lined interior, ogee sides above the shaped apron, on a bulbous turned stem, the quatreform base with scroll toes and brass casters, 20in (51cm) wide.
£600–700 *WW*

l. A Victorian walnut and ebonised work table of octagonal form, the hinged top revealing a fitted interior, raised on carved tripod base, c1880, 15½in (39.5cm) wide.
£525–575 *Ber*

Cross Reference
Colour Review

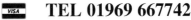

A French rococo revival rosewood work table, the serpentine-shaped top inlaid with brass, pewter, mother-of-pearl and marquetry, the lid rising to reveal a lidded interior, on cabriole legs united by an X-frame stretcher, 19thC, 23in (58.5cm) wide.
£1,000–1,100 *EH*

A kingwood and parquetry work table, by Alphonse Giroux & Co, inset with gilt-bronze mounts, the hinged crossbanded top inset with a monogram, enclosing a mirrored fitted interior above a wool box, on cabriole legs, c1865, 23½in (60cm) wide.
£3,500–4,200 *S*

Writing Tables

A George III mahogany writing table, the frieze drawer fitted with a leather-inset slide, on moulded and chamfered square section legs tied by a shaped shelf stretcher, on casters, c1765, 34in (86.5cm) wide.
£1,600–2,000 *Bon*

A Regency rosewood kidney-shaped lady's writing table, after a design by Gillows, with a beaded moulded frieze, on dual splayed legs with spindle ornament terminating in brass foliate caps and casters, 38½in (98cm) wide.
£4,000–4,500 *P*

A George III mahogany adjustable pedestal writing table, the tulipwood crossbanded sliding top with a hinged flap, the frieze with a writing drawer panelled to simulate 3 drawers, revealing a sliding baize-lined panel surrounded by divisions including a secret compartment, opposed by 3 dummy drawers, on a fluted turned column and cabriole legs ending in foliate scroll feet, 32in (82cm) wide.
£2,500–3,000 *S*

l. A George IV mahogany writing table, by Gillows of Lancaster, the inverted front with a shaped reeded edge top, above 3 frieze drawers with raised outline mouldings and turned boxwood knob handles, on ogee and ring-turned reeded tapering legs and brass casters, top formerly with a gallery, 54in (137cm) wide.
£4,000–4,500 *WW*

A George IV Anglo-Indian bowfronted writing table, on reeded tapering legs, c1825, 42in (106.5cm) wide.
£1,000–1,200 *GBr*

A Victorian rosewood and walnut writing table, the top with a gilt tooled-leather inset and 2 frieze drawers, the turned tapering legs with lappet knees ending in brass cappings and casters, restored, c1840, 42in (107cm) wide.
£1,300–1,500 *S(S)*

A mahogany writing table, by T. Willson, with three-quarter gallery, 3 frieze drawers and 2 small drawers around an arched kneehole, on reeded and turned legs ending in brass caps and casters, c1850, 42in (107cm) wide.
£1,100–1,250 *GBr*

A Victorian mahogany writing table, with a tooled-leather inset top, 4 frieze drawers to each side, on turned legs with casters, 3 knobs replaced, 96in (244cm) wide.
£2,000–2,200 *DN*

A Victorian rosewood writing table, with leather-inset top, 2 cedar-lined drawers, dual vase-turned supports on quadripartite cabriole legs acanthus carved at the knees, on casters, paper label for John Kendell & Co, 38in (96.5cm) wide.
£2,200–2,500 *P*

A Louis XV style porcelain and gilt-metal mounted kingwood *bureau plat*, the top inlaid with strapwork above a shaped frieze with an end drawer and mounted with painted porcelain plaques, on cabriole legs with foliate cast gilt-metal mounts and sabots, c1870, 40½in (103cm) wide.
£5,000–5,500 *Bon*

A Victorian walnut kidney-shaped writing table, with a floral-inlaid and leather-inset moulded top, on fluted turned tapering legs joined by flat stretchers, on casters, 46in (117cm) wide.
£1,800–2,000 *Gam*

An inlaid satinwood writing table, by Herter Brothers, the moulded frieze with a single drawer, painted throughout with bellflower banding, on turned tapered and fluted legs headed with concave capitals, the leaf-capped toupie feet joined by a curved X-stretcher, c1880, 37½in (95.5cm) wide.
£4,000–4,800 *SLM*

Herter Brothers (1865–1905)

This company was founded in New York by the half brothers Gustav and Christian Herter, who had emigrated from Germany in the mid-19thC. While Gustav concentrated on conventional and revivalist designs, Christian produced more adventurous pieces inspired by the English Aesthetic Movement, in particular the designs of E. W. Godwin and Christopher Dresser. He was also greatly influenced by the contemporary fashion for Japanese taste. In the 1870s Christian took over sole directorship of the company and Herter Brothers became one of the most progressive furniture design companies in the United States. Their pieces are rarely signed, but can usually be identified by their characteristic style as well as their high design and manufacturing standards.

A mid-Georgian style carved mahogany writing table, late 19thC, 48in (122cm) wide.
£2,200–2,500 *TMA*

l. A Sheraton revival satinwood writing table, the raised back with 2 small cupboards joined by a shelf with brass galleries, above a serpentine-fronted writing surface and 2 crossbanded drawers, on tapering legs with stretchers, c1890, 39in (99cm) wide.
£3,200–3,500 *DN*

A Louis XVI style brass-mounted *bureau plat*, by Antoine Krieger, the gilt tooled leather writing surface within a brass band, above a central frieze drawer and pair of drawers, each side fitted with a sliding writing surface, on brass channelled fluted tapering legs and toupie feet, c1900, 63in (160cm) wide.
£7,000–8,000 *S(NY)*

Antoine Krieger and his brother established their workshop in Paris in 1826. They were awarded a silver medal at the London Exhibition of 1852.

Teapoys

A Regency rosewood and brass marquetry teapoy, with stylised foliate scroll designs, the hinged top enclosing 4 lidded compartments with turned handles, on a rectangular column, quatrefoil base and splayed legs with brass paw cappings and casters, 18in (45.5cm) wide.
£1,400–1,600 *P*

A Regency chinoiserie decorated teapoy, the hinged top decorated with figures in a landscape, enclosing a red velvet compartmented interior, on a square section column and plinth, terminating in hipped outswept legs and scrolled feet, c1810, 14½in (37cm) wide.
£1,500–1,800 *Bon*

A William IV mahogany teapoy, the hinged lid opening to reveal a pair of lidded compartments centred by a recess, above a gadrooned frieze and lobed reeded column, on a conforming circular base and scrolled feet, lacking mixing bowl and slide, c1835, 18in (45.5cm) wide.
£750–850 *Bon*

A William IV mahogany teapoy, with a fitted interior, supported on a baluster column with a shaped quadripartite platform base and moulded feet, 17in (43cm) wide.
£750–850 *MAT*

Some teapoys are now used as jardinières or sewing boxes.

Trays

A mahogany butler's tray, with pierced hinged gallery, raised on a folding X-shaped base, c1845, 28in (71cm) wide.
£400–480 *GBr*

A mahogany butler's tray, mid-19thC, stand later, 25in (63.5cm) wide.
£850–950 *ANT*

A snakewood and brass-mounted tray, the pierced brass gallery fitted with scroll handles, early 19thC, 24½in (62cm) wide.
£2,300–2,500 *S*

r. A mahogany butler's tray, of serpentine form, with balustraded gallery, on a folding stand with square uprights and stretchers, late 19thC, 23in (58.5cm) wide.
£400–500 *HSS/P*

MILLER'S COMPARES . . .

I A George III mahogany butler's tray, the flush panelled base with 4 hinged and pierced flaps, the edge with reeded moulding, c1765, 36in (91.5cm) wide.
£3,500–4,000 *S*

II A George III mahogany butler's tray, the flush panelled base with 4 hinged and pierced flaps, 36½in (93cm) wide.
£2,300–2,800 *S*

A pair of butler's trays identical in design to *item I* **was supplied by Thomas Chippendale to the 5th Earl of Dumfries in 1763, which suggests that** *item I* **was also designed by Chippendale. The superior quality of this piece is immediately obvious, with its reeded edges, as opposed to the plain moulded edges of** *item II.* **The more elaborate shaping of the handholes of** *item I* **is a further desirable feature.** *S*

An Edwardian inlaid mahogany butler's tray/occasional table, on swept legs linked by an undertier, 24in (61cm) wide.
£800–900 *WL*

Wardrobes

A George III mahogany gentleman's breakfront wardrobe, with a central pair of panel doors with 2 short and 3 long drawers below, flanked by double panel doors, on reeded bun feet, 96in (244cm) wide.
£4,200–4,800 *P*

A Victorian inlaid walnut breakfront wardrobe, the central mirrored door flanked by a pair of panelled doors, on a plinth base, c1870, 81in (205.5cm) wide.
£2,300–2,600 *RPh*

A Victorian ash wardrobe, with a central mirror above 2 short and 3 graduated long drawers, flanked by hanging cupboards each enclosed by a panelled door, mid-19thC, 72in (183cm) wide.
£1,100–1,200 *SWA*

A Victorian satin birch gentleman's wardrobe, with central mirror flanked by a pair of panelled doors, 71in (180.5cm) wide.
£875–975 *MiA*

l. An Edwardian inlaid mahogany breakfront wardrobe, by Marsh, Jones, Cribb & Co, the arched pediment with satinwood fan motif and urn surmounts above a key pattern cornice and drapery frieze, the central pair of panel doors with segmented veneers and enclosing hanging space, above 2 short and 2 long drawers, flanked by a pair of conforming doors and 3 drawers each side, c1910, later alterations, 98in (249cm) wide.
£7,500–8,000 *S(S)*

Marsh, Jones, Cribb & Co were important 19thC manufacturers of furniture, based in Leeds.

Cross Reference
Colour Review

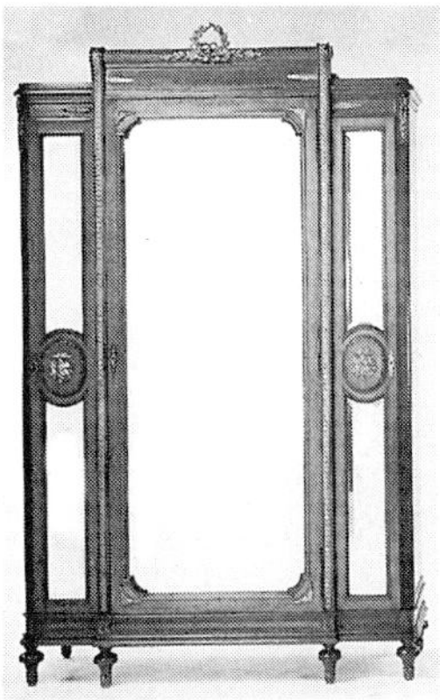

A Louis XVI style inlaid walnut and ormolu-mounted armoire, the reeded and moulded breakfront cornice centred by a ribbon and laurel crest over a mirrored door, flanked by narrow doors centred with panels depicting musical trophies, the moulded base raised on toupie feet, late 19thC, 58in (147.5cm) wide.
£1,100–1,300 *SLM*

An Italian polychrome painted serpentine-fronted wardrobe, with a broken pediment above a pair of doors decorated with figures in masks and carnival costumes, on short cabriole legs, damaged, 19thC, 32in (82cm) wide.
£850–1,000 *S(S)*

Washstands

A George III mahogany gentleman's washstand, the hinged folding top enclosing a fitted interior with a central mirror and lidded compartments, above a drawer fitted with a writing slide and 5 further drawers, on square tapered legs, restored, 29½in (75cm) wide.
£800–1,000 *Bon(N)*

A late George III mahogany and boxwood strung bowfront corner washstand, with central frieze drawer flanked by a dummy drawer either side, on square splayed legs, top replaced, 22in (56cm) wide.
£600–700 *DN(H)*

An American mahogany washstand, with hinged opening top, on square chamfered legs joined by a cross stretcher, c1780, 30in (76cm) wide open.
£2,000–2,200 *S(NY)*

A mahogany washstand, with three-quarter gallery, a dummy drawer above one long drawer, early 19thC, 31in (78.5cm) wide.
£650–750 *BUSH*

A Federal style inlaid mahogany washstand, the curved top with gallery, with one long drawer above 2 cupboard doors, on square tapering legs, American, late 19thC, 49in (124.5cm) wide.
£700–800 *SLN*

A French style mahogany gentleman's washstand, with hinged top and rising mirror, above drawers and a cupboard, 19thC, 48in (122cm) high.
£800–1,000 *RTo*

Whatnots

A George III mahogany four-tier whatnot, the base with a drawer, c1800, 15in (38cm) square.
£1,500–2,000 *SPa*

A mahogany four-tier whatnot, with turned supports, c1810, 18in (45.5cm) wide.
£1,600–1,750 *ANT*

A George IV four-tier mahogany whatnot, with concave-shaped shelves and turned supports, c1820, 19½in (49.5cm) wide.
£1,200–1,350 *HUB*

A mahogany four-tier whatnot, the top tier with a central carved medallion, the shelves with raised backs and turned supports, c1830, 21in (53.5cm) wide.
£650–750 *BUSH*

A rosewood four-tier whatnot, the lappet-carved and reeded turned supports surmounted by finials, the base with a drawer, on brass casters, c1835, back panelling later, 23in (58.5cm) wide.
£1,300–1,500 *Bon*

A rosewood three-tier whatnot, the top with three-quarter gallery and cushion-moulded drawer, on turned supports and brass casters, c1860, 17in (43cm) wide.
£1,200–1,300 *CHA*

A Victorian mahogany four-tier whatnot, the shelves supported by petal-carved uprights, on dwarf turned legs, 36½in (92.5cm) wide.
£1,300–1,500 *Oli*

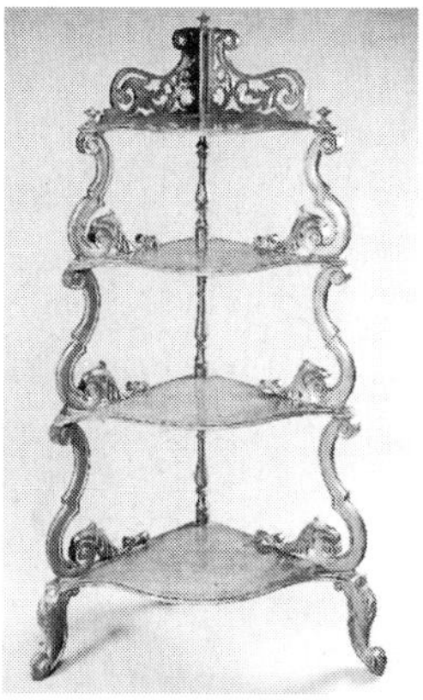

A Victorian walnut corner whatnot, the 4 serpentine graduated tiers with foliate and S-scroll supports, fretwork crest and turned finials, on scroll feet, 53in (134.5cm) high.
£700–850 *DN*

r. A Victorian walnut three-tier whatnot, the shaped shelves supported by baluster turned uprights, pierced scroll cresting, on turned legs and casters, 21½in (54.5cm) wide.
£750–850 *WL*

l. A Victorian walnut veneered whatnot, with pierced gallery back above the boxwood strung top, supported by 4 turned columns, 2 shelves below and 2 drawers in the base, on turned feet and brass-capped ceramic casters, 24in (61cm) wide.
£1,300–1,500 *Mit*

Window Seats

An Italian neo-classical painted and parcel-gilt window bench, the upholstered seat flanked by outscrolled sides with leaf-tip carved fluted top rails, on tapering fluted legs headed by paterae, late 18thC, 76in (193cm) long.
£7,000–8,000 *S(NY)*

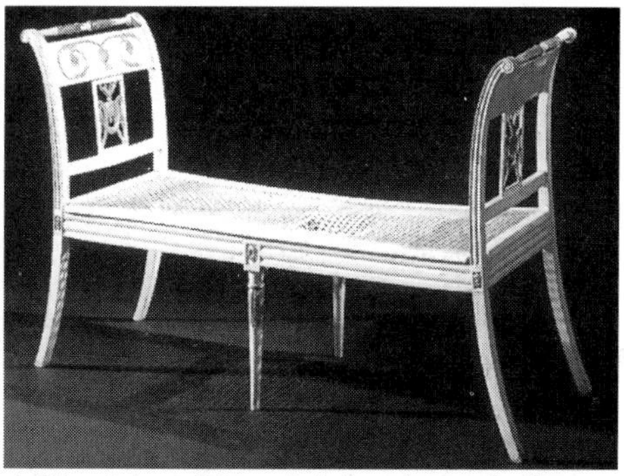

A Directoire white painted and parcel-gilt window settee, the down-curved sides carved and pierced with an urn and scrolls, on sabre side legs and rounded centre legs carved and painted with leaves, c1800, 57in (144.5cm) long.
£1,500–1,700 *S(Am)*

A William IV mahogany and upholstered window seat, with carved scroll arm facings and moulded apron, the turned legs ending in brass cappings and casters, c1835, 79in (200cm) long.
£1,000–1,200 *S(S)*

A pair of George IV rosewood window seats, in the manner of Gillows, the slightly tapered caned seats on turned tapered reeded legs, headed by carved flowerhead paterae, c1825, 40in (101.5cm) long.
£5,500–6,000 *S*

Wine Coolers

A George III mahogany and brass-bound cellaret-on-stand, the hinged top enclosing a fitted interior, with tapered body, on 4 tapering supports with brass casters, 23½in (60cm) wide.
£2,700–3,000 *Bri*

A George III mahogany cellaret, the octagonal lid inlaid with a shell on a harewood ground within parquetry and chequer strung banding, the sides with chequered ovals, on square tapered and tablet-mounted legs with fan-inlaid capitals, 18in (45.5cm) wide.
£2,000–2,200 *EH*

A Federal style satinwood-inlaid mahogany cellaret-on-stand, with hinged top, the case with central inlaid patera, the stand with one short drawer, on square tapering legs, American, 19thC, 19½in (49.5cm) wide.
£900–1,000 *SLN*

A George III mahogany and brass-bound cellaret-on-stand, the hinged crossbanded lid opening to a lined and divided interior, with brass carrying handles, on square tapering legs with brass toes and casters, 24½in (62cm) wide.
£4,500–5,000 *AH*

A mahogany cellaret, with hinged lid and brass carrying handles, on bracket feet, 18thC, 14in (35.5cm) wide.
£600–750 *LAY*

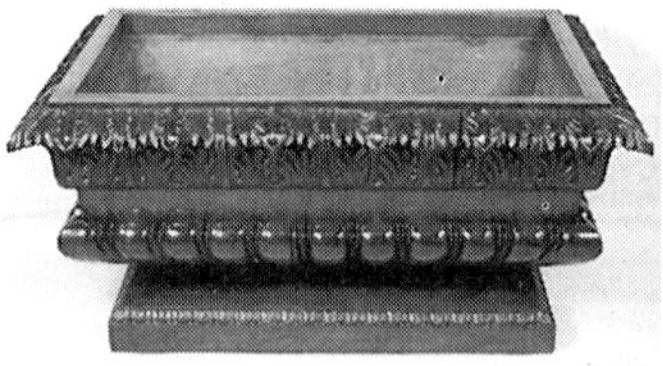

A William IV mahogany wine cooler, the open top with a later zinc tray, the edge acanthus-carved above an egg-and-dart moulded cushioned border and concave platform, the plinth with a leaf-carved edge, cracked, moulding losses, 48in (122cm) wide.
£10,000–11,000 *Hal*

This wine cooler attracted keen bidding in the saleroom because of its large size. The acanthus carving and the colour of the mahogany were also very appealing.

r. An Edwardian Sheraton revival satinwood cellaret, crossbanded with string and chequer inlay, the domed lid with marquetry patera with a trailing leaf surround, brass carrying handles, side drawer, raised on collared square tapering supports, 16in (40.5cm) wide.
£4,000–4,500 *AH*

A George III mahogany wine cooler, the top with fluted rays, on 4 outset lobed baluster turned legs, 26½in (67cm) wide.
£4,000–4,500 *L*

A mahogany and brass-bound octagonal wine cooler, on tapering legs with brass cappings and casters, c1810, 22in (56cm) wide.
£1,600–1,800 *ARE*

A Regency mahogany sarcophagus-shaped wine cooler, with ebony-edged panelled sides, lead-lined interior, on claw-and-ball feet, 28in (71cm) wide.
£2,800–3,200 *GOR(B)*

OAK & COUNTRY FURNITURE

The majority of antique oak furniture found today dates from the 17th to the 19th centuries, since earlier pieces are becoming rare and, as a result, more costly. Fortunately many of the later pieces which are available are reasonably priced. The sturdy nature of oak and country furniture makes it practical to live with as it is not as likely to show the results of knocks and rough handling. In fact everyday use together with regular polishing enhances the patina. A set of 19th century ladder-back or spindle-back rush-seat chairs represent excellent value and comfort compared with a set of 17th century Cromwellian panel-back chairs which are rarely found as an exact set and whose solid seats and backs are not designed for comfort.

The market values of oak have been subject to many vagaries. The current trend is the widening price gap between pieces of average quality and those of a more special nature. This 'added value' factor may only be a special honey colour, for example, but a late 17th century four- to six-seater gateleg table with exceptional colour and patina may be worth up to six times more than its plainer cousin. Such soaring prices also occur with rarer pieces of unusual size, because with each decade the number of such items on the market diminishes, and collectors who can afford to buy into this area will continue to see their purchases increase in demand and value.

On a more practical note, beware of oak furniture that has been made-up to order by re-assembling or cannibalising other pieces. Such items are available in large quantities and are, sadly, one of the reasons why people are frightened away from this collecting area. A further complication is the proliferation of pieces emanating from the late 19th century which saw a fashion for revival styles of early furniture such as that of the Elizabethan era. As ever, liking a particular piece is the best reason to buy, but do not expect to see such items sail into high price brackets in the near future.

Oak furniture looks best displayed with other oak pieces. It tends to clash with the reddish colours of mahogany and rosewood and the refined veneers of the 18th and 19th centuries. It sits comfortably, however, with the late 17th and early 18th century walnut furniture whose smooth golden colours offset the browns and textural tones of oak.

So good luck in your hunt for oak furniture and take advantage of the fact that competition for less special items is not too fierce at present. British buyers are currently the main takers, but European and American collectors are showing interest and, along with the South Americans now emerging as new buyers in this field, they are likely to increase the competition in the future.

Anthony Rogers

Beds & Cradles

An oak tester bed, with carved and panelled canopy, 17thC, 63in (160cm) wide.
£4,500–5,000 *AAV*

A Victorian Gothic revival oak half tester bedstead, with carved pierced brackets, the footboard with a pierced frieze and carved finials, 54in (137cm) wide.
£2,000–2,200 *WW*

An oak rocking cradle, the hinged canopy carved with animals, village scenes and flowers, dated '1671', 36in (91.5cm) long.
£1,600–1,800 *BaN*

An oak cradle, the canopy and carved floral panels decorated with turned finials, on splay feet, 17thC, 40in (101.5cm) long.
£900–1,000 *AG*

An oak cradle, c1760, 36in (91.5cm) long.
£2,500–3,000 *PHA*

A planked oak cradle, with arched shaped hood, 18thC, 35in (89cm) long.
£200–220 *DN*

Boxes

An Elizabethan painted oak desk box, with iron carrying handles, the underside of the fall with a coat-of-arms, possibly German, dated '1586', 16½in (42cm) wide.
£3,000–3,500 *FW&C*

An oak box, 17thC, 12½in (32cm) wide.
£650–750 *DaH*

These boxes are often referred to as Bible boxes although their original use was for securing paperwork and general domestic items. It was probably the Victorians who discovered their suitability for housing their large family Bibles.

An oak box, carved with leaves, later hinges, c1720, 23½in (59.5cm) long.
£250–300 *OCH*

l. A carved oak box, dated '1685', 24in (61cm) wide.
£350–400 *DaH*

An oak box, with carved double lunette front, the top with thumbnail carving each side, 17thC, on later stand, 27in (68cm) wide.
£250–275 *MSW*

A Gothic revival carved bog oak box, early 19thC, 26in (66cm) long.
£900–1,000 *REF*

Bureaux

An oak bureau, with stepped interior and a well, feet and handles replaced, c1720, 36in (91.5cm) wide.
£5,000–6,000 *PHA*

The figuring on the fall of this bureau has been caused by medullary rays which are formed at an angle to the annual growing rings of an oak tree. Their appearance in oak furniture is an attractive and valued feature.

r. A George III oak and mahogany crossbanded bureau, the fall enclosing a projecting cupboard between drawers and pigeonholes, over 2 short and 3 long drawers between line-inlaid quarter pilasters, on bracket feet, 42in (106.5cm) wide.
£1,450–1,600 *EH*

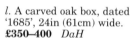

A George I oak bureau, the fall-front opening to reveal a stepped fitted interior of pigeonholes and drawers flanking a central cupboard door with a sliding well compartment below, above 2 short and 2 long drawers, raised on bracket feet, 32½in (82.5cm) wide.
£1,700–1,850 *CGC*

A fruitwood and walnut crossbanded bureau, with fitted interior, c1780, 34in (86.5cm) high.
£1,600–1,800 *RYA*

An oak bureau, with 4 graduated long drawers, on shaped bracket feet, 19thC, 35in (89cm) wide.
£650–750 *DOC*

Chairs

A Dutch Baroque walnut armchair, the shaped top rail and seat rail carved with a coat-of-arms and scrolled leaves, with columnar uprights, caned back, the arms carved with leaves, on scrolled feet, restored, late 17thC.
£2,000–2,200 *S(Am)*

A set of 6 oak dining chairs, with inverted moulded arched padded backs and upholstered seats, on turned legs and stretchers, 17thC.
£1,200–1,300 *LRG*

A Charles II joined oak panel-back armchair, with holly and ebony inlay, strapwork and chain linked carving.
£1,200–1,400 *REF*

A set of 7 oak backstools, with brass-studded leather-covered backs and seats, on bobbin-turned legs with similar front stretchers, upholstery later, some restoration, 17thC.
£1,350–1,500 *Bea(E)*

Backstools, an early form of dining chair, dating from the 17thC have naturally been subject to a long period of use. Add to this their unfashionable period during the 18thC and the majority of the 19thC it is understandable why it is rare to find a surviving set of dining chairs from the 17thC. Matched sets can often be found where there are variations to a similar design accounting for different chair makers.

l. A bow-backed primitive Windsor armchair, with solid sycamore seat and original green paint, c1780.
£1,100–1,250 *RYA*

l. A matched set of 10 walnut chairs, including 4 armchairs, each caned back and seat within a barley-twist baluster turned frame, the legs tied by conforming stretchers, on turned feet, c1680.
£4,000–4,800 *Bon*

A carved oak backstool, Lancashire, c1680.
£1,200–1,300 *KEY*

l. A Welsh oak side chair, with vase-shaped back splat, early 18thC.
£450–500 *CoA*

A George III elm corner chair.
£800–900 *SPU*

A set of 8 Chippendale style oak dining chairs, with vase-shaped splat and solid seats, 18thC.
£2,600–2,850 *LAY*

An ash rush-seated chair, late 18thC.
£130–150 *SPa*

An ash rush-seated ladder-back desk chair, c1800.
£1,400–1,800 *PHA*

l. An ash and elm rush-seated rocking chair, probably Lincolnshire, re-rushed, early 19thC.
£375–475 *MEG*

r. An elm miniature armchair, c1840.
£150–200 *MRW*

An American maple sack-back Windsor armchair, the turned curved crest rail over curved armrail continuing to arms, flanked by ring-turned armrests, with saddle seat, raised on ring-turned cylindrical tapering legs joined by turned H-stretcher, early 19thC.
£300–350 *SLN*

MILLER'S COMPARES . . .

I A yew and elm Windsor armchair, the arched spindle back with a pierced shaped splat and solid seat, on turned legs joined by a crinoline stretcher, 19thC.
£670–750 *P*

II An ash and elm Windsor armchair, the arched spindle-back with a shaped pierced splat and solid seat, on turned legs joined by an H-stretcher, 19thC.
£480–550 *P*

Both these chairs appear very similar in construction and condition, but *Item II* **is of a slightly simpler construction being made from ash and elm, with a plain stretcher and turned legs.** *Item I* **is constructed from yew and elm, and also features a crinoline stretcher –always a sought-after feature – accounting for the higher price realised when sold at auction.** *P*

A set of 6 oak Chippendale style country dining chairs, initialled 'XAV', c1800.
£3,500–4,000 *DBA*

A yew and elm wheel-back Windsor armchair, c1830.
£700–800 *KEY*

l. A fruitwood and oak chair, Pembrokeshire, c1800.
£250–300 *COM*

An ash high wheel-back Windsor armchair, c1850.
£600–650 *WELL*

A Victorian beech and fruitwood slat-back armchair, c1860.
£225–270 *CPA*

A late Victorian oak armchair, late 19thC.
£800–900 *DOC*

A matched set of 4 yew and elm Windsor armchairs, 19thC.
£1,600–1,800 *Mit*

FURTHER READING
Miller's Pine & Country Furniture Buyer's Guide, Miller's Publications, 1995

l. A pair of 17thC style carved oak armchairs, the padded arm supports and stuff-over seats upholstered in painted leather depicting figures and animals, on bobbin-turned supports united by stretchers, 19thC.
£650–750 *P*

A yew-wood stick-back Windsor chair, with pierced splats, on turned legs with crinoline stretcher, 19thC.
£650–750 *E*

A late Victorian ash and beech scroll-back carver chair, with elm seat, c1880.
£150–175 *SWN*

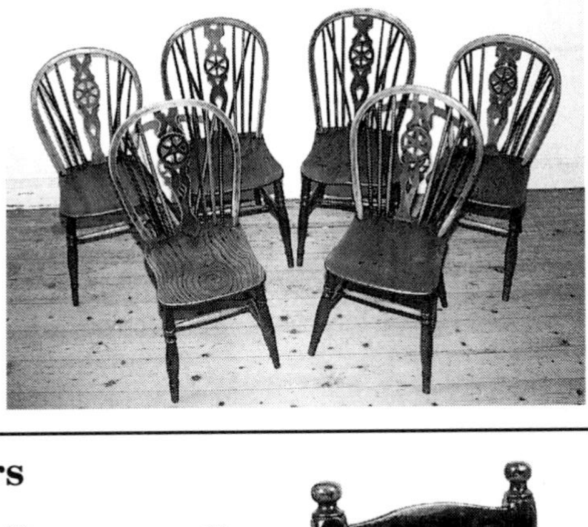

l. A matching set of 6 wheel-back dining chairs, with elm seats, c1900.
£650–750 *JH*

Children's Chairs

A child's mahogany high chair, c1800.
£650–700 *OCH*

A child's beechwood high chair, with red and brown paint, c1840.
£150–180 *A&A*

A child's country-made chair, with reddish-brown paint, c1840.
£120–150 *MTa*

A child's ash and beech rush-seated chair, with restraining bar, 19thC.
£130–150 *MLL*

Chests of Drawers

A Jacobean oak chest, the 2 short and 2 long drawers with geometric drawer fronts, between reeded pilasters, on shaped bracket feet, the carcass formed from a table frame, 46in (117cm) wide.
£600–700 *BR*

An oak chest of drawers, with geometric mouldings, c1680, handles replaced, 35in (89cm) wide.
£2,800–3,200 *DaH*

A walnut and fruitwood two-part chest of drawers, with oak sides, 4 long geometrically moulded and fielded panelled drawers with iron loop handles, on a moulded plinth base, 17thC, 43in (109cm) wide.
£6,500–7,000 *P(E)*

An oak chest of drawers, in 2 parts, with long geometrically panelled drawers, on bun feet, 17thC, 38in (97cm) wide.
£820–900 *L*

An oak chest of drawers, with 3 panelled drawers flanked by ring-turned half columns, raised on block feet, late 17thC, 38in (96.5cm) wide.
£1,100–1,200 *SLN*

Types of Construction

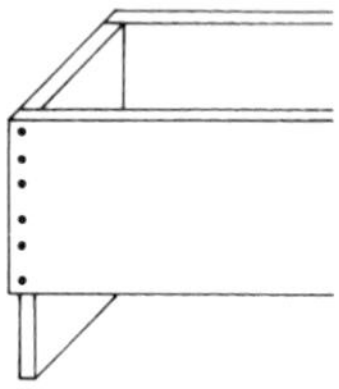

Boarded or planked construction

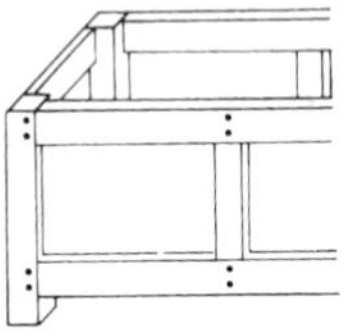

Joined construction

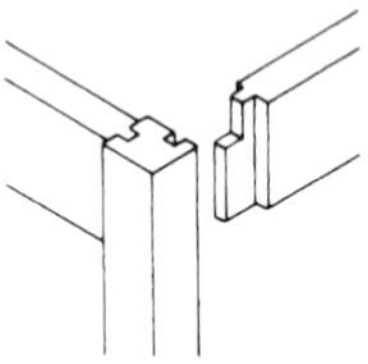

Mortice and tenon joint

Early furniture was made from planks of wood nailed together. As furniture made by joiners became slightly more refined, a framework joined by mortice and tenon joints, held in place by wooden dowel pegs or 'trenails' and filled with panels, became usual. Dowels were used less in the 18thC, as glue was improved.

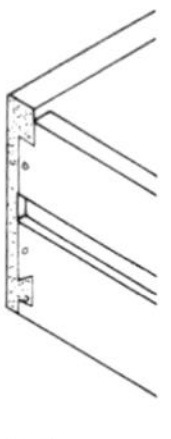

(a)

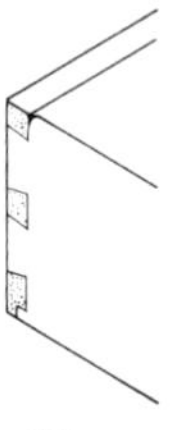

(b)

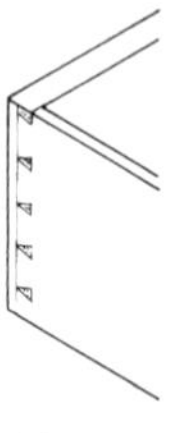

(c)

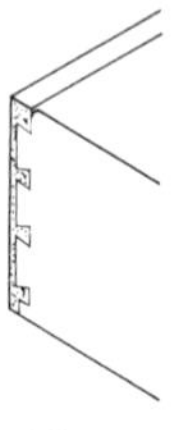

(d)

From the latter part of the 17thC dovetail joints were used in furniture such as chests of drawers and cupboards. At first drawers were crudely made, often nailed together, with a groove on each side to allow the drawer to slide (*a*). By c1700, with the influence of Dutch craftsmen, dovetails had become finer and more sophisticated (*b*). As the 18thC progressed, dovetails on top quality pieces became increasingly fine (*c*), although on country pieces of similar date they still may be relatively crude (*d*).

An oak chest of drawers, the 4 long drawers with applied mouldings, on later bracket feet, late 17thC, 36in (91.5cm) wide.
£1,350–1,500 *RBB*

An oak bachelor's chest of drawers, the fold-over cleated top with baize inset, 2 short and 3 long drawers, on later bracket feet, early 18thC, 24½in (67cm) wide.
£11,500–13,000 *S(S)*

This piece attracted high bidding as small oak bachelors' chests are seldom seen.

An oak chest of drawers, with 2 short and 3 long geometrically moulded drawers, raised on stile feet, early 18thC, 38in (97cm) wide.
£900–1,100 *Bon(C)*

A George III oak chest-on-chest, the upper part with 3 short and 3 long graduated drawers, the lower part with 3 long drawers, on ogee bracket feet, 45½in (115.5cm) wide.
£1,000–1,200 *S(S)*

An oak chest of drawers, the plank top above 2 short and 3 long pollard oak crossbanded drawers, flanked by fluted column pilasters, with fielded panelled sides, on bracket feet, mid-18thC, 36in (91.5cm) wide.
£2,400–2,800 *Bon*

l. A George III oak chest of drawers, with 2 short drawers over 3 long graduated drawers, c1780, 42in (106.5cm) wide.
£500–600 *REF*

r. An oak miniature chest of drawers, with original brasses, c1820, 10in (25.5cm) wide.
£650–800 *PHA*

Chests-on-Stands

An oak chest-on-stand, the upper part with 2 short and 3 long drawers banded in pollard oak and with boxwood and ebony chevrons, original brass handles, the base with 3 conforming short drawers around a shaped apron, on later cabriole legs, mid-18thC, 43½in (110cm) wide.
£1,200–1,350 *DN*

A William and Mary oak chest-on-stand, restoration to stand, c1790, 41½in (105.5cm) wide.
£5,000–5,500 *ANV*

r. An oak chest-on-stand, the upper part fitted with 2 short and 3 long geometrically moulded drawers, the stand fitted with a long drawer and raised on cup and baluster turned legs united by flattened stretchers, on bun feet, c1700, 41in (104cm) wide.
£5,000–5,500 *P(O)*

A Queen Anne style oak chest-on-stand, 19thC, 35½in (90cm) wide.
£900–1,000 *Ber*

Chests-on-Stands

Stands should always be closely inspected as often they are rebuilt or replaced because of the weight and movement they bear over a long period of time. Some examples have had their legs removed altogether and replaced with bracket feet.
A surviving all-original stand commands a premium.

Chests & Coffers

An oak plank chest, with chip-carved edges and zig-zag lines, the front carved with roundels and on bifurcated end supports, early 17thC, 32in (81.5cm) wide.
£700–800 *Bea(E)*

An oak mule chest, with hinged top, the panelled front above 2 drawers with geometric mouldings, 17thC, 52in (132cm) wide.
£600–700 *DN*

A carved oak coffer, the three-panel front with architectural and foliate carved decoration, on 4 stile supports, late 17thC, 51½in (131cm) wide.
£400–450 *Bri*

A Charles II oak coffer, with a triple panelled lid and a conforming front, the frieze carved with stop-fluting, 55½in (139.5cm) wide.
£350–450 *HYD*

A north Italian cedarwood chest, the top with pokerwork decorated figures to the underneath, the front with blind carved decoration, raised on a later stand with bulbous turned feet, 17thC, 72½in (184cm) long.
£2,500–3,000 *P(O)*

An oak boarded coffer, c1720, 32in (81.5cm) wide.
£700–800 *CPA*

A Continental carved fruitwood coffer, the hinged top over conforming case carved with floral motifs, on conforming shaped base with geometric carvings, 17thC, 55in (139.5cm) wide.
£1,000–1,200 *SLN*

An oak coffer, with lunette carved frieze above carved triple panels to the front, on stiles, late 17thC, 47½in (120.5cm) wide.
£650–750 *WL*

A George III oak coffer bach, with convex end panels, c1770, 20in (51cm) wide.
£2,500–3,000 *PHA*

The coffer bach originated in Wales, as its name – 'bach' meaning small – implies. Generally 24in (61cm) or less in width, they are quite rare, taking the form of a miniature mule chest with a panelled front and apron drawer or drawers. It is the unusual size that has helped their treasured survival, often having been polished and cared for while their full-size cousins became unfashionable and neglected over the passing centuries.

MILLER'S COMPARES . . .

I A carved oak coffer, the twin panelled cover above a lunette frieze, the front carved with quatrefoil motifs, late 17thC, 44½in (113cm) wide.
£900–1,000 *S(S)*

II An oak coffer, with a boarded cover, triple panel front carved with lozenge motifs, on stile feet, late 17thC, 55½in (141cm) wide.
£500–600 *S(S)*

The more unusual example of *item I*, **with its twin panelled top and front, helped to lift the price.** *Item II*, **being a more conventional three-panelled coffer, has a less desirable boarded cover. While the plainer front has attractive medullary rays it may have been plainer still in the 17thC, and the lozenge motifs added in the 19thC.** *S(S)*

A Continental oak and cast iron coffer, the domed lid with strapwork decoration, the front carved with paterae and mythical beasts, carrying handles to the sides, 18thC, 44½in (113cm) wide.
£900–1,000 *P*

Cupboards

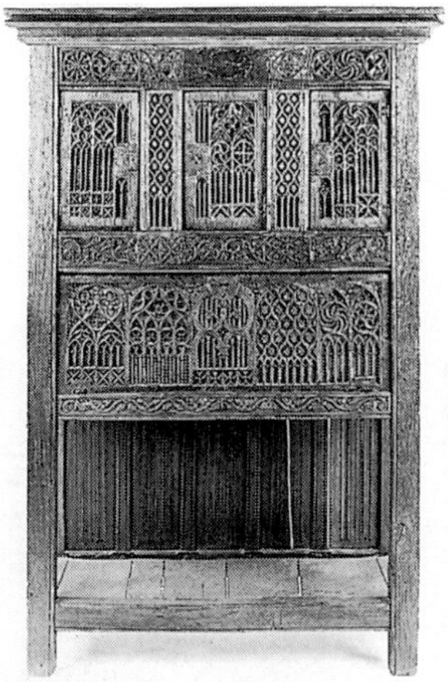

A joined oak press cupboard, with blind Gothic tracery carved frieze and 3 conforming cupboard doors, the fall-front decorated with further tracery below, on square section supports tied by a shelf stretcher, parts 16thC, reconstructed, 48in (122cm) wide.
£1,600–2,000 *Bon*

r. A Jacobean style oak livery cupboard, with dentil cornice, carved and inlaid with floral, scroll and lion mask decoration, bulbous supports, drawer and panelled door above, on square section feet, part 17thC, 45½in (115.5cm) wide.
£4,000–5,000 *Gam*

An oak wall cupboard, with fruitwood spindles and pierced panels inlaid with bog oak and holly, some restoration, c1625, 36in (91.4cm) wide.
£6,500–7,500 *PHA*

A William and Mary oak cabinet-on-stand, with a pair of glazed doors, the lower section with 3 drawers over the shaped frieze, on turned supports, flat X-stretcher with a turned central finial, 38in (96.5cm) wide.
£15,000–16,500 *RBB*

This cabinet of small proportions created enormous pre-sale interest. It came with the provenance that, having originally come from the collection of the late James Thursby-Pelham, it was sold by the London dealers S. W. Wolsey in 1948 when it was the subject of a full-page illustration in the London Antique Dealers Fair programme.

A yew wood corner cupboard, with fielded panels and fluted pilasters, c1760, 30in (76cm) wide.
£1,700–1,850 *ANV*

Yew is very rare in antique furniture, and its attractive colour and figuring make it very sought-after.

l. An oak corner cupboard, with dentil cornice, arched panelled double door opening to reveal original pine interior panelling and serpentine shaped shelves, a panelled single cupboard door under, 18thC, 48in (122cm) wide.
£1,300–1,600 *HCC*

An oak press cupboard-on-chest, the central panelled door with applied moulding, 2 short drawers below with brass swan neck drop handles, flanked by a panelled cupboard door, on a base with 6 panels above 3 cockbeaded drawers with brass drop handles, 18thC, 67in (170cm) wide.
£2,200–2,500 *Mit*

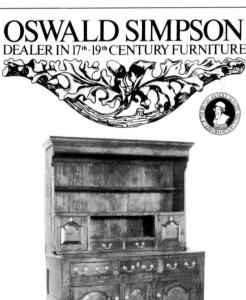

A George III oak corner cupboard, with 2 arched fielded panel doors, canted corners and moulded base, 33½in (85cm) wide.
£800–900 *AH*

A George III oak aumbry, the upper doors with pierced fret panels, the base with 2 drawers and a pair of panel doors, 42in (106.5cm) wide.
£2,600–3,000 *DOC*

The pierced panels allowed for ventilation because food was kept in the cupboard. It is not unusual to find holes in the backs of many oak pieces in which food has been stored caused by the gnawing of rats and mice.

A north Wales oak tridarn, 50in (127cm) wide.
£4,800–5,200 *REF*

A George III pale oak cupboard-on-chest, on shaped bracket feet, 53½in (136cm) wide.
£1,400–1,600 *WL*

A George III oak hanging corner cupboard, with dentil cornice, canted stiles enclosing panel door, 26in (66cm) wide.
£500–550 *HOLL*

An oak standing corner cupboard, inlaid with bog oak and pearwood, c1800, 34in (86.5cm) wide.
£5,000–6,500 *PHA*

Glazed Furniture

Always inspect glazed doors on 18thC furniture as they may originally have had plain timber or veneered panels. The use of glazing and astragals (glazing bars) may be a later enhancement using old glass obtained from antique picture frames.

A George III oak corner cupboard, with a canted front, enclosed by panelled doors, on ogee bracket feet, 35in (89cm) wide.
£3,200–3,500 *L*

A George III oak and mahogany bowfronted corner cupboard, with spice drawers, c1790, 31in (78.5cm) wide.
£1,350–1,500 *DaH*

A Dutch oak display cabinet, with a scrolling arched cornice and frieze, the foliate carved astragal glazed doors below enclosing shaped shelves flanked by similar sides, the lower part containing a pair of arched panel doors, on bracket feet, early 19thC, 63in (160cm) wide.
£4,500–5,000 *P*

Dressers

A George III joined oak dresser, with 3 shelves, 3 frieze drawers above a central column of 3 drawers, flanked by panelled cupboard doors, on bracket feet, mid-18thC, 64in (163cm) wide.
£4,200–4,800 *Bon*

Miller's is a price GUIDE not a price LIST

r. A George III elm dresser, the boarded delft rack with 2 shelves flanked by fluted pilaster uprights, above 3 central drawers, a drawer and a cupboard to either side, on block feet, 79in (200.5cm) wide.
£4,500–5,000 *AG*

An oak dresser, with original boarded back, 3 shelves and scallop-shaped side supports, raised upon a base of 3 frieze drawers, above central drawers and cupboards, 18thC, 68in (173cm) wide.
£4,200–4,800 *B*

An oak and elm dresser, the upper stage with open plate rack, the base fitted with an arrangement of 5 deep drawers, on block legs, repaired, handles altered, 18thC, 96½in (245cm) wide.
£3,500–4,000 *WL*

A George III oak crossbanded dresser, the open rack with 2 cupboards, the base with 3 frieze drawers and square section, on tapering legs, 60in (152.5cm) wide.
£1,700–2,000 *LAY*

A north Wales dresser, the superstructure of 3 open shelves flanked by flute-moulded half pillars, the base with 3 frieze drawers above a central breakfront of 3 drawers flanked by fluted quadrant pilasters, flanked by a pair of panelled doors, with brass swan neck handles throughout, raised on ogee bracket feet, late 18thC, 73in (185.5cm) wide.
£5,000–5,500 *PF*

This 18thC north Wales dresser was potentially worth £8,000–10,000, had it been in original condition. Of paramount importance to oak buyers is the colour and patination of the piece, something which is very difficult to reproduce. This particular dresser had been purchased from Harrods by the vendor in the 1940s. At that time it had been restored, undoubtedly due to its poor condition, and the restoration involved the stripping, recolouring and polishing of the piece.

An elm dresser, with shaped frieze, the base with 3 drawers with brass handles, over shaped apron and square tapered legs, c1790, 81in (206cm) wide.
£3,500–4,000 *KEY*

An American oak dresser, the upper section with 3 shelves, flanked by cupboards on either side, the lower section with 3 short drawers, over shaped apron, raised on cabriole legs ending in pad feet, 19thC, 65in (165cm) wide.
£1,100–1,300 *SLN*

An oak and mahogany crossbanded dresser, the delft rack with carved cornice, above 3 shelves and 2 crossbanded short cupboards, the 3 cockbeaded crossbanded frieze drawers with turned handles, above a shaped apron, on square tapering legs, incomplete, distressed, early 18thC, 72in (183cm) wide.
£3,200–3,500 *Hal*

An oak dresser, with rack, 3 drawers and 3 cupboards to base, c1820, 58in (147.5cm) long.
£4,750–5,250 *ANV*

Dresser Bases

A oak dresser base, with 3 frieze drawers, a central tier of 2 graduated drawers, flanked by 2 doors, with applied geometric moulding, 18thC, 66½in (169cm) wide.
£3,500–4,000 *LAY*

An oak dresser base, the 3 short drawers to the centre with brass lock escutcheons and handles, flanked by a pair of arched panelled doors, raised on bracket feet, mid-18thC, 54½in (138.5cm) wide.
£2,800–3,200 *AG*

An oak dresser base, with 4 frieze drawers, on tapering cabriole legs and pad feet, early 19thC, 76in (194cm) wide.
£1,000–1,200 *HOLL*

A George III oak dresser base, the 3 cockbeaded frieze drawers with later turned handles and oval brass lock plates, above a heart-pierced and shaped apron, on tapering cabriole front legs and hoof feet, top repaired, 74in (188cm) wide.
£7,000–8,000 *Hal*

An oak dresser base, the 4 panelled frieze drawers with turned wood handles, divided by pilasters, 4 fielded panelled cupboard doors below and panelled sides, 18thC, 117in (297cm) wide.
£4,800–5,200 *AH*

Racks & Shelves

An elm plate rack, c1800, 48in (122cm) long.
£3,000–3,500 *PHA*

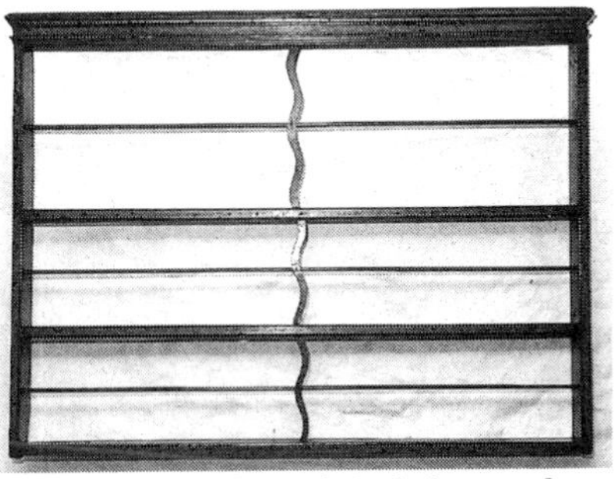

An oak plate rack, with 3 shelves and shaped front bar, Yorkshire, 18thC, 53in (134.5cm) wide.
£1,200–1,400 *ANV*

A set of George III oak corner hanging shelves, c1770, 30in (76cm) high.
£3,000–3,500 *PHA*

Settles & Settees

An oak settle, with carved panels, baluster-turned arms and legs carved with lions' masks, 17thC, 108in (274cm) wide.
£10,000–12,000 *SPa*

The reason why this particular settle received such a high price is because of its unusual length, and its exceptional condition and patina.

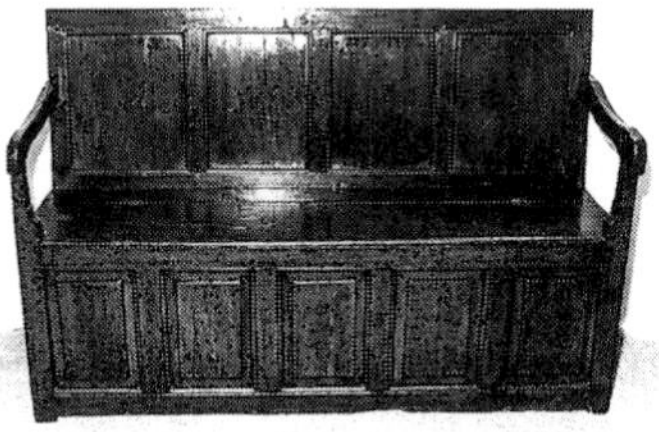

l. A box settle, with panel back and fielded panel base, early 18thC, 68in (172.5cm) wide.
£2,000–2,400 *ANV*

A Georgian oak settle, with panelled back and scrolling arms, on turned legs, 60in (152.5cm) wide.
£550–650 *AAV*

A Suffolk elm bow-shaped settle, the 5 wide elm boards flanked by winged sides with curl-over armrests, an oak front below the seat comprising 2 central drawers flanked by 2 panelled doors, minor repairs to back, 19thC, 69in (175.5cm) wide.
£2,300–2,600 *B*

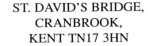

An oak monk's bench, the carved panelled back with tilting action, with hinged boarded seat above a twin panel base, 1930s, 41in (104cm) wide.
£240–280 *LF*

The origin of this item can be found in the 17thC with the oak chair-table or settle-table. The association with monks is probably a Victorian romanticism introduced during the Elizabethan revival in the late 19thC.

Stools

A joined oak upholstered stool, 17thC, 35in (89cm) long.
£3,000–3,500 *DBA*

Stools such as this, in very good original condition with excellent patina, always command high prices.

A Cromwellian oak stool, upholstered in tapestry, c1650, 15in (38cm) wide.
£1,200–1,600 *MIC*

A joined oak stool, c1670, 20in (51cm) wide.
£380–420 *WELL*

A joined oak child's stool, c1680, 12in (30.5cm) high.
£700–800 *RYA*

A joined oak stool, c1700, 18in (45.5cm) long.
£1,200–1,500 *PHA*

A sycamore dished-top stool, with hand-turned legs, early 19thC, 11in (28cm) diam.
£175–200 *MTa*

Tables

A Charles II oak side table, with frieze drawer, bobbin-turned legs and stretchers, 35½in (90cm) wide.
£2,500–2,800 *P(O)*

While side tables from the 17thC are easily found, rare examples with honey colour and special features such as this example with bobbin turning can command high prices. In addition, the conforming front and rear 'mid-height' stretcher rails make it a particularly desirable and sought-after example.

r. An oak refectory table, with replaced centre stretcher, restored top, c1660, 84in (213.5cm) wide.
£3,000–3,300 *REF*

A William and Mary oak side table, with a frieze drawer, on turned supports with flat X-stretcher, with turned finial, 30in (76cm) wide.
£1,200–1,500 *RBB*

An oak gateleg table, with turned legs and moulded stretcher, c1700, 41½in (105.5cm) wide.
£1,400–1,600 *ANV*

r. An oak refectory table, on turned and square legs, with later stretchers, early 18thC, 92in (233.5cm) long.
£2,500–3,000 *AG*

l. An oak gateleg dining table, with bow ends and oval leaves, raised on turned ring and rectangular legs with joined stretchers, on shaped feet, early 18thC, 33in (84cm) wide.
£800–900 *GAK*

An oak gateleg table, c1720, 43in (109cm) wide.
£1,200–1,500 *OCH*

An oak side table, c1730, 32in (81.5cm) wide.
£900–1,100 *WELL*

An American walnut tavern table, the removable top above a frieze fitted with one short and one long thumb-moulded drawer, on ring-turned bottle-form legs ending in pad feet, lacking pegs, some damage and repairs, c1740, 58in (147cm) wide.
£4,200–4,800 *S(NY)*

A yew tip-top tripod table, c1780, 29½in (75cm) diam.
£2,500–2,800 *DBA*

An oak side table, with frieze drawer, on turned legs united by stretchers, 18thC, 38in (96cm) wide.
£1,000–1,200 *HOLL*

A sycamore and ash cricket table, with shelf underneath held by original metalware, c1800, 26in (66cm) diam.
£650–700 *MTa*

A Welsh fruitwood and ash cricket table, c1800, 20in (51cm) wide.
£780–850 *CoA*

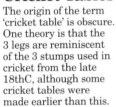

l. An oak tripod table, late 18thC, 21in (53.5cm) diam.
£450–500 *DaH*

Cricket Tables

The origin of the term 'cricket table' is obscure. One theory is that the 3 legs are reminiscent of the 3 stumps used in cricket from the late 18thC, although some cricket tables were made earlier than this.

An oak topped table, with pine frame and base, c1900, 78in (198cm) long.
£550–600 *SWN*

An oak refectory table, the cleated plank top above square chamfered and splayed end supports with scroll end friezes, 19thC, 94in (239cm) long.
£1,500–1,800 *S(S)*

French Provincial Furniture

The popularity of French provincial furniture expresses the desire for the French to understand and maintain the roots of their society and culture.

Throughout rural France the traditional family lived in one room, gathered around the farm table, surrounded by beautiful *buffets deux corps*, a painted *comtoise* clock, a *buffet bas*, and a *dressoir* or *vaisselier* in one corner. The wealthier farmer would also have a *buffet à quatre volets* (a four-door buffet) and a *bonnetière* (a cupboard with one long door) for larger quantities of linen, crockery and bonnets. As space was at a premium every piece of furniture had a specific purpose and as the family grew the room was also enlarged to accommodate more members.

To become a craftsman in France entailed not only developing the skills to build good functional furniture but also to create pieces in the style of the region for which they were intended. As such, after years of apprenticeship in his own region, the 18th century young craftsman would then travel around France and learn the principal traditions and designs of country furniture in other regions.

Every French hamlet had its busy craftsmen and the young journeyman would stay with the local master *ébéniste* (cabinet maker), bartering work for food. In rural Brittany he would make functional pieces in cherry and chestnut and improve on his oak and pine carving skills for the Normandy bourgeoisie. He would then move north and make oak furniture influenced by his Flemish neighbours and later travel to the south-east, an area rich in folk art, to learn about decorating pine in the chalets of the Alps. In Provence, his skills would be perfected as spectacular walnut commodes were demanded by his wealthy southern clientele. To complete his training the journeyman would need to be familiar with the formal designs of the Loire Atlantique, where mahogany was used for furnishing the wonderful chateaux, while *commodes tombeaux* and *armoires bombés* were a must for the Bordeaux aristocracy and rich wine merchants.

Upon completion of his *tour de France* the now seasoned craftsman would often warrant the status of master craftsman. He, in turn, would be approached by a young journeyman eager to learn the skills of his trade.

Today there is a strong demand for good rural French provincial furniture particularly from the US and Canada. Armoires and buffets made from fruitwoods are currently very popular. Despite the availability of authentic traditional French furniture there is a thriving business in reproduction pieces, made in the style of the rural designs but with a more modern element of functionality.

Pierre Farouz

l. A pair of French cherrywood benches, with turned legs and stretchers, northern Brittany, late 19thC, 78in (200cm) long.
£180–240 *MTay*

A Breton carved oak wedding bed, with original side rails, late 19thC, 54in (137cm) wide.
£1,250–1,350 *SWA*

A Louis XVI provincial oak side cabinet, the 4 doors with shaped panels, the apron carved with paterae, 18thC, 46½in (118cm) wide.
£1,100–1,200 *S(Am)*

A French oak side cabinet, with 2 drawers over a pair of panelled cupboard doors, shaped apron, on bracket feet, early 19thC, 39in (99cm) wide.
£650–700 *EH*

A French provincial chestnut buffet, with original brass handles and studs, c1850, 39in (99cm) wide.
£900–1,200 *LPA*

A French oak and cherrywood side cabinet, c1820, 50in (127cm) wide.
£1,100–1,200 *GD*

l. A Louis XV chestnut side cabinet, with 2 frieze drawers over a pair of panelled doors, northern Brittany, 19thC, 52in (132cm) wide.
£1,500–1,800 *MTay*

A set of 6 French provincial walnut chairs, with carved top-rail, seat-rail and stretcher, with rush seats, c1900.
£800–900 *LPA*

A French carved walnut chair, late 19thC.
£650–750 *GD*

A set of 6 French carved and latticework chairs, with rush seats, c1880.
£700–750 *MLL*

A French elm chair, with rush seat, c1920.
£60–75 *OLM*

A Louis XV provincial painted bergère *duchesse brisée*, with scalloped crest carved with foliage, serpentine-fronted seat, on cabriole legs ending in feet carved with foliage, mid-18thC, 72in (183cm) long.
£1,400–1,600 *S(LA)*
Ex-Marlene Dietrich collection.

A French provincial fruitwood serpentine commode, the 2 short and 2 long drawers with roundels and shaped panels, between rounded corners, shaped apron below, on scroll feet, 18thC, 49½in (126cm) wide.
£3,200–3,500 *P*

A set of 6 French beech ladder-back armchairs, with rush seats, c1930.
£800–900 *MTay*

r. A French provincial oak armoire, the 2 conforming doors with shaped moulded panels, carved with rocailles and scrolling foliage, above 2 drawers, on shaped feet, 18thC, altered and restored, 67in (170cm) wide.
£2,000–2,200 *S(Am)*

A chestnut table/coffer, Brittany, 19thC, 76in (193cm) long.
£1,000–1,200 *MTay*

A French provincial carved oak cupboard, the frieze applied with a vase of flowers and birds between ribbon-tied floral swags, the upper pair of doors enclosing 2 shelves and 2 drawers, the lower part with a pair of panelled doors enclosing a shelf, on dwarf scrolled feet, 18thC, 66in (167.5cm) wide.
£3,300–3,800 *Oli*

A French oak armoire, with a pair of panelled doors, on stile feet, c1840, 56in (142cm) wide.
£1,300–1,500 *GD*

A chestnut armoire, with a pair of carved panelled doors, Quimper, Brittany, dated '1881', 51in (129.5cm) wide.
£1,800–2,200 *MTay*

A French oak armoire, the pair of panelled doors enclosing 2 drawers, c1790, 59in (150cm) wide.
£3,000–3,250 *ANV*

A French fruitwood armoire, with a pair of panelled doors, on stile feet, c1840, 60in (152.5cm) wide.
£900–1,000 *WEE*

A French pine cupboard, the upper doors glazed, over a spindle gallery and on turned supports, the base with 2 frieze drawers and 2 cupboard doors, on bun feet, c1890, 50in (127cm) wide.
£800–1,000 *TPC*

A French yew wood cupboard, the pair of later glazed doors enclosing shelves, the base with 3 frieze drawers and a pair of panelled cupboard doors, late 18thC, 48in (122cm) wide.
£2,000–2,500 *Bon*

A French provincial Louis XV style cherrywood armoire, with original brass hinges, c1860, 58in (147.5cm) wide.
£1,000–1,200 *LPA*

A French provincial painted pine cupboard, c1880, 41in (104cm) wide.
£1,250–1,400 *MLL*

A French provincial fruitwood desk, with shaped back over 4 short drawers and open compartments, over projecting writing surface, 2 short drawers and shaped apron, on cabriole legs, early 19thC, 60in (152.5cm) wide.
£650–800 *SLN*

A French provincial oak dresser, Champagne area, c1850, 50in (129.5cm) wide.
£1,200–1,500 *LPA*

A French cherrywood dresser, with carved panelled doors and apron, late 19thC, 50in (127cm) wide.
£1,800–2,200 *MTay*

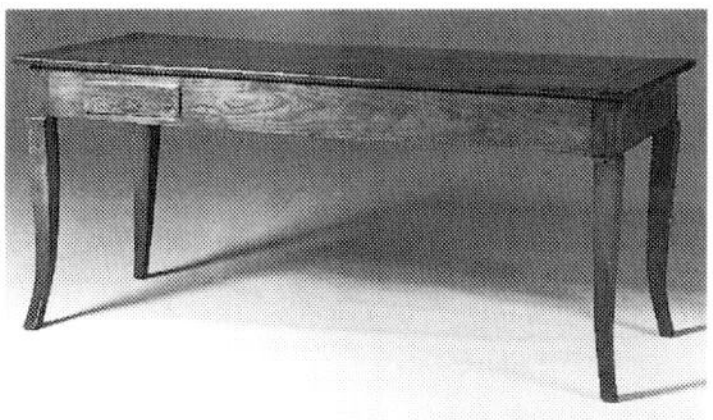

A Louis XV provincial cherrywood dining table, the plain frieze fitted with an offset small drawer, on cabriole legs, top later, feet altered, mid-18thC, 75in (190.5cm) wide.
£1,400–1,800 *S(LA)*

This table had been a gift from Ernest Hemingway to Marlene Dietrich.

A French painted pine plate rack, c1900, 36in (91.5cm) wide.
£120–150 *HRQ*

A French oak centre table, in Louis XV style, with serpentine moulded top, the apron with incised trellis and C-scroll rocaille ornament, on cabriole legs and scroll feet, 18thC, 66in (168cm) wide.
£1,400–1,800 *P*

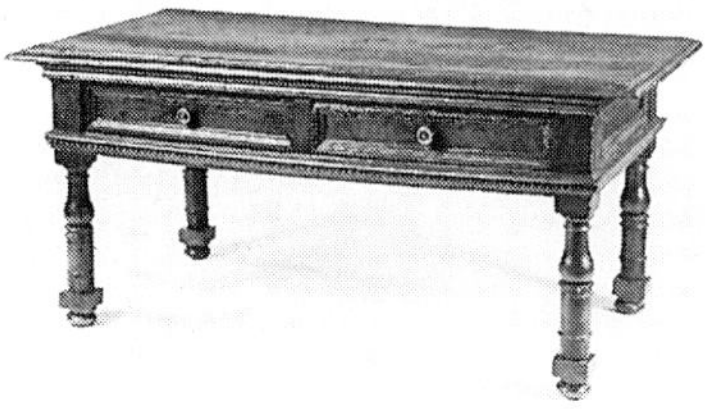

A French provincial walnut centre table, the moulded edge top over panelled apron, the frieze with 2 panelled drawers, on ring turned legs ending in flat bun feet, 18thC, 70in (178cm) wide.
£1,500–1,800 *SLN*

A French cherrywood table, with one drawer, on square legs joined by stretchers, c1830, 50in (127cm) wide.
£500–600 *GRP*

A French oak farmhouse extending table, with 2 side drawers, mid-19thC, 90in (228.5cm) long.
£2,000–2,200 *REF*

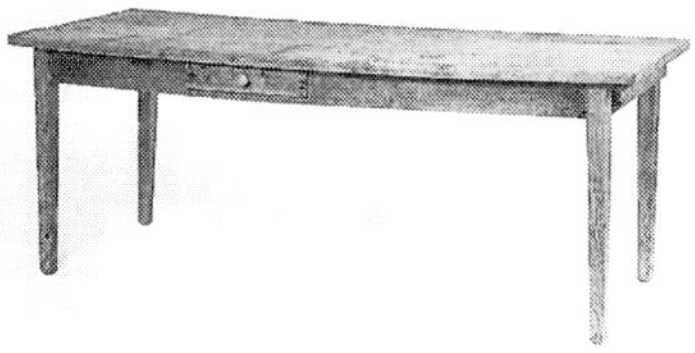

A French provincial oak and fruitwood harvest table, with one offset side drawer, on square tapering legs, 19thC, 82in (208.5cm) long.
£700–800 *SLN*

l. A French provincial elm side table, with 3 short drawers, on square moulded legs, 19thC, 79in (200.5cm) long.
£400–500 *SLN*

l. A French cherrywood farmhouse table, with one end drawer, shaped apron, on turned tapering legs, 19thC, 66in (167.5cm) long.
£750–900 *MTay*

r. A French fruitwood farmhouse table, with one side drawer, on square tapered legs, 19thC, 89in (226cm) long.
£1,750–2,000 *S(S)*

PINE
Beds & Cradles

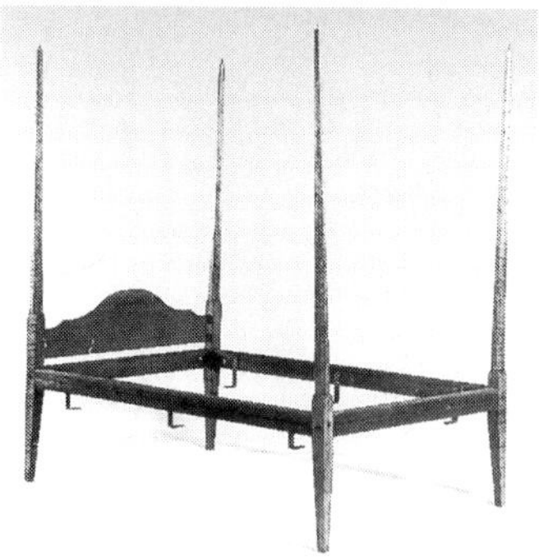

A Federal figured maple and pine 'pencil-post' bedstead, with octagonal flaring posts, arched pine headboard, on square tapering legs joined by moulded rails, with tester, New England, c1800, 51in (130cm) wide.
£7,700–8,500 *S(NY)*

A Federal birchwood and pine bedstead, the octagonal headposts centring a pitched pine headboard, surmounted by a serpentine tester, the flaring reeded footposts on urn-form drum supports joined by rails, on turned tapering legs and disc feet, painted brown, New England, c1810, 53in (135cm) wide.
£7,000–8,000 *S(NY)*

A Federal birchwood and pine bedstead, the headposts with chamfered corners centring a shaped headboard, the footposts with flaring reeded standards, on turned legs ending in peg feet, stained red, New England, c1810, 52in (132cm) wide.
£1,000–1,200 *S(NY)*

A Swiss polychrome decorated pine bed, the arched headboard painted with scrolls and flowers above an oval panel inscribed with a moral proverb, the tailboard painted with an oval vignette of a country scene, dated '1848', 70½in (179cm) long.
£2,250–2,500 *P(Z)*

A painted pine cradle, 18thC, 36in (91.5cm) long.
£380–420 *SWN*

A pine cradle, c1880, 28in (71cm) long.
£100–150 *WEE*

r. An eastern European pine sleigh bed, c1910, 73in (185.5cm) long.
£90–110 *TAN*

Benches

An Austro-Hungarian pine bench, with original paint, mid-19thC, 58in (147.5cm) long.
£550–650 *GD*

A pine bench, c1870, 41in (104cm) long.
£120–140 *MIL*

A pine and fruitwood bench, c1880, 68in (172.5cm) long.
£675–750 *MLL*

A Victorian pine bench, with traces of original paint, 60in (152.5cm) long.
£150–175 *CPA*

A painted primitive stick-back bench, decorated with floral painting, with solid seat, on faceted legs, some damage, 19thC, 74in (188cm) long.
£350–400 *S(S)*

A teak garden bench, c1920, 48in (122cm) long.
£110–130 *AL*

Bookcases

A pine astragal glazed bookcase, with raised fielded panelled base, adjustable shelves, c1840, 42in (106.5cm) wide.
£1,000–1,200 *TPC*

A pine neo-classical style bookcase, the upper section with 2 cupboard doors inset with grillework, the lower section with 2 panelled cupboard doors, 19thC, 60in (152.5cm) wide.
£1,600–1,800 *SLN*

A pine astragal glazed bookcase, c1840, 58in (147.5cm) wide.
£1,200–1,500 *TPC*

An eastern European pine glazed bookcase, c1870, 39in (99cm) wide.
£300–350 *NEW*

A pine bookcase, the upper section with 3 shelves flanked by reeded columns, the lower section with one short drawer and 2 panelled cupboard doors, flanking recessed kneehole fitted with shelves, raised on shaped bracket feet, 19thC, 61in (155cm) wide.
£850–950 *SLN*

A pine miniature bookcase, with 2 glazed doors above 4 drawers, with original paint, c1880, 19in (48.5cm) wide.
£450–500 *MIL*

A pine breakfront bookcase, made from old panelling, 1990s, 72in (183cm) wide.
£300–350 *SAU*

An oak clamped-front ark, on ogee-shaped supports, c1500, 31in (78.5cm) wide.
£3,000–3,500 *P*

A joined oak panelled coffer, candle box missing, hinges replaced, c1650, 44in (112cm) wide.
£2,100–2,400 *DBA*

An oak coffer, with carved tulip design, 17thC, 50in (127cm) wide.
£1,500–1,700 *OCH*

A William and Mary oak panelled coffer, carved with names, c1695, 52in (132cm) wide.
£2,000–2,400 *PHA*

A carved oak panelled coffer, 17thC, 43in (109cm) wide.
£1,100–1,200 *ANV*

An oak coffer, the front with 3 lozenge-carved panels, c1690, 46in (117cm) wide.
£650–750 *MIL*

A red walnut chest of drawers, with slide and original brasses, c1755, 34in (86.5cm) wide.
£7,500–9,000 *PHA*

A Charles II joined oak chest of drawers, c1680, brass handles later, 38in (96.5cm) wide.
£4,000–4,500 *DBA*

An oak chest of 4 long graduated drawers, c1795, 32in (81.5cm) wide.
£2,500–3,000 *PHA*

An oak coffer bach, inlaid with boxwood and bog oak, c1757, 21in (53.5cm) wide.
£5,500–7,000 *PHA*

Paul Hopwell Antiques

Early English Oak

Dressers, tables and chairs always in stock

A superb pair of George I oak side chairs. Excellent colour, condition and patina. English dated 1725.

A set of eight (four showing) Georgian ash wavyline ladderback dining chairs. Excellent colour, condition and patination. English c1800.

Two from a set of eight early C19th ash and alder spindle-back dining chairs. Excellent colour, condition and patina. English c1840.

An ash bobbin-turned armchair, with wing back, feet replaced, c1680.
£4,000–4,500 *DBA*

An oak armchair, with carved panel back, c1680.
£4,500–5,000 *PHA*

A set of 6 oak high splat-back chairs, early 18thC.
£4,000–4,500 *ANV*

An oak chair, with drawer beneath the seat, 18thC.
£450–500 *OCH*

A Windsor armchair, c1800.
£350–400 *SWN*

An oak and sycamore child's chair, with original paint, 19thC.
£1,100–1,200 *DaH*

A set of 6 ash chairs, with rush seats, c1840.
£1,100–1,200 *WELL*

A set of 6 elm and yew dining chairs, c1830.
£5,000–6,000 *RYA*

A turned and carved beech turner's chair, with triangular seat, 19thC.
£250–300 *MiA*

An oak press cupboard, the top with 2 doors and a central panel of geometric fielded panels, 17thC, 50in (127cm) wide.
£1,250–1,500 *MSW*

An oak press cupboard, with moulded front, c1680, 73½in (186.5cm) wide.
£7,000–8,000 *ANV*

An oak livery cupboard, with original black paint decoration, some restoration, c1690, 44in (112cm) wide.
£7,000–8,000 *PHA*

An oak press cupboard, some replacements, c1640, 58in (147.5cm) wide.
£10,000–12,000 *PHA*

An oak cupboard-on-chest, with arched panelled doors, early 18thC, 50in (127cm) wide.
£3,000–3,500 *DaH*

A George II oak dresser, the top with arcaded frieze and shaped sides, the fielded panelled base with 3 frieze drawers above 2 arched cupboard doors, c1750, 61½in (156cm) wide.
£8,000–9,000 *S(S)*

A Welsh oak press cupboard-on-chest, with fielded panels, c1740, handles later, 57in (145cm) wide.
£4,500–5,000 *DBA*

An oak panelled dresser, with moulded cornice and plain frieze, 2 shelves and cupboards, the base with 2 panelled doors, 18thC, 50in (127cm) wide.
£8,500–9,500 *CAG*

An oak breakfront dresser, with spice drawers, the base with quartered reeded columns, north Wales, c1795, 72in (183cm) wide.
£15,000–18,000 *PHA*

An oak dresser, the base with 3 frieze drawers above 2 panelled cupboard doors, 18thC, 79in (200.5cm) wide.
£9,000–10,000 *DaH*

The Refectory
38

An oak refectory table, with carved frieze and turned legs, restoration to stretchers and cleats, c1630, 96in (244cm) long.
£8,000–9,000 *DaH*

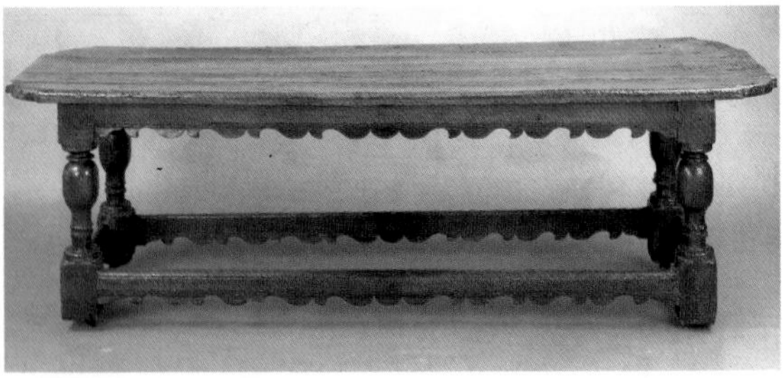

A Flemish oak refectory table, with wave-carved frieze, on ring-turned supports tied by carved stretchers, one top plank replaced, c1650, 96in (244cm) long.
£2,800–3,400 *Bon*

An oak gate-leg table, with baluster-turned supports, c1690, 52in (132cm) long.
£3,200–3,500 *ANV*

An oak side table, with single drawer, on barley-twist supports and stretchers, c1680, 22in (56cm) wide.
£9,000–10,000 *PHA*

An oak two-tier cricket table, on cabriole legs, c1750, 18in (45.5cm) diam.
£9,000–10,000 *PHA*

An oak lowboy, inlaid with boxwood and pearwood, c1745, 20in (51cm) wide.
£5,000–6,000 *PHA*

A George II oak dresser base, with chevron crossbanding and chequered stringing, above a carved apron, restored, c1750, 108in (274cm) wide.
£13,000–15,000 *S(S)*

An oak dresser base, with moulded edged top, 3 drawers over 3 smaller drawers, all with chased brass handles, shaped apron, 3 baluster-turned front legs with block feet joined by an undertier, 18thC, 60in (152.5cm) wide.
£3,200–3,500 *AH*

An oak refectory table, the baluster-turned supports joined by stretchers, 18thC, 108in (274.5cm) long.
£3,800–4,500 *REF*

A Breton chestnut bed, mid-19thC, 60in (152.5cm) wide.
£1,500–1,650 *SWA*

A French walnut cradle, 19thC, 33in (84cm) wide.
£260–320 *MTay*

A chestnut buffet base, dated '1879', 50in (127cm) wide.
£1,200–1,500 *MTay*

A Louis XV style oak bookcase, 1930s, 42in (106.5cm) wide.
£1,400–1,800 *MTay*

A carved fruitwood chair, with cane seat, c1880.
£500–550 *MLL*

A Breton oak hall chair, with turned supports, c1900.
£250–350 *MTay*

A pair of rush-seated chairs, c1930.
£75–125 *MTay*

A walnut serpentine chest of drawers, 18thC, 52in (132cm) wide.
£2,800–3,200 *P*

A pine two-door wardrobe, 18thC, 47in (119.5cm) wide.
£900–1,000 *CCP*

A pine writing table, with brass handles and square tapering legs, mid-19thC, 39in (99cm) wide.
£350–400 *GD*

A chestnut miniature armoire apprentice piece, late 18thC, 10in (25.5cm) wide.
£300–350 *MLL*

An oak armoire, with carved cornice and panelled doors, on scrolled feet, 19thC, 54in (137cm) wide.
£1,800–2,000 *SLN*

A chestnut four-door buffet, with brass studded decoration, 19thC, 56in (142cm) wide.
£1,800–2,200 *MTay*

A cherrywood armoire, with scroll panels and shaped apron, mid-19thC, 52in (132cm) wide.
£2,200–2,400 *GD*

A child's stained pine rocking chair, Cumbria, back replaced, 18thC.
£225–300 *MEG*

An Irish súgan chair, c1800.
£45–50 *TAN*

Súgan means twisted lengths of straw.

A Welsh pine carver chair, with traces of original paint, c1780.
£350–400 *CPA*

A set of 6 elm and beech chairs, with carved legs, c1880.
£280–300 *MIL*

A monk's pine chair, with plank backs, c1880.
£240–270 *CCP*

A Hungarian child's chair, early 20thC.
£40–50 *HRQ*

A pine garden chair, with a shaped frieze, c1920.
£80–90 *AL*

A child's beech and elm chair, c1920.
£30–35 *AL*

A child's pine chair, with bobbin-turned back, early 20thC.
£35–40 *TAC*

A Welsh pine box settle, early 19thC, 45in (114.5cm) wide.
£700–850 *CPA*

A pine pew, c1880, 41in (104cm) long.
£350–400 *MIL*

A Welsh box settle, Carmarthen, c1820, 56in (142cm) wide.
£700–800 *CCP*

An eastern European panelled box settle, c1890, 68in (172.5cm) wide.
£450–500 *TPC*

A pine pew, c1880, 70in (178cm) long.
£180–200 *AL*

A Georgian pine mule chest, the single drawer with brass handles, on bracket feet, 36in (91.5cm) wide.
£300–350 *TPC*

A pine box, with a drawer, c1870, 15in (38cm) wide.
£100–115 *AL*

A pine domed-top chest, with original iron carrying handles, c1850, 43in (109cm) wide.
£250–300 *CCP*

A pine chest, with brass escutcheon, carved initials and dated '1817', 45in (114.5cm) wide.
£250–300 *CPS*

A pine mule chest, with one drawer, on bracket feet, c1850, 40in (101.5cm) wide.
£280–320 *MIL*

A Georgian pine chest of drawers, with bracket feet, c1780, 34in (86.5cm) wide.
£425–475 *CPA*

A pine chest of drawers, with tray-top over 3 long drawers, c1870, 40in (101.5cm) wide.
£525–575 *AL*

A pine chest of 14 drawers, with central bookshelves, c1880, 40in (101.5cm) wide.
£400–450 *MIL*

A pine chest of drawers, with tiled back, 2 short and 2 long drawers, c1890, 42½in (108cm) wide.
£600–700 *AL*

A pine chest, with 2 short and 3 long drawers, with moulded fronts, c1810, 42in (106.5cm) wide.
£450–500 *TPC*

A Scottish pine chest of drawers, c1870, 51in (129.5cm) wide.
£1,000–1,100 *AL*

A pine chest of 4 long drawers, c1880, 36in (91.5cm) wide.
£270–300 *MIL*

A pine dressing table, with swing mirror, c1880, 42in (106.5cm) wide.
£550–650 *AL*

A painted pine chest of drawers, c1860, 47in (119.5cm) wide.
£450–500 *CPA*

An eastern European pine chest of 4 long graduated drawers, c1880, 36in (91.5cm) wide.
£450–500 *TPC*

An early Victorian pine dressing table, 39in (99cm) wide.
£550–600 *SWN*

A Victorian pine dressing table, with carved mirror supports and 4 jewellery drawers, 40in (101.5cm) wide.
£550–650 *TPC*

A Georgian pine linen press, with cockbeaded drawers, the panelled doors enclosing deep-sided slides, 52in (132cm) wide.
£1,500–1,800 *TPC*

A pine food cupboard, with 2 pairs of cupboard doors and central drawer, early 19thC, 36in (91.5cm) wide.
£1,000–1,200 *GD*

A late Georgian pine cupboard, with carved decoration, on bracket feet, 50in (127cm) wide.
£650–800 *TPC*

A pine housekeeper's cupboard, the upper part with glazed central cupboard, c1820, 62in (157.5cm) wide.
£1,300–1,500 *MIL*

A pine bookcase, with astragal glazed upper doors, c1860, 55in (139.5cm) wide.
£900–1,000 *WEE*

A pine cupboard, with 2 doors above 2 drawers, on bracket feet, c1860, 48in (122cm) wide.
£450–550 *TPC*

A pine cabinet on chest, c1860, 45in (114.5cm) wide.
£700–800 *CPS*

A Victorian pine housekeeper's cupboard, with 4 cupboard doors over 6 drawers, original painted grain finish, 84in (213.5cm) wide.
£900–1,000 *Odi*

A pine bookcase, with glazed upper doors, c1890, 48in (122cm) wide.
£680–720 *MIL*

A Georgian pine cupboard, with elm shelf, 30in (76cm) wide.
£165–185 *CCP*

A pine corner cupboard, c1800, 45in (114.5cm) wide.
£375–450 *WEE*

A late Victorian pine bedside cupboard, 16in (40.5cm) wide.
£130–145 *MiA*

A pine cupboard, c1850, 40in (101.5cm) wide.
£350–400 *CPS*

A pair of Continental cupboards, c1890, 17in (43cm) wide.
£250–280 *MIL*

A pine cupboard, with 2 doors, c1880, 43in (109cm) wide.
£300–330 *AL*

An Irish pine dresser, with moulded pediment over a carved apron, carved panelled doors, c1800, 60in (152.5cm) wide.
£2,200–2,600 *WEE*

A pine dresser, the turned legs joined by an undertier, c1830, 50in (127cm) wide.
£1,800–2,000 *AL*

A pine dresser, with delft rack, the panel-ended base with 4 drawers over 4 panelled doors, c1840, 96in (244cm) wide.
£2,000–2,500 *TPC*

An Irish pine dresser, the upper part with 3 shelves, over 2 drawers and 2 panelled doors, c1870, 60in (152.5cm) wide.
£850–1,000 *WEE*

A late Victorian pine part-glazed dresser, with shelved 'dog kennel' in base, c1890, 62in (157.5cm) wide.
£900–1,100 *TPC*

A pine dresser, with 3 shelves over 2 drawers, the base with potboard under, c1890, 49in (124.5cm) wide.
£475–525 *FOX*

A pine dresser, with 5 small and 3 frieze drawers, the base with 2 deep drawers and 2 cupboard doors, c1860, 67in (170cm) wide.
£1,800–2,000 *AL*

A pine dresser, the top with glazed doors, with brass knobs and handles, on bracket feet, c1900, 48in (122cm) wide.
£800–900 *TPC*

A pine dresser, the base with 3 deep drawers flanked by 2 cupboards, c1860, 61in (155cm) wide.
£900–1,000 *MIL*

A painted pine cricket table, with shaped frieze, c1800, 30in (76cm) diam.
£400–450 *SWN*

A Regency pine table, with 2 drawers, on turned legs, 50in (127cm) wide.
£350–400 *TPC*

A Regency pine side table, with a single drawer, on turned legs, c1810, 30in (76cm) wide.
£180–220 *TPC*

A pine farmhouse table, with a single drawer, c1810, 60in (152.5cm) wide.
£350–400 *TPC*

A pine *faux* bamboo table, c1820, 33in (84cm) wide.
£300–330 *AL*

A Victorian pine Pembroke table, 36in (91.5cm) wide.
£250–300 *TPC*

A pine scrubbed-top table, with central drawer, on turned legs, c1880, 38in (96.5cm) wide.
£300–350 *WEE*

A pine table, with mahogany top and 2 drawers either side, on fluted legs and spade feet, 19thC, 48in (122cm) wide.
£500–550 *CCP*

A pine kneehole writing table, with 4 drawers, on turned legs, c1890, 44in (112cm) wide.
£300–350 *WEE*

A Welsh pine washstand, with 2 drawers and shaped undertier, c1880, 32in (81.5cm) wide.
£300–330 *AL*

A pine table, with one drawer, on turned legs, c1890, 42in (106.5cm) wide.
£360–400 *AL*

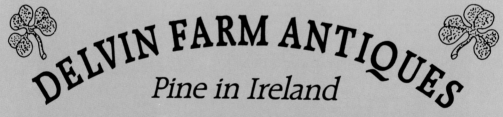

A Scandinavian painted pine doll's cradle, c1870, 21in (53.5cm) long.
£165–180 *MIL*

An east European painted pine cabinet, c1860, 35in (89cm) wide.
£350–400 *CPA*

A pine tray-top chest of drawers, with inlaid bone escutcheons, c1840, 45in (114.5cm) wide.
£500–600 *CPA*

A Romanian painted pine marriage chest, c1855, 47in (119.5cm) wide.
£300–350 *CPA*

A Romanian painted pine marriage chest, decorated with flowers, dated '1869', 59in (150cm) wide.
£300–350 *TAN*

A painted pine chest of drawers, on turned feet, 19thC, 36in (91.5cm) wide.
£500–600 *SWN*

A Victorian painted pine chest of drawers, with 2 short and 3 long drawers, 37in (94cm) wide.
£380–420 *MiA*

A Flemish pine cupboard, painted with Biblical Scenes, 17thC, 50in (129cm) wide.
£10,500–11,500 *P*

A painted pine corner cupboard, with later hinges, 18thC, 23½in (59.5cm) wide.
£825–925 *OCH*

A painted pine corner cupboard, with a panelled door, c1780, 30in (76cm) wide.
£600–650 *DaH*

A Romanian set of painted pine wall shelves, with 2 drawers, c1870, 40in (101.5cm) wide.
£300–350 *TAN*

A French champagne basket, c1880, 16in (40.5cm) wide.
£125–150 *MLL*

A wine basket, with 12 bottle capacity, c1900, 21in (53.5cm) wide.
£50–60 *WEE*

A two-tone wicker basket, c1930, 14in (35.5cm) wide.
£12–15 *UTP*

A carved wood salt box, c1880, 7in (18cm) wide.
£135–150 *MLL*

A painted pine Folk Art salt box, 19thC, 7in (18cm) wide.
£175–200 *SWN*

A Victorian copper ale jug, 16½in (42cm) high.
£325–375 *OCH*

A German biscuit mould, 19thC, 5in (12.5cm) wide.
£450–500 *AEF*

A butter mould, with 8 carved moulds in different woods, c1880, 11in (28cm) long.
£100–120 *AWT*

A copper jelly mould, shaped as a fox's mask, c1850, 6in (15cm) diam.
£125–150 *SMI*

A pottery chicken dish, c1950, 6in (15cm) high.
£20–25 *WEE*

A carved wood ginger-bread mould, c1900, 19in (48.5cm) wide.
£65–75 *MLL*

A sycamore strainer, 18thC, 8½in (21.5cm) wide.
£500–550 *AEF*

An oak cutlery tray, with shaped sides, 18thC, 17½in (44.5cm) long.
£300–330 *MTa*

An oak spoon rack, with fitted base, 18thC, 12in (30.5cm) wide.
£500–550 *ANV*

A Welsh oak spoon rack, 18thC, 16in (40.5cm) wide.
£750–850 *AEF*

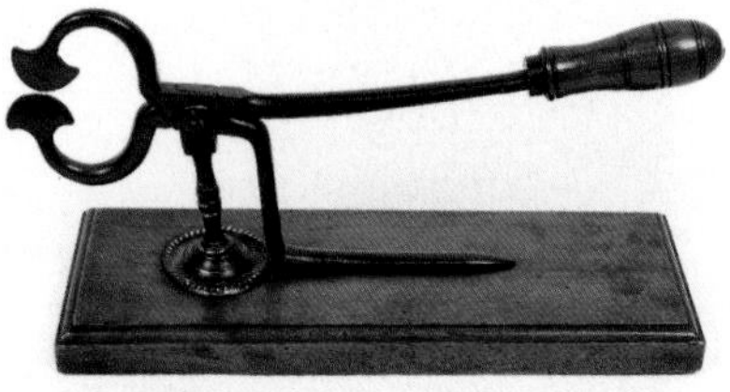

A pair of steel sugar nips, with turned wood handle, mounted on a wooden stand, 19thC, 12in (30.5cm) wide.
£150–185 *ANV*

Chairs

A pair of painted beech chairs, with rush seats, c1850.
£150–170 *SWN*

An American child's pine high chair, the shaped crest-rail over 5 turned stiles, the saddle seat on ring-turned cylindrical tapering legs joined by stretchers, early 19thC.
£180–200 *SLN*

A beech slat-back armchair, on turned legs, c1880.
£200–220 *MIL*

A late Victorian beech cane-seated chair.
£45–55 *FOX*

Pine Chairs

Many chairs popularly termed pine are, in fact, made of more durable woods such as elm or beech.

A green-painted beech chair, c1900.
£20–25 *MLL*

An Edwardian beech chair, with caned seat.
£75–85 *SAU*

A child's beech and elm chair, c1920.
£30–35 *AL*

A pair of pine folding garden chairs, c1920.
£180–200 *MSB*

Chests & Coffers

A Georgian pine mule chest, with 2 drawers and original glass handles, hinges and locks, 41in (104cm) wide.
£450–500 *CCP*

A green-painted pine coaching chest, the associated top decorated with figures and flags, inscribed 'John Miller', probably American, 18thC, 35in (89cm) wide.
£650–700 *S(S)*

Painted Pine

Originally, almost all pine furniture was painted. The techniques used for decorating were often inventive and included scumble (softening the painted finish by applying an opaque top coat of a different shade) and *faux* marbling. In recent years there has been increased demand for old pine with its original painted finish, and such pieces command a considerable premium.

l. A Federal painted pine mule chest, the hinged top opening to reveal fitted interior, over one long drawer, raised on bracket feet, American, 19thC, 31½in (80cm) wide.
£230–250 *SLN*

A late Federal painted pine blanket chest, with hinged top, raised on shaped bracket feet, with original polychrome floral decoration on yellow ground, Pennsylvania, 19thC, 67in (170cm) wide.
£220–250 *SLN*

Chests of Drawers

A pine chest of 6 drawers, on tulip bun feet, c1840, 46in (117cm) wide.
£400–450 *TPC*

A painted pine chest of drawers, with 2 short and 3 long drawers, c1860, 41in (104cm) wide.
£500–600 *AL*

A pine chest, with 7 graduated drawers, c1860, 22in (56cm) wide.
£450–500 *MIL*

A pine chest of drawers, with 3 drawers, c1870, 38in (96.5cm) wide.
£420–465 *AL*

A pine chest of drawers, with 15 drawers, c1850, 60in (152.5cm) wide.
£800–1,000 *TPC*

A Victorian pine chest of drawers, with 2 short and 2 long graduated drawers with moulded fronts, the handles inlaid with mother-of-pearl, c1860, 34in (86.5cm) wide.
£350–400 *TPC*

A pine nest of drawers, with original knobs, restored, c1860, 51in (129.5cm) wide.
£400–450 *DFA*

A pine chest of drawers, with 2 short and 2 long drawers, feet replaced, c1870, 36in (91.5cm) wide.
£420–465 *AL*

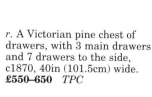

r. A Victorian pine chest of drawers, with 3 main drawers and 7 drawers to the side, c1870, 40in (101.5cm) wide.
£550–650 *TPC*

A Victorian pine chest of drawers, with 4 long drawers, c1850, 26in (66cm) wide.
£300–350 *TPC*

A Victorian pine miniature chest of drawers, with original paint, 8in (20.5cm) high.
£50–60 *CPA*

A pine chest of drawers, Yorkshire, c1870, 41in (104cm) wide.
£600–650 *AL*

A Victorian pine chest of drawers, with original boxwood handles, 36in (91.5cm) wide.
£350–400 *HRQ*

A gentleman's pine-panelled chest of drawers, with deep top hat bottom drawer incorporating plinth, c1880, 40in (101.5cm) wide.
£450–550 *TPC*

An eastern European pine chest of drawers, with 2 short and 2 long moulded front drawers, c1880, 36in (91.5cm) wide.
£400–450 *TPC*

A pine chest of drawers, with tiled splashback and 2 short and 2 long drawers, c1880, 39in (99cm) wide.
£250–300 *ByI*

A painted pine miniature chest of drawers, c1880, 20in (51cm) wide.
£120–140 *MLL*

A pine miniature chest of drawers, with 3 drawers, c1880, 18in (45.5cm) wide.
£180–200 *MIL*

A pine dressing chest, c1890, 42½in (108cm) wide.
£600–650 *AL*

A pine chest of drawers, with 10 drawers, c1900, 16in (40.5cm) wide.
£300–350 *OCP*

l. A pine Folk Art chest of drawers, with 8 drawers, painted blue, c1900, 11½in (29cm) wide.
£100–120 *MSB*

Cupboards

A painted pine corner cupboard, the 2 doors depicting an allegorical scene, early 18thC, 24in (61cm) wide.
£650–700 *Bea(E)*

A pine corner cupboard, with arched doors, c1800, 38in (96.5cm) wide.
£550–650 *WEE*

A pine cupboard, early 19thC, 16in (40.5cm) wide.
£130–150 *FOX*

A George III pine standing corner cupboard, with moulded and dentil cornice, astragal glazed door with fanlight enclosing shaped shelving, over 2 small cupboard doors and flanked by fluted pilasters, 48in (122cm) wide.
£1,100–1,200 *AH*

A pine wall cupboard, with original grain paint, early 19thC, 24in (61cm) wide.
£175–200 *CPA*

A pine corner cupboard, with shaped interior, c1830, 40in (101.6cm) wide.
£500–600 *HOA*

A painted pine standing corner cupboard, with reeded corners and 2 pairs of panelled doors, the painted interior with serpentine-fronted shelves, mid-18thC, 56in (142cm) wide.
£1,000–1,200 *S(S)*

A pine glazed corner cupboard, West Country, early 19thC, 43in (109cm) wide.
£450–500 *CPA*

A Federal grain-painted pine open corner cupboard, the upper section with 4 shelves, surrounded by shaped carving, the lower section with one long drawer, the 2 panelled cupboard doors over a shaped apron, on block feet, American, early 19thC, 44in (112cm) wide.
£550–600 *SLN*

A pine two-door cupboard, with fielded panelling, 18thC, 48in (122cm) wide.
£500–600 *TPC*

A pine linen cupboard, early 19thC, 48in (122cm) wide.
£900–1,100 *TPC*

A Federal painted pine cabinet, the glazed and mullioned cupboard door enclosing shelves, over 2 short drawers and 2 panelled cupboard doors, all flanked by reeded columns, on shaped bracket feet, American, early 19thC, 36½in (92.5cm) wide.
£1,000–1,200 *SLN*

A Scottish pine estate cupboard, with fitted interior, c1830, 60in (152.5cm) wide.
£1,100–1,250 *HOA*

A pine cupboard, with panelled doors, c1840, 52in (132cm) wide.
£1,200–1,500 *TPC*

A pine housekeeper's cupboard, with panelled doors, c1840, 80in (203cm) wide.
£1,700–2,000 *TPC*

A Scottish pine cupboard, with fitted interior, c1840, 50in (127cm) wide.
£675–750 *HOA*

A pine housekeeper's cupboard, with 2 doors above 6 short drawers, on turned feet, c1850, 60in (152.5cm) wide.
£1,000–1,200 *POT*

A late Federal painted pine corner cupboard, the upper section with glazed and mullioned cupboard door enclosing shelves, flanked by reeded carving, the lower section with 2 short drawers over 2 cupboard doors, raised on bracket feet, American, mid-19thC, 42½in (108cm) wide.
£1,700–2,000 *SLN*

A pine corner cupboard, with panelled door, c1860, 26in (66cm) wide.
£380–420 *MIL*

A European pine cupboard, with painted decoration, original handles and escutcheons, c1875, 43½in (110.5cm) wide.
£450–500 *FOX*

A pine pot cupboard, c1880, 15½in (39.5cm) wide.
£200–220 *AL*

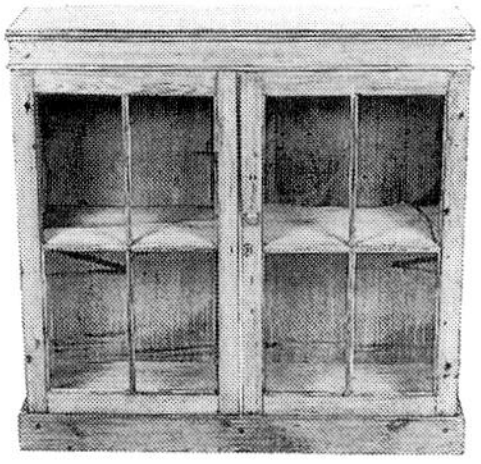

A pine glazed cupboard, with brass trim, c1880, 41in (104cm) wide.
£300–350 *AL*

A pine pot cupboard, c1880, 14in (35.5cm) wide.
£100–120 *HRQ*

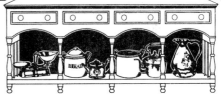

A pine linen press, with shelved interior, c1880, 46in (117cm) wide.
£800–950 *WEE*

A pine folding bed/ cupboard, c1880, 42in (106.5cm) wide.
£300–350 *WEE*

A Danish pine two-door cupboard, with serpentine top, c1880, 33in (84cm) wide.
£300–350 *BOR*

A pine two-door cupboard, c1880, 36in (91.5cm) wide.
£280–320 *AL*

A Continental pine pot cupboard, with one drawer and one cupboard, c1890, 15in (38cm) long.
£90–100 *MIL*

A pair of bedside cupboards, 19thC, 19in (48.5cm) wide.
£360–400 *CCP*

A pine two-door cupboard, c1890, 36½in (92.5cm) wide.
£160–180 *AL*

An Edwardian turned-maple and pine armoire, the *faux* bamboo turned bordered case with peaked cornice, flanked by turned finials, above a banded frieze over a mirrored door and a drawer, on turned feet, c1900, 40in (101.5cm) wide.
£1,000–1,250 *S(NY)*

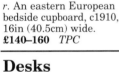

r. An eastern European bedside cupboard, c1910, 16in (40.5cm) wide.
£140–160 *TPC*

A pine pot cupboard, c1900, 17in (43cm) wide.
£90–110 *CPS*

Desks

A pine clerk's desk, the fitted interior with pigeonhole and drawer, on tapered legs, c1780, 32in (81.5cm) wide.
£500–600 *TPC*

A pine kneehole desk, with right hand cupboard, north Wales, c1850, 47in (119.5cm) wide.
£650–700 *CCP*

A pine kneehole desk, with 9 drawers on bun feet, c1880, 42in (106.5cm) wide.
£700–800 *TPC*

Cross Reference
Colour Review

l. A pine kneehole desk, the 9 drawers with brass handles, c1890, 48in (122cm) wide.
£700–800 *MIL*

Dressers

A George III pine dresser, the base with 3 frieze drawers over a shaped apron and fan spandrels, the square section legs with a low open shelf, original brass handles, 59in (150cm) wide.
£2,300–2,800 *LAY*

A pine dresser, with original paint and locks, south Wales, c1810, 58in (147.5cm) wide.
£2,000–2,300 *SWN*

A pine Welsh dresser, with 3 drawers above 3 cupboards, original hooks, c1830, 80in (203cm) wide.
£1,200–1,500 *DMA*

A pine dresser, with open delft rack over 2 drawers and 2 doors with dog kennel base, Hampshire, c1840, 78in (198cm) wide.
£1,600–1,800 *TPC*

A Victorian pine dresser, handles missing, 75in (190.5cm) wide.
£1,000–1,200 *DOR*

A Victorian pine dresser, with glazed doors, 42in (106.5cm) wide.
£650–750 *REF*

A pine dresser, with glazed doors, c1880, 60in (152.5cm) wide.
£350–400 *COP*

A pine dresser, the glazed top with shaped shelf interior, the doors flanked by turned columns, c1870, 50in (127cm) wide.
£900–1,200 *TPC*

A painted pine dresser, c1880, 42in (106.5cm) wide.
£850–950 *MLL*

A pine dresser, with arched glazed doors flanked by split columns, c1880, 48in (122cm) wide.
£800–1,000 *TPC*

A pine dresser, with glazed doors and 4 spice drawers, c1900, 40in (101.5cm) wide.
£800–900 *TPC*

Dresser Bases

A pine potboard dresser base, c1860, 84in (213.5cm) wide.
£800–900 *TPC*

The Evolution of Pine

From the late 18thC onwards, pine was either used for the backs, carcasses and drawer linings of pieces veneered with more expensive timbers, or for cheaper furniture which was then painted.

Much pine kitchen furniture was originally built into a room, and as the fashion for stripped pine grew in the 1960s numerous pieces have been removed from their original locations and converted into freestanding pieces.

Today it is rare to find a piece of pine furniture in its original condition. Most furniture has been adapted, stripped or converted to suit modern tastes. However, these pieces are often just as desirable.

A Continental pine dresser base, with 2 drawers above 2 doors, mid-19thC, 32in (81.5cm) wide.
£350–400 *CCP*

A pine dresser base, with original green paint, early 19thC, 60in (152.5cm) wide.
£650–800 *CPA*

A pine dresser base, with 2 drawers and 2 doors, c1880, 42in (106.5cm) wide.
£350–375 *WEE*

A pine potboard dresser base, c1880, 74in (188cm) wide.
£550–650 *AL*

l. A pine dresser base, with 2 drawers and 2 doors, c1880, 31in (78.5cm) wide.
£200–275 *CPS*

Racks & Shelves

A Victorian set of pine open shelves, with tray top and solid plinth base, 54in (137cm) wide.
£300–350 *TPC*

A pine wall rack, c1880, 87½in (222.5cm) wide.
£600–700 *AL*

A set of pine shelves, c1880, 20in (51cm) wide.
£70–85 *AL*

A set of pine shelves, with boarded back, c1890, 50in (127cm) wide.
£230–260 *AL*

A set of pine shelves, c1890, 23½in (59.5cm) wide.
£75–85 *AL*

A set of pine shelves, c1890, 19in (48.5cm) wide.
£65–75 *AL*

A pine plate rack, c1880, 22in (56cm) wide.
£90–100 *AL*

l. A pine book shelf, back replaced, c1880, 78½in (199.5cm) wide.
£420–460 *AL*

A pine plate rack, c1890, 66in (167.5cm) wide.
£155–175 *AL*

A set of pine hanging shelves, c1900, 26in (66cm) wide.
£70–80 *MLL*

A pine liberty shelf, c1917, 20½in (52cm) wide.
£120–140 *AL*

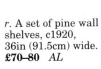

r. A set of pine wall shelves, c1920, 36in (91.5cm) wide.
£70–80 *AL*

Settles

A Georgian pine settle, with original finish, c1810, 48in (122cm) wide.
£1,000–1,200 *CPA*

A pine settle, with panelled back, c1840, 52in (132cm) wide.
£450–500 *MIL*

A Welsh pine box settle, c1840, 56in (142cm) wide.
£900–1,000 *SWN*

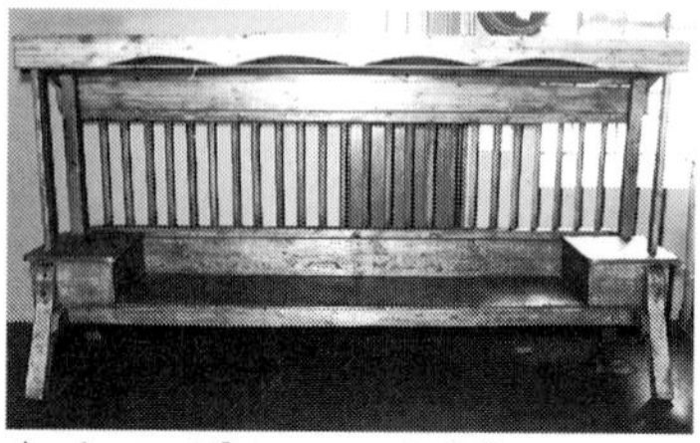

A pine settle, converted from a feeding trough, c1940, 135in (343cm) wide.
£350–450 *TAN*

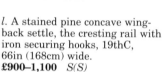

l. A stained pine concave wing-back settle, the cresting rail with iron securing hooks, 19thC, 66in (168cm) wide.
£900–1,100 *S(S)*

A high-back settle, with 2 drawers in base, 19thC, 60in (152.5cm) wide.
£500–600 *TPC*

Side Cabinets & Sideboards

An Italian painted and decorated pine commode, the pastel blue and eau-de-nil ground painted with chinoiserie design, with a single long drawer and cupboard below enclosed by a pair of doors, raised on short square tapered legs, 18thC, 30in (76cm) wide.
£1,200–1,400 *P(E)*

A pine sideboard, c1820, 34in (86.5cm) wide.
£450–500 *AL*

A pine tray top sideboard, c1840, 50in (127cm) wide.
£500–600 *TPC*

l. A carved pine sideboard, with 7 drawers and 2 cupboards, original glass handles, mid-19thC, 61in (155cm) wide.
£1,100–1,250 *CCP*

A mid-Victorian pine sideboard, North Country, c1860, 65in (165cm) wide.
£800–950 *CPA*

A pine sideboard, c1870, 54in (137cm) wide.
£850–950 *AL*

A pine sideboard, with 3 drawers and one cupboard, c1890, 48in (122cm) wide.
£560–620 *MIL*

An Edwardian Regency style pine sideboard, c1910, 41in (104cm) wide.
£250–300 *CPA*

FURTHER READING
Miller's Pine & Country Furniture Buyer's Guide, Miller's Publications, 1995

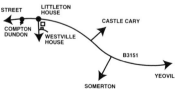

Steps

A set of pine steps, c1890, 61in (155cm) high.
£50–60 *AL*

A set of pine steps, c1880, 32in (81.5cm) high.
£120–150 *FAG*

l. A set of pine folding pine steps, c1920, 30in (76cm) high.
£35–40 *TaB*

A set of pine steps, with metal supports, c1920, 39in (99cm) high.
£35–40 *AL*

l. A set of pine steps, c1930, 44in (112cm) high.
£40–45 *AL*

Stools

A pine stool, c1860, 12in (30.5cm) wide.
£30–40 *OPH*

A pine stool, mid-19thC, 26in (66cm) wide.
£40–45 *CCP*

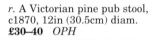

A painted pine stool, c1860, 11in (28cm) wide.
£25–35 *CPA*

An elm stool, c1870, 15½in (39.5cm) wide.
£40–50 *AL*

l. A pine beach stool, with striped fabric seat, early 20thC, 11in (28cm) high.
£40–45 *RIV*

r. A Victorian pine pub stool, c1870, 12in (30.5cm) diam.
£30–40 *OPH*

Tables

An American pine side table, the 2 long drawers over a shaped apron, on cylindrical tapering legs ending in pad feet, early 18thC, 40½in (103cm) wide.
£550–600 *SLN*

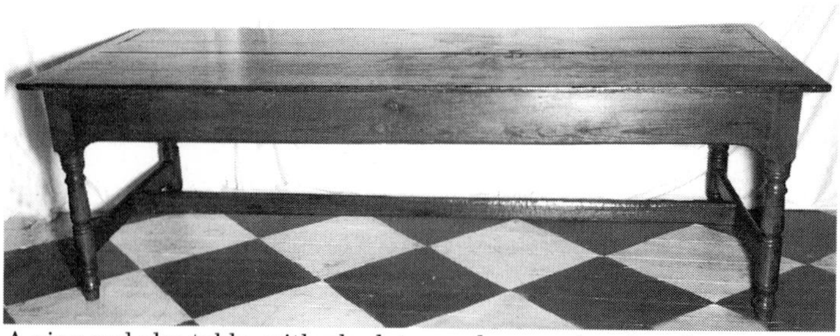

A pine and elm table, with plank top, a drawer at each end, c1800, 98in (249cm) long.
£1,500–1,700 *WEE*

An American pine tavern table, with a single frieze drawer, raised on ring and baluster-turned legs joined by a pair of plain stretchers and ending in elongated bun feet, late 18thC, 36in (91.5cm) wide.
£550–600 *S(Cg)*

A Georgian pine kitchen table, with cleated top above large end drawer, 78in (198cm) wide.
£650–800 *CCP*

r. A pine centre table, with original paint, c1830, 29in (73.5cm) high.
£400–450 *RYA*

A Welsh pine table, with original green paint, early 19thC, 48in (122cm) wide.
£400–480 *CPA*

A pine table, with pegged top and 2 side drawers, c1830, 60in (152.5cm) wide.
£450–550 *POT*

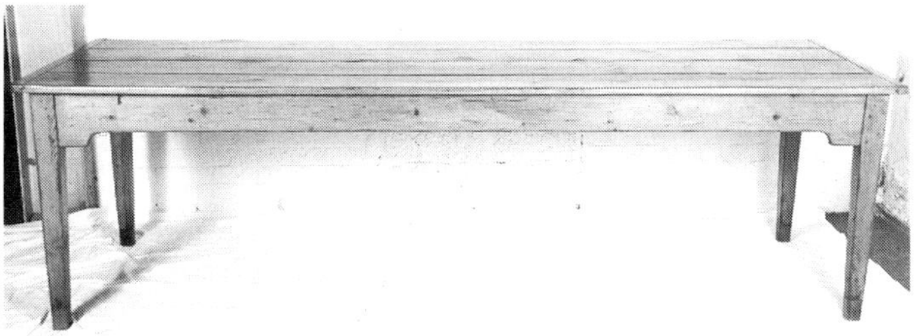

A pine farmhouse table, c1840, 96in (244cm) long.
£650–750 *HOA*

A Welsh pine X-frame tavern table, c1840, 32in (81.5cm) wide.
£270–300 *MIL*

A pine cricket table, with turned legs, c1850, 24in (61cm) diam.
£240–270 *AL*

A pine cricket table, with under-tier, c1850, 28in (71cm) long.
£420–470 *AL*

A pine cricket table, with turned legs, c1860, 29½in (75cm) diam.
£400–450 *AL*

l. A pine table, with bobbin-turned legs, c1870, 20in (51cm) diam.
£230–260 *AL*

A pine table, with plank top, c1870, 43in (109cm) long.
£180–200 *AL*

A Victorian pine kitchen table, on turned legs, c1880, 54in (137cm) wide.
£275–325 *POT*

A pine cricket table, with turned legs, c1870, 32in (81.5cm) diam.
£450–500 *AL*

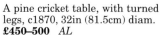

A Victorian pine drop-leaf table, on turned legs, c1880, 45½in (115cm) long.
£300–350 *POT*

A Victorian pitch pine table, with 2 drawers, 29in (73.5cm) wide.
£175–200 *CCP*

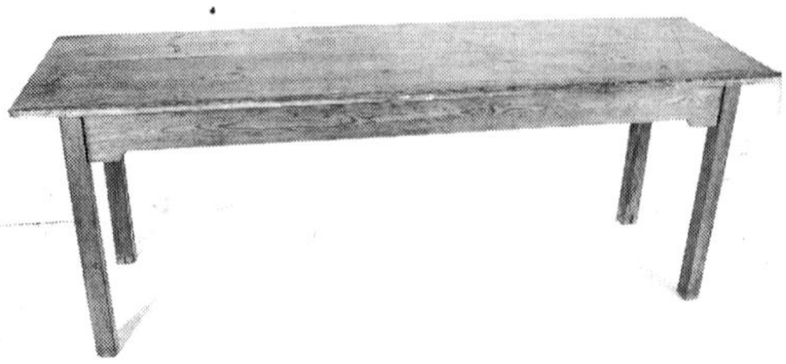

An eastern European pine cloth-cutting table, c1880, 79½in (201cm) long.
£350–400 *NWE*

A pine extending table, with 2 extra leaves, c1880, 93in (236cm) extended.
£450–550 *WEE*

A pine table, with one end drawer, on turned legs, c1880, 42½in (108cm) wide.
£360–400 *AL*

A pine table, with one drawer, legs cut down, c1880, 38in (96.5cm) long.
£100–125 *WEE*

A painted pine table, with drawer, c1880, 28½in (72.5cm) high.
£300–325 *OCH*

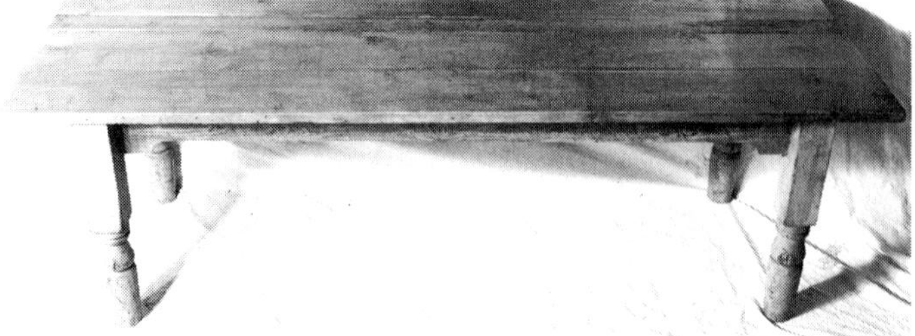

A Victorian pine coffee table, cut down from a dining table, 27in (68.5cm) long.
£250–300 *CCP*

A pine serpentine card table, c1885, 47in (119.5cm) wide.
£400–450 *BEL*

l. A pine table, with one drawer and turned legs, c1890, 42in (106.5cm) wide.
£165–185 *AL*

r. A Victorian pine writing table, with 2 drawers, 42in (106.5cm) wide.
£225–275 *AHO*

A pine drop-leaf table, with one drawer, c1890, 39in (99cm) long.
£230–260 *AL*

A pine table, with opening top, c1890, 33in (84cm) wide.
£80–120 *CPS*

A pine table, with fold-over top, on turned legs, c1890, 48in (122cm) wide.
£200–250 *OCP*

A pine extending table, with one extra leaf and winding mechanism, c1890, 53½in (136cm) long extended.
£450–500 *WaH*

A pine coffee table, one small and one large drawer, made-up from a 19thC table, 69in (175.5cm) long.
£300–350 *CCP*

r. A pine work table, with single drawer, c1880, 35in (90cm) wide.
£150–170 *AL*

A pine table,with a drawer to each end, on turned legs, 19thC, 96in (244cm) wide.
£800–1,000 *TPC*

A pine drop-leaf table, on turned legs, c1900, 48in (122cm) diam.
£130–150 *SA*

A pine dressing table, early 20thC, with one small frieze drawer, 29in (73.5cm) wide.
£300–350 *CCP*

l. A pine side table, c1910, 36in (91.5cm) wide.
£80–100 *SA*

Wall Brackets

A pair of pine wall brackets, painted in cream, mid-19thC, 30½in (77.5cm) high.
£230–260 *MSB*

l. An early George III carved pine wall bracket, in the form of an eagle standing on an asymmetrical C-scroll bordered plinth, repaired, 17½in (44.5cm) high.
£2,300–2,500 *DN*

A pair of pine wall brackets, late 19thC, 38½in (98cm) high.
£800–900 *MSB*

Wardrobes

A pine wardrobe, with a single door and bottom drawer, c1840, 40in (101.5cm) wide.
£350–400 *CPS*

A Dutch pine wardrobe, with 3 doors and 5 drawers, mid-19thC, 79in (200.5cm) wide.
£950–1,200 *GD*

A Dutch pine wardrobe, with 2 doors and a drawer, mid-19thC, 62in (157.5cm) wide.
£850–950 *GD*

Miller's is a price GUIDE not a price LIST

A Romanian pine armoire, c1870, 49½in (125.5cm) wide.
£600–650 *PEN*

A pine wardrobe, with a pair of arched panelled doors, c1880, 52in (132cm) wide.
£700–800 *TPC*

A Continental pine wardrobe, with one door and 2 drawers, split turnings to sides, c1880, 39in (99cm) wide.
£550–580 *MIL*

An eastern European pine wardrobe, with ornate moulding, one door and single drawer, c1880, 43½in (110cm) wide.
£350–400 *NWE*

A Victorian wardrobe, with Gothic arched doors, c1880, 80in (203cm) wide.
£550–600 *HOA*

A Dutch pine wardrobe, with a mirror and 2 drawers, c1880, 59in (150cm) wide.
£600–700 *AHO*

r. An eastern European two-piece pine wardrobe, the carved panelled doors with frosted glass panels above 2 drawers, 1880s, 42½in (108cm) high.
£300–350 *NWE*

A pine wardrobe, the 2 doors with glazed panels, over a single drawer, c1900, 42in (106.5cm) wide.
£350–450 *CPS*

A pine wardrobe, with 2 doors above a single drawer, c1900, 40in (101.5cm) wide.
£400–475 *CPS*

Cross Reference
Colour Review

A pine wardrobe, with arched pediment, 2 panelled doors and 2 dummy drawers, c1880, 55in (139.5cm) wide.
£500–600 *NWE*

An Edwardian pine wardrobe, with 2 doors, 2 short and 4 long drawers, 71in (180.5cm) wide.
£1,400–1,800 *AHO*

Miscellaneous

A pine revolving bookcase, c1890, 13in (33cm) square.
£170–190 *MIL*

A sycamore butcher's block, on pine base, 19thC, 41in (104cm) wide.
£800–880 *CCP*

An eastern European hand cart, c1900, 48in (122cm) wide.
£150–180 *TPC*

A painted pine chicken coop, inscribed 'Buddy Bolman's Bantams', c1920, 22in (56cm) wide.
£480–520 *MSB*

A pine commode chest, c1810, 28in (71cm) wide.
£400–500 *TPC*

An eastern European escritoire, with shaped shelf interior, c1890, 42in (106.5cm) wide.
£700–800 *TPC*

A set of painted pine letter boxes, c1890, 35in (89cm) wide.
£150–170 *MLL*

A pine overmantel mirror, with bevelled glass and plaster shell mouldings above fluted columns, c1860, 60½in (153.5cm) wide.
£400–500 *POT*

A pine swing dressing table mirror, c1880, 26in (66cm) wide.
£150–165 *AL*

A folding luggage rack, c1920, 23in (58.5cm) wide.
£40–45 *AL*

A Federal style pine overmantel mirror, surmounted by a carved gilded eagle, the tripartite mirror plate surrounded by a frame with gilt moulding, mid-19thC, 54in (137.2cm) wide.
£300–350 *SLN*

A pine swing seat, with metal fittings, c1890, 20in (51cm) wide.
£50–60 *AL*

A European pine sledge, c1900, 46in (117cm) long.
£25–30 *WEE*

A French pine trug, c1920, 16in (40.5cm) long.
£18–20 *AL*

l. A grain painted pine candle stand, with sycamore base, c1810, 29in (73.5cm) high.
£350–400 *CCP*

A Victorian pine prie dieu, with lift-up lid and shoe box in base, c1870, 26in (66cm) wide.
£200–220 *CCP*

BAMBOO, CANE & WICKER

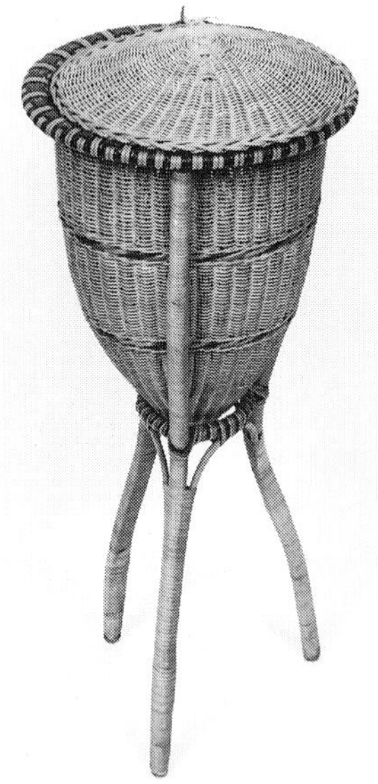

A wicker basket and stand, c1920, 29in (73.5cm) high.
£75–85 *MLL*

A Victorian child's bamboo chair.
£50–60 *WaH*

A child's wicker armchair, c1920.
£120–140 *MLL*

A pair of late George III bamboo armchairs, the backs, arms and seat rails with intricate trellis decoration, with caned seats, on circular legs with pierced angle brackets and H-shaped stretchers, painted throughout with bamboo decoration, early 19thC.
£5,200–5,800 *S*

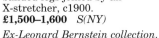

A pair of brown-painted wicker armchairs, the curved backs leading to rolled arms above caned seats, on circular banded legs joined by an X-stretcher, c1900.
£1,500–1,600 *S(NY)*

Ex-Leonard Bernstein collection.

A Lloyd Loom miniature chair, painted green, 1930s, 9½in (24cm) high.
£60–65 *SWN*

A wicker chair, c1880.
£40–45 *DaH*

A pair of American tramp's chairs, 19thC.
£330–370 *MLL*

These chairs are made from strippings of tree bark turned inside out.

An American brown-painted wicker side chair, in the manner of Heywood Wakefield, the spoon back with beaded and braided splat above a circular caned seat with beaded basketweave apron, on banded splayed legs ending in brass ferrules, early 20thC.
£500–550 *S(NY)*

Ex-Leonard Bernstein collection.

An American wicker love seat, in the manner of Heywood Wakefield, with arched tendril and braided back flanked by outscrolled arms, the seat with serpentine apron, the splayed legs joined by an X-form stretcher ending in brass ferrules, slight damage, early 20thC, 44in (112cm) long.
£600–650 *S(NY)*

Ex-Leonard Bernstein collection.

A Lloyd Loom child's chair, painted white, 1930s.
£18–20 *WCa*

An octagonal bamboo table, top replaced, c1880, 26in (66cm) high.
£40–45 *AL*

r. A double-seated wicker pram, c1900, 42in (106.5cm) long.
£160–180 *MLL*

A wicker rocking armchair, 19thC.
£280–320 *DaH*

A wicker and cane stool, c1920.
£25–30 *MLL*

A bamboo table, c1880, 18½in (47cm) square.
£40–45 *AL*

A cane chair, with curved back, c1930.
£45–50 *AL*

A bamboo and lacquer étagère, c1880, 17in (43cm) high.
£360–400 *MLL*

Two brown-painted wicker side tables, each with a circular top over a curved apron with braided edge and scrolled tendril spandrels, on curved wrapped legs joined by multiple stretchers supporting a spindle, on ball feet, early 20thC.
£2,000–2,200 *S(NY)*

Ex-Leonard Bernstein collection.

KITCHENWARE

A Victorian wire egg basket, 14in (35.5cm) high.
£35–40 *SMI*

Eggs were stored in wire baskets and hung from the ceiling of the larder to keep them away from rats and mice.

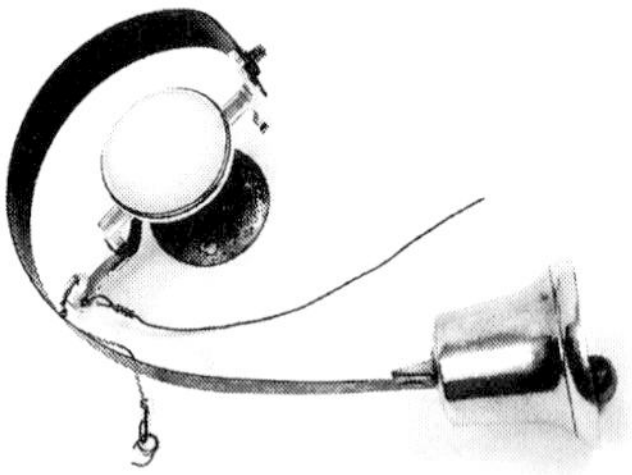

A Victorian brass servants' bell, 10in (25.5cm) wide.
£65–70 *SMI*

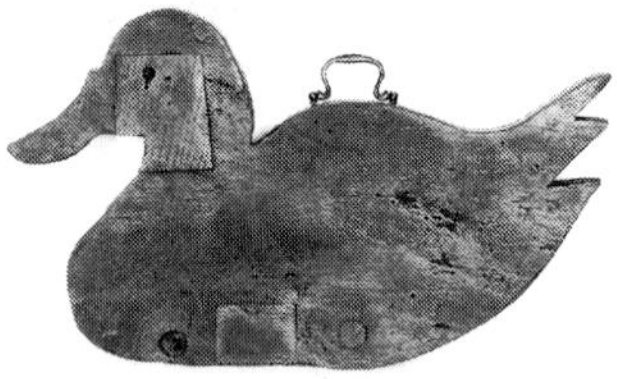

A wooden chopping board, in the form of a duck, c1900, 18in (45.5cm) wide.
£40–45 *MLL*

A painted metal bread box, the domed lid and front panel decorated with sprays of summer flowers within a gilt heightened border, with a drawer to the base, late 19thC, 12in (30.5cm) wide.
£400–450 *P*

A wooden strawberry basket, 19thC, 24in (61cm) long.
£35–40 *RIV*

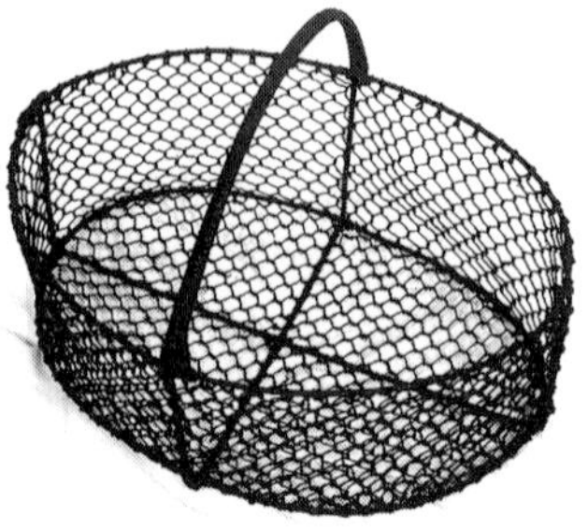

A French wire basket, c1920, 16in (40.5cm) wide.
£20–25 *AL*

A sycamore bowl, c1800, 15in (38cm) diam.
£70–85 *OCH*

An oak cutlery box, 19thC, 15in (38cm) long.
£80–100 *SWN*

An iron candlestick, 18thC, 10in (25.5cm) high.
£175–200 *OCH*

A laundry basket on wheels, c1900, 35in (89cm) long.
£40–45 *AL*

A wooden chopping block, c1860, 18in (45.5cm) high.
£180–200 *MLL*

An oak salt box, with drawer, inscribed 'J. Gaunt', c1800, 16½in (42cm) high.
£350–400 *OCH*

A set of enamel spice canisters, on a fruitwood rack, c1900, 11½in (29cm) wide.
£90–110 *SMI*

A brass and steel-banded cream can, late 19thC, 12in (30.5cm) high.
£160–180 *SMI*

A set of Cornish ware canisters, 1950s, 5½in (14cm) high.
£35–40 each *SMI*

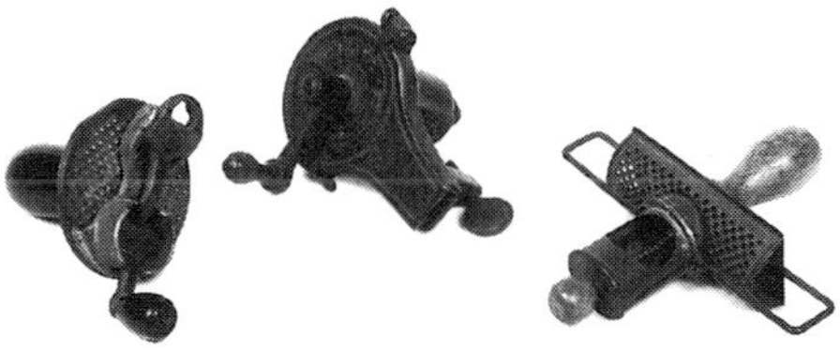

Three nutmeg graters, 1870–1920, largest 5in (12.5cm) long.
£50–60 each *SMI*

A lignum vitae coffee mill, the 3 screw-in sections and cover with iron mechanism, separate handle, 18thC, 9in (23cm) high.
£1,500–1,800 *RBB*

This piece attracted considerable interest because of its craftsmanship and rarity.

A Victorian butter churn, c1890, 20in (51cm) wide.
£80–100 *TPC*

Graters

Punched iron graters have been used in cooking for centuries, mainly for grating hard cheese or breadcrumbs from stale bread. Sheet brass graters were introduced into Britain in the 16thC with the immigration of Dutch brass workers. Early 19thC tinplate graters comprised sheets of punched metal with rolled edges around an iron or wire frame, and later the joins were machine-pressed or seamed.

Three tinplate nutmeg graters, 1900–50, largest 6½in (16.5cm) high.
£7–12 each *AL*

A cast metal marmalade cutter, by Follows & Bate, c1900, 17½in (44cm) long.
£20–25 *BBR*

A stoneware slip-decorated jar, c1880, 9in (23cm) high.
£100–120 *AWT*

r. An urn-shaped anchovy paste jar, with black and white transfer of St Paul's Cathedral, small chips to base, probably Pratt factory, c1870, 4¼in (11cm) high.
£300–350 *BBR*

A Heinz mustard jar, with cream-coloured body and blue band, transfer-printed front and rear, c1900, 4¾in (12cm) high.
£35–40 *BBR*

An Indian chutney jar, with black and white transfer print, c1890, 4¼in (11cm) high.
£130–150 *BBR*

A glass biscuit jar, inscribed 'Meredith & Drew Ltd, Biscuits', 1920s, 11in (28cm) high.
£65–70 *SMI*

A sycamore ladle, early 19thC, 14½in (37cm) long.
£80–90 *MTa*

A Cornish ware lemon squeezer, 1930s, 5in (12.5cm) wide.
£130–140 *SMI*

A sycamore butter mould, late 19thC, 8in (20.5cm) long.
£40–45 *FOX*

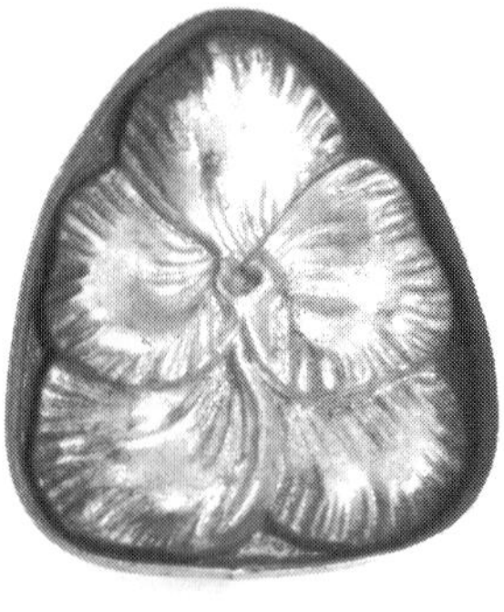

A tin ice cream mould, with pansy pattern, c1920, 6½in (16.5cm) high.
£60–70 *AWT*

A Cornish ware storage jar, 1950s, 6in (15cm) high.
£25–30 *WEE*

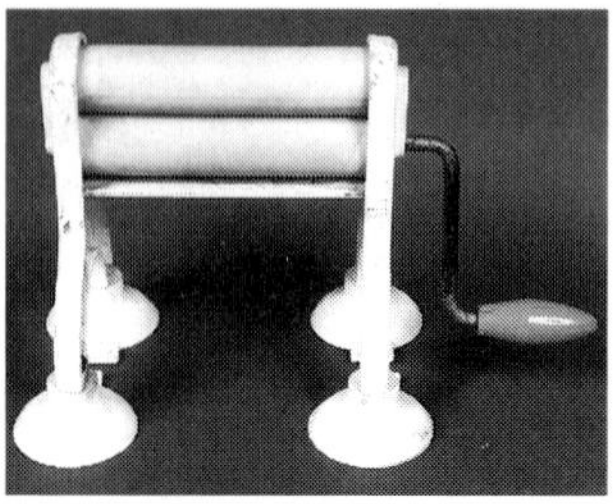

A collar mangle, 1920, 12in (30.5cm) wide.
£12–15 *UTP*

A corn measure, c1860, 13in (33cm) high.
£75–85 *MIL*

Two Hovis baking tins, 1920, 5½in (14cm) wide.
£8–10 *UTP*

A Cornish ware jug, 1950s, 3½in (9cm) high.
£10–12 *WEE*

A copper kettle, 19thC, 13in (33cm) wide.
£130–150 *OCH*

A cream measure, by J. W. Watson, Hanwell, with brass fittings and handle, late 19thC, 6in (15cm) high.
£120–135 *OCH*

A tin candy mould, reading 'Sweet Shop', early 20thC, 12½in (32cm) long.
£140–160 *MSB*

l. A wooden hexagonal butter print, with leaf pattern, c1920, 3in (7.5cm) diam.
£20–25 *AWT*

A ceramic milk pail, c1880, 13in (33cm) diam.
£200–250 *SMI*

A Raisley shortbread plate, 1920s, 9in (23cm) wide.
£50–60 *SMI*

An oak cheese press, c1860, 10in (25.5cm) diam.
£60–70 *MIL*

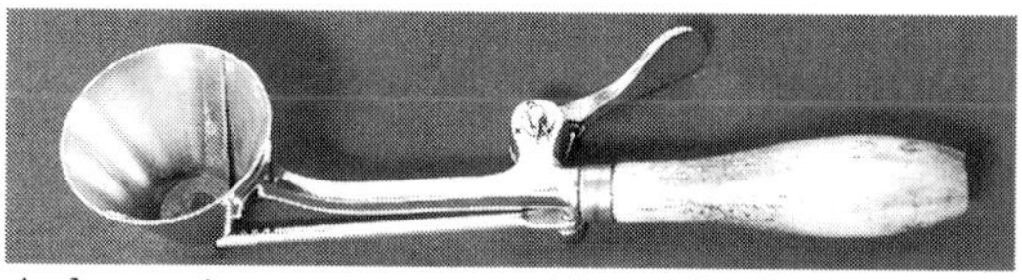
A chrome ice cream scoop, with wooden handle, c1910, 10in (25.5cm) long.
£110–120 *EKK*

Tins

By the late 19thC, biscuits and cakes were produced in increasing numbers by commercial bakers. Popular luxuries, they were often sold in attractive tins, which were re-used afterwards for storage of other items.

By 1900, it was possible to buy tins specifically for storing cakes and biscuits, often in sets comprising different-sized containers for various kinds of homemade and bought cakes. Favourite cakes included Battenburg, ginger cake, fruit cake and the favourite 19th-century delicacy, the Victoria sponge cake.

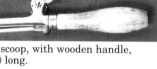

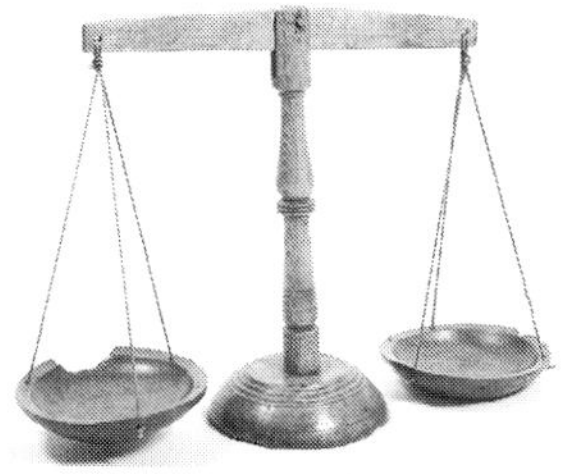
l. A set of sycamore butter scales, c1800, 18in (45.5cm) high.
£250–280 *OCH*

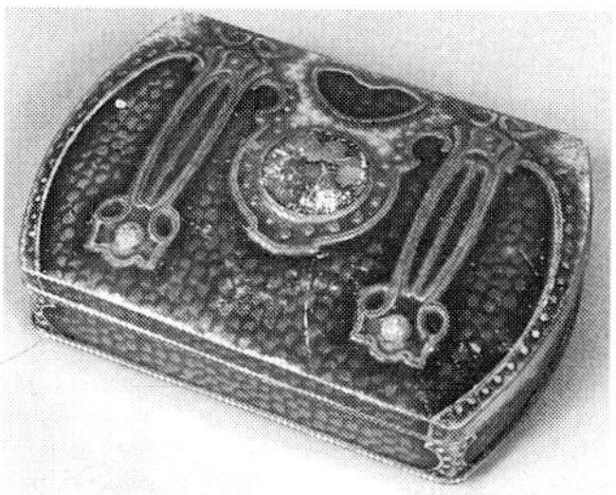
An Art Nouveau Cadbury's chocolate tin, c1900, 7in (18cm) wide.
£10–12 *UTP*

A brass pastry marker, 18thC, 7in (18cm) long.
£130–150 *SMI*

A Welsh spoon rack, with original paint, c1800, 13in (33cm) wide.
£170–200 *CPA*

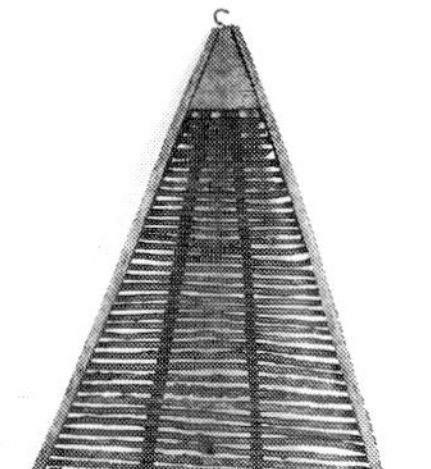
A French prune drying rack, c1920, 36in (91.5cm) long.
£40–45 *AL*

A tin, decorated with the Houses of Parliament, Westminster, c1910, 8in (20.5cm) wide.
£10–12 *AL*

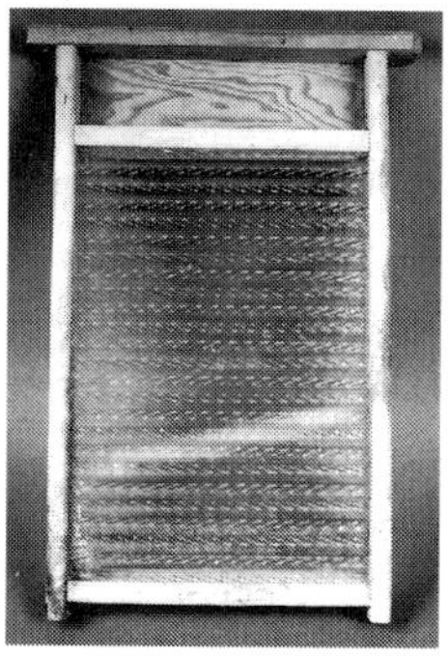
A wood and glass washboard, c1920, 17in (43cm) high.
£8–10 *UTP*

An oak oval butter tub, with iron bands, c1860, 19in (48.5cm) diam.
£120–130 *MIL*

POTTERY & PORCELAIN

As a result of new technology, the world of antiques has become one big, open marketplace. The value of Victorian majolica has risen steadily for years due to keen American buyers. Specialist dealers used to trawl the salerooms of Britain to supply American collectors, and earned well-deserved profit along the way. Today, however, auctioneers in the UK check their estimates against the catalogue of the recent sale of majolica held at Sotheby's in New York (discussed on page 270). As a result of this well-publicised sale, we all know the latest North American price for every lot, and consequently the numerous George Jones game tureens offered in sales around Britain have achieved remarkably similar prices. The American buyers get to hear about the lots on offer ahead of their London dealers, and competition can be far more direct. New York and London prices are now identical.

The Wedgwood market has been dominated by American collectors for half a century, and so when one Californian collection was auctioned recently, Sotheby's decision to offer it in London rather than New York seemed, on the face of it, quite extraordinary, especially as VAT was payable under EU regulations. The Rinaldo collection contained plenty of 19th and 20th century pieces that now attract British buyers, while at the same time the favourable pound/dollar exchange rate meant that even if English Wedgwood collectors had bid slightly less, the American consignor would still be better off. New York dealers attended the sale, but they had to compete directly with English and American private collectors and pay prices little removed from retail levels.

Observant users of *Miller's Antiques Price Guide* can spot differences in price levels between similar items photographed in auction catalogues and in dealers' stock. Nobody should begrudge dealers their profit, and naturally the auctioneer's vendor receives less after paying a commission. What seems to be happening is a narrowing of the margin between auction and shop prices, certainly as far as traditional English pottery and porcelain is concerned. Computerised auction search facilities notify collectors as well as dealers of all lots that interest them, and for standard items there is remarkably little fluctuation in the value anywhere.

As more and more people make use of price guides it is harder and harder to find a 'sleeper' or under-priced lot in any sale or antiques fair. Dealers are expressing genuine concern over stock replacement as they are paying almost the same price for new items as they made from selling similar pieces. To stay in business they have to buy, but must sell for more. I visit antiques fairs and see 19th century Meissen figures, Staffordshire flatbacks and animal groups, or Royal Worcester vases, priced at levels I am hoping to achieve for similar pieces in my next auction. The result is that something a little bit different or just a little bit special sells with ease, while a standard object can sit forlorn on a dealer's shelf or remains unsold in the auction at a reserve that seemed perfectly realistic.

Recently, keen collectors have been chasing the products of unusual English porcelain factories – the many Liverpool makers or rarities from Vauxhall, Bristol and even newly discovered Isleworth. The feeling is that such pieces are going to become increasingly difficult to find and will be even more costly next year. At a recent Phillips sale I saw obscure blue and white saucers attract fierce competition while standard Worcester, Derby and Bow was often ignored. Delft rarities are dearer than ever, while ordinary delft plates have become more modestly priced than I ever imagined. Even in such actively traded areas as majolica, the trend is much the same. Top buyers all want the three big names – Minton, Wedgwood and George Jones. When this specialist market first boomed, all kinds of majolica shot up in price, but today realistic values have returned to unattributed plates and dishes, and novelties by lesser makers; indeed, some could almost be called bargains.

The best of everything is in increasingly short supply. Enthusiastic collectors definitely have money to spend, but unless some give up their struggle to acquire the impossible and switch instead to the available, the implications are quite worrying. Thankfully, though, we are now seeing new collectors with an eye for a bargain: old Staffordshire figures, English porcelain teawares, pretty German figurines, delft dishes and blue-printed plates for display – the list could go on and on.

I believe good old-fashioned antiques offer far better potential than 20th century collectables. Take, for instance, the popular figurines from Doulton, Beswick or Hummel. Few of these ever fall in price for their value is maintained by the semi-artificial nature of the collectables market. Alongside these relatively easy fields, however, I do sense that beginners are starting to trickle back to the difficult but rewarding world of traditional collecting. I welcome them, as indeed will every dealer in 18th and 19th century ceramics, for our future needs fresh blood.

John Sandon

Animals

A Staffordshire model of a dog, c1740, 6½in (16.5cm) high.
£1,200–1,350 *JHo*

A Staffordshire model of a show horse, with docked tail, sponged in dark grey and wearing a blue and yellow saddlecloth, standing on a green washed waisted base, c1800, 6¼in (15.5cm) high.
£1,700–1,900 *CGC*

A Staffordshire model of a greyhound, on a brown and green rocky base, early 19thC, 6¼in (15.5cm) wide.
£600–700 *JHo*

A pottery model of a blue and white cow, on a green base, possibly Portobello, early 19thC, 4in (10cm) long.
£350–400 *JHo*

A Yorkshire model of a cow and her calf, decorated with black and orange, early 19thC, 7in (18cm) wide.
£600–700 *JHo*

A Staffordshire model of a lion, standing with front leg resting on a yellow ball, raised on a moulded and enamel-painted oval base, c1800, 7in (18cm) wide.
£850–950 *CGC*

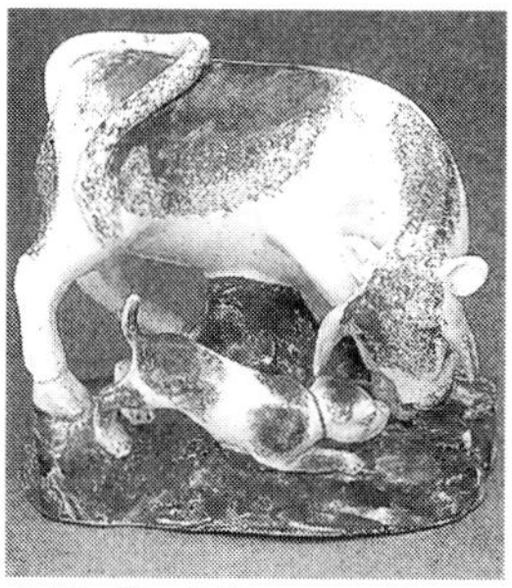

A Staffordshire pearlware bull-baiting group, the bull and hound splashed in black, on green glazed oval mound base, repaired, c1810, 5¼in (13.5cm) high.
£260–320 *DN*

A Staffordshire model of a sheep, with orange decoration, with bocage behind, c1820, 4¾in (12cm) high.
£160–180 *OCH*

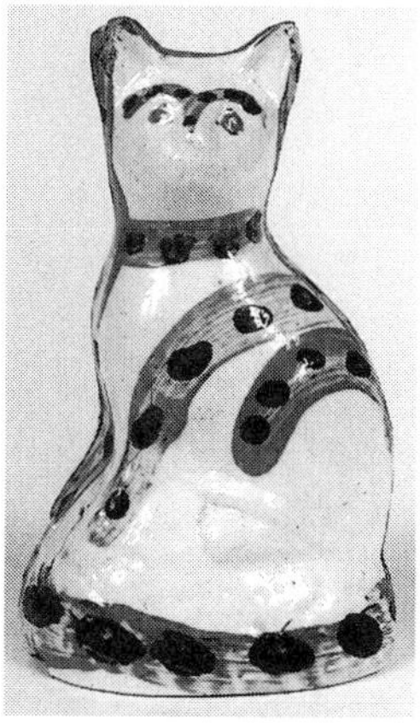

l. A Bovey Tracey model of a cat, decorated with orange and black, cracked, early 19thC, 4¼in (11cm) high.
£350–400 *JHo*

Items in the Pottery section have been arranged in date order within each sub-section.

A Staffordshire model of a dog, grey with brown markings, on a green and brown rocky base, early 19thC, 6¼in (15.5cm) wide.
£600–680 *JHo*

A Staffordshire model of a red and white deer, with bocage behind, on a brown and green base, c1820, 4in (10cm) high.
£400–450 *JHo*

A Staffordshire pearlware model of a lion, one front paw resting on a ball, with green-glazed base picked out in blue, yellow, puce and red, some damage, c1825, 6in (15cm) high.
£750–850 *DN(H)*

A Staffordshire pearlware cow creamer and cover, with a calf at its feet, boldly splashed in black, the horns picked out in yellow, on green glazed base, tail cracked, c1830–40, 4¾in (12cm) high.
£850–950 *DN*

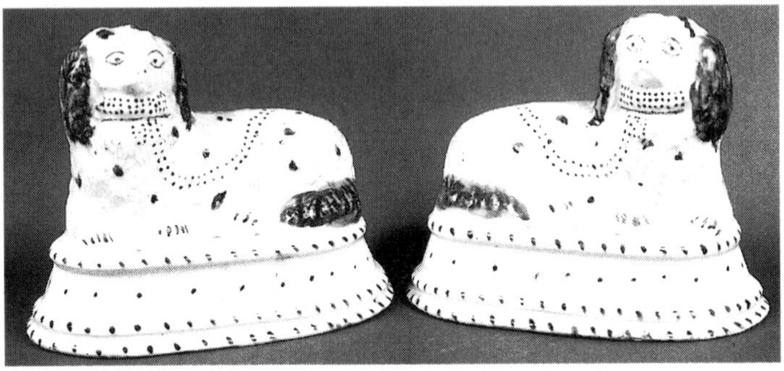

A pair of Staffordshire stoneware dogs, with brown decoration, c1830, 8in (20.5cm) high.
£800–880 *JO*

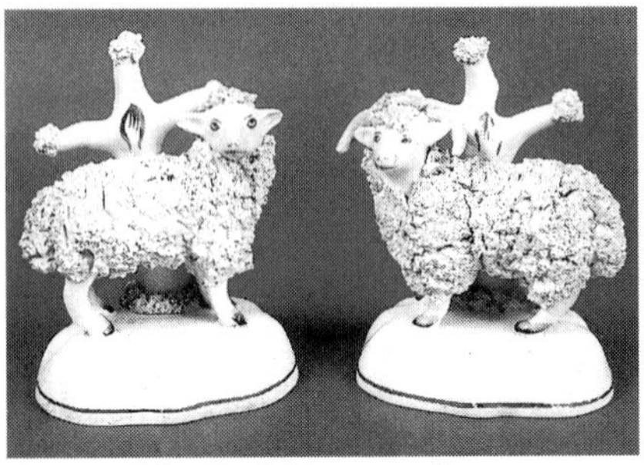

A pair of Staffordshire porcellaneous sheep, highlighted with gilt lines, restored, c1830, 4½in (11.5cm) high.
£270–320 *SER*

A Staffordshire model of a sheep, its front feet resting on a basket of flowers, c1830, 2in (5cm) wide.
£300–330 *JO*

A salt-glazed stoneware model of a spaniel, seated on a hollow cushion base, c1830, 8in (20.5cm) high.
£360–400 *CGC*

A Yorkshire treacle-glazed earthenware model of a stag, c1830, 5in (12.5cm) high.
£160–180 *SER*

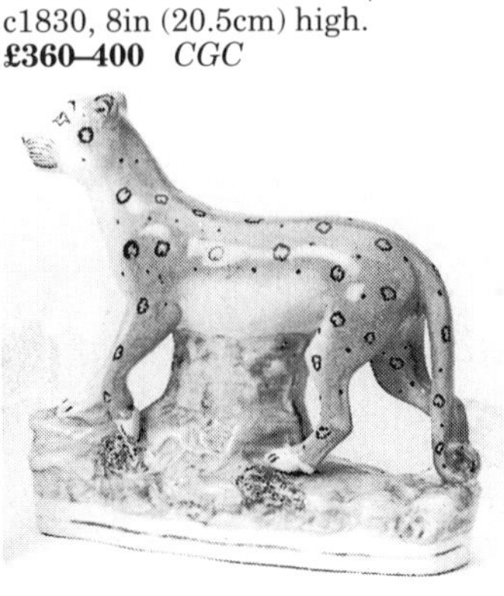

A Staffordshire model of a leopard, bright yellow with black markings, standing on a light blue washed rocky and gilt-lined base, c1840, 7½in (19cm) high.
£1,100–1,300 *CGC*

A Staffordshire model of a spaniel, with yellow eyes, gold locket and chain and black coat, free-standing front legs, c1840, 12in (30.5cm) high.
£450–500 *CGC*

A Staffordshire earthenware model of a brown and white cow, with a milkmaid, c1840, 7½in (19cm) high.
£350–400 *SER*

A Staffordshire swan group, decorated in green, yellow and red, c1850, 4½in (11.5cm) high.
£130–150 *SER*

A pair of Staffordshire porcellaneous models of spaniels, decorated with dark red/brown markings, c1840, 3¼in (8.5cm) high.
£300–360 *RWB*

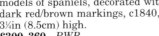

A Yorkshire pottery cow creamer, with sponged blue and ochre finish, loop tail handle, with calf standing on a platform base and blue/green matt glaze to whole, mid-19thC, 5in (12.5cm) long.
£350–400 *BIG*

A Staffordshire model of a spaniel, with a rust-coloured coat, seated on a gilt-enriched tasselled cushion base, c1840, 4¾in (12cm) high.
£380–420 *CGC*

A Staffordshire cow spill vase, with a milkmaid, decorated in brown, green and yellow, c1860, 8in (20.5cm) high.
£220–250 *GAZE*

A pair of Staffordshire spill vases, each depicting a swan family, decorated with orange and green, c1860, 5in (12.5cm) high.
£320–350 *JO*

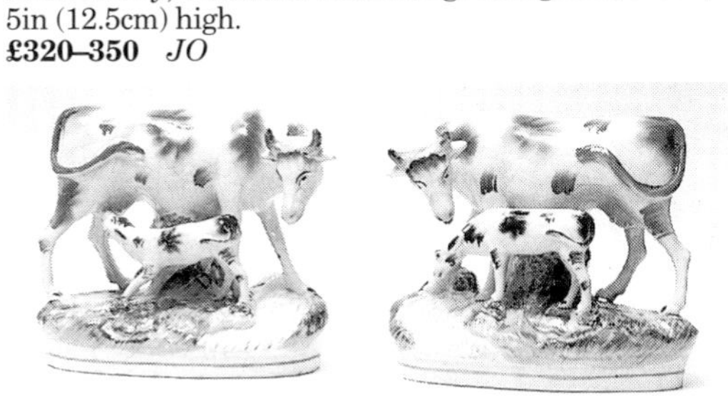

A pair of Staffordshire cow and calf groups, decorated with brown and black, c1860, 5½in (14cm) long.
£550–650 *DAN*

A pair of Staffordshire models of dogs and puppies, on blue bases, c1865, 6in (15cm) high.
£450–500 *JO*

A brown earthenware cow creamer, c1860, 7in (18cm) long.
£60–80 *SER*

A Staffordshire model of a dog, on a blue and white base, c1860, 3¾in (9.5cm) long.
£50–55 *OCH*

A Staffordshire pottery model of a rabbit, picked out in black, on green glazed oval mound base, c1860, 3¼in (8.5cm) wide.
£220–250 *DN*

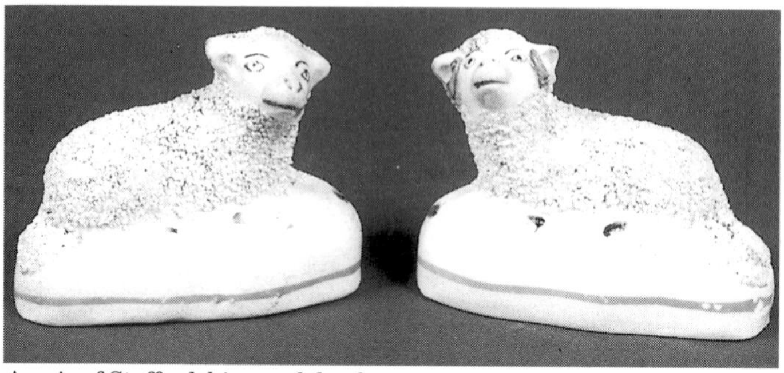

A pair of Staffordshire models of sheep, c1880, 2½in (6.5cm) high.
£200–225 *JO*

A Quimper vase, in the form of a goose, decorated in shades of green, yellow, blue and red, c1883, 10in (25.5cm) high.
£580–640 *VH*

Miller's is a price GUIDE not a price LIST

A Staffordshire model of an elephant, on a yellow base, late 19thC, 5¾in (14.5cm) high.
£1,000–1,200 *DAN*

An Austrian model of a seated fox terrier, with glass eyes and yellow collar, 19thC, 19in (48.5cm) high.
£1,300–1,500 *AH*

A Wedgwood black basalt model of a squirrel, modelled by E. W. Light, with glass eyes, impressed mark, c1913, 5¼in (13.5cm) high.
£460–500 *SK*

A pair of Staffordshire models of spaniels, standing on leaf-capped green and rustic arched pink bases, 19thC, 8in (20.5cm) high.
£2,400–2,800 *AH*

l. A Ewenny slipware model of a seated cat, its ears, eyes and whiskers incised through to the red clay, marked 'E. Jenkins, Ewenny Pottery, 1900', 15in (38cm) high.
£720–800 *WW*

The Ewenny area, near Bridgend, has been the site of a pottery industry since the early 18thC. This particular factory has been in the ownership of the Jenkins family since c1820.

Bowls & Dishes

A Dutch Delft polychrome bowl, by De Griekshe A factory, the exterior painted in iron-red, green, yellow and blue with an exotic bird perched on the branch of a prunus tree, the reverse with an insect between 2 long-tailed birds, below an iron-red trellis diaper border reserved with 6 panels, with green leaves around the rim, the interior painted with a tulip, slight damage, marked 'AK' in iron-red, c1700, 12in (30.5cm) diam.
£850–950 *S(NY)*

An English delft punchbowl, painted with kidney-shaped reserves of chinoiserie buildings on a ground of scrolling flowers in tones of iron-red, blue and green, the interior painted with a similar reserve in blue within a ring of foliate scrolls, damaged, c1730, 13¼in (33.5cm) diam.
£5,000–5,500 *Bon*

A Staffordshire glazed and gilded bowl, c1765, 5½in (14cm) diam.
£600–660 *JHo*

An earthenware dish, printed with the 'Sailor's Farewell', within lustre borders, c1880, 10in (25.5cm) wide.
£45–50 *Ber*

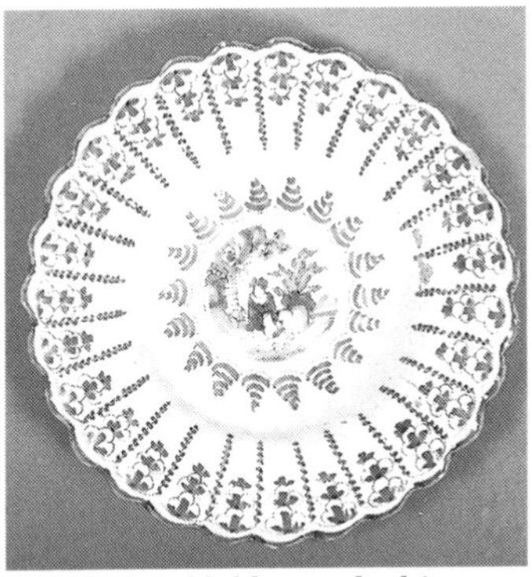

A Dutch Delft blue and white dish, c1720, 13in (33cm) diam.
£340–375 *OCH*

An English delft punch bowl, painted in blue with chinoiserie landscapes, damaged and repaired, mid-18thC, 13½in (34.5cm) diam.
£250–300 *Bon*

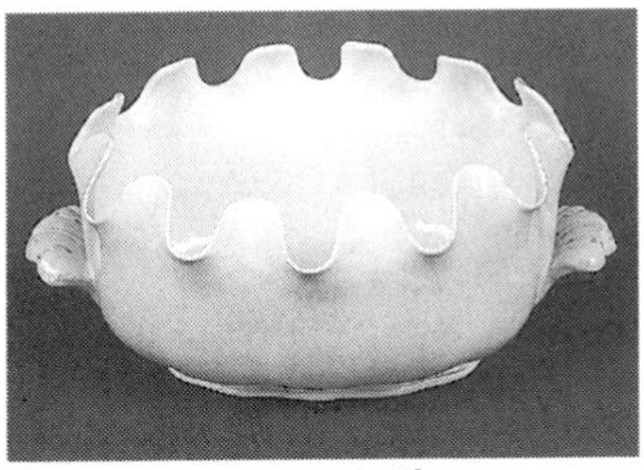

A creamware monteith, possibly Staffordshire, c1775, 13½in (34.5cm) long.
£1,750–2,000 *JHo*

A monteith is a bowl for cooling or rinsing wine glasses.

Spongeware

- Spongeware, or spatterware, was made in the 19thC mainly in the Staffordshire potteries, but it is possible to find examples of Scottish and Welsh designs.
- Bright colours were sponged through a stencil, and the design was often supplemented with painting.
- The detailed patterns were applied with potato stamps.
- The most unusual decorations are those with animals and birds and these are much sought-after by collectors.
- The pea hen design is very collectable in America.

An English delft punchbowl, inscribed 'Drink Fair, Dont Swear', enclosed by a band of trellis and rings, decorated in Chinese style with mirror and vase-shaped cartouches enclosing florets on a diaper ground, some damage, dated '1729', 11¾in (30cm) diam.
£5,000–5,500 *Bon*

A Liverpool delft blue and white bowl, the exterior painted on the front with a pair of long-necked exotic birds perched on a fence amidst flowering shrubbery, the reverse with a bird in flight pursuing an insect, and the interior with blossoms beneath a scroll-patterned blue band around the rim, c1765, 12in (30.5cm) diam.
£650–700 *S(NY)*

A spongeware bowl, decorated with red flowers and green leaves, late 19thC, 8½in (21.5cm) diam.
£60–70 *SWN*

A spongeware dish, decorated with flags and crowns, inscribed 'Are We Downhearted? No!', 1914–18, 6¾in (17cm) diam.
£85–95 *Ber*

Buildings

A Yorkshire pearlware cottage, with a blue roof, base restored, c1820, 6in (15cm) high.
£400–500 *JHo*

A pottery longcase clock money box, with a dog in front of the clock, on a green base, painted orange, green, black and blue under a pearl glaze, by J. Emerey, Mexborough, restored, c1838, 9in (23cm) high.
£250–300 *SER*

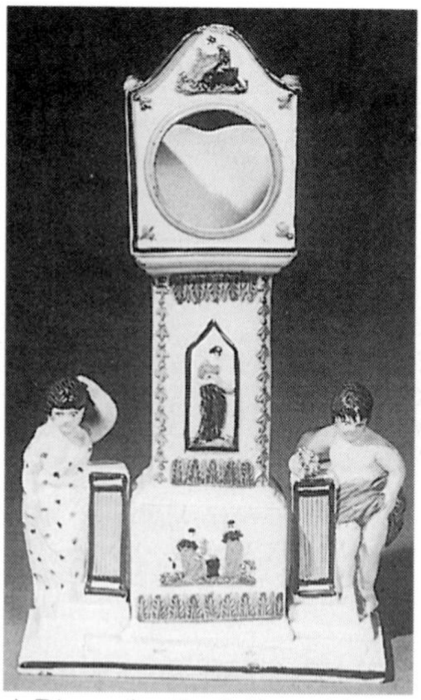

A Dixon, Austin & Co watch stand, decorated in Pratt colours, modelled as a grandfather clock, with 2 classical figures leaning against plinths on either side, slight damage, impressed mark, c1820, 11in (28cm) high.
£520–580 *P*

A Brampton type stoneware cottage-shaped box and cover, with lid, c1840, 5in (12.5cm) high.
£100–120 *OCH*

A Staffordshire two-piece pastille burner, modelled as a cottage, with flowered borders, c1835, 4¾in (12cm) high.
£220–280 *DAN*

A Staffordshire clock tower spill vase, decorated in green, pink and brown, c1850, 9½in (24cm) high.
£240–280 *GAZE*

Busts

A Staffordshire pearlware bust of Queen Charlotte, her hair in brown ringlets on her forehead and tied in a spiral bun, raised on a square purple sponged base, slight chip, c1800, 5½in (14cm) high.
£400–450 *Hal*

A Wedgwood black basalt bust of Mercury, on a waisted socle, restored, impressed mark, c1840, 17¾in (45cm) high.
£900–1,100 *SK*

A Wedgwood black basalt bust of Venus, in neo-classical style on a separate circular foot, impressed marks, late 19thC, 13½in (34.5cm) high.
£400–450 *Bon*

Covered Dishes

An English delft two-handled posset pot and lid, hand-painted in Oriental style with pavilions, rockwork and foliage, damage, early 18thC, 4¼in (10.5cm) high.
£460–500 *BLH*

A Swansea Pottery supper set, the decoration attributed to Thomas Pardoe, the borders in brown and green, finial of central dish restored, c1802, 20in (51cm) wide.
£800–900 *PF*

A Spode stone china muffin dish, decorated with Cabbage pattern, No. 2061, printed mark, c1822, 8in (20.5cm) diam.
£100–130 *JP*

r. A stoneware game pie dish and cover, chips to lid, c1830, 10in (25.5cm) wide.
£100–120 *OCH*

A Staffordshire pottery hen tureen and cover, c1860, 7½in (19cm) high.
£120–150 *Ber*

A Stephen Folch stone china supper dish and cover, c1820, 12in (30.5cm) wide.
£300–335 *VH*

l. A Savoie casserole and lid, decorated with brown on a yellow ground, c1880, 9in (23cm) diam.
£75–85 *MLL*

A spongeware cheese dish, decorated with brown, green and yellow, c1900, 7½in (19cm) wide.
£120–150 *Ber*

r. A French rabbit tureen, c1900, 8in (20.5cm) wide.
£55–60 *MLL*

Figures

A Portuguese faïence figure of a white-glazed putto, seated on a plinth, some damage, 'TB' mark in blue for T. Brunetto, Rato factory, c1767, 17¾in (45cm) high.
£2,750–3,000 *P*

A Staffordshire figure of a woman, in a brown and cream robe, c1770, 8½in (21.5cm) high.
£500–550 *JHo*

A Staffordshire creamware figure, decorated in shades of yellow and green, c1795, 7½in (19cm) high.
£240–280 *IW*

A Staffordshire figure of a Scotsman, on an orange base, early 19thC, 9¼in (23.5cm) high.
£850–950 *JHo*

Staffordshire Figures

The reference numbers included in some captions refer to the cataloguing system used by P. D. Gordon Pugh in his book *Staffordshire Portrait Figures,* published by Antique Collectors' Club, 1970. This book refers to identified portrait figures and allied subjects of the Victorian period, and does not include animals or early figures.

A Staffordshire figure of Diana, carrying a bow in her right hand and quiver of arrows in her left, early 19thC, 12in (30.5cm) high.
£200–220 *GAK*

A pair of Staffordshire pearlware figures of putti, each holding a basket of flowers, early 19thC, 4½in (11.5cm) high.
£350–400 *JHo*

A Staffordshire figure depicting the Sacrifice of Isaac, decorated in green, pink, blue and orange, bocage restored, early 19thC, 11in (28cm) high.
£1,000–1,150 *JHo*

l. A Staffordshire figure of Neptune, with his foot on a dolphin, early 19thC, 10½in (26.5cm) high.
£480–520 *TVM*

A Staffordshire figure of Rosalind, early 19thC, 7½in (19cm) high.
£1,000–1,200 *JHo*

A Prattware figure of a young girl, kneeling with her head resting on a cushioned pedestal, decorated with orange, blue, pink and yellow, c1810, 2½in (6.5cm) high.
£450–550 *RA*

A pair of Staffordshire figures, entitled 'Gardners', with bocage, c1820, 5¼in (13.5cm) high.
£600–660 *JHo*

A Staffordshire circus group, modelled as a Savoyard and his dancing bear, the trainer wearing a brightly coloured costume, c1820, 9in (23cm) high.
£2,300–2,500 *CGC*

A Staffordshire figure of a gentleman, with a dog at his feet, wearing a brown jacket and brown trousers, on a green base, damaged, c1820, 6in (15cm) high.
£300–350 *TVM*

A Staffordshire figure of Nicodemus, c1820, 11¼in (28.5cm) high.
£800–950 *JHo*

A Staffordshire figure of a hurdy gurdy player, on a brown and green base, chipped, c1825, 8¼in (21cm) high.
£300–350 *DAN*

l. A Dixon, Austin & Co lustre watch stand, modelled as a longcase clock flanked by female figures, decorated in pink lustre and bright enamels, impressed mark, restored, c1820, 11¼in (28.5cm) high.
£850–1,000 *Bon*

l. A Staffordshire pearlware figure of a boy with a dog, decorated in shades of green and yellow, c1830, 7in (18cm) high.
£350–400 *JRe*

A Staffordshire figure of Mr Van Amburgh, with a lion, lioness, cub and leopard, raised on a gilt titled base, c1835, 6¼in (16cm) high.
£3,700–4,000 *CGC*

A Staffordshire group, entitled 'Death of Nelson', c1840, 8in (20.5cm) high.
£750–850 *TVM*

A pair of Staffordshire figures, based on the story of *John Gilpin's Ride*, c1845, 8in (20cm) high, E102, Figs 205 and 206.
£650–700 *RWB*

A Staffordshire figure of the Fat Sailor, with pink shirt and blue trousers, repaired, c1840, 13½in (34.5cm) high.
£100–120 *Ber*

A pair of Staffordshire porcellaneous figures of a shepherd and shepherdess, in the style of James Dudson, wearing navy blue jackets with gilt, c1845, 6¾in (17cm) high.
£320–380 *JO*

l. A Staffordshire figure of Napoleon, with cannon and cannonballs, c1840, 12½in (32cm) high, C231, Fig.48.
£750–850 *TVM*

A Staffordshire portrait figure of Jemmy Wood, c1845, 7½in (19cm) high, G16, Fig 33.
£220–250 *RWB*

Jemmy Wood was a Gloucester draper whose disputed will was the subject of intense public interest.

A Staffordshire figure of a guardian angel, possibly watching over Princess Royal and Prince of Wales, c1845, 9in (23cm) high.
£130–170 *SER*

A Staffordshire theatrical figure of William Charles Macready as Rob Roy MacGregor, c1850, 14in (36cm) high, I6, Fig 14.
£250–300 *RWB*

A Staffordshire figure of Prince Albert, c1850, 8¼in (21cm) high.
£170–200 *SER*

A Staffordshire figure of Aunt Chloe, by Thomas Parr, c1852, 6½in (16.5cm) high, B206, Plate 28.
£300–350 *JNic*

A Staffordshire spill vase, with children playing, c1850, 11½in (29cm) high.
£160–175 *JO*

A pair of Staffordshire figures of a girl and boy holding flags on stags, c1850, 15in (38cm) high.
£275–325 *SER*

A pair of Staffordshire figures, each with a parrot and a whippet, decorated in gilt, c1850, 8in (21cm) high.
£300–350 *SER*

A Staffordshire clock face group, depicting Queen Victoria and Victor Emmanuel II, c1854, 9in (23cm) high, C38, Fig 92.
£300–350 *RWB*

A Staffordshire figure of Louis Napoleon of France, with navy blue jacket, c1854, 16in (40.5cm) high, C38, Fig 96.
£300–350 *RWB*

Louis Napoleon was President of the 2nd Republic from 1848 until 1852, when he became Emperor Napoleon III.

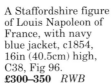

A Staffordshire figure modelled as Queen Victoria's child in a blue dress, with a goat, c1855, 6¼in (16cm) high.
£120–135 *JO*

A Staffordshire figure of the Duke of Cambridge, decorated in black, pink, mauve, green and orange, c1854, 14¼in (36cm) high.
£230–260 *TVM*

A Staffordshire porcellaneous figure of a sailor, with capstan, c1854, 8in (20.5cm) high.
£150–180 *SER*

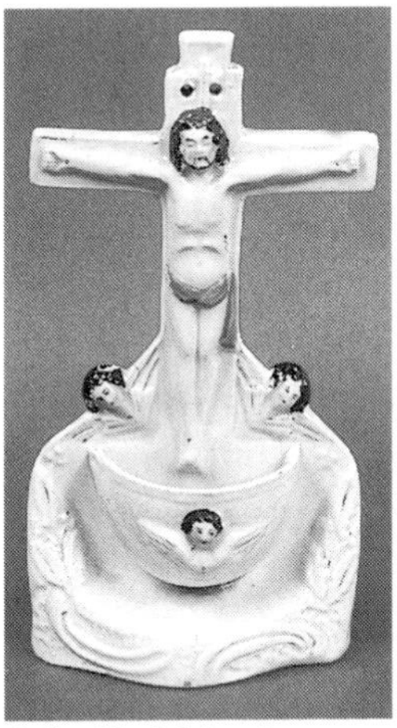

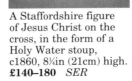

A Staffordshire figure of Jesus Christ on the cross, in the form of a Holy Water stoup, c1860, 8¼in (21cm) high.
£140–180 *SER*

A Staffordshire group, entitled 'Auld Lang Syne', wearing blue and orange jackets, c1860, 8½in (21.5cm) high.
£250–300 *JO*

A Staffordshire figure of Giuseppe Garibaldi, c1860, 10¾in (27cm) high, C102, Fig 299.
£230–250 *RWB*

A Staffordshire figure of a Private in American Civil War uniform, wearing an orange jacket and white trousers, c1861, 4½in (11.5cm) high.
£130–170 *SER*

A Staffordshire clock face group, c1860, 11½in (29cm) high.
£120–140 *JO*

A Staffordshire clock face figure of Reverend Wesley, c1860, 11¾in (30cm) high.
£240–265 *JO*

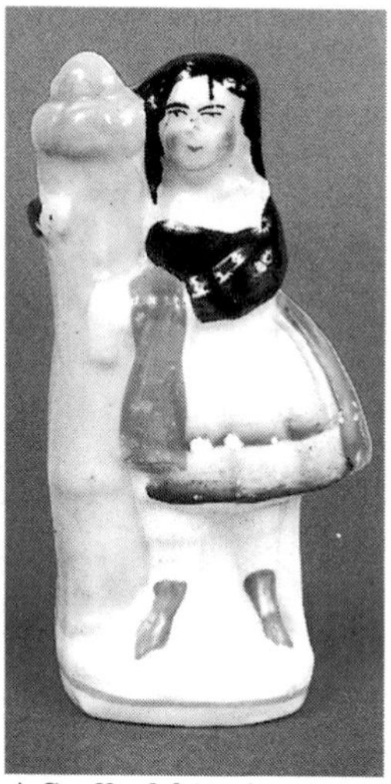

A Staffordshire figure of a girl in a blue, pink and green dress, standing next to a pump, c1870, 3¾in (9.5cm) high.
£40–50 *SER*

A Staffordshire group, depicting Paul and Virginia, decorated in yellow, pink and blue, on a white base, c1860, 9in (23cm) high.
£130–150 *JO*

Paul and Virginia were characters from a popular romantic novel published in 1787. Virginia drowned in a shipwreck because she would not take off her clothes to swim ashore. Paul died of a broken heart shortly afterwards.

A Staffordshire figure of Saint Sebastian, wearing an orange loincloth, restored, c1870, 16in (40.5cm) high.
£220–275 *SER*

FURTHER READING
Miller's Pottery Antiques Checklist
Miller's Publications, 1995

A Staffordshire group, depicting Jessica and Lorenzo from the *Merchant of Venice* at the Love Bower, c1860, 8in (20.5cm) high.
£130–150 *JO*

A Staffordshire figure of a flower girl, decorated in blue, pink, yellow and green, c1860, 10in (25.5cm) high.
£120–140 *JO*

A Staffordshire figure of a music hall star, c1870, 13¾in (35cm) high.
£130–160 *SER*

Flatware

A Gubbio maiolica moulded dish, with the infant St John in a landscape picked out in blue, green and 2 tones of lustre, the rim with a border of sunrays and stylised fruit, c1530–40, rim chips, minor hair cracks, 8½in (21.5cm) diam.
£2,300–2,500 *S*

An Hispano-Moresque copper lustre charger, with touches of blue, 17thC, 18in (45.5cm) diam.
£600–700 *SPa*

A Friesland charger, painted in blue sponged decoration with a gentleman on a rearing horse between 2 trees, 3 blue lines to the rim, minor damage, c1720, 12in (30.5cm) diam.
£575–625 *P*

An octagonal tin glazed plate, inscribed 'Weilcom my Freinds, 1661', probably London, 7½in (19cm) wide.
£8,000–10,000 *JHo*

This is the earliest date recorded on a plate of this type, and the spelling may suggest that it was decorated by a Dutchman working in London.

An English delft blue dash charger, painted in tones of manganese and ochre with Adam and Eve and the Tree of Knowledge, damaged and repaired, c1700, 13in (33cm) diam.
£1,100–1,200 *Bon*

A Dutch Delft doré dish, perhaps by Pieter Adrianensz Kocks, painted in enamels and gilding with Joseph and his brothers before the pit, probably after Hendrik Goltzius, the rim with an elaborate border of shells, peonies and turquoise foliage against an iron-red foliate ground, slight damage and restoration, early 18thC, 13½in (34.5cm) diam.
£1,800–2,000 *S*

l. A Bristol delft plate, decorated with a blue bird and flowers on a white ground, c1740, 7¾in (19.5cm) diam.
£600–680 *JHo*

An Hispano-Moresque copper lustre charger, with leaf decoration, 17thC, 20in (51cm) diam.
£600–650 *SPa*

A Staffordshire slipware saucer dish, with brown combed decoration on a cream slip ground, piecrust border, early 18thC, 8in (20.5cm) diam.
£820–900 *FW&C*

A delft plate, painted in blue with a central foliate medallion surrounded by heart-shaped panels with stylised shrubbery, alternating with 4 roundels of floral sprigs, on a manganese ground, probably Bristol, c1735, 8½in (21.5cm) diam.
£280–350 *S(NY)*

An English delft plate, decorated in blue and white on a manganese ground, c1740, 8¾in (22cm) diam.
£250–300 *JHo*

An English delft plate, painted in coloured enamels with flowers and leaves in a basket, within an iron-red border and blue line bands, probably Bristol, slight chips, c1740, 8½in (21.5cm) diam.
£400–450 *DN*

An English delft dish, decorated in blue on a white ground, cracked and chipped, c1760, 14in (35.5cm) diam.
£165–185 *OCH*

A pair of Zürich creamware plates, painted in shades of brown, grey, green, yellow, blue, puce and iron-red with a cavalry skirmish, the rim with a border of green flowerheads linked by blue dotted lozenges within brown lines and a brown band at the edge, slight wear, marked 'Z' in blue, c1790, 10in (25.5cm) diam.
£220–250 *S(NY)*

A Dutch maiolica dish, painted in shades of blue and manganese with an exotic bird perched on a rock amidst sponged woodland, within a stylised foliate wide border, minor chips, early 17thC, 11¾in (30cm) diam.
£275–300 *S(Am)*

Two faïence dishes, with scalloped rims and moulded borders, each painted in blue and yellow with figures in landscapes, probably Frankfurt, one cracked, mid-18thC, 8½in (21.5cm) diam.
£400–450 *WW*

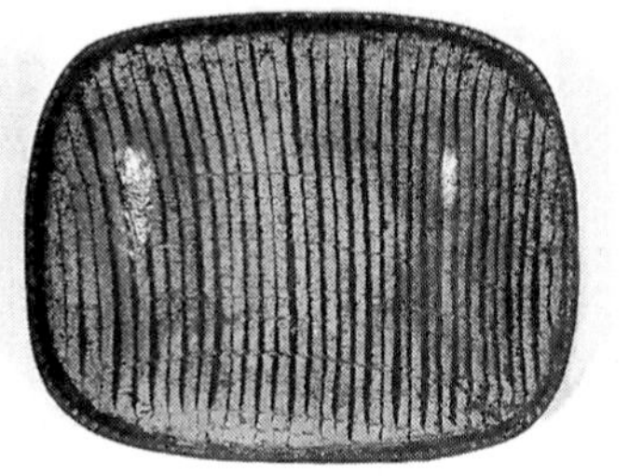

A slipware dish, with combed trailed decoration in brown on a cream ground, within a piecrust rim, late 18thC, 18in (45.5cm) wide.
£1,500–1,650 *P(F)*

The price realised for this dish was far in excess of expectations due to its extremely good condition.

Creamware

Creamware is finely potted lead-glazed earthenware which was developed over a long period in the 18thC, but brought to refinement by Wedgwood in the 1760s. The paste is a pale straw or cream colour, hence the name.

l. A pair of Wedgwood creamware platters, decorated in red and green with a central floral spray within a floral border, early 19thC, 15in (38cm) diam.
£160–180 *SWO*

An English delft plate, painted in blue, within arcaded and flowerhead panelled bands, c1740, 9in (23cm) diam.
£360–400 *DN*

An English delft dish, decorated with blue flowers on a white ground, damaged, c1760, 14in (35.5cm) diam.
£100–150 *OCH*

A Dutch blue and white dish, decorated with a central tree and leaf and flower border, flaking to rim, 18thC, 14in (35.5cm) diam.
£300–350 *BIG*

A Mason's Ironstone soup plate, decorated with Water lily pattern, impressed mark, c1815, 9½in (24cm) diam.
£140–160 *VH*

A Staffordshire ironstone chinoiserie platter, transfer-printed in black and enamelled in the centre in rose, purple, blue, iron-red, salmon, green, turquoise, yellow and black with figures, animals and birds outside a pagoda, the rim pink, gold and ochre, possibly Mason's, worn and damaged, c1815, 21in (53.5cm) wide.
£550–600 *S(NY)*

A pair of children's plates, decorated in iron-red and green with 'Symptoms of Grave Digging' and 'Symptoms of Angling', c1820, 5½in (14cm) diam.
£190–210 *OCH*

A pearlware plate, the feather-edged rim finished in underglaze blue, the centre printed in blue with a scene depicting George III presenting a book to a child, above an inscription, 1820, 6¼in (16cm) diam.
£600–650 *SAS*

Plates such as this were made in memory of George III at the time of his death and possibly distributed to the pupils of the Lancastrian School of which the King was patron.

A pottery plate, the border moulded with animals and lined in black, the centre printed in black with a portrait of William IV, commemorating his Coronation, restored, 1831, 7in (18cm) diam.
£150–170 *SAS*

A pearlware plate, painted in pink and purple lustre with a green border, c1830, 8in (20.5cm) diam.
£140–160 *OCH*

A French comport and 2 plates, decorated with green glazed ships within brown moulded borders, c1850, 9¼in (23.5cm) diam.
£270–300 *SWN*

A pottery plate, commemorating Queen Victoria's Diamond Jubilee, moulded with spirally fluted border and printed in dark blue with an equestrian portrait, dated '1837', 7in (18cm) diam.
£150–180 *SAS*

A Thomas Fell & Co child's plate, printed in green with an ice skating scene, c1840, 5½in (14cm) diam.
£50–60 *IW*

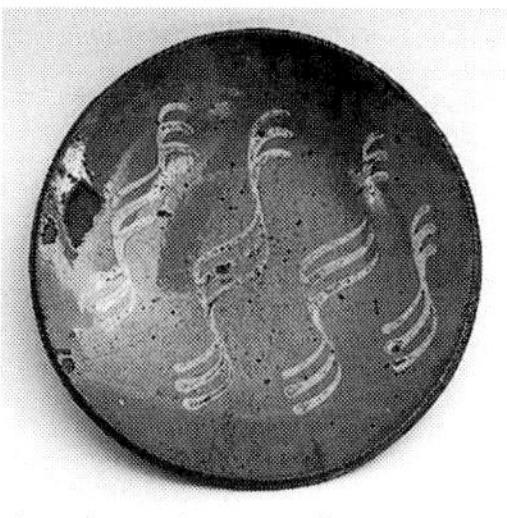

An American redware slip-decorated dish, 19thC, 9in (23cm) diam.
£200–220 *A&A*

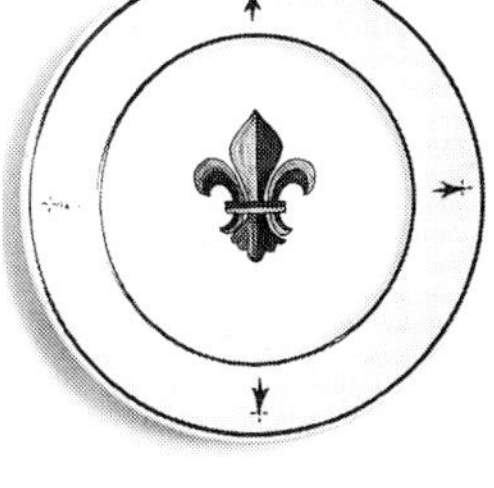

A set of 4 Quimper plates, decorated with fleurs-de-lys, c1900, 8in (20.5cm) diam.
£200–235 *MLL*

Jars

An Hispano-Moresque lustre albarello, painted in blue and gold lustre, extensively restored, late 15thC, 12in (30.5cm) high.
£2,800–3,200 *P(EA)*

A Sicilian maiolica albarello, painted with a yellow-ground medallion of a saint, the reverse with trophies, within yellow-ground borders of foliage and ribbon, probably Palermo, minor chips, 17thC, 11½in (29cm) high.
£1,800–2,000 *S*

A German bellarmine, early 17thC, 8½in (21.5cm) high.
£620–680 *JHo*

A salt-glazed stoneware jar, with an engraved silver-mounted cylindrical neck and mottled brown glaze, repaired, jug 16thC, mount probably 17thC, 8¼in (21cm) high.
£340–375 *WW*

l. A Gerace maiolica syrup jar, painted in Venetian style with scrolling foliage on a blue-washed ground, a portrait medallion of a bearded man below a broad strap handle, Calabria, chipped, 17thC, 8¼in (21cm) high.
£1,100–1,200 *S*

A Continental salt-glazed bellarmine, with impressed tulip seal, c1675, 9½in (24cm) high.
£300–350 *IW*

An English delft ginger jar, with 2 serpentine handles, painted in blue, red and green with sprays of fan-like flowers between scroll and zig-zag borders, Brislington or London, c1720, 3¾in (9.5cm) high.
£1,000–1,200 *P*

Pottery Forms

Many of the forms made by the main pottery-producing centres are very distinctive, and a familiarity with these types of wares and the areas in which they were produced, can be of help to a collector when attributing a particular piece. Illustrated here are a number of identifiable forms, together with their country of origin and a guide to the period in which they were made. Please note that these items are not drawn to scale, and comparisons between the size of the objects should not be made.

Pharmacy bottle, Italy, 16thC

Oviform albarello, Palermo, Sicily, 17thC

Campana-shaped vase, Italy, 18thC

Pharmacy jar, Savona, Italy, 17thC

Tankard, Annaberg, Germany, 17thC

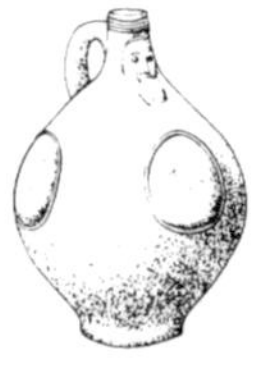

Bellarmine, Frechen, Germany, 16thC

Enghalskrug, Hanau, Germany, 18thC

Tureen, Strasbourg, France, 18thC

Delft jug, Holland, 18thC

Delft vase, Holland, 18thC

Posset pot, Bristol, England, 18thC

Agateware vase, England, 18thC

A Naples maiolica albarello, painted in manganese, blue, green and ochre with St Martin and the Beggar, in a blue-dash and line border, the reverse with crowned monogram in blue and dated '1701', hair cracks and chip to rim, 11in (28cm) high.
£4,400–4,800 *S*

This series of apothecary wares was made for the Carthusian monastery of San Martino, Naples.

A delft wet drug jar, decorated in blue on a pale blue glaze, with straight lipped spout and strap handle, with inscription, surmounted in the centre by a shell, an angel and flower spray, raised on a splayed foot, probably Lambeth, c1740, 7¼in (18.5cm) high.
£900–1,000 *FW&C*

A Penrith Pottery brown and cream tobacco jar, the cover with bird finial, beak missing, c1880, 6in (15cm) high.
£55–70 *ANV*

Miller's is a price GUIDE not a price LIST

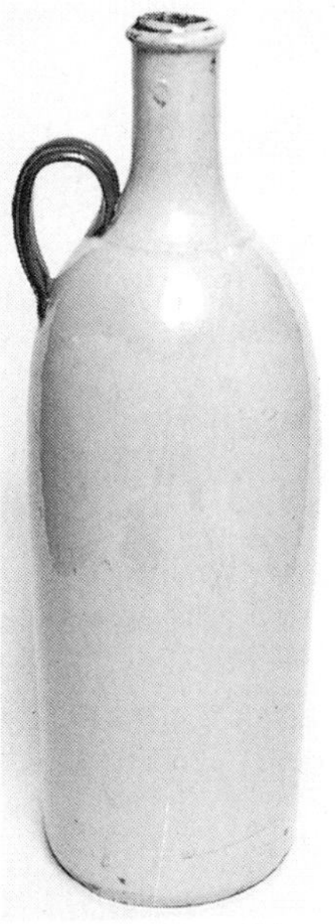

A pottery olive oil jar, cream with brown handle, c1880, 14in (35.5cm) high.
£120–130 *MLL*

Jugs

A Staffordshire glazed and gilded hot water jug, c1765, 6¼in (16cm) high.
£500–550 *JHo*

A creamware jug, Dawson & Co, Low Ford Pottery, Sunderland, with transfer print entitled 'Peace and Plenty', c1810, 8in (20.5cm) high.
£250–350 *IW*

r. A Mason's Ironstone ewer and basin, decorated in mazarine blue, and painted with enamel flowers and gilding, circular impressed mark, c1815, 8½in (21.5cm) diam.
£550–600 *VH*

A yellow glazed sgraffito harvest jug, decorated with incised slip on a darker ground, the body with the royal coat-of-arms, a heart-shaped cartouche with inscription dated '1766', Yorkshire, 13in (33cm) high.
£3,000–3,300 *PF*

Because of the brittle nature of earthenware, few of these jugs have survived into the 20thC. This piece is particularly desirable with its inscription, date, and royal coat-of-arms.

A Wedgwood jasper jug, the dark blue dip with applied green quatrefoils, white floral festoons and stiff leaf borders, damaged, impressed mark, late 18thC, 5½in (14cm) high.
£1,200–1,400 *SK*

Sgraffito

Sgraffito (literally 'scratched decoration') is the technique in which a sharp pointed tool was used to cut through a coating of slip (diluted clay) to the underlying body. This decoration is particularly effective when a pale slip overlays a dark clay body. The method was used on Chinese Cizhou wares, (10thC–13thC) and also throughout Europe on domestic eathernware and stoneware such as Bolognese pottery and English salt-glazed wares from at least as early as the 15thC. It was also used from an early date in America.

A pearlware jug, moulded and decorated with Wellington, early 19thC, 5¼in (13.5cm) high.
£150–165 *SWN*

A pearlware commemorative jug, printed in purple with Admiral Lord Nelson and his campaigns, c1810, 7in (18cm) high.
£400–450 *TVM*

A pottery jug, decorated with bands of pink lustre and printed in black with portraits, entitled 'Queen Caroline', 1821, 4¾in (12cm) diam.
£180–200 *SAS*

A Bristol pearlware documentary jug, painted by William Fifield, inscribed in black 'Ratcliff Dealer in Earthenware', inscribed in brown 'August 1824' and 'WF', 11¾in (30cm) high.
£2,700–3,000 *DN*

A blue spongeware jug and basin set, c1830, 13¼in (33.5cm) diam.
£240–265 *SWN*

A brown stoneware jug, moulded with agricultural implements and produce within bands of fruiting vines, oak leaves and acorns, on the reverse the royal coat-of-arms, crossed flags and military helmet centred by a silver escutcheon inscribed 'Presented by the inhabitants of Yeovil and its vicinity in testimony of their approval of the conduct of the Mudford Troop of Yeomanry Cavalry during the riots in that town in 1831, To Mr H. Brooks', the wavy rim mounted in silver, 9½in (24cm) high.
£900–1,000 *SAS*

On Saturday 22nd October 1831, the townsfolk of Yeovil threatened to riot following the rejection of the Second Reform Bill by the House of Lords. The Yeomanry were ordered by the Yeovil Magistrates to defend the town and a number of shots were fired injuring one rioter. The Yeomanry were judged to have acted with great professionalism and the residents of Yeovil expressed their appreciation by the presentation of an inscribed cup to each of the Troop, and an inscribed jug to each of the officers. It is thought that only 3 or 4 of these jugs have survived.

A copper lustre and enamel decorated jug, c1830, 5½in (14cm) high.
£55–70 *IW*

A pottery moulded jug, commemorating the coronation of William IV, with an all-over trellis and daisy design, printed in blue with portraits beneath panels of coronation trophies within scrolling cartouches, c1831, 7¾in (19.5cm) high.
£340–380 *SAS*

A porcelain jug, by Read & Clementson, printed in pink with 2 portraits, inscribed 'Victoria Regina, proclaimed 20th of June 1837', chip to top of handle, 5¼in (13.5cm) high.
£320–350 *SAS*

Lustreware

Lustreware is a type of decoration using metallic oxides to produce lustrous surface effects. For example, silver gives a soft golden yellow while copper appears a ruby red colour. These oxides were applied to a fired glazed piece and re-fired at a lower temperature in a reduction kiln. A successful firing would leave a deposit of virtually pure metal on the surface creating the desired lustre. The technique was probably borrowed by Mesopotamian potters from Egyptian glassmakers in the 9th century. From then on it was used on Persian, Syrian and Egyptian pottery as well as in post-medieval Spain and Renaissance Italy. The technique was revived by European potters in the 19thC.

A Mason's stoneware jug, moulded in relief and with vine-stock handle, printed crown mark and applied pad, impressed 'TOHO', c1835, 6¼in (16cm) high.
£280–320 *JP*

A stoneware jug, applied in white on a blue ground, c1820, 5¼in (13.5cm) high.
£50–70 *MEG*

A Sunderland lustre jug, with inscription and sailing boat on reverse, spout restored, c1850, 4¼in (11cm) high.
£130–160 *SER*

A Sunderland lustre pink jug, depicting the Iron Bridge, restoration to spout, c1840, 9½in (24cm) high.
£200–250 *SER*

A spongeware blue and white jug, c1840, 10in (25.5cm) high.
£180–220 *Ber*

A Sunderland lustre jug, printed *en grisaille* and painted, inscribed with verse 'The Sailor's Farewell', 19thC, 7½in (19cm) high.
£280–320 *GAK*

A Quimper jug, decorated in shades of yellow, blue and pink on a cream ground, c1920, 9in (23cm) high.
£100–115 *MLL*

A pottery jug, inscribed in brown on white with 'The Niger, The Last of the Full-Rigged Ships', c1904, 6¾in (17cm) high.
£270–300 *A&A*

Mugs & Tankards

A Staffordshire brown and cream mug, restored, chips to rim, c1765, 3in (7.5cm) high.
£400–450 *JHo*

A creamware tankard, entitled 'The happy return, Peter & Ann Scott 1797', some restoration, possibly Yorkshire, c1797, 6¼in (16cm) high.
£700–780 *JHo*

A mug, entitled 'John Gilpin', c1828, 2½in (6.5cm) high.
£85–95 *OCH*

John Gilpin is a character from George Cruikshank's novel, 'The Diverting History of John Gilpin', c1828.

r. A Copeland pottery Transvaal War commemorative tyg, decorated in colours with portraits, an allegory of Britannia, flags and inscriptions, with gilding, c1900, 5¼in (13.5cm) high.
£950–1,100 *SAS*

A creamware mug, painted in underglaze blue with a Chinese figure holding a parasol, with an ear-shaped strap handle, crack to base, c1770, 6¼in (15.5cm) high.
£550–600 *WW*

A brown and buff hunting mug, probably Mortlake, late 18thC, 8in (20.5cm) high.
£675–750 *OCH*

A two-handled loving cup, by John & Robert Godwin, Cobridge Pottery, printed in brown and coloured with the steeplechase pattern, cracked, c1850, 8in (20.5cm) diam.
£370–400 *Hal*

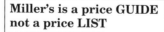

Miller's is a price GUIDE not a price LIST

A Liverpool mug, with black and white transfer print entitled 'The Gipsy Fortune Teller', c1790, 4½in (11.5cm) high.
£400–450 *JHo*

A George IV creamware coronation mug, printed in black with a bust portrait of the King encircled by an inscription, c1821, 3in (7.5cm) high.
£3,200–3,500 *Bon*

It is interesting to note the curious detailing of the incorrect date of succession, given on the mug as 1819 instead of 1820.

A Cologne faïence tankard, painted in manganese, ochre, green, yellow and brown with Adam and Eve, the pewter cover with ball thumbpiece, early 19thC, 7½in (19cm) high.
£3,700–4,000 *S*

A pearlware commemorative mug, printed in blue with an inscription, for the coronation of Queen Victoria, hairline cracks, c1838, 3in (7.5cm) high.
£500–600 *Bon*

A pearlware mug, painted in colours and with copper lustre, c1830, 5¼in (13.5cm) high.
£85–95 *OCH*

A Mocha ware mug, with moulded mark, possibly T. & G. Green, c1870, 6in (15cm) high.
£80–100 *IW*

A Heath mug, with anchor mark, 19thC, 4in (10cm) high.
£75–85 *Ber*

A yellow and brown earthenware mug, inscribed 'Sup all, eat all and pay nowt', Halifax, 19thC, 5in (12.5cm) high.
£50–55 *MTa*

An Adams pottery mug, decorated with a cockerel on a white ground, c1920, 5in (12.5cm) high.
£35–45 *Ber*

Plaques

A Castelli plaque, by Francesco Antonio Saverio Grue, painted with 3 figures, in a European harbour scene with birds in flight overhead, within an ochre and blue rim, damaged, early 18thC, 9½in (24cm) diam.
£4,000–4,500 *P*

A Dutch Delft plaque, painted in blue with a view of Ryswyk, within a manganese border, minor glaze chips, 18thC, 10½in (26.5cm) wide.
£5,000–5,500 *S(Am)*

A Pratt ware plaque, moulded with 'The Sailor's Return' within a rope-twist frame picked out in ochre, c1800, 6in (15cm) wide.
£550–600 *Bon*

A Sunderland lustre plaque, inscribed 'Prepare to meet thy God', c1840, 9¾in (25cm) wide.
£120–140 *OCH*

A plaque, moulded in relief with an equestrian portrait of the Duke of Wellington, painted in underglaze pale blue, yellow, brown and green, the reverse impressed 'Elliott', 19thC, 7½in (19cm) wide.
£150–180 *SAS*

A memorial plaque, printed with a portrait of Queen Victoria in colours, inscribed and lined in black, minor chip to rear, c1901, 6in (15cm) high.
£180–200 *SAS*

Pot Lids

'Alas! Poor Bruin', No. 1, damaged and repaired, c1850, 3½in (9cm) diam.
£40–45 *BBR*

'England's Pride', No. 149, c1850, 4in (10cm) diam.
£220–250 *SAS*

'St Paul's Cathedral and River Pageant', framed, No. 185, c1850, 4in (10cm) diam.
£80–100 *GAK*

Pot Lids

The Staffordshire pot lid is the earliest and simplest example of multi-coloured underglaze printed decoration on pottery, examples being recorded as early as 1848. They were used as containers for products such as bears grease (for rubbing into the scalp), gentleman's relish, meat and fish pastes, cosmetics etc.

The marketing impact of the pot lid owed much to the skills of Jesse Austin, a gifted artist and engraver, and Felix Edward Pratt, an entrepreneurial potter, who together traded as F. & R. Pratt of Fenton.

They were soon being copied by other pottery manufacturers, and the pictures on the lids came to be used on all manner of other items such as dessert services, plates and cups. In 1897 the first exhibition of Staffordshire pot lids and Pratt ware was held and enthusiasts started collecting.

Abe Ball wrote the comprehensive and acknowledged reference work on the subject giving to each of the pot lids a reference number and name.

Listed below are some of the most common subjects and those that the present-day collector is most likely to come across:

Pegwell Bay, Established 1760 (No. 25)
The Fishbarrow (No. 58)
The Shrimpers (No. 63)
Garibaldi (No. 169)
Trafalgar Square (No. 201)
Meeting of Garibaldi and Victor Emmanuel (No. 211)
Shakespeare's Birthplace, Exterior (No. 226)
The Village Wedding (No. 240)
The Enthusiast (No. 245)
Hide and Seek (No. 255)
The Snow Drift (No. 276)
Strasburg (No. 331)

'The Great Exhibition 1851, Closing Ceremony', No. 141, c1851, 5¼in (13.5cm) diam.
£800–900 *SAS*

'Dangerous Skating', No. 249, c1850, 4¾in (12cm) diam.
£110–120 *SAS*

r. 'The Late Duke of Wellington', No. 161, c1852, 5in (12.5cm) diam.
£500–600 *SAS*

'Chin-Chew River', framed, No. 218, c1860, 4in (10cm) diam.
£60–65 *GAK*

'Uncle Toby', No. 328, c1860, 4¼in (11cm) diam.
£35–40 *BBR*

'Ning Po River', No. 222, c1860, 4¾in (12cm) diam.
£130–150 *SAS*

Services

A Wedgwood creamware miniature tea service, comprising 15 pieces, marked, c1790, tea kettle 4¾in (12cm) high.
£900–1,000 *P*

A Neale & Bailey creamware part dessert service, comprising 24 pieces, painted with green, black and brown to the rims, the centres with blue flowers, c1800.
£1,200–1,500 *Bon*

A Wedgwood Drabware part dessert service, comprising 17 pieces, pale green with gilt rims, impressed marks, c1810.
£800–900 *Bon*

A Spode part dessert service, comprising 16 pieces, printed and brightly painted with flowers and foliage within a gilt-decorated orange rim, pattern No. 1690, c1810.
£950–1,100 *Bea(E)*

An Ironstone part dinner service, comprising 50 pieces, decorated in iron-red and blue with orange lustre details, early 19thC.
£900–1,000 *WW*

r. A Mason's Ironstone dinner service, comprising 52 pieces, decorated in iron-red and blue, c1860.
£3,300–3,600 *PAD*

l. A Mason's Ironstone part table service, comprising 17 pieces, decorated with Japan pattern, the covers surmounted by blue and gilt floral-sprig knops, c1815.
£3,200–3,500 *S(NY)*

A Mason's Ironstone dinner service, comprising 82 pieces, printed and painted in *famille verte* palette with figures and boats in a Chinese river landscape, picked out in gilt, pattern No. 1379, some damage, c1830.
£6,000–7,000 *DN*

An earthenware dinner service, comprising 44 pieces, printed and painted with flowers and leaves within an arcaded scale border picked out in brown and gilt, pattern No. 3/651, c1880.
£600–675 *DN*

Tea & Coffee Pots

A Staffordshire solid agateware pecten shell-moulded teapot and cover, minor chips, c1755, 6in (15cm) high.
£3,800–4,200 *S*

A William Greatbatch creamware tortoiseshell-glazed teapot and cover, damaged and restored, 4½in (11.5cm) high.
£1,000–1,100 *S(NY)*

A Staffordshire creamware pineapple-moulded coffee pot and cover, with a scrolling handle and leaf moulded spout, decorated with yellow and green glazes, damaged and repaired, c1765, 9¼in (23.5cm) high.
£650–750 *WW*

A treacle-glazed teapot and cover, moulded with 4 head and shoulder portraits of Admiral Lord Nelson in naval uniform, c1850, 10in (25.5cm) high.
£170–200 *SAS*

Agateware

Agateware is formed from different coloured clays which are combined to give the impression of the veining of hard stones such as agate. First developed in Roman times, it became very popular in the 18thC, when it was produced in Staffordshire by potters such as Whieldon and Wedgwood. It was revived again in late Victorian times.

A Staffordshire salt-glazed solid agateware teapot and cover, with short spout and loop handle, marbled in dark brown against a cream ground, the cover with a bun knop, restored, c1755, 3in (8cm) high.
£3,000–3,300 *S*

A William Greatbatch teapot, in the form of a cauliflower, c1770, 5½in (14cm) high.
£2,000–2,200 *JHo*

A Staffordshire salt-glazed stoneware teapot, some chips, c1745, 5½in (14cm) high.
£700–780 *JHo*

A Dixon & Austin, Sunderland, pearlware teapot, c1820, 6in (15cm) high.
£110–125 *OCH*

A Staffordshire creamware coffee pot and cover, applied in relief with a scrollwork cartouche, rocaille and floral sprigs, vines and branches, all heightened in manganese-brown, green and yellow underglaze oxides on a pale blue glaze, the domed cover applied with 4 foliate sprigs, around a pierced mushroom knop, the spout and handle coloured in green, c1755, 7in (18cm) high.
£3,200–3,500 *S(NY)*

William Greatbatch

William Greatbatch (1735–1813) served his apprenticeship with Thomas Whieldon and later set up his own pottery. He is principally known for cream-coloured pieces with transfer-printed decoration, and also for tablewares in the shape of fruit.

A William Greatbatch creamware teapot and a cover, signed, c1770, 5in (13cm) high.
£720–850 *DN*

A pearlware blue and white coffee pot, damaged, c1790, 11½in (29cm) high.
£180–200 *OCH*

A black basalt beehive-shaped teapot and cover, engine-turned around the body, cover and spout, the reeded loop handle with a foliate thumbpiece, the cover surmounted by a pierced concave knop, early 19thC, 4in (10cm) high.
£250–300 *S(NY)*

A Wedgwood black basalt beehive-shaped teapot and cover, with all-over press-moulded body, impressed mark, c1810, 5½in (14cm) high.
£700–750 *SK*

A Nove coffee pot and cover, with double scroll handle and flower finial, painted with 4 panels of brightly coloured flowers alternating with applied flower sprays, the acanthus-moulded foot and shell-moulded rim picked out in bright yellow, minor restoration, late 19thC, 9in (23cm) high.
£250–300 *P*

Tiles

Four Hispano-Moresque pottery tiles, framed, 15th/16thC, each tile 8in (20.5cm) square.
£600–650 *SLN*

A London delft tile, c1740, 6in (15cm) square.
£400–450 *JHo*

This tile is rare because of its size.

A Liverpool delft tile, c1765, 5in (12.5cm) square.
£65–75 *JHo*

A Winterthur stove tile, painted in tones of green, blue, manganese and yellow with a gardening scene, framed in an architectural panel, damaged and restored, c1700, 20½ x 14in (52 x 36cm) high.
£800–900 *P*

A Bristol delft tile, depicting the Annunciation, c1750, 5in (12.5cm) square.
£65–75 *JHo*

A Winterthur faïence stove tile, painted with a maiden in flowing drapery holding a lute, in an arched panel with acanthus motifs, crack to corner, c1700, 18½in (47cm) high.
£520–580 *P*

A London delft tile, decorated with Jacob's Ladder in manganese, c1750, 5in (12.5cm) square.
£65–75 *JHo*

l. A Dutch Delft polychrome tile, framed, early 19thC, 7½in (19cm) wide.
£50–60 *SER*

Toby & Character Jugs

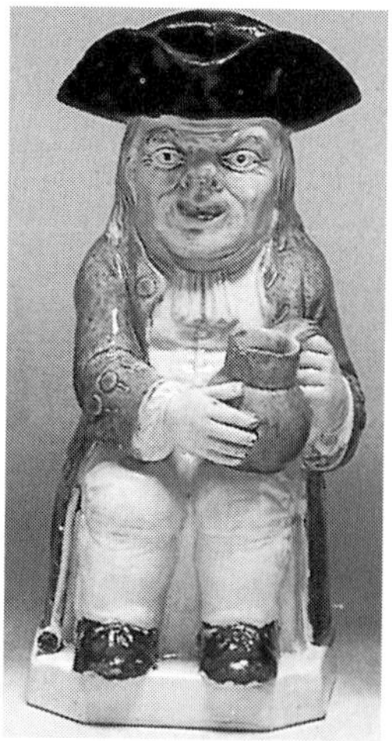

A Staffordshire pearlware Toby jug, decorated in manganese, brown and yellow, slight damage, c1780, 10in (25.5cm) high.
£800–900 *S(NY)*

A Staffordshire pearlware Toby jug, decorated in manganese, blue and yellow, c1780, 10in (25.5cm) high.
£800–900 *S(NY)*

A Staffordshire Pratt ware Toby jug, depicting Martha Gunn, c1800, 10¼in (26cm) high.
£1,800–2,000 *JHo*

This is the only known form of an 18thC female Toby jug, and is based on the 'Gin Woman of Brighton'.

A Prattware Toby jug, decorated in shades of brown, ochre and orange, 1810, 9½in (24cm) high.
£350–400 *S(NY)*

A Yorkshire type pearlware Toby jug, decorated in brown, maroon and yellow, incised E. Wood, '1794', 9¼in (23.5cm) high.
£500–550 *S(NY)*

A Staffordshire Toby jug, c1885, 9in (23cm) high.
£120–130 *JO*

A Staffordshire Toby jug, c1890, 9in (23cm) high.
£100–130 *JO*

A Wilkinson Toby jug, designed by Sir Francis Carruthers Gould, entitled 'Hell Fire Jack', printed marks, c1918, 10in (25.5cm) high.
£270–300 *SK*

Tureens

A Mason's Ironstone sauce tureen and stand, impressed mark, c1815, 7½in (19cm) high.
£450–500 *JP*

A Davenport Ironstone soup tureen and cover, decorated in Flying Bird pattern, printed mark, c1810, 12½in (32cm) wide.
£1,100–1,250 *JP*

A Brameld vegetable tureen and cover, with leaf-moulded handles and knop, printed in blue and over-painted in bright colours with 'Twisted Tree' pattern, c1835, 14¼in (36cm) wide, and 3 plates.
£180–200 *P*

l. A pair of creamware sauce tureens and covers, with integral stands and scroll knops, each painted in iron-red and green, unmarked, one slightly cracked, early 19thC, 8¾in (22cm) high.
£650–700 *WW*

Vases & Urns

A pair of Wedgwood & Bentley vases and covers, with twin handles moulded with scales, standing on square pedestals, the bodies moulded with grooves below an applied band of drapery, with circular Wedgwood & Bentley Etruria marks, some damage and repair, c1770, 11½in (29cm) wide.
£1,600–1,800 *P*

A Dutch Delft three-piece garniture, of hexagonal ribbed form, painted in blue with a chinoiserie scene, surmounted by domed covers with tear drop finials, 18thC, largest 10¼in (26cm) high.
£1,100–1,300 *S(Am)*

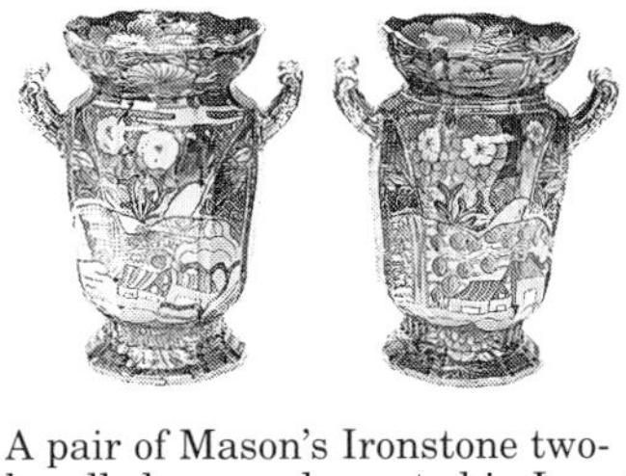

A pair of Mason's Ironstone two-handled vases, decorated in Imari style, c1815, 12in (30.5cm) high.
£3,000–3,300 *Bri*

A Staffordshire Ironstone pot pourri vase and cover, with 2 gilt loop handles, the body decorated in colours with chrysanthemums and Oriental flowers against a brick-red ground, c1820, 14in (35.5cm) high.
£850–950 *Hal*

MILLER'S COMPARES . . .

I A Wedgwood solid black jasper Portland vase, decorated in white relief with a figure wearing a Phrygian cap, impressed mark, mid-19thC, 9½in (24cm) high.
£2,000–2,500 *SK*

II A Wedgwood solid black jasper Portland vase, decorated in white relief with a figure wearing a Phrygian cap, impressed mark, large firing cracks to one side, mid-19thC, 9½in (24cm) high.
£400–450 *SK*

The damage to *item II* proved great enough to result in a considerable difference in the prices these vases achieved at auction. *Item I* was in excellent condition and therefore the price realised was far in excess of its estimate. *SK*

A Dutch Delft blue and white four-piece garniture, comprising a pair of octagonal baluster-form vases and covers, and a pair of beakers, each moulded on the front with a cartouche with a bird perched on a flowering branch above a basket of flowers, damaged and repaired, c1775, largest 14in (35.5cm) high.
£2,700–3,000 *S(NY)*

A pair of blue and white vases and covers, painted with river landscapes and figure panels within raised scroll borders, with foliate modelled handles, late 19thC, 13¾in (35cm) high.
£200–220 *P(E)*

A pair of Wedgwood rosso antico pot pourri vases and covers, each sprigged in black with stiff leaves interspersed with flowers above a similarly decorated foot, the covers pierced with holes, early 19thC, 7in (17.5cm) high.
£1,300–1,500 *Bon*

Rosso antico is a form of redware, ranging in colour from light red to chocolate brown.

A Mason's mazarine blue and gilt spill vase, c1815, 5¼in (13.5cm) high.
£120–140 *VH*

Blue & White Transfer Ware

A Spode pierced basket, decorated in Tiber pattern, c1815, 8in (20.5cm) high.
£300–350 *GN*

This basket would have formed part of a dessert service and originally would have come with a stand.

A Joshua Heath transfer-printed earthenware plate, depicting George Washington and the Arms of the United States, restored, c1780, 10in (25.5cm) diam.
£3,300–3,700 *SLN*

Joshua Heath was a Staffordshire potter who worked between c1770–1800.

A Swansea Pottery meat dish, 'Ladies of Llangollen', early 19thC, 21in (53.5cm) wide.
£850–950 *PF*

A Herculaneum pearlware meat dish, from the Indian Series, printed in blue with the Gate of a Mosque Built by Hafiz Ramut, within a broad band of vines and leaves, c1820, 20½in (52cm) wide.
£600–650 *DN*

A pearlware commemorative jubilee bowl, transfer-printed in blue with portraits and inscriptions, within a laurel leaf border, the exterior with a Willow pattern scene, c1809, 10in (25.5cm) diam.
£160–180 *SAS*

A Spode blue and white dessert comport, decorated with Lanje Lijsen pattern, c1820, 12in (30.5cm) diam.
£350–450 *GN*

A Staffordshire blue and white plate, with a view of Boston State House, Masschusetts, c1815, 18in (45.5cm) wide.
£400–450 *A&A*

A Don Pottery blue and white meat dish, decorated with a view of Corigliano, c1820, 20½in (52cm) wide.
£550–600 *TMA*

r. A Minton miniature plate, with blue and white transfer of De Gaunt Castle, c1830, 3in (7.5cm) diam.
£60–65 *OCH*

A blue and white transfer-printed bowl, with canted corners, early 19thC, 11½in (29cm) wide.
£230–260 *P(G)*

A blue and white coffee can and saucer, decorated with Bullfinch pattern, c1820, saucer 5½in (14cm) diam.
£200–220 *OCH*

A Rogers blue and white plate, depicting Boston State House, c1815, 6½in (16.5cm) diam.
£120–140 *Nor*

A Joseph Stubbs blue and white dish, decorated with a pineapple and fruit, made for the American market, c1820, 20½in (52cm) wide.
£675–750 *SCO*

A Spode blue and white Italian pattern cake stand, c1909, 6½in (16.5cm) diam.
£45–55 *TAC*

An earthenware blue and white footbath, with 2 leaf scroll-moulded handles, the interior printed in blue with flowers in a basket, the exterior with sprays of flowers and leaves, restored, c1830, 19¾in (50cm) wide.
£1,600–1,800 *DN*

A pearlware blue and white covered baluster jug, the rim printed in blue with exotic birds, scrolls and foliage, the lower body with a tower within a floral border, on a geometric floral decorated ground, 19thC, 7in (18cm) high.
£400–450 *GAK*

A blue and white transfer-printed floral mask jug, possibly Minton, c1820, 9in (23cm) high.
£230–260 *Nor*

A blue and white transfer-printed jug, c1920, 10½in (26.5cm) high.
£50–60 *Ber*

A Rogers blue and white miniature tureen, decorated in Minopteros pattern, c1820, 2in (5cm) wide.
£180–200 *AMH*

A pearlware blue and white dessert service, comprising 13 pieces, the rims pierced and moulded with leaf and scroll design, the centres printed in blue with rural landscapes, 19thC, dish 9½in (24cm) wide.
£900–1,000 *CAG*

A Spode blue and white sauce tureen and cover decorated in 'Castle' pattern, c1825, 9in (23cm) wide.
£250–275 *GN*

l. A set of 12 Wedgwood blue transfer-printed tiles, designed by Helen J. A. Miles, each titled with a month of the year, raised marks, c1877, each tile 6in (15cm) square.
£500–550 *SK*

Wemyss

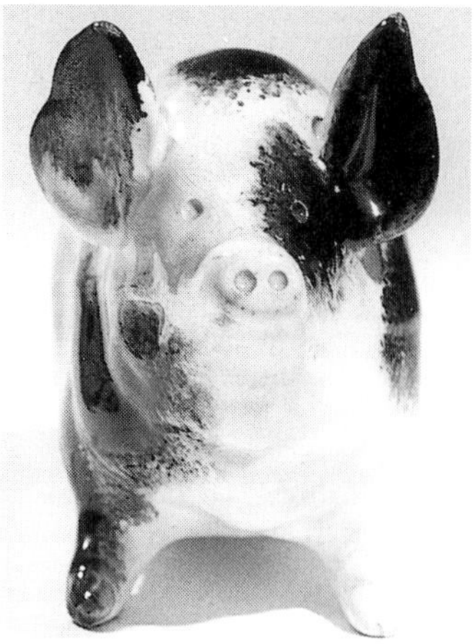

A Wemyss pig, with black and white sponged body, impressed mark, tail chipped, c1905, 6½in (16.5cm) long.
£270–300 *CAG*

A Wemyss biscuit barrel, painted with apples and green foliage, c1920, 5in (12.5cm) wide.
£150–200 *RdeR*

A Wemyss plate, painted with a beehive and green rim, c1895, 5½in (14cm) diam.
£200–250 *RdeR*

A Wemyss piglet money box, by Plichta, painted with a red flowering shamrock, c1930, 4in (10cm) high.
£200–300 *RdeR*

A Wemyss basket, painted with pelargoniums, c1900, 12in (30.5cm) wide.
£1,200–1,400 *RdeR*

A Wemyss biscuit barrel, painted with purple plums and green foliage, impressed marks and printed label for T. Goode & Co, c1920, 4¾in (12cm) diam.
£130–160 *AG*

A Wemyss plate, painted with sprigs of red flowering clover, c1895, 5½in (14cm) diam.
£150–200 *RdeR*

l. A Wemyss luggie, painted with pink pelargoniums, c1900, 8½in (22cm) high.
£1,200–1,300 *S*

A luggie is a beaker with an angled handle, produced between 1900–20 by Wemyss.

A Wemyss cat, by Plichta, painted with green shamrocks, c1930, 5¾in (14.5cm) high.
£50–60 *RdeR*

A Wemyss plate, painted with buttercups and green foliage, c1895, 5½in (14cm) diam.
£250–300 *RdeR*

A Wemyss plate, painted with brambles and autumn leaves, c1895, 5½in (14cm) diam.
£150–200 *RdeR*

A Wemyss inkwell, painted with geese and green foliage, c1900, 6in (15cm) wide.
£600–650 *RdeR*

A Wemyss jar and cover, painted with strawberries and leaves with green painted scalloped borders, impressed mark and blue printed mark of T. Goode & Co, London, c1920, 6¼in (16cm) high.
£180–200 *AG*

A Wemyss vase, painted with sweet peas in pink, mauve, yellow and green glazes, c1920, 8¼in (21cm) high.
£140–160 *P(EA)*

r. A Wemyss tankard, by Robert Heron & Son, painted with a bee skep, minor staining, c1900, 6in (15cm) high.
£400–450 *PFK*

A skep is a beehive made of straw.

A Wemyss inkwell and cover on an integral stand, painted with mauve sweetpeas with green and lemon detail, green script mark, c1910, 5in (12.5cm) diam.
£220–250 *GAK*

A Wemyss jar and cover, by Robert Heron & Son, painted with branches of purple damsons, within dark green scalloped borders, chip to base, c1920, 6¾in (17cm) high.
£200–220 *P(EA)*

A Wemyss Stuart flower pot, probably painted by J. Sharp, the flared sides with cabbage roses below a border of green spots, hair crack, c1900, 7in (18cm) high.
£275–300 *S(S)*

A Wemyss heart-shaped tray, designed by Karel Nekola, painted with a cockerell and a hen, c1900, 10in (25.5cm) long.
£450–550 *RdeR*

A Wemyss pin tray, inscribed 'Who Burnt the Table Cloth?', c1920, 5¼in (13.5cm) wide.
£75–100 *RdeR*

Majolica

The financial and decorative potential of the rich, coloured glazes of Victorian majolica (not to be confused with Italian *maiolica*) was spotted by Jeremy Cooper, an enterprising London dealer in the early 1980s. In 1982 he presented an impressive stock as a selling exhibition which acted as a catalyst and inspired wealthy American collectors to enter the market, forcing prices skywards. What is perhaps surprising is how blind many auctioneers and dealers have been ever since. Fine game tureens by Minton and George Jones have commanded thousands of pounds for years, but there are still catalogues in which the same objects are estimated to fetch just hundreds. A recent majolica auction in New York caused press excitement when prices zoomed above pre-sale estimates in a sale totalling $1.5m (£950,000). The sale contained just what the market wanted, and it acted as a new catalyst, attracting even more buyers.

The majolica pieces that are making the highest prices combine three factors: maker, quality and size. In Victorian times three factories dominated the world of majolica producing numerous pieces with high-quality modelling and careful glazing. Consequently there is plenty of superb Minton, Wedgwood and George Jones around to satisfy the gaping market (the New York sale was restricted almost entirely to these three). Some smaller makers produced competent work – Royal Worcester and Copeland, for example – but not in sufficient quantity to keep today's collectors supplied. Other firms made a great deal of less expensive majolica, copying established designs and colours, but without such attention to detail. Majolica from France, Germany and the United States has its followers, but does not stand comparison with even the simplest products of Minton and George Jones.

Shown in this section is a George Jones game tureen with a woodcock, chicks and rabbits. While the artistic merits of a tureen depicting the cuddly animals its Victorian owners were about to eat are debatable, there is no denying it is a fine piece of ceramic craftsmanship. Note especially the size of this tureen; an almost identical, smaller version is worth only one third as much. Similar large majolica tureens made in Germany are worth even less. Popular models were copied, and some of Minton's famous teapots occur in cheaper versions by unknown Staffordshire makers. In a photograph such pieces may all look the same, so do check measurements and look for makers' marks, fine modelling and the careful control of the glaze. Watch out too for modern fakes made both in England and in the Far East.

John Sandon

A Wedgwood majolica Argenta ware salad comport, decorated with a fork and spoon, framed panels with vegetables, cruet bottles surrounding the base, slight rim crack, impressed mark, c1877, 10¼in (26cm) diam.
£600–650 *SK*

A George Jones majolica teacup and saucer, decorated with raised floral and foliate decoration, the handle in the form of a lily, on turquoise blue ground with pink interior, c1875, saucer 4in (10cm) wide.
£380–420 *AG*

A George Jones majolica game pie dish, cover and liner, the cover with a woodcock and her 7 yellow chicks sitting amidst fern leaves, the sides moulded with rabbits and foliage on a dark blue ground, the handles formed as entwined oak branches, restored rim, other minor restoration, marked '3770' in black, moulded registration mark for 27th December 1873, 14¼in (36cm) wide.
£13,500–15,000 *WW*

George Jones game pie dishes in good condition have been achieving extremely high prices in the salerooms recently.

A pair of Minton majolica table salts, in the form of a young boy and girl each holding an oval basket, decorated in coloured enamels, some damage, impressed marks for 1863, 7¾in (19.5cm) high.
£650–700 *DN*

A pair of Minton majolica figures in the form of a hawker and fish wife, decorated in blue, purple, brown and green, repaired, impressed marks, c1865, largest 13¾in (35cm) high.
£900–1,000 *P*

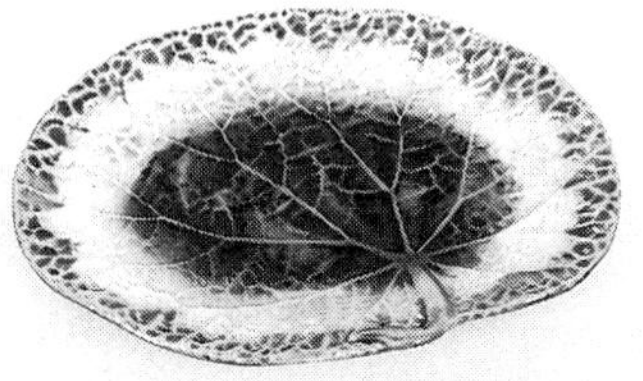

A majolica dish, in the form of a leaf, decorated in shades of green, brown and cream, c1880, 10½in (26.5cm) long.
£55–65 *Ber*

A Minton majolica vase, in the form of a putto with a scythe, seated on a corn-moulded cornucopia, a basket of grapes at his side, decorated in green and yellow, on a blue bordered mound base, shape No. 1197, some restoration, impressed marks for 1868, 11¾in (30cm) high.
£2,000–2,200 *DN*

A Royal Worcester majolica centrepiece, modelled by James Hadley, in the form of a merman and bulrushes supporting a shell, decorated in coloured enamels, the concave-sided triform base with a coral band, minor damage, c1870, 7¾in (19.5cm) high.
£1,400–1,600 *DN*

A pair of Minton majolica figural fruit dishes, each in the form of a cherub carrying a blue glazed shell and swathed in vine leaves and wheat, the shells with acanthus leaves, on mottled green bases, c1865, 11in (28cm) high.
£4,500–5,000 *AH*

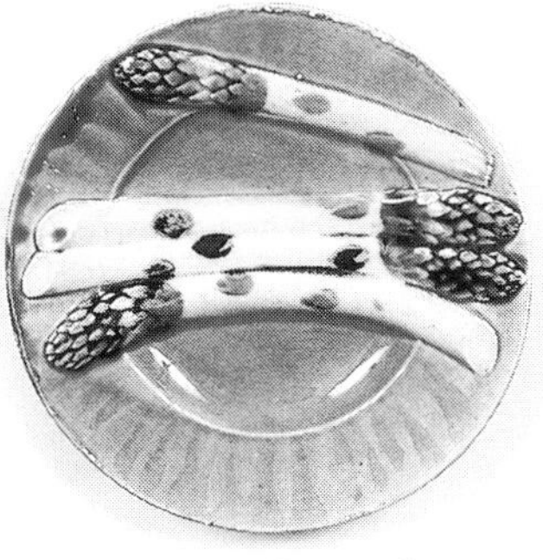

A set of 6 Lunéville majolica asparagus plates, decorated with green and white on a blue ground, c1880, 9in (23cm) diam.
£330–360 *MLL*

A pair of Minton majolica table ornaments, in the form of a boy and girl each leaning on a basket-moulded grape hod, decorated in coloured enamels, on vine-moulded mound base, some damage, c1870, 9½in (24cm) high.
£800–900 *DN*

A Portuguese majolica charger, moulded and decorated in colours with motifs of fish and eels, late 19thC, 14½in (37cm) diam.
£500–550 *GAK*

A Minton majolica jardinière, applied with garlands of fruit, pink ribbons and lions' masks, on a low pedestal supported by 3 figures of men, on a stand, impressed marks and date code for 1871, 20in (50.5cm) high.
£3,200–3,500 *Bea(E)*

A Minton majolica garden seat, moulded with florets and strapwork, set on lug feet, the top pierced with a medallion, glazed in typical colours on a turquoise ground, c1868, 17½in (44.5cm) high.
£1,500–1,800 *S*

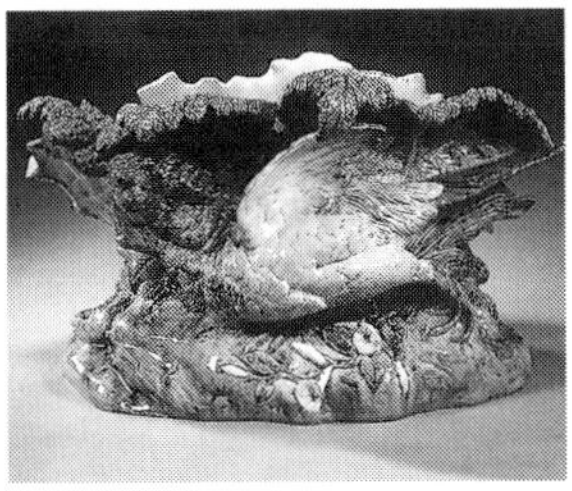

r. A Minton majolica jardinière, moulded with a pheasant on a rocky base, the flattened reverse moulded with a large thistle, indistinct date code and painted '712', c1876, 10½in (27cm) high.
£8,000–9,000 *S*

A Minton majolica jardinière, with ribbon-tied laurel wreaths applied to the sides, a moulded band of Vitruvian scrolls above Greek keys to the shoulder, the exterior turquoise-glazed with details in yellow ochre, green, dark blue, pink and rose, the interior pink, some restoration to base, c1870, 14¾in (37.5cm) high.
£950–1,100 *WW*

A Minton majolica tower jug, with vine loop handle, moulded in relief with figures dancing, within line moulded bands, cover missing, shape No. 1231, impressed marks for 1876, 9½in (24cm) high.
£250–300 *DN*

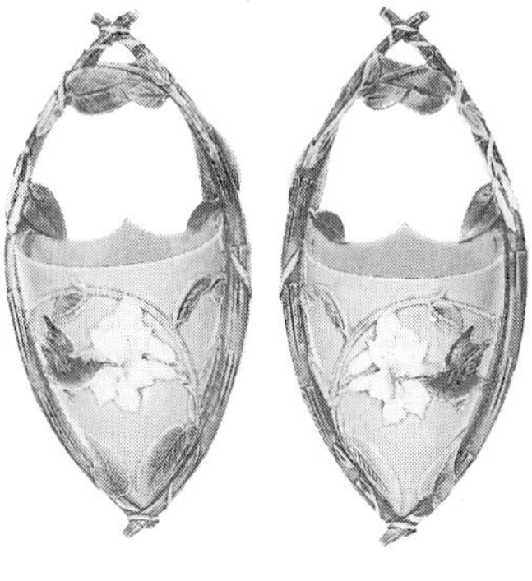

A pair of George Jones majolica wall pockets, each moulded in relief with a humming bird feeding from a white convovulus flower within a bamboo frame, on a turquoise ground, interior glazed in puce, slight damage, impressed 'GJ' monogram, c1875, 12¼in (30cm) long.
£3,700–4,000 *P*

A Sarreguemines cachepot, c1875, 8in (20.5cm) diam.
£140–160 *MLL*

An S. Fielding & Co majolica teapot and cover, decorated in yellow and blue on a brown ground, c1880, 9in (23cm) high.
£400–500 *BRT*

A Lonitz majolica tureen, decorated in shades of green, blue, yellow and red, impressed mark, No. 1461, German, c1878, 15in (38cm) wide.
£1,200–1,450 *BRT*

A majolica two-handled vase and cover, moulded with a band of flowerhead roundels within stiff-leaf and laurel swag bands, decorated in bright colours, some damage, c1860, 23½in (59.5cm) high.
£900–1,100 *DN*

An Orchies majolica cachepot, decorated with pink orchids on a green ground, c1900, 8in (20.5cm) diam.
£115–125 *MLL*

A majolica teapot, in the form of a fish, decorated in shades of green, brown and yellow, c1885, 11in (28cm) wide.
£500–600 *BRT*

A French majolica tureen and lid, decorated in shades of green and yellow, unmarked, c1900, 13in (33cm) wide.
£180–200 *MLL*

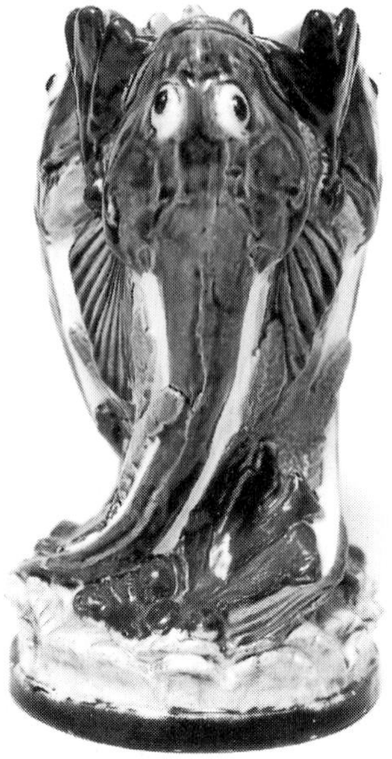

A Thomas Sargeant majolica fish vase, decorated in shades of green and blue, French, c1870, 6¾in (17cm) high.
£400–500 *BRT*

An English majolica coffee pot, c1880, 7¼in (18.5cm) high.
£250–300 *BRT*

Eight Sarreguemines plates, decorated with grapes, c1880, 8in (20.5cm) diam.
£360–400 *MLL*

A Lonitz majolica plant holder, with 2 quail in front of a tree, c1878, 12in (30.5cm) high.
£1,500–1,800 *BRT*

A Minton majolica monkey teapot, the tail forming the handle, impressed marks and numerals, slight damage, year cypher for 1877, 7in (18cm) high.
£2,000–2,200 *Hal*

A Minton majolica crab dish and cover, with seaweed handle, c1860, 15¾in (40cm) diam.
£7,000–8,000 *S*

A George Jones majolica game pie tureen and cover, cover restored, impressed 'GJ' monogram, c1875, 14in (35.5cm) long.
£11,000–12,000 *S*

A George Jones majolica afternoon tea service, decorated with the Apple Blossom pattern, 1873, tray 21¼in (51.5cm) wide.
£3,000–3,500 *AG*

A George Jones majolica sardine dish and stand, with moulded basketweave decoration, 19thC, 9in (23cm) long.
£2,600–3,000 *Mit*

A Minton game pie tureen and cover, impressed 'Minton', c1869, 17in (43cm) long.
£6,500–7,000 *S*

A Staffordshire pottery model of a water buffalo, restored, c1760, 8in (20.5cm) wide.
£8,500–9,500 *JHo*

A Staffordshire agateware cow creamer and calf, stopper renewed, c1775, 7½in (19cm) wide.
£1,500–1,750 *JHo*

A Staffordshire military group, early 19thC, 10¼in (26cm) wide.
£3,000–3,300 *JHo*

A Staffordshire pearlware model of a deer, with bocage, c1820, 6in (15cm) high.
£300–350 *OCH*

A Staffordshire cow creamer and cover, with a milkmaid, c1830, 6in (15cm) high.
£380–420 *JO*

A Staffordshire cow creamer and cover, c1835, 5in (12.5cm) high.
£550–600 *JO*

A Staffordshire model of a poodle, on an oval base decorated with sea shells, c1840, 3½in (9cm) high.
£330–360 *JO*

A Staffordshire group, possibly portraying the Prince of Wales, c1850, 9½in (24cm) high.
£400–450 *RWB*

A Staffordshire treacle-glazed lion, on an oval base, c1860, 14in (35.5cm) wide.
£800–900 *ANT*

A pair of Staffordshire models of seated spaniels, each with russet markings and gilt collars, mid-19thC, 8in (20.5cm) high.
£180–200 *AAV*

A pair of Staffordshire models of dogs, each picked out in brown on a white ground, restoration to one foot, c1885, 14in (35.5cm) wide.
£250–300 *SER*

A Le Croisic faïence gadrooned footed dish, decorated with a winged figure, 18thC, 11½in (29cm) diam.
£280–320 *BIG*

A Mocha ware pearlware bowl, decorated with Earth Worm pattern, the rim with a band of green, c1775, 7½in (19cm) diam.
£400–450 *A&A*

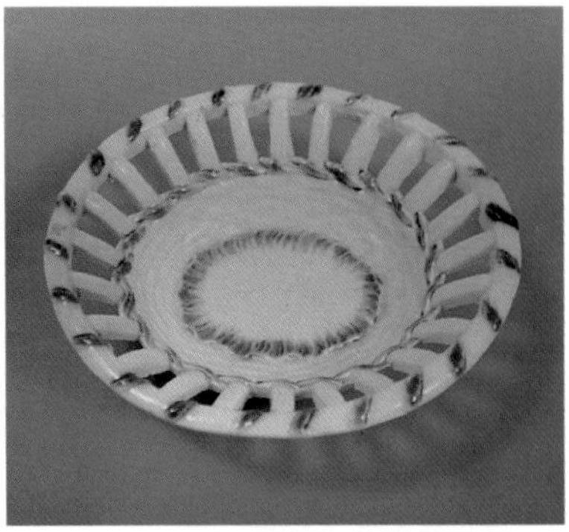

A miniature pearlware sweetmeat basket, with flared sides, probably by Turner, c1790, 3½in (9cm) diam.
£100–120 *OCH*

A Staffordshire butter dish, decorated in brown and green, the cover with a cow finial, 18thC, 6½in (16.5cm) diam.
£3,000–3,500 *JHo*

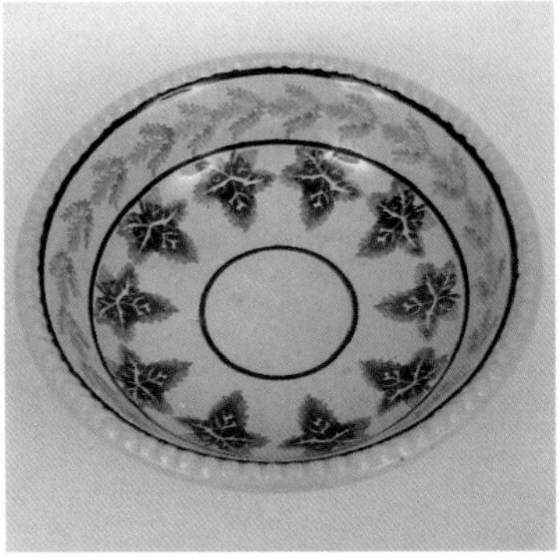

A spongeware dish, decorated with leaves in green and orange, on a cream ground, c1840, 8½in (21.5cm) diam.
£100–120 *Ber*

An ironstone punchbowl, possibly Mason's, c1845, 8in (20.5cm) high.
£350–400 *VH*

A pottery commemorative bowl, by David Lockhart & Sons, Glasgow, entitled 'Shamrock', and dated '1899', 3½in (9cm) diam.
£150–200 *BRT*

A Wemyss Audley bowl, painted with dragonflies, c1895, 7in (18cm) diam.
£1,200–1,400 *RdeR*

A Wemyss Earlshall Lincoln jardinière, of waisted bell form, early 20thC, 10½in (26.5cm) high.
£1,500–1,800 *S*

A spongeware serving dish, with central blue motif and floral border, on a cream ground, c1860, 10½in (26.5cm) diam.
£80–100 *RYA*

A Quimper egg stand, with 6 egg cups, marked, c1920, 7in (18cm) wide.
£270–300 *VH*

A Wemyss tub flower pot, painted with purple irises, c1895, 12in (30.5cm) wide.
£1,500–1,800 *RdeR*

A Dutch Delft figural gin bottle, restored, 18thC, 14¾in (37.5cm) high.
£5,200–5,800 *S(Am)*

A pair of Staffordshire figures, entitled 'Age', c1810, 6in (15cm) high.
£350–400 *JO*

A pair of Staffordshire figures, restored, c1820, 9in (23cm) high.
£350–400 *SER*

A Staffordshire figure, entitled 'The Rape of Lucretia', c1820, 13in (33cm) long.
£1,500–1,650 *JHo*

A Staffordshire figure, c1825, 8in (20.5cm) high.
£400–450 *JRe*

A Staffordshire group, damaged, c1825, 6½in (16.5cm) high.
£350–400 *DAN*

A pair of Staffordshire figures of gardeners, c1820, 6in (15cm) high.
£400–450 *TVM*

A Staffordshire group, entitled 'Tee Total', c1830, 8½in (21.5cm) high.
£3,000–3,300 *JHo*

A Staffordshire group, 'The Rural Harvest', c1880, 13in (33cm) high.
£80–100 *JO*

A Staffordshire figure, c1855, 16in (41cm) high.
£250–280 *RWB*

A Royal Dux Bohemia group, c1900, 17½in (44.5cm) high.
£1,000–1,200 *HCC*

l. A Royal Dux pottery figure of a fisherman carrying nets, applied pink triangle mark, impressed numerals '1371', c1900, 21in (53.5cm) high.
£600–650 *HCC*

A Bristol delft plate, decorated with a peacock, c1730, 7¾in (20cm) diam.
£1,200–1,350 *JHo*

An English delft plate, decorated with an Oriental landscape, mid-18thC, 11¾in (30cm) diam.
£600–700 *BIG*

A pair of Dutch Delft plates, decorated with geometric and floral pattern, c1740, 12in (30.5cm) diam.
£550–675 *ANT*

A Dutch Delft polychrome dish, 18thC, 13¾in (35cm) diam.
£400–450 *OCH*

An English slipware dish, with a pie crust rim, damaged and repaired, 18thC, 13½in (34cm) diam.
£4,500–5,000 *P*

A Mason's dessert plate, with transfer-printed decoration, c1813, 8in (20.5cm) diam.
£100–110 *JP*

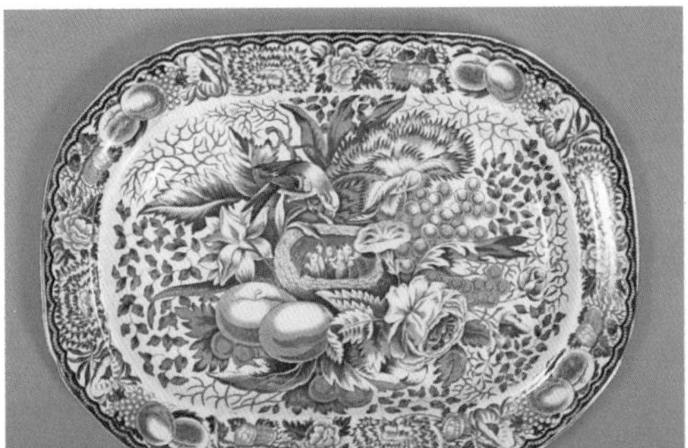

A blue and white platter, decorated with Bird's Nest pattern, c1820, 20in (51cm) wide.
£875–975 *OCH*

An Austrian dish, by Ernst Wahliss, in the form of a leaf with nuts and biscuits on a green ground, c1900, 12½in (32cm) wide.
£300–360 *BRT*

A set of 6 Longchamps asparagus plates, c1880, 11in (28cm) diam.
£350–400 *MLL*

A Wemyss plate, painted with carnations, with a green line border, c1895, 5½in (14cm) diam.
£250–275 *RdeR*

An Italian maiolica charger, with a central figure on horseback, 19thC, 25in (63.5cm) diam.
£340–380 *SWO*

A Staffordshire creamware teapot, of Whieldon type, cover restored, c1760, 3½in (8cm) high.
£400–450 *IW*

A Staffordshire teapot, decorated with an Oriental pattern, c1765, 6in (15cm) high.
£6,000–6,500 *JHo*

A Staffordshire teapot, impressed 'Wedgwood', c1770, 6¼in (16cm) high.
£2,700–3,000 *JHo*

A Sunderland earthenware tea cup and saucer, with lustre borders, c1880, cup 2¾in (7cm) high.
£45–50 *Ber*

A Staffordshire teapot and sugar bowl, by Enoch Wood & Sons, depicting Wadsworth Towers, c1818, teapot 8½in (21.5cm) high.
£750–850 *A&A*

A Staffordshire earthenware coffee pot and cover, with floral decoration on a buff ground, c1755, 8in (20.5cm) high.
£6,000–7,000 *S(NY)*

A Staffordshire salt-glazed cup, c1735, 2¾in (7cm) high.
£3,300–3,600 *JHo*

A child's blue printed pottery teaset, comprising 17 pieces, c1840, 4½in (11.5cm) high.
£180–200 *TMA*

A Mason's Ironstone jug, decorated with Table and Flowerpots pattern, c1815, 6¾in (17cm) high.
£200–225 *VH*

A Staffordshire agateware tea canister, c1755, 5in (12.5cm) high.
£4,500–5,000 *JHo*

A copper lustre beaker, c1830, 4½in (11.5cm) high.
£40–50 *SER*

A lustre goblet, c1840, 4½in (11.5cm) high.
£50–55 *BRU*

A blue and white transfer-printed loving cup, c1830, 5in (12.5cm) high.
£260–300 *Nor*

A Staffordshire Toby jug, c1885, 10½in (26.5cm) high.
£120–140 *JO*

A Victorian stoneware vase, 10¼in (26cm) high.
£165–185 *HEI*

An English delft blue and white flower brick, c1760, 9¼in (23.5cm) wide.
£900–1,000 *JHo*

A Wemyss vase, early 20thC, 21in (53.5cm) high.
£3,500–4,000 *S*

A Wemyss vase, c1920, 13in (33cm) high.
£350–400 *MSW*

A garniture of 5 Dutch Delft vases, with angel knops, damaged and repaired, mid-18thC, largest 19½in (49.5cm) high.
£7,000–8,000 *S*

A pair of Mason's Ironstone vases, impressed marks, one repaired, c1815, 10in (25.5cm) high.
£1,100–1,200 *VH*

A pair of Royal Doulton stoneware three-handled vases, commemorating the Coronation of 1911, 6½in (16.5cm) high.
£90–100 *SAS*

A Quimper vase, depicting a view of Quimper, marked, c1895, 20in (51cm) high.
£900–1,000 *VH*

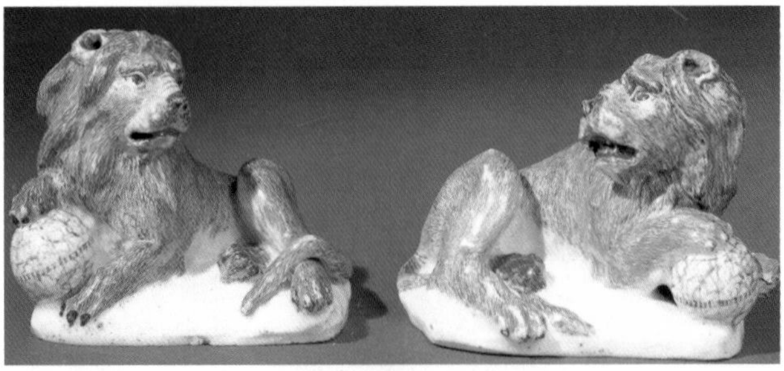

A pair of Bow models of lions, both recumbent with one paw resting on a colourful globe, c1755, 4in (10cm) wide.
£11,000–12,000 *P*

A pair of Derby models of recumbent sheep, restored, c1815, 4in (10cm) high.
£400–500 *SER*

A pair of Derby figures of 'The Ranelagh Dancers', both on rococo bases with tree stumps and leafy bocage, damaged, c1765, largest 12in (30.5cm) high.
£520–600 *TMA*

A Duesbury Derby figure of a goddess, late 18thC, 7¼in (18.5cm) high.
£230–270 *SER*

A Bloor Derby group, c1820, 9½in (24cm) high.
£1,000–1,200 *DAN*

A pair of Meissen figures of a gentleman gardener and a lady with a basket of flowers, 19thC, 14in (35.5cm) high.
£2,250–2,500 *Mit*

A pair of Sitzendorf figures, c1900, 6¼in (16cm) high.
£170–200 *P(B)*

A Meissen figure of a map seller, c1750, 7in (18cm) high.
£2,800–3,200 *BHa*

A pair of French porcelain figures of a boy and a girl, late 19thC, 9½in (24cm) high.
£280–320 *MiA*

A Meissen group of women, children and Cupid, restored, 19thC, 11in (28cm) high.
£1,000–1,200 *SWO*

A pair of Royal Worcester figures of Strephon and Phyllis, c1920, largest 6in (15cm) high.
£750–800 *TH*

A Wedgwood Fairyland lustre bowl, c1920, 8in (20.5cm) diam.
£2,800–3,200 *P*

A French porcelain box and cover, painted with landscapes, the cover with a mythological scene, late 19thC, 15¾in (40cm) wide.
£5,000–6,000 *DORO*

A Sèvres *bleu lapis* shaped jardinière, with all-over gilt decoration, date letter for 1763, 12¼in (31cm) wide.
£7,800–8,500 *S(NY)*

A Derby dish, painted in underglaze blue and coloured enamels in Imari style, with Chinese style six-character mark, c1780, 9in (23cm) wide.
£200–250 *ALB*

A Caughley kidney-shaped dish, decorated in underglaze blue with Weir pattern of a figure and pavilions in a landscape, c1785, 10½in (26.5cm) wide.
£200–250 *AAV*

An H. & R. Daniel centrepiece, from a dessert service, the claret border with flowers and gilt decoration, pattern No. 8777, c1835, 12in (30.5cm) wide.
£120–135 *BSA*

A Royal Worcester stemmed dish, signed 'H. Stinton', c1919, 7in (18cm) high.
£1,800–2,000 *TH*

A pair of Chelsea bough pots, c1753, 7¼in (18.5cm) diam.
£1,500–1,750 *S*

A Royal Worcester jardinière, by W. Powell, signed, c1907, 13½in (34cm) high.
£5,750–6,500 *S*

A Meissen sugar box and cover, with rose knop finial, crossed swords mark in underglaze blue, c1745, 3¾in (9.5cm) high.
£1,200–1,400 *S*

A Liverpool porcelain coffee pot and cover, by Richard Chaffers & Co, with Oriental decoration, c1760, 9½in (24cm) high.
£1,500–1,750 *Hal*

A Lowestoft coffee pot, c1780, 10½in (26.5cm) high.
£2,400–2,800 *DN*

A Worcester porcelain teapot and domed cover, with flowerhead finial, decorated with an Oriental scene, c1765, 6in (15cm) high.
£460–500 *CAG*

A Meissen flower-moulded part-coffee service, comprising 12 pieces, c1840.
£2,000–2,200 *S*

A Russian porcelain tea service, comprising 19 pieces, probably Imperial Porcelain Factory, 19thC, teapot 10¼in (26cm) high.
£6,500–7,500 *S*

A Lowestoft part tea service, comprising 19 pieces, decorated with a Curtis type pattern, some damage, c1790.
£2,500–3,000 *Bon*

A Worcester porcelain teapot, repaired, c1770, 6¾in (17cm) high.
£400–500 *CAG*

A Royal Worcester miniature coffee pot, signed by Roberts, with black mark, c1950, 5in (12.5cm) high.
£320–350 *DKH*

A Worcester fluted tea service, comprising 34 pieces, decorated with the Jabberwocky pattern, the teapot with double interlaced handle, some damage, c1770, tray 7¼in (18.5cm) wide.
£7,000–8,000 *P*

A Coalport cup and saucer, c1805, saucer 5in (12.5cm) diam.
£230–260 *AMH*

A Meissen teabowl and saucer, each painted in *famille verte* style, c1735, cup 2in (5cm) high.
£2,750–3,000 *S*

A Sèvres gilt-decorated cup and saucer, painted by Charles Buteux, with central medallion, c1769, cup 2⅜in (6cm) high.
£1,500–1,750 *S*

A Worcester teabowl and saucer, with workman's marks, c1756, 2in (5cm) high.
£1,000–1,250 *DN*

A set of 12 Rozenburg eggshell porcelain octagonal-shaped cups and saucers, partly painted by Sam Schellink, with birds and flowers on a white ground, marked, c1914, cups 2¼in (6cm) high.
£8,000–9,000 *S(Am)*

A Royal Worcester miniature cup and saucer, c1910, cup 1¾in (4.5cm) high.
£200–250 *DKH*

A Worcester coffee cup and saucer, decorated with Pu-Tai pattern, depicting 3 Oriental figures in an orange border, first period, c1765, cup 2½in (6.5cm) high.
£600–650 *DAN*

A Royal Worcester tea cup and saucer, with gilt and beaded borders, painted with monogram initials within a wreath of thistles, finches and a bocage of wild flowers, c1860, cup 3½in (9cm) high.
£115–130 *E*

A Royal Worcester miniature cup and saucer, decorated with grapes and peaches, with gilt borders and handle, by Roberts, with black mark, c1950, saucer 3¼in (8.5cm) diam.
£220–250 *DKH*

A pair of Ansbach soup plates, each painted with a central flowerspray, heightened with gilding, slight damage, c1767, 10in (26.5cm) diam.
£4,800–5,200 *S*

A Coalport cabinet plate, by Thomas Baxter, wear to gilding, signed and dated '1808', 9in (23cm) diam.
£3,500–3,800 *P*

A Chelsea Warren Hastings type plate, the border with rococo panels edged with gold, with lobed rim, slight chip, c1754, 11in (28cm) diam.
£2,000–2,250 *P*

A pair of Copeland blue ground cabinet plates, by J. Wallace, c1895, 9in (23cm) diam.
£2,200–2,500 *AMH*

An H. & R. Daniel comport, printed and painted with flowers on a green ground, c1835, 9in (23cm) diam.
£55–65 *BSA*

A Sèvres trembleuse saucer, c1780, 6½in (16.5cm) diam.
£130–150 *ALB*

A Swansea plate, marked, c1814–18, 8½in (21.5cm) diam.
£1,300–1,500 *DN(H)*

A pair of Royal Worcester plates, with turquoise, pink, and 'jewelled' borders, c1886, 9¼in (23.5cm) diam.
£320–350 *SLL*

A Vienna porcelain tray, painted with Apollo on a gilt ground, signed 'Joh Ferstler', slight rubbing, c1811, 16½in (42cm) wide.
£5,000–6,000 *DORO*

A set of 17 Coalport dinner plates, painted in coloured enamels on a pale turquoise ground, c1820, 10¼in (26cm) diam.
£2,000–2,200 *DN*

A Coalport part dessert service, comprising 19 pieces, by Jabey Aston, painted with flowers on a pale grey ground, within a gilt border and foliate moulded rim, gilt pattern No. 3/421, c1836.
£6,500–7,200 *S*

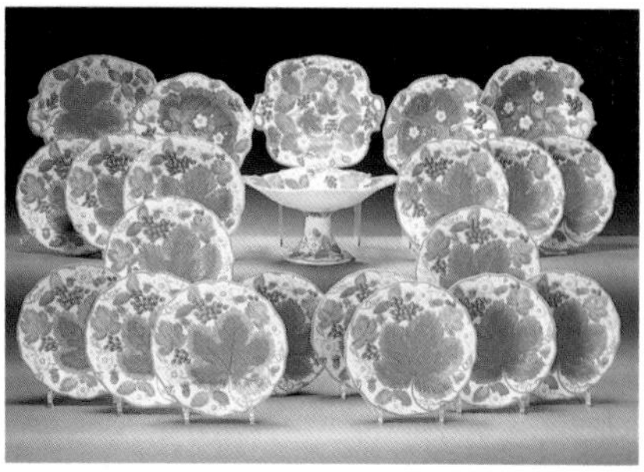

A T. J. & J. Mayer Staffordshire enamelled parian dessert service, comprising 22 pieces, each piece moulded with fruiting vine and strawberry plants, minor rim chips, printed factory mark, c1851–55.
£3,800–4,200 *S*

A Royal Doulton part dessert service, comprising 10 pieces, painted with a spray of flowers, signed 'E.W.', c1904.
£460–520 *Bea(E)*

A Bloor Derby dinner service, comprising 74 pieces, painted with flowers within gadrooned borders, some damage, c1830.
£4,000–4,500 *DN*

A Derby Crown porcelain dessert service, comprising 16 pieces, painted with Japan floral pattern and segment borders in Imari colours, with gilt finish, impressed and printed marks, c1880.
£1,500–1,750 *RBB*

A Meissen part dinner, tea and dessert service, comprising 135 pieces, slight damage, late 19thC.
£4,800–5,200 *S*

A Flight & Barr armorial part dessert service, comprising 13 pieces, painted in iron-red, blue, black and gold with the arms of Somerville, Bart, inscribed 'Crains Dieu Tant Que Tu Viveras', with gilt-edged rim, damaged, c1801.
£6,500–7,200 *S(NY)*

A Frankenthal part service, comprising 14 pieces, painted with flowersprays, scattered flowers and a purple scrollwork, against a gilt striped ground, c1775.
£9,000–10,000 *S*

A Royal Worcester jug, with gilt handle, c1903, 4½in (11.5cm) high.
£150–180 *QSA*

A Worcester mug, painted with Dalhousie pattern, c1775, 4½in (11.5cm) high.
£1,200–1,400 *AMH*

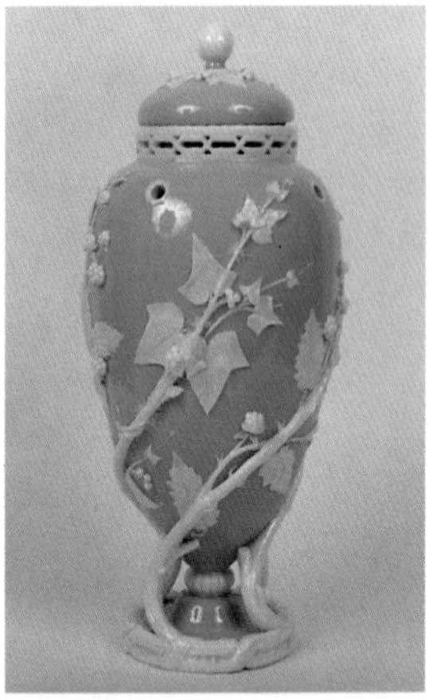

A Minton pot pourri vase, c1867, 12¼in (31cm) high.
£900–1,000 *AMH*

A Royal Worcester vase and cover, by George Owen, dated '1913', 8in (20cm) high.
£15,000–16,000 *P*

A Copeland vase and cover, painted by C. F. Hurten, with turquoise, gilt and 'jewelled' borders, c1895, 12in (30.5cm) high.
£1,800–2,000 *AMH*

A pair of French porcelain campana-shaped vases, with beaded rims, painted with Napoleonic campaign scenes and landscapes, late 19thC, 8¼in (21cm) high.
£900–1,000 *AH*

A pair of French porcelain urn vases, painted with romantic scenes, signed 'F. Bellangon', 19thC, 34½in (87.5cm) high.
£12,000–14,000 *M*

A pair of Coalport flower-encrusted vases, c1840, 14in (35.5cm) high.
£2,500–3,000 *BHa*

A Derby vase, signed 'Gregory', c1907, 10½in (26.5cm) high.
£1,700–2,000 *TH*

A pair of Minton *pâte-sur-pâte* vases, c1885, 14in (35.5cm) high.
£1,800–2,000 *Hal*

A pair of German vases and covers, damaged and repaired, 19thC, 22in (56cm) high.
£1,800–2,000 *Bon*

A pottery buffalo, painted with full harness, and cart, applied with phoenix and floret panels picked out in red, Tang Dynasty, 18in (45cm) long.
£7,000–8,000 *S*

A pair of *famille rose* figures of elephants, Jiaqing/Daoguang period, 22½in (57cm) high.
£24,000–26,000 *Bon*

A pair of *famille rose* and *café au lait* glazed bowls, c1740, 6¾in (17cm) diam.
£650–800 *GeW*

A pair of *fencai* yellow-ground bowls, on splayed foot rims, damaged and repaired, Yongzheng period, 4¾in (12cm) diam.
£11,000–12,000 *P*

A rose medallion shrimp dish, 19thC, 9½in (24cm) diam.
£500–600 *A&A*

A *sancai* censer, on 3 lions' paw feet, Tang Dynasty, 8½in (22cm) diam.
£3,500–4,000 *S*

A punchbowl and stand, 19thC, 15½in (39.5cm) diam.
£2,300–2,600 *Bon*

An enamelled figure of Buddha, wearing a black cuffed iron-red robe, decorated with areas of gilt foliate scroll-work, Qianlong/Jiaqing period, c1800, 6in (15cm) high.
£5,000–6,000 *P*

A Chinese export *famille rose* bowl, Qianlong period, 10¼in (26cm) diam.
£650–800 *GeW*

A gilt-ground bowl, painted with 9 dragons in blue enamel, iron-red and gilded, Guangxu seal mark and of the period, 4½in (11.5cm) diam.
£1,500–1,750 *S(Am)*

Two plates, decorated in underglaze blue with lotus sprays within floral scroll borders, c1500, largest 15½in (39.5cm) diam.
£4,600–5,200 *S(NY)*

A set of 6 *famille rose* plates, 3 cracked, Qianlong period, 9in (23cm) diam.
£1,500–1,700 *S*

A pair of Chinese export *famille verte* plates, depicting a phoenix and *kylin* amidst bamboo, late Kangxi period, 9in (23cm) diam.
£600–660 *ORI*

A Chinese Imari meat dish, Kangxi period, 15in (38cm) wide.
£1,000–1,200 *GeW*

A *famille verte* engraved dish, Kangxi period, 9¾in (25cm) diam.
£7,700–8,500 *S(NY)*

A pair of Chinese Imari chargers, early 18thC, 15in (38cm) diam.
£1,800–2,200 *GeW*

A pair of *famille rose* lotus-shaped dishes, c1760, 11½in (29cm) diam.
£2,000–2,500 *GeW*

A pair of *famille rose* plates, c1760, 9in (23cm) diam.
£500–600 *GeW*

A pair of *famille rose* plates, late 18thC, 10in (25.5cm) diam.
£650–750 *GeW*

A pair of Chinese export meat dishes, Qianlong period, 14½in (37cm) wide.
£1,250–1,450 *GeW*

A pair of garden seats, decorated with chrysanthemums, lotus and birds, one repaired, late 19thC, 18in (45.5cm) high.
£1,200–1,400 *PFK*

A Sancai pottery jar, Tang Dynasty, 8in (20.5cm) high.
£2,500–2,800 *S*

A Chinese provincial storage jar, Ming Dynasty, 6½in (16.5cm) high.
£150–180 *ORI*

A Transitional period jar, c1660, 18in (45.5cm) high.
£3,800–4,500 *GeW*

A Transitional period jar, cover restored, 17thC, 15in (38cm) high.
£5,750–6,500 *S*

A *famille rose* yellow-ground *deng*, Jiaqing period, 10¼in (26cm) high.
£3,500–4,000 *S*

A Yixing pottery enamelled jar, Qianlong period, 5in (12.5cm) high.
£450–500 *GeW*

A Chinese export lamp, early 20thC, 12in (30.5cm) high.
£800–900 *Wai*

A tureen and cover, with rabbits' head handles, the cover surmounted by a pomegranate knop, Qianlong period, 14in (35.5cm) wide.
£5,500–6,000 *S*

A Chinese export octagonal blue and white tureen and cover, with rabbits' head handles, c1780, 14in (35.5cm) wide.
£1,200–1,500 *GeW*

A *famille verte* vase, Kangxi period, 18in (45.5cm) high.
£4,600–5,000 *P*

A porcelain vase, decorated with scholars in a garden scene, Kangxi period, 17½in (44.5cm) high.
£1,300–1,450 *ORI*

A pair of vases, c1660, 15½in (39.5cm) high.
£4,500–5,500 *GeW*

A *meiping*, Yongzheng period, 8¼in (21cm) high.
£4,000–4,500 *S*

A pair of enamelled *fencai* bottle vases, Daoguang marks and of the period, 11¼in (28.5cm) high.
£6,000–7,000 *P*

A pair of *famille rose* temple vases, Qianlong mark and of the period, 10½in (26.5cm) high.
£20,000–22,000 *AAV*

A *famille rose* vase, Jiaqing period, 12½in (31.5cm) high.
£3,500–4,000 *S*

A *famille verte* vase, 19thC, 19in (48.5cm) high.
£5,300–5,800 *S(NY)*

A *famille rose* vase, of *hu* shape, Guangxu, Qianlong seal mark, 17½in (44.5cm) high.
£3,300–3,600 *Bon*

An Imperial dragon vase, Daoguang mark and of the period, 8in (20.5cm) high.
£2,500–3,000 *Wai*

A vase, with underglaze red dragon design on a pale celadon ground, 19thC, 7½in (19cm) high.
£200–220 *HUR*

A pair of porcelain *famille rose* baluster vases, with lotus-form handles, 19thC, 24¼in (61.5cm) high.
£13,500–15,000 *S(NY)*

A Satsuma pottery bowl, by Seikazan, signed, c1880, 9¾in (25cm) diam.
£3,000–3,500 *MCN*

A porcelain bowl, by Makuzu Kozano, Meiji period, 8in (20.5cm) diam.
£1,600–1,800 *P(C)*

A Satsuma earthenware cup, cover and saucer, marked, 19thC, saucer 7in (17.5cm) diam.
£1,800–2,200 *S(Am)*

A Satsuma earthenware figure of Hotei, c1860, 11½in (29cm) high.
£4,000–4,500 *MCN*

A Nabeshima saucer dish, c1820, 8in (20.5cm) diam.
£1,200–1,500 *Wai*

A Satsuma figure of Kannon, repaired, Meiji period, 30in (76cm) high.
£5,000–6,000 *P*

A pair of Imari armorial plates, c1740, 8¾in (22cm) diam.
£4,500–5,000 *MCN*

A pair of Imari bottle vases, c1700, 7in (18cm) high.
£2,500–3,000 *MCN*

A pair of Arita platters, c1880, 18in (45.5cm) diam.
£420–470 *BRU*

An Imari vase and cover, with a bud-shaped knop, damaged, 23½in (60cm) high.
£1,500–1,800 *P(B)*

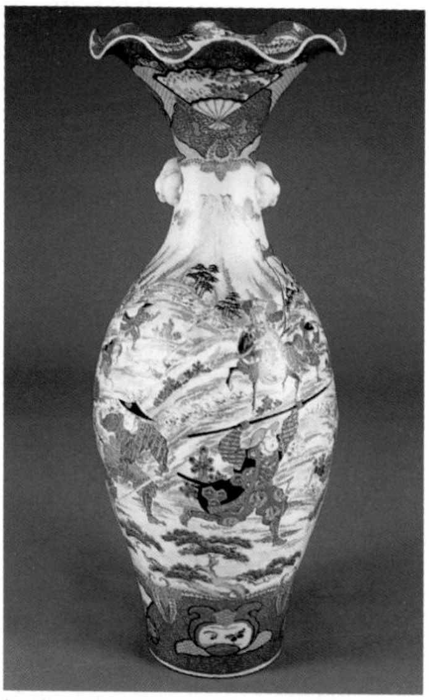

An Imari vase, with moulded rabbits' mask handles, late 19thC, 37in (94cm) high.
£850–1,000 *DN(H)*

A pair of Kutani vases, with candlestick lids, 19thC, 11¾in (30cm) high.
£300–360 *PFK*

A mallet-shaped glass decanter, with 2 neck rings, engraved 'Brandy', with lozenge stopper, c1780, 8¾in (22.5cm) high.
£400–450 *Som*

A set of 3 club-shaped blue glass decanters, with gilt labels, lozenge stoppers with gilt initials, in an iron and leather-covered stand, c1790, 7½in (19cm) high.
£1,300–1,500 *Som*

A glass decanter and stopper, c1820, 14in (35.5cm) high.
£200–250 *CB*

An amethyst glass flagon, with metal mount, cork and metal stopper, c1825, 7¾in (19.5cm) high.
£350–400 *Som*

A double-cased claret jug, with intaglio decoration, c1890, 12½in (32cm) high.
£4,000–4,500 *MJW*

A double-cased jug decanter, c1890, 10in (25.5cm) high.
£1,700–2,000 *MJW*

A silver-mounted intaglio-cut glass decanter and stopper, by Stevens & Williams, possibly cut by Joshua Hodgetts, spout inscribed 'JSC', c1896, 14½in (37cm) high.
£3,000–3,300 *S*

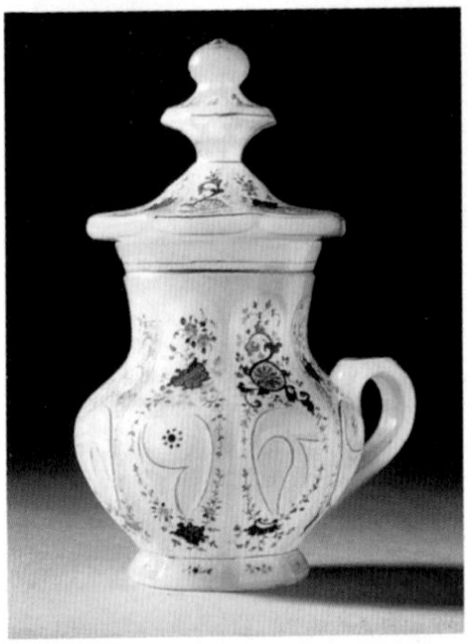

A Bohemian glass 'alabaster' jug and cover, made for the Turkish market, cut with facets and stylised leaves, with applied scroll handle and octagonal knop, c1850, 8¾in (22cm) high.
£2,000–2,200 *S*

A glass decanter, with gilt spiral decoration, early 20thC, 11½in (29cm) high.
£220–250 *JAS*

An ormolu-mounted glass scent bottle, mid-19thC, 7½in (19cm) high.
£400–475 *ANT*

Two silver-mounted scent bottles, c1860, largest 8¼in (21cm) long.
£600–650 each *Som*

A Stourbridge cameo scent bottle, c1885, 5in (12.5cm) high.
£1,200–1,400 *BHa*

A Bohemian overlaid glass comport, c1880, 8¼in (21cm) high.
£350–400 *P(B)*

A pair of silver-topped glass scent bottles, Birmingham 1896, 6½in (16.5cm) high.
£700–800 *THOM*

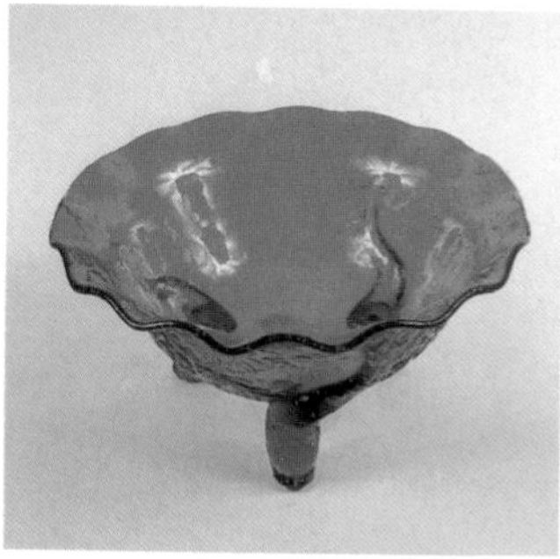

A Sowerby pressed glass bowl, moulded with flowers, on dolphin feet, c1890, 8½in (21cm) diam.
£100–120 *JHa*

A Moser style casket, enamelled with flowers and birds, gilded mounts, c1880, 8in (20.5cm) wide.
£800–900 *CB*

A turquoise opaline glass beaker, cold-enamelled and gilt with a floral band, c1860, 3¼in (8.5cm) high.
£100–120 *Som*

A Bohemian Biedermeier enamelled and cut-glass beaker, c1830, 4in (10cm) high.
£1,200–1,400 *S*

A Bohemian 'lithyalin' glass beaker, each side cut with a leaf above a lozenge boss, c1830, 4¾in (12cm) high.
£3,500–3,800 *S*

A green wine glass, with shoulder and base knops, the incised stem over a plain foot, c1760, 4½in (11.5cm) high.
£1,000–1,200 *JHa*

A pair of panel-cut green wine glasses, with conical bowls, blade and collar knop stems, c1820, 5in (12.5cm) high.
£130–150 *FD*

An electric blue wine glass, with slice-cut bowl and cut stem, c1850, 5¾in (14.5cm) high.
£100–120 *JHa*

A set of 6 blue cocktail glasses, with clear glass stems, by Webb, signed, 1930s, 6¼in (16cm) high.
£220–240 *MON*

A Bohemian glass ruby flashed goblet and scalloped cover, engraved with 4 vignettes depicting stags, late 19thC, 11½in (29cm) high.
£500–550 *WL*

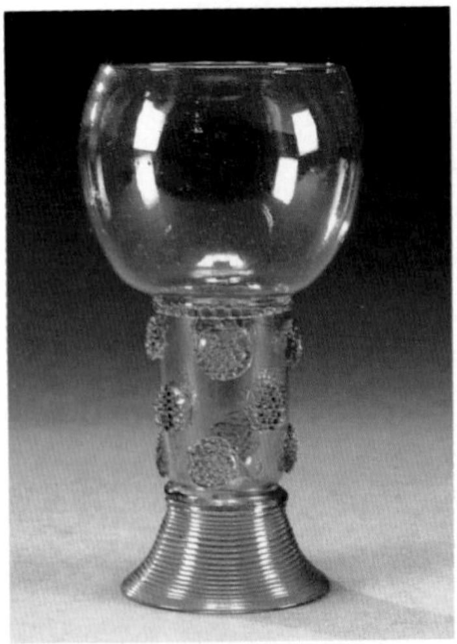

A green-tinted glass roemer, applied with 3 rows of raspberry prunts below an engrailed band, with a kick-in base and trailed everted foot, north German or Dutch, mid-17thC, 7in (18cm) high.
£1,800–2,200 *S*

A 'Nailsea' mug, with opaque white splashes and a band around the rim, c1810, 3¾in (9.5cm) high.
£400–450 *Som*

A 'Bacchus' close-packed millefiori paperweight, with star and open flower canes, within a row of white canes with green centres, some damage, mid-19thC, 3½in (9cm) diam.
£2,200–2,500 *S*

A Clichy millefiori paperweight, with muslin glass latticinio, 2 pink and green rose canes, c1850, 2¼in (5.5cm) diam.
£1,500–2,200 *STG*

A St Louis millefiori paperweight, with 5 flowerheads within a circle of canes, on an amber flashed flat base, mid-19thC, 2¾in (7cm) diam.
£850–950 *MLa*

A Clichy paperweight, the interlaced trefoils on turquoise ground, c1850, 3in (7.5cm) diam.
£2,800–3,200 *SWB*

A St Louis paperweight, with 'fruit' on latticinio, c1850, 2½in (6.5cm) diam.
£850–950 *SWB*

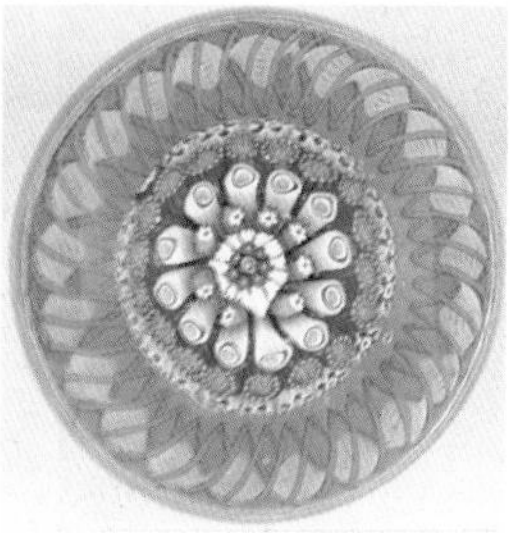

A St Louis concentric mushroom weight, with stardust centre cane within 4 rows of cogged and composite canes, dated '1848', 2¾in (7cm) diam.
£1,600–2,000 *P*

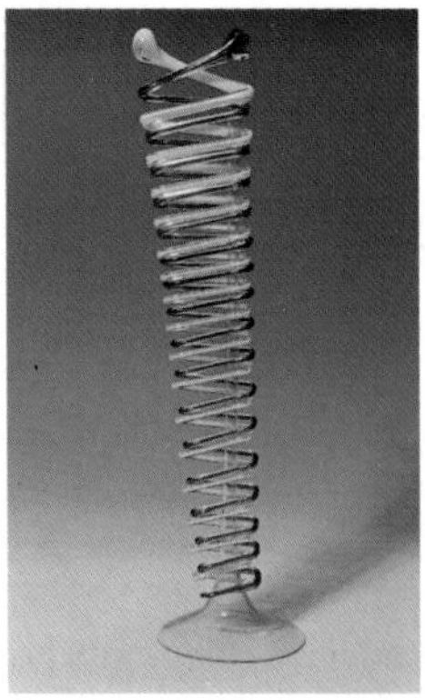

A 'Nailsea' glass ornament, c1860, 13in (33cm) high.
£160–180 *Som*

A pair of Etruscan style baluster glass vases, c1850, 15in (38cm) high.
£160–180 *FD*

A pair of Baccarat vases, c1868, 19½in (49.5cm) high.
£1,750–2,000 *S*

A Russian vase, dated '1869', 23¼in (59cm) high.
£3,500–3,800 *S*

A Lobmeyr Persian style glass vase, marked 'JLL', c1880, 17in (43cm) high.
£10,500–12,500 *S*

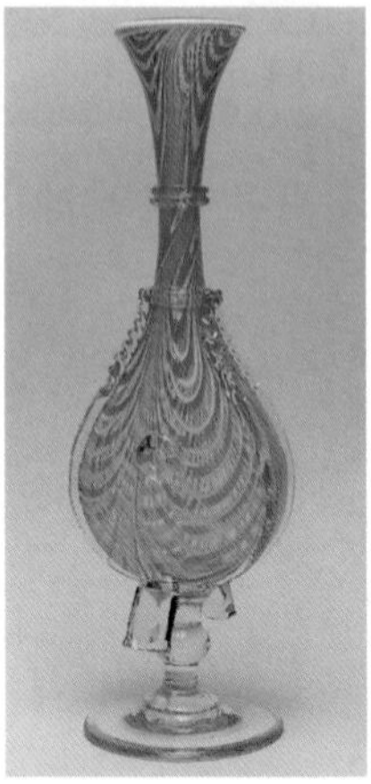

A flask-shaped glass vase, c1870, 13¾in (35cm) high.
£350–400 *MJW*

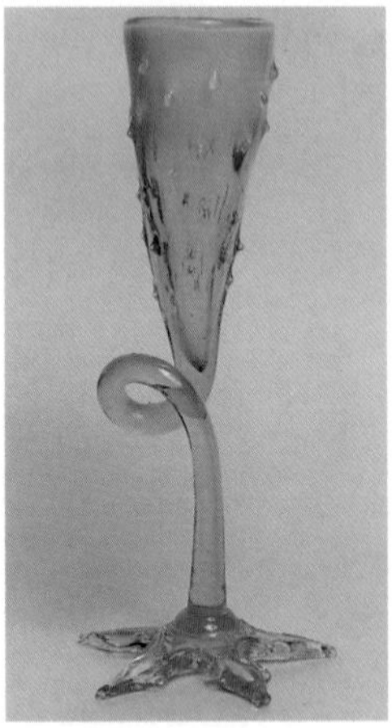

An opalescent glass vase, c1880, 8in (20.5cm) high.
£200–220 *CB*

A ruby glass vase, with acid-etched body, c1880, 6½in (16.5cm) diam.
£720–800 *MJW*

A Thomas Webb cameo glass vase, depicting Ceramia, signed 'G. Woodall', c1889, 6¼in (16cm) high.
£18,500–22,000 *P*

A pair of Bohemian glass tulip vases, c1880, 12in (30.5cm) high.
£300–350 *P(B)*

A blue-over-ivory cased glass vase, in the manner of Jules Barbe, c1890, 9¾in (25cm) high.
£250–300 *JHa*

A French glass lily vase, c1890, 23in (58.5cm) high.
£1,300–1,450 *ARE*

An American opaline glass vase, embossed with silver, c1900, 6¼in (16cm) high.
£75–85 *MON*

PORCELAIN

The last year has seen a great increase in demand for porcelain, with new buyers entering the market and existing collectors once again in buying mood. Sadly, this increase in demand has not been met by an increase in supply, and both trade and private buyers are complaining about the paucity of real quality.

As a result, prices have moved on, but not at a uniform rate. Items at the very top of the market have almost doubled in value in a year, whereas routine pieces with some damage or restoration have shown little if any appreciation. Thus collectors of 18th century English porcelain have seen the gulf between the very best and the everyday widening. With the re-discovery of the products of the obscure Isleworth Factory, whose pieces in recent years were often attributed to Derby or Lowestoft, these reassessed pieces have seen a significant rise in value and, along with the wares from Vauxhall, Limehouse and other early English factories, making them one of the strongest areas of the market.

In contrast, richly decorated English porcelain dating from 1770 to 1790 now seems undervalued, particularly set alongside price levels for comparable early 19th century pieces. It seems illogical that a decorative Worcester Imari pattern part tea service of c1770, as illustrated on page 314 can still be bought for less than a good quality modern reproduction.

The market for Belleek porcelain, produced in Fermanagh, Ireland since 1857, has also expanded in recent years, with enthusiastic European and American buyers competing for pieces. Consequently, prices have risen, particularly for large, decorative or unusual items.

As the year 2000 approaches, many pieces made at the beginning of this century seem incredibly good value. Tea and dinner services made between 1900 and 1920 by smaller factories such as Paragon are often of good quality, still useable, and less expensive than a modern alternative. This is a situation that I am sure will change shortly.

For many years now, we have been highlighting how undervalued most English porcelain figures of the 1770s and 1780s have been, and indeed still are. But perhaps this is an encouraging factor for the future of the porcelain market as pieces by household names such as Derby and Bow can be collected for relatively modest sums. A Worcester pine-cone pattern teabowl from 1770 will cost £40–50, whereas a contemporary picture or piece of furniture with a comparable pedigree would cost many thousands of pounds.

It is from such first modest purchases that many fine collections have grown, and as the Isleworth Factory has shown, there are still many rewarding discoveries to be made.

Mark Law

Animals

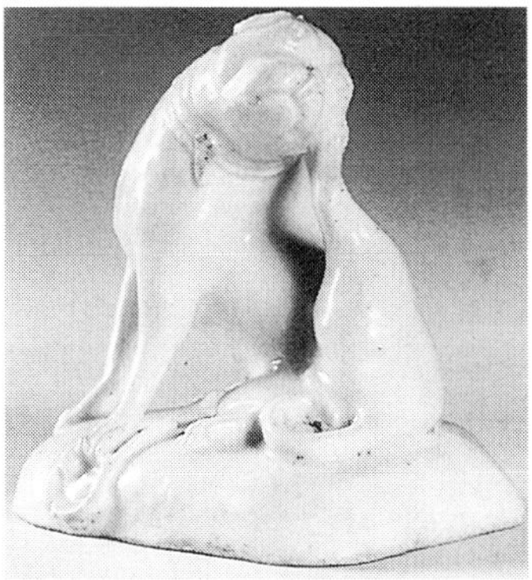

A Bow model of a pug dog, modelled in white, minor chipping, c1750, 4in (10.5cm) high.
£1,600–1,800 *P*

A Bow model of a brindle pug dog, resting on a yellow and brown cushion, wearing a collar with a flower, c1755, 4½in (11.5cm) wide.
£650–750 *Bea(E)*

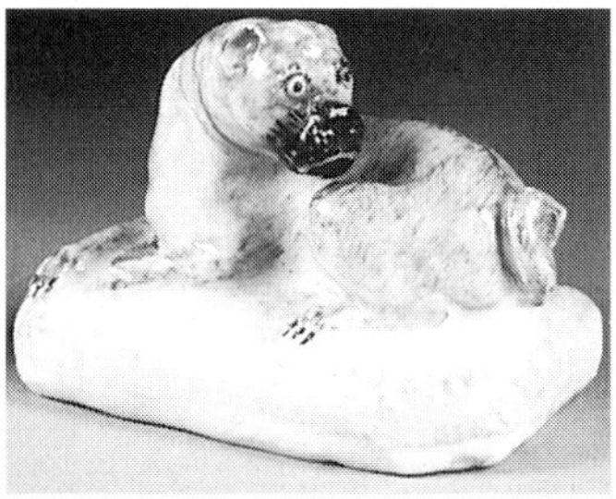

A Bow model of a reclining pug dog, naturalistically coloured in shades of brown, on a grassy base, c1758, 4½in (11.5cm) wide.
£2,300–2,500 *S*

A Derby model of a retriever, decorated in shades of beige and cream on a green base, tail restuck, c1800, 5in (12.5cm) long.
£700–800 *DAN*

A Derby model of a cow and calf, with bocage behind, tips of horns restored, c1770, 5½in (14cm) high.
£550–650 *DAN*

A porcelain model of a pug dog, after a Chinese export original, enamelled in beige with grey snout and white underbelly, minor chips, possibly Coalport, c1810, 9½in (24cm) high.
£3,700–4,200 *S*

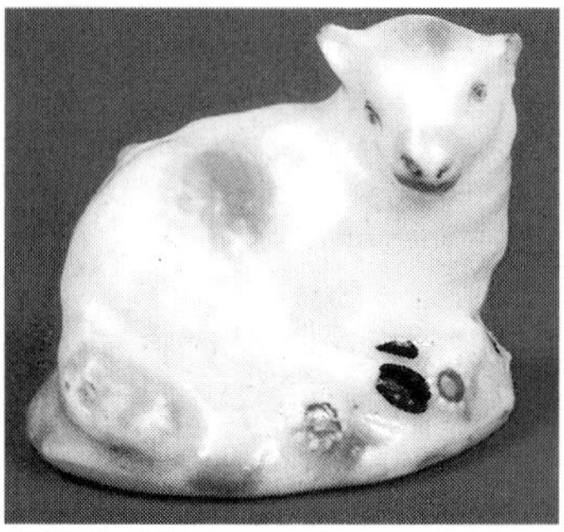

A Derby model of a recumbent sheep, on a green base, chip to one ear, c1815, 2in (5cm) long.
£230–270 *SER*

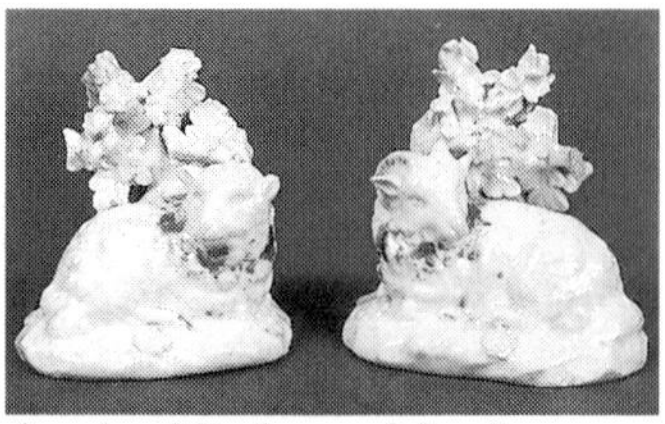

A pair of Derby models of recumbent sheep, white with traces of original gilt decoration, c1820, 2½in (6.5cm) high.
£350–400 *SER*

A pair of Meissen miniature models of a cockerel, with bright plumage, and a hen decorated in tones of brown and black, crossed swords marks in underglaze blue, c1745, cockerel 1¾in (4.5cm) high.
£1,100–1,300 *S*

A German porcelain model of a golden eagle, the plumage picked out in tones of yellow and brown, on a rocky base, broken and restored, crossed swords mark, mid-19thC, 22½in (57cm) high.
£2,000–2,200 *P*

A Lowestoft model of a pug dog, wearing a floral rosette to his collar, the base painted with puce scrolls, ear and tail restored, black firing impurities to body, c1770, 3½in (9cm) high.
£3,500–4,000 *S*

A Meissen model of a Bolognese terrier, after a model by J. J. Kändler, with brown fur, ear broken, crossed swords and incised numerals 'C76', c1880, 6½in (16.5cm) high.
£220–260 *WL*

A Nymphenburg model of a mastiff, by F. A. Bustelli, the scroll-edged flat base with tree-stump support applied with leaves, damaged and restored, c1760, 7¾in (19.5cm) high.
£1,750–2,000 *S*

A biscuit porcelain model of a sheep, standing on a rectangular base, possibly Bevington and Co, Swansea, c1820, 4¼in (11cm) wide.
£460–520 *P*

A pair of Meissen models of pug dogs, by J. J. Kändler, each wearing a puce collar, seated on a patterned cushion with gilt tassels, the Louis XVI style bases on 4 flower-bud feet with leaf terminals, one tail broken, the other repaired, c1745, 5¾in (14.5cm) high.
£9,000–10,000 *S*

A Meissen group of a pug dog and 2 other dogs, one brown, one black, painted in colours throughout, on a gilt rococo scrolled base, some damage, crossed swords mark in underglaze blue, c1860, 7in (18cm) high.
£600–700 *GAK*

A Meissen model of a white glazed lioness, modelled by A. Gaul, impressed crossed swords and marked 'Weiss', incised 'A1054', c1930, 12in (30.5cm) high.
£2,000–2,200 *S*

A German porcelain centrepiece, modelled as 2 hounds attacking a boar on a rocky outcrop with a tree stump, the base applied with various animals and game, damaged and repaired, blue crossed swords and dot, incised '402', late 19thC, 16½in (42cm) high.
£650–750 *Bon*

Baskets

A Derby flared basket, the 2 rope-twist loop handles with applied flower and leaf terminals, the interior painted in coloured enamels within a brown line rim, the exterior applied with flowerheads picked out in green and yellow, damaged and repaired, c1760, 6½in (16.5cm) diam.
£600–650 *DN*

A Derby basket, with flower encrusted openwork sides, turquoise loop handles, the interior painted with fruits and insects, c1760, 7in (18cm) wide.
£360–420 *AH*

A Fulda basket, the interior painted in iron-red, puce, blue and green with a floral spray, small chips, one handle missing, crowned 'FF' mark in underglaze blue, c1785, 3in (7.5cm) wide.
£700–800 *S(NY)*

A Rockingham square basket, with an entwined rustic handle, the central gilded motif surrounded by colourful applied flowers and leaves, some damage, puce griffin mark, c1830, 7in (18cm) wide.
£520–600 *P*

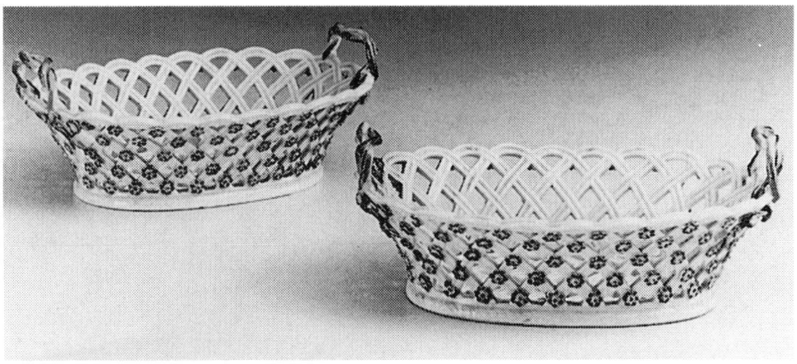

A pair of Meissen Marcolini baskets, the openwork bodies moulded with blue forget-me-nots in relief and applied with angular entwined cord-shaped handles, crossed swords above star in underglaze blue, late 18thC, 9¼in (23.5cm) wide.
£1,000–1,200 *S(Am)*

A Staffordshire porcelain basket, decorated with encrusted flowers and a blue bow, possibly by John Bevington, c1880, 10in (25.5cm) wide.
£100–120 *AAC*

r. A Rockingham octagonal basket, with an entwined and gilded handle, the border moulded in relief with primrose leaves picked out in gold and applied with flowers, damaged and restored, puce griffin mark, c1830, 9in (23cm) wide.
£800–900 *P*

Bowls

A Lowestoft wash basin, of shallow flaring form with overturned rim, painted in blue, the interior with a bird in flight enclosed within a double line cartouche, surrounded by flowering Oriental plants and flying waterfowl, beneath a flower and scroll border, the exterior with similar decoration, painter's numeral '3' for Richard Phillips, c1760, 9½in (24cm) diam.
£6,000–7,000 *P*

A Wedgwood lustre footed bowl, the interior decorated with a gilt dragon on a pearly green ground, the exterior with 2 writhing dragons in pursuit of flaming pearls, restored, printed mark, pattern No. Z4829, early 20thC, 11in (28cm) diam.
£600–700 *WW*

A Worcester documentary blue painted bowl, decorated with St George and the Dragon pattern, the interior inscribed 'A. Dunn, Birmingham 1776', small chip to rim, marked, 8¼in (21cm) diam.
£5,000–5,500 *Bon*

r. A Worcester bowl, printed in blue with a European landscape, blue crescent mark, c1770, 4½in (11.5cm) diam.
£90–110 *P(C)*

Sugar & Covered Bowls

A Chantilly Kakiemon peach-shaped sucrier and cover, painted in iron-red, yellow, turquoise, green and blue, c1740, 4in (10cm) wide.
£2,000–2,200 *S(NY)*

A Meissen silver-gilt mounted octagonal sugar box and cover, painted on each side with a chinoiserie scene, in the manner of J. G. Höroldt, marked 'K.P.M.' and crossed swords in underglaze blue, c1723, 4¼in (11cm) wide.
£7,000–8,000 *S*

A Samson porcelain sucrier, the domed lid with eagle finial, painted with floral sprays on a white ground with green and gilt banding, on paw feet, c1880, 7in (18cm) wide.
£140–160 *AH*

A Parian pot pourri bowl and pierced cover, with flowerhead knop, modelled with leaf bands, on 3 dolphin supports and concave-sided triform base, inner rim chipped, mid-19thC, 7½in (19cm) high.
£170–200 *DN(H)*

A Royal Worcester miniature sugar basin and cover, signed 'Roberts', black mark, c1950, 3in (7.5cm) high.
£160–200 *DKH*

A Helena Wolfsohn bowl, cover and stand, in Meissen style, with puce ground, 'AR' monogram, late 19thC, 9in (23cm) diam.
£350–400 *GAK*

Busts

A pair of Coalport Parian ware busts of Princess Alexandra and Edward, Prince of Wales, by John Rose, impressed and dated '18 February 1863', 13½in (34.5cm) high.
£650–750 *AH*

A Parian ware bust of Charles Dickens, by Turner & Co, c1870, 18½in (47cm) high.
£400–450 *M*

r. A Turner & Wood Parian ware bust of Queen Victoria, 1887, restored, marked, 10¾in (27.5cm) high.
£120–150 *SAS*

A white bisque porcelain bust of Princess Mary, on a tall column inscribed 'Mary', the reverse marked 'H. Tyler 1893', 10¾in (27.5cm) high.
£220–260 *SAS*

A French bisque bust of a smiling girl, decorated in pink and brown, with pink roses in her hair, c1900, 9½in (24cm) high.
£120–150 *MEG*

Candlesticks

A John Bevington two-branch candelabrum, the circular encrusted base with figure of a youth carrying a wheatsheaf, branches damaged, marked in blue with crossed sticks and 'JB', c1872, 11½in (29cm) high.
£200–220 *MSW*

A pair of Meissen two-branch candlesticks, decorated in coloured enamels, the scroll-moulded mound bases picked out in gilt, painted marks in blue and incised '1729' and '1730', 2 sconces missing, minor chips, 8in (20.5cm) high.
£500–600 *DN*

A Spode taperstick, the claret ground with raised gilding, marked 'Spode 3993', c1825, 2½in (6.5cm) high.
£375–425 *DIA*

r. A Chamberlain's Worcester chamberstick, the white ground painted with flowers, script mark, c1820, 1¾in (4.5cm) high.
£550–600 *DIA*

A pair of Chelsea candlesticks, each with a pierced sconce and drip pan, supported on bocage stems with a cherub, one holding a flaming heart, the other with a bow and arrow, painted in enamels, raised on 3 scroll-moulded feet, highlighted in gilding, minor chips and restoration, gold anchor marks, incised 'T' to bases, c1770, 8¾in (22cm) high.
£1,800–2,000 *S*

A Minton chamberstick, in 'Dresden' shape, encrusted with flowers, standing on 4 shell feet, crossed swords mark, c1830, 7½in (19cm) wide.
£400–450 *DIA*

A Spode chamberstick, the dark blue ground enhanced with gilding, marked, c1820, 1¾in (4.5cm) high.
£550–600 *DIA*

A matched pair of Meissen figural candelabra, each formed as 2 figures of Cupid in disguise, each standing before gilt-edged rococo scrolls issuing a central gnarled tree supporting 2 candle nozzles painted with *deutsche Blumen,* on a rococo scroll-moulded base heightened in gilding and applied with colourful florets and green leaves, each damaged and repaired, crossed swords marks in underglaze blue, c1755, 7½in (19cm) high.
£4,500–5,000 *S(NY)*

A pair of Sitzendorf figural three-branch candelabra, each in the form of a cherub supporting a cornucopia, on shaped bases painted with birds and insects, 19thC, 19¾in (50cm) high.
£460–520 *P(B)*

A Chamberlain's Worcester chamberstick, decorated with the Finger and Thumb pattern, c1820, 1¾in (4.5cm) high.
£600–650 *DIA*

A Worcester Flight Barr & Barr chamberstick, the pale yellow ground painted with shells, painted script marks, c1820, 1¾in (4.5cm) high.
£730–800 *DIA*

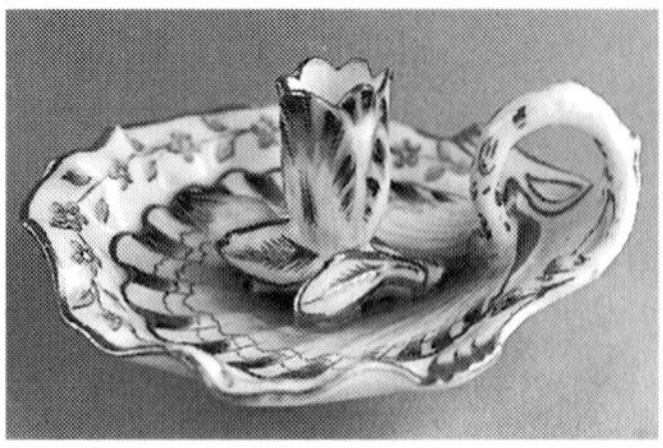

A Grainger's Worcester chamberstick, decorated with roses and enhanced with gilding, painted script mark 'Grainger, Lee & Co, Worcester', c1825, 2in (5cm) high.
£400–450 *DIA*

l. A porcelain chamberstick, the base formed as a scallop shell, unmarked, c1830, 2in (5cm) high.
£400–450 *DIA*

A pair of Royal Worcester two-branch candlesticks, modelled by James Hadley, picked out in green, orange and gilt, on mound bases, one with some damage to branches, moulded signatures, printed marks in green for 1901 and shape No. 1125, 8¾in (22cm) high.
£650–750 *DN*

Centrepieces

A Minton centrepiece, modelled as an urn, turquoise with white and gilt Greek key design rim, a gilt stretcher carried by 2 putti with turquoise loincloths, gilt, white and turquoise base, crowned globe mark, factory mark and '1517' to base, mid-19thC, 12½in (32cm) high.
£2,000–2,200 *RTo*

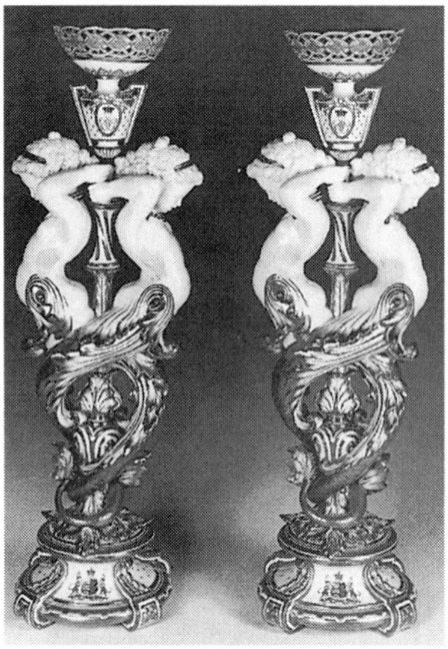

A pair of Minton dessert centrepieces, from the Abercromby service, designed by Albert Carrier de Belleuse, the composite columns supported by 2 mermaids, the urn bearing a floral cypher and barons coronet, dated '1871', converted from candelabra, 26in (66cm) high.
£2,000–2,500 *P(E)*

l. A Sèvres biscuit porcelain centrepiece, modelled in sections to represent a fruitful harvest, the central pillar hung with grapes and vine leaves surrounded by 2 cornucopiae, bowl and other accessories, the cylindrical support moulded in relief with children representing the 4 seasons, damaged, incised 'A.B', and dated for 8th November 1816, 20in (51cm) high.
£4,600–5,200 *WW*

r. A German porcelain centrepiece, in the form of a young boy and girl flanking a flower encrusted tree stump, supporting a pierced basket painted and encrusted with flowers and leaves, on pierced domed base, late 19thC, 16¼in (41.5cm) high.
£500–550 *DN(H)*

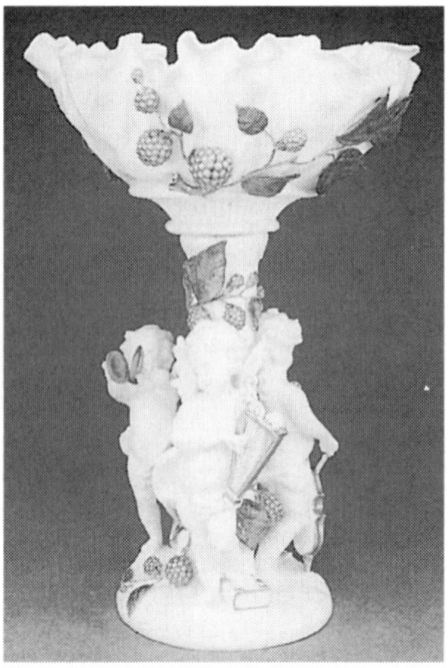

A porcelain centrepiece, in the form of putti playing musical instruments around a tree stump, supporting a fluted dish applied with fruiting vines and picked out in green and gilt, on mound base, probably by Moore Brothers, restored, c1890, 15in (38cm) high.
£700–800 *DN*

Coffee, Tea & Chocolate Pots

An Ansbach bullet-shaped teapot and cover, with animal head spout, moulded with fine fluting, painted in puce, iron-red, yellow, brown and green on either side with a floral spray and sprigs, c1765, 3in (7.5cm) high.
£850–950 *S(NY)*

A Pennington's Liverpool teapot and cover, printed in blue in Chinese style, c1780, 8in (20.5cm) high.
£200–250 *GAK*

A Lowestoft teapot, painted with flowers in underglaze blue, c1780, 5in (12.5cm) high.
£300–350 *MSW*

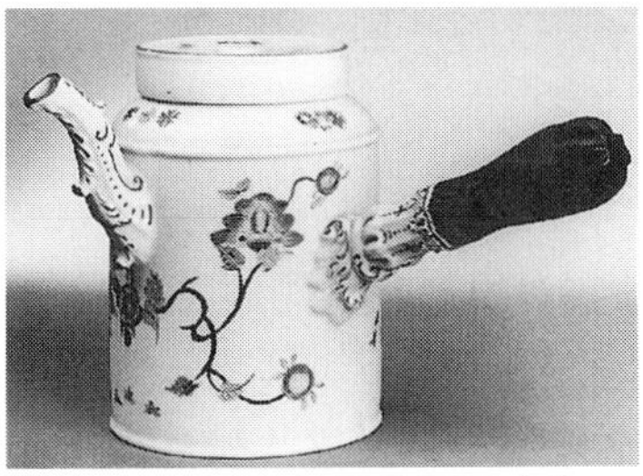

A Meissen chocolate pot, brightly painted in Kakiemon style with flowers, leaves and sprigs, the flat cover with a central hole, the spout and handle shaft moulded with scrolls and detailed in puce, the wood handle carved with flutes, gilded details, crossed swords to the base in blue, mid-18thC, 5½in (14cm) high.
£2,200–2,500 *WW*

A Crown Staffordshire miniature teapot and cover, decorated with violets, c1906, 1½in (4cm) high.
£55–65 *WAC*

l. A Meissen pear-shaped coffee pot and cover, with double scroll handle and a mask head to base of the spout, painted in polychrome with scattered *deutsche Blumen*, enamelled details and chocolate brown line rims, minor chips, crossed swords in underglaze blue, chips, mid-18thC, 7in (18cm) high.
£2,000–2,200 *WW*

Coffee & Tea Services

An Amstel 14-piece porcelain part tea service, painted with blue, red and green flowers and gilt-edged rims, marked in underglaze blue, 18thC, teapot 4½in (11.5cm) high.
£850–950 *S(Am)*

A Coalport 7-piece miniature cabaret set, decorated all-over with graduated turquoise 'jewels' on solid gilt ground, c1912, tray 5in (12.5cm) diam.
£4,000–4,500 *P*

A Copeland 33-piece part tea service, heavily gilt with stylised scrolling foliage, with deep blue detail on pale puce reserve, printed marks, c1860.
£450–500 *GAK*

A Royal Crown Derby 17-piece tea service, decorated in iron-red, blue, green and gilt with the Japan pattern, factory marks, pattern No. 2898, c1898.
£600–700 *WW*

A Pinxton 24-piece tea and coffee service, painted with a wide band of stylised flowers and gilt leaves, the letter 'R' inscribed in gold on each piece, some damage, pattern No. 312, c1805.
£1,400–1,600 *P*

A Spode 26-piece part tea service, decorated with an orange band and gilt leafy sprays on a white ground, some damage, c1815.
£200–250 *LF*

A Copeland Spode 36-piece part tea service, decorated with the Brompton pattern, printed and impressed marks, c1900.
£140–160 *GAK*

A Staffordshire 31-piece tea service, the white ground painted in gilt with roses and other floral sprays, pattern No. 143, painted in iron-red to underside, early 19thC.
£200–250 *M*

Miller's is a price GUIDE not a price LIST

A Worcester part tea service, decorated in Imari style, c1770.
£1,600–1,800 *SK*

A porcelain 22-piece part tea service, richly painted with flowers and leaves in iron-red, blue and gilt, pattern No. 2/473, some cracks, c1815.
£600–700 *WW*

A teapot, sucrier and milk jug, painted with shaped panels of floral sprays in pink and red, within an elaborate gilt, buff and blue border, pattern No. 2/9271 in red, mid-19thC.
£500–550 *P(NE)*

Cups

A Chelsea octagonal tea bowl and saucer, decorated in Kakiemon style with Lady in a Pavilion pattern, gilt highlights, c1750, saucer 4¾in (12cm) diam.
£750–850 *Bon*

A Höchst cup and saucer, painted in puce with landscape scenes, gilt-edged rims, marked, c1760, saucer 5in (12.5cm) diam.
£220–250 *S(NY)*

A set of 6 Royal Crown Derby coffee cans and saucers, by W. E. J. Dean, each painted with ships within gilt borders, slight damage, signed and marked, c1938, cans 2½in (6.5cm) high.
£2,300–2,600 *S*

William Edward James Dean worked at the Derby factory from the late 1890s until shortly before his death in 1956. He is especially known for his marine subjects.

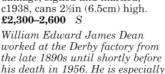

A Meissen tea bowl and saucer, the interior painted in Kakiemon style, the exterior with *indianische Blumen*, gilt line rims, crossed swords in underglaze blue, impressed star marks, c1735, saucer 5in (12.5cm) diam.
£750–850 *WW*

l. A Miles Mason tea bowl and saucer, transfer-printed in underglaze blue with Veranda pattern, seal mark, c1810, 5in (12.5cm) diam.
£100–115 *JP*

A Hilditch & Sons cup and saucer, decorated in blue and white with an Oriental scene, c1825, 5½in (14cm) diam.
£25–30 *OCH*

A Miles Mason coffee can and saucer, moulded and painted with flowers on a pale blue ground, c1808, saucer 4in (10cm) diam.
£125–140 *VH*

A Miles Mason teacup, coffee can and saucer, brightly decorated in Imari style, c1810, saucer 4in (10cm) diam.
£250–300 *VH*

A Meissen cup and saucer, painted with a landscape view in colours and decorated with gilt shells, rocailles and leaves, underglaze blue swords mark, c1840, saucer 6in (15cm) diam.
£500–600 *DORO*

A Sèvres style coffee can and saucer, the can painted with a fisherman and companion, the saucer with a putto and dolphin, reserved on a blue, white and gilt design with turquoise 'jewelling' within borders of 'pearls' and 'rubies', marked, mid-19thC, saucer 5in (12.5cm) diam.
£950–1,100 *P*

A Worcester coffee cup, with grooved loop handle, painted in iron-red, green, puce and brown with a pheasant and flowering peony, enriched with gold, c1755, 2½in (6.5cm) high.
£1,800–2,200 *P*

A Meissen chocolate cup, cover and *trembleuse* saucer, painted with figures on a blue ground, crossed swords mark in underglaze blue, mid-19thC, cup 4¾in (12cm) high.
£850–1,000 *CGC*

A Spode Bute shape coffee can, brightly decorated in Imari style, c1815, 2½in (6.5cm) high.
£200–250 *AnS*

A Swansea beaker, with a turned foot and everted rim, painted with blue flowers and gilt foliage, gilt line to rim and foot, c1820, 2½in (6cm) high.
£180–220 *P*

A cup and saucer, each printed with a portrait of the Duke of York, within a band of brightly enamelled flowers and foliage, lined in red, slight damage, 1827, saucer 5½in (14cm) diam.
£260–300 *SAS*

l. A porcelain tea cup and saucer, printed in black to commemorate the Great Exhibition of 1851, within green and gilt borders, cup 3in (7.5cm) high.
£140–170 *W&S*

A Nantgarw coffee can, attributed to Thomas Pardoe, decorated with a green woodpecker, the reverse with roses, convolvulus and a gilded moth, gilding to rim worn, c1821, 2¼in (6cm) high.
£750–850 *P*

A set of 6 Royal Worcester coffee cups and saucers, painted with Highland cattle, by Harry Stinton, c1913.
£1,700–2,000 *SWO*

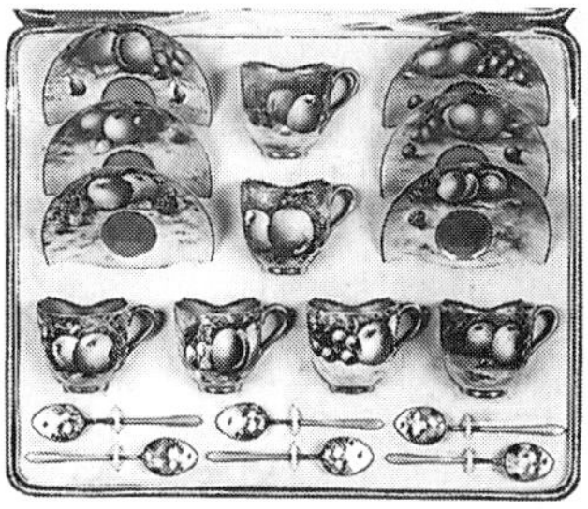

A set of 6 Royal Worcester coffee cups and saucers, painted with autumn fruits, by Harry Stinton, William Hale, Jack Stanley, William Bagnall, Raymond Rushton, Edward Townsend and Charlie Twilton, signed, dated '1920', and 6 silver-gilt spoons enamelled on the back of the bowls, with importation marks of Henry James Hulbert, c1933, in Mappin & Webb fitted box.
£2,200–2,500 *P*

A porcelain tea cup and saucer, printed and painted with Victoria and Albert, picked out in purple lustre, c1840, saucer 5½in (14cm) diam.
£45–55 *SER*

Dessert & Dinner Services

A late Caughley or early Coalport dessert service, comprising: 2 stands, 2 dishes and 7 plates, painted with Welsh landscapes, within gilt borders, some wear, c1796, dishes 8½in (21.5cm) wide.
£720–800 *P*

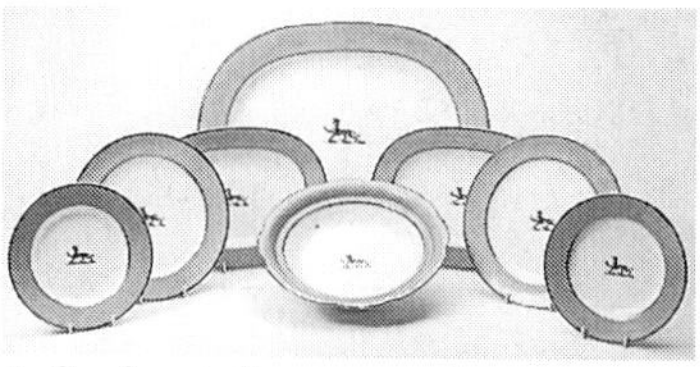

A Coalport dinner service, comprising 52 pieces, painted with a central crest within a blue and gilt-lined border, c1810.
£1,700–2,000 *CGC*

A Coalport part dessert service, comprising 27 pieces, brightly painted in Imari style within gilt-line borders, some damage, c1820.
£750–1,000 *DN*

A Coalport dessert service, comprising 27 pieces, with gilt decorated scrolling borders, brown printed foliage and polychrome enamel flowers, some pieces damaged, pattern No. 3/521, c1835.
£400–450 *WW*

A Davenport part dessert service, comprising 10 pieces, decorated with landscapes within floral and vine borders, pattern No. 963, printed marks, slight damage, c1820.
£300–350 *SK*

A Davenport dessert service, comprising 18 pieces, decorated with Japan pattern in iron-red and blue with gilt, late 19thC.
£1,200–1,400 *AH*

A Minton dessert service, comprising 17 pieces, decorated in Japanesque taste on a yellow ground, some damage, impressed marks, dated '1874', '1875' and '1878'.
£2,200–2,500 *P*

A set of 12 Derby Crown dessert plates, each printed and hand-coloured after designs by John Joseph Brownsword with children at play, in the style of Kate Greenaway, surrounded by wreaths of flowers and leaves on a claret ground, 'jewelled' border and gilt dentil rim, marks in red, pattern No. 998, c1884.
£2,000–2,500 *P*

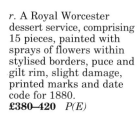

A Spode dessert service, comprising 18 pieces, decorated with Peacock pattern, the border with flowers, some damage, marks and pattern No. 2083 in red, c1820.
£1,000–1,200 *P*

A Royal Worcester Aesthetic style dessert service, comprising 18 pieces, painted with Oriental flowers, factory marks, dated '1887' and '1888'.
£450–500 *P*

A Royal Worcester dessert service, comprising 11 pieces, painted in colours with butterflies and stylised foliage on a white ground within ochre rims, printed marks and date cypher for 1881.
£150–180 *GAK*

r. A Royal Worcester dessert service, comprising 15 pieces, painted with sprays of flowers within stylised borders, puce and gilt rim, slight damage, printed marks and date code for 1880.
£380–420 *P(E)*

Ewers & Jugs

A Caughley documentary sparrow beak cream jug, enamelled with a spray of pink, purple and orange flowers, signed with monogram 'H.E.C.', dated '1782', 4¼in (10.5cm) high.
£1,000–1,200 *S*

Although examples of inscribed and dated Caughley porcelains are known, this appears to be the only recorded piece with a date and apparent artist's monogram. Only a few names of Caughley factory artists are known.

A New Hall cream jug, polychrome decorated with a boy chasing a butterfly, pattern No. 421, c1795, 4½in (11.5cm) high.
£100–120 *HYD*

A Vienna jug and cover, painted with flower-sprays under a slanting black ribboned shoulder, on 3 scroll feet, date code, shield mark in underglaze blue, c1793, 6¼in (16cm) high.
£220–250 *RTo*

A Caughley cabbage-leaf jug, from The Duke of York service, c1790, slight damage, 9in (23cm) high.
£5,600–6,000 *S(NY)*

A John Pennington Chelsea jug, painted in colours with Chinese figures, the interior with loop and dot border, with scroll handle, on feather-moulded base, c1780, 3¼in (8cm) high.
£450–500 *P*

A Worcester cabbage leaf-moulded jug, painted with chinoiserie scenes in puce and *indianische Blumen* on a yellow ground, minor scratches, c1760, 10½in (26.5cm) high.
£2,500–3,000 *Bon*

A Worcester sparrow beak cream jug, c1775, 3½in (9cm) high.
£400–450 *S*

A Fontainebleau Toby jug, holding a snuff box, decorated in purple and blue, underglaze blue Jacob Petit mark, c1830, 9¼in (23.5cm) high.
£900–1,100 *DORO*

r. A Sèvres pear-shaped milk jug, painted with floral sprays between gilt-edged cartouches patterned with blue and gilt trelliswork, on 3 legs, marked, date letter for 1759, 4in (10cm) high.
£1,600–1,800 *S(NY)*

A pair of Rockingham jugs, with rustic handles, the rims and feet moulded with scrolls and picked out in gold, one painted with flowers, the other with fruit, on green grounds with yellow flowers picked out in gold, both inscribed, one restored, slight wear to gilding, puce griffin marks, c1831, 5in (12.5cm) high.
£700–800 *P*

A pair of Worcester Kerr & Binns hand-painted ewers, c1855–60, 11½in (29cm) high.
£2,250–2,500 *AMH*

A Meissen silver-mounted hot water jug and cover, painted with peasants by buildings after Teniers, on a sea-green ground, date marks for 1750–56, crossed swords in underglaze blue, 9in (23cm) high.
£3,500–4,000 *S*

Cross Reference
Colour Review

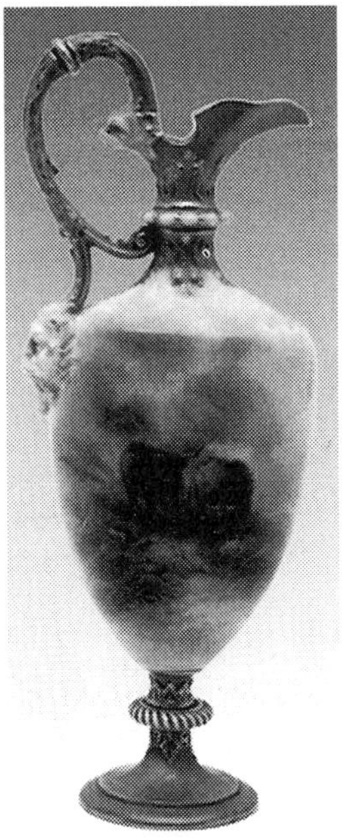

A Royal Worcester ewer, painted by John Stinton, on one side with cattle in a Highland setting, the other side with a view of a lake, the foliate moulded scroll handle terminating in mask heads, shape No. 789, printed mark and date code for 1908, 13in (33cm) high.
£2,200–2,500 *Bea(E)*

Figures

A Bow white figure, depicting Kitty Clive as Mrs Riot, with a dog under one arm, cap restored, c1750, 10½in (26.5cm) high.
£3,700–4,200 *S*

A Bow figure of a flower seller, with pink skirt and blue hat, impressed mark, c1750, 6in (15cm) high.
£1,800–2,000 *BHa*

A pair of Bow allegorical figures of Spring and Autumn, each wearing a turquoise hat and colourful clothes, standing amidst colourful flowers and leaves, the scroll-footed bases heightened in blue, turquoise and gilding, c1765, largest 7¾in (19.5cm) high.
£1,600–1,800 *S(NY)*

A Bow figure, emblematic of Earth, decorated with bright polychrome enamels and gilt highlights, dressed in a robe, holding a cornucopia and an apple, a lion at her feet, on a high scroll-moulded base, damaged and repaired, c1770, 10¾in (27.5cm) high.
£300–350 *Bon*

A Bristol figure of Milton, after the Derby model, with his arm on a pile of books and a scroll on a high plinth moulded with the Expulsion from Paradise, slight damage and restoration, c1770, 7¾in (20cm) high.
£1,000–1,200 *S*

A Continental parcel-gilt figural group, dressed in flowing drapery on a base decorated with anthemia, restored, c1900, 14¼in (36cm) high.
£2,000–2,500 *S(NY)*

A pair of Conta & Boehme table ornaments, each with a putto riding a sleigh, decorated in coloured enamels and gilt, late 19thC, 4in (10cm) wide.
£60–70 *MiA*

A Copeland Parian candle extinguisher and stand, in the form of a Bluecoat School boy, c1860, 4½in (11.5cm) high.
£270–300 *TH*

A Copeland Parian figure of Musidora, by W. Theed, c1867, 17½in (44.5cm) high.
£550–650 *JAK*

A pair of Derby dry edge figures of Chinese boys, emblematic of Air and Water, each painted in coloured enamels with flowers and leaves, picked out in gilt, restored, c1752, decoration later, 4¾in (12cm) high.
£680–750 *DN*

Dry edge is a characteristic of early Derby figures, whereby the base was wiped clear of glaze, hence the name given to this production period.

A Derby model of a child, wearing a pink and yellow jacket, sitting on a turquoise chair, stroking a cat, restored, patch marks beneath base, c1765, 5¾in (14.5cm) high.
£400–450 *WW*

A Derby biscuit group of 2 virgins awakening Cupid, patch marks, incised 'N195', c1780, 12½in (31.5cm) high.
£950–1,100 *P*

A pair of Derby figures, from the Piping Shepherds series, each before flowering bocage and on volute scroll-edge tricorn bases, c1770, 8¾in (22cm) high.
£600–700 *Bon*

Derby Porcelain

The Derby factory was founded in 1750 by a Frenchman, André Planché. In 1756 it was bought out by John Heath and his partner William Duesbury, who had until then been decorating pieces for Chelsea. In 1770 they also bought the Chelsea factory, and for the next 14 years in a phase known as Chelsea-Derby, the 2 concerns operated together. In 1811 the business was acquired from Heath and Duesbury's successors by Robert Bloor who, despite the fact that he went mad in 1826, continued to manage the declining factory until it closed in 1848. Several other factories were established in Derby in the 19thC. The most successful was the so-called 'Crown Derby' company, which survives today as the Royal Crown Derby Porcelain Company.

A Derby figure of Britannia, decorated in pink, brown and green, chips to leaves, c1780, 14in (35.5cm) high.
£850–1,000 *DAN*

A Derby model of James Quinn as Falstaff, richly decorated in coloured enamels and gilt, on a scroll-moulded base, some damage, incised 'No. 291' and '3', c1780, 11½in (29cm) high.
£250–300 *WW*

A set of 4 Derby biscuit figures, depicting Fire, Earth, Air and Water, shape No. 48, slight damage, c1790, 8½in (21.5cm) high.
£1,500–1,800 *HAM*

It is believed that c1900 these figures were painted white, hence their grey flaking appearance. When new they would have cost £3 4s 0d, due to their superior quality, as opposed to £2 12s 6d for enamelled and gilded examples.

r. A set of Derby biscuit figures of the French Seasons, after Pierre Stephan, slight damage, incised marks and No. 123, c1820, 7in (18cm) high.
£1,500–1,800 *Hal*

A Derby figure of a putto, decorated in gilt, holding a basket, c1800, 5in (12.5cm) high.
£150–200 *SER*

A pair of Bloor Derby figure groups, the Stocking Mender Group and the Shoe Mender Group, each with bocage support, coloured in deep enamels on pierced foliate scroll bases picked out in gilt, damaged and repaired, blue painted *faux* Meissen mark, c1820, 6½in (16.5cm) high.
£400–450 *Bon*

A Dresden group, advertising Yardley's Old English Lavender, depicting a mother and 2 children carrying baskets of lavender, polychrome decorations, early 20thC, 12in (30.5cm) high.
£450–500 *HCC*

A Fürstenberg figure of a miner, from the original series by Simon Feilner, remodelled by A. C. Luplau, dressed in black with white gaiters, c1765, 5in (12.5cm) high.
£800–1,000 *P*

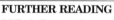

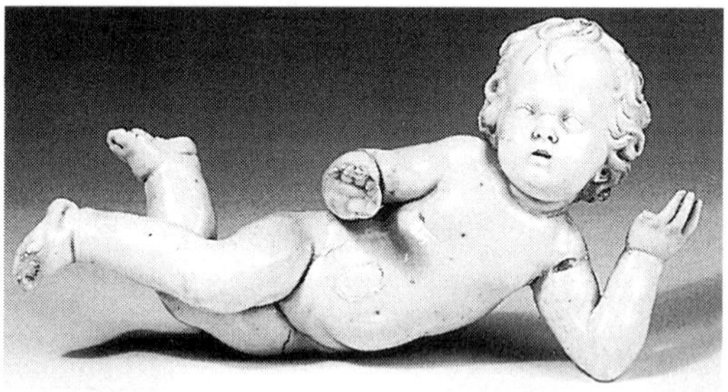

A Doccia glazed white figure of a putto, from a relief plaque or vase, damaged and repaired, c1745, 10in (25.5cm) wide.
£1,500–1,800 *P*

FURTHER READING
Miller's Pottery & Porcelain Marks,
Miller's Publications, 1995

A Meissen group, depicting lovers, on a floral mound, with a pug dog, by J. J. Kändler, c1745, 5in (12.5cm) high.
£8,000–9,000 *BHa*

A Limbach allegorical figure of Spring, decorated in purple, yellow and green, c1775, 6¾in (17cm) high.
£1,200–1,500 *S*

A Meissen figure of Bacchus, seated astride an ass, attended by a man in a cloak, the scroll-moulded base with a recumbent putto, crossed swords mark in underglaze blue, 18thC, 7¾in (19.5cm) high.
£1,000–1,200 *P(B)*

A Ludwigsburg figure of Orpheus, holding a lyre and with Cerberus at his feet, painted in colours, restored, c1770, 10½in (26.5cm) high.
£1,250–1,500 *DORO*

A pair of Meissen figure groups, one depicting a girl with a ram, the other a boy with a goat, on naturalistic bases, crossed swords mark in underglaze blue, c1870, 6in (15cm) high.
£1,000–1,200 *P(B)*

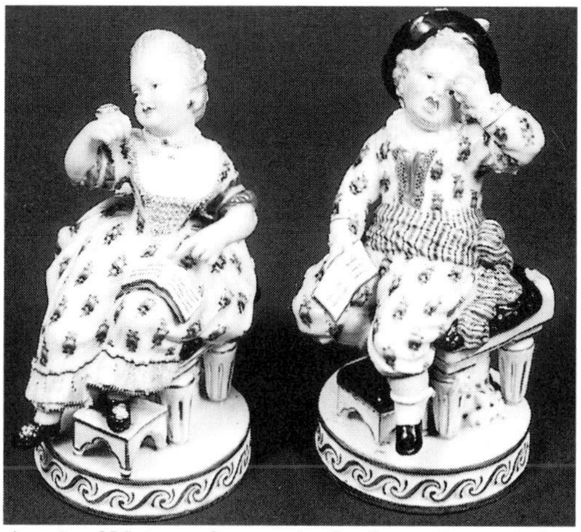

A pair of Meissen figures, in the form of a seated boy and girl, each holding a book and coloured in blue and gilt, on circular bases, crossed swords mark in underglaze blue, 19thC, 5½in (14cm) high.
£700–850 *P(B)*

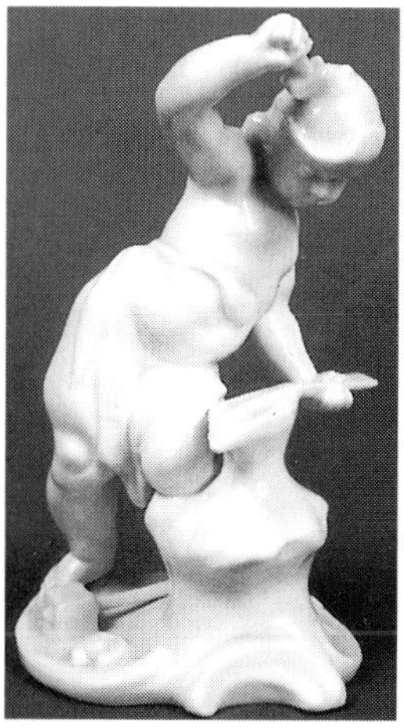

A Nymphenburg figure of a cherub blacksmith, c1870, 4in (10cm) high.
£80–100 *SER*

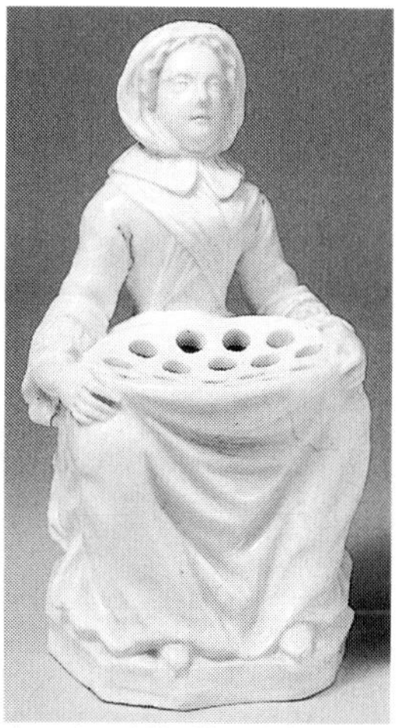

A pair of St Cloud figures of flower sellers, both supporting a pannier between their knees, on rocky mound bases, damaged and restored, c1745, 9in (23cm) high.
£2,200–2,500 *S(NY)*

A Minton Parian group, The Lion in Love, by J. B. Klagman, c1864, 16in (40.5cm) high.
£900–1,100 *JAK*

The original marble was shown at the Great Exhibition in 1851.

A Royal Dux equestrian group, depicting a soldier talking to a milk-maid, decorated in green and pink with gilt embellishment, on a floral base, early 20thC, 15¼in (38.5cm) high.
£1,000–1,200 *AH*

A Royal Worcester figure of Princess Elizabeth, wearing the uniform of Colonel-in-Chief of the Grenadier Guards, riding Tommy, by Doris Lindner, on a marbled base with black wooden plinth, printed mark, dated '1948', 13in (33cm) high.
£3,000–3,500 *P*

This model was Doris Lindner's and the Worcester factory's first equestrian limited edition. Made to commemorate Princess Elizabeth taking her first Trooping the Colour on 12 June 1948, the issue was limited to 100 models. The Princess sat for both Doris Lindner and Harry Davis, who painted the models, at Buckingham Palace.

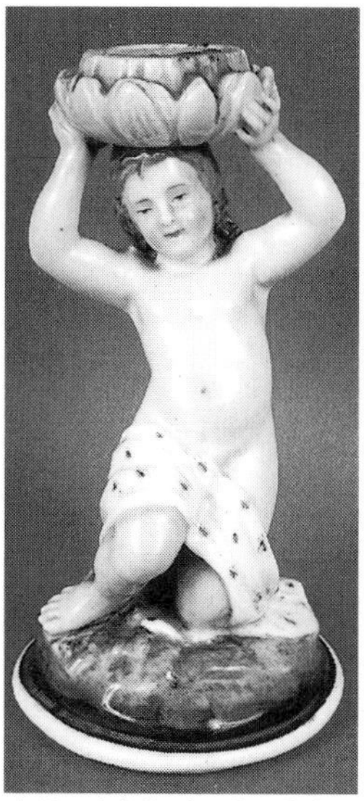

A Daniel Sutherland & Sons candlestick figure, on a rocky base, c1870, 6¾in (17cm) high.
£180–200 *HEI*

A Parian figure of Princess Alice, her hands clasping a handkerchief, on a square plinth, base initialled 'A', c1860, slight damage, 14¼in (36cm) high.
£400–450 *SAS*

l. A Parian figure, depicting Sir Henry Havelock in a three-quarter length jacket and pith helmet, walking stick replaced, base inscribed 'MacBride 1858', 14¼in (36cm) high.
£260–300 *SAS*

Sir Henry Havelock was a prominent figure in the Indian Mutiny following the relief of Lucknow in 1857.

Flatware

A set of 12 Adams plates, each transfer-printed in black and painted with a different titled scene of birds taken from *The Birds of America* by John James Audubon, c1910, 10½in (26.5cm) diam.
£1,200–1,500 *S*

John James Audubon (1780–1851), an American naturalist, began publishing Birds of America *from 1825, and today copies of his work are highly prized.*

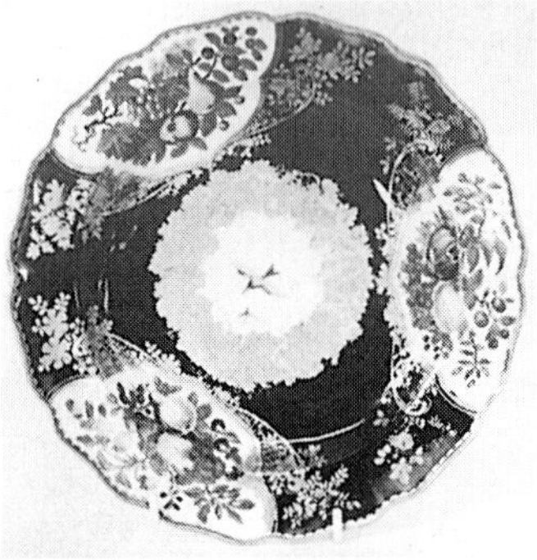

A Chelsea dessert plate, decorated with fruit and leaves, on a blue ground, slight damage, gold anchor period, c1765, 9in (23cm) diam.
£250–300 *GAK*

A set of 8 Limoges plates, by H. Mayet, each decorated with a different orchid and signed, within a scrolled gilt border, c1880, 8½in (21.5cm) diam.
£900–1,000 *SLL*

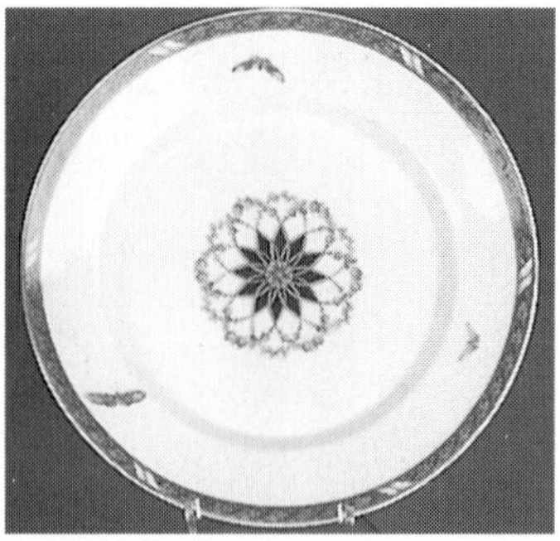

A KPM Berlin plate, decorated with red rim and green oak leaf border, painted with butterflies in colour, the centre decorated with a rosette and rose foliage, c1810, 9½in (24cm) diam.
£250–300 *DORO*

A Derby botanical dessert plate, possibly painted by John Brewer, decorated with 'Geranium Anemonefolium, Anemone Leav'd Geranium' on a yellow ground, within a circular gilded dot-and-leaf border and spirally fluted rim, marked, c1795, 9in (23cm) diam.
£1,000–1,200 *S*

A Meissen Imari dish, painted in underglaze blue, gilding and iron-red, marked, c1740, 9½in (24cm) diam.
£3,500–4,000 *S*

A Chelsea plate, painted in Hans Sloane style with a yellow puce-veined flower, buds and foliage, surrounded by a ladybird and moths, within a shaped chocolate rim, some wear, c1755, 9½in (24cm) diam.
£2,700–3,200 *S*

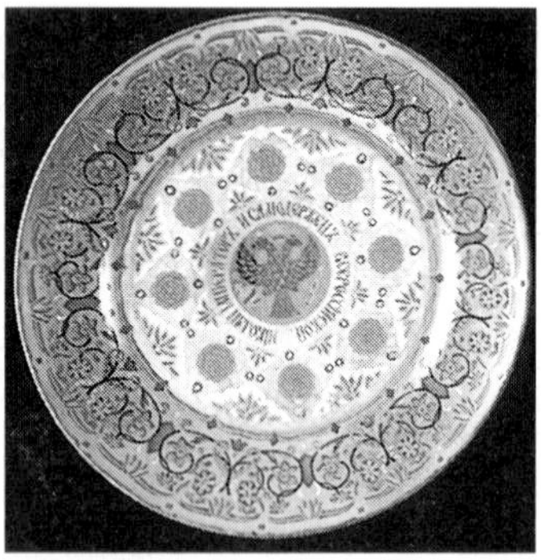

A fruit plate from the Kremlin service, Imperial Porcelain Manufactory, mark of Nicholas I Pavlovich, c1825, 8¾in (22cm) diam.
£2,200–2,500 *S*

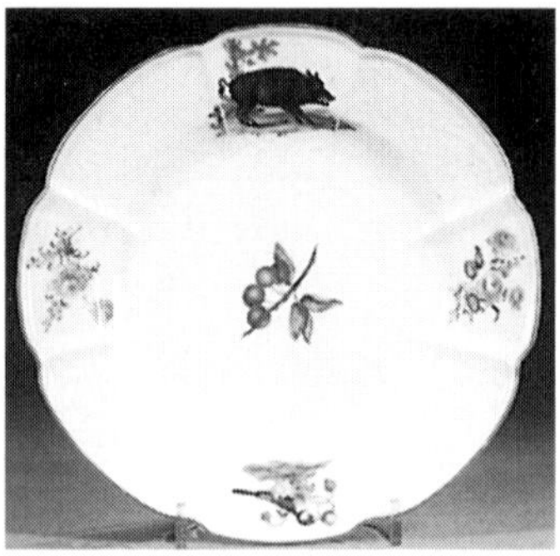

A set of 4 Meissen plates, each moulded with *Gotzkowsky-Reliefdekor* and painted in the centre with fruit, the gilt rims with alternating flowersprays, animal vignettes, a butterfly and birds perched on branches, crossed swords in underglaze blue, impressed numerals, c1750, 9¾in (24.5cm) diam.
£3,500–4,000 *S*

l. A set of 10 Meissen Academic period soup plates, painted with various birds of exotic, aquatic and domestic varieties and with insects including ladybirds, moths, and a cockroach, within narrow gilt scroll borders, 5 chipped, crossed swords and dot marks, c1770, 8¾in (22cm) diam.
£2,400–2,700 *P*

A Meissen topographical plate, painted with a named view of Dresden, within a tooled gilt band, the rim with a gilt arched border enclosing foliate motifs, titled in black on the reverse, crossed swords in underglaze blue, impressed numeral, c1820, 9½in (24cm) diam.
£3,200–3,600 *S*

A Minton pierced plate, in the Sèvres style, depicting Autumn, c1858, 9in (23cm) diam.
£800–900 *AMH*

A Moore Brothers cabinet plate, painted with flowers on a crimson and gilt ground, c1892, 9in (23cm) diam.
£70–80 *MiA*

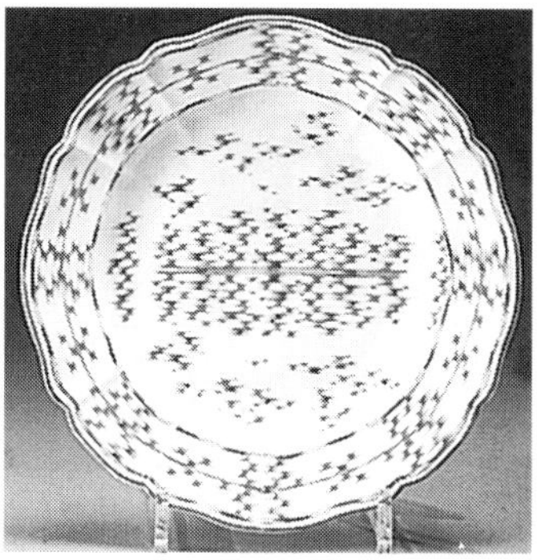

A set of 18 Nymphenburg plates, each painted with the '*Atlasmuster*' in magenta, blue and shades of green within line borders, impressed shield marks, c1770, 9¼in (23.5cm) diam.
£8,700–9,700 *S*

A Sèvres plate from the Catherine The Great Service, the central crowned floral monogram flanked by laurel and myrtle on a turquoise ground, the border with a central turquoise band gilded with scrolling foliage and reserved with 3 grisaille portrait medallions and 3 groups of classical figures, between 2 bands of flowers, damaged, marked in blue script, c1778, 10½in (26.5cm) diam.
£5,500–6,000 *WW*

A pair of Sèvres soup plates, each painted with a spray of flowers and fruit, the rims with smaller similar sprays within gilt-edged reserves against a band of gilt scrolling foliage on a blue ground, marked in purple and blue, incised numerals, c1788, 9¾in (24.5cm) diam.
£1,000–1,200 *S*

A set of 6 'Sèvres' plates, painted with battle scenes in colours within a laurel leaf gilt enamelled band, the border painted with scrolling foliage and tracery on a cobalt ground, each inscribed to the reverse, marked in blue and iron-red overglaze, c1880, 9¼in (23.5cm) diam.
£550–650 *S(Am)*

A set of 6 Spode Kakiemon soup plates, each painted in iron-red, yellow, blue, gold, lilac, turquoise and black with a flowering prunus tree and bamboo, within a narrow blue and gilt-edged border the underside with iron-red floral sprays within a zigzag border, 5 marked 'Spode', all with pattern No. 282, c1800, 9¾in (25cm) diam.
£1,000–1,200 *S(NY)*

A Spode child's dish, decorated in green, blue and yellow, pattern No. 2070, c1814, 4¼in (11cm) wide.
£55–60 *OCH*

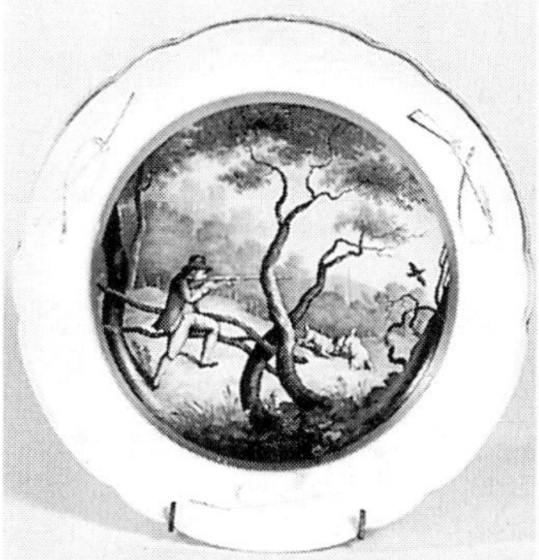

l. A porcelain plate, painted in sepia tones with a huntsman in a forest landscape shooting a woodcock, within florally moulded borders painted with gilt muskets, shaped gilt edge, c1815, 10in (25.5cm) diam.
£200–220 *Hal*

A Vienna porcelain plate, painted with the goddess Ceres seated in a wooded landscape, within a gilt border, underglaze blue beehive mark, inscribed '1811', 9½in (24cm) diam.
£1,000–1,200 *DORO*

A set of Worcester plates and dishes, comprising 11 pieces, decorated with the Jabberwocky pattern, with a red dragon among flowering plants in a chinoiserie garden, within a meandering turquoise-ground rococo border enclosing lattice panels, c1770, plates 9½in (24cm) diam.
£5,000–5,500 *S*

The Jabberwocky pattern is the name given to a Japanese Kakiemon style design, recorded in the 1769 Christie's sale catalogue as 'Fine old rich dragon pattern, bleu celeste *borders'.*

A set of 6 Royal Worcester cabinet plates, decorated with flowers and butterflies, some damage, late 19thC, 9in (23cm) diam.
£175–200 *S(NY)*

Ex-Leonard Bernstein collection.

Worcester: What's in a Name?

Worcester is classified according to the factory's owners:

1751–74 Dr Wall or First period (Dr John Wall, William Davis and other partners)
1774–83 Davis period (William Davis principal manager)
1783–92 Flight period (John and Joseph Flight)
1792–1804 Flight & Barr period (Joseph Flight and Martin Barr senior)
1804–13 Barr, Flight & Barr period (Martin Barr senior, Joseph Flight and Martin Barr junior)
1813–40 Flight, Barr & Barr period (Joseph Flight, Martin Barr junior and George Barr)
1840–52 Chamberlain & Co period (Chamberlain's and Flight, Barr & Barr amalgamated)
1852–62 Kerr & Binns period (W. H. Kerr and R. W. Binns joint owners)
1862 to present Worcester Royal Porcelain Co Ltd (known as Royal Worcester)

A Flight, Barr & Barr plate, from the Stowe service, the salmon-coloured ground decorated in gold with urns, scrolls and lyres, the centre painted with coat-of-arms, inscribed with a motto and impressed crowned 'FBB' mark, circular printed Royal Arms mark, c1813, 9½in (24cm) diam.
£2,200–2,500 *WW*

The Stowe service was made for the 2nd Marquis of Buckingham when he succeeded his father to the estate of Stowe in Buckinghamshire in 1813. Each piece was painted with the full arms of the Marquis of Buckingham within a border of gold scrollwork on a salmon ground. Most pieces are marked Flight, Barr & Barr, although many pieces also bear impressed marks of 'BFB' because the name of the factory changed in the year this service was made.

A set of 6 Royal Worcester plates, painted with game birds, within gilt-edged decorative borders with floral swags, signed with monogram, date code for 1908, slight damage, 9½in (24cm) diam.
£400–450 *MCA*

A porcellaneous tricorn plate, the border moulded with foliage in white on a blue ground with profuse gilt decoration, the centre printed in pink with a head and shoulders hatted portrait entitled 'Queen Caroline', restored, c1821, 4½in (11.5cm) wide.
£200–220 *SAS*

A porcelain plate, painted by James Copson, with playing cards, one showing the reverse inscribed 'Duty One Shilling', on a deep green border encircling the royal arms, dated '1848', 8½in (21.5cm) diam.
£650–700 *Bon*

Inkstands

A Coalbrookdale type two-handled quill stand and inkwell, with raised flower decoration, c1830, 4¾in (12cm) wide.
£250–300 *ANT*

A Minton inkstand, decorated with pink roses and gilding, c1850, 9in (23cm) wide.
£500–550 *DIA*

A Coalport inkstand, the light blue and beige ground enhanced with bright gilding, minor restoration to base, c1840, 14in (35.5cm) wide.
£700–800 *DIA*

A Chamberlain's Worcester flower encrusted inkstand, the base decorated with a floral spray, minor restoration, printed marks, c1830, 12in (30.5cm) wide.
£1,400–1,600 *DIA*

A Chamberlain's Worcester inkstand, with sarcophagus-shaped body, pierced heart-shaped handle, lift-out well and pounce pot with liner, on gilt paw feet, painted with a view of Worcester across the river Severn, on a blue ground, gilt borders and details, some damage, painted marks, early 19thC, 6in (15cm) wide.
£350–400 *WW*

Miller's is a price GUIDE not a price LIST

Jardinières

A Dresden jardinière, painted with polychrome flowers on a gilt embellished trellis ground, c1900, 8¼in (21cm) high.
£450–500 *AH*

l. A Naples jardinière, with mythological figures in relief surmounted by a band of vines flanked by parcel-gilt handles above an acanthus-cast lower section, the column with tapering stem moulded in relief with putti and classical maidens in a wooded landscape, within bands of stylised leaves, marked with crowned '4' in underglaze blue, c1880, 61in (155cm) high.
£1,000–1,200 *S(Am)*

A Vincennes jardinière, with double leaf-moulded handles picked out in puce and gilding, probably painted by Jean-Louis Morin, with one putto crowning another with a garland, the reverse painted with trophies, the rim with gilt dentil border, c1754, 11½in (29cm) diam.
£1,500–1,800 *P*

Jars

A Mennecy pomade pot and cover, moulded with 3 vertical ribs alternating with 3 flutes, painted in shades of rose, purple, yellow, iron-red, blue and green with floral sprays within a rose rim edge, the cover surmounted by a rose knop, small chips, incised 'D.V.' and 'P.' mark, c1755, 4in (10cm) high.
£220–250 *S(NY)*

A Royal Worcester blush ivory double lidded jar, with moulded wrythen wavy edge decoration to the base and floral sprays to the top, lower base with a gilt border with diamond trellis and gilt decoration Registration No. 227399, printed puce mark dating from 1896, 8in (20.5cm) high.
£460–520 *Mit*

A pair of Royal Worcester Randolph Rose jars and covers, pierced covers with gilt speckled detail, the inner covers also with gilt detail, the lobed bases decorated with panels of coloured flowers, on a blush ground, printed marks and date cypher for 1897, shape No. 1314, 5in (12.5cm) high.
£600–700 *GAK*

Items in the Porcelain section have been arranged in factory order, with non-specific pieces appearing at the end of each sub-section.

Mugs & Tankards

A Lowestoft blue and white tankard, decorated with a Chinese landscape and fence scene, marked '2' under base rim, c1765, 5in (12.5cm) high.
£2,600–3,000 *JNic*

A Chelsea Derby mug, with reeded loop handle, painted in Kakiemon style with birds and flowering branches, within blue ground bands decorated in gilt with scrolling flowerheads and leaves, painted mark in gilt, c1775, 5in (12.5cm) high.
£320–360 *DN*

A Worcester mug, with reeded loop handle, painted in Chinese style, in underglaze blue with a warbler amongst reeds, pierced rockwork and a flowering branch, the interior with a flower panelled diaper band, c1754, 3in (7.5cm) high.
£3,200–3,600 *DN*

r. A Worcester documentary mug, decorated with St George and the Dragon pattern, chips to rim, inscribed 'A. Dunn Birmingham 1776', blue open crescent mark, 3¼in (8.5cm) high.
£4,000–4,500 *Bon*

l. A Worcester blue-scale mug, painted in rose, iron-red, yellow, grey, green, brown and black on either side with birds and shrubs, the ridged loop handle reserved with a panel decorated with iron-red crosses and dots, pseudo seal mark in underglaze blue, c1770, 6in (15cm) high.
£1,300–1,500 *S(NY)*

Plaques

A Berlin plaque, brightly painted in naïve style with a country house in parkland, a pavilion and a gazebo to each side and coniferous forest behind, impressed 'KPM' and sceptre mark, incised '315–2.55', inscribed in biro on the mount 'Schloss Bellevue', late 19thC, 9¼in (23.5cm) high.
£1,800–2,000 *S*

A Limoges plaque, polychrome painted, with a scantily draped nymph seated on rockwork besides a riverbank, marked, 19thC, 9¾in (24.5cm) high.
£920–1,000 *S(Am)*

A pair of porcelain plaques, painted by Jabez Aston, each with a vase of flowers resting on a marble slab, probably Coalport, one signed 'J. Aston', c1830, 10¼in (26cm) high.
£6,000–7,000 *WW*

Jabez Aston was born at Ironbridge in about 1799. He was one of the leading flower and fruit painters and appears to have spent his whole working life at Coalport. Aston was described by Jewitt, in 1877, as one of the principal artists at Coalport.

Cross Reference
Colour Review

l. A Pountney & Goldney biscuit Parian plaque, by Edward Raby, the relief basket of flowers on a lilac ground, c1847, 9¾in (25cm) wide, in glazed box frame.
£850–1,000 *Bri*

A Flight, Barr & Barr plaque, painted with a view of Windsor Castle from the Thames, impressed 'FBB' and crown, incised cross and No. 12, c1820, 6in (15cm) wide, framed and glazed.
£980–1,100 *P*

A Royal Worcester plaque, painted by John Stinton with 'Llyn Gwyllwm', depicting 8 cattle in the shallows of the lake, mountains beyond, signed, printed and painted marks, c1920, 9¼in (23.5cm) wide, in a glazed gilt frame.
£4,000–4,500 *P(NW)*

A porcelain plaque, by Thomas Pardoe, with canted corners, painted with a bluetit perched on a branch beside a spray of garden flowers, inscribed on the reverse 'Painted by T. Pardoe', c1820, 8in (20.5cm) wide, with giltwood frame.
£2,500–3,000 *P*

Miller's is a price GUIDE not a price LIST

A Bohemian plaque, painted with a young woman in the arms of a young man, late 19thC, 16½in (42cm) diam.
£750–900 *DORO*

A pair of French bisque plates, each moulded in bold relief, one with a mounted huntsman and deer, the other with a mounted huntswoman and hound, picked out in coloured enamels and gilt, minor damage, mid-19thC, 10in (25.5cm) diam.
£600–700 *DN*

A German porcelain plaque, painted with a portrait of a young woman, 19thC, 4½in (11.5cm) high.
£200–250 *TMA*

Sauce & Cream Boats

A Derby shell-moulded sauce boat, painted in underglaze blue with scattered flower sprigs, cracked, chip to foot, c1770, 6in (15cm) long.
£180–220 *S*

Ex-William A. Gurling collection.

A pair of Worcester lettuce leaf-moulded sauce boats, each with loop handle picked out in brown and yellow, painted in *famille rose* palette with sprays of flowers and leaves and scattered flowers beneath a brown line rim, c1755, 7¼in (18.5cm) long.
£1,000–1,200 *DN*

A Worcester sauce boat, with lobed gadrooned rim and scrolled handle, the pleat-moulded body with raised scrolled panels enriched with puce scrolls enclosing sprays of flowers, the interior with further flowers and puce scrolling, c1765, 6in (15cm) wide.
£850–900 *P*

A Worcester porcelain cream boat, the leaf-moulded and spiral reeded body painted with flowers, c1768, 4¼in (11cm) long.
£450–500 *Bea (E)*

A Lowestoft blue and white cream boat, of shell form, painted with scattered flower sprigs, incised cross mark, c1770, 3½in (9cm) long.
£700–800 *S*

A Worcester cream boat, with gadrooned edge and applied strap handle, painted in blue with the Narcissus pattern, crescent mark, c1776, 4¾in (12cm) wide.
£550–600 *P*

Scent Bottles

A Berlin scent bottle, with hinged cover, painted in panels on both sides with Watteauesque figures, reserved on a moulded fluted ground picked out in celadon green, the shoulders and foot painted with flowers and insects, sceptre mark in blue, 19thC, 3¼in (8.5cm) high.
£275–300 *P*

A Coalport double scent bottle, with stoppers, decorated with a country scene and gilt border, on a pink ground, c1860, 4in (10cm) high.
£600–700 *BHa*

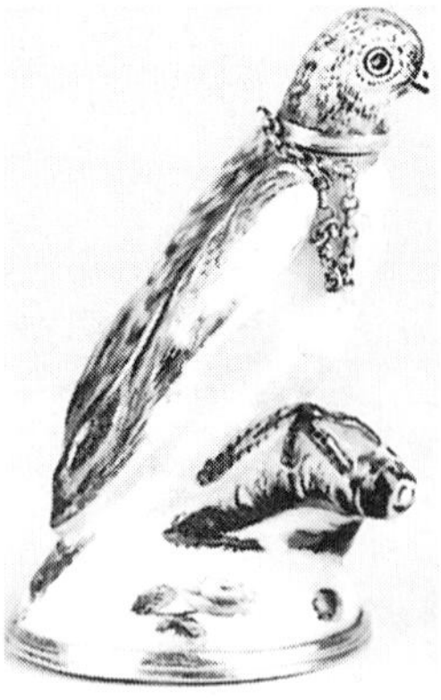

A 'Girl-in-a-Swing' scent bottle and cover, modelled as a bird, enamelled with bright polychrome plumage in tones of puce, green, yellow and manganese, *deutsche Blumen* painted base, restored, c1760, 2¼in (5.5cm) high.
£850–950 *Bon*

'Girl-in-a-Swing' pieces are principally porcelain novelties, such as scent bottles and bonbonnières, produced in the mid-18thC by the London jeweller Charles Gouyn from his house in Bennet Street, St James's. The name derives from a figure group in the Victoria & Albert Museum by the same maker.

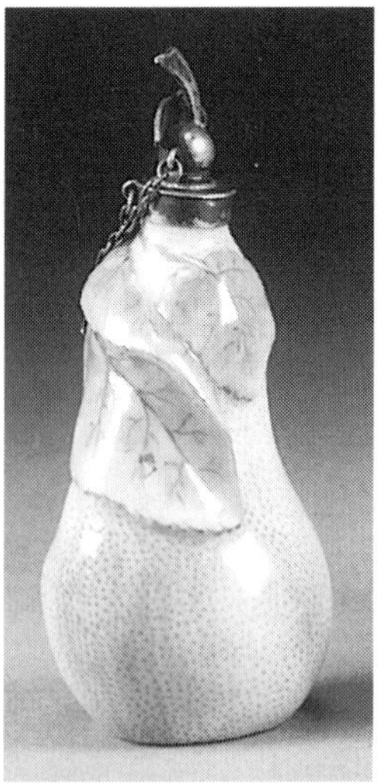

A Fürstenberg scent flask, in the form of a pear, naturalistically modelled and coloured with 2 leaves, the metal stopper as a branch with 2 leaves, attached with a short chain, traces of 'F' in underglaze blue, c1770, 3in (7.5cm) high.
£1,600–1,800 *S*

A porcelain scent bottle, in the form of a Willow pattern plate, with silver top by Samson Mordan, c1889, 1¾in (4.5cm) diam.
£180–250 *DIC*

A porcelain scent bottle, in the form of a bird's egg, by MacIntyre, with silver screw top by Samson Mordan, c1880, 2in (5cm) high.
£450–500 *BHa*

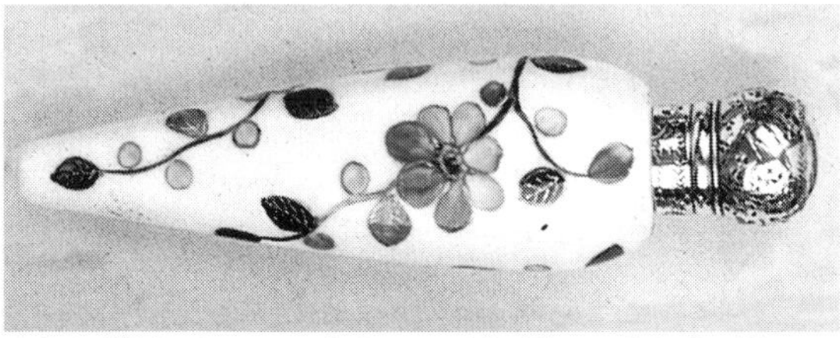

A late Victorian porcelain scent bottle, painted with trailing flowering branches with burgundy and pale pink flowers, the silver top engraved, maker's mark of Charles May, London 1884, 5in (12.5cm) long.
£320–360 *Bon*

An Edwardian porcelain scent bottle, modelled as a strawberry, with silver screw top, Birmingham 1904, 2¼in (5.5cm) long.
£350–400 *Bon*

Tea Canisters

l. A Bristol tea canister and cover, painted with leaves between bands of trailing flowers, the cover with rose finial, c1775, 4in (10cm) high.
£520–600 *P*

A Meissen tea canister and cover, in iron-red, yellow, puce, blue and turquoise on a green ground, crossed swords mark in underglaze blue, c1735, 4½in (11.5cm) high.
£2,000–2,200 *S(NY)*

A Worcester, Locke and Co tea canister and metal cover, painted by James Henry Lewis, decorated with a chaffinch perched on a branch, signed, globe mark in green, 4in (10cm) high.
£120–140 *P*

Trays

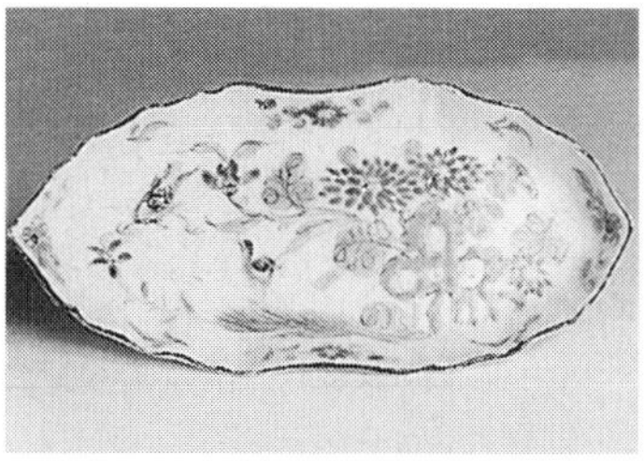

A Bow spoon tray, of lobed silver form, painted in colours with birds beside a spray of flowering peony issuing from blue pierced rockwork, the raised sides with further floral sprigs, blue line rim, c1754, 6¾in (17cm) wide.
£2,500–3,000 *P*

A Copeland & Garrett pen tray, decorated with gilt and blue border and flowers, c1840, 10¾in (27.5cm) wide.
£120–160 *DAN*

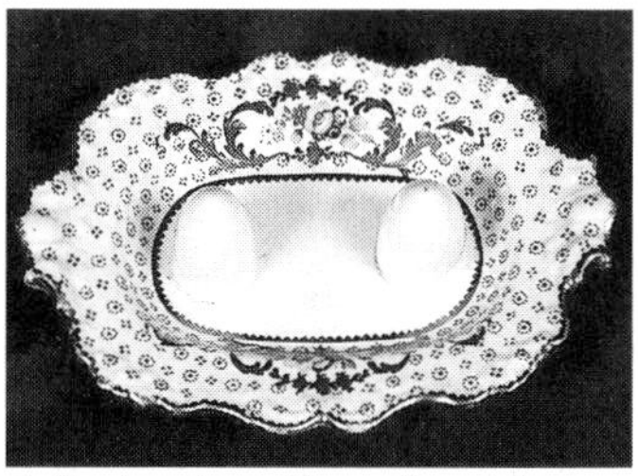

A Coalport candle extinguisher tray, painted with mock Sèvres mark, c1845, 7in (18cm) wide.
£120–145 *MiA*

A Swansea London-decorated cabaret tray, painted with a flower spray and colourful moths, the gold border with rococo scrollwork and foliage, impressed 'Swansea', c1815, 12¼in (31cm) square.
£6,000–7,000 *P*

Miller's is a price GUIDE not a price LIST

A Worcester spoon tray, painted in typical colours with a cloud-shaped panel decorated with a very early version of the 'Stag Hunt' pattern, slight damage, c1752, 5in (15cm) wide.
£550–650 *P*

Tureens

A Berlin tureen and cover, painted in colours, with sprays and bouquets of *deutsche Blumen*, surmounted by a Bacchic putto, c1880, 18½in (47cm) high.
£2,500–3,000 *S(Am)*

A tureen and cover, in Sèvres style, painted with fruit and floral sprays within gilt and blue borders, date code for 1768, 13½in (34cm) diam.
£950–1,100 *P(EA)*

A pair of Coalport sauce tureens, covers and stands and a dish, from a 'Union' dessert service, painted with exotic birds in a landscape, within a gilt-edged turquoise border and gadroon-edged rim, c1820, largest 12in (30.5cm) wide.
£450–500 *S(NY)*

A Vienna tureen and cover, painted with flowers and bouquets of flowers, rocaille handles heightened with purple, lemon twig finial, some restoration, underglaze blue beehive mark, c1772, 7in (18cm) high.
£650–750 *DORO*

A pair of Minton sauce tureens, the covers with bud finials, with gadrooned rims, gilt mask loop handles, stylised sprig decoration in green and red with blue banding and gilt embellishment, each on spreading foot, 19thC, 7in (18cm) wide.
£400–450 *AH*

A pair of English porcelain sauce tureens and covers, with berry knops, scrolling side handles and tall feet, painted in enamels and gilt with flower sprigs and sprays in the French taste, pattern No. 370, c1820, 7½in (18.5cm) high.
£300–350 *WW*

Vases

A pair of vases, with gilt rims, decorated with birds in a landscape within gilt foliate borders, on a blue ground, probably Coalport 19thC, 3½in (9cm) high.
£250–300 *GAK*

A Coalport vase, by Thomas Baxter, painted with a lady seated in a rural landscape, on a ground of red and gold vertical stripes, within gilt Greek key and floral borders, base inscribed 'T. Baxter 1804', 7in (18cm) high.
£4,500–5,000 *P*

A Coalport vase and cover, with floral painted panels, on a blue ground, supported on a square base, the cover with a triple ring finial, painted blue monogram mark, c1851, 15¾in (40cm) high.
£2,000–2,200 *P(E)*

This vase is a copy of an 18thC Sèvres shape.

A Copeland & Garrett vase and cover, painted with flowers and fruit within scrolling enamel cartouches on a gilt leaf decorated beige ground, printed mark, mid-19thC, 11in (28cm) high.
£550–600 *WW*

A Royal Crown Derby vase and cover, painted by Desiré Leroy, with gilt scroll side handles, on a gilt decorated blue ground, raised on a shaped scrolling foot, printed mark, '1133/X' incised, date code for 1897, restored, 8in (20cm) high.
£2,600–3,000 *WW*

A commemorative vase, by Copeland for Goode, printed in colours with a portrait of King Edward VII, the reverse with an allegory of Peace, inner rim with ribboned inscriptions, gilt rim, c1910, 7in (18cm) high.
£850–950 *SAS*

A pair of George Jones *pâte sur pâte* vases, decorated with nesting birds and aquatic plants below an acanthus border, moulded ring handles, gilt-lined, pattern No. 5638B, c1870, 8in (20.5cm) high.
£950–1,100 *Hal*

l. A pair of Royal Crown Derby vases and covers, with gilt rims, decorated with bellflowers on deep blue reserves, one cover missing and handles restored, signed 'Leroy', printed marks and date cypher for 1897, 6in (15cm) high.
£850–900 *GAK*

A pair of Dresden vases, painted in polychrome enamels with panels of figures and flowers, within gilt scrolling borders on turquoise grounds, 'AR' monograms, mid-19thC, 24in (61cm) high.
£1,750–2,000 *WW*

Belleek

Please see our Focus on Ireland section.

l. A pair of Longton Hall vases, the covers formed as arrangements of flowers, the bodies of rococo shape moulded with scrolls and picked out in puce, each painted with sprays and sprigs of flowers to the sides and bases, c1755, 6in (15cm) high.
£1,300–1,500 *WW*

A pair of New Chelsea vases, printed and painted with flowers within blue and gilt borders, c1919, 5in (12.5cm) high.
£110–130 *WAC*

New Chelsea is the trade name of a Staffordshire factory active from 1912–51.

A Sèvres vase, painted in the Japanese style, printed and incised marks in red and green, c1852, 12½in (32cm) high.
£1,000–1,200 *S*

A Minton vase and cover, with green rustic handles, one side painted with a view entitled 'Near Bagnall', the reverse with a flower spray, gilt line borders and details, on a matched stand, unmarked, c1830, 9¾in (24.5cm) high.
£520–580 *WW*

l. A Spode two-handled vase, decorated in Japan pattern, within bead borders, lion mask gilt loop handles, marked in red and '967', c1810, 7½in (19cm) high.
£650–750 *Hal*

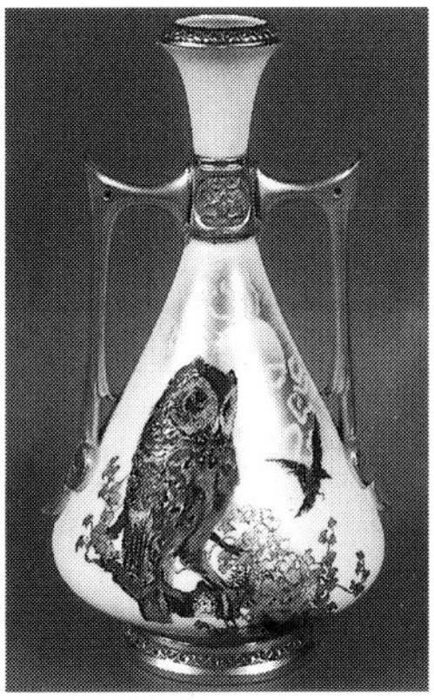

A Royal Worcester vase, attributed to Charles Baldwyn, decorated with an owl on a white and gilt background, gilt handles, c1889, 9½in (24cm) high.
£800–900 *TH*

r. A pair of Royal Worcester vases and covers, painted with hunting scenes, with gilt enamelled pink ground, late 19thC, 11½in (29cm) high.
£1,250–1,400 *AH*

A pair of vases and covers, by Helena Wolfsohn, Dresden, painted with panels of chinoiserie figures, late 19thC, 13½in (34cm) high.
£2,300–2,600 *P*

A pair of Royal Worcester two-handled stemmed vases, decorated with flowers inside a gilt border on a red ground, c1900, 4in (10cm) high.
£700–750 *TH*

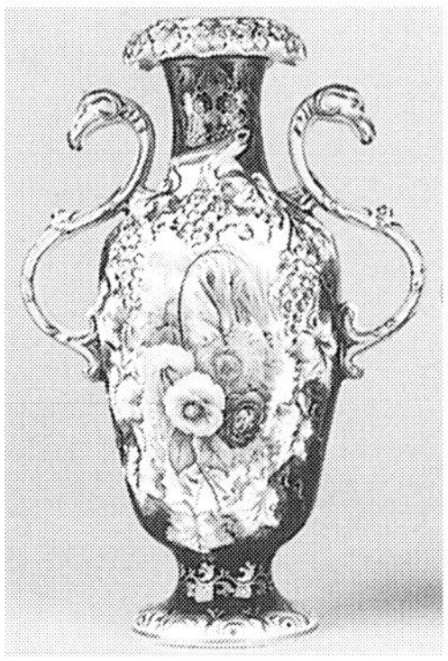

A pair of porcelain vases, with polychrome painted summer flowers on a cobalt blue ground, the rim moulded with ivy leaves, picked out in gilt on an apricot ground, c1830, 9¼in (23.5cm) high.
£450–550 *Bon*

Goss & Crested China

A W. H. Goss model of the Sandbach crosses, c1880, 10¼in (26cm) high.
£1,300–1,500 *G&CC*

A Goss candle extinguisher, in the form of a nun, c1890, 3¾in (9.5cm) high.
£100–120 *TH*

Two Goss candle extinguishers, in the form of the Welsh Lady, c1890, 4½in (11.5cm) high.
£70–80 each *G&CC*

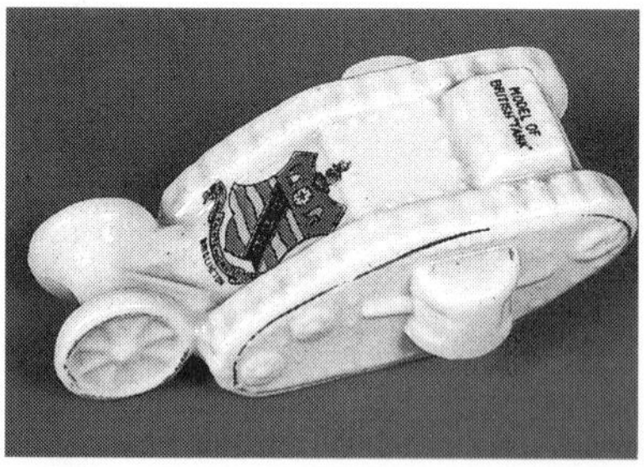

l. A Willow Art model of a British tank, inscribed 'Bridlington', c1917, 4¾in (12cm) wide.
£30–35 *JMC*

A Carlton Ware map of England, entitled 'Blighty', c1915, 4½in (11.5cm) high.
£75–85 *G&CC*

Two Crested China figures,
l. A cat, c1920, 4in (10cm) high,
r. Arcadian sergeant major pepper pot, c1920, 3¼in (8.5cm) high.
£50–60 each *G&CC*

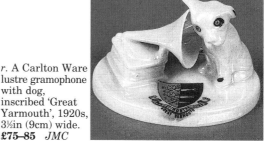

r. A Carlton Ware lustre gramophone with dog, inscribed 'Great Yarmouth', 1920s, 3½in (9cm) wide.
£75–85 *JMC*

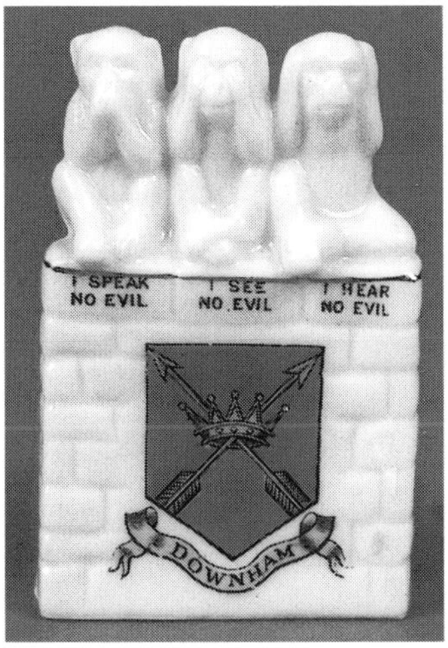

An Arcadian model of the 3 wise monkeys, inscribed 'Downham', c1920, 3in (7.5cm) high.
£15–18 *JMC*

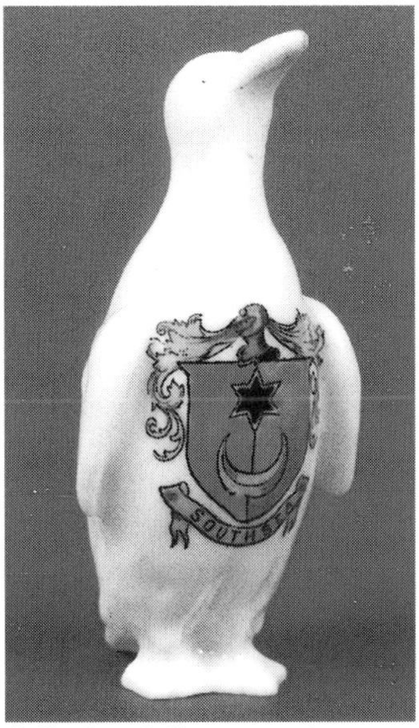

A Grafton & Sons penguin, inscribed 'Southsea', c1920, 3½in (9cm) high.
£24–28 *BCO*

A W. H. Goss Italian krater, made for the International League of Goss Collectors, c1922, 4in (10cm) high.
£125–150 *G&CC*

A Swan seesaw, with black cats, inscribed 'Ramsey Hunts', 1930s, 3¼in (8.5cm) wide.
£125–150 *JMC*

A W. H. Goss model of the Trusty Servant, c1930, 5in (12.5cm) wide.
£575–625 *G&CC*

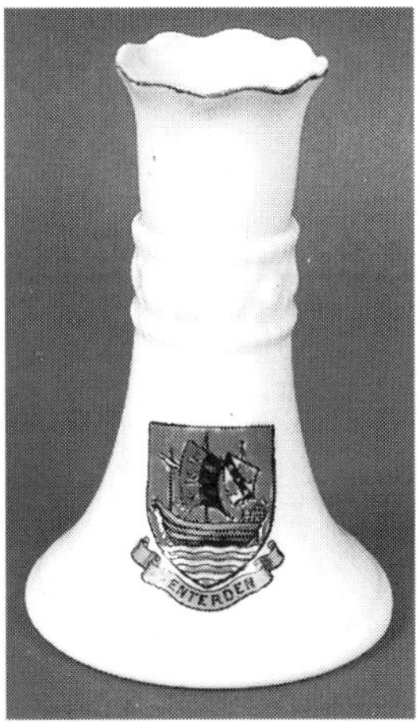

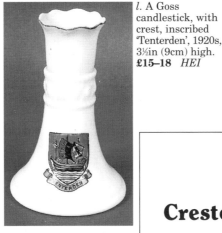

l. A Goss candlestick, with crest, inscribed 'Tenterden', 1920s, 3½in (9cm) high.
£15–18 *HEI*

r. A watering can, inscribed 'Cork', Czechoslovakia, c1940, 3in (7.5cm) high.
£15–18 *MLa*

A Goss pig, inscribed 'Belfast', c1920, 2in (5cm) high.
£18–21 *MLa*

Chinese Dynasties and Marks

Early Dynasties

新石器時代	Neolithic	10th – early 1st millennium BC	唐	Tang Dynasty	AD 618 – 907
商	Shang Dynasty	16th Century – c1050 BC	五代	Five Dynasties	AD 907 – 960
周	Zhou Dynasty	c1050 – 221 BC	遼	Liao Dynasty	AD 907 – 1125
秦	Qin Dynasty	221 – 206 BC	宋	Song Dynasty	AD 960 – 1279
漢	Han Dynasty	206 BC – AD 220	北宋	*Northern Song*	AD 960 – 1127
三國	Three Kingdoms	AD 220 – 265	南宋	*Southern Song*	AD 1127 – 1279
晉	Jin Dynasty	AD 265 – 420	西夏	Xixia Dynasty	AD 1038 – 1227
南北朝	Southern & Northern Dynasties	AD 420 – 589	金	Jin Dynasty	AD 1115 – 1234
隋	Sui Dynasty	AD 581 – 618	元	Yuan Dynasty	AD 1279 – 1368

Ming Dynasty Marks

Hongwu
1368–1398

Yongle
1403–1424

Xuande
1426–1435

Chenghua
1465–1487

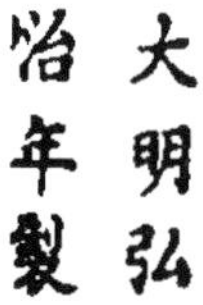
Hongzhi
1488–1505

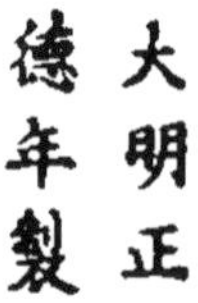
Zhengde
1506–1521

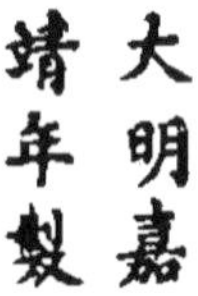
Jiajing
1522–1566

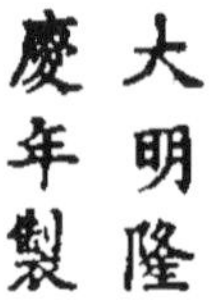
Longqing
1567–1572

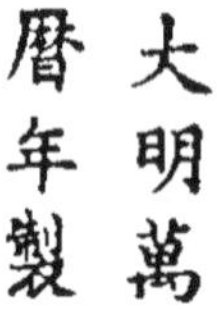
Wanli
1573–1620

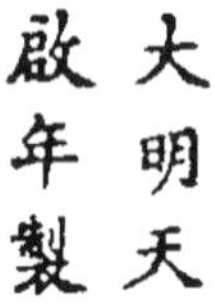
Tianqi
1621–1627

Chongzhen
1628–1644

Qing Dynasty Marks

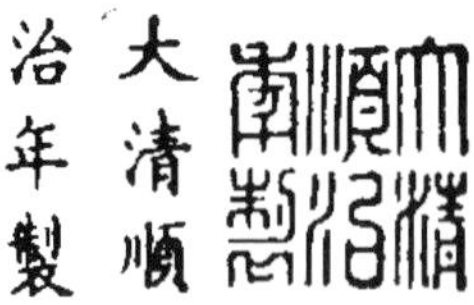
Shunzhi
1644–1661

Kangxi
1662–1722

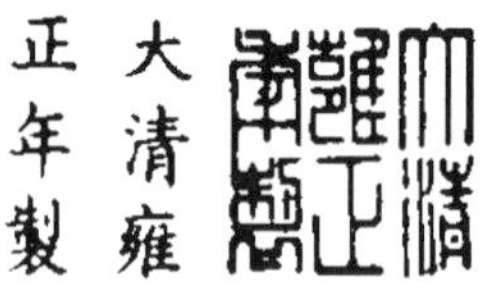
Yongzheng
1723–1735

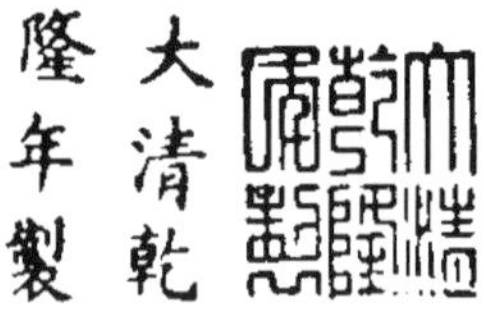
Qianlong
1736–1795

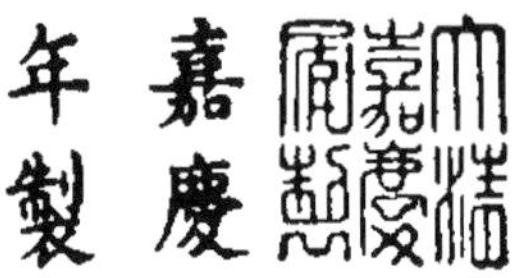
Jiaqing
1796–1820

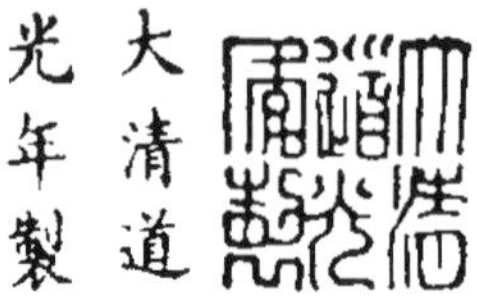
Daoguang
1821–1850

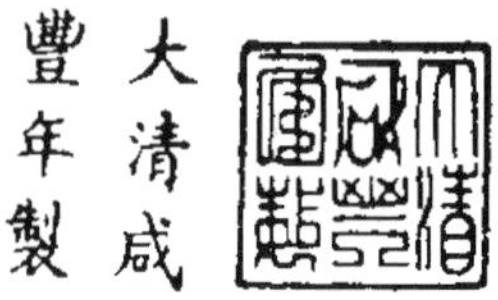
Xianfeng
1851–1861

Tongzhi
1862–1874

Guangxu
1875–1908

Xuantong
1909–1911

Hongxian
1916

ORIENTAL CERAMICS

The recent economic and political troubles in Asia have not adversely affected the market for Asian ceramics. The major buyers are Americans and Europeans. 'Although there has been some resistance to buying in Hong Kong and Japan, Taiwan buyers are still a force,' said London dealer Giuseppe Eskenazi. His two-week selling exhibition in New York recently attracted a large international group of collectors and museum curators attending the Asian sales and the International Asian Fair which, for the last three years, has made New York the centre of the market.

The entire field of Asian art, and ceramics in particular, has a bright future according to Carol Conover, specialist in Chinese works of art at the Kaikodo New York gallery. The market for Chinese ceramics is truly international. 'The Japanese are not buying now, but the Americans are on a roll and the Chinese are poised to begin,' she said. 'The market for Chinese ceramics is really two parallel markets – the porcelain buyers and the pottery collectors – and they are often different nationalities. Imperial porcelain is bought by Asians, and Han and Tang figures by Westerners. Today the hiccup in Asian economics has affected the Imperial porcelain market, making it very selective with only the top pieces selling, but it has had no effect on the earlier wares.'

The market for Japanese ceramics is not as old, as large, as international or as high-priced as the market for Chinese ceramics. There is a strong market for utility wares made for Japanese consumption, some of which are considered folk art. Rarities from the 15th and 16th centuries are hard to find and can be very expensive. 'The market for Satsuma is quiet now, except for top of the line, and at that level availability is the problem,' said Clifford Schaefer, the New York specialist in Meiji period export porcelain. 'The market for Hirado is also weak, but there is a demand for Meiji period Imari – the red, blue and gold colour scheme fits into every period of decoration.' There is also new interest in contemporary Japanese ceramics, and New York dealer Joan Mirviss has a waiting list for new items by present-day well-known artists.

The ailing Korean economy caused Sotheby's and Christie's to call off their Korean sales in New York recently. Because it is illegal to buy antique porcelain in Korea for export, the Western market consists of pieces brought out in the 1950s or pieces found in Japan where Korean ceramics have been appreciated for centuries. 'There is a demand for the rarest and highest quality,' says Suzanne Mitchell, who recently established her gallery in New York.

Lita Solis-Cohen

Animals

A pottery model of a horse, painted and with straw-coloured glaze, on a rectangular base, surface degradation, Sui Dynasty, 12¾in (32.5cm) high.
£1,400–1,600 *S(NY)*

A pottery model of a saddled horse, with buff coloured body and traces of original pigment, some restoration, Tang Dynasty, 24in (61cm) high.
£3,500–4,000 *WW*

A *famille rose* model of a hawk, perched on a tree stump, the bird brightly enamelled, slight damage, 19thC, 8¼in (21cm) high.
£400–450 *WW*

A pair of turquoise glazed ormolu-mounted figures of goats, the backs, necks and chins incised with long hair, c1800, 9½in (24cm) long.
£2,600–3,000 *Bon*

A pair of Chinese porcelain models of seated cats, each with a purple flambé glaze, 19thC, 7½in (19cm) high.
£600–700 *WW*

Bowls

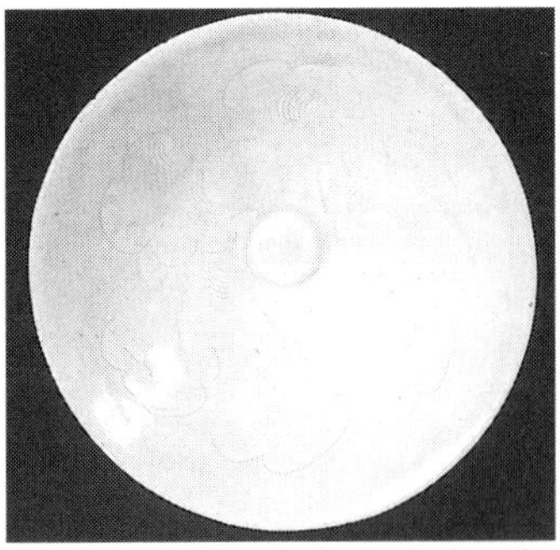

A Dingware bowl, decorated with an incised cloud-like pattern, Song Dynasty, 6¾in (17cm) diam.
£700–800 *HUR*

Dingware is the classic white-glazed porcelain from the 10th–13thC. Manufactured in northern China it was one of the first true porcelains to be made.

A *rouge de fer* decorated bowl, Kangxi period, 10in (25.5cm) diam.
£750–850 *GeW*

Rouge de fer *is an iron-red on-glaze decoration, using iron oxide.*

A punchbowl, decorated with Mandarin palette, Qianlong period, 15¾in (40cm) diam.
£2,750–3,200 *S(S)*

The Mandarin palette portrays the day-to-day life of the Mandarin class. This was very popular in the west, and is therefore common in export wares.

A *famille rose* eggshell bowl, painted in *Shining* style, the reverse with a poem, all below a *ruyi* border, the interior with a dragon roundel, blue enamel Qianlong mark, 5½in (14cm) diam.
£800–900 *S(Am)*

Shining *is named after Lang Shining, the Chinese name given to a Jesuit priest (Castiglione) who was a resident artist at the 18thC Imperial Court.*

A Longquan celadon brush washer, moulded with a recessed band around the sides, covered overall with a rich sea-green glaze, Southern Song Dynasty, 4⅓in (11cm) diam.
£5,500–6,500 *S(HK)*

A U-shaped bowl and cover, decorated in underglaze blue with panels of antiques on a prunus and cracked ice ground, chipped, Kangxi period, 8¾in (22cm) high.
£450–500 *DN*

r. A Canton *famille rose* bowl, decorated with panels of figures in interiors, with birds and butterflies amidst flowers and foliage, mid-19thC, 15¾in (40cm) diam, with wooden stand.
£900–1,000 *WW*

A *sang-de-boeuf* conical bowl, glazed with creamy-white and red, on a narrow foot, Qianlong seal mark in underglaze blue and of the period, 6in (15cm) diam.
£450–500 *P*

Sang-de-boeuf *translates literally as ox-blood, and is a bright red glaze used extensively during the Qing dynasty.*

A Nanking pouring bowl, decorated in underglaze blue with trellis pattern above panels of scenes of pagodas, late 18thC, 6in (15cm) diam.
£120–140 *GAK*

Celadon glaze

Celadon is a semi-opaque glaze, usually grey-green, applied to Chinese stoneware before firing.

The glaze is compounded with a small amount of iron-oxide which, after a 'reduced' firing, is converted from ferric oxide to ferrous oxide. In this type of firing in which the kiln is starved of oxygen at peak temperature it is impossible to control the amount of reduction, therefore no 2 pieces are ever the same.

A pair of porcelain bowls, painted with fish, on a mottled blue ground, each on a raised base and later wooden stand, Xuande mark, Kangxi period, c1700, 6in (15cm) diam.
£2,100–2,500 *Gam*

A Canton bowl, painted in *famille rose* enamels with birds and butterflies, Taoist symbols within scroll borders, mid-19thC, 14½in (37cm) diam.
£850–950 *Hal*

A pair of bowls, decorated with Yanzhi Hong red glaze, c1915, 5¾in (14.5cm) diam.
£1,000–1,200 *Wai*

Boxes

A *famille rose* box and cover, painted with multi-coloured floral scrolls, the cover with a raised panel of flowers issuing from *lingzhi* within a gilt border, iron-red seal mark and period of Qianlong, 3in (7.5cm) square.
£3,200–3,600 *S(HK)*

A seal paste box, decorated with a cicada on bamboo, by Bi Botao, signed and inscribed, c1925, 2½in (6.5cm) diam.
£800–1,000 *Wai*

The work of Bi Botao (1885–1961) is very rare. He specialised in bird, insect and flower painting.

A seal paste box, painted in He Xuren style, decorated with a winter landscape, artist base mark in iron red, c1940, 2½in (6.5cm) diam.
£950–1,100 *Wai*

He Xuren was a Chinese porcelain artist famous for his snow scene painting.

Brush Pots

A brush pot, decorated with a dignatory and 3 attendants before a pavilion in a watery landscape, Transitional period, c1640, 7in (18cm) high.
£1,100–1,300 *WW*

A brush pot, the neck incised with a flower and leaf scroll, the foot incised with waves and rockwork, painted with a groom attending to 2 tethered horses beneath a willow tree, Transitional period, c1640, 7in (18cm) high
£3,500–4,000 *WW*

A brush pot, painted in outline and wash in shades of vivid cobalt with a figure being received by an official, Transitional period, c1640, 8in (20.5cm) high, with wood stand.
£2,000–2,200 *P*

A blue and white brush pot, decorated with Master of the Rocks pattern, depicting 2 figures on a bridge in a mountainous landscape, Kangxi period, 6½in (16.5cm) diam.
£1,000–1,200 *S*

r. A part scholar's set, comprising brush pot, water jar and seal paste box, decorated with a bird and peony, by Liu Yucen, c1930, 6in (15cm) high.
£1,500–1,800 *Wai*

Censers

A green-glazed hill censer, the cover with mountain peaks moulded with riders on horseback, the body with a frieze of mythical animals and stylised figures, Han Dynasty, 9in (23cm) high.
£3,500–4,000 *S(NY)*

A celadon tripod censer, the sides carved with a band of foliate diaperwork between 'riveted' flanged borders, on lions' mask and scroll feet, early Ming Dynasty, 12½in (32cm) diam.
£400–450 *P*

A *wucai* enamelled censer, decorated in shades of green, iron-red and blue on a white ground, c1680, 9in (23cm) diam.
£900–1,100 *GeW*

Wucai *means 5 colours.*

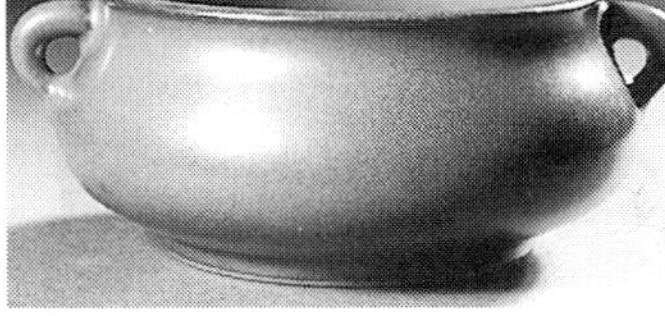

l. A censer, with 2 loop handles, covered with a green tea-leaf glaze interspersed with a fine speckling of yellow, Qianlong period, 6¾in (17cm) diam.
£3,500–4,000 *S*

Cups

A blue and white stem cup, moulded on the interior with a band of flowerheads and scrollwork, decorated in underglaze blue with 2 dragons chasing flaming pearls, scrollwork frieze on the inside lip, cracked, Yuan Dynasty, 3½in (9cm) high.
£2,500–3,000 *S(NY)*

A blue and white stem cup, Xuantong period, 6¾in (17cm) high.
£2,000–2,300 *Wai*

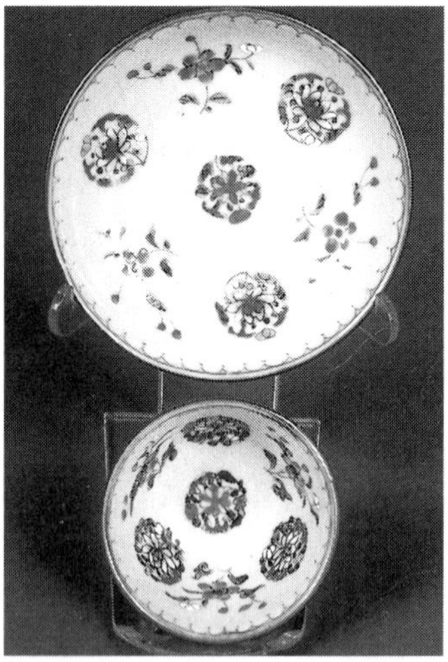

A set of 6 *famille rose* cups and saucers, with *cafe au lait* exterior glaze, Qianlong period, saucer 4¼in (11cm) diam.
£500–600 *GeW*

Three *famille rose* tea bowls and saucers, brightly decorated with a cockerel standing on rockwork amidst peonies and leaves, Yongzheng period, saucers 4½in (11.5cm) diam.
£450–500 *WW*

A *famille rose* tea cup and saucer, c1790, saucer 3¼in (8.5cm) diam.
£120–150 *ALB*

Dishes

A *kraak porselein* blue and white dish, Wanli period, 5½in (14cm) diam.
£400–500 *GeW*

A dish, decorated with a central panel of a female in a trellised garden, the border with alternating panels of figures and flowers, six-character Kangxi mark, 6¼in (16cm) diam.
£420–470 *WW*

A saucer-shaped dish, decorated with Imari colours, mid-18thC, 9½in (24cm) diam.
£250–300 *GeW*

A Chinese export Canton blue and white shrimp dish, c1820, 10½in (26.5cm) diam.
£450–500 *A&A*

A Canton leaf dish, decorated in green pink and blue enamels, c1840, 7in (18cm) wide.
£140–160 *ALB*

A dish, decorated with Imari colours, the centre panel painted as a jardinière of flowers, with foliate border and shaped rim, 19thC, 12¾in (32.5cm) square.
£300–350 *AG*

Figures

A grey pottery figure of a Western Han official, Han Dynasty, 9in (23cm) high.
£150–170 *ORI*

A *blanc de chine* group, depicting Guanyin, the goddess of Mercy, mid-17thC, 9½in (24cm) high.
£700–800 *GeW*

A *blanc de chine* figure of Guanyin, with a boy on her lap, slight damage, 18thC, 11in (28cm) high.
£2,500–2,800 *S(NY)*

r. A *blanc de chine* group of Guanyin, Dehua gourd mark, damaged, late 18thC, 15in (38cm) high.
£2,200–2,500 *S(Am)*

A painted pottery figure of a warrior, wearing an unusual helmet, traces of pigment, Northern Wei Dynasty, 14¼in (36cm) high.
£2,300–2,600 *S*

A *blanc de chine* figure of a scholar-immortal and attendant, possibly representing *Wen Qiang*, the god of Literature, with a milky-white glaze, mid-17thC, 9¼in (23.5cm) high.
£360–420 *P*

A red pottery figure of a 'Fat Lady', wearing long flowing robes, head restuck, Tang Dynasty, 13½in (34.5cm) high.
£3,500–4,000 *S*

A pottery figure of a groom, the long tunic with incised details glazed in an amber colour, the details of the face picked out in pigment, Tang Dynasty, 15in (38cm) high.
£3,500–4,000 *S*

l. A *blanc de chine* figure of a *lohan*, seated on a rock, neck and one hand restored, minor losses, 17thC, 7in (17.5cm) high.
£1,200–1,400 *S(Am)*

A figure of Guanyin, wearing a purple cloak over an iron-red dress decorated with gold flowers and holding a scroll, thumb restuck, late 18thC, 10in (25.5cm) high.
£750–850 *S*

A tilework figure of a warrior, the detail of his clothing worked in relief and enhanced with ochre, green and turquoise glazes, on a glazed square base, Kangxi period, 16¾in (42.5cm) high.
£280–320 *P*

Flatware

A pair of unglazed green biscuit decorated celadon dishes, the centre with an unglazed relief-moulded flowerhead, Yuan Dynasty, 6¼in (16cm) diam.
£2,300–2,600 *S(NY)*

An underglaze blue, iron-red and green enamelled plate, painted with a figure of a seated Buddha, Tianqi period, 7½in (19cm) diam.
£700–800 *P*

An Imari plate, Kangxi period, 8½in (21.5cm) diam.
£120–140 *ORI*

A porcelain blue and white dish, decorated with a floral design, Kangxi period, 8in (20.5cm) diam.
£150–170 *ORI*

A blue and white charger, painted in the centre with pavilions, trees and cranes, encircled on the everted rim by a band of pheonix and lotus scrolls, Ming Dynasty, 17¼in (44cm) diam.
£2,800–3,000 *S*

A charger, painted with a crane swooping towards a deer sheltering under a pine tree, encircled by 6 further cranes on the broad everted rim, Kangxi period, 15in (38cm) diam.
£2,300–2,600 *S*

A pair of plates, decorated with Long Elisa pattern, Kangxi period, 8⅛in (20.5cm) diam.
£800–900 *GeW*

A *kraak porselein* blue and white dish, Wanli period, 10¾in (27.5cm) diam.
£700–800 *GeW*

Symbols

The decoration on Chinese ceramics usually has symbolic significance:

Dragons represent authority, strength, wisdom, and the Emperor.

Pairs of ducks symbolize marital bliss.

The peony shows love, beauty, happiness and honour.

The pine, *prunus* and bamboo together denote spiritual harmony.

Cranes show longevity, and transport for Immortals.

l. A blue and white dish, decorated in the centre with a peony, the barbed rim with flowering branches, Kangxi mark and of the period, 14¼in (36cm) diam.
£550–600 *S(Am)*

A blue and white dish, decorated with Scholar Dreaming pattern, Kangxi period, 10½in (26.5cm) diam.
£300–350 *ORI*

A blue and white meat dish, 18thC, 17in (43cm) wide.
£1,400–1,600 *GeW*

A *famille rose* plate, decorated with flowers, c1790, 9in (23cm) diam.
£130–150 *ALB*

A Chinese export saucer, decorated in *rouge de fer*, c1790, 8in (20.5cm) diam.
£300–350 *DUB*

A pair of Canton meat dishes, c1840, 17¼in (44cm) diam.
£1,500–1,800 *GeW*

A Chinese Imari charger, early 18thC, 13½in (34.5cm) diam.
£800–950 *GeW*

A pair of *famille rose* chargers, decorated with peacocks amongst peony and rockwork, the border with 3 landscapes of geese beside flowers and rockwork, Qianlong period, 14¼in (36cm) diam.
£950–1,100 *Bon(N)*

A pair of Chinese export *famille rose* plates, the centres decorated with Hope, Qianlong period, 7½in (19cm) diam.
£2,300–2,600 *WW*

A blue and white charger, the centre painted with a scene of figures on an island in a mountainous landscape, the border decorated with trellis patterns, scrolls and foliage, late 18thC, 18in (45.5cm) diam.
£360–420 *GAK*

A Chinese export *famille rose* charger, sauce boat and dish, c1745, charger 13in (33cm) diam.
£3,500–4,000 *DUB*

A Chinese export plate, painted in Meissen style, hairline crack, c1775, 9in (23cm) diam.
£200–220 *Wai*

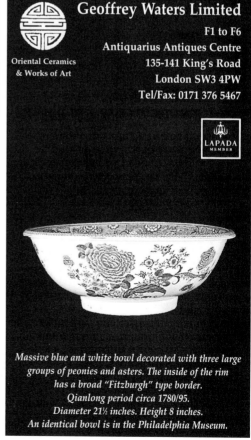

Garden Seats

A Fahua-glazed garden seat, the pierced top with a band of leafy scrolls, the side set with 4 mask handles with mock ring handles, covered overall with 2 tones of blue glaze, Ming Dynasty, 14¾in (37.5cm) high.
£2,600–3,000 *S(NY)*

A pair of carved celadon-glazed garden seats, each of a barrel form, covered overall with a sea-green glaze suffused with fine bubbles, one with stained area, Qing Dynasty, 7¼in (18.5cm) high.
£6,000–6,600 *S(HK)*

A barrel-shaped garden seat, painted with flowers and foliage, on a green ground with 2 pierced medallion pattern panels to the sides, 19thC, 18¼in (46.5cm) high.
£750–900 *AG*

r. A pair of *famille rose* garden seats, each decorated with scenes of interiors and elegantly dressed figures, reserved against a flower-strewn ground, 19thC, 18½in (47cm) high.
£3,200–3,600 *S(NY)*

A pair of *famille rose* porcelain garden seats, decorated with bird and floral pattern, Qing Dynasty, 12¼in (31cm) high.
£850–950 *SLN*

Jardinières

A Longquan jardinière, carved on the exterior with a band of scrolling foliage, within a raised rib above and below, 15thC, 9½in (24cm) diam.
£550–600 *P*

A blue and white jardinière, decorated with a broad lotus scroll, Kangxi period, 14¼in (36cm) high.
£2,800–3,200 *S(Am)*

A blue and white jardinière, decorated in Ming style with lotus heads and foliage below, Qianlong period, 16½in (42cm) high.
£1,200–1,400 *S(Am)*

A blue and white jardinière, painted around the sides with a continuous leafy lotus scroll, Qing Dynasty, 25¾in (65.5cm) diam, with wooden stand
£4,800–5,200 *S(HK)*

A blue and white jardinière, painted around the exterior with phoenix roundels enclosed by scrolling tendrils, the base pierced with a hole, Qing Dynasty, 15in (38cm) diam.
£2,400–2,700 *S(HK)*

Reign Marks

Eighty per cent of reign marks on Chinese porcelain are retrospective, intended as a tribute to Imperial ancestors. Square seal marks sometimes replace the more usual character marks. Reading from the top right down, a six-character mark includes: character for 'great'; dynasty; emperor's first name; emperor's second name and 2 characters meaning 'in the reign of'. Pieces that bear the correct mark for their period (catalogued 'mark and of the period') are more valuable than those with anachronistic marks.

Jars

A matched pair of jars, painted in underglaze blue and white with sprays of peonies, Kangxi period, 4in (10cm) high.
£300–350 *P*

A ginger jar, decorated in underglaze blue with roundels showing 3 figures on a terrace, on a ribbed ground, with carved hardwood cover and soapstone dog finial, Jiajing mark, Kangxi period, 8in (20cm) high.
£450–500 *DN*

A dragon jar, decorated with 2 dragons pursuing flaming pearls, Daoguang seal mark and of the period, 8in (20cm) high.
£1,500–1,800 *WW*

Dragons:
The Imperial dragons always have 5 claws and non-Imperial dragons have 4 claws.

Jugs

A pair of *famille verte* ewers and covers, decorated in polychrome enamels, for the Persian market, Kangxi period, 6½in (16.5cm) high.
£3,500–4,000 *S(NY)*

A blue and white ewer, decorated with 2 dignitaries in a rock garden, Transitional period, mid-17thC, 7in (18cm) high.
£2,400–2,700 *S(Am)*

A Chinese export *famille rose* jug, decorated with soldiers entering a village, damaged and repaired, Qianlong period, 12in (30.5cm) high.
£220–250 *RTo*

Mugs

A Chinese Imari bell-shaped tankard, early 18thC, 5¾in (14.5cm) high.
£650–750 *GeW*

A Chinese export mug, enamelled in polychrome and gilt with a hunting scene, Qianlong period, 5¼in (13.5cm) high.
£1,800–2,000 *HYD*

Pieces depicting European subjects are always particularly popular.

A *famille rose* tankard, decorated with a panel of Mandarin decoration, c1760, 4¼in (11cm) high.
£350–400 *GeW*

Plaques

A plaque, painted with 9 magpies, Daoguang period, 11in (28cm) diam.
£800–1,000 *Wai*

This plaque was made for setting into a piece of furniture.

A plaque, painted with 2 swallows chasing falling prunus blossom, signed 'Shi Yu Chu', c1930, 9in (23cm) wide.
£1,000–1,200 *Wai*

l. A *famille rose* plaque, decorated by Wang Yeting, with figures in a river landscape, c1930, 15in (38cm) high.
£1,700–2,000 *S(Am)*

Wang Yeting (1884–1942) was a founder member of the 'Eight Friends of Zhushan', a group of artists active 1925–1960s.

Snuff Bottles

A porcelain snuff bottle, modelled in the form of 2 boys, one dressed in blue and the other in red, their arms embracing a vase enamelled in green and incised with foliage, symbolizing peace and prosperity, Qianlong period, 2¼in (6cm) high.
£4,600–5,200 *S(NY)*

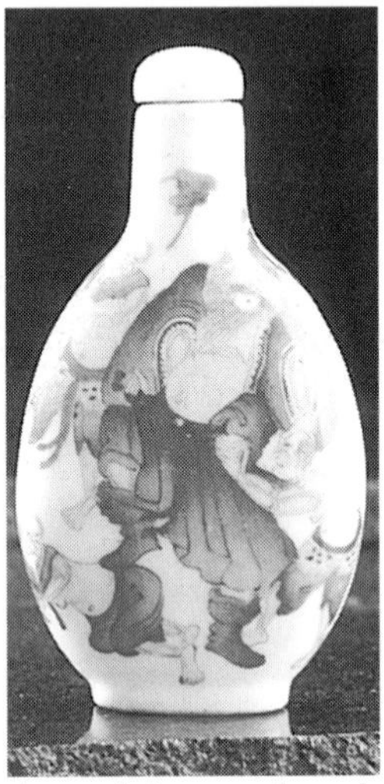

A porcelain pear-shaped snuff bottle, decorated in iron-red and white with a continuous scene of Zhonggui, surrounded by demon attendants, with jadeite stopper, 18thC, 2½in (6.5cm) high.
£1,500–1,800 *JWA*

A blue and white porcelain snuff bottle, painted with a figure and birds, 19thC, 2¾in (7cm) high.
£1,100–1,300 *JWA*

A porcelain snuff bottle, decorated *en grisaille* on a turquoise ground, iron-red four-character mark, 19thC, 2¾in (7cm) high.
£180–200 *P*

Tea Canisters

A blue and white tea canister, with silver mounts, Kangxi period, 4½in (11.5cm) high.
£650–750 *GeW*

A *famille rose* tea canister, Qianlong period, with later metal mounts, 6in (15cm) high.
£160–180 *ORI*

A blue and white tea canister, decorated with landscape and floral scenes, surmounted by a square gilt-metal mounted stopper, 18thC, 4½in (11.5cm) high.
£160–180 *P*

Tea & Coffee Pots

A blue and white teapot and cover, with fixed loop handle, Wanli period, 8in (20.5cm) high.
£850–1,000 *P*

A Yixing pottery teapot, early 18thC, 4¼in (11cm) high.
£3,200–3,600 *S(T)*

A Chinese export coffee pot, with gilt rim and entwined leaves handle, late 18thC, 10in (25.5cm) high.
£600–700 *Wai*

l. A Chinese Imari teapot, Kangxi period, c1700, 4½in (11.5cm) high.
£600–700 *GeW*

Tureens

A Chinese export *famille rose* tureen and cover, with fruit knop, decorated with scattered flowers within flower and scale borders, Qianlong period, 8in (20cm) high.
£2,800–3,200 *DN*

A Chinese export *famille rose* armorial tureen and cover, decorated with the arms of Gibbes of Tackley, with a pomegranate finial and animal head handles, Qianlong period, 14in (35.5cm) wide.
£3,500–4,000 *WW*

Philip Gibbes of Barbados (d1648) was the son of Henry Gibbes, Mayor of Bristol, and Ann Packer, cousin of Sir Thomas White, the founder of St John's College, Oxford.

A Meissen style blue and white tureen, with plumed mask handles, decorated with figures in a landscape, with a crown finial, cracked, Qianlong period, 12in (30.5cm) high.
£2,500–2,800 *S(Am)*

Vases

A blue and white miniature vase, Kangxi period, 5½in (14cm) high.
£400–500 *GeW*

A blue and white baluster-shaped vase, decorated with a mountain river landscape and figures, with a decorative border, 18thC, 18in (45.5cm) high.
£1,100–1,300 *MCA*

r. A crackle ware blue and white vase, c1900, 12in (30.5cm) high.
£60–70 *MEG*

A vase, decorated with 2 sparrows, painted and signed by Wei Xing, marked 'Jurentang zhi' in iron-red, c1940, 5in (12.5cm) high.
£1,000–1,200 *Wai*

JAPANESE CERAMICS

Japanese Chronology Chart

Jomon period (Neolithic)	circa 10,000 – circa 200 BC	Muromachi (Ashikaga) period	1333 – 1573
Yayoi period	circa 200 BC – circa 200 AD	Momoyama period	1573 – 1614
Tumulus (Kofun) period	200 – 552	Edo (Tokugawa) period	1614 – 1868
Asuka period	552 – 645	Meiji period	1868 – 1911
Nara period	645 – 794	Taisho period	1912 – 1926
Heian period	794 – 1185	Showa period	1926 –
Kamakura period	1185 – 1333		

Animals

A matched pair of Arita blue-glazed tigers, one ear restored, 19thC, 10in (25.5cm) long.
£2,000–2,200 *P*

An Hirado porcelain *suiteki*, modelled as a *minogame*, decorated in shades of blue and brown, one ear restored, 19thC, 4¾in (12cm) long.
£2,700–3,000 *S*

A minogame *is a mythical character, half turtle and half beast.*

A porcelain model of a bird, on a roof tile, decorated with brown on a white ground, signed 'Makuzu Kozan', c1900, 8in (20.5cm) wide.
£6,000–7,000 *MCN*

Bowls

An Arita blue and white bowl and cover, decorated in underglaze blue with mountainous landscapes, late 17thC, 15in (38cm) high.
£3,800–4,200 *HYD*

A porcelain blue and white leaf-shaped dish, early 19thC, 6¾in (17cm) long.
£450–500 *MCN*

An Imari barber's bowl, decorated in underglaze blue and enamelled in green, iron-red and gilt, c1800, 11in (28cm) diam.
£650–750 *HYD*

An earthenware bowl, decorated in coloured enamels and gilt, signed 'Seikozan zo', late 19thC, 9in (23cm) diam.
£1,750–2,000 *S(NY)*

r. An Imari footed dish, by Fukagawa, c1900, 10½in (26.5cm) diam.
£300–350 *MCN*

A Kakiemon style bowl, decorated in underglaze blue and iron-red with gilt flowers and green leaves, 18thC, 11in (28cm) diam.
£250–300 *WW*

A Satsuma tea bowl, with Tkugawa family crest, marked, c1880, 4¼in (11cm) diam.
£2,200–2,500 *MCN*

A Kutani porcelain bowl, decorated with figures in red, gold and brown, c1900, 9½in (24cm) diam.
£1,100–1,300 *HUR*

Figures

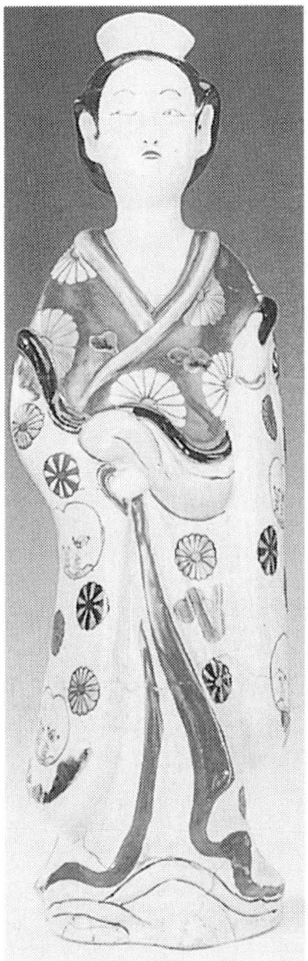

An Imari figure of a *bijin*, wearing a loose kimono, her robes gathered in her hands and with *kiku mon* decorated, damaged and repaired, c1700, 18in (45.5cm) high.
£1,300–1,500 *S(S)*

Cross Reference
Colour Review

A pottery figure of Daruma, signed 'Ryosai', c1880, 10in (25.5cm) high.
£350–400 *MCN*

A Satsuma figure of a lady with a tray and a tea bowl, on a stand, c1880, 7in (18cm) square.
£1,300–1,500 *MCN*

An Imari figure of a *bijin*, wearing a kimono, damage to comb, late 17thC/early 18thC, 15¾in (40cm) high.
£2,300–2,600 *S(S)*

A Kutani figure of a boy, decorated in blue, brown and green, c1880, 9in (23cm) high.
£270–300 *MCN*

A Satsuma earthenware figure of Ebisu, by Baizan, signed, Meiji period, 8in (20cm) high.
£800–900 *S(S)*

Kutani

Kutani is one of the most sought-after Japanese porcelains which was produced from the village of Kutani in Kaga province, Honshu. The kiln was established by 1656 and became famous for its artistic designs on large dishes. Some of the finest porcelain of the 17thC was produced there, and as pieces rarely appear on the open market some can fetch prices of up to £60,000. After a lull in the 18thC, a revivalist period took place in the early 19thC, making copies of earlier wares. These are nearly always marked under the base with the Fuku (happiness) mark. Towards the end of the 19thC a large number of wares were made for the export market. They have a predominance of finely painted on-glaze iron-red decoration and are often marked 'Kutani'.

An Imari figure of a man, large chip to base, c1700, 16in (46cm) high.
£3,500–4,000 *S(S)*

A Satsuma figure of a maiden, by Kinkozan, c1880, 17½in (44.5cm) high.
£8,000–9,000 *MCN*

Kinkozan was one of the foremost Satsuma artists of the late 19th / early 20thC, and his pieces are keenly collected.

Flatware

An Arita blue and white plate, inscribed in the centre 'VOC', for the Dutch East India Co, c1680, 9in (23cm) diam.
£2,500–3,000 *MCN*

A Kutani saucer, decorated in green, yellow, blue and aubergine enamel, base cracked, early 18thC, 5¾in (14.5cm) diam.
£2,000–2,200 *S(Am)*

An Arita blue and white hexafoil plate, painted with panels of bamboo and tied flowers within a chocolate brown rim, the centre with a *ho-o* bird, 18thC, 7¼in (18.5cm) diam.
£650–750 *P*

An Arita blue and white dish, late 17thC, 14¾in (37.5cm) diam.
£1,800–2,000 *S*

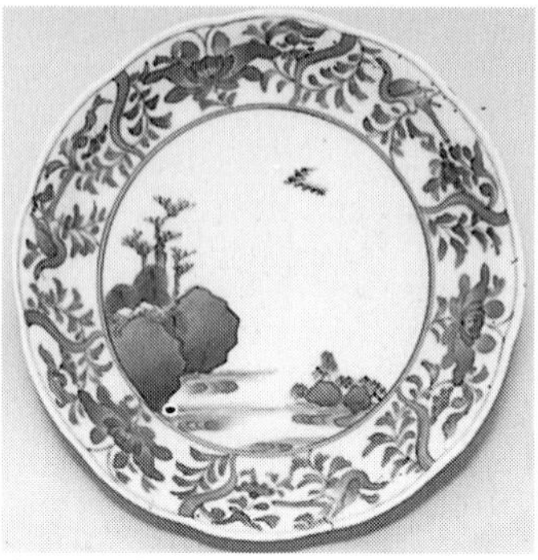

A pair of Arita blue and white porcelain dishes, early 18thC, 8½in (21.5cm) diam.
£1,100–1,300 *S(NY)*

A set of 10 Arita blue and white porcelain dishes, 18thC, 7½in (19cm) diam.
£1,100–1,300 *S(NY)*

An Imari plate, with scalloped edge, decorated with red, green and underglaze blue, damaged, 19thC, 8½in (21.5cm) diam.
£25–35 *MEG*

l. A pair of Nabeshima blue and white saucer dishes, c1870, 7¼in (18.5cm) diam.
£700–800 *Wai*

An Imari dish, decorated in coloured enamels, early 18thC, 19¾in (50cm) diam.
£1,800–2,000 *S(Am)*

An Imari octagonal dish, early 19thC, 11in (28cm) diam.
£130–150 *ALB*

A Nabeshima plate, decorated in blue and iron-red with Pineapple pattern, c1830, 6in (15cm) diam.
£1,200–1,400 *Wai*

A blue and white crackle ware plate, 19thC, 7¼in (18.5cm) diam.
£260–300 *HUR*

An Imari plate, with scalloped rim, decorated in underglaze blue and iron-red, minor fritting, 19thC, 8½in (21.5cm) diam.
£45–55 *MEG*

An Imari porcelain charger, decorated with a central blue and white motif, with surrounding panels of garden scenes, c1880, 18in (45.5cm) diam.
£350–420 *BRU*

A Kutani dish, painted in green, yellow, aubergine and blue enamels, Fuku seal mark on base, Meiji/Taisho period, 17in (43cm) diam.
£300–350 *P*

Jars

An Imari jar and cover, decorated with a garden scene, cover damaged, early 18thC, 23in (58.5cm) high.
£1,500–1,800 *Bea(E)*

A Satsuma jar, painted in gilt and finely enamelled in colours, signed in gilt within a red reserve 'Ryozan, Kyoto', Yasuda company mark, Meiji period, 9½in (24cm) high.
£1,600–1,800 *P*

A Satsuma jar, painted in gilt and coloured enamels with figures in a landscape, Meiji period, 9in (23cm) high.
£90–110 *P*

A Satsuma bell-shaped jar and cover, c1880, 4½in (11.5cm) high.
£450–500 *MCN*

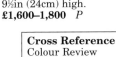

Cross Reference
Colour Review

A porcelain footed jar and cover, by Makuzu Kozan, painted with a group of penguins on a pale pink ground, signed, Meiji period, 5in (12.5cm) high.
£1,100–1,300 *S(S)*

An Imari baluster-shaped jar and cover, with 'Three Friends' decoration in iron-red, blue and gilt, repaired, 19thC, 18in (45.5cm) high.
£500–600 *PFK*

Koros

A Satsuma koro, with pierced cover, brightly decorated on each side with birds among flowering vegetation, signed on base, Meiji period, 5in (12.5cm) high.
£300–350 *P*

A Satsuma ribbed koro and cover, on 3 leaf-moulded feet, signed 'Kuzan', Meiji period, 6½in (16.5cm) high.
£1,800–2,000 *WW*

A Satsuma koro, on 3 feet, signed 'Meizan-sei', c1880, 4¼in (11cm) high.
£2,000–2,200 *MCN*

Vases

An Imari pear-shaped bottle vase, c1700, 9¾in (25cm) high.
£2,200–2,500 *MCN*

An Imari baluster-shaped vase and cover, decorated in underglaze blue, rust and gilt, damaged and repaired, cover finial missing, 18thC, 27½in (70cm) high.
£1,200–1,400 *PFK*

An Imari moon flask, decorated in underglaze blue, iron-red and gilt with *shishi* in a landscape, marked, 19thC, 10½in (26.5cm) high.
£275–300 *S(Am)*

An Imari ribbed vase, decorated in underglaze blue and overpainted in iron-red and green, 19thC, 4¾in (12cm) high.
£50–60 *MEG*

A pair of Satsuma earthenware vases, by Hattori, decorated in blue, gold and white, Meiji period, 10in (25.5cm) high.
£1,100–1,300 *S(S)*

A porcelain vase, decorated with chrysanthemums in pale yellow enamel with red and white details on a coral-red enamel ground, signed in underglaze blue 'Makuzu gama Kozan Sei', Meiji period, 11¼in (28.5cm) high.
£3,500–4,000 *S*

A pair of Kutani vases and covers, painted in red and gilt on a white ground with panels of song birds amidst flowering branches, surmounted by a teardrop-shaped knop, signed 'Kutani sei', Meiji period, 17¼in (44cm) high.
£800–1,000 *P(W)*

A Satsuma vase, by Kinkozan, decorated with birds, flowers, animals and landscapes, Meiji period, 6¾in (17cm) high.
£6,000–7,000 *Bon(N)*

This is another piece by the renowned Satsuma artist Kinkozan (see also the figure on p337). This example is in exceptional condition for a vase of this size, with microscopic detail which is always popular with Satsuma collectors.

A Satsuma vase, painted with silk brocade pattern over a band of children, on a fine dot ground, gold seal mark, Meiji period, 3½in (9cm) high.
£750–850 *EH*

A Satsuma bottle-shaped vase, the blue enamel body decorated with cloud diaper and *mon* in gilt, impressed Kinkozan mark, Meiji period, 12½in (32cm) high.
£600–700 *WW*

A Kutani vase, decorated with panels of cranes, flowers and foliage, signed to base, with Fuji mark in blue, late 19thC, 14in (35.5cm) high.
£1,000–1,200 *M*

A pair of Satsuma vases, each decorated with figures, black seal mark, c1900, 9in (23cm) high.
£300–350 *Mit*

KOREAN CERAMICS

A Korean inlaid celadon bowl, decorated with a band of 4 flowerhead medallions reserved on a foliate ground, 13thC, 7½in (19cm) diam.
£1,400–1,600 *P*

A Korean iron-decorated celadon vase, painted with chrysanthemums below a collar of stylised petals, Koryo Dynasty, 12thC, 10in (25.5cm) high.
£950–1,100 *P*

A Korean celadon vase, graduating from light brown at the foot to greyish-green at the mouth, neck restuck, Koryo Dynasty, 12thC, 9in (23cm) high.
£4,500–5,000 *S*

A Korean bottle vase, decorated in underglaze blue with a deer pursuing a crane, on a white ground, 19thC, 9¾in (25cm) high.
£850–1,000 *P*

A Korean celadon bowl, the interior decorated in white slip with pairs of cranes and stylised designs, some restoration to rim, Koryo Dynasty, 14thC, 7½in (19cm) diam.
£150–200 *Bon*

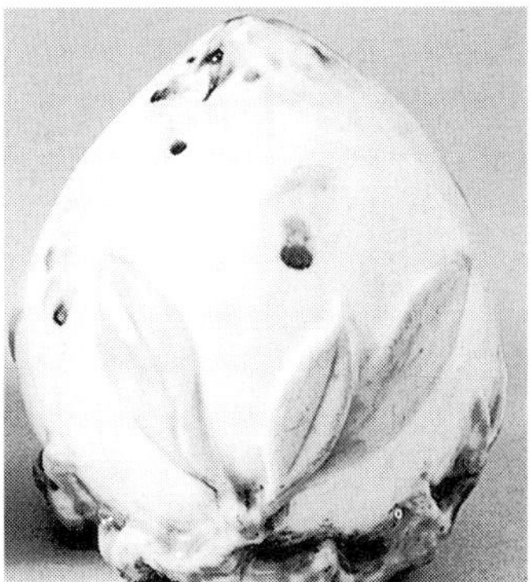

A Korean water dropper, modelled as a peach standing on a gnarled leafy branch, decorated in underglaze blue and mottled brown/grey, Yi Dynasty, late 18th/early 19thC, 3½in (9cm) high.
£800–900 *Bon*

GLASS

I wish I had a pound for every time I have been asked 'I would like to collect glass but I don't know how or where to begin.' My advice on how to start has always been to find a specialist glass dealer (most of whom are collectors whose habit has got out of control), who will be delighted to share their knowledge, let you handle pieces, as only handling develops a real feel for glass. Should you decide to buy, they will always provide a full descriptive invoice.

As to where to begin, late 18th and early 19th century drinking glasses are a good starting point. They are a pleasure to use – rummers for wine, dwarf ales for champagne, or ports and sherries – their prices compare favourably with modern glass and they provide that all-important experience of handling. The odd decanter can be another good starting point, as long as it is clean and dry as there is no easy way to clean a clouded decanter regardless of what you have heard or seen on the television.

Prices for 18th century drinking glasses have risen, stimulated by the unusually large number of named collections which have been sold this year, such as the Cranch Collection at Phillips, the Royal Brierley Crystal Sale at Sotheby's, and two parts of the Parkington collection at Christie's South Kensington. The Parkington auction also included many examples of cut, coloured, pressed and engraved items from the 19th and 20th centuries, together with a large quantity of Monart and Vasart glass.

For some time British glass made between the two World wars has been overshadowed by glass from France, Scandinavia and Italy, but is now set to 'take off'. This is due partly to the prices realised at the Royal Brierley Crystal sale, exhibitions at the Broadfield House Glass Museum, and increased interest in 20th century design generally, following a new fair in Chelsea this year.

There is still a reluctance to buy a damaged piece, however minor the flaw. It may well be better to buy an inexpensive rare example with damage than not at all, especially if such a piece, if perfect, would be outside your price range.

So my reply to the question as to how and where to start collecting glass is to buy the very best you can afford, and remember a piece does not have to be expensive to be good. Buy what you enjoy looking at or handling rather than for investment; should it go up in value, treat this as an added bonus.

Jeanette Hayhurst

Bottles, Decanters & Flasks

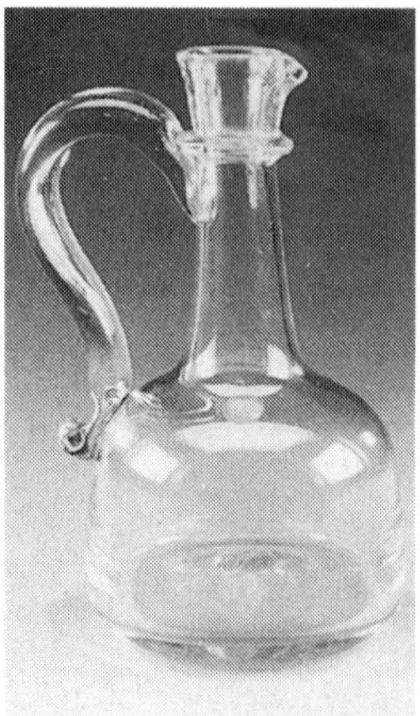

A mallet-shaped serving bottle, with slender tapering neck, the scroll handle with rolled-over terminal, c1720, 7¼in (18.5cm) high.
£1,800–2,000 *S*

A mallet-shaped decanter, engraved with swags, with bull's-eye stopper, late 18thC, 11in (28cm) high.
£220–240 *FD*

A mallet-shaped cruciform decanter, the neck with a triple ringed collar, slight damage, mid-18thC, 9in (22.5cm) high.
£170–200 *P*

A club-shaped miniature blue decanter, with snake-trailed neck ring, target stopper, c1800, 4in (10.5cm) high.
£160–180 *Som*

l. A set of 3 barrel-shaped decanters, with pinched necks and flattened stoppers, each moulded with diamond and vertical bands, on a black papier mâché stand with brass handle, mounts and feet, early 19thC, 10¼in (26cm) high.
£250–280 *DN*

r. A pair of decanters, with prism-cut necks, the bodies cut with diamonds and flutes, cut cushion stoppers, c1820, 10¼in (26cm) high.
£600–700 *GS*

A mallet-shaped magnum decanter, cut with bands of flutes, prism and diamonds, c1810, 11in (28cm) high.
£700–800 *Som*

Two blue flagons, of compressed round shape, with loop handles, metal mounts and cork and metal stoppers, c1830, 7½in (19cm) high.
£300–360 *Som*

An onion-shaped amber glass whisky decanter, c1830, 10in (25.5cm) high.
£220–240 *JAS*

r. A pair of decanters, the silver mounts by William Comyns, London 1896, 10in (25.5cm) high.
£1,100–1,300 *THOM*

The value of these decanters is enhanced by the identifiable silver mounts, and original stoppers

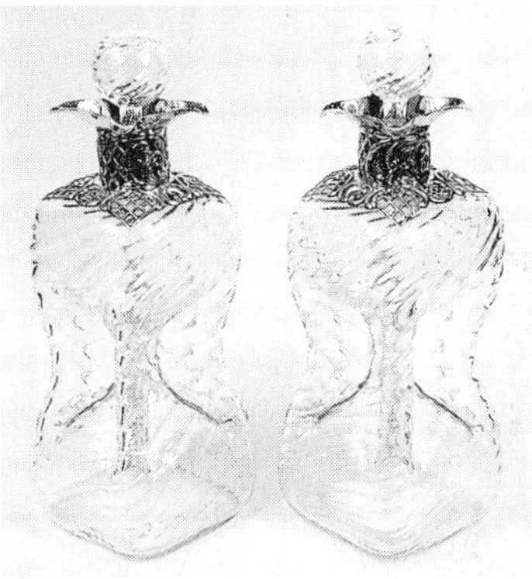

l. A green jug decanter, with clear handle and stopper, c1880, 9in (23cm) high.
£70–90 *MJW*

A glass decanter, with applied cranberry prunts, c1870, 10½in (26.5cm) high.
£580–650 *ARE*

An American blown glass three-mould decanter, c1830, 11in (28cm) high.
£220–240 *A&A*

A waisted cylindrical decanter, the silver mount with a tricorn spout, London 1909, 13in (33cm) high.
£270–300 *WeH*

Bowls

A two-piece bowl, with step, diamond and flute cutting, c1820, 12in (30.5cm) diam.
£800–1,000 *JHa*

This type of bowl has to be made in 2 pieces as it is impossible to cut the base of the bowl and the stem in one piece. Bases which have lost their bowls are sometimes called ham stands.

A set of 4 amber-coloured finger bowls, flute-cut with flared rims, moulded bases, c1850, 3¼in (8cm) high.
£250–300 *Som*

A Sowerby Patent Ivory Queen's Ware pressed glass 'new bowl', moulded with a band of panels enclosing floral and foliate sprays, with 2 comb-shaped handles, 1879, 6in (15cm) wide.
£230–260 *P(NE)*

A cut glass fruit bowl, with silver rim, c1886, 8¼in (21cm) diam.
£180–200 *CB*

A pressed glass bowl, simulating cut-glass, by George Davidson, Gateshead, registration No. 96945, c1888, 8in (20.5cm) diam.
£50–60 *JHa*

The use of registration marks in the form of diamonds ceased in February 1884. Five-figure numbers were used from 1884 to May 1888, and six-figure numbers thereafter.

l. A glass rose bowl, with green lustre leaves, c1900, 6in (15cm) high.
£75–85 *DKH*

Centrepieces

An early George III sweetmeat tree, with a panel-moulded ogee-shaped bowl, the tapering stem with 3 tiers of 4 scroll branches, on a domed and folded foot, repaired, one basket missing, 2 replaced, c1760, 16¼in (41.5cm) high.
£7,500–9,000 *DN*

This item realised a considerable sum at auction despite the damage, as it is extremely rare. Only a few have survived, and almost all have 'mix and match' baskets.

A Whitefriars/Powell iron-mounted table centrepiece, with wavy rim, c1880, 5in (12.5cm) high.
£200–250 *JHa*

A Lobmeyr Persian style enamelled sweetmeat dish, painted in turquoise and gilt with a rosette within a scroll pattern, gilt line rim, on a spreading foot, marked 'JLL', c1880, 8¾in (22cm) wide.
£1,600–1,800 *S*

A Bohemian or Stourbridge cranberry-tinted épergne, the shallow bowl with crimped rim and high centre with gilt-metal mount, supporting a tall slender trumpet cased in clear glass, flanked by 2 similar trumpets and 2 pendant baskets, minor chips, c1880, 19¼in (49cm) high.
£650–750 *S*

Drinking Glasses
Beakers & Tumblers

A Bohemian beaker, each panel engraved with an allegorical figure of the Continents between line banding, c1700, 4½in (12cm) high.
£950–1,100 *S*

The engraving of the 4 allegorical figures of Europe, Asia, Africa and America contribute to the value of this piece.

A north Bohemian beaker, with 4 cut panels, one engraved with Jesus Christ within an oval medallion, rosette-cut base, c1830, 5in (12.5cm) high.
£800–1,000 *S*

A Davidson's pearline pressed glass beaker, c1890, 5½in (14cm) high.
£25–30 *CSA*

r. A Bohemian tumbler, the red overlay cut through to clear glass, late 19thC, 5in (12.5cm) high.
£140–160 *CB*

A tapered beaker, engraved with 'ICA' within a floral cartouche, the reverse with a bird in flight, c1780, 4¼in (11cm) high.
£140–160 *Som*

A Bohemian beaker and cover, possibly by Anton Simm, engraved with The Last Supper after Leonardo da Vinci, inscribed, the lower section cut with panels of fine diamonds, the domed cover cut with raised diamonds, c1825, 7½in (19cm) high.
£3,200–3,600 *S*

This subject was very popular in the Biedermeier period, and was used by a number of different glass engravers.

A tumbler, engraved 'Ford for Ever', c1790, 4in (10cm) high.
£350–400 *BrW*

The initials on this tumbler appear to relate to Sir Francis Ford, who became Member of Parliament for Newcastle-under-Lyme in 1792.

A Bohemian commemorative transparent glass beaker, engraved with a train, engine driver and carriage on a red ground, c1830, 5¼in (13.5cm) high.
£250–300 *DORO*

A Bohemian transparent enamelled beaker, attributed to Carl von Scheidt, of faceted bell-shape with leaf panels around the middle, on a heavily cut scalloped foot, painted with 8 Chinese figures, slight wear, mid-19thC, 5¾in (14.5cm) high.
£650–750 *P*

A pair of conical beakers, engraved with naval inscriptions, c1800, 5in (12.5cm) high.
£580–650 *Som*

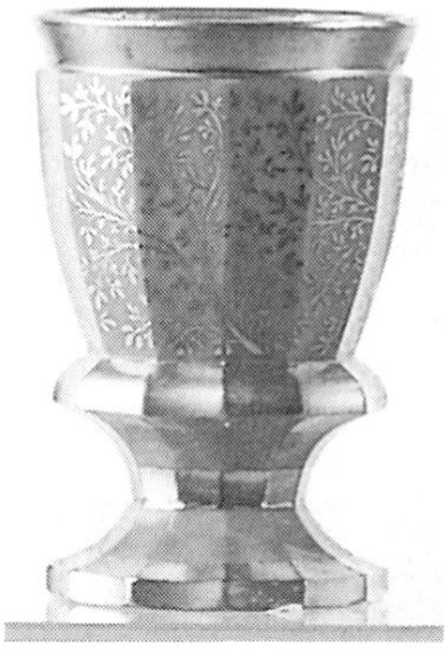

A Bohemian light blue marbled glass beaker, painted with gilded foliage, slight rubbing, c1840, 4½in (11.5cm) high.
£1,400–1,600 *DORO*

A pair of amberina glasses, with diamond quilted pattern, c1840, 4in (10cm) high.
£70–80 each *A&A*

A Viennese transparent enamelled and gilt beaker, with a diamond-cut base, painted in the Kothgasser manner with a view of Vienna, some damage, mid-19thC, 4¼in (11cm) high.
£950–1,100 *P*

Wine Glasses & Goblets

A heavy baluster goblet, the funnel bowl with solid base over a teared wide angular knop and basal knop, bowl scratched, c1710, 8½in (21.5cm) high.
£1,600–1,800 *S*

An ale glass, the deep funnel bowl with multiple spiral double knopped air-twist stem, on a plain conical foot, c1750, 7¾in (19.5cm) high.
£800–900 *Som*

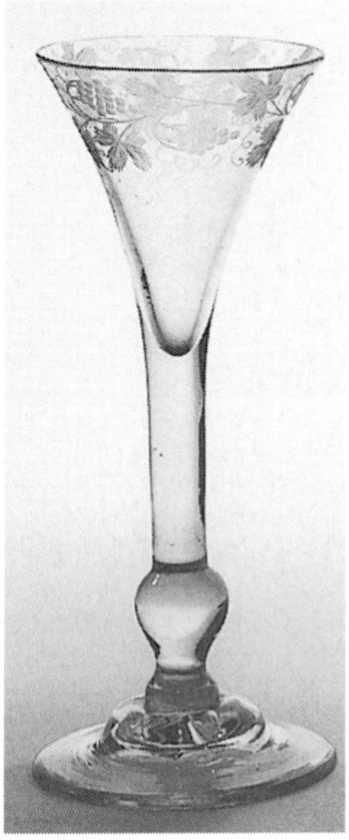

A 'Kit-Kat' type glass, with drawn trumpet bowl engraved with fruiting vine, on a plain stem terminating in a knop and domed foot, c1730, 6¾in (17cm) high.
£600–700 *P*

'Kit-Kat' refers to a painting by Keller depicting members of the Kit-Kat Club drinking out of glasses of similar shape.

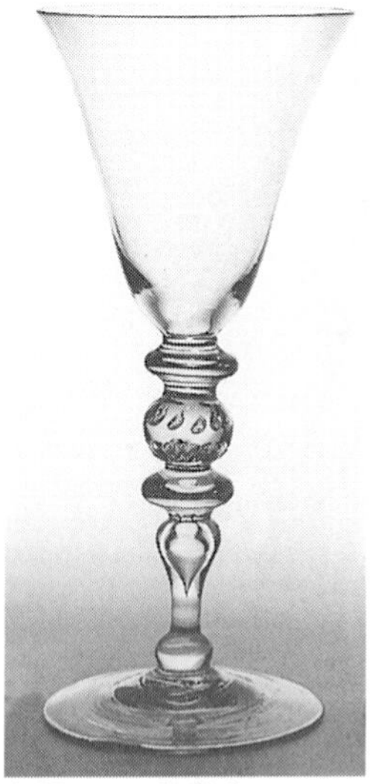

A Newcastle light baluster goblet, with deep bell-shaped bowl, on an air-beaded ball knop between 2 angular knops, above an inverted baluster with a tear, basal knop and conical foot, c1740, 8½in (21.5cm) high.
£1,000–1,200 *P*

Newcastle light baluster glasses were made in the north-east of England between c1730 and 1755. They are distinctive by the lightness of the glass of which they were made. These glasses often had knops with tears in them to create the impression of light within the stem.

l. A composite stem wine glass, the bell-shaped bowl supported on a multi-spiral air-twist stem with a beaded basal knop over a short plain section, c1755, 6¾in (17cm) high.
£450–550 *GS*

A composite stem is one which includes elements of all the popular stem types which were made between 1745 and 1775. Opaque twists in composite stems are rare.

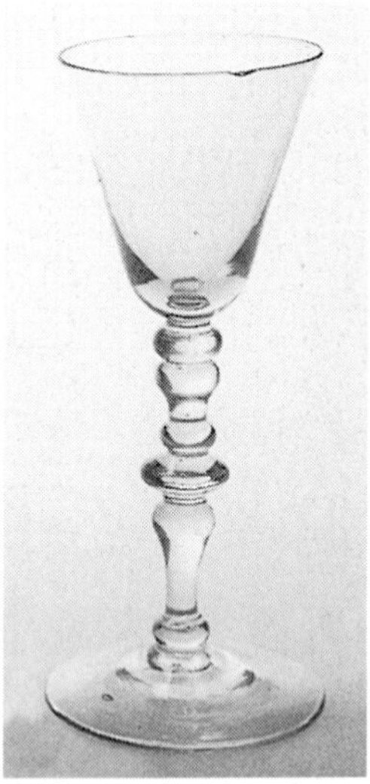

A Newcastle wine glass, with rounded funnel-shaped bowl, on multi-knopped stem with flattened central knop, rim chip, c1740, 7in (18cm) high.
£350–450 *DN*

The damage to this glass affected its price quite considerably when sold at auction.

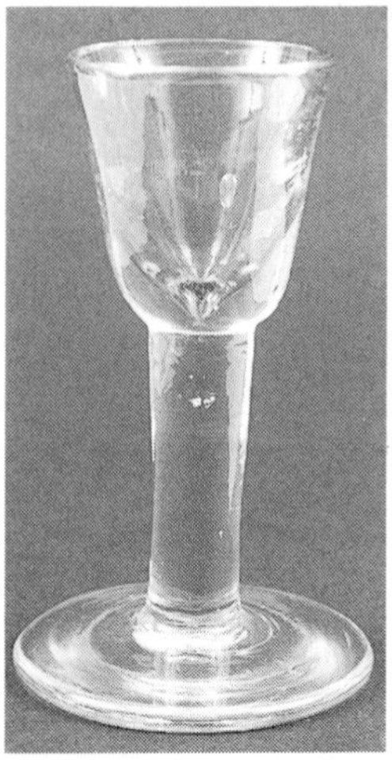

A dram glass, with plain stem, round funnel bowl and heavy foot, c1750, 4in (10.5cm) high.
£200–220 *BrW*

Types of Drinking Glass

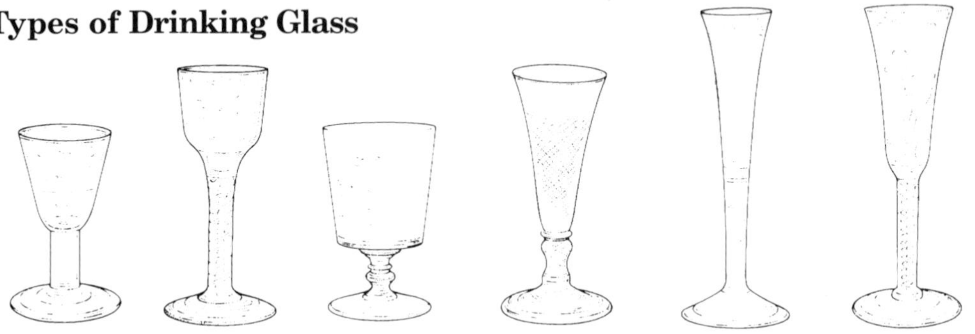

Dram glass 4in (9.5cm) | Wine glass 6in (15cm) | Rummer 5in (13cm) | Dwarf ale glass 5in (13.5cm) | Ratafia glass 7in (18.5cm) | Ale glass 8in (20.5cm)

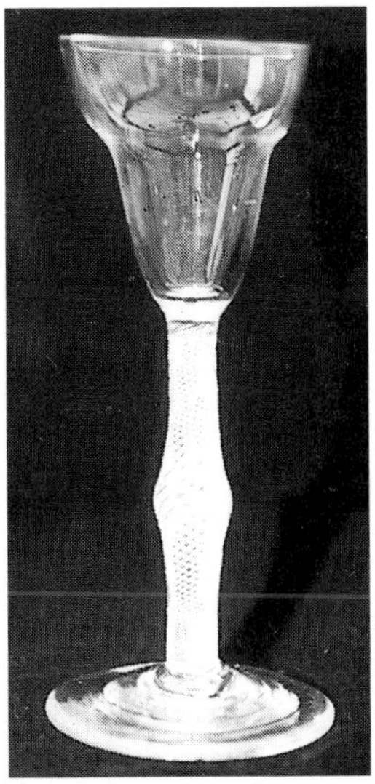

A pan-top wine glass, on a multi-spiral air-twist stem with swelling knop and conical foot, c1755, 5¾in (14.5cm) high.
£320–380 *GS*

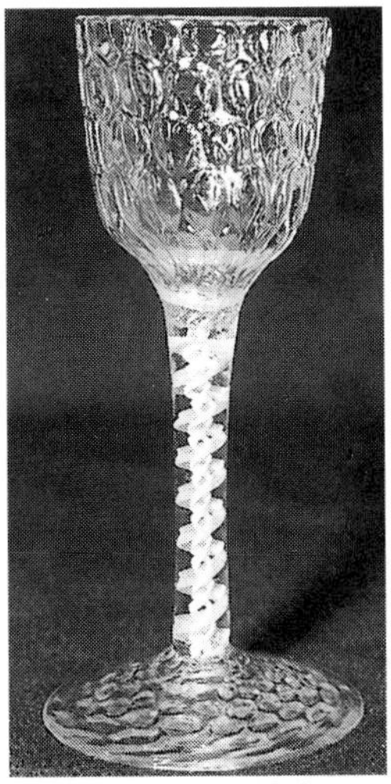

A wine glass, with honeycomb moulded ogee bowl and foot, on a double series opaque twist stem, c1760, 6in (15cm) high.
£500–600 *Som*

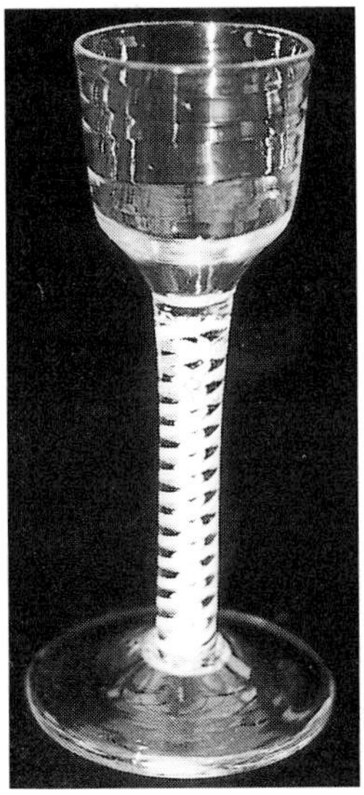

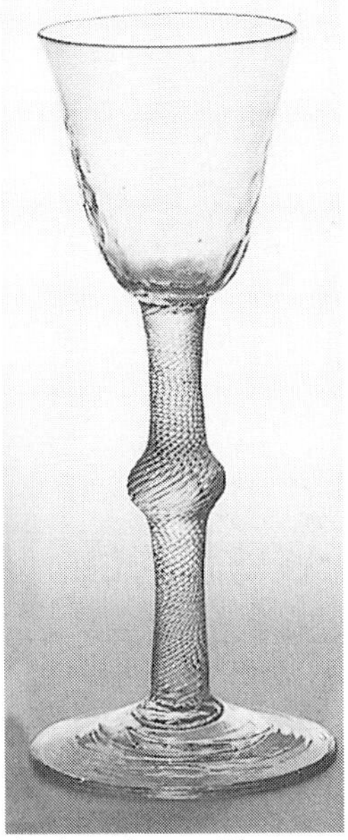

A wine glass, with hammered rounded funnel bowl, on a centre-knopped incised twist stem and conical foot, c1755, 6¼in (16cm) high.
£800–900 *P*

Incised twist stems incorporating knops are rare.

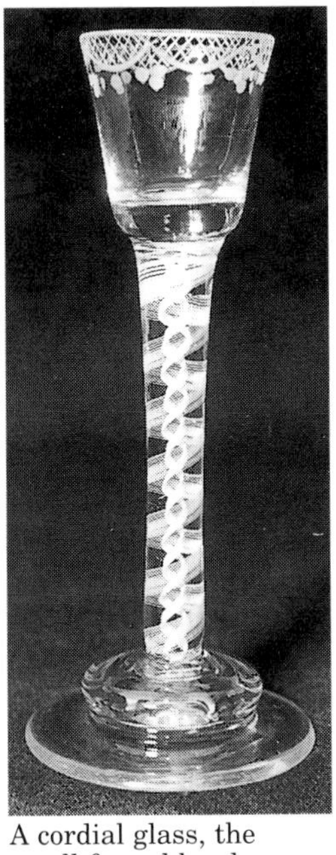

A cordial glass, the small funnel bowl engraved with a drapery border, on a double series opaque twist stem, and domed foot, c1760, 6¾in (17cm) high.
£800–900 *Som*

l. A 'Lynn' wine glass, the six-band ogee bowl supported on a double series opaque twist stem, c1765, 5½in (14cm) high.
£800–900 *GS*

A wine glass, with flared funnel bowl with moulded basal flutes, single series air-twist stem, c1760, 6¼in (16cm) high.
£340–380 *BrW*

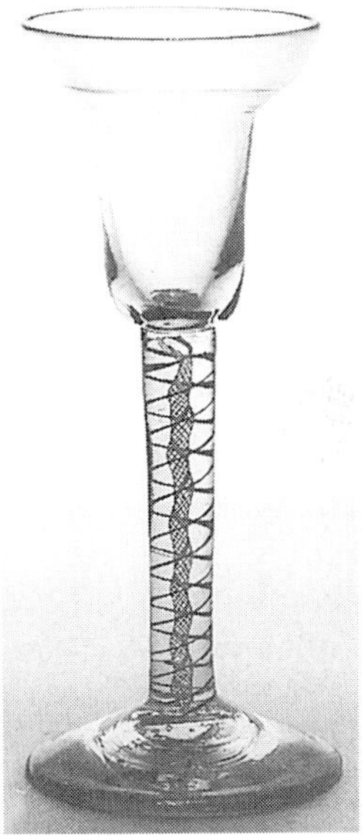

A wine glass, with pan-topped bowl, the stem with opaque central gauze cable encircled by 2 solid spiralling strands, c1760, 6½in (16.5cm) high.
£450–500 *P*

r. A Beilby enamelled wine glass, the funnel bowl painted in opaque white with fruiting vine, traces of gilding, set on a double series opaque twist stem and conical foot, chipped, c1765, 6in (15cm) high.
£1,400–1,600 *S*

The Beilby family, particularly William and his sister Mary, were renowned glass enamellers in Newcastle-upon-Tyne from c1762–78.

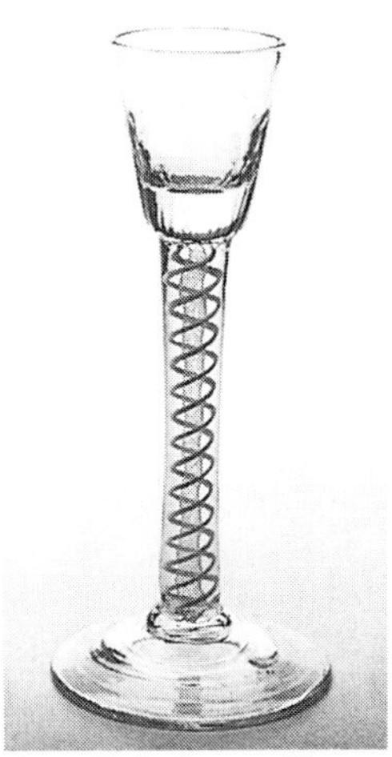

A cordial glass, with basally fluted bucket-shaped bowl, on double spiral opaque twist stem with central gauze, c1760, 6¾in (17cm) high.
£600–700 *DN*

A wine glass, on diamond facet cut stem with centre knop, on a conical foot, c1760, 5¼in (13.5cm) high.
£160–180 *JHa*

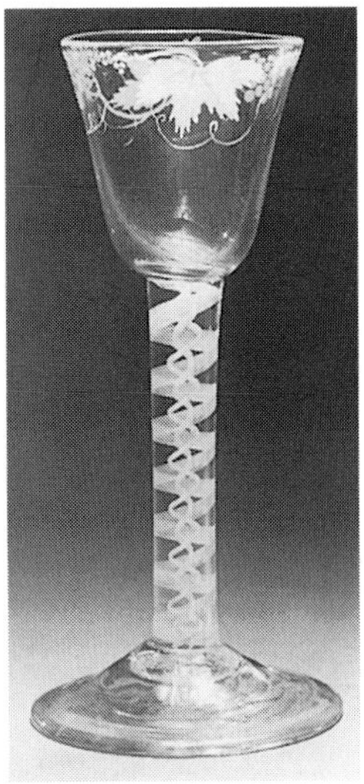

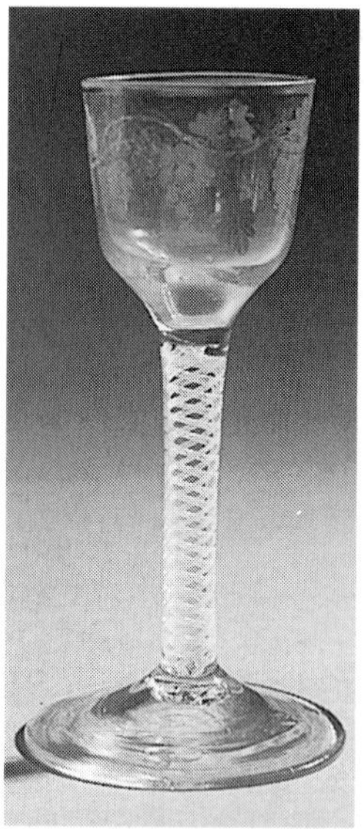

A wine glass, from the studio of James Giles, the ogee bowl gilt-decorated with a continuous branch of fruiting vine below a gilt line to the rim, on an opaque twist stem of 4 gauze spirals, on a conical foot, gilding rubbed, c1770, 5½in (14cm) high.
£600–700 *P*

James Giles (1718–80) had a workshop in Berwick Street, London, producing high quality gilding and enamelling. The slight rubbing to the gilding on this glass reduced the value by about 25 per cent.

A rummer, the ovoid bowl engraved 'Queen Caroline 1820' surrounded by birds, the reverse with a crown and initials, on a short stem and circular foot, 6in (15cm) high.
£330–370 *P*

Caroline of Brunswick was married to the Prince Regent. He became King in 1820, but at his Coronation in 1821 he refused Caroline entry to the Abbey. She died in the same year.

A wrythen ale glass, on a folded foot, c1770, 5in (12.5cm) high.
£60–70 *JHa*

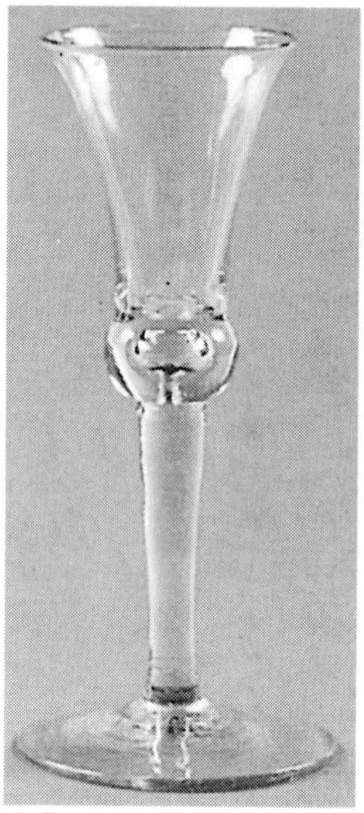

A Continental wine glass, the thistle bowl with tear, plain stem and foot, late 18thC, 6in (15cm) high.
£90–110 *PFK*

A port or sherry glass, cut with arch and feather design, on slice and step cut stem, c1820, 4in (10cm) high.
£25–30 *JHa*

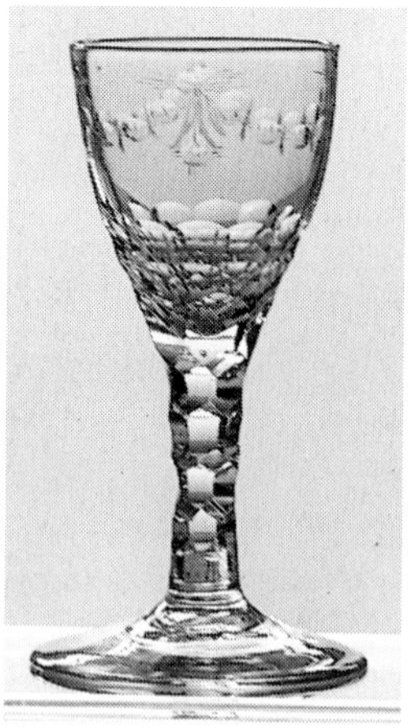

A wine glass, with funnel bowl engraved with swags, on a facet cut stem, c1780, 5in (12.5cm) high.
£100–120 *FD*

A Masonic firing glass, with engraved ogee bowl, double series opaque twist stem, terraced firing foot, c1765, 3¾in (9.5cm) high.
£500–600 *JHa*

A blue cased glass goblet, enamelled with gold, on a plain facet stem, c1860, 6¼in (16cm) high.
£175–225 *CB*

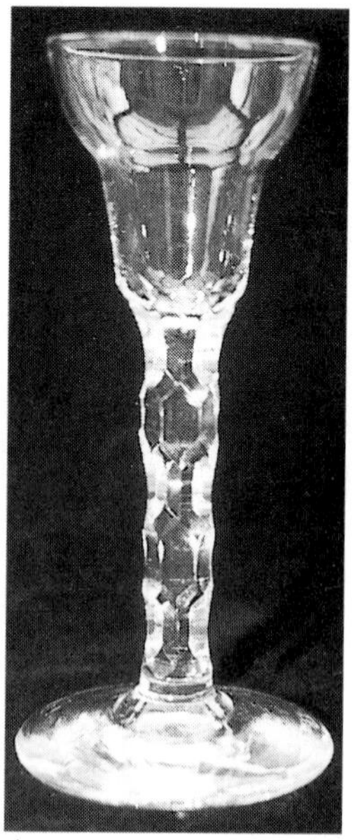

A pan-top wine glass, on a hexagon-cut facet stem, the facets extending into the bowl base, c1780, 5½in (14cm) high.
£280–330 *GS*

An amethyst tinted wrythen dwarf ale glass, with trumpet bowl, the stem with 2 ball knops, on a plain foot, c1800, 5in (12.5cm) high.
£250–280 *Som*

A pair of water goblets, acid-etched with Flaxman type gods and goddesses, c1870, 7in (18cm) high.
£300–350 *BrW*

Jugs

A heavy cut-glass jug, with bands of prisms and small diamonds, heavy strap handle, the pedestal foot star-cut underneath, c1810, 7½in (19cm) high.
£400–450 *Som*

A claret jug, cut with flutes, bands of strawberries and raised diamonds, notched cut spout, strap handle, c1820, 8½in (22cm) high.
£450–500 *Som*

A claret jug, with flute-cut neck and base, bevelled lip and strap handle, cut mushroom stopper, c1830, 9½in (24cm) high.
£450–500 *Som*

A baluster jug, cut with panels of diamonds between fan cutting, 'stick-up' handle, c1890, 11in (28cm) high.
£180–200 *JHa*

From 1860–70 the way the handles were applied changed from 'stick-down' to 'stick-up'. This type of handle appears to be stronger than the 'stick-down' type.

A claret jug, flute-cut with single neck ring and cut spout, strap handle, star cut base, c1830, 9¾in (25cm) high.
£350–400 *Som*

A baluster jug, with slice cut neck and leaf-cut body, 'stick-down' handle, c1850, 9in (23cm) high.
£120–140 *JHa*

This jug can be dated from the way the handle has been applied. The gather of glass was attached at the top and pulled over and down.

A cranberry glass jug, with clear handle, c1890, 6¼in (16cm) high.
£100–125 *DKH*

r. A cut-glass lemonade jug, with silver mount, Birmingham 1890, 9½in (24cm) high.
£500–600 *TC*

Lustres

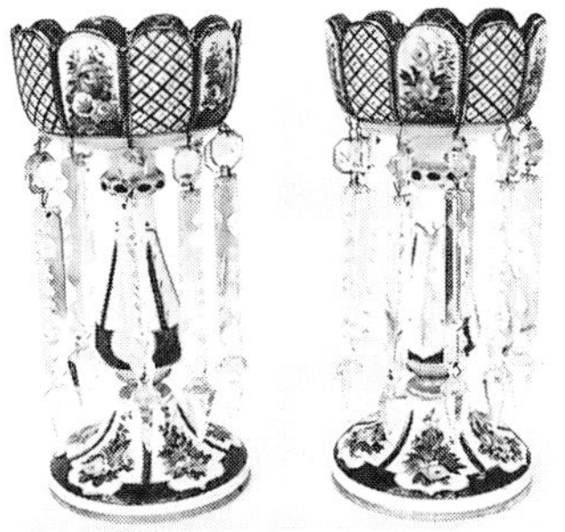

A pair of Venetian style overlaid glass lustres, with hipped gilt rims, latticed panels with gilt detail, the bowls and domed bases decorated with stylised flowers, hung with clear glass prismatic drops, 19thC, 13in (33cm) high.
£1,000–1,200 *GAK*

l. A pair of French opaque white overlay tulip-shaped lustres, with floral sprays and enriched in gilt, early 19thC, 10in (25.5cm) high.
£600–700 *L*

A pair of cut-glass and ormolu table lustres, each ormolu support formed as a temple containing an urn and pineapple, surmounted by a sconce and drip pans cut with bands of diamonds, hung with faceted button and icicle drops, some damage, 19thC, 12½in (32cm) high.
£950–1,100 *P*

Paperweights

A Baccarat close-pack mushroom faceted paperweight, c1850, 2½in (6.5cm) diam.
£1,500–1,700 *SWB*

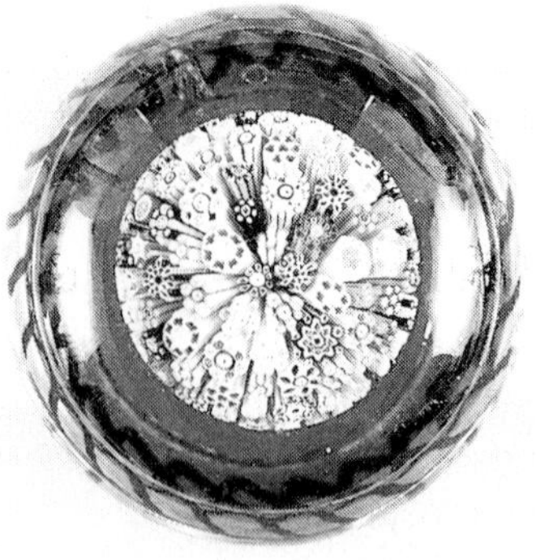

A Baccarat millefiori tuft mushroom paperweight, with central twisted torsade of white gauze and blue ribbon, on a star-cut base, c1850, 3in (7.5cm) diam.
£1,600–1,800 *STG*

A Baccarat paperweight, with central blue and white primrose, c1850, 2¼in (5.5cm) diam.
£1,100–1,350 *SWB*

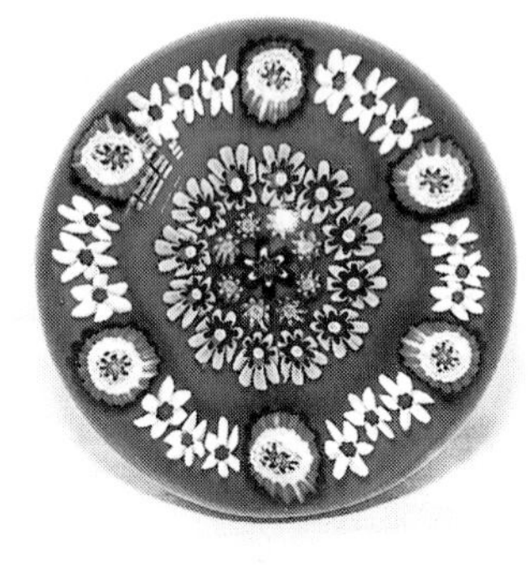

A Clichy paperweight, with concentric coloured canes on a turquoise ground, c1850, 2¼in (5.5cm) diam.
£1,100–1,350 *SWB*

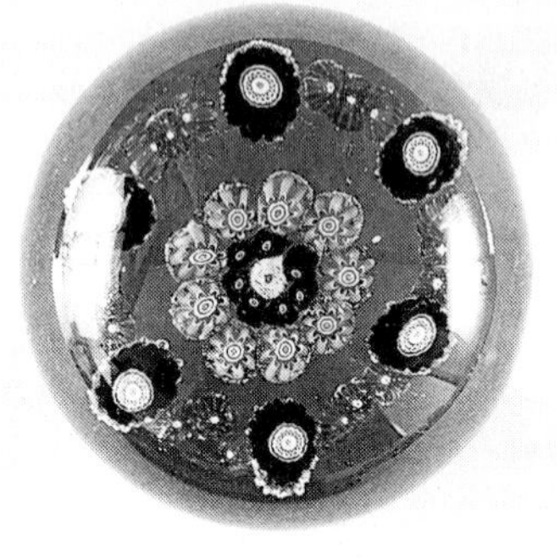

A Clichy paperweight, with small central white rose cane, c1850, 2½in (6.5cm) diam.
£550–600 *STG*

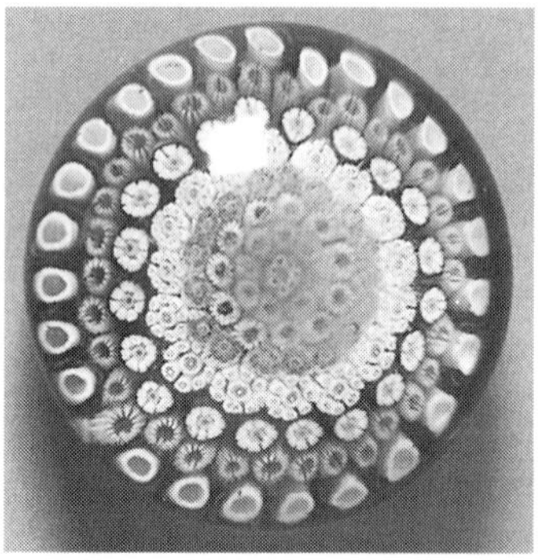

A St Louis millefiori paperweight, with green, red, white and blue canes enclosed by a basket of turquoise canes with white centres, slight damage, mid-19thC, 3in (7.5cm) diam.
£1,300–1,600 *S*

A St Louis paperweight, set with green leaves and orange, red and yellow fruit, c1850, 2½in (6.5cm) diam.
£800–950 *SWB*

A St Louis paperweight, set with garlands of clematis flowers, c1850, 3in (7.5cm) diam.
£5,500–6,250 *STG*

An example of this type with a central flower as well as an outer border is rare.

A St Louis paperweight, set with a bouquet of flowers and leaves encircled by a blue and opaque white torsade, star-cut base, slight wear, mid-19thC, 2¾in (7cm) diam.
£400–450 *WW*

l. An Italian paperweight, by Pietro Bigaglia, the canes depicting animals, birds and lyres interspersed with ribbons, signed 'B', dated '1845', 2in (5cm) diam.
£1,800–2,000 *P*

r. A New England Glass Co paperweight, with a white latticinio ground, slight damage, 19thC, 3in (7.5cm) diam.
£1,500–1,700 *S(NY)*

Scent Bottles

A clear glass scent bottle, with embossed gold mount, c1790, 4in (10cm) long, in a fitted case.
£600–700 *Som*

Two scent bottles, by Apsley Pellatt, engraved with portraits of Lord Brougham and Princess Victoria, rim chip, c1835, 4in (10cm) high.
£925–1,100 *S*

Lord Brougham was Chancellor in the Reform Parliament of 1832, and was a prime figure in the movement to abolish slavery.

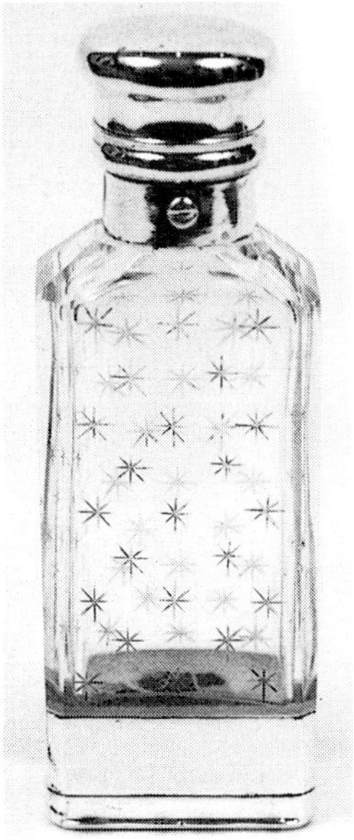

A star-cut glass scent bottle and vinaigrette, with silver mount, by S. Mordan & Co, London 1879, 4in (10cm) high.
£650–720 *THOM*

A yellow glass scent bottle, c1850, 6¼in (16cm) high.
£300–350 *MJW*

A red glass double-ended scent bottle and vinaigrette, in the form of opera glasses, with silver-gilt mounts, by S. Mordan & Co, c1880, 5½in (14cm) long, in a fitted case marked 'Face, Keen & Face, Plymouth'.
£820–920 *Som*

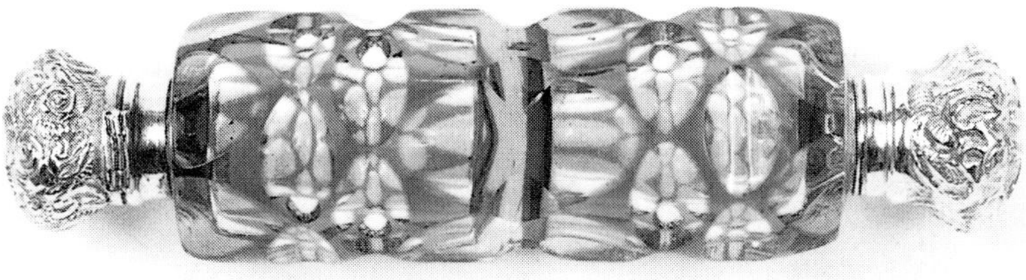

A double-ended scent bottle, with cranberry overlay, silver mounts, c1885, 4in (10cm) long.
£320–360 *THOM*

r. A Stourbridge cameo glass scent bottle, with violets and a butterfly, silver top and inner stopper, c1904, 3½in (9cm) long.
£1,000–1,250 *BHa*

l. A ruby red overlay glass scent bottle, with lozenge decoration, the hinged silver cover embossed with foliate scrolls, maker's mark of Hilliard & Thomason, Birmingham 1897, 6in (15cm) long.
£280–320 *Bon*

A Clichy scent bottle, with silver top and inner stopper, c1870, 3in (7.5cm) high.
£450–520 *BHa*

Sweetmeat & Jelly Glasses

l. A sweetmeat bowl and cover, moulded with 8 panels, the cover with an acorn finial, on a domed and folded foot with similar panel moulding, early 18thC, 8¾in (22cm) high.
£4,600–5,200 *P*

This is possibly a world record price for a sweetmeat bowl. It is an extremely rare item, especially with its original cover

A sweetmeat glass, the flared bowl with star-cut rim and facet-cut bands, c1750, 6¼in (16cm) high.
£300–350 *DN*

A jelly glass, with beaded knop and domed foot, c1770, 4¼in (11cm) high.
£300–350 *GS*

Vases

A celery vase, cut with alternating straw-berries, diamonds and stars between slice cutting, pedestal stem, star-cut foot, c1820, 8¾in (22cm) high.
£150–180 *JHa*

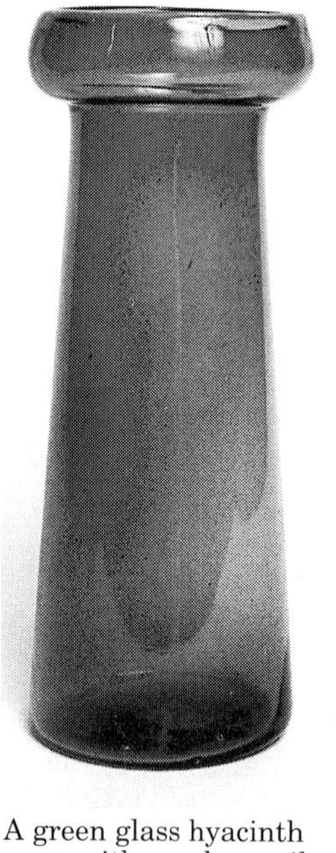

A green glass hyacinth vase, with rough pontil, c1870, 6in (15cm) high.
£40–50 *CB*

A pair of blue glass bud vases, with baluster bodies and flared lips, c1840, 7in (18cm) high.
£300–350 *JHa*

FURTHER READING
Miller's Glass Antiques Check List
Miller's Publications, 1994

A pair of Venetian style glass vases, by James Powell, Whitefriars, with hollow twisted stems, late 19thC, 6½in (16.5cm) high.
£350–400 *JHa*

An amethyst glass hyacinth vase, c1880, 5in (12.5cm) high.
£40–50 *CB*

A Thomas Webb cameo glass vase, by George Woodall, the dark brown ground overlaid in white and carved with a figure of Psyche holding a box issuing smoke, the neck and foot with leaf motifs, damaged and repaired, signed, c1889, 7in (17.5cm) high.
£3,200–3,600 *P*

This piece was severely damaged but still sold for double its pre-sale estimate. A similar example in excellent condition in the same sale realised in the region of £18,500 (see Colour Review p296).

An opaque white glass vase, polychrome painted with birds in a flower garland, with gilt line rims, probably by Richardson, slight rubbing, mid-19thC, 15½in (39.5cm) high.
£500–600 *WW*

A pair of vaseline glass vases, with spiral citrus trimming, c1890, 8in (20.5cm) high.
£200–225 *ARE*

A Bohemian glass vase, c1840, 9½in (24cm) high.
£1,200–1,450 *MJW*

A cranberry glass vase, c1890, 6½in (16.5cm) high.
£60–70 *CB*

A pair of Edwardian cut-glass and gilt-bronze mounted vases, with pierced collars and Wedgwood style ceramic plaques, raised on white stone bases, 10½in (27cm) high.
£1,200–1,500 *P*

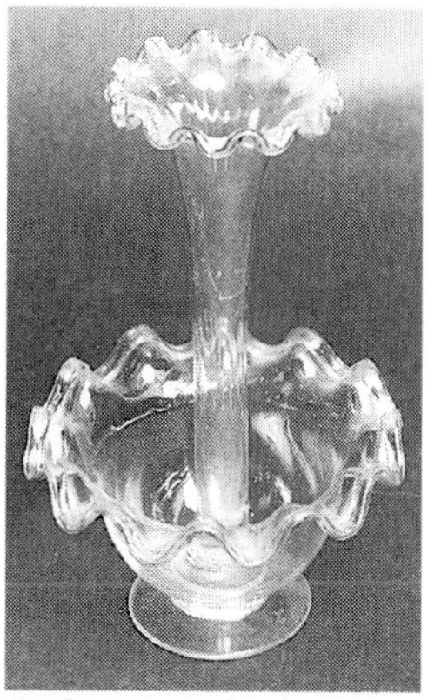

A glass posy holder, c1890, 8in (20.5cm) high.
£120–135 *ARE*

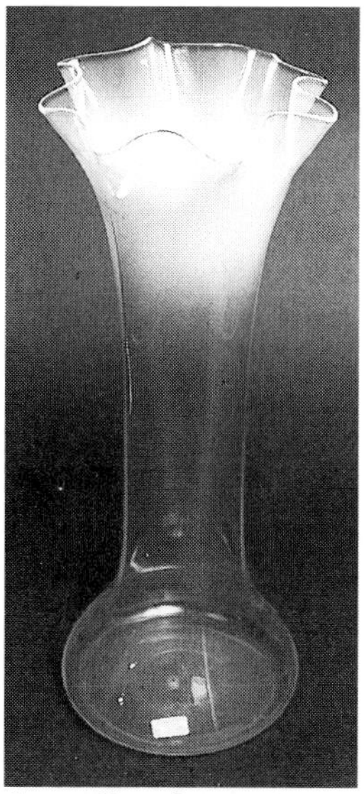

A vaseline glass vase, with frilled top, c1906, 14in (35.5cm) high.
£200–220 *ARE*

A pair of Bohemian gilt overlaid cranberry glass portrait vases, the flared rims and narrow necks above slender bodies, painted with panels of busts of maidens and flowers, on circular feet, late 19thC, 12½in (32cm) high.
£700–800 *RTo*

A Stourbridge amber glass vase, by Thomas Webb, engraved with water lilies, c1920, 8¼in (21cm) high.
£70–85 *MON*

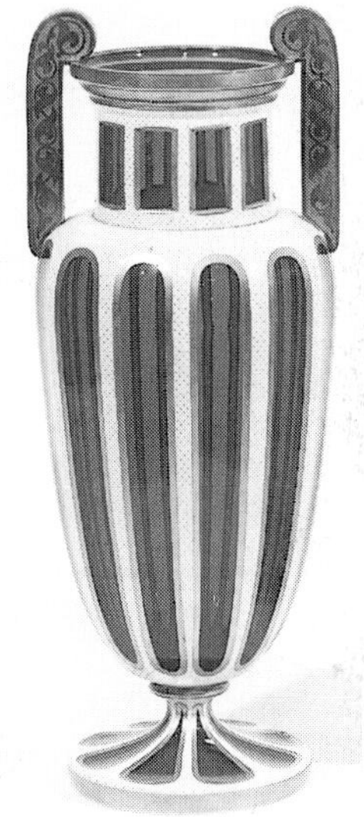

A pair of Bohemian ruby tinted glass vases, with white overlay, flared rims, chased gilt metal scrolled handles, on circular feet, 19thC, 13½in (34.5cm) high.
£700–800 *AH*

A vaseline glass vase, by Walsh of Birmingham, with opalescent 'brocade' design, c1900, 6½in (16.5cm) high.
£170–200 *JHa*

A cranberry glass hyacinth vase, early 20thC, 7in (18cm) high.
£150–200 *CoHA*

Miller's is a price GUIDE not a price LIST

A Bohemian turquoise glass vase, by Moser, engraved with pheasants, c1920, 6½in (16.5cm) high.
£120–150 *Mon*

SILVER

As in all markets, silver prices are dictated by the law of supply and demand and these two factors are playing an increasingly critical role today.

The supply of silver items for sale is noticeably reduced and appears to be limited. It is a harsh and undeniable fact that goods are drying up fast, and this trend is going to continue. This is not a new phenomenon, but what is alarming is the rate at which the supply is deteriorating.

What of demand? There appears to be a distinct watershed of what collectors are prepared to pay for. Out of fashion is 'commercial' silver, namely everyday items such as tea sets, coffee pots, salvers etc. Today an unexceptional George III coffee pot can be bought for as little as £1,000: 20 years ago the same pot might have cost £1,500. Despite the dwindling supply, the demand for this type of silver appears proportionately even weaker. As a result this section of the market is considerably reduced and prices are chalked down accordingly.

What is in demand? Anything of noticeably good quality, the exceptional, the unusual, the decorative, the amusing and something different. There are new demands developing for specialist pieces within the silver market, for example provincial Scottish and Irish silver (see Focus on Ireland section page 746), novelty items relating to cocktails and cigars, and certain 20th century makers. The worldwide demand for Georg Jensen silver, for example, is particularly strong with prices sometimes two or three times higher than English Georgian silver counterparts. Cartier, Tiffany and Puiforcat silver all continue to attract a determined following. The sustained boom of Georg Jensen silver is mainly for second-hand items which are attracting strong international interest.

What of the immediate future? There is little control over such external risk factors as fluctuations in international economies, and political crises. What is more predictable is the demise of small-margin/volume-trading. Fewer more carefully selected goods will be chased by a more determined demand. As the supply shrinks, the silver business becomes more global, and although London may remain the centre of the market, the market itself is having to operate in a truly international sphere.

Alastair Crawford

Baskets

A George II cake basket, by Edward Aldridge & John Stamper, with spiral beaded flutes and pierced panels, on mask and scroll feet, 1758, 15in (38cm) wide, 46oz.
£4,300–4,800 *P(WM)*

A George III sugar basket, by William Plummer, the wirework sides with trailing vine leaves, London 1770, 3in (8cm) diam.
£360–400 *DN*

A George III gilt-lined sugar basket, by Solomon Hougham, engraved with a band of bright-cut foliate decoration beneath the fluted rim, with 2 shield-shaped cartouches between reeds, on a raised foot, engraved with initials 'JEM', 1797, 6¾in (17cm) high, 8oz.
£420–480 *L*

A silver sweetmeat basket, by David Darling, Newcastle, chased with ribbon-tied flower festoons, reeded borders, swing handle, engraved with a monogram, c1803, 7½in (19cm) high, 6oz.
£380–420 *S(Am)*

An early Victorian cake basket, with a shaped raised border, the repoussé foliage with pierced hatched paterae panel to a matt ground, scrolling edge, pierced engraved swing handle, on pierced repoussé shell scroll panel feet, retailed by Hunt & Roskell, London 1847, 15in (38cm) high, 38oz.
£1,200–1,500 *WW*

An Edwardian silver sweetmeat basket, by Goldsmiths & Silversmiths Co Ltd, with reeded swing handle, on a pedestal foot, London 1907, 7in (18cm) wide.
£400–450 *HofB*

Beakers

A German parcel-gilt beaker, by Paulus Schütte, with embossed floral decoration, inscribed on base 'N4' and name, c1670, 5½in (14cm) high, 8oz.
£4,200–4,800 *P*

A Charles II silver beaker, by John Spackman, engraved with a coat-of-arms within plume mantling, on moulded skirt foot, London 1681, 4in (10.5cm) high, 7¾oz.
£3,200–3,600 *S*

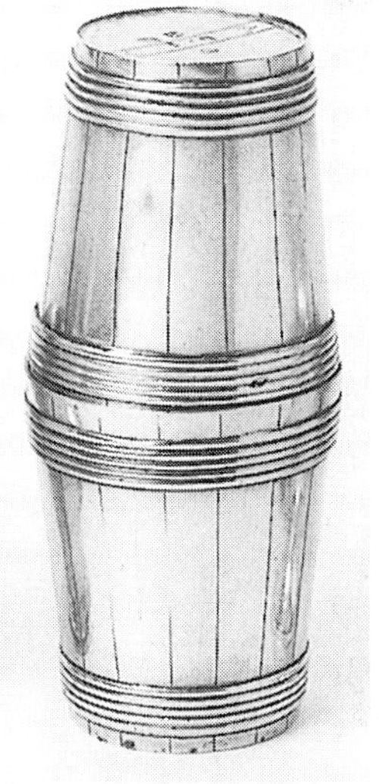

A pair of George III provincial double beakers, with reeded hoops and engraved staves, attributed to Joseph Walley of Liverpool, Chester 1779, 5½in (14cm) high, 7¾oz.
£4,300–4,800 *P*

A Guatemalan silver beaker, with flared moulded rim and gilt interior, marked on base with crowned tax stamp and Guatemala mark, c1800, 4in (10cm) high, 9½oz.
£2,000–2,200 *S(NY)*

A German parcel-gilt silver beaker, repoussé with a band of scroll and foliage on a matted ground above the spreading foot, chased with similar decoration under the reeded rim, early 18thC, 4¼in (11cm) high, 3½oz.
£1,400–1,600 *SLN*

A George III tapered beaker, by John Lambe, with fluted decoration and a band of chased and embossed baskets of flowers, engraved coat-of-arms within a C-scroll cartouche, gilt interior, the foot with scalloped engraving, later inscription to base, 1786, 4in (10cm) high, 4½oz.
£220–260 *P(EA)*

Prices

The price ranges quoted in this book reflect the average price a purchaser would expect to **pay** for a similar item. When selling as an individual expect to receive a lower figure. The price will fluctuate according to the condition, rarity, size, colour, provenance and restoration of the item and these must be taken into account when assessing values.

A George III flared beaker, by Thomas Ray, lightly embossed and chased with a wooded scene, on a flared base, the interior gilt, 1763, 5in (12.5cm) high, 5oz.
£220–260 *P(EA)*

Biscuit Boxes

A late Victorian ivory and silver-mounted biscuit box, by John Round & Son, with engraved crest, the part fluted silver cover with an ivory finial, Sheffield 1890, 4¾in (12cm) high.
£550–600 *P(E)*

l. A frosted glass biscuit box, with silver mounts, by Martin Hall & Co, Sheffield 1867, 7in (18cm) high.
£900–1,100 *TC*

A silver biscuit box, decorated with Gothic panels around the sides, the lid with ring handle, on 3 ball feet, by Roberts & Belk, Sheffield 1902, 6in (15cm) high.
£600–650 *THOM*

Bowls

A Swiss silver-gilt bowl, by Hans Rudolph Mayer, decorated with an engraved armorial below a reeded rim, the domed foot embossed with foliage, c1680, 5in (12.5cm) diam, 5½oz.
£2,250–2,750 *S(G)*

The St John mazer, the silver-mounted maple bowl with a double moulded band, the rim mount with a central plaited wire, the upper strapwork bands with 3 rows of hyphens, later applied ox-eye handles, 4 hinged straps to the flared foot rim with egg-and-tongue border and lappets moulded to the wood, the rim and foot fully hallmarked, maker's mark a caltrap, London 1585, 7in (18cm) diam.
£55,000–60,000 *WW*

This silver-mounted mazer (hardwood drinking vessel) was found in a country house by Rev St John in Victorian times. Because it had been stored for such a long time it was in pristine condition, although the body was cracked due to shrinkage through lack of use. The non-original handles were added in c1630.

A Dutch silver brandy bowl, by Hendrik van Manen, Sneek, engraved at the rim 'AE/1777', 1772, 10in (25.5cm) high, 6½oz.
£850–950 *S(Am)*

Miller's is a price GUIDE not a price LIST

A Victorian sugar bowl, by Robert Harper, with folded borders, repoussé with deep band of foliate diaper pattern between beading, on a pedestal foot, 1871, 4¾in (12cm) diam, 6oz.
£140–180 *P(EA)*

A Victorian rose bowl, with gadrooned and shell rim, lion mask drop ring handles, leaf embossed body on flared base, with pierced and scrolled bracket feet, London 1890, 15in (38cm) wide, 53oz.
£1,650–1,850 *AH*

A silver bowl, chased with foliate swags on a matted ground divided by winged putti masks and 2 double scroll handles, on a pedestal foot, import marks for London 1890, 4in (10cm) diam.
£250–300 *HofB*

A silver sugar basin, London, c1901, 4in (10cm) high.
£135–150 *RAC*

A silver strawberry set, Birmingham 1909, largest 6in (15cm) wide.
£200–240 *CoHA*

r. A silver quaiche, Sheffield 1928, 4in (10cm) diam.
£110–130 *JAS*

An Edwardian silver punch bowl, with shaped mask, scroll and bead decorated rim, the fluted body with embossed blind cartouche and scrolling foliate banding, on moulded circular foot, London 1902, 12¼in (31cm) wide, 44½oz.
£1,600–1,800 *AH*

An American silver centrepiece bowl, by Shreve & Co, San Francisco, with wide rim cast and pierced with classical foliage and arches, c1910, 24¼in (61.5cm) long.
£2,800–3,200 *S(NY)*

Boxes

A William III silver tobacco box, by John Sutton, with moulded and corded borders, the cover engraved with contemporary arms under a foliate mantle, the base engraved 'Joshua Powell', marked on body and cover, London 1699, 3½in (9cm) diam, 3oz.
£2,800–3,500 *S(NY)*

A George II tobacco box, by Edward Cornock, the stepped and moulded cover engraved with an armorial within a foliate cartouche, maker's mark, London 1727, 4in (10cm) long.
£3,700–4,200 *DN*

A Victorian silver trompe l'oeil box, by John Samuel Hunt of Hunt & Roskell, formed as a dinner plate with a folded damask napkin bearing the cypher 'CR VIII', London 1844, 11in (28cm) diam, 59oz.
£5,750–6,500 *S*

The cypher is that of Christian VIII of Denmark. Hunt & Roskell made a number of such boxes for European royal and noble families. This box is traditionally said to have been a gift from Queen Victoria who commissioned Hunt & Roskell to supply many of the gifts sent to European households.

A pierced silver jewellery box, London 1900, 6in (15cm) wide.
£650–750 *SHa*

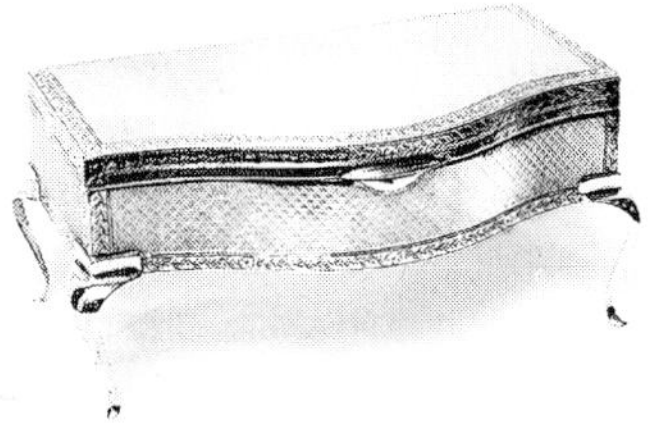

A silver jewellery casket of serpentine shape, by Goldsmiths & Silversmiths Co Ltd, with engine-turned decoration and foliate borders, on high scroll supports, London 1919, 5½in (14cm) wide.
£400–450 *HofB*

A silver box, with small drawer, on cabriole legs, 1875, 5½in (14cm) wide.
£300–340 *SSW*

Caddies

A George III tea caddy, with urn-shaped finial, bright-cut engraved foliate detail, London 1786, 5¾in (14.5cm) wide, 13oz.
£650–700 *WL*

A Dutch silver tea caddy, maker's mark 'H' with a figure and sword in shield, early 18thC, 4in (10cm) high, 4oz.
£1,500–1,700 *S(Am)*

A miniature Dutch tea caddy, die stamped with 3 vignettes of gardeners, putti at play and a horse and figures in a landscape, c1885, 3½in (9cm) high.
£220–250 *HofB*

Caddy Spoons

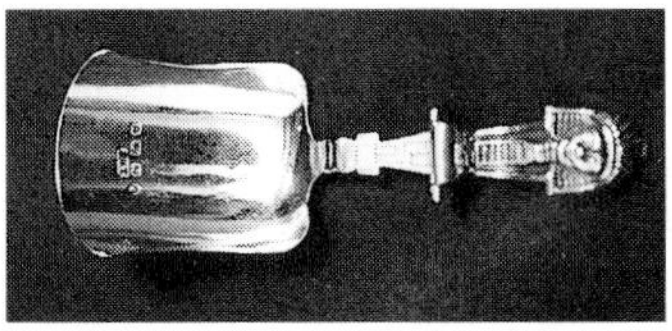

A silver caddy spoon, by Hilliard & Thomason, Birmingham 1881, 3½in (9cm) long.
£130–150 *DIC*

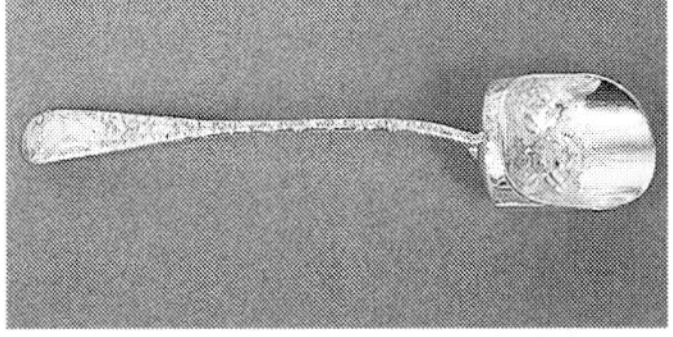

A silver caddy spoon, with foliate decoration, Birmingham 1894, 4¼in (11cm) long.
£110–130 *AMH*

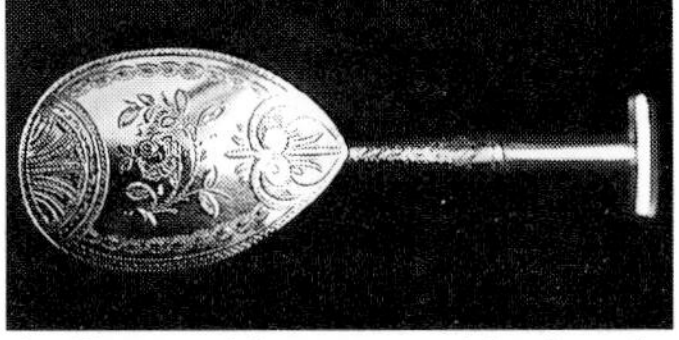

A silver caddy spoon, with shovel handle, Birmingham 1895, 3½in (9cm) long.
£120–140 *DIC*

Candlesticks & Chambersticks

A pair of George II silver candlesticks, by James Gould, with shaped circular bases, double knopped stems, detachable sconces with wavy edges, London 1734, 8in (20.5cm) high, 28oz.
£2,300–2,700 *GAK*

A set of 4 George III candlesticks, by John Green & Co, with plain columns, circular bases and detachable nozzles, Sheffield 1796, 6¼in (16cm) high.
£1,500–1,750 *PFK*

A pair of Victorian desk-top candlesticks, by Hawksworth, Eyre & Co, with octagonal bases, knopped baluster stems and detachable nozzles, Sheffield 1900, 6¾in (17cm) high.
£250–300 *Bea(E)*

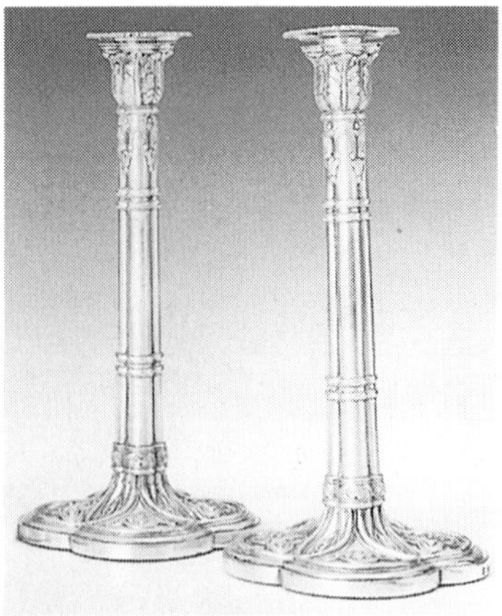

A set of 4 early George III style candlesticks, by Ebenezer Coker, the acanthus leaf decorated candleholders with gadroon edge detachable nozzles, London 1766–67, 11½in (29cm) high.
£3,500–4,000 *WW*

A George III chamber candlestick, by John Crouch I and Thomas Hannam, with reeded borders engraved with crests, with extinguisher and nozzle, London 1796, 5¾in (14.5cm) diam.
£450–500 *DN*

A set of 4 American silver table candlesticks, by Marshall Field & Co, with baluster stems, detachable nozzles, decorated with putti and rococo ornament, Chicago, early 20thC, 9in (23cm) high.
£2,100–2,300 *S(NY)*

l. A pair of Edwardian chamber candlesticks, by Charles Henry Townley and John William Thomas, the circular base with conical snuffer rest, gadrooned borders, engraved with crests, London 1904, 4in (10cm) high, 28oz.
£1,200–1,400 *P(NE)*

A pair of George III fluted baluster candlesticks, by William Abdy, with roundel and reeded borders, on fluted bases, London 1785, 11½in (29cm) high.
£900–1,100 *AG*

A pair of late Victorian candlesticks, by Hawksworth, Eyre & Co, of baluster form with shell decoration, on stepped square, scroll bases, 11in (28cm) high.
£550–600 *P(EA)*

A pair of Edwardian three-light candelabra, by William Hutton & Sons Ltd, the circular drip-pans and nozzles with fine gadroon edging, with reeded scrolling branches and detachable flame finials, Sheffield 1903, 20½in (52cm) high, loaded.
£2,500–3,000 *Bea(E)*

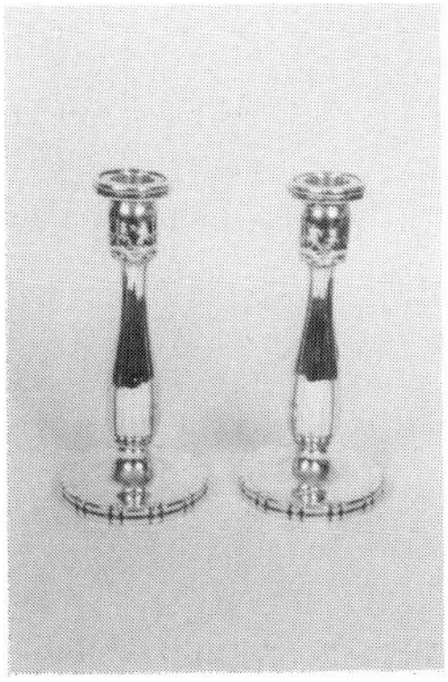

Centrepieces

A George IV épergne, the central bowl supported by 4 scroll acanthus supports, baluster stem, with 4 foliate scroll branches, each supporting a glass bowl, on a shaped tapering square base, with shell and foliate decoration, on paw feet, crested, Birmingham 1823, 17½in (44.5cm) high, 92oz.
£6,500–7,500 *Bon*

An early Victorian comport, decorated with lattice-work design and with applied fruiting vine, on an oval stem foot, engraved inscription, maker Chas Reily & George Storer, London 1842, 11½in (29cm) high, 33oz.
£850–950 *AG*

An Edwardian table centrepiece, by J. Davis & Son, composed of 4 intersecting open scroll branches supporting a central oval basket, with pierced foliate sides and floral scrolling rim, 2 smaller baskets similarly decorated, and 2 trumpet-shaped vases, all with green glass liners, Sheffield 1907, 14½in (37cm) high, 91½oz.
£6,000–6,750 *P(WM)*

l. A Tiffany & Co sterling silver pierced comport, maker's mark of Edward Moore, c1880, 9in (23cm) diam.
£1,000–1,200 *SHa*

Coffee Pots & Teapots

A George II silver teapot, by John Rowe, with rococo swan neck spout, the shoulder engraved with a band of strapwork, marked on base and cover, London 1750, 5in (12.5cm), 12½oz.
£1,600–1,800 *S(NY)*

A George III coffee pot, the domed lid with urn finial, embossed with drapes and tassels and engraved with a crest, leaf capped spout, later loop handle and spreading foot with beaded edging, maker Daniel Smith and Robert Sharp, London 1775, 13in (33cm) high, 35oz.
£3,000–3,500 *AH*

A George II coffee pot, by John Wirgman, embossed with shells and a crest, the hinged domed lid with pineapple finial, London 1755, 10in (25.5cm) high, 31oz.
£1,600–1,800 *P(G)*

A George III baluster coffee pot, with a crest within a surround of scrolls, flowers and foliage, maker's mark 'T.E.', London 1774, 9¼in (23.5cm) high, 26oz.
£500–550 *Bea(E)*

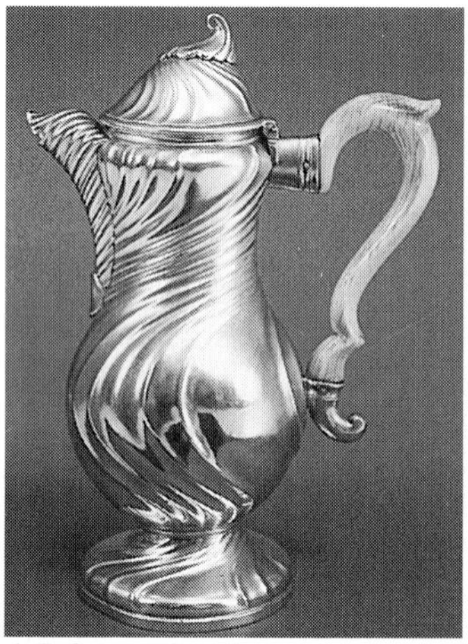

A Belgian silver coffee pot, with conforming foot, the cover with scroll finial and carved ivory handle, Liège 1764, 8¼in (21cm) high, 17oz.
£8,600–9,000 *HAM*

Belgian silver of this period is rarer than German or Swiss silver. The Belgian market for antiques is also currently very strong.

A Dutch silver teapot, by Jan de Wal II, Leeuwarden, with ivory scroll handle and finial, hinged cover, 4 leaf supports, 1784, 15in (38cm) high, 14½oz.
£3,700–4,200 *S(Am)*

Teapot Marks

Teapots are marked in a group on the base, apart from some early 19thC ones which are marked in a line near the handle. Lids bear the lion passant, maker's mark and, after 1784, the sovereign's head and date letter.

A George IV coffee pot, by George Burrows II and Richard Pearce, with gadrooned border, leaf-chased handle and spout, on a circular foot, London 1826, 7in (18cm) high, 27½oz.
£600–700 *DN*

A George III coffee pot, by Wakelin & Garrard, with tapering sides and scalloped leaf-capped spout with shell motif at base, engraved with crest of Henderson, 1797, 11½in (29cm) high, 39½oz.
£2,700–3,000 *P*

A George III urn-shaped coffee pot, by Richard Cooke, London 1800, 11½in (29cm) high, 32½oz.
£2,250–2,500 *TC*

An early Victorian silver teapot, maker's mark 'IM&S', London 1839, 6in (15cm) high.
£1,000–1,200 *SHa*

A Victorian pear-shaped teapot, by E. J. & W. Barnard, the hinged lid with flower finial, London 1839, 6in (15cm) high, 22oz.
£320–350 *P(NE)*

An American silver tea kettle-on-stand, lamp missing, marked on base of stand 'Ball Black and Co, W. F., New York', c1850, 17¼in (44cm) high, 91oz.
£1,400–1,600 *S(Cg)*

A Victorian silver teapot of octagonal baluster form, with wavy rim, hollow scrolled handle, engraved with panels of flowers and vacant cartouches, octagonal foot, floral finial to lid, maker J. M., Glasgow 1857, 7in (18cm) high, 25oz.
£370–420 *GAK*

A silver tea kettle, with burner and stand, by Mappin & Webb, Sheffield 1911, 11in (28cm) high, 38oz.
£800–1,000 *CoHA*

A late Victorian coffee pot, of waisted form with half-lobed decoration, maker SWS, 1896, 6in (15cm) high, 13½oz.
£130–150 *L*

Coffee & Tea Services

A Regency three-piece tea service, the part ribbed boat-shaped bodies engraved with an initial, with gadroon flange borders, on ball feet, by Michael Starkey, London 1810, 45½oz.
£720–800 *WW*

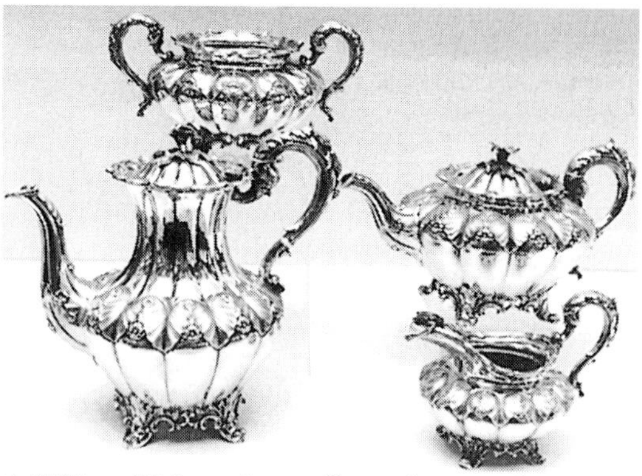

A William IV four-piece coffee and tea set, by Messrs Barnard, of compressed segmented form, with leaf-capped shoulders, handle and spout, on scroll bracket feet, 1836, 77½oz.
£1,700–2,000 *P(C)*

A William IV Scottish three-piece tea service, with leaf-chased rims and feet, scroll handles, engraved with monograms, maker's mark 'AW', Edinburgh 1832, 49½oz.
£800–900 *DN*

A William IV four-piece coffee and tea set, by John Fraser, with acanthus leaf-capped scroll handles and flower finials, foliate scroll feet and stylised stiff-leaf borders, engraved with armorials, c1835, 83½oz.
£1,800–2,200 *P*

A Russian silver four-piece tea service, by Carl Siewers, St Petersburg, fluted into panels, with ivory-fitted scroll handles and finials, gilt interiors, 1859, 64½oz.
£1,600–1,800 *S(Am)*

An American silver five-piece coffee and tea set, by Eoff & Shepherd for Ball, Black & Co, New York, with bright-cut borders, monogrammed 'JCS', c1860, 86½oz, and a silver-plated tray.
£2,100–2,400 *S(NY)*

A Victorian silver four-piece coffee and tea set, by Smith, Nicholson & Co, decorated with Cellini pattern, initialled, in a fitted oak case with carrying handles, London 1866, 77oz.
£2,300–2,600 *S(S)*

A Victorian silver five-piece coffee and tea set, by William Smily for A. B. Savory & Sons, in George II style, London 1864, 77½oz.
£1,300–1,500 *CGC*

An American sterling silver medallion coffee and tea set, by William Gale & Son, New York, c1862.
£7,500–8,500 *YAN*

A Victorian silver six-piece coffee and tea set, maker's mark of Stephen Smith, London, 1866 and 1867, 168oz.
£3,200–3,600 *Bon*

A silver four-piece coffee and tea set, with butterfly finials, by J. R. Callwell & Co, c1880.
£1,600–1,800 *SFL*

A German silver five-piece coffee and tea service, by Deyhle, with bone-fitted loop handles and hinged covers, c1900, 86oz.
£880–1,000 *S(Am)*

A George V silver four-piece coffee and tea service, with thread edging, on 4 bun feet, maker's mark 'H.A.', Sheffield 1918, 56oz.
£350–400 *Bea(E)*

Coffee & Chocolate Pot Marks

Coffee and chocolate pots are marked in a group below the handle or in a line to the right of it. The lids should also be marked with the lion passant, except on some pots from the 1740s, on tuck-in bases. After 1784 lids should also be struck with the sovereign's head duty stamp.

An American silver part coffee and tea set, each on 6 paw feet, bases monogrammed and dated '1893', marked on bases with maker's mark of a seahorse above initial 'S', 1893, 232oz.
£3,500–4,000 *S(NY)*

An Edwardian silver three-piece tea service, the teapot with a winged lion finial, on fluted pedestal bases, by W. Hutton & Sons Ltd, 1902, 61½oz.
£850–1,000 *P(E)*

A George V silver four-piece coffee and tea service, by Goldsmiths & Silversmiths Co, each circular body with vertical reeding and textured foliate borders, London 1926, 69oz.
£680–740 *Bea(E)*

l. A George V silver three-piece globular tea service, on stepped circular bases, maker's mark 'B & S', Sheffield 1935, 34oz.
£350–400 *Bea(E)*

Cruets

A Queen Anne silver cruet, by Charles Adam, the stepped frame with 5 pillar supports, scroll handle and simple ring holders, with 3 casters and glass oil and vinegar bottles with detachable caps, London 1708/09, 7¾in (20cm) high, 30½oz.
£7,000–8,000 *S*

A George I silver cruet stand, by John Hugh le Sage and Thomas Bamford, in the form of 3 conjoined octagonal frames holding 2 cut-glass bottles with silver caps and an octagonal caster, engraved with a contemporary cypher, the stand with maker's mark on base, London 1724, 7in (18cm) long, 27oz.
£2,800–3,200 *S(NY)*

A George III silver cruet, by John Schofield, London 1792, bottles later, 14¼in (36cm) wide, 25oz.
£400–500 *P(G)*

A silver cruet stand, by Edward Barnard Jnr and John William Barnard, with gadrooned border, on 4 scroll feet, London 1833, 23oz.
£500–550 *HOLL*

A Victorian silver four-piece cruet set, by Thomas Hayes, in George III style, pierced with birds amidst foliage below gadrooned rims, with blue glass liners, Birmingham 1898/1900, 3in (7.5cm) wide.
£550–650 *HofB*

Cups & Goblets

A Charles I silver wine cup, with bell-shaped bowl and baluster stem, maker's mark, London 1635, 6in (15cm) high, 6½oz.
£4,000–4,500 *S(NY)*

A German silver-gilt wine goblet, the tapering bowl with panelled corners, on a fruit engraved panelled foot, 18thC, 6in (15cm) high.
£1,300–1,500 *WW*

l. A George I silver cup and cover, the bell-shaped body with a girdle moulding, on a moulded spreading foot, London 1714, 11in (28cm) high, 47oz.
£3,000–3,500 *WW*

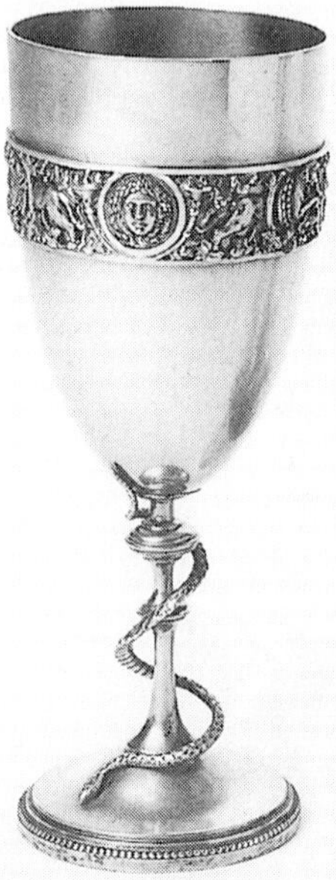

A set of 4 Victorian silver-gilt goblets, by Stephen Smith, the elongated vase-shaped bodies applied with a frieze of lions jumping through vine tendrils, the stems entwined with snakes, 1865, 8¼in (21cm) high.
£1,600–1,800 *P*

A French parcel-gilt, enamelled and garnet set neo-Gothic chalice, by Placide Poussielgue-Rusand, Paris, c1852, 10½in (26.5cm) high, 44oz.
£3,600–4,000 *S*

This chalice illustrates the resurgence of fine craftsmanship in French religious silver which occurred in the middle of the 19thC. Placide Poussielgue-Rusand is considered to be the principal goldsmith of this movement.

Cutlery

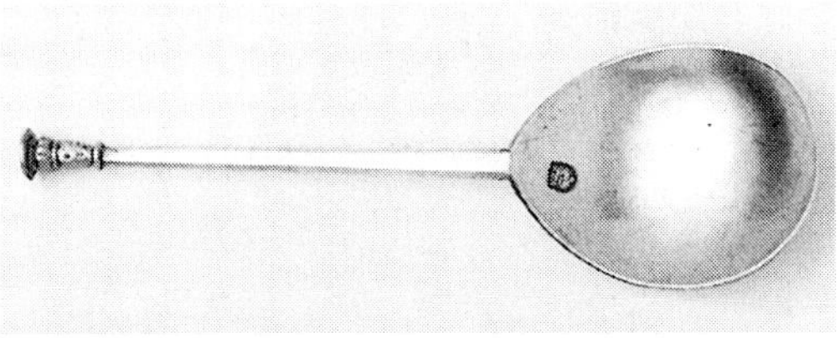

A Charles I silver seal-top spoon, the fluted and foliate baluster seal with traces of gilding, the terminal engraved with 'pricked' initials 'AB AW', London 1638, 6in (15cm) long.
£500–600 *P*

A James II silver trefid spoon, the oval bowl with a plain rat-tail, repaired, maker's mark probably Wm Mathew, London 1685, 7¼in (18.5cm) long, 1oz.
£260–300 *Bon*

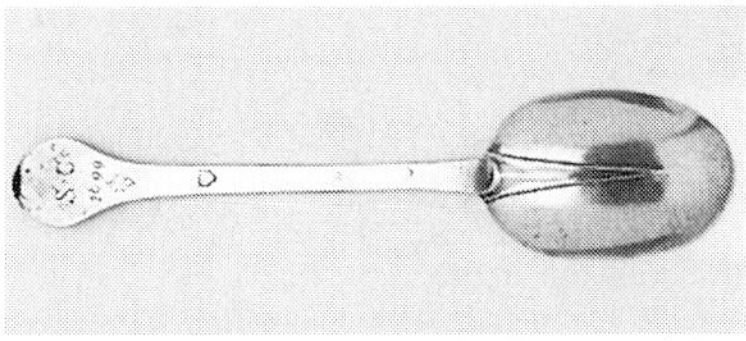

A William III provincial silver trefid spoon, with rounded terminal, ribbed rat-tail bowl, the front of the stem decorated with foliate scrolls, the reverse engraved '*S*G*' above '1699', maker's mark stamped twice 'C A', 8½in (21.5cm) long.
£350–400 *P*

Seven silver dog-nose tablespoons, with rat-tail bowls, engraved with wing and coronet crests, London 1701 and c1720, 17½oz.
£820–900 *DN*

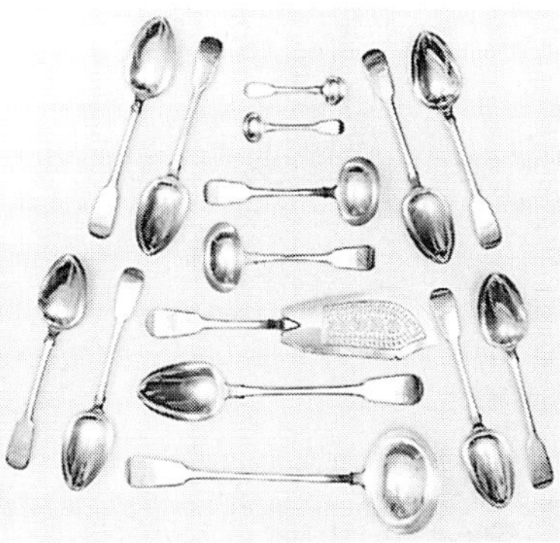

A George IV silver fiddle pattern table service, engraved with monograms, various makers, c1820, 194½oz.
£2,400–2,800 *P(EA)*

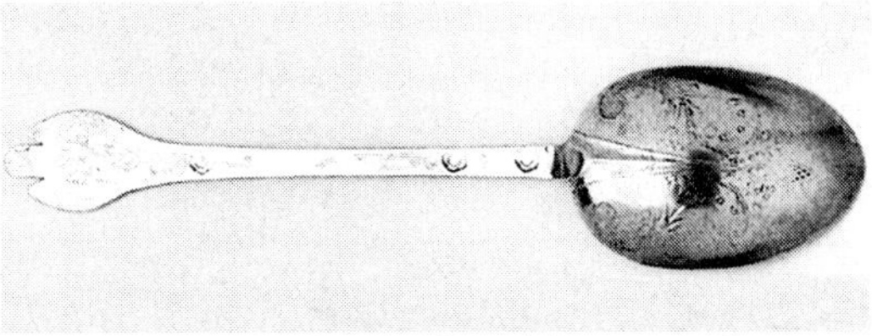

A Charles II silver lace-back trefid spoon, with flared terminal, the back of the stem engraved with prick-dot initials 'ME', the bowl with ribbed rat-tail, West Country, c1680, 7¾in (19.5cm) long.
£550–600 *P*

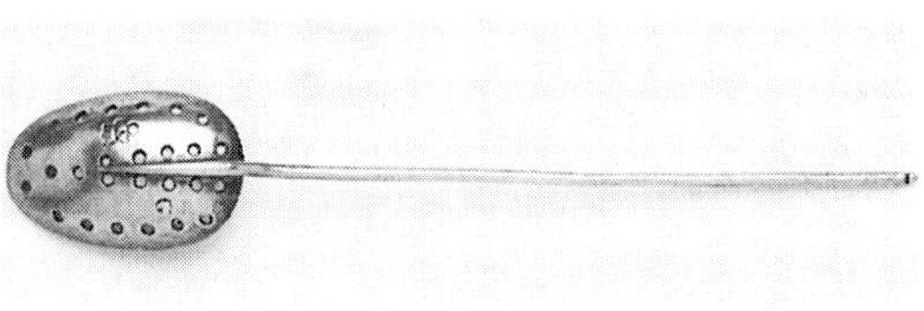

A silver mote spoon, the plain oval bowl with narrow rat-tail, pierced with holes, maker's mark 'AH' with crown above and cinquefoil below, c1690, 5in (12.5cm) long.
£400–450 *P*

A mote spoon was used for straining tea leaves.

Hallmarks

British silver has been struck with hallmarks applied at the Goldsmiths Hall (hence the word hallmark) since 1478. Most English silver bears a minimum of 4 marks which, historically, guaranteed that a piece of silver was of the required legal standard. The use made today of the date letter and maker's mark in identifying antiques is an unintended by-product. Hallmarks are a good guide to age and authenticity, but should not be regarded as definitive, as they can be worn to the point of illegibility, faked, or even let-in from other pieces of silver.

Standard set of marks

The main marks are:

1. **The sterling guarantee**
Sterling is the British term for silver that is at least 92.5% pure. From 1300 the mark was a leopard's head, by 1478 it had a crown. In 1544 it was a lion passant walking to the left, and from 1820 the lion was uncrowned.

Britannia standard
This was a higher standard of silver required between 1697 and 1720. On this standard of silver the town and sterling marks were replaced by Britannia and a lion's head in profile.

2. **The town mark**
This varied according to the assay office of the individual town.

Birmingham Chester

Norwich Sheffield

3. **The date letter**
This appeared in London from 1478, later in other parts of the country. It is unique from year to year and assay office to office, but usually follows an alphabetical sequence. The letter is always enclosed by a shield.

1721 1741 1781 1801

4. **The maker's mark**
Used on silver from 1363, the early marks were signs or symbols, as few people could read; this remained the case until the late 17thC when initials and symbols were combined, the symbols falling from use during the next 100 years. The initials are those of the Christian name and surname, except on Britannia standard wares (between 1697 and 1720), where the first 2 letters of the surname are used instead.

Ayme Videau c1739–1747 Paul Storr c1792–1834

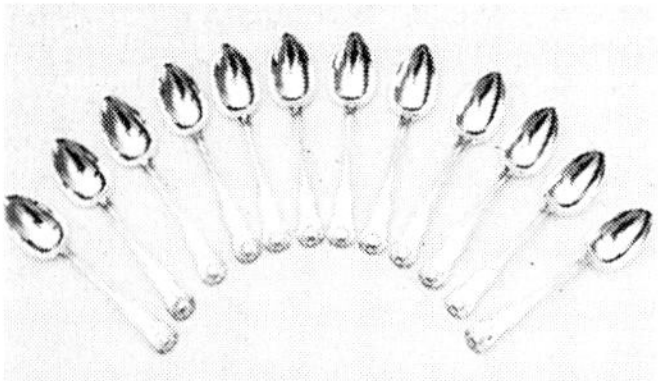

Twelve George III silver hour-glass pattern teaspoons, by Thomas Wallis and Jonathan Hayne, initialled 'R', London 1817, 12½oz.
£150–180 *Bea(E)*

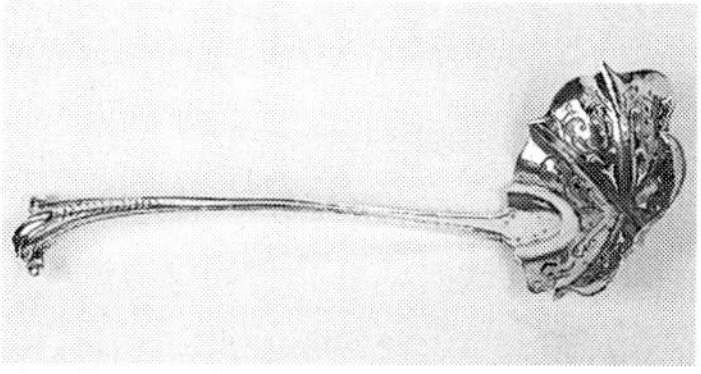

A silver sifter spoon, by Lias, London 1845, 6in (15cm) long.
£200–230 *AMH*

Four silver salt spoons, with twisted handles, London 1861, 2¾in (7cm) long.
£90–100 *AMH*

A Victorian silver canteen of 12 pairs of dessert cutlery, Sheffield 1839, case 14in (35.5cm) wide.
£1,600–1,800 *CoHA*

A Tiffany & Co silver flatware set, comprising 120 pieces, engraved 'F.S.F.', stamped on stems 'John Polhemus and Patent 1860'.
£3,500–4,000 *S(NY)*

A silver beaded-pattern service, engraved with a crest, comprising 116 pieces, maker's mark of George Adams, London 1867, 236oz.
£6,000–7,000 *Bon*

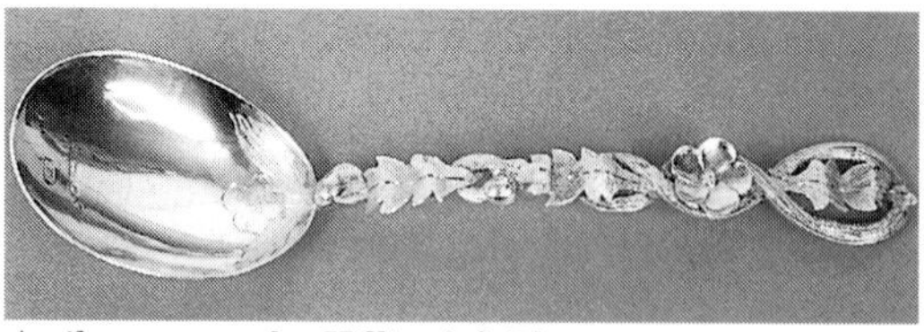

A silver spoon, by Hilliard & Thomason, Birmingham 1876, 5in (12.5cm) long.
£250–300 *AMH*

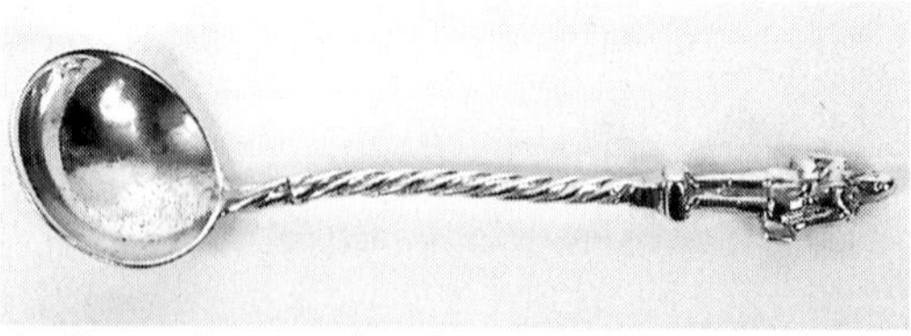

A silver salt spoon, London 1885, 3½in (9cm) long.
£25–30 *AMH*

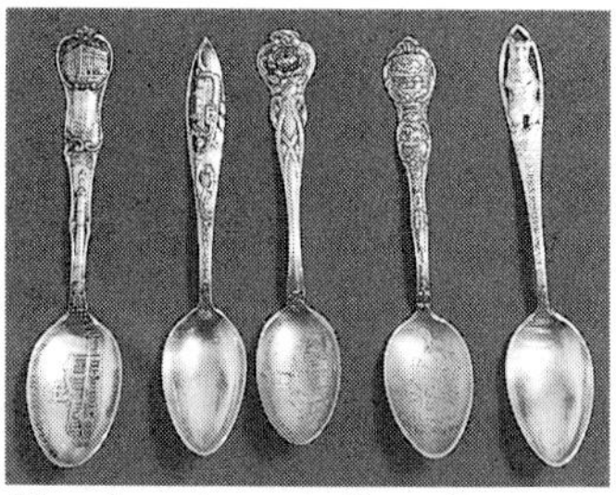

Five American sterling silver souvenir spoons, c1915, 4in (10cm) long.
£30–40 each *YAN*

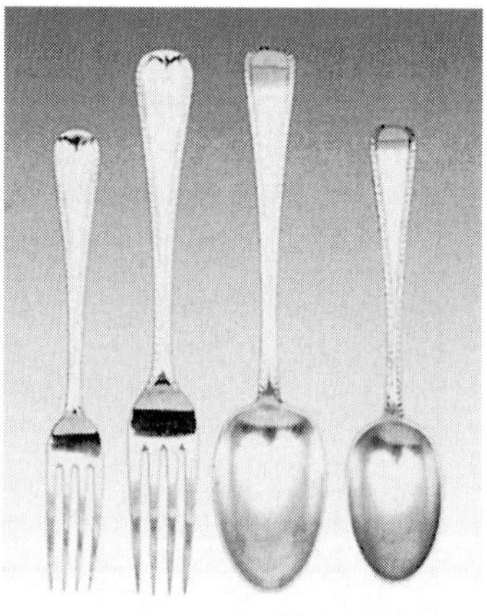

A George V silver feather-edge Old English pattern part service, by Mappin & Webb, comprising 39 pieces, London 1920, 83½oz.
£800–900 *Bea(E)*

A silver Hanoverian pattern table service, each engraved with crest, the majority Sheffield 1933, 180oz, in a fitted mahogany canteen.
£3,600–4,200 *Gam*

l. A canteen of cutlery, comprising 12 place settings, the knives with mother-of-pearl or ivory handles, Sheffield 1933, 200oz.
£3,000–3,500 *JNic*

A George VI Hanoverian pattern table service, by Goldsmiths & Silversmiths Co, Sheffield 1941, London 1935 and 1940, 56oz.
£550–600 *Bea(E)*

Dishes

A George III silver pap boat, London 1806, 5in (12.5cm) wide.
£120–150 *PSA*

A pair of silver bonbon dishes, by Mappin & Webb, London 1910, 3in (7.5cm) high.
£600–650 *AMH*

A pair of late Victorian silver dishes, embossed and chased with medallions of amorini beside trees, maker's mark 'T.S.', London 1882, 6½in (16.5cm) diam, 11oz.
£260–300 *P(F)*

r. Two silver dessert dishes, by Alfred, James, Francis and Arthur Walter Pairpoint, the open basketwork sides applied with grape vines and a gadrooned edge, on a panelled skirt foot, London 1912 and 1922, 10in (25.5cm) diam, 44½oz.
£1,800–2,000 *WW*

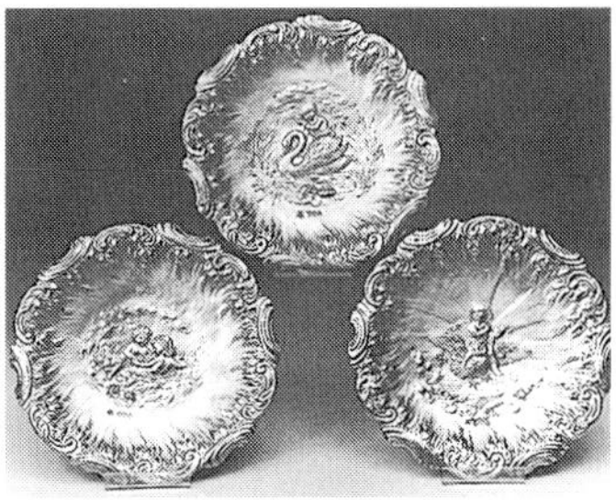

A set of 3 late Victorian silver-gilt dessert dishes, the centres decorated with repoussé putti figures, scroll borders, on bun feet, maker W. J. Connell, London 1897, 8½in (21.5cm) diam, 28oz.
£2,000–2,400 *WW*

Covered Dishes

A set of 4 George III silver entrée dishes and covers, by Thomas Robinson, with gadrooned borders and detachable foliate ring handles, the covers engraved with crests, 1812, 11¾in (27.5cm) long, 237oz.
£6,000–6,500 *P*

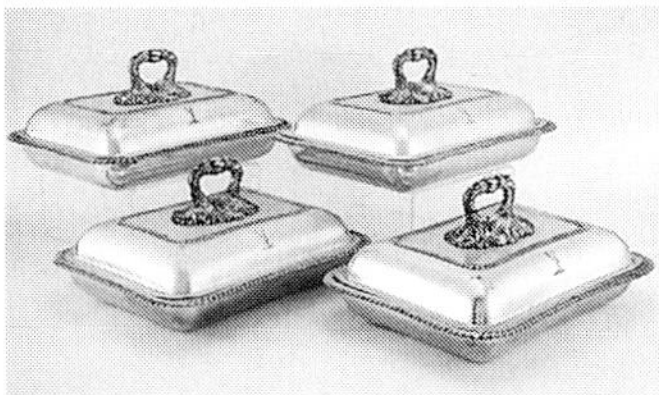

A set of 4 silver entrée dishes, with gadrooned borders and crests, foliate handles, 19thC, 11in (28cm) wide.
£650–750 *DN*

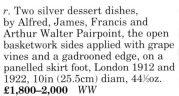

A silver muffin dish, by Sebastian Crespel, London 1836, 7½in (19cm) diam.
£800–1,000 *AMH*

A pair of American silver covered vegetable dishes, by Samuel Kirk & Son Co, repoussé and chased with Gothic scenes amidst flowers and foliage on a matted ground, similar ring handles, engraved on bases 'Gladys Heald Watts', marked and No. '243L', 1903–24, 10½in (26.5cm) wide, 64oz.
£2,800–3,200 *S(NY)*

l. A pair of silver entrée dishes, covers and handles, maker W.H.P., London 1908, 10in (25.5cm) wide, 80oz.
£900–1,100 *SWO*

r. A George V shaped silver entrée dish, by James Deakin & Sons, with gadroon edging, the cover with detachable handle, Sheffield 1918, 12in (30.5cm) wide, 60½oz.
£450–500 *Bea(E)*

A pair of American silver vegetable dishes and covers, by Dominick & Haff, New York, chased all-over with flowers on a matted ground, bases with contemporary monograms, 1886, 11½in (29cm) wide, 85oz.
£2,800–3,200 *S(NY)*

An Edwardian silver muffin dish and cover, with central scroll handle, scroll and shell border, maker's mark of James Dixon & Sons, Sheffield 1906, 8in (20.5cm) high, 14½oz.
£180–200 *Bon(C)*

Egg Stands

A silver egg stand, Sheffield 1818, 9in (23cm) high.
£900–1,000 *DIC*

A George IV silver egg stand, by Edward Barton, with central foliate carrying handle and pierced leaf spoon holders, on a domed lobed base with stiff-leaf decoration, 1829, the spoons of fiddle pattern engraved with crests, by William Troby, 1828, 8in (20.5cm) diam, 30oz.
£600–700 *P(EA)*

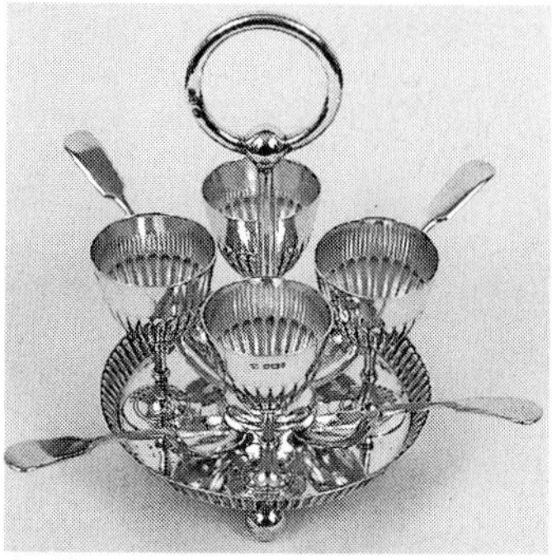

A silver four-piece egg stand, Sheffield 1901, 7½in (19cm) high.
£250–300 *PSA*

Frames

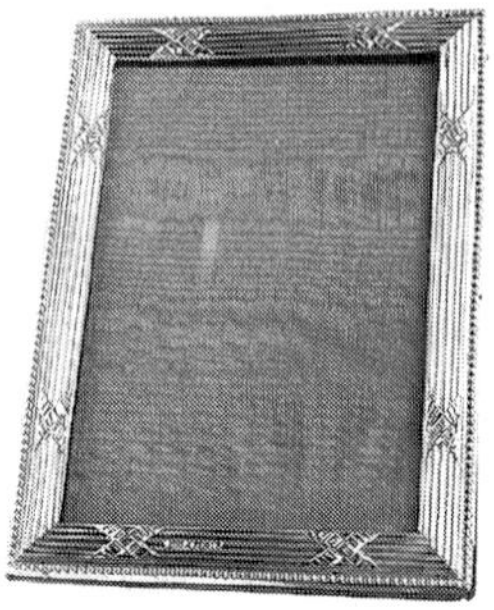

A silver photograph frame, by H. Matthews, Birmingham 1907, 6½in (16.5cm) high.
£320–360 *THOM*

A silver photograph frame, by Saunders & Shepherd, Birmingham 1892, 6¾in (17cm) high.
£600–650 *THOM*

A late Victorian embossed silver-mounted photograph frame, Birmingham 1899, 8in (20.5cm) high.
£250–300 *GAK*

An Edwardian silver photograph frame, Chester 1908, 6½in (16.5cm) high.
£225–250 *ATQ*

Inkstands & Wells

A Victorian silver boat-shaped inkstand, engraved with a mermaid crest, with 2 pen trays and 2 moulded globular glass inkwells with silver covers, the central pierced container holding a cranberry glass jar and surmounted by an embossed taperstick with extinguisher, Birmingham 1846, 13½in (34.5cm) wide, 21oz.
£1,700–2,000 *P(EA)*

A Victorian silver inkwell, by W. & J. Barnard, in early 18thC style, with a pewter capstan-shaped well and a ring of quill holders, London 1890, 2in (5cm) high.
£300–350 *HofB*

A silver scallop-shaped inkstand, by Pairpoint Brothers, in the form of a James I spice box, the cover with chased decoration and egg-and-dart flange border, engraved with initials, on shell feet, overstruck by D. & J. Wellby, London 1922, 5in (12.5cm) wide, 20¼oz.
£500–600 *WW*

Jugs & Ewers

A George III silver helmet-shaped cream jug, by Thomas Hallows, on a raised circular foot, 1783, 4¼in (11cm) high, 3oz.
£100–120 *L*

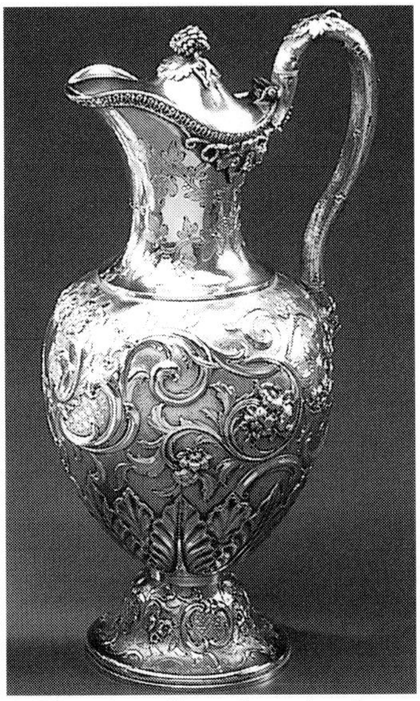

A Victorian silver claret jug, by Robert Gray & Son, the domed cover with grape bunch finial, vine bough loop handle, Glasgow 1840, 12in (30.5cm) high, 29oz.
£2,000–2,200 *S*

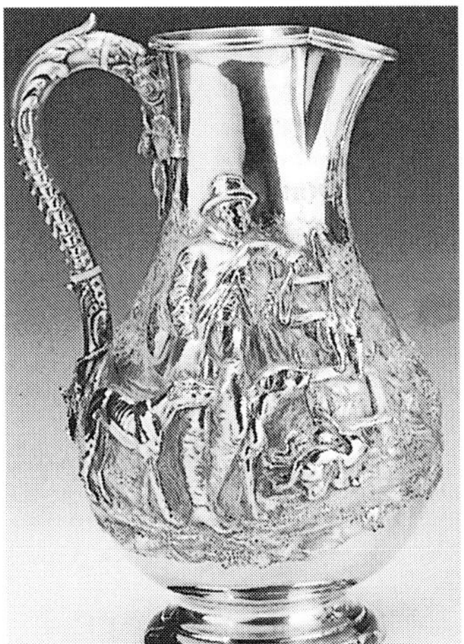

A Victorian silver ewer, by Robert Hennell, embossed with a scene of 2 huntsmen resting after the hunt, engraved with a crest and inscribed, London 1872, 11in (28cm) high, 38oz.
£2,000–2,300 *Bon*

A George III silver cream jug, with scroll and acanthus handle, on pedestal foot, London 1799, 5in (12.5cm) high.
£200–250 *PSA*

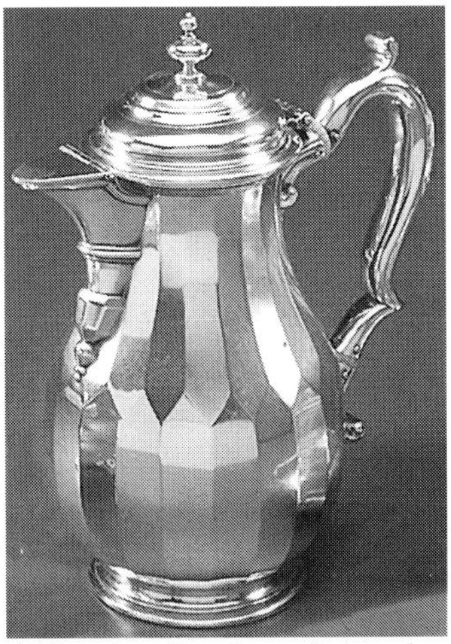

A Victorian silver jug and cover, by Robert Hennell & Sons, the spout with hinged flap, London 1844, 8in (20.5cm) high, 24oz.
£3,000–3,500 *S*

A Tiffany & Co silver ewer, by Young & Ellis, decorated with grape vines, c1860, 16in (40.5cm) high.
£2,000–2,500 *SFL*

A Regency silver hot water jug, by William Burwash, with gadrooned rim, treen handle, probably London 1816, 4½in (11.5cm) high, 24oz.
£220–250 *GAK*

Cream Jug Marks

Early cream jugs are marked in a group on the base. Later examples are marked in a line to the right of the handle or, particularly at the end of the 18thC, below the lip.

A South American silver pitcher, the branch handle entwined with a serpent, probably Bolivian, mid-19thC, 13¼in (33.5cm) high.
£1,400–1,600 *S(NY)*

An American silver pitcher, by Gorham Mfg Co, Providence, RI, with a broad die-rolled band of stylised foliate ornament, with contemporary cypher on the front 'RMT', 1885, 10in (25.5cm) high.
£1,400–1,600 *S(NY)*

Mirrors

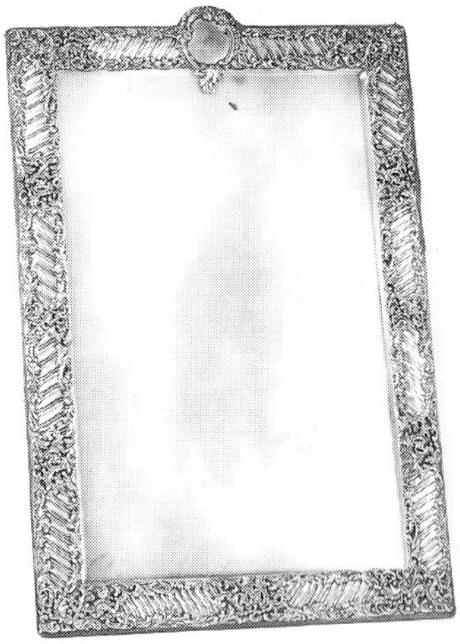

An Edwardian silver mirror, with bevelled oblong plate and embossed scrolling foliate surround, centred by scrolling cartouche, on strut support, London 1903, 22in (56cm) high.
£450–500 *AH*

An Edwardian silver dressing table mirror, by William Comyns, with heart-shaped glass, the surround pierced and embossed with putti, masks, birds and scrolls, with blue velvet easel back, London 1905, 11in (28cm) high.
£460–500 *GAK*

A George V silver dressing table mirror, with bevelled glass and plain frame, maker's mark worn, Birmingham 1917, 18¼in (46.5cm) high.
£300–350 *Bea(E)*

FURTHER READING
Miller's Silver & Plate Antiques Checklist,
Miller's Publications, 1994

Mugs & Tankards

A Queen Anne silver tankard, by Benjamin Pyne, the hinged cover with chair-back thumbpiece, the body engraved with a coat-of-arms, London 1709, 8¾in (22cm) high, 48oz.
£8,500–9,000 *P(NE)*

A George II silver plain baluster tankard, the domed lid with pierced thumbpiece attached to scroll handle, the body with moulded girdle and engraved armorial with motto and crest, stepped base, maker's mark 'PE' (Peter Elliott), Exeter 1759, lid maker JK (John Kidder), London 1786, 7½in (19cm) high, 27oz.
£900–1,100 *PFK*

A silver tankard, by Henry Green, London 1794, 7¾in (19.5cm) high.
£1,800–2,000 *AMH*

A Victorian silver christening mug, by Harry Atkin, engraved with flowers and leaves, Sheffield 1899, 3in (7.5cm) high.
£220–250 *BEX*

A Victorian silver christening mug, by F. D. Dexter, embossed with figures, a cartouche with monograms, on scroll feet, London 1844, 3¾in (9.5cm) high.
£280–320 *DN*

l. A silver half pint christening mug, by William Hutton & Sons, Birmingham 1932, 3½in (9cm) high.
£220–250 *BEX*

Pincushions

A silver pincushion, by Levi & Saloman, in the form of a hedgehog, Birmingham 1903, 1½in (4cm) high.
£480–520 *THOM*

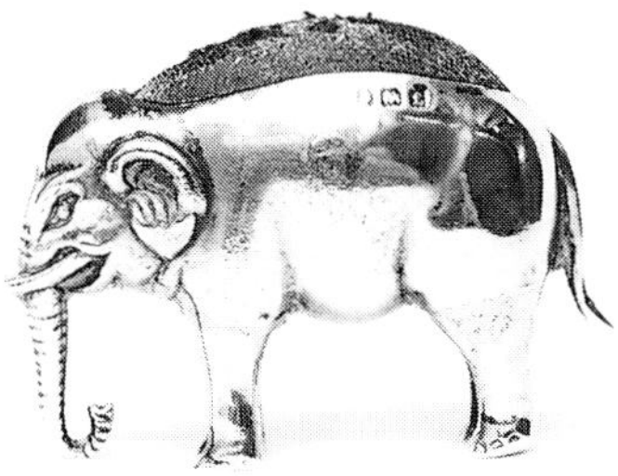

An Edwardian silver pincushion, by Adie & Lovekin Ltd, in the form of an elephant, Birmingham 1905, 2in (5cm) long.
£250–280 *HofB*

A silver pincushion, by Saunders & Shepherd, in the form of a camel, Birmingham 1906, 2¼in (5.5cm) high.
£500–650 *THOM*

A silver pincushion, in the form of a goat pulling a mother-of-pearl cart, maker A & LL, Birmingham 1909, 6½in (16.5cm) long.
£320–360 *GH*

A silver pincushion, in the form of a rollerskate, registered No. 535766, maker C & N, Birmingham 1909, 2½in (6.5cm) long.
£220–250 *GH*

Salts

A pair of silver cauldron salts, with gadrooned rims, embossed and chased rococo cartouches and flowers, rococo scroll feet, gilt interiors, marked 'Storr * Mortimer', London 1830, 3in (7.5cm) diam, 7½oz.
£420–480 *P(S)*

l. A pair of coin silver salts, by Jones, Ball & Co, Boston 1840, 2¼in (5.5cm) diam.
£300–350 *A&A*

A set of 3 Victorian silver salts, with pierced leaf rims, the sides pierced and chased with animals and fences, each with 3 shell feet headed by Chinamen, maker IW, London 1841, 1842 and 1844, 2¼in (5.5cm) diam, 10oz, with liners.
£520–560 *DN*

A set of 4 American silver salts, by J. E. Caldwell, with shell-shaped bowls each raised on a pedestal foot modelled as a tortoise, 3 marked on base, one marked on underside of bowl, late 19thC, 2¾in (7cm) high, 29½oz.
£3,500–4,000 *S(NY)*

A pair of silver and gilt salts, Sheffield 1911, 2¼in (5.5cm) diam.
£80–100 *WAC*

Salvers & Trays

A George III silver salver, by Robert Ross, London 1785, 6¾in (17cm) diam.
£700–800 *CoHA*

A late Victorian silver salver, with beaded rim, pierced wavy border and foliate motifs, the centre engraved with swags and scrolls, on 3 bun feet, Sheffield 1894, 12in (30.5cm) diam, 30oz.
£450–500 *WL*

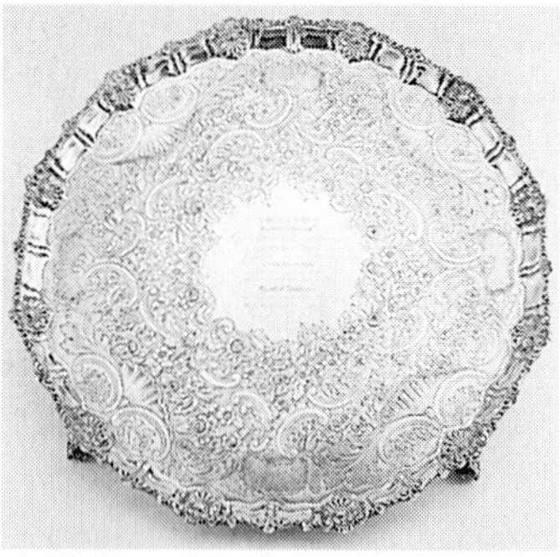

A William IV silver salver, with a raised shell and leaf scroll border and a wide band flat chased with shells, C-scrolls and flowers, engraved with a presentation inscription, on 4 leaf-chased claw-and-ball feet, sponsor's mark 'RG' untraced, Sheffield 1832, 21in (53cm) diam, 121oz.
£2,000–2,300 *DN*

A late Victorian silver two-handled tray, with leaf-capped handles, gadroon and shell border, the centre with engraved decoration and crest, maker's mark of William Gibson and John Langman, London 1898, 29¼in (74.5cm) wide, 172oz.
£2,200–2,500 *Bon*

An early Victorian silver tray and salver service, the tray decorated with engraved armorials, motto, trellis, baskets of fruit and foliate scrolls, with chased, fluted, floral and leaf border and C-scroll handles, with 2 matching salvers, on fluted scroll feet, all inscribed on the bases 'B. Smith, Duke Street, Lincoln's Inn Fields', London 1844, tray 23¾in (60.5cm) diam, 181oz, in original oak baize lined box.
£4,500–5,000 *AG*

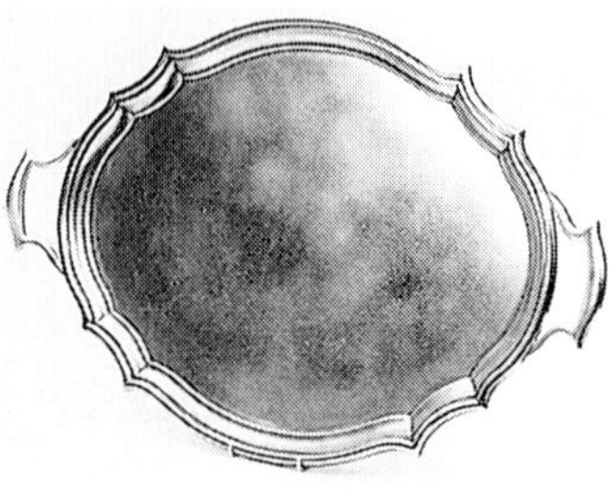

A George V tea tray, by Goldsmiths & Silversmith Co, of oval barbed outline with ogee moulded rim and scroll handles, 1920, 29in (74cm) wide, 141oz.
£1,200–1,400 *P(G)*

Sauce Boats

A George II silver sauce boat, by George Wickes, with double scroll acanthus leaf capped handle, with a crest beneath the spout, on 3 legs ending in claw-and-ball feet with lion mask terminals at top, London 1742, 5¾in (14.5cm) high, 19oz.
£1,300–1,500 *B&B*

A silver sauce boat, London 1769, 3¼in (8.5cm) high.
£400–450 *AMH*

A Georgian silver sauce boat, on 3 shell feet, later embossed with floral design, maker 'SM', London 1753, 6in (15cm) long, 4oz.
£200–250 *GAK*

A pair of George III silver sauce boats, by William Grundy, with gadrooned borders and acanthus leaf-capped double scroll handle, on shell feet, engraved on one side with armorial shield, 1770, 8¾in (22cm) long.
£2,000–2,500 *P*

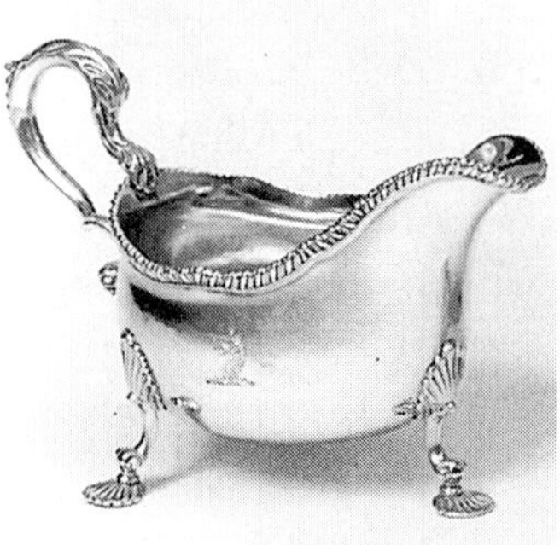

A pair of early George III silver sauce boats, engraved with a crest, moulded shaped gadrooned edge, on cast shell applique scroll legs to shell feet, by Daniel Smith and Robert Sharp, London 1769, 6in (15cm) wide, 24¼oz.
£2,200–2,500 *WW*

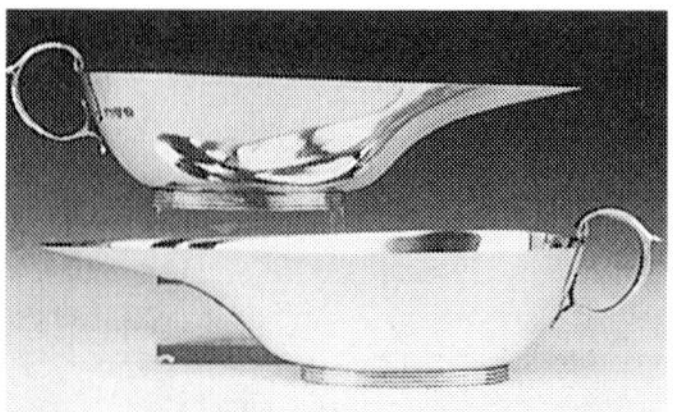

A pair of silver sauce boats, with scroll handles, on reeded oval bases, Chester 1938, 7in (18cm) wide, 4oz, with fitted case.
£220–250 *Bon(C)*

Scent Bottles

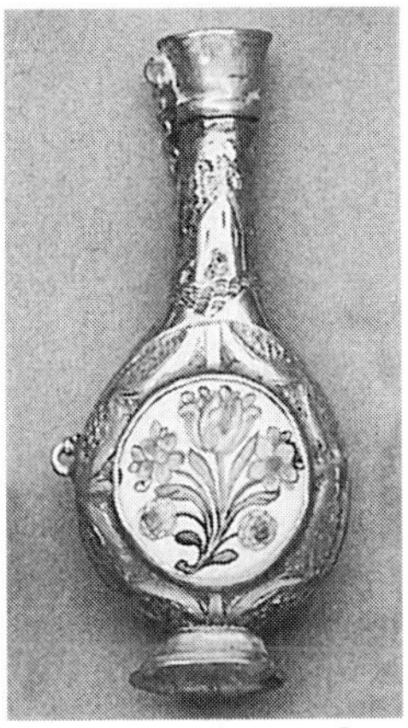

A German silver and enamel scent bottle and stopper, with tall neck engraved with buildings, the body inset on both sides with a circular enamel plaque painted in bright colours with a flowerspray, within an engraved border of swags, the stopper attached by a chain, 18thC, 2¾in (7cm) long.
£400–440 *P*

A mid-Victorian silver-gilt and cobalt blue glass scent bottle, maker's mark of Abraham Brounett, London 1864, 3¼in (8.5cm) high.
£450–500 *Bon*

A pair of silver-mounted glass dressing table scent bottles, of faceted square form, the glass with lozenge decoration, with hinged tops and stoppers, maker's mark 'H & A', Birmingham 1885, 5¼in (13.5cm) high.
£600–700 *Bon*

An enamelled silver scent bottle, with hinged cover, painted on one side with a condor eagle perched on a grassy rock, in shades of brown and grey, maker's mark 'H & A', Birmingham 1884, 4¼in (11cm) long.
£600–650 *P*

r. A silver scent bottle and stopper, repoussé on both sides, the screw cover engraved with a flower, on a circular foot, London 1890, 2¾in (7cm) high.
£220–250 *P*

l. A late Victorian silver scent bottle, with hinged cover and glass stopper, some damage, maker's mark 'H & A', Birmingham 1893, 4½in (11.5cm) high.
£320–360 *Bon*

Snuff Boxes

A Continental parcel-gilt silver snuff box and watch, chased with trailing flowers, one side with hinged lid over snuff compartment, the other side with twin covers opening to reveal a verge watch with white enamel dial signed 'Pet Barth', marked on rim with 'H' crowned and a script 'T', possibly Belgian, c1760, 3in (7.5cm) wide.
£1,400–1,600 *S(NY)*

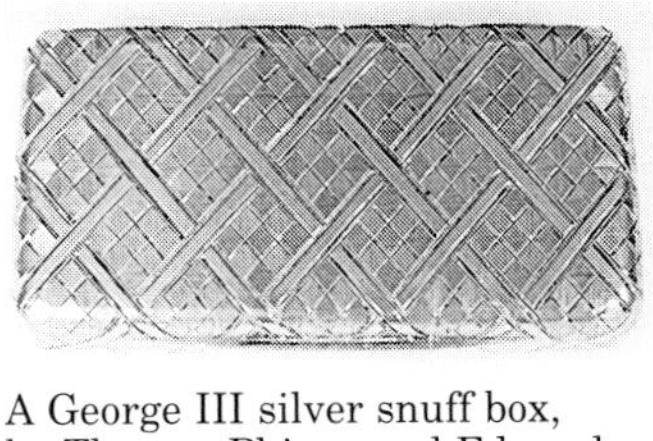

A George III silver snuff box, by Thomas Phipps and Edward Robinson, with trellis and diaper engraving, London 1801, 3in (7.5cm) wide.
£500–550 *CGC*

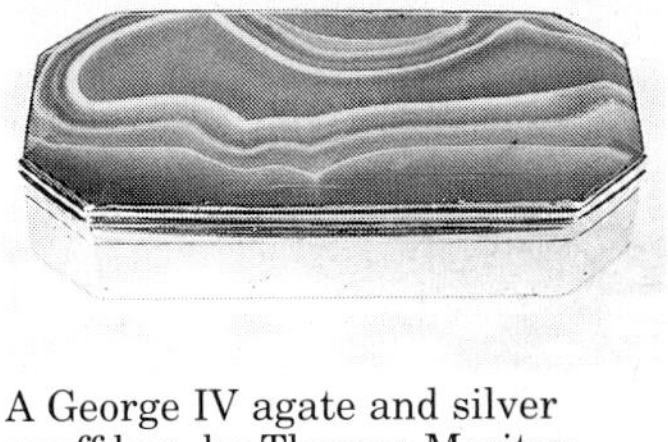

A George IV agate and silver snuff box, by Thomas Meriton, London 1822, 3in (7.5cm) wide.
£500–550 *CoHA*

Miller's is a price GUIDE not a price LIST

A George IV silver-gilt snuff box, by Nathaniel Mills, the cover engine-turned within a broad floral and foliate border, Birmingham 1827, 3¼in (8.5cm) wide, 3¾oz.
£400–450 *CGC*

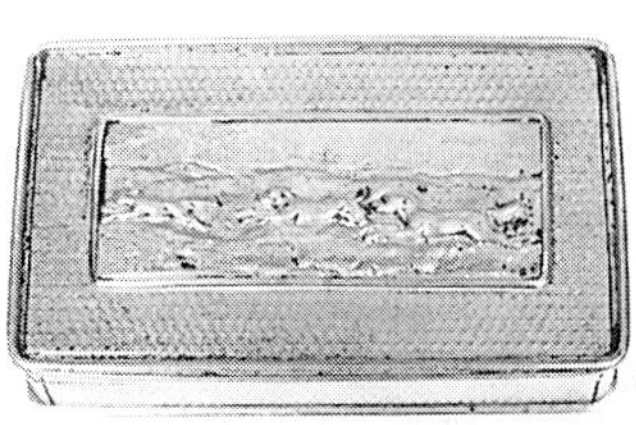

A William IV silver snuff box, by Nathaniel Mills, the cover engine-turned and applied with a scene of chasing hounds, Birmingham 1830, 3¼in (8.5cm) wide, 3¼oz.
£240–280 *CGC*

l. A George IV silver snuff box, by Edward Smith, Birmingham 1827, 3in (7.5cm) wide.
£300–350 *CoHA*

Sugar Casters

A set of 3 American silver sugar casters, by Samuel Edwards, mounted in an English silver frame, by Samuel Wood, with 2 cut-glass bottles, the casters monogrammed 'TEA', marked 'SE' beneath a crown and within a shield, the frame with scrolled handle on 4 double scrolled legs and shell-form feet, London 1750, frame 8½in (21.5cm) high, 44oz.
£2,200–2,500 *S(Cg)*

Samuel Edwards began silversmithing in Boston in 1725. He probably made the 3 casters to replace or complete the English set.

l. A George III silver sugar caster, by Thomas and George Hayter, with reeded band, on square foot, 1816, 5½in (14cm) high.
£110–140 *L*

A pair of Dutch silver sugar casters, with spirally fluted bodies, the covers pierced with scrolls and flowers, and capped by wrythen knop finials, c1895, 12in (30.5cm) high, 44oz.
£1,200–1,400 *P*

A silver sugar caster, by Goldsmiths & Silversmiths Co Ltd, London 1916, 7in (18cm) high, 5oz.
£250–300 *TC*

l. A silver sugar caster, in early 18thC style, with quarter-fluted decoration, on a stepped circular foot, London 1924, 6½in (16.5cm) high, 8½oz.
£170–200 *GAK*

Vinaigrettes

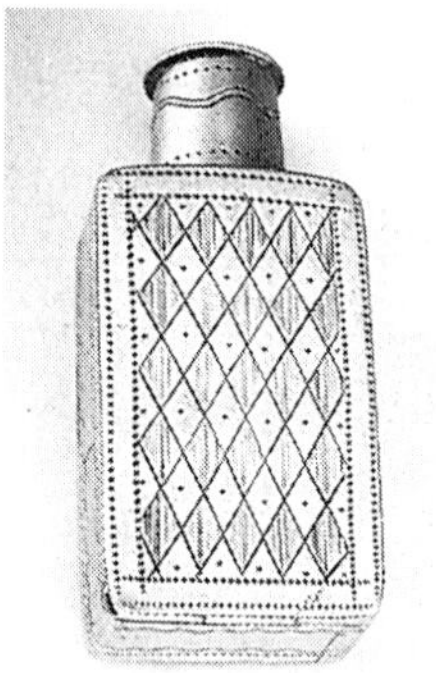

A George III silver vinaigrette, by Cocks & Bettridge, in the shape of a scent bottle, the hinged cover and base engraved with a lozenge diaper panel border, engraved sides and screw stopper, Birmingham 1801, 2in (50mm) high.
£2,500–3,000 *DN*

A William IV silver-gilt vinaigrette, by Nathaniel Mills, the cover ornately foliate scroll chased with floral border, engine-turned body, the grille decoratively pierced and engraved, Birmingham 1835, 1½in (38mm) high, 1oz.
£400–450 *CGC*

A George III silver vinaigrette, by Samuel Pemberton, the cover engraved with floral basket, Birmingham 1809, 1¼in (30mm) diam.
£180–220 *CGC*

A Victorian silver vinaigrette, by Nathaniel Mills, Birmingham 1844, 1¼in (32mm) wide.
£250–300 *CoHA*

A George IV silver 'castle-top' vinaigrette, by Nathaniel Mills, Birmingham 1827, 1¾in (45mm) wide.
£850–950 *CGC*

l. A Victorian silver 'castle-top' vinaigrette, by Joseph Willmore, the cover depicting Beverley Minster, Birmingham 1843, 1¾in (45mm) wide.
£1,000–1,200 *CGC*

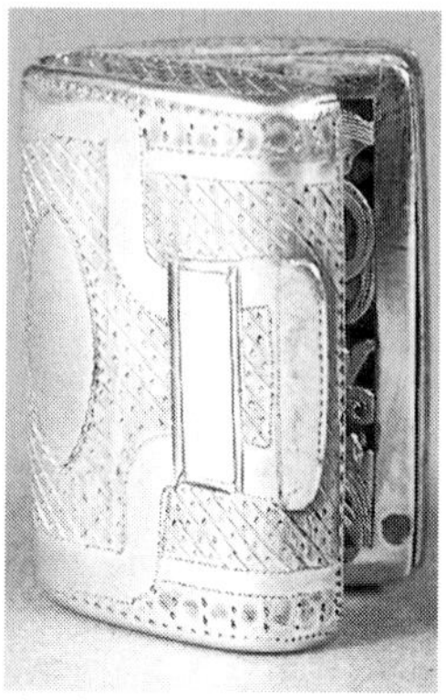

A silver vinaigrette, Birmingham, late 19thC, 2in (50mm) high.
£120–140 *MRW*

SILVER PLATE

A silver-plated on copper telescopic candlestick, 1810–20, 11in (28cm) high extended.
£90–120 *CoHA*

A silver plated two-handled trophy, inscribed 'The West Heath Dancing Cup, presented by Betty Vacani', on turned stem, circular foot, and on an ebonised plinth, 1958, 6½in (16.5cm) high.
£7,000–8,000 *GOR*

This cup was awarded to Lady Diana Spencer in 1976.

A Sheffield plate entrée dish and cover, the gadroon rim with scroll acanthus at intervals, scroll leaf ring handle, c1810, 10in (25.5cm) diam.
£250–300 *HofB*

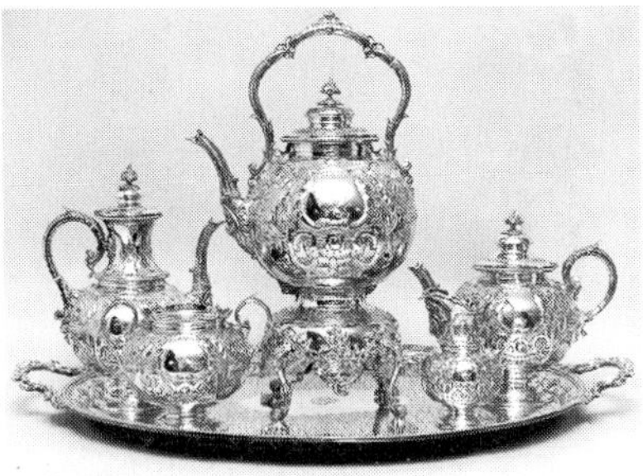

r. A late Victorian electroplated tea and coffee service, possibly by Stacy, Henry & Horton of Sheffield, inscribed mark on underside, 19½in (49.5cm) wide.
£1,400–1,600 *HCC*

An electroplated tobacco jar, by Elkington & Co, c1880, 9in (23cm) high.
£400–450 *DIC*

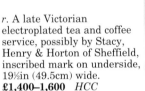

Sheffield Plate Marks

Much early Sheffield plate was marked with imitations of silver hallmarks which were surprisingly deceptive at first glance. The Birmingham and Sheffield assay offices opened in 1773, and one of the provisions of opening was that makers of plate should not mark their objects at all. However, in 1784 the Sheffield office managed to pass a law allowing plate made in Sheffield to be marked with the maker's name or initials, and from this time many marks were registered from this city. Few were registered from Birmingham. An item marked Sheffield Plate on the bottom is modern plate that has been made in Sheffield.

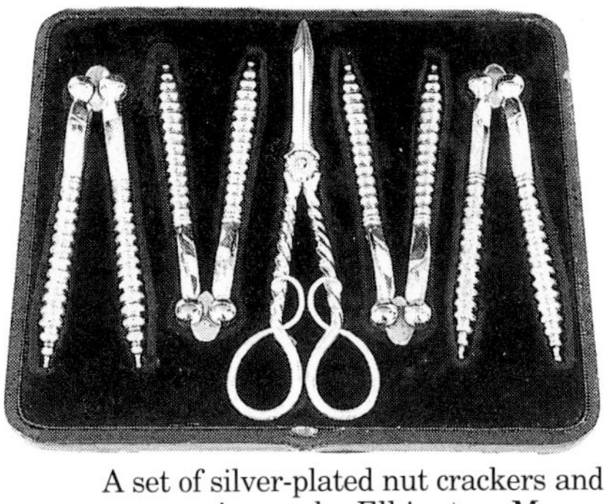

A set of silver-plated nut crackers and grape scissors, by Elkington, Mason & Co, c1860, box 9in (23cm) wide.
£200–250 *CoHA*

A pair of electroplated urns, of compana form, relief-decorated with swags and gadrooning, on cylindrical rouge marble bases, late 19thC, 11¾in (30cm) high.
£180–200 *P(B)*

A pair of Sheffield plate Regency style wine coolers, fluted and with a band of shells and palmettes, reeded handles, c1820, 9¼in (23.5cm) high.
£3,000–3,500 *B&B*

A late Victorian silver-plated vesta case, in the form of a half hunter pocket watch, 2in (50mm) diam.
£70–90 *CoHA*

WINE ANTIQUES

An olive green onion-shaped sealed wine bottle, applied with seal inscribed 'R. Hayne 1717', 6¼in (16cm) high.
£2,000–2,500 *S*

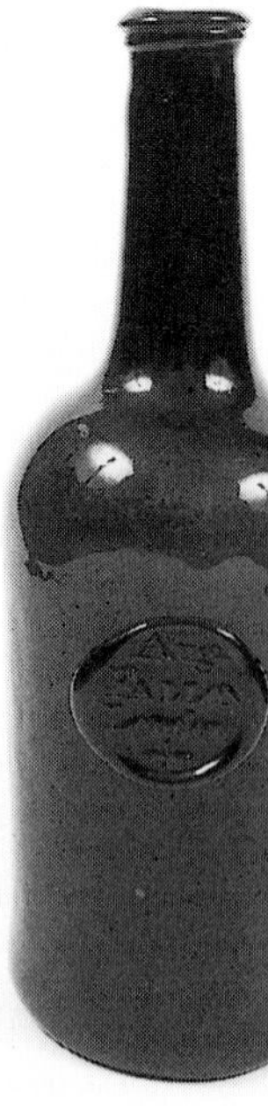

A wine bottle, applied with seal inscribed 'Aug-Fallon London', c1770, 11in (28cm) high.
£200–250 *NWi*

A French green glass wine bottle, c1730, 8¼in (21cm) high.
£250–300 *NWi*

A pair of Sheffield plate wine ewers, decorated with floral and leaf scrolls, early 19thC, 12in (30.5cm) high.
£850–950 *AAV*

A silver-mounted claret jug, with barley-twist handle, cut and engraved with flowers, with star-cut base, c1860, 9½in (24cm) high.
£1,500–1,800 *CB*

r. A Russian cut-glass claret jug, by Pavel Ovchinnikov, the mount decorated with stylised flowers, c1896, 10½in (26.5cm) high.
£750–1,000 *P*

An American silver-mounted cranberry glass claret jug, the body panelled and cut with branches of prunus, the silver neck chased with a collar of flowers, with hinged cover, Gorham Mfg Co, Providence, RI, 1888, 10½in (26.5cm) high.
£3,500–4,000 *S(NY)*

A French silver-mounted cut-glass claret jug, with domed cover and pomegranate finial, maker's mark 'H. Fres & Cie', c1880, 10in (25.5cm) high.
£1,800–2,000 *S*

l. A claret jug, engraved with birds and flowers, with silver-plated mount, c1870, 12in (30.5cm) high.
£900–1,000 *CB*

A pair of silver-mounted claret jugs, the cut-glass bodies with hobnail decoration, scroll handles and plain hinged lid, some damage, Birmingham 1899, 8½in (21.5cm) high.
£450–500 *Bon(C)*

An Edwardian silver-mounted cut-glass claret jug, by Thomas Webb, with plain glass loop handle and silver spout, stopper and mount, London 1904, 8½in (21.5cm) high.
£460–500 *Bea(E)*

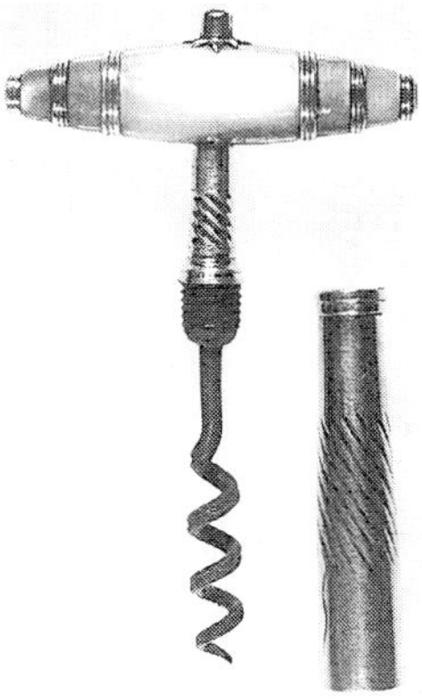

A silver travelling corkscrew, by Samuel Pemberton, with mother-of-pearl barrel-shaped handle and silver bands, c1790, 3¼in (8.5cm) long.
£120–140 *CS*

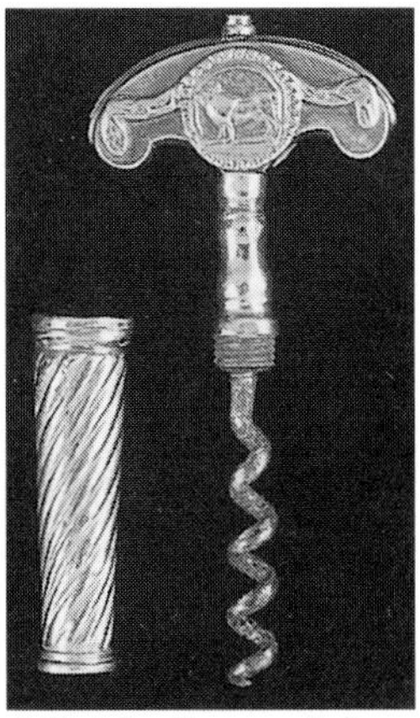

A Dutch silver pocket corkscrew, the handle applied with swags, late 18thC, 3¼in (8.5cm) long.
£1,500–1,800 *S(S)*

A double-action corkscrew, with bone handle and brass barrel embossed with 'Gothic window' pattern, c1810, 8½in (21.5cm) long.
£330–350 *CS*

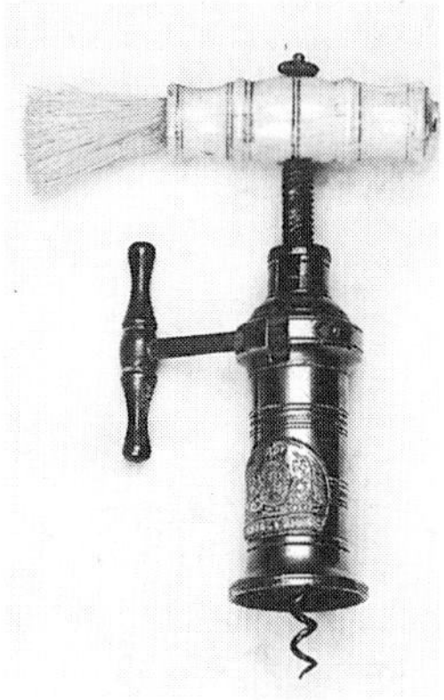

A Heeley & Sons brass King's corkscrew, the turned bone handle with ring and later brush, late 19thC, 6in (15cm) long.
£260–300 *Bon*

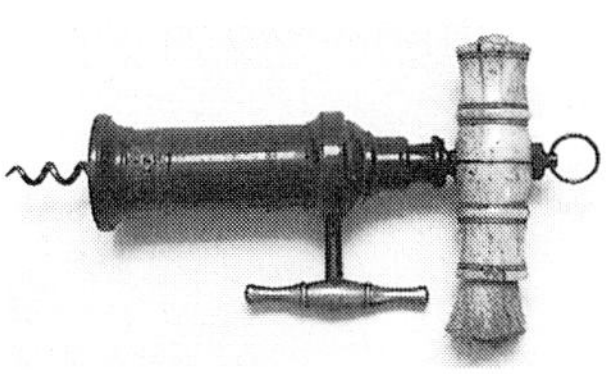

A King's Screw corkscrew, with bronze barrel and bone handle, maker's plate 'Joseph Rodgers & Sons, Sheffield', early 19thC, 5in (12.5cm) long.
£300–350 *DD*

r. Four compound folding bow corkscrews, clockwise from left: faceted bow with 8 tools, c1810, 3in (7.5cm) wide. **£75–95** folding bow with 8 tools including carriage key, c1820, 2¾in (7cm) wide. **£75–95** faceted bow with 6 tools, c1840, 2¾in (7cm), **£55–75** folding bow with corkscrew and hoof pick, c1880, 2¼in (5.5cm) wide.
£10–15 *CS*

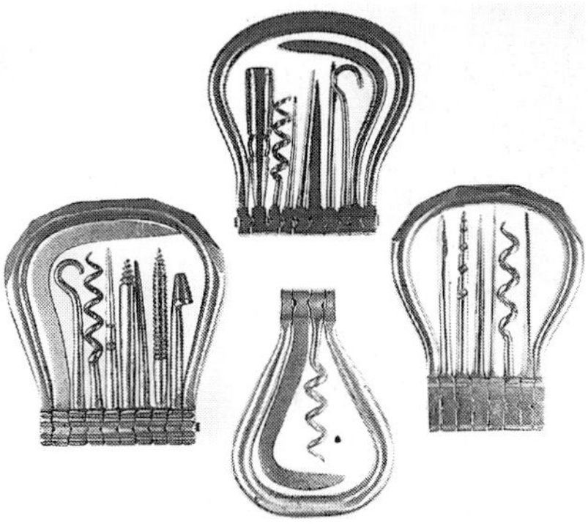

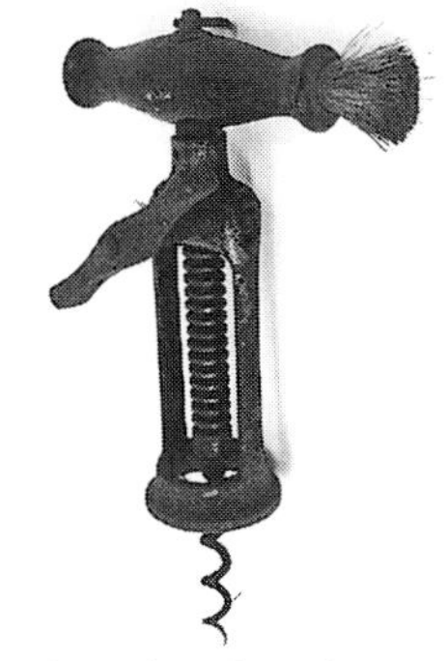

A barrel and ratchet corkscrew, with brush, late 19thC, 6½in (16.5cm) long.
£70–90 *GAK*

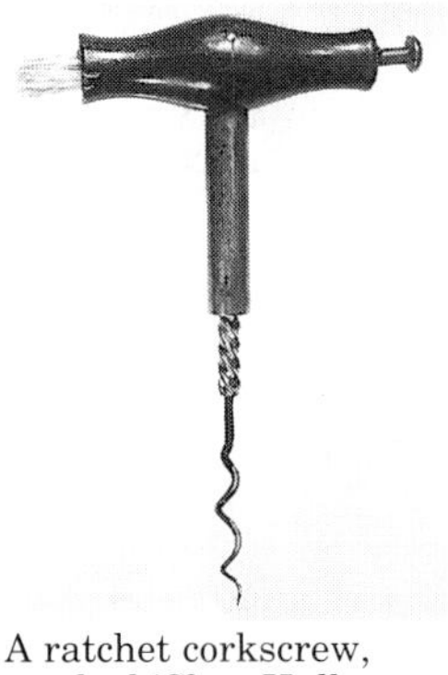

A ratchet corkscrew, marked 'Chas Hull Corkscrew Patent Presto', c1860, 6½in (16.5cm) long.
£400–450 *CS*

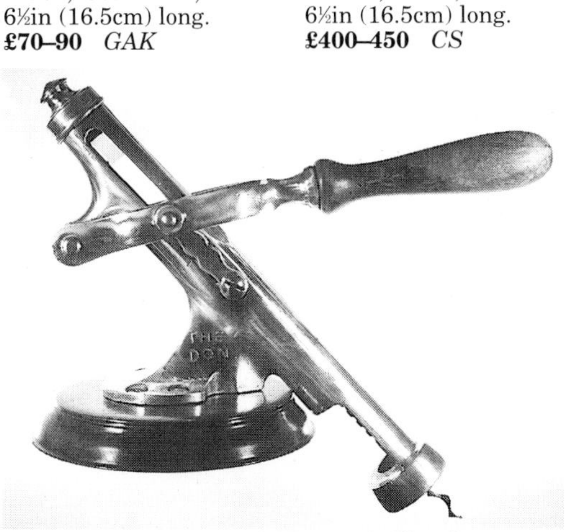

A bar corkscrew, named 'The Don', Chambers English patent 1903, 12in (30.5cm) long.
£85–95 *CS*

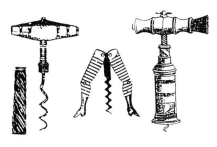

A French silver wine taster, with fluted sides and reverse-punched beading, the serpent ring handle with scaled finish, inscribed around side 'J. Richards' & 'F. Cacussey', Paris 1750, 3in (7.5cm) diam, 3½oz.
£800–900 *P*

A French provincial silver wine taster, the sides chased with bunches of grapes, the ring handle formed by eagles' heads and terminating in an arrow head, inscribed 'Antoine Mouseron 1776', maker's mark, 2½in (6.5cm) diam, 3oz.
£700–800 *P*

A George III silver wine funnel, Sheffield 1803, 6in (15cm) long.
£1,250–1,500 *SHa*

A George III wine funnel, with detachable sieve and lobed funnel, maker's mark rubbed, 1803, 5½in (14cm) high, 4oz.
£280–320 *L*

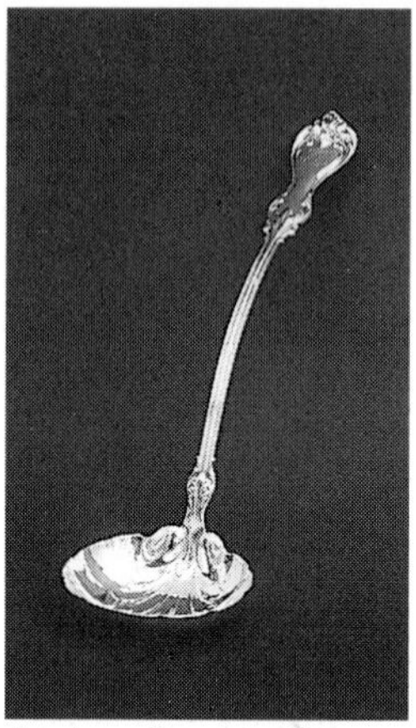

An American sterling silver punch ladle, by Shreve, Crump & Low, 1868, 12¼in (31cm) long.
£250–300 *A&A*

Two silver wine labels, inscribed 'Port' and 'Claret', c1820, 2½in (6.5cm) wide.
£40–50 *CS*

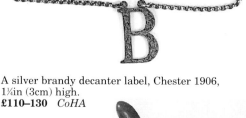

A silver brandy decanter label, Chester 1906, 1¼in (3cm) high.
£110–130 *CoHA*

A silver-plated wine pourer, early 19thC, c1825, 3in (7.5cm) high.
£125–150 *JAS*

A silver-plated bottle label, 19thC, 1½in (4cm) wide.
£55–70 *JAS*

r. An early George III brandy saucepan, of baluster form, with baluster wood handle at right-angles to spout and a heart-shaped junction, maker's mark indistinct, 1762, 3¼in (8cm) diam.
£620–680 *P*

r. Two pairs of George IV silver wine labels, inscribed 'Sherry', 'Port', 'Marsala' and 'Claret', London 1828, maker's mark of William Eaton, and London 1830, maker's mark of Charles Reily and George Storer, 2½in (6.5cm) wide.
£200–250 *(Bon)*

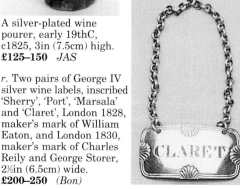

A silver-plated claret label, 19thC, 1½in (4cm) wide.
£35–45 *JAS*

A silver gin label, marked, London 1968, 1¾in (4.5cm) wide.
£55–65 *JAS*

A Victorian electroplated wine cooler, by W. & G. Sissons, the cylindrical body engraved with a frieze of classical figures, with rope-twist swing handles folding down to form the rim, c1865, 12in (30.5cm) diam.
£3,200–3,600 *S(S)*

A pair of Victorian coasters, by Hy Wilkinson & Co, decorated in relief with grapes and vine leaves, with turned wood bases, Sheffield 1847, 9in (23cm) diam, 30oz.
£1,850–2,000 *Bea(E)*

A William IV tulipwood, gilt-bronze and silver-gilt liqueur casket, the quarter-veneered box with hinged top and flanked by 2 handles, enclosing 4 octagonal decanters each with a silver-gilt cover in the form of an 8 pronged coronet interposed by shamrocks and thistle finials, London 1832, 10¼in (26cm) high.
£5,500–6,000 *S*

A multi-faceted glass ice bucket, by Goldsmiths & Silversmiths Co Ltd, with silver mounts, Birmingham 1929, 8½in (21.5cm) high, and a pair of silver tongs, Sheffield 1934.
£550–600 *TC*

A pair of Victorian silver-plated bottle coasters with mask and pierced rims, 8in (20.5cm) diam.
£170–200 *CaC*

A French ebonised and brass-inlaid liqueur cabinet, the interior with 4 square decanters with stoppers and glasses, c1860, 12in (30.5cm) wide.
£800–900 *WeH*

r. An etched glass and gilt-bronze tantalus, with 4 fitted decanters and 16 liqueur glasses within a vine-etched glass body fitted with bamboo-cast banding and legs, late 19thC, 14½in (37cm) high.
£4,200–4,600 *S(NY)*

A Sheffield plate wine coaster, with ogee sides and gadrooned rim, on a mahogany base, c1815, 6in (15cm) diam.
£150–180 *JAS*

A pair of Sheffield plate wine coasters, early 19thC, 5in (12.5cm) diam.
£350–400 *ANT*

A mid-Victorian cold-painted cast iron gin camel, the saddle carrying 2 enamelled glass gin barrels and 12 enamelled glass tumblers, on an oval ebonised plinth, beneath a glass dome, 17in (43cm) high.
£850–1,000 *Bon(N)*

CLOCKS

Over the last few years there has been a steady increase in clock prices which have been recovering from the fall in prices of the early 1990s. Top makers such as Thomas Tompion and George Graham are the most sought after, and generally there is now a demand for high quality and precision clocks.

Novelty clocks are making far more at auction than a lot of high quality English bracket clocks – a case of fashion dictating the price. This has resulted in the appearance on the market of a number of fake Black Forest and swinger timepieces from the Far East, which are often sold for the same price as the originals. The fakes are generally easy to spot because of their inferior quality and the use of modern movements. As with all collecting areas, buyers must be aware of these fakes.

There have been a number of sales devoted to one type of clock, such as carriage clocks. With carriage clocks, the more decorative designs with ornate cases and porcelain panels are keenly collected. Most sought after are clocks with the factory mark on the backplate. These marks are generally quite small and hidden beneath the gong. Each factory has its own trademark: Henri Jacot's mark was a parrot on a perch with the letter JH; Drocourt's stamp was a picture of a carriage clock between the letters DC. Value is increased by the presence of the original travelling box and, with Drocourt clocks, the original numbered key.

The current French clock market reflects the fluctuating economic situation in Europe and may offer good value. Longcase clocks with colourful painted dials and rolling moon faces are popular at the moment although, as with all longcases, it is important to check that they have not been married to a later case.

There has been increased demand for 17th century marquetry longcase clocks. The name on the dial will not necessarily add to the value of the clock unless it is that of a top maker. Do bear in mind that they have often had their cases reduced in size and that restoration can be quite extensive.

The finest French clocks were made in the 18th and early 19th century, with superb quality castings and original fire gilding. Porcelain panels were popular on later examples and these need to be checked for damage. Porcelain panels were also used on less desirable and less expensive spelter clocks. The type of metal can be identified by scratching under the foot: spelter will look silver, and ormolu will look gold in colour and is much more difficult to mark. Glass domes on skeleton clocks and some clock garnitures are often broken and can be very difficult to replace if they are an unusual size.

Oliver Saunders

Bracket Clocks

l. A walnut bracket clock, by Bennett, London, the brass dial with Roman numerals, the 5 pillar twin fusee bell striking movement with anchor escapement, bell and pendulum missing, restored, early 19thC, 14¾in (37.5cm) high.
£500–550 *Bri*

A mahogany bracket clock, by Barrie of Edinburgh, the domed cover with central pineapple finial, applied with gilt-metal mounts, with silvered chapter ring, strike/silent, late 19thC, 11½in (29cm) high.
£1,700–2,000 *GAK*

r. A Regency mahogany bracket clock, by J. J. Dison, Cambridge, with brass acorn finial above an architectural pediment, brass-strung domed case, enamelled dial, 8-day striking movement, 18in (45.5cm) high.
£1,300–1,500 *Mit*

An ebonised and ormolu-mounted bracket clock, with inverted bell top and brass carrying handles, the brass dial signed Birch & Gaydon, with strike/silent and regulator dial, the triple fusee movement striking the quarters on gongs, c1880, 17in (43cm) high.
£3,600–4,000 *GH*

An ebonised bracket clock, the painted dial signed Cragg, Southampton, with Roman and Arabic numerals and strike/silent dial, the twin fusee movement with 5 turned pillars, with verge escapement striking on a bell, late 18thC, 17in (43cm) high.
£1,300–1,500 *P*

A carved rosewood bracket clock, by Deane Dray & Co, London Bridge, the engraved dial with scroll ornament, strike/silent and regulation dials, 3 train fusee movement quarter striking on 8 bells and a gong, early 19thC, 26¾in (68cm) high.
£2,000–2,200 *P(EA)*

An ebonised bracket clock, by Conys Dunlop, London, the arched brass dial with silvered chapter ring and mock pendulum, twin fusee movement with 5 ringed pillars, verge escapement striking on a bell, engraved backplate, mid-18thC, 18in (45.5cm) high.
£3,000–3,500 *P*

A late Regency mahogany and brass-inlaid bracket clock, the silvered dial signed Ellicott & Smith, London, twin fusee movement and anchor escapement, the door with canted brass corners, inlaid with flowerheads, on a plinth base, with ball feet, 16in (40.5cm) high.
£3,200–3,600 *P*

A mahogany bracket clock, by French, Royal Exchange, London, with domed hood, the arched dial with black chapter ring and strike/silent dial, 8-day movement, early 19thC, 11in (28cm) high.
£1,600–1,800 *GAK*

A mahogany bracket clock, by Thomas Gray, London, with pierced brass spandrels, 8-day fusee repeater movement, mid-18thC, 20in (51cm) high.
£1,750–2,000 *AH*

l. An ebonised bracket clock, by Henry Hester, London, the inverted bell top with brass handle, silvered chapter ring, matted centre with mock pendulum aperture and calendar, 5 pillar movement with engraved backplate, verge escapement with bob pendulum, repeating on 2 bells with single hour bell, case restored, c1700, 16in (41cm) high.
£2,500–3,000 *Bon*

A Regency mahogany bracket clock, by Jacob Jackson, Bristol, with 8-day 2 train fusee movement and anchor escapement striking on a bell, c1800, 17in (43cm) high.
£1,500–1,800 *DN(H)*

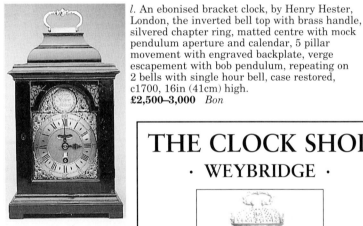

A mahogany bracket clock, by Francis Hobler, London, the arched brass dial with silvered chapter ring, strike/silent and date aperture, mid-18thC, 20in (51cm) high.
£4,500–5,000 *P(G)*

An ebonised and brass-mounted bracket clock, the brass dial with silvered chapter ring, signed J. & H. Jump, London, with moonphase, signed twin fusee movement with anchor escapement and ting-tang quarter chiming on 2 gongs, 19thC, 15in (38cm) high.
£4,500–5,000 *P*

A George III mahogany bracket clock, the arched engraved silvered dial signed W. Langlois, with subsidiary date and strike/silent dials, twin fusee movement with engraved backplate, now converted to anchor escapement, 18in (45.5cm) high.
£1,800–2,000 *P*

A mahogany pad-top bracket clock, the painted dial signed Jeffreys & Ham, London, the twin fusee movement with engraved backplate, striking on a bell, repeating cord, strike/silent, c1820, 17½in (44.5cm) high.
£2,500–3,000 *Bon*

An Edwardian oak musical bracket clock, by Pearce, Leeds, Huddersfield and Leicester, with arched gilt-brass dial and silvered chapter ring, striking the hours and chiming the quarters on a coiled gong and 8 bells, 24in (61cm) high.
£1,800–2,000 *HSS/P*

r. A walnut bracket clock, signed Jasper Taylor, with silvered chapter ring, verge escapement and bob pendulum with pull repeat on 2 bells, late 17thC, 17in (43cm) high.
£6,000–7,000 *HAM*

l. An ebonised bracket clock, signed Scrivener, Cockspur St, the arched brass dial with silvered chapter ring, matted centre and gilt-brass spandrels and subsidiaries, triple fusee movement with anchor escapement striking on 9 bells and a gong, foliate engraved backplate and pendulum, late 19thC, 18in (45.5cm) high.
£1,300–1,600 *P*

Bracket Clocks

Bracket remains the umbrella description for spring-driven clocks with a short pendulum designed to stand on a surface, such as a table, shelf or wall bracket. Originally only a few bracket clocks were ever displayed on a separate wall bracket. They are sometimes referred to as table clocks. The clockmakers themselves often preferred to describe bracket clocks as 'spring' clocks, as all examples are driven by a coiled steel spring rather than hanging weights. In the United States, where they were produced in large numbers, bracket clocks are commonly known as shelf clocks.

A mahogany bracket clock, signed Rentzsch, London, the cream painted dial with calendar aperture and subsidiaries, triple fusee movement quarter striking, exposed anchor escapement on engraved backplate, early 19thC, 25½in (65cm) high.
£2,600–3,000 *L*

A late Regency mahogany bracket clock, the white enamel dial inscribed W. Vaughan, Newport, the twin fusee movement with anchor escapement and pull repeat mechanism striking on a gong, 18¾in (47.5cm) high.
£950–1,100 *P(C)*

A rosewood bracket clock, with silvered chapter ring signed E. J. Vokes, Bath, triple fusee movement with anchor escapement chiming on 8 bells and 5 gongs, late 19thC, 16½in (42cm) high.
£1,600–2,000 *P*

A mahogany bracket clock, by William Welch, Plymouth, with domed hood, silvered chapter ring, the sides applied with gilt-metal trellis apertures, striking movement, c1800, 12in (30.5cm) high.
£1,600–2,000 *GAK*

A green lacquer and chinoiserie-decorated bracket clock, by Windmills, London, with silvered chapter ring, mock pendulum and date apertures, 5 pillar twin fusee movement with verge escapement, movement restored, early 18thC, 32in (81.5cm) high.
£9,000–10,000 *P*

A Regency mahogany bracket clock, with arched top, brass inlay and carrying handle, white enamel dial, 2 train fusee movement, 17in (43cm) high.
£1,300–1,500 *RBB*

An ebonised bracket clock, the 2 train fusee movement quarter chiming on 8 bells, with anchor escapement, the pendulum with regulation screw, enamel dial indistinctly signed, early 19thC, 19¾in (50cm) high.
£700–800 *DN*

l. An ebonised bracket clock, the arched dial with Roman chapter ring and subsidiary dials, late 19thC, 16in (40.5cm) high, and matching bracket.
£2,200–2,500 *GAK*

An Edwardian walnut and brass-mounted bracket clock, with arched brass and silvered dial, strike/silent 8-day movement, 15½in (39.5cm) high.
£1,300–1,600 *M*

A carved oak bracket clock, by Winterhalder & Hofmeier, with silvered chapter ring, subsidiary dials, triple fusee movement striking on 4 wire gongs, c1900, 33in (84cm) high.
£1,000–1,200 *Bon*

Carriage Clocks

A French brass repeating alarm carriage clock, with silvered dial, striking on a bell, sliding rear door, c1860, 6in (15cm) high.
£800–1,000 *GH*

A gilt-brass repeating carriage clock, with gilt engine-turned dial on a champlevé surround, gong striking movement signed with stamp of Drocourt and with fine club tooth lever escapement, c1885, 6in (15cm) high.
£2,500–3,000 *S*

A French brass carriage timepiece, with replaced lever platform escapement, ivorine chapter ring with Arabic numerals within a cast floral scroll mask, similar side panels and reeded columns, 19thC, 6¼in (16cm) high.
£300–350 *P*

A French brass repeating 8-day carriage clock, the bevelled glass platform viewer engraved 'N' over an ivory dial with Arabic numerals, signed Drocourt, Paris, enclosed by fret cut foliate scrollwork, in a beaded gorge case, 19thC, 7in (18cm) high, with original travelling case.
£1,750–2,000 *GOR(B)*

FURTHER READING
Miller's Clocks & Barometers Buyer's Guide, Miller's Publications, 1997

l. A miniature brass alarm carriage timepiece, c1890, 4in (10cm) high, with carrying case.
£450–500 *BED*

A combination carriage clock and aneroid barometer, c1890, 8in (20.5cm) high.
£1,200–1,500 *BED*

A French silvered-metal carriage clock, late 19thC, 10in (25.5cm) high.
£300–350 *TMA*

A French carriage clock and barometer, with visible escapement, 8-day movement with hour and half-hour strike, c1900, 10½in (26.5cm) high.
£1,600–1,800 *BED*

A French gilt-brass and champlevé enamel carriage clock, with thermometer and compass, enamel dial with visible club tooth lever escapement, 2 train gong striking movement, c1900, 9in (23cm) high.
£950–1,100 *S*

A French striking carriage clock, signed Mappin & Webb Ltd, Paris, c1900, 6½in (16.5cm) high, with original carrying case.
£550–700 *BED*

A striking and repeating carriage clock, by Mappin & Webb Ltd, London, with gun-metal case, 8-day movement, c1920, 5½in (14cm) high.
£800–1,000 *BED*

A French alarm carriage clock, the serpentine gilt-brass case decorated with bands of foliage, with cream enamel dial and subsidiary alarm dial, decorated with floral swags, backplate stamped DH, c1900, 6¼in (16cm) high.
£300–350 *GH*

A French carriage clock, the off-white enamel chapter ring with Arabic numerals on a frosted gilt mask, the polished brass movement with 2 going barrels for the strike and going trains, the silvered platform with lever escapement, uncut bimetallic balance with spiral hairspring, polished steel regulator, c1910, 5¾in (14.5cm) high.
£700–800 *PT*

Cartel Clocks

A Louis XV style gilt-bronze cartel clock, the white enamel dial signed Martinot à Paris, the movement with outside countwheel stamped HMF Paris 2869, c1880, 39in (99cm) high.
£3,000–3,500 *S*

l. A gilt-bronze cartel clock, the white enamel dial signed Robin H'lger du Roy, the case surmounted by a ribbon-tie and eagles' heads, flanked by laurel leaves, the movement striking on a bell, c1880, 34¾in (88.5cm) high.
£3,600–4,000 *S*

A French carved cartel clock, with white Roman numerals, c1870, 40in (101.5cm) high.
£500–550 *OT*

A French gilt-bronze cartel clock, the dial cast in relief with white enamel cartouche numerals, flanked by rams' heads, above a lion's mask, surmounted by an urn, c1870, 32in (81.5cm) high.
£1,800–2,000 *S*

Garnitures

A French gilt-bronze and porcelain clock garniture, with Japy movement, 19thC, clock 16in (40.5cm) high.
£2,300–2,600 *P(NE)*

A French gilt-metal and porcelain clock garniture, with 8-day movement and painted porcelain dial, the backplate inscribed Lagard à Paris, the inset panels decorated with lovers and floral sprigs, 19thC, clock 13¼in (33.5cm) high.
£1,500–2,000 *AH*

A French ormolu and white marble clock garniture, the blue painted clock case with applied stars and gilt numerals, signed for H. Luppens & Cie, Bruxelles, 19thC, clock 15in (38cm) high.
£1,700–2,000 *P*

r. A French gilt-brass and porcelain-mounted clock garniture, the case surmounted by a twin-handled urn, applied with swags and foliage with scrolls to the sides, applied with panels depicting lovers, the dial signed Hry Marc, Paris, the twin train movement with anchor escapement striking on a bell, 19thC, clock 16in (40.5cm) high.
£2,500–3,000 *P*

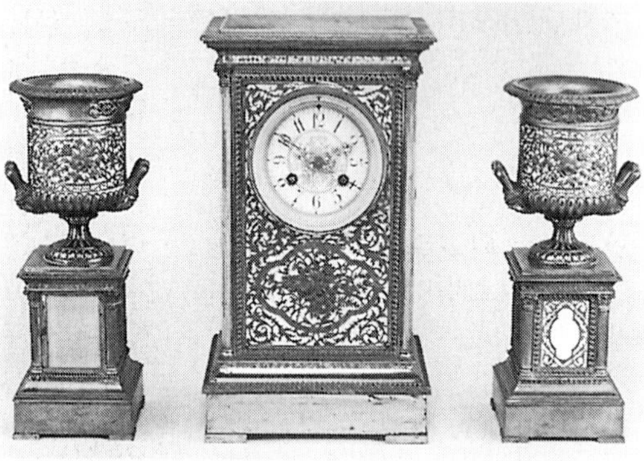

A French gilt-brass clock garniture, the 8-day striking clock with fret-cut and embossed flower and acanthus leaf panels, on turquoise porcelain grounds, 19thC, clock 13in (33cm) high.
£1,100–1,300 *EH*

A French marble clock garniture, with Egyptian style obelisks, bronze sphynx and hieroglyphics, c1870, clock 17½in (44.5cm) high.
£1,000–1,200 *CHe*

A French brass and porcelain-mounted clock garniture, the gong striking movement with Brocot suspension, c1880, clock 16½in (42cm) high.
£2,000–2,200 *S(S)*

A French spelter clock garniture, the clock surmounted by a lady with a cherub, with a pair of urns with cherubs, c1880, clock 16in (40.5cm) high.
£1,200–1,400 *HAC*

A French gilt-spelter and porcelain-mounted clock garniture, the bell striking movement by Japy Frères, c1885, clock 20½in (52cm) high.
£1,300–1,600 *S*

A French gilt ormolu clock garniture, the enamel dial with Roman and Arabic numerals, bell striking movement, c1890, clock 15½in (39.5cm) high.
£1,500–1,800 *Bon*

A Continental carved walnut figural clock garniture, the case surmounted by a figure of a hunter, late 19thC, clock 38½in (98cm) high.
£8,500–9,500 *S(NY)*

A French bronzed spelter clock garniture, with 8-day movement and outside countwheel strike, on black marble bases, late 19thC, clock 27in (68.5cm) high.
£500–600 *DN*

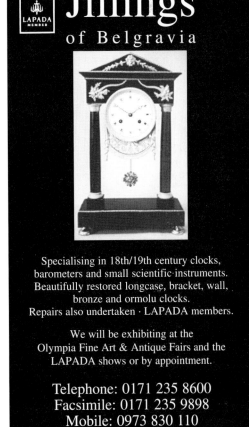

A French slate clock garniture, with 8-day striking movement, c1901, clock 17in (43cm) high.
£800–900 *BWC*

A French gilt-brass, champlevé enamel and porcelain-mounted clock garniture, by Samuel Marti, early 20thC, clock 15in (38cm) high.
£2,200–2,500 *PF*

Lantern Clocks

A brass lantern clock, signed J. Booth, London, the chapter ring with Roman numerals, with twin fusee bell striking movement, on ball feet, late 19thC, 16in (40.5cm) high.
£800–1,000 *Bon*

A winged lantern clock, by Henry Chaple, Bridgwater, the posted movement with divided trains, verge escapement with centrally oscillating pendulum, later anchor-shaped bob, wings and top mounted bell, c1700, 15in (38cm) high.
£3,400–3,800 *S*

A brass lantern clock, by George Clarke, London, for the Turkish market, with broken arch dial, the posted bell striking 2 train movement with verge escapement and bob pendulum, c1760, top finial later, 13½in (34.5cm) high.
£1,000–1,200 *S*

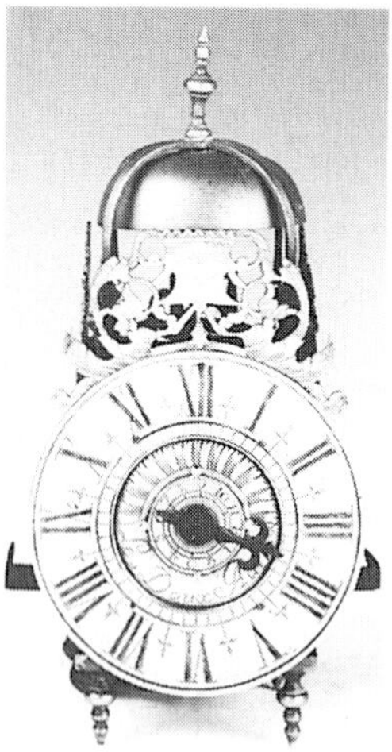

A French brass lantern timepiece, with alarm, the engraved dial signed Le Doux A Paris, alarm set to centre, single steel hand, movement with verge bob pendulum escapement and hoop and spur mounting, 18thC, 10in (25.5cm) high.
£2,000–2,200 *P*

Winged Lantern Clocks

On winged lantern clocks the pendulum is situated in the centre and at the front rather than behind the movement. A long arc terminates at either end in an arrow, replacing the conventional pendulum bob, and this appears and disappears alternately in the glazed wings on either side of the clock.

The wings may have been incorporated to accommodate the large swing of this particular type of pendulum, or may merely be a decorative feature – opinion is divided.

A brass lantern clock, with flower-chased brass dial, inscribed William Sellwood at ye Merymade in Lothbury, with 30-hour birdcage movement, anchor escapement, 18thC, 13¾in (35cm) high.
£1,500–1,800 *AH*

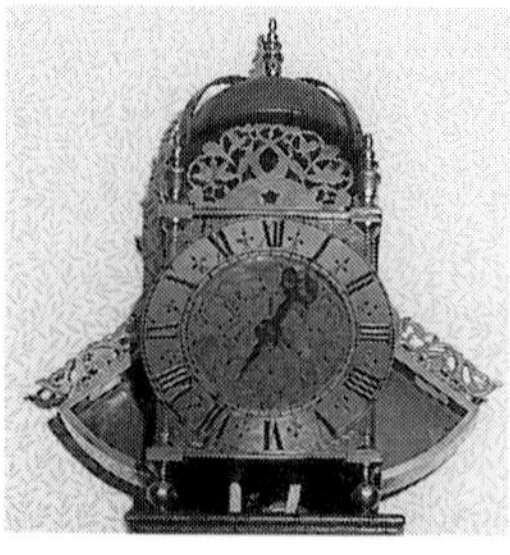

A brass lantern clock, dated 1710, double fusee movement c1880, 15in (38cm) high.
£650–750 *CHe*

l. A brass lantern clock, with verge escapement, original frets, c1680, 15¾in (40cm) high.
£4,800–5,800 *DSP*

A lantern clock, the dial signed Thomas Marston, Ashby, engraved with flowers and leaves, the posted movement with rebuilt verge and balance escapement, 17thC, top mounted bell later, 15¼in (38.5cm) high.
£2,500–3,000 *S*

A winged brass lantern clock, by Joseph Windmills, London, with single hand and central alarm disc surrounded by foliate engraving, the posted rope and weight driven bell striking movement with verge escapement, late 17thC, wings later, 15½in (39.5cm) high.
£3,000–3,500 *S*

Joseph Windmills is a highly regarded and prolific maker whose long career covers the early years of English clockmaking. He was made free of The Clockmaker's Company in 1671 and was still working in 1720. He would probably have made this lantern clock c1685 while working at Mark Lane End, Tower Street, London.

Longcase Clocks

A flame mahogany longcase clock, by Robert Allam, London, the 12in (30.5cm) brass dial with strike/silent to the arch, 8-day 5 pillar movement, break-arch top, brass reedings to hood columns, c1780, 86in (218.5cm) high.
£7,250–7,750 *ALS*

A flame mahogany longcase clock, by G. Anderson, Aberdeen, with painted dial, 8-day regulator movement, deadbeat escapement, maintaining power and wood rod pendulum with massive brass bob, striking the hours on a bell, c1835, 90in (228.5cm) high.
£4,500–5,000 *PAO*

l. A mahogany longcase clock, by Henry Adams, Hackney, with silvered brass dial, 8-day 5 pillar movement striking on a bell, c1805, 81in (205.5cm) high.
£6,000–6,500 *PAO*

Small London longcase clocks are rare.

r. A mahogany and chinoiserie decorated 8-day longcase clock, the painted 13in (33cm) dial indistinctly signed Armstrong, Newcastle, with subsidiary dials, c1800, 82in (209cm) high.
£2,250–2,500 *S(S)*

A mahogany 8-day longcase clock, by James Barlow, Northwich, the brass and silvered dial with moonphases, with swan neck pediment and brass eagle orb finial, late 18thC, 90in (228.5cm) high.
£2,700–3,200 *MAT*

l. An oak 8-day longcase clock, the painted 12in (30.5cm) break-arch dial signed Wm Barrow, Ross, subsidiary dial, moonphase to arch, the hood with swan neck pediment and Corinthian pilasters above a shaped trunk door with star inlay, on a plinth base and bracket supports, requires restoration, early 19thC, 94½in (240cm) high.
£1,600–1,800 *Bri*

An oak 8-day longcase clock, by Robert Beets, Lynn, the brass dial with centre seconds and moonphase, the 5 pillar movement with shaped plates and striking the hours on a bell, c1775, 82in (208.5cm) high.
£5,800–6,500 *PAO*

A George III oak 30-hour longcase clock, by Basford, Wem, 77in (195.5cm) high.
£1,100–1,300 *DOC*

An inlaid mahogany longcase clock, by Bright, Saxmundham, c1800, 85in (216cm) high.
£1,500–1,800 *Bon(C)*

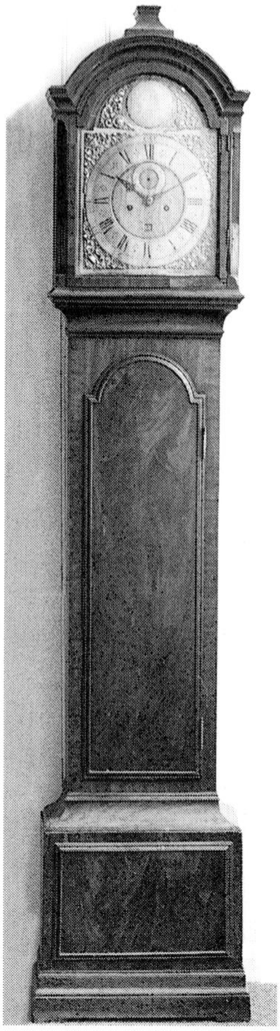

A mahogany longcase clock, by Aaron Brown, Erith, parts missing, c1770, 85in (216cm) high.
£7,000–8,000 *CAG*

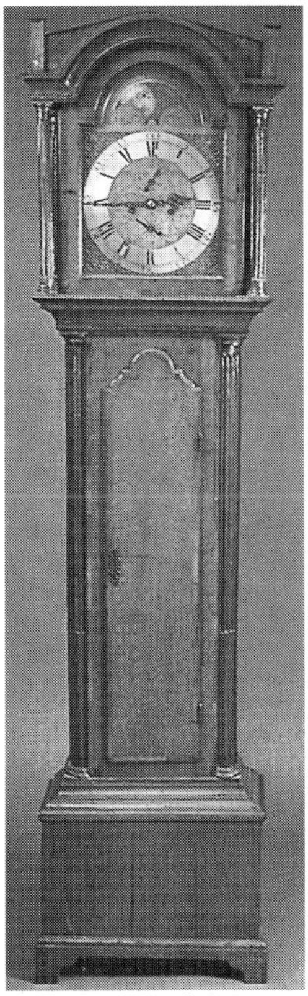

A George III oak longcase clock, by John Bunting, Long Buckby, the 11½in (29cm) arched brass dial with painted moonphase and month indicator, the centre engraved with foliate decoration and scrolls, subsidiary dials and silvered chapter rings, case later, 75in (190.5cm) high.
£2,200–2,500 *DN*

A George III mahogany longcase clock, by John Carne, Penzance, the 12in (30.5cm) arched brass dial with silvered chapter ring, the twin train movement with anchor escapement, 86in (218.5cm) high.
£2,700–3,200 *P*

An oak 8-day longcase clock, by Thomas Burges, Gosport, the brass dial with silvered brass chapter ring, the 5 pillar movement striking the hours on a bell, c1750, 80½in (204.5cm) high.
£4,500–5,500 *PAO*

Miller's is a price GUIDE not a price LIST

r. A painted tortoiseshell and chinoiserie longcase clock, by Wm Carter, Southwark, the 12in (30.5cm) brass dial with subsidiary dials, the 4 pillar movement striking on a bell, mid-18thC, 87in (221cm) high.
£1,600–1,800 *Bon(C)*

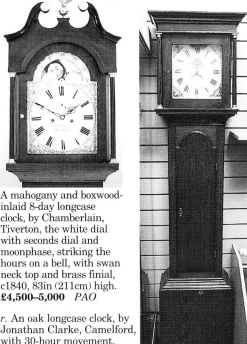

A mahogany and boxwood-inlaid 8-day longcase clock, by Chamberlain, Tiverton, the white dial with seconds dial and moonphase, striking the hours on a bell, with swan neck top and brass finial, c1840, 83in (211cm) high.
£4,500–5,000 *PAO*

r. An oak longcase clock, by Jonathan Clarke, Camelford, with 30-hour movement, c1810, 78in (198cm) high.
£1,200–1,400 *BWC*

A mahogany 8-day longcase clock, by Dobbie, Edinburgh, the white dial with subsidiary seconds dial, c1810, 78in (198cm) high.
£4,500–5,200 *PAO*

Cross Reference
Colour Review

l. An oak longcase clock, by John Chambley, W. Hampton, with 13in (33cm) painted dial, 4 pillar movement striking on a bell, c1800, 83in (211cm) high.
£700–800 *Bon(C)*

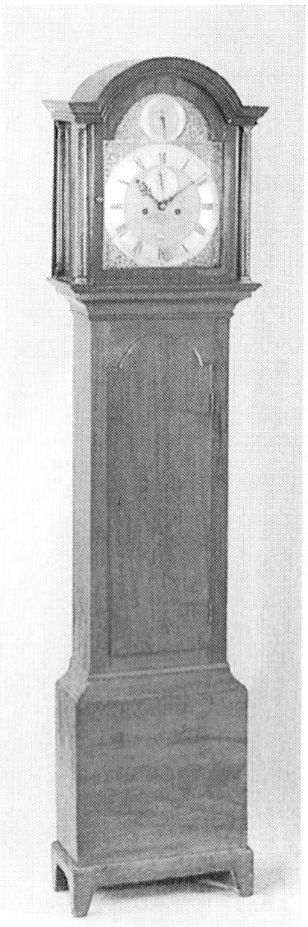

A George III mahogany 8-day longcase clock, by E. P. Dent, London, with silvered chapter ring, seconds dial, strike/silent and date aperture, 82in (208.5cm) high.
£2,500–3,000 *JNic*

A walnut 8-day longcase clock, the 12in (30.5cm) break-arch dial signed Fra Dorrell, London, the 5 pillar movement striking on a bell, the case with arched top and foliate fretwork frieze, base altered and rebuilt, c1740, 83½in (212cm) high.
£3,000–3,500 *S(S)*

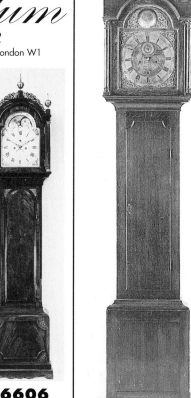

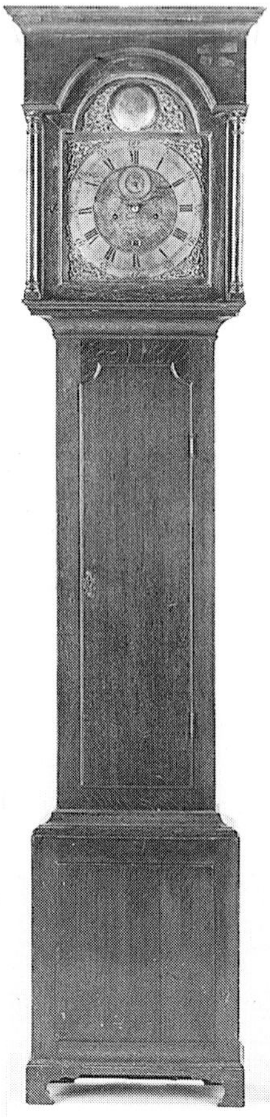

An oak 8-day longcase clock, by W. Drury, Banbury, the arched white dial with moonphase, with painted ladies to each corner depicting the 4 seasons, c1805, 77in (195.5cm) high.
£4,500–5,000 *PAO*

l. An oak longcase clock, by J. Gordon, Perth, the 12in (30.5cm) brass dial with silvered numerals, 4 pillar bell striking movement, on a stepped base with bracket feet, c1800, 87in (221cm) high.
£1,300–1,500 *Bon(C)*

A silver basket, by H. Bateman, London 1774, 5in (13cm) high.
£1,100–1,300 *AMH*

A sterling silver basket, by Tiffany & Co, with pierced scrolled border and central monogram, c1890, 10½in (26.5cm) wide.
£650–800 *SFL*

A silver pierced and scrolled miniature basket, Chester 1896, 4in (10cm) wide.
£140–160 *AMH*

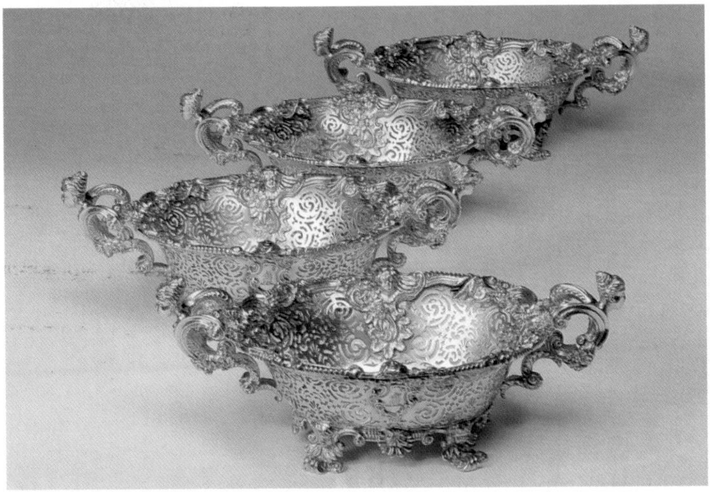

A set of 4 silver-gilt dessert baskets, with pierced fret sides, London 1899, 1905 and 1906, 12½in (32cm) wide, 180oz.
£11,000–13,000 *WW*

A silver sweetmeat dish, by Odiot of Paris, late 19thC, 5½in (14cm) high.
£1,750–2,000 *SHa*

A silver-gilt engraved shallow bowl, late 17thC, 5¼in (13.2cm) diam.
£4,500–5,000 *S(G)*

A silver-gilt historismus tazza, with vase-shaped stem, c1860, 7in (18cm) diam, 20oz.
£2,400–2,600 *S(G)*

A George V pierced silver centrepiece, by William Hutton & Son, with applied border of scrolls, London 1910, 9¼in (23.5cm) high.
£3,500–4,000 *B&B*

A pair of American sterling silver repoussé vegetable dishes, by William Holmes, c1850, 10in (25.5cm) diam.
£4,800–5,200 *YAN*

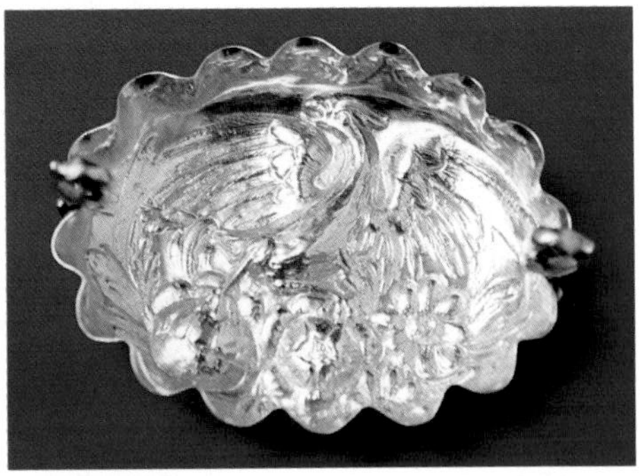

A silver dish, decorated with a bird and foliage, import marks for London 1896, 4in (10cm) wide.
£225–275 *HofB*

A pair of silver-gilt candlesticks, c1700, 25in (63.5cm) high.
£3,000–3,750 *DBA*

A set of four silver-plated on copper candlesticks, 19thC, 10¼in (26cm) high.
£800–950 *CoHA*

A pair of silver taper sticks, London 1890, 5in (12.5cm) high.
£400–450 *PSA*

A pair of close plate candle snuffers, c1800, 8in (20.5cm) long.
£125–150 *CoHA*

Close plate is a method of applying a layer of silver foil to steel.

A Sheffield plate cruet stand, by Bolton & Fothergill, c1769, 7in (18cm) high.
£350–400 *CoHA*

A silver engraved coffee pot, by W. & J. Priest, London 1766, 11½in (29cm) high.
£2,800–3,200 *DIC*

A pair of silver candlesticks, Sheffield 1894, 7in (18cm) high.
£1,100–1,300 *THOM*

An American coin silver tea service, by Woodward & Grosjean, c1847, large pot 8in (20.5cm) high.
£6,800–7,600 *YAN*

A late Victorian silver four-piece tea set, by C. S. Harris, London 1899, 10¼in (26cm) high, 65oz.
£800–1,000 *HAM*

A silver tea caddy, Birmingham 1890, 5in (12.5cm) high.
£350–400 *CoHA*

A Victorian four-piece electro-plated Britannia metal tea service, of tapering oval form, by Mappin & Webb, c1880, large jug 9in (23cm) high.
£250–300 *HofB*

A silver-plated egg stand, on claw feet, c1920, 9in (23cm) high.
£120–140 *CoHA*

A pair of silver frames, by William Comyns, 1893, 4in (10cm) wide.
£600–700 *AMH*

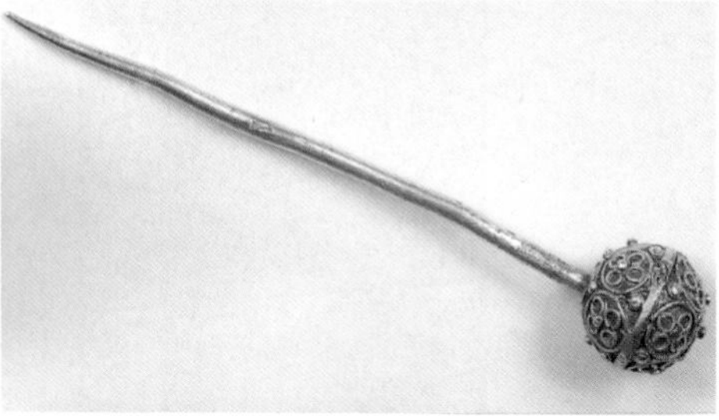

A silver-gilt dress pin, with quatrefoil decoration, 16thC, 3½in (9cm) long.
£120–150 *FW&C*

A silver stamp case, Birmingham 1910, 1¼in (32mm) wide.
£45–50 *PSA*

A silver engraved stamp case, Chester 1914, 1¾in (45mm) wide.
£80–90 *PSA*

A silver salt, by Paul Storr, London 1813, 4¾in (12cm) wide.
£6,000–7,000 *S(NY)*

A silver mustard pot and spoon, Birmingham 1877, 2½in (6.5cm) high.
£500–550 *AMH*

A set of 4 lily pattern salts, by Martin Hall, London 1874, 4in (10cm) diam.
£1,000–1,250 *AMH*

A pair of Victorian silver salts, with matching spoons, by Henry Hyams, London 1863, 1¾in (45mm) diam.
£250–300 *CoHA*

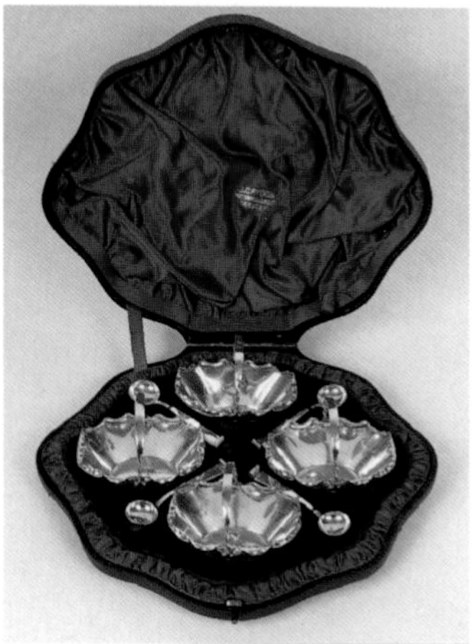

A set of 4 salts and spoons, by Hukin & Heath, London 1883, 3¼in (8cm) wide.
£1,000–1,100 *AMH*

A silver vesta, inset with gold flowerheads and a shield, Birmingham 1920, 1¾in (45mm) high.
£100–125 *GH*

A French silver snuff box, the engine turned case with symmetrical scroll and floral decoration, 19thC, 3in (7.5cm) wide.
£225–250 *WeH*

A Georgian Scottish silver-mounted stag's horn vinaigrette, with original sponge, 2¼in (5.5cm) long.
£1,000–1,200 *CoHA*

A Regency silver-mounted horn-shaped vinaigrette, chased with flowerheads, with a frosted and cut-glass body, c1830, 3in (7.5cm) long.
£350–400 *HofB*

A George III mahogany bell-shaped musical bracket clock, signed Wllm Barker, London, c1800, 22in (56cm) high.
£4,200–4,800 *GH*

A red lacquered musical bracket clock, signed James Chater, London, with twin fusee movement and verge escapement, 18thC, 22in (56cm) high.
£6,000–7,000 *GH*

An inlaid mahogany lancet-top bracket clock, by Martin of London, with 8-day fusee movement, on brass ball feet, c1870, 17in (43cm) high.
£800–1,000 *BED*

A red tortoiseshell and gilt-bronze-mounted bracket clock, by Thos Best, London, 18thC, 14½in (37cm) high.
£6,500–7,500 *P*

A mahogany bracket clock, by Dwerrihouse, Berkeley Square, with twin fusee movement, c1800, 16¾in (42.5cm) high.
£3,800–4,200 *Bon*

A Regency mahogany and brass-inlaid bracket clock, by Shotter, Drury Lane, London, with twin fusee movement, c1825, 21in (53.5cm) high.
£4,000–4,500 *BED*

An ebonised bracket clock, by James Boyd, London, with twin fusee movement and verge escapement, late 18thC, 20in (51cm) high.
£1,300–1,500 *TMA*

A mahogany bracket clock, by John Green, London, with 2 train fusee movement and verge escapement, mid-18thC, 21in (53.5cm) high.
£11,000–13,000 *DN*

A mahogany and line-inlaid bracket clock, by Morath Bros, Liverpool, the dial with Roman numerals, c1820, 14in (35.5cm) high.
£600–700 *SPa*

A fruitwood and ebonised bracket clock, by Thomas Wagstaffe, London, with triple fusee movement and verge escapement, c1780, 21¾in (53.5cm) high.
£3,800–4,200 *Bon*

A George IV bracket clock, with twin fusee movement and anchor escapement, striking the hours on a bell, 13¾in (35cm) high.
£2,200–2,500 *DN(H)*

A late Victorian mahogany 8-day bracket clock, with brass and silvered dial, the 3 train fusee movement striking the hours on a gong, c1860, 19in (48.5cm) high.
£2,000–2,500 *BED*

A late Victorian ebonised chiming bracket clock, with silvered dial, matted centre and subsidiary dials, on brass bracket feet, 18in (46cm) high.
£900–1,100 *MSW*

A French Louis XV boulle bracket clock, the movement signed Dumier, early 18thC, 37½in (95.5cm) high.
£1,500–1,800 *S(Z)*

A French Regency style brass-inlaid bracket clock, with 8-day movement, on brass bracket feet, c1900, 7in (18cm) high.
£280–300 *CHe*

A German walnut bracket clock, by Junghams, with cushion top and boxwood floral scroll inlays, the brass dial and 2 subsidiary dials in the arch indicating chime/silent and pendulum control, late 19thC, 17½in (44.5cm) high.
£650–700 *TMA*

A German walnut bracket clock, by R. Schneckenburger, with foliate and shell carving, brass and silvered dial, 8-day movement with Westminster chimes, 19thC, 25½in (65cm) high.
£600–700 *M*

A Dutch musical bracket clock, signed Gt ter Vooren, Amsterdam, brass-mounted and lacquered, fusee movement and verge escapement striking on 13 bells, 18thC, 22in (56cm) high.
£10,000–12,000 *P*

An enamelled strike/repeat carriage clock, the dial with Roman numerals, late 18thC, 7in (18cm) high.
£2,000–2,500 *BED*

A French carriage clock, the 8-day movement with lever escapement, c1880, 6in (15cm) high.
£1,400–1,600 *PAO*

A *grande sonnerie* carriage clock, made for Benson of London, c1880, 10½in (26.5cm) high.
£2,750–3,250 *BED*

A French brass carriage clock, with painted porcelain panels, late 19thC, 5½in (14cm) high.
£2,800–3,200 *SWO*

A brass repeating carriage clock, inscribed J. W. Benson, London, late 19thC, 7in (18cm) high.
£1,300–1,500 *P(C)*

A French Louis XV bronze and parcel-gilt cartel clock, signed Verdier à Paris, mid-18thC, 13½in (34.5cm) high.
£2,250–2,500 *S(Z)*

A Louis XVI ormolu cartel clock, with white enamel dial, late 18thC, movement later, 18in (45.5cm) high.
£5,600–6,000 *S(NY)*

A Victorian brass skeleton clock, with 8-day striking single fusee movement, alabaster base, and glass dome, 22in (56cm) high.
£500–550 *DN*

A walnut wall clock, by Joseph Knibb, London, late 17thC, later pierced fret, 12½in (32cm) high, with walnut weight case.
£22,000–25,000 *P*

A walnut and floral marquetry longcase clock, signed Peter Abbott, London, the 11in (28cm) brass dial with silver chapter ring, base restored, 18thC, 80in (204cm) high.
£6,500–7,500 *P*

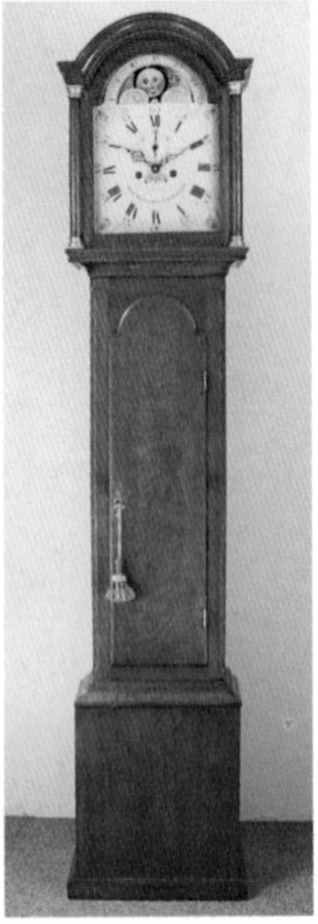

An oak longcase clock, by Alexander, Chippenham, with seconds, date and moonphases to arch, late 18thC, 81¼in (207cm) high.
£3,750–4,250 *ALS*

A walnut marquetry longcase clock, by Jonas Barber, London, the silvered chapter ring with Roman numerals, c1690, 82in (208cm) high.
£4,800–5,200 *Bon*

A mahogany 8-day longcase clock, by Jonathan Beake, London, the brass dial showing seconds and date with strike/silent feature, c1735, 89in (226cm) high.
£9,000–10,000 *PAO*

A mahogany longcase clock, by Joseph Clark, London, c1770, 100in (254cm) high.
£12,000–13,000 *PAO*

A George III mahogany 8-day longcase clock, by Gimblett & Vale, Birmingham, the 13in (33cm) brass and silvered arch dial with a moonphase in the arch, beneath a foliate engraved band, the 4 pillar movement with rack strike, c1770, 97in (247cm) high.
£6,500–7,500 *DN*

A red lacquer and chinoiserie decorated musical longcase clock, signed Claudius du Chesne, London, the 12in (30.5cm) dial with brass chapter ring, 18thC, 115in (292cm) high.
£19,000–21,000 *P*

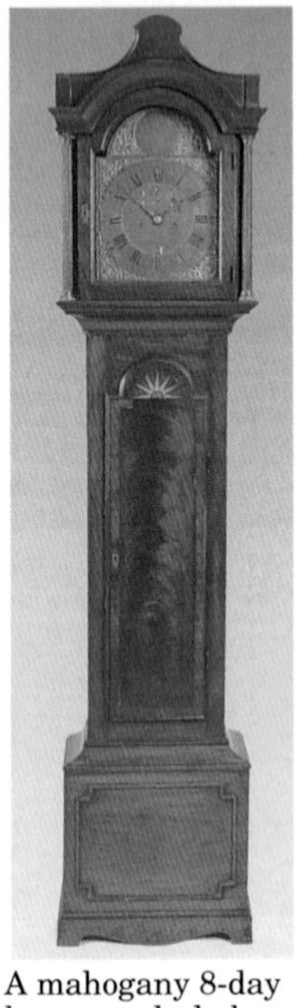

A mahogany 8-day longcase clock, by John Farley, 18thC, 89¾in (228cm) high.
£2,000–2,250 *Bea(E)*

l. A lacquered longcase clock, by William Ericke, London, the 5 pillar movement striking the hours on a bell, c1755, 87in (221cm) high.
£6,500–7,500 *PAO*

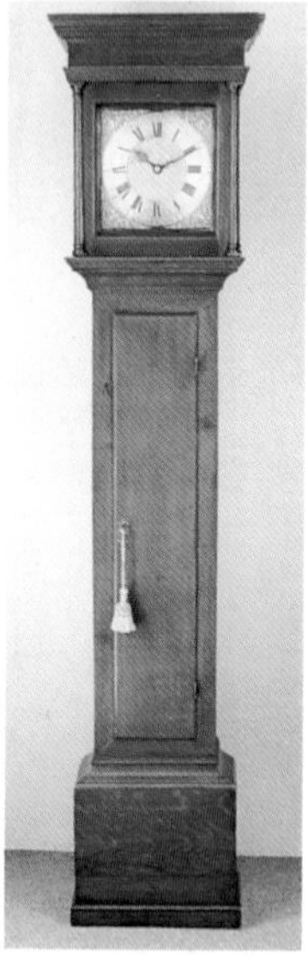

An oak longcase clock, by Thos Hine, c1770, 81in (205.5cm) high.
£2,250–2,500 *ALS*

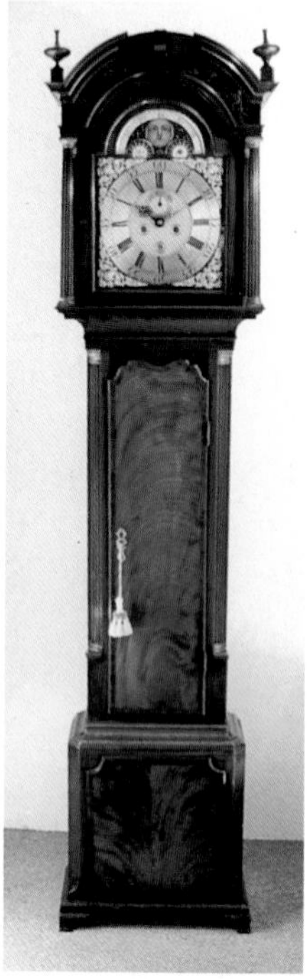

A flame mahogany longcase clock, by Rowland Johnson, c1765, 90in (228.5cm) high.
£7,500–8,250 *ALS*

A mahogany longcase clock, by J. B. Jenkins, Crickhowell, with an automaton of a butcher and a bull, c1832, 86in (218.5cm) high.
£5,000–5,500 *ALS*

A mahogany longcase clock, by Charles Hains, Swindon, the arch painted with Furness Abbey, Ulverston, c1840, 89in (226cm) high.
£4,000–4,500 *PAO*

A mahogany 8-day longcase clock, c1810, 88in (223.5cm) high.
£3,500–4,000 *SO*

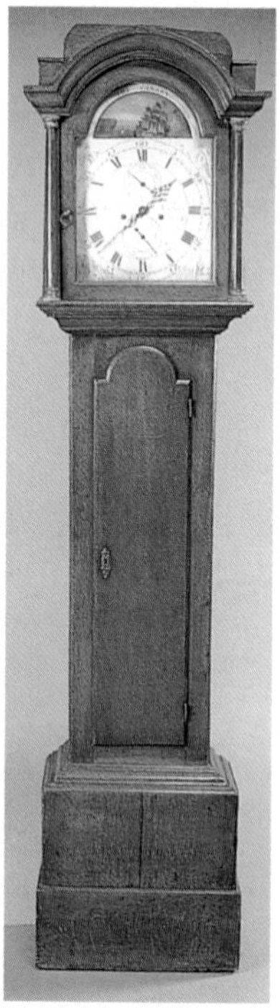

An oak longcase clock, by Anthony Lynch, Newbury, with an automaton sailing ship in the arch, c1760, 81in (205.5cm) high.
£2,300–2,600 *DN*

An inlaid mahogany longcase clock, by Andrew Lawley, Bath, with moonphase to the arch, c1825, 91in (231cm) high.
£6,500–7,000 *PAO*

A red japanned long-case clock, by David Murray, Edinburgh, with subsidiary seconds, c1780, 92in (233.5cm) high.
£4,200–4,800 *Bon*

l. A mahogany longcase clock, by Martin Platts, London, with 5 pillar rack and bell-striking movement, c1775, 86in (218.5cm) high.
£4,000–4,500 *S*

A regulator longcase clock, by William McGregor, Edinburgh, with deadbeat escapement, Harrison's maintaining power, c1850, 79in (200.5cm) high.
£5,500–6,000 *PAO*

A Scottish mahogany longcase clock, c1840, 94in (239cm) high.
£3,200–3,600 *S*

An oak longcase clock, c1800, 78in (199cm) high.
£3,250–3,750 *ALS*

A walnut 8-day longcase clock, by Thos Shindler, Canterbury, mid-18thC, 86in (218.5cm) high.
£2,800–3,200 *TMA*

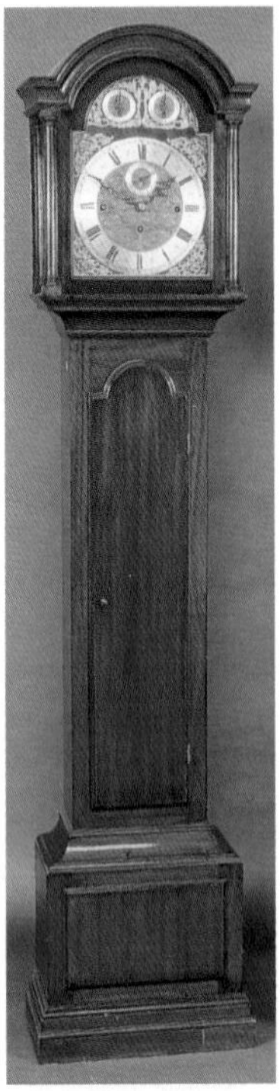

A George III style mahogany longcase clock, by Jno Smith, with arched brass dial and silvered chapter ring, late 19thC, 79in (200.5cm) high.
£2,800–3,200 *P(WM)*

A mahogany longcase clock, by James Sutton, c1820, 90in (228.5cm) high.
£6,500–7,000 *PAO*

An oak longcase clock, by Moses Trugard, c1780, 72in (183cm) high.
£4,750–5,250 *PAO*

An inlaid mahogany 8-day longcase clock, by James Walker, Montrose, c1835, 80in (203cm) high.
£4,750–5,250 *PAO*

l. An inlaid mahogany 8-day longcase clock, by Wood, Stroud, the 12in (30.5cm) break-arch dial with moonphases to the arch, the trunk with reeded quarter pillars, c1810, 80¾in (205cm) high.
£5,250–5,750 *ALS*

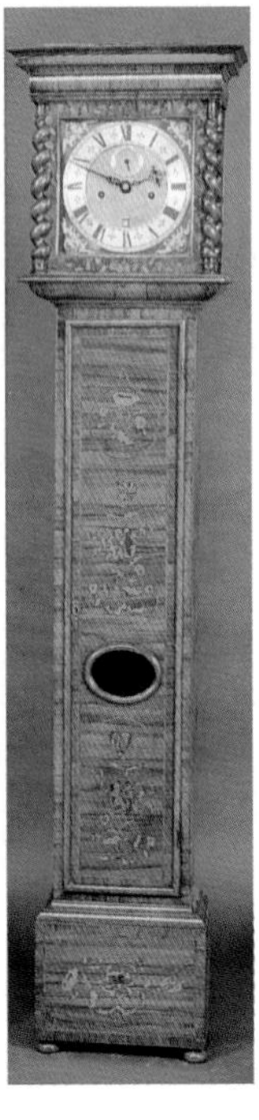

r. An inlaid walnut longcase clock, by Joseph Windmills, the 10in (25.5cm) brass dial with silvered chapter ring, the cherub head spandrels with scored line border, the movement with 5 ring-turned pillars, restored, late 17thC, 74¼in (186.5cm) high.
£7,200–8,000 *P(WM)*

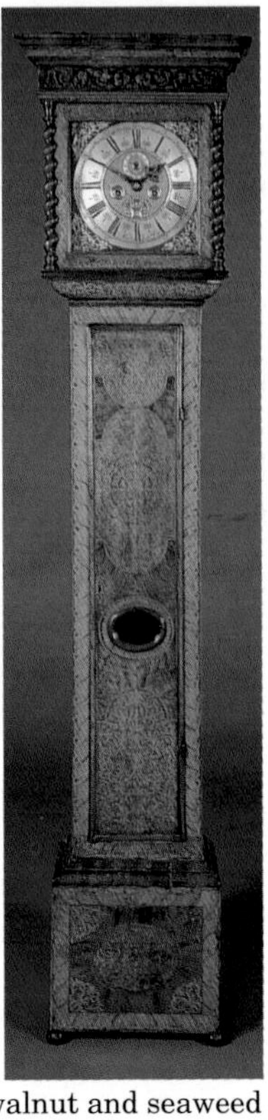

A walnut and seaweed marquetry longcase clock, by Benji Willoughby, with 11in (28cm) brass dial, possibly associated, restored, early 18thC, 81in (206cm) high.
£6,800–7,500 *P*

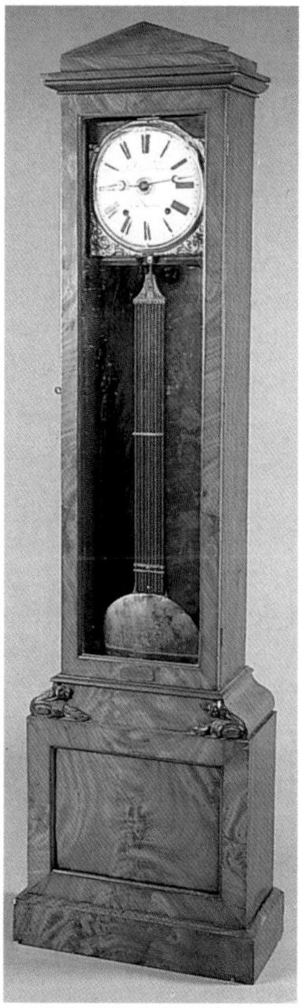

A French mahogany longcase clock, by Clement Bourgois, c1850, 77½in (197cm) high.
£1,600–1,800 *DN*

A marquetry-inlaid and ormolu-mounted month duration longcase clock, by Gasparo Astori, Rome, with 6 pillar movement, c1700, 87in (221cm) high.
£14,000–16,000 *SO*

A Scandinavian mahogany longcase clock, the dial painted with a rural scene at the centre, with 3 train quarter-striking movement, c1800, 86in (220cm) high.
£3,200–3,600 *S*

A carved mahogany Gothic style longcase clock, with Westminster chimes, the arched crest centred by a winged female bust holding an armorial tablet, on stylised bracket feet, early 20thC, 108in (274.5cm) high.
£5,000–5,500 *B&B*

A French gilt-bronze mantel clock, the enamel dial signed Ravrio, Bronzier, Mesnil Hn, on a *verde antico* base and claw-and-ball feet, c1800, 9½in (24cm) wide.
£3,700–4,200 *S*

A French ormolu mantel clock, the dial signed Hunziker, the case surmounted by figures of Cupid and Psyche, c1820, 18in (45.5cm) high.
£1,250–1,500 *GH*

A French rosewood mantel timepiece, signed Malecot à Paris, inlaid with birds and foliage, c1840, 10in (25.5cm) high.
£700–800 *SO*

A French ormolu-mounted mantel clock, signed Raingo Frères à Paris, with 8-day movement, c1860, 18½in (47cm) high.
£1,500–1,800 *BED*

A French ormolu striking mantel clock, surmounted by an urn with scroll handles, c1870, 13½in (34.5cm) high.
£750–1,000 *BED*

A French four-glass gilded mantel clock, with mercury pendulum and reeded columns, c1860, 9in (23cm) high.
£1,400–1,600 *BWC*

A French ormolu striking mantel clock, surmounted by an urn, with porcelain panels and gilt presentation plaque, c1860, 18in (45.5cm) high.
£1,000–1,100 *CHe*

A French green boulle striking mantel clock, by Samuel Marti, Paris, surmounted by a vase with flowers, on paw feet, c1870, 13in (33cm) high.
£1,100–1,300 *SO*

A French gilt-bronze 8-day bell-striking mantel clock, surmounted by an urn with scroll handles, inset with porcelain panels, c1870, 10½in (26.5cm) high.
£1,200–1,500 *SO*

A French ormolu mantel clock, inset with porcelain panels and flanked by flaming torches, the dial supported by a female figure, late 19thC, 19in (48.5cm) high.
£500–550 *TMA*

A mahogany table clock, c1795, 18in (45.5cm) high.
£6,000–6,750 *PAO*

A mahogany table clock, c1780, 19in (48cm) high.
£4,000–4,500 *S*

A mahogany 8-day mantel clock, with brass mouldings, 18thC, 18¾in (47.5cm) high.
£1,400–1,600 *CAG*

A Regency mantel timepiece, 8¾in (22cm) high.
£1,150–1,300 *DN*

A French calendar clock, by Japy Frères, c1870, 11in (27.9cm) high.
£2,500–3,000 *SO*

A German rosewood mantel clock, c1890, 13¼in (33.5cm) high.
£250–280 *CHe*

A gilt-metal hexagonal table clock, by Benedict Engelschalk Thorn, 17thC, 4in (10cm) high.
£8,000–9,000 *S(Z)*

A silver-gilt and enamel mantel clock, late 18thC, 7in (18cm) high.
£4,000–4,500 *BHa*

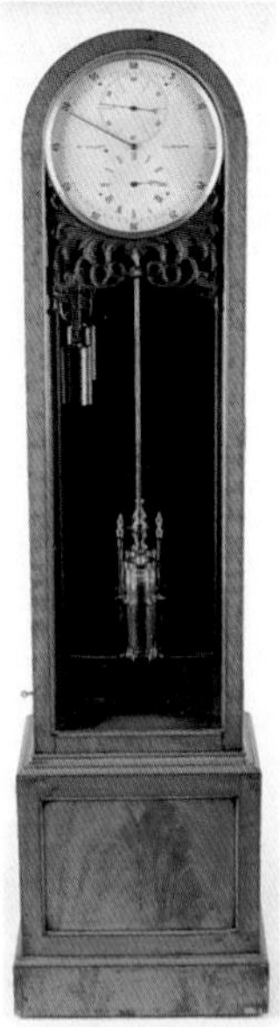

A mahogany longcase regulator, signed Wm Sharp, Glasgow, c1880, 72in (175cm) high.
£4,800–5,200 *Bon*

A longcase regulator, by John Todd, Glasgow, with wooden rod pendulum, c1820, 77in (195.5cm) high.
£5,500–6,250 *DRA*

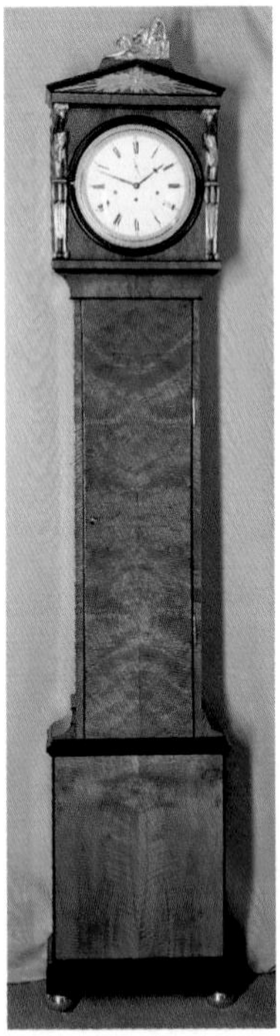

A Viennese walnut veneered *grande sonnerie* striking clock, with ebonised moulding and gilded applied decorations, c1810, 90in (228cm) high.
£35,000–40,000 *GeC*

A Viennese regulator timepiece, by Anton Janartchek, with enamel dial, c1840, 46in (117cm) high.
£7,500–8,500 *GeC*

r. A mahogany longcase 8-day regulator, by David Whitelaw, Edinburgh, the silvered-brass dial with Roman chapters and strike/silent facility, c1835, 80in (203cm) high.
£4,200–4,650 *PAO*

A gilt and shagreen verge pocket watch, by George Etherington, London, the champlevé dial with Roman and Arabic numerals, fusee and chain with worm and wheel barrel set-up between the plates, pierced and engraved cock with mask, pierced and engraved foot and plate for the silver regulator disc, signed, late 17thC, 51mm diam.
£1,600–1,800 *PT*

An 18ct gold and enamel pair cased pocket watch, by Ilbery, London, the white enamel dial with Roman numerals, subsidiary seconds dial, the outer case polychrome enamelled, 1802, 59mm diam.
£5,500–6,000 *S(G)*

A gold and enamel pocket watch, by Moulinie & Co, Geneva, made for the Turkish market, with white enamel dial, the case decorated with flowers on a shagreen ground, signed, later bow, c1820, 47mm diam.
£2,500–3,000 *S(G)*

An 18ct gold half hunter pocket watch, with Roman numerals and English lever movement, 1913, 50mm diam.
£450–500 *PSA*

A gold open face verge pocket watch, by Racine, Geneva, with engine-turned silver dial, full plate gilt fusee movement, the case with applied three-colour gold decoration set with turquoises and amethysts, c1820, 39mm diam.
£700–780 *PT*

A lady's 14ct gold fob watch, with Roman numerals and cylinder movement, 1920s, 32mm diam.
£180–200 *BWC*

A Swiss gold quarter repeating open face pocket watch, with polychrome enamel dial, the silver regulator dial with blue steel Breguet hands, full plate fusee movement, c1810, 57mm diam.
£3,500–4,000 *PT*

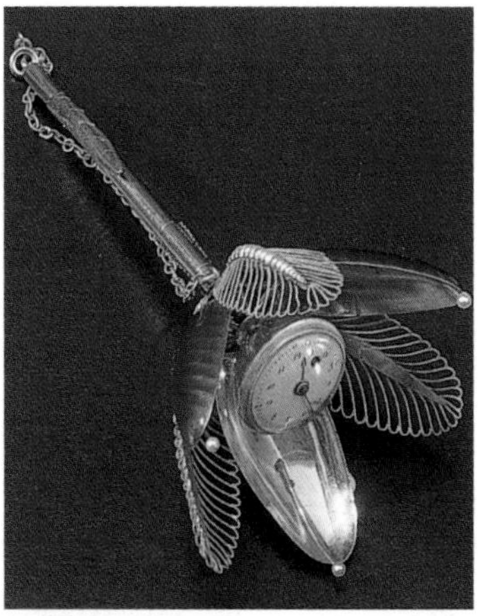

A lady's gold, enamel and pearl tulip-shaped watch, the enamel dial with Arabic numerals, with gilt fusee verge movement, minor damage, probably Swiss, c1820, 4¾in (12cm) long, in a fitted case.
£8,500–9,000 *S(Am)*

A Swiss 18ct gold minute repeating pocket watch, retailed by Tiffany & Co, with white enamel dial and blue steel Breguet hands, signed, c1900, 50mm diam.
£2,200–2,500 *B&B*

A Cartier lady's 18ct gold and enamel wristwatch, with gilt lever movement, signed, c1915, 26mm diam.
£3,500–4,000 *S(NY)*

An Audemars Piguet 18ct gold jump hour wristwatch, with silvered dial, rhodium-plated lever movement, signed, c1920, 37mm diam.
£4,400–4,800 *S*

A Rolex lady's 14ct gold and diamond bracelet wristwatch, with 17 jewels, signed, c1960, 21mm diam.
£1,500–1,750 *S(HK)*

A lady's 18ct gold bracelet wristwatch, by Jaeger LeCoultre, with nickel lever movement, signed, c1955, 19mm diam.
£700–800 *S(NY)*

A Patek Philippe lady's gold and emerald bracelet wristwatch, with nickel lever movement, mono-metallic compensation balance, signed, c1935, 20mm diam.
£2,500–2,750 *S(HK)*

A Rolex lady's 18ct gold and diamond bracelet wristwatch, with 17 jewels, signed, c1960, 18mm diam.
£1,200–1,500 *S(NY)*

An 18ct gold single-button chronograph wristwatch, by Ulysse Nardine, the white enamel dial with subsidiary dials for seconds and 30 minute register, bimetallic compensation balance, nickel lever movement, signed, c1925, 33mm diam.
£3,500–4,000 *S(NY)*

A Rolex Oyster 'bubbleback' 9ct gold automatic wristwatch, the black dial with Arabic numerals, the screw on the back stamped RWC Ltd, signed, c1937, 32mm diam.
£1,800–2,000 *Bon*

A Vacheron & Constantin 18ct gold wristwatch, with 15 jewels, signed, c1950, 33mm diam.
£1,500–1,750 *S(G)*

An Omega lady's 9ct gold dress wristwatch, with baton markers, fitted with bark finish bracelet, c1964, 12mm diam.
£370–400 *BWC*

A Rolex Oyster Perpetual lady's 18ct gold bracelet self-winding wristwatch, with date aperture, nickel lever movement, 26 jewels, c1959, 24mm diam.
£2,600–3,000 *S(NY)*

A lady's 18ct white gold dress watch, with diamond bezel, on a wide bracelet, c1960, 14mm diam.
£1,500–1,800 *BWC*

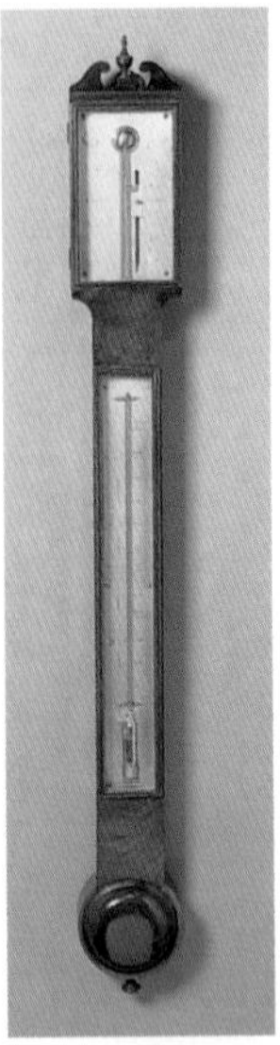

A mahogany stick barometer, by George Adams, London, with swan neck cresting and urn finial, the concealed tube with silvered plate and vernier, signed, c1790, 39¼in (99.5cm) high.
£4,800–5,200 *S*

A light oak-cased Polytechnic barometer, by J. Davis, London, with silvered card scales, the case with pointed pediment and carved scroll decoration, c1890, 39in (99cm) high.
£1,200–1,400 *AW*

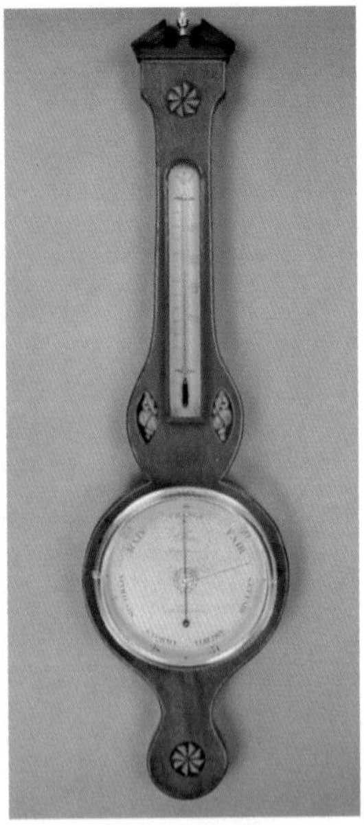

A Regency mahogany wheel barometer, by T. Bates, Market Harborough, with 8in (20.5cm) silvered brass scale and thermometer, with weather notations, the case inlaid with shells and with an architectural top, c1820, 37in (94cm) high.
£1,000–1,100 *PAO*

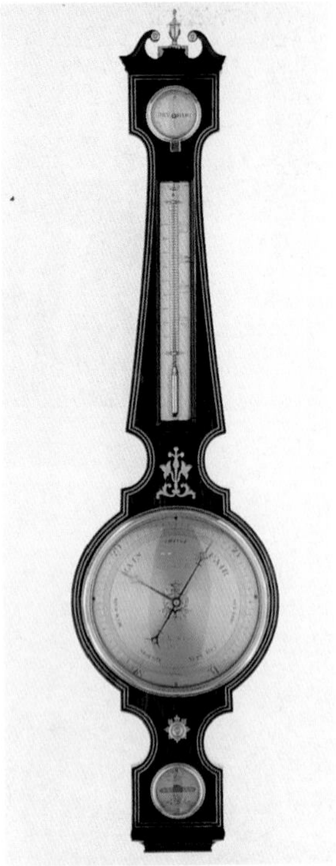

A rosewood and brass-inlaid wheel barometer, by Francis Amadio, London, with 8in (20.5cm) dial, signed, c1830, 39in (99cm) high.
£2,400–2,700 *AW*

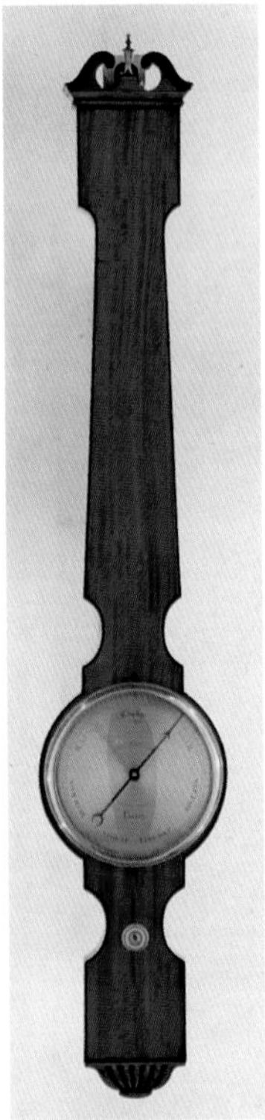

A satinwood veneered and ebony-strung wheel barometer, by Thos Rubergale, London, with 5in (12.5cm) dial, with swan neck pediment, c1825, 34in (86.5cm) high.
£3,000–3,500 *AW*

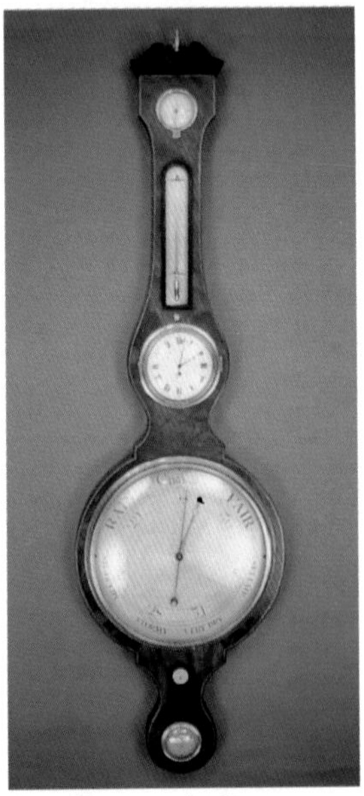

A mahogany clock barometer, by Lione & Somalvico, London, with 12in (30.5cm) silvered brass barometer scale, hygrometer, spirit level and clock, the verge clock movement by William Terry, London, c1805, 44in (112cm) high.
£2,700–3,000 *PAO*

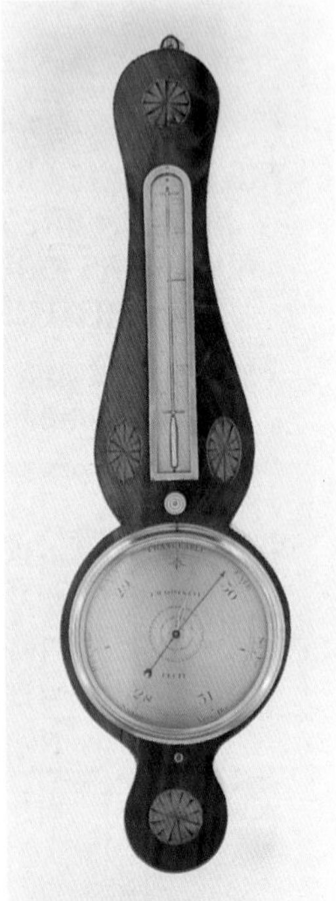

A figured mahogany wheel barometer, by J. M. Ronketti, London, the case inlaid with fan paterae and chequer stringing, inset with brass-framed thermometer and barometer dial, c1790, 38in (96.5cm) high.
£2,500–3,000 *AW*

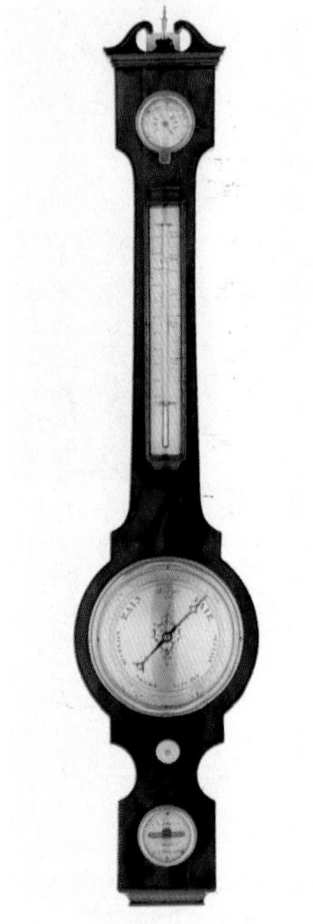

A flame mahogany four-dial wheel barometer, by Tognoni, Bristol, with 6in (15cm) dial and square base, c1825, 35in (89cm) wide.
£1,200–1,500 *AW*

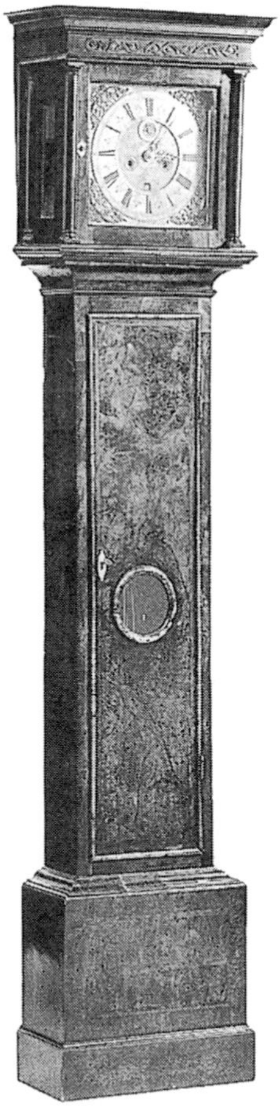

A burr walnut and feather-banded 8-day longcase clock, the brass dial engraved Chr Gould, Londini Fecit, on a plinth base, mid-18thC, 83in (211cm) high.
£7,000–8,000 *AG*

A mahogany 8-day longcase clock, the arched chased brass dial with silvered chapter ring, signed Hugh Gordon, Aberdeen, the top with scroll pediment and blind fret frieze on fluted quarter columns, panel base and bracket feet, c1780, 86in (218.5cm) high.
£4,000–4,500 *AH*

A *faux* walnut longcase clock, by Holmes, Cheshire, c1830, 78in (198cm) high.
£1,500–1,800 *SWN*

l. An early Victorian mahogany and rosewood crossbanded 8-day longcase clock, the 14in (35.5cm) enamelled and painted dial with subsidiary dial, signed Heywood, Wrexham, the trunk with Tunbridge ware style inlay, 90in (229cm) high.
£1,400–1,800 *P(NW)*

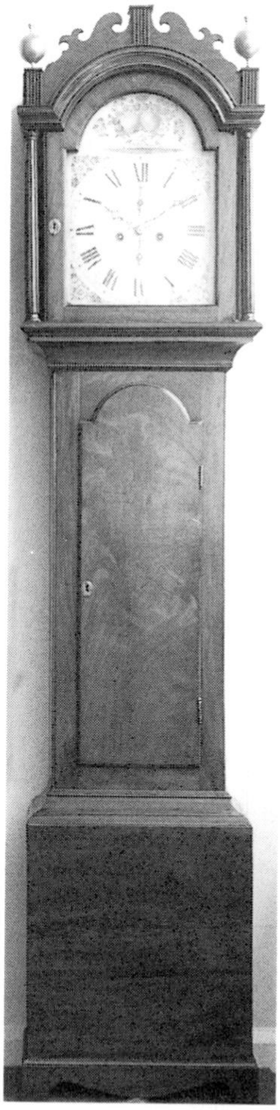

l. A mahogany 8-day longcase clock, by Greenwood, Canterbury, the 12in (30.5cm) arched painted dial with subsidiary seconds and date dial, glass cracked, finials later, over-painted, 19thC, 84in (213.5cm) high.
£2,000–2,200 *CAG*

An oak 8-day longcase clock, by Hardeman & Son, Bridge, the 12in (30.5cm) arched painted dial with subsidiary dials, plinth reduced, 19thC, 82in (208.5cm) high.
£1,500–2,000 *CAG*

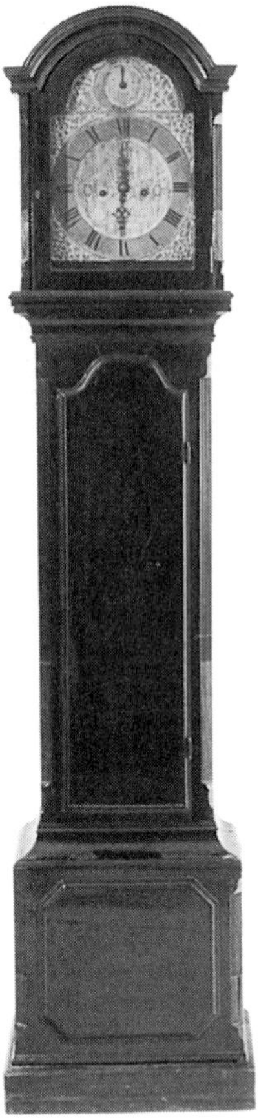

A mahogany 8-day longcase clock, by Jessop, London, the arched brass and silvered dial engraved with oval medallions and foliage, striking on a bell, c1780, 85in (216cm) high.
£1,600–1,800 *Bea(E)*

Parts of the Dial

The basic parts of the dial of an 18th century longcase clock include:

- **A** chapter ring
- **B** subsidiary dial
- **C** calendar aperture
- **D** applied corner spandrels
- **E** winding holes
- **F** hour hand
- **G** minute hand
- **H** dial arch
- **I** strike/silent lever
- **J** dial centre

A George III figured and faded mahogany 8-day longcase clock, by James Leslie, London, the 12in (30.5cm) arched silvered brass dial with strike/silent to the arch, subsidiary date and seconds dials, 5 pillar movement, anchor escapement and rack strike on bell, 85in (216cm) high.
£5,000–5,500 *JM*

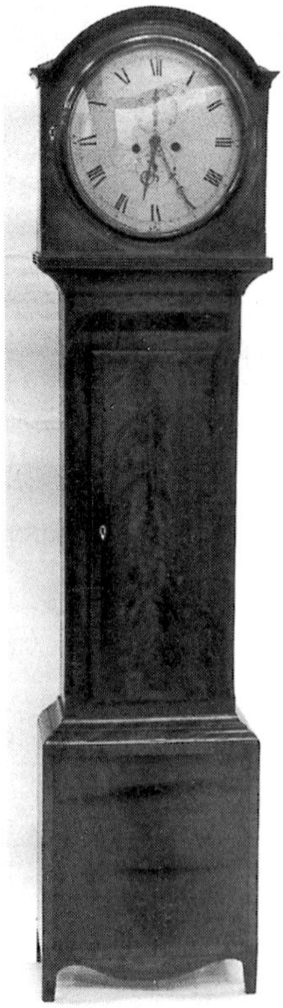

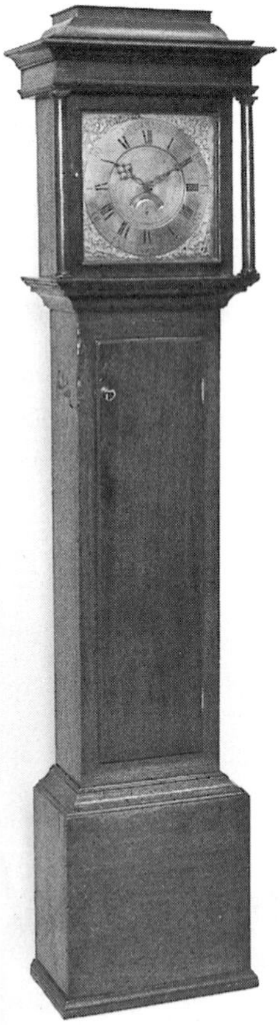

An oak longcase clock, by Gilbert Kidd, Malton, the 11in (28cm) brass dial with calendar indicator, 30-hour movement, c1800, 78in (198cm) high.
£2,200–2,500 *HCC*

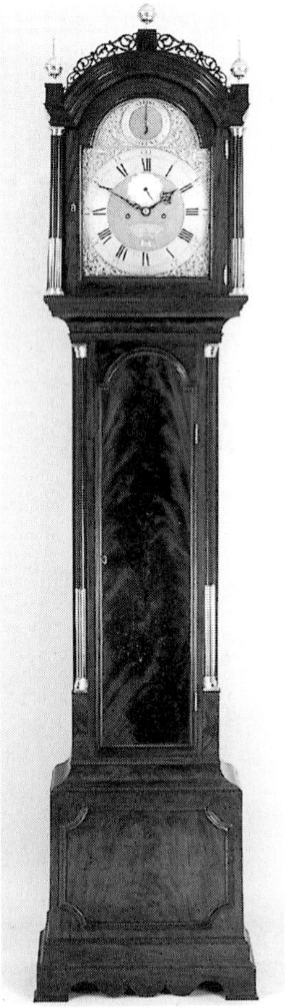

A mahogany and brass-inlaid 8-day longcase clock, by Richard Marsh, Watford, with 5 pillar movement striking the hours on a bell, c1770, 94in (239cm) high.
£10,000–12,000 *PAO*

l. A George III Scottish mahogany and crossbanded 8-day longcase clock, by MacFarlane, Perth, the painted dial with seconds and date indicators, 77in (195.5cm) high.
£1,250–1,500 *E*

An oak longcase clock, by Charles Miller, Reigate, the 11in (28cm) painted dial with seconds, 30-hour movement, pagoda top, early 19thC, 77in (196cm) high.
£1,500–1,750 *ALS*

A Scottish light oak 8-day longcase clock, by John McAnsh, Crieff, with silvered brass dial, c1790, 88in (223.5cm) high.
£3,500–4,000 *PAO*

r. An oak longcase clock, by Monkhouse, Carlisle, the 13in (33cm) arched brass dial with polished brass chapter ring and painted phases of the moon to arch, subsidiary date dial, twin dummy winding holes, 30-hour striking movement, late 18thC, 91in (231cm) high.
£1,000–1,200 *CAG*

A Scottish mahogany 8-day longcase clock, by David Norrie, Leith, the white dial with subsidiary dials, painted with country scenes, c1800, 83in (211cm) high.
£4,500–5,000 *PAO*

l. An inlaid mahogany 8-day longcase clock, the 14in (35.5cm) painted dial signed Moore, Birmingham, subsidiary seconds dial and date aperture, moonphase in arch, c1840, 93½in (237cm) high.
£3,800–4,200 *S(S)*

An oak longcase clock, by Pearson, Halifax, the 13in (33cm) break-arch dial with moonphases and date indicators, 30-hour movement, the hood with swan neck top, c1800, 91in (231cm) high.
£2,400–2,750 *ALS*

l. A George III oak longcase clock, by J. Ochlee, Luton, with 11in (28cm) white dial, 30-hour movement, 83in (211cm) high.
£550–600 *DOC*

An inlaid mahogany longcase clock, by Ortelli, Buckingham, early 19thC, 91in (231cm) high.
£3,500–4,000 *Oli*

A mahogany 8-day longcase clock, the arched dial signed Osbourne, painted with a harvest scene, early 19thC, 98½in (250cm) high.
£1,600–1,800 *P(WM)*

A Scottish oak 8-day longcase clock, by John Pinkerton, Haddington, striking the hours on a bell, c1810, 74in (188cm) high.
£2,500–2,800 *PAO*

l. A mahogany longcase clock, signed C. Packer & Co, London W, the 12in (30.5cm) break-arch dial with silvered chapter ring, subsidiary seconds dial, the 3 train movement chiming on 8 tubular bells, c1900, 101in (256.5cm) high.
£2,800–3,200 *S(S)*

A Scottish mahogany 8-day longcase clock, by Reid, Edinburgh, the 13in (33cm) white dial with seconds and date dials, c1805, 79in (201cm) high.
£4,800–5,200 *PAO*

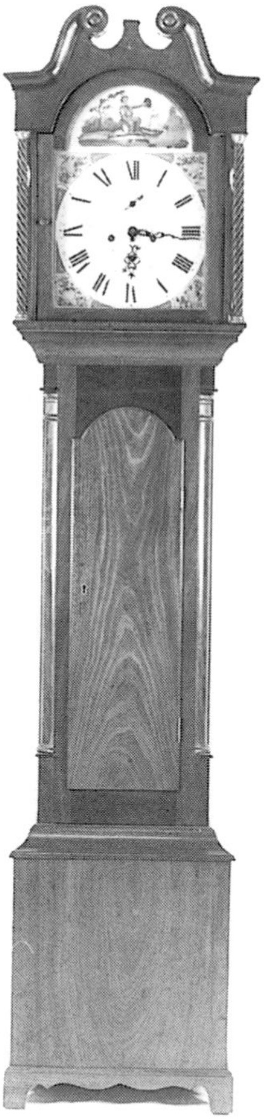

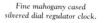

l. A mahogany 8-day longcase clock, by Proctor-Garland, the 12in (30.5cm) dial painted with a sailor to the arch, subsidiary date and seconds dial, 19thC, case later, 85½in (217cm) high.
£850–950 *WL*

An oak and mahogany crossbanded 8-day longcase clock, by Henry Richards, Somerton, the 12in (30.5cm) brass dial with subsidiary seconds dial and date aperture, c1770, 77in (195.6cm) high.
£4,800–5,200 *PAO*

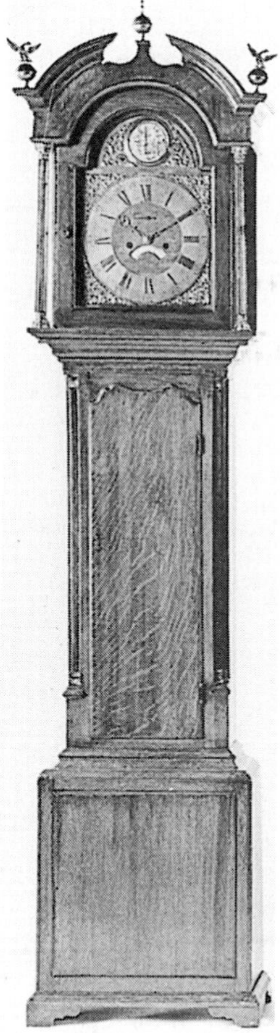

l. An oak longcase clock, by Thomas Radford, Leeds, with subsidiary seconds and date apertures, early 19thC, 86½in (220cm) high.
£1,250–1,500 *P(NE)*

A mahogany 8-day longcase clock, by John Roger, Leominster, the arched brass dial with moonphase and silvered chapter ring, late 18thC, 89in (226cm) high.
£3,000–3,500 *AH*

l. An oak longcase clock, by Francis Robinson, London, with brass 12in (30.5cm) dial, 4 ringed pillar movement striking on a bell, c1720, 77in (196cm) high.
£900–1,000 *Bon(C)*

Condition of Clock Cases

All clocks should have their original finish and decorative features intact although some restoration is acceptable if carried out sympathetically. Cases in need of extensive repair and reconstruction should be avoided. Changes in temperature and humidity cause veneers to lift and for longcase clock trunk doors to warp. Mouldings may loosen as the original glue dries out and bubbles may appear under lacquer.

Clocks should be kept out of direct sunlight, as this causes the finish to bleach. Other problems include missing finials, damaged mouldings, broken glass on the hood, and scratching or damage to the polish.

A George III oak 8-day longcase clock, by James Scholefield, London, the 11in (28cm) brass dial with silvered chapter ring and subsidiary dials, restored, 96½in (245cm) high.
£1,700–2,000 *DN*

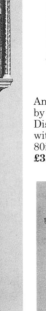

An oak longcase clock, by Benjamin Shuckforth, Diss, the painted dial with moon roller, c1755, 80in (203cm) high.
£3,500–4,000 *GAZE*

r. An oak and mahogany crossbanded 8-day longcase clock, by J. Simcock, Nantwich, with 14in (35.5cm) painted dial, c1830, 87in (221cm) high.
£1,800–2,000 *S(S)*

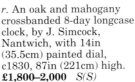

An oak 8-day longcase clock, by John Smith, Betley, the brass dial with silvered brass chapter ring, c1710, 79in (201cm) high.
£3,800–4,200 *PAO*

r. A mahogany 8-day longcase clock, by Emanuel Solomon, Canterbury, the 12in (30.5cm) silvered dial with subsidiary seconds dial and date aperture, 5 pillar striking movement, reduced in height, 18thC, 84in (213.5cm) high.
£2,200–2,500 *CAG*

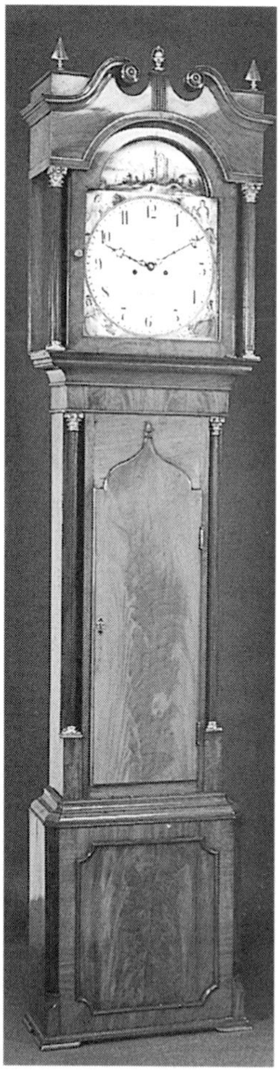

l. A mahogany longcase clock, the painted arched dial inscribed F. Thomas Halesowen, painted with a lakeside scene, early 19thC, 96½in (245cm) high.
£2,000–2,200 *P(WM)*

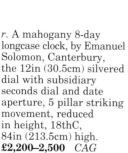

An oak and mahogany crossbanded 8-day longcase clock, by James and John Thristle, Stogursey, the arched white dial with painted seashells to the corners, c1810, 87in (221cm) high.
£3,500–4,000 *PAO*

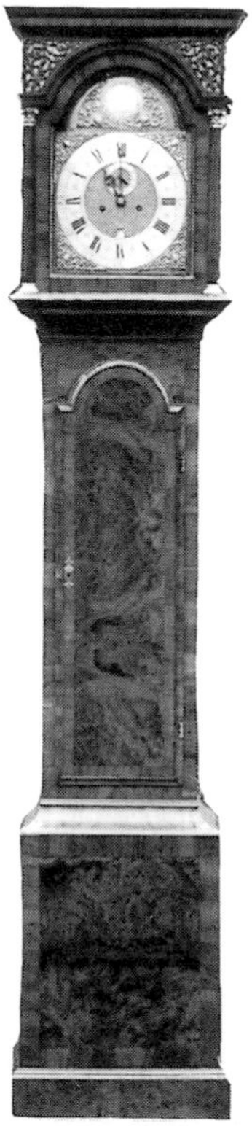

Fine London clock by William Barron in walnut case

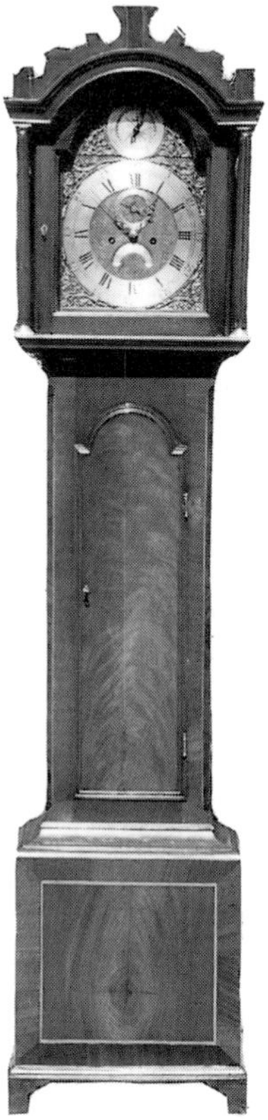

John Marsh with strike/silent lever in mahogany case

An oak 8-day longcase clock, by Richard Wallis, Truro, the chapter ring with matted centre and chased gilt spandrels, base reduced, 18thC, 78½in (199.5cm) high.
£1,600–1,800 *LAY*

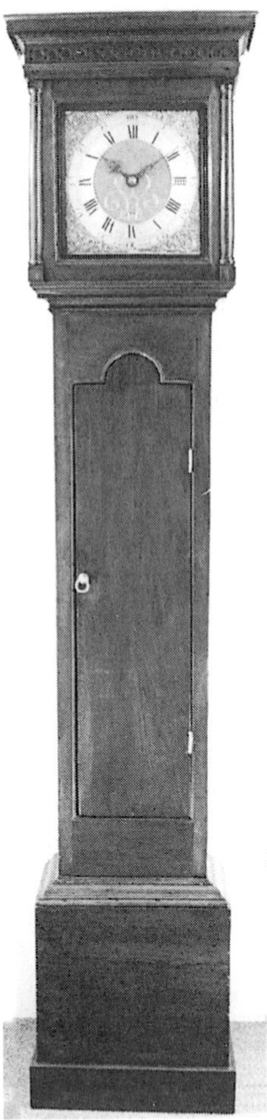

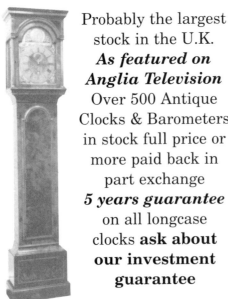

l. An oak longcase clock, by Humphrey White, Fairford, with 11in (28cm) brass dial, 30-hour birdcage movement, c1760, 85in (216cm) high.
£2,200–2,600 *ALS*

MILLER'S COMPARES . . .

I An oak and mahogany longcase clock, by John Wilson, Peterborough, with ship automaton above 12in (30.5cm) painted dial, 4 pillar rack and bell striking movement, late 18thC, 81in (205.5cm) high.
£3,500–4,000 *Bon*

II A mahogany and fruitwood strung longcase clock, by Richard Morland, Kirby Malzard, the 14in (35.5cm) dial with subsidiary dials, 4 pillar movement striking on a bell, c1820, 90in (228.5cm) high.
£1,200–1,500 *Bon(C)*

Item I **sold for almost 3 times the price of** *Item II* **because it has a number of particularly desirable features. The smaller dial of** *Item I* **is more popular than the 14in (35.5cm) dial of** *Item II.* *Item I* **also looks more refined than** *Item II* **with its narrow trunk and long door, its finer mouldings and its fluted corner columns, rather than the chamfered columns of** *Item II.* **Furthermore,** *Item I* **has an extremely well painted harbour scene in the arch above the dial.** *Bon*

An oak 8-day longcase clock, by Richard Winch, Maidenhead, the white dial with subsidiary dials painted with flowers, c1795, 85½in (217cm) high.
£3,500–4,200 *PAO*

An oak and mahogany crossbanded 8-day longcase clock, by J. Winstanley, Holywell, the 13in (33cm) painted break-arch dial with moonphase, early 19thC, 87in (221cm) high.
£4,000–4,500 *ALS*

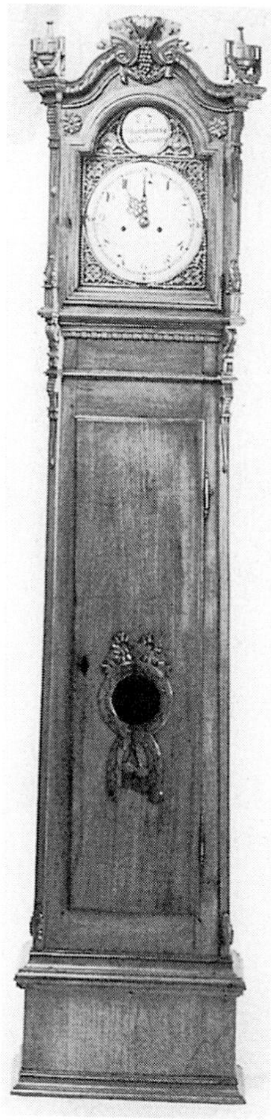

l. A French carved walnut longcase clock, with German movement, the arch inscribed P. J. Blumenberg in Remagen, 19thC, 69½in (176.5cm) high.
£1,800–2,000 *SLM*

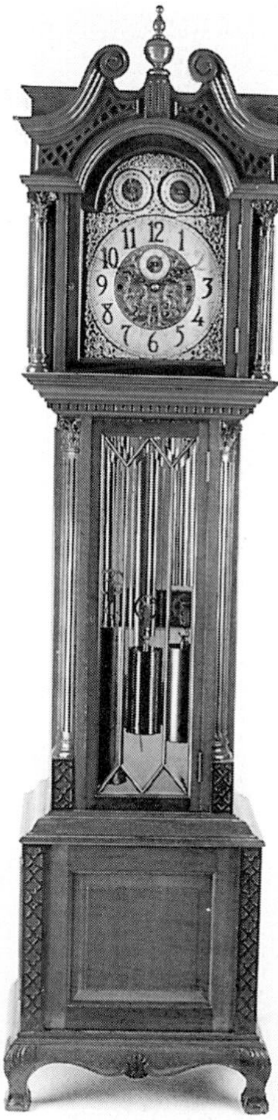

r. A mahogany longcase clock, the 12in (30.5cm) dial with silvered chapter ring and subsidiary dials, the movement chiming on 8 tubular gongs, c1890, 93in (236cm) high.
£2,600–3,000 *Bon*

A Scottish mahogany longcase clock, with painted dial, the hood with a foliate surmount above a fluted tapering trunk, on a bowed plinth base, mid-19thC, 80¾in (205cm) high.
£1,400–1,600 *P(NE)*

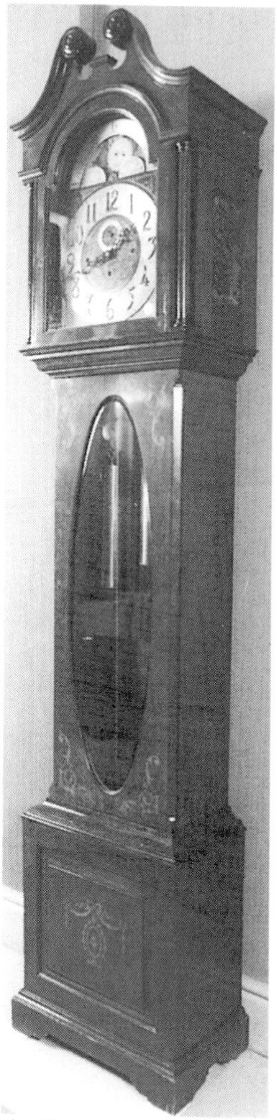

An Edwardian mahogany musical 8-day longcase clock, by Winterhalder & Hofmeier, with brass and silvered dial, 94in (239cm) high.
£3,500–4,000 *M*

l. A Continental bombé longcase clock, with gilt-metal mounts, painted with Vernis Martin style decoration on a gilt ground, the lacquered-brass arch dial with silvered chapter ring and ornate spandrels, late 19thC, 94½in (240cm) high.
£1,600–1,800 *P(G)*

Mantel Clocks

A mahogany mantel clock, by Camerer Kuss & Co, the 5in (12.5cm) shaped arch dial with silvered chapter ring, the 3 train fusee movement with anchor escapement, chiming on 8 bells and striking on a gong, c1900, 15¼in (39cm) high.
£2,800–3,200 *S(S)*

A goncalo alves four-glass library clock, by E. J. Dent, London, with engraved 3½in (9cm) silvered dial, 8-day chain fusee movement, anchor escapement, pendulum with locking screw, c1840, 9in (23cm) high.
£3,500–4,000 *JIL*

r. A rosewood four-glass mantel clock, by E. J. Dent, with single fusee movement, c1840, 9in (23cm) high.
£2,000–2,500 *SO*

Mantel or Table Clocks

The mantel or table clock is second in popularity to the carriage clock, and the choice is wide as most European countries have produced them in large numbers since the mid-19thC. In France from 1780 to 1880 they appeared in large numbers in a wide range of highly decorative cases with figural decoration. As a rule, those of the 1830 to 1950s are a little more subtle and of better quality and, as with garnitures, the movements are of a fairly standard type and not therefore of great importance.

A mahogany table clock, by Hardeman & Son, Bridge, with striking fusee movement, c1810, 16½in (42cm) high.
£2,500–3,000 *SO*

An Edwardian mahogany table clock, the 5¾in (14.5cm) silvered and engraved dial signed Dent, Maker to HM the King, London, similarly signed 5 pillar 2 train gong striking fusee and chain movement with spotted plates and anchor escapement, c1905, 15½in (39.5cm) high.
£1,800–2,000 *S*

l. A mahogany mantel clock, by Payne, New Bond Street, with striking fusee movement with repeat, c1820, 11in (28cm) high.
£2,500–3,000 *SO*

A mahogany table timepiece, the 6¾in (17cm) dial with subsidiary seconds dial, inverted fusee and chain movement with visible pendulum controlled detent escapement, c1900, 17¾in (45cm) high.
£1,300–1,600 *S*

An inlaid satinwood, ebony and bronze chiming table clock, the 8in (20.5cm) enamel dial signed Grimalde & Johnson, 431 Strand, with 6 pillar 3 train trip repeating fusee movement, the case inlaid with an armorial figure on a stylised lion, c1810, 23¾in (60.5cm) high.
£7,500–8,500 *S*

An Edwardian oak mantel clock, with brass dial, 8-day movement, 11in (28cm) high.
£300–350 *GAK*

An inlaid mahogany mantel clock, c1910, 11in (28cm) high.
£320–350 *CHe*

A Louis XVI style gilt-bronze and marble mantel clock, signed E. Barrard, Rue Memilmontant, Paris, late 19thC, 22½in (57cm) high.
£2,800–3,200 *S(NY)*

A French bronze mantel clock, with silk suspension, striking movement, bronze by Bradler, c1830, 19¾in (50cm) high.
£1,500–1,800 *DSP*

A French ormolu mantel clock, by Denière of Paris, the dial with enamel cartouche numerals, the anchor movement rack striking on a bell, similarly signed and marked Cailleaux, c1860, 31½in (80cm) high.
£3,500–4,000 *S(Am)*

The firm of Denière et Fils is recorded as working at the Rue Charlot in Paris between 1860 and 1890.

A French mantel clock, probably by A. Dumas, Paris, the 3¼in (8.5cm) porcelain dial painted and with turquoise and gilt numeral cartouches, 8-day striking movement, 19thC, 13¾in (35cm) high.
£900–1,000 *CAG*

r. A silvered, parcel-gilt and lapis lazuli mantel clock, by Elkington & Co, with platform escapement, c1880, 25¼in (64cm) wide.
£10,000–11,000 *S*

A French porcelain-mounted two-colour ormolu chariot clock, the 4¼in (11cm) twelve-piece enamel dial forming the wheel of the chariot, the bell striking Japy Frères movement signed Futvoye A Paris, c1850, 17¼in (44cm) high.
£3,500–4,000 *S*

A French gilt ormolu pillar mantel clock, the 3½in (9cm) enamel dial signed Dutertre, Paris, base signed Osmond, 19thC, 14in (35cm) high.
£2,500–3,000 *Bon*

A French provincial wood religieuse table clock, indistinctly signed Gautron, the green painted iron dial with pewter chapter ring, damaged, c1737, 18in (46cm) high.
£350–400 *S(Am)*

Early clocks of the Louis XIV period were known as 'religieuses', and were influenced by the sober Protestantism of the Dutch taste.

A French bronze and gilt-bronze mantel clock, the enamel dial inscribed Guillemin à Paris, the movement with outside countwheel striking on a bell, 19thC, 17½in (44.5cm) high.
£3,000–3,500 *P(E)*

A Vienna porcelain clock, the Japy Frères movement striking on a gong, the 3in (7.5cm) silvered dial inset into the porcelain and ormolu case painted with panels of maidens, late 19thC, 20in (51cm) high.
£2,200–2,500 *GH*

l. A French gilt-bronze figural mantel clock, the dial signed Leroy et Fils, Palais Royal 114–115, Galerie de Valois, mid-19thC, 19in (48.5cm) high.
£6,500–7,500 *S(NY)*

A French red tortoiseshell boulle mantel clock, with gilt-metal mounts, by Japy Frères, the gilt dial with white enamel cartouches and blue Roman numerals, 8-day striking movement, the arched top surmounted by a bowl of fruit, late 19thC, 12in (30.5cm) high.
£550–600 *LF*

A French inlaid mahogany mantel clock, by Japy Frères, with striking movement, c1900, 12½in (32cm) high.
£450–500 *SO*

A French ormolu figural mantel clock, the 3½in (9cm) enamel dial signed Lopin, Palais Royal, No 143, the bell striking movement with silk suspension, bell missing, c1840, 14in (36cm) high.
£650–750 *Bon*

A French porcelain-mounted ormolu mantel clock, the 4¼in (11cm) enamel dial signed Julien Leroy à Paris, with bell striking Japy Frères movement, c1855, 19¾in (50cm) high.
£2,800–3,200 *S*

A French Empire ormolu mantel clock, the dial signed L. Mallet, H & MDD Orleans, with 8-day movement in outside countwheel striking on a bell, c1800, 14in (35.5cm) high.
£800–900 *DN(H)*

A Louis XVI style gilt-bronze-mounted mantel clock, inscribed Maple & Co Ltd, Paris, with champlevé enamel columns and green and white Wedgwood jasperware plaques, c1900, 16in (40.5cm) high.
£1,600–2,000 *B&B*

A rosewood mantel clock, inlaid with brass and mother-of-pearl, the white enamel dial inscribed Henri Marc, Paris, the 8-day movement striking on a bell, mid-19thC, 12¼in (31cm) high.
£500–550 *Bea(E)*

A French mantel clock, the rims applied with ebonised scrolled mounts, interspersed by inlaid mother-of-pearl and boulle panels, the striking movement by Hy Marc, Paris, 19thC, 15½in (39.5cm) high.
£650–750 *GAK*

A French ormolu and malachite-mounted mantel clock, with 4in (10cm) gilt dial, the bell striking movement signed Pons Medaille d'Argent 1823, with silk suspension, c1840, 24½in (62cm) high.
£5,500–6,500 *Bon*

A French Oriental style gilt-brass mantel clock, with 5in (12.5cm) enamel dial, 2 train gong striking movement stamped GV 4634 64 Marti et C, with Brocot escapement, c1890, 21in (53cm) high.
£1,600–2,000 *S*

r. A French spelter mantel clock, by Moreau, in the form of a cherub lying on a grassy bank, entitled 'L'Amour en Fête', c1880, 15in (38cm) high.
£700–800 *HAC*

A French Louis XVI ormolu and white marble mantel clock, the enamel dial signed Rouviere A Paris, the twin train movement with silk suspension and outside countwheel strike, 19¼in (49cm) high.
£7,000–8,000 *P*

A French Directoire gilt and patinated bronze 'au bon sauvage' mantel clock, surmounted by figures of Paul and Virginie, with enamel dial, silk suspension, anchor movement with outer countwheel striking on a bell, restored, c1800, 18½in (47cm) high.
£14,000–16,000 *S(Am)*

A French Empire gilt patinated and silvered bronze sculptural mantel clock, the enamel dial signed à Paris, with silk suspension, anchor movement striking on a bell, c1810, 17in (43cm) high.
£3,500–4,000 *S(Am)*

A French ormolu mantel clock, the 8-day 2 train bell striking movement with silk suspension, mid-19thC, 20in (51cm) high.
£400–450 *Bri*

A French alabaster and brass mantel clock, with swinging cherub pendulum and 8-day striking movement, c1870, 13½in (34.5cm) high.
£850–950 *BED*

A French gilt-brass mantel clock, with enamel dial, Brocot escapement, the 8-day movement striking the hour and half-hour on a coiled gong, c1870, 13in (33cm) high.
£2,000–2,500 *PAO*

Transporting a Clock

The spring from which the pendulum is suspended is fragile, and may break when a clock is moved. Spring-driven clocks with a short pendulum, such as English bracket and mantel clocks, and most 19thC French clocks, should be held upright when carried. The pendulum, if detachable, should be removed or the back should be packed with tissue paper. When transporting a longcase clock, remove the weights and pendulum. The hood should be taken off, and the dial and movement packed separately.

A French four-glass mantel clock, with Brocot escapement, and striking movement, c1870, 12½in (32cm) high.
£800–900 *SO*

A French ormolu mantel clock, with decorated porcelain panels, c1880, 12in (30.5cm) high.
£1,600–1,800 *TUR*

A French brass-cased four-glass mantel clock, the 3¾in (9.5cm) enamel dial with visible escapement, gong striking movement, c1880, 13in (33cm) high.
£450–500 *Bon*

A French tortoiseshell and gilt-metal mantel clock, with white enamel dial and 8-day movement, 19thC, 13½in (34.5cm) high.
£2,000–2,500 *AH*

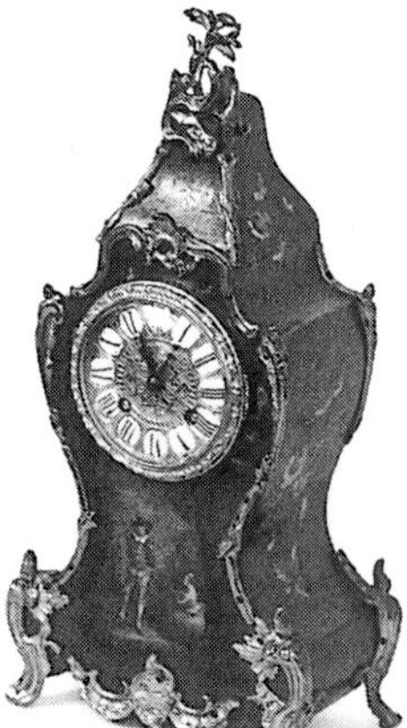

A French painted mantel clock, applied with gilt-metal foliage and scrolled mounts, 19thC, 13½in (34.5cm) high.
£400–450 *GAK*

A French gilt-metal mantel clock, with blue porcelain dial, 8-day movement, 19thC, 16in (40.5cm) high.
£1,000–1,200 *AH*

A French ormolu and porcelain-mounted mantel clock, with floral painted dial and 8-day bell striking movement, 19thC, 14in (35.5cm) wide.
£900–1,000 *P(S)*

A French gilt-metal and marble mantel clock, with white enamel dial and 8-day movement, 19thC, 22¼in (56.5cm) high.
£850–950 *AH*

A chromium-plated clock and barometer set, with gilt cherubs, c1890, 18in (45.5cm) high.
£550–650 *DKH*

Insurance Values

Always insure your valuable antiques for what it would cost to replace with a similar item, regardless of the original price paid. Both dealers and auctioneers will provide a valuation service for a fee.

A fruitwood 8-day table clock, by Ignatius Fliry, Thannhausen, with verge escapement and striking on 2 bells, c1770, 19in (48cm) high.
£3,000–3,500 *S*

A Black Forest oak mantel clock, carved with a ram and a dog, striking on the hour and half-hour, c1850, 8in (20.5cm) high.
£1,600–1,800 *REF*

A French red boulle mantel clock, of waisted form, with gilt mounts, c1895, 12in (30.5cm) high.
£1,400–1,600 *TUR*

A carved oak mantel clock, by Winterhalder & Hofmeier, with brass arched dial and silvered chapter ring, subsidiary dials for strike/silent, chiming on 8 gongs, 19thC, 26½in (67.5cm) high.
£300–350 *M*

A Venetian rococo giltwood and etched glass mantel clock, with a white enamel dial, mid-18thC, 29in (73.5cm) high.
£3,000–3,500 *S(NY)*

A French inlaid mahogany lancet mantel clock, with 8-day striking movement, c1900, 11½in (29cm) high.
£320–350 *CHe*

A French brass-cased mantel clock, with a black and gilt chapter ring, 8-day movement striking on a bell, late 19thC, 11¾in (30cm) high.
£350–400 *WW*

l. A German mahogany mantel clock, by Winterhalder & Hofmeier, with twin fusee movement and quarter-chiming, late 19thC, 10in (25.5cm) high.
£450–550 *TPA*

Mystery & Novelty Clocks

A Directoire gilt-bronze, marble and enamel annular clock, the blue enamel celestial globe with white chapter ring painted with Roman and Arabic numerals, late 18thC, 12in (30.5cm) high.
£5,200–5,800 *SLM*

A gilt-bronze group of the 3 graces supporting a clock, the chapter ring with Roman numerals, marked d'Après Germain Pilon, early 19thC, 40in (101.5cm) high.
£8,000–9,000 *S(S)*

A French ormolu, marble and bronze globe clock, with a winged cherub standing to one side, on a stepped base, c1860, 10½in (26.5cm) high.
£800–900 *GH*

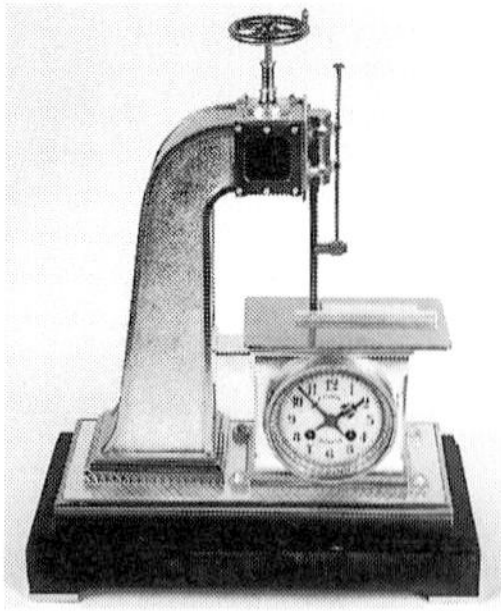

A French gilt and silver metal clock, in the form of a bandsaw, c1820, 15in (38cm) high.
£3,000–3,300 *CHe*

A Viennese *grande sonnerie* picture clock, with 56-hour striking and repeating movement, c1840, 17¼in (44cm) wide.
£800–900 *TPA*

r. A mystery clock, by Ansonia, New York, with a spelter figure, with 8-day movement, c1887, 28in (71cm) high.
£800–900 *CHe*

An automaton picture clock, oil on metal, with 8-day timepiece movement powering a windmill and watermill, c1860, 24in (61cm) wide.
£2,250–2,500 *DSP*

The Mystery Clock

One of the most popular 19thC novelties is the mystery clock. The most common style shows a female figure holding a pendulum, which seems otherwise unconnected to the clock. However, the movement causes the figure to rotate almost imperceptibly to the left and right. The motion set up causes the pendulum to swing, apparently unaided. Other mystery variations include a figure holding up a timepiece, and an elephant holding a timepiece in his trunk.

A French mystery clock, c1890, 78in (198cm) high with pedestal.
£8,000–9,500 *BED*

A French bronze and white marble figural clock, the figure by Barbedienne Foundry, Paris, the works by Mascuraud, minor damage, c1900, 37½in (95.5cm) high.
£1,400–1,600 *SK(B)*

l. A French globe mantel clock, with silvered chapter ring around a paper printed globe signed Richards Chronosphere Patent 19460, the base containing a lever movement, early 20thC, 12in (30cm) high.
£2,500–3,000 *Bon*

Skeleton Clocks

A brass skeleton clock of triple steeple form, with double fusee movement striking on a bell, stepped base on marble plinth, early 19thC, 18in (45.5cm) high.
£600–700 *PFK*

A brass skeleton timepiece, with pierced and silvered 8in (20.5cm) chapter ring, the fusee movement with anchor escapement and wood rod pendulum with pewter bob, passing strike on the top mounted bell, probably by Evans of Handsworth, c1870, 17¾in (45cm) high, with a glass dome.
£1,600–1,800 *S(S)*

Quality of Skeleton Clocks

The quality of skeleton clocks is of paramount importance. The wheelwork should be finely executed and better clocks may have 5 or 6 spokes to each wheel instead of the usual 4 found on a bracket clock. Other signs of quality include well executed pendulums, finely turned pillars, decorative collet work, and well laid out dials.

An Edwardian brass skeleton timepiece, the silvered chapter ring inscribed R. Donaldson, 8 Hinde Street, W1, under a glass dome with an oak base, on ball feet, 15in (38cm) high.
£380–420 *WW*

A Victorian cathedral skeleton clock, with 7½in (19cm) pierced chapter ring, 2 train gong striking fusee and chain movement with deadbeat escapement, gridiron pendulum, 5-spoke wheels, bolt type stopwork, c1870, 30½in (77.5cm) high.
£3,700–4,200 *S*

l. A skeleton timepiece, with engraved scissor-shaped frame, white enamel chapter ring, with glass dome, on ebonised base stamped 'Ms Honorables, Paris, Londres', 19thC, 7in (18cm) high.
£400–450 *Oli*

Travel Clocks

An Austrian green stained and ivory travel clock, signed François Syré, Vienne, with enamel dial, the shaped movement with duplex escapement, 19thC, 3¾in (9.5cm) high, in a fitted leather travelling case.
£1,300–1,500 *P*

A Victorian silver travel clock, with embossed design, the dial marked A. Jones, 154 Regent St, on a wooden and leather base, Birmingham 1902, 3in (7.5cm) high.
£140–160 *GAK*

r. A Swiss travel clock, signed Albert Barker, London, the white dial with Roman numerals, c1900, 6¾in (17cm) square, in original case.
£400–450 *TPA*

Wall Clocks

A mahogany wall clock, signed E. Emanuel, The Hard, Portsea, with white painted dial and fusee movement, c1860, 23½in (60cm) diam.
£2,000–2,200 *L*

A mahogany and brass-inlaid wall clock, by William Loof, Tunbridge Wells, with 8-day fusee movement, c1840, 7in (43cm) high.
£2,000–2,200 *PAO*

A mahogany weight-driven striking tavern clock, by Sam Thorpe, Abberly, with 18in (45.5cm) painted dial and alarm mechanism, early 19thC, 66in (168cm) high.
£1,600–1,800 *Bon*

r. An ebonised drop dial wall clock, with 11in (28cm) blue painted dial, twin fusee movement, c1900, 37in (94cm) high.
£260–320 *Bon(C)*

A Regency mahogany and brass-inlaid wall clock, by Frodsham, London, with fusee movement, c1820, 15in (38cm) diam.
£1,800–2,200 *BED*

A mahogany wall clock, by G. Staples, London, with 8in (20.5cm) engraved dial, verge escapement, c1800, 10in (25.5cm) high.
£2,750–3,250 *DSP*

A hook and spike pantry alarm wall timepiece, attributed to John Whitehurst, the 6in (15cm) brass dial signed W. Sleigh Stockton, with 30-hour movement, c1840, 6in (15cm) high.
£460–520 *S*

A mahogany and brass-inlaid wall clock, by Halfhide, London, with 8-day fusee movement, c1825, 17in (43cm) diam.
£1,200–1,400 *BED*

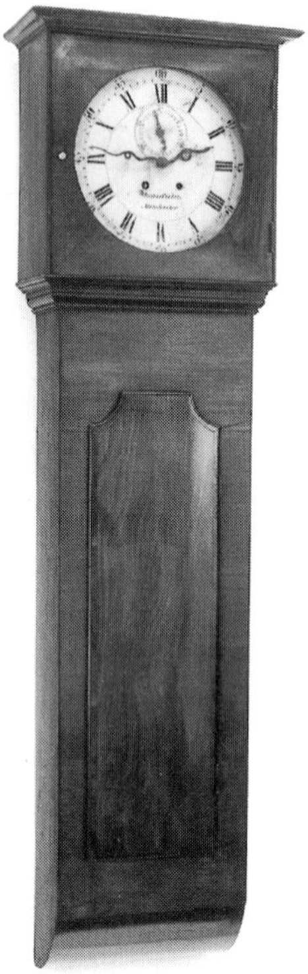

A Georgian mahogany wall clock, the enamel dial marked James Porter, Manchester, 58in (147.5cm) high.
£400–450 *LRG*

A Victorian walnut and mother-of-pearl wall clock, with 12in (30.5cm) painted dial and fusee movement, 29½in (75cm) high.
£280–320 *DOC*

A mahogany weight-driven tavern wall clock, by Handley & Moore, the dial painted with Roman numerals, single train movement, c1800, 49½in (125.5cm) high.
£1,600–1,800 *Bon*

A George III oak wall timepiece, by Henry Tory, Hale, with 10in (25.5cm) square silvered dial, 30-hour weight driven movement, 4 ringed pillars, anchor escapement and alarm, 30in (76cm) high.
£1,200–1,400 *DN*

A black chinoiserie Act of Parliament clock, by Daniel Vauginon, London, the dial with turned finials and gilt chapters, late 18thC, 62¼in (158cm) high.
£6,500–7,500 *P(NE)*

A Dutch provincial mahogany wall clock, the 8-day movement striking on a bell, the arched painted dial with rural scenes and allegorical figures, the domed hood surmounted by the figure of Atlas, the pendulum bob aperture surmounted by a cockerel, 19thC, 58in (147.5cm) high.
£650–800 *WW*

A Black Forest carved wood flute wall clock, with 9in (23cm) wooden dial, 3 train brass-plated weight driven movement, playing one of two tunes on 8 pipes, in an oak case, c1885, 46in (117cm) high.
£2,800–3,200 *S*

At the commencement of the music a pair of doors below the dial open to reveal a brightly painted flautist in Bavarian costume.

A Dutch *staartklok*, with 30-hour weight-driven movement, 11½in (29cm) painted dial with Roman numerals and arcarded floral minute ring, centre brass alarm setting disc, moonphase in arch, 19thC, 50in (127cm) high.
£360–400 *Bon*

A Dutch walnut and marquetry *staartklok*, the movement with turned corner posts, anchor escapement and outside countwheel strike, 19thC, 49in (125cm) high.
£1,400–1,600 *P*

A staartklok *is a 19thC bracketed wall clock made in Friesland in the Netherlands.*

American Clocks

An American multi-wood inlay wall clock, by Ansonia Watch & Clock Co, with hourly strike movement, c1870, 38in (96.5cm) high.
£550–600 *BWC*

An American mahogany veneered banjo clock, by Geo. Hatch, Attleboro, Mass, for Riggs & Bro, Philadelphia, with 8-day weight driven movement, c1880, 33in (84cm) high.
£800–900 *OT*

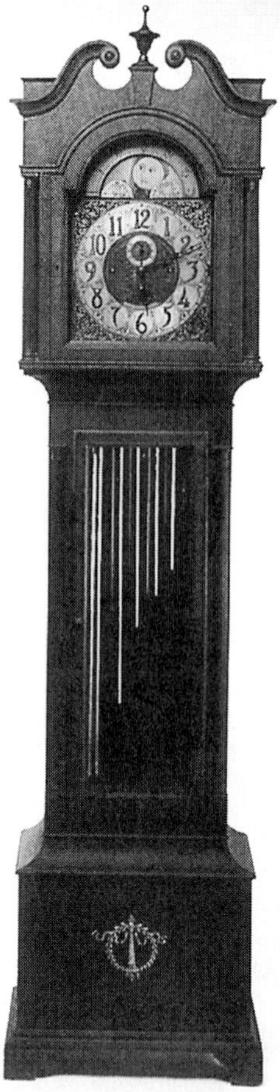

An American mahogany tallcase clock, by Colonial Mfg Co, Zeeland, Mich, early 20thC, 96in (244cm) high.
£1,500–1,800 *SLM*

An American mahogany tallcase hall clock, by Walter H. Durfee, retailed by Tiffany & Co, New York, with a John Elliot of London 8-day precision quarter-hour chime on gongs, hour strike movement and precision mercury compensating pendulum, c1890, 96in (244cm) high.
£5,500–6,500 *JAA*

l. A Federal mahogany tallcase clock, inscribed Wasbrough, Duggan & Co, Bristol, pediment and feet reduced, c1800, 99in (251cm) high.
£3,000–3,500 *S(NY)*

A walnut gingerbread shelf clock, by Ingraham Clock Co, c1895, 12in (30.5cm) high.
£150–200 *OT*

An American mahogany shelf clock, by Daniel Pratt, with mirror glass panel, c1837, 33¾in (85.5cm) high.
£900–1,000 *A&A*

l. An American walnut shelf clock, by E. N. Welch Clock Co, with 8-day time and strike mechanism with alarm, c1870, 20in (51cm) high.
£200–250 *OT*

An oak 8-day drop dial clock, by Sessions Clock Co, c1895, 32in (81.5cm) high.
£300–350 *OT*

English Regulators

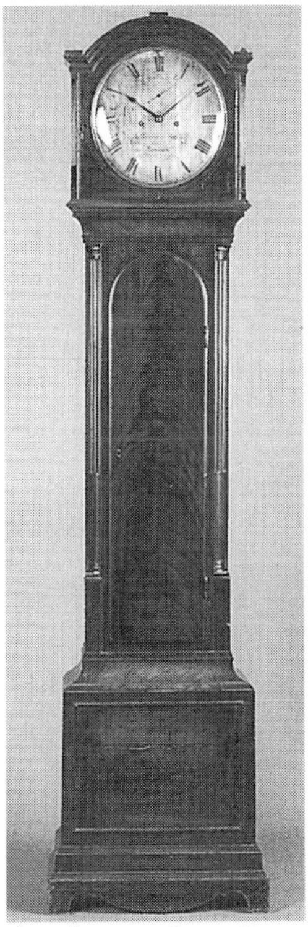

A mahogany domestic regulator, signed Barwise & Sons, London, with silvered 12in (30.5cm) dial, the 2 train 5 pillar 8-day movement with deadbeat escapement, c1820, 80in (203cm) high.
£5,800–6,200 *S(S)*

An oak railway longcase regulator, signed Dent, London, Clock Maker to The Queen, No. 939, the 4 pillar movement with deadbeat escapement, beat setting and maintaining power, c1850, 76in (194cm) high.
£3,000–3,500 *Bon*

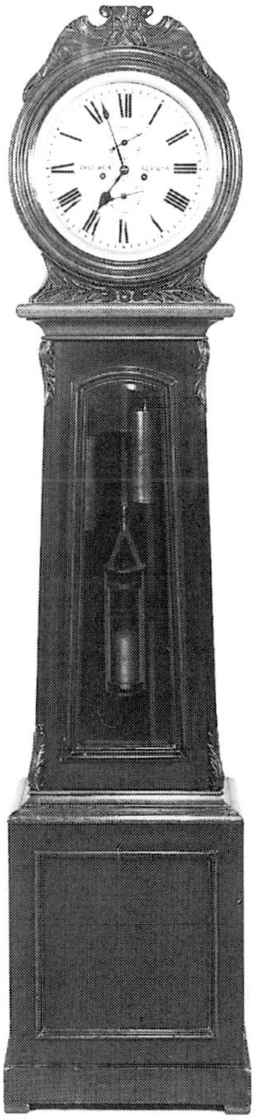

A teak wall regulator, by J. W. Benson, London, with white dial, c1860, 47¼in (120cm) high.
£1,600–1,800 *TPA*

l. A mahogany longcase regulator, inscribed James Weir, Glasgow, with mercury-filled brass and steel pendulum, 19thC, 83½in (212cm) high.
£1,600–2,000 *P(S)*

Vienna Regulators

A burr-walnut and ebonised Vienna regulator, by Gustav Becker, with weight-driven movement, 19thC, 53½in (136cm) high.
£1,400–1,600 *AH*

A Vienna walnut and ebonised regulator, the weight-driven 2 train deadbeat movement with rack striking on a gong, trapezoid plates, maintaining power and beat adjustment on the crutch, late 19thC, 51¼in (130cm) high.
£450–500 *S(Am)*

Pocket Watches

A Swiss nickel pocket watch, the cream dial marked Aeonicloc, with stop and alarm button, 30-hour movement, 1930s, 64mm diam.
£160–180 *TIH*

A 14ct gold full hunter watch, signed Elgin Natl Watch Co, with enamel dial, gilt full plate lever movement, c1900, 50mm diam.
£400–480 *Bon(C)*

A Swiss silver keyless lever watch, signed Rolex, with enamel dial, the movement jewelled to the centre with micrometer regulation, Birmingham 1940, 51mm diam.
£350–400 *P*

A Swiss gold full hunter watch, signed Narcisse Dreyfus, Paris, with enamel dial, the nickel movement under a glazed cover, the case with applied initials, c1900, 50mm diam.
£300–350 *Bon(C)*

A gilt pair cased verge pocket watch, signed Thos Garnier, the enamel dial with owner's initials in place of numerals, c1780, 48mm diam.
£950–1,000 *PT*

A 18ct gold open-face five-minute repeating watch, by Tiffany & Co, New York, c1900, 40mm diam.
£2,200–2,500 *S(G)*

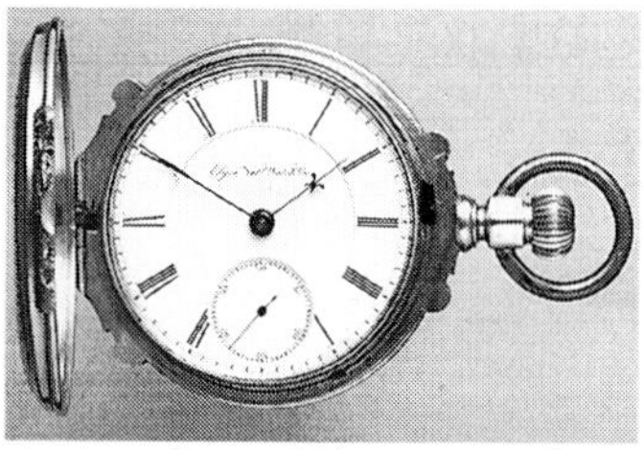

An American gold hunter watch, the white enamel dial signed Elgin Natl Watch Co, the keyless gilt full plate movement with going barrel, marked 'Mermod & Jaccard Jewelry Co - Warranted 18 Carat Fine', c1885, 52mm diam.
£750–850 *PT*

An Ingersoll chrome-cased Mickey Mouse pocket watch, by Ingersoll, with Albert chain, T bar, and enamelled fob, c1940, 50mm diam.
£250–300 *BWe*

A silver pocket watch, by Kendal & Dent, with key wind fusee movement, restored, Birmingham 1891, 50mm diam.
£150–170 *TIH*

A silver pair cased verge stop watch, the champlevé dial signed Tho Rayment, London, 18thC, 52mm diam.
£2,000–2,200 *P*

An 18ct two-tone gold open-face digital watch, by Van Cleef & Arpels, dial and movement signed, c1930, 42mm diam.
£1,800–2,000 *S(HK)*

An 18ct gold open-face watch, by Simon Willard Jnr, Boston, dial, movement and dust cover signed, stamped with Chester hallmarks and casemaker's mark 'E.I.', c1830, 52mm diam.
£2,500–3,000 *S(NY)*

A Swiss silver quarter-repeating automaton verge open-face watch, with blue enamel dial, fusee movement, c1810, 58mm diam.
£2,500–2,750 *PT*

An 18ct four-colour gold pocket watch, with Roman numerals, c1814, 64mm diam.
£2,000–2,200 *BWC*

A Victorian silver lady's fob watch, 32mm diam.
£40–50 *HEI*

A Swiss white metal triple calendar moonphase pocket watch, c1890, 78mm diam.
£700–800 *B&B*

A Swiss 12ct gold fob watch, with engraved bezel and case back, c1908, 32mm wide.
£80–100 *PSA*

A Swiss 18ct gold half hunter watch, with enamel dial, in a plain polished case, c1929, 45mm diam.
£280–320 *Bon(C)*

A Swiss 9ct gold pocket watch, with Arabic numerals and 17 jewels, c1921, 50mm diam.
£200–250 *PSA*

l. A Swiss gold-plated hunter pocket watch, with quarter repeat mechanism, 15 jewels, c1920, 50mm diam.
£400–450 *PSA*

Miller's is a price GUIDE not a price LIST

Wristwatches

A 9ct gold manual dress wristwatch, by J. W. Benson, c1971, 28mm diam, with original box and documents.
£220–250 *BWC*

A Breitling 18ct pink gold wristwatch, the silvered dial and movement signed, 17 jewels, 1940s, 26mm square.
£680–750 *S(Am)*

A Buren wristwatch, with green dial and mechanical stainless steel case, Swiss, c1949, 25mm diam.
£80–100 *TIH*

A Cartier platinum and diamond wristwatch, signed, with fine mesh bracelet and diamond set clasp, c1920, 22mm wide.
£3,500–4,000 *S*

An Ingersoll lady's dress wristwatch, decorated with marcasites, c1920, 83mm wide.
£40–50 *HEI*

An Eberhard & Co 18ct gold single button chronograph wristwatch, dial and movement signed, c1940, 40mm diam.
£2,000–2,200 *S*

A Jaeger LeCoultre stainless steel centre seconds military wristwatch, marked 6B/346, 3987/48, c1948, 32mm diam.
£360–400 *Bon*

A Lemania British military issue two-register chronograph, 1950s, 42mm diam.
£400–450 *BWC*

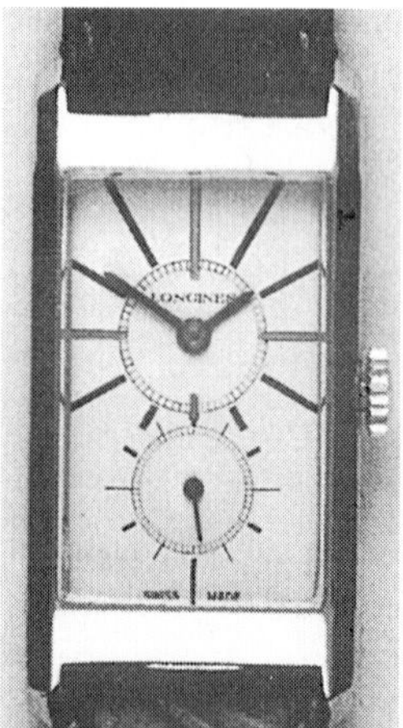

A Longines steel duo-dial wristwatch, with black crocodile strap, c1931, 32mm long.
£1,400–1,600 *PT*

An Oris gold-plated watch, with black dial, 17 jewels, Swiss, c1950, 32mm diam.
£80–100 *TIH*

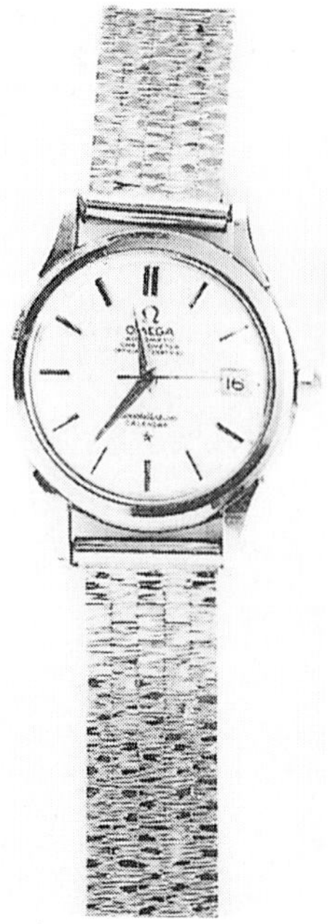

An Omega 18ct gold automatic centre seconds calendar watch, fitted on a non-factory bracelet, 1959, 34mm diam.
£800–900 *Bon*

A Swiss 18ct gold chronograph wristwatch, by Ulysse Nardin, with 2 subsidiary dials, c1910, 33mm diam.
£3,000–3,500 *S(HK)*

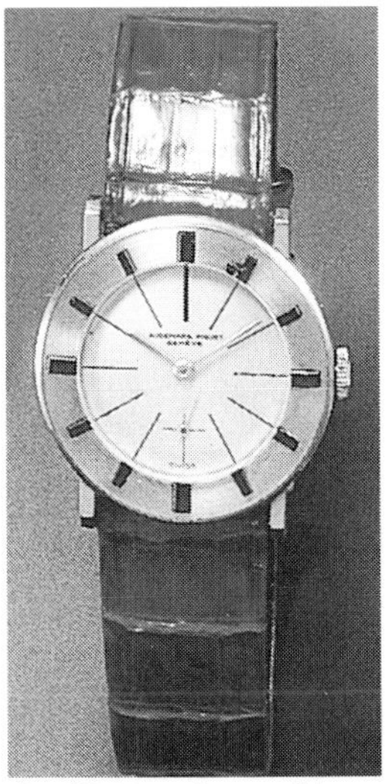

An 18ct two-tone gold and sapphire wristwatch, dial and movement signed Audemars Piguet, No. 55649, c1949, 29mm diam.
£5,000–5,500 *S(NY)*

A Revue stainless steel wristwatch, with automatic date, 21 jewels, Swiss, restored, 1960s, 38mm wide.
£80–100 *TIH*

A Rolex 9ct gold wristwatch, Birmingham 1960, 30mm wide.
£450–500 *Bon*

A Scopas 18ct gold 2 register chronograph, with 17 jewels, Swiss, 1960s, 45mm diam.
£350–400 *BWC*

A Vacheron & Constantin steel centre seconds automatic wristwatch, with blue crocodile strap, c1960, 35mm diam.
£3,000–3,500 *PT*

A Sicura wristwatch, with chrome case and black dial, Swiss, c1960, 38mm wide.
£80–100 *TIH*

A Rotary stainless steel watch and bracelet, with automatic day and date, Swiss, 1950s, 38mm wide.
£80–100 *TIH*

A Universal 14ct gold chronograph calendar wristwatch with registers, moonphases and tachometer, Swiss, c1945, 35mm diam.
£1,500–1,800 *S(G)*

A platinum and diamond wristwatch, on platinum expanding bracelet, 15 jewels, Swiss, c1920, 38mm long.
£800–950 *PSA*

A Zodiac automatic wristwatch, with power reserve indicator, Swiss, c1960, 29mm diam.
£180–200 *BWC*

BAROMETERS
Stick Barometers

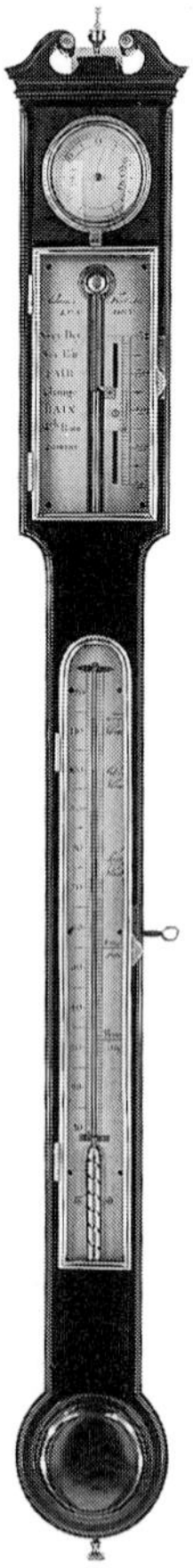

A mahogany stick barometer, by George Adams, London, c1810, 42in (106.5cm) high.
£6,800–8,000 *AW*

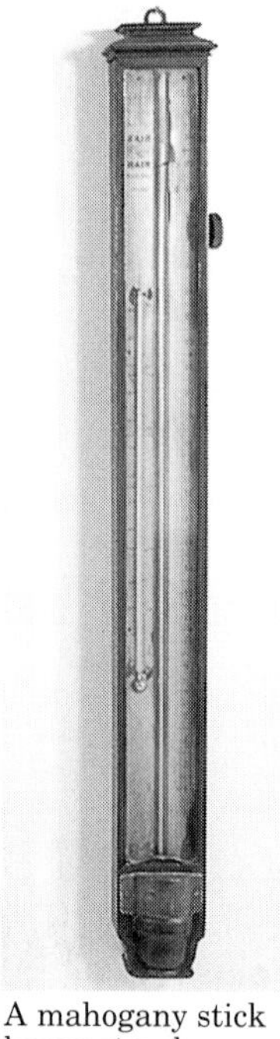

A mahogany stick barometer, by J. Hughes, 19thC, 38in (96.5cm) high.
£2,000–2,400 *JNic*

A mahogany and chequer-strung angle barometer, the silvered dial signed H. Banister, Lichfield, late 18thC, 32in (81.5cm) high.
£2,500–3,000 *P*

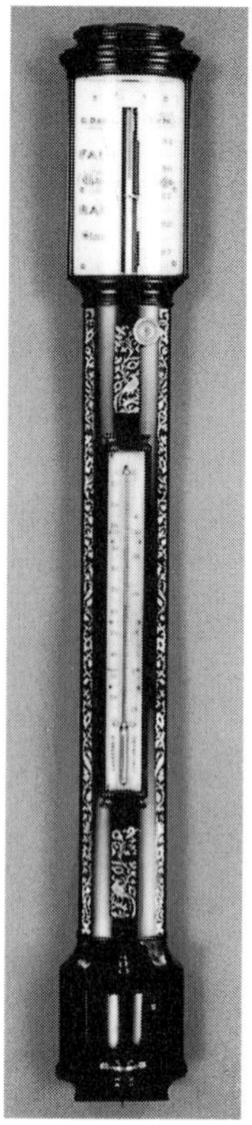

r. An ebony and mother-of-pearl bowfront stick barometer, by G. Davis, Leeds, with ivory scale, c1840, 39in (99cm) high.
£4,200–4,700 *PAO*

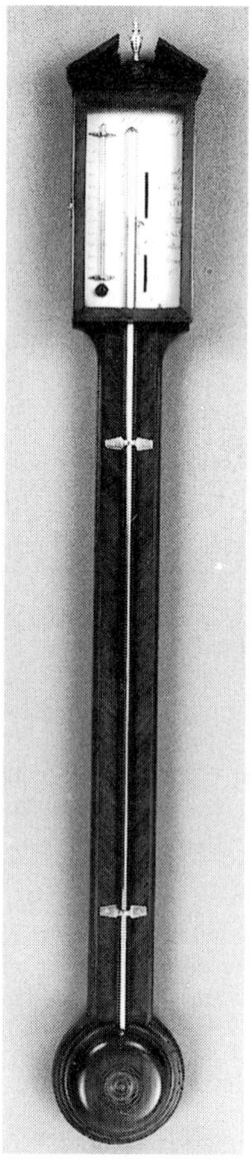

A mahogany stick barometer, by P. Donegan & Co, London, with exposed mercury tube and broken architectural top, c1820, 39in (99cm) high.
£1,750–2,000 *PAO*

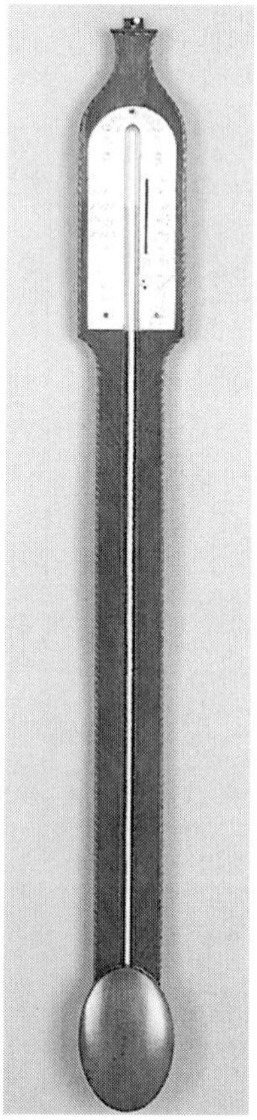

A mahogany stick barometer, by Balthazar Knie, Edinburgh, signed, with chequered stringing and oval cistern cover, c1800, 39¼in (99.5cm) high.
£2,500–3,000 *S*

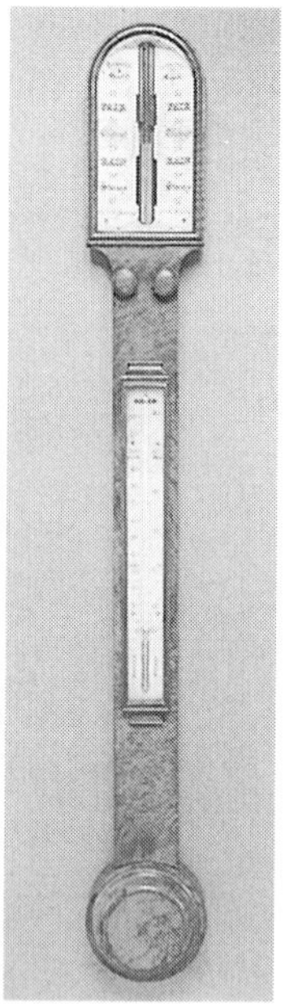

A Victorian walnut-cased stick barometer, by Carpenter & Westley, London, with ivory register plate, the case with an arch top and turned cistern cover, 37in (94cm) high.
£900–1,000 *DN*

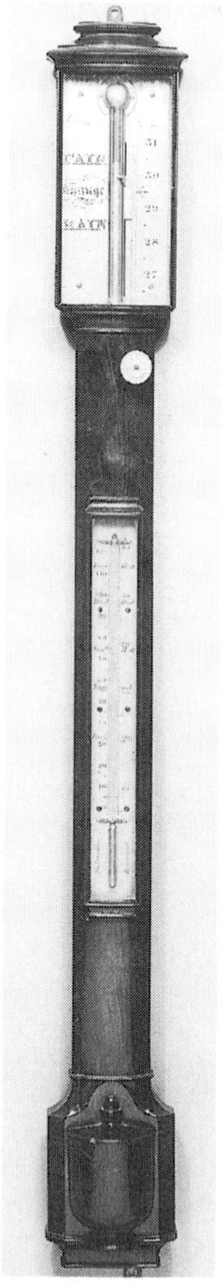

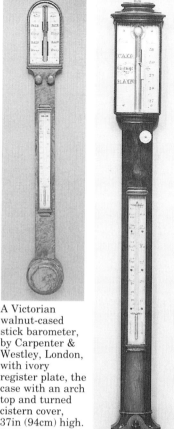

A mahogany bowfront stick barometer, by Dollond, London, the signed silvered dial with vernier, the trunk set with a mercury thermometer with silvered scale above an urn-shaped cistern cover, c1840, 38in (96.5cm) high.
£4,200–4,600 *P*

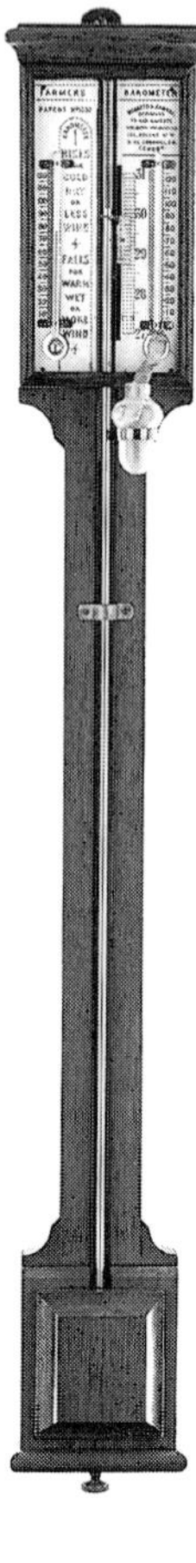

l. An oak farmers' barometer, by Negretti & Zambra, London, with porcelain plates, wet and dry bulb thermometer, c1880, 42in (106.5cm) high.
£1,200–1,600 *AW*

The wet and dry bulb thermometer would enable farmers to calculate the relative humidity, enabling them to make informed decisions on storage and planting of crops.

l. An oak miner's barometer, by Negretti & Zambra, London, with silvered brass scale, c1880, 36in (91.5cm) high.
£1,000–1,200 *AW*

This type of barometer was made obligatory equipment under the Mines Act of 1872. Miners needed to locate areas of low pressure, where combustible gases tended to concentrate.

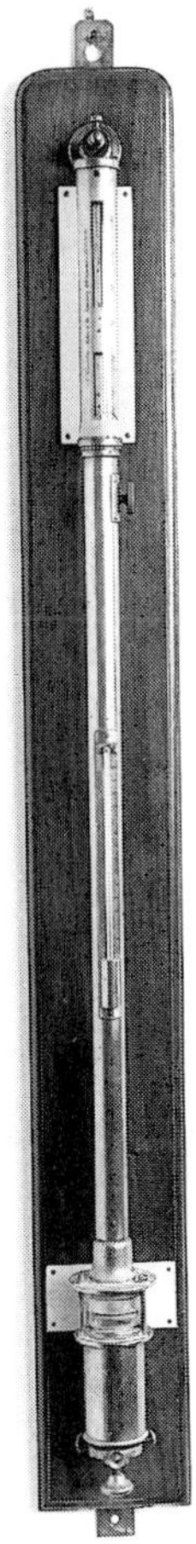

l. A Fortin barometer, by Negretti & Zambra, London, with brass case, mounted on a mahogany board, c1880, 44in (112cm) high.
£1,100–1,400 *AW*

The Fortin barometer was invented by Nicholas Fortin, and has been used in science laboratories since about 1870 because of its high degree of accuracy.

Bulb-Cistern Tube

In early English barometers the tube and the cistern for storing the mercury were separate components. The bulb-cistern tube, introduced in the early 18thC, incorporated both elements, but was not an immediate success as it made the barometer less accurate and more difficult to move. With the increase of mass-production in the 19thC, the inexpensive bulb-cistern became better established.

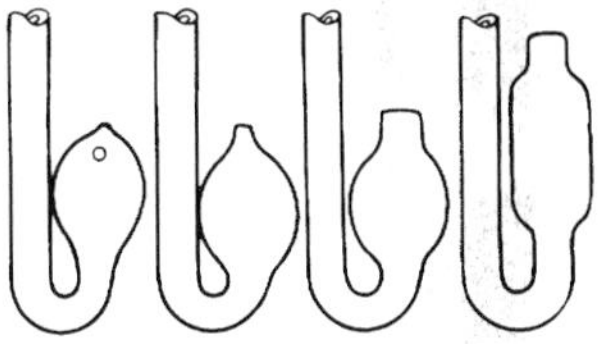

Above Bulb-cistern tubes with their approximate date of introduction.

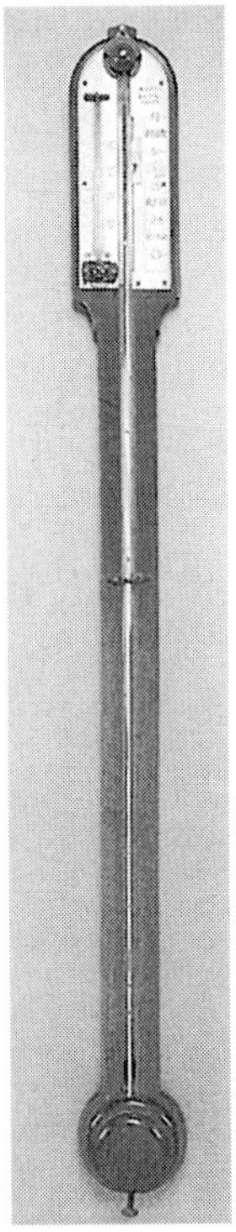

r. A rosewood stick barometer, by Negretti & Zambra, the ivory register plate with thermometer and vernier scale, signed, c1880, 36in (91.5cm) high.
£460–500 *DN*

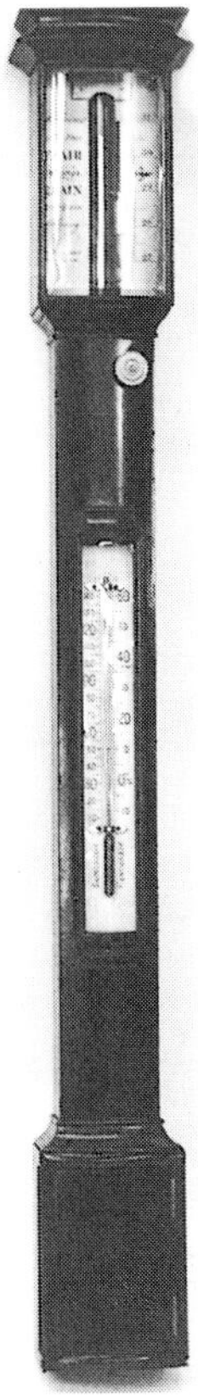

A mahogany bowfront stick barometer, signed Twaddell, Glasgow, with ivory register plate, inset thermometer on trunk, c1870, 38in (96.5cm) high.
£1,600–2,000 *GAK*

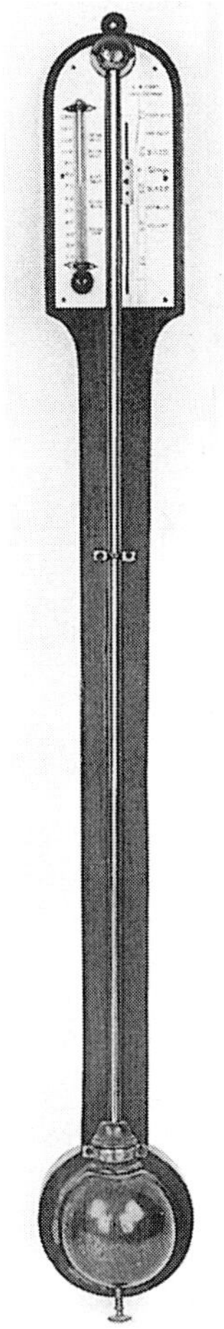

l. A Victorian rosewood stick barometer, the bone register signed 'I. D. Vent, Cheltenham', set with thermometer, the trunk with exposed tube and turned cover, c1860, 35¾in (91cm) high.
£300–350 *Bon(C)*

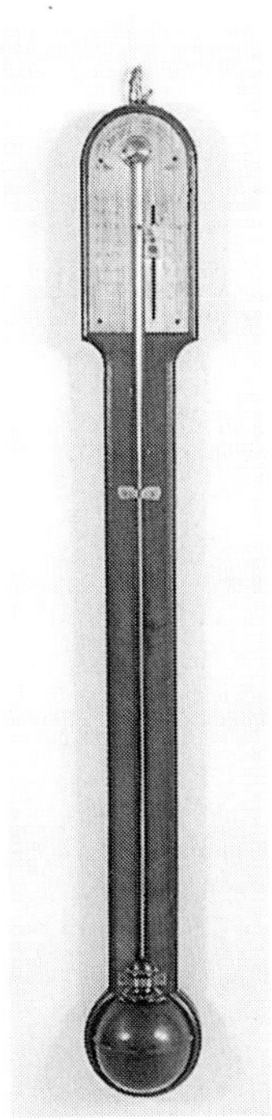

A George III mahogany stick barometer, by J. & W. Watkins, London, the feather crossbanded case with domed top and ball base, c1790, 36in (91.5cm) long.
£1,800–2,000 *JNic*

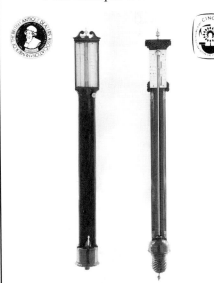

Wheel Barometers

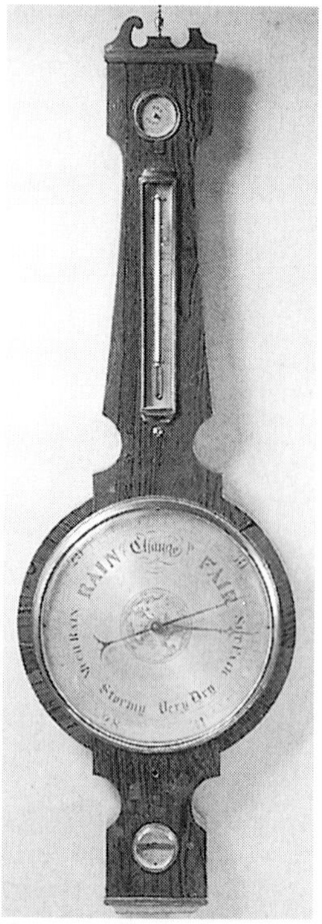

A rosewood wheel barometer, by Abraham, Bath, with 12in (30.5cm) silvered dial, thermometer, hygrometer and level, c1840, 45in (114cm) high.
£450–550 *DN*

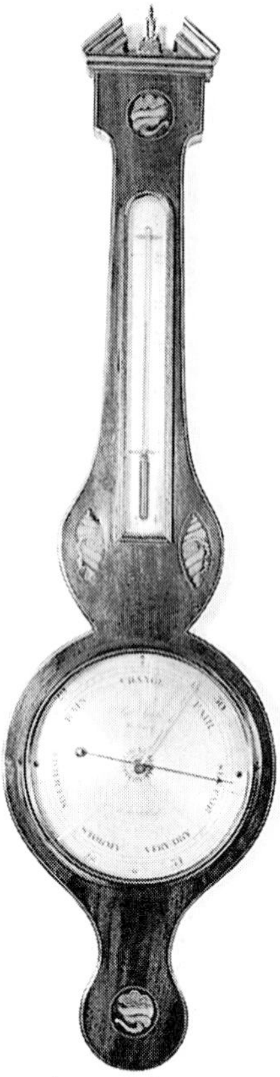

A mahogany barometer, by Josh Aprile, Sudbury, with conch shell inlay, c1830, 36in (91.5cm) high.
£500–550 *Oli*

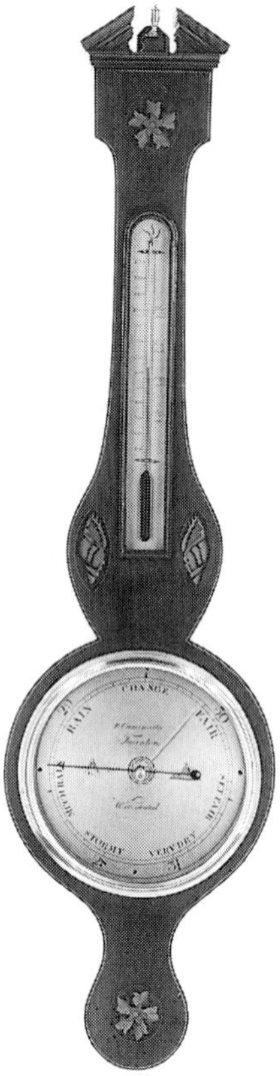

A mahogany wheel barometer, by Caminada, Taunton, boxwood and ebony-strung, inlaid with shell and flowerhead paterae, c1830, 36in (91.5cm) high.
£750–900 *AW*

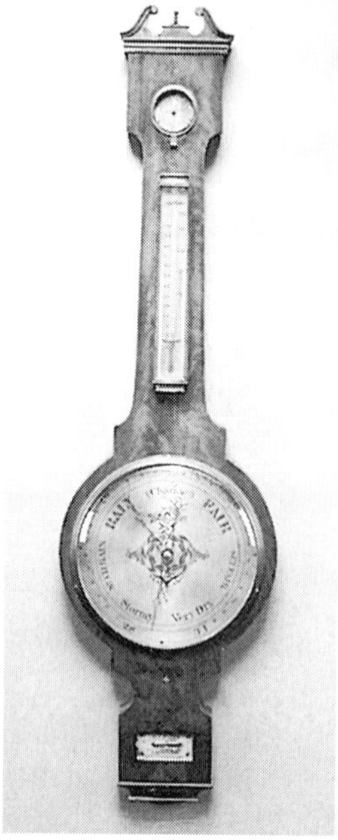

A mahogany wheel barometer, by G. J. Bates, Catfield, c1840, 42½in (108cm) high.
£300–350 *DN*

A flame mahogany five-dial wheel barometer, signed Della Torre, Perth, c1840, 38in (96.5cm) high.
£600–750 *AW*

A flame mahogany wheel barometer, signed Franklin & Co, Manchester, c1830, 45¾in (116cm) high.
£700–800 *Bon(C)*

A walnut veneered wheel barometer, inscribed Gardner & Co, c1860, 43¼in (110cm) long.
£450–550 *P(Sc)*

A mahogany wheel barometer, signed James Gatty, London, inlaid with fan paterae, engraved thermometer and dials, c1800, 37in (94cm) high.
£1,500–1,800 *AW*

A rosewood and mother-of-pearl inlaid wheel barometer, by C. Gerletti, Glasgow, with silvered barometer dial, dry/damp dial and thermometer, signed, 19thC, 45¾in (116cm) high.
£350–400 *P(Sc)*

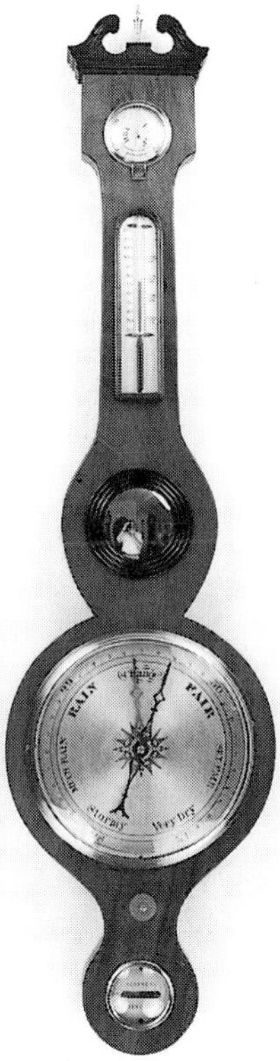

A mahogany five-dial wheel barometer, signed Hartnell, Cirencester, c1840, 38in (96.5cm) high.
£650–750 *PAO*

A mahogany 'upside-down' five-glass wheel barometer, by Laffrancho, Ludlow, c1840, 39in (99cm) high.
£1,000–1,200 *AW*

A mahogany five-dial wheel barometer, by Martinelli, London, c1830, 38in (96.5cm) high.
£650–750 *PAO*

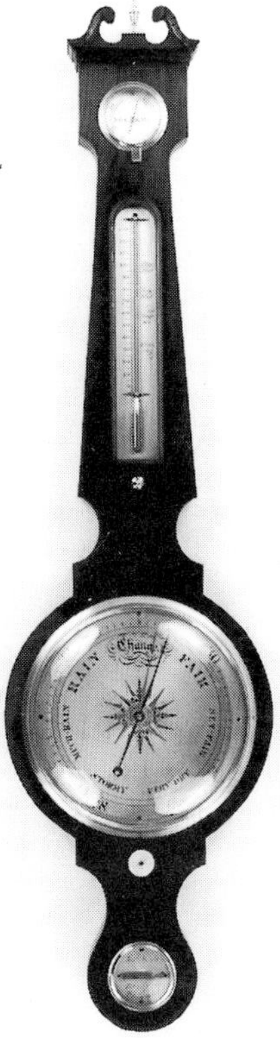

A mahogany four-dial wheel barometer, by Jos Riva, Bridport, c1840, 38in (96.5cm) high.
£750–850 *PAO*

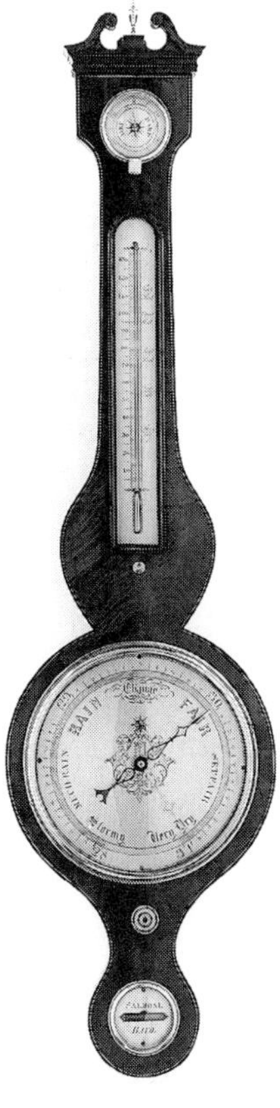

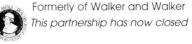

An inlaid mahogany wheel barometer, by Salmoni, Bath, c1830, 39in (99cm) high.
£750–900 *AW*

A mahogany five-dial wheel barometer, c1845, 39in (99cm) high.
£650–750 *AW*

A mahogany five-dial wheel barometer, with swan neck pediment, hygrometer, alcohol thermometer, convex mirror and spirit level, 19thC, 38in (97cm) high.
£400–450 *L*

A French Louis XVI giltwood barometer, the paper dial signed Besombes, Paris, surmounted by a jasperware medallion with putto, thermometer below, late 18thC, 39in (99cm) high.
£800–1,000 *S(Am)*

A French Louis XVI style carved giltwood barometer, with painted and enamelled dial signed Chevallier, the elaborately carved case with doves, garlands, ribbons and emblematic cornucopia, 19thC, 44in (112cm) high.
£1,500–1,750 *SLM*

Aneroid Barometers

Aneroid Barometers

The aneroid barometer, invented in 1843, consists of a small chamber evacuated of air, which rises and falls with changes in atmospheric pressure. From c1865 some aneroid barometers were made to imitate wheel barometers, which were more expensive. A long door in the back of the case indicates a mercury wheel system, whereas an aneroid barometer will have a small hole through which the mechanism can be adjusted. Surveying instruments, for use by surveyors and mining engineers, were made from c1870. Many are equipped with a magnifying glass to help read the small scale divisions.

A silver-cased pocket travelling barometer, signed Callow of Mount Street, Park Lane, with engraved silvered dial, inset thermometer, c1900, 3¼in (8.5cm) square.
£360–400 *Bon(C)*

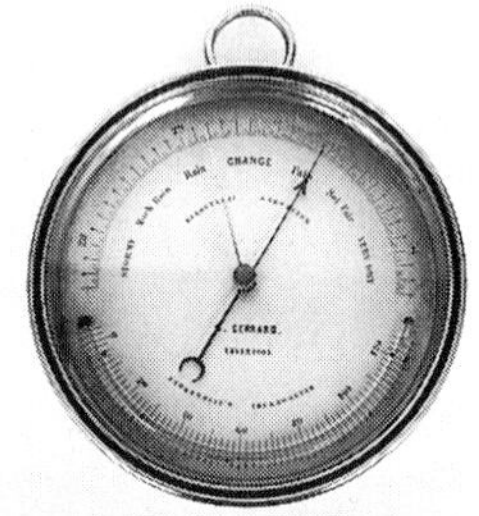

A brass-cased aneroid barometer, signed W. Gerrard, Liverpool, c1865, 5in (12.5cm) diam.
£250–275 *JIL*

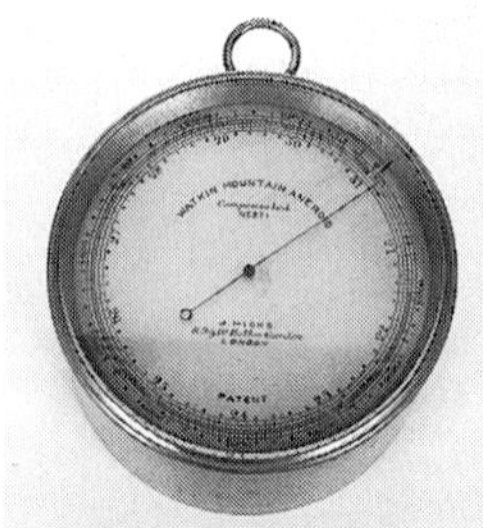

l. An aluminium-cased Watkin Mountain aneroid barometer, by J. Hicks, London, c1900, 5in (12.5cm) diam.
£240–265 *JIL*

A travelling barometer, signed Harrods, with silvered dial and engraved scale, c1930, 6¾in (17cm) square, in a folding leather travelling case.
£80–120 *Bon(C)*

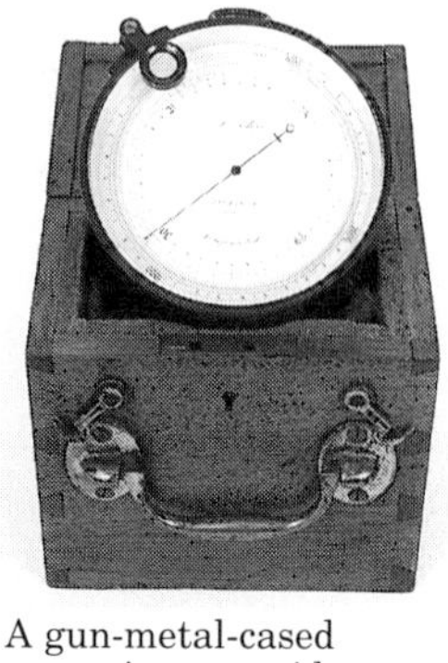

A gun-metal-cased surveying aneroid barometer, by Stanley, London, c1865, 5in (12.5cm) diam.
£750–850 *JIL*

An oak-cased aneroid barometer, 1930s, 12in (30.5cm) high.
£16–20 *CaC*

A brass-cased aneroid barometer, with card dial and exposed movement, c1870, 5in (12.5cm) diam.
£250–300 *AW*

Barographs

An oak-cased barograph, by Negretti & Zambra, London, with bevelled glass and chart drawer, c1900, 9in (23cm) wide.
£1,100–1,200 *AW*

A rosewood-cased barograph, by M. W. Dunscombe, Bristol, c1930, 15in (38cm) wide.
£650–750 *RTw*

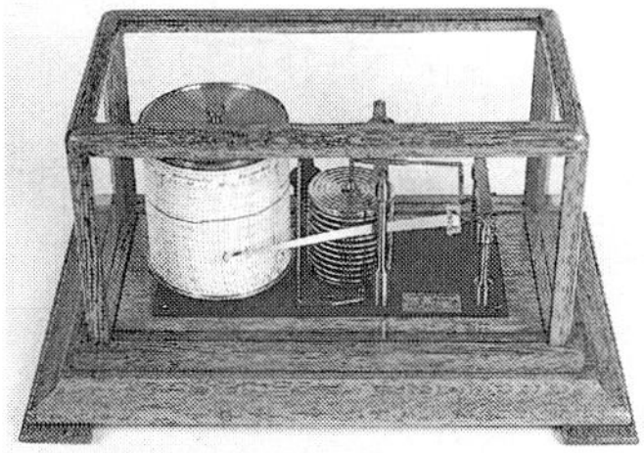

An oak-cased barograph, by Negretti & Zambra, c1930, 15in (38cm) wide.
£500–600 *GeM*

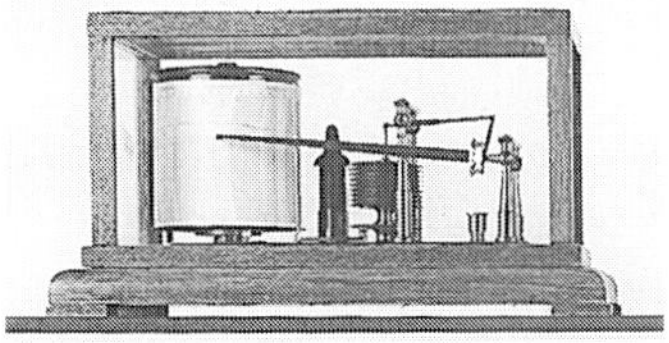

An oak-cased barograph, signed Negretti & Zambra, London, with 9 aneroid bellows, lacquered-brass mechanism, and clockwork recording drum in a glazed case, c1930, 13½in (34.5cm) wide.
£350–400 *Bon(C)*

A mahogany-cased barograph, by Short & Mason, in Meterological Office style box, with hinged lid and pen drawer, c1937, 12in (30.5cm) wide.
£350–400 *RTw*

A copper-cased barograph, by Negretti & Zambra, London, on cast iron base, c1935, 10in (25.5cm) wide.
£250–300 *RTw*

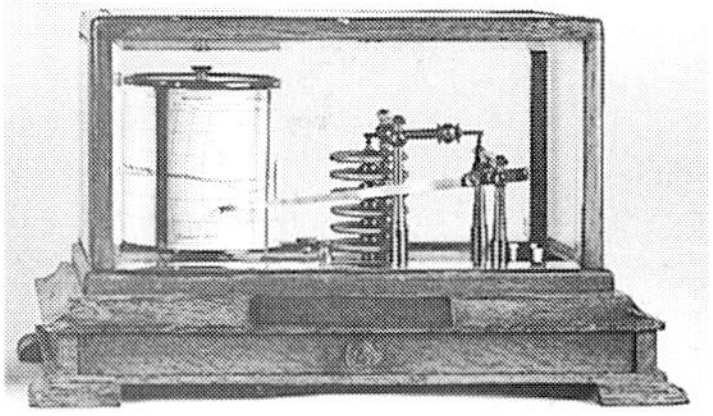

r. An oak-cased barograph, with clockwork recording drum, lacquered-brass mechanism and 6 aneroid bellows, in a glazed case with drawer to base, c1920, 13¾in (35cm) wide.
£400–500 *Bon(C)*

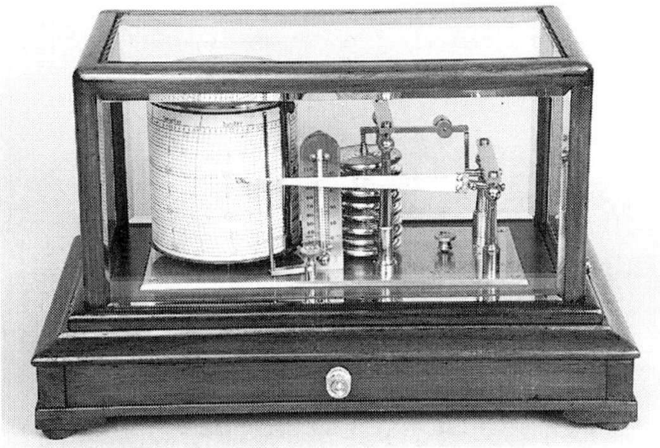

A mahogany-cased barograph and thermometer, with chart drawer, c1900, 15in (38cm) wide.
£1,000–1,200 *AW*

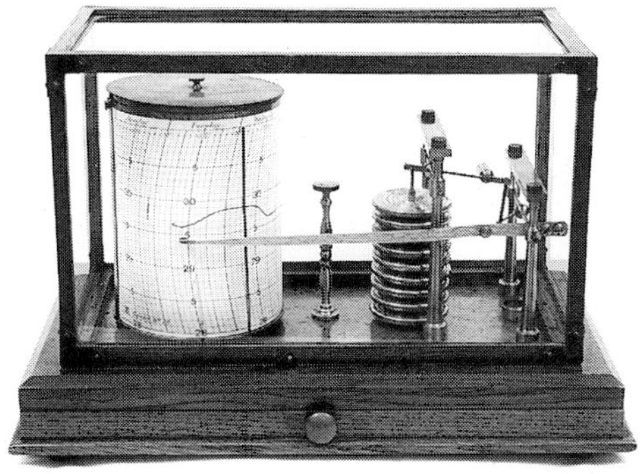

An oak-cased barograph, with chart drawer, c1920, 19in (48.5cm) wide.
£800–900 *RTw*

DECORATIVE ARTS
Arts & Crafts Furniture

An Arts and Crafts rosewood display cabinet, designed by C. A. Lion Cachet, with 2 glass doors, the interior fitted with 3 shelves, above a protruding lower part enclosing a curved drawer, decorated with carved figures by Anton Fortuin, c1910, 39½in (100cm) wide.
£2,200–2,500 *S(Am)*

An Arts and Crafts music cabinet, the serpentine top with pierced gallery, above a single frieze drawer with heart-shaped drop handles, the openwork brass door with applied floral motifs, supported on block feet united by a shaped apron, c1910, 39½in (100cm) high.
£420–460 *P(B)*

l. A painted oak side chair, by Charles Rohlfs, the slender back with stylised piercings above a shaped plank seat raised on a pierced base, impressed maker's mark 'R' within a bow saw, c1904.
£6,500–7,500 *S(NY)*

Charles Rohlfs opened his practice in Buffalo, New York, c1890. His style is unmistakably Arts and Crafts influenced, with extensive use of exposed joinery. Rohlfs worked almost exclusively in dark oak, sometimes stained black, and made a feature of hand-wrought iron or copper hardware. Most pieces bear an incised monogram.

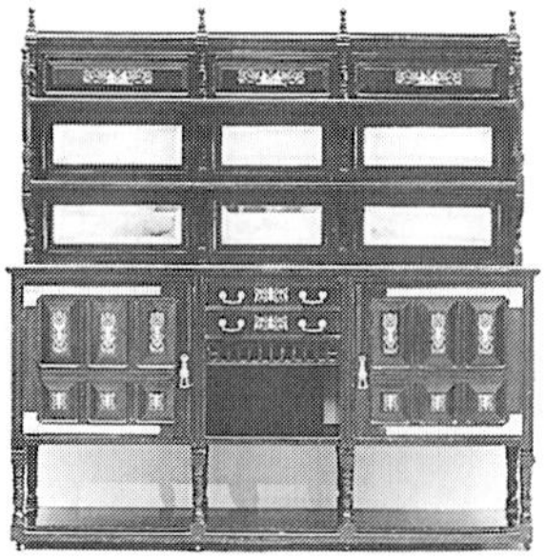

l. An Aesthetic Movement ebonised sideboard, with ivory marquetry inlay, c1880, 78in (198cm) wide.
£2,500–3,000 *WW*

An Arts and Crafts coromandel and ebony cabinet-on-stand, designed by Charles Spooner, framed at the front edge with ebony, c1910, 37½in (95.5cm) wide.
£9,500–10,500 *P*

An ebonised wood canterbury, by Philip Webb for Morris & Co, with 3 open shelves above a deep open-fronted cabinet and 2 further shelves, with panelled sides and spindle turned galleries, c1880, 17in (43cm) wide.
£2,100–2,300 *S*

l. An Arts and Crafts mahogany-framed elbow chair, with spindle turned back supports, raised on turned legs joined by stretchers, c1890.
£400–450 *AAV*

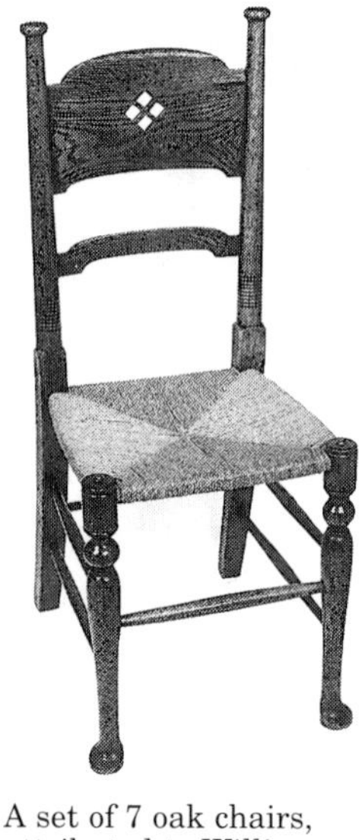

A set of 7 oak chairs, attributed to William Birch, the arched backs with pierced lozenge motifs, above sisal seats, on tapered legs and pad feet joined by stretchers, c1890.
£550–650 *P(B)*

A Danish Faaborg solid oak tub chair, by Kaare Klint, with crescent-shaped back-rail, 1914–23.
£600–700 *Bon*

This chair is one of several variations on a chair originally designed in 1914 by the architect Kaare Klint for the Faaborg museum, Funen, a folk art museum designed by Klint & Carl Peterson.

Gustav Stickley

In 1884 Gustav started a furniture business in New York with his 2 younger brothers to make original furniture with an Arts and Crafts feel. The firm used mainly American white oak, stained either rich or light brown, or grey, using a fuming process developed at the factory. Traditional construction methods were used, as well as handmade hardware, often with a hammered surface. The upholstery is mainly leather and typically brown, red or green.

An oak settle, by Gustav Stickley, with slatted back and arms, worn, c1910, 77in (196cm) long.
£4,200–4,600 *S(NY)*

r. An American Aesthetic Movement walnut centre table, inlaid with a Greek key and stylised floral band, late 19thC, 48in (122cm) wide.
£3,000–3,500 *S(NY)*

A Mission oak taboret, c1915, 12in (30.5cm) square.
£150–200 *EKK*

Mission furniture refers to a style used by a few American furniture makers during the early part of the 20thC, the most well-known being Gustav Stickley of New York. Mission furniture celebrated the architectural style of the American south west and followed the heavy, severe furnishings of the southern Spanish missions.

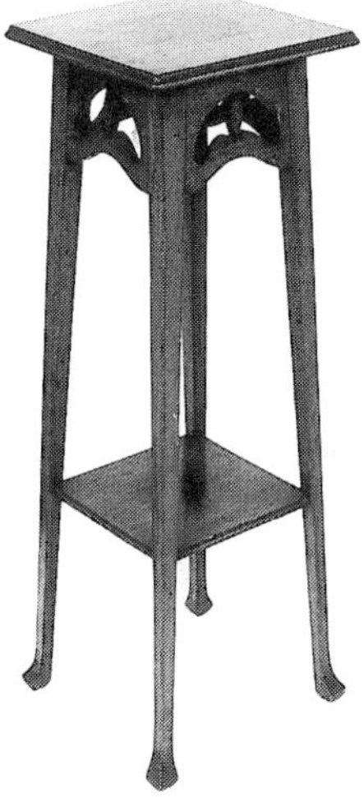

An Arts and Crafts jardinière stand, with a pierced shaped apron, on sweeping legs united by a second tier, c1900, 36in (91cm) high.
£130–150 *P(B)*

l. A Thebes stool, by Liberty & Co, the beech frame with dished tooled-leather seat and brass studs, on ring-turned legs united by stretchers and spindles, c1885, 22in (57cm) wide.
£900–1,000 *DN*

A mahogany dining table, supported on a turned wood simulated bamboo frame of 6 vertical legs radiating from one central support, c1880, 58½in (148.5cm) diam.
£10,500–11,500 *TMA*

This table was probably made to a design by Philip Webb, furniture designer with William Morris.

An oak library table, by L. & J. G. Stickley, with 2 frieze drawers raised on square legs headed by curved brackets, some wear, c1915, 36in (91.5cm) wide.
£1,200–1,500 *S(NY)*

Leopold & J. George Stickley were brothers of Gustav Stickley. Their company made simple, solid home and office furniture such as bookcases and tables, and many pieces bear a branded signature or brass plate.

A Heal's limed-oak refectory table, with twin barrel turned end supports, on a stretchered base, 1950s, 78in (198cm) long, and 6 limed-oak dining chairs.
Table £2,700–3,000
Chairs £2,500–2,800 *WW*

A Limbert oak centre table, on pierced trestle supports joined by a lower shelf, branded with maker's mark, refinished, c1915, 44in (112cm) wide.
£1,300–1,500 *S(NY)*

Miller's is a price GUIDE not a price LIST

A Heal's oak drop-leaf sewing table, 1930s, 47½in (120.5cm) wide, open.
£180–200 *P(Ba)*

A Heal's limed-oak wardrobe, the plain top with rounded ends, the central mirrored door flanked by panelled doors enclosing hanging space and drawers, raised on turned supports united by chamfered stretchers, c1930, 72½in (184cm) wide.
£480–520 *P*

Art Nouveau Furniture

An Art Nouveau oak bookcase, with a pair of leaded and stained glass doors, panelled doors below, on a plinth base, c1900, 39¾in (101cm) wide.
£500–550 *P(C)*

A Dutch Art Nouveau oak buffet cupboard, attributed to Jac van den Bosch or H. P. Berlage, the upper part with 3 glazed doors flanked by open compartments, the lower part with 4 doors with inlaid geometrical ornament of stained and ebonised wood, the doors with brass mounts, c1910, 83in (211cm) wide.
£3,500–4,000 *S(Am)*

FURTHER READING
Miller's Art Nouveau & Art Deco Buyer's Guide, Miller's Publications, 1995

An Art Nouveau inlaid mahogany cabinet, the central cupboard with broad cornice and inlaid apron below, over a leaded glass door, flanked on either side by a plain gallery partly enclosing a shelf with angled doors below inlaid in coloured woods, mother-of-pearl and pewter, 3 drawers below, plated handles, c1900, 46in (117cm) wide.
£3,500–4,000 *P*

An Art Nouveau inlaid display cabinet, with mirrored gallery over a shelf with inlaid apron, with bowed and bevelled-glass cupboard and sides with tapered supports, the base with leaded and coloured glass doors, with panels inlaid in coloured woods, copper and pewter, c1900, 51¼in (130cm) wide.
£2,200–2,500 *P*

Prices

The price ranges quoted in this book reflect the average price a purchaser would expect to **pay** for a similar item. When selling expect to receive a lower figure.

An Art Nouveau oak dresser, in the manner of Liberty, the raised back with 3 leaded glazed doors, the pierced supports enclosing a central mirror plate, the base with bowfront top and 2 frieze drawers with bulbous stylised tulip handles stamped 'L & C', above a pair of panel doors with inlaid lozenge motifs, on stepped block feet, c1900, 66in (167.5cm) wide.
£1,000–1,200 *DN*

An Art Nouveau mahogany side cabinet, with mother-of-pearl and wood inlay, the pierced arched back and bevelled mirror above a bowed leaded glazed door and recess flanked by cupboards, on square legs and pad feet, c1900, 62in (157.5cm) wide.
£1,500–1,800 *LRG*

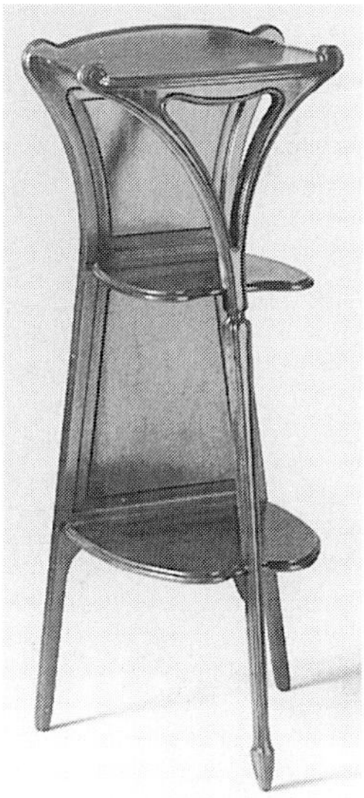

A carved fruitwood and burr mahogany étagère, stamped 'L. Majorelle, Nancy', c1900, 49in (125cm) high.
£2,300–2,600 *S(NY)*

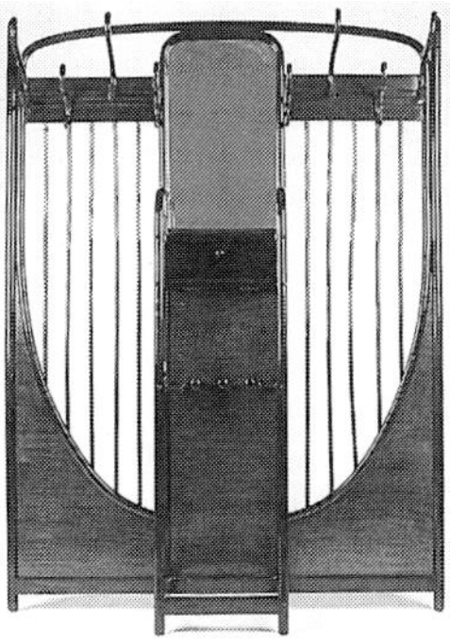

A Thonet beechwood coat stand, stained brown, with faceted mirror, No. 10906, c1900, 58in (147.5cm) long.
£1,500–1,800 *DORO*

An Art Nouveau mahogany drawing room chair, re-upholstered, c1890.
£60–80 *MEG*

An American enamelled leaded glass and carved wood firescreen, c1900, 37in (94cm) wide.
£3,000–3,500 *S(NY)*

An Art Nouveau oak sideboard, the raised open shelf back with a central cupboard enclosed by a leaded astragal door, the base with canted wings, the 2 long drawers flanked by a pair of panelled doors, on tapered square legs and knopped feet, c1905, 66in (167.5cm) wide.
£550–650 *S(S)*

A pair of Thonet chairs, designed by Adolf Loos, red-brown stained and polished, restored, early 20thC.
£3,000–3,500 *DORO*

These were made for the Café Capua in Vienna.

A French Art Nouveau walnut pedestal stand, restored, c1900, 42½in (108cm) high.
£2,800–3,200 *S(NY)*

An American Art Nouveau walnut occasional table with inward curving canted corners, the undertier with pierced legs and angles, late 19thC, 24in (61cm) square.
£80–100 *AP*

Arts & Crafts Metalware

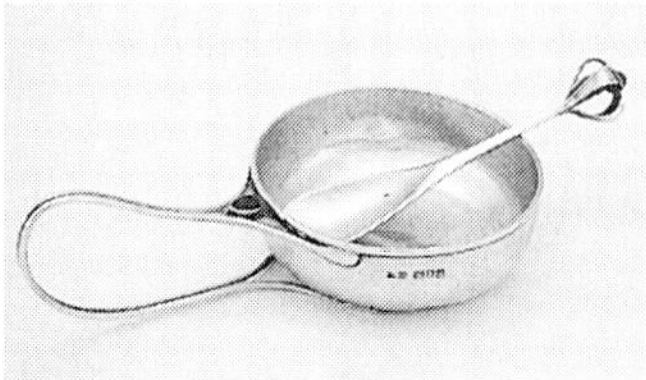

A Guild of Handicrafts Ltd silver bowl and spoon, designed by C. R. Ashbee, the hammered round bowl with reeded loop handle set with a green quartz cabochon, London 1902, 3in (7.5cm) diam.
£1,600–2,000 *HOLL*

A pair of Arts and Crafts dishes, by Martin & Hall, with stylised hoof feet, Birmingham 1906, 3¼in (8.5cm) diam.
£400–450 *P*

An Arts and Crafts silver cigar box, London 1907, 10in (25.5cm) wide.
£320–350 *Doc*

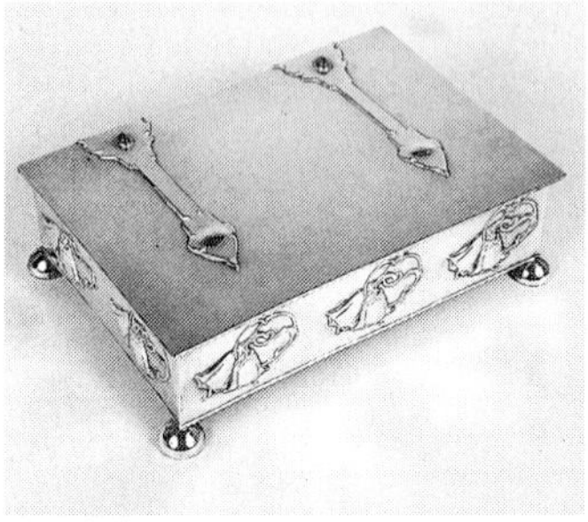

An Arts and Crafts silver casket, by William Hutton & Sons, probably designed by Kate Harris, with shaped hinged straps, set with pink tourmaline cabochons, maker's mark for London 1905, 9½in (24cm) wide.
£1,300–1,600 *P*

A Liberty & Co Cymric silver butter dish, designed by Archibald Knox, the domed cover with loop handle set with a turquoise cabochon, and a butter knife, marked 'L & Co', Birmingham 1904, butter dish 7½in (19cm) long.
£5,500–6,500 *P*

An Arts and Crafts silver-plated chalice, by Philip Ashberry & Sons, c1890, 7½in (18cm) high.
£70–80 *WeH*

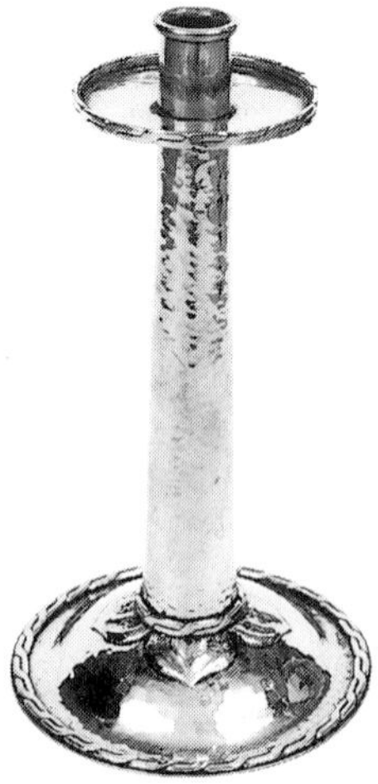

An Arts & Crafts copper candlestick, by Bernard Wood, 1890s, 9in (23cm) high.
£110–125 *WAC*

A German silver coffee pot, designed by Emmy Roth, the handle with 2 ivory bands and an ivory finial, signed and stamped, 1920s, 11½in (29cm) high.
£1,000–1,200 *P*

A pair of Arts and Crafts steel fire dogs, decorated with oak leaves and scrollwork, 1890s, 23¾in (60.5cm) high.
£460–520 *P(Sc)*

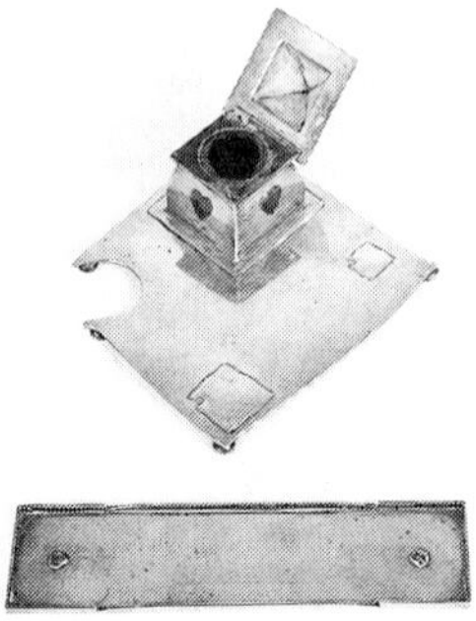

A Liberty & Co Cymric silver and enamel inkstand, the inkwell with 3 heart-shaped motifs in green and blue enamel, stamped maker's marks, Birmingham 1904, and a pen tray marked Birmingham 1905, 7¾in (19.5cm) long.
£1,200–1,500 *P*

r. An Arts and Crafts copper photograph frame, attributed to Keswick School of Industrial Arts, c1900, 9in (23cm) high.
£325–375 *SHa*

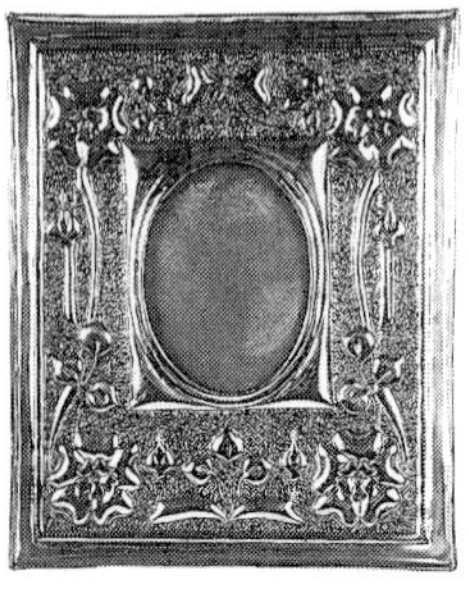

r. An Arts and Crafts copper photograph frame, set with pottery plaques by Ruskin, c1900, 11½in (29cm) high.
£400–450 *SHa*

Art Nouveau Metalware

A Tiffany sterling silver bowl, the edge embellished in relief with an openwork design of clover and foliage, c1905, 12in (30.5cm) diam.
£1,200–1,400 *SFL*

An Art Nouveau silver photograph frame, decorated with honesty motifs, Birmingham 1903, 6½in (16.5cm) high.
£550–650 *SHa*

An Art Nouveau vase, by William Hutton & Sons, set with Ruskin pottery plaques, c1900, 7in (18cm) high.
£500–550 *SHa*

A German Art Nouveau pewter punch bowl and cover, c1900, 17¼in (44cm) high.
£460–520 *Bri*

A nickel-brass electric kettle, by Peter Behrens for AEG Berlin, 1909, 8¾in (22cm) high.
£500–600 *DORO*

An Art Nouveau silver paperweight, by William Hutton & Sons, Birmingham 1902, 3½in (9cm) wide.
£200–250 *RAC*

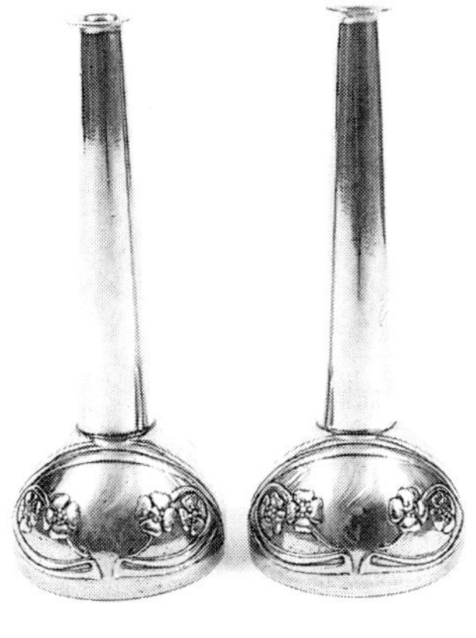

r. A pair of Liberty & Co pewter spill vases, with slender necks, the bases decorated with flowers, c1905, 6in (15cm) high.
£350–400 *ASA*

A pair of Tiffany bronze four-branch candelabra, 1892–1902, 12½in (31.5cm) high.
£2,500–3,000 *S(NY)*

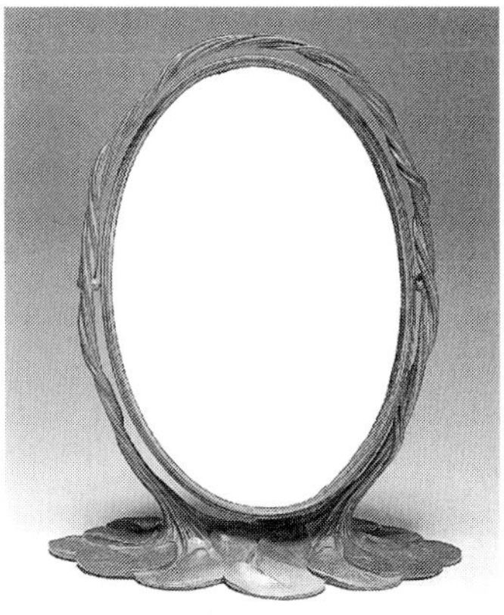

A Tiffany lily pad mirror, impressed, 1899–1918, 19in (48.5cm) high.
£700–750 *S(NY)*

A pair of Art Nouveau silver flower vases, by Elkington & Co, on circular bases, Birmingham 1902, 6in (15cm) high.
£350–400 *GAK*

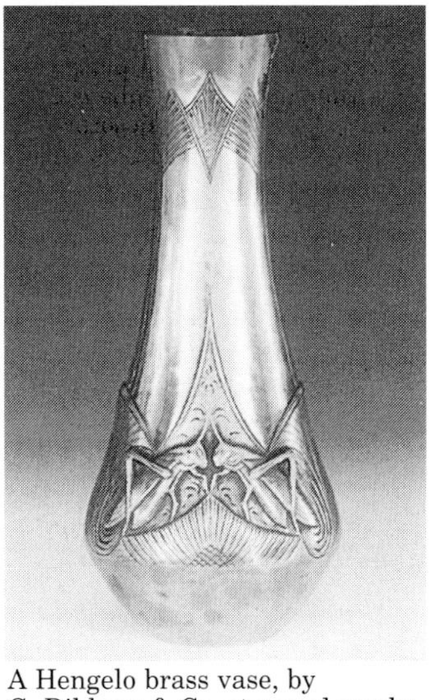

A Hengelo brass vase, by G. Dikkers & Co, stamped marks 'DH' and windmill, imperfections, c1905, 9¼in (23.5cm) high.
£480–520 *S(Am)*

Art Nouveau Glass

A pair of Baccarat gilt-decorated blue and green glass vases, moulded with daisies, supported by a grasshopper on a wheat moulded mound, early 20thC, 8¼in (21cm) high.
£1,200–1,400 *S(NY)*

A Daum carved cameo and martelé glass anemone vase, internally streaked with light blue at the top and rust towards the base, decorated in *marqueterie sur verre* technique with 3 carved anemones with etched stems on carved ground, engraved mark, c1900, 7in (18cm) high.
£3,000–3,500 *S(Am)*

A glass vase by Burgun Schverer & Co, applied with a hammered silver mount, the grey glass enclosing deep reddish-brown swirling decoration and cut with 3 curving martelé swirls, early 20thC, 6¾in (17cm) high.
£600–700 *S(NY)*

A Daum internally decorated glass dish, etched and painted in naturalistic colours with continuous bellflowers and gold borders, painted gold mark, c1905, 5in (12.5cm) wide.
£1,000–1,200 *DORO*

A Gallé cameo glass vase, amber tinted and overlaid with blue and amethyst glass, acid-etched with marguerites, signed, c1900, 9in (23cm) diam.
£2,500–3,000 *PSG*

l. A Gallé cameo glass vase, the amber tinted body overlaid with amethyst and pale blue, acid-etched with marsh plants and grasses, c1910, 5½in (14cm) high.
£1,400–1,600 *ART*

A Daum etched, gilt and enamelled perfume bottle and stopper, decorated with purple and green layers, branches and berries, printed mark, 1890–96, 3¾in (9.5cm) high.
£700–850 *S(Am)*

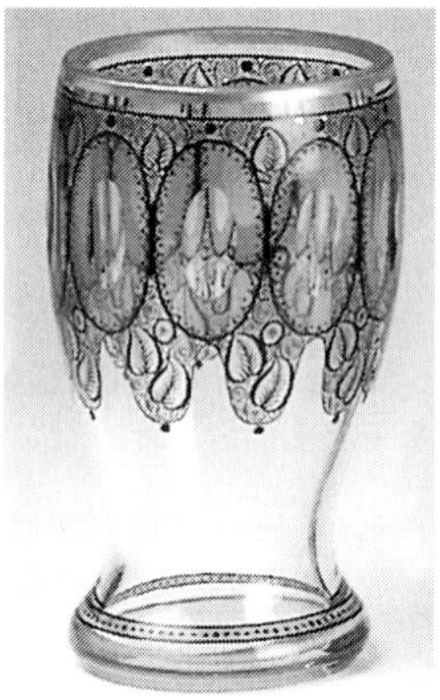

A Fachschule Steinschönau vase, the clear glass decorated with yellow tinted oval medallions surrounded by leaves in spirals in black enamel and gold, c1915, 6in (15cm) high.
£500–600 *DORO*

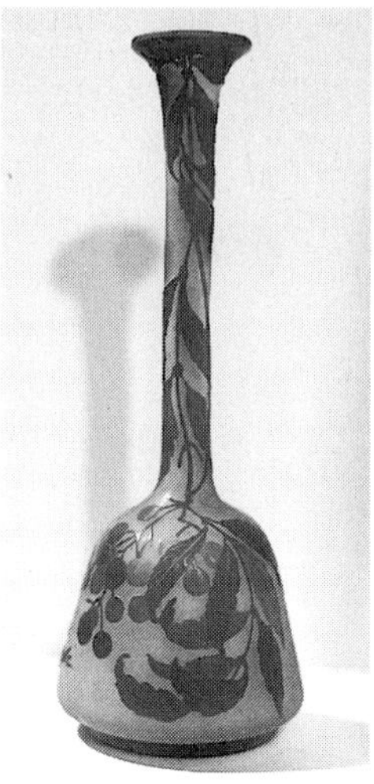

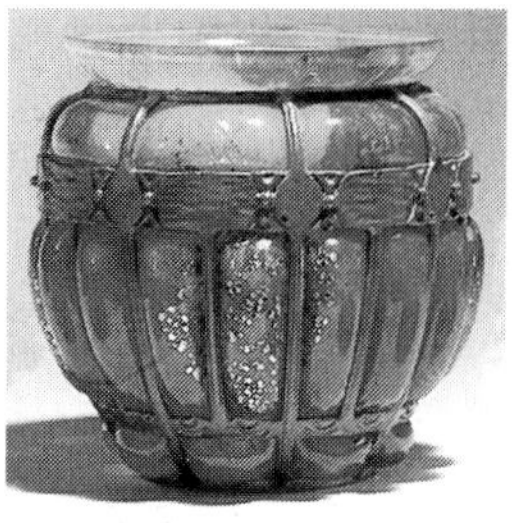

A Daum grey and blue glass vase, internally streaked with amber and infused with gold foil inclusions, within a wrought iron mount, by Majorelle, inscribed marks, c1900, 10in (25.5cm) high.
£3,500–4,000 *S(NY)*

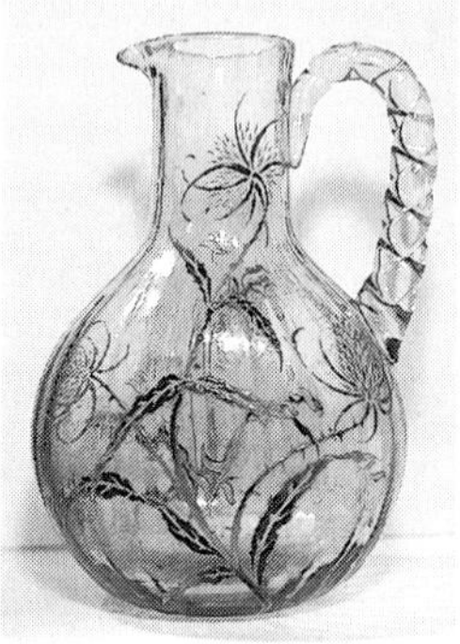

A Gallé glass ewer, decorated with enamelled thistle design and gilded details, signed, c1895, 8¼in (21cm) high.
£1,800–2,000 *PSG*

A Gallé colourless glass vase, overlaid in pink and purple and etched with prunus blossom, fire-polished, c1900, 11¾in (30cm) high.
£2,200–2,500 *S(Am)*

l. A Gallé cameo glass *solifleur* vase, decorated with red overlaid on amber, acid-etched with berries and leaves, signed in cameo, c1900, 8¼in (21cm) high.
£1,000–1,200 *PSG*

A pair of Leune enamelled glass vases, the orange glass degrading into grey, enamelled with a riverscape and trees, painted mark, c1910, 16in (40.5cm) high.
£520–580 *S(Am)*

An internally decorated cameo glass vase, by Ernest Leveille, internally decorated with lemon and coral-red patches, overlaid with a deep reddish-brown glass, acid-etched and wheel-carved with fish swimming, signed, dated '1890', 7in (18cm) high.
£16,000–18,000 *P*

A Loetz iridescent glass vase, with pinched rim, decorated with peacock-blue swags on a green ground, overlaid with silver stylised flowers, 2 pieces of silver lacking, c1900, 7in (18cm) high.
£1,000–1,200 *RTo*

A Loetz iridescent vase, covered with a light peacock blue spotting on a dark blue ground, c1900, 8¼in (21cm) high.
£400–450 *RTo*

Loetz (Austrian 1836–1939)

This glassmaking firm, founded at Klostermühle by Johann Loetz, specialised in making high quality art glass. The firm was known as Glasfabrik Johann-Loetz Witwe after 1848, when Loetz died and his widow Suzanne took over the directorship.

Loetz took the Art Nouveau spirit to heart and their iridescent wares combine finely controlled surface decoration with highly inventive glass forms. At the Vienna Jubilee Exhibition of 1898, Loetz showed a group of iridescent wares which soon rivalled the products of Louis Comfort Tiffany in popularity. Although many collectors view Loetz glass as the Austrian attempt to emulate Tiffany, it was actually Tiffany who was impressed by the Loetz wares shown at the various international exhibitions.

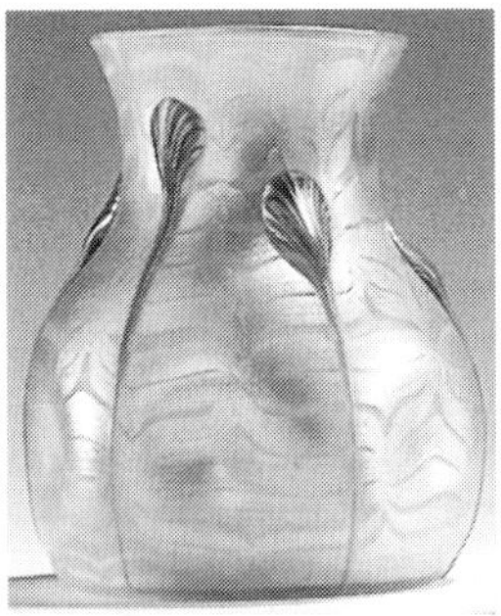

A Loetz glass vase, the dimpled amber glass decorated with iridescent silvery-blue bands and applied with butterscotch glass drips with iridescent silvery-blue streaks, inscribed 'Loetz/Austria', c1900, 7in (18cm) high.
£3,000–3,500 *S(NY)*

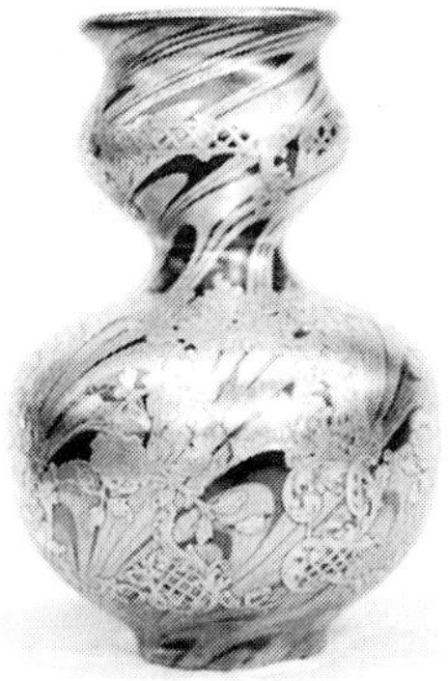

A Loetz iridescent glass vase, decorated with swirling bands of green-blue iridescence and silver applique of flowers and foliage, inscribed 'Loetz Austria', c1900, 9in (22.5cm) high.
£1,400–1,600 *BIG*

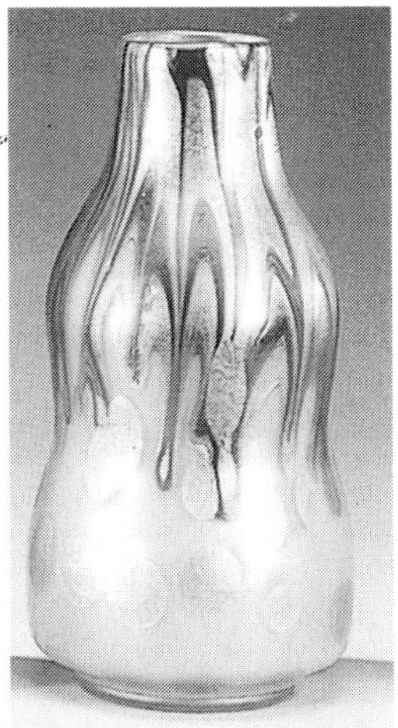

A Loetz vase, internally decorated with yellow and washed with violet, peacock blue/green and gold iridescence, etched mark 'Loetz Austria', c1902, 9in (23cm) high.
£3,500–4,000 *S*

r. A Moser clear glass vase, with tinted amethyst at the top and deeply wheel-carved with tulips, c1900, 8in (20.5cm) high.
£80–100 *MON*

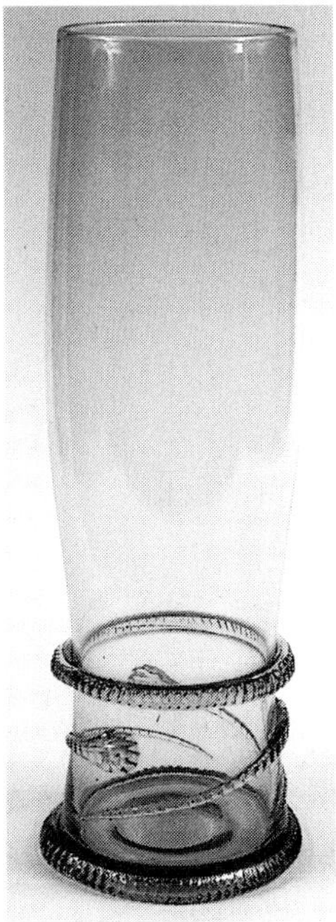

A Tiffany Favrile crocus vase, decorated in yellow with green and amber foliage, the interior in subtle iridescence, inscribed 'L. C. Tiffany-Favrile 3357 G.', c1912, 4½in (11.5cm) high.
£3,800–4,200 *S(NY)*

l. A Powell's Whitefriars serpent vase, in sea-green glass, c1910, 9¼in (23.5cm) high.
£250–300 *JHa*

Arts & Crafts and Art Nouveau Jewellery

An Arts and Crafts bracelet, by Bernard Instone, the circular plaques of green-stained chalcedony, carnelian labradorite, snowflake obsidian and others, divided by links of Oriental inspiration, stamped 'BI' and 'Silver', c1920, 8¼in (21cm) long.
£220–250 *P*

A conch pearl, natural pearl and diamond brooch, by Tiffany & Co, styled as thistles, signed, some diamonds missing, late 19thC.
£5,000–5,500 *S(HK)*

An Art Nouveau gold symbolist brooch/pendant, depicting a lakeland scene with 2 flamingos matt-enamelled in pink, within a ruby and diamond scrolling frame, c1900.
£3,500–4,000 *P*

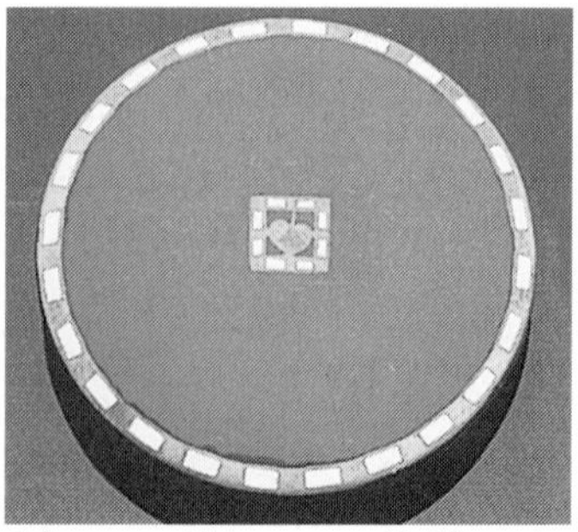

A brass and blue enamelled brooch, by Josef Hoffman for the Wiener Werkstätte, with a stylised leaf motif, a border of white enamelled dashes, monogram 'WW', c1910, 1½in (4cm) diam.
£2,500–3,000 *S*

An Arts and Crafts enamelled and moonstone necklace, c1900, 15in (38cm) long.
£700–800 *P*

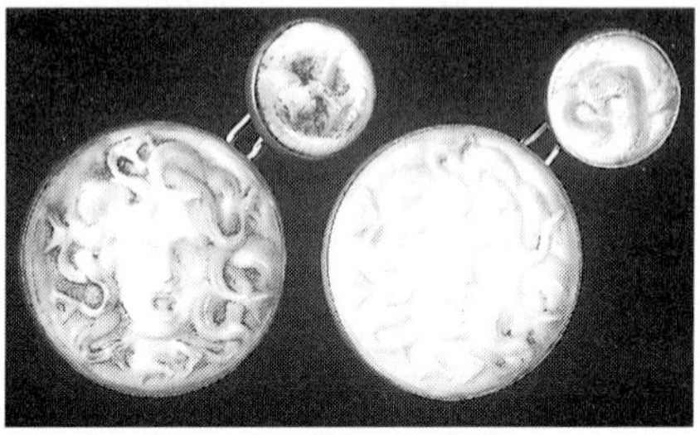

A pair of French foil-backed glass cuff links, set in gilt-metal, signed 'R. Lalique', c1912.
£3,000–3,500 *JES*

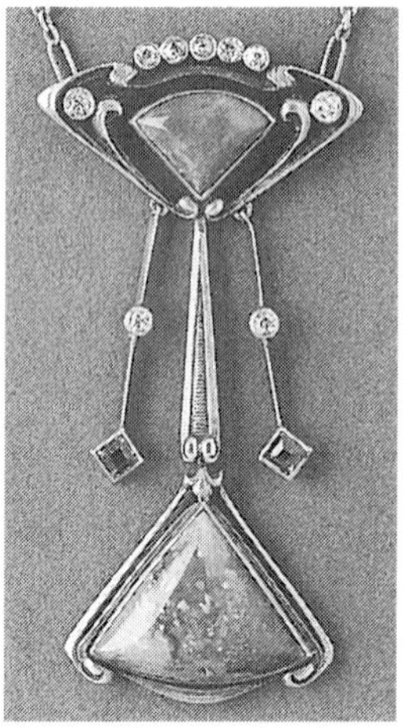

An Art Nouveau black opal, diamond, demantoid garnet and 14ct gold necklace, c1900.
£2,600–3,000 *SLM*

An Art Nouveau pearl and enamel pendant, with a spray of chrysanthemums of green and orange translucent enamel against a polychrome *plique-à-jour* enamel background supporting a pearl diamond drop, on a detachable chain, c1900.
£5,200–5,800 *S*

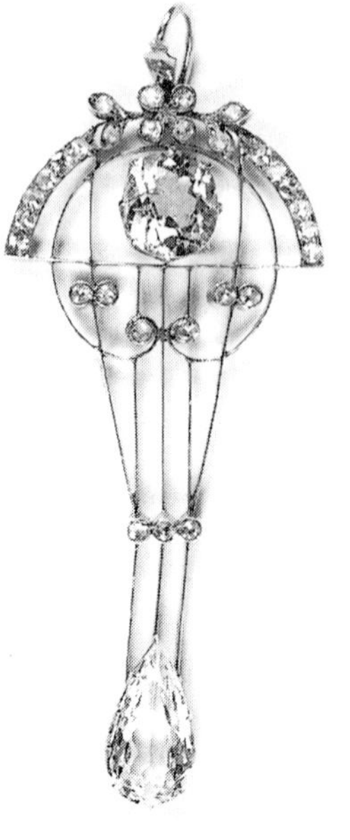

r. A Russian Art Nouveau pendant, the openwork top centred with a pale aquamarine flanked by diamonds, a tear drop aquamarine below, suspended from articulated mount, marked 'AT' and standard marks '583', c1900, 2¾in (7cm) long.
£750–850 *P*

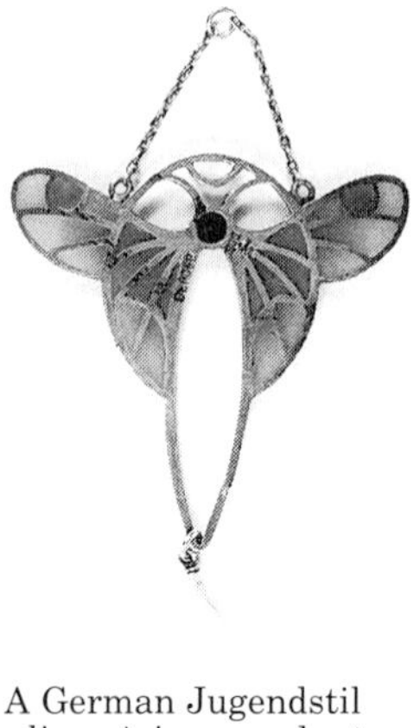

A German Jugendstil *plique-à-jour* pendant, with mauve and green translucent enamels, freshwater pearl drop below, maker's mark '900' and 'Déposé', c1900, 1¾in (4.5cm) wide.
£700–800 *P*

A German Jugendstil pendant necklace, designed by Otto Prutscher and made by Heinrich Levinger, the reverse with maker's monogram 'HL' and 'Déposé', 1901–02, 1½in (4cm) high.
£2,500–3,000 *S*

Clocks

A Doulton Lambeth stoneware mantel clock, by Eliza Simmance, with Japy gong-striking movement, in an Indian inspired architectural case, c1886, 16¼in (41.5cm) high.
£1,600–1,800 *Bri*

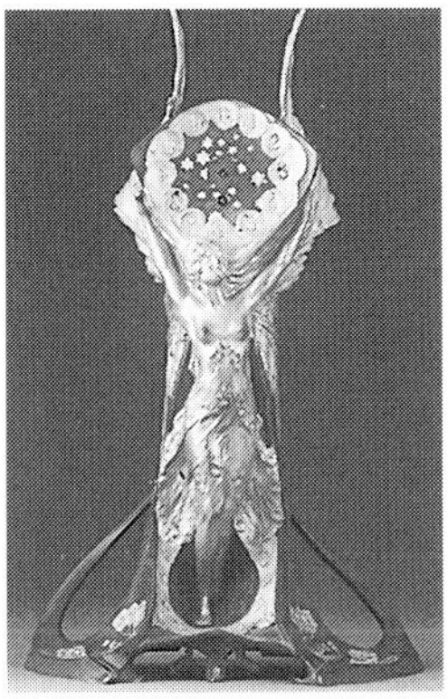

A French parcel-gilt and patinated-bronze figural mantel clock, modelled as a winged female figure, c1900, 20in (51cm) high.
£1,600–1,800 *S(NY)*

A Liberty pewter clock, designed by Rex Silver, c1900, 9in (23cm) high.
£2,000–2,250 *SHa*

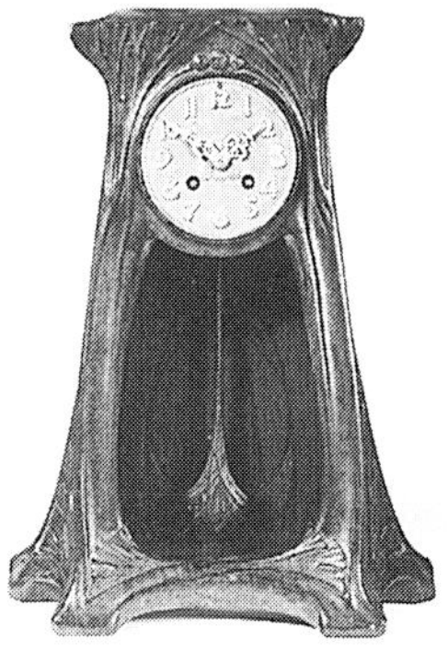

An Art Nouveau mahogany clock, with a bronze pendulum, probably from the School of Nancy, c1900, 16¼in (41.5cm) high.
£1,100–1,300 *P*

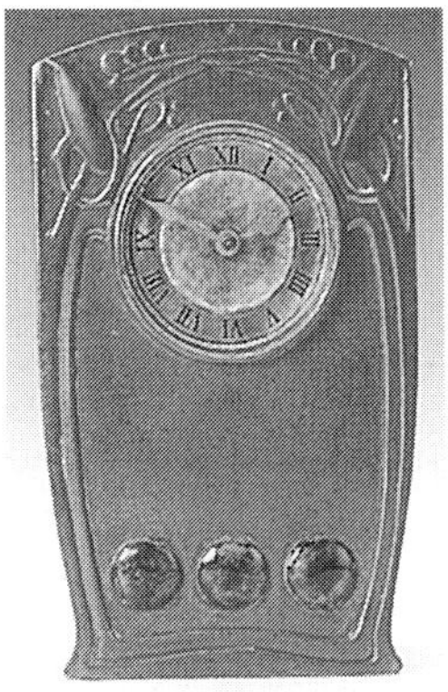

A Liberty Tudric pewter mantel clock, designed by Archibald Knox, the dial of copper and enamel, mounted with 3 turquoise coloured enamelled bosses, the move-ment stamped 'Lenzkirch AGU', the base inscribed 'Tudric', c1910, 7¾in (19.5cm) high.
£2,800–3,200 *S(S)*

A French spelter sculptural clock, c1920, 12in (30.5cm) high.
£350–400 *CIR*

An Almaric Walter table clock, the green *pâte-de-verre* enamelled in turquoise, blue, yellow and green, oval brass face with black numerals, inscribed 'A. Walter, Nancy', c1925, 4¼in (11cm) high.
£1,100–1,300 *DORO*

Don't Forget!
If in doubt please refer to the 'How to Use' section at the beginning of this book.

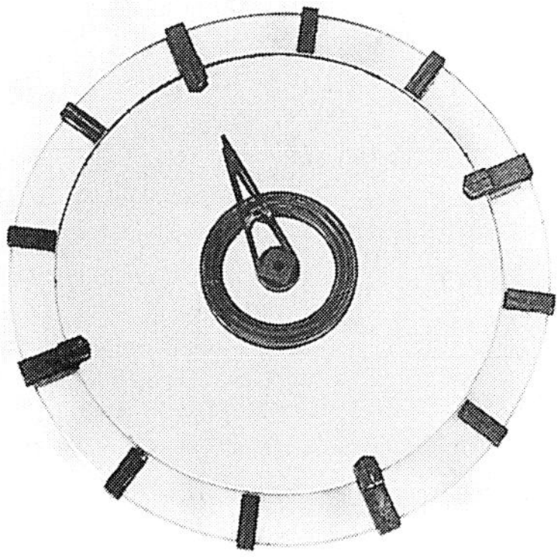

An Art Deco wall clock, with steel hands, the electric movement by Tyme Ltd, c1930, 12¼in (31cm) diam.
£200–250 *P(F)*

An Art Deco oak wall clock, with chrome Roman numerals, 1930s, 14¼in (36cm) wide.
£60–80 *P(B)*

A Swiss Art Deco chrome and leather digital clock, with 8-day movement, 1930s, 4in (10cm) square.
£175–200 *TIH*

An Art Deco acid-cut and gilt decorated mantel clock, with electric mechanism and fitted for illumination, 1930s, 18½in (47cm) high.
£900–1,000 *Bon*

An Art Deco mantel clock, by Metamec, 1940s, 12in (30.5cm) wide.
£20–30 *MiA*

Lighting

A pair of Arts and Crafts copper and enamel wall lights, each inset with a blue and turquoise enamel plaque, 1890s, 14in (35.5cm) high.
£750–900 *P*

A Tiffany two-light bronze candlestick, with green opaque glass and copper patina, impressed 'Tiffany Studios New York', 1899–1920, 8½in (21.5cm) high.
£1,250–1,500 *DORO*

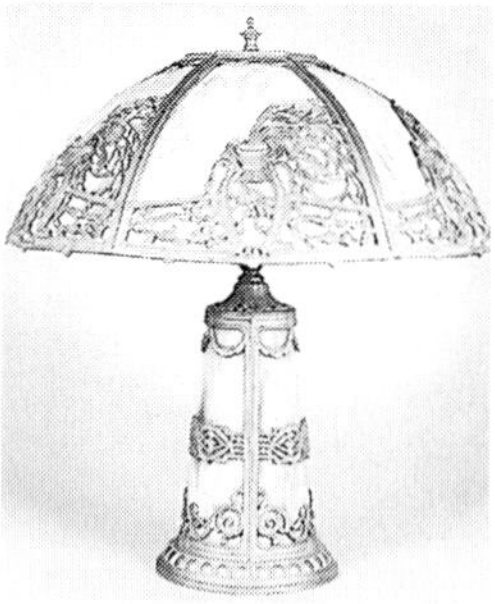

An American table lamp, the blue, mauve and white glass enclosed within a pierced gilt-metal mount cast with flora radiating from swan neck vases and birds perched amid foliage, c1900, 21¾in (55.5cm) high.
£750–900 *P*

A Tiffany Favrile patinated-bronze and glass three-light lily table lamp, 1899–1920, 8½in (21.5cm) high.
£2,300–2,500 *S(NY)*
Ex-Leonard Bernstein collection.

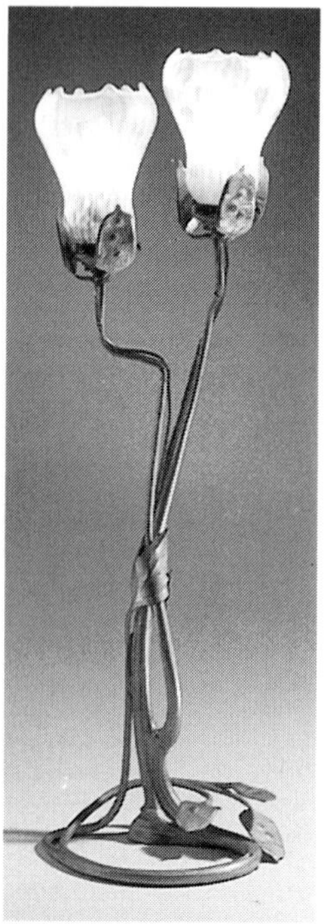

A Daum Nancy cameo glass and Majorelle gilt-iron lamp, the shades in grey glass overlaid in lime green and pale peach and cut with a pattern of blossoms, c1903, 27½in (70cm) high.
£6,000–7,000 *S(NY)*

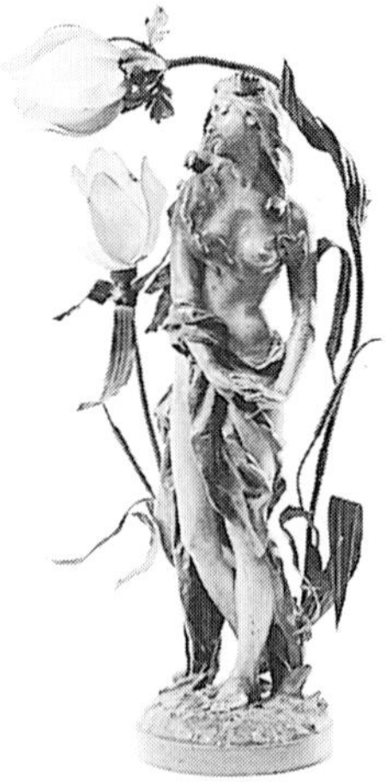

An Art Nouveau patinated spelter figural lamp, the naked maiden standing against rushes and water plants, c1900, 33in (83cm) high.
£1,000–1,200 *P(O)*

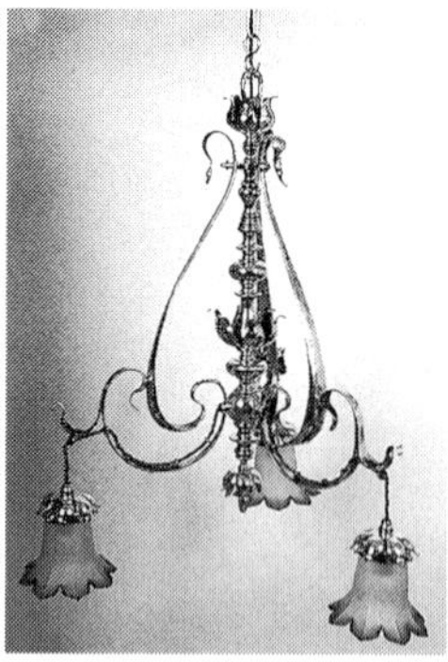

An Art Nouveau brass electrolier, with original shades, probably by Hinks & Son, c1900, 29in (73.5cm) high.
£1,400–1,600 *CHA*

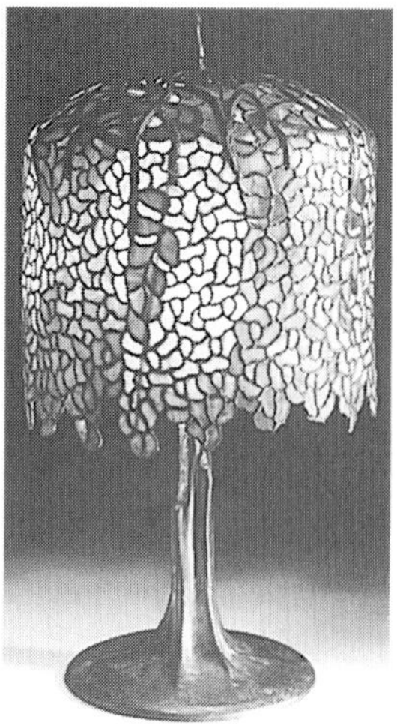

A Wisteria lamp, by A. Hart, composed of light and dark blue wisteria blossoms cascading from an openwork branch upper section, on patinated bronze tree trunk form base, minor losses, c1900, 21½in (54.5cm) high.
£1,100–1,300 *S(NY)*

A set of 12 Otto Wagner silvered-bronze and aluminium light sconces, c1911, 8½in (21.5cm) high.
£5,000–5,500 *S(NY)*

A Pairpoint reverse-painted moulded glass boudoir lamp, the shade in grey glass moulded with clusters of flowers, painted on the interior with yellow, white, black, purple and crimson, gilt-metal base, c1920, 14½in (37cm) diam.
£3,500–4,000 *S(NY)*

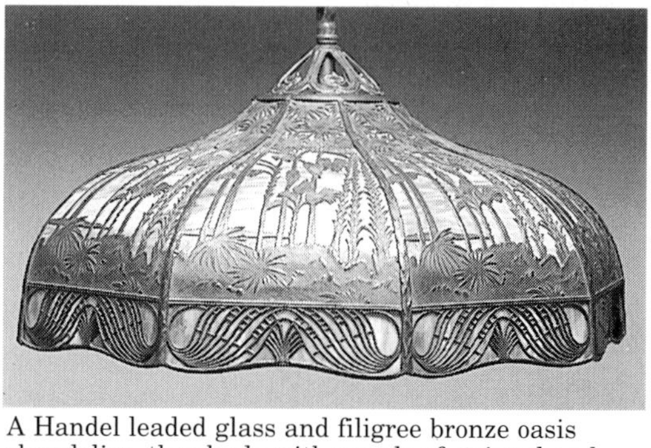

A Handel leaded glass and filigree bronze oasis chandelier, the shade with panels of striated and swirled glass in shades of red, white, amber and green overlaid with an elaborate bronze filigree, No. 5381, c1915, 13½in (34.5cm) diam.
£5,000–5,500 *S(NY)*

A Wiener Werkstätte patinated brass eight-light ceiling lamp, designed by Dagobert Pêche, with white silk shade, marked, c1920, 49¼in (125cm) high
£11,000–13,000 *DORO*

This piece realised a high price because the Wiener Werkstätte, for whom it was designed by Dagobert Pêche (himself a leading light within the design workshops), is internationally well-known and highly appreciated by collectors and museums alike.

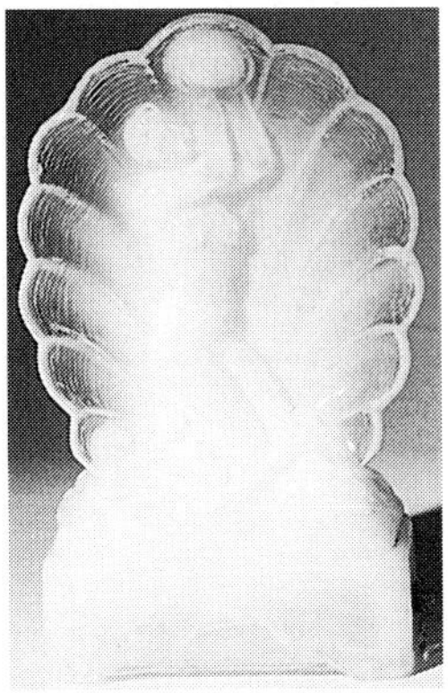

An Art Deco opalescent glass lamp, in the form of an upright seashell, c1925, 10¾in (27.5cm) high.
£500–550 *P*

An Art Deco chromium-plated and glass chandelier, in the manner of Desny, 1930s, 26in (66cm) diam.
£600–700 *P*

A Lalique frosted glass plafonnier, entitled 'Charmes', with moulded leaves, signed, c1920, 15in (38cm) diam.
£1,500–1,800 *ASA*

A Paul Kiss lamp, the lamp shade composed of alabaster panels within a wrought iron frame, above a bronze figure, impressed 'Paul Kiss/Paris', c1925, 10¾in (27.5cm) high.
£4,200–4,600 *S(NY)*

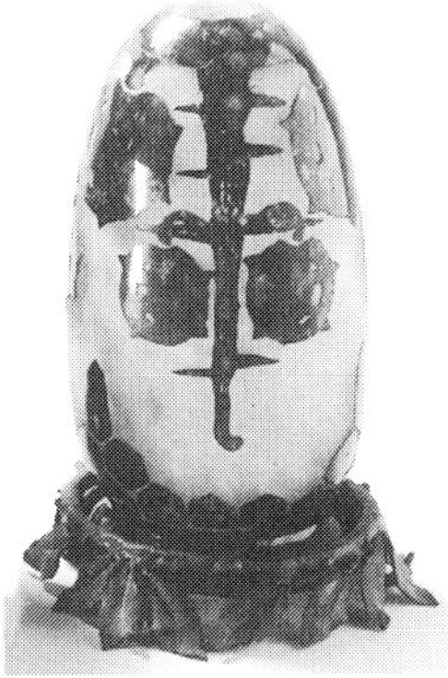

A Le Verre Français cameo glass veilleuse, the grey glass tinted with yellow and orange, overlaid with red and green and cut with a branch and berry design, inscribed, c1925, 7¼in (18.5cm) high.
£580–620 *S(NY)*

r. A Lalique frosted glass lamp, entitled 'Six Danseuses', the underside of the base with stencilled mark 'R. Lalique France', c1932, 10in (25.5cm) high.
£5,600–6,000 *S*

A pair of glass chandeliers, in the style of Emile-Jacques Ruhlmann, each with fluted silvered-bronze standard conjoining strings of pendant glass beads, c1925, 32in (81.5cm) high.
£6,000–7,000 *S(NY)*

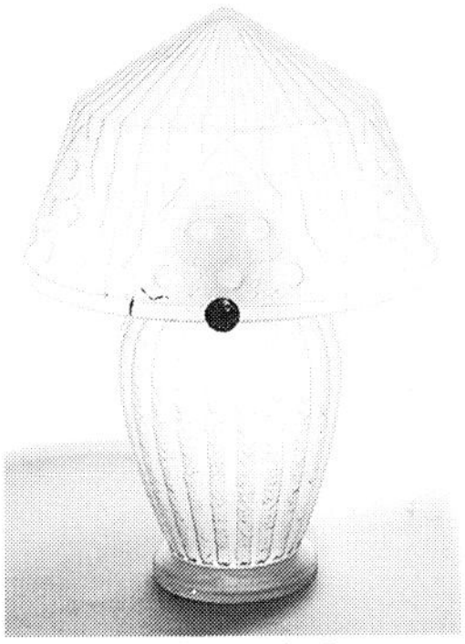

A Daum frosted glass table lamp and shade, acid-etched in high relief, etched marks, small crack to shade, c1925, 15in (38cm) high.
£1,200–1,500 *P*

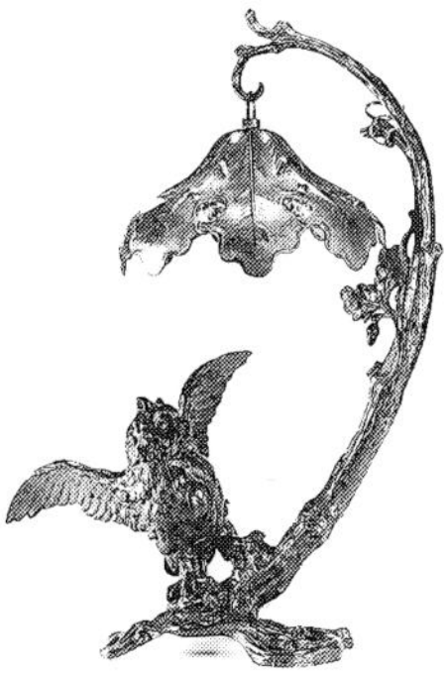

An Art Deco bronzed-metal table light, formed as an owl with illuminating eyes, the hanging petal shade set with coloured glass roundels, c1930, 24in (61cm) high.
£900–1,100 *MAT*

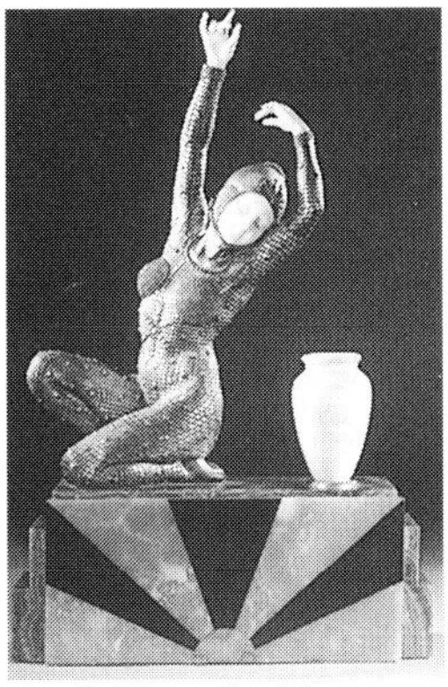

An F. Rigaud cold painted bronze and ivory figural lamp, modelled as a girl in a studded and jewelled cat suit and headdress, with a sunburst of green and black onyx, restoration to one finger, c1920, 23½in (59.5cm) high.
£4,000–4,500 *S*

A pair of Art Deco bronzed-metal and glass light fittings, c1930, 18in (45.5cm) wide.
£1,000–1,200 *ASA*

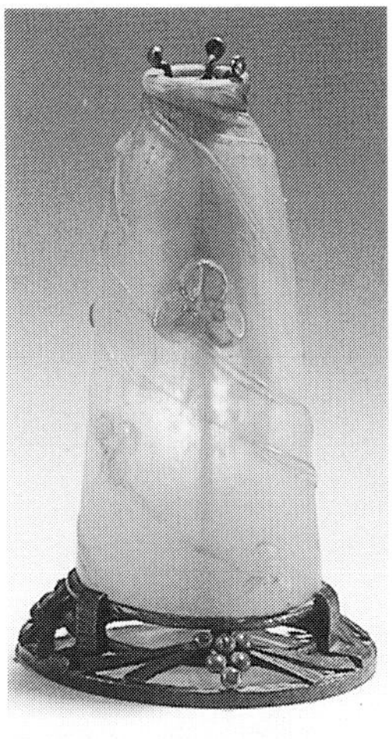

An Almeric Walter *pâte-de-verre* and wrought iron lamp, moulded in low and medium relief with blossoms and tendrils in shades of amber, orange-brown and green, raised on a wrought iron base cast with stylised mistletoe, moulded 'A. Walter/Nancy', c1920, 8½in (21.5cm) high.
£2,000–2,200 *S(NY)*

Ceramics

Decorative Arts Ceramics

This year we have taken a fresh approach to the diverse subject of Decorative Arts ceramics. Rather than divide it into Art Nouveau and Art Deco sections, as in the past, we have decided to arrange the items chronologically, so that it can be seen how styles and designs developed and changed over a period of about 70 years. The output of the studio potters such as Martin Brothers, will be seen alongside the Art Nouveau pieces which were being produced at the same time. Special sections are allocated to Doulton, Moorcroft, Poole Pottery, Clarice Cliff and Susie Cooper, since they have their own specialist collectors. For this reason Doulton figures, which one would not normally expect to find under the Decorative Arts umbrella, are shown here with other examples from that prolific and versatile factory whose output encompassed domestic table and sanitary ware, studio pottery and collectors' items.

A Martin Brothers stoneware egg cup, with incised decoration on a brown ground, c1873, 2¼in (5.5cm) high.
£150–170 *AMH*

A Wedgwood Art Pottery vase, probably by George Marsden, of broad baluster shape, decorated in autumnal coloured slips with scrolling foliage against black, restored, c1885, 11in (28cm) high.
£175–225 *DSG*

A William de Morgan ruby lustre bowl, decorated with fish amongst leaves and scrolls, c1890, 13¼in (33.5cm) diam.
£700–800 *P(G)*

A Minton tile, designed by John Moyr Smith, c1875, 9in (23cm) square.
£100–125 *DSG*

A Minton porcelain box and cover, probably designed by Christopher Dresser, decorated with butterflies and scarab beetles in enamelled colours outlined in gilt on a rose pink ground, marked 'Mintons', c1880, 3¼in (8.5cm) long.
£300–350 *P(Ba)*

A Burmantofts pottery jardinière, the sides incised with 3 pairs of brightly coloured blue dogs wearing yellow collars running between stylised trees, impressed marks, c1890, 9¾in (25cm) high.
£1,000–1,200 *S(S)*

l. A Burmantofts faïence pottery vase, painted with a Persian style design of flora and leaves in turquoise, brown, green and blue on a white ground, impressed mark, c1890, 9½in (24cm) high.
£360–400 *P*

A Linthorpe pottery vase, shape No. 24, c1883, 9½in (24cm) high.
£250–300 *NCA*

Shape No. 24 is probably the most common of the Linthorpe shapes. It was designed by Christopher Dresser and has 3 or 4 'dimples' impressed into the vase. Only early pieces carry Dresser's facsimile, such as the piece illustrated here. Without the facsimile signature the value is reduced. Prices also depend upon the quality and brilliance of the glaze.

A French lustreware vase, by Clement Massier, decorated with dense foliage, on a bronze mount, c1892, 11in (28cm) high.
£1,100–1,200 *SUC*

A Rozenburg earthenware wall plate, decorated with thistles in front of a spider's web, in shades of blue, green and brown, painted factory mark and date code 'L', 1894, 10¾in (27.5cm) diam.
£1,100–1,300 *S(Am)*

A Martin Brothers baluster-shaped vase, modelled in relief with starfish, on a matt blue ground, incised marks for January 1896, 11in (28cm) high.
£400–450 *DN*

A Martin Brothers salt-glazed stoneware vase, incised with medallions enclosing masks and fruit-filled urns, in brown and pale blue, incised and dated '8-1894', 13½in (34.5cm) high.
£2,000–2,200 *S(NY)*

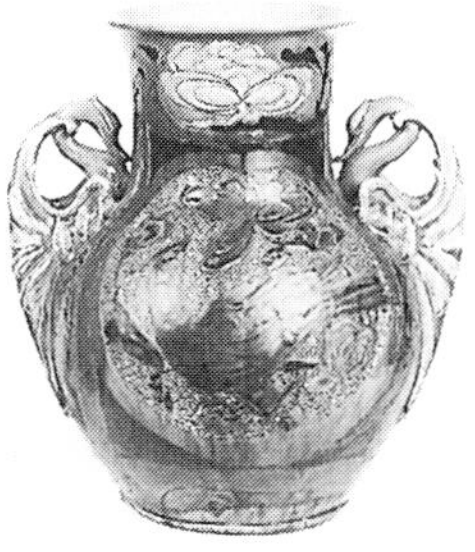

A Brannam pottery twin-handled vase, by James Dewdney, the body sgraffito-decorated with 2 panels each with a bird perched amid flora, in blue, green and brown, incised to base 'C. H. Brannam, Barum' and 'J. D. 1898', 16¾in (42.5cm) high.
£450–500 *P*

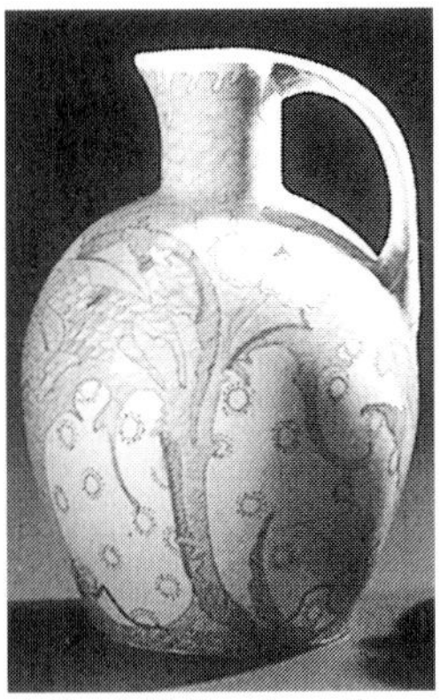

A Zuid-Holland earthenware jug, painted by J. Th. Stam, in shades of blue, green, yellow and purple on a cream ground, c1899, 5¾in (14.5cm) high.
£330–360 *S(Am)*

l. A Martin Brothers salt-glazed stoneware vase, moulded as a ribbed six-sided pod with striations glazed in brown and black, set with 3 handles cast in the form of lizards with only hind legs, incised 'Martin Bros/London & Southall' and '11-1900', 11in (28cm) high.
£2,500–2,800 *S(NY)*

A Brannam pottery vase, with loop handles, decorated in sgraffito with coloured slips in Art Nouveau style and with panels of fish, c1900, 19in (48.5cm) high.
£675–750 *DSG*

A Bretby Pottery vase, the base and collar simulating bronze, a central ivory-coloured band with Oriental style mice and rabbits, c1900, 8½in (21.5cm) high.
£100–120 *AAC*

A Watcombe pottery oviform vase, with twin handles, painted in brown, black and pink with flowers and foliage on a white ground, c1900, 7¾in (19.5cm) high.
£60–70 *DSG*

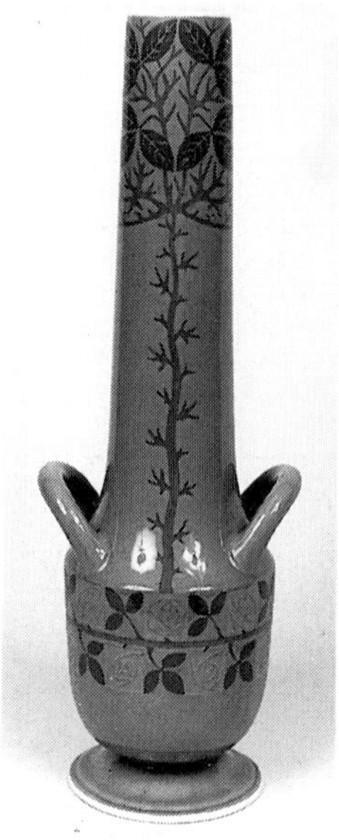

An Art Nouveau vase, by Villeroy & Boch, with stylised orange and brown rose pattern, on celadon green ground, c1900, 19¾in (50cm) high.
£400–450 *ANO*

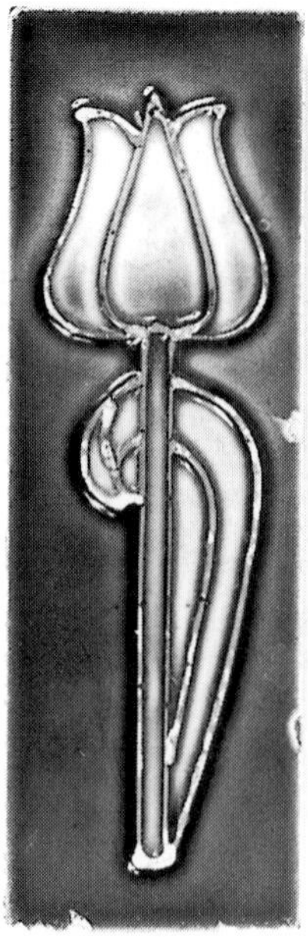

An Art Nouveau tube-lined tile, c1900, 6in (15cm) high.
£20–25 *HIG*

A Royal Bonn pottery wall charger, decorated with a young maiden surrounded by flowering poppies and holding a cigarette issuing a thin cloud of grey smoke across the pale green ground, framed within a brown edged rim, factory marks, c1900, 19¾in (50cm) diam.
£500–550 *S(NY)*

The decoration on this charger is after a design by Alphonse Mucha for Job cigarette papers, c1896.

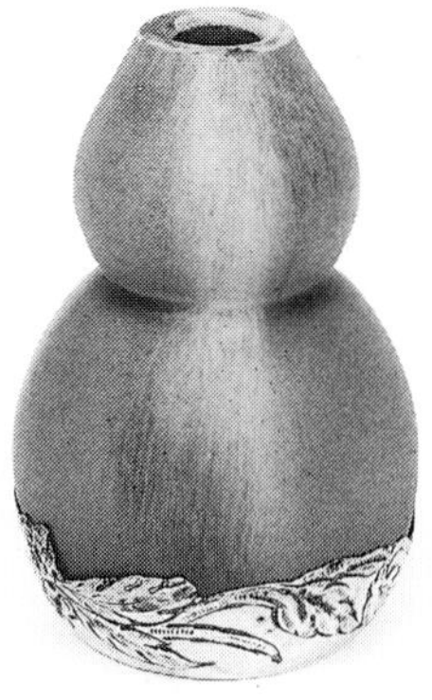

An Art Pottery vase, of double-gourd shape, decorated with streaked matt glaze with embossed floral mount on base, possibly French, c1900, 4in (10cm) high.
£140–160 *SUC*

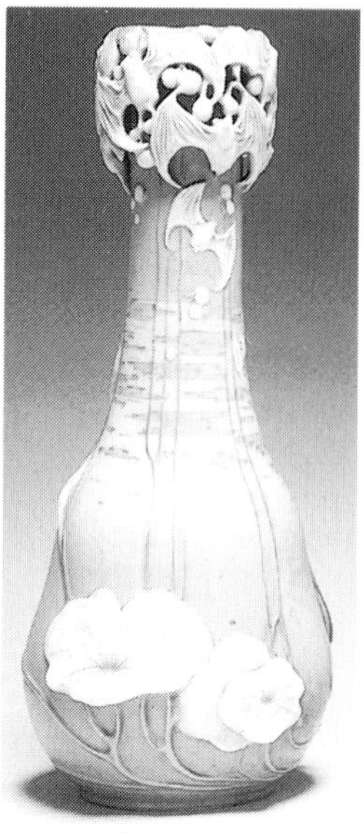

An Amphora earthenware vase, the rim modelled in high relief with bats, glazed in shades of tan, yellow, green, brown and ivory heightened in gilt, impressed, c1900, 21in (53.5cm) high.
£4,000–4,500 *S(NY)*

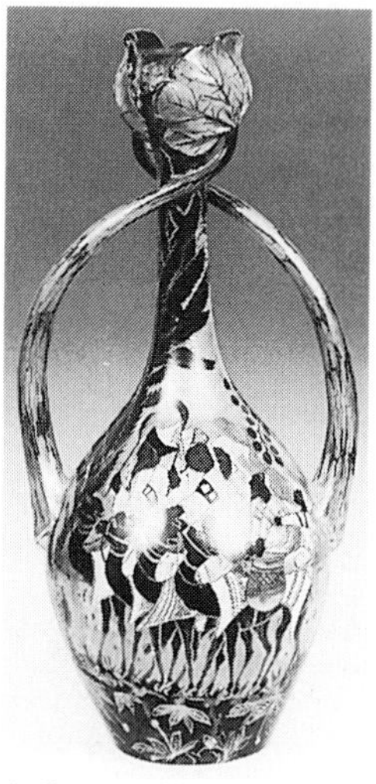

A Cantagalli lustre pottery vase, painted with a procession of Eastern figures on camels and figures seated at a table in a rural setting, in purple, grey, yellow, blue and white, paper label to base, painter's cockerel monogram, c1900, 20in (51cm) high.
£1,200–1,500 *P*

An Amphora earthenware vase, applied with a large dragon with outspread wings, with a landscape of leafy trees glazed in shades of tan, ivory and gold on a lavender and white ground, impressed, c1900, 21in (53.5cm) high.
£3,200–3,600 *S(NY)*

A German earthenware tile, the design attributed to C. S. Luber, depicting a young girl with a bouquet of daisies in a landscape, within a wooden frame, painted mark, c1902, 18in (45.5cm) wide.
£1,200–1,500 *S(Am)*

l. A Weller 'Sicardo' lustre vase, by Jacques Sicard, American, c1901, 5in (12.5cm) high.
£500–550 *YAN*

This vase was retailed through Tiffany's in New York.

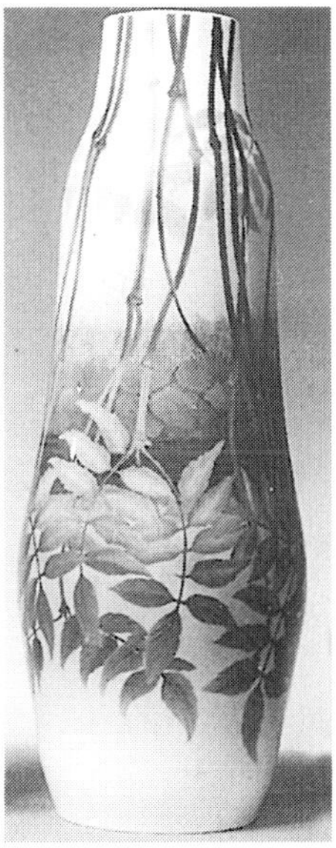

A Royal Copenhagen vase, decorated by Jonny Mayer, signed and dated '1904', factory mark, green printed mark, '212/A' incised, 23¼in (59cm) high.
£1,500–2,000 *WW*

A Hampshire pottery oviform vase, designed by Cadmon Robertson, modelled with stylised tulips below a matt olive-green-glaze, American, 1904, 9in (23cm) high.
£700–800 *YAN*

This vase bears the mark 'M' inside a circle, said to be a tribute to Robertson's wife, Emmoretta.

An Arts and Crafts pottery vase, possibly by Bernard Moore, with pewter mounts and hand-beaten finish, c1905, 7in (18cm) high.
£80–100 *P(B)*

A Martin Brothers salt-glazed stoneware bird, with removable head, glazed in white, brown, blue, black and ochre, incised, dated '1906', 9in (23cm) high.
£5,000–5,500 *S(NY)*

A Weller pottery vase, decorated in sunken relief with floral panels, picked out in colours, American, c1910, 8½in (21.5cm) high.
£145–165 *DSG*

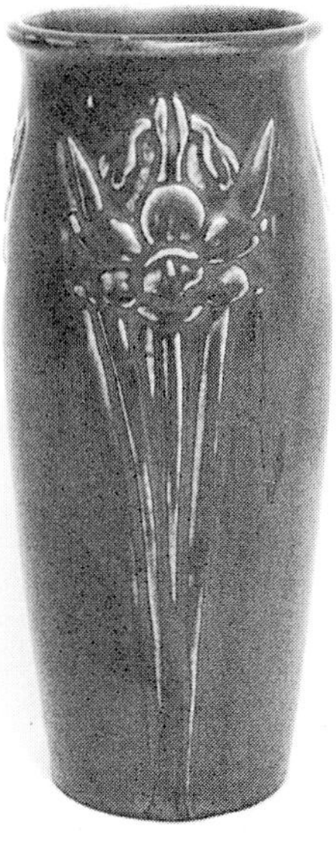

A Rookwood pottery oviform vase, decorated in relief with daffodils beneath a matt and muted blue glaze, 1912, 9in (23cm) high.
£220–260 *YAN*

Rookwood

Rookwood was the leading American 'Art Pottery'. It employed the novel technique of encasing pottery in silver deposits by an electrolytic process that allows silver to be attracted to the pottery surface. Until 1910 the wares were usually signed by the artist and carried a date and shape number.

A Pilkington's Royal Lancastrian shallow bowl, covered with a vivid flecked orange glaze, 1914–38, 10½in (26.5cm) diam.
£75–85 *RAC*

A Roseville pottery vase, decorated in shallow relief with wisteria picked in naturalistic colours against streaky brown, American, c1915, 6in (15cm) high.
£300–350 *MSB*

A Gouda twin-handled pottery bowl, painted with flowers and stylised foliage against white, c1918, 12in (30.5cm) wide.
£400–450 *OO*

A Zuid-Holland earthenware wall plate, designed and painted by H. L. A. Breetvelt, matt glaze, decorated with an abstract floral pattern in shades of blue, yellow and brown, painted factory mark, 1920–23, 18¾in (47.5cm) diam.
£1,700–2,000 *S(Am)*

A Wedgwood pottery vase, by Louise Powell, painted with an all-over decoration of foliage in blue and red lustre on a white ground, painted artist's monogram and impressed factory mark, c1925, 21¾in (55.5cm) high.
£1,000–1,200 *P*

A Sèvres tête-à-tête, designed by Suzanne Lalique-Haviland, painted with stylised leaves and fruit outlined in grey, comprising 10 pieces, c1921.
£2,000–2,200 *S*

Suzanne Lalique-Haviland, the daughter of the celebrated glassmaker and designer René Lalique, married Paul Haviland of Limoges, the porcelain manufacturer. She was a noted designer of porcelain and theatre sets and worked for Sèvres 1914–30.

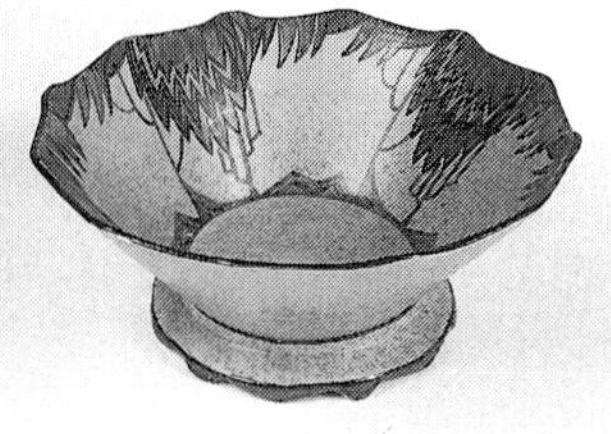

An Art Deco Phoenix ware bowl, decorated in muted greens, brown and amber tones with stylised pendant foliage and slender stems, with separate stand, c1925, 11in (28cm) diam.
£40–50 *DSG*

A Shelley three-piece 'Boo Boo' tea set, designed by Mabel Lucie Attwell, in the form of mushrooms, 1926–45, teapot 5½in (14cm) high.
£450–500 *WWY*

A Wedgwood pottery trial group, designed by John Skeaping, in straw-coloured glaze, stamped mark, 1927, 8in (10.5cm) high.
£1,100–1,200 *P*

r. A Rookwood pottery oviform vase, with a simple border around the shoulders beneath a muted blue glaze, American, 1928, 6in (15cm) high.
£150–180 *YAN*

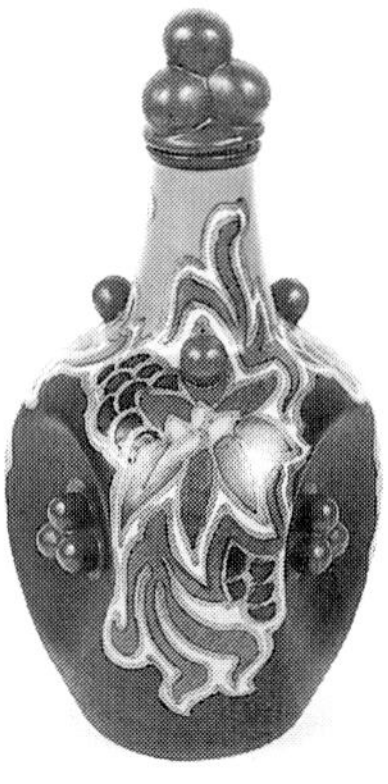

A pair of Gouda decanters, designed by Nadro, c1927, 10in (25.5cm) high
£450–500 *OO*

A Ruskin high-fired flambé vase, with 4 lug handles, decorated with a red and grey flecked glaze, dated '1927', 11½in (29cm) high.
£1,600–1,800 *BWe*

An Adnet pottery group of doves, with crackleware glaze, on a square base, indistinct monogram, c1930, 17¾in (45cm) wide.
£120–150 *P(B)*

A Gouda matt-glazed covered box, c1930, 5in (12.5cm) diam.
£30–40 *ZEI*

An Art Deco New Chelsea Coraline coffee service, decorated with floral sprays, comprising 15 pieces, c1930, coffee pot 9in (23cm) high.
£60–80 *P(B)*

A Crown Ducal part tea and breakfast service, decorated with Orange Tree pattern, printed marks, c1930.
£350–400 *WL*

l. A Denby Regent Pastel 'penguin' vase, designed by Donald Gilbert, early 1930s, 10½in (26.5cm) high.
£300–330 *KES*

A Gray's pottery Brocade water jug, hand-painted in bright colours, c1930, 4½in (11.5cm) high.
£30–40 *RAC*

l. A Wedgwood pottery bowl, designed by Keith Murray, with horizontal rubbing beneath a crackled white glaze, on a spreading circular foot, 1930s, 10in (25.5cm) diam.
£160–180 *AAV*

Keith Murray

Keith Murray is now regarded as one of the most important Art Deco ceramics designers. His work, although still affordable today, is likely to become more expensive. His output included pale-coloured geometric wares and a range of vases in darker colours. Genuine pieces are marked with his facsimile signature, and later, 'KM' combined with the Wedgwood mark.

A Crown Ducal vase, by Charlotte Rhead, decorated in green, orange, red and gilt on a pale mottled green ground, with a dragon chasing an eternal pearl, printed factory marks and facsimile signature, c1930, 12¼in (31cm) high.
£70–90 *P(E)*

l. A Shelley Regent shape trio, decorated with Bands and Line pattern, c1934, plate 7in (18cm) diam.
£25–30 *CSA*

Doulton

A pair of Doulton stoneware jardinières and stands, decorated with Natural Foliage pattern in shades of brown on a mottled grey/green ground, some chips, impressed marks, c1880, 29½in (75cm) high.
£800–1,000 *S(S)*

A Doulton Lambeth stoneware jardinière, by George Tinworth, incised and glazed with a band of seaweed between lappet borders on an ochre ground, with coiled serpent handles, incised monogram, dated '1881', 9¼in (23.5cm) high.
£1,300–1,500 *S*

A Doulton Lambeth stoneware bowl, decorated with a band of flowers and leaves in blue and white by Frances E. Lee, beneath silver-mounted rim, Birmingham 1881, printed mark and impressed date '1881', 9in (23cm) diam.
£300–350 *Oli*

A pair of Doulton faïence baluster-shaped vases, decorated by Helen A. Arding with apple blossom on a pale turquoise ground, impressed mark, c1889, 9½in (24cm) high.
£260–300 *CAG*

A Doulton Lambeth owl jug, the silver rim with coat-of-arms and engraved initials, 1894, 9½in (24cm) high.
£1,200–1,450 *POW*

A Doulton Lambeth stoneware vase, by Hannah Barlow, with incised decoration, rim restored, impressed date '1883', 16in (40.5cm) high.
£500–600 *EH*

A Doulton Burslem earthenware figure of a man, signed 'Noke', restored, printed mark, c1895, 17½in (44.5cm) high.
£400–450 *SK*

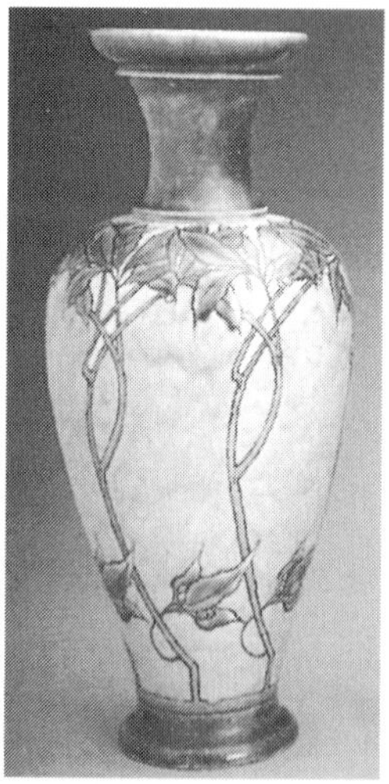

l. A Royal Doulton vase, decorated by Eliza Simmance, with impressed and incised mark, c1903, 13¾in (35cm) high.
£600–700 *DN*

A pair of Royal Doulton stoneware vases, decorated in muted colours with continuous landscape panels, on a dark blue ground, 1902–22, 7½in (19cm) high.
£225–250 *POW*

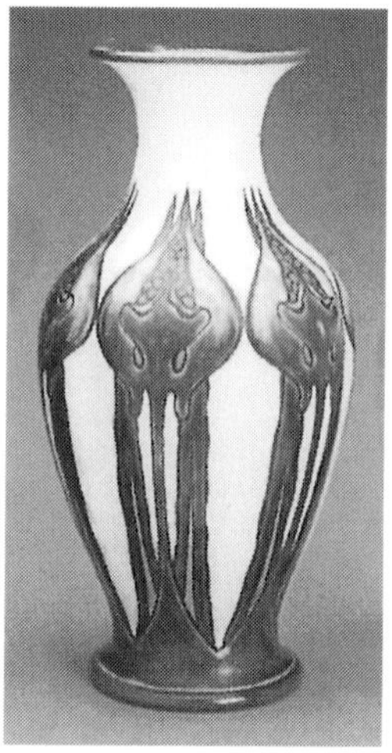

A Royal Doulton lobed baluster-shaped vase, with flared rim, decorated by Eliza Simmance in coloured enamels with stylised flowers and leaves, on a white ground, impressed and incised marks, c1903, 11¼in (28.5cm) high.
£600–700 *DN*

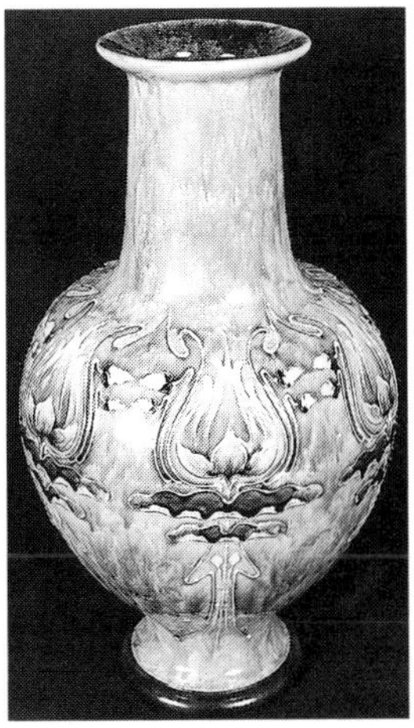

A Royal Doulton stoneware vase, decorated with a tube-lined Art Nouveau design by Eliza Simmance, c1903, 15¼in (38.5cm) high.
£950–1,100 *BWe*

A Royal Doulton commemorative loving cup, to celebrate 25 years of the reign of King George V and Queen Mary, with moulded decoration of St George outside Windsor Castle, signed 'H. Fenton', 1935, 10¼in (26cm) high.
£400–450 *P(B)*

A Royal Doulton figure of a Victorian lady, dressed in mauve shawl, repair to head, 1932–45, 4in (10cm) high.
£60–70 *MAC*

A Royal Doulton stoneware figure of Admiral Lord Nelson, on a square base, entitled 'Nelson 1805–1905', impressed and incised marks, c1905, 8in (20.5cm) high.
£400–450 *DN(H)*

A Royal Doulton figure, 'The Bride', HN1600, holding a bouquet of yellow roses, signed, 1930s, 9in (23cm) high.
£300–350 *CDC*

A Royal Doulton tobacco jar, 'Paddy', D5845, by Harry Fenton, 1939–42, 5½in (14cm) high.
£370–420 *BBR*

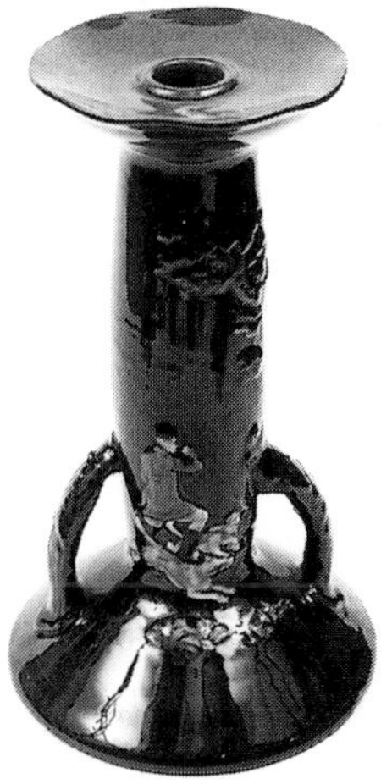

A Royal Doulton Kingsware candlestick, decorated with a huntsman and hounds against a treacle-brown ground, 1930s, 9¾in (25cm) high.
£85–95 *SnA*

A Royal Doulton stoneware oviform vase, decorated in relief with swags of fruit and flowers, picked out in amber, dark blue and pale blue glazes, c1910, 4¾in (12cm) high.
£45–55 *RAC*

r. A Royal Doulton plate, decorated in underglaze blue with the head and shoulders of William Shakespeare encircled by characters from his plays, 1920, 10½in (26.5cm) diam.
£60–70 *BRU*

Moorcroft

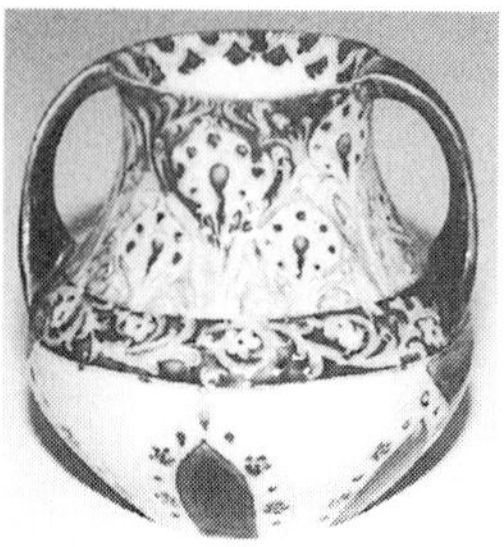

A Moorcroft MacIntyre Florian ware vase, printed mark in brown and green, 1898–1905, 4in (10cm) high.
£300–350 *RTo*

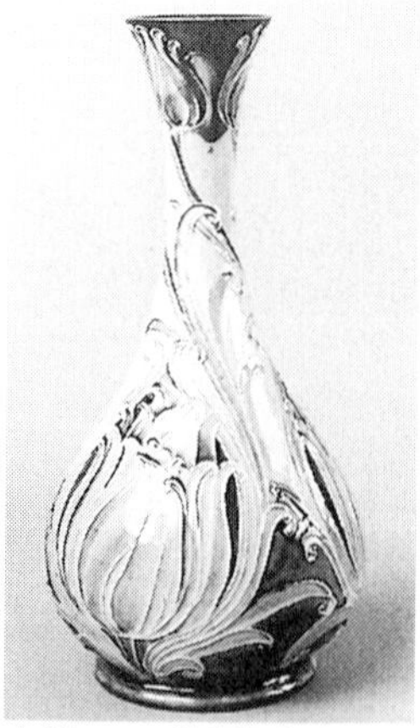

A Moorcroft MacIntyre Florian ware vase, the bottle-shaped body tube-line decorated and painted in shades of blue with stylised iris and scrolling leaves, printed and painted marks, c1900, 8in (20.5cm) high.
£650–700 *EH*

A pair of Moorcroft MacIntyre Florian ware spill vases, decorated in shades of cornflower blue with flowers and foliage, printed mark and signed 'W. Moorcroft Des' in green, c1900, 7in (18cm) high.
£1,300–1,500 *GAK*

A Moorcroft MacIntyre Florian ware jardinière, decorated with scrolling cartouches of orchids and foliage in pale and dark blue, c1900, 8in (20.5cm) high.
£850–1,000 *BIG*

A Moorcroft square two-handled biscuit box and cover, tube-lined with Claremont pattern, in red, purple and white on a green ground, restored, impressed and signed in blue, c1910, 6in (15cm) high.
£600–700 *DN*

Tube-lining

Tube-lining is applied as runny slip (liquid clay) through a fine nozzle or tube, much as one would ice a cake. Its function is to help keep the various colours in the decoration separate.

A Moorcroft two-handled vase, decorated with Cornflower pattern, impressed mark, signed and dated '1927', 12¾in (32.5cm) high.
£3,000–3,500 *SK*

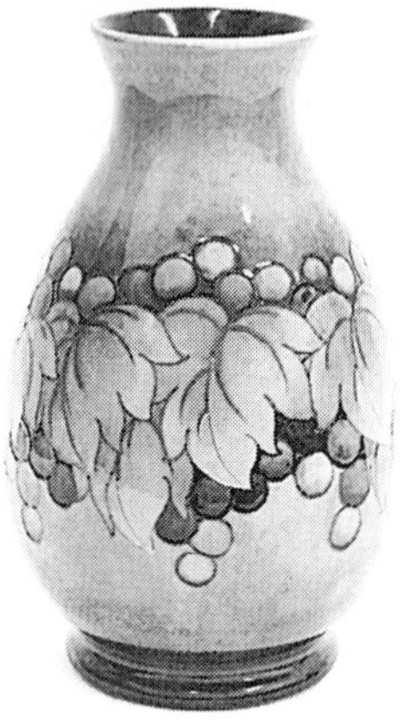

A William Moorcroft vase, decorated with purple grapes and green vine leaves on a green ground, signed and inscribed, 1920s, 14½in (37cm) high.
£550–600 *Mit*

A Moorcroft pottery bowl, the interior tube-lined with fish and plants on a mottled blue/green ground, inscribed, impressed and marked, 1930s, 9½in (24cm) diam.
£450–500 *Hal*

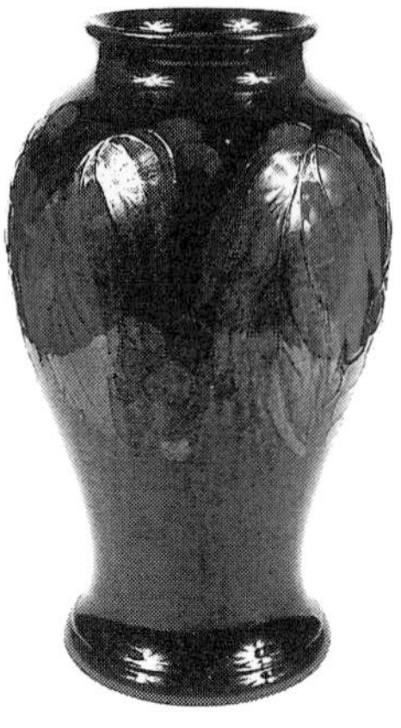

A Moorcroft Flambé vase, decorated with vine leaves and berries, in red tones, c1950, 13in (33cm) high.
£1,850–2,200 *DSG*

r. A Walter Moorcroft vase, decorated with Spring Flowers pattern, c1950, 13in (33cm) high.
£1,300–1,500 *RUM*

Poole Pottery

Established in 1873 as Carter & Co, the company expanded in 1921, taking the combined names of its partners to become Carter, Stabler & Adams. It was in 1963 that the trade name of Poole Pottery emerged.

The pottery began life manufacturing tiles and architectural faïence. By the 1880s, Poole was becoming increasingly well known, not just for this, but also for making ornamental garden pottery as well. With the help of designer and artistic potter, James Radley Young, Owen Carter's deep interest in decorative ware was to lead the company in a completely new direction. By 1920, the company was gaining a reputation for decorative ware and attracted many leading artists, including Harold and Phoebe Stabler, whose figures and models can be seen in the Poole Pottery museum.

The pottery flourished in the 1920s and 1930s under the inspired leadership of John Adams. Designer Truda Carter created the fresh floral patterns from which the distinctive modernist style emerged. Poole gained a worldwide reputation for originality and its Art Deco and traditional hand-painted wares became (and remain) fashionable and collectable.

Despite the restrictions of the war years, John Adams produced Streamline table wares, which were either decorated with the simple designs of Truda Carter or finished in a two-colour glaze known as Twintone. In the 1950s Poole was characterised by freeform shapes and abstract patterns developed by Alfred Read. The 1960s saw the expansion of both domestic and studio wares under the guidance of Robert Jefferson, Tony Morris and Guy Sydenham. The Delphis range was developed, followed by the Leslie Elsden-inspired Aegean range, demonstrating the creativity of the new, art-school-trained, paintresses.

The collectability of Poole continues to soar, with rare items reaching hundreds, even thousands, of pounds. While Art Deco ware by Ruth Pavely and Ann Hatchard commands extremely high prices, traditional 1920s and 1930s Poole has also become very collectable. The early Delphis range also continues to be increasingly desirable and new approaches to studio collections developed throughout the 1990s are expected to become the antiques of the future.

With the value of Poole's historical pieces now increasing daily, the Collectors' Club is going from strength to strength with over 1,000 members.

Lucy Lafferty

Poole Pottery

l. A Carter, Stabler & Adams vase, decorated by Margaret Holder, with stylised plant forms and geometric motifs in mushroom, brick-red, black and white, 1928–34, 7¾in (19.5cm) high.
£650–700 *ADE*

A Carter, Stabler & Adams vase, by Truda Carter, painted with stylised geometric design in blue, brown and white, marked, c1930, 7in (18cm) high.
£600–700 *P*

A Carter, Stabler & Adams two-handled globular baluster vase, painted in typical colours with Bluebird pattern, foliage and trellis pattern, on an off-white ground, c1929, 7in (18cm) high.
£450–500 *BKK*

A Carter, Stabler & Adams jug, with loop handle, painted in coloured enamels by Ann Hatchard, with a broad band of stylised tulips and leaves, beneath a wave and roundel band, slight damage, impressed and painted marks, c1930, 14½in (37cm) high.
£300–350 *DN*

A Carter, Stabler & Adams oviform vase, covered overall with a tin-glaze and painted in naturalistic colours, marked 'Carter & Co', 1915–21, 13in (33cm) high.
£280–350 *HarC*

r. A Carter, Stabler & Adams covered bowl, designed by Dora Batty, with 2 children playing and birds in flight above, c1934, 4in (10cm) high.
£75–100 *RDG*

r. A Carter, Stabler & Adams Sylvan oviform vase, with horizontal banding beneath a muted green glaze with brown speckling, 1934–37, 9in (23cm) high.
£120–150 *ADE*

A Carter, Stabler & Adams vase, decorated in blues, pale browns and pale orange and grey with geometric flowers, foliage and chevrons, by Ruth Pavely, 1938–42, 10½in (26.5cm) high.
£800–900 *ADE*

A Carter, Stabler & Adams plaque, modelled by Harold Brownsword, to commemorate the Coronation of Edward VIII, Prince of Wales, in 1936, 11in (28cm) high.
£250–300 *HarC*

This type of commemorative item was produced even though the coronation did not take place. Due to production schedules these pieces were in the pipeline as King George V was failing in health.

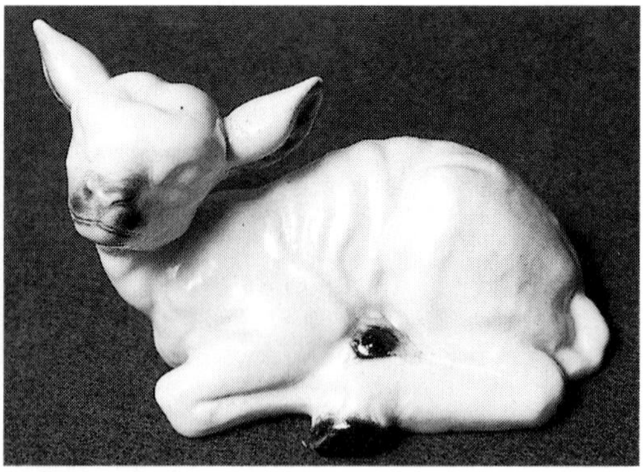

A Carter, Stabler & Adams model of a recumbent lamb, modelled by Marjorie Drawbell, 1940s, 5in (12.5cm) long.
£75–90 *HarC*

A Carter, Stabler & Adams jug, decorated in cream with a green interior, c1950, 4in (10cm) high.
£8–10 *UTP*

l. A Poole Pottery green plate, with blue and yellow decoration, shape No. 4, c1970, 10½in (26.5cm) diam.
£70–80 *PrB*

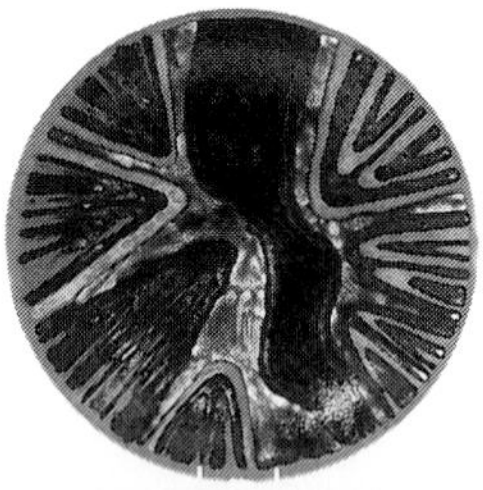

l. A Poole Pottery Delphis range charger, decorated by Shirley Campbell, 1966–69, 16in (40.5cm) diam.
£350–400 *ADE*

A Poole Pottery impressed brown plate, decorated in Oriental manner in brick-red and black, with 3 girls sitting beneath a flowering tree, 1970s, 9½in (24cm) diam.
£40–50 *HarC*

A Poole Pottery vase, by Chris White, decorated with orange swirls, shape No. 83, c1976, 6¼in (16cm) high.
£40–50 *PrB*

A Poole Pottery vase, painted in tones of green, ochre and beige with leaves and flowers, signed by Gwen Haskins, marked 'ZB', c1980, 15¾in (40cm) high.
£250–300 *MCA*

These are known as 'spot edged' patterns.

A Poole Pottery model of a bird, designed by Barbara Linley Adams, 1970s, 4in (10cm) high.
£10–12 *HarC*

Clarice Cliff

A Clarice Cliff Tankard shape coffee service, decorated with Crocus pattern, comprising 21 pieces, c1928.
£1,250–1,450 *HCC*

A Clarice Cliff Fantasque Dover jardinière, painted with Pebbles pattern, c1929, 7¼in (19cm) high.
£400–450 *GAK*

A Clarice Cliff Bizarre polychrome hand-painted bowl, decorated with Rhodanthe pattern, with yellow ground interior, 1930s, 9¾in (23.5cm) diam.
£200–220 *MCA*

A Clarice Cliff Bizarre Fantasque Stamford tureen and cover, decorated with Solomon's Seal pattern, c1930, 5½in (14cm) diam.
£170–220 *GH*

A Clarice Cliff Bizarre tea set, decorated with Gayday pattern, comprising 29 pieces, with facsimile signature, c1930.
£2,200–2,500 *P*

A Clarice Cliff Conical shape teapot, decorated with Farmhouse pattern, c1931, 5¾in (14.5cm) high.
£900–1,000 *CSA*

r. A Clarice Cliff Bizarre two-person tea set, painted with Crocus pattern, facsimile signature in black and impressed date code for 1933.
£550–600 *P(NE)*

A Clarice Cliff Biarritz plate, decorated with Blue Firs pattern, c1933, 10½in (26.5cm) wide.
£200–240 *GH*

A Newport Pottery Clarice Cliff Bizarre Fantasque octagonal plate, decorated with Secrets pattern, c1933, 10in (25.5cm) diam.
£220–250 *MCA*

A Newport Pottery Clarice Cliff Bizarre Fantasque vase, decorated with Solitude pattern, shape No. 360, with green and yellow ringed rim and base, black printed mark, c1933, 8in (20.5cm) high.
£1,600–1,800 *JM*

l. A Clarice Cliff Bon Jour hot water jug, decorated with Cabbage Flower pattern, c1934, 7in (18cm) high.
£650–700 *BKK*

A Clarice Cliff Conical sugar sifter, painted with Oasis pattern, above a blue painted foot rim, c1935, 5¼in (13.5cm) high.
£450–500 *Bea(E)*

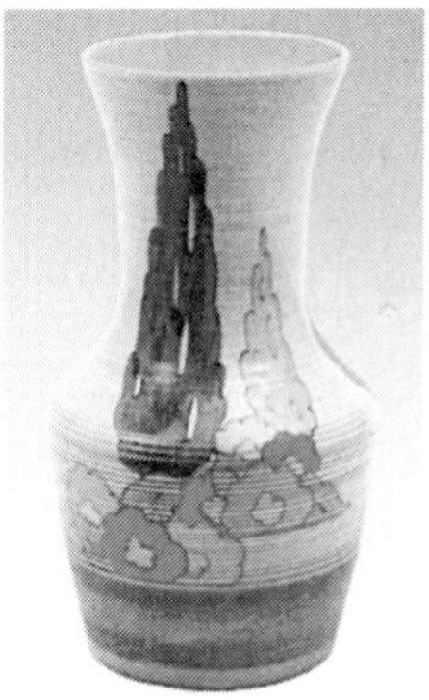

A Clarice Cliff pottery vase, painted with Capri pattern, shape No. 386, slight damage, c1935, 12¼in (31cm) high.
£280–320 *Bea(E)*

A Clarice Cliff Bizarre wall mask, Flora, fascimile signature, c1935, 6¾in (17cm) high.
£250–280 *P(Ba)*

A Wilkinson's Pottery Clarice Cliff octagonal plate, decorated with Taormina pattern, c1936, 9in (23cm) diam.
£220–250 *MCA*

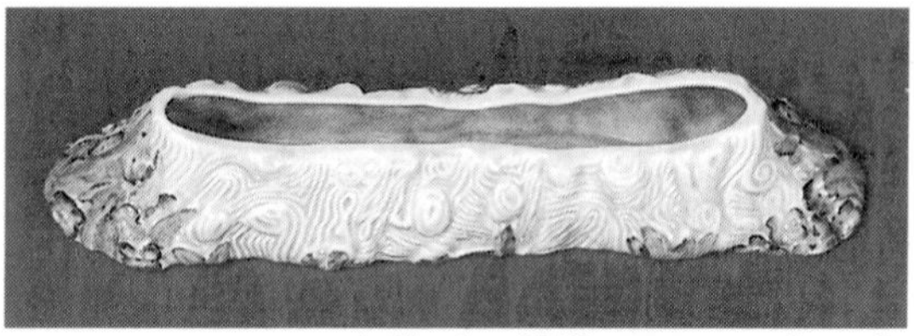

A Clarice Cliff posy vase, shaped as the gnarled base of a tree, decorated at each end in colours with groups of flowers amid grasses, late 1930s, 11in (28cm) long.
£70–80 *RAC*

A Clarice Cliff Windsor shape teapot, decorated with Sundew pattern, c1937, 5in (12.5cm) high.
£50–60 *CSA*

l. A Clarice Cliff Celtic Harvest biscuit barrel, c1938, 7¼in (18cm) high.
£170–200 *CSA*

Susie Cooper

A Susie Cooper dinner service, by Gray's Pottery, comprising 70 pieces, c1925.
£500–600 *P(G)*

A Susie Cooper hand-decorated plate, by Gray's Pottery, pattern No. 8034, c1928, 9in (23cm) diam.
£160–180 *BKK*

A Susie Cooper coffee service, comprising 16 pieces, incised with stylised leaves, on a dark brown ground, printed marks in brown, coffee pot rivetted, 1930s.
£200–220 *DN*

A Susie Cooper Classic Vista coffee set, comprising 24 pieces, decorated in pale brown, blue and yellow, 1970, plate 8½in (21.5cm) diam.
£5,000–5,500 *MAV*

Classic Vista is a rare pattern.

Figures & Models

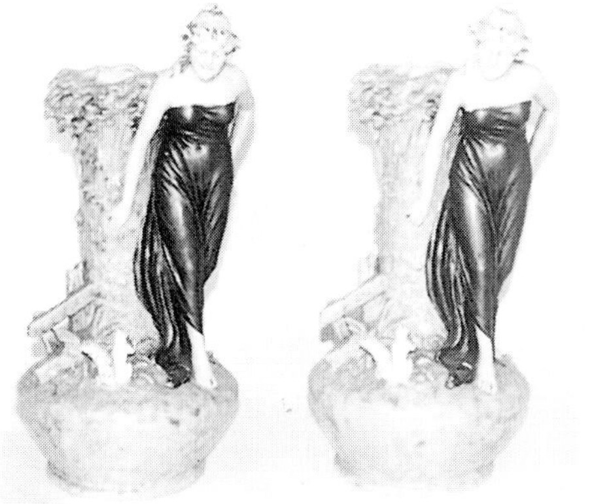

A pair of green mottled figural vases, each with gold draped maidens, squirrels and flower detail, c1900, 14in (35.5cm) high.
£240–280 *AP*

A pair of Goldscheider busts, after Carrier Belleuse, one with a lion, the other with an eagle, c1900, 27½in (70cm) high.
£3,700–4,200 *P*

A Berlin Art Nouveau style porcelain figural vase, enamelled on 3 sides with sinuous flower stems, the front with a maiden scantily clad in a pale green robe, probably modelled by Martin Fritzsche, red printed orb mark and 'K.P.M.', c1900, 19¼in (49cm) high.
£3,300–3,800 *S*

l. A French Art Deco crackle glazed pottery figure, depicting Diana and hound, unsigned, c1930, 8in (20.5cm) high.
£200–240 *CIR*

A Hutschenreuther figure of a naked maiden, juggling 2 gilt balls, signed 'C. Werner', 1930–50, 8in (20.5cm) high.
£450–500 *AAV*

A carved ivory bust of a young woman, in the manner of Alphonse Mucha, her hair painted in orange-red, wearing a golden diadem, c1910, 5in (12.5cm) high.
£200–240 *WeH*

A Myott Son & Co Goldscheider figure of Edith Sitwell, wearing a jester's turquoise hat with bells, and a yellow short cape decorated with blue, green and ochre, black printed mark, 1930s, 9in (23cm) high.
£160–180 *Hal*

This type of Goldscheider figure was made under licence in the Myott factory, the parent factory being in Vienna.

Cross Reference
Colour Review

A carved marble figure of an Amazon, with a bronze bow, on a marble base, c1920, 15½in (39.5cm) long.
£2,800–3,200 *S(NY)*

An Art Deco carved marble figure of a naked bathing girl, seated on a rocky base with seashells, signed 'J. Vichy, Florence', 1930s, 10¾in (27.5cm) high.
£260–300 *P(Ba)*

l. A Lenci figure of a naked girl, kneeling on top of the world, wearing a chequered beret, the globe decorated with the continents and their indigenous animal species, marked, 1930s, 18in (46cm) high.
£4,000–4,500 *WW*

A gilt-bronze lamp, by François-Raoul Larche, depicting Loië Fuller, marked, c1900, 17½in (44.5cm) high.
£16,000–18,000 *S(NY)*

This lamp is by a very well known and respected sculptor, the subject being a famous American dancer. The piece is very fluid in its execution, giving a marvellous sense of movement. An ingenious and attractive feature is that the light fittings and bulbs are concealed within the veils above the dancer's head, which casts light on to the figure.

A bronze figure of a naked dancer, after F. Ouillon-Carrère, entitled 'Sword Dance', on a square marble base, parts missing, signed and dated '1919', 21½in (54.5cm) high.
£850–1,000 *HYD*

r. An Art Deco bronze and ivory figure, by Lorenzl, entitled 'Pyjama Girl', c1930, 10in (25.5cm) high.
£1,200–1,400 *ASA*

A cold-painted and gilt-bronze figure of a bat dancer, by Professor Poertzel, dressed in a short tunic, on a green and black veined marble base, marked, 1920s, 23½in (60cm) high.
£4,600–5,000 *S*

A gilt-bronze and ivory figure of a dancer, cast and carved from a model by D. H. Chiparus, with outstretched arms, in a jewelled tunic skirt and headress heightened with coloured enamels, on a black marble base, c1925, 10¾in (27.5cm) high.
£4,500–5,000 *P*

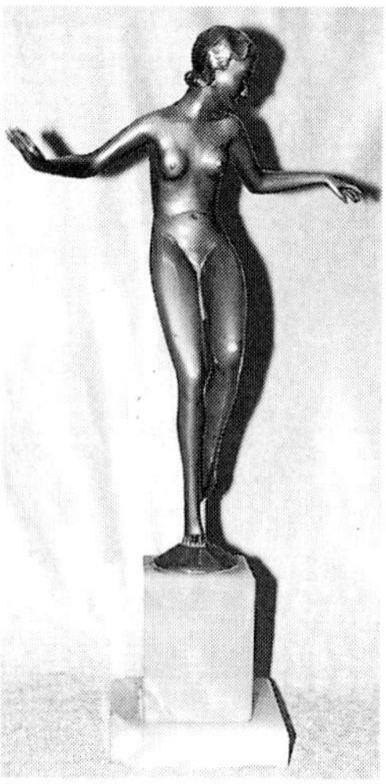

An Art Deco bronze figure of a dancer, by Adolph, c1930, 16in (40.5cm) high.
£1,300–1,500 *ASA*

An Art Deco spelter figure of a semi-naked female, holding a globe, in the form of an electrical table lamp, on an alabaster base, c1930, 20in (51cm) high.
£550–600 *M*

A cold-painted bronze figure of a dancing girl, cast from a model by Lorenzl, with green patination, on a circular marble base, signed, c1930, 10½in (26.5cm) high.
£850–1,000 *P*

Art Deco Furniture

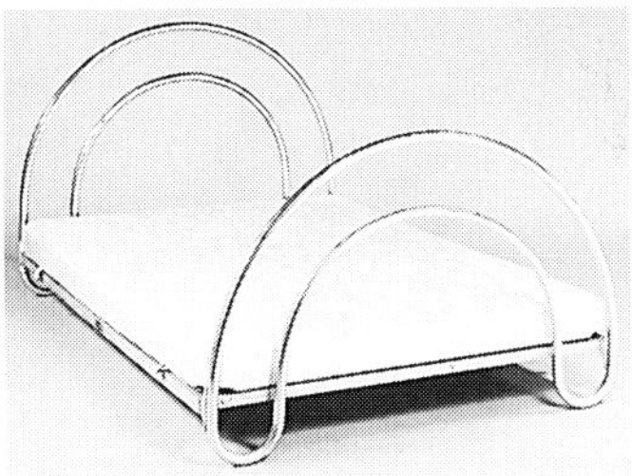

An Art Deco chromium-plated bed, with head and footboard of rounded tubular form united by bed irons and hinged bed base, probably made by PEL, c1930, 54in (137cm) wide.
£450–500 *P(Ba)*

A Pierre Chareau rosewood and mahogany cabinet, the cabinet opening to 2 short drawers above shelves, raised on a plinth, c1930, 59in (149cm) wide.
£13,500–15,000 *S(NY)*

An Art Deco walnut veneered display cabinet, on a platform base, c1930, 45in (114.5cm) wide.
£320–380 *DA*

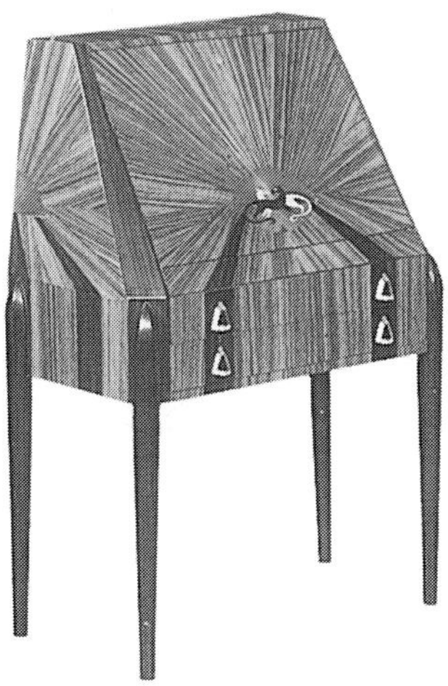

A French Art Deco bronze-mounted *ébène-de-macassar* cabinet, attributed to Dominique, the bowed top with canted corners above a glazed door opening to a shelved interior, above 2 short drawers, flanked by 2 doors opening to shelves, the whole raised on tapering legs trimmed in bronze, c1928, 59in (150cm) wide.
£2,600–2,900 *S(NY)*

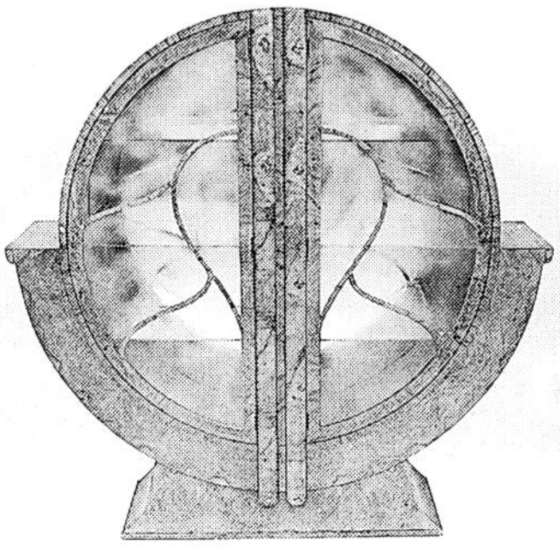

An Art Deco walnut circular-shaped display cabinet, the interior with 3 glazed shelves, enclosed by a pair of glazed and moulded panel doors, on sweeping shaped base, c1930, 57in (144cm) wide.
£720–800 *P(F)*

A Donald Deskey armchair, the upholstered back and seat flanked by curved arms with upholstered rests continuing to front legs, c1931.
£3,200–3,500 *S(NY)*

A model of this chair was shown at the Brooklyn Museum's 1931 AUDUC Exhibit of Modern Industrial & Decorative Art.

l. An Art Deco desk, inlaid with brass, ebony and ivory, with sycamore and bird's-eye maple interior, the fall-front with a design of entwined panthers, above 2 drawers, on tapering legs, 1920s, 29in (74cm) wide.
£2,000–2,500 *S*

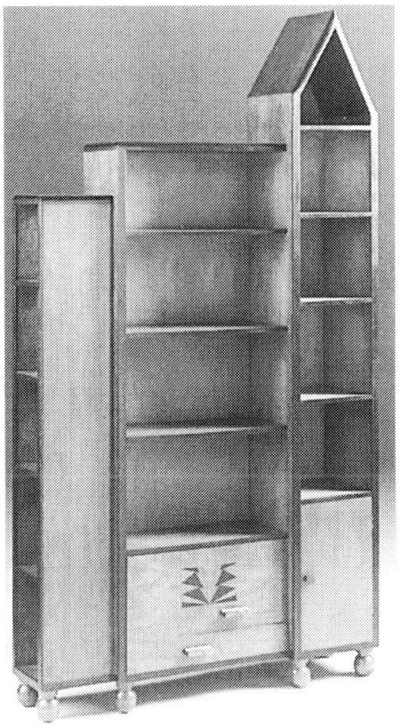

An American Art Deco birch and stained mahogany skyscraper cabinet, in the manner of Paul T. Frankl, with an irregular arrangement of shelves, drawers and cabinet doors raised on ball feet, the lower drawers inlaid with geometric design, mounted with nickelled-bronze hardware, c1930, 40in (102cm) wide.
£2,500–3,000 *S(NY)*

A French Art Deco ivory-inlaid ébène-de-macassar chest of drawers, the top painted with *faux* ivory craquelures, above 3 central drawers with ivory pulls flanked by panels inlaid in ivory, raised on carved tapering feet, c1925, 36in (91.5cm) high.
£3,200–3,500 *S(NY)*

A French Art Deco ébène-de-macassar, celluloid and leather desk, the top drawers and panels on the reverse clad in celluloid moulded with stylised flower-heads, the remaining drawer fronts, side and reverse panels veneered and inlaid with diamond pattern stringing, raised on shaped legs with celluloid sabots, c1925, 52in (132cm) wide.
£10,000–12,000 *S(NY)*

An Art Deco burr-walnut lady's dressing table, the interior fitted with triptych mirror, a well and swing-trays, the fittings with initials 'HC', the frieze with a central secret frieze drawer flanked by smaller drawers, the apron continuing into square-section tapered legs, crossbanding and ebony stringing throughout, c1930, 22½in (57cm) wide.
£3,500–4,000 *SLM*

A Jules Leleu burr walnut sofa, raised on a flaring base above ball feet, c1927, 80in (203cm) long.
£8,000–9,000 *S(NY)*

A pair of French Art Deco consoles, each with *verde antico* marble top, raised on 3 scrolling hammered iron supports ending in pendant leaf-form clusters, beneath a panel carved in low relief with stylised flowers, each back with a mahogany panel flanked by conforming wrought iron brackets, the stepped base clad in marble, c1925, 43½in (109cm) high.
£9,000–10,000 *S(NY)*

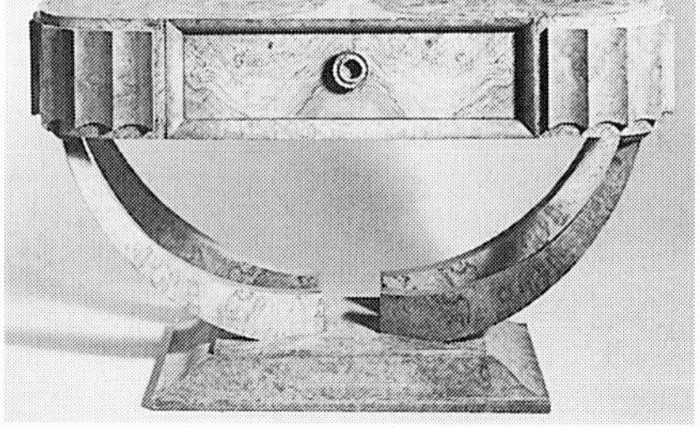

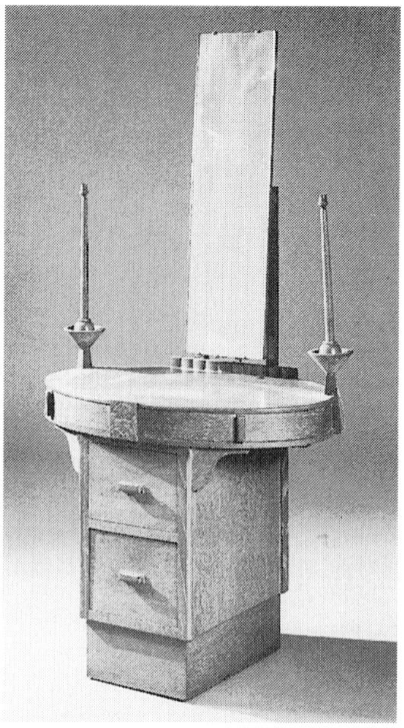

An Art Deco oak dressing table, with a mirror above an oval top with 'candlestick' light fitments on either side, the apron with carved and painted floral panels flanked by hinged drawers, the single pedestal base with 2 drawers, c1930, 30in (76cm) wide, and a limed oak wardrobe.
£320–400 *P(Ba)*

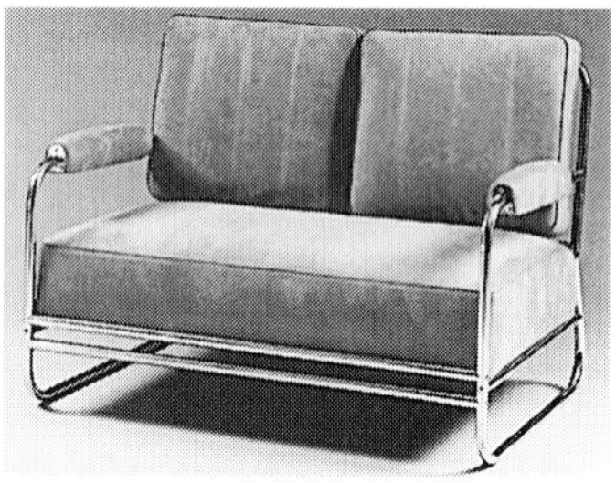

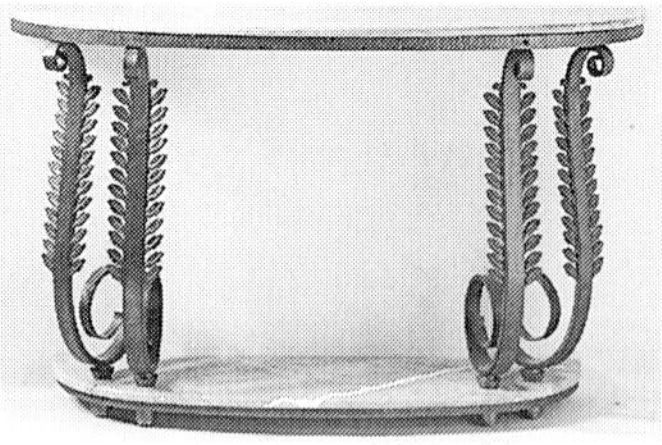

An Edgar Brandt wrought iron and marble console, the marble top raised on 4 scrolled legs wrought with leafage above a marble base, on a hammered iron support, impressed 'E. Brandt', c1925, 59in (150cm) high.
£11,500–13,000 *S(NY)*

Cross Reference
Art Deco Ceramics

l. A Hille walnut serving table, the top rounded and fluted at the front corners, with glass back panels, raised on 4 curved and angled supports, on a shaped rectangular base, c1935, 54in (137cm) wide.
£750–900 *P*

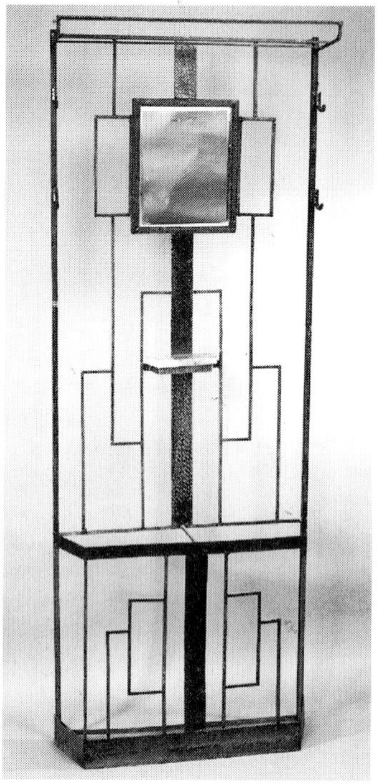

A Belgian Art Deco wrought iron mirror-back hall stand, the square bevel-edged mirror plate over a veined marble short shelf, c1930, 28½in (72.5cm) wide.
£500–600 *TMA*

l. A Howell chromed-steel settee, upholstered in olive green suede, c1930, 48in (122cm) long.
£1,750–2,000 *S(NY)*

An Asprey cocktail table, with mirrored and chrome front and top, maker's label to reverse, c1930, 23in (58.5cm) wide.
£380–420 *BKK*

An Art Deco walnut nest of tables, the tops veneered in triangular segments, each raised on 4 plank supports on cruciform bases, c1930, 31in (80cm) diam.
£420–500 *P*

Art Deco Metalware

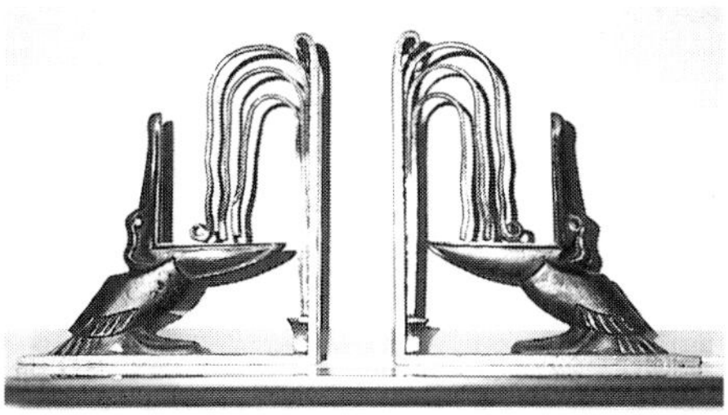

A pair of wrought iron bookends, by Edgar Brandt, c1925, 10in (25.5cm) high.
£1,500–2,000 *CIR*

A Dutch silver beaker, by Gerritsen & van Kempen, Zeist, with 2 wooden handles, 1933, 7½in (19cm) high.
£250–300 *S(Am)*

A Lustre Art iridescent glass bowl, on an Oscar Bach bronze base, modelled as 3 nude men, fitted with a flaring glass dish in golden iridescence shading to purple and green, dish signed 'Lustre Art/1142', base stamped 'Obaso-Bronze/Oscar B. Bach Studios', c1930, 14¾in (37.5cm) diam.
£2,500–2,800 *S(NY)*

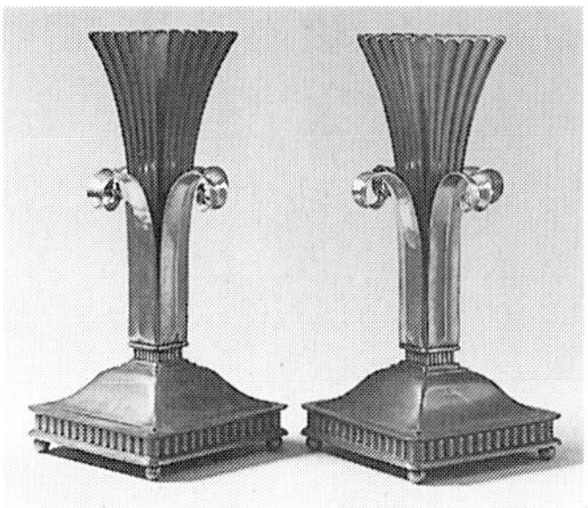

A pair of French Art Deco bronze and steel candlesticks, attributed to Raymond Subes, each with recessed candle cup within a flaring fluted support, wrought with curling leaves, above a reeded support, raised on ball feet, c1925, 18¼in (46.5cm) high.
£3,200–3,600 *S(NY)*

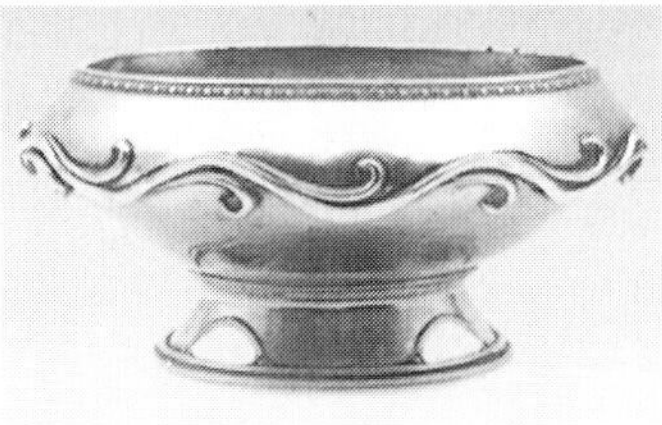

An Omar Ramsden silver fruit bowl, with lightly hammered decoration, applied with scrolls below a beaded rim, on a pierced spreading circular base, 1938, 8¾in (22cm) diam.
£900–1,000 *Bea(E)*

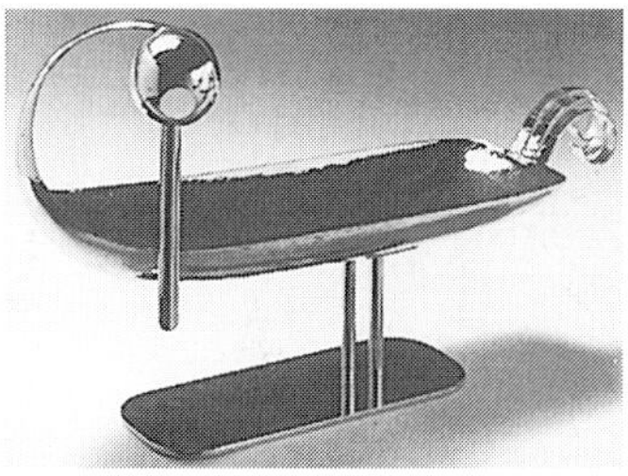

A Hagenauer chromed-metal figural centerpiece, modelled as a stylised bird, impressed 'Franz Hagenauer Wien', c1930, 18¼in (46.5cm) wide.
£1,400–1,700 *S(NY)*

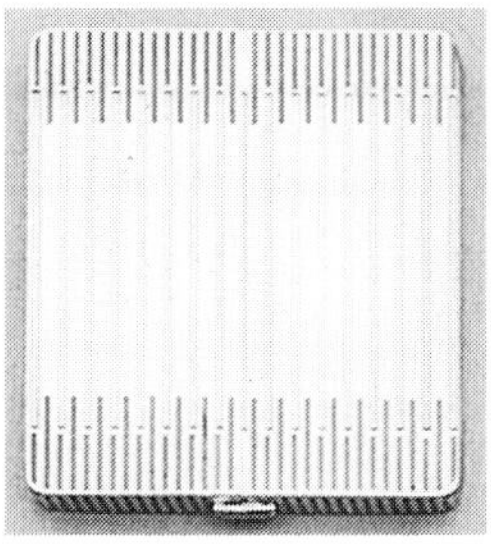

An Art Deco 18ct gold compact, with black enamel geometric decoration, the pop-up cover opening up to reveal a mirror, signed 'Cartier', London 1933, 2½in (66.5cm) square, in a fitted case.
£800–1,000 *Bon(C)*

An Art Deco chrome crumb tray, surmounted by a figure, based on a design by Lorenzl, c1934, 7¾in (19.5cm) high.
£40–50 *BKK*

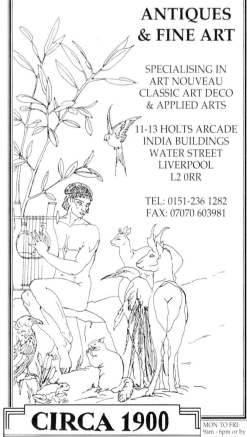

An Art Deco dressing table centrepiece, the alabaster base surmounted by a pair of spelter nudes, with a pair of scent bottles and an oval tray, each with fitted gilt mounts, and a small mirror mounted on a pair of columns, c1925, 15in (38cm) long.
£280–320 *P(B)*

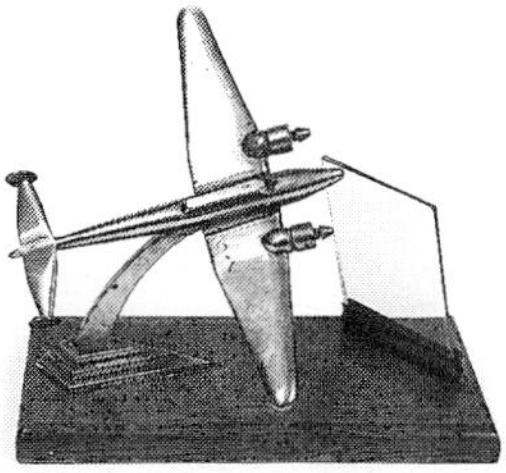

An Art Deco desk photograph frame, supported on a wooden plinth, surmounted by a brass aeroplane, 1940s, 11¾in (30cm) long.
£70–80 *P(B)*

Art Deco Glass

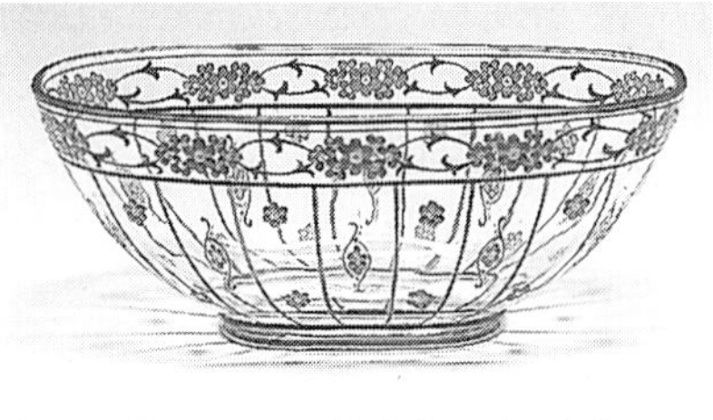

An Art Deco enamelled glass bowl, by Marcel Goupy, enamelled in tones of blue with forget-me-nots and scrolls, signed in script, c1925, 11¾in (30cm) long.
£260–300 *B&B*

A Lalique glass bowl, entitled 'Gui', decorated with moulded mistletoe pattern, the base with moulded signature and etched 'France', c1940, 9¼in (23.5cm) diam.
£420–500 *L&E*

A Lalique opalescent glass shallow dish, entitled 'Rosheim', decorated with stylised shell motifs, c1935, 13in (33cm) diam.
£300–350 *HYD*

A Lalique opalescent glass figure of Thais, signed 'R. Lalique', c1925, 8½in (21.5cm) high.
£5,800–6,500 *SLN*

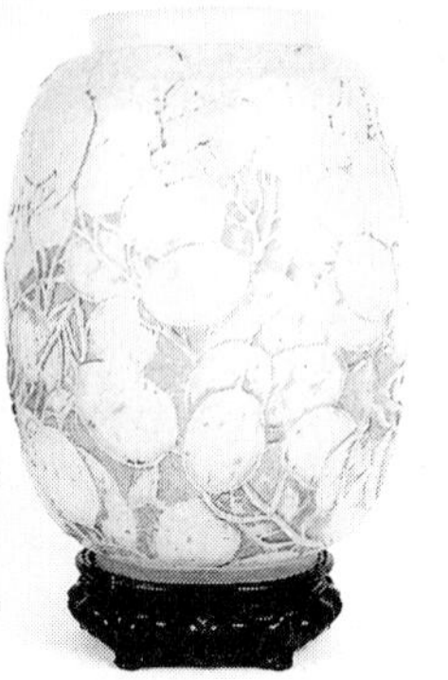

A Lalique opalescent glass vase, entitled 'Monnaie du Pape', moulded with stems of honesty, heightened with blue staining, on a wooden stand, etched 'R. Lalique France', c1915, 9¼in (23.5cm) high.
£1,300–1,500 *P*

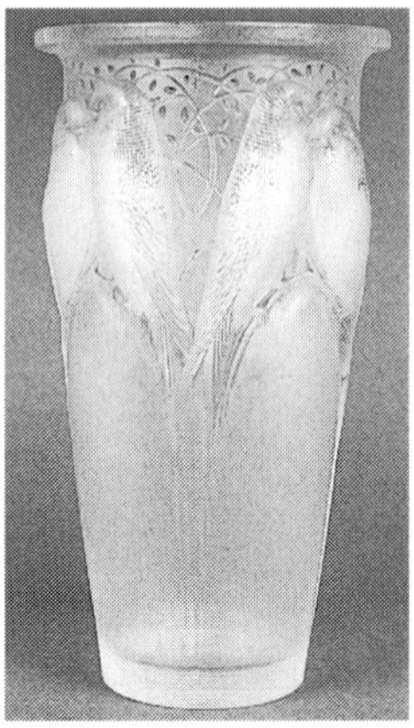

A Lalique opalescent glass vase, entitled 'Ceylan', moulded in relief with pairs of lovebirds perched amidst boughs of prunus blossom, engraved 'R. Lalique, France', c1922, 9½in (24cm) high.
£2,000–2,200 *P*

A Lalique opalescent glass vase, entitled 'Laurier', moulded in bold relief with berries and leaves, etched mark and 'No. 947', c1925, 7in (18cm) high.
£450–500 *DN*

A Schneider clear glass vase, internally decorated with air bubbles, applied with a band of clear glass discs with olive-green spirals, each centring a red cabochon glass sphere, inscribed, c1925, 8¼in (21cm) high.
£10,000–12,000 *S(NY)*

A Daum Nancy vase, the smoky topaz glass deeply acid-etched with geometric design, signed in intaglio, c1925, 20in (51cm) high.
£2,200–2,500 *S(NY)*

An André Hunebelle glass vase, of compressed globular shape, moulded with densely packed stylised sunflowers and foliage, heightened with green-blue staining, 1928, 4¼in (11cm) high.
£450–550 *BKK*

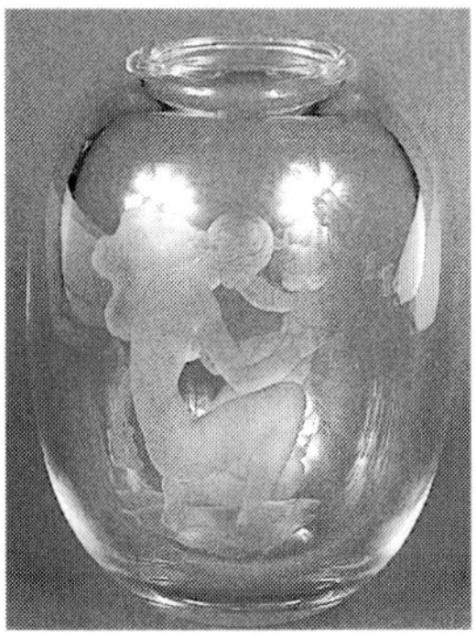

An Orrefors glass vase, engraved with a young mother holding a baby, c1930, 6½in (16.5cm) high.
£750–900 *SHa*

A Stevens & Williams globular light blue glass vase, designed by Keith Murray, with sand-blasted surface texture, decorated with vertical ribbing, signed, 1932–39, 9¾in (25cm) high.
£450–500 *ADE*

r. A Powell's Whitefriars amethyst ribbon-trailed vase, c1935, 9in (23cm) high.
£70–80 *JHa*

Art Deco Jewellery

An Art Deco diamond bracelet, set with a scrolling centrepiece and ruby cabochon endstones, c1935.
£6,000–7,000 *P*

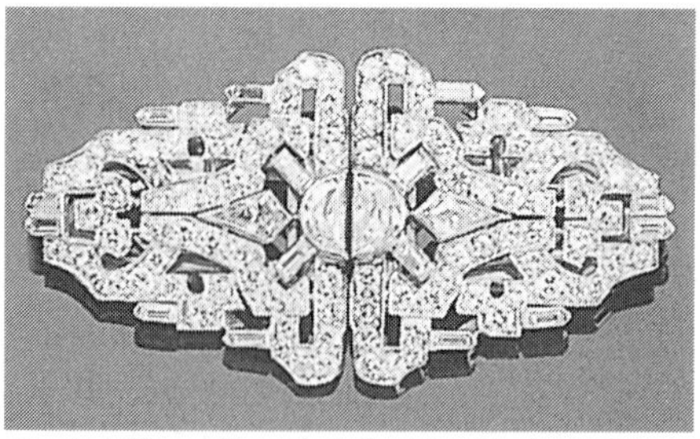

An Art Deco diamond double clip brooch, of openwork geometric design, set with demi-lune, kite, brilliant and baguette-cut diamonds, 1930s.
£1,200–1,400 *Bon(C)*

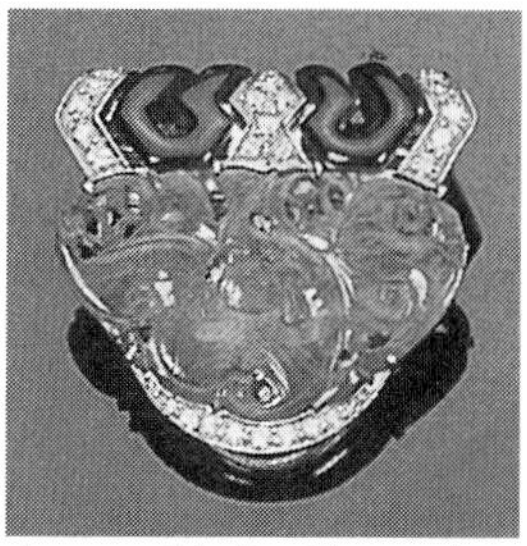

A carved jade, diamond and black enamelled dress clip, the jade carved in a foliate design, 1930s.
£950–1,100 *S(S)*

An Art Deco diamond double clip brooch, each clip designed as a stylised scroll, some diamonds missing, c1935.
£3,500–4,000 *Bon(C)*

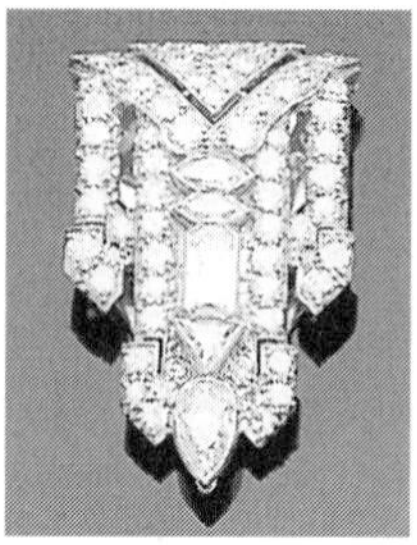

An Art Deco diamond clip, set with a channel of fancy-cut diamonds in a geometric diamond cartouche cluster frame, c1935.
£2,000–2,200 *P*

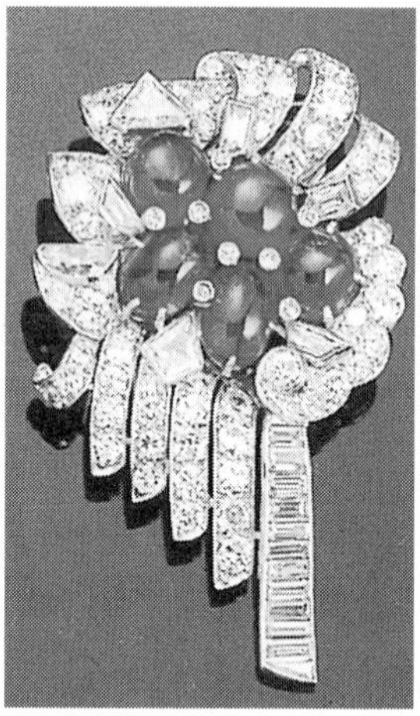

An Art Deco ruby and diamond clip brooch, c1935.
£4,000–4,500 *Bon*

r. A pair of diamond ear pendants, set with baguette-cut diamond stepped sections, c1925.
£3,000–3,300 *P*

l. A Georges Fouquet frosted rock crystal, platinum and diamond necklace, composed of 48 elongated beads supporting a ring conjoined by diamond encrusted links, further supporting a carved rock crystal pendant, signed, c1925, 15in (38cm) long.
£4,200–4,800 *S(NY)*

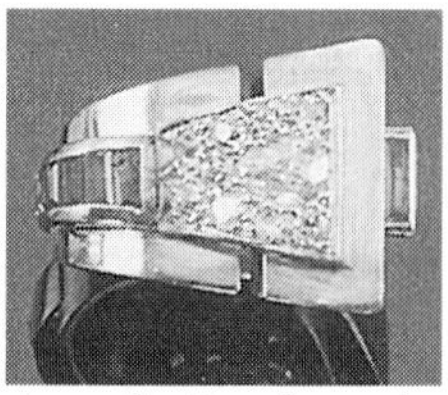

A synthetic ruby and diamond cocktail ring, the tapered geometric front pavé-set with cushion-shaped diamonds and channel-set with calibré-cut synthetic rubies.
£660–700 *S(Am)*

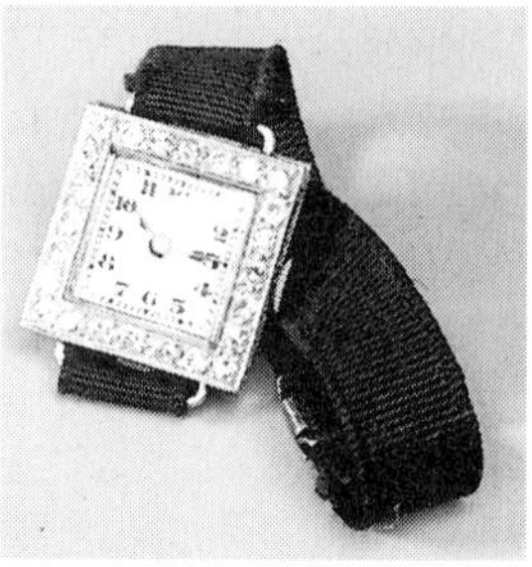

An Art Deco platinum and diamond lady's wristwatch, by Libela Watch Company, with a Swiss 17 jewel movement, 1930s.
£780–880 *TMA*

r. An Omega silver and enamel lever dress watch, the silvered dial with Arabic numerals, case, dial and movement signed, c1920.
£800–900 *S(Am)*

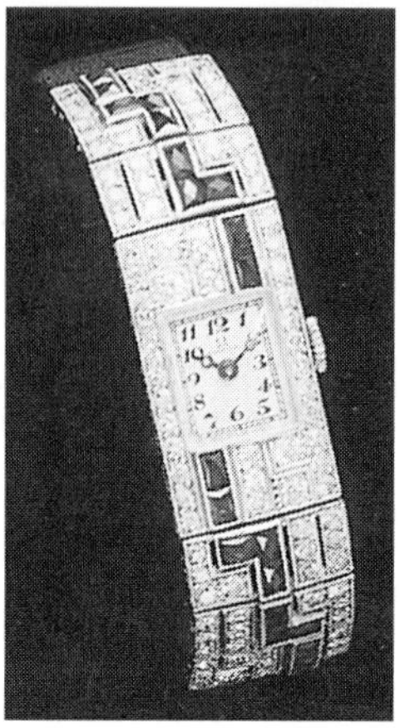

l. An Omega lady's platinum, diamond and sapphire wristwatch, with cream matt dial with Arabic numerals, 17 jewels, dial and movement signed, c1925.
£2,500–3,000 *S(HK)*

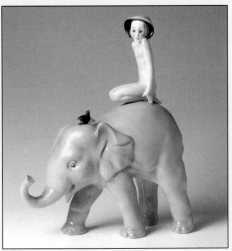

An oak revolving bookcase, by Liberty & Co, c1900, 25½in (65cm) square.
£1,800–2,000 *S*

A carved oak bureau, probably German, restored, c1910, 24½in (62cm) wide.
£1,800–2,000 *DORO*

A mahogany and fruitwood inlaid vitrine, c1905, 54in (137cm) wide.
£1,850–2,200 *S*

A pair of Arts and Crafts oak armchairs, with pierced decoration, c1900.
£120–140 *P(B)*

A Morris & Co ebonised beech Sussex chair, with rush seat, c1900.
£180–200 *FOX*

An Arts and Crafts oak open armchair,with slat back and rush seat, stamped 'J. M. Bristow', c1900.
£650–800 *DN*

An Aesthetic Movement fire surround, tiles by W. B. Simpson & Sons, c1875, 84in (213.5cm) wide.
£12,000–14,000 *S*

A beechwood chair, designed by Josef Hoffmann, with brass feet, one missing, c1901.
£1,500–1,700 *DORO*

An ebonised wood and painted parchment settee, by Carlo Bugatti, c1900, 51in (129.5cm) wide.
£5,500–6,000 *S(NY)*

An Arts and Crafts oak work table, stamped 'Liberty & Co', c1890, 28in (71cm) wide.
£625–685 *GBr*

A Majorelle gilt-bronze and ormolu-mounted mahogany sideboard, carved with poppies, c1900, 80in (203cm) wide.
£4,000–4,500 *S(NY)*

A five-panel screen, attributed to Frederick Hollyer, entitled 'Les Six Jours de la Création', in a giltwood frame, c1890, 24½in (62cm) high.
£2,000–2,200 *S*

An Arts and Crafts oak dining table, by John P. White, Bedford, designed by M. H. Baillie Scott, c1901, 71in (180.5cm) wide.
£10,500–12,000 *S*

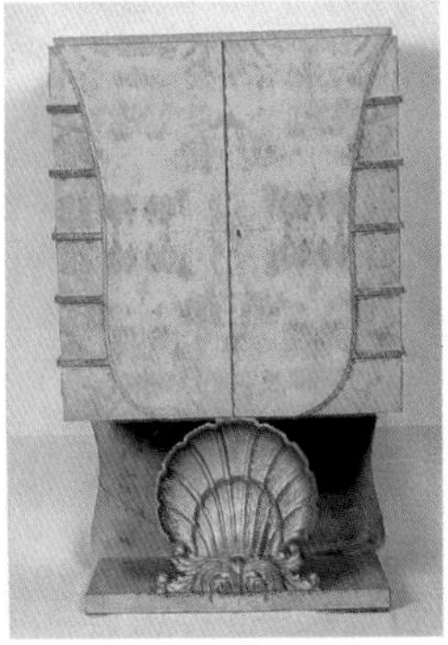

An Art Deco bird's-eye maple cocktail cabinet, with shell motif, by Hille, 1930s, 37in (94.5cm) wide.
£2,400–2,800 *Bri*

An Art Deco walnut bowfronted drinks cabinet, in 2 sections, with roller doors, the top enclosing a mirrored interior, 1930s, 36in (91cm) wide.
£380–420 *P(B)*

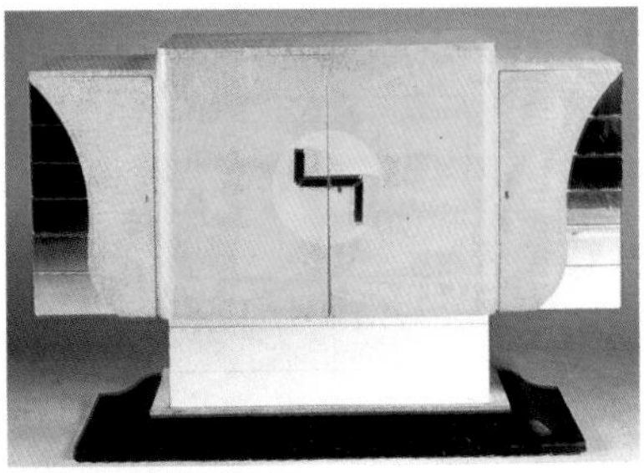

An Art Deco satin maple and ebonised cocktail cabinet, attributed to Hille, the breakfront with 2 central doors enclosing fitted satin birch and mirrored interior, c1930, 63¾in (162cm) wide.
£1,700–2,000 *P*

An amboyna and blonde wood cocktail cabinet, by Maurice Adams, c1934, 48in (122cm) wide.
£3,700–4,000 *S*

A padouk dining table, by Joseph Emberton of Bath, the end supports on stepped bases, 1930s, 105in (266.5cm) long.
£2,000–2,200 *S*

A red lacquered occasional table, by Jules Leleu, the top raised on 4 bow-fronted block legs, on a circular base, branded reference number on underside '3213', c1930, 35¼in (89.5cm) diam.
£7,000–8,000 *S*

An Art Deco children's desk and chair, the design attributed to H. Wouda, painted in red and black, Dutch, c1930, table 19in (49cm) high.
£750–900 *S(Am)*

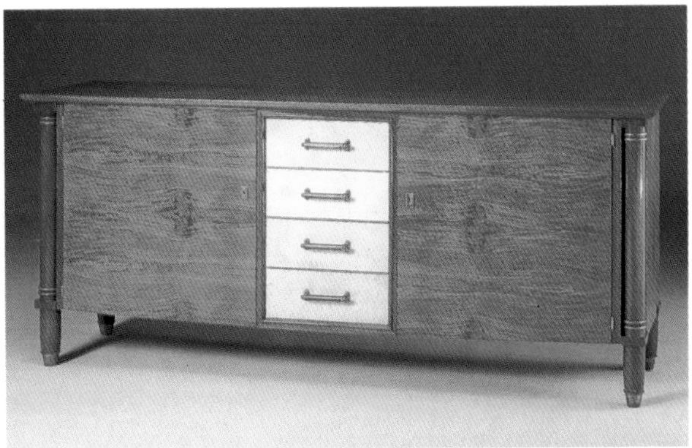

A satinwood sideboard, by Jules Leleu, with 4 central parchment-covered drawers with bronze pulls, flanked by 2 doors opening to shelved interiors, c1930, 84in (218cm) wide.
£4,250–4,750 *S(NY)*

An Art Deco oak three-tier coffee table, supported on block feet, c1930, 41¼in (105cm) high.
£50–60 *P(B)*

A parchment-covered wood writing desk, by André Arbus, c1935, 43in (52.5cm) wide.
£6,200–6,800 *S*

An Art Deco Magnolia No. 5 and ebonised dining table and chairs, designed by Ray Hille, with extension leaf, c1935, 83¾in (213cm) long.
£2,200–2,400 *P*

A Thun pottery charger, Switzerland, c1885, 14¾in (37.5cm) diam.
£300–350 *DSG*

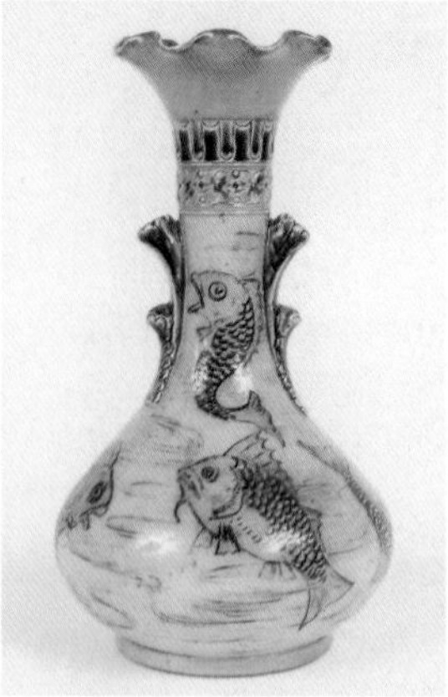

A Martin Brothers stoneware vase, incised with comical fish, dated '25.5.79', 10¾in (27cm) high.
£600–700 *P*

An Art Pottery lustre charger, possibly designed by Walter Crane, c1880, 12¼in (31cm) diam.
£400–450 *P(B)*

A Burmantofts faïence vase, with twin handles, decorated with florets in roundels, c1885, 8in (20.5cm) high.
£140–160 *DSG*

A Barnstaple pottery jardinière, possibly by Alex Lauder, c1890, 11½in (29cm) high.
£140–160 *P(B)*

A William de Morgan vase, decorated by Joe Juster, c1890, 7in (18cm) high.
£3,100–3,500 *HAM*

A pair of J. Stiff & Sons, Lambeth, stoneware vases, c1890, 5in (12.5cm) high.
£100–120 *SnA*

A Langley Pottery jardinière, decorated in coloured slips, c1900, 8in (20.5cm) high.
£200–250 *DSG*

A Della Robbia pottery charger, signed with ship monogram 'DR', c1894, 15in (38cm) diam.
£330–360 *P(B)*

A Scottish *faux bois* lustre jug, with a pewter lid, c1900, 8in (20.5cm) high.
£30–40 *OD*

A North Devon Pottery twin-handled vase, by W. L. Baron, c1895, 5½in (14cm) high.
£120–140 *DSG*

An Art Nouveau pottery jardinière, by Ravissant, coloured in orange and honey glaze, c1900, 8¼in (21cm) high.
£80–100 *P(B)*

A Van Briggle Pottery vase, entitled 'Lorelei', c1901, 11in (28cm) high.
£750–850 *EKK*

A Minton Secessionist vase, designed by L. V. Solon and J. W. Wadsworth, c1902, 17½in (44.5cm) high.
£600–675 *DSG*

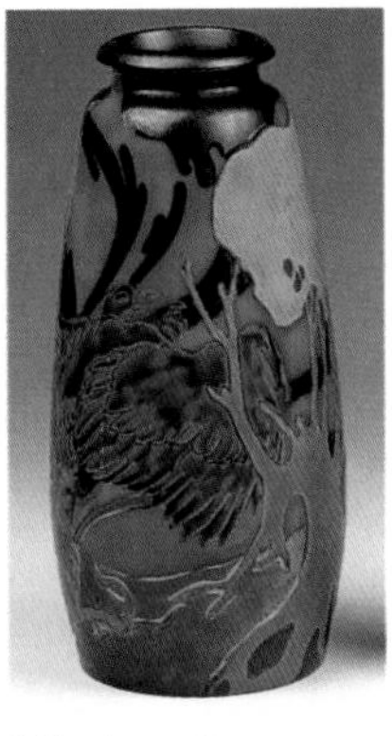

A Zsolnay faïence lustre vase, painted with a bird of prey, impressed mark, c1905, 9¾in (24.5cm) high.
£2,500–3,000 *DORO*

A Martin Brothers stoneware model of a bird, dated '1911', 8in (20.5cm) high.
£2,800–3,400 *P*

A Zuid-Holland pottery rose bowl, with a pierced metal cover, c1905, 6in (15cm) diam.
£350–380 *OO*

A Longwy painted pottery sandwich dish, decorated with stylised daffodils and clematis, France, c1910, 15in (38cm) wide.
£145–175 *DSG*

A K. K. Fachschule Znaim floor vase, decorated with grapes, marked, c1905, 15¼in (38.5cm) high.
£800–900 *DORO*

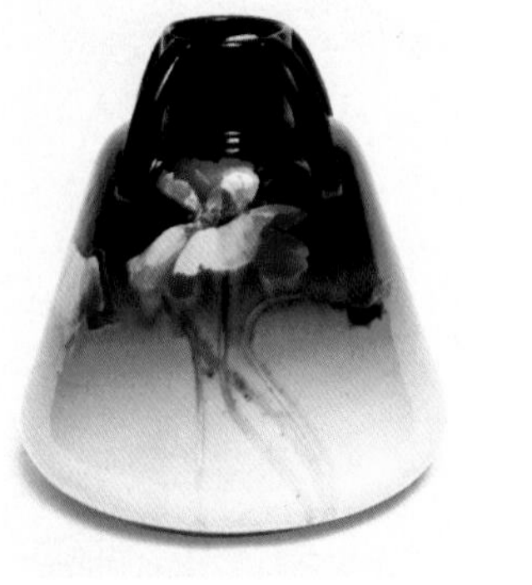

A Weller pottery vase, American, c1915, 8in (20.5cm) high.
£180–200 *EKK*

A Shelley lustre vase, by Walter Slater, c1920, 15in (38cm) high.
£1,200–1,500 *DSG*

A Quimper Art Deco style jardinière, c1920, 6in (15cm) high.
£220–250 *MLL*

A Bauer ringware pottery jug, c1920, 8in (20.5cm) high.
£130–150 *EKK*

A pair of Gouda plates, painted with nasturtiums, c1924, 7½in (19cm) diam.
£45–50 *OO*

A Gouda pottery oviform vase, decorated in colours in batik manner with stylised flowers, c1920, 8¼in (21cm) high.
£150–180 *DSG*

An Austrian earthenware vase, by Otto Prutscher, c1923, 15in (40.5cm) high.
£2,500–3,000 *DORO*

A Rubian baluster vase, with transfer-printed decoration, c1920, 8¼in (21cm) high.
£120–140 *DSG*

A Gouda Srebo vase, c1920, 7½in (19cm) high.
£120–140 *OO*

A pottery jug, probably Crown Ducal, decorated by Charlotte Rhead, with tube-lined flowers, 1930s, 8½in (21.5cm) high.
£150–170 *PrB*

A Susie Cooper Kestrel shape coffee set, decorated with green stars and green and orange banding, pattern No. 1530, c1930, coffee pot 7¼in (18.5cm) high.
£650–750 *MAV*

Two Susie Cooper horizontally ribbed tankards, with inset handles, decorated in various colours on a cream ground, printed crown works mark, c1930, 5in (12.5cm) high.
£75–85 each *CDC*

A Crown Ducal Charlotte Rhead charger, with tube-lined decoration, c1930, 12in (30.5cm) diam.
£280–300 *MAV*

A Charlotte Rhead dish, tube-lined and painted with stylised foliage, c1930, 12in (30.5cm) wide.
£160–190 *PrB*

A Chameleon ware oviform vase, c1930, 5¾in (14.5cm) high.
£50–60 *PrB*

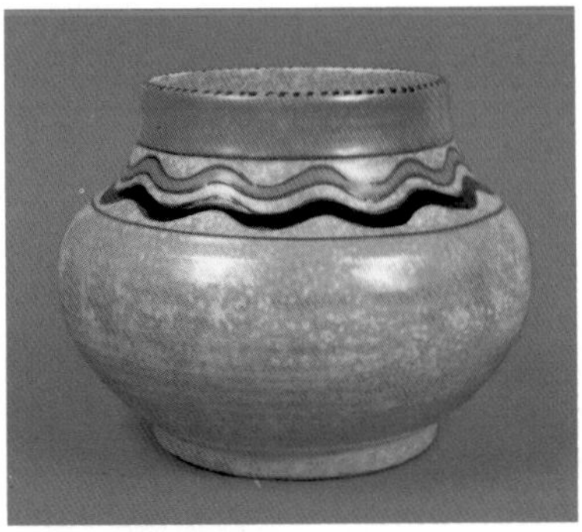

A Charlotte Rhead pottery vase, with tube-lined decoration, probably Crown Ducal, c1930, 6in (15cm) diam.
£150–170 *PrB*

A Crown Ducal Charlotte Rhead pottery vase, decorated with flowers and foliage, c1935, 12½in (32cm) high.
£380–430 *DSG*

A Rookwood pottery baluster vase, American, c1930, 9in (23cm) high.
£550–600 *EKK*

A Chameleon ware pottery vase, base stamped, c1935, 10¼in (26cm) high.
£140–160 *P(B)*

A Myott & Sons bowl, decorated with red, brown and green banding and floral sprays, on a stepped base, c1930, 11in (28cm) wide.
£50–60 *CSA*

A Pilkington Lancastrian monochrome twin-handled vase, covered overall with an orange glaze, 1930s, 5½in (14cm) high.
£55–65 *DSG*

A Burleigh ware vase, in the form of 2 interlocking lozenge shapes with double angle poised handles, 1930s, 7in (18cm) high.
£350–400 *P(B)*

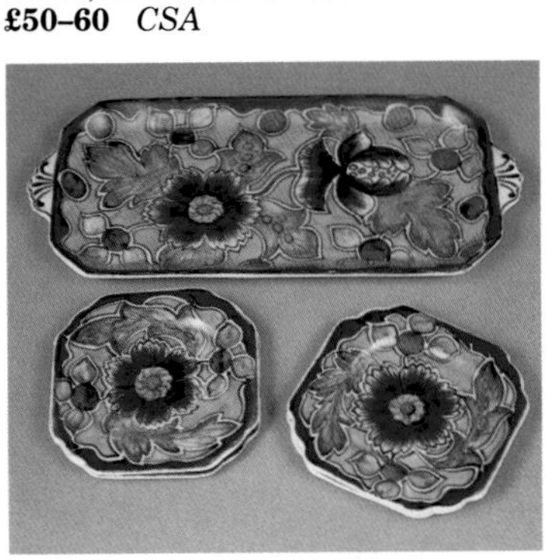

A Chameleon ware sandwich set, comprising 5 pieces, decorated with stylised blue flowers and foliage, on a beige ground, 1930s, plate 4½in (11.5cm) wide.
£80–100 *MRW*

A Carlton Ware jug, with a black handle, decorated with orange, yellow, green and red bands, with a black interior, 1930s, 3in (7.5cm) high.
£40–50 *MRW*

A pair of Doulton Lambeth stoneware vases, decorated by Hannah Barlow, c1885, 35in (89cm) high.
£1,250–1,400 *HAM*

A pair of Doulton Lambeth tube-lined stoneware vases, c1890, 12½in (32cm) high.
£170–200 *P(B)*

A Royal Doulton flambé vase, possibly by Arthur Eaton, c1925, 18½in (47cm) high.
£4,000–4,500 *S*

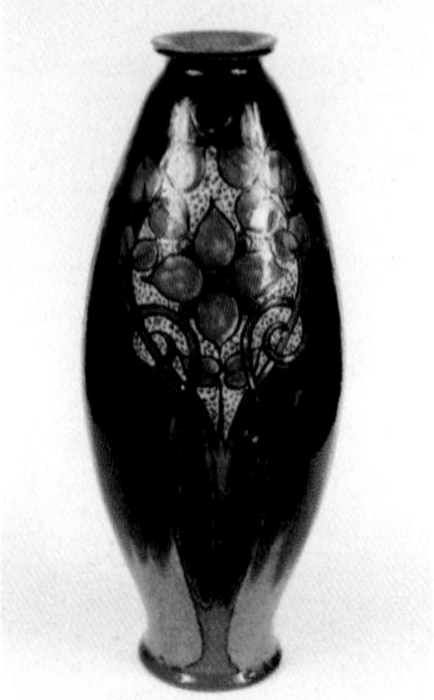

A Doulton Lambeth stoneware vase, by Francis C. Pope, c1900, 15in (38cm) high.
£650–700 *DSG*

A Royal Doulton Chrysanthemum pattern trio, c1908, cup 2in (5cm) high.
£40–50 *HEI*

A Royal Doulton vase, decorated by Mark V. Marshall, c1902, 16in (40.5cm) high.
£2,200–2,400 *POW*

A Moorcroft Fish pattern vase, impressed mark, c1930, 9¼in (23.5cm) high.
£1,500–1,700 *P*

A Royal Doulton Chang ware vase, with thick crackled glaze, signed 'Noke', dated '9.27', 12in (30.5cm) high.
£1,300–1,500 *CDC*

A Moorcroft pottery Flambé vase, decorated with irises, c1925, 8in (20.5cm) high.
£280–320 *CDC*

A Moorcroft vase, painted with pansies, signed, c1920, 6½in (16.5cm) high.
£400–500 *CEX*

A Moorcroft salt-glazed vase, decorated with Cornflowers pattern, c1915, 6½in (16.5cm) high.
£1,000–1,250 *DSG*

A Moorcroft plate, decorated with Leaf and Blackberry pattern, c1930, 8in (20.5cm) diam.
£260–280 *NP*

A Carter, Stabler & Adams model, entitled 'The Galleon', by Harold Stabler, c1925, 20½in (52cm) high.
£1,600–1,800 *RDG*

A Carter, Stabler & Adams vase, by Ruth Pavely, c1928, 10in (25.5cm) high.
£600–700 *ADE*

A Carter, Stabler & Adams 'Leaping Stag' vase, designed by Truda Carter, c1930, 9½in (24cm) high.
£700–800 *HarC*

A Carter, Stabler & Adams pottery charger, decorated with a stylised tree, c1935, 11½in (29cm) diam.
£230–260 *P(B)*

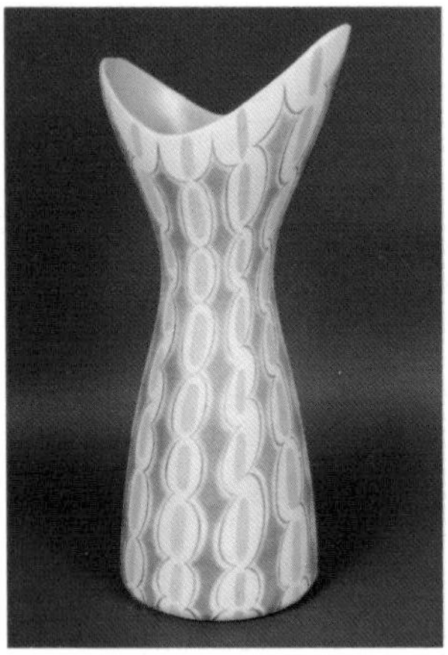
A Carter, Stabler & Adams 'Free-form' vase, decorated by Gwen Haskins, c1955, 14in (35.5cm) high.
£700–800 *ADE*

A Carter, Stabler & Adams vase, with narrow rim, c1960, 6¼in (16cm) high.
£50–60 *P(B)*

A Carter, Stabler & Adams bowl, painted by Christine Tate, marked and signed, c1960, 16in (40.5cm) diam.
£250–300 *HarC*

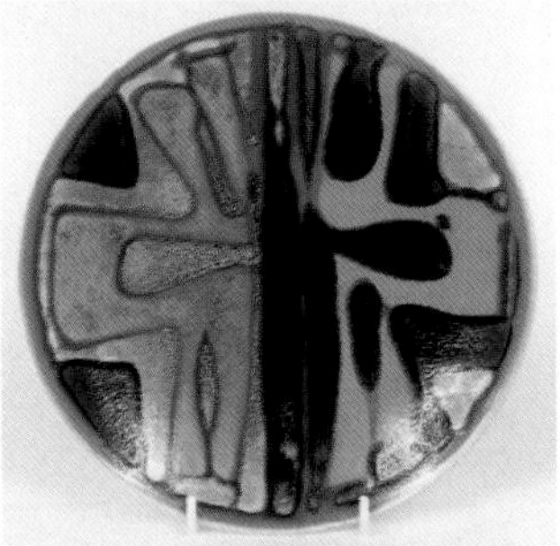
A Poole Pottery Delphis range plate, c1965, 8in (20.5cm) diam.
£70–85 *ADE*

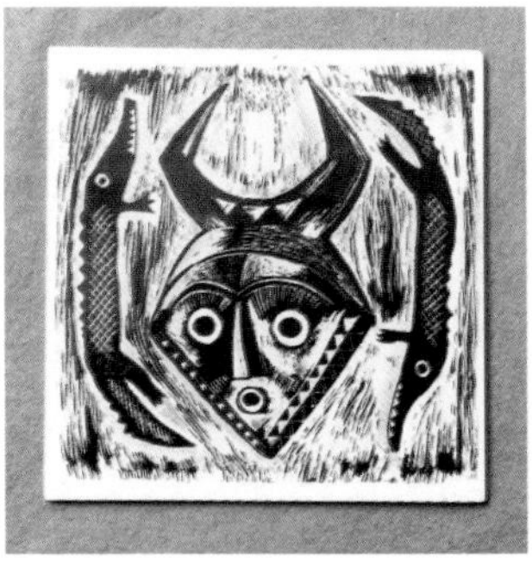
A Carter, Stabler & Adams tile, 1960s, 6in (15cm) square.
£20–25 *HarC*

A Poole Pottery vase, by Lynn Gregory, shape No. 15, c1972, 8½in (21.5cm) high.
£45–50 *PrB*

A Poole Pottery Delphis range vase, decorated in brown and black, 1960s, 4½in (11.5cm) high.
£30–35 *HarC*

A Poole Pottery plate, by Jane Brewer, with 'Jaçana and Lilies' pattern, c1972, 12¾in (32.5cm) diam.
£400–450 *DSG*

A Clarice Cliff Fantasque Bizarre Conical bowl, decorated with Orange Alpine pattern, c1930, 7½in (19cm) high.
£550–600 *P*

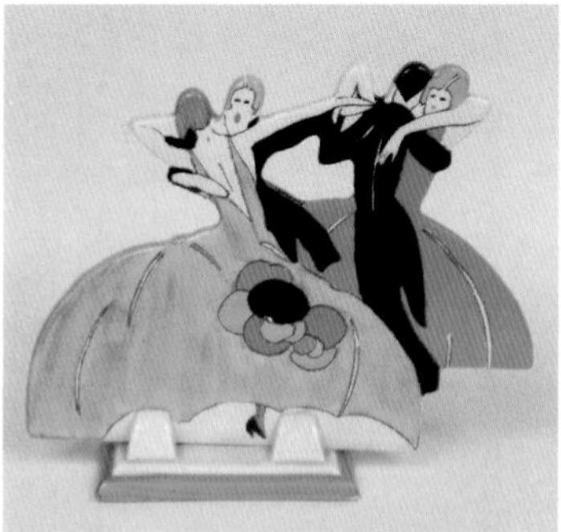

A Clarice Cliff pottery group, from the Age of Jazz series, c1930, 7in (18cm) high.
£15,000–17,000 *MAV*

A Clarice Cliff Bizarre jardinière, decorated with Autumn pattern, c1930, 6¾in (17cm) high.
£400–450 *P(B)*

A Clarice Cliff Bizarre bowl, decorated with Gayday pattern, c1930, 8½in (21.5cm) diam.
£200–250 *GSP*

A Clarice Cliff Fin dish, decorated with Idyll pattern, shape No. 475, c1931, 12¾in (32.5cm) wide.
£1,000–1,200 *MAV*

A Clarice Cliff Fantasque Lotus shape twin-handled jug, decorated with Orange Gardenia pattern, c1931, 11¾in (29.5cm) high.
£1,200–1,400 *P*

A Clarice Cliff globular jug, shape No. 634, decorated with Delecia Pansies pattern, c1932, 7in (18cm) high.
£600–675 *MAV*

A Clarice Cliff Tankard shape coffee pot, c1935, 7½in (19cm) high.
£500–600 *DSG*

A Clarice Cliff Fantasque Bizarre cigarette and match holder, decorated in Blue Chintz pattern, c1930, 2¾in (7cm) high.
£320–360 *HCC*

A Clarice Cliff Fantasque single-handled Isis vase, decorated with Circle Tree pattern, c1930, 9½in (24cm) high.
£1,400–1,600 *AG*

A Clarice Cliff Globe shape vase, decorated with Trees and Houses pattern, shape No. 370, c1929, 7in (18cm) high.
£2,200–2,400 *MAV*

A Clarice Cliff vase, c1930, 8in (20.5cm) high.
£3,200–3,500 *BKK*

A Clarice Cliff Lotus jug, c1934, 7in (18cm) high.
£700–800 *IM*

A Clarice Cliff Bizarre Trieste shape tea-for-two, painted in Orange Capri pattern, c1930.
£1,300–1,500 *AH*

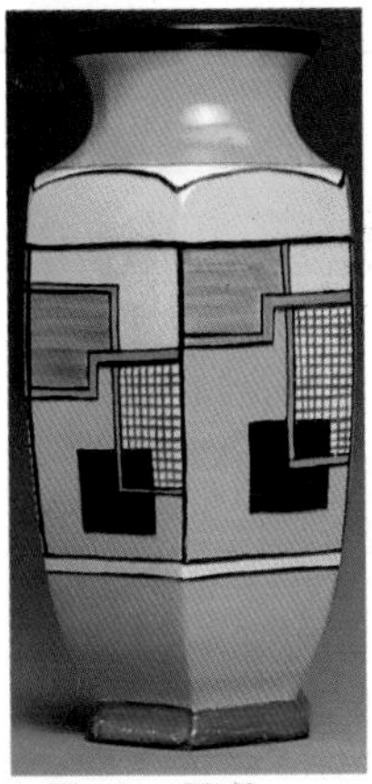

A Clarice Cliff vase, c1930, 15in (38cm) high.
£2,500–3,000 *AG*

A Clarice Cliff Bizarre vase, c1934, 8in (20.5cm) high.
£720–800 *IM*

A Clarice Cliff sugar sifter, c1934, 5in (12.5cm) high.
£250–280 *BKK*

A Clarice Cliff Bizarre Dover shape jardinière, and Isis shape jug, c1930s, jug 9½in (24cm) high.
£300–350 *HYD*

A German three-panel stained glass window, the upper part painted with foliage and blossoms in brown and beige, the lower part painted with a rural scene, late 19thC, 78in (200cm) wide.
£7,500–9,000 *DORO*

A glass lily stem vase, of bifurcated form, with an applied green stem and opalescent flowerhead, c1890, 13½in (34cm) high.
£260–300 *P(B)*

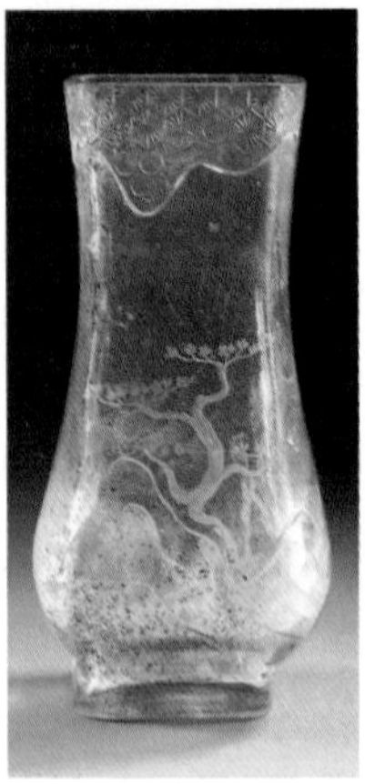

A François Eugène Rousseau 'Japonisant' vase, moulded with stylised flowerheads, c1880, 9in (23cm) high.
£2,000–2,200 *S*

A Tiffany Favrile glass vase, decorated with links, c1895, 11½in (29cm) high.
£2,800–3,200 *S(NY)*

A Eugène Feuillâtre silver-mounted enamelled vase, on a three-footed base, c1900, 9½in (24cm) high.
£7,700–8,500 *S(NY)*

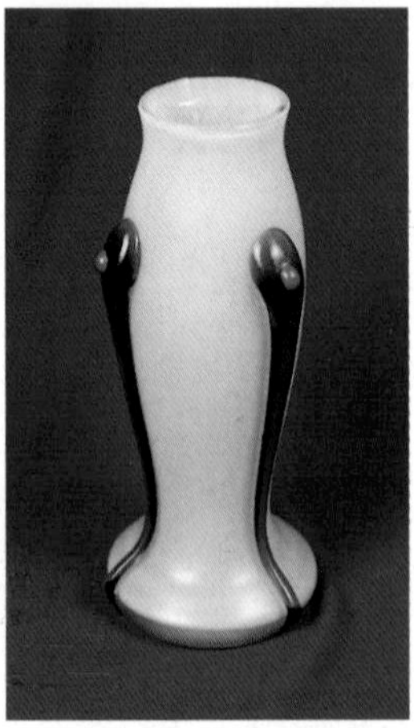

A Bohemian iridescent glass vase, c1900, 8in (20.5cm) high.
£90–100 *MiA*

A pair of American glass vases, with silver overlay, marked 'Quezal' on base, c1900, 15¼in (38.5cm) high.
£12,000–14,000 *SFL*

A Daum Nancy enamelled 'Solifleur' vase, painted with violets, c1900, 5in (12.5cm) high.
£1,300–1,500 *ART*

A Daum Nancy cameo glass vase, acid-etched and painted with poppies, c1900, 24¾in (65.5cm) high.
£3,800–4,200 *S(NY)*

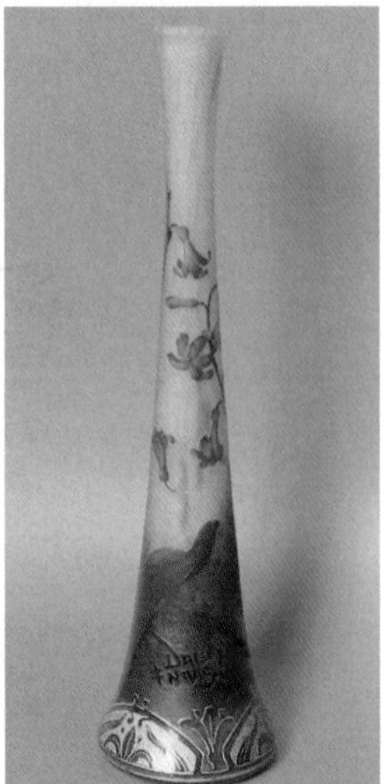

A Daum Nancy enamel vase, acid-etched with blue lilies, and painted in naturalistic colours, c1900, 9in (23cm) high.
£2,600–2,800 *ART*

A Gallé cameo glass vase, overlaid with blue and amethyst glass acid-etched with anemones, c1910, 8in (20.5cm) high.
£4,000–4,500 *ART*

A Loetz iridescent glass vase, in a pewter mount, c1900, 12in (30.5cm) high.
£300–350 *P*

A Bohemian glass decanter, with blue dot decoration, c1925, 10½in (26.5cm) high.
£150–180 *DSG*

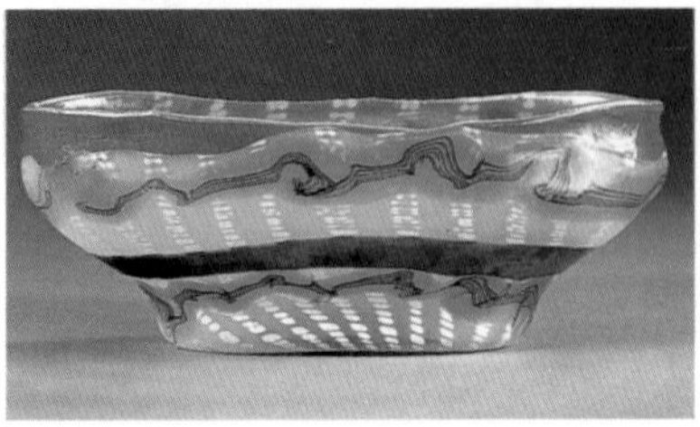

A Loetz milky glass bowl, for J. & L. Lobmeyr, internally decorated with bands of green and blue-mauve, washed with purple/gold iridescence, 1900, 4in (10cm) wide.
£9,500–11,000 *S*

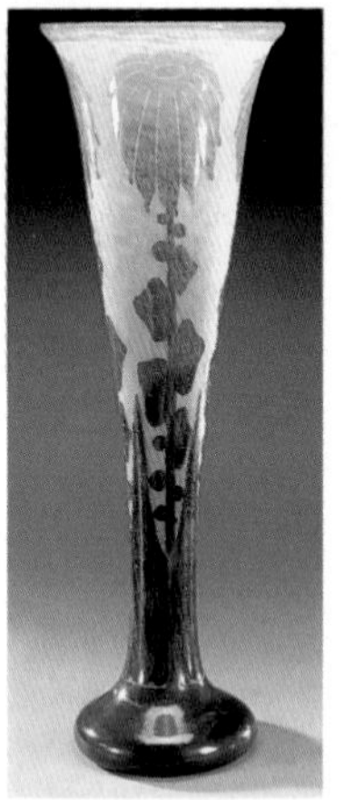

A Le Verre Français dahlia vase, c1925, 29in (73.5cm) high.
£2,000–2,200 *S*

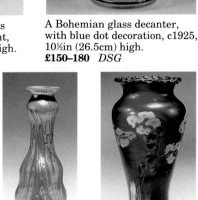

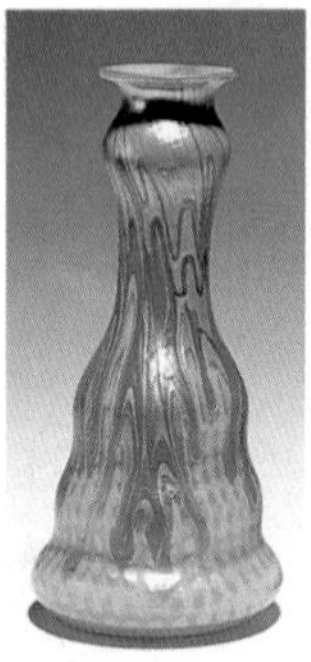

A Loetz iridescent glass vase, designed by Franz Hofstatter, c1900, 8¼in (21cm) high.
£8,500–10,000 *S(NY)*

An Artisti Barovier murrhines glass vase, decorated with roses, c1920, 9in (23cm) high.
£4,500–5,000 *S(NY)*

A Tiffany Favrile glass compote, with original label, c1905, 4in (10cm) high.
£650–750 *ANO*

A Loetz cobalt blue vase, etched with a lozenge pattern, c1907, 7in (17.5cm) diam.
£4,500–5,000 *DORO*

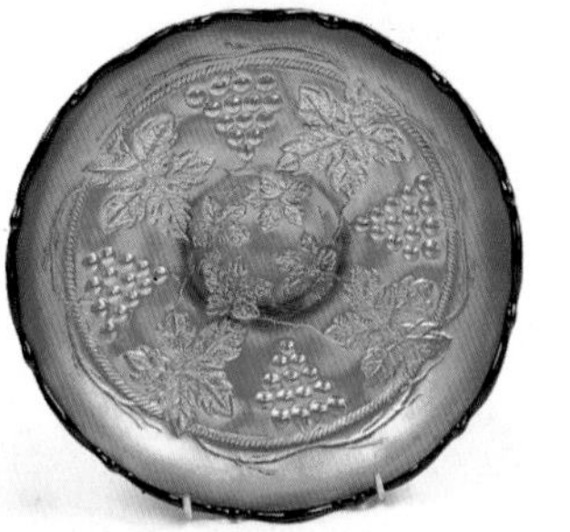

A Fenton carnival glass bowl, with a red base, c1925, 7in (18cm) diam.
£300–350 *ASe*

A WMF Myra Cristal glass vase, with golden iridescence, c1925, 5½in (14cm) high.
£100–125 *MON*

A Tiffany Favrile paperweight glass vase, decorated with convolvulus blossoms, c1915, 7½in (19cm) high.
£22,000–25,000 *S(NY)*

A Stevens & Williams 'Rainbow' vase, c1930, 6in (15cm) high.
£80–90 *JHa*

An Arts and Crafts style copper and brass basin, and a similar copper and brass kettle, c1890, kettle 11in (28cm) high.
£150–180 *P(B)*

A Marie Zimmermann hammered gilt-copper and jade two-handled bowl-on-stand, marked, c1910, 23½in (59.5cm) wide.
£8,000–9,500 *S(NY)*

A Liberty & Co enamelled pewter bowl, designed by Archibald Knox, marked 'Tudric 0229', c1905, 6½in (16.5cm) high.
£1,000–1,200 *P*

A pair of Arts and Crafts copper candlesticks, c1900, 9in (23cm) high.
£160–175 *WAC*

A Liberty & Co pewter and enamel timepiece, c1905, 6¾in 17cm) high.
£2,000–2,200 *P*

A Russian silver and lapis lazuli frame, c1900, 3½in (9cm) high.
£2,000–2,200 *SHa*

A glass and silver overlay jug, c1900, 7¼in (18.5cm) high.
£2,500–3,000 *SFL*

A copper and cloisonné enamelled vase, c1890, 6½in (16.5cm) high.
£350–400 *SUC*

A pair of Art Nouveau pewter candlesticks, by Orivit, c1900, 14in (35.5cm) high.
£2,500–2,750 *SHa*

A spelter mantel clock, possibly by WMF, c1900, 10½in (26.5cm) high.
£300–330 *P(B)*

An Orivit pewter claret jug, c1900, 11½in (29cm) high.
£450–500 *SUC*

A bronze vase, with ivory faces, by Jompliers, c1900, 6in (15cm) high.
£1,500–1,700 *ART*

A gilt-bronze and carved ivory figure, by Louis Ernest Barrias, c1900, 10in (25.5cm) high.
£7,000–8,000 *ART*

A gilt-bronze figure, by Raoul Larche, entitled 'Nude in Rushes', marked on base, No. 928B', c1900, 29in (73.5cm) high.
£3,800–4,200 *S*

A cold-painted bronze figure of a harem dancer, by Frans Bergman, her skirt hinged at the front, early 20thC, 14½in (37cm) high.
£2,000–2,200 *MAT*

A bronze figure of a dancing girl, cast from a model by Lorenzl, with gilt-coloured and green patination, on a marble base, c1925, 7in (18cm) high.
£600–700 *P*

An Art Deco bronze figure of Diana, with three-colour patination, signed 'Bouraine', c1925, 28in (71cm) high.
£4,000–4,500 *ART*

A gilt, green-patinated and cold-painted bronze figure entitled 'Dancer with Thyrsus', by Pierre Le Faguays, on a stepped beige veined black marble base, c1920, 22in (56cm) high.
£4,600–5,000 *S*

A bronze and ivory figure of Diana, signed 'F. Preiss', on a marble base, bow and arrow replaced, c1925, 9¾in (24.5cm) high.
£7,200–8,000 *P*

A Goldscheider pottery figure of a dancer, designed by Stefan Dakon, minor chips, inscribed 'Dakon', c1927, 18¾in (47.5cm) high.
£1,400–1,600 *DORO*

A Royal Dux pottery figure of a girl, with 'Royal Dux Bohemia' triangle to base, c1930, 11¾in (29.5cm) high.
£400–500 *P*

A green-patinated bronze figure of a girl, by Bouraine, with a skirt that billows in a spiral, c1930, 13in (33cm) high.
£2,800–3,200 *ART*

Antique Galleries
26 Broad St., Pendleton, Salford
Manchester, M6 5BY, Tel: 0161 737 5938
AUDREY STERNSHINE
Specialist in Art Nouveau & Art Deco

A Tiffany Favrile glass and bronze prism lamp, base impressed, c1910, 20¼in (51.5cm) high.
£4,200–4,600 *S(NY)*

A Pairpoint reverse painted glass and gilt-metal lamp, c1910, 23in (58.5cm) high.
£9,000–10,000 *S(NY)*

A Tiffany Favrile glass and gilt-bronze dragonfly lamp, impressed marks, c1910, 25¾in (65.5cm) high.
£15,500–17,000 *S(NY)*

A Daum Nancy acid-etched glass lamp, signed, c1925, 24¾in (63cm) high.
£1,200–1,500 *S(NY)*

A Tiffany Favrile glass and bronze dogwood lamp, impressed marks, c1910, 25½in (65cm) high.
£14,500–16,000 *S(NY)*

A Tiffany Favrile glass and bronze 'jewelled' feather lamp, damaged, impressed marks, c1910, 22in (56cm) high.
£3,500–4,000 *S(NY)*

A Daum Nancy cameo glass table lamp, acid-etched with tobacco flowers, wheel-carved details, c1920, 13in (33cm) high.
£6,000–7,000 *ART*

r. A Handel cameo-cut and reverse-painted glass and metal lamp, enamelled and gilded with peacocks, designed by George Palme, with finial, c1924, 23½in (59.5cm) high.
£7,000–8,000 *S(NY)*

A Tiffany Favrile glass and bronze daffodil lamp, base impressed, c1919, 27in (68.5cm) high.
£25,000–28,000 *S(NY)*

A Tiffany Favrile glass and bronze clematis lamp, impressed marks, c1910, 22in (56cm) high.
£21,000–24,000 *S(NY)*

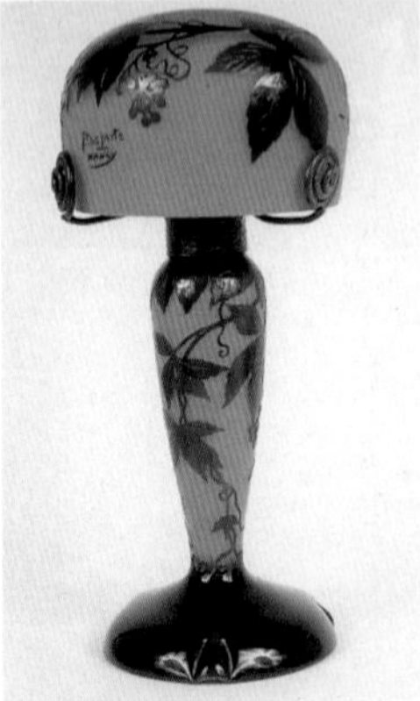

A Delatte Nancy cameo glass table lamp and shade, acid-etched and polished with vines, signed, c1900, 13¼in (33.5cm) high.
£1,200–1,400 *P*

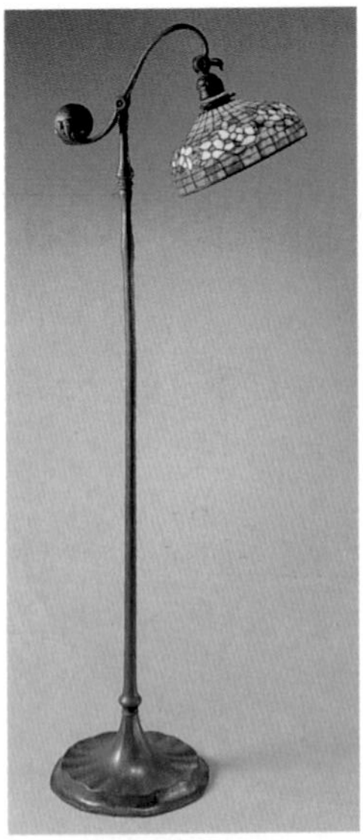

A Tiffany Favrile glass and bronze counter-balance bridge lamp, c1910, 52in (132cm) high.
£5,500–6,500 *S(NY)*

An Austrian Art Nouveau glass shade lamp, by Loetz, c1900, 23in (58.5cm) high.
£7,000–8,000 *ART*

A marble and onyx table lamp, in the form of an eagle, on a rocky hard-stone base, c1930, 20½in (52cm) high.
£320–360 *P(B)*

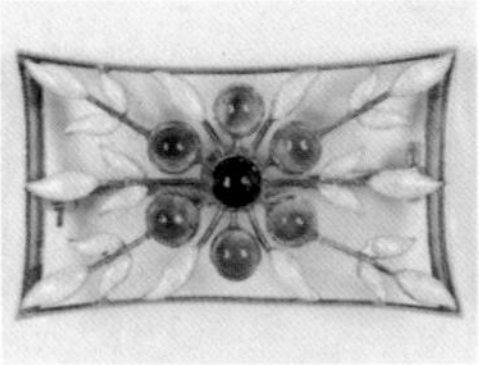

An enamelled and amethyst brooch, by Mrs P. Newman, c1890, 1¾in (4.5cm) wide.
£360–400 *P*

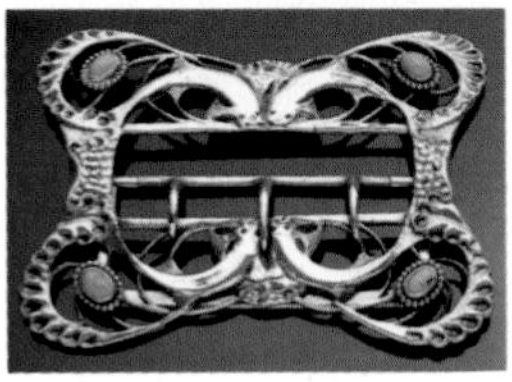

A silver buckle, by C. R. Ashbee, with a turquoise at each corner, c1897, 3¼in (8.5cm) wide.
£4,000–4,500 *S*

An Arts and Crafts brooch, with 2 carnelians and a moonstone, c1910, 2¾in (7cm) long.
£170–200 *P*

A silver buckle, by Georg Jensen, designed as a pierced dragonfly, with a cabochon opal, c1895.
£3,000–3,300 *S(Am)*

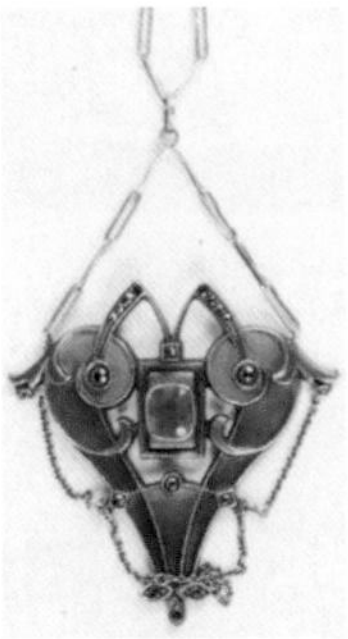

A Jugendstil *plique-à-jour* pendant, c1900, 2in (5cm) long.
£750–850 *P*

An Arts and Crafts enamelled and wirework pendant, some damage, c1900.
£100–120
Bon(C)

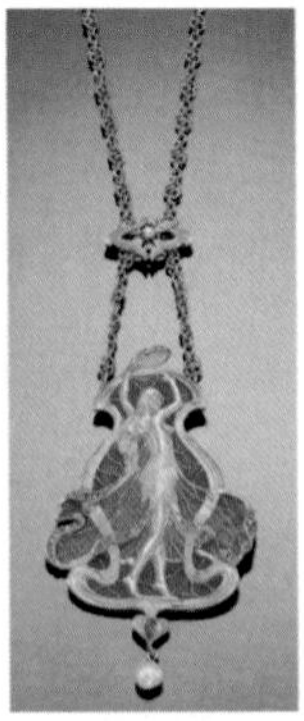

A French *plique-à-jour* enamel, gold, diamond, ruby and pearl pendant, c1900.
£2,800–3,200
S(NY)

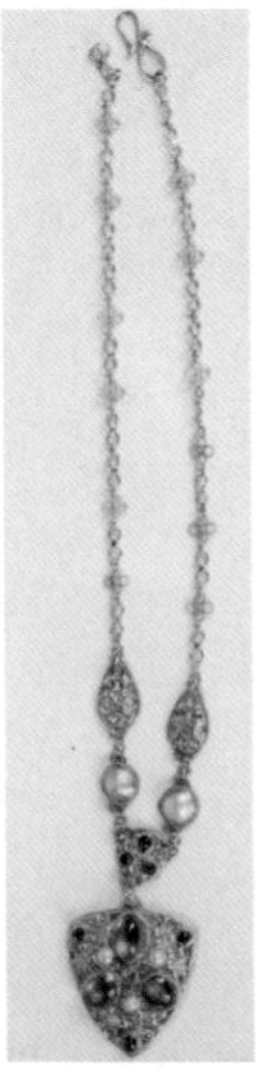

An Arts and Crafts pendant necklace, c1910.
£1,200–1,400
P

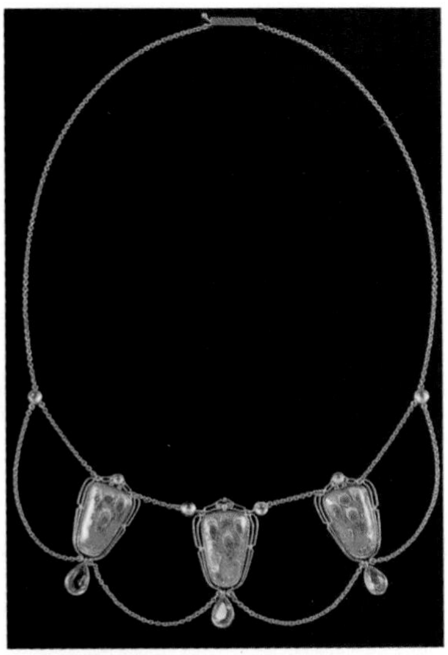

A Guild of Handicraft Ltd peacock necklace, the chain set with 6 green cabochons, the enamelled pendants hung with peridots, c1900.
£5,500–6,500 *S*

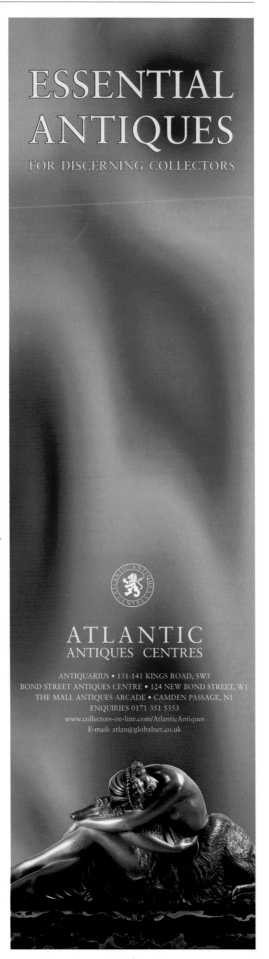

An Art Deco sapphire and diamond bracelet, designed as a series of pavé-set diamond buckle panels with calibré-cut sapphire detail, c1925, 7in (18cm) long.
£10,000–12,000 *S(G)*

An Art Deco diamond, onyx and emerald cocktail bracelet, the flexible narrow band with stirrup connections, pavé-set with single, brilliant, baguette and marquise cut diamonds, c1925, 7in (18cm) long.
£6,000–7,000 *Bon*

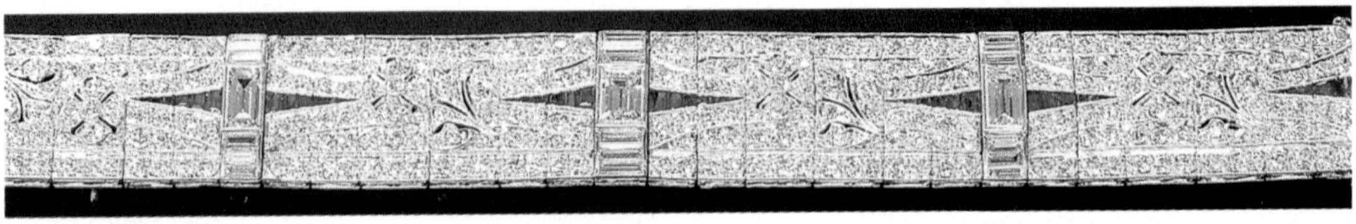

A diamond and emerald bracelet, the articulated band decorated with 4 floral sprigs against a ground of pavé-set diamonds, framed by step-cut and baguette diamonds and calibré-cut emeralds, c1925, 7in (18cm) long.
£13,000–15,000 *S(G)*

A French diamond bracelet, the articulated band decorated with oval openwork links, the centres with collet-set circular-cut diamonds, on a ground of round stones, mounted in platinium, c1930, 7in (18cm) long.
£5,000–6,000 *S(G)*

An emerald and diamond bracelet, designed as a tapered band alternately set with step-cut emeralds, brilliant-cut and baguette diamonds, on a similarly set diamond clasp of buckle design, c1930, 6in (15cm) long.
£12,500–14,000 *S*

An Art Deco diamond plaque brooch, with central cabochon sapphire, c1930.
£1,800–2,000 *Bon*

An Art Deco sapphire and diamond brooch, c1935.
£3,600–4,000 *P*

A Cartier diamond bar brooch, set with rectangular amethysts, citrines and tourmalines, outlined with black onyx, c1925.
£6,500–7,000 *S(G)*

An Art Deco 18ct gold and enamel watch, c1925, 49mm diam.
£2,500–3,000 *S(NY)*

An Art Deco emerald and diamond strap bracelet, mounted with a rectangular collet set emerald, within a geometric diamond set surround, to similarly set openwork arched and panel articulated sides, c1935, 7in (18cm) long.
£4,600–5,000 *P*

A cultured pearl and enamel brooch, by Ramond Sunyer Clará, in the form of a stylised cluster of leaves, mounted with a citrine, slight damage, 1940s.
£950–1,100 *S*

A ruby and diamond dress ring, by Sterlé, in a corded wire mount, signed, 1950s.
£5,300–5,800 *S*

A Giardinetto multi-gem flower basket brooch, c1950.
£650–750 *Bon*

A 14ct gold brooch, by Tiffany & Co, with prong-set spinel, peridot, diamond, sapphire, citrine and amethyst flowers, signed, c1950.
£4,200–4,800 *SK*

A ruby and diamond brooch, with wirework cascade, c1950.
£850–1,000 *P*

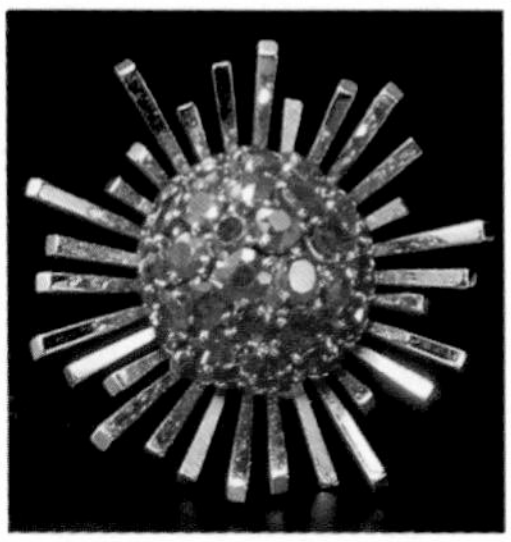

A French 18ct gold and ruby clip, c1950.
£4,000–5,000 *S(HK)*

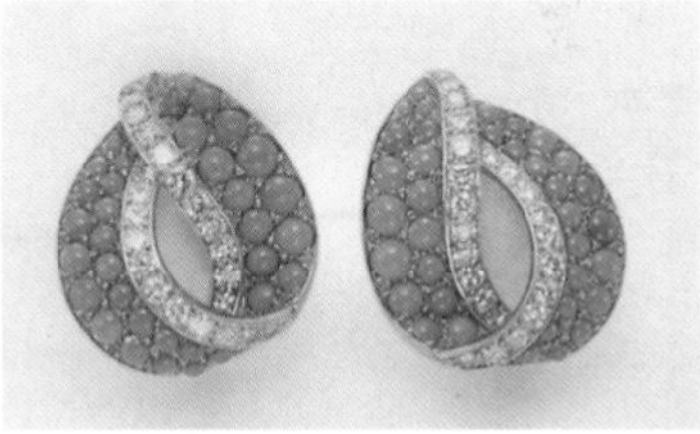

A pair of Cartier 18ct gold, turquoise and diamond ear clips, designed as overturned ribbons, signed, c1950.
£5,000–6,000 *S(HK)*

A French 18ct gold necklace, the scroll wire front claw-set with clusters of brilliant-cut diamonds, c1950.
£1,300–1,500 *S(Am)*

A rose quartz and cabochon ruby brooch, by John Donald, 1967.
£650–750 *Bon*

A diamond whorl brooch, set with emeralds, c1960.
£2,600–3,000 *P*

A coral, diamond and 18ct yellow gold floral spray brooch, by Kutchinsky, 1970.
£1,500–1,800 *Bon*

An amethyst, emerald and diamond brooch, by Andrew Grima, 1972.
£3,000–3,500 *Bon*

A sapphire and diamond bracelet, by John Donald, the 18ct gold band composed of textured square-shaped links, randomly set with sapphires and brilliant-cut diamonds, maker's mark, 1968, 6½in (16.5cm) long.
£1,000–1,200 *Bon*

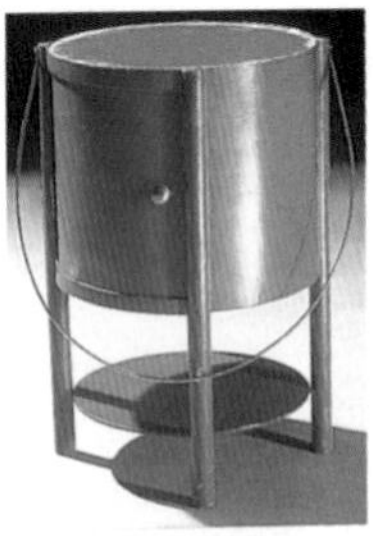

A wooden sewing table, designed by Gerrit Thomas Rietveld, c1936, 21½in (54.5cm) high.
£3,500–4,000 *S(Am)*

Three 'Universale' plastic chairs, by Joe Colombo, c1967, 28½in (43.5cm) high.
£1,000–1,100 *S*

An oak chest, designed by Frank Wardel Knight, c1930, 49in (124.5cm) wide.
£1,500–1,750 *E*

A 'Mini Kitchen', by Joe Colombo, with laminated pull-out surface, c1963, 44in (113cm) wide.
£2,300–2,600 *S*

A set of 4 white metal and plastic chairs, by Pierre Paulin for Artifort, c1960, with a wool circular rug.
£720–780 *S*

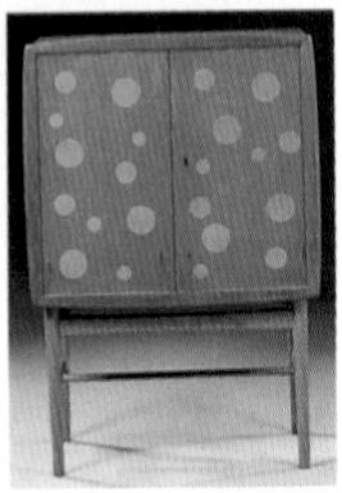

A teak and beech drinks cabinet, by Tove & Edvard Kindt-Larsen, 1955, 32¼in (82cm) wide.
£1,250–1,500 *S*

An 'Oxford' dining table and 4 chairs, by Fritz Hansen, designed by Arne Jacobsen, c1960, table 57½in (146cm) diam.
£3,600–4,000 *S*

A yellow fabric and grey leather tennis ball chair, by De Sede, c1980, 31in (78cm) high.
£850–1,000 *S*

An Intarsio grey stained glass vase, designed by Ercole Barovier, c1960, 13½in (31cm) high.
£1,500–1,750 *DORO*

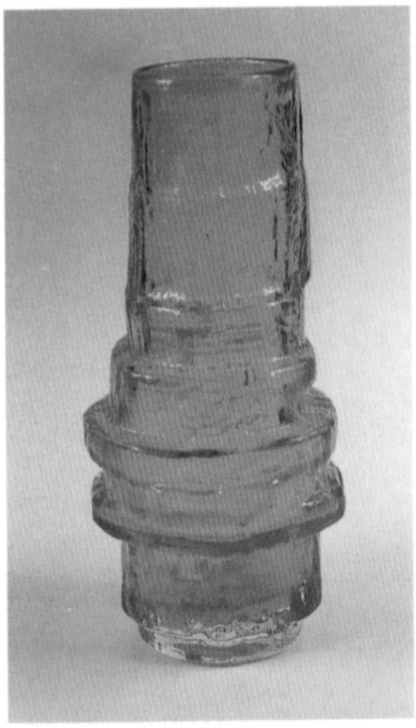

A Whitefriars hooped vase, designed by Geoffrey Baxter, c1966, 11in (28cm) high.
£120–140 *JHa*

A semi-transparent glass vase, designed by Giulio Radi, for AVEM, c1950, 10½in (27cm) high.
£4,000–4,500 *S*

A Whitefriars forked vase, designed by Wilson, c1955, 10in (25.5cm) high.
£100–120 *JHa*

A Leerdam Unica glass vase, designed by A. D. Copier, imprinted with fishes and seaweed, c1942, 11in (28cm) diam.
£5,000–5,500 *S(Am)*

A studio pottery jug, in the manner of Leach, with fish-tail strap handle, c1950, 9½in (24cm) high.
£30–35 *P(B)*

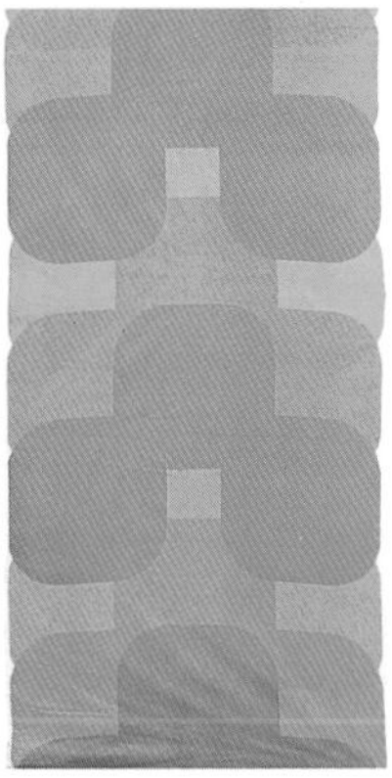

A 'Motus' length of fabric, by Gaetano Pesce for Collezione Expansion, 1970, 787in (2000cm) long.
£950–1,100 *S*

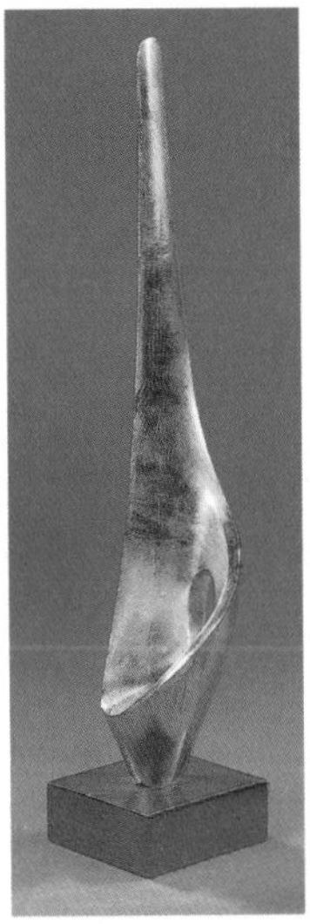

A bronze sculpture, entitled 'Praze', by Denis Mitchell, on a black stone base, 1964, 16in (41cm) high.
£500–550 *RTo*

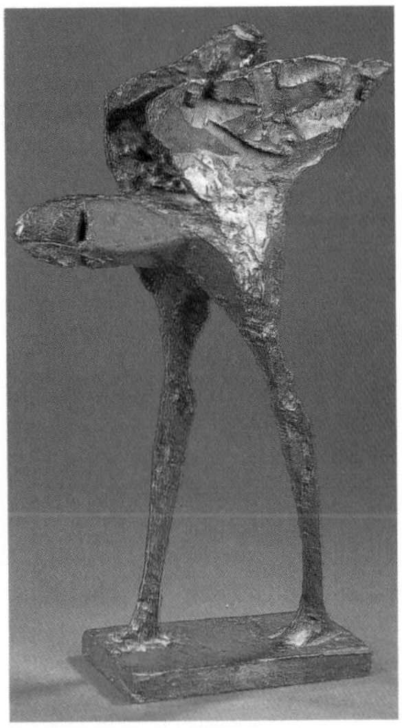

A bronze sculpture, entitled 'Firebird', by Dame Elizabeth Frink, signed, marked '3/8' on base, 1962, 16½in (42cm) high.
£5,000–5,500 *RTo*

An 'Oriented' wool rug, by Alessandro Mendini for Alchimia, designed 1980, 94 x 66in (239 x 186cm).
£1,400–1,600 *S*

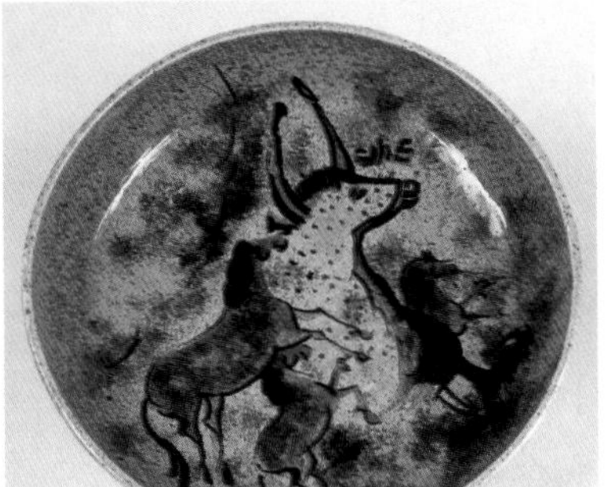

A Rye Pottery vase, decorated with brown and black leaves, 1950s, 6¼in (16cm) high.
£30–35 *ADE*

l. A pottery dish, with Lascaux style decoration, c1950, 11½in (29cm) diam.
£65–75 *DSG*

A Rye Pottery jug, decorated with yellow stripes and black lines on a white ground, 1950s, 6½in (16.5cm) high.
£30–35 *ADE*

An Italian bottle vase, by Marcello Fantoni, with funnel top, brown drip glaze over dark blue, c1960, 9in (23cm) wide.
£250–275 *DSG*

Four tiles, designed by Salvador Dali, c1954, each 8in (20.5cm) square.
£225–250 *GIN*

A stoneware vase, by Shoji Hamada, signed, c1957, 10in (25.5cm) high.
£6,200–6,800 *Bon*

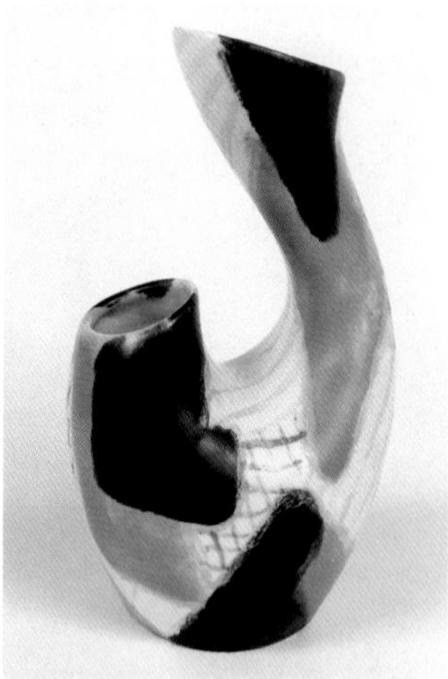

A Beswick double-funnel vase, decorated in blue, black and yellow, c1950, 8in (20.5cm) high.
£30–40 *GIN*

A Royal Tudor ware cup, saucer and coffee pot, c1960, coffee pot 10in (25.5cm) high.
Cup and saucer £7–8
Coffee pot £15–18 *UTP*

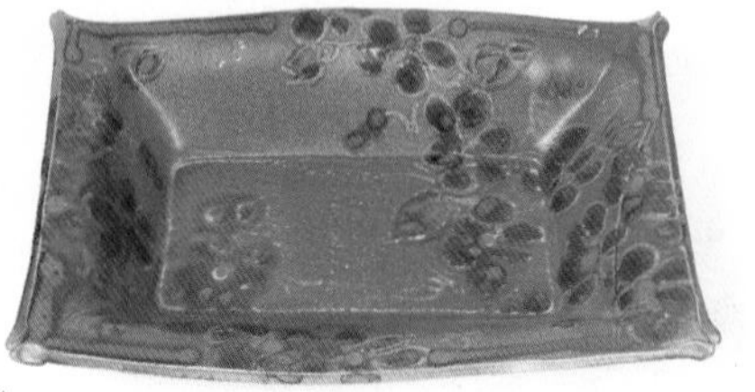

A studio pottery dish, by Michael Smith, decorated with brown flowers on a blue ground, Western Australia, c1960, 12in (30.5cm) long.
£60–70 *RAC*

An 'American' stoneware yellow bowl, by Dame Lucie Rie, c1962, 5½in (14cm) diam.
£2,400–2,600 *Bon*

A porcelain footed bowl, by Dame Lucie Rie, dark pink with inlaid decoration, running bronze rim, with a bronze foot, impressed 'LR' seal, c1974, 7in (18cm) diam.
£1,500–1,750 *Bon*

A porcelain vase, by Dame Lucie Rie, 1964, 5in (13cm) high.
£3,400–3,800 *Bon*

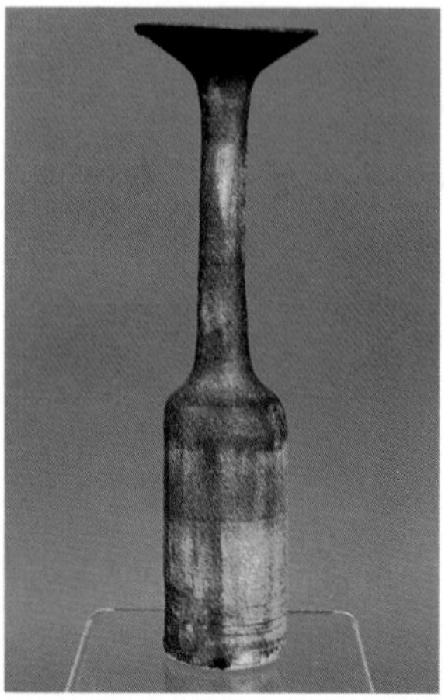

A stoneware vase, by Dame Lucie Rie, with a wide top, c1970, 8in (20.5cm) high.
£1,500–1,750 *SWO*

A porcelain bowl, by Dame Lucie Rie, c1978, 7½in (19cm) high.
£10,000–11,000 *Bon*

TWENTIETH CENTURY DESIGN

Plastic Furniture

Man-made plastics were first produced at the end of the 19th century as a by-product of the petro-chemical industry. One of the most famous was Bakelite, developed by the Belgian chemist Dr Leo Baekland, which was used for a host of household products during the 1920s and 1930s. Bakelite is hard-wearing, and many of these products have survived and are recognisable by their distinctive brown colour. The investment required to produce plastic artefacts was enormous, and consequently the plastic objects made were small-scale and aimed at the mass-market. A few pieces of Bakelite furniture are known from the 1930s, but the heyday of plastic furniture came after WWII.

The expansion of the aerospace industry during the war provided the capital investment required to make large-scale plastic products a possibility; it was a small step from moulded aircraft parts to Baroque-style bedroom suites moulded from Lucite. The American designer Charles Eames was amongst the first to experiment with moulded furniture, first in plywood and subsequently in plastics.

In the 1950s plastics were developed in a range of bright, often primary, colours and became identified in the public imagination with the creation of Utopian suburbs in the USA, Britain and Europe. This process continued during the 1960s when plastics were seen as the first space-age materials and were used in futuristic NASA projects and on the set of Stanley Kubrick's film *2001: A Space Odyssey*.

During the 1960s, many designers and architects experimented with the moulded structures and modular forms that plastic made possible. Italian designers such as Joe Colombo, Ettore Sottsass and Vico Magistretti designed products for Artemide and Cassina that would fit together to form a new kind of interior. The results often defy categorisation, being part furniture, part architecture. The foam sculptures and plastic inflatables from this period are also part of this creative flux.

The oil crisis of the early 1970s postponed the economies of scale that had been the spur of so much experimentation, and by the mid-1970s the petro-chemical industry and its plastic products had been identified as a potential environmental and ecological problem. In the 1980s and 1990s, however, new products by the Italian design company Alessi and the French designer Philippe Starck have helped to rehabilitate plastics as an authentic high-tech material for the new millennium.

The major auction rooms of London, Europe and the USA have continued to promote the growing market for post-war design. Large plastic pieces are often prototypes and appear in relatively small numbers, often commanding very high prices.

Paul Rennie

Furniture

A laminated birch, lead and glass coffee table, probably Italian, signed 'Velone' or 'Melbine', probably Italian, c1930, 43¼in (110cm) long.
£5,300–6,000 *S(NY)*

A laminated wood chair, by Gerald Summers, for Makers of Simple Furniture, c1935.
£1,800–2,000 *S*

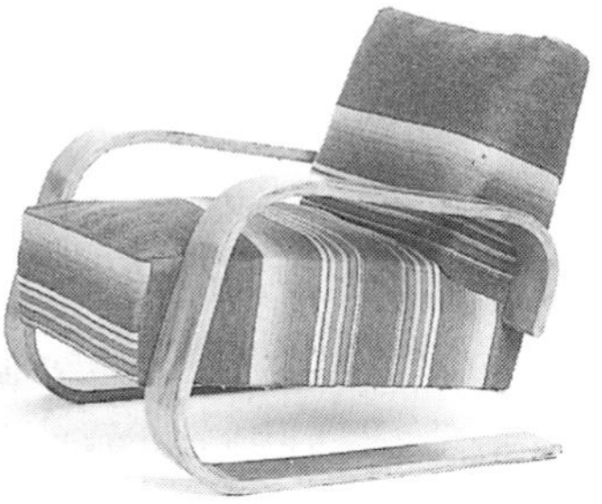

A No. 400 easy chair, by Alvar Aalto, for Finmar, with birch laminated cantilevered supports, the seat and back sprung, c1935.
£1,200–1,400 *Bon*

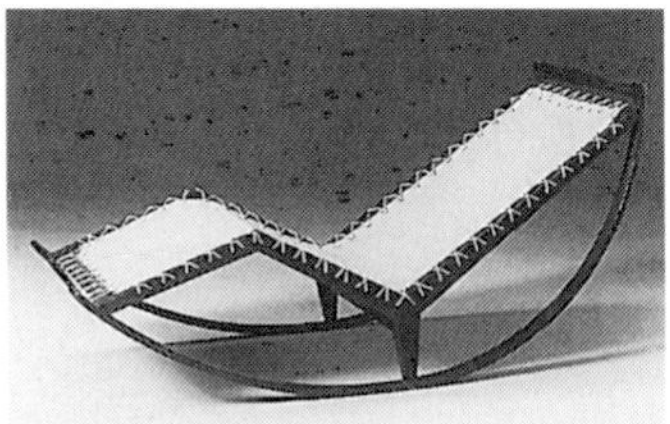

A Franco Albini rocking chaise longue, the angular wooden frame laced with a stretched canvas seat, above an arched base, c1940, 63in (160cm) long.
£4,200–4,800 *S(NY)*

r. A Charles and Ray Eames steel, moulded plywood and painted Masonite storage unit, c1950, 47in (119.5cm) wide.
£5,500–6,000 *S(NY)*

A white painted metal rod rocking chair, designed by Ernest Race for Race Furniture, with mahogany armrests, designed 1948.
£350–400 *S*

A limed oak side cabinet, designed by James Mont, the doors with hammered metal ring pulls, maker's mark, c1948, 52in (132cm) wide.
£2,500–3,000 *S(NY)*

A Charles Eames chair, for Herman Miller, with white plastic-coated metal and white fibreglass, covered with vinyl, designed c1950.
£230–260 *S*

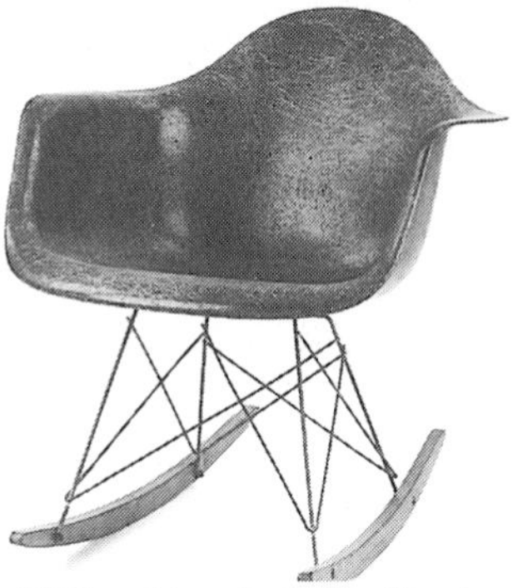

A DAR rocking chair, by Charles Eames, for Herman Miller, with grey fibreglass seat, designed 1950.
£650–750 *Bon*

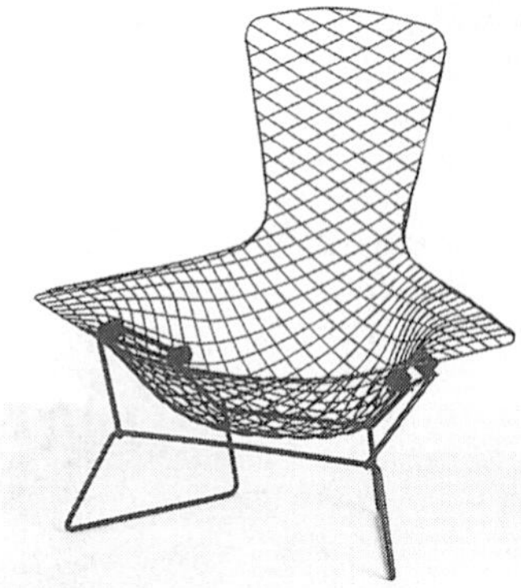

A 'bird' chair, designed by Harry Bertoia for Knoll Associates, with black plastic welded coated steel rod frame, 1950–52.
£250–300 *Bon*

Charles Eames

Charles Eames (1907–78) was the first person to explore the use of the new materials developed in the mid-20thC and the techniques used in car and aeroplane manufacture and apply them to furniture design. He was an advocate of the new vogue for open plan designs in architecture, which is reflected in his famous house in Santa Monica, California, which he designed in 1949. This movement in architecture had an effect on the furniture of the period, placing it away from the walls of a room and into the centre, where it became the focal point, being seen in the round like a free-standing sculpture. Eames' furniture designs moved away from the angular designs popular in the 1920s and 1930s to more organic, sculptural forms. The so-called 'Eames Chair', designed in 1946 for Herman Miller Inc, is made of moulded plywood on a metal rod frame. Although particularly well-known for his chairs, Eames also designed many other types of furniture, including collapsible tables, screens and radio cabinets.

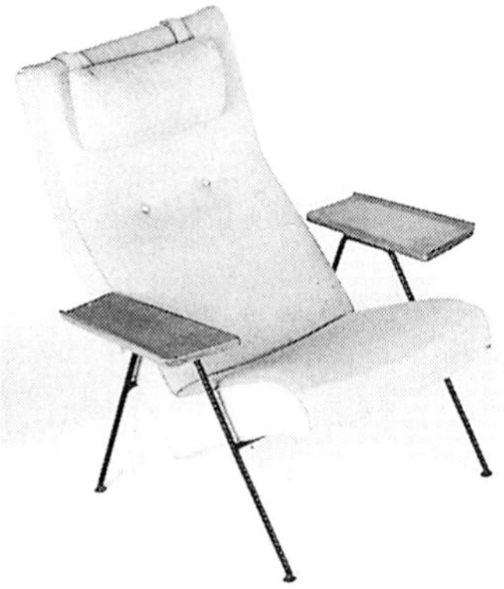

A reclining chair, designed by Robin Day for Hille, the one-piece hardwood framed seat with button-back and adjustable headrest, with ash table arms, 1952.
£800–1,000 *Bon*

A laminated and solid wood writing desk, with glass top, single drawer to the right, 1950s, 55in (140cm) wide.
£1,200–1,400 *S*

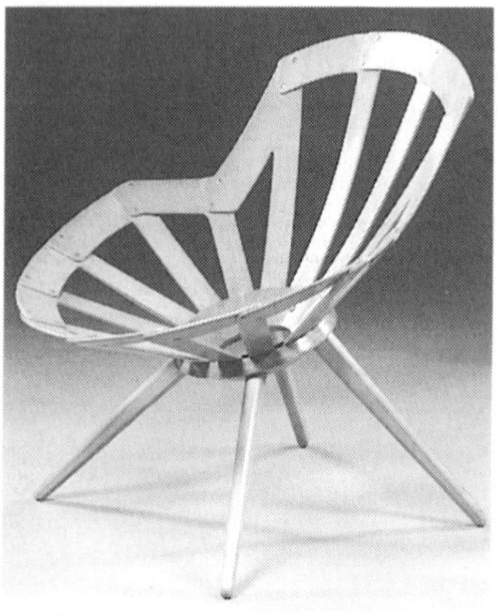

A plywood chair, designed by Gregotti, Meneghetti and Stoppino for SIM, designed 1954.
£4,800–5,200 *S*

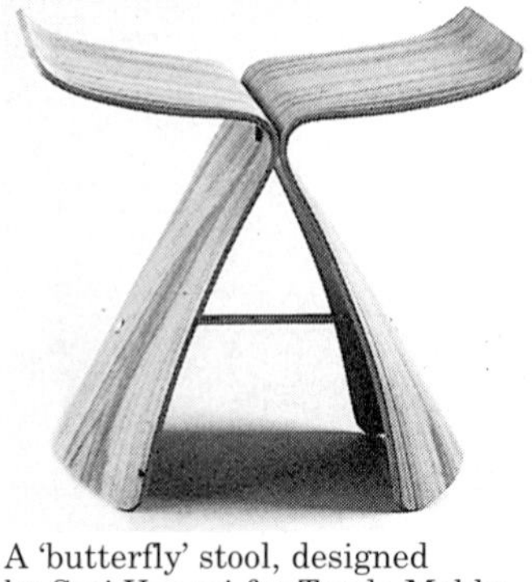

A 'butterfly' stool, designed by Sori Yanagi for Tendo Mokko, the 2 bent rosewood veneered plywood forms attached together with a brass rod, designed 1954.
£850–1,000 *Bon*

An aluminium chair and stool, designed by Charles and Ray Eames for Herman Miller, 1915.
£620–700 *SLN*

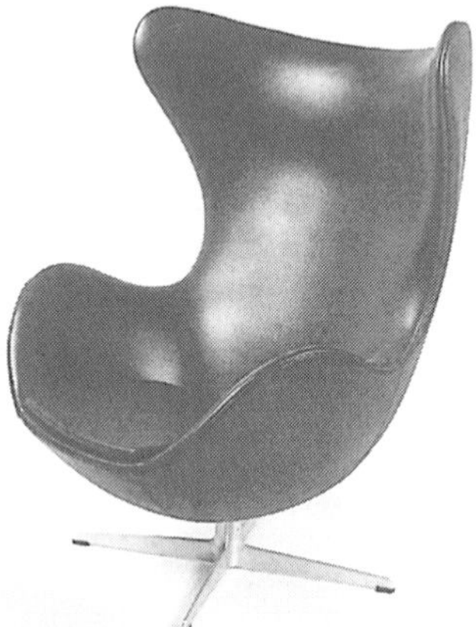

r. An Egg chair, by Arne Jacobsen for Fritz Hansen, 1958.
£850–1,000 *Bon*

A '692' malacca and reed rocking chair, designed by Franco Bettonica for Vittorio Bonacina, 1964.
£300–350 *S*

A Kartell blue polyester dining table, designed by Ferrieri and Gardella, blue reinforced polyester resin with chromed metal, designed 1967.
£250–300 *S*

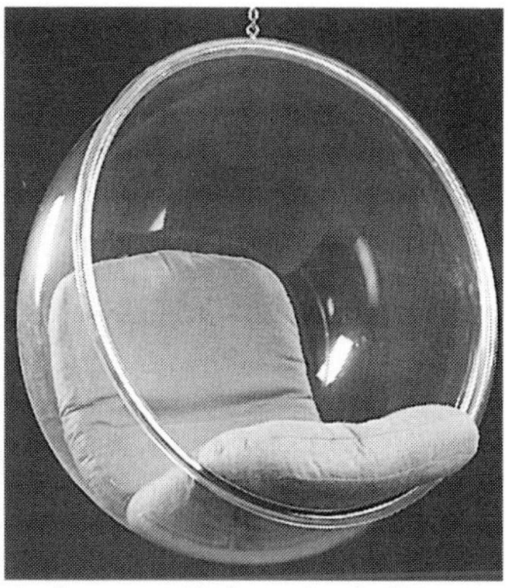

A clear acrylic hanging ball chair, designed by Eero Aarnio for Asko, 1966.
£3,500–4,000 *S*

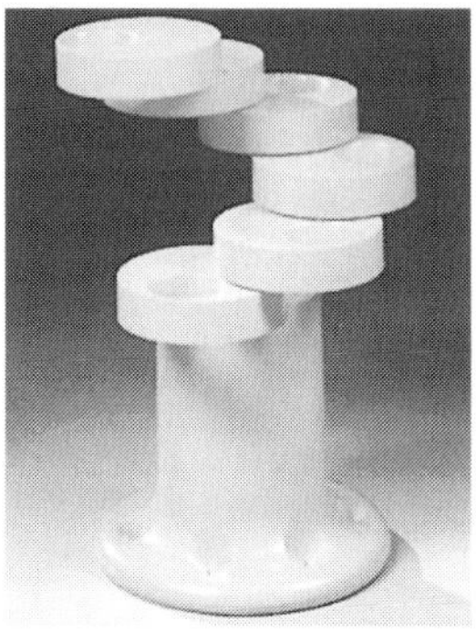

A Castelli 'Pluvium' umbrella stand, designed by Gian Carlo Piretti, in orange/yellow plastic, c1968, 19½in (49.5cm) high.
£60–80 *S*

r. A lacquered wood and metal miniature cupboard, 'Gli Animali', by Hans von Klier for Planula, designed 1969, 14in (35.6cm) wide.
£2,800–3,200 *S*

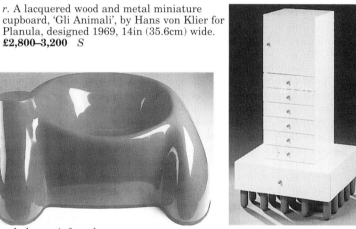

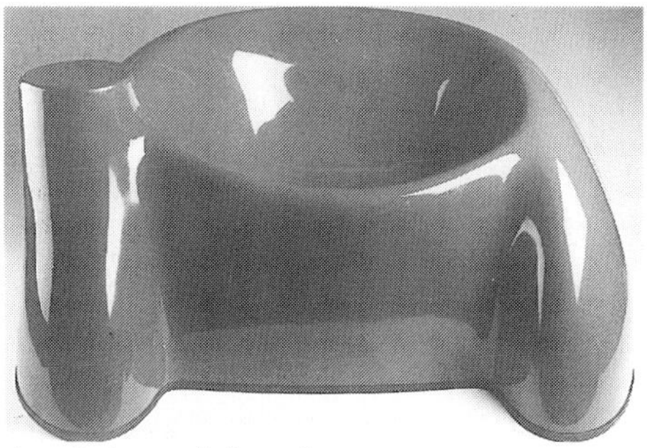

A red glass reinforced polyester Castle chair, by Wendell Castle, American, c1969.
£500–600 *Bon*

A 'Primate' stool, by Achille Castiglioni for Zanotta, black PVC on grey plastic base, designed c1969, 18¼in (46.5cm) high.
£720–800 *S*

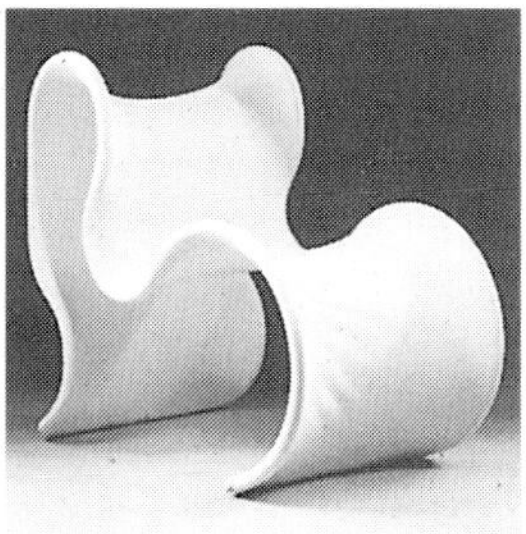

A tubular metal and yellow fabric Fiocco chair, designed by Group G 14 for Busnelli, frame with yellow synthetic stretch fabric, 1970.
£2,000–2,250 *S*

A pair of dark green plastic shell chairs, by Steen Ostergaard for Cado, Norway, upholstered in yellow, maker's mark, 1972.
£130–150 *DORO*

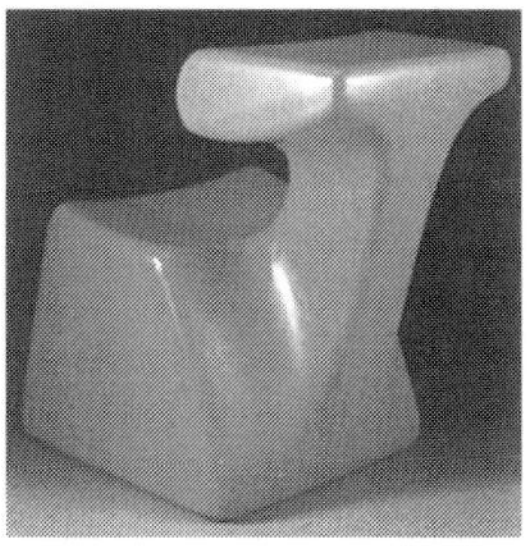

A 'Zocker' child's chair/desk, designed by Luigi Colani for Top System, in orange rigid polyurethane, 1972.
£180–200 *S*

Ceramics

A St Ives stoneware bowl, by Shoji Hamada, the thick olive-green glaze incised with chrysanthemum decoration, impressed marks, c1923, 6¼in (16cm) diam.
£1,600–1,800 *Bon*

A Swedish stoneware vase, by Carl Harry Rostrand, c1950, 4½in (11.5cm) high.
£45–50 *SnA*

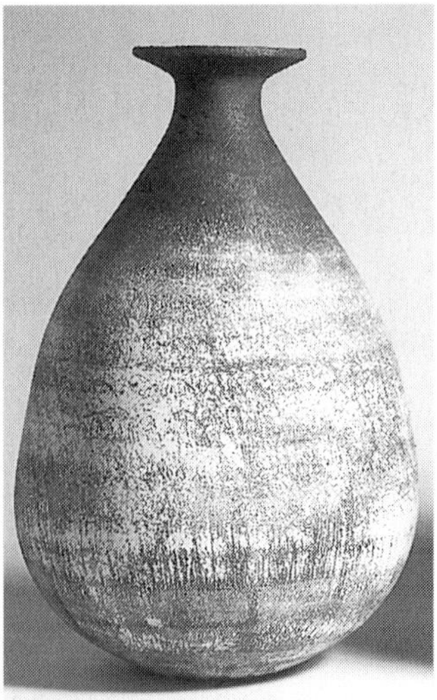

A stoneware pear-shaped pot, by Hans Coper, the buff textured base curving upwards to dark brown neck and flattened rim, impressed 'HC' seal, c1952, 13½in (34.5cm) high.
£3,000–3,300 *Bon*

A pair of Crown Ducal vases, decorated with Stitch pattern, 1940s, 7in (18cm) high.
£45–50 *RAC*

A celadon crackle-glazed vase, by James Walford, c1950, 4¼in (11cm) high.
£80–100 *IW*

An earthenware teapot, by Stig Lindberg, Sweden, for Gustavsberg, decorated in blues, purples, green and yellow with a hand-painted glazed bust of a woman, and other motifs, marked, 1952, 10in (25.5cm) high.
£230–260 *Bon*

r. An earthenware shallow dish, by James Tower, with shiny brown and cream glaze decoration, marked, 1953, 22in (56cm) long.
£600–700 *Bon*

A Roseville pottery vase, American, c1945, 7in (17.5cm) diam.
£135–155 *DSG*

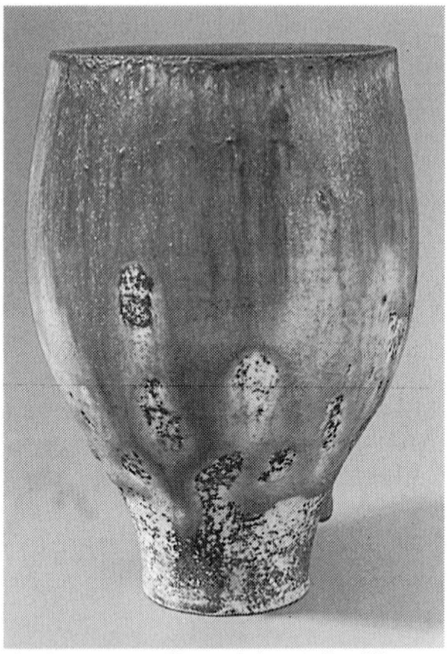

A stoneware 'treacle' pot, by Hans Coper, with shiny amber coloured glaze running over buff and brown tapering body, impressed 'HC' seal, early 1950s, 6in (15cm) high.
£4,500–5,000 *Bon*

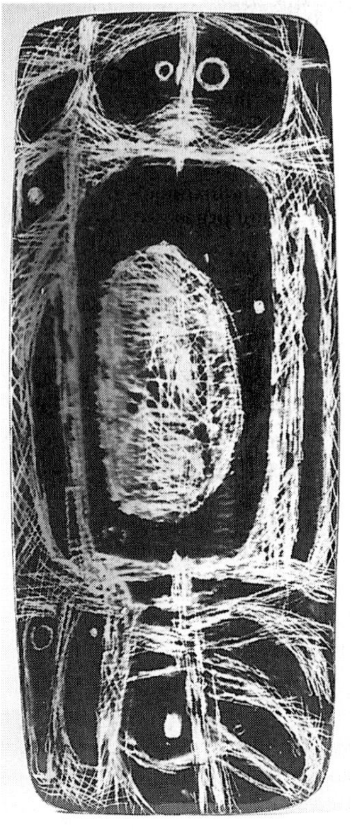

A 'tripot', by Hans Coper, with beige and brown geometric decoration and indications of carmine, c1956, 7¾in (20cm) high.
£5,200–6,000 *Bon*

Four Rye Pottery egg cups, c1950, 2in (5cm) high.
£45–50 *DSG*

A Portmeirion coffee set for 6, with plates, c1960s, pot 13in (33cm) high.
£70–80 *GIN*

An earthenware goblet vase, by Ettore Sottsass for Bitossi, glazed red with a grey band, signed, c1960, 13in (33cm) high.
£2,600–3,000 *Bon*

A stoneware footed bowl, by Dame Lucie Rie, white with inlaid criss-cross decoration, the well with radiating lines, impressed 'LR' seal, c1978, 7¼in (18.5cm) diam.
£4,200–4,800 *Bon*

A Meissen white porcelain vase, 1950s, 10in (25.5cm) high.
£30–35 *RCh*

l. A stoneware salad bowl, by Dame Lucie Rie, with brown running flecks on a ground of matt off-white glaze, an extending lip to one side, impressed 'LR' seal, c1968, 11¼in (28.5cm) wide.
£1,800–2,000 *Bon*

Glass

A Maastricht Kristalunie Coquille amber glass vase, designed by W. J. Rozendaal, with iridescent burst-open crackle, 1938, 5¾in (14.5cm) high.
£1,000–1,200 *S(Am)*

This vase was produced for only one year, and only two copies are known. It is a variation of the very popular Coquille glass charger of which large quantities were produced between 1938 and 1959.

A Leerdam Unica glass vase, designed by A. D. Copier, internally decorated with a graduated opal layer and with blue colour powders, engraved marks, c1940, 7in (18cm) high.
£500–550 *S(Am)*

Miller's is a price GUIDE not a price LIST

A Leerdam Unica glass vase, designed by A. D. Copier, internally decorated with a yellow layer graduating into yellow swirls, engraved marks, 1944, 8in (20.5cm) high.
£1,500–1,800 *S(Am)*

A Leerdam Unica glass vase, designed by A. D. Copier, covered with a blue layer and imprinted with seaweed, air bubbles and a layer of colourless glass, engraved marks, 1944, 10¼in (26cm) diam.
£2,800–3,200 *S(Am)*

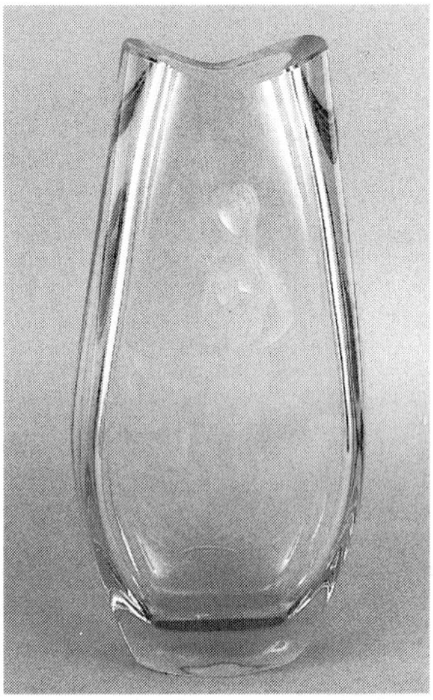

An Orrefors glass vase, etched with a mermaid standing in a shell, Swedish, c1950, 12½in (32cm) high.
£340–380 *WeH*

A Whitefriars 'knobbly' vase, 1963, 8in (20.5cm) high.
£65–80 *JHa*

An Italian art glass blue-green vase, decorated with an aquarium pattern, c1950, 11¾in (30cm) high.
£400–450 *SLM*

A Leerdam Unica glass vase, designed by A. D. Copier, the interior enamelled with flowers, marked, 1950, 6¾in (17cm) high.
£1,200–1,400 *S(Am)*

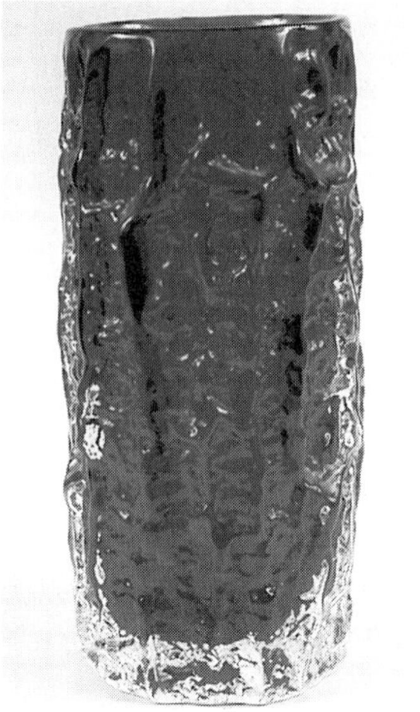

A Whitefriars red textured bark vase, designed by Geoffrey Baxter, c1967, 9in (23cm) high.
£50–60 *JHa*

A Venini Fazzoletto glass handkerchief vase, decorated with white latticinio stripes, acid stamped, c1950, 9in (23cm) high.
£800–900 *S(NY)*

A Seguso Vetri d'Arte glass vase, with everted rim, internally decorated with a pink layer with gold foil inclusions, on applied foot, 1950s, 13in (33cm) high.
£1,000–1,200 *S(Am)*

A Leerdam Unica glass vase, designed by Floris Meydam, with yellow, brown and cream layers, covered with a layer of colourless glass, 1959, 5in (15cm) diam.
£1,300–1,500 *S(Am)*

A Whitefriars cinnamon-coloured textured bark vase, c1966, 7in (18cm) high.
£50–60 *JHa*

Jewellery

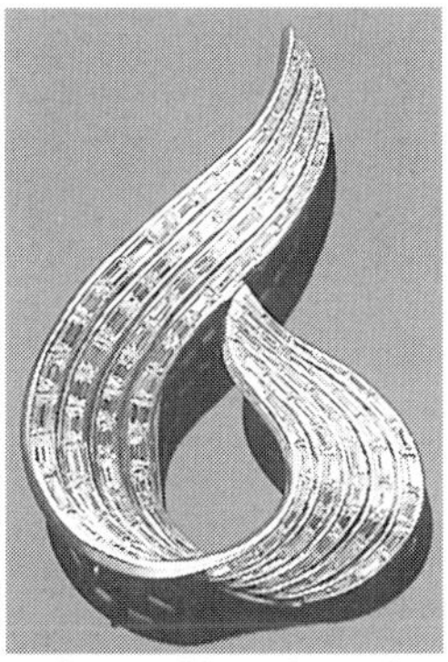

A diamond brooch, in the form of a curled ribbon, set with vertical waved lines of baguette diamonds, c1950.
£2,800–3,200 *P*

An emerald and diamond brooch, designed as a bunch of flowers, pavé-set with circular-cut emeralds and brilliant-cut diamonds, one emerald and one diamond missing, c1950.
£500–550 *S(Am)*

An 18ct gold and sapphire brooch, designed as a blossoming peony, the blue enamel decorated petals opening to reveal the cabochon sapphire set stamens, c1950.
£1,500–1,800 *S(Am)*

A brooch, with green baguette cut stones and green rhinestone drops, on a gilt setting, 1950s, 2¼in (5.5cm) long.
£60–70 *PGH*

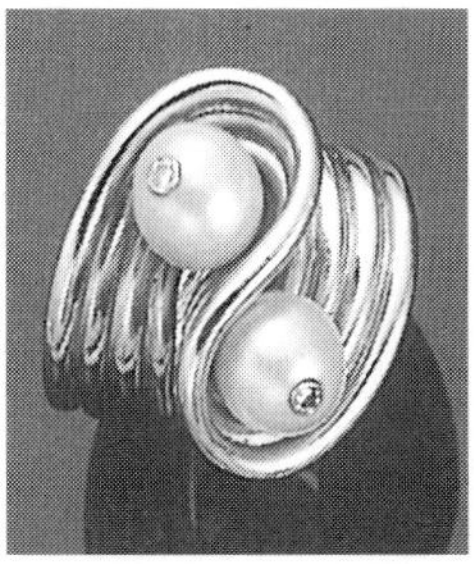

l. A cultured pearl and diamond dress ring, of reeded cross-over design set with 2 cultured pearls, each with a single brilliant-cut diamond to the centre, c1955.
£360–400 *Bon*

r. A yellow metal brooch, by Napier, set with white glass cabochon to the centre, surrounded by marquise-shaped white glass stones, signed, c1950, 4in (10cm) long.
£75–85 *PKT*

A yellow metal brooch, by Mirium Haskell, of flower design with *faux* turquoise blue centres, c1955, 2in (5cm) diam.
£100–125 *PKT*

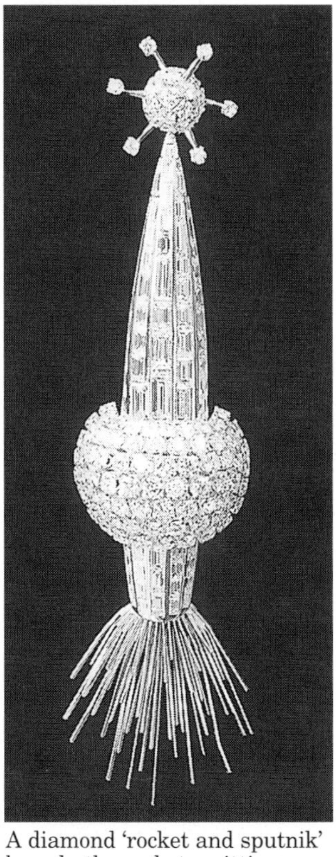

A diamond 'rocket and sputnik' brooch, the rocket emitting flames from its tail, decorated with vertical rows of baguette diamonds, a bombé segment of round diamonds around the centre, the tip with brilliant-cut stones, mounted in platinum, late 1950s.
£11,250–13,000 *S(G)*

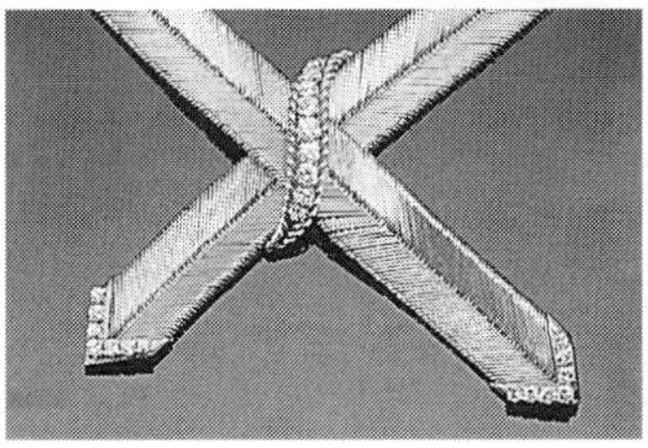

A gold and diamond necklace, designed as a woven crossed ribbon, with lines of brilliant-cut diamonds, c1950, 16½in (42cm) long.
£1,500–1,800 *S(Am)*

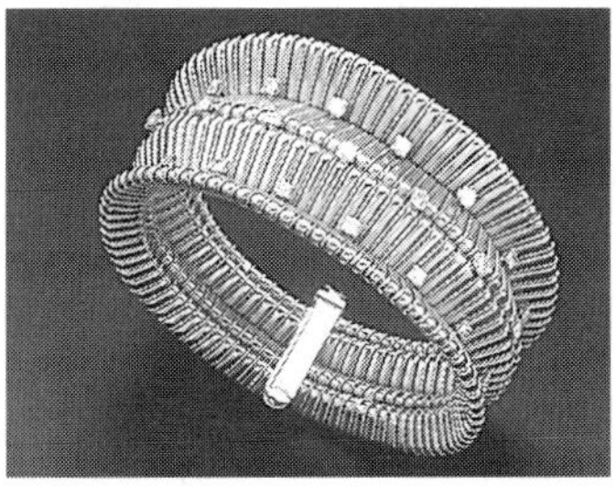

A diamond bracelet, by Mauboussin, designed as 4 tapered bands of flattened gas-pipe linking, decorated at the front with brilliant-cut diamonds, 1950s.
£3,200–3,600 *S*

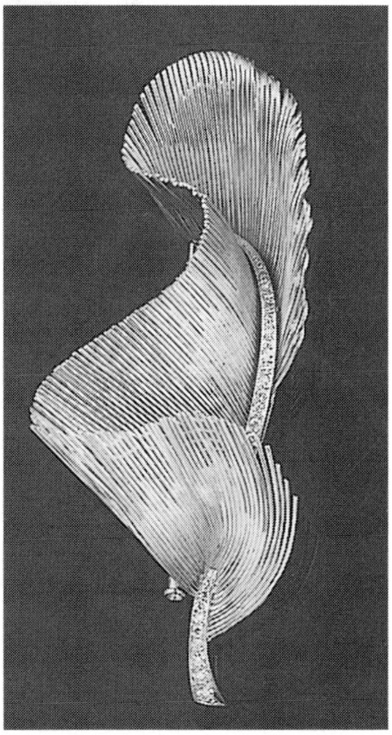

A gold and diamond scrolled feather brooch, set with diamonds, London import marks for 1957, French control marks, in a Wartski fitted leather case.
£2,000–2,200 *Bon*

A japanned-metal brooch, by Capri, in the form of a flower, set with a white diamanté, with round green and marquise blue diamanté, signed, c1960, 2in (5cm) long.
£35–40 *PKT*

Two yellow metal brooches, by Marcel Boucher, in the form of bunches of flowers, each with white diamanté on the front, and a single, half round, dark translucent stone set in the top, c1960, largest 2in (5cm) long.
£200–225 *PKT*

A yellow metal brooch, by Kramer, with open centre, surrounded by 4 rows of yellow diamanté, c1960, 2in (5cm) diam.
£75–85 *PKT*

A diamond dress ring, of abstract textured design, the bombé front claw-set with a line of graduated brilliant-cut diamonds, c1960.
£750–850 *S(Am)*

A turquoise and diamond ring, by Cartier, Paris, pavé-set with 8 brilliant-cut diamonds and cabochon turquoise, signed, c1960.
£3,700–4,200 *S*

A gem-set dress ring, the abstract openwork bezel randomly set with a single marquise cut diamond, circular-cut rubies and emeralds, and marquise-cut sapphires, c1965.
£130–150 *Bon*

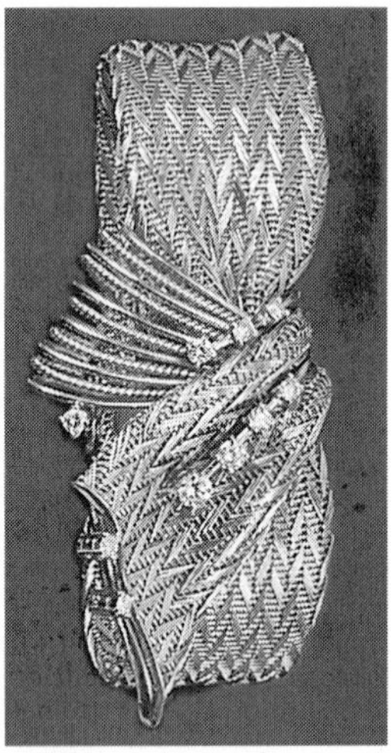

A diamond bracelet, of tapering woven herringbone design, with a central tie motif set with graduated brilliant-cut diamonds, c1960, 7in (18cm) long.
£800–900 *S(Am)*

A brooch, by Eisenberg Ice, set with various shades of pink, round and baguette-shaped diamanté with small white stone leaves, signed, c1965, 2in (5cm) diam.
£240–280 *PKT*

A yellow metal necklace, designed by Christian Dior, made by Henkel & Grosse, set with autumn-coloured diamanté, with small pearl drops, c1962, 14in (35.5cm) long.
£200–220 *PKT*

l. A garnet and diamond cluster ring, the step-cut garnet within an openwork and textured square pattern surround, randomly set with brilliant-cut diamonds, one diamond missing, c1965.
£250–300 *Bon*

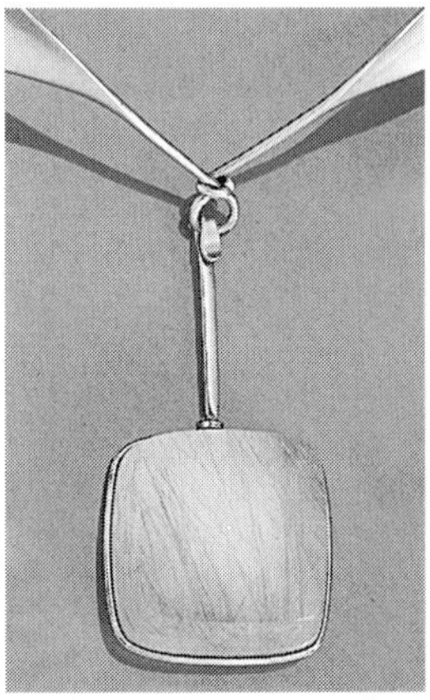

A silver and quartz collar necklace, by Torun for Georg Jensen, the quartz drop suspended from a tapering silver collar, signed, 1970.
£1,500–1,800 *Bon*

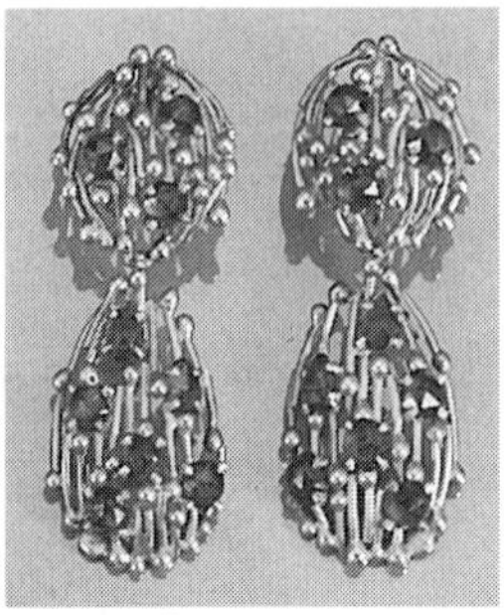

A pair of garnet ear pendants, by Tom Scott, the double tiered openwork drops randomly set with rose-cut garnets, maker's mark, c1975.
£130–150 *Bon*

A diamond cocktail ring, the lozenge-shaped abstract front claw-set with brilliant-cut diamonds, c1970.
£800–1,000 *S(Am)*

An aquamarine and diamond pendant, by John Donald, the aquamarine within an 18ct white gold textured radiating surround, set with brilliant-cut diamonds, maker's mark, 1969.
£700–800 *Bon*

Lighting

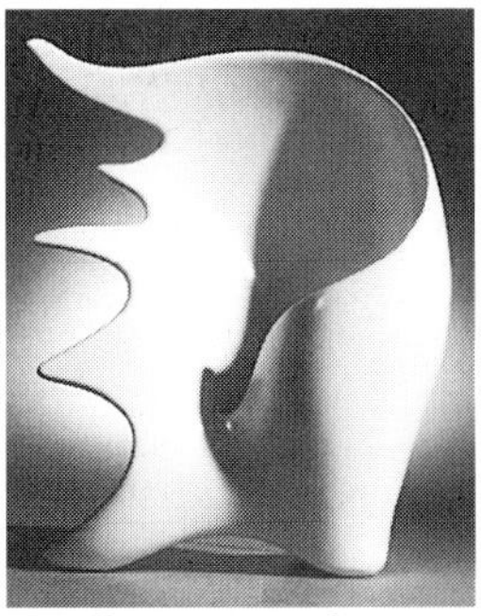

A yellow ceramic lamp, by Antonia Campi, for Lavenia, stamped, c1952, 11¼in (28.5cm) high.
£460–520 *S*

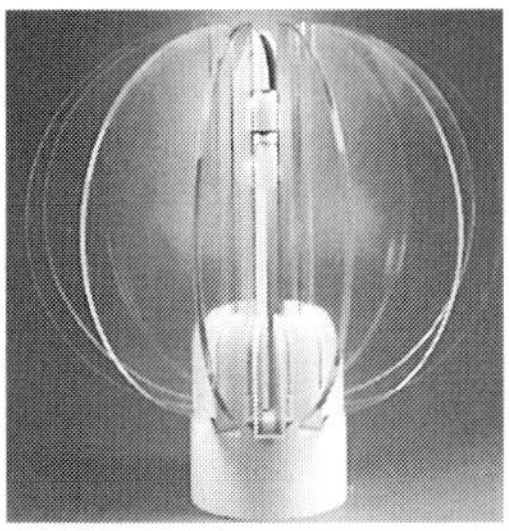

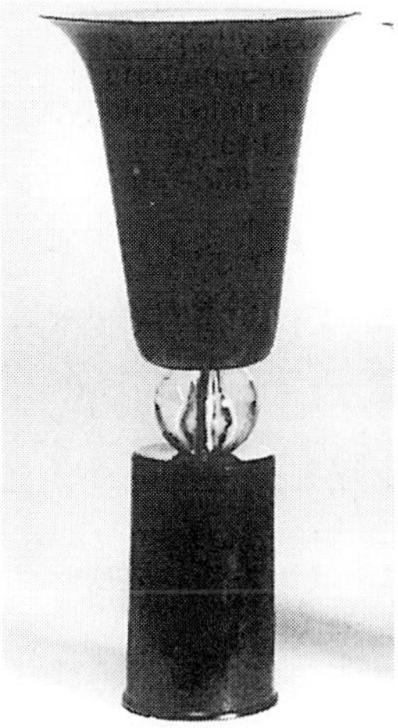

A pair of black enamelled aluminium and plastic lamps, c1950, 17¼in (44cm) high.
£280–320 *SLM*

l. A King Sun lamp, by Gae Aulenti, for Kartell, the clear perspex with white laquered cast aluminium, 1967, 27½in (70cm) high.
£1,200–1,400 *S*

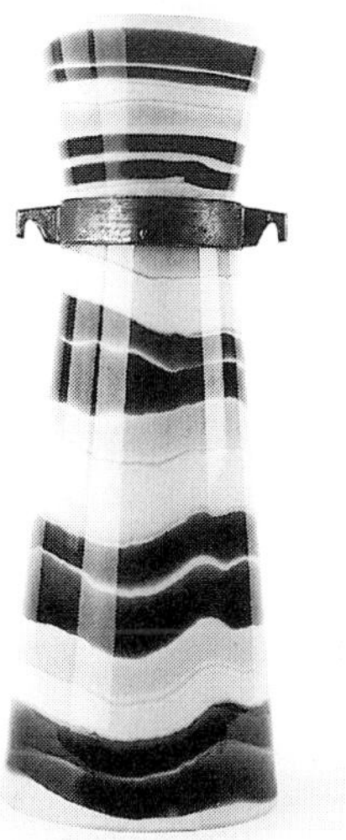

A Venini hanging lamp, by BBPR Design Group for Olivetti, the body in opaque glass with purple, lilac, yellow or green irregular band decoration and brass fixing around waist, 1954, 26¼in (66.5cm) high.
£1,000–1,200 *Bon*

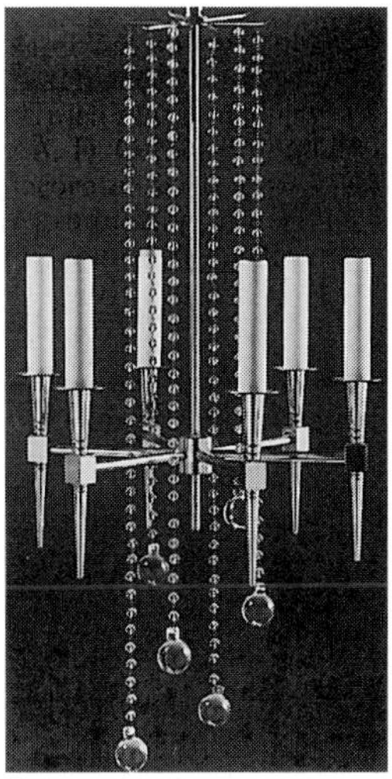

A polished brass and glass six-light chandelier, by Tommy Parzinger, composed of brass rods, hung with strings of glass beads, c1958, 39in (99cm) high.
£2,000–2,200 *S(NY)*

Each arm was originally fitted with a glossy paper shade.

A chandelier, by A. V. Mazzega, with acid-treated glass discs, the metal frame with central fitting for 12 small bulbs, 1950s, 25in (64cm) cube.
£230–260 *S*

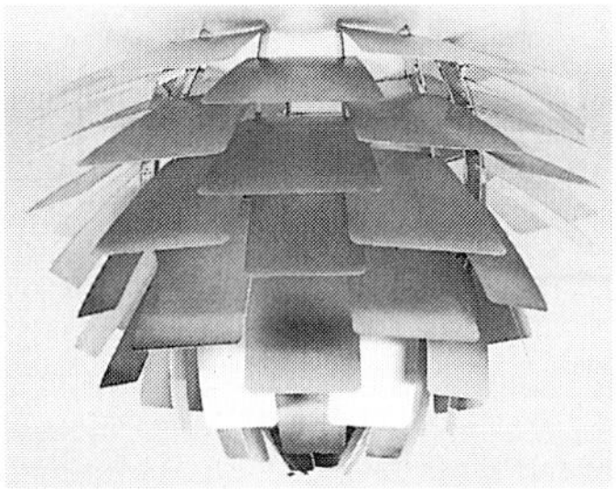

A copper-plate and aluminium ceiling Artichoke lamp, by Poul Henningsen, Denmark, for Louis Poulsen, partially painted white, 1958, 19¾in (50cm) high.
£750–850 *DORO*

A pair of Italian glass ceiling lights, each of dual undulating handkerchief form, in clear glass with green glass piping to the rim, c1960, 19¾in (50cm) diam.
£600–700 *P*

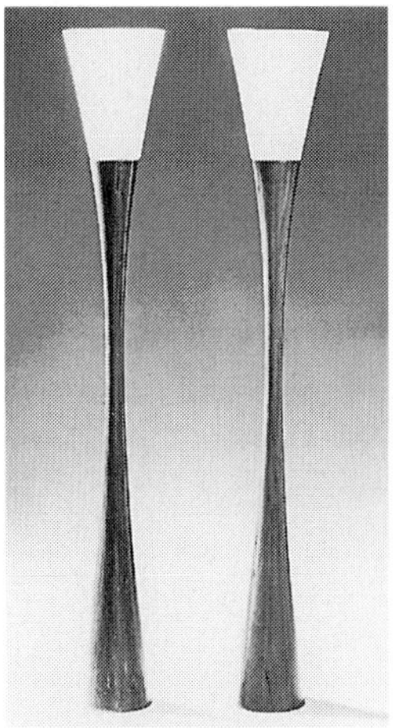

A pair of Disderot laminated turned-mahogany and frosted opaque glass standing lamps, each with a flaring opalescent glass shade, c1965, 62in (157cm) high.
£3,800–4,200 *S(NY)*

Two 'Boalum' floor lights, by Castiglioni and Frattini, for Artemide, the flexible 2 section structure with plastic skin over spiralling metal tubular elements and internal lighting, moulded marks to end, 1970, 72in (183cm) long.
£900–1,000 *Bon*

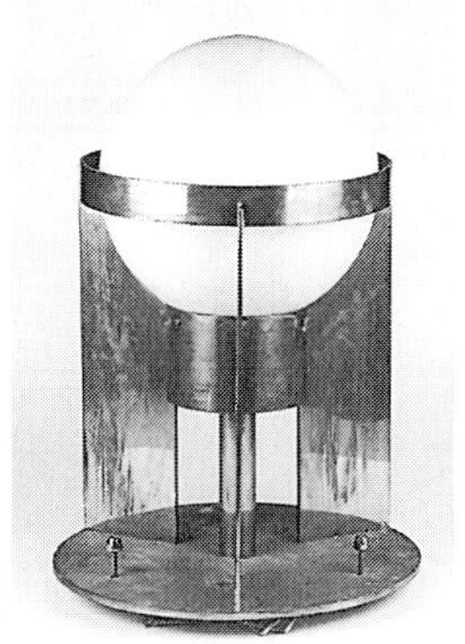

r. A wall light, by Walter Pichler, for a student hostel, the brass frame with an opaque glass ball, c1970, 15¾in (40cm) diam.
£1,500–1,800 *DORO*

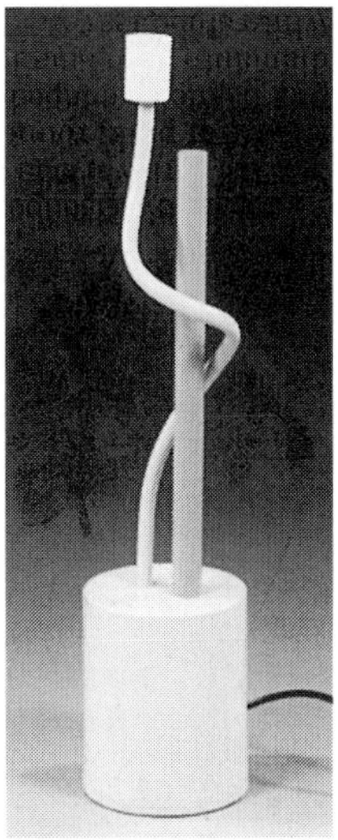

A 'Sinerpica' lamp, designed by Michele de Lucchi, for Alchimia, with blue, green and pink painted metal, 1979, 28¾in (73cm) high.
£780–880 *S*

LAMPS & LIGHTING
Ceiling & Wall Lights

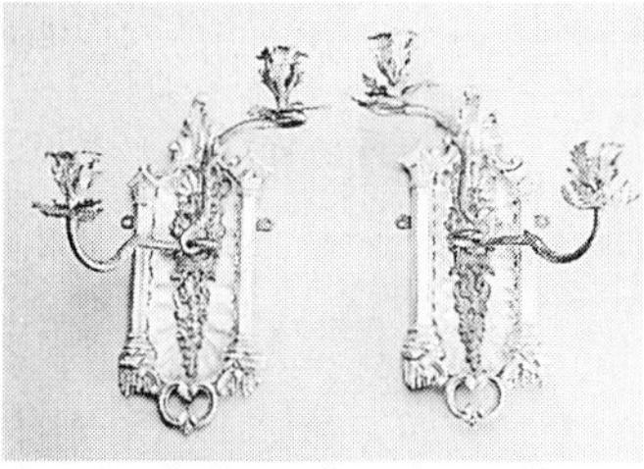

A pair of giltwood and ormolu wall brackets, the scrolling foliate branches with leaf-chased candleholders, each on a backplate chased with profile masks and a shell, 18thC, 15in (38cm) high.
£1,000–1,200 *DN*

A pewter two-tier chandelier, the stem with ball terminal, the upper tier with 6 scrolled foliate reflector arms, the lower tier with 6 scrolled candle arms, Scandinavian or German, mid-18thC, 24¾in (63cm) high.
£2,200–2,500 *S(Am)*

A pair of painted copper hanging lights, the glazed panels within moulded frames, with pierced central bands and hinged doors, openwork tops with brass ring supports, c1800, 22¾in (58cm) high.
£3,700–4,200 *S*

A Venetian gessoed and giltwood carved lantern, with acanthus and scroll carvings, moulded glazed doors with metal-lined interior, early 19thC, 22in (56cm) high.
£1,000–1,200 *SLM*

A Restauration bronze chandelier, the leaf-capped reeded standard rising from a five-sided base with gilt-bronze dolphin-form candle branches, ending with a flaming finial, c1820, 17½in (44.5cm) high.
£1,000–1,200 *SLM*

A gilt-bronze four-light chandelier, cast with berried foliage centering a foliate and shell cast urn fitted with nozzles, signed 'Carleton, Boston', replacements, mid-19thC, 52in (132cm) high.
£5,000–5,500 *S(NY)*

A Victorian lamp, the cranberry glass shade on a polished brass frame with peacock medallions, cranberry glass font with Venus burner, clear cut crystal prisms, 18in (45.5cm) high.
£700–800 *JAA*

A bronze hexagonal hanging lantern, fitted with a corner mounting bracket, with scrolled pierced top and shaped base, 19thC, 30¾in (78cm) high.
£2,300–2,600 *S*

r. A brass hall lantern, the moulded fish scale corona with 3 double brass rope suspenders, supporting a lantern with glass panels, converted to electricity, 19thC, 56in (142cm) high.
£1,500–1,800 *MEA*

A Victorian brass hanging lantern, with leaf-capped wrythen stem, foliate finials, bevelled glass panels and turned feet, 32in (81.5cm) high.
£1,400–1,600 *AH*

A Continental silvered-bronze chandelier, with a bird's head corona and biscuit porcelain Greek female figure, fitted for electricity, 19thC, 40¾in (103.5cm) high.
£2,500–2,800 *S(NY)*

A French parcel-gilt and iron hexagonal hall lantern, the glazed facets surmounted by a cresting pierced with quatrefoils and scrollwork, applied with flowers and scrolling acanthus leaves, c1870, 68½in (174cm) high.
£7,000–8,000 *S*

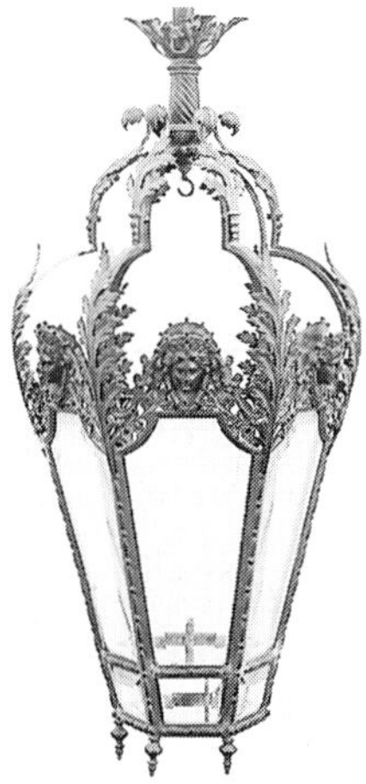

A Victorian bronze and glass gas lantern, the corona issuing 6 brackets with acanthus clasp, the bevelled glass surmounted by female masks, traces of original gilding, late 19thC, 28½in (72.5cm) high.
£1,200–1,400 *Bon(C)*

A brass ceiling light, with 4 etched glass panels, foliate chains and motifs, c1890s, 35½in (90cm) high.
£400–450 *LRG*

A gilt-bronze and cut-glass hanging lamp, the tapering shade below a pierced anthemion cast corona, late 19thC, 19¼in (49cm) high.
£200–250 *P*

l. A glass and metal light, in the form of a star, early 20thC, 12in (30.5cm) diam.
£150–180 *ASM*

r. A Viennese cut-glass eight-light chandelier, with glass shaft and glass ball top, fitted for electricity, late 19thC, 35½in (90cm) high.
£1,250–1,500 *DORO*

A pair of brass candle wall sconces, c1900, 14in (35.5cm) long.
£300–330 *DRU*

An Edwardian brass three-light electrolier, with etched glass shades, 32in (81.5cm) high.
£1,200–1,450 *CHA*

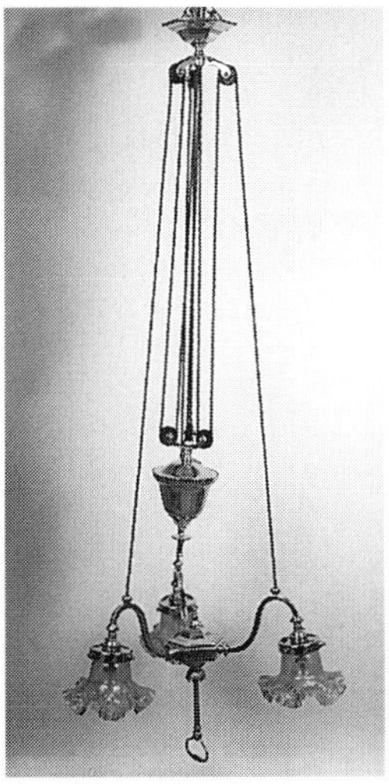

An Edwardian brass three-branch light, with vaseline glass shades, c1910, 48in (122cm) high.
£950–1,100 *CHA*

Table & Standard Lamps

A pair of George III ormolu-mounted porcelain and cut-glass two-light candelabra, each centred by a faceted spire with crescent and pagoda finial flanked by a pair of scrolled arms decorated with faceted drops, raised on a square stepped blue and gilt-decorated porcelain plinth, on bun feet, late 18thC, 23½in (59.5cm) high.
£4,500–5,000 *S(NY)*

A pair of ormolu table lamps, each with a fluted and quarter-reeded column with Corinthian capital, on a stepped and panelled base, applied with wreaths and bows, on paw feet, converted to electricity, early 19thC, 28in (71cm) high.
£3,200–3,500 *MEA*

An Empire marble table with adjustable oil lamp, c1800, 16½in (42cm) diam.
£1,100–1,300 *DOR*

A pair of George III gilt-bronze and cut-glass candelabra, with thistle-shaped nozzles and star-shaped drip pans, on blue glass bases and gilt-metal plinths on ball feet, 24in (61cm) high.
£4,500–5,000 *P*

r. A Sandwich glass astral lamp, the wheel-cut and acid-etched shade with Gothic arches, damaged, 19thC, 33in (84cm) high.
£2,200–2,500 *SK(B)*

This lamp was originally owned by Deming Jarvis, owner of Boston Sandwich Glass Company.

l. A pair of bronzed and gilt-metal candelabra, each with a bunch of flowers incorporating 6 candle branches held by a putto, on a white marble plinth with swags of flowers and scroll feet, 19thC, 27in (69cm) high.
£1,300–1,500 *DN*

A pair of Regency ormolu and glass two-branch lustres, on circular bases and paw feet, 13¾in (35cm) high.
£4,000–4,500 *GH*

A lace maker's glass lamp, with hollow baluster stem and handle, 19thC, 8¾in (22cm) high.
£220–250 *P*

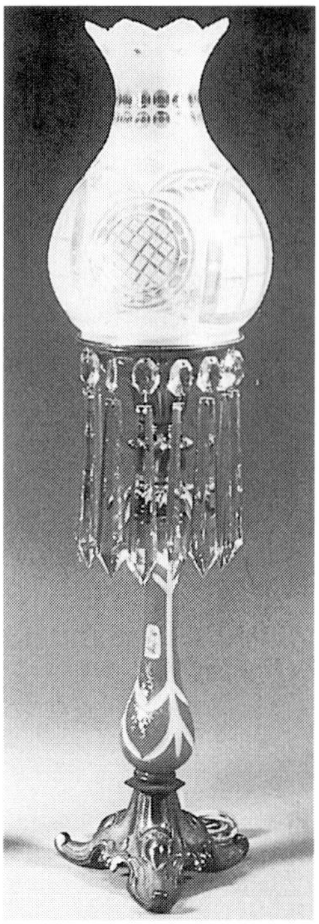

A pair of Regency bronze oil lamps, the fluted reservoirs of cornucopia form, with foliate decorated covers and boar's head terminals, on swept fluted plinths and winged paw feet, 11in (28cm) high.
£4,600–5,000 *P(EA)*

A pair of glass lustres, on coloured marble socles, 19thC, 12in (30.5cm) high.
£1,200–1,400 *GH*

A pair of glass and gilt-bronze lamp stands, the blue glass vases cast with bacchic masks linked by vined garlands, on reeded bases with flower garlands, 19thC, 29in (73.5cm) high.
£3,000–3,500 *P*

A carved and gilded oak table lamp, 19thC, 26in (66cm) high.
£130–150 *ASM*

A pair of French white marble and gilt-bronze lamps, fitted for electricity, c1880, 26in (66cm) high.
£2,300–2,500 *S(S)*

A brass two-branch table lamp, with cut and etched shades, converted for electricity, c1890, 26in (66cm) high.
£750–850 *CHA*

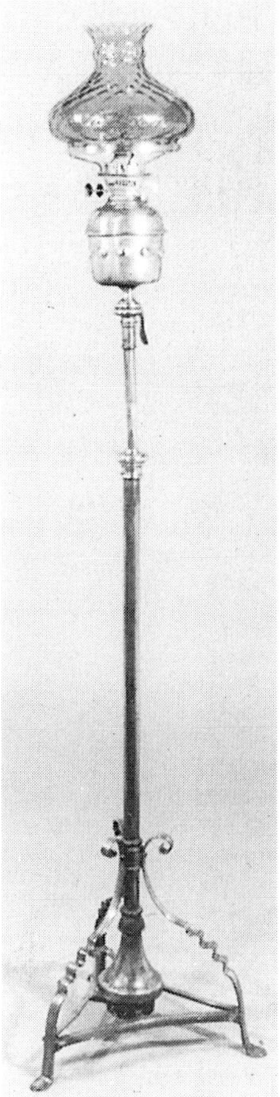

A Victorian oil lamp, with cranberry glass shade, telescopic action, on 3 scroll supports and triangular base, 72in (183cm) high.
£250–300 *WBH*

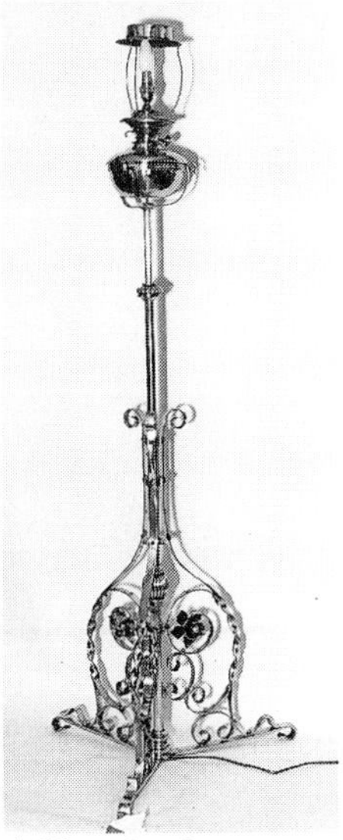

A Victorian brass telescopic adjustable lamp, with copper reservoir and 3 brass scroll supports, late 19thC, 60in (152.5cm) high.
£400–465 *LCA*

A silver-plated oil lamp, with cranberry glass tinted shade, in original working condition, c1890, 32in (81.5cm) high.
£1,000–1,100 *CHA*

A late Victorian oil lamp, with cranberry glass shade, on fluted brass support, black slag socle, 23in (58.5cm) high.
£450–500 *GAK*

A French tin lamp, 19thC, 17in (43cm) high.
£300–330 *RIV*

A tin and glass lantern, late 19thC, 17½in (44.5cm) high.
£70–80 *RIV*

Electric Lighting

Always check that electric lighting conforms to the current safety regulations.

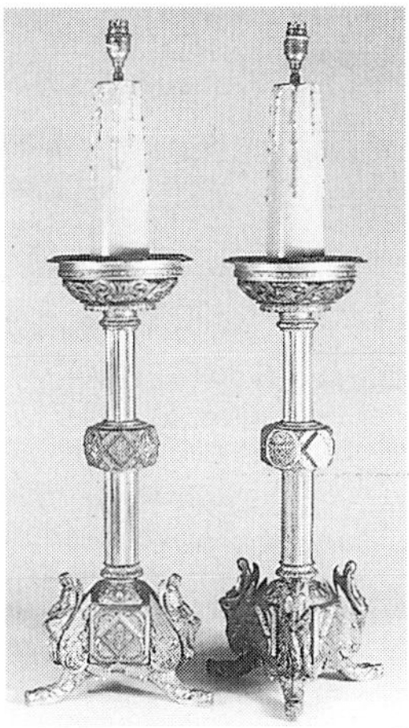

A pair of French gilt-metal altar candlesticks, each reeded stem with a multi-faceted knop and pierced foliate cast drip pan, on a triform base, fitted for electricity, late 19thC, 31in (78.5cm) high.
£900–1,100 *P*

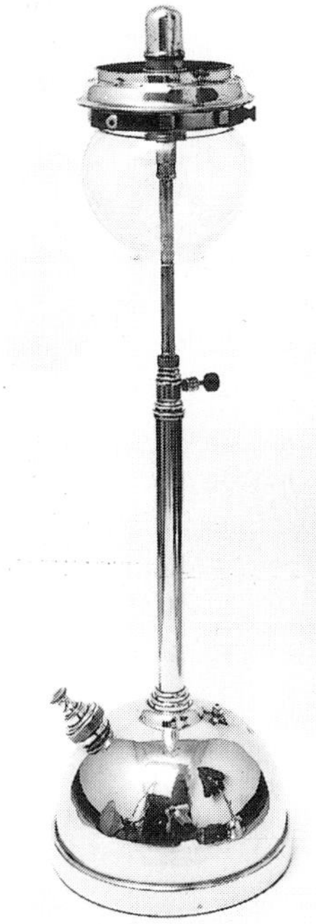

A brass Tilley lamp, 1940s, 23in (58.5cm) high.
£80–90 *HEM*

RUGS & CARPETS

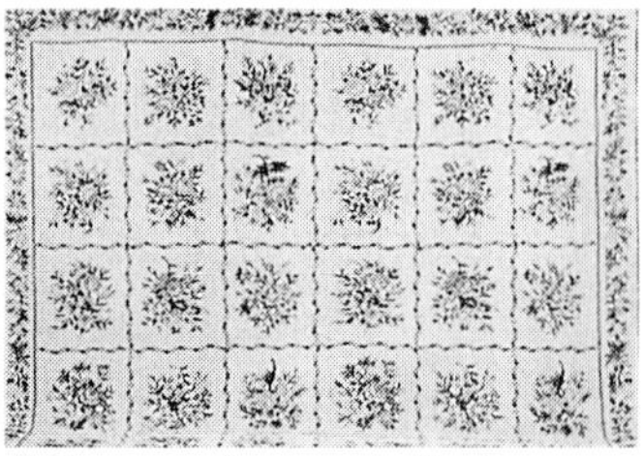

A Savonnerie carpet, the ivory compartmented field containing floral sprays enclosed by simple meandering vine borders, French, c1925, 212 x 144in (538.5 x 366cm).
£1,200–1,500 *SLN*

A French needlepoint carpet, with all-over lattice design containing cruciform motifs, in pale blue and coral red, the borders of cartouches interspersed with scrolling vines, c1860, 204 x 201in (518 x 510cm).
£9,000–10,000 *P*

A Bessarabian kilim, the ivory field with sprays of flowers, the ice-blue main border of trailing flowers and foliage within narrow pale brown guards, Moldavian/Romanian border, early 20thC, 106 x 73in (269 x 186cm).
£2,200–2,800 *WW*

r. An Anatolian prayer rug, the ivory field with a vase of flowers flanked by buildings, framed by a striped *mihrab* supported by columns, the ivory spandrels filled with flowers, enclosed by lemon yellow foliate borders, 1875, 79 x 48in (200 x 122cm).
£450–500 *P*

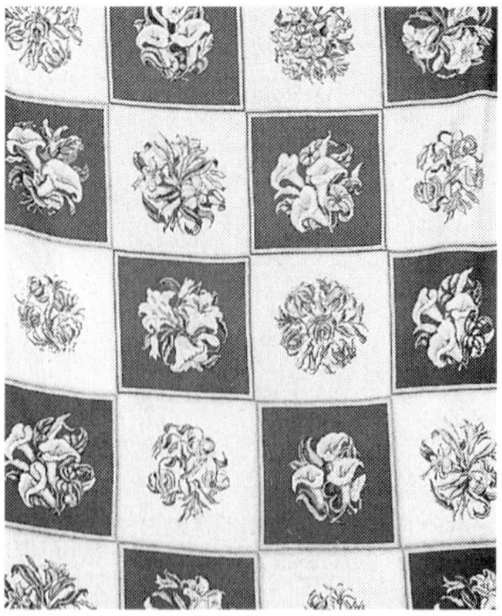

An English needlework carpet, divided into squares depicting white lilies on a red ground alternating with pink lilies on a cream ground, all within tan, beige and yellow borders, label on reverse marked 'Women's Home Industries' and 'Hand Made in Great Britain', late 19thC, 168 x 96in (426 x 244cm).
£550–650 *S(Cg)*

An Aubusson carpet, the walnut brown field centred by an ivory medallion containing floral sprays framed by rococo scrolls, with similar spandrels, enclosed by simple rosette borders, restored, French, 19thC, 188 x 162in (478 x 412cm).
£6,500–7,000 *Bon*

The rugs in this section have been arranged in geographical sequence from west to east, in the following order: Europe, Turkey, Anatolia, Caucasus, Persia, Turkestan, India and China.

An Aubusson carpet, with foliate scrolls and flowerheads on a dark field, French, c1860, 163 x 117in (415 x 297cm).
£5,750–7,000 *S*

An Ushak carpet, the faded peach field with columns of stylised flowerheads and vines enclosed by indigo borders flanked by saffron guard stripes, minor damage, west Turkey, c1900, 201 x 147in (510 x 375cm).
£2,700–3,200 *Bon*

Carpet Weaving

Although it is not known exactly when the first piled weavings were produced, the craft is thought to have been practised many centuries before the birth of Christ, and was probably begun by nomads as an attempt to insulate their tents against the cold. Over the centuries carpet weaving was carried across Asia by invading armies, traders and migrating nomads. Today carpet weaving has developed into a huge multi-million pound business.

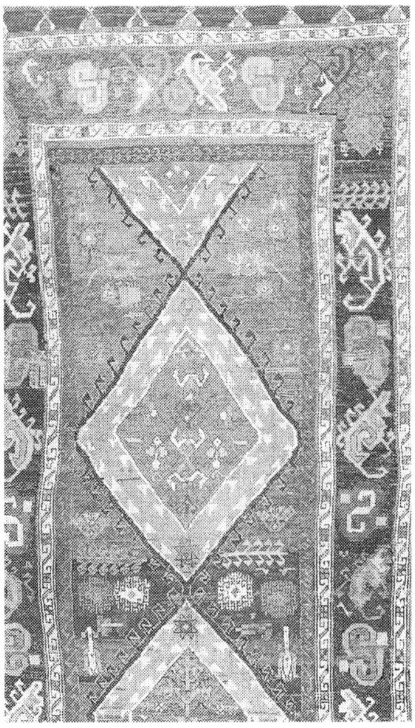

A Konya rug, the abrashed walnut ground with 3 latch hook *guls*, enclosed by indigo borders of geometric devices, central Anatolia, slight wear and repair, 1804, 125 x 52in (317 x 137cm).
£5,000–5,500 *S(NY)*

A Daghestan prayer rug, the ivory lattice field containing stylised plants beneath the *mihrab*, flanked by spandrels and bird borders, north east Caucasus, late 19thC, 57 x 48in (145 x 122cm).
£1,500–1,800 *SLN*

A Shirvan kilim, with bands of hexagons and S motifs in royal blue, red, gold, tan, ivory, brown and blue/green, east Caucasus, slight damage, late 19thC, 120 x 69in (305 x 175.5cm).
£450–500 *SK(B)*

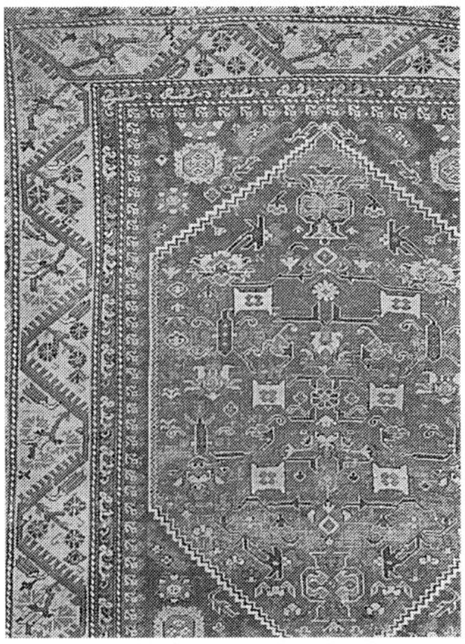

A Kula village rug, the dark terracotta field with overall flowering plants, blue flowerhead spandrels and broad soft yellow flowering vine border, west Anatolia, 1890, 61½ x 56½in (156 x 143cm).
£620–750 *S(S)*

A Kuba rug, with royal blue, red, ivory, black and pale blue/green shield motifs and rosettes on a gold field, ivory border, north east Caucasus, late 19thC, 58 x 48in (147.5 x 122cm).
£550–650 *SK(B)*

A Bergama rug, the tomato red field with a central blue hooked panel, pendant blue, red and ivory hooked octagons, blue border of diced, octagon and star *guls*, west Anatolia, early 19thC, 76 x 66in (193 x 167cm).
£8,000–9,000 *S*

The 5 medallion mid-19thC Bergama design is a direct descendant of Anatolian 'Holbein' rugs of the 16thC, such as those in the Museum of Turkish and Islamic Art, Istanbul.

A Shirvan rug, the dark blue field with scattered florettes and jewels, woven with a string of 4 stepped lozenge or peony-shaped medallions, some damage, east Caucasus, mid-19thC, 97 x 45in (246.5 x 114.5cm).
£400–500 *L*

l. A Chajli rug, the brick field with 3 polygons in pale blue and ivory with contrasting central octagons and filled with anthropomorphic motifs, the ivory main border with spaced octagons, flowerhead secondary borders, pale gold, brick and ivory striped guards, south Caucasus, late 19thC, 98 x 42in (249 x 107cm).
£1,600–1,800 *WW*

A Karabagh Khelleh, the indigo field of polychrome palmettes and flowerheads enclosed by madder turtle borders and pale lemon guard stripes, Caucasus, 19thC, 228 x 83in (570 x 208cm).
£3,500–4,200 *Bon*

A Kazak rug, the brick field with 3 large lobed cruciform medallions, surrounded by scattered animals and people and small geometric motifs, ivory main border of scrolling geometric motifs, dark brown and brick scrolling floral guards, Caucasus, c1900, 95 x 56in (241 x 142cm).
£720–800 *WW*

FURTHER READING

Rugs & Carpets, Andrew Middleton, Mitchell Beazley, 1996

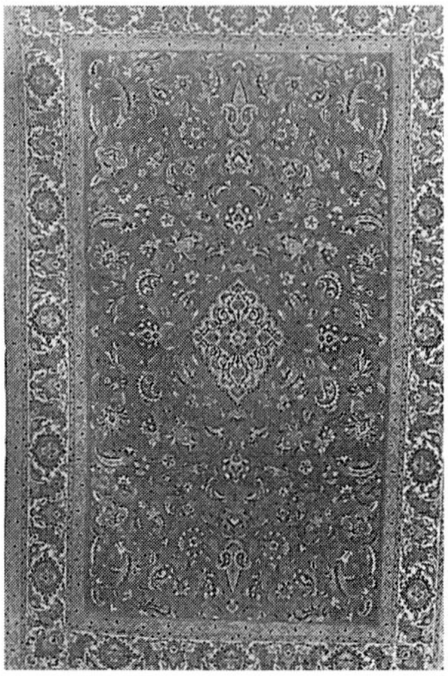

A Dorush carpet, the beige field with columns of large rosettes and meandering vines enclosed by similar indigo borders, east Persia, c1880, 157 x 101in (397 x 256cm).
£7,000–8,000 *S*

An Isfahan prayer rug, with trees on an ivory field and blue corners, one wide red ground border and 2 narrow borders, Persia, c1930, 78 x 54in (198 x 137cm).
£420–500 *DN*

l. A pair of Isfahan rugs, each with a central medallion surrounded by floral vines enclosed by ivory flowerhead borders, central Persia, c1930, 83 x 58in (210 x 148cm).
£800–1,000 *RTo*

l. A Sewan Kazak rug, the strawberry field centred by typical shield medallion, with rosettes enclosed by an indigo hooked motif border, Caucasus, late 19thC, 92 x 76in (234 x 192cm).
£4,600–5,000 *Bon*

A Kurdish rug, with Mina Khani design on a dark blue field, one pale ground and 2 red ground borders, west Persia, c1880, 94½ x 50in (240 x 127cm).
£800–900 *DN*

Carpets of Mina Khani design (a stylised floral lattice which is also found on Belouch and Kurdish piled weavings) have been produced in the town of Veramin in central Iran for at least 100 years. Veramin carpets are made in workshops, on a cotton foundation and with a Turkish knot. They are good quality rugs, but are rarely found outside Iran.

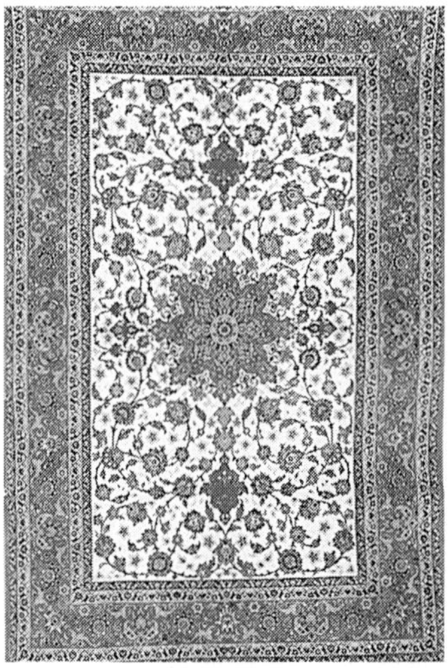

An Isfahan Sayrafiyan rug, the beige field centred by a medallion surrounded by scrolling vines and palmettes enclosed by madder borders of meandering vines, central Persia, c1940, 89 x 59in (227 x 150cm).
£9,000–10,000 *S*

The inscription cartouche on this rug reads 'Woven [in] Iran, Isfahan, Sayrafiyan'.

A Lori/Bakhtiyari soumac weave saddlebag, with ivory cross-hatching panels, animal head medallion sides with traditionally piled weave decorations, west Persia, c1900, 79 x 29½in (200 x 75cm).
£675–750 *AWH*

A Tafrish rug, the mid-blue field with centre medallion and cream inner medallion, filled with scrolling flowers and foliage, quarter medallions in each spandrel, ivory trailing floral and palmette main border, red floral guards, west Persia, 1930s, 79 x 55in (201 x 140cm).
£400–450 *WW*

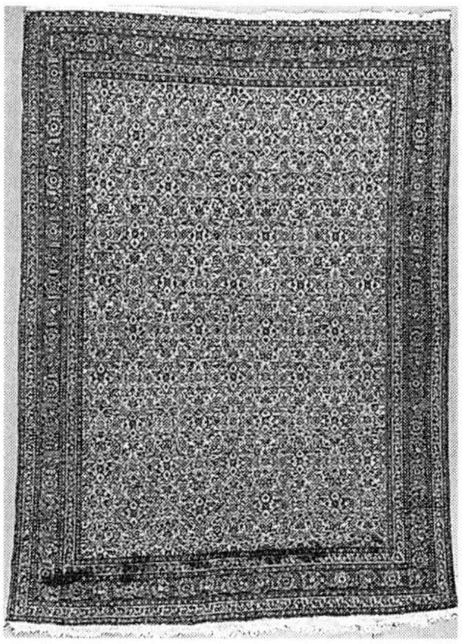

A Senneh rug, the ivory field filled with the *herati* design in rose, light brick, pale blue and pale gold, light brick trailing vine and flowerhead main border, pale gold floral guards and twin narrow indigo floral stripes, silk foundation, west Persia, c1900, 68 x 48in (173 x 122cm).
£7,500–8,500 *WW*

A Sarouk rug, with floral sprays and blossoming vines in blue, gold, ivory, tan and blue/green on a wine red field, midnight blue border, west Persia, early 20thC, 77 x 50in (195.5 x 127cm).
£1,100–1,200 *SK(B)*

A Ziegler Mahal carpet, the ivory *herati* field centred by an indigo medallion framed by spandrels and madder samovar borders, west Persia, 163 x 142in (413 x 359cm).
£7,200–8,000 *S*

The samovar motif is found on the borders of many western Persian weavings, although it is by no means exclusive to this area. It is also used to a limited extent by the weavers of Kuba and the Beshir tribe in Turkestan.

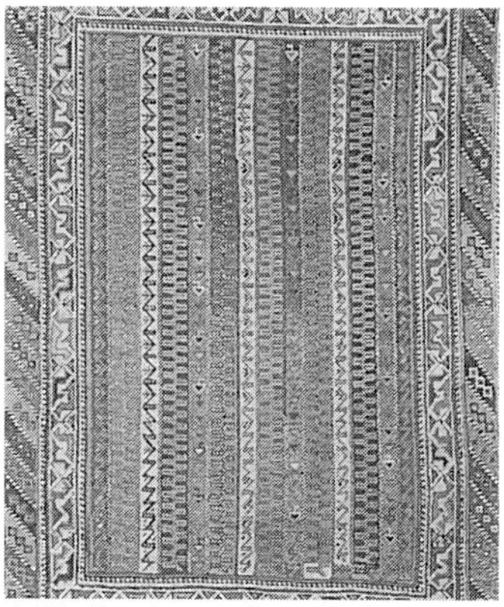

A Kashgai rug, the polychrome columned field within ivory bird and tulip inner border and diagonal striped outer border, south west Persia, c1900, 56 x 42in (142 x 106cm).
£550–650 *S(S)*

A Kashgai rug, the blue field with 5 diamond medallions and overall flowerheads and birds, yellow flowering vine border and multiple guard stripes, south west Persia, 1910, 73 x 51in (186 x 130cm).
£650–750 *S(S)*

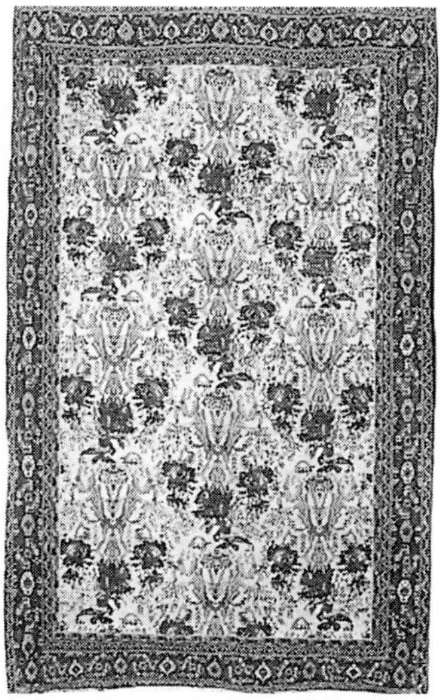

A Senneh rug, the ivory field with all-over design of stylised plants with roosting birds enclosed by a hazelnut border, cotton foundation, restored, west Persia, c1920, 106 x 98in (269 x 173cm).
£1,750–2,000 *Bon*

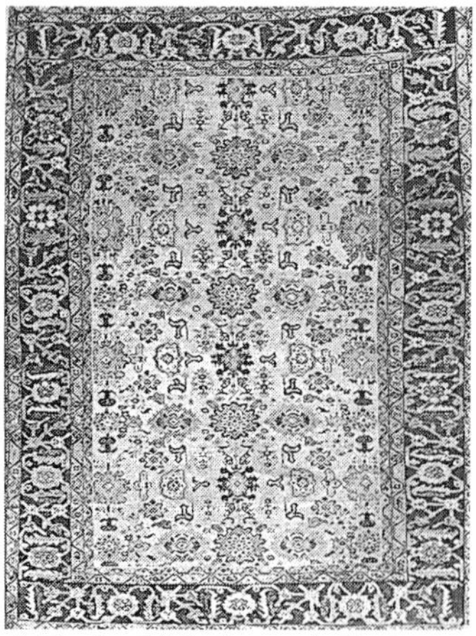

A Ziegler Mahal carpet, the honey field woven with scattered palmettes, the broad pale brick main border with a palmette meander, Persia, c1890, 125 x 97in (317 x 246cm).
£3,500–4,200 *L*

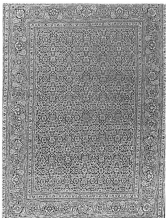

A Mahal carpet, the brick field with tiny animals scattered all-over in the Shah Abbas design, repeated in the indigo main border, pale brick and ivory *boteh* and trailing floral guards, c1890, central Persia, 159 x 119in (404 x 302cm).
£7,000–8,000 *WW*

The Shah Abbas is a design of large palmettes and floral scrolling vines.

Knots

The type of knot can be useful when one seeks to identify a carpet. Some designs were used by weavers in more than one area, and if the dyes used are also similar then the structure must be examined in order to determine the carpet's origin. Fringes, selvedges (side cords), knots, warps and wefts all provide useful clues to the origin of the weaving.

As a general rule, the Turkish, or symmetrical, knot is used throughout Turkey, exceptions being Isparta, Sivas and some Herekes. It is also common in much of west Persia and may be found in weavings of many nomadic tribes of both Persia and central Asia. The Persian, or asymmetrical, knot is used throughout much of central or eastern Persia and by some Turkoman tribes.

Finely knotted rugs are prized by some, but a high knot count may not be indicative of high value. Currently, Ushak carpets which are crudely knotted are fetching very high prices.

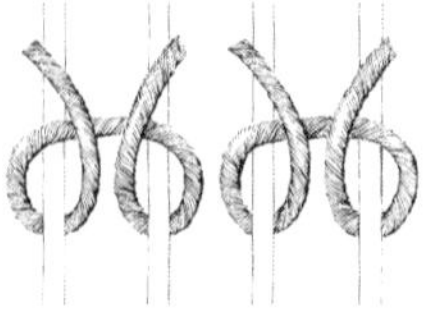

The Turkish , Ghiordes or symmetrical knot

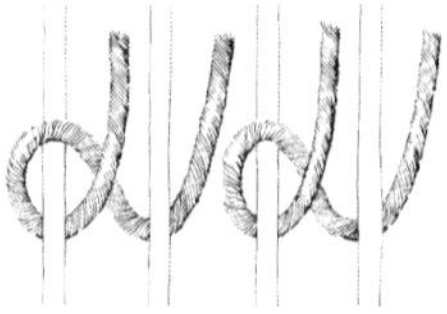

The Persian, Senneh or asymmetrical knot

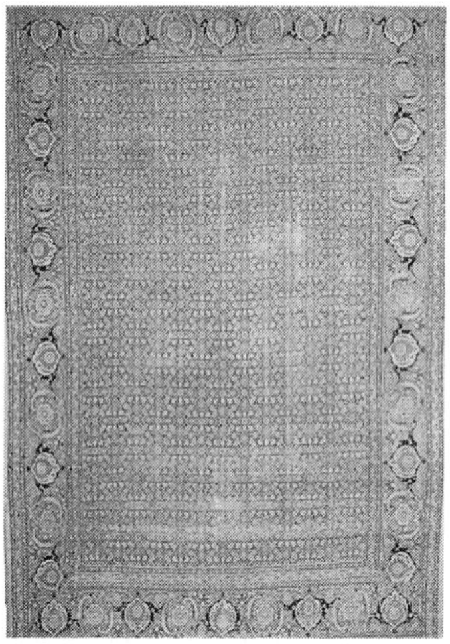

A Tabriz carpet, the field of *herati* design enclosed by wide madder samovar and leaf border, north west Persia, c1900, 265 x 165in (650 x 414cm).
£9,000–10,000 *Bon*

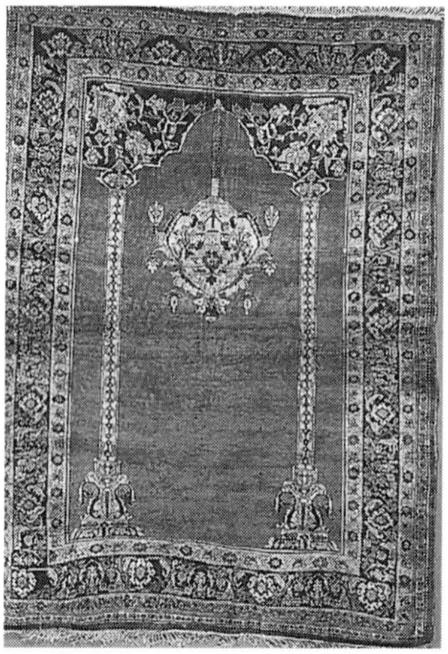

A silk Tabriz prayer rug, the rust *mihrab* with a cream floral column to each side with a floral hanging lamp in the arch, indigo floral spandrels, main border of scrolling floral vines and palmettes, pale green scrolling floral guards, north west Persia, early 20thC, 68 x 53in (173 x 135cm).
£2,000–2,200 *WW*

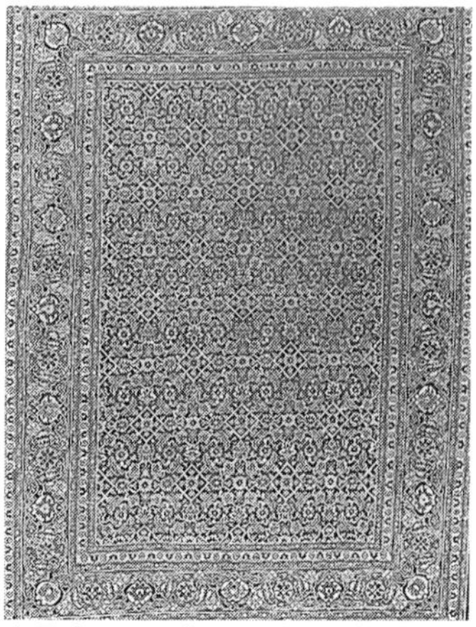

A Tabriz wool rug, the indigo field with all-over *herati* design within a main madder border, north west Persia, early 20thC, 74 x 55in (188 x 139cm).
£700–800 *CGC*

A Bakshaish rug, the indigo ground centred by a madder and mint green lozenge enclosed by borders of stepped geometric devices and multiple minor borders, north Persia, c1880, 67 x 51in (170 x 129cm).
£4,500–5,000 *S(NY)*

A Tabriz carpet, the large floral medallion with a dark blue ground on a rust field with floral angles inside 4 borders, north west Persia, early 20thC, 224 x 143in (569 x 363cm).
£6,250–7,000 *MEA*

A Heriz carpet, the brick red field of angular vines centred by an ivory and indigo cruciform medallion framed by ivory spandrels and samovar borders, north west Persia, c1900, 150 x 120in (382 x 304cm).
£4,600–5,000 *S*

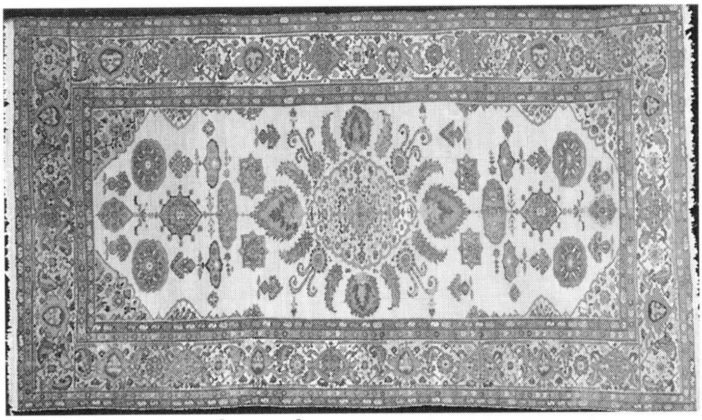

A Sultanabad carpet, the camel field with stylised flowerheads, central Persia, c1890, 183 x 104in (465 x 265cm).
£3,600–4,000 *Bon*

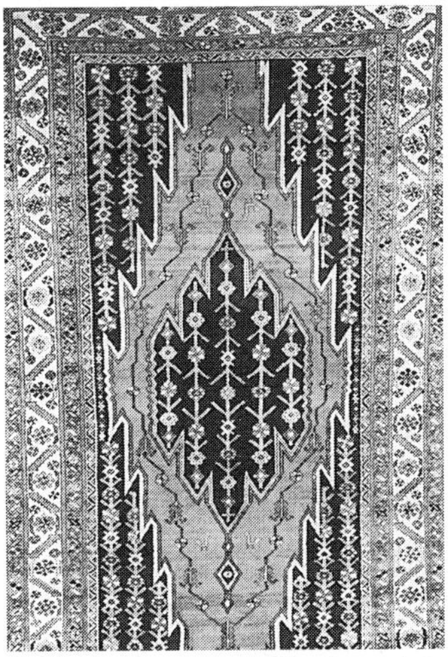

A Maslaghan rug, with elongated 'lightning' medallions and columns of rosettes in red, sky blue, rose, pale gold, camel and blue/green on a midnight blue field, ivory border, north west Persia, early 20thC, 86 x 54in (218.5 x 137cm).
£850–950 *SK(B)*

A Kurdish village rug, with 4 geometrical medallions on a dark blue field with 3 borders, north west Persia, c1900, 85 x 40in (216 x 102cm).
£200–250 *DN*

A Karaja carpet, the field of large angular vines centred by a medallion framed by stepped spandrels and borders of samovar motifs and meandering vines, north west Persia, late 19thC, 71in (180.5cm) square.
£900–1,100 *SLN*

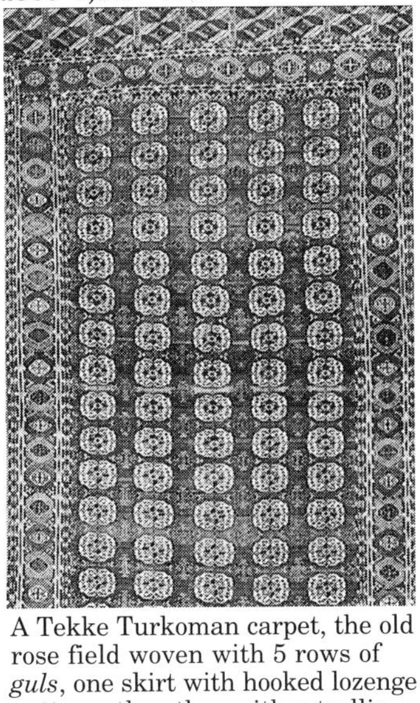

A Tekke Turkoman carpet, the old rose field woven with 5 rows of *guls*, one skirt with hooked lozenge pattern, the other with a trellis pattern, west Turkestan, c1920, 165 x 86in (419 x 219cm).
£2,500–3,000 *L*

l. A Chodor chuval, the pale aubergine diamond lattice field of Ertmen *guls* within borders of latch hook motifs, central Turkestan, 19thC, 33 x 51in (83 x 128cm).
£2,750–3,000 *S*

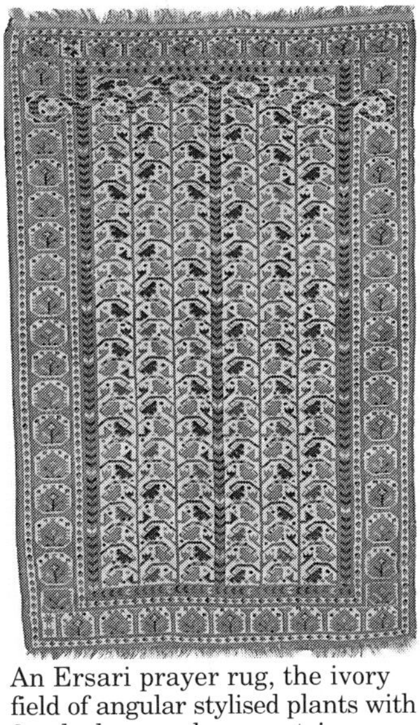

An Ersari prayer rug, the ivory field of angular stylised plants with 3 polychrome chevron stripes terminating in ram's horn motifs, enclosed by a compartmented border of madder shield motifs, Emirate of Bokhara, slightly reduced in length, west Turkestan, 19thC, 83 x 52in (201 x 133cm).
£4,500–5,500 *P*

A Beshir carpet, the pale blue field with all-over palmettes and flowers, outlined in pale gold, pale blue panelled flowerhead main border, pale gold medallion guards and brick panelled octagon outer border, west Turkestan, late 19thC, 99 x 47in (251 x 120cm).
£400–450 *WW*

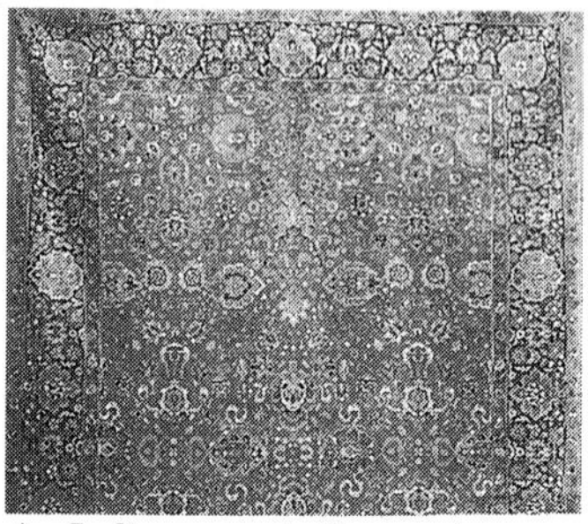

An Indian carpet, the cassis field with an all-over design of flowering vines, cloud bands and palmettes enclosed by an indigo palmette border, c1910, 215 x 143in (543 x 363cm).
£3,400–3,750 *Bon*

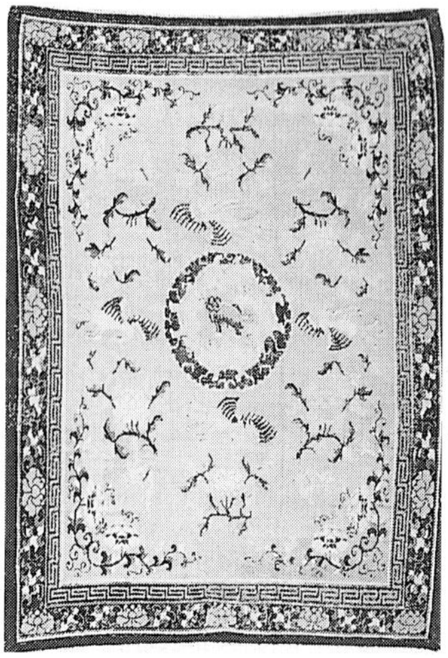

An Agra carpet of unusual size, the beige field with an all-over *herati* design, framed by cartouche borders and meandering vine guard stripes, north India, extensively repiled, early 20thC, 104 x 94in (264 x 239cm).
£5,500–6,500 *S(NY)*

A Chinese carpet, the field sparsely decorated with floral motifs centred by a roundel medallion framed by spandrels and meandering vine borders, probably Ningshia, mid-19thC, 116 x 93in (294.5 x 236cm).
£450–500 *SLN*

A Chinese carpet, the ivory lattice field centred by a roundel medallion, the spandrels with blooming flowers enclosed by meandering vine borders, c1910, 118 x 94in (300 x 239cm).
£1,800–2,000 *Bon*

l. A Ningshia carpet, the beige field of floral motifs surrounding a roundel medallion containing a Fo dog, the spandrels with flowering vines, enclosed by indigo rosette borders and Greek key guard stripes, west China, rewoven and replied areas, 126 x 94in (320 x 239cm).
£5,500–6,500 *S(NY)*

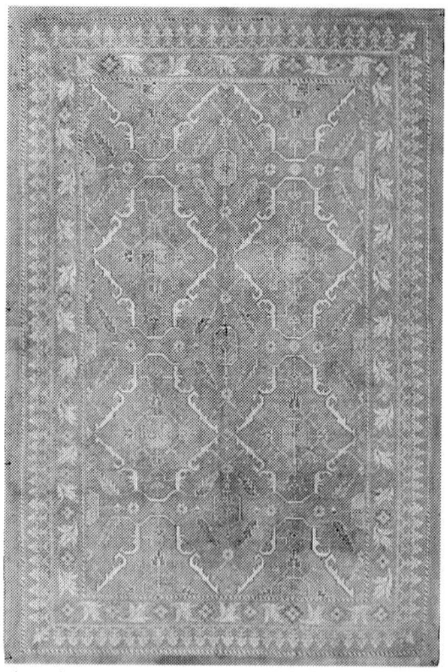

An Agra cotton rug, the beige field with an all-over lattice containing leaves and vines enclosed by borders of rosettes and meandering vines, north India, early 20thC, 106 x 70in (269 x 178cm).
£3,800–4,200 *S(NY)*

A Chinese dragon carpet, the abrashed indigo field centred by a large dragon and a flaming pearl, moth damage, late 19thC, 93 x 60in (236 x 152.5cm).
£6,500–7,500 *S(NY)*

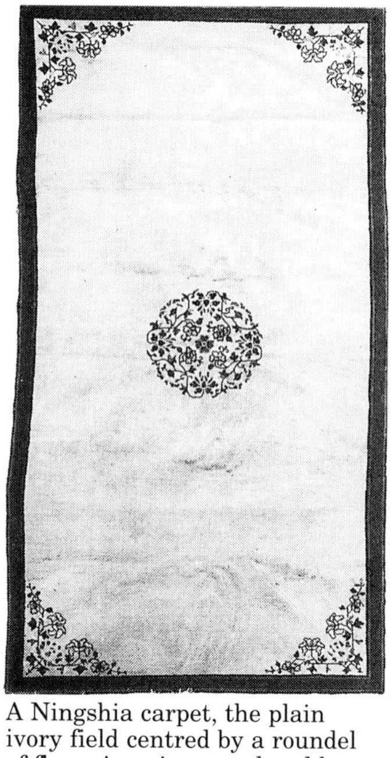

A Ningshia carpet, the plain ivory field centred by a roundel of flowering vines, enclosed by floral spray spandrels within a plain indigo border with sky blue guard stripes, west China, c1890, 115 x 64in (292 x 162cm).
£1,100–1,200 *P*

TEXTILES
Covers & Quilts

A quilted linen pillow cover, worked with a central vase of flowers surrounded by a ribbon-tied trellis enclosing flowers within a trailing floral border, fine gathered lawn frill, 18thC, 31½ x 18½in (80 x 47cm).
£400–450 *WW*

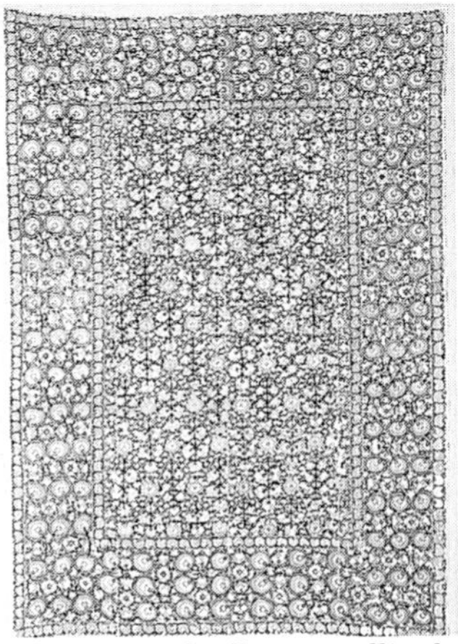

A *susani*, with all-over trellised floral motifs in dark brown, pink, apricot and green, with pink flowerhead guards, Uzbekistan, mid-19thC, 96 x 70in (244 x 178cm).
£950–1,100 *WW*

Susanis
A Susani is a central Asian hand-embroidered bridal bed cover.

An American pieced and appliqué quilt, in Californian Rose design, composed of pink and yellow ochre flowerheads and buds on sea green stylised stems, the ground quilted with central motif, possibly late 19thC, 90 x 80in (228.5 x 203cm).
£500–550 *WW*

A patchwork quilt, in brown, orange and fawn, c1820, 100 x 92in (254 x 234cm).
£800–1,000 *TT*

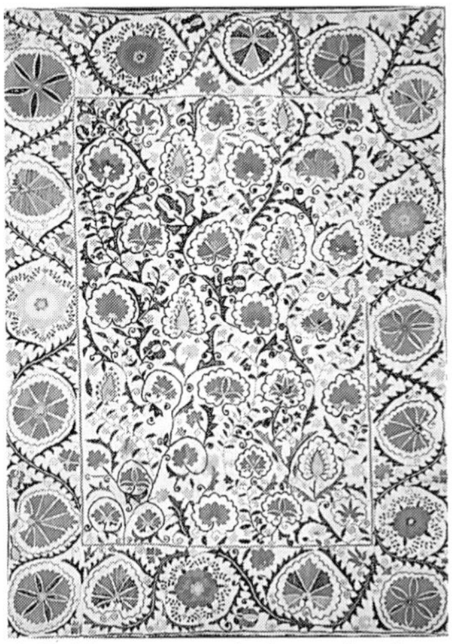

A Bokhara *susani*, the undyed cotton ground embroidered with coloured silks in chain, laid and couched stitches, Uzbekistan, late 19thC, 88 x 45½in (224 x 116cm).
£700–800 *P*

An American quilt, appliquéd in pink and green floral design, c1890, 71 x 78¾in (180.5 x 200cm).
£200–250 *TT*

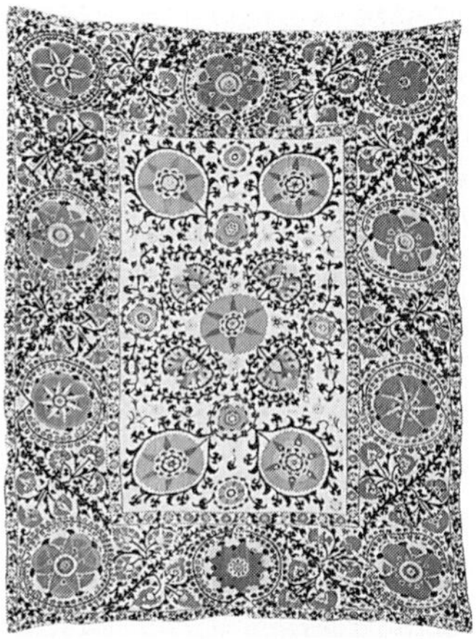

A *susani* embroidery, with all-over floral and foliate motifs in red, orange and blue, Uzbekistan, small stains, mid-19thC, 94 x 74in (239 x 188cm).
£7,700–8,500 *S(NY)*

A *susani*, embroidered with all-over flowers and foliage, the field with a centre rosette within a diamond shape medallion, wide border of rosettes, flowerheads and foliage, probably Bokhara, late 19thC, 58 x 39in (147.5 x 99cm).
£1,300–1,500 *WW*

A red satin cover, with block printed fabric, late 19thC, 34 x 32in (86.5 x 82cm).
£100–120 *TT*

l. A Welsh hand-stitched quilt, with a floral design, c1910, 32½ x 35½in (92.5 x 90cm).
£130–150 *SUS*

Embroidery & Needlework

A tapestry panel, the crimson velvet ground applied with 2 ivory silk squares embroidered in satin stitch with fruit and flowers and 4 oval embroideries with figures representing virtues, probably French, early 17thC, 68½ x 17in (174 x 43cm).
£1,300–1,500 *P*

A needlework picture, worked in petit point and rococo stitch with coloured silks, entitled 'The Flight of Lot', depicting Lot and his daughters being escorted by angels from the burning city of Sodom, with Lot's wife turned into a pillar of salt to one side, some stitches missing, mid-17thC, 8 x 10¾in (20.5 x 27.5cm).
£1,200–1,500 *WW*

A blue and beige crewelwork and petit point panel, depicting Rebecca at the well, damaged, c1700, 10 x 9½in (25.5 x 24cm).
£520–600 *SK(B)*

An embroidered picture, worked in couched metal thread on a satin ground, depicting a noble couple, possibly King Charles II and his Queen, and 2 other figures, enhanced with seed pearls, a moonstone and chenille, faded and worn, in a walnut frame, mid-17thC, 8 x 10in (20.5 x 25.5cm).
£800–900 *Bon(C)*

An embroidered panel, worked in tent stitch, depicting Charles I and his Queen surrounded by courtiers, a palace, and a battle field, remounted on felt, mid-17thC, 12¾ x 15in (32.5 x 38cm).
£550–600 *Bon(C)*

A needlework picture, worked in coloured silks, purl and metal thread on an ivory satin ground, entitled Susannah and the Elders, depicting Susannah bathing in a pool with an elaborate fountain, the Elders in attendance, repaired, in a later gilt gesso frame, 17thC, 13¼ x 17½in (33.5 x 44.5cm).
£1,200–1,500 *WW*

A silk needlework picture, depicting Charles I and Henrietta Maria, framed and glazed, mid-17thC, 13½ x 16½in (34.5 x 42cm).
£1,200–1,500 *Bon(C)*

A Charles II lady's toilet case, decorated in stumpwork and needlework, the rising top revealing a fitted interior lined in quilted silk, with small drawers and 2 scent bottles, damaged, 20½in (52cm) wide.
£2,100–2,400 *RBB*

This case was by repute once the property of Lucy Walter, mistress of Charles II. Stumpwork embroidery incorporates distinctive areas of raised decoration, formed by padding certain areas of the design.

A pair of needlework petit point panels for sofas, depicting Bacchus in his chariot drawn by goats accompanied by attendants, a farmyard scene nearby, both with gros point borders of brightly coloured serrated leaf forms and flowers, early 18thC, 28 x 67in (71 x 170cm).
£1,800–2,200 *Bon(C)*

l. A French needlework fire screen, worked in petit point, depicting a party of musicians, within a later gros point foliate border, c1720, 26 x 23in (66 x 58cm), in a gilt frame.
£1,000–1,200 *S*

A silkwork and chenille picture, depicting a shepherdess, worked in blue, green, brown, ochre, red, cream and black, watercolour and ink on a silk ground, c1750, 15 x 12¾in (38 x 32.5cm).
£1,100–1,300 *S(Cg)*

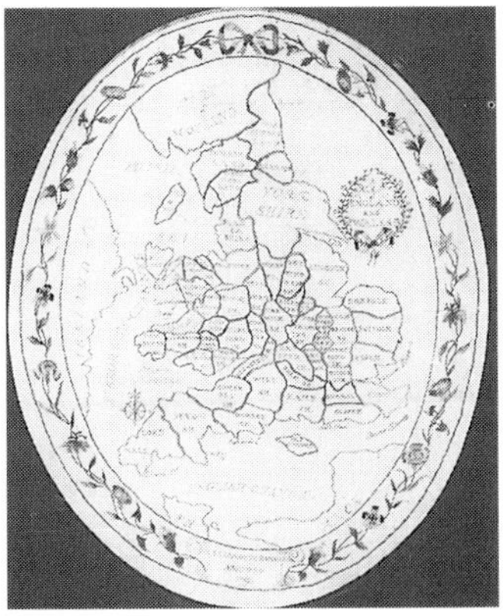

A George III embroidered map of England and Wales, worked in coloured threads on a cream silk ground and bordered with a garland of flowers, by Elizabeth Banks, Ashford, framed, 1791, 14 x 11in (35.5 x 28cm).
£350–400 *HYD*

A pair of silkwork and paper portraits of Emperor Napoleon and Lord Nelson, framed and glazed, early 19thC, 4 x 3in (10 x 7.5cm).
£135–150 *TMA*

r. A painted needlework picture, the ivory ground worked with silk, depicting a Georgian house in parkland with a shepherd and his flock in the foreground, with *verre eglomisé* mount, framed, 19thC, 9¾ x 12in (25 x 30.5cm).
£160–175 *WW*

A pair of George III needlework pictures, worked in gros and petit point, depicting scenes from La Fontaine's fables, in giltwood frames, damaged, 18thC, 15 x 19in (38 x 48.5cm).
£2,800–3,200 *S(NY)*

An embroidered silk picture, depicting a young woman carrying a basket and fishing rod, on the banks of a river, late 18thC, 8¼in (21cm) wide, mounted and framed.
£260–300 *P(WM)*

A needlework picture, depicting 2 children and rabbits, in a gilt frame, c1820, 13 x 12in (33 x 30.5cm).
£250–300 *MTa*

A George III needlework map, entitled 'Europe', worked in coloured silks on a cream silk ground, within an acorn and oak leaf border, 19¼in (49cm) long.
£650–750 *P(WM)*

An embroidered silk picture, worked in coloured wools, depicting Rachel and Jacob discovered by Laban, early 19thC, 13¾in x 18½in (35 x 47cm).
£160–180 *DN*

A Regency silkwork picture, depicting a girl with a lamb with painted features, c1820, 8¼ x 7½in (21 x 19cm), framed.
£620–680 *S(S)*

A set of 4 Victorian petit point woolwork pictures, worked in brown, red, black and white depicting country scenes, 11¾ x 13½in (34.5 x 30cm), in glazed maple frames.
£950–1,150 *P(WM)*

Lace

A flounce of Flemish bobbin lace, worked with flowering plants arranged in columns with scrolling foliage and blossom between, incorporating the Louis XIV cypher surmounted by a coronet in 2 places, c1690, 123 x 21¼in (314 x 54cm).
£750–850 *P*

A panel of bobbin lace, the scrolling pattern with oversize blooms, a variety of fillings and maglia mesh ground, probably Spanish, late 17thC, 157 x 10¼in (400 x 26cm).
£110–120 *P*

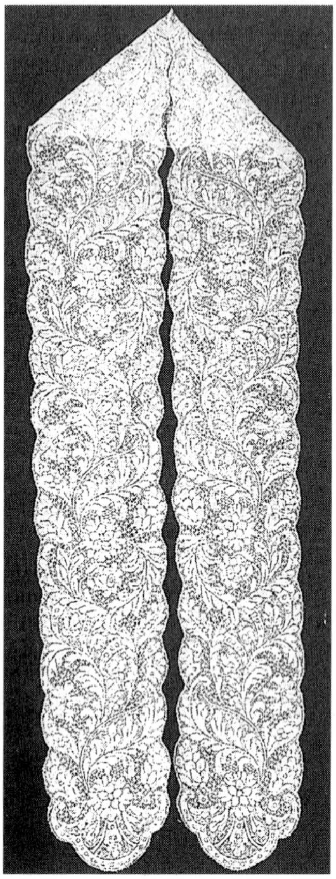

l. A pair of Flemish Valenciennes bobbin lace lappets, worked with scrolling foliage and flowers with snowflake fillings, joined, c1730, 22½in (57cm) long.
£600–700 *P*

A Belgian bobbin lace bridal veil, worked with lace flowers applied to spot net, arranged in bouquets to the corners and in sprays to the border, with scattered sprigs, late 19thC, 78¾ x 74in (202 x 188cm).
£1,000–1,100 *P*

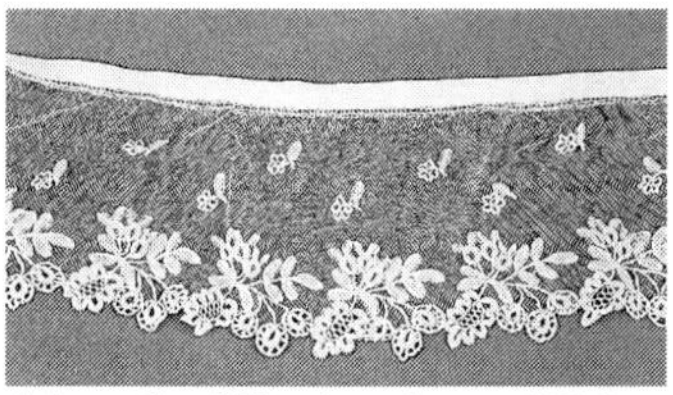

A length of Honiton lace, c1880, 86in (218.5cm) long.
£60–70 *LB*

A lace collar, c1900, 19in (48.5cm) long.
£60–70 *LB*

Samplers

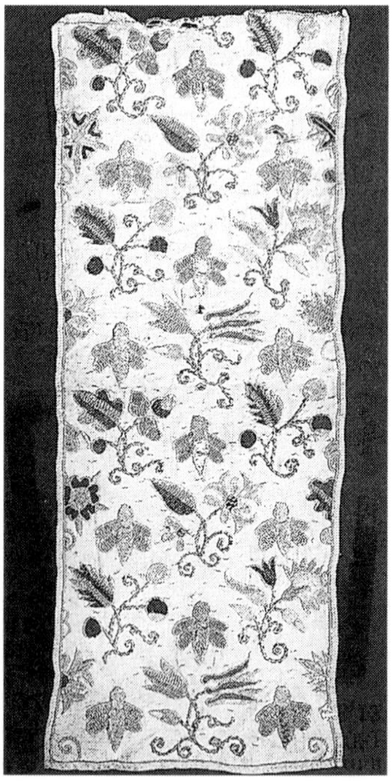

A needlework sampler, by Martha Beck, with bands of the alphabet and a verse above trees and 2 deer, within a broad floral meander, 1749, 13in (33cm) square.
£1,000–1,100 *L*

l. A linen sampler, worked in applied silk with embroidered slips, oak leaves and acorns, cherries, honeysuckle, carnations and insects, damaged, early 17thC, 13½ x 5¼in (34.5 x 13.5cm).
£350–400 *P*

A needlework sampler, worked in satin, cross stitch, French knot and long and short stitches in coloured silks on a linen ground with bands of flowers and leaves, geometric patterns, birds and the alphabet, early 18thC, 15¾ x 12in (40 x 30cm), framed and glazed.
£850–950 *P*

Miller's is a price GUIDE not a price LIST

A needlework sampler, by Sarah Cotton, aged 8, worked in cross stitch with coloured silks on a linen ground, the top with alphabet, numbers and 2 verses, with bands of floral motifs, slight damage, late 18thC, 13 x 11in (33 x 28cm).
£260–300 *WW*

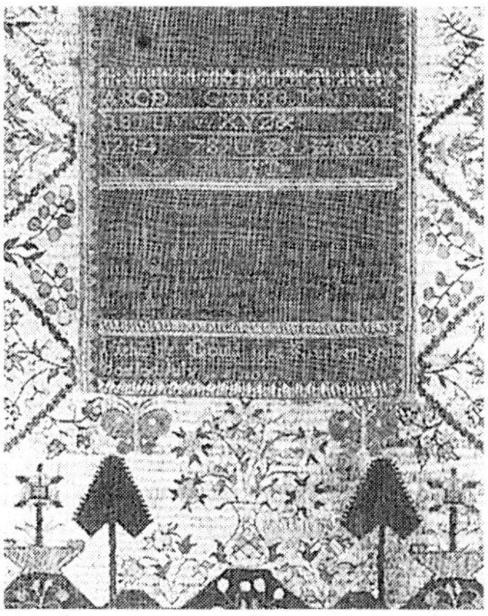

An American needlework sampler, by Mehitable Gould, worked in blue, green, yellow, and white silk on a linen ground with verses and bands of alphabets and numerals, flowers and trees, the sides with a border of flowers and berries, some discolouration and losses, 1805, 20 x 16¾in (51 x 42.5cm).
£850–950 *S(NY)*

A needlework sampler, by Catherine C. Gibbins, aged 12, worked in silks with a stag between 2 trees, birds, flowers and animals, within a scrolling floral border, 19thC, 16½ x 12½in (42 x 32cm), in a gilt painted frame.
£520–580 *WW*

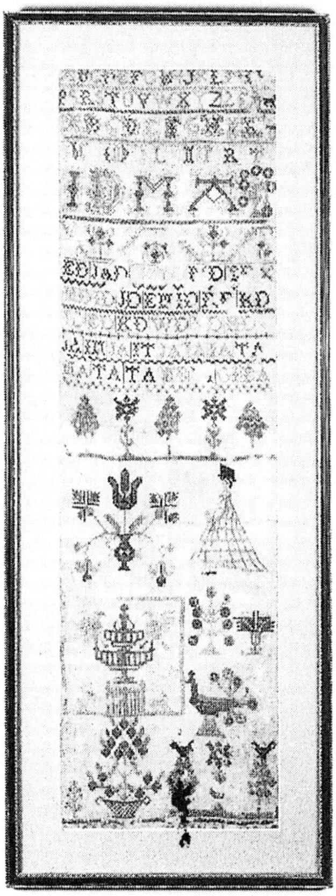

A cross stitch sampler, worked in red and light brown wool on a linen ground, designed with bands of numerals and the alphabet, vases of flowers, trees and birds, early 19thC, 24½ x 7in (62 x 18cm), mounted, framed and glazed.
£320–380 *P*

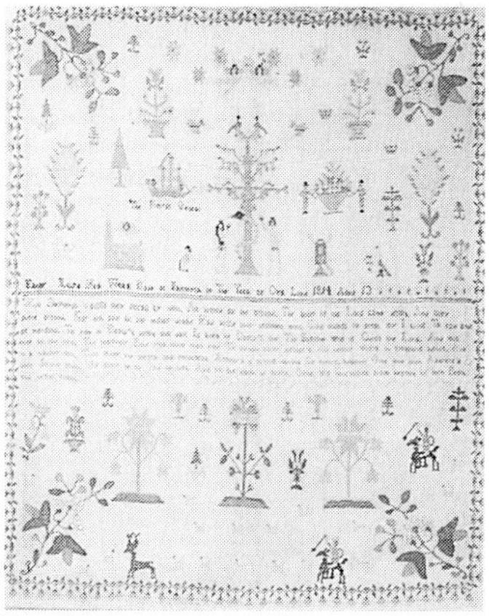

A needlework sampler, worked in cross stitch on a linen ground with figures, a church, the Royal George, Adam and Eve and a passage from the Bible, with a floral spray in each corner, 1814, 24 x 20½in (61 x 52cm).
£1,100–1,200 *S(S)*

r. A needlework sampler, by Elizabeth Evans, worked in coloured threads, depicting Pool Church and reflections on the death of unknown children, slight wear, 1823, 15¼ x 14in (38.5 x 35.5cm), framed.
£280–350 *Bon(C)*

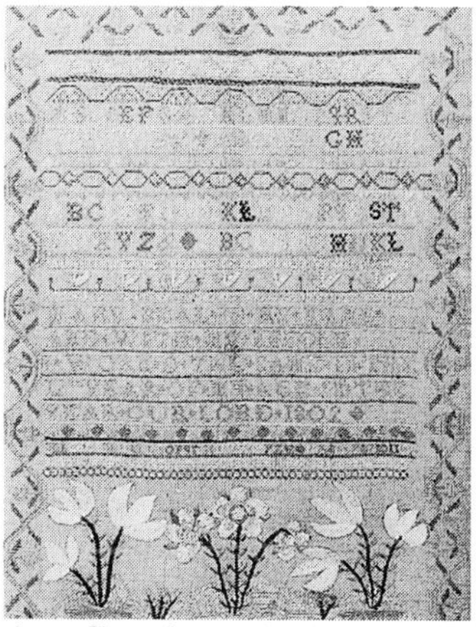

A needlework sampler, by Mary Beal, worked in colours and white silk on a linen ground, within a meandering floral vine border, 1802, 20½ x 15in (52 x 38cm).
£1,300–1,500 *S(NY)*

A needlework sampler, by Mary Ratton, worked in coloured threads with the alphabet, numbers, flowers, animals, buildings and a poem, 1808, 12 x 15in (30 x 38cm).
£270–300 *DDM*

A needlework sampler, by Elizabeth Royce, aged 13, with figures, birds, flowers, symbols and a poem, 1822, 17¼ x 12¼in (44 x 31cm), framed.
£750–825 *DDM*

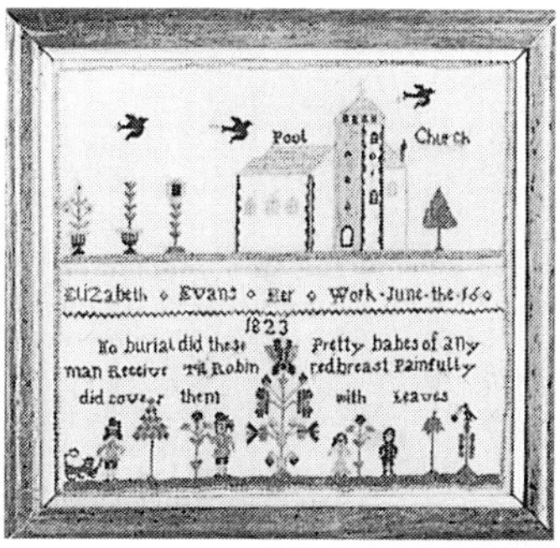

A cross stitch sampler, by M. A. Elgar, worked in silks on a linen ground with a pavilion, birds and a verse, 1824, 18 x 13in (45.5 x 33cm), framed.
£450–500 *WW*

A needlework sampler, by Lucy Green, aged 11, 1832, 13 x 12in (33 x 30.5cm), in a rosewood frame.
£380–420 *DD*

A needlework sampler, by Ann Morton, worked in coloured threads, 1835, 16½in (42cm) square, framed.
£250–300 *PFK*

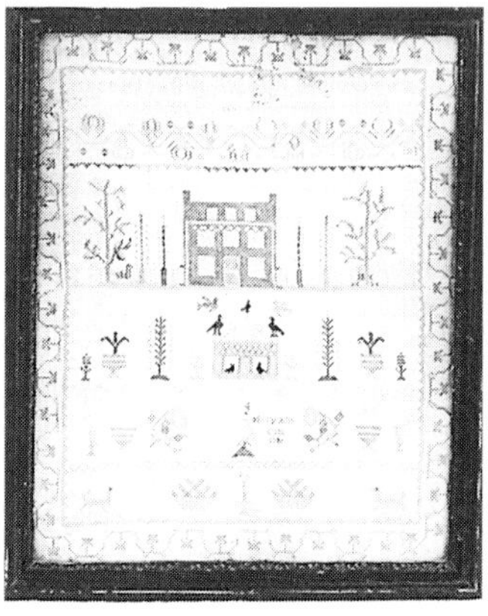

A needlework sampler, by Jane Oliver, aged 13, with a verse surrounded by a foliate and butterfly border, slight damage, framed, 1825, 19 x 13in (48.5 x 33cm).
£350–400 *SK(B)*

A needlework sampler, by Elizabeth Green, worked in coloured threads with text, trees and bird motifs, 1833, 13 x 12in (33 x 30.5cm), in a rosewood frame.
£500–550 *DD*

A needlework sampler, by Isabel Broomfield, aged 11, worked in red and green threads, 1835, 15½ x 16¼in (39 x 41cm), in a modern glazed gilt frame.
£400–450 *P(WM)*

l. A needlework sampler, by Mary Ann, within a floral border, 1885, 16½ x 14in (42 x 35.5cm), framed.
£400–450 *Bon(C)*

r. A needlework map sampler, by Esther James, aged 11, worked in blue, red, green and yellow thread, framed and glazed, 12½ x 16½in (32 x 42cm).
£90–100 *LF*

A needlework sampler, by Sarah Morris, worked in coloured threads, 1825, 12½in (32cm) square.
£280–320 *LF*

A needlework sampler, by Merina Patten, worked in coloured silks, with a verse entitled 'What is Life?', 1835, 16½ x 12¾in (42 x 32.5cm).
£1,000–1,100 *LAY*

A needlework sampler, by Hannah Dees, worked with a verse, church, Adam and Eve, flowers and birds, 1845, 18¼ x 18½in (46.5 x 47cm).
£300–350 *AH*

Tapestries

A Flemish tapestry, depicting beasts of prey and birds in scrolling foliage, a town in the distance, within a border of flowers and figures, late 16thC, 124 x 106in (315 x 270cm).
£3,750–4,250 *S(Z)*

A Flemish tapestry, depicting a landscape with trees and a chateau, c1600, 94in (239cm) square.
£2,300–2,500 *SLN*

An Aubusson tapestry, woven with figures in a wooded landscape within brown and blue borders, 17thC, 110 x 130in (279 x 330cm).
£7,200–8,000 *WW*

A Flemish tapestry border, probably from a hunting tapestry, depicting a boar's head and hunting trophies at each end, with a central trophy of fruit and musical instruments, c1660, 30 x 180in (77 x 460cm).
£3,200–3,500 *S*

An Aubusson tapestry, attributed to Antoine Grellet, depicting Judith and her maid in four-sided floral surround with golden foliage and shell motifs on a blue ground, some minor repairs and later selvage, c1680, 110 x 55in (180 x 140cm).
£3,500–3,800 *S*

The Grellet family was one of the leading families of weavers at Aubusson.

A Flemish tapestry panel, probably depicting Alexander the Great, surrounded by soldiers and attendants, 17thC, 97 x 89in (247 x 226cm).
£3,500–3,800 *P*

l. An Aubusson tapestry panel, depicting a heraldic coat-of-arms with floral swags and acanthus leaves, late 17thC, 101 x 69in (256.5 x 175.3cm).
£3,500–4,000 *SLN*

A tapestry cushion, depicting Judith and her handmaiden, within a border of flowers and butterflies, some damage and repair, Dutch or north German, c1680, 20in (50cm) square.
£575–625 *S*

A Flemish tapestry panel, woven with the goddess Ceres, enclosed by an egg-and-dart border, 17thC, 48 x 35in (120 x 89cm).
£2,300–2,500 *P*

An Aubusson tapestry, worked in blue and gold with a landscape, within a border of flowers and leaves, late 17thC, 104 x 67in (265 x 170cm).
£2,250–2,500 *S(Z)*

l. A Continental tapestry panel, depicting neo-classical figures flanked by flower filled-vases, restored, 17thC, 19½ x 68in (49.5 x 172.5in).
£1,200–1,500 *SK(B)*

A Flemish tapestry, depicting huntsmen and hounds in pursuit of deer in the grounds of a palace, enclosed by a border of flowering plants and fruit, c1700, 138 x 76in (351 x 194cm).
£8,700–9,500 *P*

A Flemish tapestry, depicting a monarch attended by his court, lacking borders, c1700, 74 x 133in (187 x 337cm).
£3,800–4,200 *Bon*

A Flemish tapestry, depicting Procris and her husband Cephalus with his hunting dog and magic spear, with a city in the distance, c1700, 111 x 97in (282 x 247cm).
£7,000–8,000 *P*

An Aubusson tapestry, woven in tones of green, rose, blue and brown, depicting Demeter in a landscape with harvesters, c1700, 100 x 139in (254 x 350.5cm).
£6,000–7,000 *SK(B)*

A Flemish tapestry, woven with the infant Ganymede carried away by the eagle, in a wooded landscape with a distant building, lacking border, some wear and minor repairs, early 19thC, 76 x 58in (184 x 147cm).
£3,500–3,800 *S*

According to classical mythology the infant Ganymede, a beautiful child, was abducted by Zeus to serve as his cup bearer on Mount Olympus, the home of the gods. Astronomers immortalised the youth as the constellation Aquarius and the eagle as Aquila.

A Flemish 'Teniers' tapestry fragment, woven with 2 men in the foreground, with a distant village, part of a larger tapestry, some rewoven repairs, c1730, 85 x 49in (215 x 125cm).
£3,500–4,000 *S*

A Felletin tapestry, woven with a bird perched on a tree-stump in the foreground and a distant building, within a floral border, small repairs, c1730, 106 x 73in (270 x 186cm).
£3,000–3,500 *S*

Insurance Values

Always insure your valuable antiques for what it would cost to replace with a similar item, regardless of the original price paid. Both dealers and auctioneers will provide a valuation service for a fee.

A set of 4 Aubusson tapestry panels, depicting foliate scrolled arabesques, exotic birds, flower-filled urns and lappets, each within a carved, painted and parcel-gilt frame, early 18thC, each panel 57½ x 22in (156 x 56cm).
£5,500–6,500 *S(NY)*

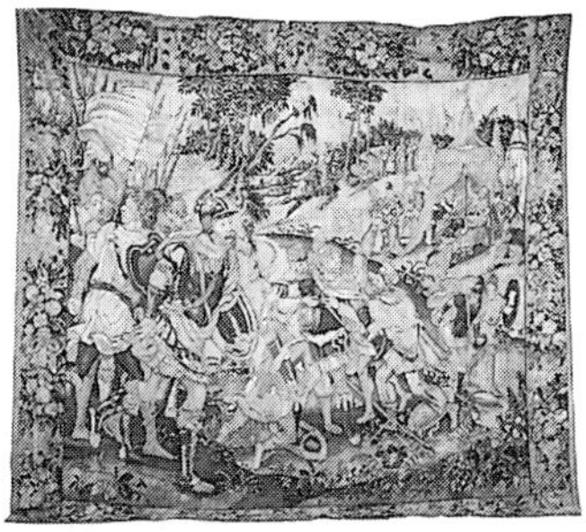

A Flemish tapestry, worked in shades of blue, green, red, brown and cream, depicting a Greco-Roman battle scene with a village, trees and tents in the distance, all within a wide border of fruit, flowers and birds, 18thC, 136 x 144in (286.5 x 366cm).
£11,000–12,000 *S(Cg)*

A Mortlake tapestry, worked in shades of brown and cream, depicting a village surrounded by a landscape setting, all within a flower and leaf border, worn, 18thC, 120 x 102½in (305 x 260.5cm).
£1,300–1,500 *S(Cg)*

A French tapestry, woven in shades of blue, green, brown and cream, depicting a shepherdess, seated beside a youth playing a horn within a pastoral setting, within an aubergine border, possibly Aubusson, 18thC, 69½ x 68¼in (176.5 x 174cm).
£3,500–4,000 *S(Cg)*

A Continental needlepoint wall hanging, woven in shades of blue, green, crimson and brown, depicting an exotic bird standing beneath an apple tree with a villa in the background, all within a flowering vine border, 19thC, 74 x 54in (188 x 137cm).
£1,300–1,500 *S(Cg)*

r. An Aubusson tapestry panel, depicting a panoramic scene of figures in a landscape with ruins and a tower, slight damage, 19thC, 32 x 58in (81.5 x 147.5cm).
£500–600 *SK(B)*

A Flemish tapestry, depicting a hunter and his dogs in pursuit of a wild boar in a woodland setting, with a castle and lake in the distance, 19thC, 71¼ x 90½in (181 x 230cm).
£4,000–4,500 *P(W)*

A Berlin woolwork tapestry, depicting 2 Mediterranean gentlemen with a rearing black stallion, with buildings, mountain and sea in the background, 19thC, 24½ x 22½in (63 x 57cm).
£1,000–1,100 *Mit*

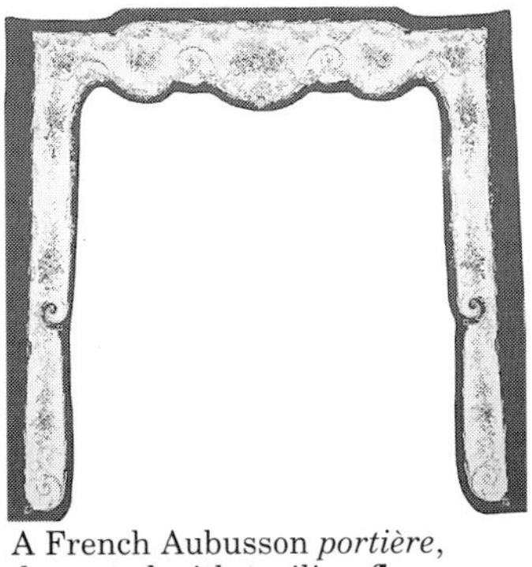

A French Aubusson *portière*, decorated with trailing flowers, within a red border, late 19thC, 158 x 163in (401 x 414cm).
£1,800–2,000 *S(NY)*

This piece was by repute purchased from the collection of Queen Mother Olga of Greece in 1932, and until that time had hung in the Royal Palace in Athens.

A French tapestry wall hanging, woven in gros and petit point in cream, brown and green wools, depicting a pastoral scene of figures in a garden, a boat on a lake in the background, late 19thC, 78¾ x 72½in (200 x 184cm).
£700–800 *P*

An Aubusson pastoral tapestry, depicting a young girl and a youth in a landscape, late 19thC, 84¾ x 72in (215 x 183cm).
£3,500–4,000 *S*

COSTUME

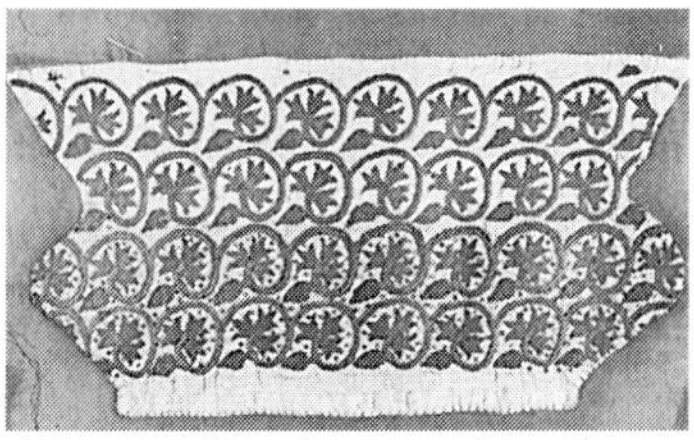

A linen coif, embroidered in silver-gilt thread in buttonhole stitch, 2 rows worked with spangles, c1700, 8½ x 16in (21.5 x 40.5cm), mounted and framed.
£800–1,000 *Bon(C)*

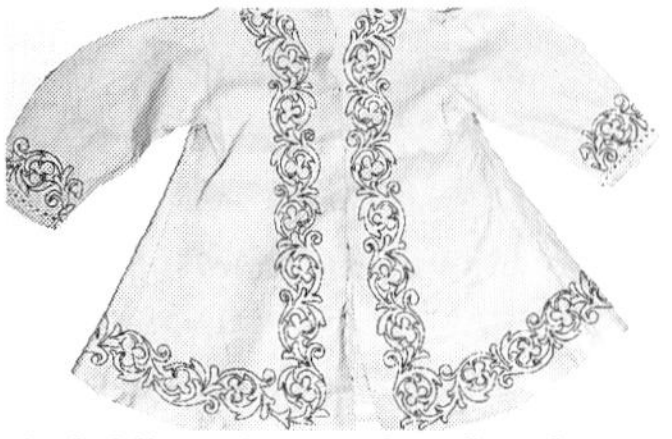

A child's jacket, embroidered with black thread on a cream ground, 19thC.
£45–50 *CCO*

Costume: Condition

- Condition of costume is critical since stitching, fastenings and laundering details are an important part of the appeal to the collector.
- Beware of areas that have obviously been treated, cleaned or repaired, in case important historical evidence has been lost.
- Ancient repairs or alterations can add interest to a piece.

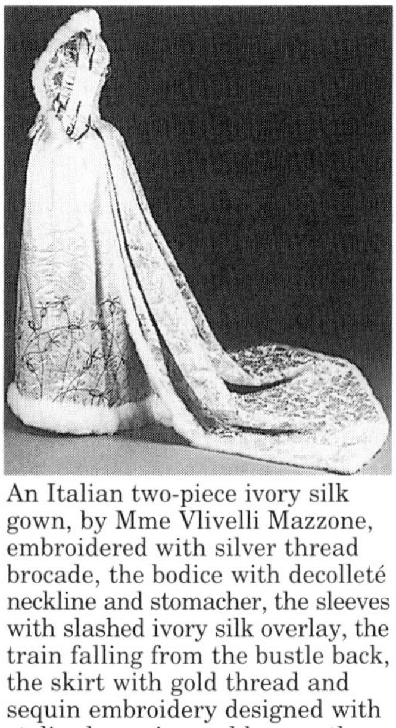

An Italian two-piece ivory silk gown, by Mme Vlivelli Mazzone, embroidered with silver thread brocade, the bodice with decolleté neckline and stomacher, the sleeves with slashed ivory silk overlay, the train falling from the bustle back, the skirt with gold thread and sequin embroidery designed with stylised poppies and leaves, the whole with swansdown trim, c1890.
£800–900 *P*

A silk sack-back gown, the ivory silk brocaded in coloured silks with sprigs of flowers and leaves, with pinked fur below and neckline trim, 2 small buttons at the hips to draw up the train, lace trim later, c1770.
£1,500–1,800 *P*

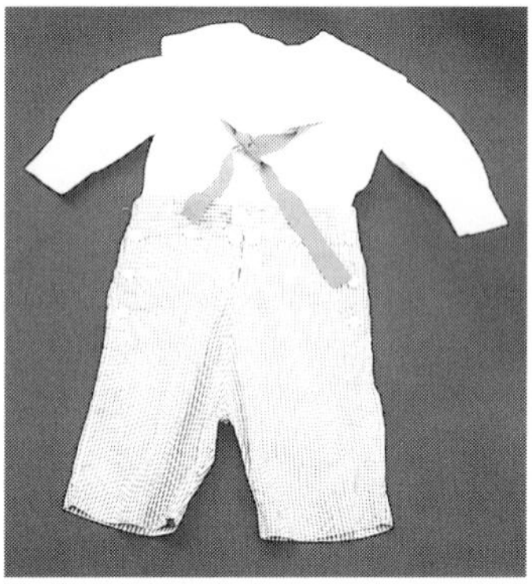

A Victorian boy's sailor suit, with white blouse and brown and white striped trousers.
£65–75 *RRA*

r. A girl's brown satin afternoon dress, trimmed with a lace edge, 1880s.
£80–100 *Har*

An Athenian court dress, embroidered with gold thread appliqué to the border, with loop fastening to the front, the open sleeves, side seams, high collar and front with pleated and frilled trim, c1820.
£320–350 *P*

A pair of Victorian plaid velveteen and black leather baby's boots, with side pearl buttons, 3½in (9cm) high.
£180–200 *RRA*

A pair of baby's blue leather shoes, with blue ribbon ties, 19thC, 5in (12.5cm) long.
£45–50 *BaN*

An Indian wool shawl, with black centre section, red, turquoise, yellow and black fringed embroidered border, 19thC, 78in (193cm) square.
£380–420 *DN(H)*

A baby's long dress, with embroidery, appliqué and pin tucks, c1880, 42in (106.5cm) long.
£50–55 *Ech*

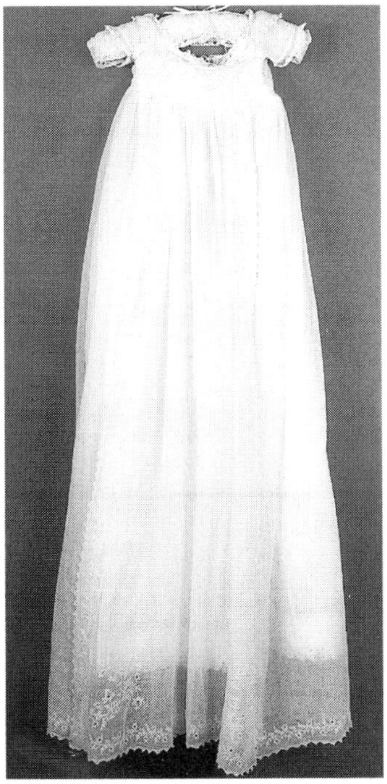

A white lawn christening gown, embroidered with flowers, c1900, 39in (99cm) long.
£130–150 *LB*

An Edwardian lady's wool and velvet embroidered jacket, by Amy Linker & Co, Paris.
£150–175 *TT*

A two-piece dress, by Mme Milliory Robes, the blue silk brocaded with silver grey bubbles, the high necked side fastening boned bodice with velvet V-front insertion and leg-o'-mutton sleeves, the skirt gathering to the back, c1890s.
£450–500 *P*

An Edwardian lady's silk velour hat, trimmed with a feathered bird.
£120–140 *Ech*

A peach satin wedding dress, embroidered with crystal and pearl beads to scoop neckline, sleeves, waist and train, the bodice and sleeves with pin tuck detailing, with drop waist, long train and underskirt, 1920s.
£170–190 *WW*

A child's crocheted bonnet, c1900.
£22–25 *CCO*

An Edwardian white cotton child's day dress, embroidered with flowers and trimmed with lace, 18½in (47cm) long.
£16–18 *MAC*

A baby's white cotton dress, c1920, 16in (40.5cm) long.
£25–35 *LB*

A black hat, trimmed with a ribbon, 1940s.
£25–30 *Ech*

Insurance Values

Always insure your valuable antiques for what it would cost to replace with a similar item, regardless of the original price paid. Both dealers and auctioneers will provide a valuation service for a fee.

A Chanel black crêpe knee length dress, the bodice embroidered with beads, gold thread and mother-of-pearl designed as falling blossom and tendrils, with round neckline and short sleeves, altered, 1930s.
£280–300 *P*

A black silk velvet evening jacket, by Jacques Fath, with white mink collar and silk satin bow, diamanté-covered buckle, c1950, 16½in (42cm) long.
£2,000–2,200 *S(NY)*

A pair of gold leather evening sandals, by Codreano, Paris, together with black and white publicity still from 'Gilda' with Rita Hayworth wearing a similar pair of shoes, c1940.
£780–850 *S*

These shoes were given to the manager of the Carlton Hotel in Cannes in 1949 after a stay by Rita Hayworth and her lover, Aly Khan.

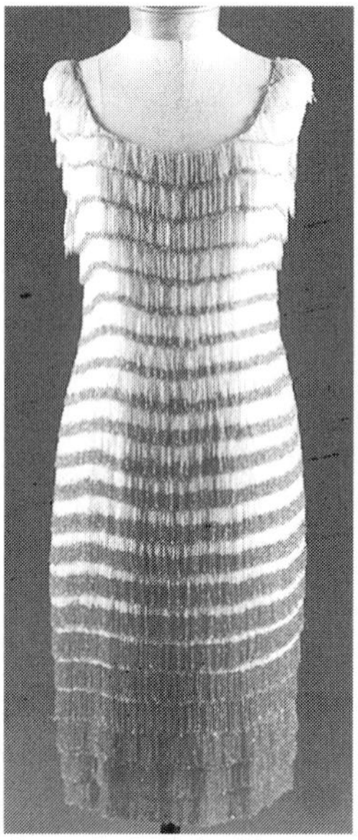

An ombré pink silk chiffon cocktail dress, by Jean Dessès, with clear and pink crystal fringe beadwork, graduating to tones of dark rose at hem, 1961.
£2,600–3,000 *S(NY)*

l. A orange double-knit cotton pant suit, by Courrèges, with princess style jacket and flared trousers, c1960.
£1,300–1,500 *S(LA)*

Ex-Marlene Dietrich collection.

r. A chocolate brown velour trouser suit, by Jean Bouguin, with front ring-pull closure, c1970.
£350–380 *S(LA)*

Ex-Marlene Dietrich collection.

A blue silk velvet and satin evening ensemble, by Christian Dior, with silk satin cummerbund mounted on buckram belt, 1948, 41½in (105.5cm) long.
£1,800–2,000 *S(NY)*

A Balenciaga ivory wool day coat, with a roll collar, kimono sleeves and curved hip pockets, c1950.
£280–320 *S(LA)*

Ex-Marlene Dietrich collection.

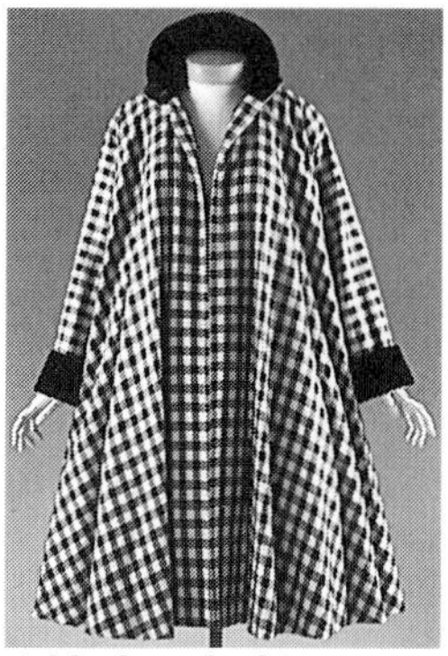

A black and white checked wool day coat, by Jacques Fath, with a velvet Peter Pan collar and wide folded cuffs, 1951, 38¾in (98.5cm) long.
£1,200–1,300 *S(NY)*

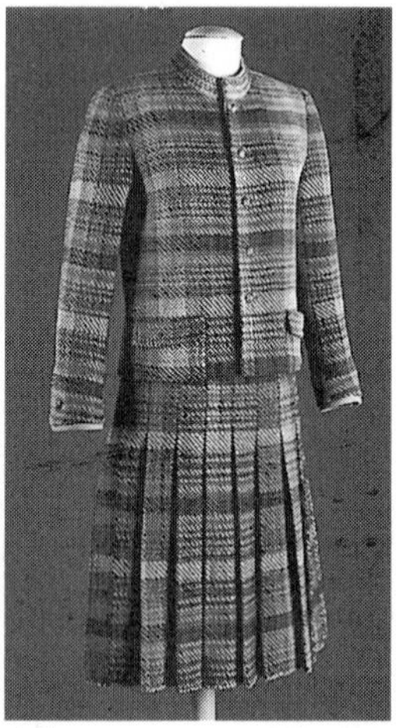

A brown, green and orange plaid suit, by Chanel, with green collar and cuff edges, c1960.
£1,100–1,200 *S(LA)*

Ex-Marlene Dietrich collection.

r. A poppy red silk taffeta strapless ball gown, by Christian Lacroix, for Jean Patou, with crisscross lacing down the left side and a boule-shaped skirt, 1987.
£1,400–1,600 *S(NY)*

FANS

A Dutch ivory brisé fan, painted and lacquered with a scene depicting Europa and the Bull with attendants, the guards and gorge of chinoiserie design, the reverse with a house in a landscape, c1720, 8¼in (21cm) wide.
£600–650 *P(NY)*

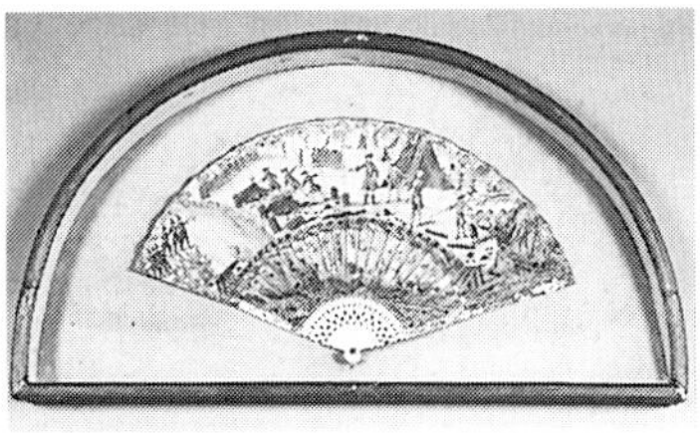

A French fan, with carved and painted ivory sticks, the paper leaf painted with a French battle scene, c1740, 10¼in (26cm) wide, in a glazed frame.
£1,400–1,600 *P*

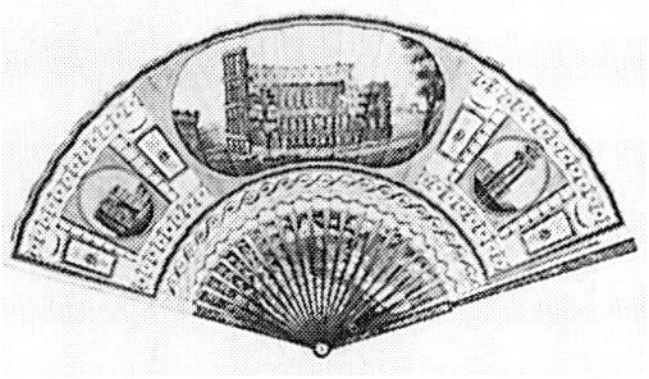

A Grand Tour fan, the chickenskin leaf painted with a central vignette of the Coliseum flanked by 2 small views, the black lacquered sticks clouté with mother-of-pearl, c1770, 10¾in (27.5cm) wide.
£750–900 *Bon(C)*

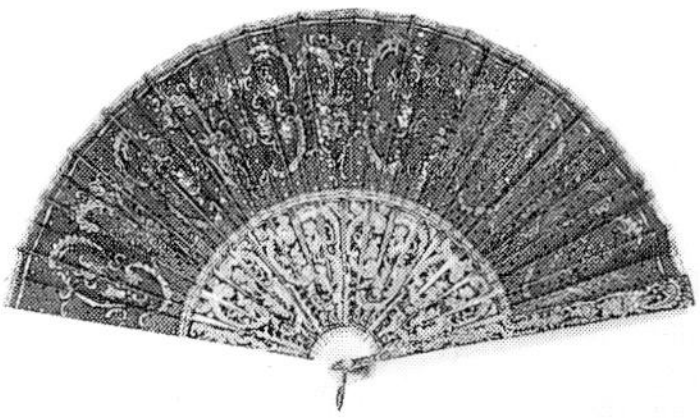

A green silk leaf fan, decorated with sequins, with carved, painted and gilt ivory sticks and guard, probably French, c1770, 10in (25.5cm) wide.
£100–120 *ALD*

An articulated fan, the ivory and mother-of-pearl guardsticks each with a lever moving a tinsel curtain opening to reveal a seated lady with a hovering Cupid, the silk leaf painted with vignettes of battle scenes, some damage, c1770, 11in (28cm) wide.
£450–550 *Bon(C)*

An ivory brisé fan, the centre panel painted with Juno in her chariot being drawn by peacocks, c1780, 9¾in (25cm) long, with a red leather box.
£1,000–1,200 *P*

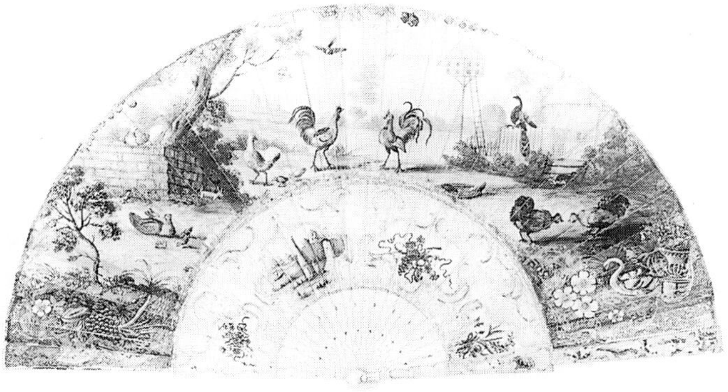

A fan, the leaf painted with a variety of farmyard fowl, animals and exotic birds, with pierced and carved ivory sticks and guardsticks with painted vignettes, c1780, 11in (28cm) wide.
£1,700–2,000 *Bon(C)*

A French fan, the vellum leaf painted in bright colours with figures in a landscape, the sticks and guards enamelled, c1780, 6½in (16.5cm) wide.
£1,700–2,000 *ALD*

A Chinese export silver filigree brisé fan, painted in blue and green enamels with central shield depicting a bird and flower, the reserves with oval medallions with houses and trees, c1820, 7½in (19cm) wide.
£1,350–1,500 *P(NY)*

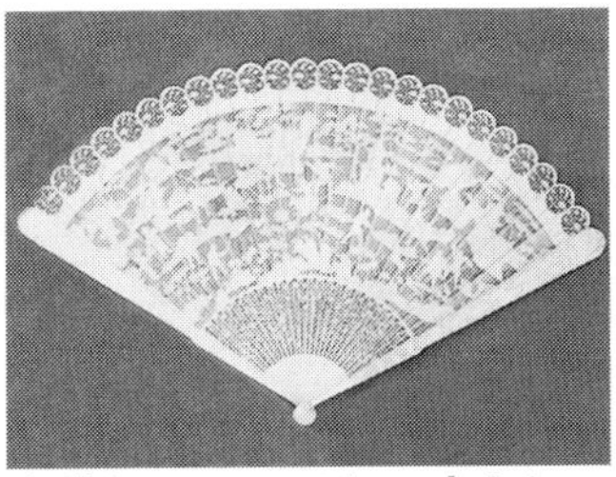

A Chinese export ivory brisé fan, carved with warring figures brandishing weapons, amid pagodas and palaces, slight damage, late 18thC, 10in (25.5cm) wide.
£450–500 *Bon(C)*

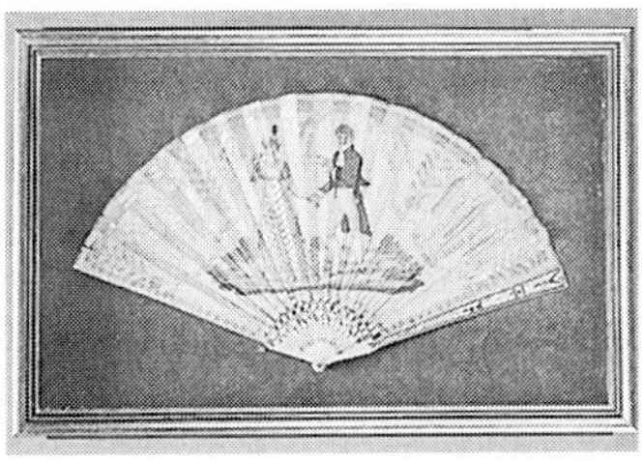

A Regency fan, the leaf painted with a lady and gentleman in a landscape, the bone sticks inlaid with silver, decorated with sequins and spangles, in a glazed case, 7in (18cm) wide.
£75–100 *DN*

l. A French pierced horn puzzle fan, the central panel painted with a girl in a garden, the reserves with flowers and leaves, c1810, 6in (15cm) wide.
£700–800 *P(NY)*

A Cantonese fan, the vellum leaf painted with 3 rural scenes, with lacquered wood sticks and guard, c1830, 10in (25.5cm) wide.
£400–450 *ALD*

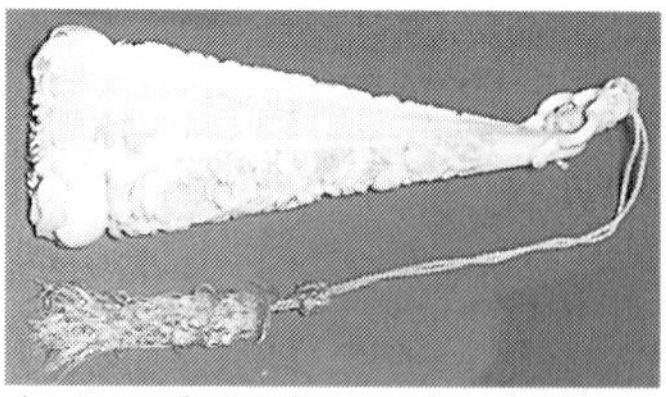

An ivory brisé fan, each guard carved in high relief with ribbon-tied clusters of flowers, with trilobe ivory ring and silk tassel, probably Erbach, slight damage, c1860, 8¾in (22cm) long.
£2,000–2,200 *S*

A tortoiseshell and parchment fan, painted with central cartouches of pastoral scenes, all within gilt scrollwork, mounted on tortoiseshell sticks within a conforming carved frame, 19thC, 20in (51cm) wide.
£370–400 *SLM*

An American fixed fan, depicting the opening of Brooklyn Bridge, the reverse with lists of trustees, engineers, etc, with wooden handle, 1883, 17¾in (45cm) long.
£600–700 *P(NY)*

r. A French fan, with blue stained mother-of-pearl sticks of plume design, the black gauze leaf painted with a family group in pierrot costume and Arlecchino from the *Commedia del'Arte*, lacking one guard stick, c1910, 10¼in (26cm) long.
£1,500–1,800 *P(NY)*

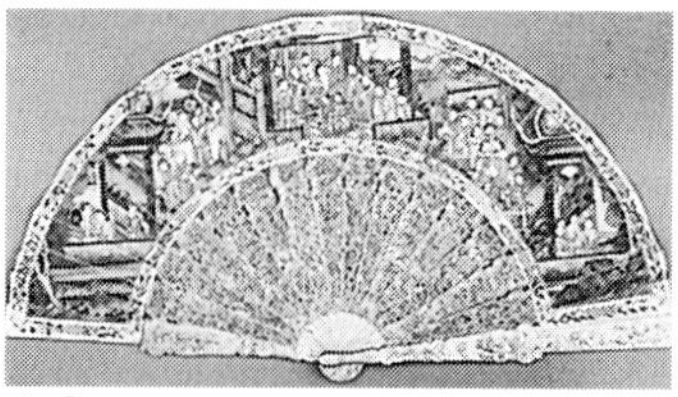

A Cantonese carved ivory fan, the leaf and ivory painted with Thousand Faces pattern, with carved, pierced and enamelled filigree sticks, mid-19thC, 11in (28cm) wide, with box.
£700–800 *Bon(C)*

A Chinese export fan, with carved and pierced shaped bone sticks, the painted paper leaf with ivory and silk appliqué depicting a seated dignitary and attendants, the reverse with a central panel of a landscape scene, c1860, 10¾in (27.5cm) long.
£750–825 *P*

A Shaker fan, the woven straw leaf with a horizontal and vertical striped pattern in undyed and plum coloured straw, with turned wooden handle, American, c1890, 13½in (34.5cm) long.
£120–150 *P(NY)*

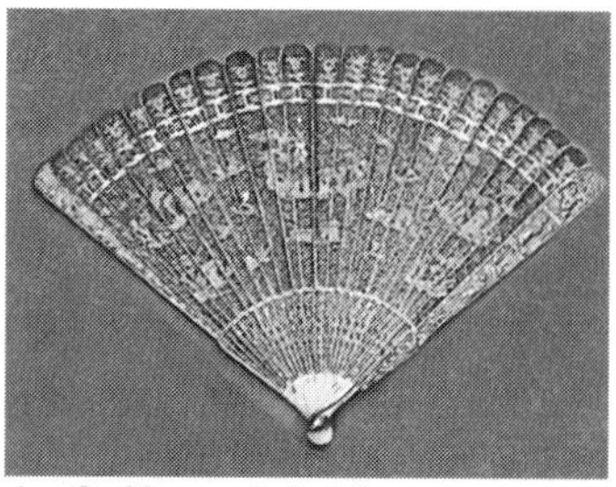

A gilt filigree brisé fan, enamelled in blue and green with vignettes of a pagoda and other buildings, ribbon missing, mid-19thC, 7½in (19cm) wide.
£620–700 *Bon(C)*

A marriage fan, the mother-of-pearl guard stick gilded with foliage swags, the leaf painted with a pastoral scene reserved on a floral ground, 19thC, 9¾in (25cm) wide.
£200–220 *DN*

A fan, with carved mother-of-pearl guards, the vellum leaf painted with nymphs and doves by a pond, c1880, 11in (28cm) long.
£700–800 *P*

A Brussels *point de gaze* lace fan, the leaf worked with various chinoiseries, with tortoiseshell sticks, late 19thC, 11in (28cm) wide.
£900–1,000 *Bon(C)*

A Brussels *point de gaze* lace fan, with pierced bone sticks and mother-of-pearl guards, the leaf worked with sprays of roses, late 19thC, 12¾in (32.5cm) long.
£260–300 *FW&C*

JEWELLERY
Bangles & Bracelets

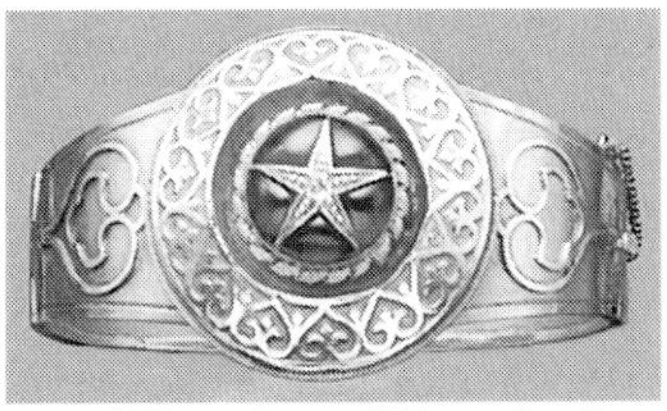

A mid-Victorian gold bangle, the central plaque set with a cabochon garnet and single diamond star motif, the shoulders with applied Moorish style decoration, a later inscription to the reverse 'To Clara Novello Davies', a locket to the reverse containing a photograph of Clara Novello.
£300–330 *P*

Clara Novello Davies was a well known choral conductor and mother of Ivor Novello, the famous British composer.

r. A Victorian 15ct gold bangle, the hinged band set with 15 graduated half pearls in a boat-shaped mount, c1870.
£550–600 *HofB*

A Victorian gold half hoop bangle, set with diamonds and turquoises, c1870.
£1,250–1,400 *HofB*

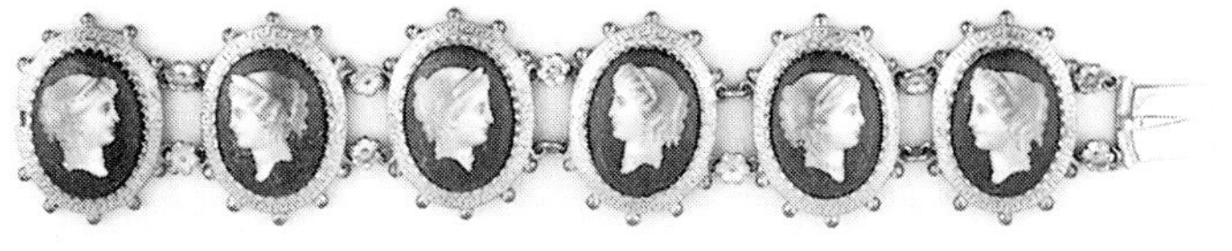

A Victorian yellow metal bracelet, decorated with profiles of Grecian ladies, backed with abalone.
£120–150 *FHF*

Bracelet Styles

- Mid-19thC: substantial in appearance, although usually made of pressed-out hollow gold and, therefore, pieces feel lightweight. Archaeological motifs such as sphinxes, lotus heads or scarabs became popular. Bracelets were the most common form of jewellery, with several often being worn at one time.
- Late 19thC: enormous demand for inexpensive bracelets – vast numbers were mass-produced in centres such as Birmingham. Designs were often Japanese-inspired or sentimental motifs such as ivy (for fidelity) or forget-me-nots.
- Edwardian period: bracelets typically delicate and were much thinner than previously. Usually worn singly.

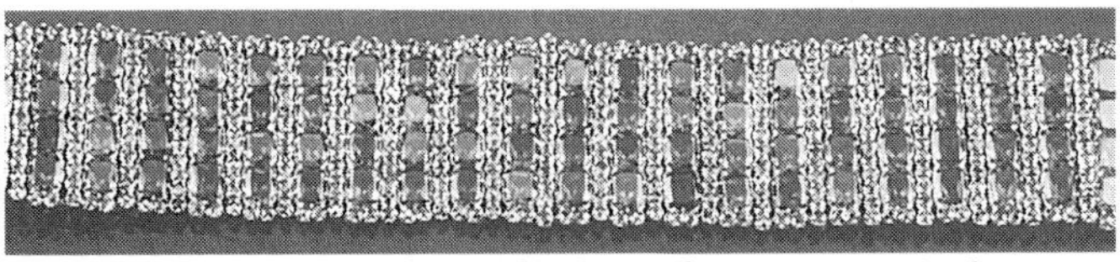

A Victorian garnet bracelet, with silver-gilt mount, repaired.
£525–575 *SK*

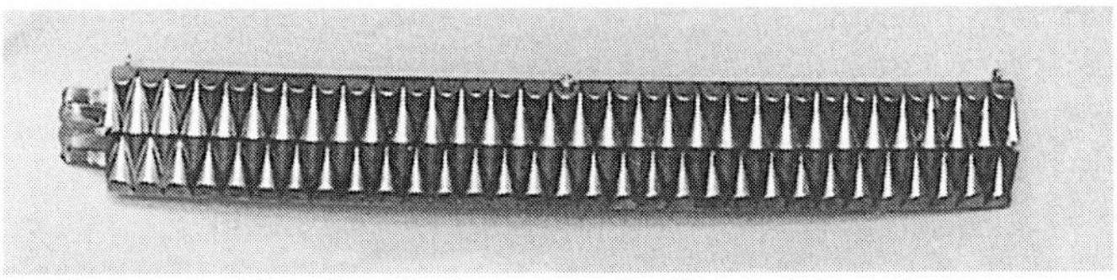

A Victorian gold archaeological revival collar and bracelet, the necklet of alternate long and short shaped pipkin drops, the articulated bracelet of diamond-shaped links.
£5,500–6,000 *P(C)*

A Victorian gold hinged bangle, set with 9 oval rubies and 18 brilliant-cut diamonds.
£3,800–4,200 *WW*

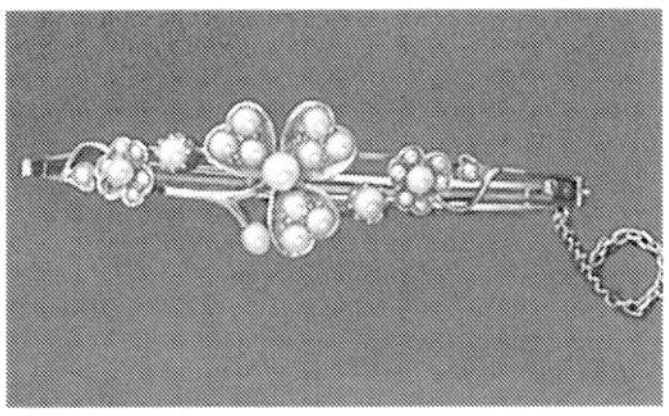

A late Victorian gold and half pearl hinged bangle, with flower and foliate motifs, one small half pearl missing.
£400–450 *P*

An Edwardian bracelet, centred by a flexible platinum plaque with collet and bead-set diamonds on a seed pearl, rose-cut diamond and platinum bracelet, French hallmark.
£4,500–5,000 *SK*

A 9ct gold bangle, set with a front panel of 3 red stones and 2 small diamonds, Chester 1911.
£150–175 *GAK*

A bracelet, composed of 5 carved and pierced jade plaques of fruits and vines bordered by floral links enhanced with small diamonds, mounted in platinum, c1920, 7½in (19cm) long.
£1,600–1,800 *S(NY)*

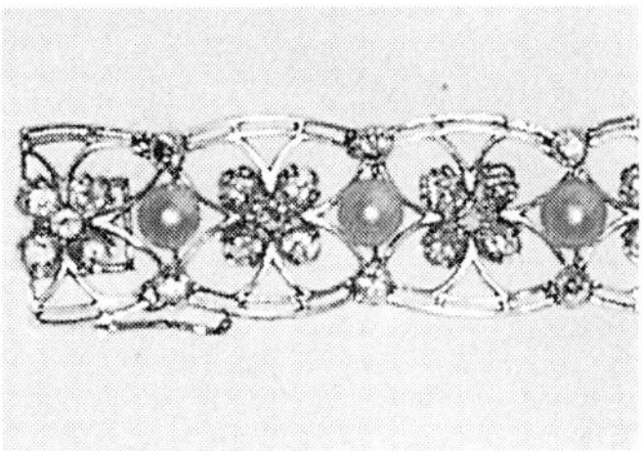

A platinum bracelet, with wirework panels set with 77 diamonds designed in flowerheads, interspersed with cultured pearls, 1920s.
£1,500–1,700 *DD*

Brooches

A brooch, the applied seed pearl motif of doves by a fountain beneath the motto 'l'amour et l'amitié', within a pearl border, mounted in gold, late 18thC.
£380–420 *P*

A gold-mounted enamel brooch, painted with Venus laying a garland of flowers around the neck of Mars with Cupid looking on, late 18thC, 3¼in (8cm) wide.
£1,200–1,400 *P*

A citrine and gold brooch pendant, early 19thC, in original fitted case.
£300–330 *WW*

An amethyst brooch, in goldwork surround, c1825, 2in (5cm) long.
£650–750 *HofB*

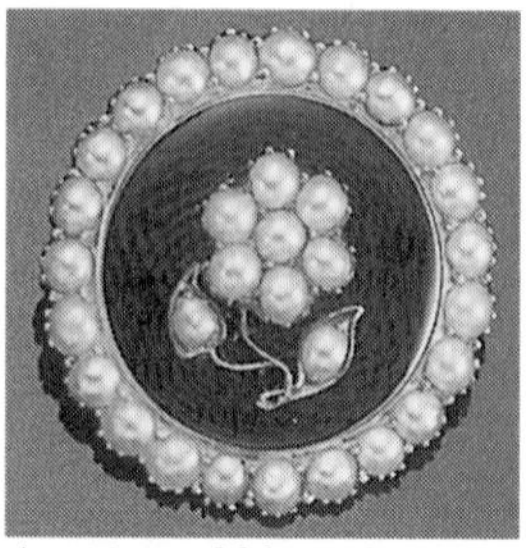

An 18ct gold brooch, by Child & Child, with a central pearl flowerspray on a blue enamelled ground, within a half pearl border, later brooch fitting, mid-19thC.
£320–350 *Bon(C)*

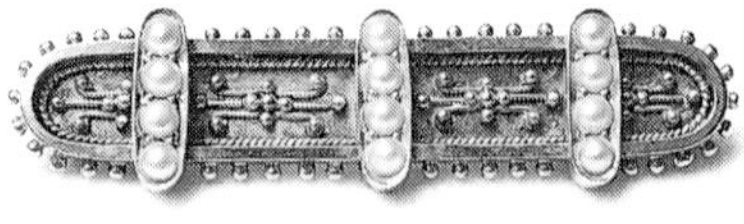

A Victorian Etruscan revivalist gold brooch, set with half pearls, c1870, 2in (5cm) long.
£400–450 *HofB*

r. A Victorian gold brooch/pendant and earrings, decorated with raised scroll and shell borders and central aquamarines, the earrings each set with 3 aquamarines.
£900–1,000 *AG*

A Victorian carbuncle brooch, with central red cabochon surrounded by alternating green and white enamel on a gold mount, glazed to reverse.
£500–550 *HAM*

A brooch/pendant, the small centre diamond set in a surround of 6 heart-shaped opals in a diamond border, with an outer surround of alternating heart-shaped opals and diamonds, late 19thC.
£800–900 *S(S)*

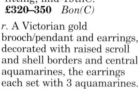

A Victorian heart-shaped brooch, with an emerald border enclosing an openwork flower design of diamond-set leaves and pearl flowerheads centred with small diamonds, with locket back.
£1,800–2,000 *DN*

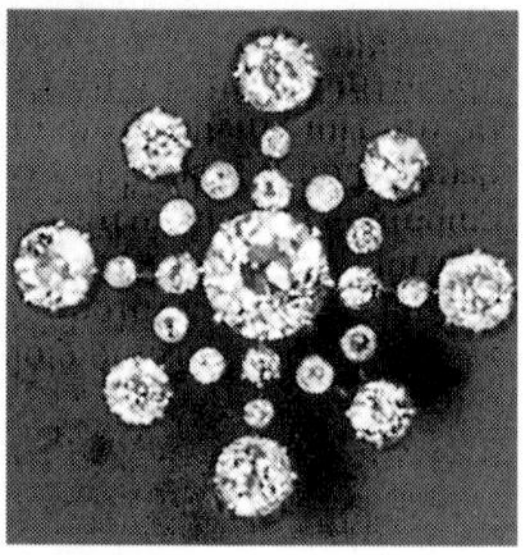

A Victorian diamond snowflake brooch, the centre brilliant-cut diamond surrounded by numerous smaller stones, set in white metal with a yellow gold mount and fine link safety chain.
£6,200–6,800 *HYD*

A Victorian half pearl swallow brooch, with small cabochon ruby eyes, on a gold knife bar with pearl terminal, c1880, 2in (5cm) long.
£120–150 *HofB*

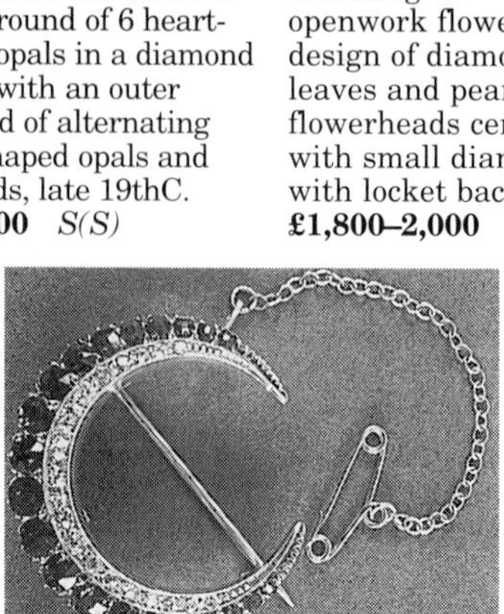

A Victorian crescent-shaped brooch, set with cornflower blue sapphires and old-cut diamonds.
£700–800 *WL*

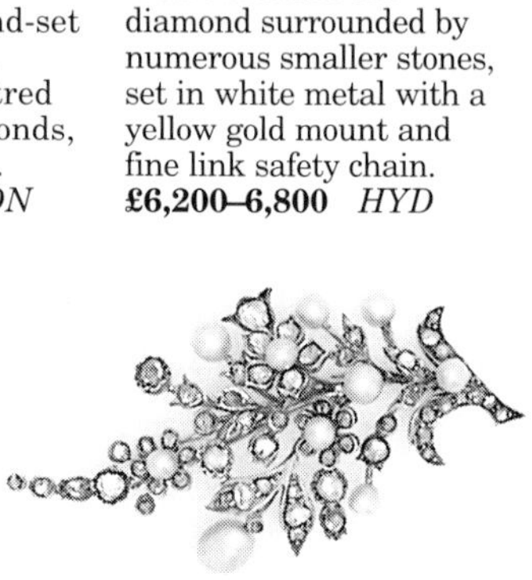

A Victorian diamond and pearl flowerspray brooch, the silver collet set with rose-cut diamonds and pearls.
£1,000–1,100 *P(WM)*

A diamond and turquoise mounted brooch, of openwork scroll design, 19thC.
£1,350–1,500 *Bea(E)*

A late Victorian diamond brooch, in the form of a pansy, set with old and rose-cut stones.
£820–900 *P(WM)*

A late Victorian gold and enamel open circle brooch, depicting a steeplechaser, surrounded by the words 'All Round', set with diamonds and turquoises.
£420–460 *WW*

A dragonfly brooch, set with amethysts within rose and diamond borders, with ruby eyes and diamond body and tail, the 4 wings mounted on springs, c1900.
£9,000–10,000 *HAM*

A dragonfly brooch, set with 29 diamonds and 2 rubies, with blue enamel wings, c1900.
£1,700–1,850 *RBB*

A platinum openwork brooch, pavé-set with rose diamonds, later brooch fitting, c1920.
£2,200–2,500 *S(Am)*

A swallow brooch, the head, outstretched wings and tail pavé-set with circular-cut diamonds, with pale blue and white enamel decoration, rubies to the eyes, mounted in silver and gold, some enamel damage and repair, c1900.
£2,750–3,000 *P*

Buckles

A buckle, set all-round with oval and round topaz, early 19thC.
£1,000–1,100 *WW*

A Dutch silver buckle, from the Province of Zeeland, 19thC, 7in (18cm) wide.
£75–85 *JBB*

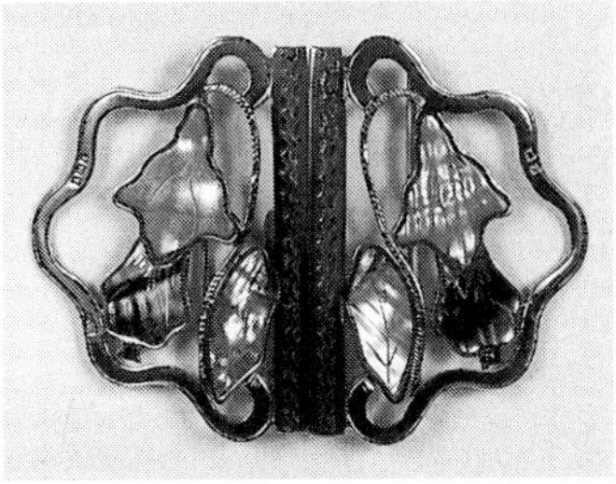

A silver pierced and engraved buckle, by Marshall Brothers, inset with purple, yellow and cream mother-of-pearl, Birmingham 1910, 3½in (9cm) wide.
£300–325 *TC*

FURTHER READING
Miller's Jewellery Antiques Checklist
Miller's Publications 1997

r. An enamel buckle, decorated in multi-coloured designs, c1920, 2in (5cm) wide.
£15–20 *MRW*

Cameos

A Georgian shell cameo brooch, the oval panel depicting a classical scene of a woman feeding an eagle, with 14ct yellow gold snake motif frame, cracks to cameo.
£175–200 *SK*

A shell cameo brooch, depicting the profile of a Bacchante, the husk-link mount with a beaded border, mid-19thC.
£520–570 *Bon(C)*

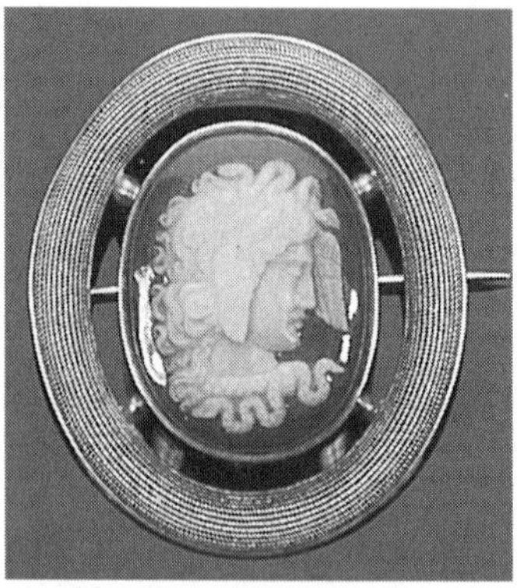

A gold and sardonyx cameo brooch, depicting the head of Medusa, in an oval surround with a wirework finish, beaded at intervals, mid-19thC.
£800–900 *S(S)*

Hardstone Cameos

Hardstone is a term used to cover opaque stones such as agate, sardonyx and carnelian. A hardstone cameo looks and feels different from a shell cameo: it is colder, harder and heavier, and also has a deeper, glassier appearance. Hardstone cameos are generally more expensive than shell versions, because the material is more costly and more difficult to carve.

A gold and sardonyx cameo brooch, by Castellani, depicting a putto, the gold frame with ropework and beaded decoration in white and black spot enamel disc motifs, c1850.
£5,200–5,800 *P*

A Victorian gold-mounted shell cameo brooch, carved with Hebe and the eagle of Jupiter, c1860, 1½in (4cm) high.
£250–300 *HofB*

l. A shell cameo brooch/pendant, depicting Athena and an owl, within a gold border, c1900.
£1,100–1,200 *S(S)*

Locate the Source

The source of each illustration in Miller's can be found by checking the code letters below each caption with the Key to Illustrations.

r. A sardonyx cameo brooch, depicting a profile bust of a girl, within a diamond octagonal pierced foliate frame, c1920.
£800–900 *P*

A hardstone cameo brooch, by Amastini, the white/grey agate carved in high relief, mounted in a foiled chrysolite-set gold frame, early 19thC.
£720–850 *P*

An Italian shell cameo, carved with Cupid being crowned with a wreath, watched by his mother Venus, in a gold engraved rope-twist brooch mount, mid-19thC.
£400–450 *Bon(C)*

A Victorian shell cameo brooch, depicting Hebe and the Eagle, within a gold filigree and cannetille frame.
£460–500 *P*

Cuff Links

A pair of Celtic silver cuff links, c1900, 15mm wide.
£30–40 *JBB*

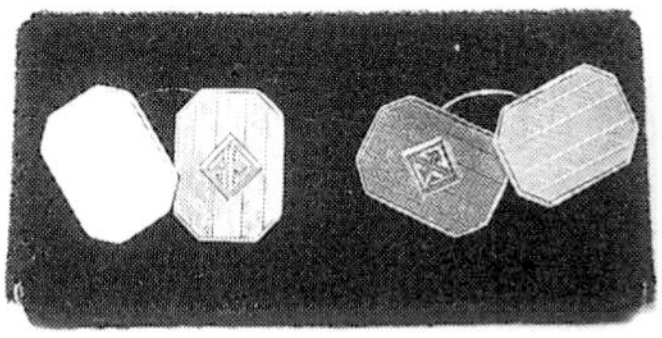

A pair of American 14ct gold cuff links, c1940, 15mm wide.
£85–95 *JBB*

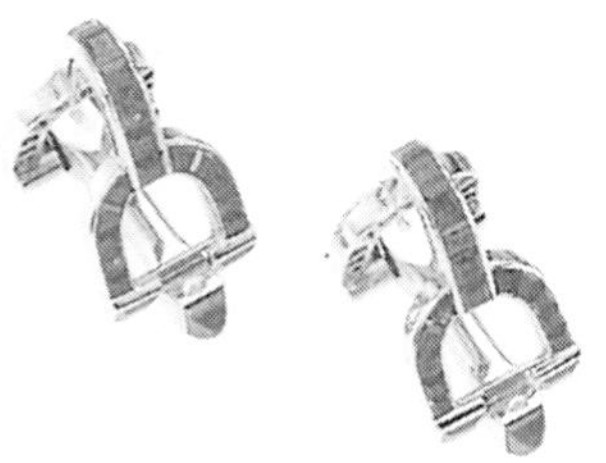

r. A pair of 18ct gold and calibré-cut ruby cuff links, by Jean Ferrière, c1950.
£4,500–5,000 *S(G)*

Earrings

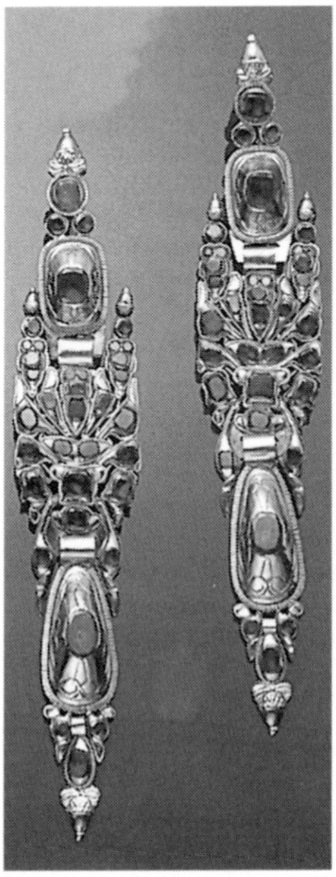

A pair of Iberian gold earrings, set with flat table-cut garnets in a domed collet and cluster formation, c1800.
£1,200–1,500 *P*

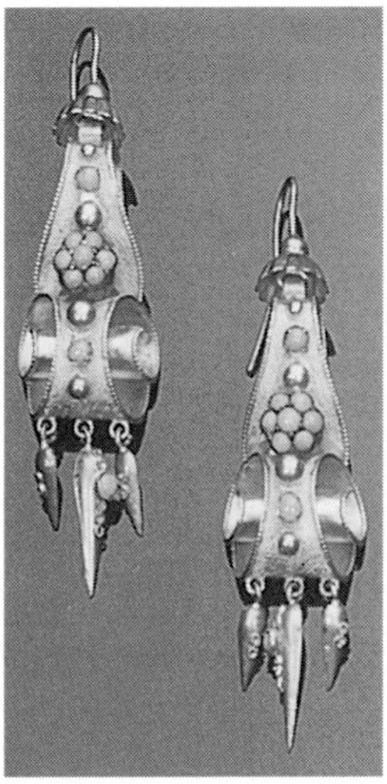

A pair of gold pendant earrings, each in a scrolled design with a turquoise cluster at the centre, the front with 3 drops, the tops with capped wires, c1860.
£550–650 *S(S)*

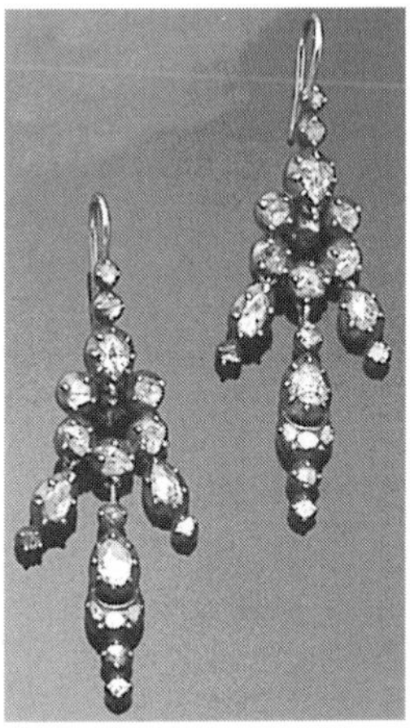

A pair of pendant earrings, set with rose-cut diamonds, on a silver and gold mount, early 19thC.
£1,200–1,300 *P*

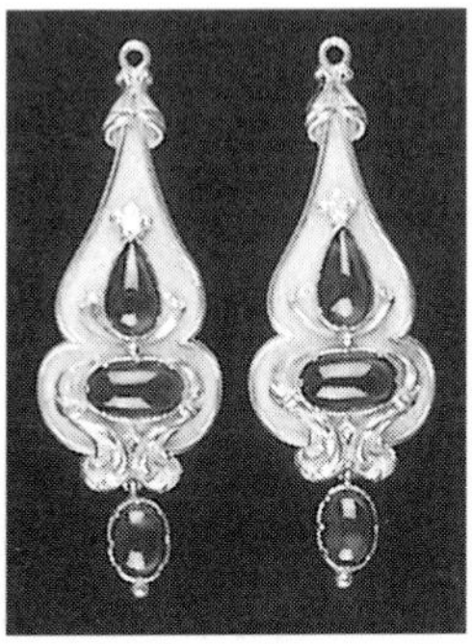

A pair of earrings, each set with 3 cabochon garnets on gold scroll mounts, missing suspension loops, 19thC.
£900–1,000 *L*

A pair of archaeological revival gold earrings, of curved panel design, with granulated and wirework decoration, surmounted by shells, one slightly damaged, 19thC.
£800–900 *Bon(C)*

Micro-mosaic

Micro-mosaic was an Italian technique perfected specifically to provide expensive souvenirs for the growing tourist trade. The plaques were literally tiny mosaics of coloured glass usually backed by black glass, and could be bought unmounted in various shapes. The mosaics usually depicted ancient ruins, local landscapes or figures in national dress.

A pair of earrings, each mounted with a drop-shape polished old-mine emerald bead suspended from rose diamond foliate cluster tops with single diamond connections, c1845.
£9,000–10,000 *P*

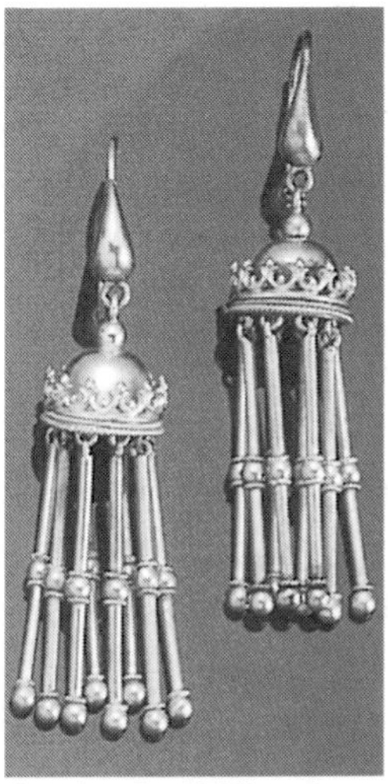

A pair of mid-Victorian gold Gothic revival pendant earrings, the domed terminals within a coronet surround, suspending 8 baton drops, each with spherical terminals.
£1,100–1,200 *Bon*

A pair of micro-mosaic pendant earrings, each with 2 graduated oval panels depicting views of Roman ruins, set in black glass, in gold wirework mounts with spindle links, mid-19thC.
£750–825 *Bon(C)*

A pair of earrings, with graduated circular bands suspending pear-shaped gem stones, one pendant detached, some minor damage, one stone missing, marked 'Storr & Mortimer', 156 New Bond Street, 19thC.
£4,800–5,300 *L*

Necklaces

A garnet choker and pendant, of pierced foliate cluster motif close-set with oval shaped garnets, supporting a ribbon bow and pear-shaped pendant, set in gilt-metal, late 18thC.
£2,000–2,200 *P*

A garnet necklace, of festoon and drop design, early 19thC.
£1,400–1,600 *WW*

A *demi parure* necklace, set with 7 micro-mosaic plaques depicting birds and baskets of flowers within gold frames connected by fine gold chains, with a pair of matching pendant earrings, c1800.
£2,500–2,750 *S*

An Egyptian revivalist gold necklace, the knitted linked chain with gold attachments c1865, 16¼in (41cm) long.
£2,000–2,200 *P*

A diamond and pearl necklace, set throughout with cushion-shaped diamonds and decorated with pearl drops, the later back chain interspersed with pearls, c1890, 17in (43cm) long.
£5,200–5,800 *S*

This was formerly a tiara.

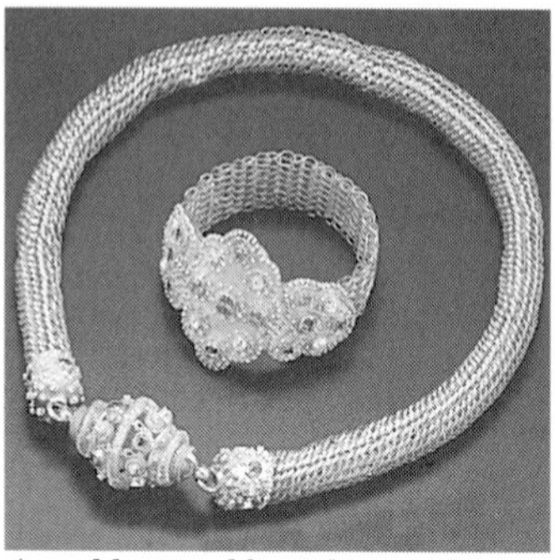

A necklace and bracelet set, the flexible multi-link tubular pattern necklace terminating in mounts decorated with rope and beadwork and set with cushion-shaped diamonds and mixed-cut emeralds, with similarly decorated bracelet, c1830.
£3,000–3,300 each *S*

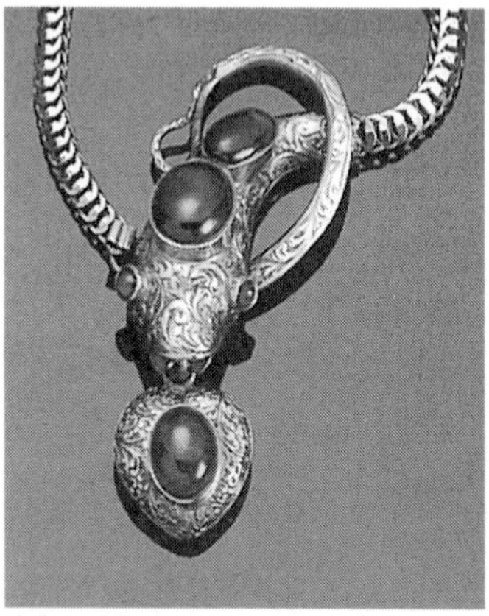

A late Victorian gold snake necklace, with a heart-shaped pendant, set with garnets.
£680–750 *Bon*

A pendant necklace, the 13 amethysts set within repoussé pink and yellow gold scrollwork frames, with detachable pear-shaped amethyst pendant within a similar gold setting, c1840, 16in (40.5cm) long.
£3,000–3,300 *S(NY)*

A late Victorian gold and half pearl necklace, the front with 3 flowerheads with graduated cusp drops between, on a similarly set backchain.
£1,100–1,200 *P*

l. An Edwardian pearl necklace, with ruby and diamond round cluster clasp, centred with an emerald within an old-cut diamond single line border and suspending a single collet.
£5,000–5,500 *DN*

Pendants

A Victorian heart-shaped pendant, with central banded agate surrounded by split pearls with a rose diamond below a pearl-set ribbon bow.
£380–420 *FHF*

A pendant necklace, set with an amethyst in a surround of rose-cut diamonds, the top designed as a bow and with linen-fold scrollwork pierced sides, further set with rose diamonds on a trace link neckchain with a bolt ring clasp, late 19thC.
£1,400–1,600 *S(S)*

A late Victorian micro-mosaic pendant/brooch, of quatrefoil design, the centre with dove motif, enclosed by panels of flowers, grapes and an anchor, with beaded frame.
£550–600 *P(WM)*

A zircon and diamond pendant, set with an orange/brown zircon, with rose-cut diamond surround and within a frame of seed pearls and brilliant-cut diamonds in a gold collet setting, late 19thC.
£1,400–1,600 *Bea(E)*

A gold pendant, set with a central cushion-shaped diamond surrounded by 6 opals and with small rubies set at intervals, all in a pierced scrollwork mount set with half pearls, c1900.
£450–500 *S(S)*

An Edwardian openwork pendant, with detachable brooch mount, set with a centre cluster of aqua-marine and diamonds.
£1,800–2,000 *WL*

An Edwardian 9ct gold cross pendant, engraved with scroll foliage, Chester 1904.
£90–100 *HofB*

A pendant, the woven seed pearl latticework necklace with rose-cut diamond finials and aquamarine and diamond cluster pendant, c1915.
£2,300–2,500 *P*

Rings

A gold posy ring, converted to a mourning ring with the addition of an engraved cranium, inscribed inside, maker's mark 'I.E.', 17thC.
£300–330 *FW&C*

'Posy' is a corruption of the word poesie, and refers to a short inscription which is often found engraved on the inside of gold hoop rings dating from the late 16thC to the early 18thC. Sometimes a skull or extended skeleton would be added after a loved one had died, converting the piece into a mourning ring.

An 18ct gold and diamond ring, c1890.
£1,250–1,400 *GEM*

A diamond cocktail ring, the 7 graduated old brilliant-cut diamonds with a fluted mount, with French control marks, c1930.
£1,100–1,200 *Bon*

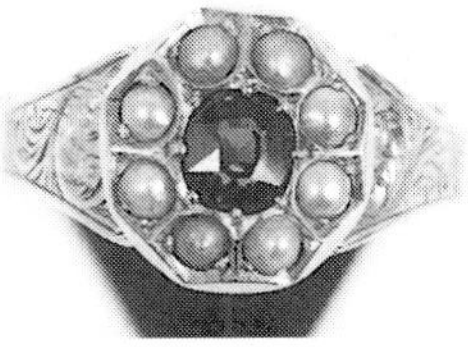

A late Victorian sapphire and pearl ring, c1900.
£150–180 *PSA*

An Edwardian 18ct gold buckle ring, set with a diamond, Birmingham 1901.
£200–220 *HofB*

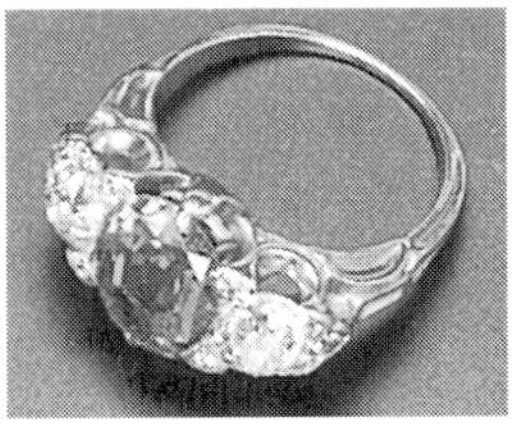

l. A sapphire and diamond ring, set with a cushion-shaped sapphire between 2 diamonds, the mount decorated with small diamonds, late 19thC.
£6,700–7,500 *S*

An 18ct gold ring, set with a single diamond, Birmingham 1918.
£120–150 *HofB*

A brilliant-cut diamond ring, with 3 stones, c1935.
£850–900 *HofB*

ENAMEL

An enamel beaker, produced to commemorate the coronation of Tsar Nicholas II, 1896, 4in (10cm) high.
£85–95 *W&S*

A green enamel patch box, the lid decorated with a black and white transfer print of a lady harvester, with original mirror, south Staffordshire, c1780, 2in (5cm) long.
£350–400 *BHa*

Don't Forget!
If in doubt please refer to the 'How to Use' page at the beginning of this book.

An enamel and silver box, by Heinrich Levinger, Birmingham, 1899 import mark, 3in (7.5cm) diam.
£1,500–1,750 *SHa*

A enamel mask *bonbonnière*, modelled as a mastiff with staring eyes, the later lid painted as the back of the beast's head, with original metal mounts, restored, Bilston, c1770, 2¼in (6cm) diam.
£1,500–1,800 *S*

An enamel quatrefoil trinket box, the lid painted in colours with a scene of dancing figures in a garden, Bilston, c1900, 3½in (9cm) wide.
£300–330 *GAK*

A pair of white enamel table candlesticks, painted with flower sprigs, south Staffordshire, late 18thC, 9in (23cm) high.
£500–550 *MSW*

A silver and enamel dressing table set, with 2 bowls on a glass and silver tray, Birmingham 1936, tray 10½in (26.5cm) long.
£850–950 *SHa*

r. An Austrian silver and enamel presentation photograph frame, inset with ducal crest, c1900, 7in (18cm) high.
£5,000–5,500 *SHa*

An enamel box, decorated with a Palladian scene to the lid, the white base decorated with a floral design, Birmingham, c1770, 2½in (6.5cm) diam.
£900–1,000 *BHa*

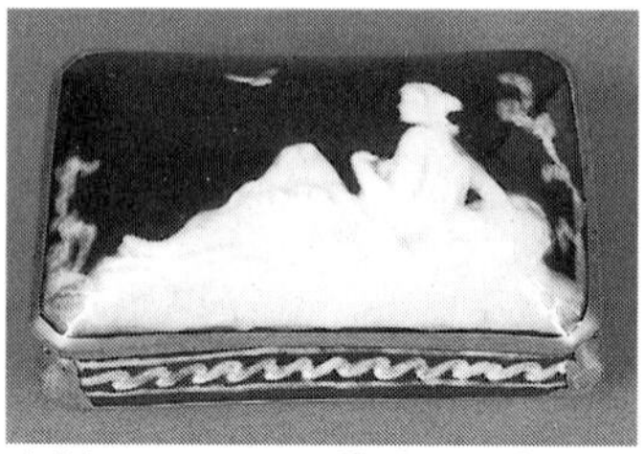

A Limoges enamelled porcelain box, with a classical scene on a blue ground, c1890, 6½in (16.5cm) long.
£200–250 *SER*

A Victorian enamel card case, decorated with a floral bouquet surrounded by an acanthus leaf border on a green ground, the green back inset with gold, silver and green, with a pink silk lining, 6in (15cm) long.
£300–330 *BIG*

FABERGE

A Fabergé gold bangle, enamelled in translucent *rose Pompadour* over ruched engine-turning, the baton-shaped clasp with enamelled ball terminal, workmaster Henrik Wigström, St Petersburg, 1908–1917.
£10,000–12,000 *S(G)*

A Fabergé silver-gilt and blue *basse taille* enamel cigar cutter, painted with trailing leafage in white, with beaded rim and cast foliage thumbpiece to the cutter, Moscow, c1905, 1½in (38mm) diam.
£7,200–8,000 *RBB*

A Fabergé silver-gilt overlaid and rose-diamond set nephrite vase, decorated with a floral pattern, c1900, 5in (15cm) high.
£17,000–20,000 *HAM*

The Fabergé workshops were seldom influenced by styles and this piece, with its Art Nouveau appearance, is consequently

r. A Fabergé vase, with original glass liner, marked, c1910, 8¾in (22cm) high.
£3,400–3,750 *SHa*

A Fabergé brooch, set with a golden brown cushion-shaped sapphire surrounded by diamonds, with similarly set tied bow surmount, 1908–1917.
£8,500–10,000 *P*

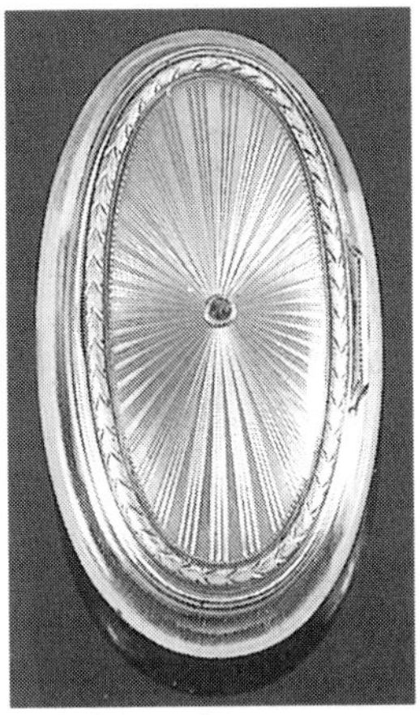

A Fabergé glass snuff box, the lid enamelled blue over an engine-turned ground and centred by a garnet, workmaster Fedor Affanassiev, St Petersburg, 1899–1908, 2¾in (7cm) wide.
£5,750–7,000 *S*

A Fabergé sugar bowl, the spiral fluted sides chased with a scroll-edged rococo cartouche flanked by flowers and bulrushes, on a collet foot, Moscow, c1895, 5¼in (13.5cm) diam, 6½oz.
£800–900 *P*

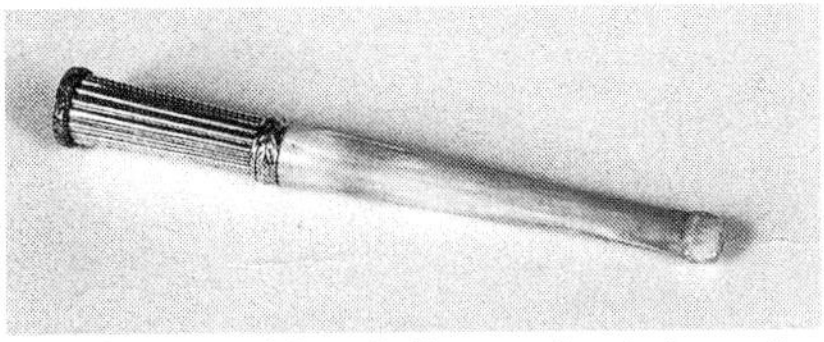

A Fabergé gold and diamond-set cigarette holder, by Henrik Wigström, St Petersburg, c1900, 3½in (9cm) long.
£1,300–1,500 *SHa*

A Fabergé silver and gold cigarette holder, decorated with a hound pursuing a wild boar, the two-colour gold tip chased with leaf-tips, St Petersburg, c1910, 3½in (9cm) long.
£2,000–2,200 *S(NY)*

GOLD

A Cartier 18ct gold, enamel and diamond-set gentleman's cigarette case, with vesta, signed and dated '1911', 4¾in (12cm) wide.
£5,000–5,500 *SHa*

A French tortoiseshell snuff box, decorated with gold and silver inlay, c1700, 3½in (9cm) long.
£3,200–3,500 *EMC*

A gold-mounted tortoiseshell snuff box, the lid inset with a micro-mosaic plaque depicting a fight between a dog and a cat, with scrolled gold thumbpiece and gold lining, early 19thC, 3¼in (8cm) wide.
£4,000–4,500 *S*

A 9ct gold snuff box, with the cypher of Edward VII on the lid, London 1909, 1½in (38mm) long.
£2,500–2,750 *SHa*

r. A gold toothpick case, by André-Pierre Lebrun, the lid later engraved with the cypher of Edward, Prince of Wales, marked, Paris 1783, 3⅓in (8.5cm) long.
£4,800–5,300 *S*

A gold cigarette case, by Van Cleef & Arpels, engraved with horizontal linear motifs, the silvered interior with a signed picture of Marlene Dietrich, mid-20thC, 3in (7.5cm) long.
£1,400–1,600 *S(LA)*
Ex-Marlene Dietrich collection.

A black lacquered and gold snuff box, by Jacques Lebrun, the cover set with a miniature of a lady, attributed to Richard Cosway, Paris, 1769, 3½in (9cm) long.
£2,750–3,000 *P*

A Continental gold snuff box, the central panels engine-turned with wavy decoration within engraved and chased foliate borders, the sides similarly decorated, early 19thC, 3¾in (9.5cm) long.
£550–650 *Bon*

A Victorian gold-mounted red glass scent bottle, maker's mark 'BK & Co', c1870, 3in (7.5cm) high.
£700–800 *HofB*

A gold presentation snuff box, decorated with a central blue enamel panel applied in rose-cut diamonds with a spray of flowers, the ground engraved and picked out in blue enamel with floral and foliate decoration, by C. M. Weishaupt & Söhne, Hanau, c1883, 3⅓in (8.5cm) wide.
£2,000–2,500 *S*

r. A two-colour gold and glass flacon vinaigrette, with a spring lid, slight damage, Paris, late 19thC, 2½in (63mm) high.
£700–800 *S*

A gold musical toothpick case, applied with turquoise-coloured beads and a central rose diamond amid chased flowers and foliage, the base containing the musical movement, pinned disc, the comb with 17 tines, Geneva, c1820, 2½in (6.3cm) wide.
£3,000–3,300 *S(G)*

ORIENTAL

Oriental arts are very popular. Collectors generally concentrate on one area; archaic Chinese bronzes, or objects from a scholar's study – scholars' rocks and brush pots, and calligraphy. Collectors of snuff bottles rarely collect jade; textile enthusiasts ignore cloisonné.

'There is enormous interest in a broad range of Chinese works of art,' said James B. Godfrey, who heads the Chinese department at Sotheby's in New York. 'Well over half of the buyers at my sales are Americans, and the core of the market seems to be in New York. It is a comfortable environment, the import and export process is straightforward and the tax structure attractive, encouraging people to send works to New York for sale. Asians, Europeans and North and South Americans like to come to New York to buy.' According to James Godfrey, the market for archaic jade is strong while the market for later jadeite carving has levelled off: it is a Far Eastern taste and economic difficulties in Asia have had an effect. The market for textiles has been buoyed by the recent exhibition of Chinese silk at the Metropolitan Museum of Art which provided an opportunity for study and scholarship. Chinese painting is the most demanding field, a field dominated by scholars; prices can be inconsistent.

It is essential to buy Chinese archaic bronzes from reliable sources. 'It is rare to find a piece with a patina that has not been doctored and common to find an old piece with new inlays' said Edith Frankel, a New York dealer.

Collectors of Chinese furniture have nearly exhausted the supply of 17th and early 18th century chairs and tables made of *huanghuali* wood. 'The market is belatedly turning its attention to furniture made of a variety of other woods used in the same period, said Marcus Flacks, the New York dealer. 'I know of more than 24 different woods commonly used on high quality furniture: *nanmu*, from the cedar family, *jichimu* (chicken feather wood), walnut and elm are generally less costly than *huanghuali* wood, although in the last two years the prices of furniture made of these woods have tripled as people become aware of their rarity.' Watch out for container loads of Chinese furniture made of soft wood in traditional styles in the 19th and early 20th century. Chairs, some with traces of paint, are sold as exotic decoration for as little as £275 each and cabinets, most of them with new hardware and often repainted, for £1,500–3,000.

With the Japanese economy in recession the buying power of the dollar in Japan is the best in eight years according to New York dealer Joan Mirviss. 'The drop in the value of the yen has made things more affordable, and some good things are beginning to come out, especially in the area of Japanese paintings in an acquisition hungry market,' she said.

Lita Solis Cohen

Cloisonné

A Chinese polychrome cloisonné enamel bowl, decorated on the exterior with a design of 6 meandering flowering lotuses, reserved on a pale blue ground, the interior lined in gilt-metal, late 17thC, 6¾in (17cm) diam.
£620–680 *P*

A Japanese silver-mounted and inlaid cloisonné enamel box and cover, by Namikawa Yasuyuki, decorated with blossoms and leaves on a midnight blue ground, the interior in lemon yellow, signed, c1890, 3in (7.5cm) wide.
£5,500–6,000 *FW&C*

A Chinese cloisonné incense burner, the cover surmounted with a gilt Buddhistic lion with a ribbon in its mouth, late 19thC, 39in (99cm) high.
£1,800–2,000 *SK(B)*

A Chinese export white metal cloisonné enamel cup, decorated with birds on a green ground, c1905, 6½in (16.5cm) high.
£600–650 *SHa*

A Japanese cloisonné bowl, decorated with panels of birds and flowers with foliage on a powder blue ground, late 19thC, 14½in (37cm) diam.
£75–85 *AG*

r. A pair of Chinese cloisonné floor vases, decorated with bamboo entwined with convolvulus, late 19thC, 34in (86cm) high.
£1,300–1,500 *Bon(M)*

A Japanese vase, with flared rim, cloisonné enamelled with lilies on a rich blue ground, 19thC, 9½in (24cm) high.
£400–450 *WL*

Namikawa Yasuyuki

Namikawa Yasuyuki (1845–1927) was one of only two cloisonné makers appointed to the Imperial Household Arts and Crafts Department during the Meiji period in Japan. By chance, they were both surnamed Namikawa, but were unrelated. Namikawa Yasuyuki helped to develop the deep black transparent enamel which features extensively in late 19thC cloisonné. Working in Kyoto, he was one of the most talented makers of the Meiji period, producing extremely complex and minutely detailed designs. He won many prizes at international exhibitions, where his work was very much in demand, and still is today.

A Japanese silver wire cloisonné enamelled vase and cover, by Namikawa Yasuyuki, decorated to one side with a bird in flowering branches against a mirror black ground, the reeded turned finial as a flowerhead, on a conforming hardwood stand, Meiji period, 7¼in (18.5cm) high.
£20,000–22,000 *Hal*

This piece, by one of the foremost craftsmen of the period, is in perfect condition and of striking appearance. Its value is increased because of its solid silver body.

A Japanese cloisonné enamel vase, worked with purple and white irises, with pendant border to the neck, on a dark blue ground, Meiji period, 12½in (31.5cm) high.
£430–480 *P(W)*

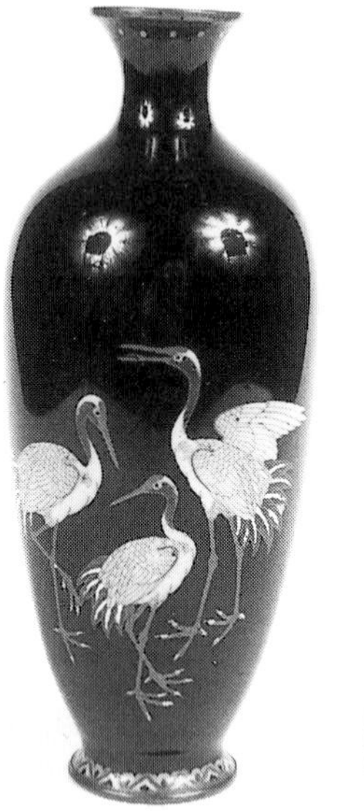

A pair of Japanese cloisonné vases, decorated with cranes, c1880, 6½in (16.5cm) high.
£500–600 *MCN*

A Japanese silver cloisonné vase, signed 'Namikawa', c1880, 5in (12.5cm) high.
£12,000–14,000 *MCN*

Enamel

A Chinese Canton enamel box and cover, painted with 2 ribbon-tied trumpets and a harp amid flowers and fruit, the sides with gilt-bronze scrolls reserved on a turquoise ground, minor chips, mark and period of Qianlong, 2¾in (7cm) wide.
£4,800–5,300 *S*

l. A Chinese gilt-copper champlevé enamel *meiping* and stand, cast with a broad band of bats and lotus scrolls entwined around stylised *wan* and *shou* symbols, brightly coloured with enamel infill, with a matching stand and pierced finial, Qing Dynasty, 11in (28cm) high.
£4,000–4,500 *S*

r. A pair of Japanese enamelled silver and ivory-inset bottle vases, signed 'Genyu', with curled dragons at the shoulders, decorated with oval panels inlaid with birds and a basket of peonies, on trefoil bracket feet, Meiji period, 8in (20.5cm) high.
£3,000–3,300 *P*

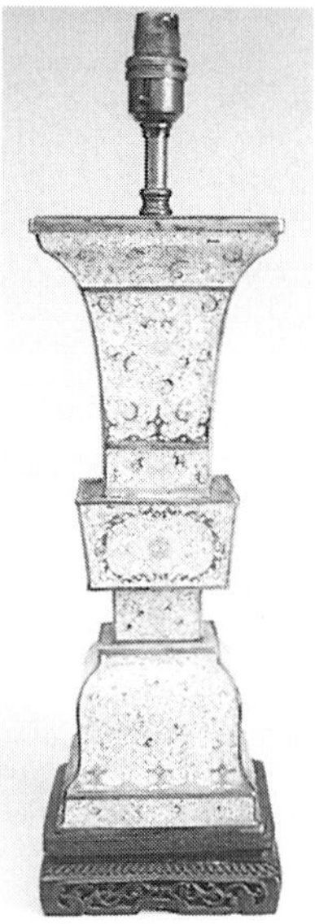

A Chinese Canton vase, enamelled in famille rose colours with scrolling lotus on a blue ground, the central panels with *shou* medallions on a yellow ground, now fitted as a lamp, Qianlong period, 12½in (32cm) high.
£2,800–3,200 *DN*

Glass

A Chinese green glass disc, one side carved all-over with lines of raised bosses in low relief, restuck from pieces, Western Han Dynasty, 5in (12.5cm) diam.
£1,200–1,500 *S*

This item is a tomb object, representing the sky.

A Chinese yellow Peking glass brush washer, with waisted neck and rounded rim, incised Qianlong mark, 18thC, 6¼in (16cm) diam.
£4,200–4,800 *S(NY)*

r. A Chinese turquoise Peking glass vase, with a faint swirl pattern, on a short slightly flared foot, Qianlong, 9½in (24cm) high.
£4,600–5,000 *B&B*

Jade

A Chinese jade model, carved as 2 ducks amongst lotus, Southern Song Dynasty, 3in (7.5cm) wide.
£3,500–4,000 *Wai*

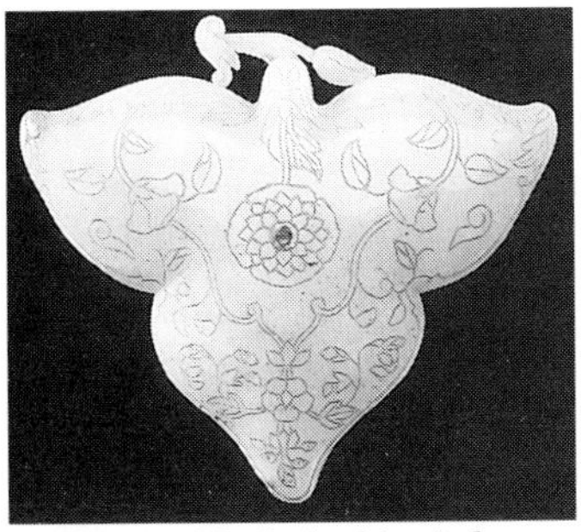

A Chinese Moghul white jade leaf-shaped box and cover, incised with stylised scrolling prunus and hibiscus around a chrysanthemum, the interior with 3 compartments, Qing Dynasty, 18thC, 4¼in (11cm) wide, on a wooden stand.
£4,500–5,000 *S*

A Chinese celadon jade model of a swooping crane, with a floral sprig in the mouth serving as a hanging loop, Yuan/Ming Dynasty, 3¼in (8.5cm) wide.
£3,000–3,300 *S*

A Chinese jade model of a goat, on a wooden stand, Ming copy of Tang Dynasty, 2½in (6.5cm) high.
£1,800–2,000 *Wai*

l. A Chinese yellowish-green jade carving of a crab, seated among sprigs of millet, its 8 legs neatly folded, Qing Dynasty, probably 19thC, 4in (10cm) wide.
£1,800–2,000 *P*

A Chinese Moghul style greenish-grey jade two-handled cup, the sides flanked by pendant buds against leaves, on a lotus flower-head footrim, Qing Dynasty, probably 18thC, 5in (13cm) diam.
£1,800–2,000 *P*

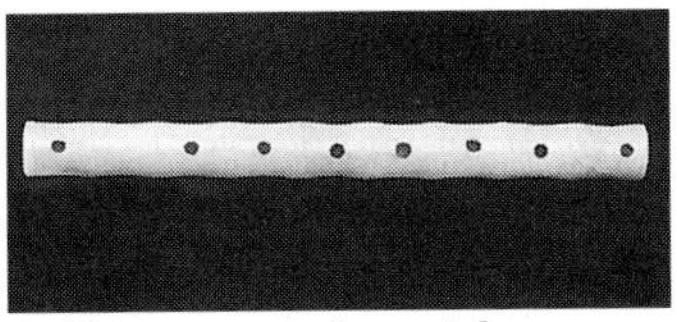

A Chinese carved greyish-green jade flute, imitating a bamboo stalk, Qianlong period, 11½in (29cm) long.
£1,500–1,800 *S*

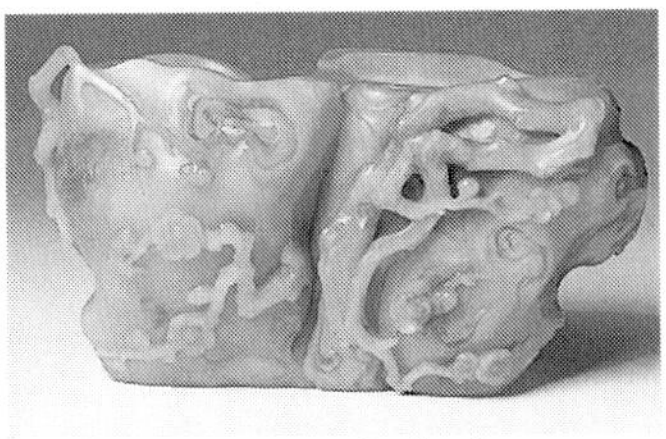

A Chinese russet-flecked green jade double vase, carved and pierced in relief as 2 hollow pine trunks, with flowering branches on the sides, a bird perched on one branch, 18thC, 8¾in (22cm) wide, on a wooden stand.
£5,500–6,000 *P*

r. A Chinese spinach jade censer and cover, carved with lattice-work, the cover with intertwined scrolls surmounted by a splayed multi-faceted knop, on 4 feet, 18thC, 4¼in (11cm) diam.
£5,000–5,500 *S(NY)*

Lacquer

A Japanese lacquer document box, decorated in gold and silver *hiramakie*, 19thC, 19¼in (49cm) long.
£1,800–2,000 *S(NY)*

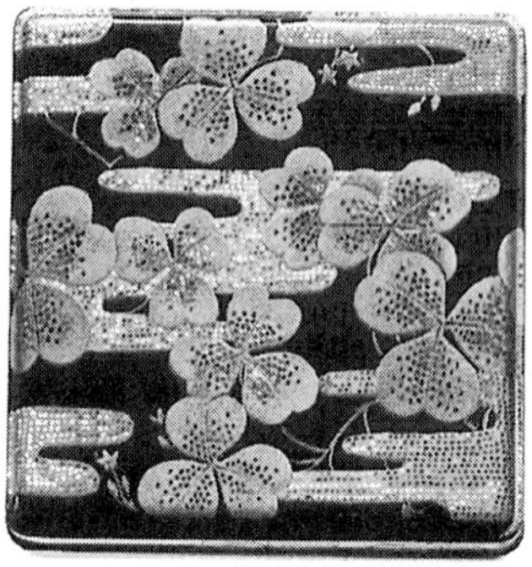

A Japanese black lacquered incense box, decorated with wood sorrel in gold and silver *hiramakie* and green, yellow and mauve, 19thC, 2¼in (6cm) square.
£1,300–1,500 *S*

A Chinese gilt lacquer and wood figure of Buddha, with blue topknot and robe tie, red and gilt crown, 19thC, 37in (94cm) high.
£1,000–1,100 *SLN*

A Japanese four-tiered gold lacquer box and cover, of double flowerhead form, decorated in *hiramakie* and *takamakie* with textile design borders, the interior red lacquered, 19thC, 8in (20.5cm) high.
£1,800–2,000 *S(Am)*

A Japanese gilt lacquer box and cover, decorated with a house by a stream at the foot of a hill, the interior with a fitted tray, slight damage, Meiji period, 7in (17.5cm) wide.
£600–700 *P*

A Japanese lacquered wood incense box, by Morikawa Shizan, the cover decorated with a hare, the interior with autumn grasses, signed, early Showa period, 3in (7.5cm) diam.
£2,800–3,200 *S*

A Japanese lacquer box, the cover decorated with floral designs, c1860, 3½in (9cm) wide.
£1,800–2,000 *MCN*

A Japanese lacquer box, decorated with blossoming cherry trees, Meiji period, 10in (25.5cm) wide.
£1,400–1,600 *SK(B)*

A Japanese gold lacquer and enamel dish, by Yukoku, inlaid with ducks by a stream within impressed silver panels partly enamelled with flowers, some inlay missing, Meiji period, 11¾in (30cm) wide.
£2,500–2,750 *S*

A Japanese lacquer tray, by Shibayama, signed, c1880, 9in (23cm) square.
£3,000–3,500 *MCN*

l. A Chinese export black lacquer tea caddy, decorated with vignettes of figures in pavilions, surrounded by foliage and flowers, on dragon-form feet, the interior with a pewter canister, 19thC, 5¾in (14.5cm) wide.
£500–550 *B&B*

Metalware

A Japanese bronze model of a cockatoo, perched on a tree trunk, signed 'Nikko', Meiji period, 20¼in (51.5cm) high.
£21,000–23,000 *MCA*

This is a particularly fine example of a rare subject, since Japanese sculptors usually made models of animals and birds which were indigenous to Japan.

A pair of Japanese parcel-gilt bronze incense burners, in the form of caparisoned elephants, with howdah-like platforms, Meiji period, 19¾in (50cm) high.
£2,300–2,500 *P*

A Chinese patinated bronze censer, the cover with a finial in the form of a lion, with scrolling handles, on hoof feet, 17thC, 10½in (26.5cm) high.
£170–200 *P(EA)*

r. A Sino Tibetan gilt-bronze figure of a seated Buddha, 18thC, 4in (10cm) high.
£450–500 *AAV*

A Japanese bronze model of a dromedary and rider, Meiji period, 14½in (37cm) high.
£950–1,100 *HYD*

Two Japanese bronze models of an Indian elephant and her calf, late 19thC, largest 10in (25.5cm) high.
£750–850 *CAG*

A Chinese bronze brush rest, in the form of a pair of entwined lizards, their necks providing the support for the brushes, late Ming Dynasty, 6¾in (17cm) wide.
£750–850 *P*

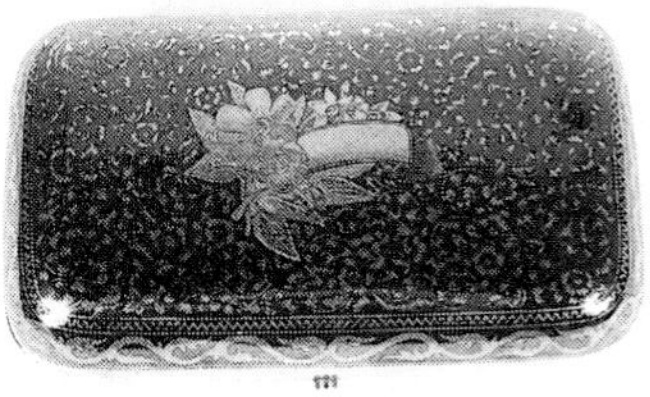

A Chinese silver box, a presentation piece for the Mosquito Yacht Club, c1900, 4¼in (11cm) wide.
£350–400 *ELI*

A pair of Chinese bronze models of deer, 17thC, largest 10¾in (27cm) high.
£5,500–6,000 *S*

A Japanese silver bowl, decorated with irises, on a rim base, early 20thC, 10¼in (26cm) diam.
£1,650–1,800 *Bea(E)*

A Chinese parcel-gilt copper censer, decorated in relief with bands of mythical animals and stylised foliage on a wave and punch-decorated ground, with 2 gilded cast bronze loop handles formed as monsters' heads with scrolled pendant drops, c1600, 8½in (21.5cm) diam.
£6,000–6,500 *FW&C*

A Japanese bronze *koro* and pierced cover, with hoofed Kirin finial, the body with tripod feet and separately cast three-clawed dragon handles, damaged, Meiji period, 13in (33cm) high.
£550–600 *Bon*

A Chinese gilt-bronze figure of Buddha, with a flammiform aureole, seated on a rectangular base, Qianlong period, 8in (20.5cm) high.
£350–400 *WW*

A pair of Japanese bronze vases, decorated around the neck with a separately cast three-clawed dragon, Meiji period, 13in (33cm) high.
£600–700 *Bon*

A Chinese bronze figure of Budai with children, on a bronze stand in the form of a sack with 2 boys to one side, Qing Dynasty, 17/18thC, 24in (61cm) wide.
£8,000–9,000 *S*

A Chinese silver mug, with presentation inscription, dated '1899', 3¼in (8.5cm) high.
£340–375 *ELI*

l. A Chinese export mug, embossed with scenes of warriors and a temple, the scroll handle formed as a dragon, 19thC, 8¼in (21cm) high.
£750–825 *P(WM)*

A pair of Japanese bronze vases, inlaid with silver and gold, late 19thC, 7¼in (18.5cm) high.
£530–585 *ELI*

A Japanese bronze figure of a sleeping boy, slumped against a drum with a cat perched on his shoulder, decorated with incised patterns highlighted in gilt, plaque signed 'Miyao', with a fitted wooden stand, Meiji period, 4¾in (12cm) high.
£3,000–3,300 *P*

A Chinese export silver three-piece tea service and matching tongs, by Wang-Hing, Shanghai, c1900, teapot 5⅛in (13cm) high.
£850–950 *B&B*

A Japanese bronze bottle vase, applied in relief with a lizard and spray of flowers, signed 'Kazumas', Meiji period, 13¾in (35cm) high.
£1,100–1,200 *P*

l. A Chinese bronze wine vessel, with taotie mask decoration, late Qing Dynasty, 10¾in (27.5cm) high.
£180–220 *SLN*

A taotie is a type of mythical animal who devours wrongdoers.

Wood

A Chinese export brass-bound travelling dressing box, inlaid with mother-of-pearl, the interior with a rising mirror, drawers and trays, 19thC, 21in (53.5cm) high when open.
£750–900 *CORO*

A Chinese wooden panel, carved in deep relief with a scene of an Emperor receiving gifts from a visiting emissary, surrounded by warriors and courtiers in a palace interior, 19thC, 56 x 81in (142 x 206cm) framed.
£1,200–1,400 *P*

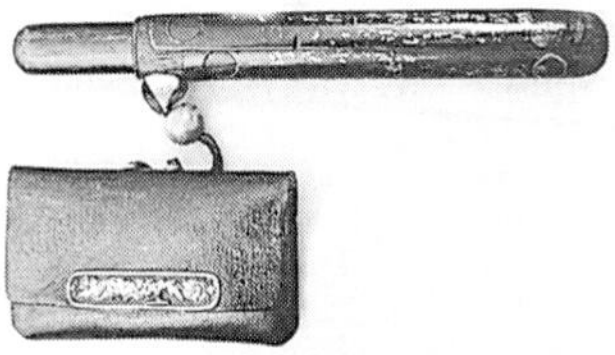

A Japanese carved wood pipe set, attached to a leather pouch with silver and gilt-metal clasp and agate *ojime*, and a silver-mounted brass pipe with bamboo body, 18thC, pipe 7in (18cm) long.
£200–220 *EH*

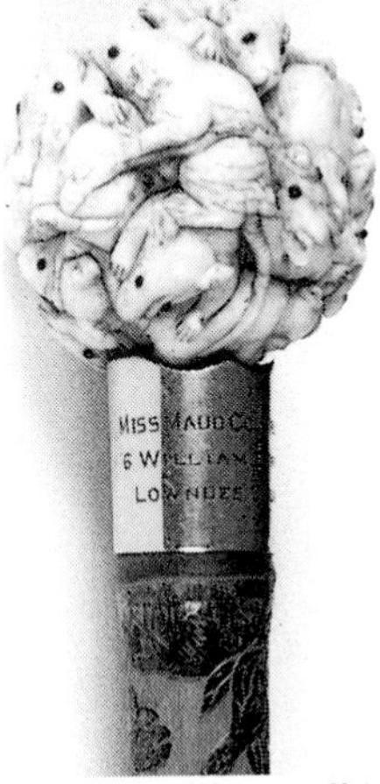

A Japanese bamboo walking stick, with carved ivory handle, late 19thC, 36in (91.5cm) long.
£1,100–1,250 *SHa*

A Japanese boxwood keepsake box, carved with rats amongst corn, their eyes in ebony, signed 'Ikko', Meiji period, 3¼in (8cm) high.
£1,100–1,200 *Bea(E)*

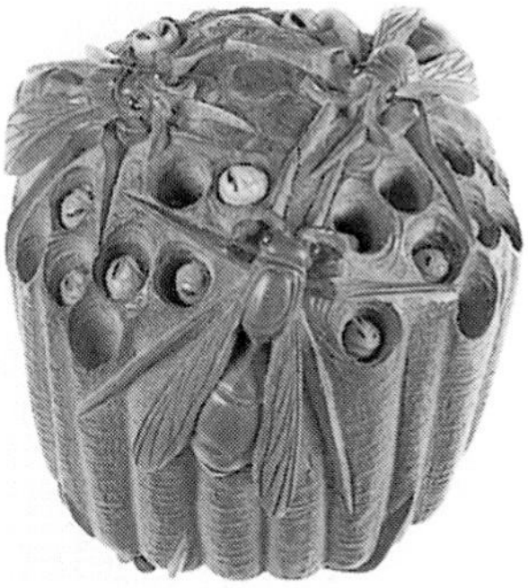

A Japanese boxwood study of a wasps' nest, by Tadakazu, with a wasp perched on the top and 3 more on the side, the underside with several inlaid grubs, c1900, 2in (5cm) high.
£1,800–2,000 *S*

A Chinese wooden vase, the sides carved in imitation of bronze with landscape panels enclosed by keyfret borders, reserved on archaistic scroll grounds, Qianlong period, 16¼in (41.5cm) high.
£4,000–4,500 *S*

A Chinese bamboo brush pot, carved with 2 ladies standing by a table, 17thC, 5¾in (14.5cm) high.
£1,650–1,800 *S(HK)*

A Chinese bamboo libation cup, pierced and carved in varying relief as a gnarled pine trunk, Qing Dynasty, 6in (15cm) wide.
£1,750–2,000 *P*

A Japanese wooden sake vessel, c1880, 29in (73.5cm) high.
£350–400 *MLL*

A Japanese shop sign, in the form of a carved wood carp covered in negoro lacquer, 19thC, 39in (99cm) long.
£850–950 *SK(B)*

Negoro lacquer was originally made by the monks of Negoro temple, and is now the term for black and red lacquer of worn appearance.

Arms & Armour

A Japanese partial *tosei gusoku*, the 62 plate *suji kabuto* with three-lame *shikaro*, each side double-hinged and the interior partially lined in red lacquered leather, dated '2nd month 3rd era of Kyoho', 1718.
£8,500–9,500 *B&B*

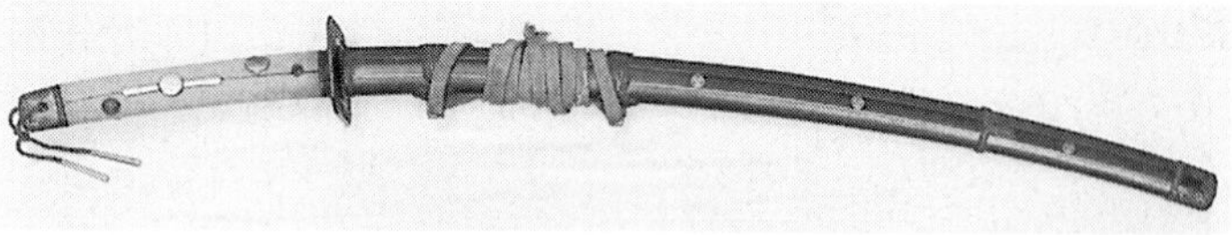

A Japanese sword *tachi*, with chamfered iron *tsuba* chiselled in relief with a dragon in clouds, signed 'Moriiye Tsukuru', possibly Hatakeda School, Bizen, 1190–1420, blade 27½in (70cm) long.
£2,500–2,750 *WAL*

A Japanese *tanegashima*, by Shigehide, engraved along its whole length with a dragon, clouds and a *Kaga-umebachi-mon* and inscription, the stock lacquered black and decorated with gold *hiramakie*, signed, slight damage, 18thC, 30½in (77.5cm) long.
£5,000–5,500 *S*

Tanegashima *is a matchlock musket.*

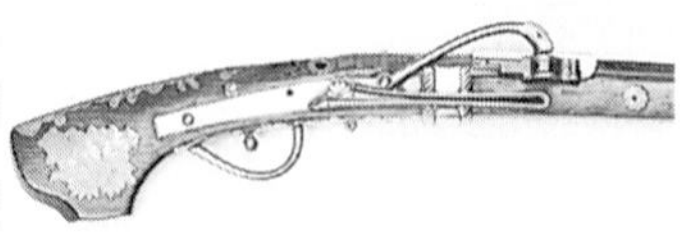

l. A Japanese matchlock gun, the sighted barrel with bulbous muzzle with brass foliage, minor damage, 19thC, barrel 41¼in (105cm) long.
£1,200–1,500 *Bon*

A Japanese black-lacquered retainer's hat *jingasa*, decorated with a red-lacquered dragon in carved relief, slight damage, 19thC, 17½in (44.5cm) diam.
£350–400 *WAL*

A Japanese bone-mounted *tanto* blade, 19thC, 7½in (19cm) long.
£120–140 *Bon*

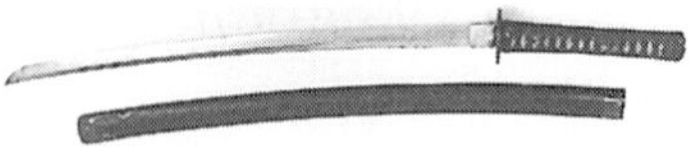

A Japanese *katana*, with silver *habaki*, the *tsuba* with gilt marine foliage, the signed gilt copper *fuchi-kashira* with dragons, 2 gilt floral *menuki*, in lacquer scabbard with gilt dragon *kojiri*, 19thC, 36in (91.5cm) long.
£1,300–1,500 *GSP*

A Japanese lacquered wood sword stand, Meiji period, late 19thC, 18in (45.5cm) wide.
£600–700 *HYD*

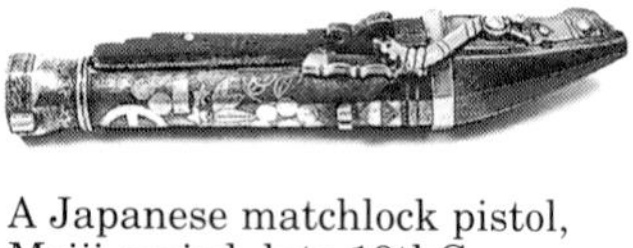

A Japanese matchlock pistol, Meiji period, late 19thC, 4½in (11.5cm) long.
£2,500–2,750 *GV*

A Japanese *tanto* blade, by Nagakatsu, 19thC, 8¾in (22cm) long.
£3,400–4,000 *S*

Tsuba

A Japanese *haruta tsuba*, in the form of a cartwheel with trailing leaves, Momoyama period, c1600, 3in (7.5cm) wide.
£520–600 *S*

A Japanese *higo tsuba*, in the form of a crane, its carved and pierced wings outstretched, the tips meeting at the head, making a floriform rim, Hayashi school, Edo period, 19thC, 3¼in (8cm) wide.
£350–400 *S*

A Japanese gold lacquer *tsuba*, decorated with 3 devils beating a gong and a drum by a tree, the edge and *seppadai* decorated in gold *hirame*, late 19thC, 4in (10cm) long.
£2,000–2,200 *CGC*

Furniture

A pair of Chinese elm cabinets, in 2 parts, both sections with 2 cupboard doors, Qing Dynasty, 18thC, 38in (96.5cm) wide.
£1,800–2,200 *SLN*

A Japanese black-lacquered *shodana*, with a cupboard between open shelves to the top and base, the corners and feet with carved brass mounts, decorated overall with scrolling peony and *yamashiro* and *kuwana* mon in gilt, with 3 boxes and covers all with the same decoration, late 19thC, 30in (76cm) wide.
£850–950 *WW*

A Japanese lacquer and parquetry table cabinet, Meiji period, late 19thC, 11½in (29cm) wide.
£450–500 *SPa*

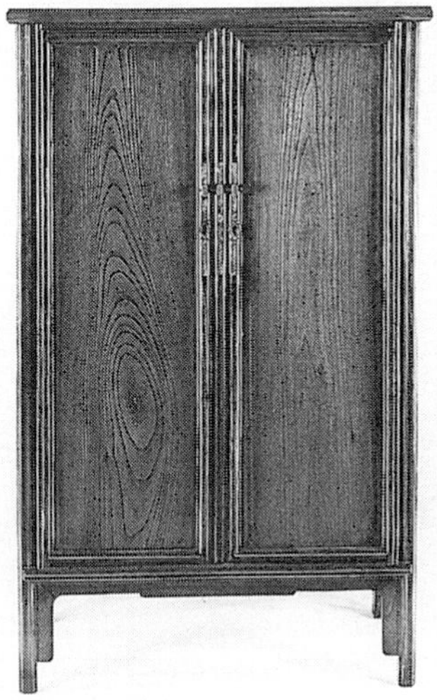

A Chinese elm cabinet, with 2 figured panelled doors opening to an interior with shelves and a pair of drawers, the doors separated by a removable stile, 18thC, 36in (91.5cm) wide.
£550–650 *SLN*

Please refer to pages 324 & 336 for Chinese and Japanese chronology charts.

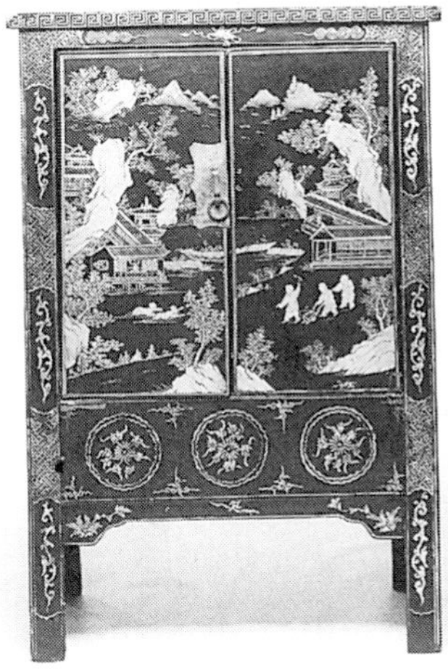

A Chinese black-lacquered and chinoiserie decorated cabinet, with 2 cabinet doors and raised on square legs, early 20thC, 39¾in (98.5cm) wide.
£450–550 *SLM*

A Chinese *zitan baitong* mounted table cabinet, with a pair of doors opening to an arrangement of short drawers, probably late 17thC, 13¾in (35cm) wide.
£5,500–6,500 *S(NY)*

A Japanese lacquered wood *shodana*, the shallow compartment across the top with 4 small doors and a deeper one across the bottom with 2 doors, 2 stepped shelves between, some damage, early 19thC, 38in (96.5cm) wide.
£2,500–3,000 *S*

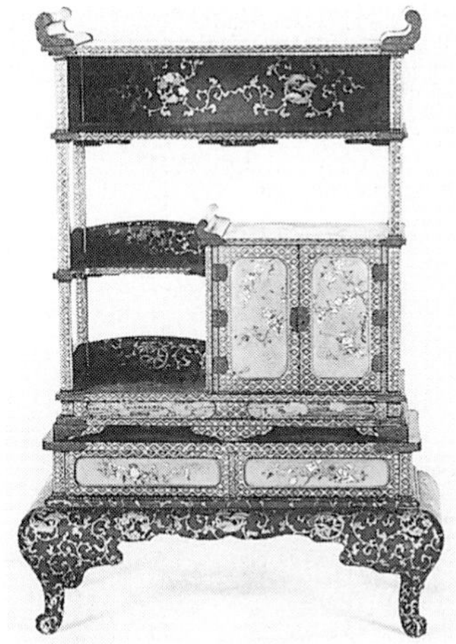

A Japanese gold-lacquered netsuke cabinet-on-stand, with shelves and a cupboard enclosed by a pair of panelled doors, carved and applied with birds perched in branches of wisteria in mother-of-pearl and stained bone, the stand with 2 drawers to the frieze similarly decorated, the whole painted with bamboo, prunus blossom and scrolling leaves in red and gilt, late 19thC, 29in (74cm) wide.
£800–900 *HSS/P*

A pair of Chinese *nanguan maoyi* elm chairs, with traces of original lacquer, c1800.
£1,500–2,000 *SK(B)*

Nanguan maoyi *are reception chairs for officials to meet guests and talk over business.*

A Chinese marble-inset hardwood armchair, with a rattan seat, the aprons carved with simple scrolls, the back and sides composed of scrolled bars with a mottled marble panel, 19thC.
£700–800 *P*

A Chinese *zitan* stand, the front and back with sunken panels, the top lifting off to reveal 2 small trays on either side of the central drawer, one forming the face of a central partitioned drawer, carved in relief with stylised *chilong* confronting *yin-yang* symbols, flanked by panels of single beasts, 19thC, 12½in (31.5cm) long.
£750–800 *P*

A Chinese hardwood side table, early 19thC, 35in (89.5cm) wide.
£1,100–1,250 *SPa*

A Chinese brown and gilt lacquer artist's painting table, decorated overall with landscape scenes with foliate motifs, each pedestal with a single drawer and a pair of doors, 19thC, 73in (185.4cm) wide.
£3,500–4,000 *S(NY)*

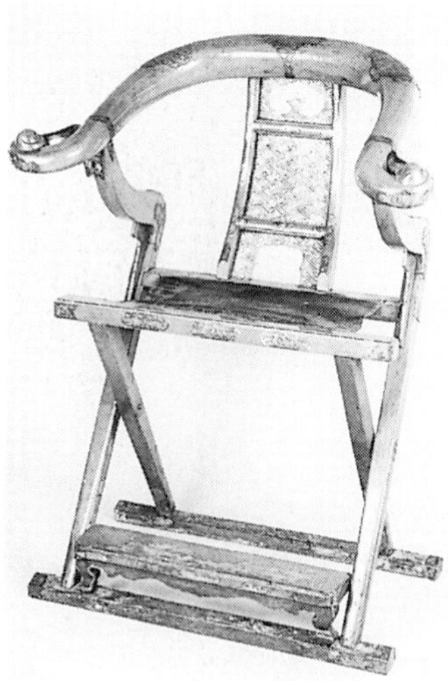

A Chinese priest's gilt-metal mounted red-lacquered wooden yoke-backed folding chair, the top-rail supported by a gilt back-splat carved with basketwork, the applied shaped mounts chased and chiselled with scrolling foliage reserved on a dotted ground, with a leather seat attached to straight legs pivoting to form an X-frame, with a platform foot-rest at the front, damaged, 19thC.
£650–750 *P*

A Chinese padouk wood jardinière stand, the marble top with mother-of-pearl inlay, c1890, 21in (53.5cm) wide.
£400–450 *ANT*

A Chinese export hardwood side table, the top with pierced flowerhead and branch frieze, with central carved recoiling dragon within a roundel, late 19thC, 38in (96.5cm) wide.
£450–500 *DN(H)*

A pair of Chinese bamboo corner shelves, with black lacquer surface, 19thC, 37in (94cm) wide.
£5,000–6,000 *S(NY)*

Insurance Values

Always insure your valuable antiques for what it would cost to replace with a similar item, regardless of the original price paid. Both dealers and auctioneers will provide a valuation service for a fee.

A pair of Chinese rosewood vase/plant stands, c1860, 13in (33cm) square.
£1,000–1,250 *BUSH*

A Chinese hardwood table, the incurved legs reinforced by brackets at their junctions with the double-edged top, inset with a panel of white-streaked reddish marble, late Qing Dynasty, early 19thC, 38in (96.5cm) diam.
£1,100–1,200 *P*

Inro

A Japanese black lacquer four-case *inro*, by Hara Yoyusai, decorated in *takamakie,* inlaid pewter and *aogai* with a maple tree on undulating ground, the interior of matt gold lacquer, similar design to reverse, c1800, 2½in (6.5cm) high.
£650–750 *S*

A Japanese lacquer *inro*, c1850, 3in (7.5cm) high.
£1,350–1,500 *MCN*

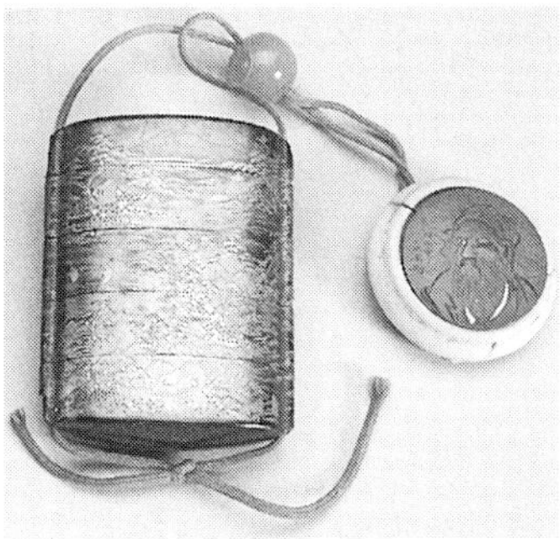

A Japanese *inro*, decorated in gold and coloured lacquer, 19thC, 3½in (9cm) long, with a signed *netsuke* and a carnelian *ojime*.
£400–500 *SK(B)*

A Japanese *inro*, inlaid in mother-of-pearl with peacocks on a cherry tree, 19thC, 4in (10cm) long, with an ivory *netsuke* in the form of a pair of pomegranates.
£600–700 *SK(B)*

Lacquer

The art of lacquering originated in China in Neolithic times, coming to the fore from the 5th century BC. It was exported to Japan from the 7th century AD. It is a highly skilled craft which is particularly suited to the decoration of small items such as inro.

l. A Japanese gold lacquer four-case *inro*, by Tachibana Gyokuzan, decorated in coloured *takamakie* with an octopus, ray and 2 large fish, 19thC, 3in (8cm) high, with wood *netsuke* of a *fugu*, the tail and fins incised.
£3,200–3,800 *S*

A Japanese lacquer four-case *inro*, the *saku* with pot-form seal, embellished in gold and silver *togidashi, hiramakie, takamakie, kirikane* and gold foil, one side with shaped panels containing landscapes, the reverse with a group of drums and drumsticks, signed Kajikawa, 19thC, 3½in (9cm) long, with a coral *ojime*.
£1,400–1,800 *S(NY)*

Netsuke

r. A wooden *netsuke* of a *sake* bottle, carved with the figure of Hotei in low relief on one side, signed 'Tanaka Minko', 18thC, 1½in (3.5cm) high.
£900–1,000 *S(NY)*

A Japanese ivory *netsuke*, comprising 11 puppies, each with inlaid eyes, tumbling over and chewing on an old straw hat and sandals, 19thC, 2in (5cm) long.
£1,200–1,300 *S(NY)*

A Japanese amber *netsuke*, depicting Hotei with a fan, covered with finely aged engravings, 19thC, 2in (5cm) high.
£280–320 *SK(B*

A Japanese ivory *netsuke* of a dog with a bell, 19thC, 1¼in (32mm) high.
£850–950 *SK(B)*

A Japanese wood *netsuke* of a *tengu* emerging from a cracked egg, signed 'Shigekatsu', 19thC, 1¾in (45mm) wide.
£4,200–4,600 *JWA*

A Japanese ivory *netsuke* of a *shishi*, 19thC, 1¾in (45mm) high.
£1,200–1,350 *HUR*

A shishi *is a Japanese mythical lion dog*

A wood, ivory and mother-of-pearl *netsuke*, depicting a Sambaso dancer, signed 'Hojitsu', 19thC, 1¾in (45mm) high.
£3,500–4,000 *JWA*

A Japanese ivory *netsuke*, depicting Raiden with his thunderdrum, 19thC, 2¼in (5.5cm) high.
£1,100–1,200 *HUR*

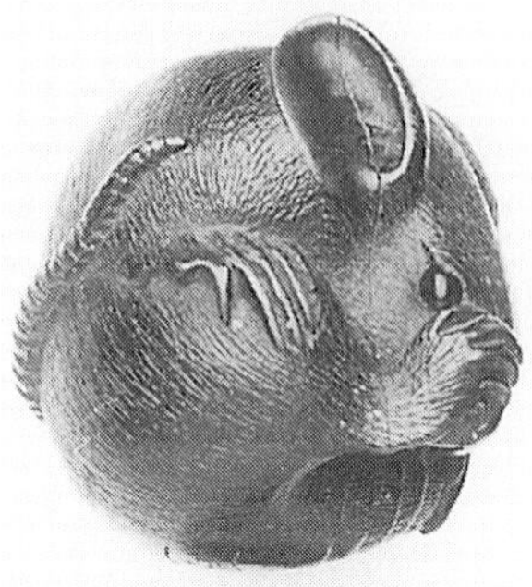

A Japanese carved wooden *netsuke*, in the form of a curled rat, his tail wrapped around his body and with one paw resting against his nose, the eyes inlaid, signed 'Masanao', Meiji period, late 19thC, 1½in (4cm) diam.
£600–700 *P*

A Japanese wood and ivory *netsuke*, depicting Hoeti in a relaxed posture, signed 'Akishige', late 19thC, 1½in (4cm) high.
£4,500–5,000 *JWA*

A Japanese lacquered wood *netsuke*, in the form of a flautist, with a gilt flute wearing a brightly coloured gown, with a separate purse hung from his waist forming a plug to one hole, Meiji period, late 19thC, 1½in (4.5cm) high.
£900–1,000 *P*

Snuff Bottles

A glass snuff bottle, with blue overlay curled vines, double gourds and furled leaves, with a butterfly, c1800, 2¼in (59mm) high.
£900–1,100 *S(HK)*

l. A green overlay glass snuff bottle, attributed to the Yangzhou School, carved on the front with a cat amongst flowers, a bird flying overhead, the reverse with geese, c1800, 2½in (6.5cm) high.
£1,500–1,700 *JWA*

r. A chalcedony snuff bottle, carved in low relief with a phoenix, perched on rocky outcrops beside tall pine, a full moon amongst wispy clouds overhead, mid-19thC, 2¼in (5.5cm) high, with glass stopper and green jade collar.
£950–1,100 *JWA*

An opaque black glass snuff bottle, attributed to the Beijing Palace workshops, painted in pastel enamels in a continuous scene of a flowering prunus tree, the neck further decorated with stylised waves, the coral stopper carved with a *chilong*, the base bearing a Guyuexuan mark, 18thC, 2in (52mm) high.
£3,500–4,000 *JWA*

A jade snuff bottle, the nephrite of greyish-green tones with a large deep brown coloured inclusion on front, carved from a natural pebble shape to represent a fruit, 18thC, 2½in (65mm) high.
£1,350–1,500 *JWA*

A scent wood snuff bottle, relief carved with 2 sages playing chess, and a scholar chanting poems by rocks, all set in a landscape of pine and bamboo, Daoguang period, 1821–50, 2¼in (5.5mm) high, with matching stopper.
£2,800–3,200 *S(NY)*

Scent wood, or sandalwood, is sometimes mistaken for bamboo. The strong fragrant smell is the key element that distinguishes it from other materials.

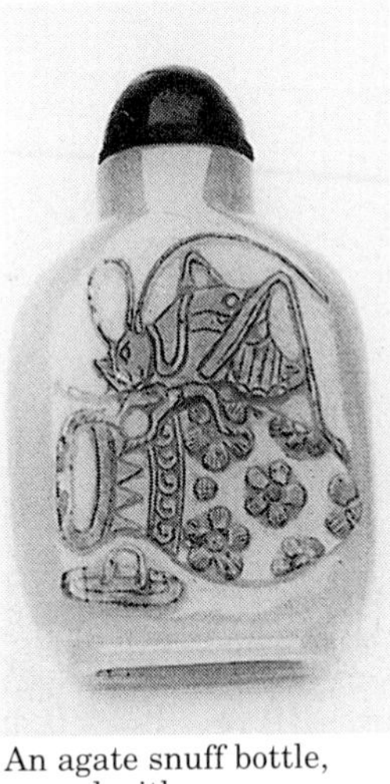

An agate snuff bottle, carved with a grasshopper perched on an overturned wine vat on a brown and off-white ground, 19thC, 2½in (6.5cm) high, with stopper.
£500–600 *P*

r. An inside-painted sepia glass snuff bottle, by Ye Zhongsan, painted on one side with Huang Chenyen riding a mule followed by a boy attendant, the reverse painted with a fisherman in a sampan, with red glass stopper, signed and dated '1924', 3in (7.5cm) high.
£260–300 *Bon*

A cinnabar lacquer double gourd-shaped snuff bottle, carved in relief on the lower lobe with 2 men in a sampan, below a phoenix emerging from clouds on the upper lobe, all reserved on a diaperwork ground, divided by a simulated looped cord at the waist, 19thC, later stopper, 2in (5cm) high.
£480–530 *P*

A blue overlay glass snuff bottle, carved to the milky-white ground with a prunus tree, a willow and *lingzhi* fungus in a landscape of rocks and distant mountains, 19thC, 2¼in (5.5cm) high.
£1,300–1,500 *S(NY)*

A caramel and milky-grey agate snuff bottle, the front carved from a caramel coloured inclusion with a bannerman riding a galloping horse, 19thC, 2½in (6.5cm) high, with matching stopper.
£850–1,000 *P*

A quartz snuff bottle, carved in relief on one side with a pine tree, the other carved to depict a bird among blossoms, late 19thC, 2¾in (7cm) high.
£275–350 *P*

A Japanese ivory snuff bottle, with a raised panel on either side depicting landscape scenes, all reserved on a red lacquer ground, four-character Qianlong mark, late 19thC, 2¾in (7cm) high.
£1,300–1,400 *S(NY)*

r. A clear quartz inside-painted snuff bottle, by Ye Zhongsan, painted with a scene of children dancing around a tree, signed and dated '1923', 2½in (6.5cm) high, with reticulated silver stopper.
£1,400–1,600 *JWA*

A Beijing glass snuff bottle, the bright yellow transparent body overlaid with opaque yellow vine and double gourd designs, with rose quartz stopper, 19thC, 3in (7.5cm) high.
£2,000–2,200 *P*

A Chinese inside-painted quartz snuff bottle, by Ye Zhongsan, with carved amethyst stopper, signed and dated for 1915, 2¾in (7cm) high.
£1,800–2,000 *JWA*

Robes

A Chinese man's semi-formal robe, the mid-blue ground woven in purple, white and green embroidered with dragons, cranes, Taoist and cosmic symbols in silk and gold thread, c1880.
£1,500–1,700 *P*

Storing Costume

Period costume should be stored flat, and shoulders, sleeves and folds padded with acid-free tissue paper.

A Japanese white silk kimono, decorated with blue flowers, 1930s.
£80–100 *ASG*

A Chinese woman's red silk semi-formal robe, embroidered in blue, white, green and black silk with gold thread butterflies, with pink silk lining, c1890.
£550–600 *P*

A Chinese woman's semi-formal robe, the purple damask silk with ivory silk border and sleeve bands embroidered in purple, blue and green silks, lined, c1890.
£400–450 *P*

A Japanese blue silk *haori*, decorated with white *shiburu* flowers, 1940s.
£275–325 *ASG*

Shiburu means tie-dyed.

A Chinese woman's informal robe, the blue silk ground embroidered with dragons, late 19thC.
£400–450 *S(S)*

A Japanese silk formal sash, embroidered with eagles in gold, red and green, 1940s, 77in (195.5cm) long.
£300–350 *ASG*

Textiles

A Chinese silk hanging, the yellow ground embroidered with 2 pairs of dragons and a flaming pearl, amid Buddhist emblems, precious objects, cloud scrolls and florets, Qing Dynasty, 18thC, 105½in (268cm) long.
£4,500–5,000 *S*

A Chinese Imperial embroidered silk panel, with a couched metallic gold dragon, the flaming pearl of wisdom, bats and clouds, Qing Dynasty, 1880–95, 34in (86.5cm) long.
£450–550 *SLN*

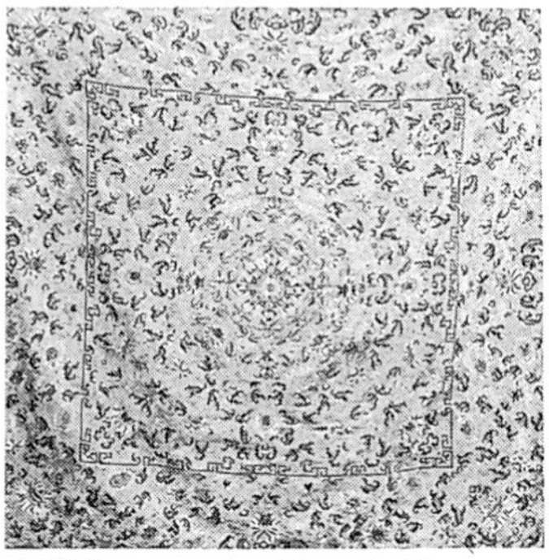

A Chinese embroidered silk panel, decorated with flowers on a yellow ground, Qing Dynasty, 1880–95, 32in (81.5cm) square.
£850–950 *SLN*

ISLAMIC

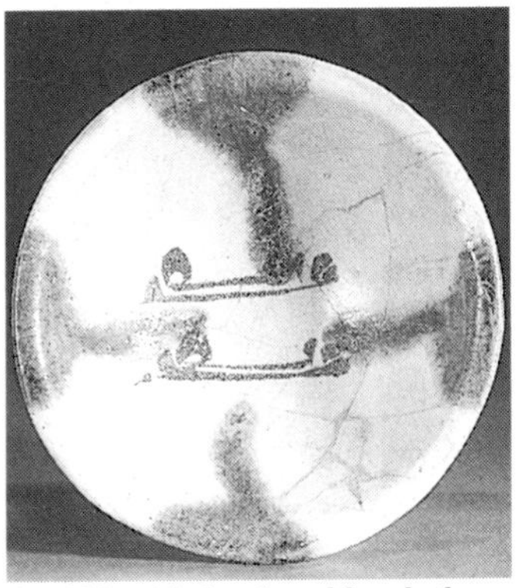

An Abbasid tin-glazed bowl, the interior grey ground painted in cobalt blue with the *kufic* inscription *baraka* (blessing) repeated twice, on a short foot, repaired, Mesopotamia, 9th century, 6in (15cm) diam.
£2,800–3,200 *C*

A Kashan turquoise model of a lion, with a single horn, some restoration, central Persia, early 13thC, 7in (18cm) high.
£2,200–2,500 *C*

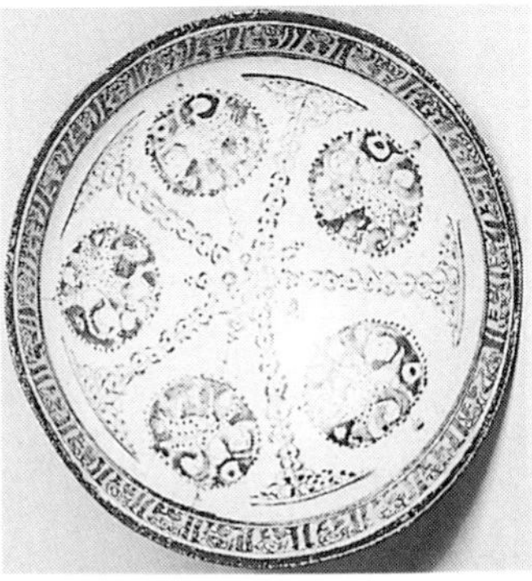

A Kashan lustre bowl, the interior painted with roundels of stylised harpies, divided by radiating strapwork, below a border of stylised *kufic* script, the exterior with a band of open scrollwork, repaired, circa 13thC, 8¾in (22cm) diam.
£1,600–1,800 *P*

r. A pottery jar, underglaze painted in cobalt blue with a design of vertical stripes, Persia, 13thC, 7¼in (18.5cm) high.
£1,800–2,200 *Bon*

A Nishapur bowl, the interior painted in manganese, yellow, white and tomato red slip with spiralling arabesques forming a stylised bird, repaired, north east Persia, 9th century, 8½in (21.5cm) diam.
£2,000–2,500 *C*

A Kashan pottery dish, the interior painted with an overall design of black, blue and green on a white ground depicting scrolling leafy tendrils issuing circular flower-heads, repaired, central Persia, early 13thC, 8½in (22cm) diam.
£8,000–9,000 *C*

A Raqqa lustre condiment dish, the 5 circular recesses grouped around a central hexagonal recess, each painted in yellow-brown lustre with spiralling foliage, chequer boards and stylised calligraphy, Syria, 13thC, 9¼in (23.5cm) diam.
£4,000–5,000 *C*

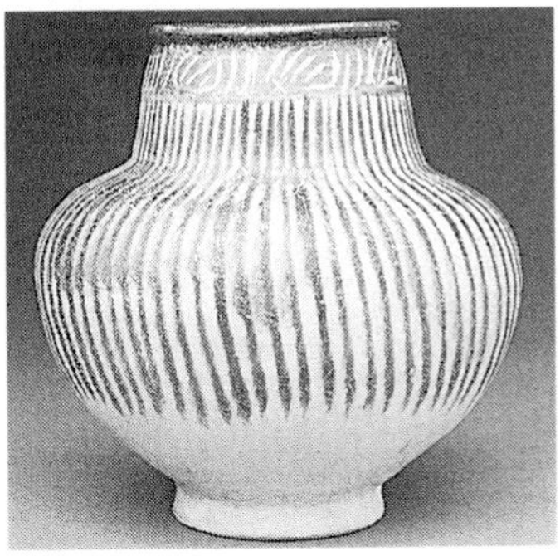

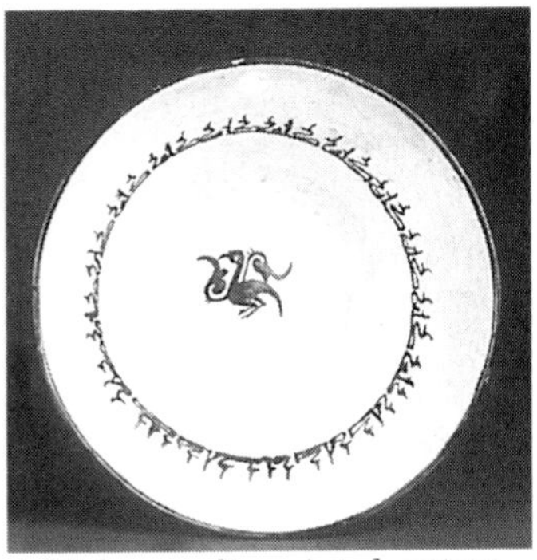

A Nishapur slip-painted pottery bowl, decorated in manganese and brown on a cream ground with a central bird motif, the sides with a continuous band of *kufic* inscription, Persia, 9th century, 9½in (24cm) diam.
£700–800 *Bon*

A Kashan tile, decorated with a single line of moulded cobalt blue calligraphy on a moulded ground of spiralling floral meander, highlighted with turquoise, the upper register with a moulded band of split palmettes, central Persia, mid-13thC, 12¼ x 11¼in (31 x 29cm).
£4,200–5,000 *C*

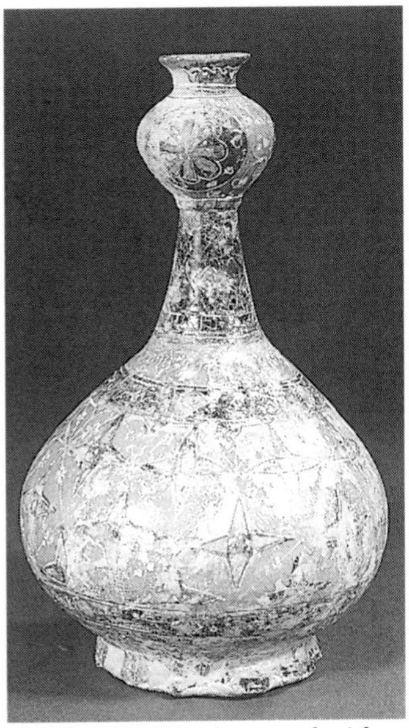

A pottery bottle, decorated with a broad band of linked stellar motifs, surface covered with a turquoise glaze, repaired, central Persia, late 13thC, 12in (30.5cm) high.
£3,800–4,200 *C*

A Timurid bowl, underglaze painted in cobalt blue, black and turquoise, the centre decorated with concentric rings, the sides with panels of abstract motif, Persia, late 14th/early 15thC, 7½in (18.5cm) diam.
£300–350 *Bon*

An Iznik pottery tankard, decorated in relief-red, cobalt blue and olive green outline on a turquoise ground, decorated with interlacing palmettes, the collar with a band of petal motifs, Turkey, c1590, 9in (23cm) high.
£6,000–6,500 *S*

An Iznik pottery dish, painted in blue, green, black and red with 2 confronting leaves enclosing a central tree motif and 2 carnations on leafy stems, the border with an ammonite scroll design, chips, early 17thC, 12¼in (31cm) diam.
£1,800–2,000 *WW*

Iznik ceramics

Iznik pottery appeals to both serious collectors of Islamic art and to those attracted by its obvious decorative appeal. Rarity and condition are still the most important factors for determining prices at the top end of the market, but even at the lower end prices have increased in recent years.

A Safavid blue and white pottery bowl, decorated with mythological beasts and flowerheads, the interior with a medallion reserved with a crane in flight, Persia, early 17thC, 13in (33cm) diam.
£2,200–2,500 *Bon*

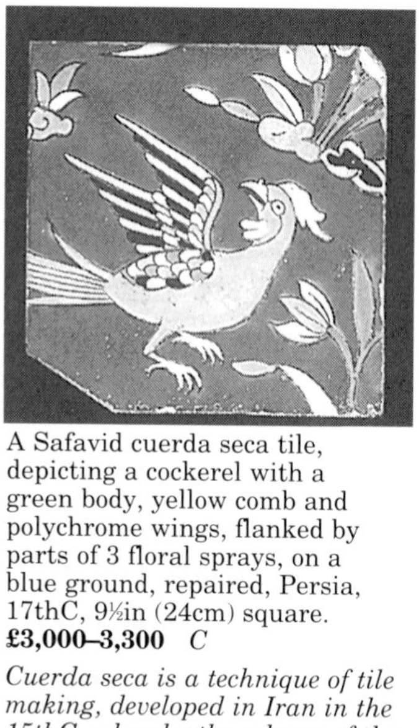

A Safavid cuerda seca tile, depicting a cockerel with a green body, yellow comb and polychrome wings, flanked by parts of 3 floral sprays, on a blue ground, repaired, Persia, 17thC, 9½in (24cm) square.
£3,000–3,300 *C*

Cuerda seca is a technique of tile making, developed in Iran in the 15thC, whereby the colours of the design were separated by an oily substance which leaves a brownish outline.

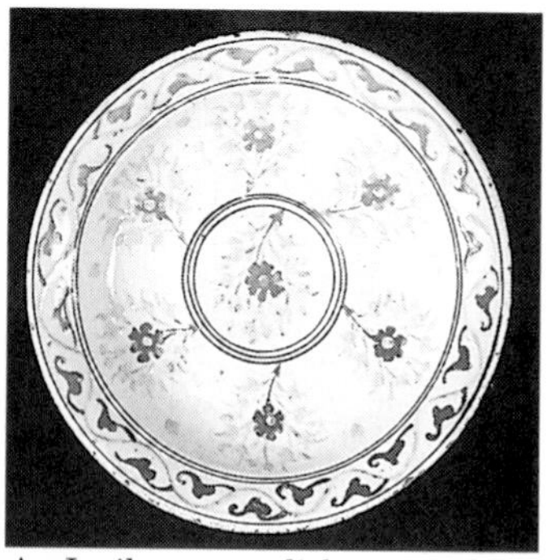

An Iznik pottery dish, painted in lavender-blue and brown slip on a white ground, the rim decorated with a garland of half palmettes, Turkey, c1575, 12in (30.5cm) diam.
£4,500–5,500 *S*

A Safavid polychrome dish, the interior decorated in cobalt blue, ochre, green, tomato red and black on a white ground, depicting a flowering tree and other plants, with a dotted lattice motif around the rim and cavetto, Kubachi, early 17thC, 13½in (34.5cm) diam.
£1,400–1,600 *S(NY)*

A Qajar pottery flask, painted with sprays of vivid coloured flowers on a white ground, late 19thC, 6¼in (16cm) high.
£100–120 *FW&C*

l. A Kütahya pottery pilgrim flask, decorated in cobalt blue with stylised floral motifs and circular abstract designs, Turkey, early 18thC, 5¾in (17.5cm) high.
£4,500–5,000 *S*

Prices for Kütahya have increased in the past 12 months, particularly for pieces from the 18thC.

MILLER'S COMPARES . . .

I An Iznik pottery jug, decorated in cobalt blue, green and red, depicting tulips interspersed with small blue flowers, above and below a stylised border, Turkish, 17thC, slight damage, 9¾in (25cm) high.
£1,800–2,000 *P*

II An Iznik pottery jug, decorated with floral sprays in red, green and cobalt blue above and below narrow borders, restored rim chip, Turkish, 17thC, 8¾in (22cm) high.
£500–550 *P*

The output of the Iznik potteries declined in quality during the 17thC as they became swamped with orders from palaces and mosques. An example of this is illustrated by the 2 items pictured above. *Item I* **is more elegantly potted, has a white ground and the flowers are clearly painted without colour run. The floral design on** *Item II*, **on the other hand, does not stand out as clearly from the ground and the colours have run. The broken rim further affects the value.** *P*

A Qajar polychrome tile, moulded in relief, reserved in white and finely painted in aubergine, turquoise, grey and black on a cobalt blue ground, depicting a prince on horseback, a bird in flight above him, Teheran, late 19thC, 13¾ x 10½in (35 x 26.5cm).
£1,600–1,800 *S(NY)*

Two Qajar polychrome tiles, moulded in relief depicting robed figures on the scrolling foliate ground, with inscribed border at the base, each fitted with metal mounts forming hinges, 19thC, 7¾ x 17½in (19.5 x 44.5cm).
£900–1,000 *P*

A post-Sassanian wheel-cut clear glass flask, the body with a honeycomb lattice of oval depressions, one rim chip, north east Persia, 8th century, 3½in (9cm) high.
£4,000–5,000 *C*

A Khorassan bronze inkwell, the sides engraved and inlaid with a lattice of copper and silver inlaid strapwork enclosing small floral panels, the underside engraved with animals around a central bird roundel, north east Persia, 12thC, 4in (10cm) high.
£5,000–6,000 *C*

l. A Seljuk brass mortar, with a single bovine mask handle, the sides decorated with 6 lotus buds in relief and engraved with floral medallions, with a guilloche motif on the base and rim, 12th/13thC, 7¼in (18.5cm) diam.
£3,000–3,300 *S(NY)*

A Khorassan bronze double spouted oil lamp, with red and green patination to the lobed and domed cover, the handle with finial in the form of a standing lion, foot probably associated, north east Persia, 12thC, 7in (18cm) high.
£3,200–3,800 *C*

A Persian polychrome enamel gold-covered Kalian cup, decorated with 2 oval panels depicting scenes of maidens and children, divided by large clusters of flowers, above and below narrow bands of floral swags, damaged and repaired, 19thC, 2in (50mm) high.
£2,000–2,200 *P*

A Kalian cup is part of a hookah, or hubble-bubble pipe.

'The Battle of the Clans' an illustrated page from Nizami's *Layla va Majnun*, gouache with gold on paper, Turkoman, c1500, 7 x 4in (18 x 10cm).
£10,000–12,000 *S*

This Turkoman miniature is notable for the highly unusual manner in which the vegetation in the background has been painted with the flat foliate forms of a piece of illumination, rather than a more realistic respresentation.

An Ottoman gilt-copper bowl, the exterior decorated in relief with interlaced radiating buds, reserved scrolling vines against a stippled ground encircling the rim, an engraved and stippled rosette in the centre, 19thC, 5in (12.5cm) diam.
£3,500–3,800 *S(NY)*

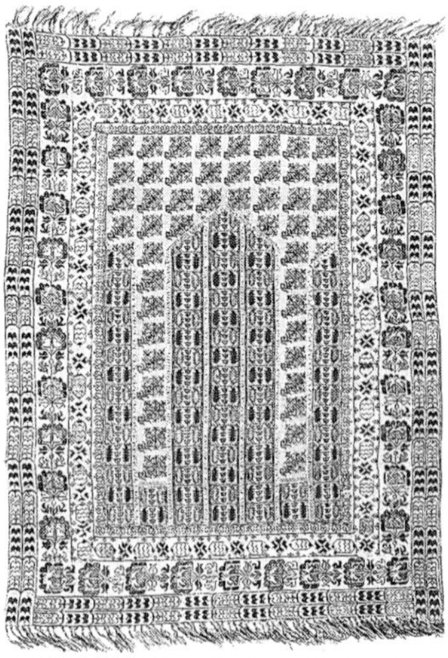

A Qibleh niche design cloth, the embroidered linen and cotton strips and pieces designed with stylised flower and leaf motifs, Turkish, c1890, 49¾ x 37¾in (126 x 96cm).
£320–350 *P*

l. An Ottoman embroidered turban cover cloth, the wool ground worked in silk chain stitch and flat silver metal thread strip, probably palace workshop, Istanbul, Turkey, c1800, 47in (118cm) square.
£8,000–9,000 *S*

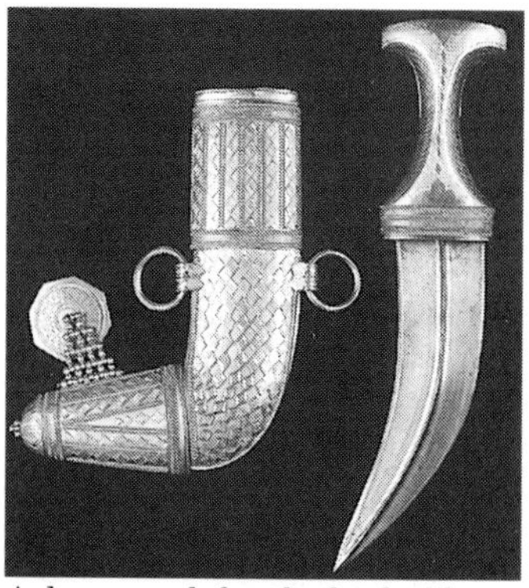

A dagger and sheath, the double-sided curving blade with central ridge, solid gold hilt engraved with bands of diamond shapes on the grip, signed on reverse 'Muhammad b. Banu', the red leather sheath mounted with bands of applied gold lozenges divided by gold beading and bands of filigree, gold attachment bands, southern Arabia, early 20thC, 10½in (27cm) long.
£9,500–10,500 *C*

l. A Qur'an manuscript on paper, with gold and polychrome illumination, decorated with flowers and pagodas framing prayers, in original morocco binding, restoration to page edges, China, 18thC, 7¾ x 5¼in (19 x 13.5cm).
£7,000–8,000 *C*

Although prices for Qur'ans are quite low at present, unusual and highly decorated examples, such as this Chinese piece, can make very good prices.

A bone-inlaid wood hinged games board, the exterior with inlays forming a chess board, the interior decorated as a backgammon board, with motifs of stylised chrysanthemum heads, leafy tulip tendrils and flower motifs, stained green inlaid details, Turkey, 18thC, each panel 20½in (52cm) long.
£11,000–12,000 *S*

This is an extremely rare and fine example of Ottoman woodworking. The decorative motifs do not display any trace of the later Ottoman baroque taste and the games board can therefore be dated prior to the second half of the 18thC, which saw the wholesale arrival of this European influence. The floral inlays are reminiscent of the stylised motifs of the 17thC.

ARCHITECTURAL ANTIQUES

Brass

A pair of brass finials, 19thC, 6½in (16.5cm) high.
£90–110 *ASM*

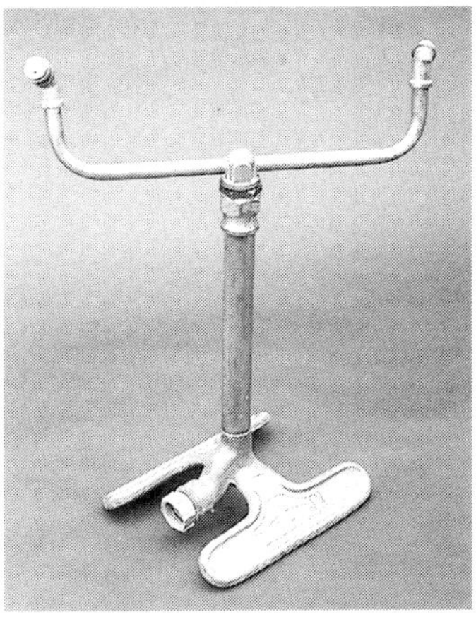

r. A brass and iron sprinkler, with green paint to base, 19thC, 13in (33cm) high.
£40–50 *Riv*

A brass sundial, the square plate decorated with Biblical figures, c1920, 13in (33cm) high.
£300–350 *Riv*

Bronze

A pair of Napoleon III bronze and gilt-bronze chenets, each with a lion recumbent upon a draped base, with pine cone finials, turned feet and wrought iron fire bars, 17½in (44.5cm) wide.
£2,600–3,000 *AH*

A bronze figural fountain, in the form of a pelican with wings outstretched, stamped 'Bruno Neri', late 19thC, 28½in (72.5cm) high.
£3,800–4,200 *S(NY)*

Miller's is a price GUIDE not a price LIST

A patinated bronze sundial, late 18thC, 13in (33cm) square.
£425–475 *SPU*

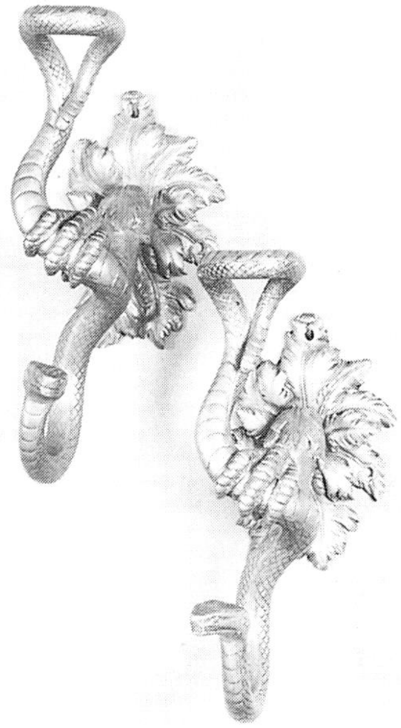

A pair of gilt-bronze curtain ties, each in the form of a cockerel's foot clutching a writhing serpent, late 19thC, 12in (30.5cm) high.
£350–400 *P*

A set of 4 William IV bronze newel post lights, the stems fluted and decorated with acanthus leaf and bead collars, the centre decorated with anthemia, on leaf-cast octagonal bases, c1835, 26¾in (68cm) high.
£3,200–3,500 *S*

A French bronze group, depicting 3 putti and a dog supporting a shallow reeded urn, late 18thC/early 19thC, 32in (81.5cm) high.
£9,200–10,000 *SWO*

A bronze sundial plate, signed 'Tho Eayre, Kettering', 18thC, 14in (35.5cm) diam, on a Portland stone pedestal, 19thC.
£5,000–5,500 *S(S)*

Iron

A cast iron Renaissance style fountain, c1850, 46½in (118cm) high.
£1,700–2,000 *NOA*

A cast iron balcony, the uprights pierced with flowerheads flanking panels pierced with fairies holding baskets on their heads, late 19thC, 121in (302cm) wide.
£1,600–1,800 *S(S)*

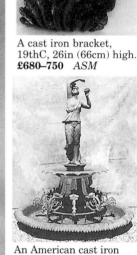

A cast iron bracket, 19thC, 26in (66cm) high.
£680–750 *ASM*

A cast iron boot scraper, c1900, 10in (25.5cm) wide.
£50–55 *OCH*

l. A French Gothic style cast iron door, of lancet form, with panelled lower section beneath tracery decoration, c1860, 79in (200cm) high.
£750–820 *S(S)*

A Victorian cast iron fountain, in the form of a neo-classical monument surmounted by an urn, on a plinth moulded with a spray of flowers, 105in (267cm) high.
£1,600–2,000 *DN*

Ex-Lord Lloyd-Webber collection.

An American cast iron figural fountain, the basin with stiff-leaf decoration on a base of scrolling volutes, surmounted by a smaller basin topped by a semi-draped female figure, c1880, 58in (147cm) high.
£2,800–3,200 *S(NY)*

A pair of wrought iron gates, the 2 arched panels within a border of flowering scrolls decorated with figures of squirrels, birds, monkeys and panthers, c1910, 72in (183cm) high.
£5,500–6,000 *S(NY)*

r. A pair of French cast iron lamp posts, the fluted columns with stiff-leaf decoration and cast with masks, surmounted by replaced tapering cylindrical lanterns, pierced with foliage and with crenellated castle chimney, c1870, 197in (500cm) high.
£7,000–8,000 *S*

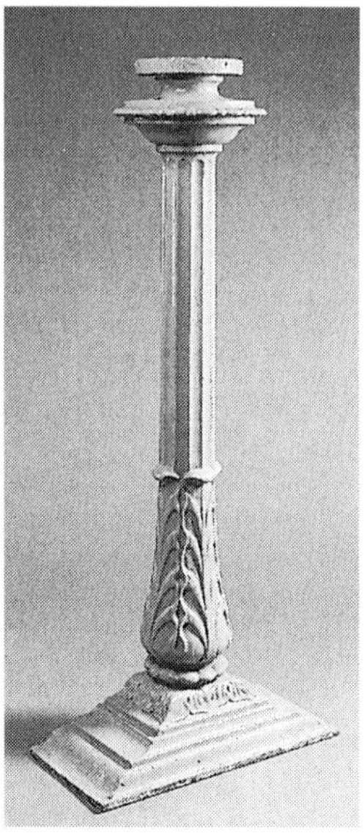

r. A set of 7 cast iron gas light supports, each with a fluted column and leaf-cast base, on a stepped plinth, 19thC, 55½in (140cm) high.
£600–700 *DN*

Five cast iron architectural masks, comprising 3 classical female and 2 bearded male masks, late 19thC, 21in (53.5cm) high.
£3,500–4,000 *S(NY)*

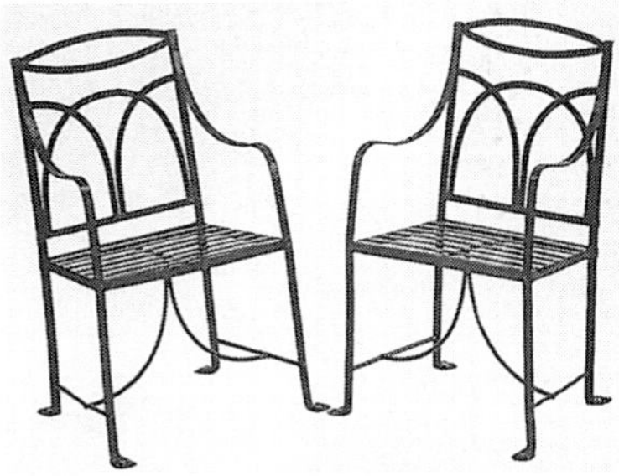

A pair of Regency iron garden armchairs, with slatted metal seats and stylised paw pattern feet, 38in (96.5cm) high.
£600–700 *CAG*

A Coalbrookdale cast iron garden seat, with Fern and Blackberry pattern, c1880, 60in (152.5cm) wide.
£800–900 *RAW*

A pair of cast iron campana-shaped garden urns, with mask headed scrolled handles, the body with a frieze of cornucopiae within scrolled surrounds, on foliate socle, late 19thC, 24in (61cm) high.
£750–850 *AH*

A Victorian cast iron garden seat, with branch and leaf design, 36in (91.5cm) wide.
£1,000–1,100 *RBB*

A Victorian cast iron plant stand, with 4 graduated semi-elliptical tiers pierced with scrolling leaves, on lion mask and paw feet, 99in (251.5cm) high.
£3,200–3,500 *DN*

Lead

l. A William and Mary lead cistern, cast with a fruiting vine over 2 cartouche-shaped panels, dated '1694', 26in (66cm) wide.
£1,100–1,200 *HYD*

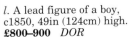

A lead cistern, with bead-and-reel border, the panelled front cast with cornucopiae and flowers above a sun mask and the figure of St George slaying the dragon, above a satyr mask, damaged, 18thC, 24in (61cm) wide.
£1,750–2,000 *DN*

l. A lead figure of a boy, c1850, 49in (124cm) high.
£800–900 *DOR*

Marble

A white marble figure of Lucretia, plunging a dagger into her naked breast, c1700, 41in (102cm) wide.
£3,200–3,500 *S(S)*

A marble figure of a spaniel, seated beside a basket amidst roses, wearing a collar inscribed 'Jessie', signed 'M. Muldoon & Co Lou L.N.', late 19thC, 29in (73.5cm) high.
£7,700–8,500 *S(NY)*

A French statuary marble bust of a lady, by Charles Henri Joseph Cordier, wearing a bandeau and with her hair in ringlets, weathered, dated '1856', 30in (76cm) high.
£900–1,100 *Bon(C)*

A white marble fountain, in the form of a cherub and a sea creature, c1860, 41in (104cm) high.
£4,250–4,750 *DRU*

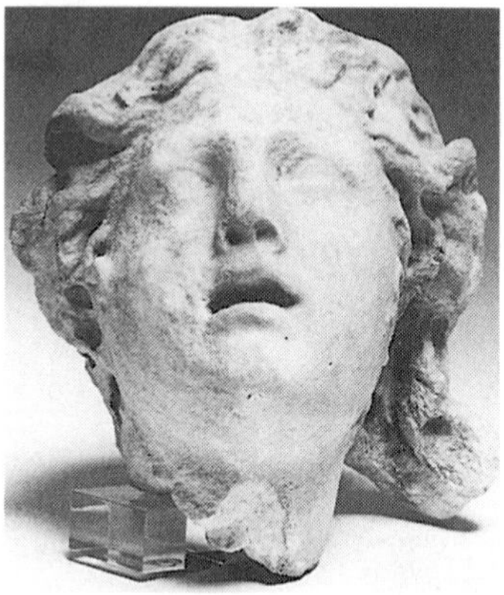

An Italian white marble carved head of a young woman, with flowing locks, weathered, early 19thC, 8¾in (22cm) high.
£520–580 *P*

r. A white marble classical garden urn, with plain bulbous body and turned footrim, on an octagonal pedestal, c1900, 53in (134.5cm) high.
£1,700–2,000 *CAG*

Pottery

Two treacle-glazed stoneware figures of seated bears, with paws outstretched, perhaps to support a log as a seat, damaged, 19thC, 42½in (108cm) high.
£500–600 *DN*

A Victorian stoneware architectural frieze, decorated in high relief with masks and ribbon-tied swags of fruit beneath facsimiles of Victorian pennies, dated '1882', 134in (340cm) wide.
£1,300–1,500 *S(S)*

This frieze is reputed to have come from Old Scotland Yard in London.

l. A pair of glazed earthenware sphinxes, each wearing elaborate headdress, signed 'Emil Muller', early 20thC, 45in (104cm) wide.
£7,500–9,000 *S(S)*

r. A Victorian brown glazed stoneware planter, moulded with laurel swags on spiral lobed column, impressed mark 'T. Knowles Ltd, Darwen', 35½in (90cm) high.
£200–250 *P(G)*

Stone

A stone model of a reclining lion, on a rectangular base, 17thC, 30½in (77.5cm) wide.
£1,600–1,800 *SLM*

A carved stone model of a lion, with flowing mane, standing on a rocky outcrop, on a rectangular base, 19thC, 60in (152.5cm) long.
£10,000–12,000 *DRU*

A pair of sandstone models of a seated cat and dog, on rectangular plinths and block bases, 19thC, 27¼in (69cm) high.
£380–420 *WL*

A stone capital, carved with leaf scrolls above egg-and-tongue beading and foliage, damaged, early 19thC, 51¼in (130cm) wide.
£650–800 *P(W)*

A Cotswold stone capital, 18thC, 34in (86.5cm) diam.
£340–360 *RAW*

A carved stone head of a man wearing a cap, damaged, 18thC, 20in (61cm) high.
£600–650 *DN*

A pair of limestone columns, 19thC, 127in (322.5cm) high.
£3,500–4,000 *RECL*

A reconstituted stone figure of a putto astride a drum, 19thC, 36in (91.5cm) high.
£2,800–3,200 *DRU*

A pair of reconstituted stone harpy eagles, c1920, 20in (51cm) high.
£750–850 *RAW*

A pair of limestone roof bosses, each carved in the form of a grotesque beast, on square bases, 19thC, 11in (28cm) high.
£1,400–1,600 *S(S)*

Terracotta

A Victorian terracotta roof finial, 23in (58.5cm) high.
£60–80 *DOR*

A terracotta garden orb, 19thC, with a wrought iron base, 20thC, 22½in (57cm) high.
£200–240 *ASM*

A terracotta grotto chair, 19thC, 42in (106.5cm) high.
£1,100–1,200 *Riv*

r. A terracotta garden urn, on a pedestal base moulded with laurel wreaths, 19thC, 39in (99cm) high.
£320–380 *EH*

A pair of terracotta garden seats, the supports in the form of 4 winged lions, 19thC, 15¾in (40cm) square.
£2,600–3,000 *P(NE)*

Wood

A pair of Victorian wooden porch brackets, with applied fretwork, 36in (91.5cm) high.
£220–250 *ASM*

A pair of carved wood capitals, mid-19thC, 9in (23cm) high.
£220–240 *Riv*

A carved elm heraldic mount, with the coat-of-arms of the Royal House of Stuart, late 17thC, 17¼in (44cm) wide.
£1,600–1,800 *P*

A stack of oak parquet floor blocks, c1930, each block 3in (7.5cm) wide.
£15–20 per sq yd *RECL*

l. A wooden door head, 19thC, 85in (216cm) wide.
£550–650 *RAW*

Bathroom Fittings

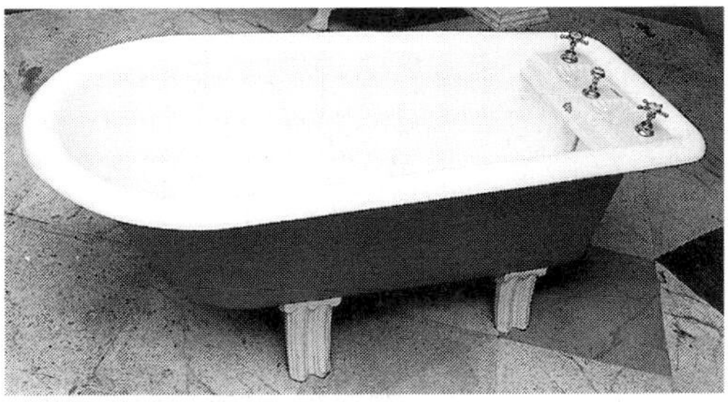

A Victorian roll-top bath, with porcelain soap dishes, and plunger waste, 62in (157.5cm) long.
£1,500–1,800 *WRe*

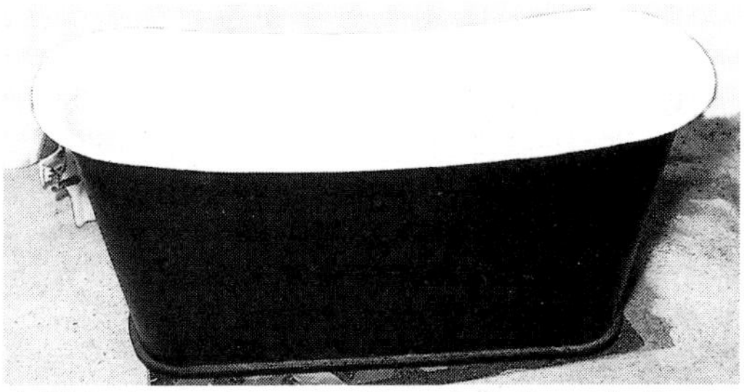

A Victorian cast iron double-ended slipper bath, 60in (152.5cm) long.
£2,500–3,000 *WRe*

A cast iron roll top bath, with lion's paw feet, c1880, 64in (162.5cm) long.
£1,200–1,300 *DOR*

A Shank's bath, with canopy shower, c1910, 72in (183cm) long.
£7,000–8,000 *POSH*

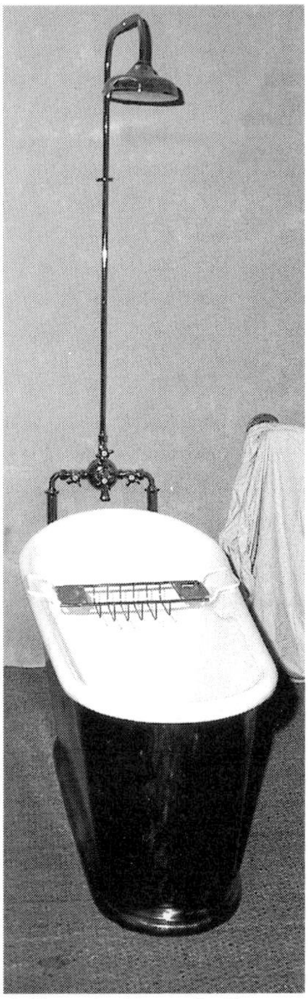

A French slipper bath with shower, c1900, 60in (152.5cm) long.
£2,500–3,000 *POSH*

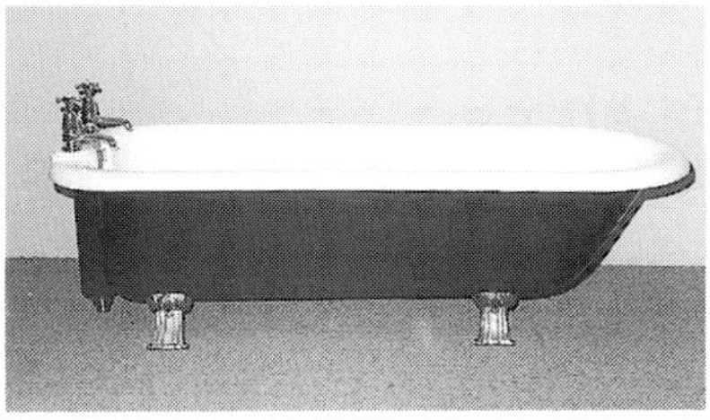

A cast iron bath, by John Bolding, c1920, 82in (208.5cm) long.
£1,800–2,000 *POSH*

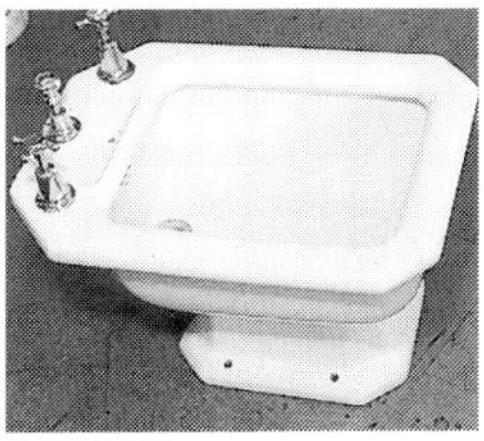

A Pyramid white porcelain bidet, with brass taps, c1930, 21in (53.5cm) wide.
£200–250 *NOST*

A Wedgwood blue and white earthenware washbasin, transfer-printed with Chinese Temple pattern, with brass drain collar, impressed mark, slight damage, c1830, 13¾in (35cm) diam.
£230–280 *SK*

A Johnson Bros Pyramid bidet, c1930, 22in (56cm) wide.
£250–300 *POSH*

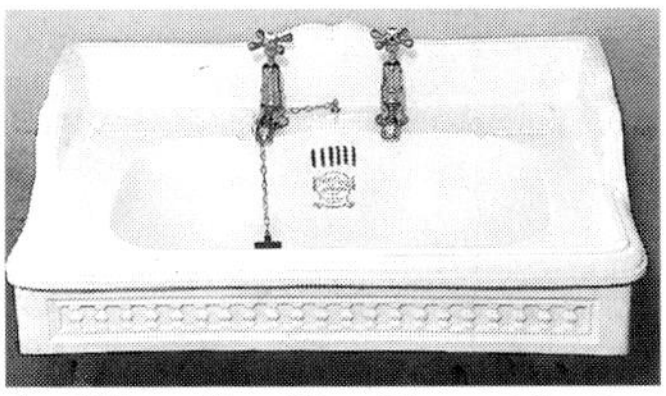

An Edwardian Shank's washbasin, with brass taps, on a cast iron bracket, 27in (68.5cm) wide.
£700–800 *NOST*

l. A French barber's marble sink top, with oak and pine base, c1900, 43in (109cm) high.
£1,500–1,600 *DOR*

A Simplicitas blue and white transfer-printed lavatory pan, by Doulton & Co, London and Paisley, c1890, 17in (43cm) high.
£450–500 *NOST*

A marble-topped mahogany washstand, with original brass fittings, c1910, 32in (81.5cm) wide.
£1,000–1,100 *NOST*

An Ogee porcelain washbasin, c1920, 29in (73.5cm) high.
£110–140 *RAW*

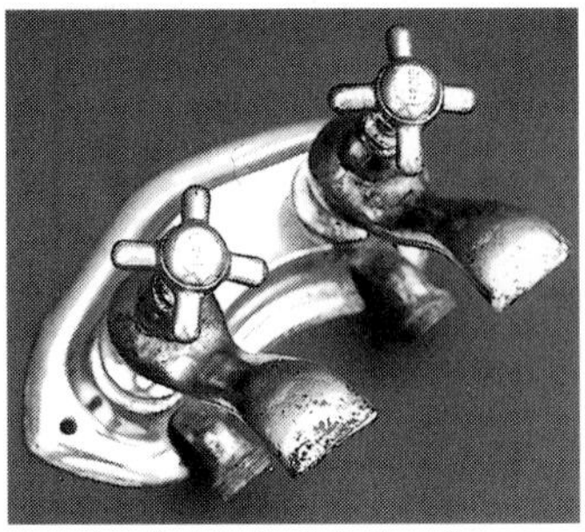

A pair of nickel-plated and ceramic bath taps, late 19thC, 9in (23cm) wide.
£80–90 *Riv*

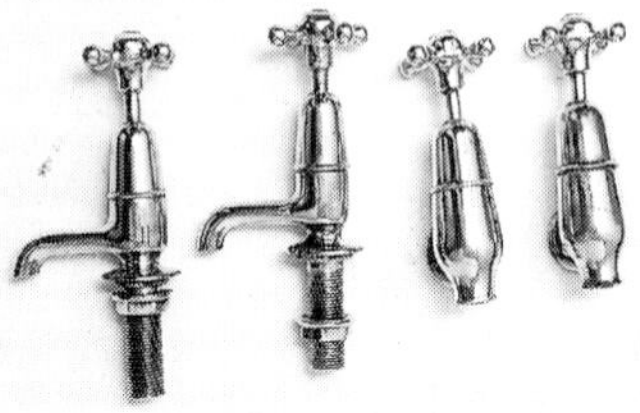

Two pairs of brass bath and wash basin taps, with pottery heads, c1920, 6in (15cm) high.
£80–90 per pair *HEM*

A royal blue bathroom suite, comprising a bidet, lavatory and wash basin, late 19thC, wash basin 25in (63.5cm) wide.
£600–700 *DOR*

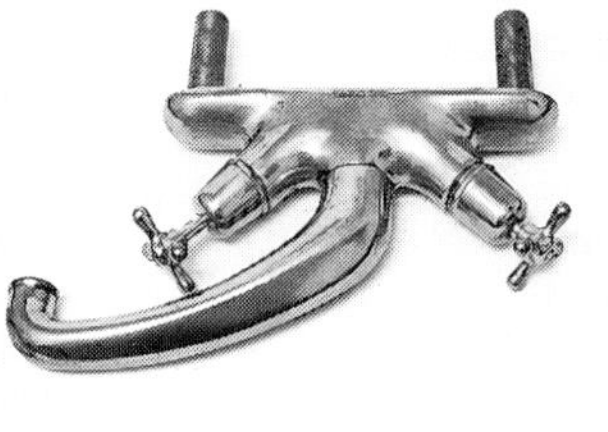

A set of kitchen mixer taps, on a block base, c1960, 9in (23cm) wide.
£60–65 *HEM*

A walnut towel rail, c1880, 19in (48.5cm) wide.
£90–100 *MLL*

A pair of brass and copper long reach pillar taps, c1930, 10in (25.5cm) high.
£65–75 *HEM*

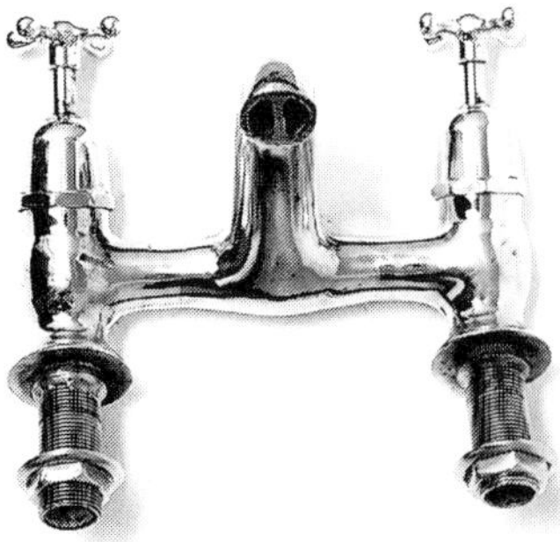

A set of brass mixer taps, c1930, 6in (15cm) wide.
£60–65 *HEM*

Doors & Door Furniture

A Georgian pine six-panelled door, 78in (198cm) high.
£120–130 *RAW*

A Georgian pine six-panelled door, 85in (216cm) high.
£130–160 *DOR*

A carved oak six-panelled door, the upper panels with portraits in Elizabethan dress, above 2 carvings of the Rock of Ages, with dragon scroll carved panel above 2 further bust portraits, 19thC, 77¼in (196cm) high.
£650–720 *P(NW)*

A Victorian pine plank door, 71in (180.5cm) high.
£45–55 *RAW*

A late Victorian wooden screen door, 80in (203cm) high.
£330–360 *A&A*

A pair of brass door knobs, c1860, 2½in (6.5cm) diam.
£80–90 *HEM*

r. A brass hinge, c1890, 4¼in (11cm) wide.
£45–50 *DRU*

A Victorian brass bell pull, 4½in (11.5cm) diam.
£140–160 *DOR*

A brass bell push, c1890, 3½in (9cm) wide.
£30–40 *HEM*

A cast iron door knocker, c1860, 9in (23cm) high.
£50–60 *HEM*

A rimlock, key and keep, c1890, 4¼in (11cm) wide.
£40–50 *HEM*

Fireplaces & Accessories

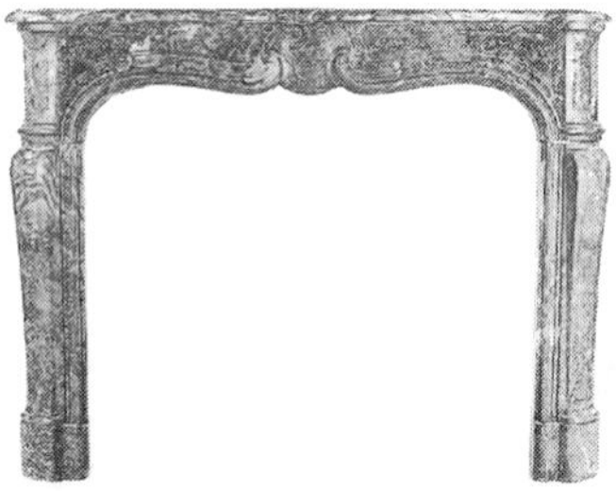

A Louis XV marble fire surround, the panel moulded frieze centred by a rococo cartouche, the jambs modelled as scrolled panel pilasters, some damage, mid-18thC, 56¼in (143cm) wide.
£3,000–3,300 *Bon(C)*

A Georgian pine overmantel, the breakfront top with the frieze carved in high relief with fruit and foliage flanked by bellflowers, the dog-leg uprights above carved volutes and flowerheads, c1770, 55in (140cm) wide.
£4,200–4,650 *S(S)*

A George III marble fire surround, with early Victorian cast iron grate, fire surround 71in (180.5cm) wide.
Fire surround £7,000–8,000
Grate £1,400–1,500 *NOST*

A Bath stone Gothic revival fire surround, the inverted breakfront shelf above the Tudor arch aperture, the jambs modelled as half columns with faceted tapered capitals, raised on block feet, mid-19thC, 74¾in (190cm) wide.
£2,500–3,000 *Bon(C)*

A pine fire surround, c1860, 48in (122cm) wide.
£280–320 *TPC*

A Victorian rococo style red marble fire surround, 71in (180.5cm) wide.
£1,700–1,900 *BIG*

A Victorian carved oak fire surround, with swan neck pediment over mirrored shelving supported by caryatids, the surround with dentil and acanthus moulding on carved Ionic jambs, 84in (215cm) wide.
£3,000–3,300 *EH*

A carved pine fire surround and overmantel, with mirror back, c1880, 62in (157.5cm) wide.
£1,200–1,500 *BAS*

A late Victorian brick fire surround, 42in (106.5cm) wide.
£240–280 *TPC*

A pine fire surround, with mirror back, late 19thC, 68in (172.5cm) wide.
£1,500–1,800 *RAW*

A late Victorian decorated slate fire surround, with cast iron grate and original tiles, 62in (157.5cm) wide.
Fire surround £450–550
Grate £350–450
Tiles £150–200 *NOST*

A Victorian white and red marble fire surround, with cast iron grate and original tiles, 69in (175.5cm) wide.
Fire surround £1,000–1,200
Grate £350–400
Tiles £150–200 *NOST*

A Victorian pine fire surround, with cast iron grate, 63½in (161.5cm) wide.
Fire surround £550–650
Grate £450–500 *NOST*

A cast iron hob grate, with serpentine bars, 18thC, 39in (99cm) wide.
£800–900 *WRe*

A cast iron hob grate, with splayed jambs, c1820, 36in (91.5cm) wide.
£900–1,000 *WRe*

A George III cast iron and brass fire grate, the railed serpentine basket above a pierced frieze decorated with birds of paradise and scrolling foliage, flanked by square tapering uprights with urn finials, 32¼in (82cm) wide.
£900–1,100 *P*

A fire grate, by Alfred Stevens, the railed front above a pierced foliate frieze flanked by acanthus cast uprights, below a canopy, mid-19thC, 24½in (62cm) wide.
£450–500 *P*

Prices
The price ranges quoted in this book reflect the average price a purchaser would expect to **pay** for a similar item. When selling expect to receive a lower figure.

A cast iron grate, c1850, 61in (155cm) wide.
£600–700 *WRe*

A late Victorian cast iron combination grate, by Coalbrookdale, with a shelf above foliate cast frieze, the aperture flanking the railed basket, raised on block feet, 34in (86.2cm) wide.
£450–500 *Bon(C)*

An Arts and Crafts style cast iron combination fire surround, late 19thC, 31in (78.5cm) wide.
£200–250 *RAW*

A Victorian arched fire grate, c1870, 38in (96.5cm) wide.
£650–750 *DRU*

A pair of bright-cut brass and wrought iron fireplace andirons, Philadelphia, c1780, 20in (51cm) high.
£550–600 *S(NY)*

A pair of French Gothic style silver-plated andirons, the fronts with fleur-de-lys shields, early 20thC, 32¼in (82cm) high.
£1,000–1,200 *Bon*

A gilt-metal fire screen, the fan-shaped grilles with central female mask, raised on a scroll base, late 19thC, 29¼in (74cm) high.
£500–550 *P*

An Art Nouveau style brass fender, c1900, 52in (132cm) wide.
£300–350 *NOST*

A cast iron fire surround, c1900, 40in (101.5cm) wide.
£300–350 *NOST*

A pair of George III steel andirons, engraved with floral wreaths, with urn finials, 15in (38cm) wide.
£400–450 *CGC*

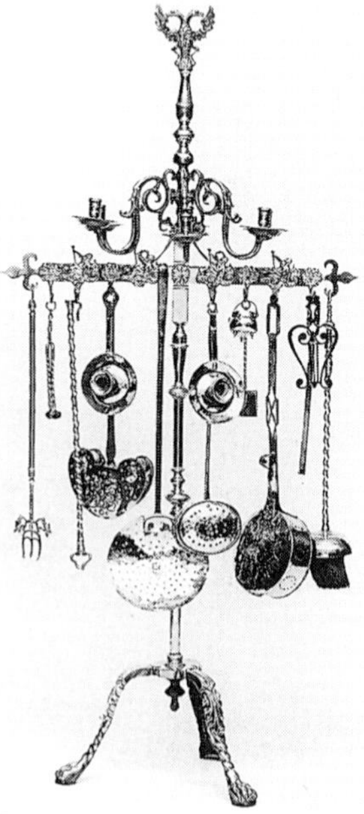

A brass companion stand, the turned column supporting a bar with hooks for fire irons, and 6 candle branches, a double-headed eagle finial, on a tripod base with paw feet, now hung with various brass utensils including a pair of chambersticks, 3 chestnut roasters and a milk skimmer, 19thC, 62in (157cm) high.
£1,400–1,600 *P(O)*

An Edwardian cast iron combination fire surround, and a Victorian rococo style fender, fire surround 41in (104cm) wide.
Fire surround £250–300
Fender £60–80 *RAW*

A pair of brass andirons, the scrolled supports centred by a lion's mask and a ring, on claw-and-ball feet, late 19thC, 25in (64cm) high.
£1,600–1,800 *S*

A set of fire irons, adapted from bayonets, dated '1878', shovel 26in (66cm) long.
£175–200 *NOST*

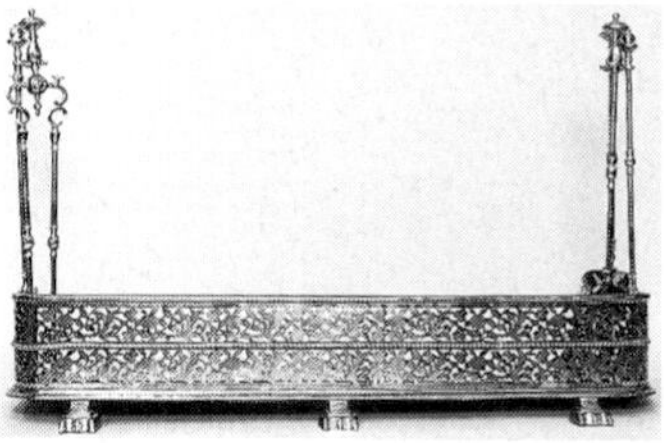

A Victorian brass fender, with pierced and engraved foliate decoration, on stylised paw feet, with original companion stand either end and matching set of 3 fire irons, 48in (122cm) long.
£750–850 *DD*

METALWARE
Brass

l. A brass candlestick, with iron pricket, the tapering stem with rims and discs, south German, early 16thC, 15¾in (40cm) high.
£900–1,000 *S(Am)*

A pair of brass candlesticks, with re-entrant corners and side pushers, mid-18thC, 7½in (19cm) high.
£475–525 *ANT*

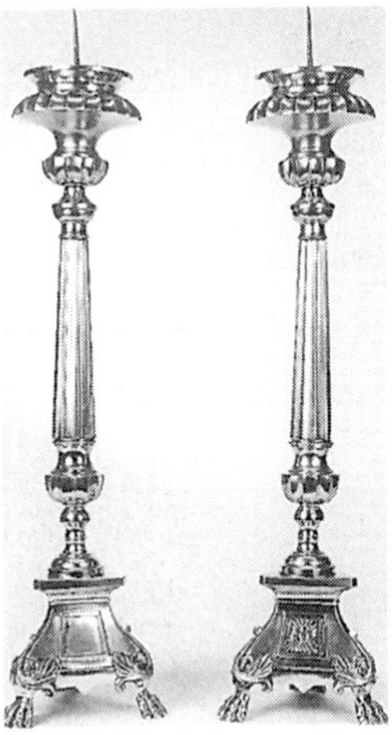

A pair of gilt-brass altar candlesticks, the reeded stems on triform bases with lion's paw feet, 19thC, 24½in (62cm) high.
£370–400 *P*

A brass chamber stick, c1900, 4½in (11.5cm) high.
£200–235 *CHe*

Cleaning

Obstinate marks on brass can be cleaned with a little paraffin mixed with jeweller's rouge and 2 drops of ammonia to form a thick paste. Gently apply the paste with a rag until the marks have gone.

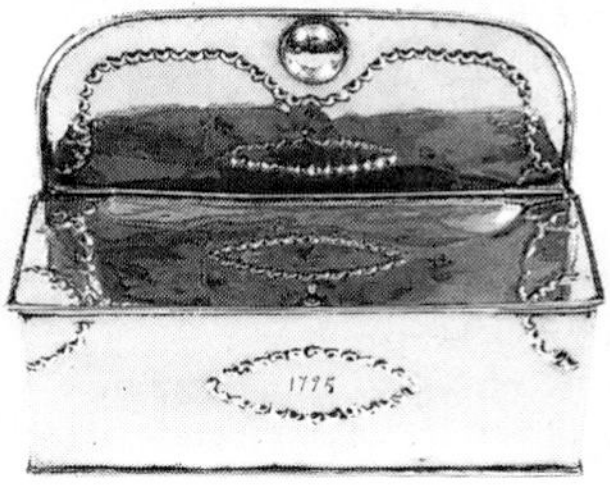

A brass candle box, dated '1795', 13½in (34.5cm) wide.
£300–330 *ANV*

A pair of brass photograph frames, the tops with pomegranate motifs, c1860, 6¾in (17cm) high.
£150–180 *MSB*

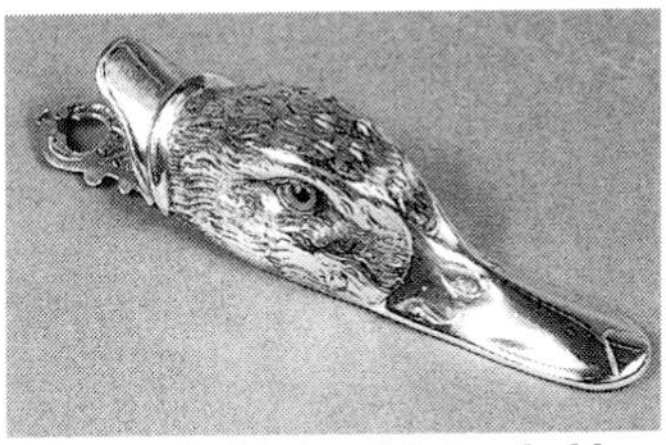

A brass duck's head letter holder, c1850, 6in (15cm) wide.
£220–245 *EMC*

A brass butterfly letter rack, c1910, 5in (12.5cm) wide.
£45–50 *CHe*

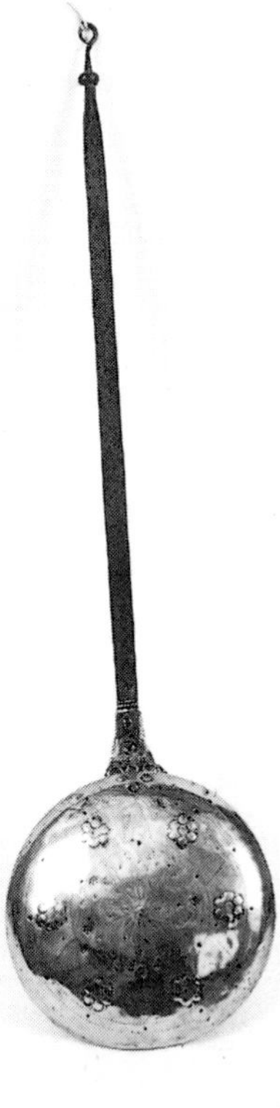

A brass warming pan, with wrought iron handle, c1690, 41in (104cm) long.
£420–470 *DaH*

A Victorian brass trivet, with paw feet, 10in (25.5cm) wide.
£50–60 *DKH*

A Victorian brass watch magnifier, c1880, 4¼in (11cm) high.
£250–275 *SHa*

A brass watering can, c1900, 11in (28cm) high.
£50–60 *FOX*

Bronze

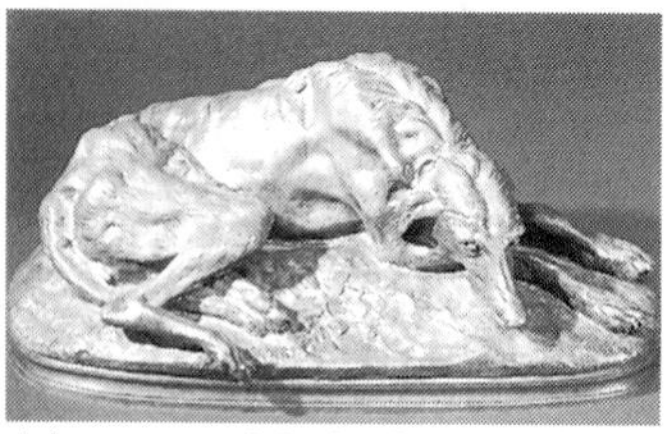

A bronze model of a deerhound, by Paul Gayrard, base incised and dated '1848', 12in (30cm) wide.
£800–1,000 *HAM*

A bronze model of a wild bear with a cub, on a marble plinth, c1870, 7½in (19cm) wide.
£650–750 *ANT*

A pair of French cast bronze Marley horses, on naturalistic bases, stamped 'Coustou', 19thC, 13in (33cm) high.
£220–250 *PFK*

A pair of bronze chickens, c1910, cockerel 16in (40.5cm) high.
£630–700 *WeH*

A pair of French Empire gilt and bronze candelabra, c1780, 21in (53.5cm) high.
£6,500–7,500 *ART*

A pair of gilt-bronze candelabra, each in the form of a cherub supporting a cornucopia of scrolling branches, on satyr and rams' head mounted plinth bases, 19thC, 23in (58.5cm) high.
£700–800 *WL*

Don't Forget!

If in doubt please refer to the 'How to Use' page at the beginning of this book.

A pair of bronze figures, in the form of a bacchante and a faun, each supporting 2 ormolu candle sconces, on fluted marble plinths with ormolu edged bases, 19thC, 17in (43cm) high.
£1,850–2,000 *MCA*

A bronze figure of Arthur, Duke of Wellington, on horseback, by Cotterell, on a bronze plinth, 19thC, 25in (63.5cm) high.
£1,500–1,650 *P*

A life-sized bronze bust of a young girl, after Houdon, 19thC, 24in (61cm) high.
£2,200–2,400 *SPa*

l. A bronze figure of a sphinx, c1850, 7in (18cm) long.
£420–465 *ANT*

Two bronze figures, Queen Elizabeth I and Mary Queen of Scots, by Albert Ernest Carrier de Belleuse, both signed 'Denière', c1860, 27in (69cm) high.
£8,300–9,000 *S(S)*

Denière was a Parisian foundry active from 1820 to the end of the 19thC, producing not only furnishing bronzes but also art bronzes for Carrier de Belleuse and others. Following their success at the Exposition Universelle of 1855 and 1874 the Duc d'Orléans commissioned them to make various bronze figures.

A bronze group of Cupid and Psyche, after Chaudet, by the Barbédienne Foundry, on a veined marble socle with ormolu panels of putti and ormolu claw feet, c1880, 18in (45.5cm) high.
£1,800–2,000 *GAK*

A pair of Austrian cold-painted bronze figures of dervishes mounted on camels, by Franz Bergmann, c1890, 8¼in (21cm) high.
£750–900 *P(B)*

A bronze figure of Napoleon riding Marengo, mounted on a base, 19thC, 17in (43cm) high.
£950–1,150 *AH*

A pair of Italian bronze figures of Diana Chasseresse and Apollo Belvedere, after the antique, mounted on marble bases, late 19thC, 16½in (42cm) high.
£1,200–1,300 *AH*

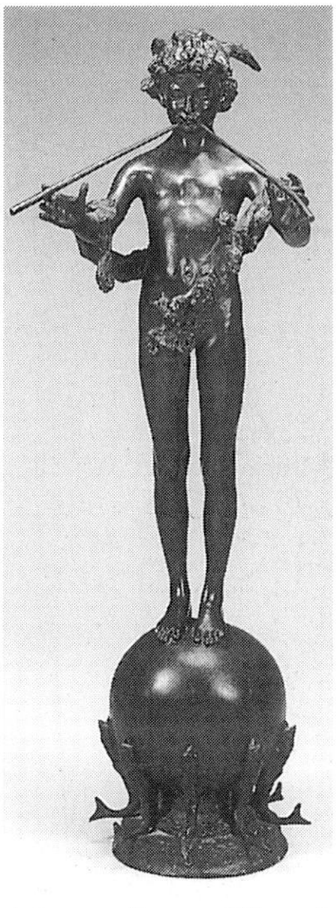

A bronze figure of Pan of Rohallion, by Frederick William MacMonnies, inscribed and dated '1890', 30in (76cm) high.
£4,500–5,000 *B&B*

r. A gilt-bronze rococo style inkstand, in the form of a huntswoman and hounds, the inkwells with ceramic liners, late 19thC, 9in (23cm) wide.
£850–950 *P(B)*

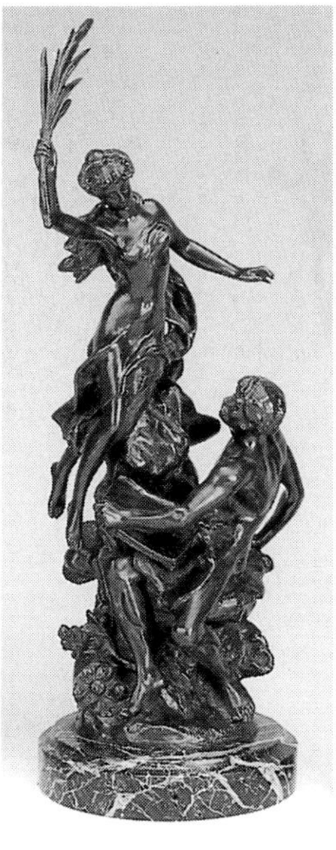

r. A French bronze group, depicting Nature and Science, from the model by Mathurin Moreau, on a marble plinth, signed and inscribed, c1900, 16¾in (42.5cm) high.
£1,000–1,200 *Bon*

A bronze figure of a boy and a turtle, by Henri Crenier, on a wooden pedestal, signed and dated '1916', 11½in (29cm) high.
£1,000–1,100 *SLN*

A pair of French gilt-bronze urns, on grey marble bases, c1800, 16in (40.5cm) high.
£2,500–3,000 *ART*

Copper

An embossed copper alms box, the panelled lid and sides decorated with stylised rose motifs, with elaborate locking plate, 17thC, 15¾in (40cm) wide.
£500–600 *P*

A Greek copper ecclesiastical plaque, painted with the figures of Emperor Constantine and the Empress Helena, on a gilt ground, c1800, 7¼in (18.5cm) diam.
£700–800 *P*

A copper watering can, with brass handles and rose, c1900, 12in (30.5cm) high.
£55–60 *OCH*

Use the Index!
Because certain items might fit easily into any of a number of categories, the quickest and surest method of locating any entry is by reference to the index at the back of this book.

l. A copper and brass watering can, early 20thC, 9½in (24cm) high.
£50–55 *OCH*

An American copper weathervane, in the form of an eagle perched on an orb, with traces of gold paint, late 19thC, 15¾in (40cm) wingspan.
£3,500–4,250 *A&A*

Iron

A German painted iron strongbox, with elaborate strapwork and large loop handles to each end, lock mechanism missing, 17thC, 24½in (62cm) wide.
£700–800 *P*

A French forged iron eagle, with outstretched wings and tail, c1700, 63in (160cm) wide.
£2,000–2,200 *S(Am)*

An American wrought iron boot scraper, in the form of a Scotty dog, early 20thC, 9in (23cm) wide.
£65–75 *MSB*

A cast iron doorstop, in the form of a seated greyhound supporting a tapering shield, on a stepped plinth, 19thC, 19¾in (50cm) high.
£1,100–1,200 *P*

A pair of cast iron stands, one with an iron top for use downstairs, the other with a brass top for use upstairs, marked and dated '1844', largest 11in (28cm) high.
£350–400 *CoHA*

A cast iron and painted figural stick stand, in the form of the adventurer Stanley, mounted on a moulded base, late 19thC, 31in (78.5cm) high.
£800–950 *S*

Pewter

A pewter saucer, the rim with 'CAI' in Lombardic script, the reverse with a horseshoe, c1400, 7½in (19cm) diam.
£3,200–3,500 *S(S)*

This piece was excavated from the River Thames.

A pewter ceremonial or alms dish, the border chased with 2 portraits in cartouches, bordered by elaborate floral scrolls, the central bowl chased with a heraldic crest, 17thC, 17in (43cm) diam.
£230–250 *GAK*

A Charles II pewter candlestick, with octagonal dished base and matching drip tray, c1675, 8½in (21.5cm) high.
£6,200–7,000 *S(S)*

A pewter quart mug, with crown WR verification mark, engraved and inscribed 'At the White Hart Inn, Parshore', c1680, 7in (17.5cm) high.
£3,500–4,000 *P(NW)*

A Scottish pewter lidded 'potbelly' measure, with domed lid, c1700, 10½in (26.5cm) high.
£2,200–2,500 *P(NW)*

A German pewter wine jar, with a cast dragon head spout, inscribed with names and places above a date, the moulded domed hinged cover engraved with crossed fish, early 18thC, 13½in (34.5cm) high.
£500–600 *WW*

A pewter two-handled jardinière, with lion's mask mounts and ring handles, on claw-and-ball feet, c1800, 19in (48cm) diam.
£820–900 *GAK*

Spelter

A pair of spelter military figures in 16thC costume, both carrying halbards, on hexagonal bases, 19thC, 21in (53.5cm) high.
£180–200 *M*

A spelter figure of William Shakespeare, beside a pile of books, early 20thC, 13½in (34cm) high.
£60–70 *Bon*

l. A Victorian spelter figure group of a maiden holding a torch above her head, with 2 Cupids at her feet, 28in (71cm) high.
£250–300 *P(G)*

ALABASTER

A French alabaster tazza, with later ormolu scrolled handles, 19thC, 15¾in (40cm) diam.
£3,300–3,600 *S(NY)*

A Renaissance style carved alabaster bust of a young girl, on a white marble base, c1900, 15¾in (40cm) high.
£1,400–1,600 *P(G)*

r. An Italian white and grey mottled alabaster bust of a young lady, inscribed 'Nello Panto', on a veined brown alabaster socle, early 20thC, 19in (48.5cm) high.
£2,500–2,750 *S*

Two Neapolitan alabaster figures of the Continents, polychrome decorated, on socles painted with 'Europa' and 'Africa', 19thC, 7¾in (19cm) high.
£370–400 *P*

An Italian alabaster figure of a seated woman holding an urn, on a grey marble slab, 19thC, 22in (56cm) high.
£950–1,100 *AP*

An alabaster group of 2 tiger cubs, with glass eyes and black painted noses, on a naturalistic base and plinth, c1920, 21in (53.5cm) wide.
£850–950 *S(S)*

MARBLE

A white marble bust of Lady Ogle, by Henry Behnes Burlowe, signed and dated 'Rome 1837', 27¾in (70.5cm) high.
£1,700–2,000 *S*

An Italian carved Carrara marble bust of a Renaissance maiden, with a laurel wreath in her hair, on a brick-coloured base, c1880, 16½in (42cm) high.
£650–750 *SK(B)*

A white marble bust of Queen Victoria, 19thC, bust 17¾in (45cm) high, on an ebonised column base.
£700–800 *P*

A Continental marble bust of woman holding opera glasses, on a pedestal base, 19thC, 62in (157.5cm) high.
£1,650–2,000 *SLN*

r. A pair of marble tomb figures of winged putti, one wiping tears from his eye, Netherlands, early 18thC, 27in (69cm) high.
£2,400–3,000 *DN*

Marble

There are hundreds of types of marble, due to mineral deposits which cause enormous variations in colour and pattern. White Carrara marble is particularly prized for its smoothness, even colour and almost translucent appearance.

A white marble figure of Paris, wearing a Phrygian cap and holding an apple in his right hand, a staff in his left, his right elbow resting on a tree stump draped with his cloak, c1800, 74in (188cm) high.
£9,000–11,000 *DN*

A carved white marble figure of Cupid, by Cesare Fantacchiotti, with a broken arrow held in one hand, the other resting on a quiver and bow, on a column carved with bands of berried leaves, shells and dolphins, believed to be titled 'The Divine Regret', minor damage, 19thC, 28¾in (73cm) high.
£9,000–10,000 *P(WM)*

r. A marble and granite decorative urn, draped in a grey marble cloth, late 19thC, 29½in (75cm) high.
£440–480 *P*

A mid-Victorian white marble figure of a cherub, reclining against a tree stump and caressing a dove, 19¾in (50cm) high.
£850–950 *RTo*

A white marble figure of a lady, signed 'Pugi', c1900, 24in (61cm) high.
£1,000–1,200 *ART*

A French white marble figure of a nude, perching on a rocky outcrop with doves below, inscribed 'Delpech' and 'Boudet, Paris', 19thC, 30in (76cm) high.
£4,000–4,500 *RTo*

A Continental marble sculpture of Una and the Lion, 19thC, 26½in (67.5cm) high.
£3,400–3,800 *SLN*

A carved statuary marble vase and cover, the lid with raised vine decoration, the body decorated with leaves, Greek key and laurel branches, the bronze handles of looping briars, 18thC, 33in (84cm) high.
£23,000–25,000 *B*

This vase, which was modelled on the 2nd century Roman original in the Vatican Museum, is the epitome of the classical revival period of the late 19thC. Pieces such as this rarely appear on the market and therefore attract great interest when they do.

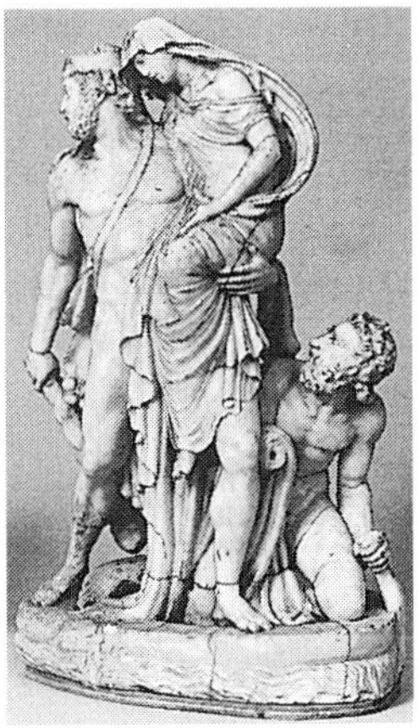

A white marble figure group of Hercules carrying Deianira, with Ialaos crouching behind them, on an oval base, repaired, 19thC, 25½in (65cm) high.
£900–1,000 *M*

A white marble figure of Cleopatra kneeling, by C. F. Holbech, dated '1897', 31½in (80cm) high.
£5,200–5,700 *P(NW)*

Carl Frederik Holbech worked as the sculptor Thorvaldsen's assistant in Rome for a number of years, and was known for his neo-classical figure groups, much in the manner of his one-time master.

A white marble figure of a veiled girl, kneeling on a green marble cushion, by Alessandro Ruga, on a portoro marble base, signed and dated '1901', 13in (33cm) high.
£1,100–1,200 *S(S)*

PAPIER MACHE

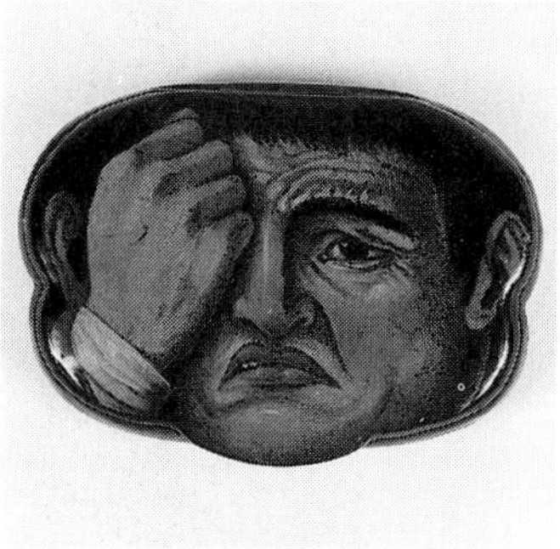

A Victorian papier mâché snuff box, depicting a man rubbing his eye, c1860, 3¼in (8.5cm) wide.
£350–450 *RdeR*

A Victorian papier mâché and mother-of-pearl inlaid stationery box, the shaped lid hinged to reveal a fitted interior, with a drawer below, 9¾in (25cm) wide.
£140–160 *P*

A George III papier mâché red and black japanned tray, with floral borders and rounded corners, repaired, 30½in (77cm) wide.
£950–1,100 *DN(H)*

Miller's is a price GUIDE not a price LIST

A papier mâché tray, painted with a floral spray within a green and gilt border with floral pendants and foliate scrolls, 19thC, 31in (79cm) wide.
£600–700 *Oli*

A papier mâché tray, by William S. Burton, London, painted with a vase of flowers flanked by birds on a green lacquered ground, with gilded border, 19thC, 32in (81.3cm) wide.
£620–680 *AH*

r. A Continental chinoiserie lacquered papier mâché urn, decorated with bamboo and flowers, and 4 cartouches depicting Chinese characters, fitted with a tin liner, 19thC, 19in (48.5cm) diam.
£4,000–4,500 *S(NY)*

TERRACOTTA

l. A pair of Italian painted terracotta models of sheep, with glass eyes, one eye missing, early 19thC, 7½in (19cm) wide.
£420–460 *P*

l. An Austrian terracotta figure of a gnome, the bearded figure standing holding a basket on one shoulder, some damage, c1900, 32in (81cm) high.
£450–500 *S(S)*

A pair of terracotta pug dogs, one standing, the other seated, tails curled, each wearing a studded wide collar, both with glass eyes, late 19thC, 19¾in (50cm) high.
£3,000–3,300 *S(Am)*

A Flemish terracotta figure of a dancing female dwarf, 18thC, 22in (56cm) high.
£3,500–4,000 *S*

r. An Italian terracotta oil lamp, the spout and handle moulded with acanthus leaves, the top applied with a classical figure beside a flaming urn, the sides with scrolling foliage, damaged and repaired, 19thC, 13in (33cm) long.
£100–120 *WW*

TREEN

A French engraved tobacco box, 18thC, 6¾in (17cm) wide.
£850–950 *AEF*

A sycamore ladle, early 19thC, 13½in (34.5cm) long.
£75–80 *MTa*

A Scottish provincial Celtic revival quaiche, by Ferguson & MacBeam, the oak body carved with strapwork, with 2 lug handles, silver rim and foot, the boss engraved 'Squab-Asi, Inverness', Birmingham marks, c1903, 4in (10cm) wide.
£250–275 *HofB*

Squab-Asi means 'sweep it up'.

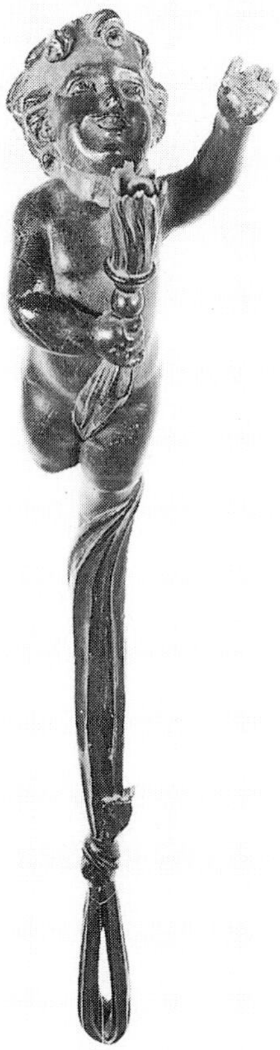

An Edwardian carved and painted wooden cherub, holding a torch in his right hand and flying astride a ribbon, 37¼in (95cm) long.
£350–400 *P*

A Dutch maple turned container, by Jacob Kortebrant, with turned cups, the rimmed container with screwable lid and fine chip carving patterns, with a turned engraved cup containing 29 very thin smaller cups, dated '1755', 9½in (24cm) high.
£1,100–1,200 *S(Am)*

A carved hardwood snuff box, in the form of a dog's head, 19thC, 2½in (6.5cm) high.
£1,100–1,250 *SHa*

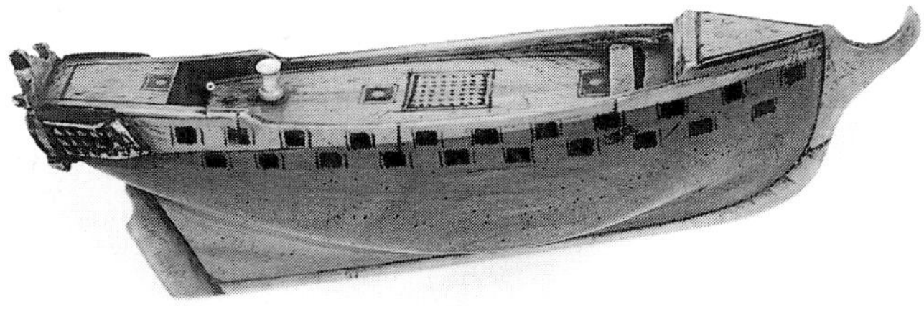

A wood and bone snuff box, in the form of a boat, c1820, 6½in (16.5cm) long.
£850–950 *AEF*

A Scandinavian carved oak tankard, 18thC, 7in (18cm) high.
£1,000–1,250 *AEF*

A fruitwood tea caddy, in the form of an apple, early 19thC, 4¼in (11cm) high.
£2,200–2,500 *LAY*

r. A French pocket watch stand, c1800, 13in (33cm) high.
£850–950 *AEF*

TUNBRIDGE WARE

A Tunbridge ware games box, the lid with central star burst motif, c1840, 8in (20.5cm) wide.
£800–880 *AMH*

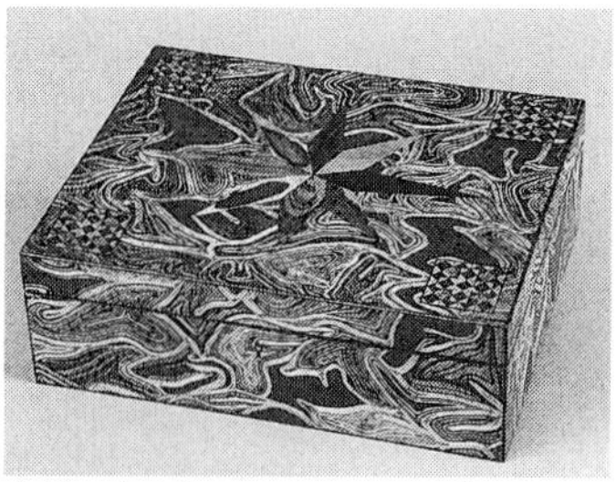

A Tunbridge ware games box, by Wise, the lid with central marquetry star and half-square mosaic corners, c1850, 10½in (26.5cm) wide.
£1,450–1,600 *BR*

To create this marbled effect, which is a rare form of Tunbridge ware, wood shavings were rolled up, clamped and compressed into a block. This was then cut into veneers and applied to the carcass of the box.

A rosewood fitted sewing box, the domed lid with a central view of Hever Castle, with tessera bandings to sides, c1850, 10½in (26.5cm) wide.
£1,000–1,100 *BR*

A Tunbridge ware coromandel workbox, by Edmond Nye, the lid with central rose spray within tessera flower bandings, label on base, c1850, 10½in (26.5cm) wide.
£500–550 *BR*

A Tunbridge ware five-drawer cabinet, the lid with a view of Tonbridge Castle, c1860, 11in (28cm) wide.
£2,200–2,500 *AMH*

A Victorian Tunbridge ware yew wood sewing cabinet, the top and doors with panels of cubed parquetry, 3 graduated drawers to the interior, 11¼in (28.5cm) wide.
£950–1,000 *P(G)*

l. A Tunbridge ware silk skein holder, c1860, 8¾in (22cm) long.
£350–400 *AMH*

A rosewood tea caddy, the domed cover with a tessera lily spray between conch shells, the interior with central panel depicting mice, with 2 canisters, c1850, 13in (33cm) wide.
£1,250–1,400 *BR*

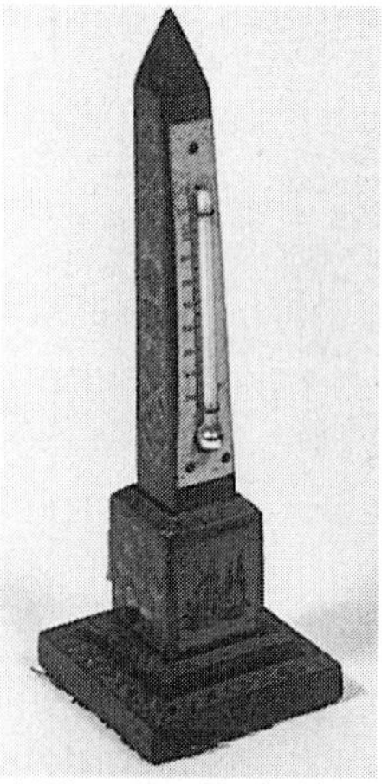

A Victorian Tunbridge ware obelisk desk-top thermometer, the tapered sides inlaid with flowers, the square stepped plinth with a windmill, parquetry and mosaic border, 8in (20.5cm) high.
£200–220 *P(F)*

r. A Tunbridge ware scent casket, decorated with geometric borders, containing 2 glass scent bottles, early 19thC, 4in (10cm) wide.
£400–450 *P*

A rosewood sarcophagus-shaped tea caddy, by Alfred Talbot, the lid with a central view of St Helena cottage within tessera Berlin work bandings, the interior fitted with a moulded glass mixing bowl between 2 canisters, c1850, 12in (30.5cm) wide.
£1,000–1,100 *BR*

A Tunbridge ware rosewood writing slope, the hinged fall-front with inlaid floral border enclosing a central panel of Battle Abbey cloisters, opening to reveal a fitted interior, c1840, 14in (36cm) wide.
£450–500 *DN(H)*

WOOD

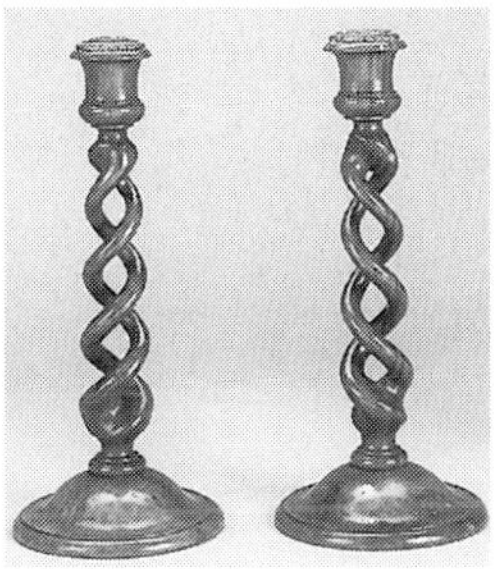

A pair of Victorian walnut candlesticks, each pierced carved barleytwist-turned columnar standard with an urn-form nozzle over a domed foot, 12in (30.5cm) high.
£700–800 *B&B*

A carved oak figure of a bearded philospher in robes, Netherlands, c1700, 60in (152.5cm) high.
£3,600–4,000 *B*

An inlaid mahogany letter rack, c1900, 7½in (19cm) high.
£225–250 *GeM*

r. A Scandinavian style burr wood tankard, the hinged lid with central leaf boss and pine cone thumbpiece, with double scroll handle, supported on 3 carved feet, engraved 'J.K.' to base of handle, 18thC, 7in (18cm) high.
£700–800 *BWe*

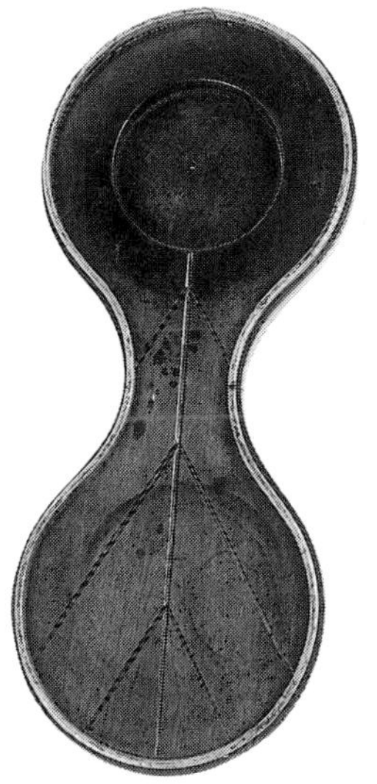

A walnut ale coaster, 18thC, 21in (53.5cm) long.
£1,200–1,350 *AEF*

Don't Forget!
If in doubt please refer to the 'How to Use' section at the beginning of this book.

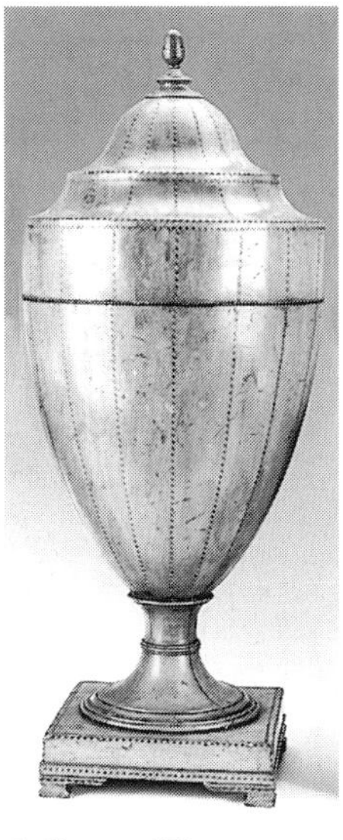

A George III mahogany knife urn, with an acorn finial and barber's pole stringing, enclosing a fitted interior, on a square plinth, c1790, 23½in (60cm) high.
£1,400–1,600 *Bon*

A Spanish polychrome painted and carved wood group of the Education of the Virgin, 17thC, 9½in (24cm) high.
£875–975 *DBA*

A Spanish carved wood figure of the Virgin Mary, 17thC, 21in (53.5cm) high.
£400–450 *OCH*

r. A Betjeman's Patent partners' oak inkstand, c1895, 14½in (37cm) wide.
£500–550 *GeM*

BOXES

A mahogany and elm heart-shaped swear box, with coin aperture at the top painted, with a banner inscribed 'Swear Not At All', the back with indistinct inscription and later inscribed date, 18thC, 6in (15cm) wide.
£2,100–2,300 *S(NY)*

A George III mahogany candlebox, the shell-inlaid canted top above a front inlaid with an urn of flowers, c1790, 6¾in (17cm) wide.
£600–660 *Bon*

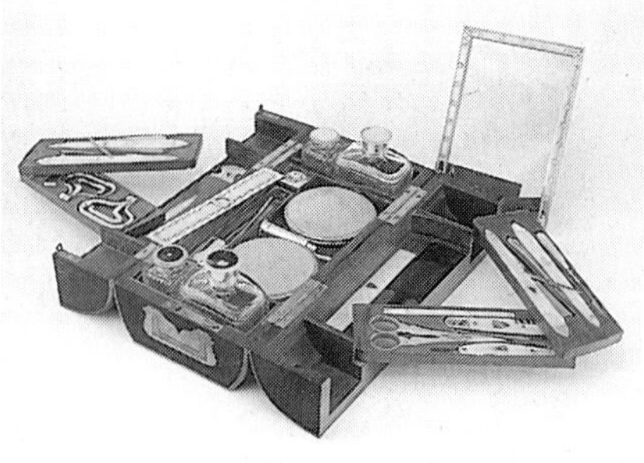

A gentleman's mahogany and brass-bound dressing case, by Pierre-Noel Blaquiere, with glass, mother-of-pearl and silver-gilt mounted fittings, the 2 hinged covers revealing swivelling compartments and containing shaving accoutrements, early 19thC, 12in (30.5cm) wide.
£8,500–9,500 *DN*

A mahogany fan-shaped writing slope, with dogs' tooth marquetry border, opening to reveal a red leather document pouch, and a green baize interior with fitted compartments, c1820, 19¾in (50cm) wide.
£1,650–1,800 *HAM*

An ebony-mounted, maple and rosewood writing slope, by William Fisk, with a paper holder, 2 brass-mounted locking inkwells and implement compartments, a later leather writing surface below, the upper section opening to 4 short drawers and a well, the sides fitted with brass carrying handles, c1815, 16in (40.5cm) wide.
£1,750–2,000 *S(NY)*

A West Indian green micro-mosaic and ivory-bound fitted needlework box, with silver carrying handles, c1820, 13in (33cm) wide.
£1,800–2,000 *CORO*

A Regency rosewood and brass-inlaid writing box, 20in (51cm) wide.
£450–500 *SPU*

l. A Scottish penwork tea caddy, the top decorated with a rural scene, 19thC, 9in (23cm) wide.
£900–1,100 *BWA*

A Regency burr yew wood tea caddy, c1820, 7½in (19cm) wide.
£340–385 *ANT*

r. A rosewood dressing case, with brass banding and monogrammed plaque, the red velvet interior with 3 trays and 2 short drawers under compartments for 9 cut-glass and engraved silver-lidded containers, London 1846, 13in (33cm) wide.
£700–800 *Bri*

A tea caddy, with 2 interior lids, painted with floral, shell and fruit decoration, c1830, 7½in (19cm) wide.
£780–850 *GSP*

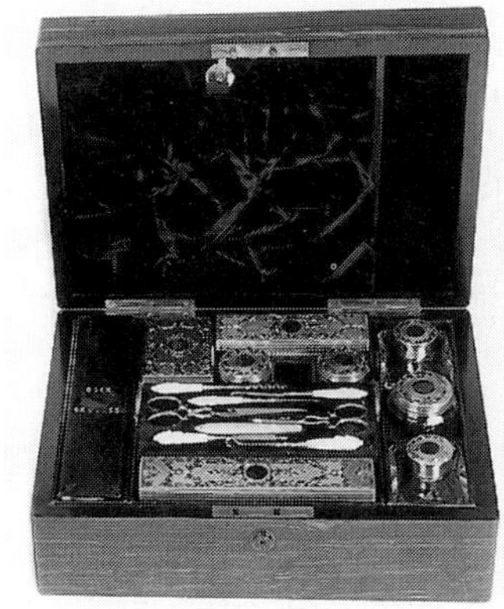

A coromandel dressing case, with scroll engraved silver and ivory mounted fittings, stamped 'Mechi, Leadenhall St & 112 Regent St', London 1858, 12in (30.5cm) wide.
£1,200–1,350 *RBB*

A coromandel and brass-mounted travelling case, with silver-gilt, cut-glass and other fittings, by Howell, James & Co, London, mid-19thC, 14¼in (36cm) wide.
£4,700–5,200 *P(WM)*

A paper and cardboard hatbox, by Hannah Davis, decorated with a Napoleonic scene, c1860, 15¾in (40cm) high.
£550–600 *A&A*

A Victorian oak writing box, with double fall-front, the interior fitted with 3 short drawers, 6 compartments, inkwells, pen tray, gilt tooled black leather insets to lid and slope, brass side carrying handles, 16in (40.5cm) wide.
£400–480 *LF*

A Victorian walnut writing box, with broad parquetry bands to lid and front, fitted interior, 20in (51cm) wide.
£110–120 *WBH*

A coromandel inlaid stationery box, with secret drawer and original contents, c1880, 15in (38cm) wide.
£650–750 *STK*

An oak smoker's cabinet, with revolving door and Doulton Lambeth tobacco jar, c1900, 14in (35.5cm) wide.
£240–270 *GBr*

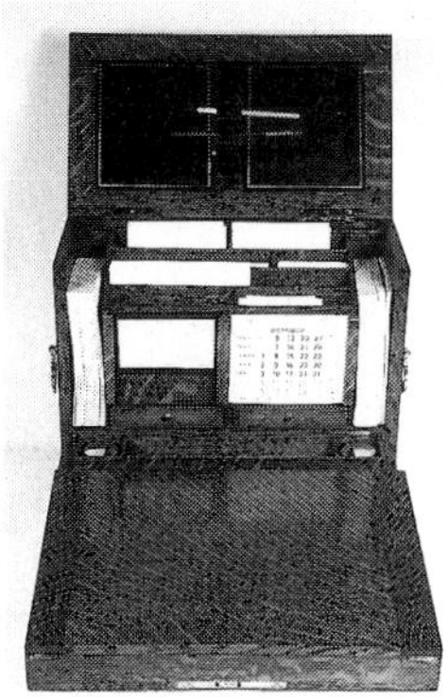

An oak fall-front travelling stationery cabinet, with writing slope, c1890, 12in (30.5cm) high.
£630–700 *GeM*

r. A smoker's compendium, painted to look like coromandel, c1901, 12in (30.5cm) wide.
£750–850 *GIO*

MUSIC
Cylinder Musical Boxes

A Victorian cylinder musical box, by Mermod, in an inlaid rosewood case, 24in (61cm) wide.
£550–600 *JH*

A Swiss musical box, the 9¼in (23.5cm) cylinder playing 8 airs, contained in a rosewood case, the lid inlaid with mistletoe, 19thC, 18in (45.5cm) wide.
£420–460 *AAV*

A musical box, by Nicole Frères, with 13in (33cm) cylinder, contained in a rosewood veneered and marquetry inlaid case, the top boxwood strung and inlaid with a classical design to the centre, late 19thC, 20in (51cm) wide.
£1,500–1,650 *Mit*

A Swiss musical box, with 6in (15cm) cylinder playing 8 airs, contained in a rosewood veneered case, boxwood strung and crossbanded and with painted musical instrument motif to the lid, late 19thC, 19in (48.5cm) long.
£620–700 *Mit*

A Swiss mandolin cylinder music box, with 17in (43cm) cylinder playing 6 airs, contained in an ebonised wood case inlaid with pewter, tulipwood and brass geometric designs, c1880, 33in (84cm) wide.
£7,000–8,000 *S*

A Swiss musical box, by B. H. Abraham, with 6¼in (16cm) cylinder playing 10 airs, contained in a transfer-decorated case with carrying handles, late 19thC, 18in (45.5cm) wide.
£520–620 *Bon(C)*

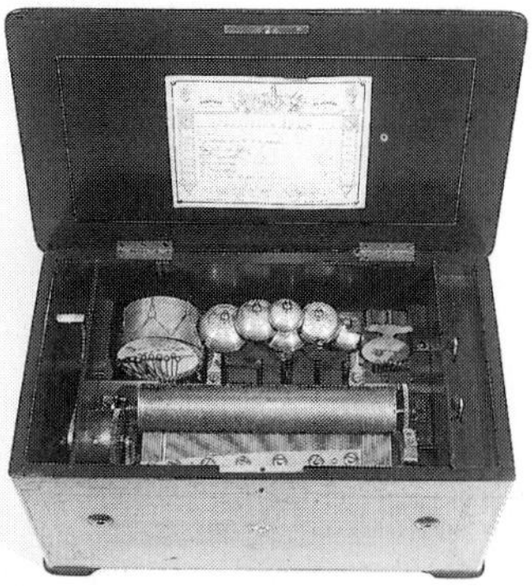

A Swiss cylinder musical box, with 11½in (29cm) comb and drum movement, contained in a walnut and ebonised case with string and marquetry inlay, 19thC, 20in (51cm) wide.
£1,400–1,600 *AH*

l. A Swiss musical box, with 13in (33cm) cylinder playing 12 airs, contained in a rosewood case inlaid with musical trophies and flowers, crossbanded in kingwood and with boxwood stringing and ebonised borders, mid-19thC, 27½in (70cm) wide.
£1,500–1,650 *MSW*

A Swiss musical box, by B. A. Bremond, with 17in (43cm) organocliede cylinder playing 6 airs, contained in a rosewood veneered case inlaid with central medallion flanked by sphinxes, c1880, 28in (71cm) wide.
£4,500–5,000 *S(NY)*

The organocliede style of movement is similar to that of the mandolin, having repeated notes throughout the length of the comb but with particular emphasis being placed on the bass notes, which pitches the tonal scale an octave lower than that of a normal musical box.

A musical box, with 11in (28cm) cylinder playing 8 airs, contained in a buffet style case with zither attachment and inlay decoration to the doors, c1905, 22in (56cm) wide.
£2,000–2,200 *P(Ba)*

Disc Musical Boxes

A Symphonion 12in (30cm) disc musical box, contained in a walnut case inlaid with flowers, mid-19thC, 20in (51cm) wide.
£1,500–1,800 *MSW*

A Symphonion 13½in (34.5cm) disc musical box, late 19thC, 20½in (52cm) square.
£820–900 *Doc*

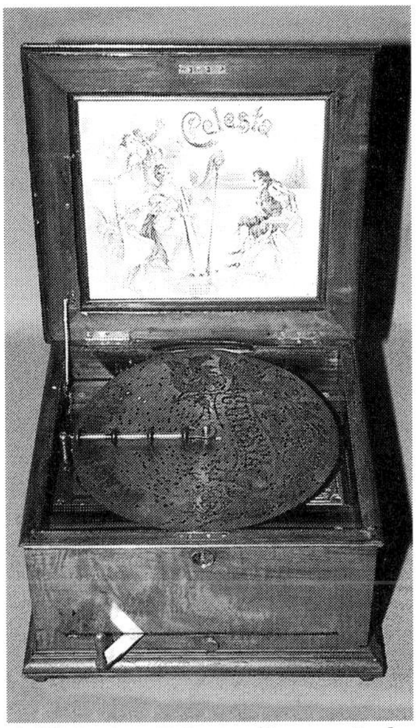

A Victorian Celesta disc musical box, with picture in lid, 15in (38cm) square.
£450–500 *JH*

A Nicole Frères 11in (28cm) disc musical box, contained in a walnut case, Swiss, c1900, 23¾in (60cm) high.
£2,200–2,400 *Bon(C)*

l. A Symphonion Imperial 15¾in (40cm) disc musical box, contained in a mahogany case, American, c1900, 23in (58.5cm) wide.
£2,800–3,200 *S(NY)*

The Imperial Symphonion Manufacturing Company was founded c1897 at the Bradley Beach, near Asbury Park in New Jersey. Records indicate that the company closed down soon after 1902 and it is estimated that between 5,000 and 10,000 musical boxes were made.

Mechanical Music

A Karl Czech barrel orchestrion, the weight-driven 48 key movement with pinned wooden barrel, in a mahogany case with glazed doors over covered doors, Bohemian, c1900, 47in (119.5cm) wide.
£2,100–2,300 *S(NY)*

A chamber barrel organ, with 3 interchangable 17¼in (44cm) wooden barrels each playing 10 airs, c1790, 22¾in (58cm) wide.
£1,350–1,500 *Bon*

Don't Forget!

If in doubt please refer to the 'How to Use' page at the beginning of this book.

A Triola mechanical zither, the hand-cranked mechanism mounted above a shaped zither and one paper roll, German, c1905, 17in (43cm) wide.
£630–700 *S(NY)*

Phonographs

An Edison Fireside Model A phonograph, No. 5147, combination gearing '4 minute 2' oak base with domed lid and metal horn, c1900, 23in (58.5cm) wide.
£165–185 *AP*

A Edison Standard phonograph, with blue painted horn, No. 5142961, American, c1901, 12¾in (32.5cm) wide.
£260–300 *Bon*

A Thomas Edison Triumph phonograph, c1905, 18in (45.5cm) wide.
£700–800 *ET*

l. An Edison Fireside phonograph, with 2 and 4 minute Combination Model K reproducer, original red-painted fluted metal horn, c1905, 14in (35.5cm) wide.
£600–700 *WAL*

An Edison 2 minute home phonograph, with witch's hat horn, c1906, 16in (40.5cm) wide.
£500–600 *ET*

Gramophones

A Gramophone and Typewriter Monarch gramophone, with single spring motor, exhibition soundbox and carved oak base with brass-mounted metal horn, c1905, 11½in (29cm) wide.
£670–800 *S*

A Victor horn gramophone, with exhibition sound box, 10in (25.5cm) diameter turntable, double spring motor, oak case, American, c1905, 12in (30.5cm) wide.
£1,700–2,000 *S(NY)*

A Fullotone gramophone, with mahogany cabinet, c1928, 40in (101.5cm) high.
£120–180 *OTA*

Locate the Source

The source of each illustration in Miller's can be found by checking the code letters below each caption with the Key to Illustrations.

r. An HMV Intermediate Monarch gramophone, with Ionic wood horn, c1917, 15in (38cm) wide.
£1,500–1,800 *ET*

Musical Instruments

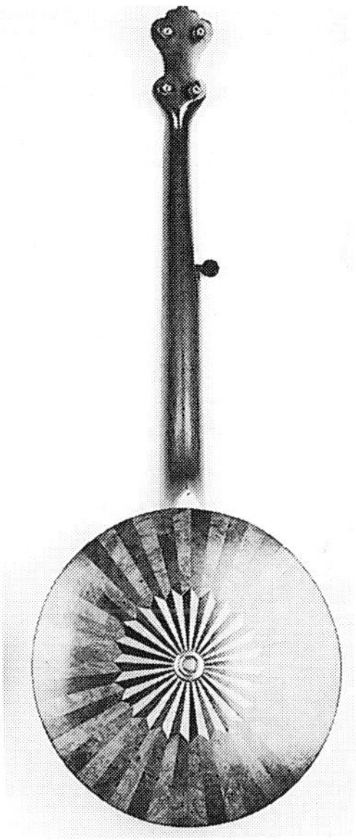

A 5-string zither banjo, by A. Cammeyer, the back inlaid with different woods, the neck, fingerboard and head inlaid with mother-of-pearl, c1900, 34¾in (88cm) long.
£180–220 *Bon*

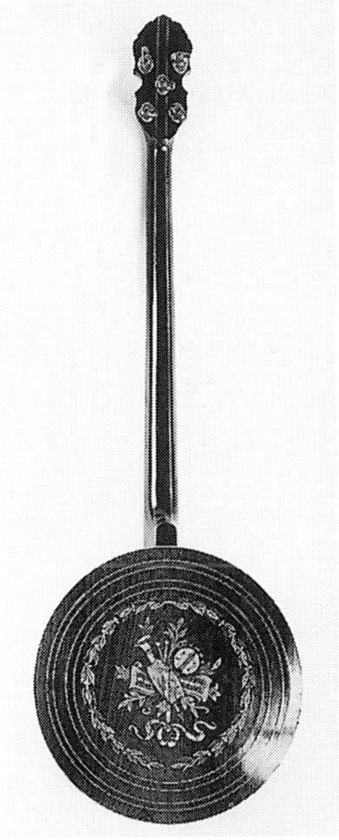

A 4/5 string G banjo, by Windsor, Birmingham, the head inlaid with a metal shape, 1928, 37½in (95cm) long in original case.
£1,000–1,200 *Bon*

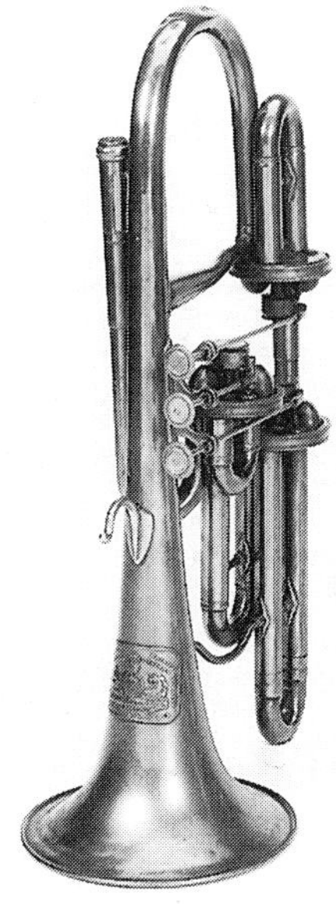

A brass cornet or cornopean, by Kohler, London, c1870, bell 4¾in (12cm) diam.
£1,100–1,200 *P*

A double bass, probably Italian, c1750, string length 41in (104cm).
£3,500–4,200 *Bon*

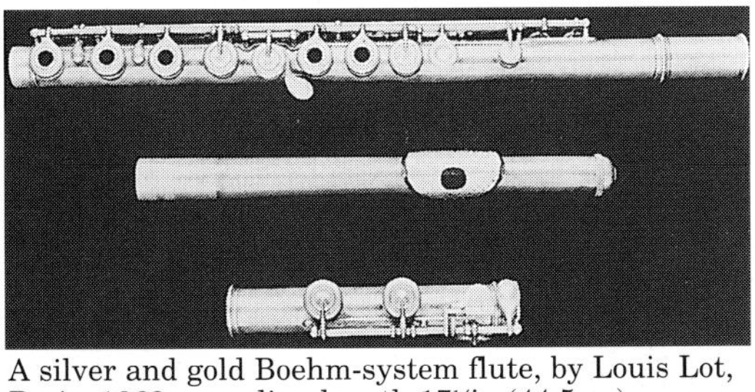

A silver and gold Boehm-system flute, by Louis Lot, Paris, 1862, sounding length 17½in (44.5cm), with original case.
£5,200–6,000 *Bon*

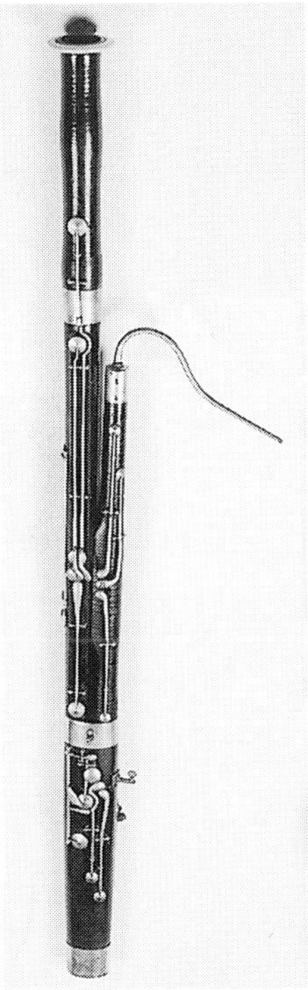

A single-action 48 button concertina, by Wheatstone, No. 19300, with rosewood ends and case, c1873, 9in (23cm) wide.
£680–750 *Bon*

l. A German bassoon, by Heckle, Biebrich am Rheim, with stained wood body, metal mounts and keywork, ivory sole, c1870, 50in (127cm) long, with crook and fitted case.
£1,700–2,000 *Bon*

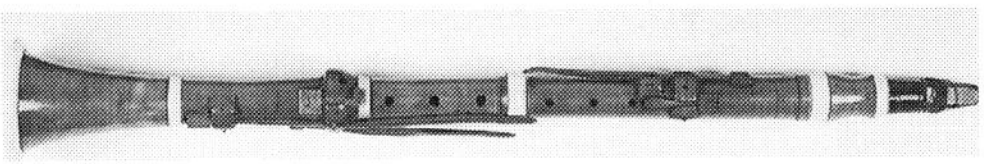

A six-keyed boxwood clarinet, by Goulding, with bone mounts and square brass keys, c1810, 23½in (60cm) long.
£450–550 *Bon*

A silver flute, by Rudall Carte & Co, London, the mouthpiece decorated with floral engravings, c1875, sounding length 23½in (59.5cm), with original case.
£400–450 *Bon*

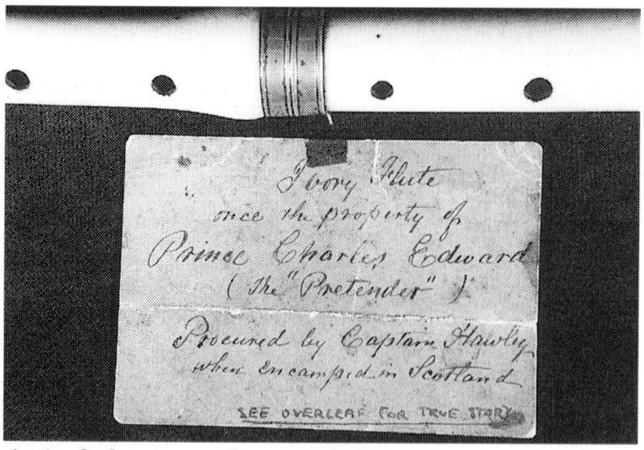

A single key ivory flute, 18thC, 34in (86.5cm) long.
£3,000–3,500 *B*

The inscription on the period card that accompanies the piece states 'once the property of Prince Charles Edward, (The "Pretender"), procured by Captain Hawley when encamped in Scotland'.

A Herman Hauser guitar, the spruce soundboard with maple back and sides, pine back bracing and top fan bracing, rosewood bridge, rosette of inlaid wood in concentric patterns, cedar neck and head and ebony fingerboard, Munich, c1928, scale length 25½in (64.5cm), in case.
£7,000–8,400 *Bon(C)*

A Gibson EB2 No. 68080 Sunburst guitar, with semi-hollow body and rosewood fretboard, 1964 scale length 30½in (77.5cm).
£450–500 *Bon(C)*

Cross Reference
Colour Review

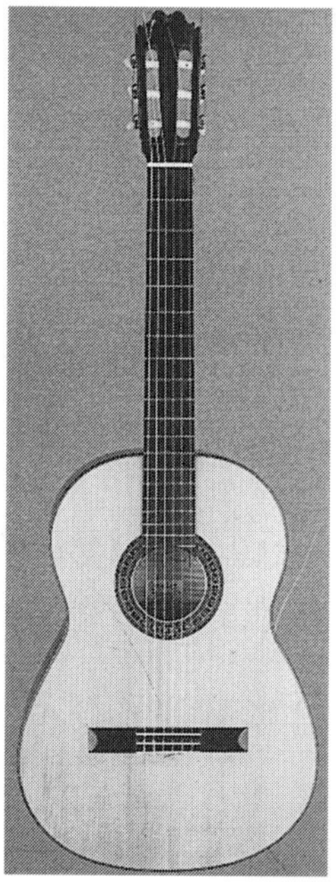

l. A George Love guitar, the Swiss pine sound-board with flamed Bosnian maple back and sides, cedar neck and head, ebony fingerboard, Rio rosewood bridge, the rosette inlaid with butterfly patterns, 1976, scale length 25½in (65cm).
£700–800 *Bon(C)*

A freestanding Dital harp, by Edward Light, the chinoiserie-decorated body with 2 sound holes on the back, early 19thC, 34in (86.5cm) high, in a fitted case.
£1,000–1,100 *P*

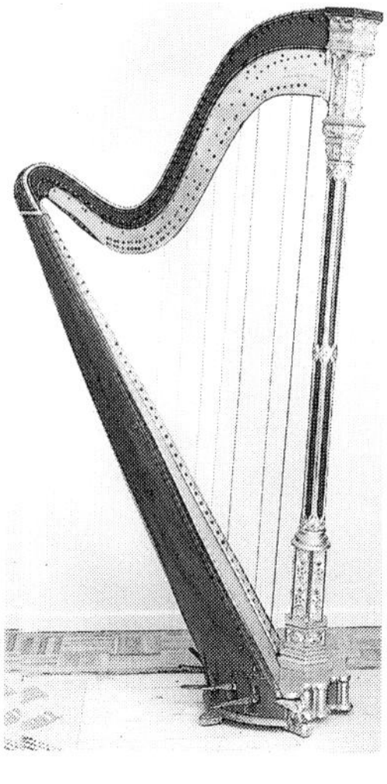

A giltwood and rosewood harp, No. 2103, with 8 pedals, signed 'Erard', 19thC, 70in (178cm) high.
£3,100–3,500 *Doc*

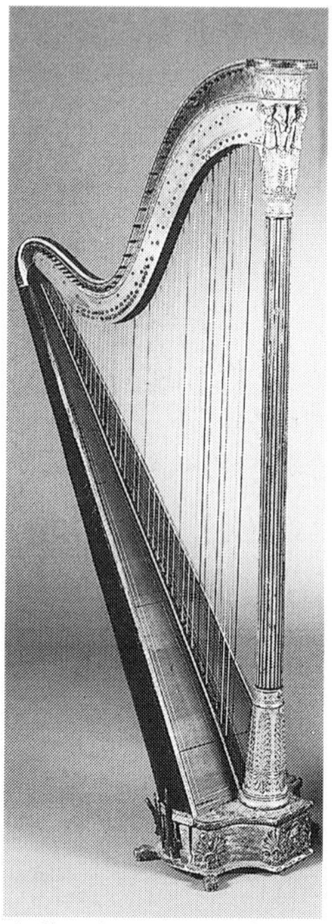

A Grecian concert harp, by Sebastian Erard, the capital of the column with gilded caryatid figures and foliate decoration with further fluting and anthemion leaves, raised upon a decorated base, c1820, 67in (170cm) high.
£3,500–4,000 *P*

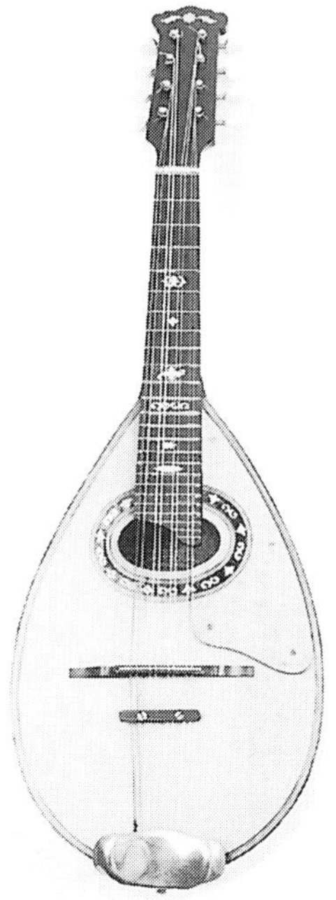

A flat-backed mandolin, by Clifford Essex, London, the back and ribs of rosewood, the table of spruce, the edging of bone, the soundhole, fingerboard and headpiece decorated with mother-of-pearl, c1928, 23¾in (63cm) long, in a fitted case.
£320–380 *Bon*

A John Broadwood & Sons rosewood grand piano, c1850, 53¼in (135.5cm) wide.
£2,000–2,200 *NOA*

A John Broadwood & Sons satinwood and ormolu-mounted upright piano, the keyboard surround applied with festoons and guilloche scrolls, raised on fluted tapering cylindrical legs, c1880, 63in (160cm) wide.
£2,500–3,000 *Hal*

A Broadwood carved oak grand piano, with trailing foliate frieze and cherub masks, c1890, 96in (244cm) long.
£7,500–9,000 *P(Ba)*

A Misdale & Misdale rosewood square piano, with part gilded and transfer-printed frame featuring musical trophies, with lyre-shaped pedestal, 19thC, 70in (178cm) wide.
£625–700 *AH*

A Bechstein rosewood grand piano, with marquetry case and double legs, c1900, 78in (167.5cm) long.
£5,000–6,000 *PEx*

A Kranich & Bach burr walnut grand piano, the music stand pierced and carved with stylised foliage, with leaf-capped flared reeded legs and bun feet, 19thC, 55in (139.5cm) wide.
£5,500–6,000 *S(Cg)*

l. A John Broadwood & Sons grained mahogany and parcel-gilt boudoir grand piano, the sides applied with gilt gesso guilloches, swags of husks and Vitruvian scrolls, c1902, 66in (168cm) long.
£2,100–2,300 *P(O)*

r. A C. Bechstein ebonised grand piano, on square tapering legs with brass cappings and casters, c1902, 70in (178cm) long.
£3,250–3,600 *P(Z)*

l. A Karl Hamburger mahogany boudoir grand piano, with tapered legs and brass-mounted casters, Vienna, c1910, 55in (139.5cm) wide.
£1,000–1,200 *PFK*

A Challen chinoiserie-decorated baby grand piano, with matching duet stool, c1920, 54in (137cm) long.
£3,000–3,600 *PEx*

An Art Deco Evestaff ebonised 'Minipiano' and stool, the side columns with rounded edges and parallel bands of chromium-plated metal, c1935, 51¾in (131cm) wide.
£360–450 *P(Ba)*

A D'Almaine mahogany baby grand piano, on square tapering supports and brass casters, late 1940s, 57in (145cm) long.
£650–700 *HCC*

r. A Steinway & Sons grand piano, in ebonised case, c1960, 90in (228.5cm) long.
£21,000–23,000 *GOR*

Ex-West Heath School, Kent, where it was played by Lady Diana Spencer.

A Weber black polyester grand piano, c1900, 57½in (146cm) wide.
£8,500–9,300 *SI*

A Blüthner black-lacquered grand piano, with matching stool, 1964, 75in (191cm) long.
£6,700–7,500 *S(LA)*

Ex-Marlene Dietrich collection.

The piano was acquired as payment for Marlene Dietrich's appearances behind the Iron Curtain, for which Burt Bacharach arranged some of her most famous songs.

l. A Bösendorfer baroque style white grand piano, c1985, 88½in (225cm) wide.
£25,000–30,000 *PEx*

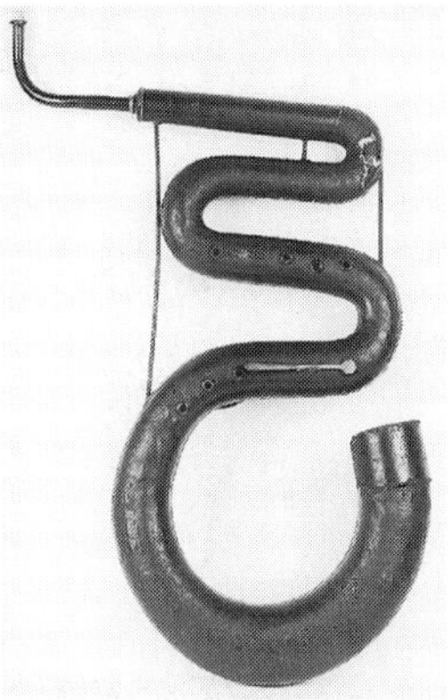

A serpent, with 3 brass keys, the wooden body covered by restored hide or canvas, London, c1825, bell 3¾in (9.5cm) diam.
£1,150–1,250 *P*

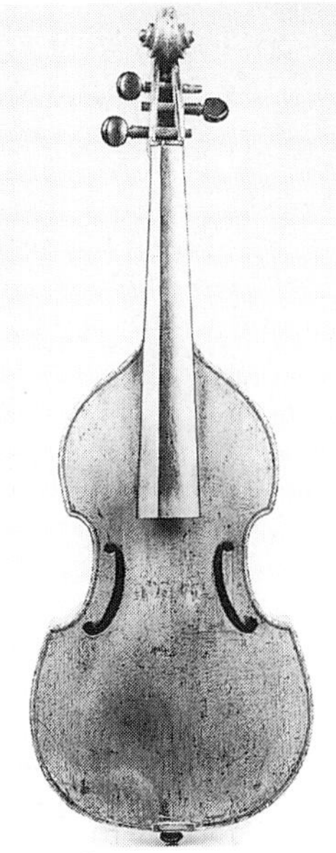

A pardessus, or quinton, Paris School, c1760, length of back 14¾in (37.5cm).
£2,000–2,200 *P*

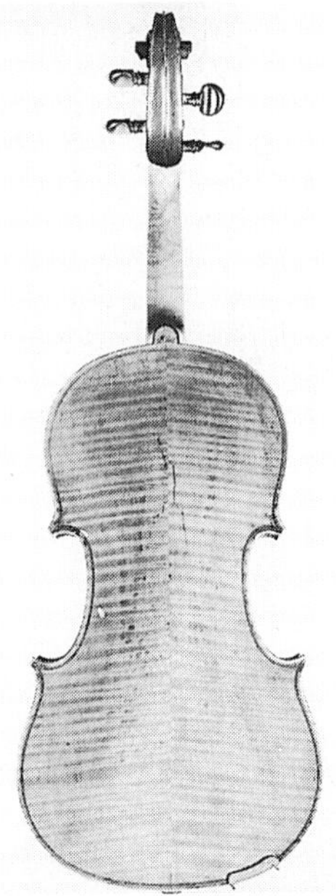

A viola, by J. M. Somny, 1896, London, length of back 16in (40.5cm).
£1,500–1,650 *Bon*

A viola, by J. Hill, London, 1770, length of back 15¾in (40cm).
£12,000–14,500 *Bon*

A viola, by Enrico Marchetti, Turin, 1908, length of back 15¾in (40cm).
£13,000–15,000 *S*

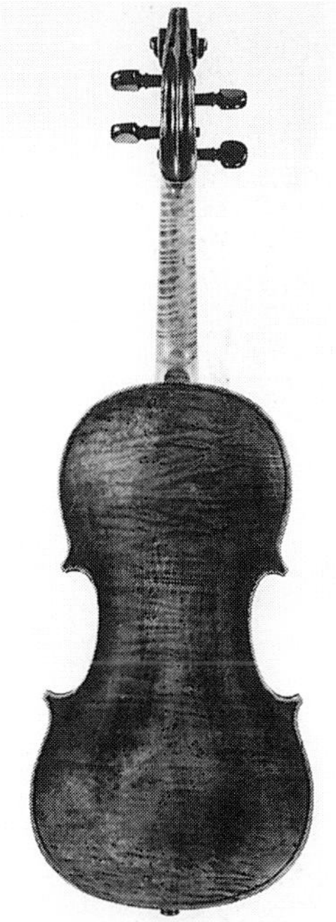

A Flemish child's violin, mid-18thC, length of back 13½in (34.5cm).
£7,800–8,500 *S*

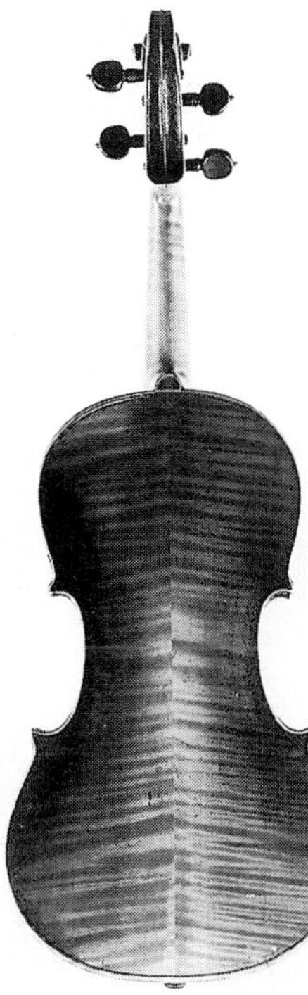

A German violin, by N. Seitz, Mittenwald, the varnish of a red colour on a golden ground, labelled, c1825, length of back 14in (35.5cm).
£700–800 *Bon*

A violin, by G. Craske, the varnish of a red, orange, brown colour, labelled, c1845, length of back 14¼in (36cm).
£3,000–3,500 *Bon*

A French violin, by Hippolyte Chretien Silvestre, Paris, c1900, length of back 14in (35.5cm).
£9,500–11,500 *P*

A violin, by G. Pyne, London, 1912, length of back 14in (35.5cm).
£2,000–2,400 *Bon*

A gold and tortoiseshell-mounted violin bow, by James Tubbs, London, c1860, 64g.
£6,000–7,000 *Bon*

A half-size violoncello, by B. Norman, London, 1719, length of back 26in (66cm).
£1,600–2,000 *Bon*

l. A silver-mounted violin bow, by Eugène Sartory, Paris, c1920, 58g.
£6,500–7,500 *S*

A violoncello, by Joseph Hill, London, c1770, length of back 29½in (74.5cm).
£15,000–16,500 *P*

A violoncello, by a maker of the Betts School, late 18thC, length of back 29in (73.5cm), with bow and wooden case.
£8,500–10,000 *LAY*

Music Stands

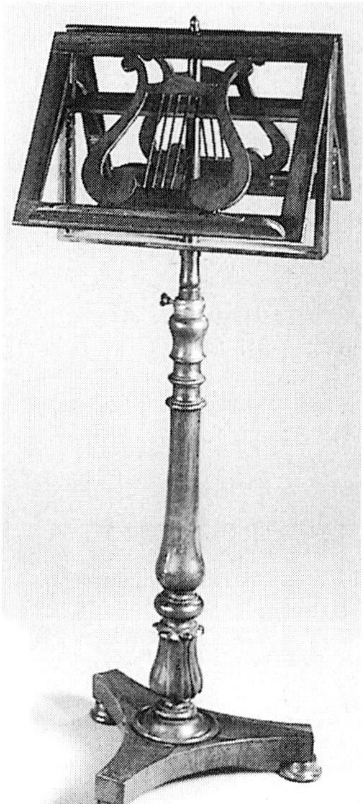

A William IV rosewood duet stand, the adjustable sheet rest with pierced lyre decoration, on turned and lappet-carved height-adjustable support, 44½in (113cm) high.
£1,750–2,000 *DN(H)*

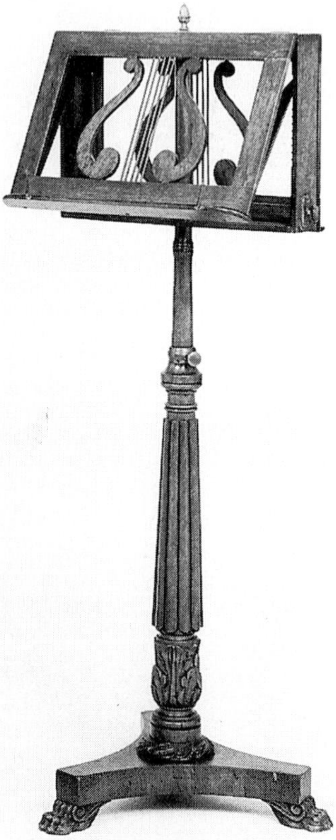

A Regency carved mahogany music stand, with opposing pierced lyre scroll ratcheted slopes, candle sconces to the sides, on adjustable tapered reeded column, 54in (137cm) high.
£1,350–1,500 *P(EA)*

A Victorian walnut music stand, on a turned and fluted column and carved tripod base, 16½in (42cm) wide.
£650–720 *HYD*

A French Empire bronze and ormolu six-branch chandelier, surmounted by a coronet supporting chains with masks, c1800, 15¾in (40cm) high.
£3,000–3,500 *P*

A Baltic neo-classical gilt-metal, green glass and cut-glass chandelier, the pendant drops centred by a stylised vase of flowers within a circular border, fitted with 10 scrolled candle branches hung with pendants, late 18thC, 40in (101.5cm) high.
£17,000–18,500 *S(NY)*

An ebonised wood and iron four-light chandelier, 18thC, 9¾in (25cm) high.
£4,000–4,500 *S(NY)*

A Gothic revival gilt-bronze chandelier, c1810, 130in (330cm) high.
£35,000–40,000 *Hal*

A pair of rococo style ormolu girandoles, each with 3 candle sconces, mid-19thC, with 18thC porcelain flowerheads and figures, 23in (58.5cm) high.
£5,000–5,500 *GH*

A pair of brass and copper wall lights, the frosted glass shades with Edwardian swag decoration, mounted on shaped blocks of wood, c1915, 13¾in (35cm) high.
£150–180 *P(B)*

A Victorian brass hall lantern, with stained-glass panels, 24in (61cm) high.
£570–650 *TMA*

A Victorian Gothic style bronzed gas lantern, with original stained glass, c1880, 34in (86.5cm) high.
£1,800–2,000 *CHA*

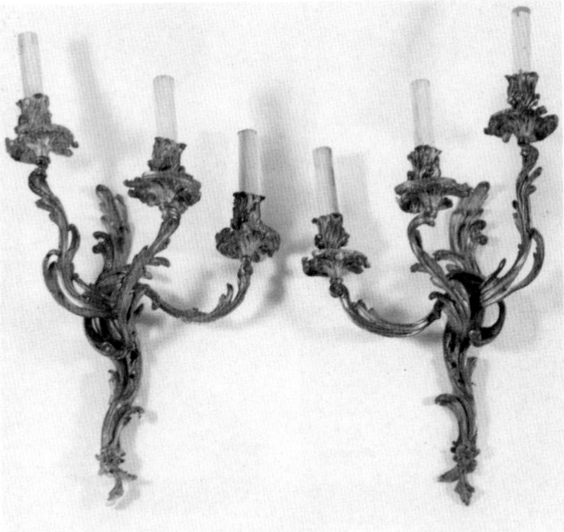

A pair of gilt-brass three-branch wall lights, with rococo leaf scrolls, leafy sconces, and electric candle fitments, c1920, 21in (53.5cm) high.
£400–450 *CAG*

A Louis XV style gilt-bronze 'birdcage' chandelier, hung with tear-shaped drops, late 19thC, 45in (114.5cm) high.
£5,800–6,400 *Bon*

A gilt-bronze candelabrum, with 3 candleholders, c1760, 12½in (32cm) high.
£2,500–2,800 *ART*

A pair of Louis XVI ormolu-mounted marble candlesticks, each flanked by cockerels' heads, late 18thC, 13¼in (33cm) high.
£5,600–6,200 *S(NY)*

A Charles X gilt-bronze mounted oil lamp, cast with angels and flowers, later domed shade, c1830, 32½in (82.5cm) high.
£5,750–6,250 *S*

A pair of French Empire bronze candlesticks, c1820, 11¾in (30cm) high.
£380–430 *SSW*

A Russian gilt-bronze six-branch candelabrum, the shaft with 3 caryatids, applied heads to the base, c1810, 23in (58.5cm) high.
£2,500–3,000 *S(Z)*

A brass oil lamp, with etched glass shade and coloured glass well, c1870, 29in (73.5cm) high.
£700–800 *BERA*

A glass oil lamp, the frosted glass shade with crimped rim, on a brass foot, c1880, 29in (74cm) high.
£220–250 *P(B)*

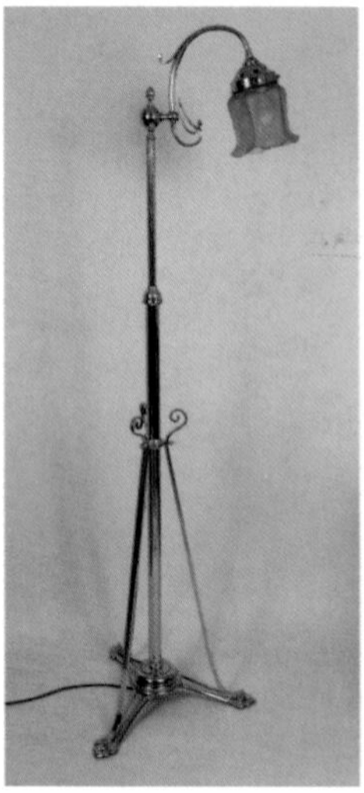

An adjustable brass lamp, with etched cranberry glass shade, c1890, 61in (155cm) high.
£950–1,100 *CHA*

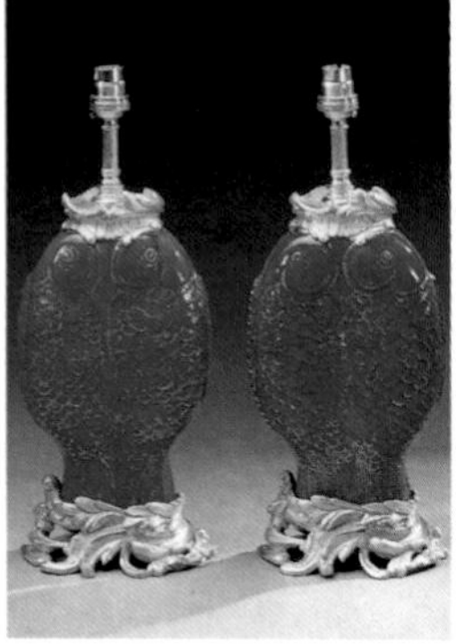

A pair of French gilt-bronze and porcelain lamps, each in the form of 2 fishes with gilded scales, with foliate mounts, c1880, 15in (38cm) high.
£2,300–2,500 *S*

A pair of Empire gilt-bronze and patinated lamps, applied with foliate wreaths, c1800, with later milk-glass shades, 32¼in (82cm) high.
£2,250–2,500 *S(Z)*

A rose and butterfly decorated carnival glass oil lamp, with brass fittings, c1910, 16in (40.5cm) high.
£3,500–4,000 *ASe*

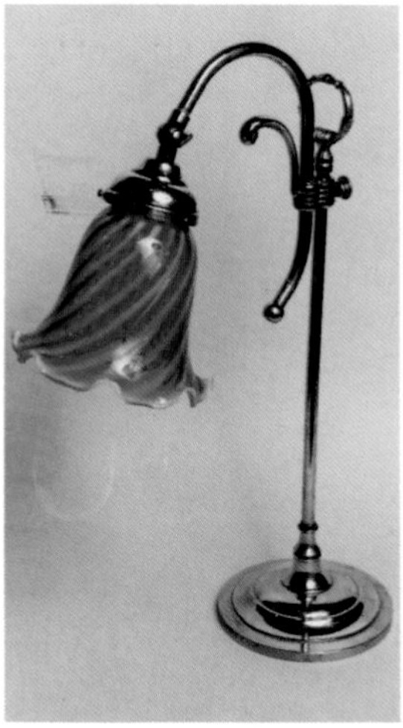

A brass table lamp, with ribbed cranberry glass shade, c1920, 15in (38cm) high.
£150–200 *CB*

A Louis-Philippe Aubusson carpet, French, repaired, mid-19thC, 261 x 224in (663.5 x 568cm).
£10,500–12,000 *S(NY)*

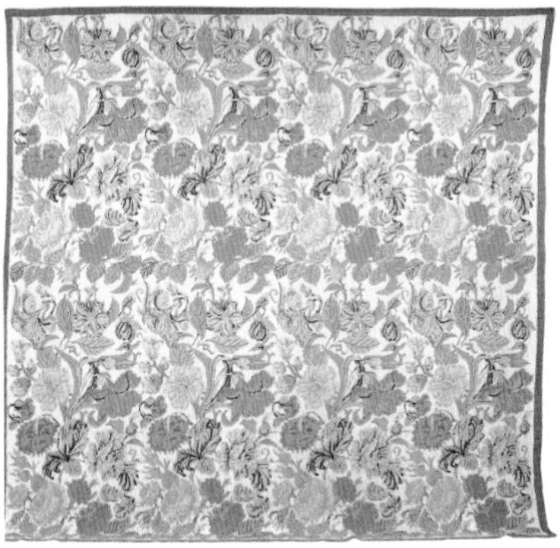

A Portuguese needlework carpet, c1920, 147in (373.5cm) square.
£4,600–5,200 *S(NY)*

A Balkan kilim, rewoven areas, late 19thC, 113 x 94in (287 x 239cm).
£4,600–5,200 *S(NY)*

An Aubusson carpet, late 19thC, French, border later, 136 x 105in (345.5 x 266.5cm).
£8,500–9,000 *S(NY)*

A Spanish carpet, by Real Fàbrica de Tapices, Madrid, 1859, 270 x 217in (687 x 552cm).
£10,500–12,000 *S*

A Bessarabian kilim, small repairs, c1900, 155 x 117in (394 x 297cm).
£8,500–10,000 *S(NY)*

A Kuba rug, north east Caucasus, late 19thC, 45 x 65in (114.5 x 165cm).
£1,600–1,800 *FW&C*

An Anatolian prayer rug, c1800, 67 x 49in (170 x 125cm).
£17,500–19,000 *P*

A needlepoint rug, minor repairs, possibly Russian, mid-19thC, 66 x 78in (168 x 198cm).
£9,000–10,000 *S(NY)*

An Ushak carpet, western Turkey, c1900, 148 x 142in (378.5 x 362cm).
£5,600–6,000 *Bon*

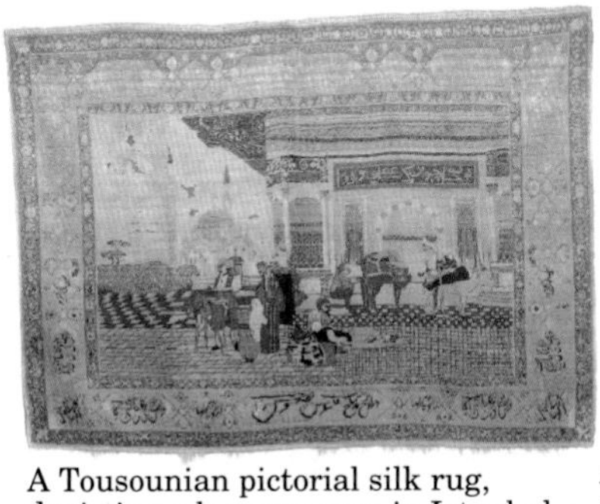

A Tousounian pictorial silk rug, depicting a bazaar scene in Istanbul, western Turkey, c1900, 59 x 81in (149 x 205cm).
£6,000–7,000 *S*

A Karabagh rug, south Caucasus, late 19thC, 91 x 41in (231 x 104cm).
£1,850–2,000 *P*

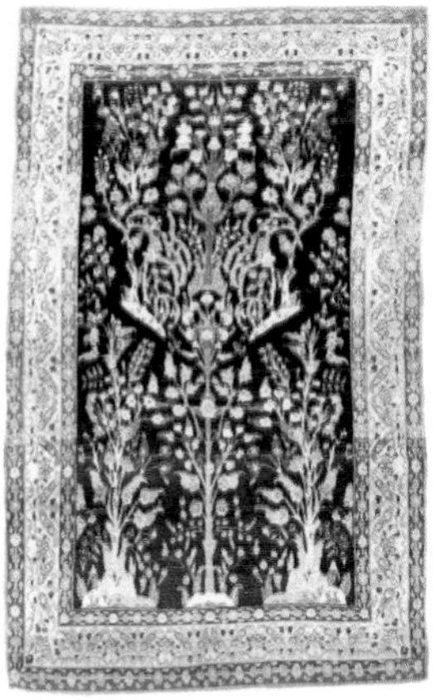

A Motashem Kashan rug, central Persia, late 19thC, 84 x 55in (214 x 139cm).
£3,000–3,500 *P*

A Kashan rug, with lobed terracotta pole medallion and spandrels, central Persia, c1920, 84 x 52in (214 x 131cm).
£1,650–1,850 *AWH*

A Heriz carpet, c1880, 222 x 144in (563 x 366cm).
£5,750–6,250 *P*

A Ziegler Mahal carpet, west Persia, late 19thC, 318 x 133in (810 x 337cm).
£7,000–8,000 *P*

A Bakshaish carpet, late 19thC, 130 x 97in (330 x 246cm).
£7,000–8,000 *S(NY)*

A Persian carpet, with Tree of Life design, c1900, 147 x 112in (373 x 284cm).
£8,750–10,000 *S(NY)*

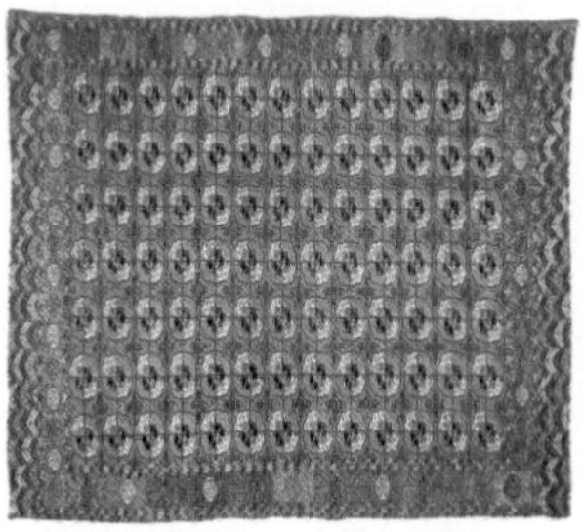

A Tekke carpet, with 7 columns of quartered *guls*, west Turkestan, c1890, 122 x 106in (310 x 269cm).
£3,000–3,500 *P*

An Agra carpet, centred by an Ardebil medallion, late 19thC, 166 x 126in (421 x 320cm).
£5,300–5,800 *P*

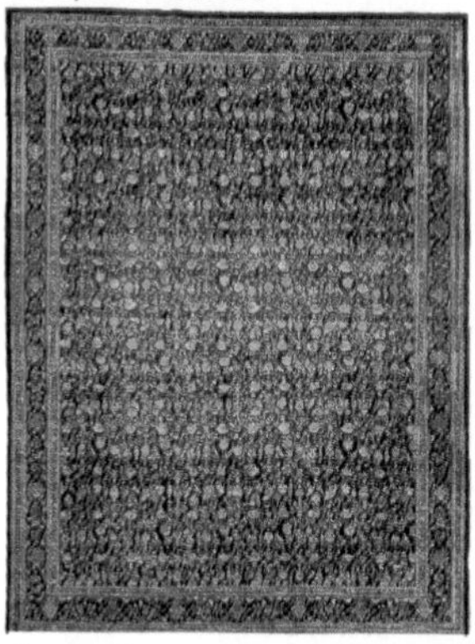

An Indian carpet, c1900, 237 x 180in (600 x 457cm).
£10,500–12,000 *B&B*

A Gabbeh rug, with 4 semi-naturalistic camels, south west Persia, c1900, 69 x 53in (175 x 135cm).
£3,200–3,800 *S(NY)*

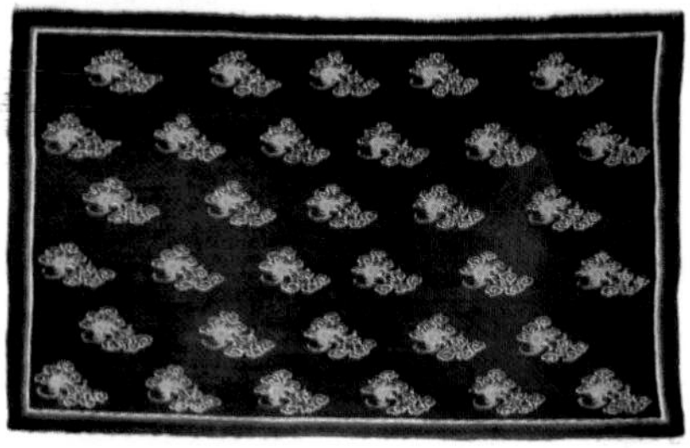

A Chinese rug, with coral red bats amongst stylised clouds, framed by linear borders, c1900, 98 x 60in (249 x 152cm).
£2,400–2,600 *P*

A Kansu carpet, west China, some areas repiled, early 19thC, 140 x 74in (356 x 188cm).
£11,500–13,000 *S(NY)*

A needlework picture, probably depicting Adam and Eve, repaired and with patches, early 18thC, 22½ x 24¾in (57 x 63cm).
£6,300–7,000 *S(NY)*

A set of 4 Italian silk cushions, with a silver thread border and boldly scrolling foliage, embroidered with flowers, butterflies and birds, on a cream ground, with later backs, part 18thC, 17¼ x 13in (44 x 33cm).
£9,000–10,000 *S*

A stumpwork embroidery, worked in silk, depicting the Judgement of Solomon, dated in beads '1654', 9 x 13in (23 x 33cm).
£20,500–23,000 *SWO*

A beaded picture, in original maple frame, early 19thC, 14½in (37cm) square.
£250–300 *MTa*

An embroidered picture, depicting a stylised beast in a landscape, early 19thC, 8 x 9in (20 x 23cm).
£1,700–1,850 *DaH*

A woolwork picture, c1880, 28 x 23in (71 x 58.5cm).
£100–120 *TMA*

A woolwork picture, depicting Red Riding Hood, formerly a polescreen, 19thC, 16 x 17in (40.5 x 43cm).
£225–265 *MTa*

A French allegorical tapestry, depicting the robed figure of Europe holding a mace, a key and a crown with other regal emblems, and putti, 18thC, 99 x 127in (251.5 x 322.5cm).
£12,000–14,000 *P*

A Louis XV Aubusson verdure landscape tapestry, depicting a dog catching a rabbit in a forest landscape with a distant chateau, in a floral border with central reserves of fountains, c1730, 111 x 165in (282 x 424cm).
£11,500–13,000 *S*

A Flemish tapestry, depicting Chinese pagoda-style buildings and water birds surrounded by trees and foliage, within a floral and spandrel design border, 18thC, 111 x 124in (282 x 315cm).
£8,500–10,000 *S(Cg)*

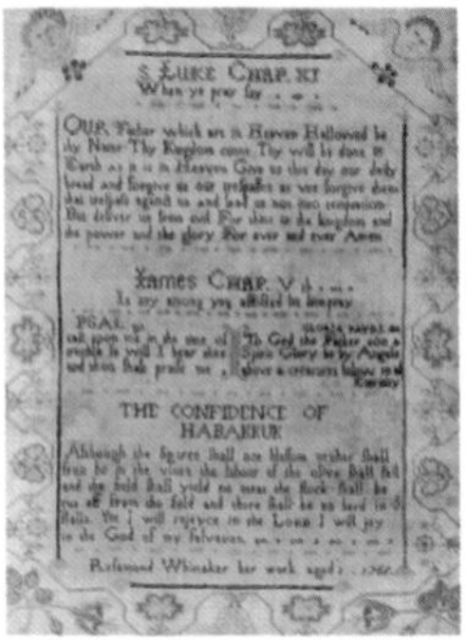

A linen sampler, dated '1765', 12 x 9in (30.5 x 23cm).
£950–1,100 *S(S)*

A needlework sampler, worked in coloured silks on linen, by E. Watts, dated '1775', 12¼ x 18in (31 x 46cm).
£620–700 *P(WM)*

A sampler, by Mary Blackwell, worked with the alphabet and verse, dated '1791', 16½in (42cm) square.
£500–600 *Bea(E)*

A linen sampler, dated '1781', 14 x 11½in (36 x 29cm).
£500–600 *S(S)*

A needlework sampler, by Sarah Ruskin, with a panel depicting a shepherd and a windmill, dated '1802', 17 x 12¼in (43 x 31cm).
£3,500–4,000 *P(WM)*

A sampler, by Ann Jeffery, c1825, 16½ x 14in (42 x 35.5cm).
£300–330 *OCH*

A linen sampler, by Sarah Sole, dated '1856', 18 x 13¼in (46 x 34cm).
£850–950 *S(S)*

A needlework sampler, by Elizabeth Berryman, c1840, 18 x 15in (45.5 x 38cm).
£250–285 *OCH*

A linen sampler, worked in cross stitch, with a windmill, verse and a floral border, 17¾ x 13¼in (45 x 33.5cm).
£800–900 *S(S)*

A needlework sampler, attributed to Elizabeth Taylor, New Jersey, c1840, 33 x 17¾in (84 x 45cm).
£3,500–4,000 *S(NY)*

A William IV needlework school sampler, worked with a 'Representation of Solomon's Temple', within a geometric strawberry border, dated '1832', 15¾ x 22½in (40 x 57cm).
£350–400 *P(WM)*

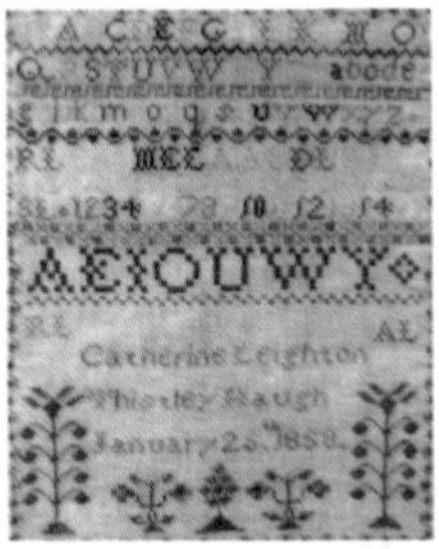

A woolwork sampler, by Catherine Leighton Thistley Waugh, 1885, 15 x 12in (38 x 30.5cm).
£360–400 *AP*

An inlaid gold and hardstone visiting card case, mid-19thC, 4in (10cm) high.
£3,200–3,500 *S(G)*

An enamel box, decorated with basket weave pattern and flowers, Birmingham, c1780, 2in (5cm) diam.
£550–600 *BHa*

A Continental polychrome enamel serpentine box, with silver mounts and hinge, painted with figures in landscapes, 18thC, 3½in (9cm) wide.
£550–600 *CDC*

A Limoges enamel plaque, in a gilt-bronze frame, 16thC, 6¾ x 5¼in (17 x 13.5cm).
£2,500–3,000 *S(Z)*

A Bilston enamel egg-shaped nutmeg grater, c1800, 2in (5cm) long.
£1,000–1,100 *BHa*

A Bilston enamel bird bonbonnière, slight damage, c1770, 2in (5cm) high.
£1,000–1,100 *BHa*

A Limoges enamel plaque, depicting the Nativity, in a gilt-metal frame, 19thC, 5 x 4in (12.5 x 10cm).
£520–580 *TMA*

An enamel card case, by Samson, Paris, decorated with figures in a landscape, late 19thC, 3in (7.5cm) high.
£650–750 *BHa*

A Russian cloisonné purse, decorated in red, blue, green and white with floral motifs, late 19thC, 3¼in (8.5cm) wide.
£400–450 *GH*

A Fabergé silver and gilt cloisonné enamel dish, painted with a traditional abstract design, c1900, 3½in (9cm) square, in a maple case.
£5,300–5,800 *HAM*

An Austrian enamel vase, decorated with a bust of a lady, the top in the form of a flower, c1900, 6in (15cm) high.
£1,000–1,250 *SHa*

An Imperial fan, the jewelled gold mounts by Fabergé, with cypher for the Queen of Prussia, inscribed and stamped, c1910, 8½in (21.5cm) long.
£19,500–22,000 *S(G)*

An enamel and gem-set bracelet, designed as a series of plaques each depicting a Swiss girl in regional costume, within a two-colour gold surround with applied gold rosettes and gem-set detail, the reverse with enamel plaques denoting each Swiss canton, c1840, 7in (17.5cm) long. **£3,000–3,500** *Bon*

A French enamelled gold and diamond-mounted bracelet, the hinged sections with engraved strapwork design, 19thC.
£1,100–1,200 *Bea(E)*

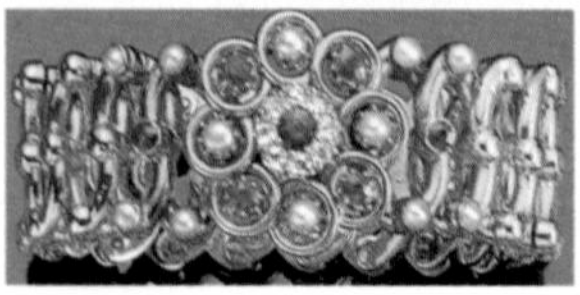

A late Victorian gold and multi-gem expanding bracelet, with central ruby and diamond flowerhead cluster, the border of rubies and half-pearls.
£1,400–1,600 *Bon(C)*

A cameo brooch, c1800, 1¼in (33mm) wide.
£1,000–1,100 *Bea(E)*

A hinged gold bangle, mounted with an Italian sardonyx cameo by Amastini, in a half-pearl surround, 19thC.
£3,800–4,200 *P*

A pavé-set coral and diamond bangle/brooch, the front designed as a detachable star, the bangle decorated with twisted wire trelliswork, brooch fitment missing, c1880.
£2,800–3,200 *S(Am)*

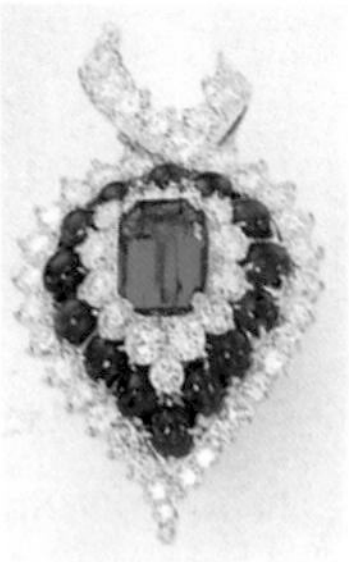

A sapphire, diamond and emerald brooch, by Bulgari, c1950.
£15,000–18,000 *S(G)*

A gold and imperial-foiled topaz suite of brooch and earrings, of scroll and bead openwork design, c1840, some fitments missing, in a fitted case.
£2,000–2,200 *DN*

A Cartier Mogul jade brooch, set with emeralds and rubies, 1920s.
£8,000–9,000 *FHF*

A gold and agate set cameo brooch, the gold setting with wirework, beaded and scrollwork decoration, late 19thC.
£1,200–1,400 *S(S)*

A gold and turquoise set brooch, with wirework and beaded decoration, locket back, c1860.
£300–330 *S(S)*

An emerald and diamond brooch, of scrolled cartouche design, late 19thC.
£2,200–2,500 *Bon*

A gold, blue enamelled and shell cameo brooch, carved with 3 figures with ruins in the background, c1860.
£650–750 *S(S)*

A gold, garnet and diamond pendant/necklace, mid-19thC, 16in (40.5cm) long.
£1,200–1,400 *S(NY)*

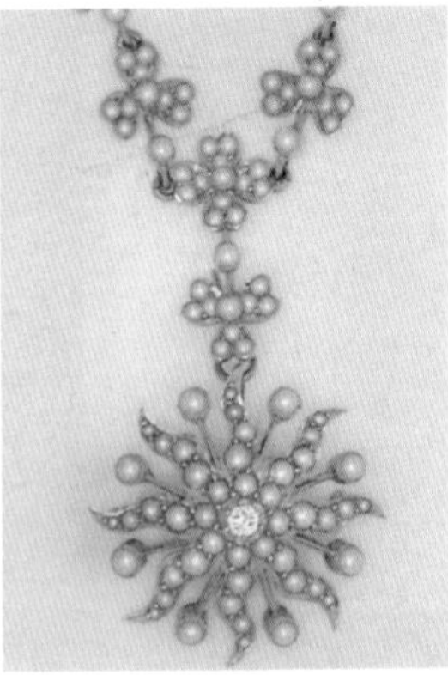

A late Victorian gold necklace, with half-pearl set clover leaf front, the pendant with diamond set centre.
£1,300–1,500 *P(WM)*

An Iberian finely pierced gold and diamond pendant/brooch, late 18thC, with later brooch fitting.
£1,000–1,200 *Bon*

A gold pendant, with seed pearl floral spray under glass, with half-pearl surround, c1800.
£750–850 *P*

An enamel, opal and rose diamond pendant/brooch, with monogram, c1820.
£2,500–3,000 *S(Am)*

An Edwardian fire opal necklace, the stones suspended from an old-cut diamond collet with trace link swags, the centre stone with a further drop.
£1,650–1,800 *DN*

An emerald and diamond pendant/brooch, of ribbon and garland design, with a pear-shaped emerald drop, late 19thC.
£3,300–3,600 *S*

A diamond, ruby and five-strand pearl necklace, c1880.
£6,500–7,500 *Bon*

La Fortune, a gold, enamel, diamond and pearl pendant, by Bapst & Falize, c1880.
£26,000–30,000 *P*

A polychrome enamel, sapphire, pearl and diamond pendant with openwork scrolling framework, with 5 pearl drops, c1895.
£2,300–2,600 *DN*

An 18ct gold cluster ring, with inset turquoise, c1840.
£220–250 *DIC*

A topaz and enamel pendant, edged with diamonds, c1895.
£1,500–1,700 *P*

A William IV amethyst five-stone dress ring, engraved with inscription and dated '1834'.
£450–500 *HofB*

An Edwardian 18ct gold sapphire five-stone half-hoop ring, the stones divided by pairs of diamond chips, Birmingham 1902.
£600–700 *HofB*

A Chinese cloisonné enamel box and cover, Ming Dynasty, 2in (5cm) diam.
£3,500–4,000 *S*

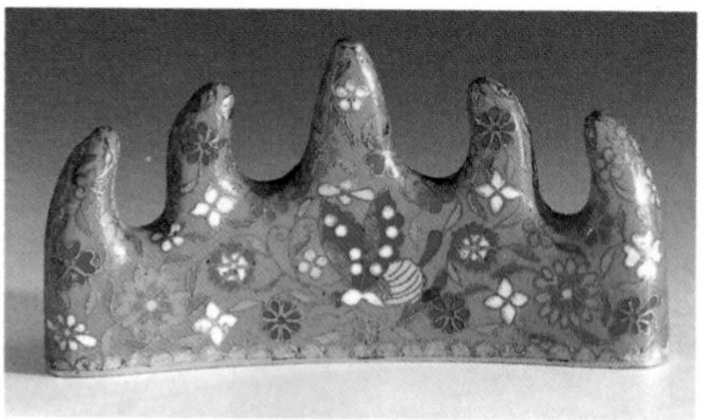

A Chinese cloisonné enamel brush rest, in the form of a five-peak mountain range, 18thC, 4½in (11.5cm) wide.
£2,000–2,200 *S(Am)*

A Chinese Imperial enamel mallet vase, Kangxi seal mark and period, 7½in (19cm) high.
£10,000–11,000 S

A Chinese Canton enamel punch bowl, polychrome decorated with figures in a landscape, Qianlong period, 14¾in (37.5cm) diam.
£2,500–3,000 *GeW*

A Chinese cloisonné *hu* and cover, late Qianlong period, 16¾in (42.5cm) high.
£2,100–2,500 *S(NY)*

A Japanese Ginbari cloisonné enamel *koro*, with Kumeno Teitaro mark, late 19thC, 7in (18cm) diam.
£3,000–3,300 *S(NY)*

A Chinese cloisonné enamel ram, bearing a pear-shaped vase on its back, with a saddle blanket, 19thC, 15in (38cm) high.
£5,000–5,500 *S(NY)*

A Chinese Canton enamel vase, decorated in blue and lime-green, c1800, 7in (18cm) high.
£250–300 *GeW*

A Japanese cloisonné plate, late 19thC, 12in (30.5cm) diam.
£140–160 *ELI*

A Japanese cloisonné vase, c1880, 4½in (11.5cm) high.
£450–500 *MCN*

A pair of Japanese cloisonné plates, each with different chrysanthemum decoration, c1900, 12in (30.5cm) diam.
£350–400 *ELI*

A pair of Chinese cloisonné vases, decorated with geometric roundels, and a matching bowl, late 19thC, vases 12½in (32cm) high.
£250–300 *E*

A Chinese inlaid bronze mirror, circa 200 BC, 5in (12.5cm) wide.
£21,000–25,000 *S(NY)*

A Chinese repoussé decorated gold box and cover, with a gold lining, Yuan Dynasty, 3in (7.5cm) wide.
£10,500–12,000 *S*

A Japanese gilt and bronze tobacco box and cover, possibly for the Dutch market, 18thC, 5¾in (14.5cm) high.
£3,000–3,300 *P*

A gilt-bronze figure, Wanli period, 8¾in (22cm) high.
£1,300–1,500 *P*

A Japanese silver and gilt *kogo*, signed 'Setsuho Hidetomo', Meiji period, 2¾in (7cm) diam.
£5,600–6,200 *Bea(E)*

A Chinese gold splashed bronze *hu*, Xuande mark, 18thC, 12¼in (31cm) high.
£4,000–4,500 *S(NY)*

A Japanese bronze and mixed metal vase, signed 'Miyabe Atsuyoshi', late 19thC, 12in (30.5cm) high.
£2,300–2,500 *S(NY)*

A lacquer mirror stand, 19thC, 15in (38cm) high.
£2,500–3,000 *S(NY)*

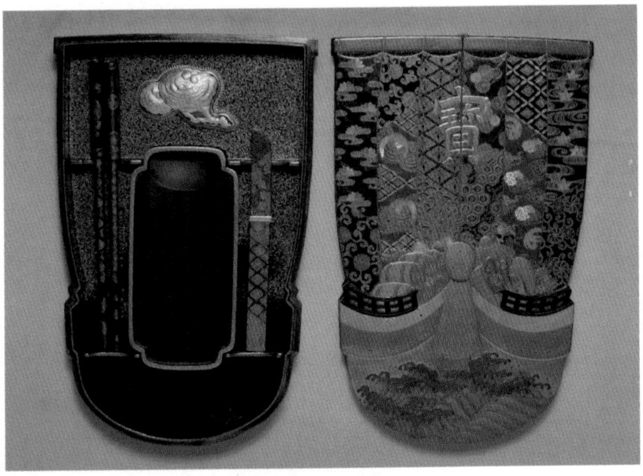

A Japanese lacquer writing box, with fitted interior, the rims reinforced with silver, 19thC, 8¼in (21cm) high.
£5,300–6,000 *P*

A Chinese carved cinnabar lacquer double box and cover, Qing Dynasty, 7in (18cm) wide.
£3,500–4,000 *S*

A Japanese lacquer and mother-of-pearl inlaid presentation box, with Imperial crest, c1900, 10in (25.5cm) wide.
£9,000–10,000 *MCN*

A Japanese inlaid lacquer tea caddy, by Bunjusai Chosetsu, covered with platinum bands, signed, 19thC, 3in (7.5cm) high.
£3,700–4,000 *S*

A Japanese lacquer vase, by Shibayama, c1880, 12in (30.5cm) high.
£3,500–4,000 *MCN*

A Chinese reverse mirror painting, Qianlong period, in a giltwood frame, 14¼ x 24¼in (36 x 61.5cm).
£10,500–11,500 *Bon*

Three Chinese barrel-shaped glasses, carved with scrolling dragons, 18thC, largest 4in (10cm) high.
£6,000–6,600 *S(NY)*

A pair of Chinese glass vases, c1800, 8¾in (22cm) high.
£2,400–2,700 *S(HK)*

A pair of Chinese glass bowls, carved with figures in a landscape, on carved openwork ivory stands, 19thC, 6in (15cm) diam.
£3,400–3,700 *S(NY)*

A Chinese spinach green jade vessel and cover, Qing Dynasty, 6in (15cm) high.
£3,200–3,500 *S*

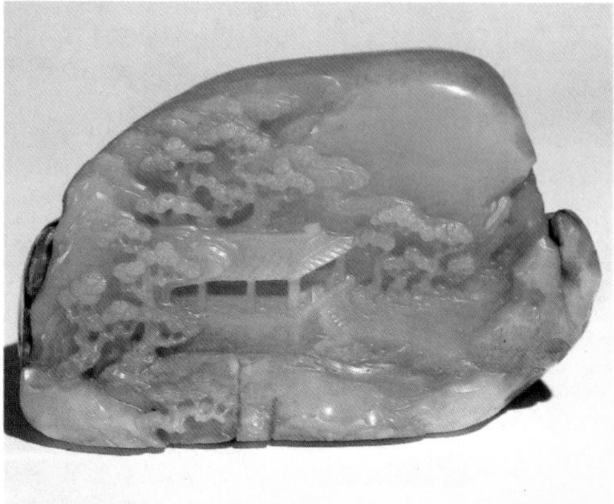

A Chinese jade boulder carving, Yangzhou school, Qianlong period, 6½in (16.5cm) long.
£5,500–6,000 *P*

A pair of Chinese polychrome stucco figures of temple guardians, damaged and restored, Ming Dynasty, 14½in (37cm) high.
£5,300–5,800 *S(NY)*

A Japanese giltwood figure of Amida Nyorai, 18thC, 23in (58cm) high.
£1,500–1,800 *S(Am)*

A Chinese celadon jade carving of a horse, recumbent amongst waves, holding 2 scrolls, 18thC, 5in (13cm) wide.
£2,700–3,000 *S(Am)*

A Chinese jadeite figure of a maiden Immortal, with a crane and spray of *lingzhi,* Qing Dynasty, 10½in (26.5cm) high.
£3,500–3,800 *S*

A Chinese carved figure of an Immortal, c1850, 35in (89cm) high.
£675–750 *MiA*

A Japanese carved wood model of a crab, c1900, 4½in (11.5cm) wide.
£700–800 *MCN*

An enamelled silver snuff bottle, Kangxi/Yongzheng period, 2¾in (7cm) high.
£8,000–9,000 *JWA*

A Chinese glass snuff bottle, Yangzhou school, 1780–1850, 2in (5cm) high.
£1,250–1,400 *JWA*

A Chinese amber snuff bottle, 19thC, 2½in (6.5cm) high.
£600–700 *P*

A Japanese inro, signed 'Seichi', c1800, 4in (10cm) high.
£7,500–8,500 *MCN*

A Japanese silk wedding kimono, machine embroidered, 1960s.
£400–460 *ASG*

A Japanese kimono, with woven flower pattern, 1940s.
£75–85 *ASG*

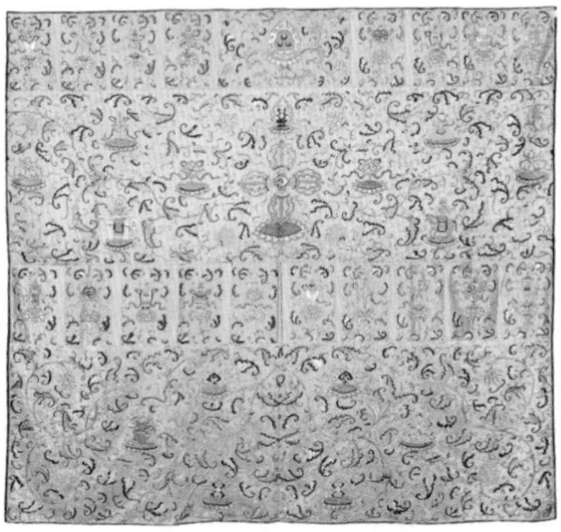

A Chinese silk embroidered altar frontal, with Buddhist and other emblems, 18thC, 68 x 78in (172.5 x 198cm).
£4,200–4,700 *S(NY)*

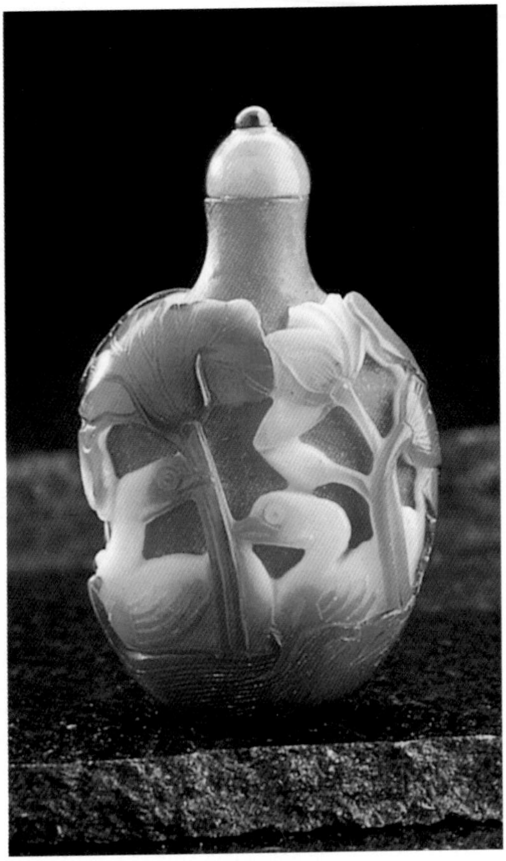

A Japanese Nanban style inlaid lacquer cabinet-on-stand, restored, 17thC, 18in (45.5cm) wide.
£3,800–4,200 *S(NY)*

A Japanese inlaid lacquer cabinet-on-stand, with hinged and sliding doors, late 19thC, 42¼in (107.5cm) high.
£5,000–5,500 *S(NY)*

A Japanese carved hardwood side cabinet, on cabriole legs, 19thC, 39in (99cm) wide.
£800–900 *TMA*

A Japanese lacquer and ivory inlaid *shodana*, late 19thC, 42½in (108cm) wide.
£2,200–2,500 *P(WM)*

A pair of Chinese *zitan*, hardwood and ivory curio cabinets, the removable double-tiered book stack with disguised drawers, 19thC, 16½in (42cm) wide.
£8,500–9,500 *S(NY)*

A Japanese black and gold lacquer table cabinet, damaged, Meiji period, 17in (43cm) wide.
£400–450 *Bea(E)*

A Chinese bamboo throne, with fretwork panels, 18th/19th century.
£3,300–3,600 *S(NY)*

A Chinese mahogany reclining armchair, with adjustable back and hinged footrest, 19thC.
£2,500–2,750 *S(NY)*

A Chinese carved mahogany nest of 4 tables, late 19thC, largest 20in (51cm) wide.
£1,100–1,250 *ANT*

A Chinese red lacquer long desk, with 4 short frieze drawers, on slightly flared legs, 18thC, 65in (165cm) wide.
£4,200–4,800 *S(NY)*

A Chinese export carved hardwood stand, with a rouge marble top, late 19thC, 23in (58.5cm) high.
£180–220 *MEG*

A pair of Chinese bamboo D-form tables, with lattice aprons, joined by low stretchers, 19thC, 40½in (103cm) wide.
£6,000–6,600 *S(NY)*

A Kashan moulded lustre pottery tile, with an inscription in cobalt blue *naskh* script, Persia, 13thC, 14 x 13in (35.5 x 33cm).
£3,000–3,300 *Bon*

A Mamluk painted jar, with stylised inscription, 14thC, 8in (20.5cm) high.
£2,300–2,500 *S(NY)*

A Kubachi pottery dish, Safavid Persia, slight damage and restoration, early 17thC, 13½in (34.5cm) diam.
£9,000–10,000 *C*

A Safavid underglaze-painted pottery ghalian base, Persia, late 17thC, 11¾in (30cm) high.
£8,500–9,500 *Bon*

A Safavid style tile panel, comprising 12 tiles, Qajar Persia, mid-19thC, 37¼ x 28in (94.5 x 71cm).
£6,500–7,500 *C*

A Tunisian pottery tile panel, comprising 50 tiles, early 18thC, 63 x 33in (160 x 84cm).
£4,000–4,500 *C*

A Qur'an, on polished buff paper, 19thC, text 7 x 4¼in (18 x 11cm), in red morocco binding.
£18,000–20,000 *C*

An Ottoman ruby and emerald-set jade plaque, mounted as a mirror, Turkey, 18thC, 8½in (21.5cm) high.
£12,700–14,000 *S*

A pair of Qajar enamelled gold earrings, slight damage, Persia, 19thC, 2in (5cm) long.
£1,000–1,100 *C*

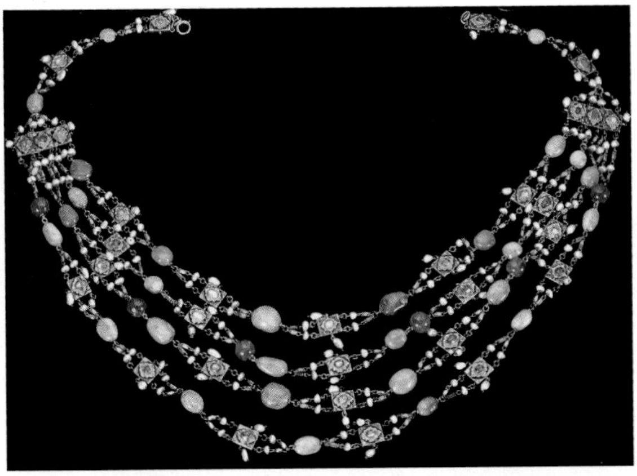

A Qajar necklace, the 4 gold chains with aventurine quartz beads and enamelled ruby-set gold plaques, the chain strung with baroque pearls, Persia, 19thC, 25½in (65cm) long.
£8,000–9,000 *S*

A Persian lacquer mirror case, signed 'Kazim Ibni Najaf Ali', c1855, 10 x 7in (25.5 x 18cm).
£2,300–2,500 *JFG*

The signature is that of the son of a famous Persian painter.

A Turkish linen quilt facing, embroidered with silks in laid and couched stitches, c1700, 86 x 51in (218 x 130cm).
£1,400–1,600 *P*

l. An Ottoman silk thread panel, each medallion bordered by carnations, Turkey, 16thC, 19¾ x 12½in (50 x 32cm).
£2,000–2,200 *Bon*

A gilded sheet copper lion weathervane, with applied mane and acanthus brackets, 18thC, 60in (152cm) long.
£8,000–9,000 *S(S)*

A pair of carved marble busts, depicting a miser and a drunkard, on pedestals incised with text, early 20thC, 44in (112cm) high.
£6,500–7,500 *WW*

A pair of Victorian cast iron campana-shaped urns, 30in (76cm) high.
£300–350 *GAZE*

A terracotta urn, on a plinth, c1880, 37in (94cm) high.
£1,500–1,800 *RAW*

A terracotta urn, c1900, 37in (94cm) high.
£650–750 *DOR*

An oval-shaped reeded and turned walnut towel rail, c1880, 19in (48.5cm) wide.
£80–100 *MLL*

A pair of oak cupboard doors, c1535, 68in (172.5cm) high.
£5,800–6,400 *FW&C*

A Puritas washdown closet, c1890, 16in (40.5cm) high.
£650–700 *NOST*

A pair of brass fingerplates, with geometric pattern, c1820, 11in (28cm) long.
£100–120 *DRU*

A pair of brass fingerplates, with foliate and scroll pattern, c1900, 15½in (39.5cm) long.
£180–200 *DRU*

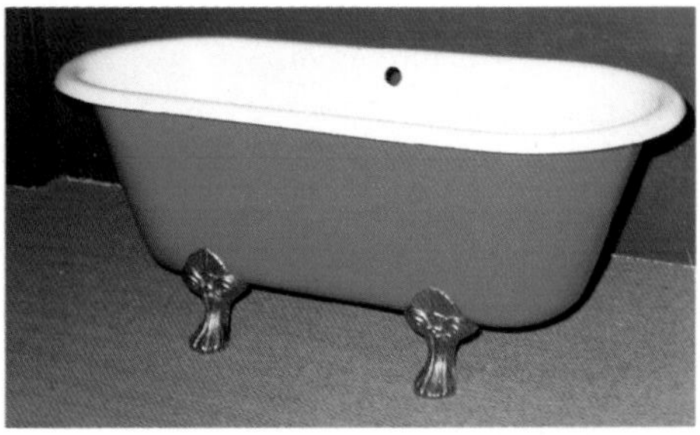

A French double-ended bath, with Empire style feet, early 20thC, 65in (165cm) long.
£800–1,000 *POSH*

A pine chimneypiece, the centre carved with urns, swags, leaves and flowers, c1770, 83in (211cm) wide.
£7,000–8,000 *S*

A lime wood chimneypiece, carved with eagles' heads and foliate scrolls, with later oak slips, c1790, 55in (140cm) wide.
£3,200–3,500 *Hal*

A Victorian Jacobean style carved oak fire surround, 77in (195.5cm) wide.
£2,500–3,000 *RAW*

A Victorian pine fire surround, with tiled insert, 54in (137cm) wide.
£500–600 *RAW*

A Regency fire basket, with brass finials and serpentine frieze, 24in (61cm) wide.
£300–350 *GAZE*

An Edwardian cast iron fire surround and fender, with tiled insert, c1900, 41in (104cm) wide.
£800–900 *NOST*

A steel railed fender, with bronze mounts, c1840, 49in (124.5cm) wide.
£450–500 *NOST*

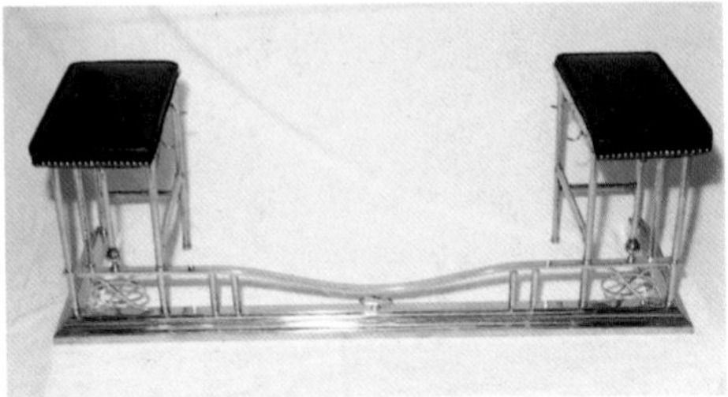

A brass club fender, with leather seats on a moulded base, c1905, 51in (129.5cm) wide.
£1,000–1,200 *LCA*

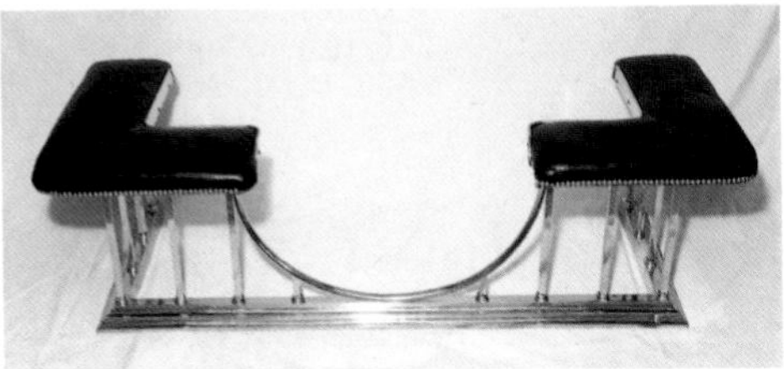

A brass club fender, the leather seats with rear brass heat protectors, c1905, 54in (137cm) wide.
£2,000–2,200 *LCA*

A steel and brass fire grate, the arched back cast with a pair of griffins and a brazier, on cabriole legs with pad feet, late 19thC, 22in (56cm) wide.
£1,850–2,000 *S*

A Welsh brass and steel footman, with cabriole front legs, c1880, 15in (38cm) wide.
£350–400 *DBA*

A pair of brass andirons, each with knopped urn-shaped finials on a lobed sphere and spreading scrolling plinth centred by a lion's head mask, on lions' paw feet, 19thC, 28¾in (73cm) high.
£2,000–2,200 *P*

A bronze model of a mastiff, signed 'L. Bureau', c1900, 18in (45.5cm) wide.
£1,150–1,275 *WeH*

A pair of French parcel-gilt bronze figures of a Persian king and queen, converted to lamps, mid-19thC, 17¼in (44cm) high.
£2,000–2,200 *Bon*

A bronze group of a Merino ram and ewe, on a naturalistic base, by Jules Moigniez, signed, c1870, 12½in (32cm) wide.
£2,000–2,200 *M*

A pair of French gilt-bronze candlesticks, with shell-decorated nozzles, 18thC, 5in (13cm) high.
£2,500–3,000 *P*

A bronze model of an elephant, signed 'J. V. Badin', early 20thC, 7in (18cm) wide.
£5,750–6,500 *S*

A pair of bronze models of cranes, late 19thC, 24in (61cm) high.
£850–1,000 *MRW*

A pair of gilt-bronze candlesticks, the bases with canted corners, c1900, 7¾in (19.5cm) high.
£700–800 *ART*

A bronze, gilt-bronze and ivory figure, entitled 'La Liseuse', by A. E. Carrier de Belleuse, late 19thC, 24½in (62cm) high.
£4,000–4,500 *S(S)*

A bronze inkwell, in the form of 3 bulls surmounted by a cherub, on a marble plinth, c1860, 7½in (19cm) high.
£450–500 *ANT*

A pair of Napoleon III gilt-bronze tazzas, each cast in the form of a putto, c1870, 14½in (37cm) high.
£3,000–3,500 *S*

A bronze group of Perseus with the head of Medusa, after Benvenuto Cellini, on a marble plinth, 19thC, 38½in (98cm) high.
£1,000–1,200 *AH*

A brass circular birdcage, with 2 perches and an ebony handle, c1890, 22in (56cm) high.
£450–500 *LCA*

A Dutch copper and brass tobacco box, the lid depicting William of Orange, c1690, 6¼in (16cm) wide.
£1,400–1,600 *S(NY)*

A brass desk calendar, with elaborate foliate decoration, c1890, 10in (25.5cm) high.
£100–120 *CHe*

A pair of brass candlesticks, on square bases, late 18thC, 11in (28cm) high.
£450–500 *ANT*

A pair of Georgian brass candlesticks, with stepped square bases, 9½in (24cm) high.
£165–185 *SPU*

A brass and copper log bin, the rim applied with star motifs and paterae, 19thC, 23½in (60cm) diam.
£3,000–3,500 *S*

A copper and brass-mounted coffee pot, mid-18thC, 11in (28cm) high.
£380–420 *OCH*

A copper and brass vase, with leaf decoration and pierced rim, c1880, 15in (38cm) diam.
£240–265 *MLL*

A cast iron doorstop, in the form of a woodcutter and his dog, with original paint, 19thC, 15½in (39.5cm) high.
£120–135 *MTa*

A French spelter figure of a girl, signed, on original base, c1870, 18in (45.5cm) high.
£110–125 *MiA*

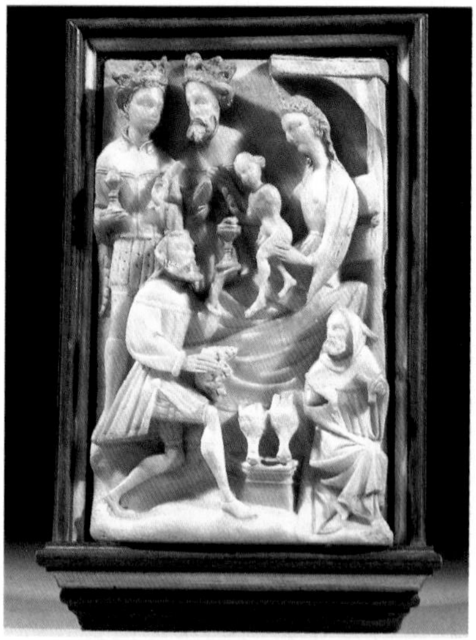

An alabaster relief of the Adoration of the Magi, Nottingham, 15thC, 17in (43cm) high.
£9,000–10,000 *S(Am)*

A French alabaster figure of an Arabian water carrier, signed 'L. Madrassi', early 20thC, 31¾in (80.5cm) high.
£4,000–4,500 *S*

An alabaster bust, by Antonio Frilli, late 19thC, 27½in (70cm) high.
£2,000–2,200 *Bon*

An Italian polychrome terracotta group of the Virgin and Child, early 15thC, 19in (48cm) high.
£10,500–12,500 *S*

A pair of French Siena marble tazzas, mid-19thC, 19¼in (49cm) diam.
£6,500–7,500 *S(NY)*

A gilded terracotta model of a lion, early 19thC, 4½in (11.5cm) high.
£130–145 *ANT*

A carved marble bust of Apollo, 18thC, on a later socle, 36in (91.5cm) high.
£2,200–2,500 *DN*

A terracotta figure of a water carrier, by Giuseppe Vaccaro of Caltagirone, c1850, 12½in (32cm) high.
£600–685 *ANT*

A wall-mounted terracotta model of a dog's head, fitted with loops for hanging, c1890, 8in (20.5cm) high.
£800–900 *ARE*

A Goldscheider terracotta figure of a boy, with impressed and printed factory marks, early 20thC, 21½in (54.5cm) high.
£600–700 *AH*

A Dutch walnut group of St Anne with the Virgin and Child, probably Brabant, late 15thC, 21¾in (55cm) high.
£6,500–7,500 *S(Am)*

A gilded carved figure of a saint, c1600, 12½in (32cm) high.
£1,200–1,500 *DBA*

A pair of Continental carved and polychromed giltwood figures of angels, damaged, 18thC, 17¼in (44cm) high.
£2,300–2,500 *B&B*

A walnut and ebonised serpentine inkstand, c1860, 13½in (34.5cm) wide.
£600–675 *GeM*

A carved boxwood snuff box, in the form of a lion, possibly Dutch, slight damage, c1700, 4¼in (11cm) long.
£4,750–5,250 *S(NY)*

A lignum vitae combined wassail bowl and pestle, 17thC, bowl 6in (15cm) high.
£1,500–1,650 *AEF*

A carved wooden box, with a ship on top, c1880, 11in (28cm) wide.
£180–200 *MLL*

A yew-wood screw type nutcracker, carved as a double head in a nightcap, 19thC, 6½in (16.5cm) high.
£160–175 *TMA*

A Tunbridge Ware tea caddy, with views of Eridge Castle and Holy Trinity Church, c1840, 14in (35.5cm) wide.
£2,200–2,500 *AMH*

An Austrian wooden stirrup cup, carved with a hound's head, c1800, 3¼in (8.5cm) high.
£675–750 *AEF*

A Tunbridge Ware needlework box, fitted with spools, tape and thimble, c1845, 9in (23cm) wide.
£1,400–1,550 *AMH*

A French oyster kingwood and brass-mounted coffret, with fleur-de-lys decoration, enclosing a later lidded strong box, late 17thC, 14¼in (36cm) wide.
£1,250–1,500 *P*

An inlaid mahogany octagonal tea caddy, c1770, 5¼in (13.5cm) high.
£600–700 *GeM*

A German oyster walnut and mother-of-pearl veneered box, with brass mounts, late 17thC, 10½in (26.5cm) wide.
£400–450 *CORO*

A Georgian gold-mounted ivory patch box, with green and blue enamel panels, one depicting a classical lady, 4in (10cm) wide.
£360–400 *RBB*

A George III mahogany knife box, the inside of the lid inlaid with a star, 14in (35.5cm) high.
£360–400 *JH*

An ivory tea caddy, with tortoiseshell facings, c1790, 4in (10cm) high.
£2,000–2,300 *GeM*

A tortoiseshell veneered tea chest, late 18thC, with 17thC silver and gilt-metal mounts, and 2 plain oval silver caddies, marked 'SW', London 1778, tea chest 8¾in (22cm) wide.
£6,500–7,500 *DN*

A staw-work casket, depicting naval scenes, with a fitted interior, early 19thC, 12in (30.5cm) wide.
£400–450 *Odi*

A hexagonal curled paper tea caddy, with original colour, c1800, 5in (12.5cm) high.
£850–950 *GeM*

A Regency mahogany tea chest, with brass carrying handle, with 3 carved boxwood caddies, 8¾in (22cm) wide.
£4,200–5,000 *P*

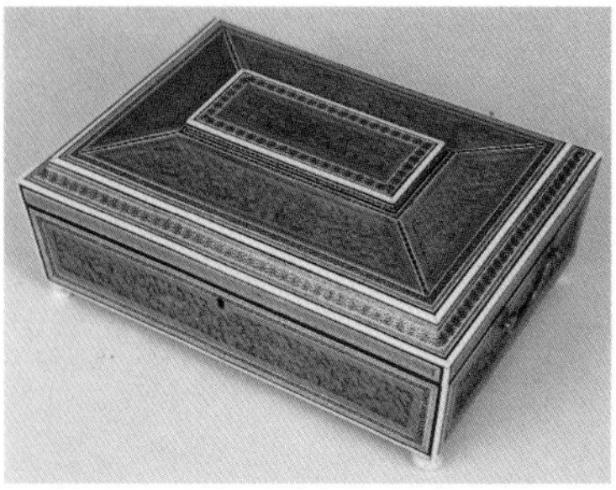

A carved sandalwood and micro-mosaic sewing box, c1840, 12½in (32cm) wide.
£600–700 *CORO*

A mother-of-pearl writing slope, dated '1866', 14in (35.5cm) wide.
£850–950 *SPa*

A burr walnut lady's dressing case, c1842, 14in (35.5cm) wide.
£1,650–1,850 *GeM*

A malachite and ormolu jewel box, late 19thC, 14in (35.5cm) wide.
£4,200–4,700 *S(NY)*

An engraved brass document box, with carrying handles and internal letter holder, Ceylon, c1870, 16in (40.5cm) wide.
£500–600 *CORO*

l. A burr walnut and brass edged writing box, with secret drawers, c1860, 14in (35.5cm) wide.
£450–500 *GeM*

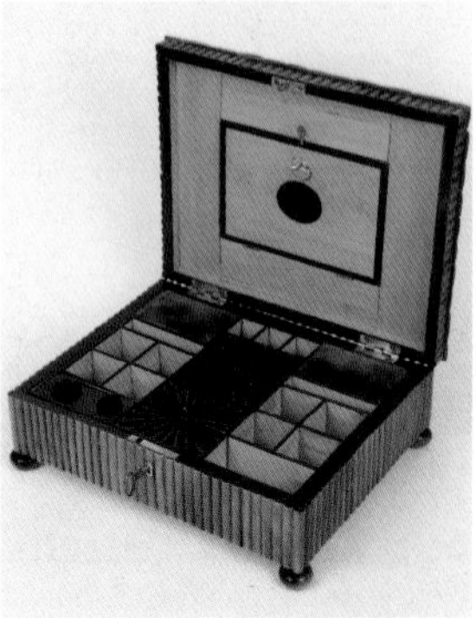

An Indian sandalwood sewing box, the exterior with reeded horn, c1860, 10¾in (27.5cm) wide.
£1,500–1,800 *CORO*

ICONS

A Russian icon of The Mother of God of Smolensk, painted on an olive green ground and encased in a later gilt-metal oklad, the garments with a covering of seed pearls and semi-precious stones, 17thC, 10¾ x 9½in (27.5 x 24cm).
£1,600–2,000 *S*

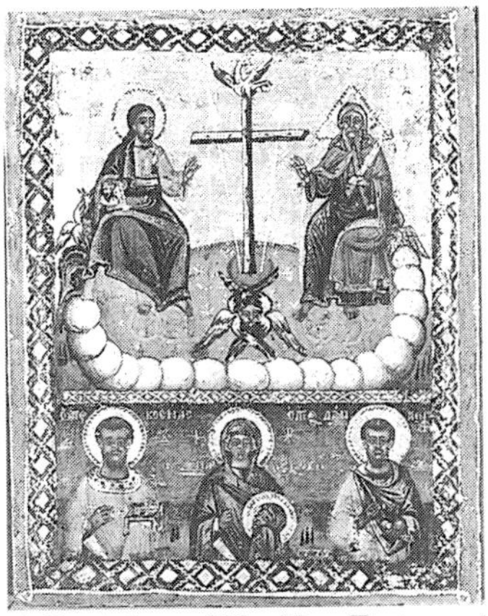

A Greek icon of The New Testament Trinity, the lower register with Saint Paraskeva, flanked by Saint Cosmos and Saint Damian, dated '1773', 9¾ x 8in (25 x 20cm).
£750–825 *P*

Icons

The first icons were produced in Byzantium – present-day Istanbul – in early Christian times, appearing further afield, such as in the Balkans and Russia, as Christianity spread.

A Russian icon of Saint Nicholas of Mozhaisk, c1700, 20 x 13in (51 x 33cm).
£4,500–5,000 *RKa*

A Greek icon of Saint Nicholas, seated on a stone bench, holding the Gospels, 18thC, 13¾ x 10½in (35 x 27cm).
£580–650 *P*

A Russian icon of The Crucifixion, the panel inset with a brass cross embellished with blue enamel, the panel painted with the Baptism of Christ and Saints, 18thC, 12¼ x 10¼in (31 x 26cm).
£700–800 *P*

l. A Russian icon of The Coronation of Mary, 18thC, 12¼ x 10¼in (31 x 26cm).
£1,150–1,300 *JAA*

A Russian icon of The Nativity of Christ, incorporating subsidiary scenes including the Adoration of the Magi, 17thC, 12½ x 10¾in (31.5 x 27cm).
£2,300–2,800 *S*

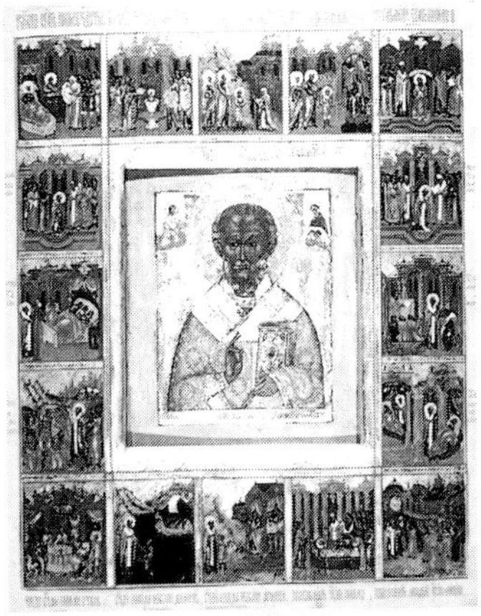

A Russian icon of Saint Nicholas, the panels inset with 16 important events in his life, 18thC, 27¼ x 23¼in (62 x 59cm).
£3,300–3,600 *JAA*

A Russian icon of The Crucifixion, the brass cross set in a panel painted with the Mother of God and Saint John at the foot of the cross, with winged seraphs above, 18thC, 10½ x 6in (27 x 15.5cm).
£850–950 *P*

A Russian icon of The Descent into Hell and Principal Feasts, early 19thC, 14 x 11¾in (35.5 x 30cm).
£3,000–3,500 *RKa*

A Russian icon of Christ Pantocrator, with silver-gilt riza, in hinged cartouche-shaped box-frame, 19thC, 7 x 5¾in (18 x 14.5cm).
£300–350 *SLM*

A Russian icon of The Guardian Angel, painted by A. Glazunov, 1909, 12¼ x 10½in (31 x 26.5cm).
£1,500–1,800 *JAA*

A Russian icon of Saint Sophia, The Divine Wisdom of God, the borders with repoussé silver covering, early 19thC, 12½ x 10½in (31.5 x 27cm).
£1,600–2,000 *S*

A Russian icon of Saint John the Evangelist, depicted with his scribe, Prokhor, 19thC, 21 x 17½in (53.5 x 44.5cm).
£1,100–1,200 *S(NY)*

l. A Russian icon of the Three Hierarchs, painted on a gilt incised ground, c1900, 12¼ x 10½in (31 x 26.5cm).
£500–600 *JAA*

A Russian icon of The Pokrov, encased in a repoussé and chased silver-gilt oklad, the garments of the Virgin and Roman the Melodist decorated with filigree applied with silver pellets, maker's mark 'I.S.', St Petersburg, 1886, 12¼ x 10½in (31 x 26.5cm).
£900–1,000 *S*

A near Eastern icon of The Enthroned Mother of God with the Infant Saviour, the gilded crowns in shallow relief with paste gems, the top and bottom registers painted with saints, 19thC, 29¼ x 19¼in (74 x 49cm).
£1,800–2,000 *P*

A Russian icon of the Madonna and Child, with silver-gilt and enamel frame, painted in oil, framed in polychrome cloisonné enamels with formal leaf and scroll motifs, c1896, 4¾in (12cm) high.
£800–900 *S(G)*

A Russian icon of Saint Nicholas, contained in a repoussé and engine-turned silver oklad, with cloisonné enamel halo and corners, c1908, 8¾ x 7in (22 x 18cm).
£600–700 *P*

PORTRAIT MINIATURES & SILHOUETTES

A silhouette miniature of a lady, by William Alport, in an oval hammered brass frame, c1810, 4½in (11.5cm) high.
£70–85 *Bon*

A French portrait miniature of a young child, attributed to Julie Corneo, wearing a white dress with blue ribbon trim, holding a posy of red flowers, signed and dated 'J. C. 1796', 2¾in (70mm) diam, in a gilt-mounted wood frame.
£700–800 *P*

A portrait of a child, entitled 'John Russell', by Annie Dixon, in a gilt-metal frame with ribbon cresting and scroll motif, signed and dated '1872', 5¾in (15cm) high, with velvet lined fitted leather carrying case.
£3,500–4,000 *P*

r. A silhouette of Lt Edward M. Yard 'US Navy Boston', by Auguste Edouart, dated '1st March 1842', 11¾in (30cm) high.
£450–550 *SK(B)*

A silhouette miniature of an officer of the 10th North Lincolnshire Regiment of Foot, picked out in scarlet, blue and gold, by Charles Buncombe, c1805, 4¼in (11cm) high, in a gilt-metal and ebonised frame.
£750–900 *DN*

A portrait miniature of a gentleman, by Richard Cosway, embroidered with silver thread, the reverse by John Smart, set either side in a gold frame with plaited border, c1760, 1½in (38mm) high.
£5,500–6,000 *Bon*

A portrait miniature of Captain Frederick Spencer, later 4th Earl Spencer, wearing a blue uniform with gold lace, by Henry Pierce Bone, signed, inscribed and dated '1835', in a gilt-metal mount, 4½in (11.5cm) high.
£4,200–4,600 *S*

A portrait miniature of a young gentleman, by Abraham Daniel, in a gold locket frame with split pearl surround and hair back, c1790, 2in (50mm) high.
£2,400–2,700 *BHa*

A portrait miniature of a gentleman, wearing a black cloak and white lawn collar, by Richard Gibson, in gilt-metal frame, c1650, 2in (50mm) high.
£5,800–6,500 *Bon*

A portrait miniature of Charles Earl, by Thomas Hargreaves, c1820, 6 x 4in (15 x 10cm) high.
£1,200–1,500 *BHa*

A portrait miniature of Lord Loftus, by Andrew Plimer, in a gold frame with hair back, c1790, 3in (7.5cm) high.
£2,000–2,200 *BHa*

Locate the Source

The source of each illustration in Miller's can be found by checking the code letters below each caption with the Key to Illustrations.

A portrait miniature of Arthur Wellesley, first Duke of Wellington, wearing a major general's uniform with gold epaulettes, in gesso frame in the form of a Duke's coat-of-arms, above an oblong glazed velvet aperture, by Robert Home, c1804, 3¼in (8.5cm) high.
£6,000–7,000 *Bon*

A portrait miniature of Lord William Osborne Elphinstone, in officer's uniform of the 10th Hussars, the gilt-metal frame with cast foliage border, by Simon Jacques Rochard, signed and dated '1829', 6in (15cm) high.
£2,500–3,000 *P*

A portrait miniature of a young man, wearing a blue coat, by E. Weser, signed and dated '1829', 2½in (6.5cm) high, in an ivory and wooden frame.
£380–420 *P(EA)*

l. A portrait miniature of a young lady, with dark curly hair, by John Wright, c1805, 3in (7.5cm) high.
£1,100–1,250 *BHa*

A portrait miniature of Lady Strangways, wearing a blue dress with diamond brooch, by Joseph Pastorini, c1810, 3in (7.5cm) high, with fitted leather case.
£650–700 *Bon*

A portrait miniature of a lady, wearing a white turban and black dress with a fichu, by Thomas Richmond, gilt frame, c1810, 3in (7.5cm) high.
£1,100–1,200 *Hal*

Thomas Richmond was born in Kew in 1771. He was a pupil of his cousin George Engleheart and exhibited at the Royal Academy from 1795–1829.

A portrait miniature of a lady, wearing a white dress with blue sash and a black choker, the reverse with plaited hair, English School, c1790, 3in (7.5cm) high.
£550–600 *CGC*

A pair of portrait miniatures of a lady and gentleman, members of the Piarritz family, English School, c1790, 2½in (64mm) high.
£600–700 *HYD*

A portrait miniature of a lady, wearing a buff coloured dress with lace trim, red cloak and pearl and enamelled jewellery, c1840, 4in (10cm) high.
£600–700 *WeH*

A portrait miniature of a gentleman, c1810, 2¼in (55mm) high, in a plaster gilt frame.
£160–180 *P(NW)*

A silhouette of Jean Pierre Blanchard, reserved against a balloon, in a gilt-metal mount, French School, early 19thC, 3in (7.5cm) high.
£800–900 *S*

A portrait miniature of an officer in tartan, Scottish School, c1810, 2¾in (70mm) high.
£850–950 *BHa*

A French portrait miniature of Napoleon, on porcelain, in a heavy gilt-brass frame, 19thC, 2¼in (57mm) high.
£450–500 *MEA*

l. A silhouette of the Stéavenson family, cut-out and bronzed on card, maple wood frame with inner ebonised wood border, English School, dated '1840', 14in (35.5cm) high.
£300–330 *Bon*

Two portrait miniatures of ladies, in gilt frames, 19thC, 12in (30.5cm) high.
£320–375 each *GAZE*

ANTIQUITIES

The antiquities market saw some big changes during 1997. Prominent was the change in attitudes towards unprovenanced pieces that come on to the market, many said to be from illicit excavations, or illegal exports, from the southern European countries rich in cultural heritage; Italy and Greece, or from the Near East, principally Turkey, Iran, Iraq and Egypt. This has led, in the course of the year, to quite a substantial part of the trade in important antiquities that would normally have been offered in Britain being transferred to the New York salesrooms. The other major element in Britain affecting antiquities was the Treasure Act that came into force on September 24, 1997. This gives much wider protection to antiquities found in England and Wales with a requirement to report and record; the old Treasure Trove legislation only protected items of gold and silver.

Overall, the general impression is that antiquities are still remarkably good value in comparison with other collecting areas. Many ancient items can still be bought for under £500, although good pieces in fine condition still command a premium. In the upper echelons of the market, some remarkable sales were held last year, notably the dispersal by Sotheby's of 33 pieces of ancient glass from the British Rail Pension Fund which realised just over £4 million. At Christie's, another impressive piece of Roman glass sold was the Constable-Maxwell chariot skyphos, which realised £496,500. Their like will not be seen again for a very long time. More middle range ancient glass was also strong at Bonham's, where there was also a lot of interest in British Bronze Age items on offer.

The main London antiquities sales now take place in June and November, with little else in between. With the movement of a great deal of trade to New York, one wonders how antiquities sales will fare in the coming years. There is a great deal of paperwork, such as export licences, proof of provenance, etc, which worries many middle range collectors of antiquities. They should not be too concerned so long as proper business ethics are followed in their collecting: buying from reputable dealers, obtaining invoices and as much information about the piece as possible. Many antiquities have been circulating for years, even centuries, and therefore do not have 'chapter and verse' behind them, and even provenanced pieces can lose that information after changing hands several times. An antiquity's history can add to its interest and therefore its monetary and information value. Hence, proper records are not only necessary but of inestimable value to both dealers and collectors.

Peter Clayton

An Egyptian pre-Dynastic laurel leaf-shaped flint, circa 4000 BC, 2½in (6.5cm) long.
£40–45 *ANG*

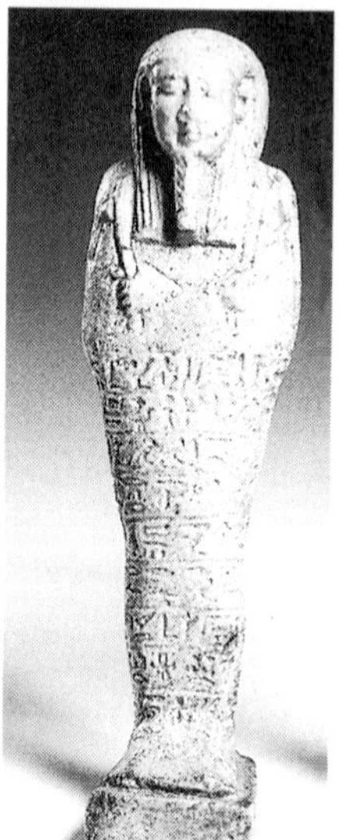

r. An Egyptian green-glazed ushabti figure, the front inscribed with the Sixth Chapter of the Book of the Dead, the back pillar clearly impressed for General Ank-wah-ibre-sa-nit, late XXVI Dynasty, circa 550 BC, 6½in (16.5cm) high.
£900–1,000 *P*

l. A Mesopotamian bronze male figure, wearing a knee-length garment, holding a club in his left hand, his right arm supporting a ring on top of his head, circa 2000–1750 BC, 4¾in (12cm) high.
£5,750–6,250 *S*

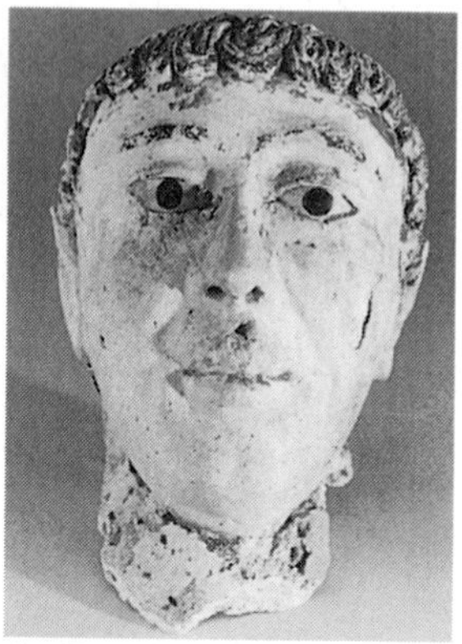

An Egyptian plaster mummy portrait of a man, the inset glass eyes with black-painted lashes and eyebrows, Roman Period, circa 2nd century AD, 8in (20.5cm) high.
£1,500–1,650 *S(Am)*

Ushabti figures

Ushabti means, literally, 'answerer' and the purpose of these figures was to work in the afterworld in the place of the dead person they represent. They often hold a pick and hoe and have a basket slung over their shoulder, because these were the tools used in the fields to keep the irrigation canals clean. Ushabtis usually bear the name of the deceased, his mother's name and sometimes his occupation. Larger examples also carry a version of Chapter Six of the Book of the Dead, which is a spell invoking the figure to work for the deceased in the next world.

Antiquities

The items in this section have been arranged in sequence of civilisations, namely Egyptian, Near Eastern, Greek, Roman, Byzantine, Western European, British, Anglo-Saxon and medieval European.

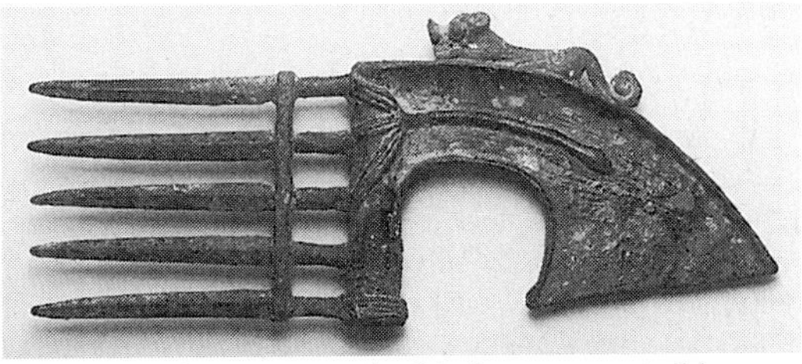

A Luristan bronze axe, the blade surmounted by a couchant feline, decorated in relief with a palm-like frond to the shaft hole, 5 long spikes on the back, circa 1200–900 BC, 9½in (24cm) long.
£1,700–1,850 *S(NY)*

A Persian pottery cup, painted with geometric designs in red slip on a pale orange fabric, with a zoomorphic handle, 1000–800 BC, 5¼in (13.5cm) high.
£250–275 *FW&C*

A Cypriot bichrome-ware jug, painted over a buff slip in red and black with concentric circle designs, circa 7th century BC, 13in (33cm) high.
£3,200–3,500 *S(NY)*

An indigo blue core-formed alabastron, with 2 bands of feathered sky blue, yellow and white decoration between white trails, with applied opaque yellow lug handles, eastern Mediterranean, 4th–3rd century BC, 5½in (14cm) high.
£900–1,000 *P*

A Hellenistic dark blue core-formed glass amphoriskos, decorated in opaque blue and yellow trailed decoration combed into a feather pattern, translucent colourless glass looped handles attached to the shoulder and neck, circa 2nd–1st century BC, 4in (10cm) high.
£1,400–1,700 *Bon*

A Corinthian pottery alabastron, decorated with a bearded male siren with outstretched wings, the base with a large rosette, circa 600 BC, 8in (20.5cm) high.
£4,800–5,300 *S*

A Boeotian hand-modelled terracotta standing votive dog, decorated with geometric decoration in added red-brown, minor cracks, circa 6th century BC, 4in (10cm) high.
£480–530 *Bon*

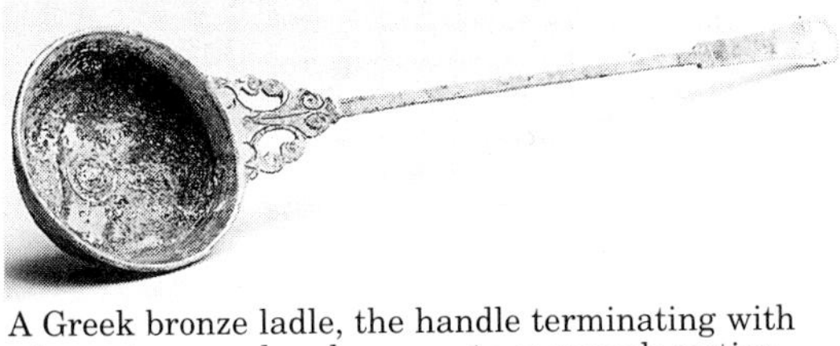

A Greek bronze ladle, the handle terminating with a loop at one end and an ornate openwork section adjoining the bowl, engraved decoration, 4th–3rd century BC, 15¾in (40cm) long.
£2,400–2,800 *Bon*

An Etruscan terracotta head of a grinning satyr, wearing a wreath on his head and animal skin tied around his neck, 4th–3rd century BC, 8¼in (21cm) high.
£450–550 *Bon*

l. A Graeco-Roman terracotta lamp holder, in the form of an actor's mask with wide open mouth, repaired, circa 1st century AD, 6in (15cm) high.
£1,800–2,200 *Bon*

A small lamp would be placed inside this lamp holder through the gaping mouth.

A Hellenistic bronze head oinochoe, eyes originally inlaid, ancient Berytus, Phoenicia, 1st century BC–1st century AD, 4½in (11.5cm) high.
£4,000–4,500 *SAnt*

MILLER'S COMPARES . . .

I A Roman marble head of Hermes, (Mercury), late 1st century BC–early 2nd century AD, after a Greek 4th century BC prototype, 8¼in (21cm) high.
£25,000–28,000 *SAnt*

II A Roman marble head of a muse, goddess or votary, wearing a himation over a floral garland, 1st century AD, 6in (15cm) high.
£10,000–12,000 *SAnt*

Both pieces pictured above are pleasing carved marble heads, very close in date and size. The fact that *item I* is more than twice the price of *item II* relates to its being recognisable as a Roman copy based on an earlier, well-known Greek original, as well as being a representation of an identifiable god. *Item II* is appealing, with its downcast gaze, but it lacks the presence and excellent antecedents of *item I*. *SAnt*

A Roman marble head of a woman, the deeply drilled hair bound in a diadem and swept back in unruly waves to a small circular chignon, the face probably re-cut, circa late 1st century AD, 12in (30.5cm) high.
£2,600–3,000 *S(NY)*

A Byzantine high tinned-bronze reliquary cross, engraved on one side with a saint, on the other with 5 recessed concentric circles, hinged at both ends, 5th–7th century AD, 2¼in (5.5cm) high, attached to a lapis lazuli and tinned-bronze necklace.
£950–1,100 *Bon*

A Roman bronze finial, styled as a duck's head, with details of feathers incised, circa 2nd century AD, 2½in (6cm) high.
£600–700 *Bon*

A Roman green glass 'snake thread' sprinkler flask, blown, decorated with applied undulating trailing, 2nd–3rd century AD, 3¾in (9.5cm) high.
£10,000–11,000 *S*

Ex-British Rail Pension Fund.

A Sasanian cut-glass bottle, with 4 rows of hexagonal and pentagonal facets, the neck hexagonal in shape, circa 6th century AD, 3in (7.5cm) high.
£1,100–1,200 *Bon*

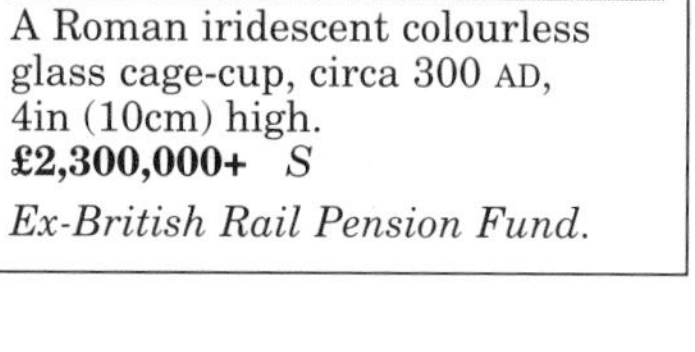

A Roman iridescent colourless glass cage-cup, circa 300 AD, 4in (10cm) high.
£2,300,000+ *S*

Ex-British Rail Pension Fund.

A Neolithic stone ball, divided into 6 flattened disc-like sections, 3rd millennium BC, 3in (7.5cm) diam.
£6,000–7,000 *Bon*

Stone balls such as this one are said to have been found chiefly in Aberdeenshire, Scotland. Their use is unknown, although it is thought that they had a symbolic function.

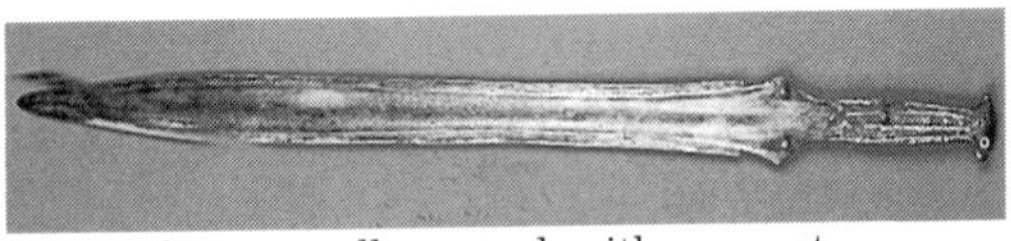

A British copper alloy sword, with crescent pommel, Late Bronze Age, circa 10th century BC, 20½in (52cm) long.
£1,600–1,750 *Bon*

This sword is probably from southern or eastern England.

A dagger, with rapier-shaped blade, Middle Bronze Age, 1450–900 BC, blade 5½in (14cm) long.
£110–120 *FW&C*

A Romano-British black carinated ware angular baluster urn, 1st–2nd century AD, 5in (12.5cm) high.
£130–145 *FW&C*

An old inscription under the base suggests a Kent origin.

An Anglo-Saxon gilded bronze button brooch, the stylised face mask with hair indicated by vertical grooves, 5th–6th century AD, 1in (23mm) diam.
£85–95 *ANG*

This item was found in south-east England.

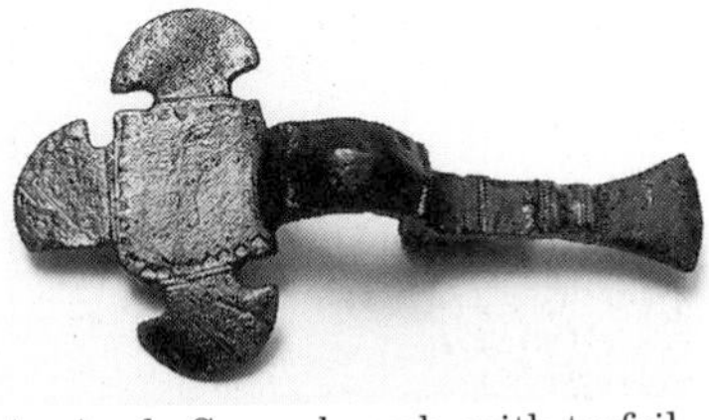

An Anglo-Saxon brooch, with trefoil head-plate around a central square with punched annulets around the centrepiece, part of top foil and iron pin missing, Lincolnshire, 6th century AD, 2½in (65mm) long.
£65–75 *ANG*

A late Anglo-Saxon silver dress fastener, the grooved linear pattern inlaid with niello, Dorset, 8th–9th century AD, 1in (25mm) long.
£45–50 *ANG*

A Romanesque silver finger ring, with engraved and punched decoration depicting 3 crosses, representative of the Holy Trinity, 11th century AD.
£90–100 *FW&C*

A lead seal matrix, with central eight-pointed star and legend, decoration on reverse, 13th century AD, 1½in (38mm) long.
£25–30 *ANG*

r. A champlevé enamel on copper figure of Christ on the cross, Limoges, early 13th century AD, 6¾in (17cm) high.
£4,200–4,600 *S(NY)*

Ex-Keir Collection of Medieval Works of Art.

A Romanesque large bronze casket key, with pierced quatrefoil terminal, 11th century AD, 3in (7.5cm) long.
£80–90 *FW&C*

TRIBAL ART

A Cree beaded pouch, with floral motifs on both sides in shades of pink, white, green, yellow and blue, the borders of pink silk piping, with red wool tassels, the loom woven bead strap of polychrome geometric designs, Native American, 7¼in (18.5cm) long.
£440–480 *P*

A pair of hide and sinew moccasins, probably Northern Cheyenne, with Morning Star pattern, decorated with iridescent purple beads, and terraced pattern in orange, blue, red, yellow and green, Native American, c1890, 9½in (24cm) long.
£1,100–1,350 *HUR*

A Chippewa birch bark and quill hinged basket, Michegan, 19thC, 6¼in (16cm) long.
£200–250 *HUR*

A Navajo Yei rug, woven in natural and aniline dyed wools in shades of brown, grey, red, purple, orange and yellow, depicting 6 dancers wearing kilts and holding feathers, framed by an angular meander border, Native American, 79 x 52½in (200x 133cm).
£1,700–2,000 *P*

A late Transitional Navajo rug, Native American, c1890, 77 x 51in (195.5 x 129.5cm).
£1,000–1,200 *SLN*

A mountain goat horn spoon, the handle carved with a hawk's head, surmounted by a kneeling figure and a bird, north west coast of America, 9½in (24cm) long.
£800–900 *Bon*

A Plains woman's parade saddle, the wood frame stretched with hide, decorated with hide pommels each ornamented with hemispherical brass tacks, trimmed with long twisted hide fringe, Native American, 19½in (49.5cm) long.
£1,500–1,800 *S(NY)*

An old label remains, identifying the piece as northern Cheyenne, 1880, collected 1901, by A. P. Proctor.

A Native American trade tomahawk, the head of French origin, probably early 19thC, 25in (63.5cm) long.
£340–380 *ASB*

Trade blades, introduced from England and France, replaced earlier stone heads. Often the blades combine a pipe bowl with a hollow wood handle which serves as the pipe stem.

l. A Dogon shrine door, 19thC, Mali, 16in (40.5cm) wide.
£750–850 *LHB*

The traces of figures carved in relief on this door are figures of ancestors.

r. A Ivory Coast Baule mask, with elongated nose and pierced slit eyes, surmounted by a carved bird, with red and black patina, African, probably early 20thC, 20in (51cm) high.
£360–400 *CGC*

Miller's is a price GUIDE not a price LIST

Tribal Art

When looking at tribal art, the collector needs to establish whether something is:

- a genuine tribal artefact
- 'tourist art', ie made for European taste
- a reproduction

A genuine tribal artefact will be an object of functional or ritual significance. Valuable pieces usually date from the 19th and early 20thC. A good provenance that explains when and how an item was collected also enhances value. The majority of tribal art in circulation is 'tourist art', or reproductions of older examples. These should be avoided by the collector. This includes purely decorative pieces such as masks that are impractical to wear and wood busts – the idea of the head and shoulders sculpture is purely a European concept.

A Kuyu head, surmounted by a spotted lizard, with yellow, black, white and indigo pigments, Nigerian, 36¾in (93.5cm) high.
£6,500–7,500 *S(NY)*
Ex-Vincent Price collection.

A Nigerian carved wooden ritual mask, with large eye slits and mouth with pointed teeth, 11in (28cm) high.
£450–500 *ASB*

A Cameroon stool, the openwork geometric motif in the form of numerous abstract interlocking spiders, with dark brown patina, 15¾in (40cm) high.
£850–950 *S(NY)*

A Kongo wood figure, with inset coloured eyes, wearing a domed headdress and wire hoop earrings, golden patina, 11½in (29cm) high.
£7,000–8,000 *P*

A Yoruba headdress, carved with a head with striated coiffure, the face with cheek and forehead scarification, traces of yellow ochre pigment, Nigerian, 9½in (24cm) high.
£150–180 *Bon*

A Yoruba helmet mask, carved as a bearded man with long animal ears, with tension drum to the front and monkey grasping an okra vegetable to the rear, the forehead with a row of gourds, painted mustard, brown and black, Nigerian, 13½in (33cm) high.
£250–300 *Bon*

A wicker-covered shield carried by the Ganda and Soga tribes of Uganda, around the edges of Lake Victoria, the two halves flexed along the vertical axis with central projecting wooden boss, minor damage, 39in (99cm) long.
£270–300 *ASB*

l. A Sakyara sect wooden book cover, Tibet, 14thC, 24½in (62cm) long.
£500–550 *LHB*

A Songo comb, the handle composed of 4 standing couples, the 2 facing inwards holding a rifle and baby, central Africa, 13½in (34.5cm) long.
£180–220 *Bon*

An African ivory oliphant, or trumpet, carved in hollowed tapering form with a diamond-shaped opening at one end for playing, decorated with a geometric pattern composed of repeating circle and dot motif, honey-brown to dark brown patina, 16in (40.5cm) long.
£1,500–1,800 *S(NY)*
This item was collected c1885.

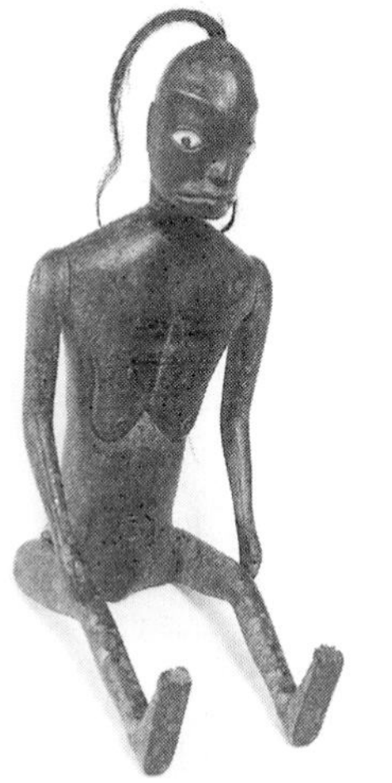

A Shaman carved wood medicine box, with human hair, Lombok, Indonesia, 18in (45.5cm) long.
£500–550 *LHAr*

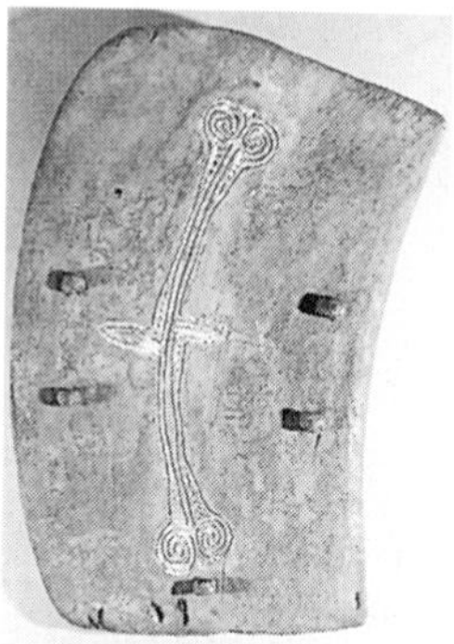

A Lumi shield, the centre carved with a curvilinear motif, infilled with kaolin, fibre straps to the reverse, Melanesia, 38in (97cm) high.
£200–240 *Bon*

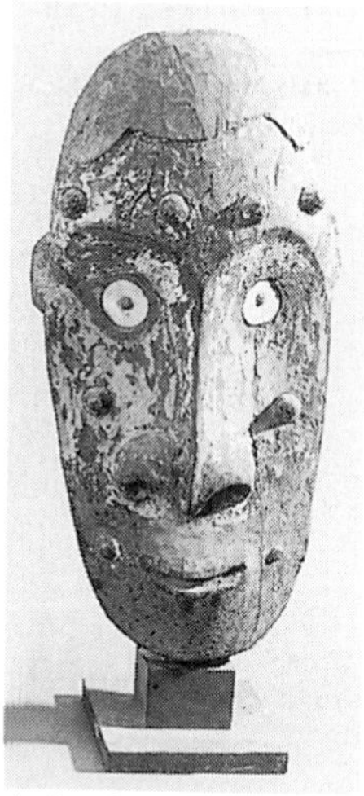

A Sepik gable mask, the forehead, cheeks and mouth corners with carved bosses, the face with shell set eyes, traces of red-ochre pigment to face, New Guinea, 26in (66cm) high.
£440–480 *Bon*

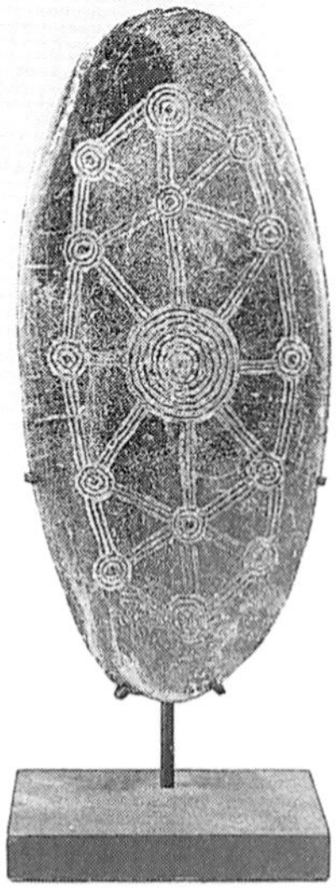

An Aborigine Aranda People stone tablet, the mottled green stone incised on both sides with a network of parallel lines linking small concentric medallions, around a larger medallion, 7¼in (18.5cm) high.
£2,600–3,000 *Bon*

The images on stone tablets such as this serve as records of mythological stories.

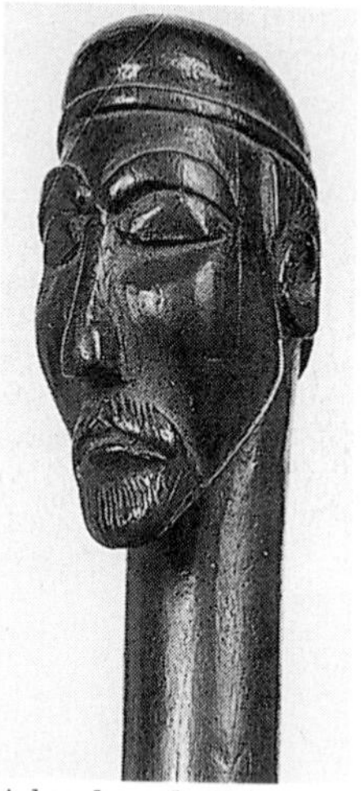

A hardwood stick, with carved terminal in the likeness of Paul Gauguin, 22in (56cm) long.
£2,100–2,300 *FW&C*

Paul Gauguin, the French artist, left for Tahiti in 1891 in search of simplicity and primitive values. In 1901 he moved to the Marquesas Islands, where he died in 1903. Gauguin is known to have carved walking sticks and according to family tradition, this stick was recovered from his house after his death.

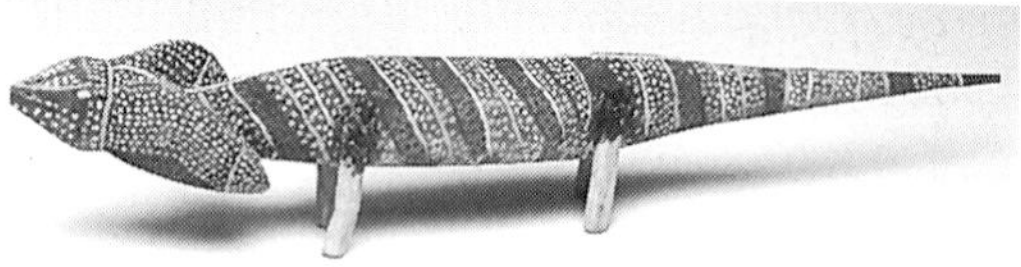

An Australian carved ironwood model of a frilled neck lizard, by Jimmy Kantilla, with natural earth pigments, the softwood legs attached with bush gum, 1950s, 24¾in (63cm) long.
£900–1,000 *S(A)*

A Fiji wooden gunstock club, the grip side of the butt carved in shallow relief with panels of circles and zig-zags, 42in (107cm) long.
£1,500–1,800 *P*

Fijian warriors used a wide variety of clubs which imitated various forms including the gunstock, pineapple, lotus, paddle and rootstock. The heads of these clubs are shaped accordingly and are popular with collectors. The more valuable clubs are often inset with marine ivory motifs.

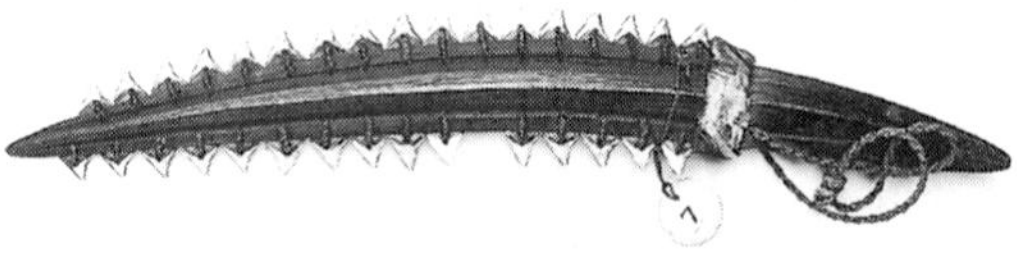

A Gilbert Islands shark's tooth dagger, the hardwood stem set with 2 rows of teeth, bound with sennit, the handle with wrist loop and pandanus guard, 14in (36cm) long.
£520–580 *Bon*

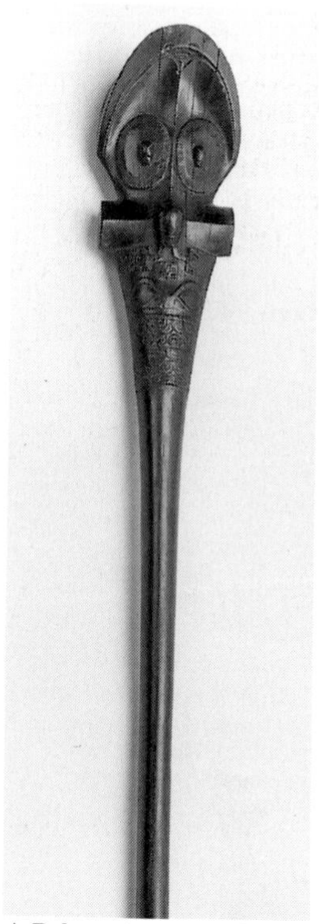

A Polynesian carved hardwood ceremonial club, from the Marquesas Islands, 19thC, 54¾in (144cm) long.
£1,450–1,600 *L&E*

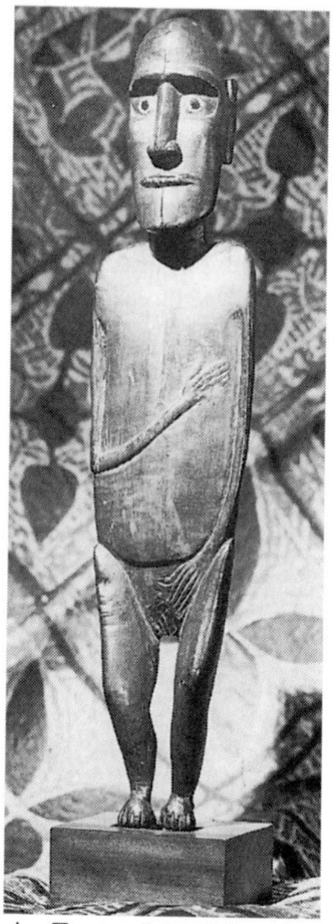

An Easter Island female figure, the pronounced brow overshadowing the obsidian and fish-bone eyes, 19thC, 23¼in (59cm) high.
£5,000–5,500 *P*

BOOKS & BOOK ILLUSTRATIONS

The past two years have been exciting, with greater competition amongst trade and auction houses and new buyers coming into the market at all levels.

Some remarkable prices were achieved at Sotheby's during 1997, such as £297,000 for *Oiseaux remarquables de Brésil*, c1840, against an estimate of £8,000–12,000; £353,500 for a picture album compiled by Hans Andersen in 1852 for his god-daughter, which had been estimated at £40,000–60,000; and £14,375 – over three times its top estimate – for an inscribed copy of Mark Twain's *Adventures of Huckleberry Finn*.

Sotheby's also held the first of a series of sales from the archive of the Enid Blyton Company, offering a selection of the artwork for the Noddy books. The original picture letter in which Noddy and friends are seen for the first time was sold for £40,000 (estimate of £15,000–20,000), and the original water-colours were selling between £200 and £7,000. The majority of the buyers had never before bought at auction, let alone from a dealer.

Theme sales and single-owner collections proved popular with the auction houses, with sales devoted to cookery, mountaineering, the Antarctic, the Ottoman Empire, science, fine Continental books, and authors such as Graham Greene and Beatrix Potter.

One of the most enduring areas of interest has been fantasy books and illustrations. Pictures by Arthur Rackham, Edmund Dulac, Kay Nielsen, Harry Clarke, William Timlin and contemporary artists such as Alan Lee and Brian Froud sold exceptionally well. Arthur Rackham has continued to do well both at auction and with dealers. A copy of Hans Andersen's *Fairy Tales* with a presentation inscription and drawing by Rackham to his publisher sold at Christie's for £8,050. Provenance such as this will always command a higher price and copies with inscriptions from the author or artist are always worth looking for. The copy of Kate Greenaway's illustrated edition of Robert Browning's *The Pied Piper of Hamelin*, with a watercolour drawing and presentation inscription of her friend and mentor John Ruskin that sold for £3,600, would be worth £60–80 at auction for an ordinary copy.

As collectors become more discerning the condition of books becomes more important. The copy of the *Wind in the Willows*, that sold for £1,520 would be worth £300–400 if the binding was soiled and stained. Charles Darwin's *On The Origin of Species* that sold for £14,000 due to the fine condition of the binding and internal cleanliness, would be worth £2,000–3,000 if rebound.

Catherine Porter

The History of the University of Cambridge, Its Colleges, Halls and Public Buildings, Rudolph Ackermann, London 1815, 2 vols, 4°, with contemporary gilt stamped calf.
£2,300–2,500 *DN*

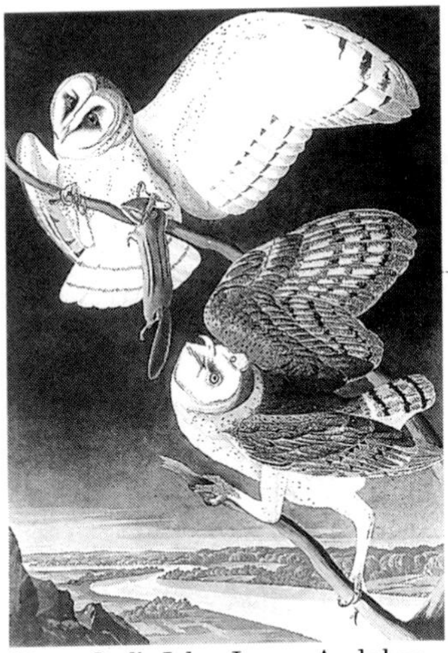

'Barn Owl', John James Audubon, Plate No. 35, engraved, printed and coloured by R. Havell, 1883, 37½ x 24½in (95.5 x 52cm).
£7,500–8,250 *NOA*

Richard Adams, *Watership Down*, published by Penguin Books, 1976, first illustrated edition with plates by John Lawrence, 8°, signed and dedicated to publisher by author and artist.
£130–150 *HAM*

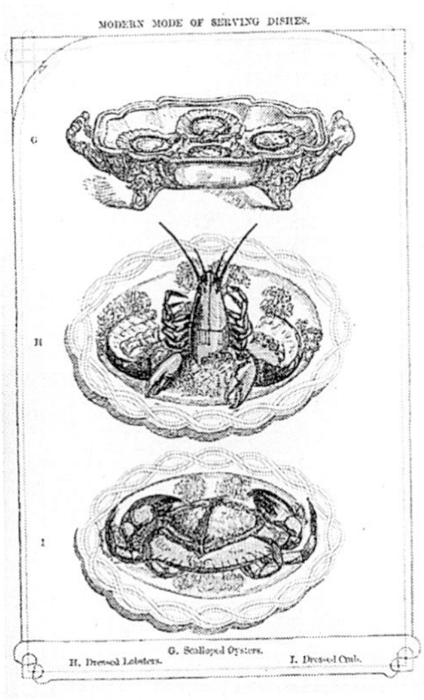

l. Mrs Isabella Beeton, *The Book of Household Management*, 8°, 1861, first edition, contemporary half-calf, worn.
£1,000–1,100 *S*

FURTHER READING
Catherine Porter, *Miller's Collecting Books* Miller's Publications. 1995

E. F. Benson, *Mapp and Lucia*, published by Hodder & Stoughton 1931, first edition, cover design in brown pen and ink and white highlights, titles in blue, 18¼ x 14¼in (46.5 x 36cm).
£420–500 *P*

A James I copy of the Holy Bible, contained within a stumpwork cover with panels of mythical beasts and flowers worked in silver wire and coloured silks, dated '1631', 6 x 3½in (15 x 9cm) high.
£340–375 *TMA*

A letter addressed to Enid Blyton, signed by Harmsen van der Beek, illustrated in pencil and watercolour with Noddy, Big-Ears and friends, browned and frayed at edges, dated '4 May, '49', 10¾ x 8in (27.5 x 20.5cm).
£40,000–45,000 *S*

A. Burgess, *A Clockwork Orange*, first edition, 1962, first issued in black cloth boards, 7½ x 5in (19 x 12.5cm).
£470–530 *WW*

A silver-mounted leather-bound copy of the Holy Bible, published by John Bill, Thomas Newcomb, and Henry Hills, London, c1680, 12°, gilt stamped with acorn and grape tools, silver clasps and corners, engraved 'MW' in the upper central medallion and '1687' in the lower.
£1,500–1,650 *S(NY)*

Robert Browning, *The Pied Piper of Hamelin, Routledge*, 1888, 4°, coloured illustrations by Kate Greenaway, inscribed by the artist to Lionel Hallam Tennyson.
£3,600–4,000 *Bon*

In the inserted accompanying letter the artist apologises for the quality of the drawing, explaining that the paper was not fit to draw on, continuing with references to her stay at Freshwater and with Helen Allingham in Pinner.

M. J. Cazabon, *Views of Trinidad*, oblong folio, c1851, modern half calf, oblong folio with 17 hand-coloured views of Trinidad.
£3,700–4,000 *P*

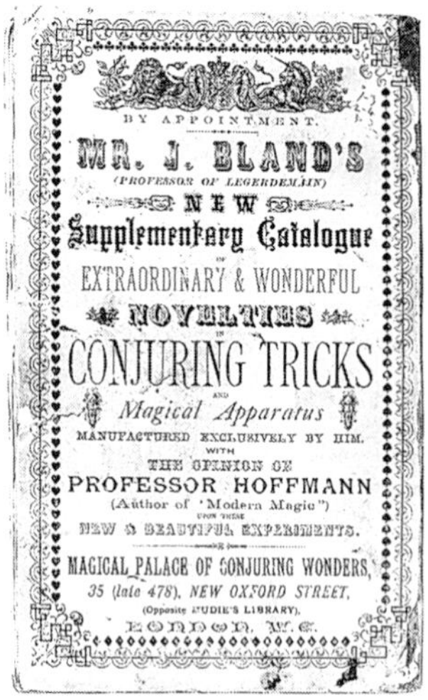

BY APPOINTMENT.
MR. J. BLAND'S
(PROFESSOR OF LEGERDEMAIN)
NEW
Supplementary Catalogue
OF
EXTRAORDINARY & WONDERFUL
NOVELTIES
IN
CONJURING TRICKS
AND
Magical Apparatus
MANUFACTURED EXCLUSIVELY BY HIM.
WITH
THE OPINION OF
PROFESSOR HOFFMANN
(Author of "Modern Magic")
UPON THESE
NEW & BEAUTIFUL EXPERIMENTS.
MAGICAL PALACE OF CONJURING WONDERS,
35 (late 478), NEW OXFORD STREET,
(Opposite MUDIE'S LIBRARY),
LONDON, W.C.

J. Bland, *New Supplementary Catalogue of Extraordinary & Wonderful Novelties in Conjuring Tricks and Magical Apparatus*, 1883, 8°, cloth-backed boards.
£450–500 *Bon*

John Bruce, *Views of Brighton*, 1833–34, 2°, with 14 hand-coloured aquatint plates and one hand-coloured engraved plan, contemporary aubergine half morocco.
£2,000–2,200 *BBA*

A coloured etched frontispiece and 12 coloured plates, by Salvador Dali, for Lewis Carroll's *Alice's Adventures in Wonderland*, published by Maecenas Press, New York, 1969, 2°, loose as issued in original cloth wrappers, morocco-backed fitted case.
£1,700–1,850 *Bon*

Limited to 2,700 copies, of which this is No. 986, signed by the artist on title page. A mint copy, in the original packaging.

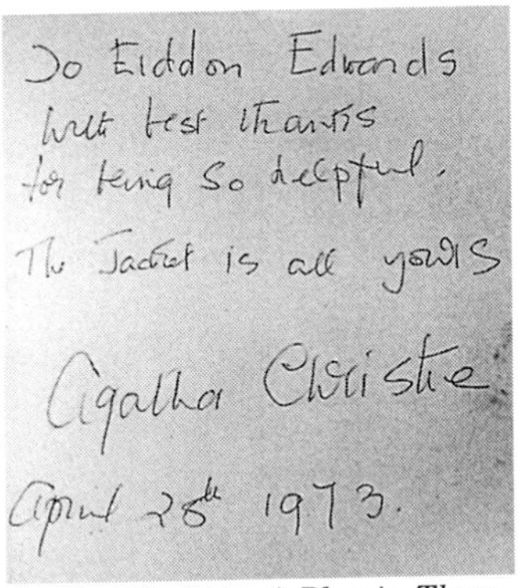

Agatha Christie, *A Play in Three Acts*, 1973, first edition, 8°, signed and inscribed by the author to Eiddon Edwards, original boards.
£1,000–1,200 *BBA*

Captain James Cook, *A Voyage Towards the South Pole, and Round the World*, published by R. W. Strahan and T. Cadell, 1777, first edition, 2 vols, 4°, with engraved frontispiece portrait, 13 maps and charts, 50 plates, folding language table.
£750–900 *BBA*

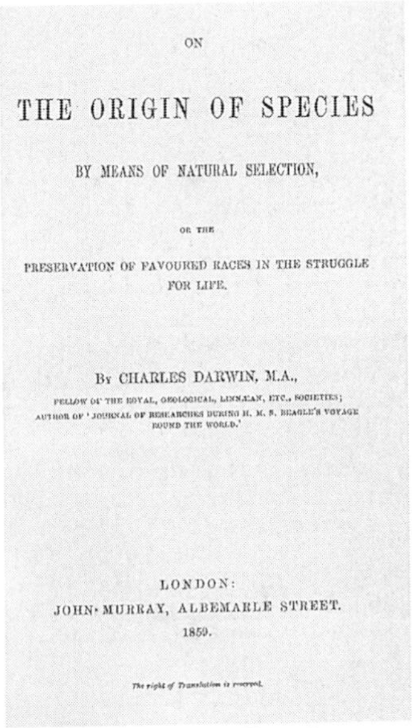

ON

THE ORIGIN OF SPECIES

BY MEANS OF NATURAL SELECTION,

OR THE

PRESERVATION OF FAVOURED RACES IN THE STRUGGLE FOR LIFE.

By CHARLES DARWIN, M.A.,

FELLOW OF THE ROYAL, GEOLOGICAL, LINNÆAN, ETC., SOCIETIES;
AUTHOR OF 'JOURNAL OF RESEARCHES DURING H. M. S. BEAGLE'S VOYAGE ROUND THE WORLD.'

LONDON:
JOHN MURRAY, ALBEMARLE STREET.
1859.

The right of Translation is reserved.

Charles Darwin, *The Origin of Species*, 1859, first edition, 8°, original green blind-stamped cloth, uncut, spine gilt.
£14,000–16,000 *BBA*

Edward Donovan, *The Natural History of British Insects*, 1802–13, 16 vols, 8°, 576 engraved plates, 569 hand-coloured plates, contemporary half calf, edges uncut.
£1,500–1,650 *BBA*

John Gould, *The Birds of Great Britain*, 1873, 5 vols, 2°, 367 lithographs with hand colouring, published by the author.
£25,000–28,000 *AG*

This is one of the classic illustrated works on ornthology.

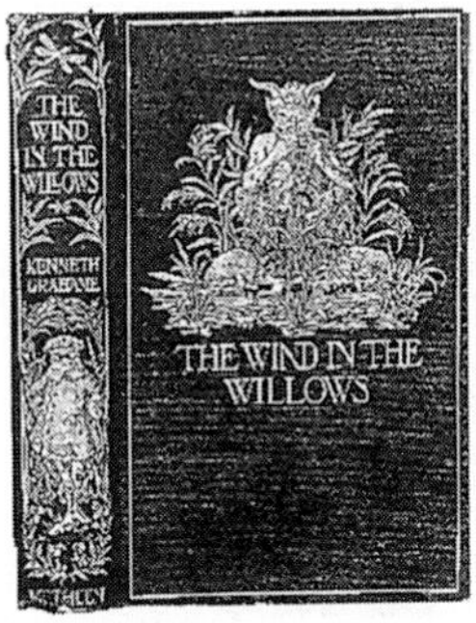

l. Kenneth Grahame, *The Wind in the Willows*, first edition, 1908, 8°, original cloth gilt.
£1,500–1,650 *DW*

Ernest Hemingway, *In Our Time*, published by Three Mountains Press, Paris, 1924, first edition, small folio, frontispiece woodcut portrait of Hemingway after Henry Starter, original pictorial boards of an overall newspaper collage printed in red and black on brown paper.
£6,500–7,000 *S(NY)*

This copy is No. 35 of 170 numbered copies printed on Rives handmade paper.

Horticultural Society of London (The) Transactions, 1820–48, first series 7 vols, 2nd series 3 vols, vol 1 and 2 third editions, vol 3 second edition, the rest first editions, 4°, 175 engraved plates, 93 hand-coloured, contemporary half diced russia, gilt.
£4,400–4,800 *BBA*

A watercolour depicting a procession of 16 children carrying flowers down a village street past timber-framed houses, by Kate Greenaway, framed and glazed, 5¼ x 14½in (14 x 37cm).
£7,000–8,000 *Bon*

The drawing is in its original frame and has various autograph and printed labels indicating that it was exhibited at the Dudley Gallery in 1876. It was produced as a studio watercolour when the artist was working on her drawings for her children's book, Under the Window, *and is possibly the earliest of all her processional pictures.*

Book Sizes

The size or format of a book is expressed by the number of times a single sheet of paper is folded into the sections which, when gathered and sewn, make up the finished volume.
Shown below are some of the usual descriptions of sizes:

Folio:	1 fold	2 leaves	Fo or 2°
Quarto:	2 folds	4 leaves	4to or 4°
Octavo:	3 folds	8 leaves	8vo or 8°
Duodecimo:	4 folds	12 leaves	12mo or 12°
Sextodecimo:	5 folds	16 leaves	16mo or 16°
Vicesimo-quarto:	6 folds	24 leaves	24mo or 24°
Tricesimo-secundo:	7 folds	32 leaves	32mo or 32°

J. Swift, *Gulliver's Travels*, 1909, No. 68 of 750 copies, 4°, illustrated by Arthur Rackham, white buckram, gilt titles and motif, 13 colour plates.
£220–250 *HAM*

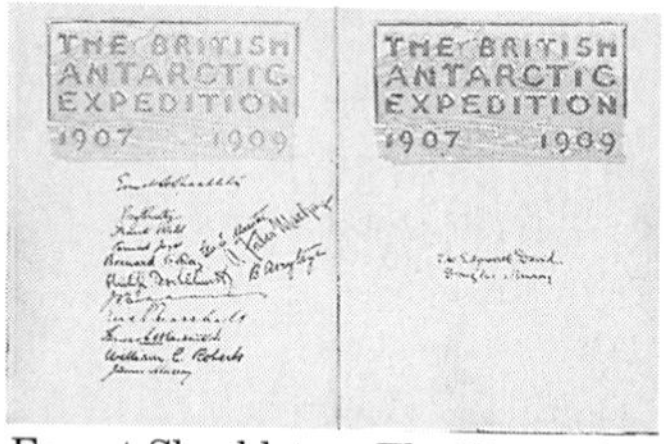

Ernest Shackleton, *The Heart of the Antarctic,* published by William Heinemann, London, 1909, first edition, 4°, No. 150 of 300 copies signed by every member of the shore party and with additional contributions in the 3rd volume, *The Antarctic Book*, numerous coloured and plain plates, illustrations, vols. 1 and 2 in original vellum gilt, vol. 3 in original vellum-backed boards.
£4,800–5,300 *S*

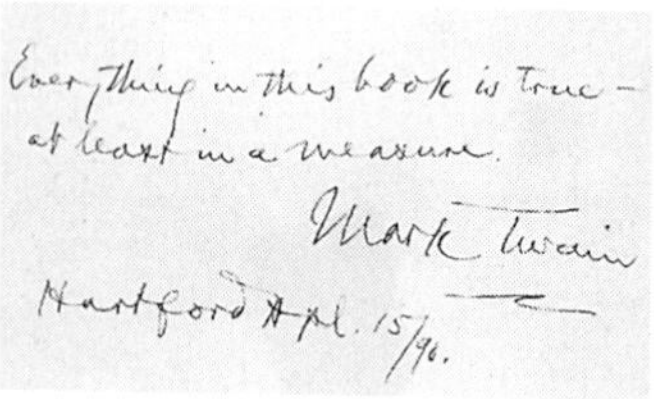

Mark Twain, *Adventures of Huckleberry Finn*, first American edition, inscribed, published by Charles L. Webster, 1885, 8°, repaired, speckled sheep binding.
£14,500–16,000 *S*

Magna Carta Regis Johannis XV, published by John Whittaker, 1816, large folio, 14 leaves printed in gold on vellum, comprising title, dedication to the Prince Regent, list of barons and 11 leaves of text, all elaborately illuminated in gold and colours by J. Harris and Thomas Willement, contemporary red morocco with triple fillet border.
£4,600–5,000 *BBA*

Miller's is a price GUIDE not a price LIST

Louis Wain and Charles Morley, *Peter, A Cat o' One Tail, His Life and Adventures*, published by Pall Mall Gazette Extra, 1892, 4°, numerous black and white illustrations to text, original picture cloth.
£280–320 *DW*

A watercolour drawing depicting a rabbit with umbrella and basket stepping from his doorway watched by his wife, by Beatrix Potter signed with initials 'H.B.P.', c1890, 6¼ x 4in (16 x 10cm).
£34,000–38,000 *Bon*

The drawing is believed to date from around 1890 and was probably intended as a Christmas card design. It was bought by an American dealer who commented that it was the finest sketch by Beatrix Potter that he had seen in 28 years' dealing in children's books and illustrated art.

Samuel Wesley, *Maggots, or Poems on Several Subjects*, 1685, first edition, 12°, woodcut frontispiece, mottled calf by Bickers & Son.
£1,100–1,300 *HAM*

The author, father of John and Charles Wesley, was only 19 when these poems appeared, published by his brother-in-law John Dunton.

DOLLS
Unknown Makers

A Grödnertal doll, the painted and gessoed shoulder head with black painted hair, on a carved wood body with pegged joints, c1820, 14in (36cm) high, holding bisque baby doll, c1900.
£500–600 *S*

Grödnertal dolls are wooden European dolls made in and around densely forested mountainous regions, such as Grödnertal in Austria. They were made during the 18th and 19thC, in response to the demand in England for less expensive dolls.

A German shoulder-headed china doll, with glazed blue eyes, the gusseted leather body in original pale blue and white printed cotton gown, c1845, 27in (69cm) high.
£700–800 *S*

A Biedermeier shoulder-headed papier mâché doll, with painted blue eyes, the gusseted leather body with wooden hands and lower legs, in original figured silk gown, c1835, 17in (44cm) high.
£1,150–1,250 *S*

Most Biedermeier dolls, so called because they date from the Biedermeier period in Germany, were made between c1820–30. They are also referred to by collectors as 'milliners' models'.

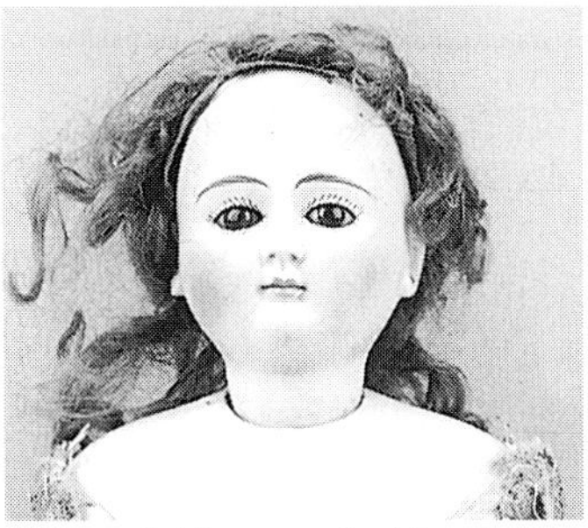

A French bisque swivel-headed fashion doll, with fixed blue glass eyes, closed mouth, cork pate with blonde mohair wig, on a bisque shoulder plate, the leather over wood body jointed at the thighs and knees, replaced cloth arms with composition hands, c1870, 12¾in (32.5cm) high.
£350–400 *Bon(C)*

r. A poured wax shoulder-headed doll, with brown rooted hair wig, fixed blue glass eyes and closed mouth, on a cloth filled body with poured wax lower limbs, dressed in original cream satin and lace frock with matching hat, original shoes and socks, c1880, 21in (53cm) high.
£700–800 *P(Ba)*

A poured wax shoulder-headed doll, with fixed black pupil-less glass eyes, brown wig, cloth body with wax lower arms, in original costume, c1840, 13in (33cm) high.
£250–300 *S(S)*

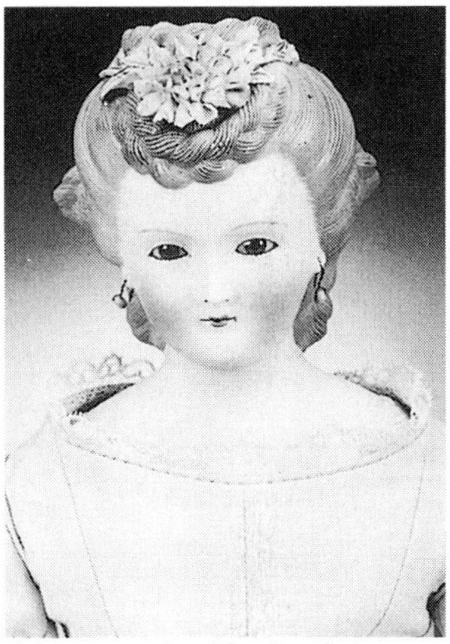

A German shoulder-headed Parian bisque doll, with elaborate blonde coiffure and moulded plaits, inset with blue glass eyes and closed mouth, the white kid body with glazed porcelain lower arms and hands, in pale blue 1850s style gown, restored, c1870, 21½in (55cm) high.
£500–600 *S*

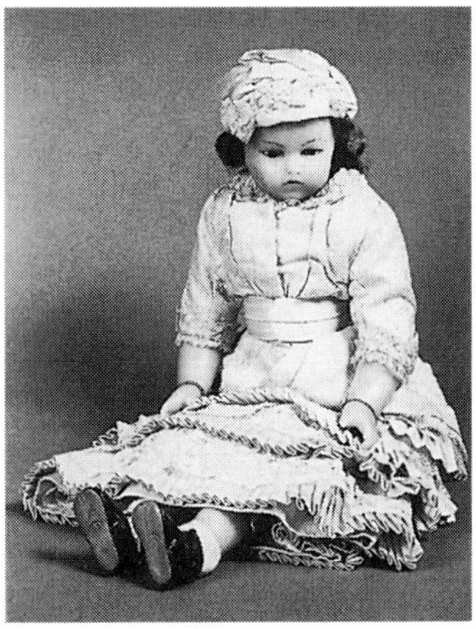

l. A German swivel-necked shoulder bisque doll, with fixed brown eyes, closed mouth, blonde wig, gusseted fabric body with celluloid lower arms, original boned eau de nil satin laced-up bodice and brown leather ankle boots, c1880, 20in (51cm) high.
£600–700 *S*

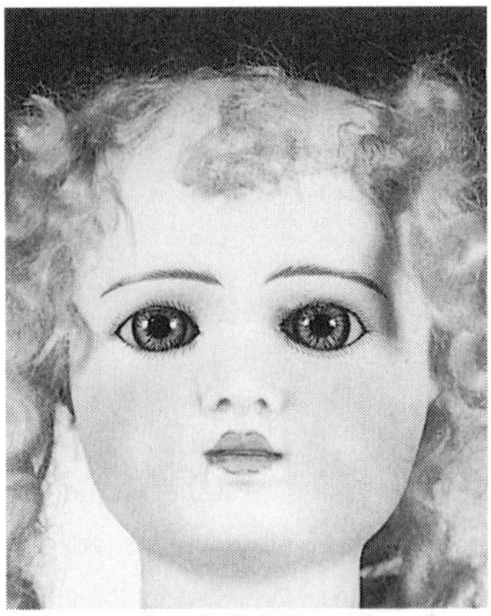

A bisque-headed doll, with pale blue paperweight eyes, open/closed mouth, the remains of replacement yellow crimped mohair wig, on ball-jointed wood and composition body, the head German, the body French, 1880s, 20½in (52cm) high.
£1,000–1,200 *S*

A bisque-headed portrait doll, depicting Uncle Sam, the moulded face with fixed blue eyes and loose brown wig, on composition ball-jointed body, dressed with painted card top hat, felt jacket, cotton shirt, waistcoat and trousers, c1900, 13¾in (35cm) high.
£1,200–1,400 *Bri*

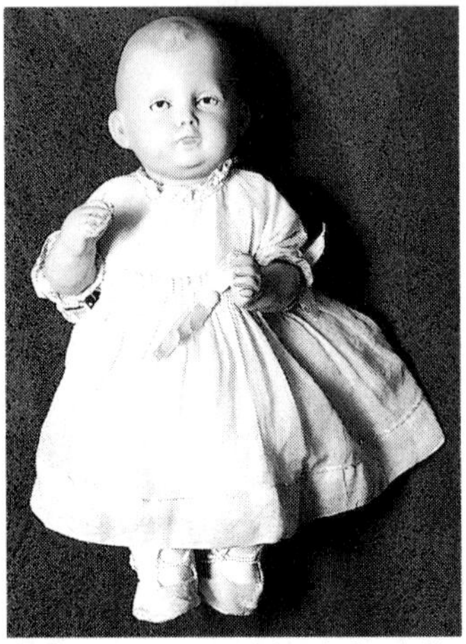

A German composition baby doll, with original clothes, c1920, 18in (45.5cm) high.
£120–150 *DOL*

A pot manual walker doll, in original box, 1930s, 22in (56cm) high.
£75–85 *DOL*

FURTHER READING
Miller's Dolls & Teddy Bears Antiques Checklist, Miller's Publications, 1992

l. A French celluloid doll, 1930s, 4½in (11.5cm) high.
£20–25 *DOL*

A German celluloid doll, 1930s, 4¼in (11cm) high.
£35–40 *DOL*

Selected Makers

A Bru bisque-headed *bébé* doll, with fixed brown eyes, closed mouth showing tip of tongue, cork pate and blonde wig, kid leather body with jointed wooden lower legs, bisque lower arms, head and one hand restored, c1870, 21in (53cm) high.
£2,200–2,500 *S*

An EFFanBee doll, depicting Susan B. Anthony, c1980, 15in (38cm) high.
£80–90 *EKK*

EFFanBee Toy Co (1910–present) is one of America's top manufacturers of 'unbreakable' composition dolls.

Gaultier

Gaultier was an exception in marking most of its fashion dolls on the shoulder and/or back of the crown of the head. It is important when checking a doll to be sure that the head and body belong together.

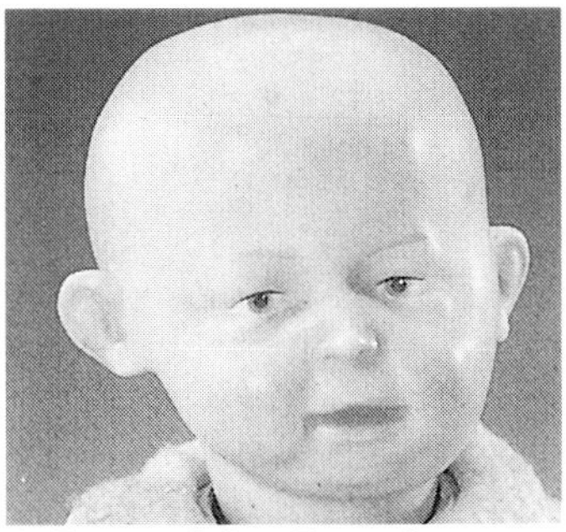

A Cuno and Otto Dressel character bisque-headed doll, with open/closed mouth, painted eyes and curved limb composition body, impressed 'B6', c1909, 13¼in (34cm) high.
£450–550 *S(S)*

r. An F. Gaultier bisque-headed bébé doll, with blue stationary paperweight eyes, closed mouth, brush stroke eyebrows, long brown mohair wig, swivel wrist fully-jointed wood and composition body, wearing a blue dress, incised '9, F. G.' in scroll, c1895, 24in (61cm) high.
£1,000–1,200 *Bon(C)*

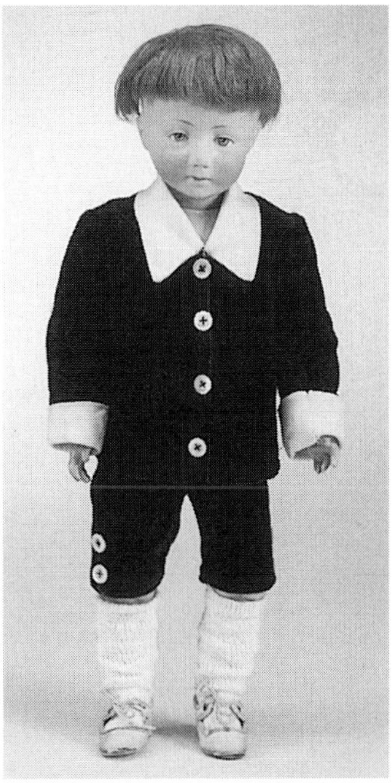

A Catterfelder Puppenfabrik bisque-headed character boy, with blue intaglio eyes, closed mouth, jointed wood and composition body, impressed 'C. P. 212 94', c1910, 13½in (35cm) high.
£3,500–4,200 *S*

l. An F. Gaultier bisque swivel-headed fashion doll, with fixed pale blue eyes, closed mouth, original cork pate applied with spartan blonde wig, gusseted kid leather body, in a blue silk bodice and skirt, c1875, 15in (41cm) high.
£600–700 *S*

A Hertel, Schwab & Co bisque-headed googly-eyed doll, with closed mouth, silver blonde wig and blue paperweight glass eyes, on composition bent limb body, impressed '165.5', c1910, 13¾in (35cm) long.
£2,500–3,000 *Bea(E)*

A Gebrüder Heubach bisque piano baby doll, repair to chair, c1890, 15in (38cm) high.
£800–900 *STK*

A Gebrüder Heubach grinning baby doll, with original clothes, c1910, 12in (30.5cm) high.
£900–1,000 *DOL*

A Gebrüder Heubach bisque-headed baby doll, with closed mouth, blue sleeping eyes, blonde mohair wig, bent limbed composition body, dressed in original outfit, impressed with square Heubach logo, c1910, 9in (23cm) high.
£700–800 *EW*

Gebrüder Heubach

This firm was founded by the Heubach brothers in 1820 in Thuringia, Germany, originally to make porcelain. By 1905, the company was manufacturing whole dolls. Distinctive, usually pink, bisque heads with exaggerated facial expressions are their strong point. In comparison the bodies are often crudely modelled.

Look for highly realistic intaglio eyes, moulded with an indented pupil and iris and then painted, often with a white dot added to the iris for the illusion of extra depth.

Gebrüder Heubach was also known for all-bisque figurines of babies intended for display on a piano, hence the name 'piano babies'. These and larger mantelpiece babies should bear the Heubach mark.

A Gebrüder Heubach whistling boy doll, mould No. 7679, c1910, 13½in (34.5cm) high.
£850–950 *DOL*

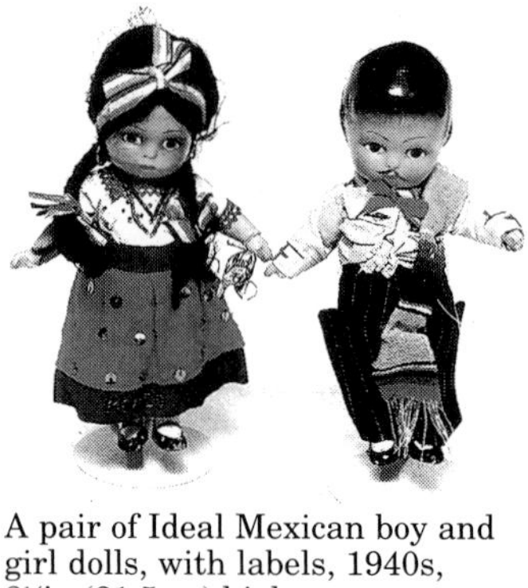

A pair of Ideal Mexican boy and girl dolls, with labels, 1940s, 8½in (21.5cm) high.
£30–35 *DOL*

A Gebrüder Heubach 'Petulant Boy' character doll, with moulded blond curly hair, brown weighted eyes, closed mouth, on jointed wood and composition toddler body, in Austrian lederhosen outfit, impressed '8', with square Heubach logo, c1910, 19in (48.5cm) high.
£11,000–12,000 *S*

This doll is believed to be unique, the only known similar example having intaglio rather than glass eyes. It may be that the doll's stylised face made it more appealing to adults than children, making it less of a commercial success. Furthermore, since a bisque head is easily broken, fewer examples would have survived.

A Jumeau bisque-headed *bébé* doll, with fixed blue paperweight eyes, moulded mouth, blonde mohair wig on a ball-jointed composition body, wearing a crimson and sage green silk dress, jacket and hat, marked '5', c1900, 13in (33cm) high.
£1,800–2,200 *DN*

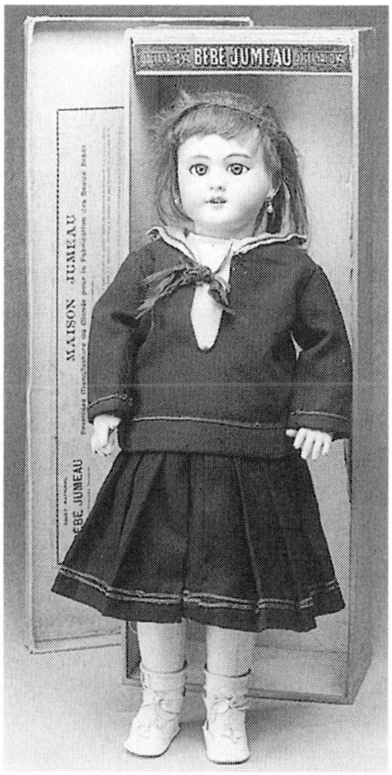

A Jumeau bisque doll, with weighted blue eyes, open mouth, light brown wig, jointed wood and composition body, inoperative pull-cord voice mechanism, in original red, white and blue sailor suit, white leatherette shoes, head impressed 'DEP 8' and marked in red 'Tête Jumeau', c1900, 19½in (50cm) high.
£1,400–1,600 *S*

A Kestner bisque doll, with sleeping blue eyes, painted brows and lashes, closed mouth, blonde mohair wig, on a composition bent limbed body, wearing a blue dress, white kid shoes and a straw hat, marked 'D8 169', c1900, 17½in (44.5cm) high.
£850–950 *DN*

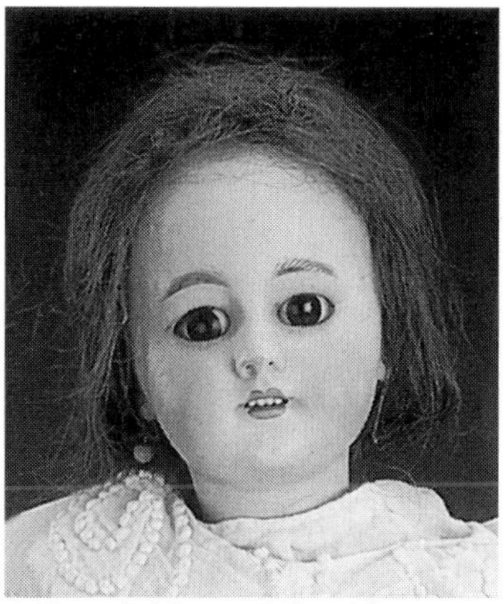

A French bisque doll, with open mouth, brown glass eyes, auburn wig over cork pate and jointed wood and composition body, in embroidered muslin costume, red velvet fur trimmed cape and bonnet, pull-string voice box detached, replacement voice box within body, impressed 'DEP 7' and stamped in red 'Tête Jumeau', c1900, 17¾in (45cm) high.
£500–600 *S(S)*

A Kestner bisque-headed baby doll, with sleeping blue eyes, open mouth, composition body, dressed in a cotton lawn embroidered dress and petticoat, wool cape and bonnet, impressed mould No. 257, c1927, 19¾in (49cm) high, in original box.
£500–550 *DN*

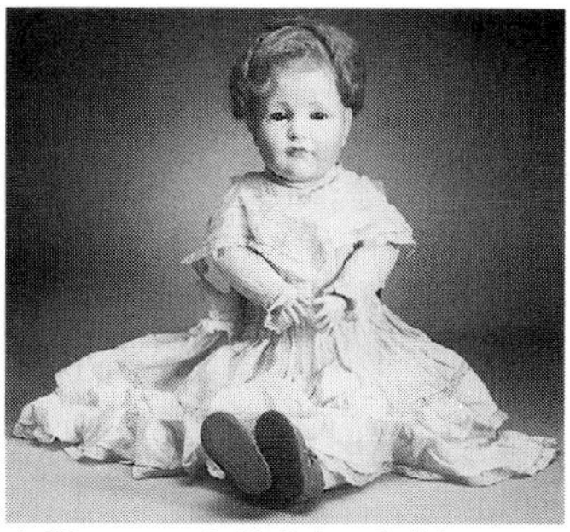

A Kämmer & Reinhardt bisque-headed character doll, with closed mouth, brown glass eyes, fully jointed composition body, replaced wig, impressed '114' mark, c1909, 24in (61cm) high.
£7,000–8,000 *SK(B)*

A German bisque-headed doll, probably Kestner, with brown glass sleeping eyes, closed mouth, blonde mohair wig, jointed wood and composition limbs and body, dressed in original peach and cream muslin gown and bonnet, marked 'E made in Germany 9', c1910, 17½in (44.5cm) high, with original cardboard box.
£1,200–1,300 *AH*

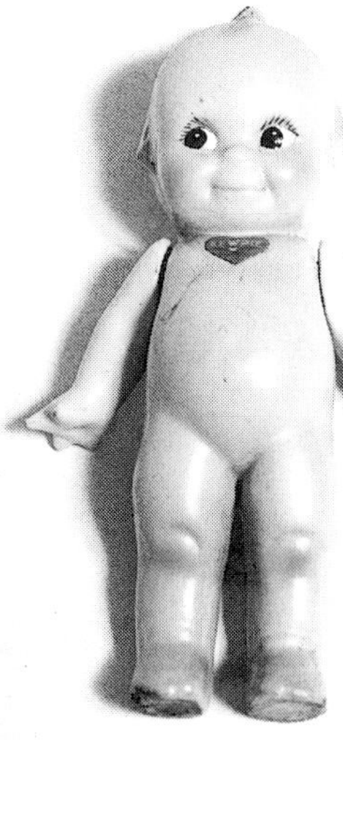

r. A German composition Kewpie doll, 1930s, 11in (28cm) high.
£70–80 *EKK*

Kewpies (c1913–present)

Kewpie dolls were the inspiration of American illustrator Rose O'Neill and were supposedly the guardian angels of children. The first bisque Kewpies were made in 1913 at the Kestner factory, but they were soon being produced at several other factories in Germany and the United States.

They were made from many materials including bisque, celluloid, fabric, rubber and composition, bisque being the most sought-after today. They may have a heart-shaped or circular label attached to their chest or back.

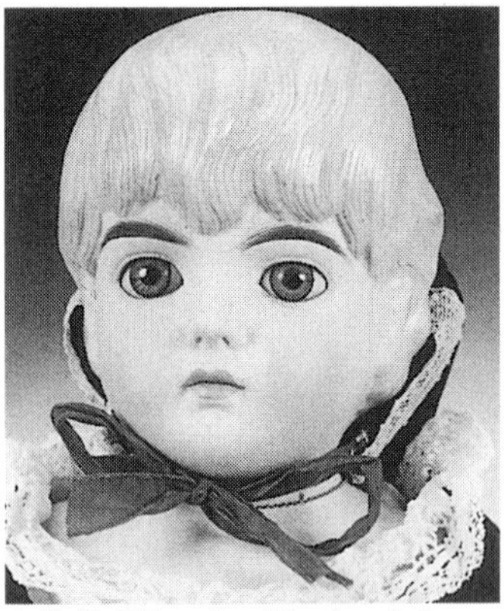

A C. F. Kling shoulder-headed bisque doll, with moulded blonde hair, blue eyes and closed mouth, on gusseted kid leather and fabric body with bisque lower arms, composition lower legs, in original national costume, impressed '131–11', c1880, 22in (56cm) high.
£800–900 *S*

A Gebrüder Kuhnlenz bisque-headed doll, on a five-piece body, c1890, 10in (25.5cm) high.
£700–800 *STK*

An Armand Marseille bisque-headed doll, the hard stuffed body with composition hands, in antique clothes, c1920, 14in (36cm) high.
£250–350 *EW*

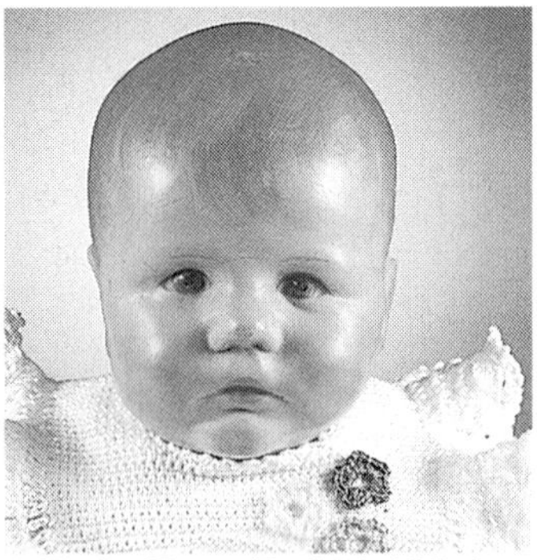

A Käthe Kruse 'Du Mein' fabric doll, with sand-weighted silk stockinette body, the head with painted brown hair, brown eyes, in a later pink Käthe Kruse baby outfit, c1920, 19½in (50cm) high.
£1,750–2,000 *S*

A Limoges Lanternier bisque-headed *bébé* doll, with brown paperweight eyes and fully jointed body, c1890, 20in (51cm) high.
£750–850 *STK*

An Armand Marseille bisque swivel-headed doll, with sleeping blue eyes, on a kid gusset body, bisque lower limbs, original scarlet silk skirt, jacket, bonnet, and leather shoes, marked 'S9H 719', c1900, 17½in (44.5cm) high.
£950–1,150 *DN*

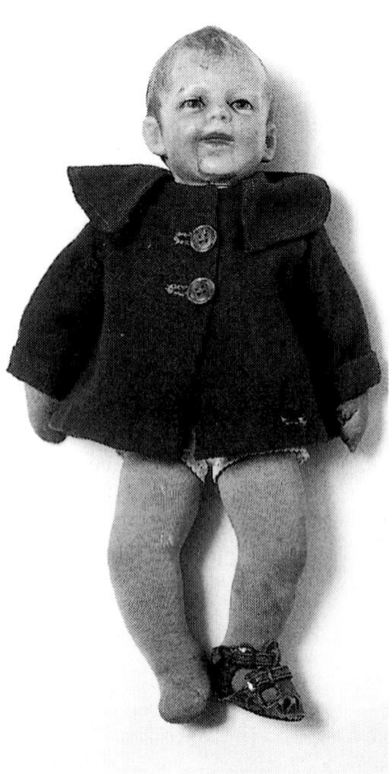

A Käthe Kruse Schlenkerchen cloth doll, c1922, 13in (33cm) high.
£2,500–3,000 *DOL*

This is the only type of doll Käthe Kruse made with an open/closed mouth. Schlenkerchen means 'little dangle limbs'.

FURTHER READING
Miller's Collecting Teddy Bears and Dolls
Miller's Publications, 1996

Two Madame Alexander hard plastic dolls of Prince Charles and Princess Anne, with weighted eyes, real hair wigs, jointed bodies, together with a quantity of clothes, c1958, dolls 8in (20cm) high, boxed.
£700–800 *Bon(C)*

Madame Alexander is among the best-known makers of early plastic and vinyl dolls. Based in North America, Beatrice Behrman, the daughter of Russian-born toymaker Maurice Alexander, first designed and helped her father to make Red Cross nurse dolls during WWI. In 1923 she set up the Alexander Doll Co, trading as Madame Alexander, but she only became famous for her hard plastic and vinyl dolls after 1945.

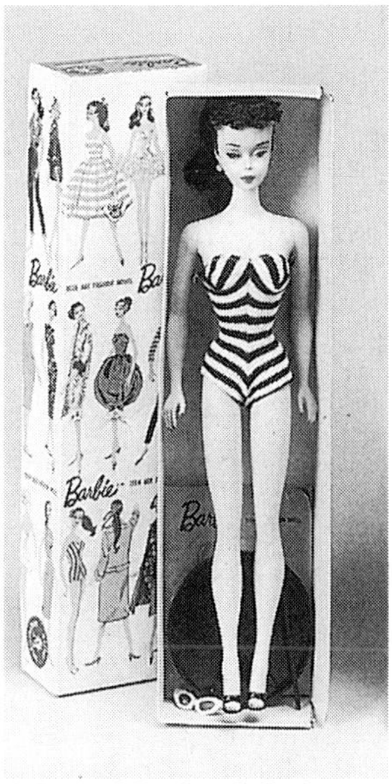

A Mattel Barbie doll, the vinyl solid body with black hair in a ponytail, black and white striped bathing suit, with accessories, 1959–60, 11in (28cm) high, with original box.
£250–300 *S(NY)*

A poured wax shoulder doll, probably by Montanari, with closed mouth, fixed blue glass eyes, inserted blonde wig and cloth body with poured wax lower limbs, in original costume, c1880, 21¾in (55cm) high.
£500–600 *S(S)*

A Mothereau bisque *bébé* doll, with fixed brown eyes, closed mouth, cork pate with brown wig, jointed wood and composition body with fixed wrists, in original scarlet muslin gown, impressed 'M2B', c1880, 13in (33cm) high.
£5,750–7,000 *S*

A wax over composition shoulder-headed doll, probably by Pierotti, with blue spiralled glass eyes, inserted lashes, inserted curling blonde wig, poured wax arms and lower legs, gusseted fabric body, in original challis gown, cream shawl and straw bonnet, black leather ankle boots, hands restored, c1865, 23in (59cm) high, with a trunk of accessories.
£1,100–1,200 *S*

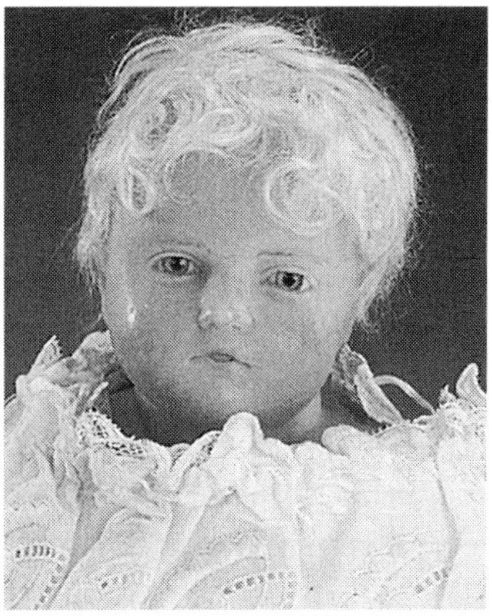

A poured wax shoulder-headed doll, probably by Pierotti, with closed mouth showing tip of tongue, fixed blue glass eyes, inserted blonde hair, and cloth body with poured wax lower limbs, in original costume and bonnet, c1880, 20¾in (53cm) high.
£500–600 *S(S)*

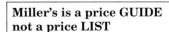

Miller's is a price GUIDE not a price LIST

A Rabery & Delphieu bisque-headed doll, with brown paperweight eyes, hair wig and jointed body, c1880, 28in (71cm) high.
£3,500–4,500 *STK*

r. A poured wax doll, probably by Pierotti, with closed mouth, fixed blue glass eyes, inserted long brown hair and cloth body with poured wax lower limbs, in original red wool dress, red velvet cape, hat, underclothes, socks and shoes, with a quantity of other clothes, c1860, 24¼in (64cm) high, in original wooden box.
£8,000–9,000 *S(S)*

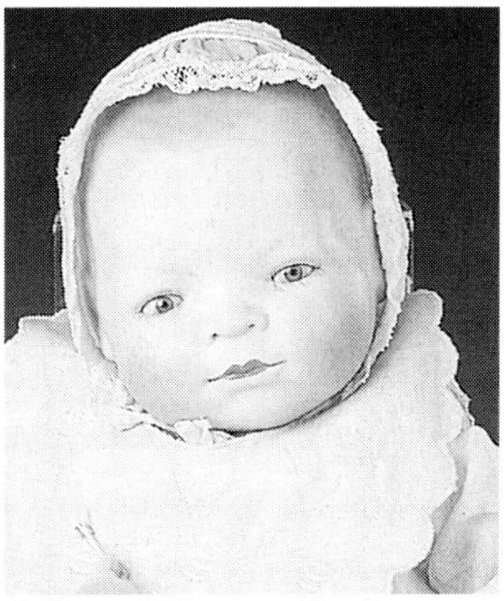

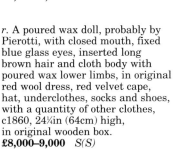

A Grace S. Putnam Bye-Lo bisque baby doll, with closed mouth, weighted blue eyes, cloth body and celluloid hands, impressed 'Copr by Grace S. Putnam', c1923, 13¾in (35cm) high.
£500–600 *S(S)*

A Rosebud hard plastic doll, 1950s, 14½in (37cm) high.
£65–75 *CMF*

This doll was made by the Northamptonshire doll maker T. Eric Smith, who registered under the trademark Rosebud. The company is so-named because of a little girl who was presented with a doll after visiting his factory, Nene Plastics. Asked what she most liked about the doll, she replied: 'What lovely rosebud lips the doll has.' The firm merged with American Mattel Inc in 1967.

A Schoenhut wooden doll, the head with bobbed moulded hair, pink painted headband, blue intaglio eyes, fully articulated spring-jointed wooden body, in pink and white spotted dress with white leather shoes, German or American, bearing blue transfer 'Schoenhut, Pat.Jan 17th, 1911, U.S.A.', 16½in (42cm) high.
£700–800 *S*

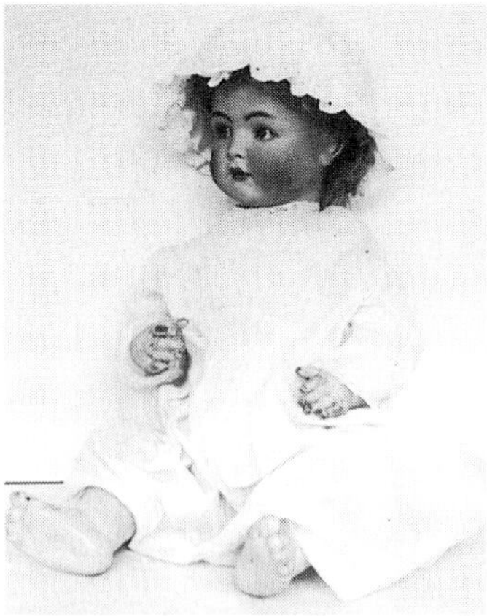

A Franz Schmidt porcelain-headed doll, with weighted blue eyes, open mouth and upper teeth, on a jointed composition body, impressed '1225 F. S. & C, 19thC, 25in (63.5cm) high.
£350–400 *DA*

An S.F.B.J. Jumeau mould bisque-headed doll, with fixed blue paperweight eyes, open mouth, blonde wig, jointed wood and composition body, original clothes, c1907, 13in (33cm) high.
£1,500–2,000 *EW*

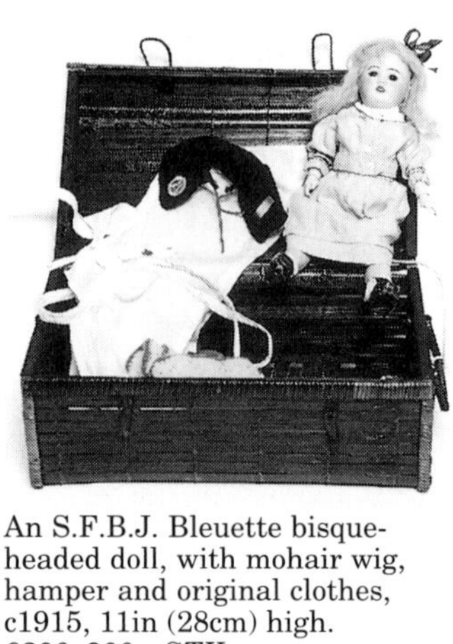

An S.F.B.J. Bleuette bisque-headed doll, with mohair wig, hamper and original clothes, c1915, 11in (28cm) high.
£800–900 *STK*

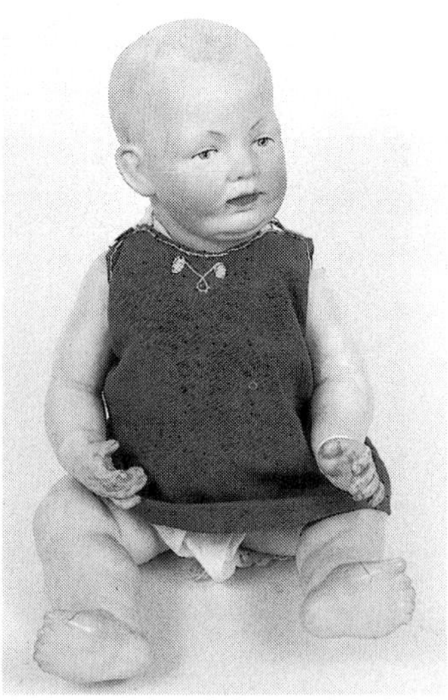

A Franz Schmidt bisque-headed doll, c1912, 13¾in (35cm) high.
£500–600 *YC*

A moulded bisque character doll, probably by S.F.B.J, with open/closed mouth showing white between lips, fixed brown glass eyes, red-brown real hair wig and joined wood and composition body, in peach dress with net covering and matching bonnet, c1915, 20in (50cm) high.
£600–700 *S*

A pair of S.F.B.J. twin dolls, with basket of extra clothes, c1920, 18in (45.5cm) high.
£1,000–1,150 *DOL*

A picture of the original twin owners accompanies these dolls.

A Simon & Halbig bisque china-headed doll, with closing brown glass eyes, open mouth, white kid body with bisque arms and soft lower limbs, original clothes, impressed 'S.H.18. 949', early 20thC, 36in (90cm) high.
£2,600–2,800 *Bea(E)*

A Simon & Halbig black bisque-headed doll, mould No. 1358, with weighted brown eyes, open mouth, black mohair wig, on a fully jointed wooden/composition body, incised '1358, Germany, Simon & Halbig S & H8', c1910, 22in (56cm) high.
£2,200–2,800 *Bon(C)*

A Simon & Halbig Oriental bisque-headed doll, with brown glass sleeping eyes, open mouth, mohair wig, jointed composition and wood limbs, marked 'SH1129, Germany, Dep 5½', c1910, 14½in (37cm) high.
£1,500–1,650 *AH*

An F. Simonne pressed bisque swivel-headed doll, with blue glass paperweight eyes, blonde real hair wig over original cork plate, closed mouth, and gusseted kid leather body, clothes frail, body stamped in blue 'Simonne Paris', c1870, 18in (45.5cm) high.
£2,500–3,500 *EW*

A Jules Steiner bisque-headed *bébé* doll, with blue glass eyes, closed mouth, blonde mohair wig, composition and wood fully jointed body with straight wrists, original clothes, marked 'A1 Paris', c1890, 8½in (21.5cm) high.
£2,500–3,500 *EW*

A Jules Steiner bisque doll, with fixed blue glass eyes, closed mouth, purple card pate with long blonde wig, jointed wood and composition body, dressed in ivory damask satin and lace trimmed gown, impressed 'Steiner Fre A 6', c1890, 20in (51cm) high.
£1,600–2,000 *S*

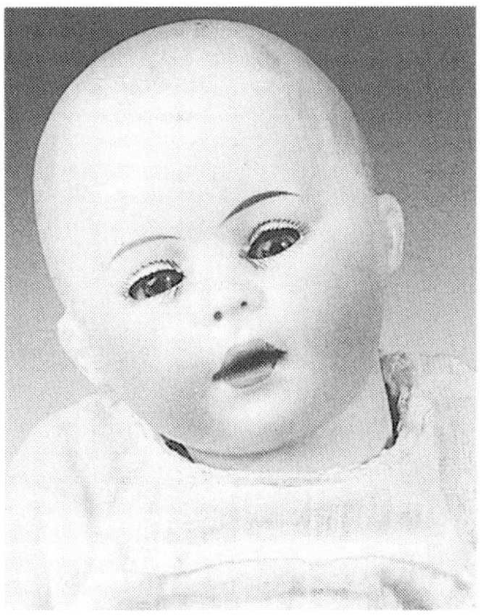

l. A Swaine & Co character bisque doll, with weighted blue eyes, open/closed mouth, curved limb body, in a white shift, impressed 'D 5 1', c1910, 9in (23cm) high.
£400–450 *S*

A pair of Norah Wellings Maori dolls, 1930s, 8½in (21.5cm) high.
£60–65 each *DOL*

DOLLS' FURNITURE & ACCESSORIES

A bone dressing table, corner unit and desk, made by Napoleonic prisoners of war, early 19thC, desk 5in (12.5cm) wide.
£200–350 each *HOB*

A rosewood commode, with kingwood and boxwood details, decorated with floral and armorial marquetry, with gilt-metal handles, 19thC, 26½in (30cm) wide.
£650–750 *S*

A mahogany and beech half-tester bed, with crimson drapes, c1870, 17¾in (45cm) wide, with quilt, pillows, bolster and bedspread.
£370–450 *S(S)*

A cast iron bed, 19thC, 22¼in (56.5cm) long.
£350–400 *ASM*

A hickory wood and twig toy settee, c1880, 8in (20.5cm) high.
£200–220 *YAG*

A Viennese Renaissance revival five-piece silver and enamel set of urns, ewers and a vase, painted with classical figures, late 19thC, 3½in (9cm) high.
£850–1,000 *EH*

A German painted tin pram, with cloth hood, c1880, 5in (12.5cm) long.
£80–90 *MSB*

Six pieces of Waltershausen doll's house furniture, lithographed in gold to imitate inlay, late 19thC, wardrobe 6¼in (14cm) wide.
£550–650 *S*

A green-painted high chair, c1900, 17in (43cm) high.
£100–120 *MLL*

A Waltershausen sideboard, with marble top, c1890, 6½in (16.5cm) wide.
£130–150 *HOB*

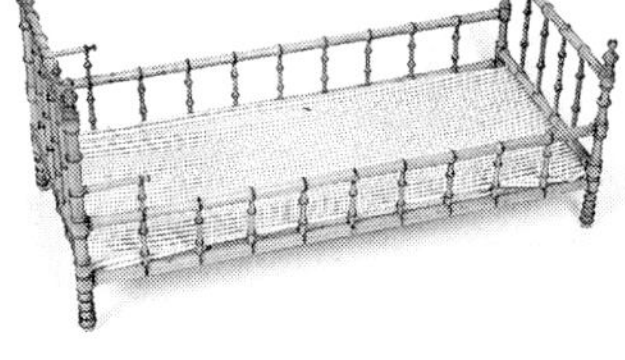

r. A *faux* bamboo bed, c1900, 28in (71cm) long.
£120–140 *MLL*

A tinplate stove, probably by Märklin, enamelled black with embossed nickel plated doors and sides, brass hand-rail with 4 copper pans, kettle, water heater, internal spirit burners, c1910, 22in (56cm) long.
£850–1,000 *S*

DOLLS' HOUSES

A Regency painted pine dolls' house, 11in (28cm) wide.
£550–600 *SWN*

A Victorian wooden dolls' house, the exterior painted red with brick effect, the hinged façade opening in 2 sections revealing 4 rooms, staircase and landing, with a quantity of furniture and a bisque doll, 46in (117cm) wide.
£600–700 *S(S)*

A wooden dolls' house, c1900, 38in (96.5cm) high including chimney.
£400–450 *Riv*

A Georgian dolls' house, with cream painted simulated stonework, a flat roof and imitation balustered rail, each room with a chimney breast and fireplace, the kitchen with a fitted dresser, stove, hanging shelf and towel rail, slight damage, 42½in (108cm) wide.
£2,500–3,000 *P(Ba)*

A Victorian mansard roof dolls' house, comprising 2 storeys with 2 rooms on each floor, an attic, staircases, cast iron fence and a wooden outhouse, late 19thC, 25in (63.5cm) wide.
£1,750–2,000 *SK(B)*

A wooden dolls' house, the front opening in 2 hinged sections revealing 4 large rooms, hall, landing and backstairs, c1917, 45¾in (116cm) wide.
£700–800 *S(S)*

The Galsworthy cabinet dolls' house, with glazed front opening door and 8 partitioned rooms, based on a platform, c1850, 47in (120cm) wide.
£5,000–6,000 *P(Ba)*

A late Victorian dolls' house, the hinged front opening to reveal 3 floors with 2 rooms on each floor, each room containing filigree metal and wooden furniture, dolls and accessories, divided by a central staircase, 44in (112cm) high.
£2,500–3,000 *RTo*

A dolls' house, the double opening front revealing 4 interior rooms fitted with furniture and accessories with a *faux* tiled pebble dashed roof, 1920s, 15in (38cm) wide.
£380–420 *M*

l. A Lines Brothers Triang dolls' house, with three-bay front, the centre section opening to reveal a large upstairs room and a smaller one downstairs, fitted with wiring for lighting, c1950, 24in (61cm) wide.
£55–65 *DN*

TEDDY BEARS

A Chad Valley teddy bear, 1950s, 16in (40.5cm) high.
£120–150 *Ber*

A Merrythought mohair teddy bear, with velvet snout and cloth paws, glass eyes and bells in his ears, c1957, 11in (28cm) high.
£150–175 *STK*

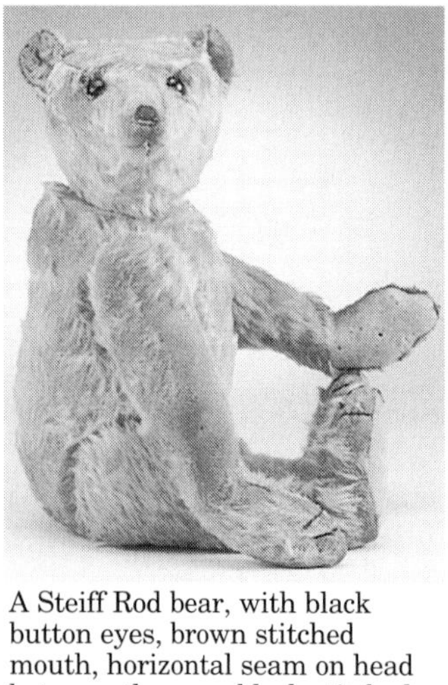

A Steiff Rod bear, with black button eyes, brown stitched mouth, horizontal seam on head between the ears, black stitched claws, elephant button to ear, c1904, 15½in (39.5cm) long.
£5,200–6,000 *S*

This bear is one of the earliest produced by the Steiff company and is also believed to be the only Rod bear in existence with the very scarce elephant button. The unusual seam on the head allowed the bear to be filled from above.

A Chiltern mohair teddy bear, with glass eyes, 1920s, 25in (63.5cm) high.
£500–550 *STK*

Care & Restoration

Restoration can be vitally important to the conservation of a teddy bear and it is always best to consider carefully before doing anything. Dirty bears should be cleaned by a specialist; if they are left untreated the dirt can cause the fabric to rot. Holes in a bear can be mended without detracting from the bear's value. When patching, always try to use similar, preferably old, fabric, and leave as much of the original fabric as possible. Paw pads made from felt often suffer wear badly so it is always much better to patch them than to replace them completely. How much the value of a bear may be affected by pad replacement varies considerably, so it is better to check first.

Two Schuco miniature mohair teddy bears, with fully jointed bodies, 1930s, 3in (7.5cm) long.
£220–250 each *CMF*

A Zotty mohair teddy bear, by Hermann, 1950s, 14in (35.5cm) long.
£80–100 *CMF*

A Pedigree mohair teddy bear, with glass eyes and a yellow ribbon, c1950, 17in (43cm) high.
£125–150 *CMF*

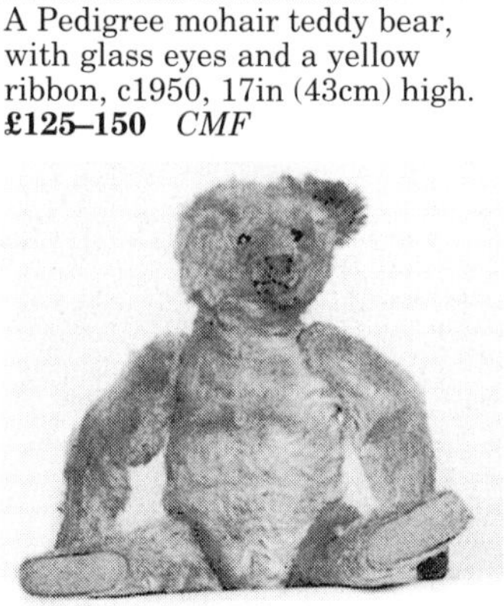

A Steiff blonde plush teddy bear, button in ear, with black boot button eyes, black stitched snout and claws, lacking right ear, growler inoperative, c1905, 12in (31cm) high.
£850–950 *S*

l. A Steiff teddy bear, with curly cinnamon mohair plush on an excelsior filled body, working growler and swivel joints, wearing original leather muzzle, c1905, 24in (61cm) high.
£9,000–10,000 *P(Ba)*

A teddy bear, probably by Steiff, with a long nose and hump back, c1906, 15in (40.5cm) high.
£900–1,000 *DD*

A black burlap bear, probably by Steiff, c1912, 19in (48.5cm) high.
£1,000–1,200 *TED*

Burlap is a coarse cloth made with single jute yarns, often used in the manufacture of early bears.

A Steiff yellow plush teddy bear, with black stitched snout, brown and black glass eyes, swivel joints and excelsior stuffed, c1920, 17in (43cm) high.
£1,400–1,600 *S*

An Edwardian gold plush teddy bear, possibly by Steiff, with black stitched snout, black and brown glass eyes, long arms, leather pads to feet and paws, with straw filling, c1908, 13in (33cm) high.
£200–220 *HCC*

A teddy bear, possibly by Steiff, with light golden mohair, black boot button eyes, black vertically stitched nose and mouth, with wood-wool filled body fitted with a sound box, early 20thC, 20in (51cm) high.
£2,800–3,200 *Bea(E)*

A Steiff caramel mohair teddy bear, wired limbs and jointed head, chest tag, 1960s, 2¾in (7cm) high.
£50–60 *TED*

A Steiff style sailor teddy bear, with dark golden mohair, dark glass eyes and black stitched nose, lacking button in ear, pads repaired, c1910, 23in (58.5cm) high.
£2,800–3,200 *CAG*

A Steiff pocket teddy bear, with glass eyes, 1914–18, 4in (10cm) high.
£220–250 *CMF*

These pocket teddy bears were given to service men as mascots in WWI.

A Dutch cotton teddy bear, with blue bow, early 1950s, 16½in (42cm) high.
£55–65 *CMF*

SOFT TOYS

A stuffed parrot, embroidered over tricot in green and gold silk blanket stitch, with fringed cotton tail and silk bound iron legs, possibly 18thC, 9in (23cm) long.
£300–330 *TMA*

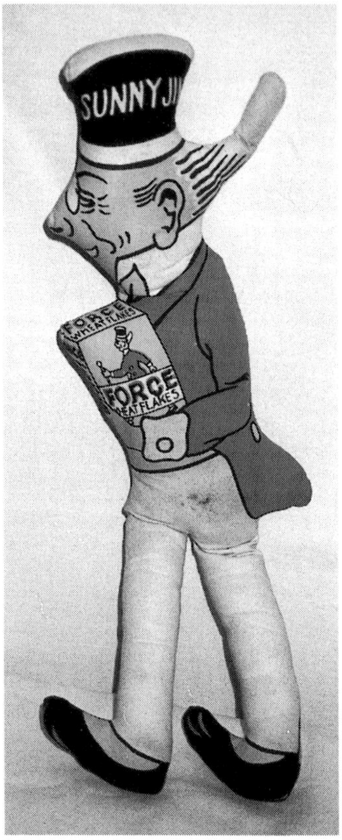

A cloth figure of Sunny Jim, advertising Force Wheat Flakes, c1940, 16in (40.5cm) high.
£30–40 *LF*

Steiff soft toy animals: owl, bison, goat and pig, 1950s–60s, pig 6in (15cm) long.
£30–40 each *CMF*

A Steiff cloth bear, 1920s, 4½in (11.5cm) high.
£80–90 *MSB*

What to Look For

- Named makers, as most animals of any value have manufacturers labels.
- Known animal characters. These are the most likely to rise in value, especially if they are favourites from the world of films.
- Particularly cute or cuddly examples.

A Dean's Child's Play Toys golly, 1940s, 13in (33cm) high.
£60–70 *DOL*

A Steiff tiger, 1960s, 3in (7.5cm) long.
£100–110 *MSB*

A Merrythought cat, entitled 'Dear Pussy', with pale old gold plush and glass eyes, early 1930s, 12½in (32cm) high.
£110–120 *CAG*

A Steiff tiger hand puppet, 1950s, 9in (23cm) high.
£65–75 *MSB*

A Chad Valley golly, with yellow shirt and red trousers, 1960s, 17in (43cm) long.
£28–32 *CMF*

TOYS

Boats

A Leonhard Uebelacker tinplate clockwork riverboat, *Niagara*, with Neptune motor, painted windows and doors, the forward deck with canopy above a group of lead flat figures, the hull finished in red, cream and black, c1895, 17¼in (44cm) long.
£600–700 *S(S)*

A Märklin tinplate clockwork battleship, the hull hand-painted in white with green portholes, red and black below the waterline, with key-wind to forward funnel, the deck with 6 gun turrets, cast tiller operating rudder and four-blade screw, c1905, 20½in (52cm) long.
£6,700–7,500 *S(S)*

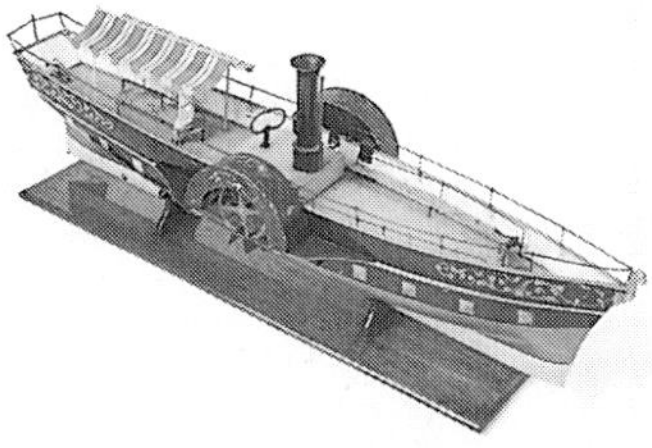

A side-wheel clockwork Paris river boat, by Maltête et Parents, c1900, 29½in (75cm) long.
£7,250–8,000 *BKS*

A Märklin clockwork first series battleship, *New York*, the masts and upper deck painted grey over white trimmed hull, painted brown/red below water line, c1900, 30in (76cm) long.
£23,000–25,000 *S(NY)*

A Radiguet live steam gunboat, c1900, 18in (45.5cm) long.
£7,500–8,500 *BKS*

A Märklin clockwork first series battleship, HMS *Victory*, hand-painted in grey, some damage, and parts missing, c1909, 28in (72cm) long.
£15,500–17,000 *S*

r. A Hornby 'Racer II' clockwork speedboat, cream with blue door, with key and book, c1934, 14in (35.5cm) long.
£75–90 *CDC*

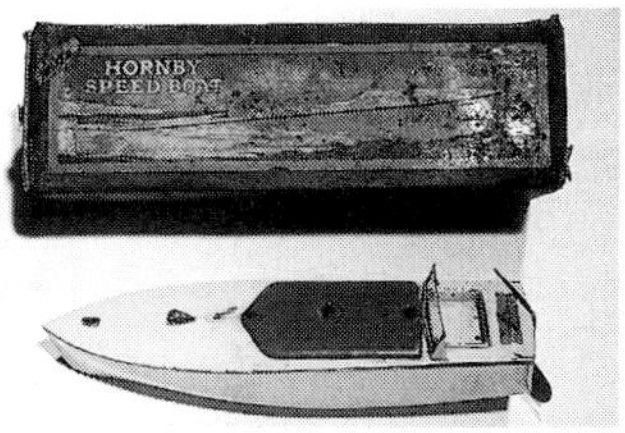

Trains

A Bassett-Lowke 0 gauge 'Royal Scot' LMS locomotive and tender, with clockwork mechanism, c1933, engine 11½in (29cm) long.
£400–450 *WaH*

A Bassett-Lowke 0 gauge 'Duchess of Montrose' locomotive and tender, the electric 4-6-2 engine and six-wheel tender finished in LMS maroon livery, minor paint retouching, 1940s.
£1,450–1,600 *Bon(C)*

A Bing station building, consisting of 2 separate structures with opening doors and central area with a canopy supported by 4 cast pillars enamelled in yellow and orange, c1900, 22in (56cm) wide.
£1,800–2,200 *P(Ba)*

A Bing gauge 2 guard's van, with a suburban coach, c1910, 14in (35.5cm) overall.
£2,000–2,200 *Doc*

A Bing Great Western bogie restaurant car, with lifting roof and interior chairs and tables, No. 3295, c1925, 12¼in (31cm) long overall, with a similar Bing corridor/baggage car and dining car, both unlettered, all finished in brown and cream.
£120–140 *BKS*

A Bond's 0 gauge 'Princess Royal' electric tender locomotive, finished in LMS red, 1936–39.
£900–1,000 *WaH*

A Brimtoy 0 gauge mechanical train set, with red and yellow tinplate 0-4-0 tender locomotive and four-wheeled coach, late 1950s.
£50–60 *WaH*

Four Exley 0 gauge carriages, finished in brown and cream, c1935.
£180–280 each *HOB*

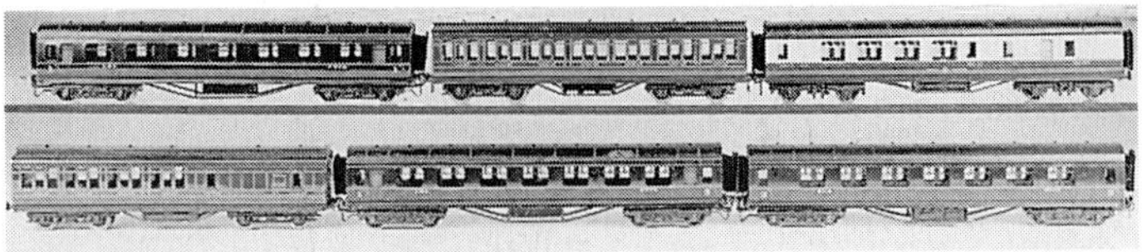

Seven Exley 00 gauge tinplate and diecast coaches, including GWR brown and cream side corridor brake/third, 2 dark red MR coaches, and 4 maroon LMS coaches, 1950s.
£160–200 *Bon(C)*

A Hornby train set, comprising locomotive and tender finished in black, 2 tinplate carriages finished in brown and cream, with a quantity of track, a pair of signals and a pedestrian bridge, 1930s, engine and tender 10in (25.5cm) long, in original distressed box.
£300–330 *DW*

A Hornby 0 gauge Metropolitan coach, lithoprinted in browns, c1927, 13in (33cm) long.
£100–125 *WaH*

l. A Hornby 0 gauge station, with electric operating lamps, 1938, 17in (43cm) wide.
£120–150 *WaH*

A Hornby 4-6-2 'Princess Elizabeth' locomotive, finished in LMS red with gold lining and lettering, 1945–50, 17in (43cm) long, in green lined wooden case.
£1,800–2,000 *AH*

Train Glossary

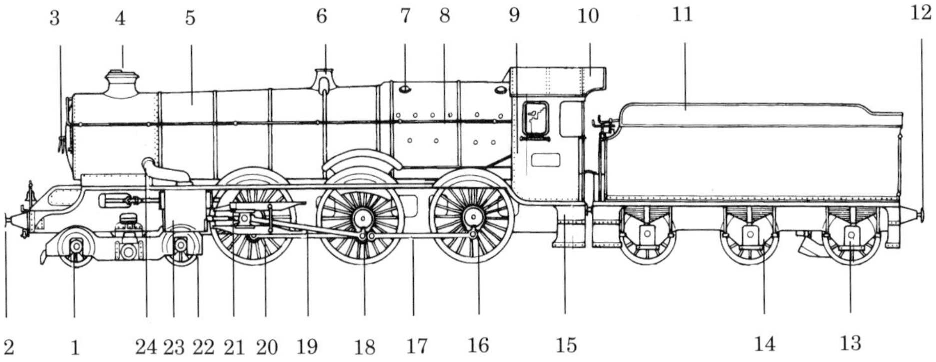

KEY TO ILLUSTRATION

1. Bogie wheel
2. Buffer and buffer beam
3. Smokebox door
4. Chimney
5. Boiler
6. Safety valve
7. Firebox
8. Handrail
9. Cab
10. Backhead (controls)
11. Tender
12. Coupling
13. Axle box
14. Axle guard
15. Cab step
16. Trailing wheel
17. Coupling rod
18. Driving wheel
19. Connecting rod
20. Leading wheel
21. Crosshead
22. Outside cylinder and piston
23. Valves
24. Main steam pipe to cylinder

A Hornby 0 gauge No. 1 level crossing, c1955, 9½in (24cm) wide.
£20–25 *AAC*

Miller's is a price GUIDE not a price LIST

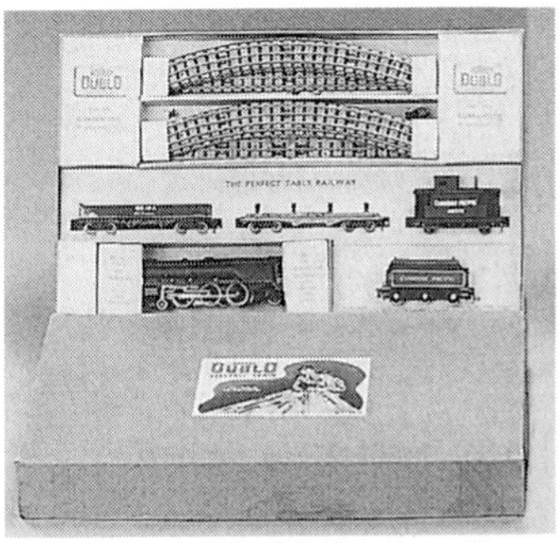

A Hornby-Dublo EDG 3 Canadian Pacific freight train set, locomotive No. 1215, with six-wheeled tender, high capacity brick wagon, caboose and bogie bolster wagon, 1956–57.
£1,250–1,400 *S(S)*

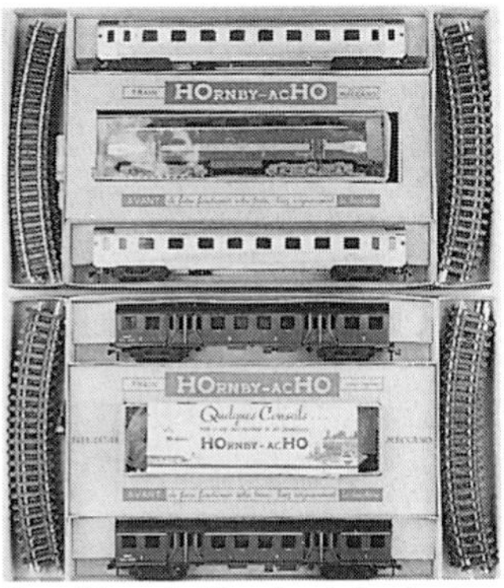

Two French Hornby Acho train sets, HO gauge, both in original green boxes, c1964.
£130–150 *Bon(C)*

An Ives 0 gauge Miniature Railway System, with wind-up black cast iron engine, lithographed tin No. 11 black tender, red Limited Vestibule Express parlour car, 'Harvard' red Limited Vestibule Express Baggage/Mail car, early 20thC.
£2,500–2,750 *SK(B)*

A Lionel Lines gauge one three-rail electric train set, comprising a tinplate BO-BO locomotive No. 402, 3 New York Central Lines tinplate bogie coaches, and a quantity of straight and curved track, c1920.
£500–550 *DN*

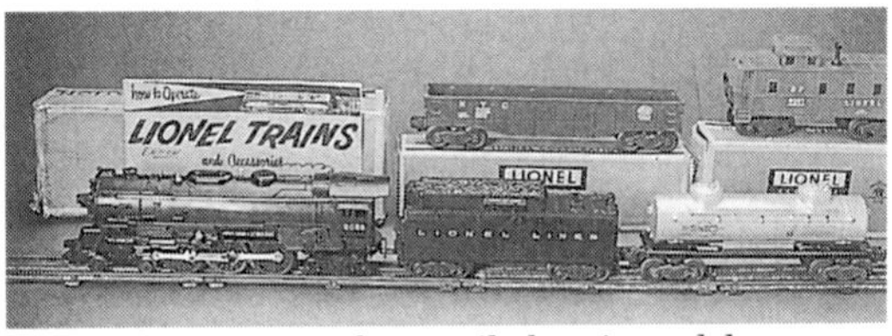

A Lionel 027 gauge three-rail electric model railway, comprising No. 2055 4-6-4 locomotive and 6026 tender, 6456 hopper car, 6462 gondola car, 6465 tank car, 6357-25 caboose and 6019 remote control track set, 1950s, all in original boxes.
£280–320 *DN*

A Lionel 0 gauge 'City of Portland' streamlined diesel train set, with 4 cars, finished in yellow and brown, 1950s.
£370–400 *S*

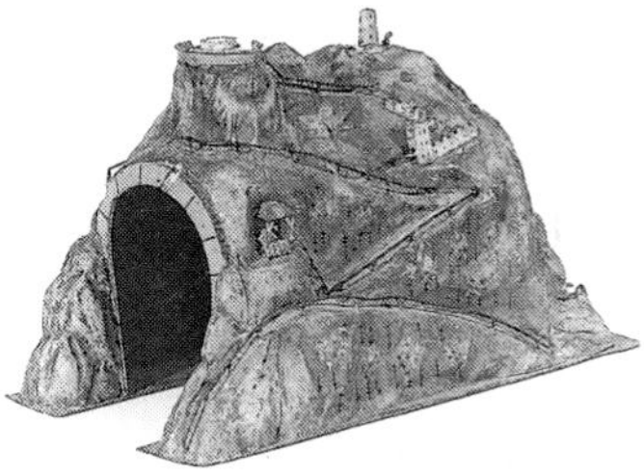

A Märklin gauge one pressed tin tunnel, the hand-painted sides with castle and light house, parts missing, early 20thC, 11in (28cm) wide.
£250–275 *AH*

A Märklin gauge one 20 volt DR 4-6-4 tank locomotive, finished in black, repainted, c1937.
£1,750–2,000 *S*

A Märklin bogie gauge 2 GNR dining car, painted in brown with cream roof and detailed interior, repainted, c1904, 15in (39.5cm) long.
£850–950 *S*

A Rock & Graner gauge one hospital car, hand-painted in blue with orange lined windows, the hinged roof revealing a fitted interior, c1902.
£3,400–3,750 *S*

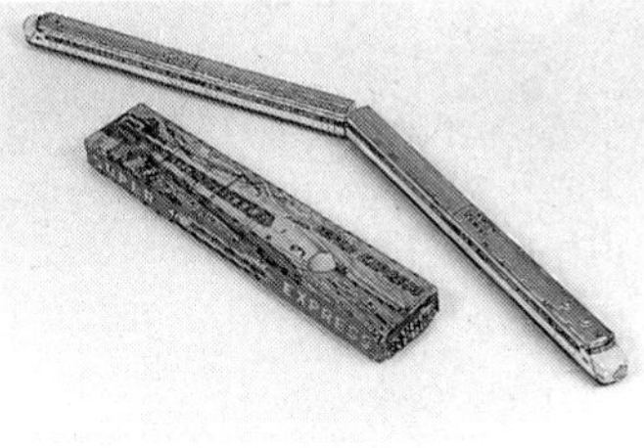

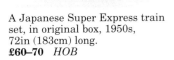

A Japanese Super Express train set, in original box, 1950s, 72in (183cm) long.
£60–70 *HOB*

A Wells o' London Mickey Mouse Circus train set, consisting of a tinplate circus tent brightly lithographed, clockwork silver link locomotive with tender and wagon, c1935, tent 5½in (14cm) high, in original box.
£2,300–2,500 *P(Ba)*

Vehicles

A Dinky Supertoys No. 512 Guy Flat Truck, c1947, 52¼in (133cm) long, mint and boxed.
£130–150 *OTS*

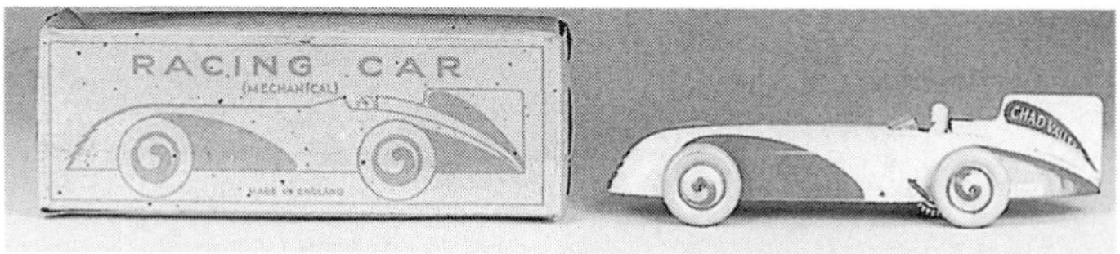

A Chad Valley clockwork racing car, lithographed in cream with red flashes, grey wheels with red and cream swirl hubs, 1930s, 11½in (29cm) long.
£250–275 *Bon(C)*

A Dinky Supertoys 935 Leyland Octopus Flat truck, with chains, early 1960s, 8in (20.5cm) long.
£750–850 *WAL*

An Eberl key-wind lithographed tinplate limousine, with driver, finished in yellow with gold and blue decoration, c1912, 10in (25.5cm) long.
£700–800 *S(NY)*

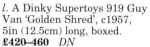

l. A Dinky Supertoys 919 Guy Van 'Golden Shred', c1957, 5in (12.5cm) long, boxed.
£420–460 *DN*

A Dinky Toys 173 Pontiac Parisienne, with retractable aerials, late 1960s, 5in (12.5cm) wide, mint and boxed.
£35–40 *WaH*

l. A Lines Bros painted wood and metal Bullnose Morris pedal car, with aluminium radiator cover, painted in green with red lines, with first aid box and petrol can, 1930s, 48in (122cm) long.
r. A Eureka painted metal Bugatti Type 35 pedal car, with chain drive, adjustable seat and hand brake, in blue and red, 1930s, 61in (155cm) long.
£650–700 each *AH*

An Ever Ready Austin A70 plastic battery-operated saloon car, c1953, 7in (18cm) long.
£40–50 *CDC*

A Günthermann Bluebird record car, the litho tinplate finish in blue with yellow and white, play wear and spot rusting, c1930, 22in (56cm) long.
£300–330 *WAL*

An Opel child's car, with maroon paintwork and original lamps, lacking wheels, c1909, 51¼in (130cm) long.
£2,000–2,500 *BKS*

A Sturditoy green, black and red pressed steel US Mail truck, some scratching to paint, 1920–30, 25½in (65cm) long.
£1,400–1,600 *SK(B)*

Soldiers & Army Vehicles

A British Army 'Review' set of toy soldiers, and a set of flat figures with some civilians, staff tent, tents, flag, trees and cavalry, some damage, c1840, all in original wooden box.
£180–200 *P(Ba)*

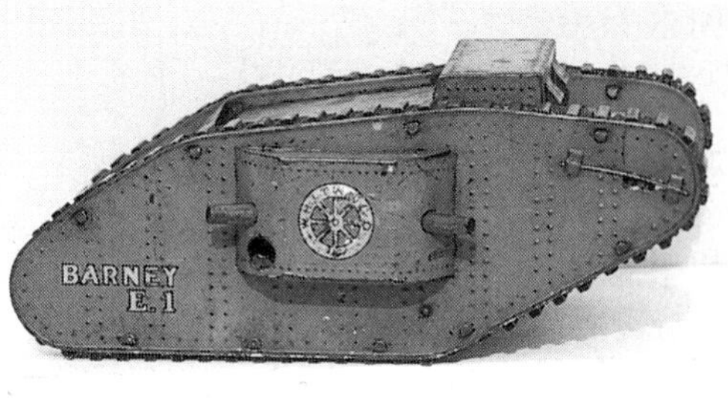

A Whitanco WWI clockwork tank, 'Barney E1', c1915, 8in (20.5cm) long.
£150–165 *RAR*

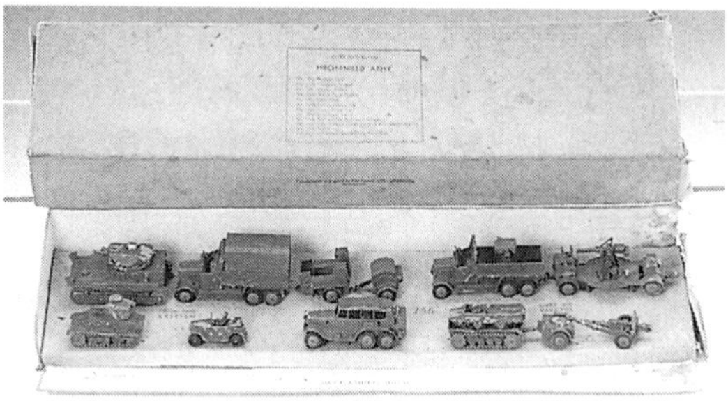

A Dinky Toys No. 156 mechanised army set, comprising 12 pieces, slight wear, c1935, in original box.
£400–450 *S(S)*

A Heyde 45mm scale British WWI trench raiding party, c1923.
£370–400 *P(Ba)*

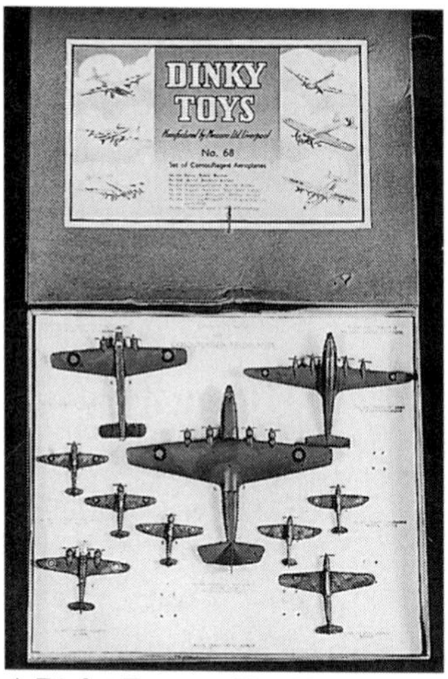

A Dinky Toys set No. 68 camouflaged aeroplane set, comprising an Ensign, Frobisher, Whitley, Fairy Battle, Blenheim, Spitfire, and Hawker Hurricane, late 1930s, 14in (35.5cm) long.
£1,600–2,000 *P(Ba)*

r. A Britains set No. 211 heavy howitzer with 10 horse Royal Field Artillery team, some damage, c1920–41.
£500–600 *Bon (C)*

A Britains set No. 135 Japanese Cavalry with officer, in dark blue jackets, c1939, horses 4in (10cm) long.
£650–700 *P(Ba)*

r. A Dinky Toys No. 623 army covered wagon, 1950s, 4¼in (11cm) long.
£45–55 *NTM*

A Britains set No. 255 The Green Howards, with officer, colour bearer and drummer, 1937, in original Whisstock box.
£2,100–2,300 *P(Ba)*

A Matchbox Gift Set G-5 Army Set, comprising 8 pieces, 1950s.
£165–180 *Bon(C)*

Mechanical Toys

A Leopold Lambert musical automaton of a lady, with a Jumeau head and blue paperweight eyes, the right hand raises the hinged egg to reveal a chick, French, late 19thC, 20in (51cm) high.
£2,000–2,200 *S(NY)*

A Simon & Halbig mechanical bisque-headed doll, with galloping horses and trolley, c1890, 15in (38cm) long.
£1,500–1,800 *YC*

A blacksmith and farrier automaton, the sand-powered mechanism operating 4 figures, each with an articulated arm, set within a three-storey forge, hand-coloured, late 19thC, 11¾in (30cm) wide.
£350–400 *S(S)*

An Edwardian toy donkey, with wooden stable, when the door opens the donkey moves out and heehaws, 7in (18cm) wide.
£170–185 *DD*

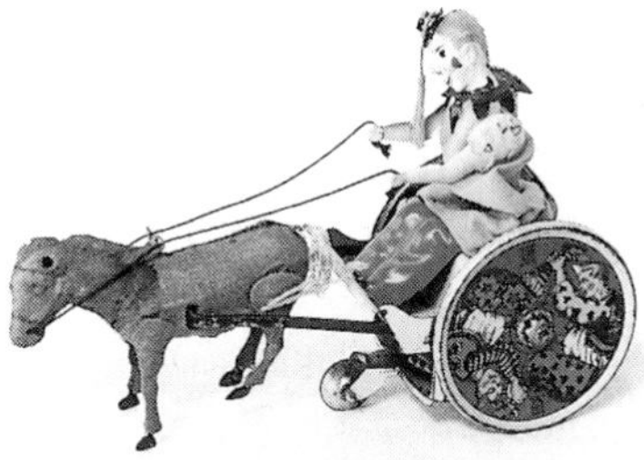

A Lehmann clockwork tinplate toy, c1920, 8in (20.5cm) long.
£160–180 *EKK*

A French automaton knitting cat, probably by Renou, covered in white rabbit fur, the keywound stop-start mechanism causing the head to lift and the paws to twist, early 20thC, 13½in (34cm) high.
£1,600–1,750 *S*

A German tinplate clockwork figure of Charlie Chaplin, dressed in felt tailcoat and trousers with black metal bowler hat and orange walking stick, c1930, 6½in (16.5cm) high, with original box.
£450–500 *MSW*

r. A Triang gyro cycle clockwork toy, c1930, 10in (25.5cm) long, with original box.
£75–85 *LF*

A German carousel, with 7 horses and riders, lamps inside base, spray painted in various colours, with music box, c1930, 17in (42cm) high.
£950–1,150 *P(Ba)*

A Chein & Co tinplate clockwork clown with spinning umbrella, American, c1930, 8in (20.5cm) high.
£75–85 *MSB*

l. An Arnold MAC 700 clockwork motorcycle, c1950, 6in (15cm) wide.
£420–460 *RAR*

A tinplate clockwork L'il Abner band, by Unique Art Manufacturing Co, 1945, 10in (25.5cm) wide.
£550–600 *YAN*

Prices
The price ranges quoted in this book reflect the average price a purchaser would expect to **pay** for a similar item.

Money Boxes

l. A J. & E. Stevens cast iron bulldog money bank, the coin is placed on the snout, the tail pulled back and the coin falls into the mouth, Amercian, patented 1880, 5½in (14cm) long.
£1,000–1,100 *S*

A J. & E. Stevens Shoot the Chute money bank, designed by Charles A. Bailey, with nickel-plated boat, American, c1906, 9½in (24cm) high, in original box.
£15,000–16,500 *S(NY)*

This piece is in excellent condition and still in its original box. It is impressive because of the faster than average speed of its motion.

A J. & E. Stevens owl money bank, painted cast iron with a turning head and inset glass eyes, perched upright on a log, American, patented 1880, 7½in (19cm) high.
£320–380 *S(S)*

l. A Shepard Hardware Co Trick Pony money bank, painted cast iron brown horse with black mane and tail, brown plinth highlighted with gold and black mouldings, lever-operated head motion towards opening trap, patented 1885, 8in (20.5cm) wide.
£1,400–1,600 *S(S)*

Rocking Horses

A rocking horse chair, ears and bridle missing, c1860, 37½in (94cm) long.
£220–250 *MSB*

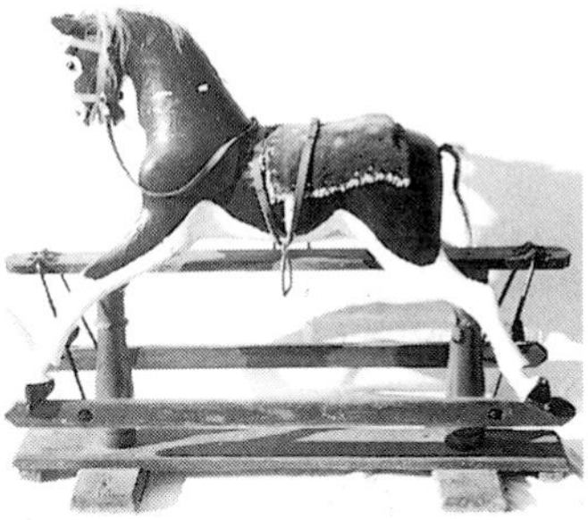

A Victorian rocking horse, with flared nostrils and pointed ears, the wood and plaster body repainted brown and white, on trestle rockers, 54in (137cm) long.
£450–500 *LF*

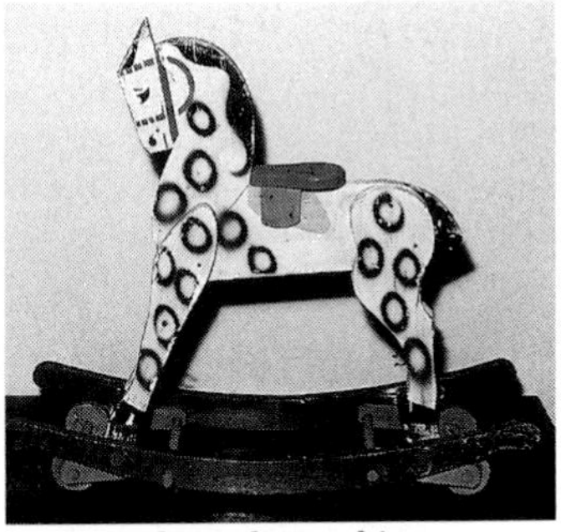

A painted wooden rocking horse, with wheels, c1900, 31in (78.5cm) long.
£100–125 *MLL*

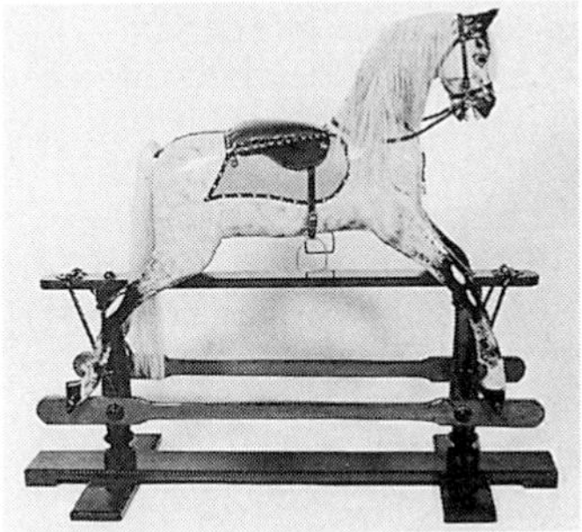

A late Victorian dapple grey rocking horse, 53½in (136cm) high.
£1,000–1,200 *HYD*

A wicker rocking horse, c1900, 22in (56cm) long.
£20–25 *MLL*

A wooden rocking horse, on pine twin-pillar safety stand, the grey-painted body with remains of original leather tack, mane missing, early 20thC, 50in (127cm) long.
£600–700 *DN*

l. A pony skin rocking horse, c1905, 50in (127cm) wide.
£300–350 *JUN*

Rocking Horses

Basic carved wooden horses are among the earliest surviving toys, possibly dating back to early civilisation. By the Middle Ages there are several references to hobby horses in contemporary manuscripts, although rocking horses are not mentioned until the 17thC, when they appear as simple structures with flat board sides instead of legs. By the 19thC rocking horses had become a regular feature in most Victorian nurseries. As the century progressed, more attention was given to safety and so rockers became shallower, and by the 1870s rockers were often replaced with a swing 'safety' stand, where the horse is hung on metal bars from a secure wooden base. The most popular colour for rocking horses is dapple grey.

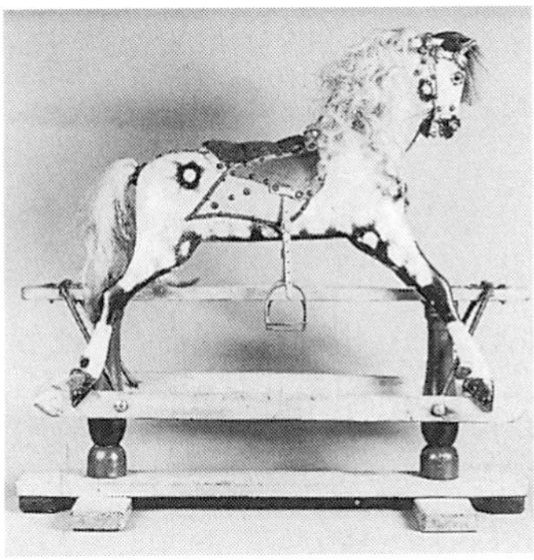

l. A carved wooden rocking horse, painted dapple grey with horsehair mane and tail, glass eyes, open mouth and flared nostrils, plush saddle with stirrups, leather bridle, c1920, 34in (86cm) long.
£500–550 *P(Ba)*

CAROUSEL ANIMALS

Steam roundabouts with carved animals (usually pine) were made from the 1880s until the 1920s, the middle 20 years being the heyday of fairground baroque carving. Most of the carved fairground rides were broken up, and replaced with faster modern machines in the early 1960s, and subsequently carousel animals became available to British collectors. Since then the prices have risen steadily, and a well-carved horse that cost £10 in 1965 is now worth around £2,000.

Most English full-size (adult) carousels and the small hand-cranked juvenile roundabouts carried horses, but some were produced with chickens and other farmyard animals. The French favoured domestic and farm animals, while the Germans chose wild beasts and fantastic creatures as well as the ubiquitous horse. It is easy enough to identify English animals because roundabouts were the only ones to turn clockwise and it is the more visible left-hand side of the mount that is most heavily ornamented. European or American animals have the extra decoration on the right-hand side. The animals from the outside of a ride are larger and more embellished than those from the inner rows, and generally more valuable.

The main manufacturers of carved animals were Orton & Spooner, Anderson, and Savage in Britain; Bayol, Limonaire, and Chanvin in France; and Heyn and Müller in Germany. Heyn also made left-facing horses for the English market. American animals are very rarely found in Europe, but the very large and heavily carved mounts by Dentzel, for example, can be worth at least £15,000, so they are certainly worth looking for.

Original carousel animals turn up in auctions and a few specialist antique shops, but beware of the reproductions and fakes which are appearing in growing numbers. Most old animals would have been repainted every few years, and could have accumulated as many as 30 layers of paint over the original colour and gold leaf. This is hard to fake convincingly, as is the sort of wear and damage acquired from decades of use. Nearly all original animals were hollowed out for lightness, so peer inside for signs of new wood, and look underneath for evidence of new paint which has escaped the 'distressing' wax.

When buying carousel animals it is usually best to go for quality of workmanship and decoration. Rarer subjects are more likely to increase in value, but many of the simpler and less expensive pieces have an appealing character and individual charm that make them a delight to collect. Being hand-finished, no two are exactly alike so there is plenty of variety and scope for the collector.

Grierson Gower

A carved and painted wood roaring lion, carved by Daniel Müller, from the Dentzel workshop in Philadelphia, late 19thC, 69in (175.5cm) long.
£15,000–18,000 *CSK*

Having been taught the skill by his German father, Gustav A. Dentzel (1840–1909) began making carousels soon after his arrival in America in the 1860s and is now the best known of American carousel manufacturers.

A Victorian carved wood carousel horse, painted white with pale green and blue saddle, slight damage, c1880, 55½in (141cm) long.
£500–600 *S(S)*

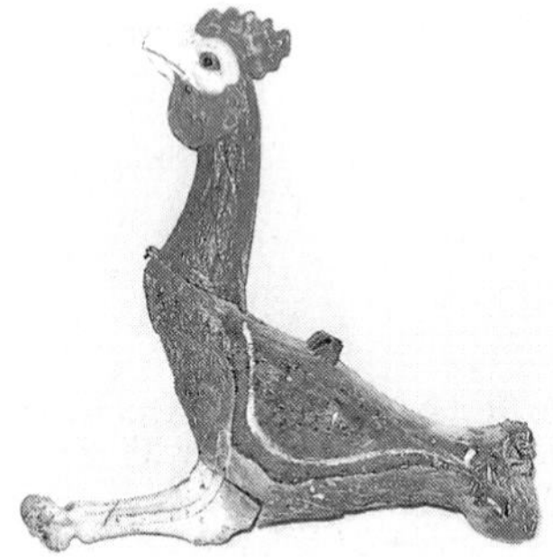

A carved wood galloper cockerel, painted red with blue back and yellow beak and legs, c1890, 58in (147.5cm) wide.
£700–800 *JUN*

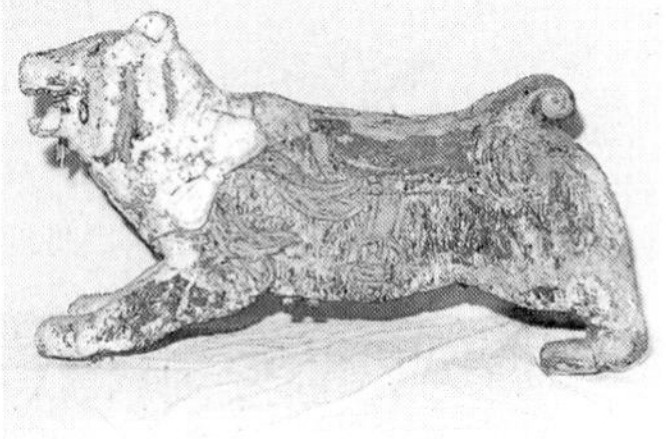

l. An Anderson carved wood carousel bear, with red, green and yellow saddle, c1890, 35in (89cm) long.
£1,000–1,200 *JUN*

r. A Savage carved wood carousel cockerel, painted brown with red and blue saddles, c1890, 64in (162.5cm) long.
£1,300–1,500 *JUN*

A Savage carved wood carousel ostrich, painted yellow with green, red and blue, c1890, 68in (172.5cm) long.
£1,500–1,800 *JUN*

A carved and painted wood camel, with inset glass eyes, labelled 'C. W. Parker, Leavenworth, Kansas', c1890, 53in (135cm) long.
£10,500–11,500 *S(NY)*

A carved wood galloper peacock, painted yellow, tail removed, damaged, c1890, 44in (112cm) long.
£1,200–1,500 *JUN*

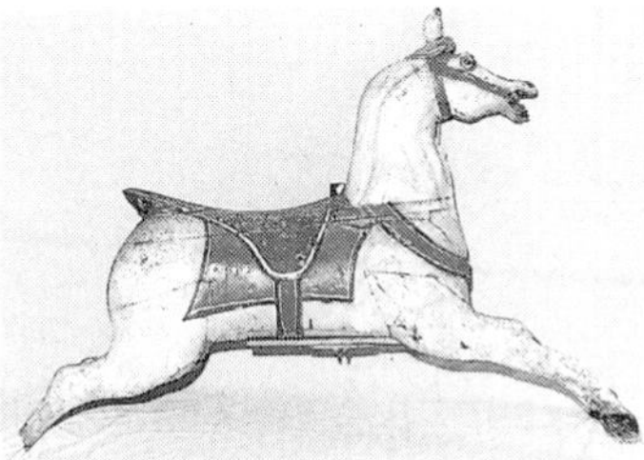

A German carved wood galloper horse, painted white with red and blue saddle, c1900, 59in (150cm) long.
£450–500 *JUN*

A carved carousel horse, c1910, repainted in yellow, green and mauve, c1960, 60in (152.5cm) long.
£800–900 *JUN*

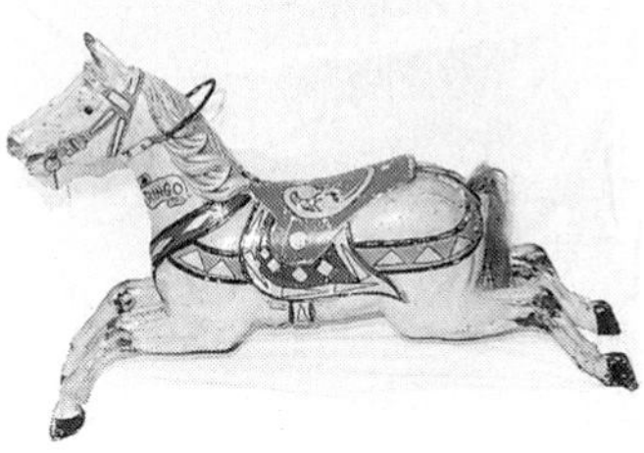

An American carved wood outside row goat, damaged, late 19thC, 65in (165cm) long.
£3,000–3,300 *S(NY)*

A carved wood carousel cockerel, painted yellow, by Orton & Spooner, c1900, 58in (147.5cm) long.
£1,200–1,500 *JUN*

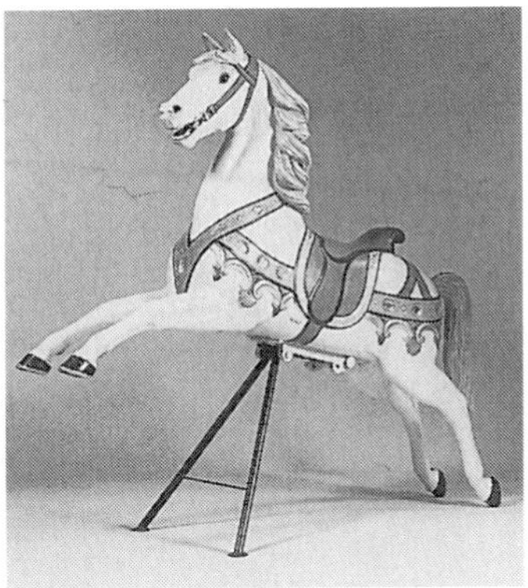

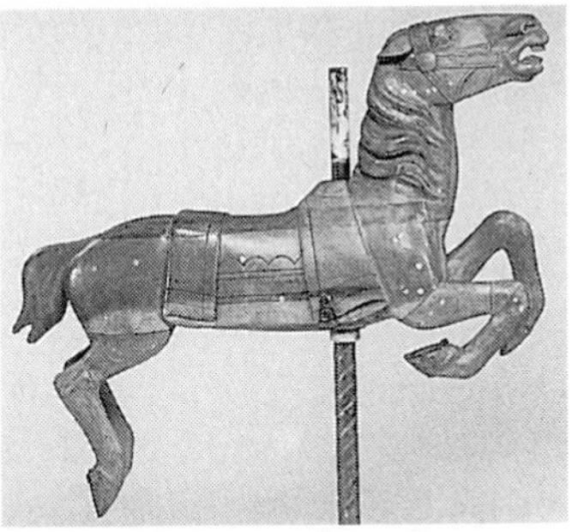

An American carved wood carousel horse, by Herschell, c1920, 48in (122cm) long.
£275–325 *SLN*

l. A carved wood carousel horse, painted cream with a red and green saddle, c1910, 45in (114.5cm) long.
£500–600 *JUN*

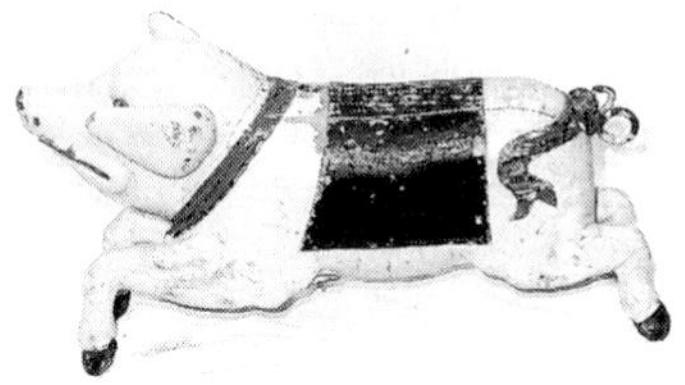

A French carved wood carousel pig, painted pink with a black saddle, c1890, 43in (109cm) long.
£700–800 *JUN*

A carved wood carousel horse, with red and green saddle, c1900, 76in (193cm) long.
£1,800–2,000 *JUN*

Two carved wood polychrome painted carousel horses, 19thC, 36in (91.5cm) high.
£850–950 *SLM*

l. A Hubner carved and painted wood fairground galloper, with inset bevelled glass panels, c1900, 66in (168cm) long.
£900–1,100 *S(NY)*

A carved wood carousel lion, painted in yellow with a green and brown mane, c1900, 39½in (100cm) long.
£450–500 *S(Am)*

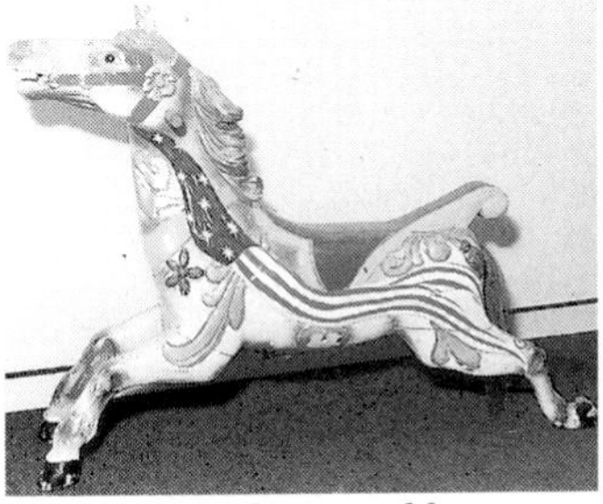

A carved wood carousel horse, painted red, yellow, green and blue, c1950, 40in (101.5cm) long.
£500–550 *JUN*

EPHEMERA

Annuals, Books & Comics

The New Adventures of Rupert, first Rupert annual, illustrated by Alfred Bestall, 1936.
£2,500–2,750 *P*

Ugly Duckling, Walt Disney, published by Collins, c1939.
£55–65 *CBP*

Father Noah's Ark, published by Birn Bros, c1940.
£65–75 *CBP*

The New Rupert Book, illustrated by Alfred Bestall, c1946.
£70–85 *HAM*

The Beano Book, 1957.
£60–70 *CBP*

Captain Marvel 85 comic, 1948.
£120–150 *CBP*

Batman 155 comic, 1963.
£70–80 *CBP*

Blue Peter, the first Blue Peter annual, BBC TV, 1965.
£60–70 *CBP*

Autographs

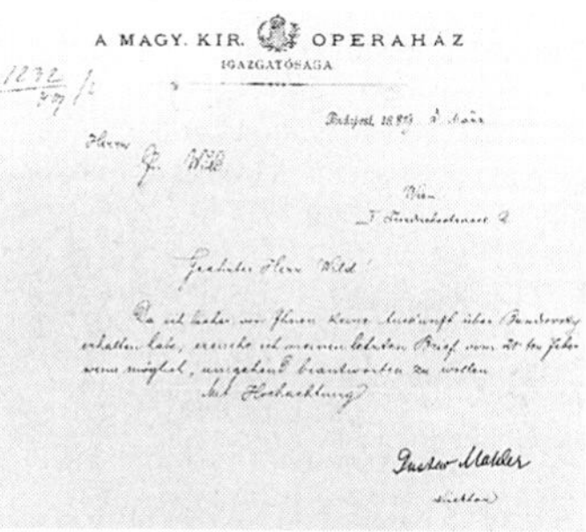
A. MAGY. KIR. OPERAHAZ
IGAZGATÓSÁGA

A written letter by Gustav Mahler, when Director of the Budapest Opera, to Herr J. Wild requesting an answer as soon as possible to his earlier letter, dated '3 March 1889'.
£1,400–1,600 *S(NY)*
Ex-Leonard Bernstein collection.

Sarah Bernhardt, a signed sepia cabinet photo, 1903.
£80–100 *VS*

Clark Gable, a signed portrait photograph, 1930s.
£180–220 *DW*

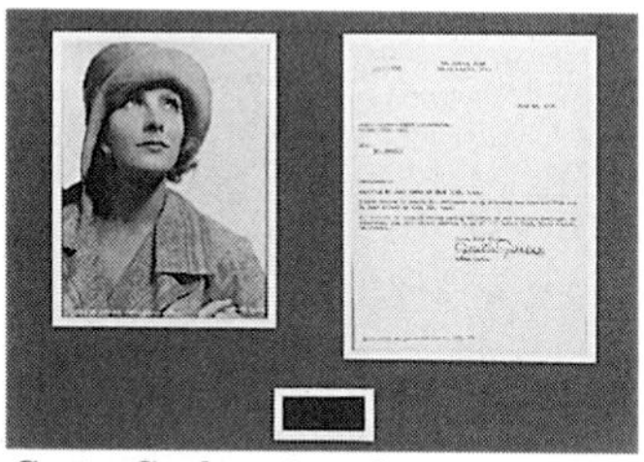

Greta Garbo, signed typewritten letter addressed to Metro-Goldwyn-Mayer, framed with an MGM black and white publicity still, dated 'June 23, 1936', 19½ x 24½in (49.5 x 62cm).
£550–650 *S(NY)*

Two Christmas cards, signed by Beatrix Potter, 1934 and 1936.
l. **£420–480**
r. **£280–340** *PFK*

King George VI, Queen Elizabeth, Princesses Elizabeth and Margaret, signed coronation photograph, dated by the King '1937'.
£1,000–1,100 *P*

Marlene Dietrich and Maurice Chevalier, signed photograph, c1940, 10 x 8in (25.5 x 20.5cm).
£1,400–1,600 *S(LA)*
Ex-Marlene Dietrich collection.

Elizabeth Taylor, signed publicity photograph, 1940s, 10 x 8in (25 x 20cm).
£300–350 *S*

Albert Schweitzer, signed album page, with 3 newspaper photos, dated '1955'.
£55–65 *VS*

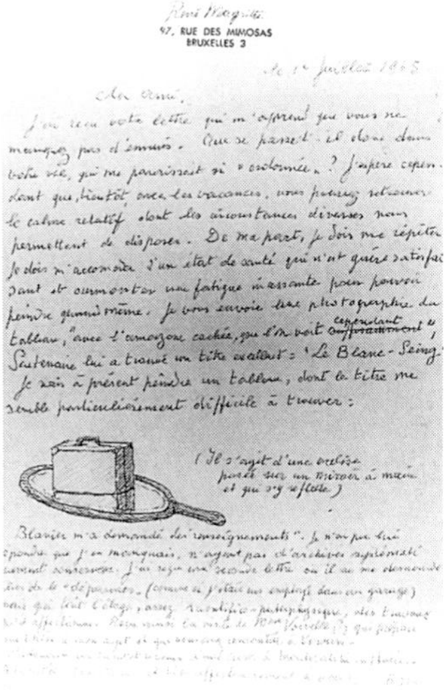

René Magritte
97, RUE DES MIMOSAS
BRUXELLES 3

le 1er juillet 1965

Cher ami,

J'ai reçu votre lettre qui m'apprend que vous ne manquez pas d'ennuis. Que se passe-t-il donc dans votre vie, qui me paraissait si « ordonnée » ? J'espère cependant que, bientôt, avec les vacances, vous pourrez retrouver le calme relatif dont les circonstances diverses nous permettent de disposer. De ma part, je dois me répéter je dois m'accommoder d'un état de santé qui n'est guère satisfaisant et surmonter une fatigue harassante pour pouvoir peindre quand même. Je vous envoie une photographie du tableau, "avec l'amazone cachée, que l'on voit cependant", Scutenaire lui a trouvé un titre excellent : 'Le Blanc-Seing'. Je suis à présent peindre un tableau, dont le titre me semble particulièrement difficile à trouver :

(Il s'agit d'une valise posée sur un miroir à main et qui s'y reflète.)

Blavier m'a demandé des "renseignements". Je n'ai pu lui répondre que j'en manquais, n'ayant pas d'archives ...

r. René Magritte, signed letter in French, with a sketch in the text, Brussels, 1 July 1965, 11 x 7¼in (28 x 18.5cm).
£1,600–1,800 *S(NY)*

Cigarette Cards

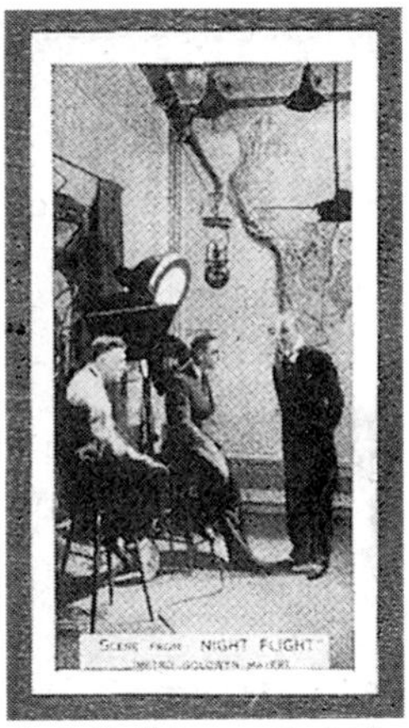

Ardath Tobacco Co Ltd, Scenes from Big Films, set of 100, 1935.
£95–105 *VS*

Collins' Cigarettes, Homes of England, set of 24, 1924.
£55–60 *VS*

W. F. Faulkner Ltd, Police Terms, set of 12, 1899.
£105–120 *VS*

W. Duke Sons & Co, Terrors of America and Their Doings, set of 50, c1900.
£60–65 *WAL*

r. Kinney, National Dances, set of 50, c1900.
£50–55 *WAL*

Postcards

A postcard showing log cutting, with traction engine and horse-drawn water cart, 1900–14.
£18–25 *VS*

A postcard showing the opening of the Shirley recreation ground, dated 'September 10th', early 1900s.
£10–12 *MRW*

A postcard showing 7 men in front of a steam roller, possibly taken in Monmouthshire, Wales, 1904.
£55–60 *VS*

A postcard showing George Ohr, Pork Butchers, corner shop, Yorkshire, published 1911.
£70–80 *VS*

A Jungnickel Art Deco postcard, 1911.
£35–40 *VS*

A postcard of the Titanic, 1912.
£40–50 *VS*

Six humourous postcards of Mickey Mouse and other characters, 1930s.
£50–55 *DW*

A postcard of L&NW Manchester Express at Rugby platform, 1920s.
£10–12 *MRW*

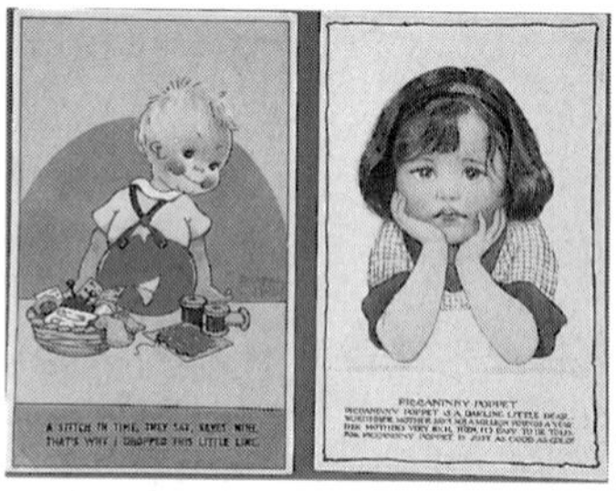

l. Two postcards of children, 1930s.
£2–3 each *MRW*

Posters

A poster depicting Picturesque Dover, overprinted with *Chemins de Fer de L'Etat Belge*, on linen, c1906, 40 x 25in (102 x 64cm).
£500–600 *ONS*

A German poster depicting Charlie Chaplin in *The Kid*, by Eckert, 1921, 56 x 37in (142 x 94cm).
£4,500–5,500 *S*

A Farman Airlines poster, by Albert Solon, 1926, 35½ x 24in (90 x 61cm).
£380–450 *ONS*

A poster depicting Lyme Regis, by Lambert, 1926, 40 x 25 (102 x 64cm).
£450–550 *ONS*

Displaying Posters

Posters should be mounted on linen or japan paper, using vegetable paste. They are best displayed in plain, lightweight frames and glazed with perspex.

r. An LNER poster, by Brien, depicting the East Coast, c1930, 38 x 46in (96.5 x 117cm).
£750–850 *HAM*

A London Underground poster, 'Travel Underground for all the Theatres', by E. McKnight Kauffer, lithographed in colours, 1930, 40 x 23¾in (101.5 x 63cm).
£180–220 *Bon(C)*

A poster advertising Warmond Watersport, by William Ehrenfeld, c1930, 36¾ x 25in (63.5 x 93cm).
£375–425 *VSP*

A poster advertising Marconi Super-hets, 1934, 40 x 30in (101.5 x 76cm).
£40–50 *OTA*

A poster advertising Guinness, by Frank H. Allen, watercolour and body colour over pencil, 1939, 30 x 22in (76 x 55.5cm).
£520–600 *P(EA)*

l. A poster depicting Humphrey Bogart and Ingrid Bergman in *Casablanca*, Warner Bros, 1942, 81in (205.5cm) square.
£50,000–55,000 *S*

This poster is one of only 2 known to exist, although it is rumoured there is a third copy in a private collection.

A poster depicting James Stewart and Donna Reed, in *It's A Wonderful Life*, British half-sheet, linen backed, 1946, 22 x 28in (56 x 71cm).
£1,200–1,400 *S*

A poster advertising Suchard Milka chocolate, by Herbert Lenpin, 1952, 50½ x 35½in (128 x 90cm).
£100–120 *VSP*

An Air France poster depicting *Amérique du Nord*, by Guy Arnoux, 1946, 39 x 24½in (99 x 62cm).
£400–450 *VSP*

r. An American poster for *Hair*, 1968, 30 x 40in (76 x 101.5cm).
£80–100 *Bon(C)*

ROCK & POP

A souvenir tour programme of Buddy Holly and the Crickets, signed on the back cover by Buddy Holly, Joe Mauldin and Jerry Allison, also signed inside by Des O'Connor presenter of the show, 1958.
£650–750 *Bon(C)*

A black and white promotional photographic card, signed in ballpoint pen on the back by The Rolling Stones, c1964, 5 x 4in (12.5 x 10cm).
£650–750 *S(NY)*

Don't Forget!
If in doubt please refer to the 'How to Use' section at the beginning of this book.

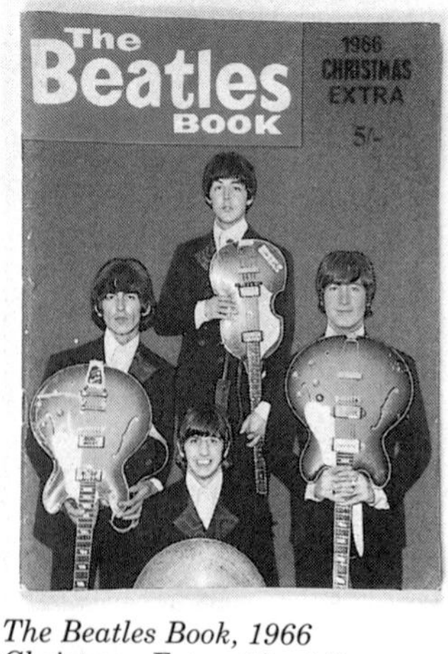

The Beatles Book, 1966 Christmas Extra, 12 x 10in (30.5 x 25.5cm) high.
£15–20 *BTC*

l. A Beatles photograph, with Pete Best, signed on reverse by John Lennon and Paul McCartney, 5th April 1962, 4 x 6in (10 x 15cm).
£340–400 *VS*

A ticket for The Who at the Marquee Club, with a typed band schedule from the club, Tuesday 29th December, 1964, 5 x 8in (13 x 20.5cm).
£350–400 *S*

George Harrison's Monarch Stereogram, by Ferguson, 1960s, 51in (130cm) wide.
£1,750–2,000 *S*

A black and white photograph of The Rolling Stones, signed by all members, late 1960s, 5½ x 4½in (14 x 11.5cm).
£450–500 *VS*

r. A signed copy of 'Hey Joe', by The Jimi Hendrix Experience, 1966.
£1,100–1,200 *S*

John Lennon's two-tone blue and grey silk tailored jacket, by Doug Millings & Co, London, c1960.
£800–1,000 *Bon(C)*

This jacket was made for John Lennon for the film production of Help!, *and is accompanied by a letter of authenticity and amended invoice for the jacket from Gordon Millings.*

Paul McCartney's wool stage suit, by D. A. Millings & Son, with collarless jacket and matching trousers, with label sewn into lining, c1963.
£11,000–12,000 *S(NY)*

A poster, Steve Miller Band at the Fillmore and Winterland, by Lee Conklin, January 1967, 20 x 13½in (51 x 34.5cm).
£180–200 *Bon(C)*

A poster, Dantalians Chariot, Jeff Beck and Ten Years After At the UFO Club, September 1967, details in fluorescent pink, red and orange with silver/gold ground, 30 x 20in (76 x 50.5cm).
£950–1,100 *S*

A poster, Jefferson Airplane, Fantasy Unlimited, The Crazy World of Arthur Brown, Fillmore East, May 1968, 20 x 13½in (51 x 35cm).
£140–170 *Bon(C)*

A Jimi Hendrix pop concert hand bill, on double card, c1969, 7 x 4in (18 x 10cm).
£125–150 *CTO*

A poster, Traffic in concert, by Gunther Kieser, Frankfurt, Germany, 6.2.71, 33 x 23in (84 x 58.5cm).
£180–220 *Bon(C)*

l. A Private Eye magazine, featuring Paul McCartney on the cover, 26th February 1971, 12 x 10in (30.5 x 25.5cm) long.
£13–15 *BTC*

An R.C.A. Records LP cover of Elvis Presley, signed on the front cover in black ink, c1975, 12in (30.5cm) square.
£400–450 *Bon(C)*

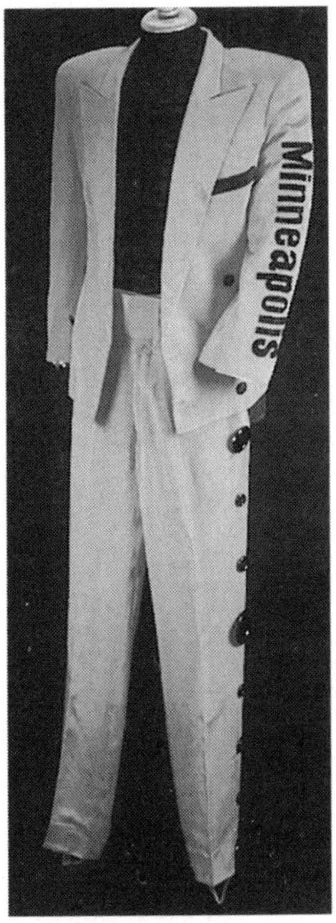

Prince's two-piece orange suit, worn on the Sign O' The Times tour, the left arm lettered 'Minneapolis', the high waisted trousers decorated with black buttons down the seams, 1987.
£4,000–4,500 *S*

A silver print photograph of Sting, by Terry O'Neill, signed by photographer, early 1980s, 11¾ x 11in (30 x 28cm).
£130–150 *Bon*

A signed colour photograph of Diana Ross, 1993, 10 x 8in (25.5 x 20.5cm).
£50–55 *VS*

SCIENTIFIC INSTRUMENTS

Prices at the upper end of the market have been guided by the exceptional quality of items on offer this year. As original period pieces become increasingly rare, that illusive combination of scarcity and condition have fuelled an already buoyant market in scientific instruments. Many auction houses hold specialist auctions dealing solely with scientific instruments.

At a recent Christie's sale there were some fascinating entries, with most lots making well in excess of estimate. The star of the sale was a fine rare Ptolemaic armillary sphere signed and dated 'Antonius Costa Mirandulanus Fecit; 1667', realising £265,000 against an estimate of £200,000–250,000. Similarly at a recent Phillips auction, a pair of globes by Cary in excellent condition, which had been stored in an attic for over 70 years, exceeded their estimate and sold for £26,000.

Collectors of more modest means are turning their attentions to 20th century scientific instruments, which continue to rise in prominence. Items of particular interest are early Zeiss optical equipment. Military instruments such as clinometers, if in pristine condition with original cases, are also sought after. It should be remembered that the 1940s saw a very rapid period of development of military instruments, and in two or three years many advances were made in these technologies, examples of which are set to become as sought after as anything that came before. Amongst the most prolific makers in these areas were companies such as Carl Zeiss and Carl Plath, both innovators at the forefront of their technologies.

The more commonplace scientific instruments have generally made modest gains. One area of strong demand is early 20th century brass instruments which are eagerly sought by those wishing to exploit their commercial value as brightly polished curios. The fact that they are polished has, I fear, ruined many would-be highly collectable pieces, since polishing should only be done after consulting an expert, as it could seriously damage its patina and reduce its value. The market in this, as in many other sectors, seems increasingly driven by rarity and quality, which if combined with historical interest has seen prices rise beyond the plausible. This is a reflection on the specialist collector and connoisseur where simply only the best will do. This pattern in buying will undoubtedly become ever more accentuated as the supply of better items dwindles.

Mark Jarrold

Calculating Equipment

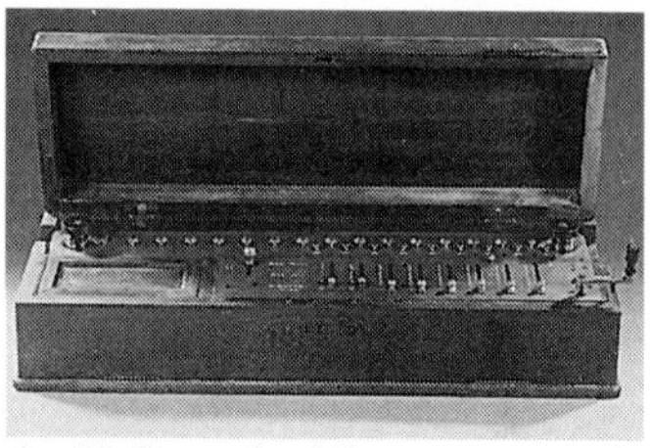

An H. Bunzel arithmometer, with 16 digit displays, sliding numeric cursors, addition/multiplication, subtraction/division switch, and operating handle, in a mahogany case, late 19thC, 23½in (60cm) long.
£1,800–2,200 *S*

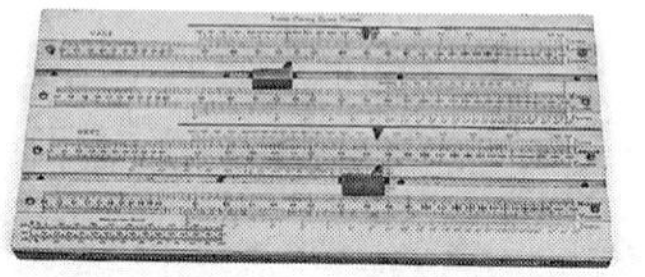

A boxwood Lord's patent cotton cloth coster, by Asto & Mander, in a mahogany box, c1880, 15in (18cm) wide.
£200–250 *TOM*

A pocket watch type calculator, designed by Boucher, made by H. Chatlain, Paris, c1890, 2in (5cm) diam.
£65–80 *TOM*

A Customs officer's calculating kit, by L. Lumley & Co, in a leather pouch, c1880, 13in (33cm) long.
£100–120 *TOM*

An Otis King cylindrical slide rule, c1920, 6in (15cm) long closed.
£15–20 *TOM*

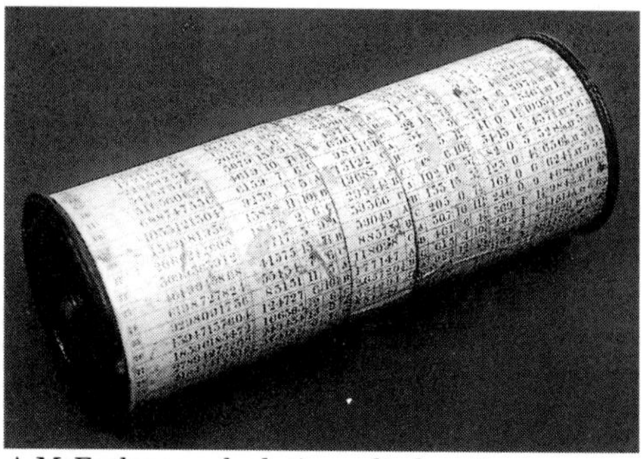

A McFarlanes calculating cylinder, the 3 revolving cylinders with engraved paper scales and mahogany ends, c1890, 6in (15cm) long.
£100–120 *TOM*

Dials

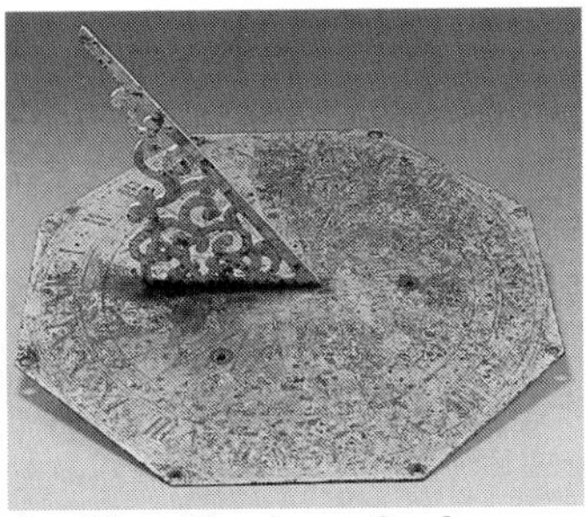

An Elias Allen brass fixed latitude horizontal sundial, the brass plate with engraved 32-point compass rose, the gnomon decoratively cut and engraved with scrolling leaf forms, early 17thC, 17¼in (44cm) diam.
£7,000–8,000 *S*

Elias Allen, the leading English instrument maker of the first half of the 17thC, was born near Tonbridge, Kent, c1588 and was apprenticed to Charles Whitwell in 1602 and instruments signed and dated by Allen are known from as early as 1606. Thereafter until his death in 1653 a stream of well made instruments emanated from his workshop, many of them realisations of new ideas by leading mathematicians of the period.

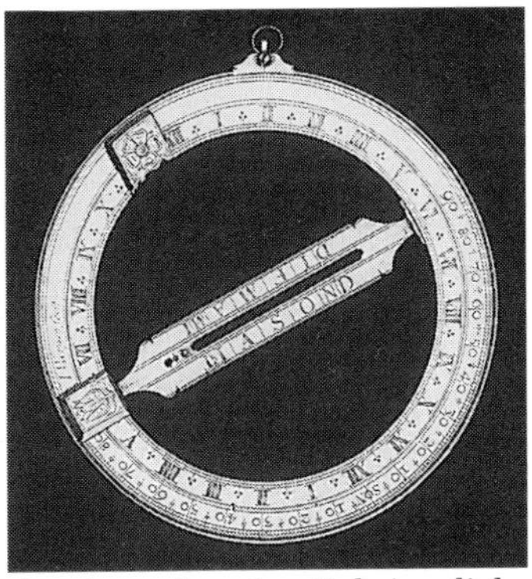

A universal equinoctial ring dial, signed 'I. Worgan', the 7¼in meridian ring with later sliding suspension ring, late 17thC.
£5,300–6,000 *P*

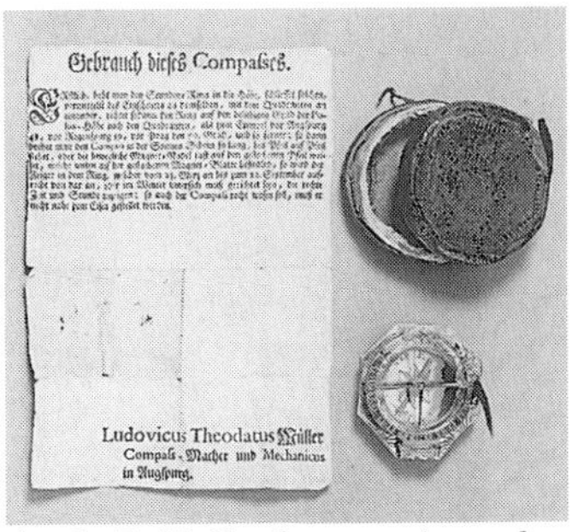

An L. T. Müller brass universal equinoctial dial, German, early 19thC, 2in (50mm) wide, in original card case, with printed latitudes on separate sheet.
£750–825 *S*

A Continental pocket sundial, signed 'And Vogl', with engraved brass case housing a glazed compass, c1730, 2¼in (57mm) diam.
£800–880 *PT*

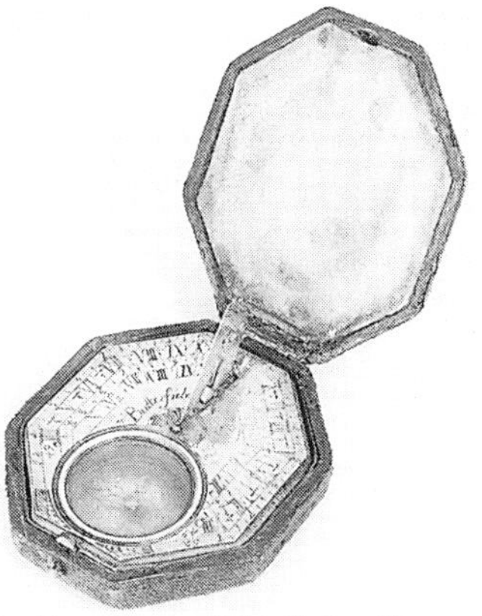

A silver Butterfield dial, with folding bird gnomon, engraved double chapter ring, and recessed compass, the underside engraved with the names and latitudes of 21 French cities, 18thC, 3in (8cm) long, in original leather-covered box.
£900–1,100 *P*

A French silver Butterfield dial, set with a compass and radially engraved with times for 3 latitudes and adjustable gnomon, the underside listing the latitudinal bearings of European cities, 1717–22, 3in (8cm) wide overall.
£2,300–2,600 *S*

l. A French silvered-brass portable equinoctial dial, the rosewood fitted case containing an inset compass, c1810, 4¾in (12cm) square.
£1,000–1,100 *S*

Globes & Spheres

A Beuler 2¾in (7cm) diam pocket globe, in fishskin covered case printed with the signs of the zodiac, slight damage, c1819.
£1,100–1,200 *Bea(E)*

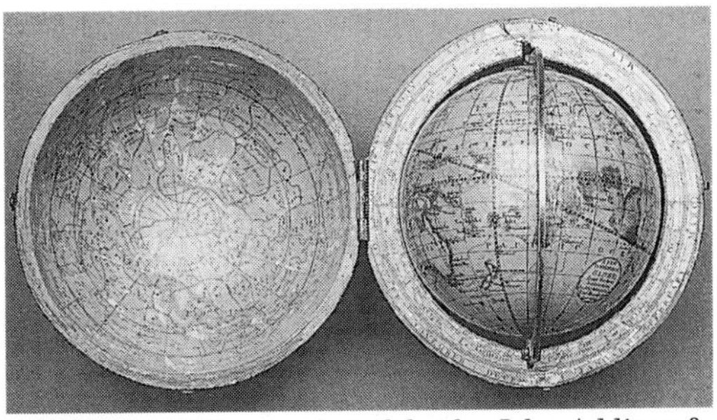

A 3in (7.5cm) diam pocket globe, by John Addison & Co, depicting the voyages of Cook, Perouse, Gore, Vancouver and Bois, with metal pinions, engraved hour circle, brass meridian ring, in an imitation fishskin case, 1822–25.
£1,600–2,000 *Bon(C)*

A J. & W. Cary terrestrial globe, on a mahogany stand, with discoveries made by Captain Cook, Captain Vancouver, and M. de la Perouse, 1815, 48in (122cm) high.
£4,000–4,500 *SLN*

A pair of 18in (45.5cm) diam standing celestial and terrestrial globes, by Cary, on mahogany stands with baluster turned and reeded legs, early 19thC, 45in (114.5cm) high.
£26,000–30,000 *P(S)*

These globes were in excellent condition, and having been stored in an attic for over 70 years, they were fresh to the market.

A 15in (38cm) diam terrestrial globe, published by G. & J. Cary, the meridian circle engraved in four quadrants, the horizon ring printed with zodiac and calendar scales, with 4 supports on a baluster-turned column and incurved tripod base, 1824.
£5,500–6,500 *P(B)*

An Italian neo-classical style walnut terrestrial standing globe, by Guido Cora, c1888, 30in (76cm) diam.
£5,000–5,500 *S(NY)*

A French terrestrial globe, by Delmarche, on a wooden stand, 1844, 19¾in (50cm) high.
£1,600–1,800 *S(Am)*

A French 9¾in (25cm) diam terrestrial table globe, by Charles Dien, with hand-coloured print, engraved brass meridian ring and steel horizon ring, mounted on a stained beech stand, published 1831, 18¾in (48cm) high.
£800–1,000 *S*

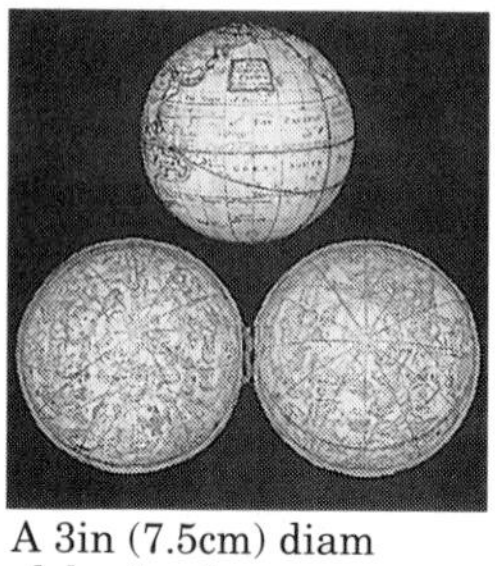

A 3in (7.5cm) diam globe, by James Ferguson, the 12 hand-coloured and engraved gores showing California as a peninsula, with Anson's track marked, in a fishskin case inlaid with printed and hand-coloured celestial gores, c1750.
£2,300–2,600 *Bon*

An American miniature terrestrial globe, by Joslin, revolving in a brass support over a turned wood baluster standard, on a slightly domed circular foot, c1845, 9¼in (23.5cm) high.
£1,600–1,800 *B&B*

l. A celestial floor globe, by W. & A. K. Johnston, London, painted blue and green, raised on a tripartite cast-iron base, late 19thC, 46in (117cm) high.
£1,400–1,800 *S(NY)*

A pair of 2¾in (7cm) diam globes, the terrestrial globe with cartouche inscribed 'Minschulls', with brass meridian rings and mounted on wooden stands, both restored and some damage, published 1816, 5½in (13cm) high.
£2,200–2,500 *S*

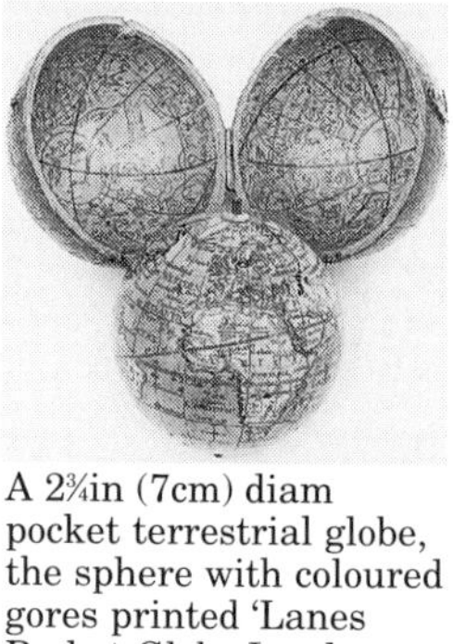

A 2¾in (7cm) diam pocket terrestrial globe, the sphere with coloured gores printed 'Lanes Pocket Globe London 1815', in a fishskin case with coloured print of the heavens.
£2,400–2,800 *P(G)*

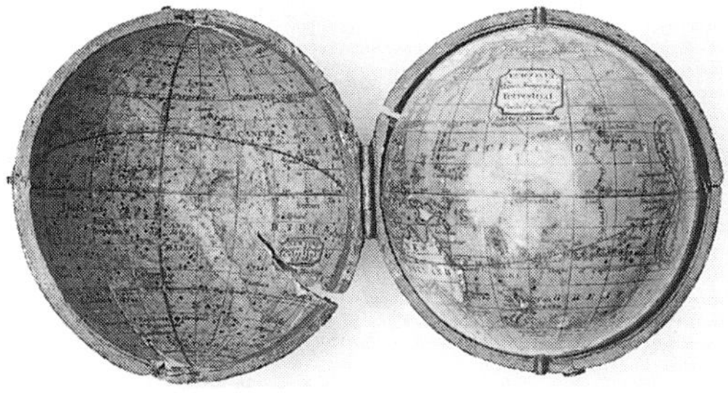

A 3in (7.5cm) diam terrestrial pocket globe, by Newton, composed of 12 hand-coloured engraved gores, showing tracks of Cook's second and third voyages, contained in original imitation fishskin covered case, c1817.
£1,700–2,000 *Bon(C)*

Two 2in (5cm) diam terrestrial globes, by Newton, each composed of printed and hand-coloured gores, showing the tracks of Cook's third voyage and Gore's voyage of 1780, 1818 and 1836 editions, on later stands.
£600–700 *Bon(C)*

A 12in (30.5cm) diam celestial globe, the mahogany stand with 3 turned supports joined by a stretcher, restored, 19thC.
£1,100–1,300 *S(NY)*

l. A 12in (30.5cm) celestial globe, by John Smith, made up of 12 printed and hand-coloured gores, with engraved hour circle, meridian ring engraved on one face, printed and coloured horizon circle, on a stand, c1820, 17¾in (45cm) high.
£900–1,100 *Bon(C)*

A 23½in (60cm) diam terrestrial globe, by Newton, on a mahogany stand with reeded baluster column and tripod base with scroll feet, published 1853, 51¼in (130cm) high.
£11,500–12,500 *Bea(E)*

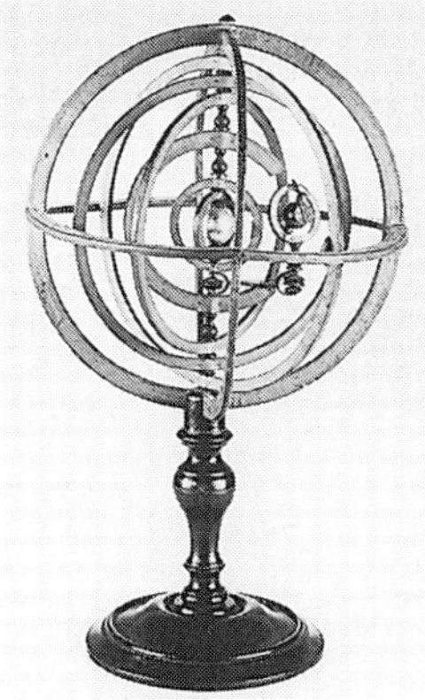

l. A pasteboard armillary sphere, the gilded sun set within revolving printed circles with an orbiting earth linked via a pulley, raised on a turned ebonised stand, early 19thC, 18½in (47cm) high.
£2,000–2,200 *P*

A 1½in (4cm) diam terrestrial globe, made up of 12 coloured paper gores, with folding chart printed with colour and illustrating 32 people of various nations, contained in a fitted box, 19thC, 2½in (6.5cm) wide.
£900–1,100 *Bon(C)*

A Charles X ebonised and brass Copernican armillary sphere, representing the sun, earth and moon, within concentric moveable bands, 14in (35.5cm) diam.
£4,000–4,500 *S(NY)*

Hourglasses

r. An hourglass, in a walnut case, 19thC, 7½in (19cm) high.
£550–600 *CAT*

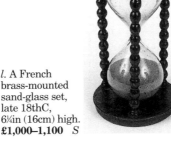

l. A French brass-mounted sand-glass set, late 18thC, 6¼in (16cm) high.
£1,000–1,100 *S*

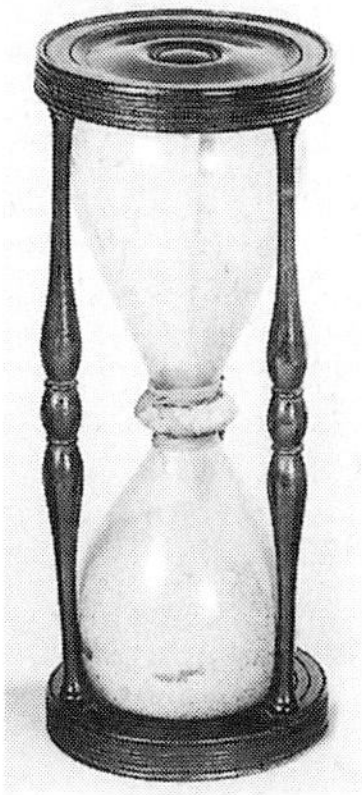

r. An hourglass, with turned mahogany ends and side supports, 19thC, 8in (20.5cm) high.
£530–580 *P*

Medical & Dental

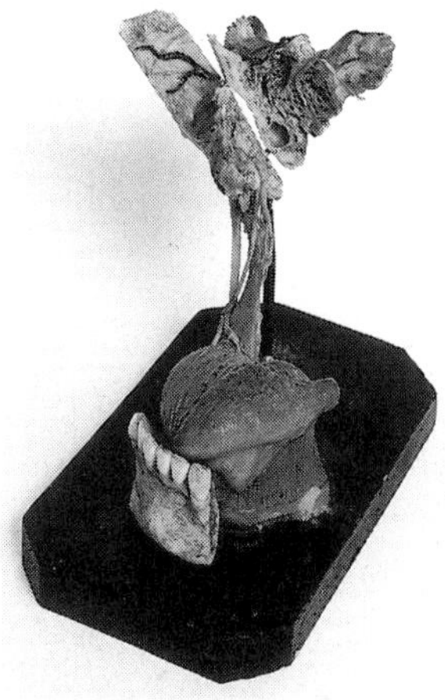

An anatomical model of the tongue and nerves, in wax and human bone, signed 'Valpeur à Paris', c1830, 6in (15cm) high.
£700–800 *ET*

A George III mahogany brass-mounted apothecary's chest, enclosing glass bottles and fitted compartments above 3 short and 2 long mahogany-lined drawers, with ebony stringing, fitted to the rear with a sliding compartment enclosing a series of jars, 12in (30.5cm) wide.
£720–820 *Mit*

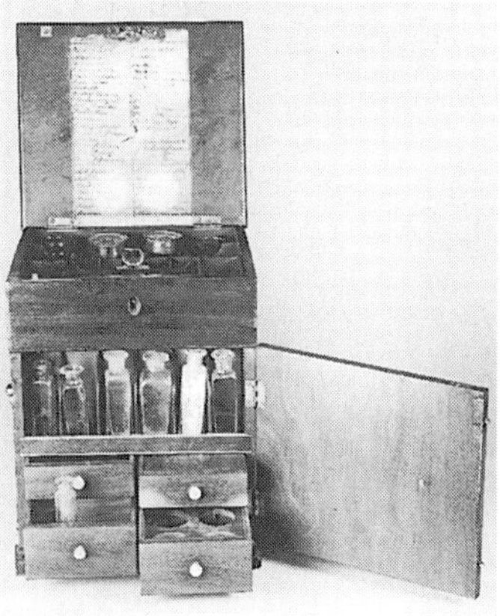

A mahogany medicine chest, the hinged top opening to reveal a fitted interior containing 5 glass bottles and a pair of beam scales, above a single door with a gallery for 6 bottles, above 4 drawers with ivory handles, 19thC, 11in (28cm) high.
£500–600 *P*

r. A surgeon's field kit, by P. Harris & Son, Birmingham, early 20thC, 6in (15cm) long.
£80–100 *ET*

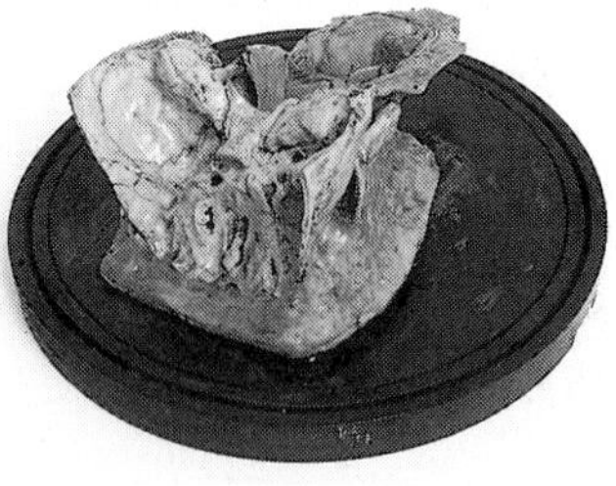

A French anatomical model section through the back of head and neck, in wax and human bone, c1840, 9in (23cm) wide.
£700–800 *ET*

A mahogany domestic medicine chest, the hinged lid revealing 15 glass bottles, the doors open at the front to reveal a small drawer containing weights, glass bottles and other glass medical equipment, c1860, 11½in (29cm) wide.
£420–480 *S*

Did You Know?

You should never attempt to polish an old scientific instrument of any type without checking with an expert first. If you do so you may seriously damage its patina, and reduce its value.

A Victorian surgeon's field kit, with 2 trays of instruments, in a mahogany and brass-bound box, 18in (45.5cm) wide.
£2,000–2,400 *ET*

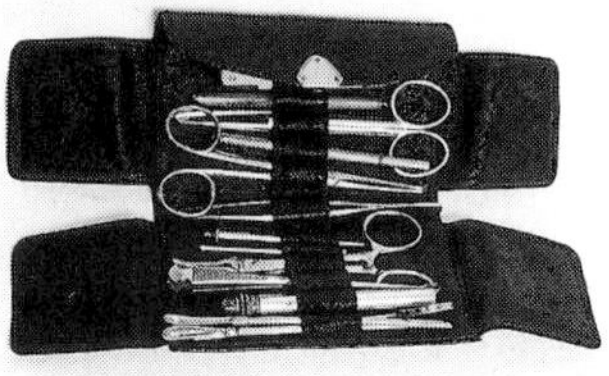

A mahogany medicine chest, with double doors at the front and back, with racks and shelves displaying glass bottles, 5 accessory drawers containing scales, spatulas and flasks, c1790, 13¼in (33.5cm) wide.
£1,750–2,000 *S*

A mahogany domestic medicine chest, the hinged front opening to reveal compartments for bottles and 3 short and 2 long drawers, a poison compartment in the back with flush brass handle, c1870, 25¼in (64cm) wide when open.
£1,250–1,400 *Bon*

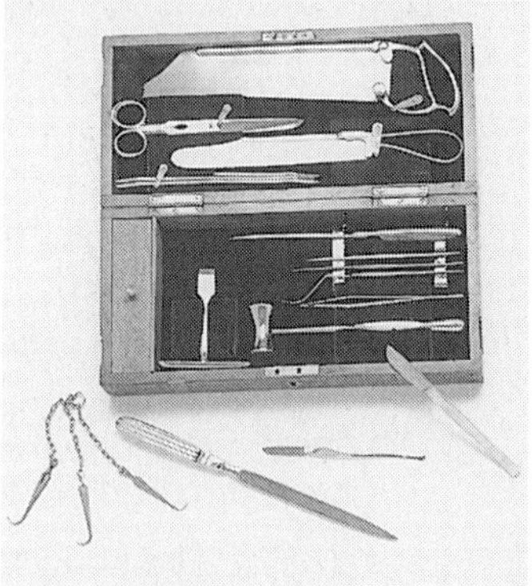

A set of medical instruments, in a mahogany and brass-bound box, late 19thC, 18in (45.5cm) wide.
£1,300–1,500 *BOS*

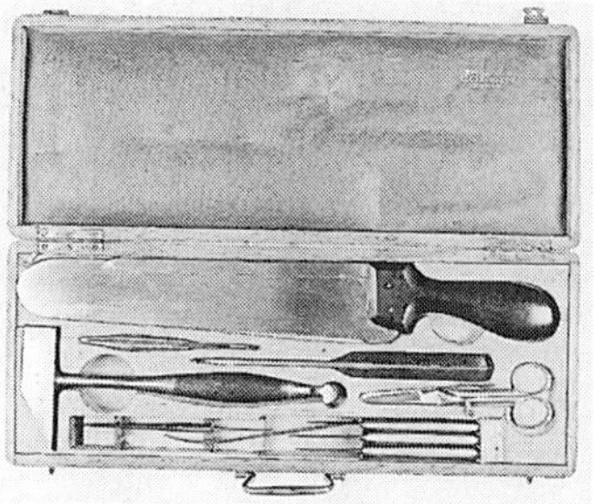

A post mortem set, by Collin, with ebony handles, in a fitted mahogany case, French, early 20thC, 16½in (42cm) wide.
£220–240 *Bon*

A chemist's mahogany cabinet, the 10 labelled drug drawers flanked by 2 cupboard doors, c1880, 104in (264cm) wide.
£1,000–1,100 *S*

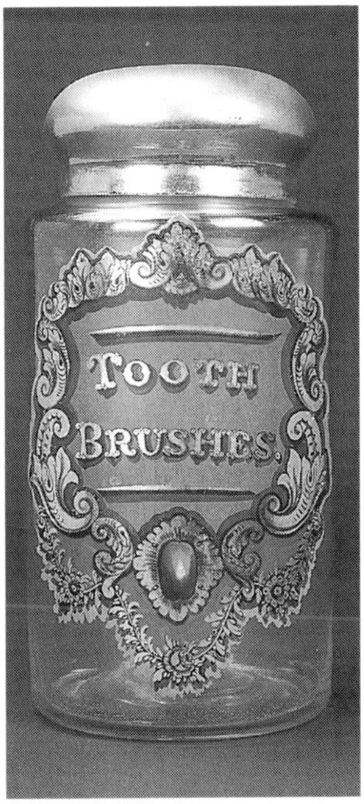

r. A chemist's glass jar, with a gilt cover, the blue ground cartouche with gilt, red and green border, inscribed 'Tooth Brushes', 19thC, 11in (28cm) high.
£650–750 *TEN*

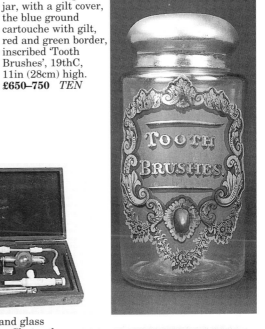

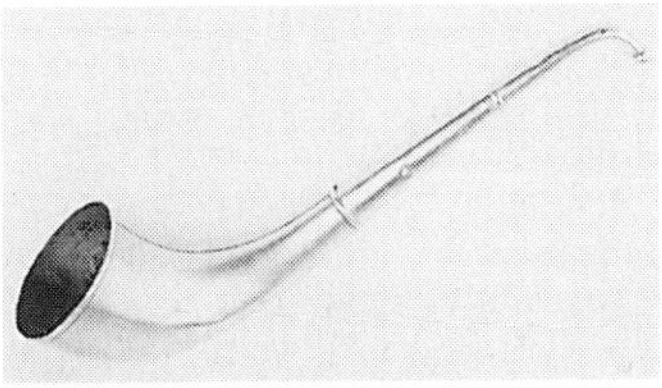

A Hausmann Prof Siebemann pattern brass euphometa, German, early 20thC, 13¾in (35cm) long.
£260–290 *Bon*

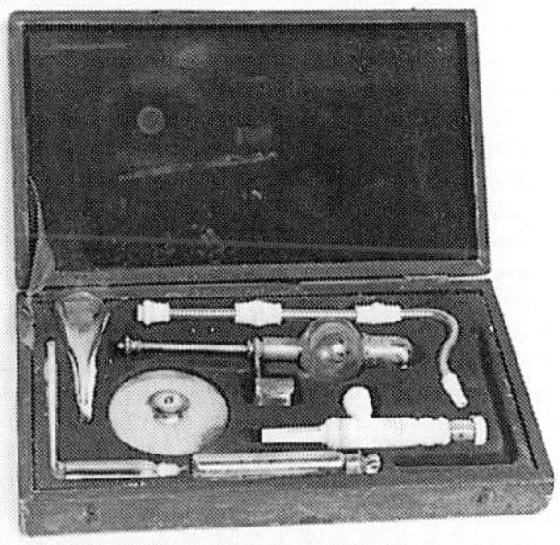

A French ivory and glass iodine inhaler, by Chatroule, in a wooden case, patented c1860, 11in (28cm) wide.
£750–820 *ET*

A pair of tortoiseshell spectacles, with case, c1890, 7½in (19cm) long.
£60–65 *CHe*

Miller's is a price GUIDE not a price LIST

A lacquered brass scarificator, by S. Maw & Son, with 12 blades and adjusting screw, c1860, 2¼in (5.5cm) wide.
£110–120 *Bon*

A scarificator is a surgical instrument for use in puncturing the skin or other tissue.

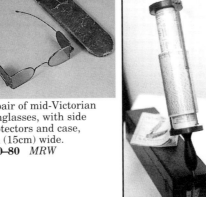

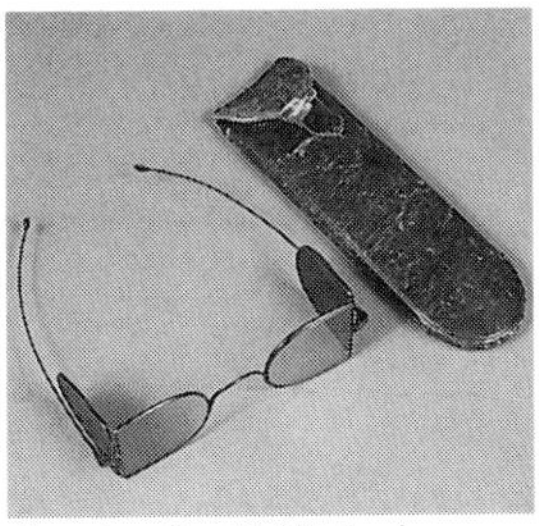

A pair of mid-Victorian sunglasses, with side protectors and case, 6in (15cm) wide.
£70–80 *MRW*

l. A portable X-ray machine, by Harry W. Cox, London, with X-ray tube, c1915, 23in (58.5cm) wide.
£750–900 *ET*

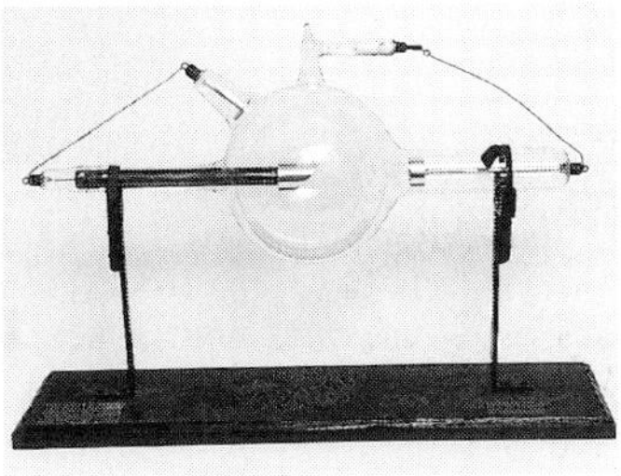

r. An X-ray tube, by Watson & Sons, for the Ministry of Munitions, c1915, 22in (56cm) long.
£300–360 *ET*

Microscopes

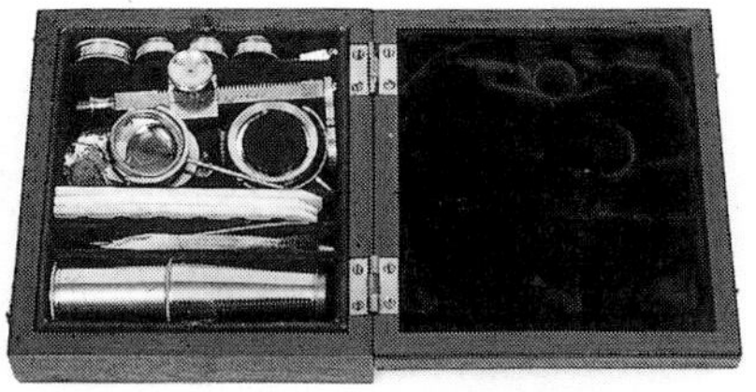

A compound monocular botanical microscope, by Cary, London, in mahogany box, c1820, 5in (12.5cm) wide.
£500–600 *TOM*

l. A lacquered-brass and japanned monocular microscope, by Casartelli & Son, Manchester, in a mahogany case, c1890, 12in (30.5cm) high.
£120–150 *TOM*

A John Cuff brass compound monocular microscope, with sliding cover to the eyepiece, fine focusing to the stage, the mahogany stand with a drawer containing accessories, in a mahogany pillar case, c1760, 13in (33cm) high.
£2,300–2,800 *S*

A Dollond silver simple microscope, with extending pillar and 2 folding lenses, c1820, 2⅜in (6cm) extended, with leather case.
£360–400 *Bon(C)*

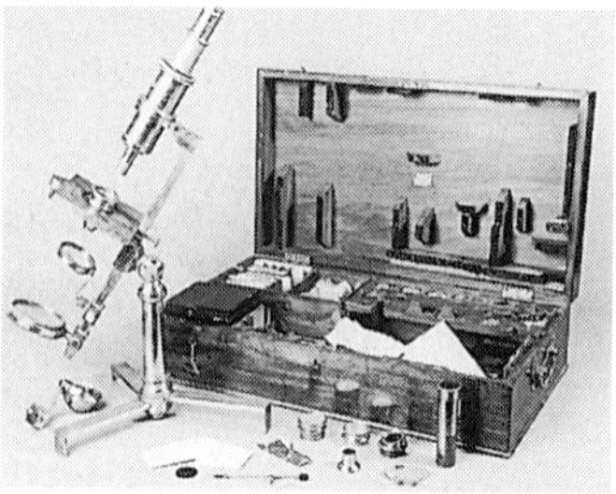

A Dollond lacquered-brass compound monocular microscope, the body tube with screw fine focusing, the square stage with mechanical movement to the circular centre via 2 knurled knobs, above a hinged bull's-eye lens and 3in (7.5cm) piano concave mirror, signed, mid-19thC, 21in (54cm) high, in original mahogany fitted box, with some accessories.
£2,300–2,500 *P*

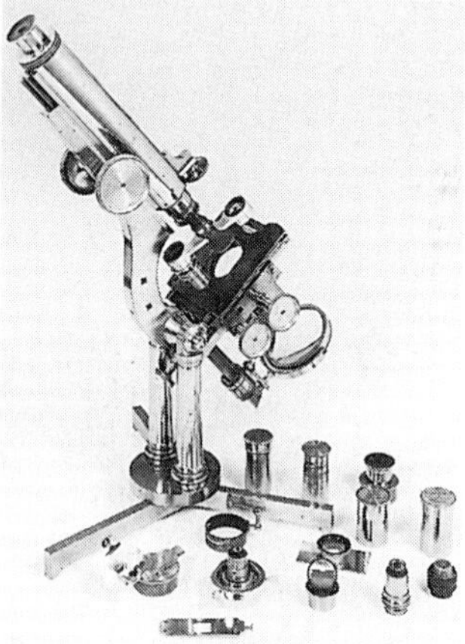

A lacquered-brass compound monocular microscope, by Smith & Beck, with coarse and fine rack-and-pinion focusing, twin nosepiece, mechanical stage and plano concave mirror, 19thC, 18in (46cm) high, in a fitted mahogany box, with some accessories.
£750–900 *P*

A Challenge brass monocular microscope, by J. Lizars, Glasgow, with rack-and-pinion focusing, in a fitted mahogany case, late 19thC, 11½in (29cm) high, with accessories.
£150–200 *DW*

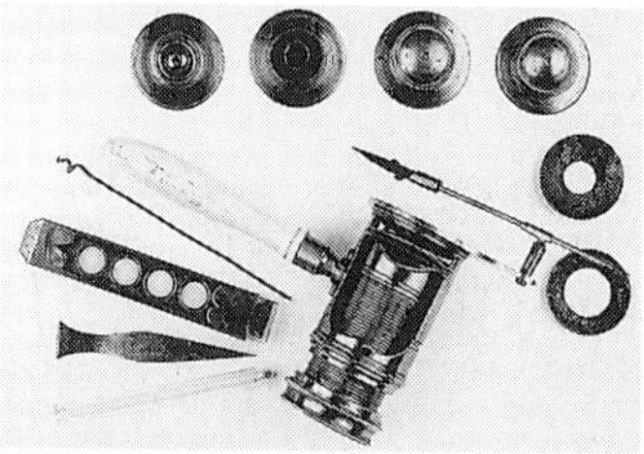

A brass screw barrel microscope, with ivory handle, 4 brass-mounted objectives, 2 leiberkuhns, threaded holder and other accessories, unsigned, mid-18thC, 2⅜in (6cm) long, in a green plush-lined fishskin case.
£680–750 *Bon(C)*

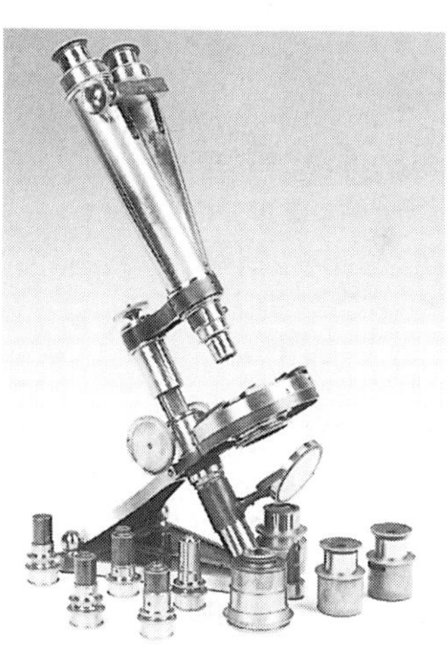

l. A lacquered-brass compound binocular popular microscope, by Smith, Beck & Beck, with rack-and-pinion focusing, mechanical circular stage and piano concave mirror, signed, 19thC, in a fitted mahogany box, 16in (40cm) wide, with accessories in a lift-out tray.
£420–500 *P*

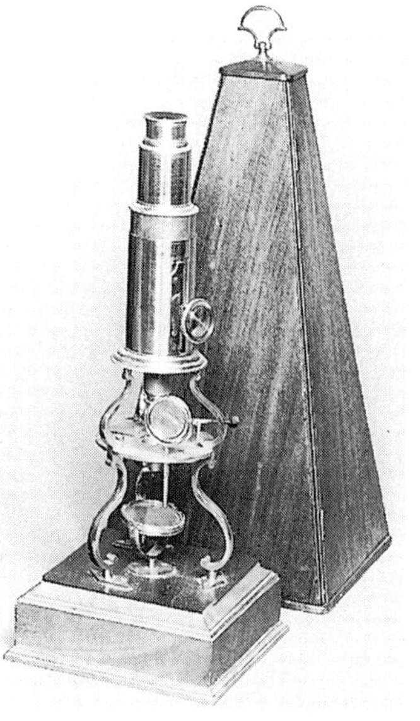

r. A Culpeper type compound monocular microscope, with rack-and-pinion focusing, the mahogany base set with concave mirror and drawer containing accessories, 19thC, 16in (40cm) high, in a mahogany pyramid shaped box.
£950–1,100 *P*

Surveying & Drawing

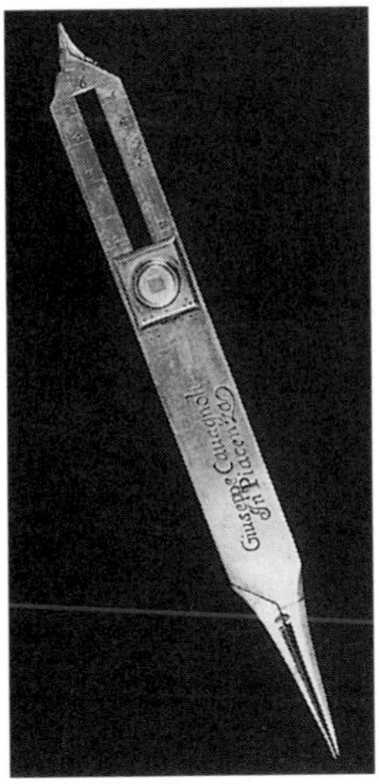

An Italian brass proportional surveying compass, with steel tips, engraved 'Giuseppe Cauagnoli In Piacenza', mid-18thC, 7in (17cm) long.
£480–530 *S*

r. A lacquered-brass drainage level, by Gardner & Co, with 12¼in (31cm) telescope on a hinged arm with screw adjustment, silvered scale, c1860, 12½in (32cm) wide, in a mahogany case.
£180–220 *Bon*

l. A French lacquered-brass and steel meridian dipleidoscope, by R. Mailhat, the telescope eyepiece on adjustable armature, transverse mounting, the cylinder with green glass prism, scale and vernier, mid-19thC, 15¾in (40cm) high.
£750–900 *Bon*

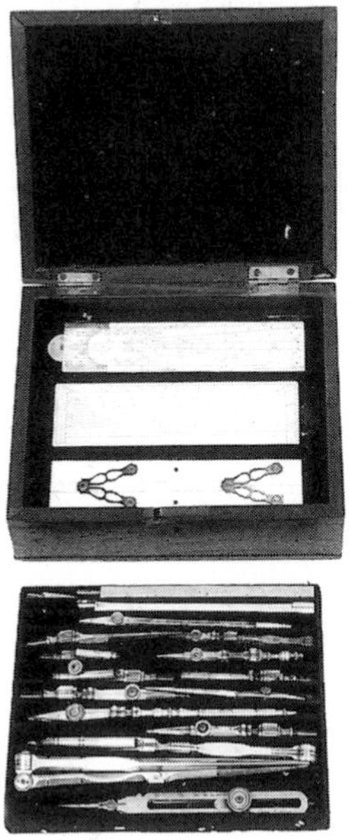

A set of drawing instruments, by Cary, London, in a brass-bound mahogany box, c1790, 8in (20.5cm) wide.
£700–800 *TOM*

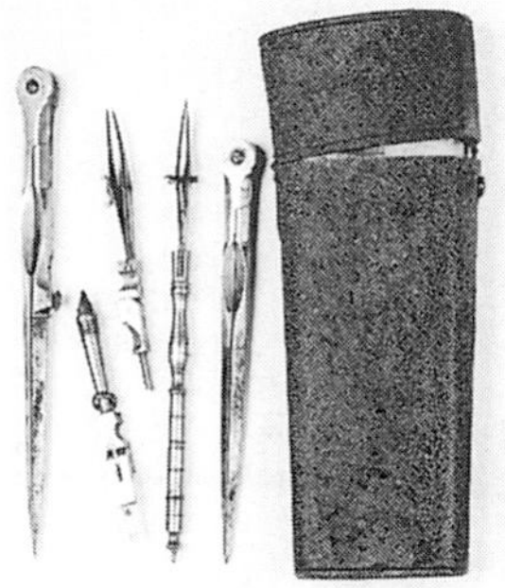

A pocket case of brass and steel drawing instruments, in a black fishskin case, early 19thC, 6¾in (17cm) long.
£140–160 *Bon*

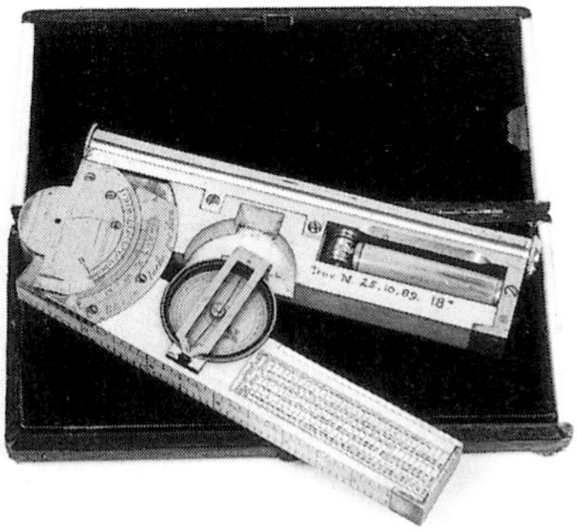

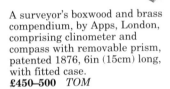

A surveyor's boxwood and brass compendium, by Apps, London, comprising clinometer and compass with removable prism, patented 1876, 6in (15cm) long, with fitted case.
£450–500 *TOM*

Miller's is a price GUIDE not a price LIST

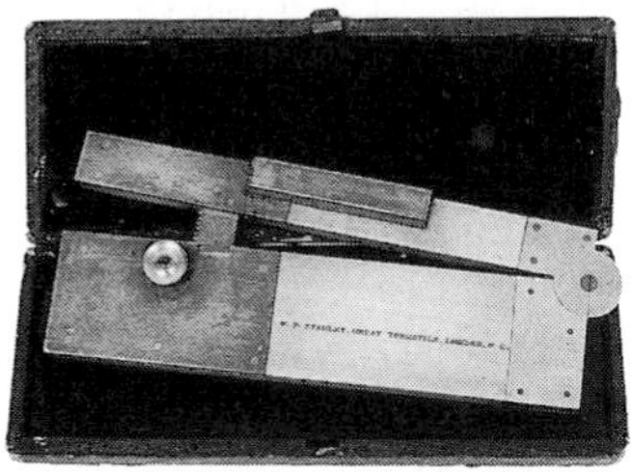

A boxwood and brass adjustable clinometer, by W. F. Stanley, London, c1883, 7in (18cm) long.
£125–150 *TOM*

l. An American lacquered-brass telescopic hand level, by W. & L. E. Gurley, late 19thC, 3¼in (8cm) long.
£200–220 *Bon*

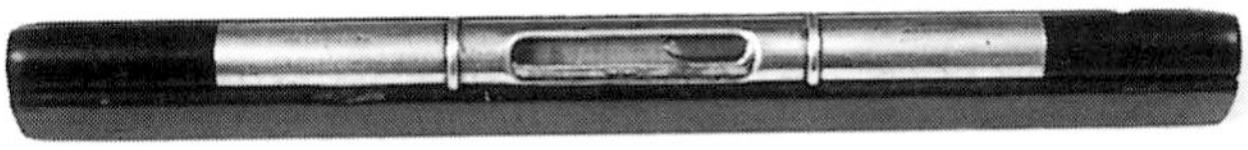

A rosewood and brass rolling cover level, by Mathieson, Glasgow, c1900, 12in (30.5cm) long.
£60–75 *MRT*

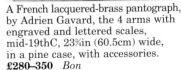

A French lacquered-brass pantograph, by Adrien Gavard, the 4 arms with engraved and lettered scales, mid-19thC, 23¾in (60.5cm) wide, in a pine case, with accessories.
£280–350 *Bon*

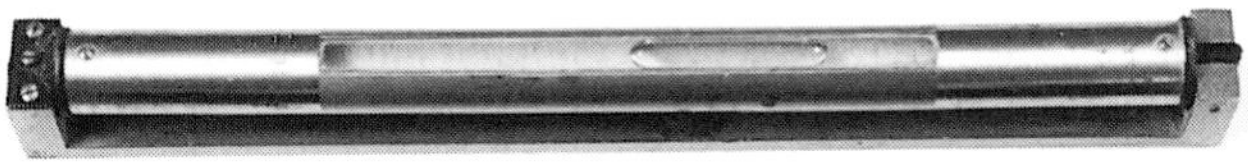

A brass level, with graduated tube, c1900, 12in (30.5cm) long.
£35–45 *MRT*

A brass sector, by T. Heath, 1740, 9in (23cm) long.
£500–600 *TOM*

An oxidised and lacquered-brass theodolite, by L. Casella, London, the 4in (10cm) vertical silvered scale and the 4¼in (11cm) horizontal scale each with 2 verniers, tangent screw and clamp and level, 1870, 11½in (30cm) telescope with lens hood, in a mahogany fitted case.
£450–500 *DN*

A French brass transit level, 18thC, 8in (20.5cm) wide.
£180–220 *ET*

A theodolite, by Adie, Edinburgh, c1830, 14in (35.5cm) high.
£60–80 *BWA*

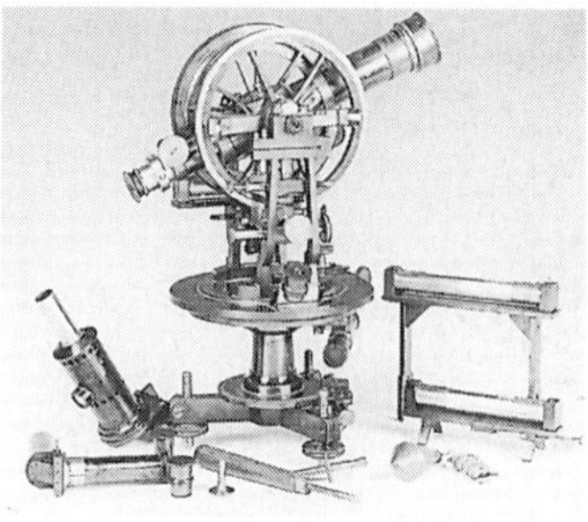

An oxidised and lacquered-brass transit theodolite, by H. Morin, Paris, the 9in (24cm) telescope with rack-and-pinion focusing and cross-wire adjusters set within six-spoke wheels with silvered scale and 2 verniers, 19thC, 13½in (34cm) high, in fitted box, with accessories.
£820–900 *P*

Locate the Source
The source of each illustration in Miller's can be found by checking the code letters below each caption with the Key to Illustrations.

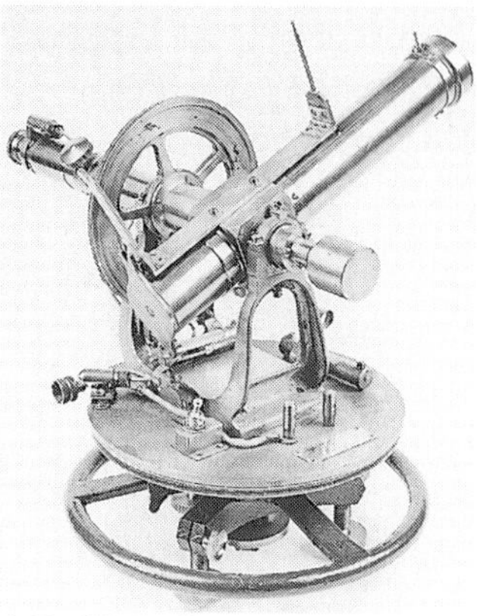

A Buff & Buff type ML 47 theodolite, with 12¼in (31cm) telescope, folding sites, silvered vertical scale, enclosed horizontal scale with silvered vernier, tangent screw level and bubble above a green enamel wheel, American, dated '1932', 13in (33cm) high.
£520–620 *Bon*

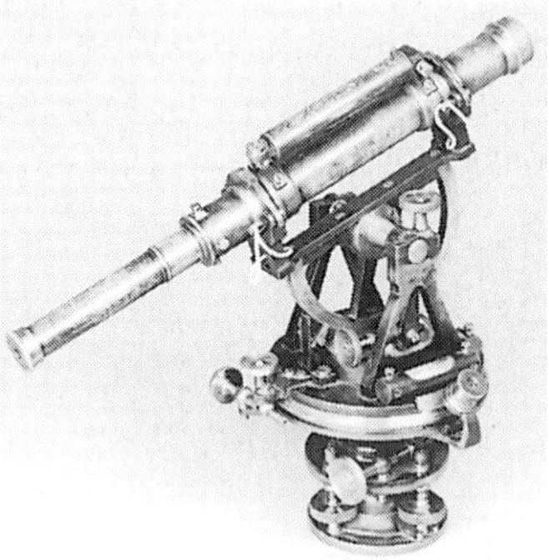

An oxidised-brass A-frame theodolite, by Troughton & Simms, London, the 9½in (24cm) telescope with rack-and-pinion focusing with bubble level below, the vertical half circle with silver scale and vernier, 19thC, in original mahogany box.
£460–520 *P*

Telescopes

A silver-mounted seven-draw telescopic monocular, signed Adams, Fleet St, London, late 18thC, 3½in (9cm) high.
£1,300–1,500 *P*

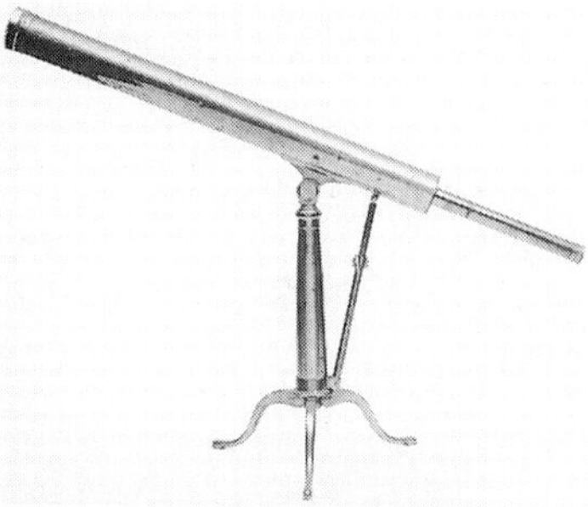

A brass 3in (7.5cm) refractory telescope, signed 'M. Berge, London', with rack-and-pinion focusing, with spare lenses, in a fitted mahogany box, early 19thC, 39¾in (101cm) long.
£1,500–1,650 *P(E)*

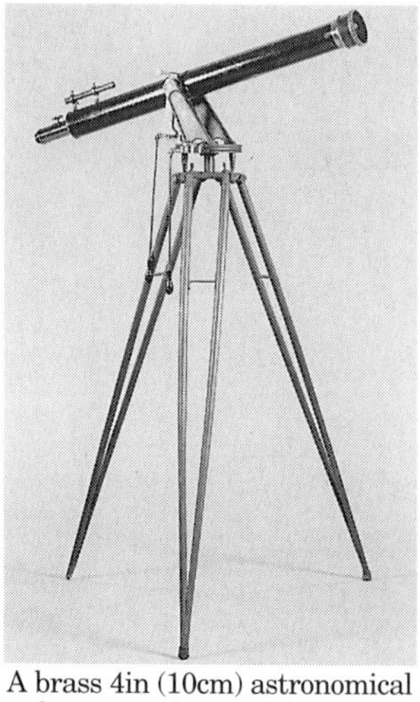

A brass 4in (10cm) astronomical refracting telescope, by John Browning, London, with rack-and-pinion focusing, fitted with a star finder, in a mahogany case, with accessories, c1900, 56in (142cm) long.
£1,500–1,800 *S*

l. A lacquered-brass Y-level, signed Cail, Newcastle-upon-Tyne, the 17in (43.5cm) rack-and-pinion focusing telescope above a quadrantally engraved silvered compass, early 19thC.
£300–330 *P*

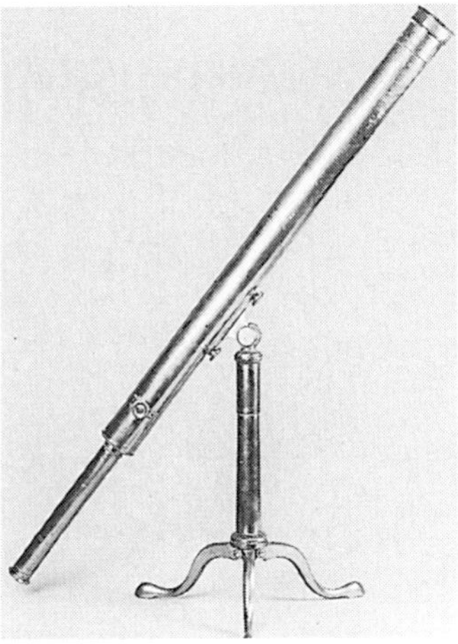

A brass 2in (5cm) telescope, signed Dollond, London, the 29in (74cm) long body tube with rack-and-pinion focusing, 19thC.
£450–550 *P*

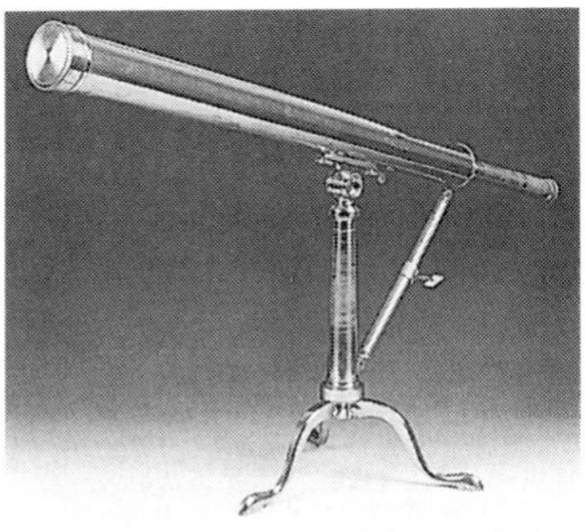

A Victorian lacquered-brass 2½in (6.5cm) refracting telescope, signed I. Ramage, Aberdeen, the 29in (73.5cm) body tube with adjusting steadying bar, with additional eyepieces, in fitted mahogany case.
£720–800 *P(Sc)*

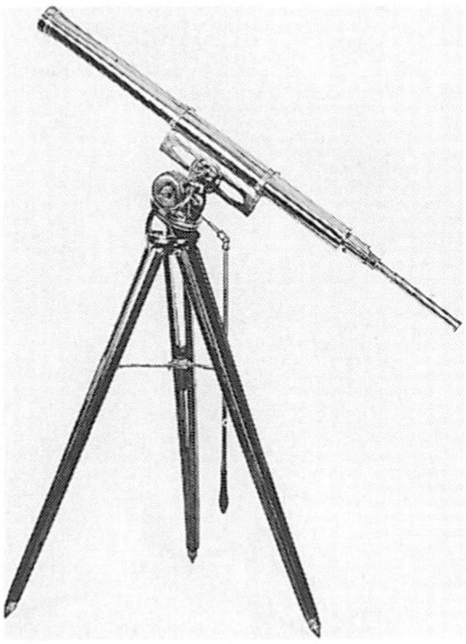

A lacquered-brass 3½in (9cm) refracting telescope-on-stand, signed Josiah T. Slugg, Manchester, the 58¼in (148cm) tube with rack focus to the eyepiece, finder tube, equatorial mount with balance, on a mahogany and brass tripod, c1860, 76in (193cm) high.
£2,200–2,500 *Bon*

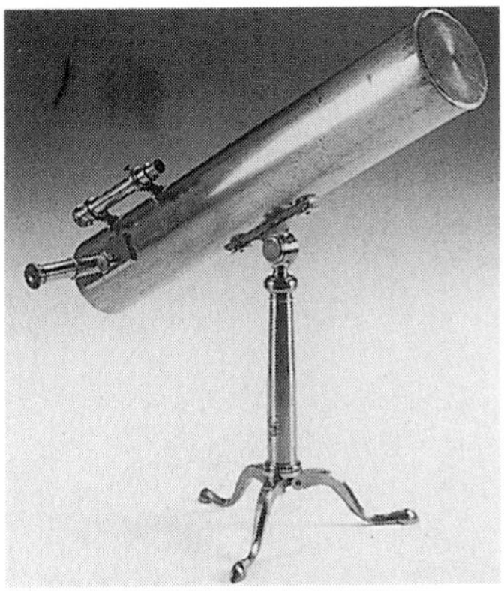

A Newtonian reflecting 5in (12.5cm) telescope, signed J. Duboscq à Paris, the 28¼in (72cm) body tube with speculum mirror, the eyepiece with pinion focusing, the viewfinder with focusing, French, 19thC, 20in (51cm) high.
£1,300–1,500 *S*

A lacquered-brass 1½in (4cm) transit telescope, by Charles Schmalcalder, London, the 21¾in (55cm) body tube with silvered scales and 2 verniers, level, tangent screw and clamp, and a lamp adapted for electricity, in a fitted case, early 19thC, 15¼in (38.5cm) wide.
£450–500 *DN*

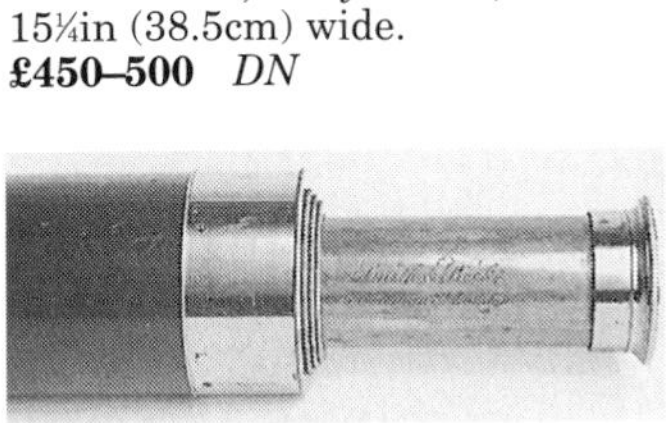

A 2¼in (5.5cm) four-draw telescope, by Smith & Beck, with mahogany bound tube, c1848, 36¼in (92cm) long, in a leather case.
£580–650 *Bon(C)*

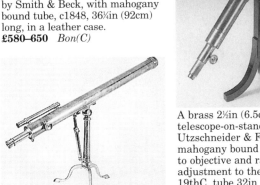

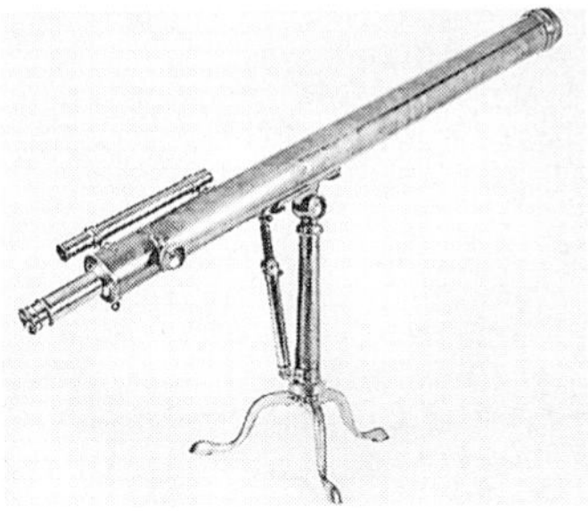

r. A lacquered-brass 2½in (6.5cm) telescope on stand, by Troughton & Simms, the 43in (109cm) finder tube with rack focus, mid-19thC, 23in (58cm) high, in a red plush-lined mahogany case.
£550–600 *Bon*

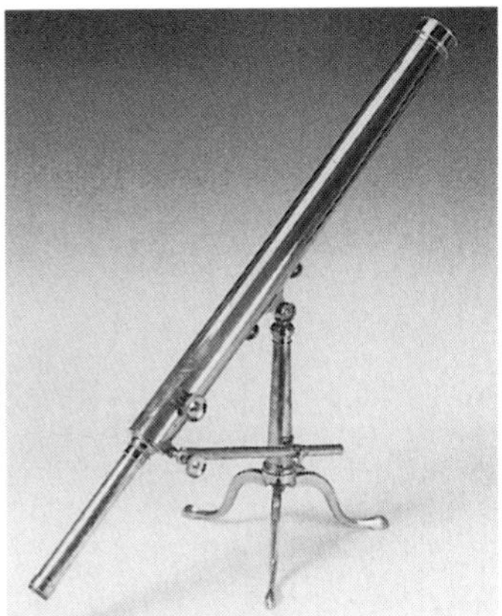

A Thomas Harris & Son brass 2½in (6.5cm) refracting telescope-on-stand, with rack-and-pinion focusing, in a wooden case, with accessories, mid-19thC, 32in (81cm) long.
£1,400–1,700 *S*

A lacquered-brass meridian transit telescope, mounted on a cast iron stand, the 10in (25.5cm) telescope stamped J. Short, London, in the original fitted box, early 20thC.
£350–400 *P*

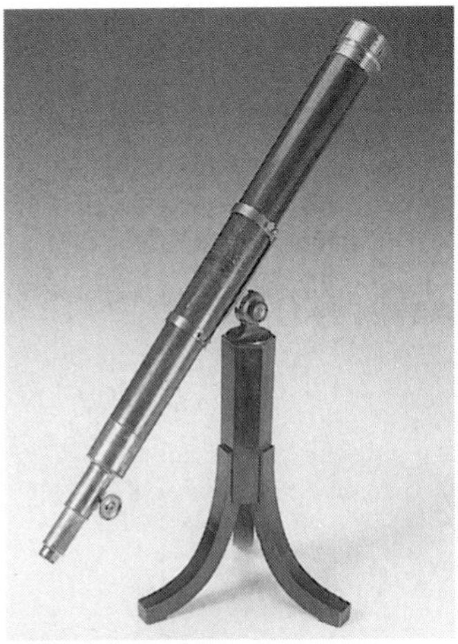

A brass 2½in (6.5cm) refractory telescope-on-stand, by Utzschneider & Fraunhofer, the mahogany bound tube with cap to objective and rack-and-pinion adjustment to the eyepiece, early 19thC, tube 32in (81cm) long.
£2,300–2,500 *S*

Weighing & Measuring Equipment

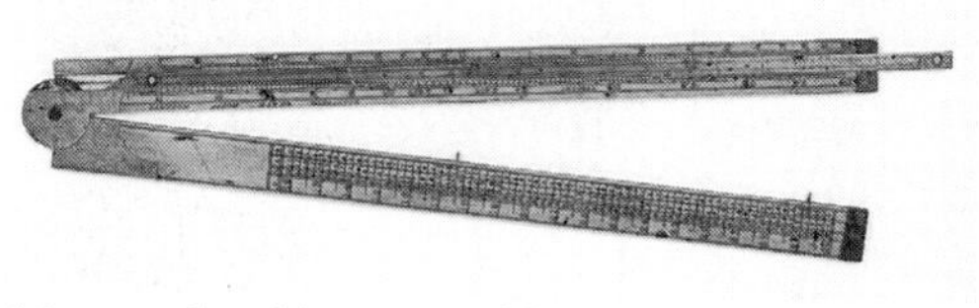

A boxwood and brass two-fold calculating rule, by Samson Aston, with sliding caliper and £ s d scales, c1840, 12in (30.5cm) long.
£40–50 *TOM*

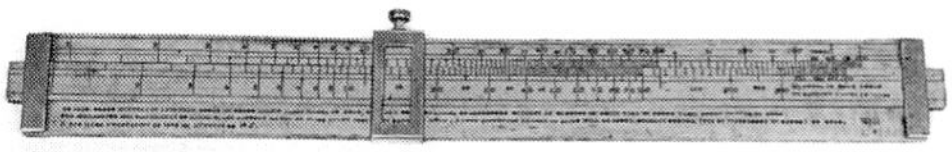

A boxwood and brass gunner's slide rule, by J. Hicks, London, c1890, 15in (38cm) long.
£50–60 *TOM*

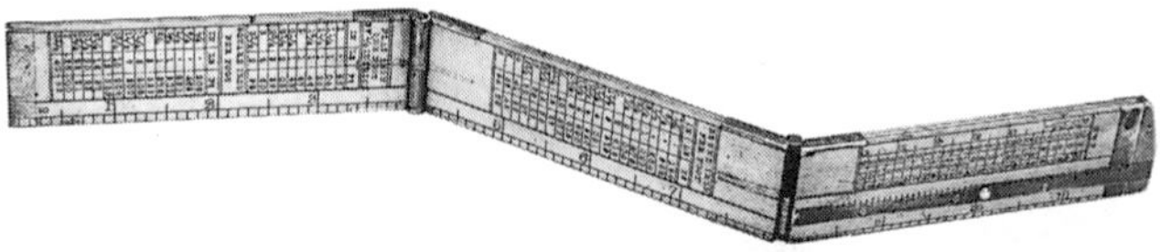

A boxwood and brass three-fold ironmonger's rule, by John Rabone & Sons, Birmingham, c1870, 12in (30.5cm) long.
£40–50 *TOM*

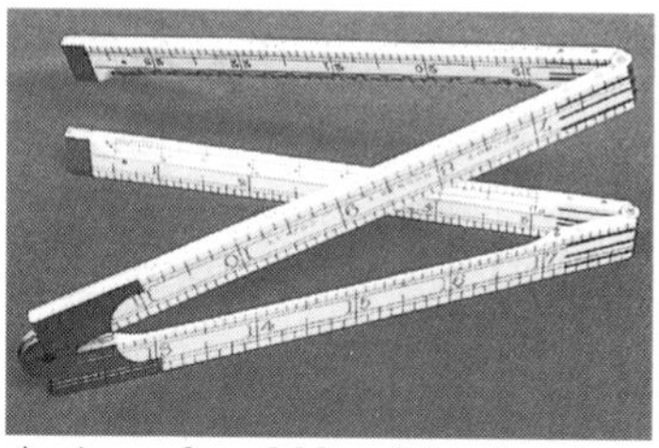

An ivory four-fold architect's rule, by Keyzer & Bendon, London, with inside bevelled edges, c1900, 24in (61cm) long.
£100–120 *TOM*

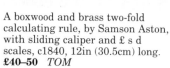

An ivory proof rule, with nickel-silver fittings, c1900, 9in (23cm) long.
£35–40 *TOM*

A County of Lincoln brass Winchester bushel measure, by Degrave, London, dated '1809', 19¼in (49cm) diam.
£850–950 *S*

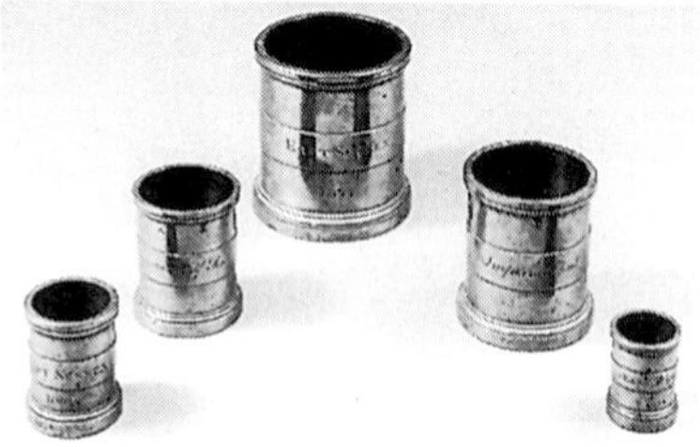

A set of 5 bronze measures, including imperial quart, pint, half-pint, gill and half-gill, signed 'Alwood & Wimble, Lewes', dated '1834', 5¼in (13.5cm) to 2½in (6cm).
£1,400–1,600 *P*

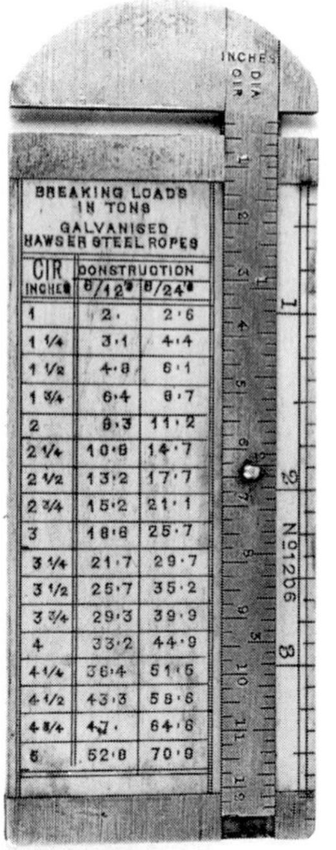

r. A brass and wood rope gauge, late 19thC, 12in (30.5cm) high.
£40–45 *BSA*

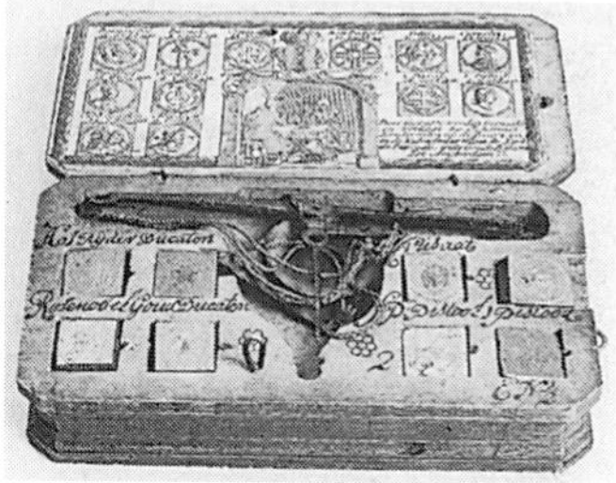

A set of Continental beam scales, with steel balance and 11 weights, the drawer below containing a further 13 weights, 18thC, 5¼in (13.5cm) wide.
£500–550 *P*

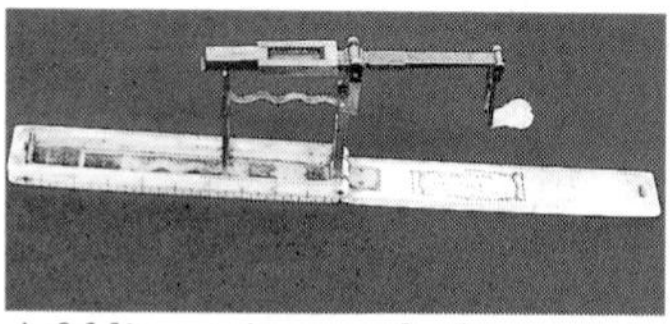

A folding guinea scale, by W. Arstall, Lancashire, c1780, 5in (12.5cm) long, in a fitted ivory case.
£450–500 *TOM*

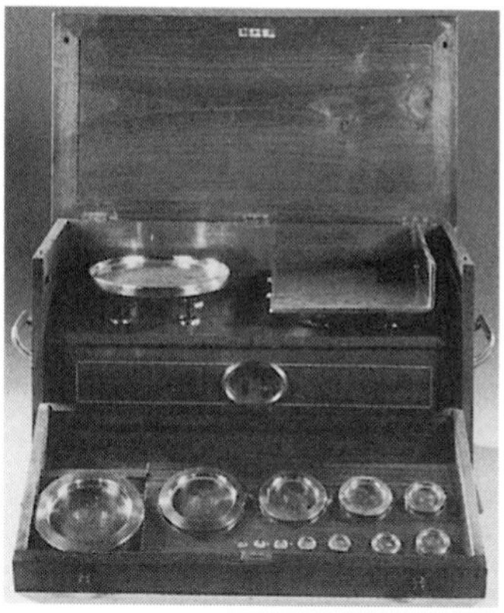

l. A set of Avery Beranger type counter scales, with 2 brass pans with scale reading window above a drawer with 12 brass weights from ½ dram to 4lbs, late 19thC, in a mahogany case, 21¼in (54cm) wide.
£450–550 *S*

A set of brass balance scales, by Hunt & Co, with 6 graduated weights, 19thC, 21in (53.5cm) high.
£180–200 *GAK*

MARINE

Barometers

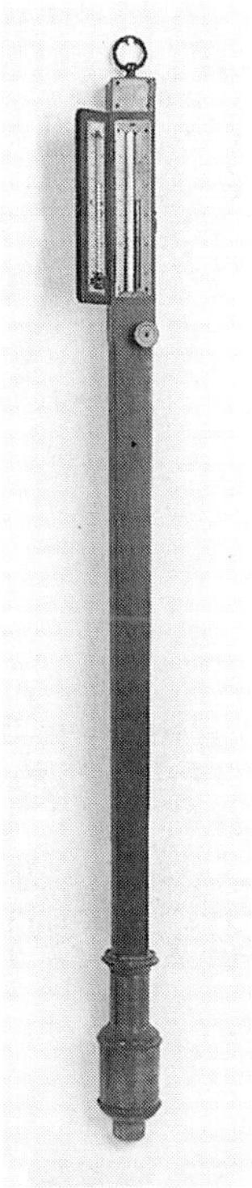

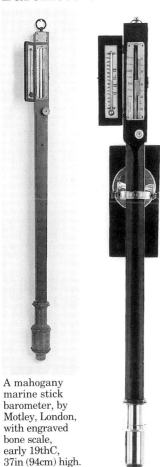

A mahogany marine stick barometer, by Motley, London, with engraved bone scale, early 19thC, 37in (94cm) high.
£1,700–2,000 *Bon*

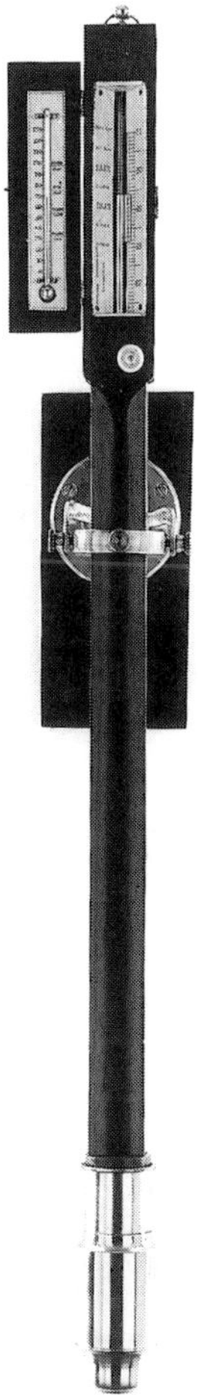

l. A mahogany marine barometer, by Bywater, Liverpool, with hinged door and ivory plates, c1850, 36in (91.5cm) high.
£1,800–2,200 *AW*

A brass aneroid ship's barometer, signed Abraham & Co, Liverpool, set with an alcohol centigrade/reamur thermometer and a mercury Fahrenheit thermometer, 19thC, 8¼in (21cm) diam.
£530–580 *P*

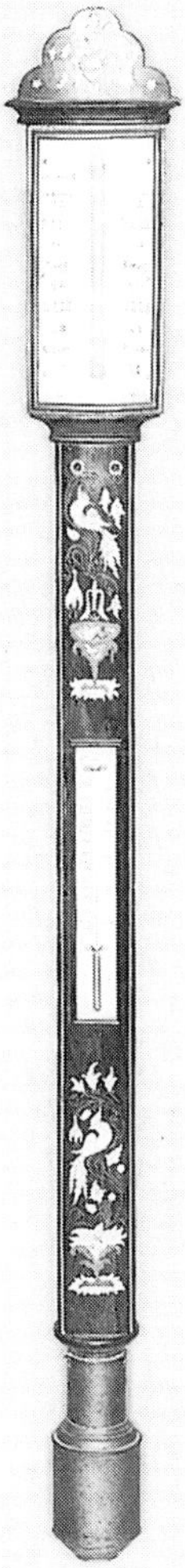

r. A rosewood, brass and mother-of-pearl inlaid marine barometer, signed H. Grimoldi & Co, London, the trunk set with a mercury thermometer and inlaid with birds and a fountain amongst scrolling foliage, the angled bone dial with twin scales and verniers for '10am Yesterday and 10am Today', 19thC, 38in (96cm) high.
£1,700–2,000 *P*

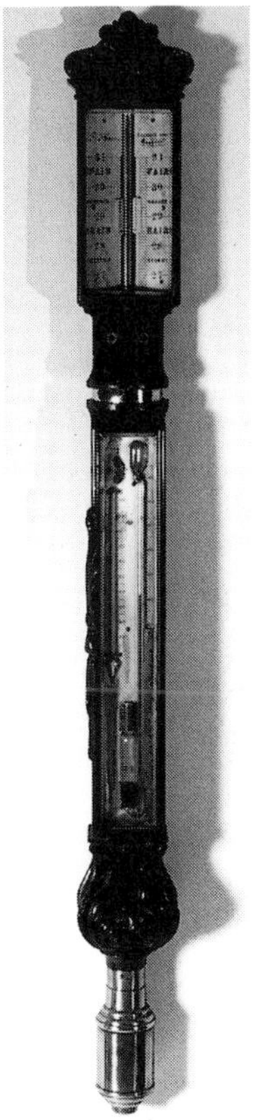

A carved rosewood marine barometer and sympiesometer, signed D. Heron, Glasgow, with bone register plate, with a brass cistern, c1830, 35in (89cm) high.
£2,300–2,500 *GH*

Chronometers & Timekeepers

A bronze 8-day deck watch, by Dent, London, with 4in (10cm) enamel dial, fusee movement and maintaining power, the under-slung ratchet tooth lever escapement with compensation balance, c1860, in oak box.
£1,500–1,700 *S*

A German WWII naval chronograph, by Dugena, 2in (5cm) diam.
£450–550 *MJa*

r. An American 56-hour marine chronometer, signed Hamilton Watch Co Lancaster, PA, the 4¼in (10.5cm) diam silvered-brass dial with subsidiaries for seconds and power reserve indication, full plate damascened nickel keywind fusee movement, c1941, in a brass-bound mahogany box.
£1,400–1,600 *PT*

A 2-day marine chronometer, by William Farquhar, London, with silvered dial, the detent escapement with compensation balance and free-spring helical spring, c1850, bezel 4in (10cm) diam, with three-tier brass-bound rosewood box.
£1,800–2,200 *S*

An 8-day marine chronometer, by David Glasgow, the silvered dial with subsidiary seconds and power reserve indicator, the spotted three-quarter plate movement with a bimetallic compensated balance, blued helical spring, diamond endstone reserve fusee, late 19thC, bezel 6in (15cm) diam.
£4,000–4,500 *Bon*

A 2-day marine chronometer, by Thos Hall, London, the movement with Earnshaw type spring detent escapement, compensated balance and helical spring with diamond endstone, dial 3¾in (9.5cm) diam, in a brass bound mahogany box.
£1,100–1,300 *P*

A Ulysses Nardin silver open-face centre-seconds deck watch, with matching slip box, the enamel 2¼in (5.5cm) dial with frosted gilt movement and precision regulator, Swiss, c1940.
£800–900 *Bon*

A 2-day marine chronometer, signed Hewitt & Son, London, the silvered 4¾in (12cm) dial with subsidiary seconds and power reserve indicator, the spotted movement with an Earnshaw spring detent escapement, bimetallic balance and a blued helical spring, in brass rosewood bound box.
£1,500–1,700 *Bon*

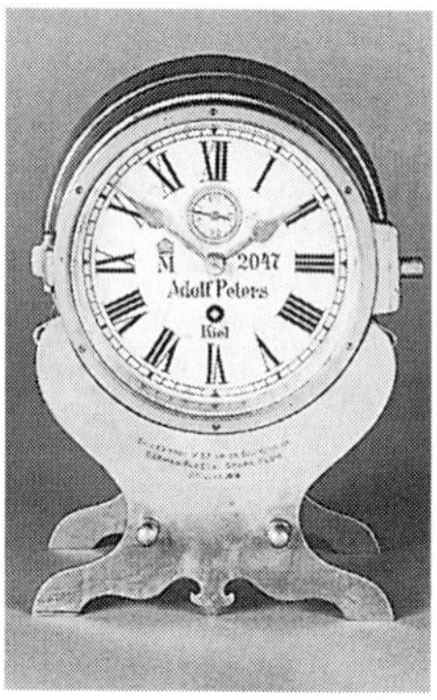

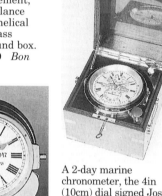

A German bulkhead timepiece, the 6in (15cm) dial signed Adolf Peters, Kiel, the circular movement with lever platform escapement, bearing inscription, with Gustav Becker mark, c1919, mounted on a brass bracket.
£1,200–1,300 *P*

The bracket bears the inscription 'Salved from VS7 after scuttling of the German fleet at Scapa Flow 21st June, 1919.

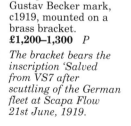

l. An 8-day gimballed deck watch, by Waltham, the silvered 2¼in (5.5cm) dial with subsidiary seconds and nickel plate movement, c1940, in a mahogany box.
£580–650 *Bon*

A 2-day marine chronometer, by Thomas Mercer, c1970, 7¼in (18.5cm) square, in a wooden box.
£700–800 *TMe*

A 2-day marine chronometer, the 4in (10cm) dial signed Joseph Sewill, Liverpool, the movement with Earnshaw type spring detent escapement, compensated balance and helical spring, 19thC, in a brass bound mahogany box.
£1,800–2,000 *P*

An 8-day marine chronometer, marked French, Royal Exchange, London, with reversed fusee, Harrison's maintaining power, blued steel helical spring, bimetallic balance with Eiffe's auxiliary compensation, bezel 5¼in (13.5cm) diam, in a brass bound mahogany box.
£3,700–4,000 *S*

An 8-day Earnshaw type marine chronometer, the 5in (12.5cm) silvered dial signed John Morton & Co, Glasgow, the spring detent escapement with Poole's auxiliary compensation and freesprung helical spring, 19thC, in a two-part brass bound mahogany box.
£3,400–3,800 *P*

An 8-day keyless deck watch, by Waltham Watch Co, the 2¼in (5.5cm) enamel dial with damascened nickel lever movement and bimetallic compensation balance, c1910, in a three-tier brass-bound mahogany box.
£800–1,000 *S*

A German WWII bulkhead timepiece, the 5½in (14cm) silvered dial stamped with an eagle and swastika, c1944.
£850–950 *P*

Model Ships

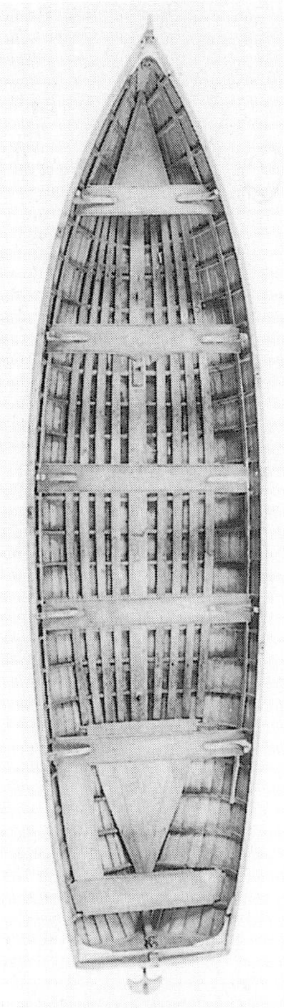

A fruitwood model of a rowing skiff, with klinker-built hull, fruitwood thwarts and shaped rudder, early 19thC, 27in (69cm) long.
£3,800–4,200 *S*

A plank on frame model of a three-masted merchant ship, mounted on dry dock stanchions, with carved wood female figurehead and rudder, rigging distressed, mid-19thC, 31in (79cm) long.
£1,600–1,800 *S*

A model of the USS *Constitution*, with mahogany deck and copper sheets below waterline, 19thC, 60in (152.5cm) wide.
£1,800–2,200 *SLN*

A shipping diorama, the painted background mounted with half-block model of a merchant ship and pilot boat in the foreground, in framed and glazed cased, mid-19thC, 43in (109cm) wide.
£1,000–1,200 *S*

A pine pond yacht, with projecting bowsprit, helm and deck houses, lacking masts and sails, mid-19thC, 70in (178cm) long.
£1,200–1,400 *S*

A pond yacht, with wooden hull and weighted keel, gaff-rigged main mast, linen sails, brass tiller, on stand, late 19thC, 86in (218cm) long.
£900–1,100 *S*

A diorama, depicting a three-masted sailing ship, *Star and Hope*, with steam tug, *Flying Mist*, 19thC, 31in (78.5cm) wide.
£450–550 *Mit*

A Scottish sailor-made painted model of the trawler *Spesmelilr of Kirkcaldy*, with hinged masts, raised bridge house with single funnel, in a glazed pine case, early 20thC, 16in (41cm) long.
£400–450 *S*

l. A model of the American clipper ship *Flying Cloud*, the copper hull sheathed from the waterline down and painted black above, in a mahogany case with brass mouldings, c1930, 36in (91.5cm) wide.
£1,350–1,500 *SLN*

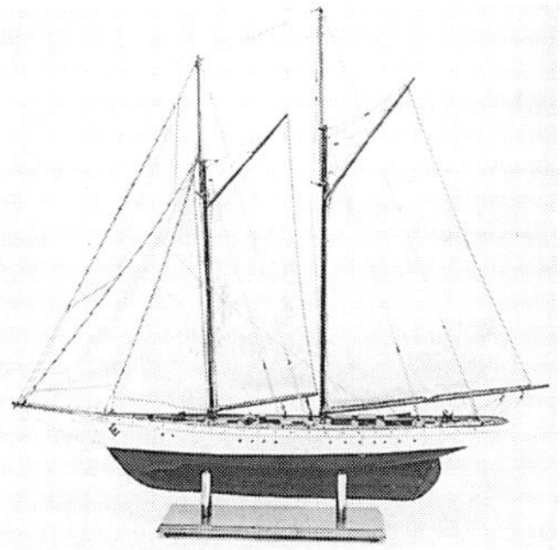

A wooden gaff-rigged pond yacht, with blue and white painted hull, on a brass and wood stand, 19thC, 63in (160cm) long.
£750–850 *Oli*

A wooden pond yacht, restored, c1930, 70in (178cm) long.
£480–530 *Doc*

A builder's model of the bulk carrier *Moorwood*, by S. P. Austin & Son Ltd, Sunderland, the hull painted iron-red below the waterline, well detailed deck fittings, also bearing light armament, mounted on turned baluster supports, 1940, 35½in (90cm) long, in a mahogany case.
£1,800–2,000 *P(G)*

Nautical Handicrafts

A French prisoner-of-war 'spinning jenny' automaton, with traces of red, yellow and blue paint, c1800, 5½in (14cm) high.
£1,200–1,300 *S*

A woolwork picture, depicting a three-masted ship, early 19thC, 21 x 20in (53 x 51cm), in a walnut frame.
£1,000–1,100 *Bea(E)*

A French prisoner-of-war display case, the double doors opening to reveal a mirror-backed interior, decorated overall with geometric straw work designs, c1800, 14in (38cm) wide.
£800–900 *S*

A picture of *The Sea Witch*, attributed to Thomas Willis, the embroidered textiles applied to a painted canvas, c1860, 22 x 41in (56 x 104cm) wide, in a carved giltwood frame.
£1,200–1,500 *NOA*

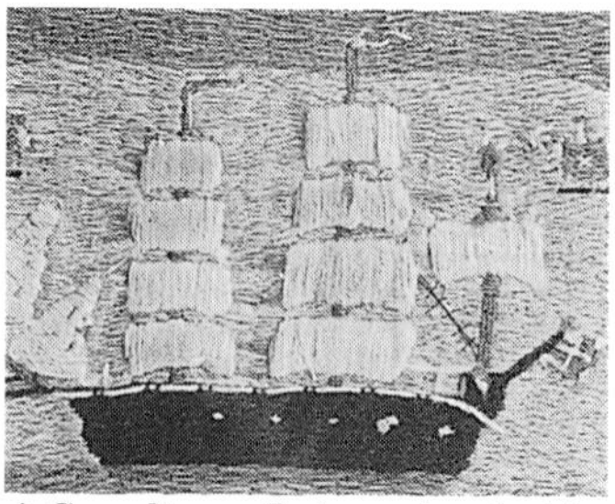

A Canadian sailor's woolwork ship picture, 1860s, 7 x 9in (18 x 23cm).
£80–100 *Bon*

A sailor's woolwork picture, depicting a twin funnel three-masted paddle steamer, HM Yacht *Victoria & Albert*, below a moon and star sky, mid-19thC, 19in (48cm) square.
£500–550 *P(WM)*

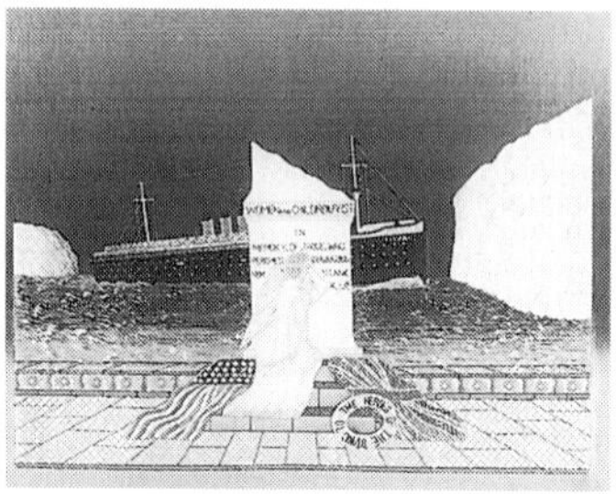

An embroidered silk picture of RMS *Titanic*, worked in polychrome silks on a grey silk background, c1914, 15 x 20in (38 x 51cm) wide.
£1,250–1,400 *S*

A sailor's woolwork picture, depicting a three-masted man o' war flying the White Ensign, Royal Ensign and the Union Jack, worked with coloured wools and silk details, late 19thC, 9½ x 12½in (24 x 32cm), in a burr maple frame.
£480–550 *WW*

A scrimshawed whale's tooth, depicting a Scottish lady and gentleman, both in Highland costume, mid-19thC, 6½in (16.5cm) high.
£700–800 *S*

A scrimshawed whalebone busk, the central whaling scene flanked by portraits of a mansion and a classical folly, mid-19thC, 15¼in (39cm) long.
£850–1,000 *S*

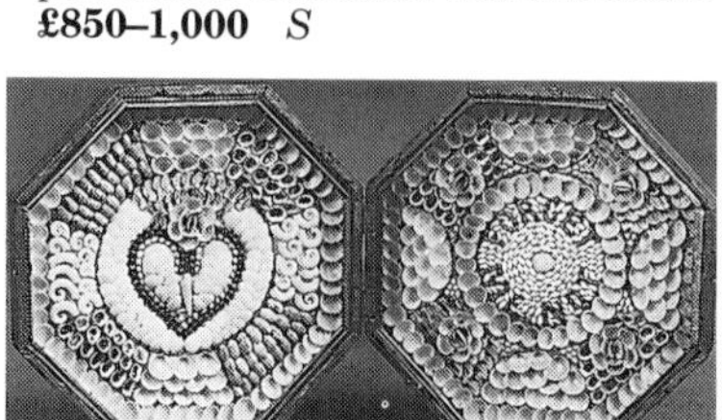

A pair of sailor's valentine greetings, made up from Caribbean shells, contained in 2 mahogany hinged boxes, 19thC, 9in (23cm) wide.
£1,000–1,200 *WW*

A scrimshawed sperm whale tooth, etched with typical scenes of a three-masted brig and whaling boats, 18thC, 7½in (19cm) long.
£1,700–2,000 *GAK*

Navigational Instruments

A lacquered-brass circumferentor, signed J. Search, London, the quadrantally divided silvered compass mounted above a 6in (15cm) diameter horizontal scale, in original fitted box, late 18thC, box 6¼in (16cm) square.
£1,100–1,200 *P*

A Severn's Patent warning compass, by Lilley & Son, London, in a mahogany box, early 20thC, 10½in (27cm) wide.
£370–400 *P*

First patented in 1879, the compass could be set by 2 knurled knobs in the centre of the glass so that a bell would sound if the helmsman wandered more than a few degrees off course.

l. A German WWII spherical magnetic compass, by Carl Plath, Hamburg, 12in (30.5cm) high.
£450–500 *MJa*

A Canadian Hughes, Owens & Co compass binnacle, with floating compass, gimballed mount, brass binnacle with side illuminant and wooden drum base, early 20thC, 18½in (47cm) high.
£350–400 *Bon*

l. A ship's binnacle, from the *Toronto*, by McGregor & Co, Glasgow & Greenoch, with turned oak pedestal, brass compass and gimbal, mid-19thC, 12in (30.5cm) high.
£800–900 *HCC*

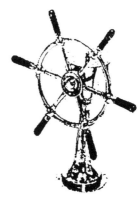

An ARG-1 German naval issue WWII navigation apparatus, by Carl Zeiss, c1944, 8½in (21.5cm) diam, with fitted case.
£250–280 *MJa*

This was removed from a U-boat upon its surrender in 1945.

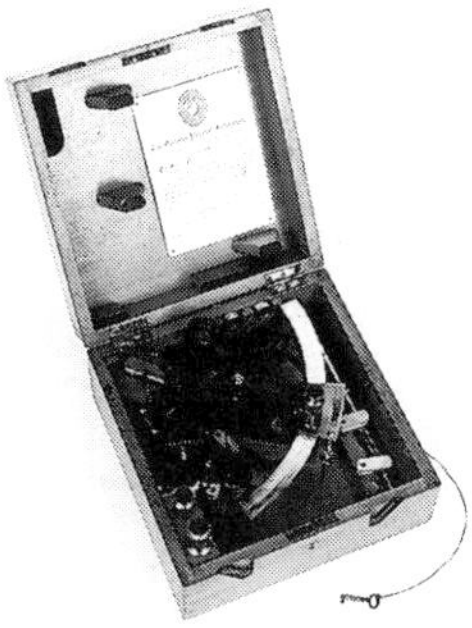

A three circle vernier sextant, by H. Hughes & Sons, c1915, 10in (25.5cm) square.
£600–700 *NC*

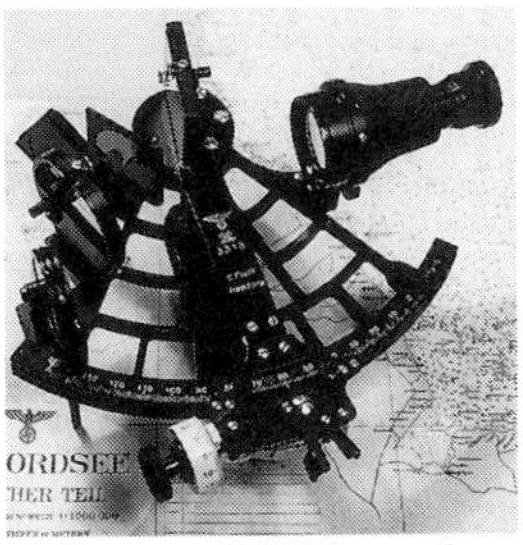

A German WWII naval alloy sextant, by Carl Plath, Hamburg, dated '1941', 9¼in (23.5cm) wide, with original case.
£500–600 *MJa*

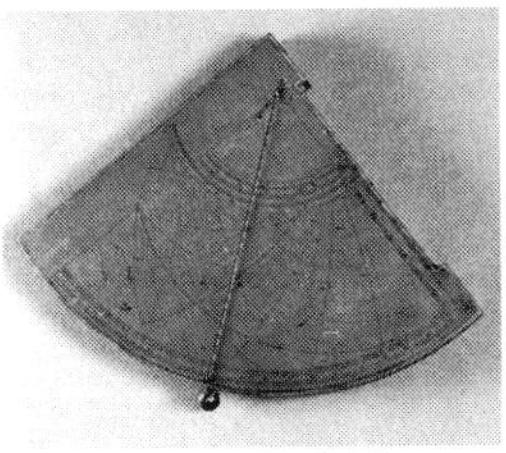

An Ottoman-Turkish lacquered wood quadrant, red and orange with scales drawn in red, black and gold pointing, early 19thC, 6in (15cm) radius.
£2,300–2,500 *S*

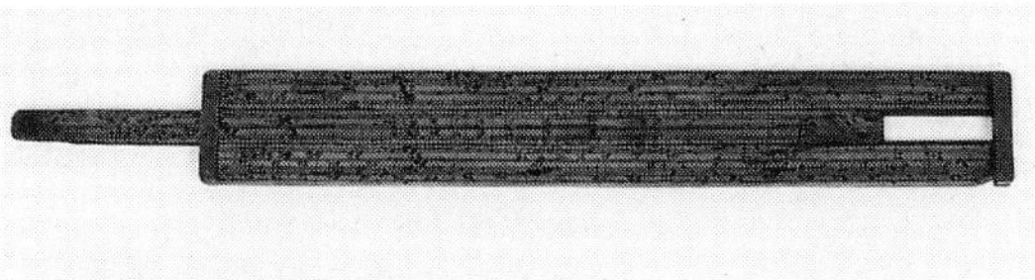

A navigator's boxwood and brass slide rule, early 18thC, 12in (30.5cm) long.
£120–150 *TOM*

Ships' Fittings

A cast iron starting cannon, the barrel mounted on a trunnion between 2 cast side supports with lion head finials, 19thC, 25in (64cm) long.
£1,200–1,500 *S*

l. A brass bell from HMS *Wallace*, 1919, 13in (33cm) high.
£950–1,150 *P*

HMS Wallace *served with distinction throughout WWII, including Dunkirk.*

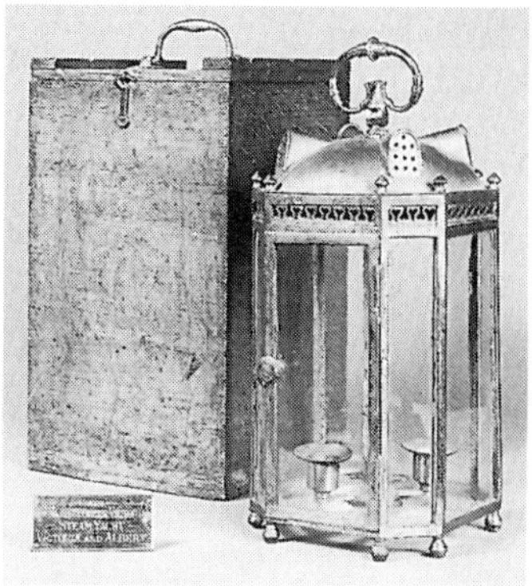

A gilt-brass lamp, with a domed top and 4 ventilation chimneys, a gilt and lacquered-brass plaque reading From Her Majesty Queen Victoria's Steam Yacht *Victoria and Albert*, 19thC, 16¼in (41.5cm) high.
£2,800–3,200 *P*

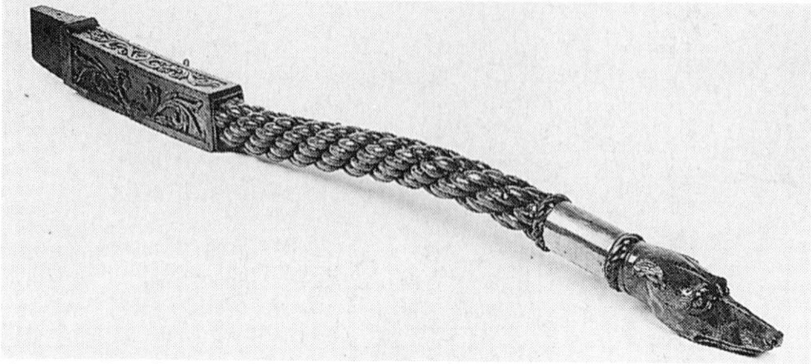

A carved and stained beech tiller from the HMS *Greyhound*, the terminal in the form of a greyhound's head, wide brass neck ring on to a four-spun carved rope handle terminating in a rectangular block carved with acanthus scrolls, early 19thC, 73¾in (187cm) long.
£550–650 *P*

An oak and mahogany ship's wheel, with central brass boss, mid-19thC, 42in (122cm) diam.
£700–800 *S*

Miscellaneous

l. A Royal Navy rating's straw hat, with original cap tally for HMS *Lion*, late 19thC.
£270–300 *BOS*

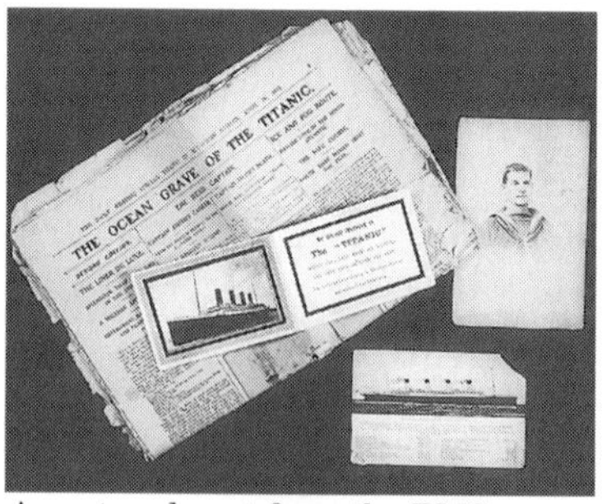

A postcard sent from the RMS *Titanic*, posted from Queenstown, dated 'April 11th, 1912', together with a sepia photograph of the sender and an official memorial card, with *The Daily Graphic Special Titanic Memoriam*, dated 'April 20th, 1912'.
£3,200–3,500 *S*

The postcard was sent from Mr Ernest King to his son Tom, shortly before the Titanic *sank on April 15th, 1912. Mr King was a purser clerk on board the ship and was one of approximately 1,500 people who tragically lost their lives.*

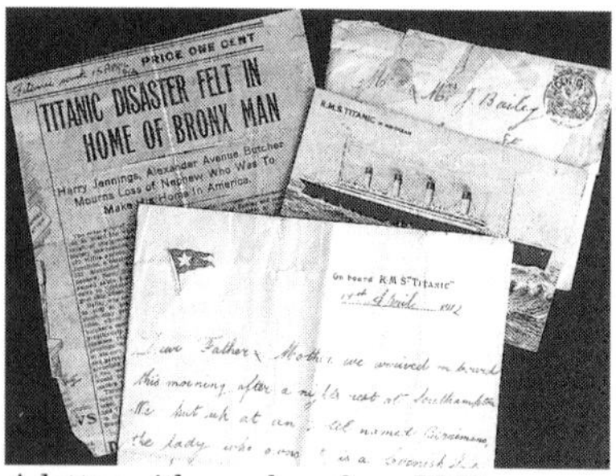

A letter with envelope from RMS *Titanic*, written by 19-year-old Percy Bailey of Penzance on 11th April, 1912, with printed *White Star* flag and heading, with a postcard from Southampton, dated '10th April', and a cutting from an American newspaper.
£2,700–3,000 *LAY*

Percy Bailey wrote 'I have never seen such a sight in all my life, she is like a floating palace'.

l. A Continental white metal naval dirk, the worked hilt in the form of a boat with fighting sailors, the scabbard with a battle scene, possibly Dutch, mid-19thC, 12in (31cm) long.
£2,000–2,200 *DN(H)*

A mahogany barrel organ, by Longman & Broderip, London, with a painted giltwood front panel, on a stand, c1790, 21½in (55cm) wide.
£2,500–3,000 *S*

A Gasparini Butel 52-key pipe organ, with 3 automated carved wood figures, the painted wood façade in 3 sections, early 20thC, 103in (262cm) wide, with a collection of music books.
£11,000–12,000 *S*

A Symphonion 13⅝in Eroica, in a walnut case, late 19thC, 73in (186cm) high.
£21,000–23,000 *S*

An interchangeable 9-cylinder musical box, playing 6 airs on 2 combs, with tune indicator, in a burr walnut veneered case, Swiss, c1880, 35½in (91cm) wide, on a later stand.
£3,700–4,500 *S*

A Gavioli & Co marquetry-inlaid street barrel organ, playing 10 tunes, the hand-cranked movement with pinned wooden barrel, c1880, 23in (58.5cm) wide.
£6,700–7,500 *S(NY)*

A Gramophone Co Intermediate Monarch gramophone, with tin horn, on an oak base, c1913, 24in (61cm) wide.
£700–800 *ET*

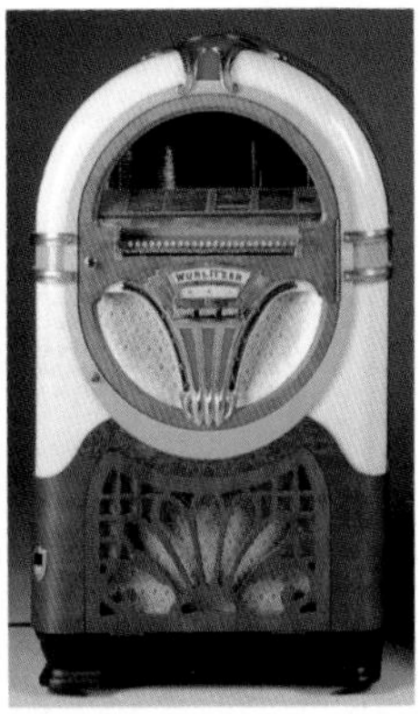

A Wurtlitzer Model 750 jukebox, with a walnut case and stylised floral motif, 24 song selection, c1941, 55¾in (142cm) high.
£3,200–3,500 *S(NY)*

An American Rock-Ola 1426 magic glow jukebox 323, playing 20 selections, with walnut veneered case, c1947, 56in (142cm) high.
£2,500–3,000 *S*

A double bass, by Bernhard Simon Fendt, the flat two-piece back of medium curl, inscribed by restorer, c1820, 41½in (105.5cm) long.
£19,000–21,000 *Bon*

A Spanish violin, by Jose Contreras, the back of medium curl, ribs and scroll of similar figure, restored, label dated '1767', 14¼in (36cm) long.
£15,000–16,500 *P*

An Italian violin, by S. Scarampella, Mantova, the varnish of a red/orange colour, c1895, length of back 14in (35.5cm).
£28,000–32,000 *Bon*

A violoncello, probably by Peter Wamsley, London, the bridge stamped 'Forster', c1780, length of back 29¼in (74cm).
£15,000–18,000 *Bon*

A two manual harpsichord, by William Dowd, Boston, inscribed, painted green and red with gilt bands, 1969, 37in (94.5cm) wide.
£11,000–12,000 *S(NY)*

A French mahogany and parquetry grand piano, signed 'Erard', the top with a diaper motif, with jasperware panels centred with classical figures, parcel-gilt borders, c1900, 61in (155cm) wide.
£21,000–25,000 *S*

A Steinway marquetry-inlaid grand piano, with carved music rest, reconditioned, c1890, 72in (183cm) wide.
£15,000–18,000 *PEx*

A Steinway satinwood and marquetry-inlaid grand piano, with inlaid medallions of classical figures, c1904, 59in (150cm) wide.
£22,000–25,000 *Bon*

A Bechstein satinwood, sycamore and mother-of-pearl inlaid baby grand piano, the design attributed to G. M. Ellwood, the case by J. S. Henry, c1904, 55½in (141cm) wide.
£8,500–9,500 *P*

A Brinsmead grand piano, with 6 cabriole legs, c1920, 72in (183cm) wide.
£4,000–5,000 *PEx*

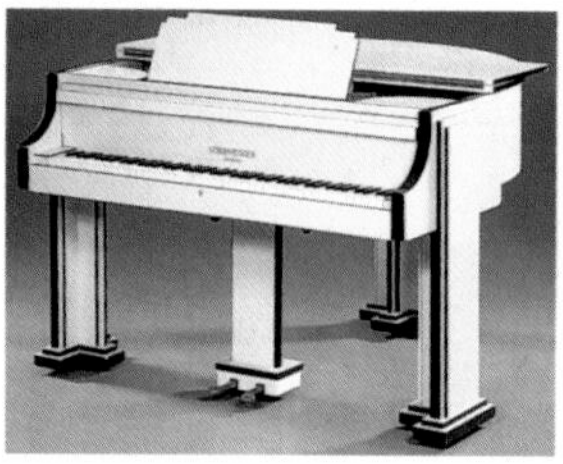

A Strohmenger painted baby grand piano, 1930s, 54in (138cm) wide, and a stool.
£2,000–2,200 *S*

r. A walnut and marquetry-inlaid spinet, by Stephen Keene, repaired, 1685, 61in (155cm) wide.
£17,000–18,500 *WW*

A Bösendorfer semi-concert grand piano, with ebonised case, the pedal lyre with 3 pedals, on 3 tapered legs, 1987, 61in (155cm) wide.
£236,000–250,000 *S(NY)*

This piano bears the signature of Leonard Bernstein, with the device of a heart, on its iron frame.

A Russian icon of The Birth of the Virgin, depicting St Anna resting on the bed where the midwife and a servant prepare to bathe the newborn infant, with Judith and another servant, 16thC, 12½ x 10⅛in (32 x 26.5cm).
£9,000–10,000 *RKa*

A Bulgarian icon of St Marina, 16thC, 14⅜ x 11in (36.5 x 28cm).
£5,500–6,000 *RKa*

Marina is the protectress against evil and demonic powers.

A Russian icon of an Apostle, holding a copy of the Gospels, 17thC, later overpainted, 45 x 18¼in (114.5 x 46.5cm).
£1,400–1,800 *S(NY)*

A Russian icon of the Dormition of The Mother of God, with Christ standing behind Mary receiving her soul, c1600, 12¼ x 9¾in (31 x 25cm).
£2,800–3,200 *JAA*

A Russian icon of The Mother of God of the Burning Bush, painted on an olive green ground, the raised borders with gilt inscriptions, 18thC, 12 x 10¼in (31 x 26cm).
£2,000–2,200 *S*

A Russian icon of John the Baptist, pointing to the infant Christ contained in a diskos and symbolising the Lamb of God, inscribed 'Holy John the Forerunner', 19thC, 21 x 17½in (53.5 x 44.5cm).
£750–900 *JAA*

A Russian icon of the Nativity of Christ, with the three Wise Men and animals, 18thC, 26 x 20in (66 x 51cm).
£1,600–1,800 *S(NY)*

A Russian icon of the Anastasis, painted with the Resurrection and Descent into Hell, late 17thC, 41½ x 23in (105.5 x 58.5cm).
£6,000–6,750 *S(NY)*

A Russian icon of The Lord Almighty, egg tempera overlaid with silver-gilt riza, enamel halo and plaques, c1900, 12¼ x 10¼in (31 x 26cm).
£3,000–3,300 *JAA*

A Russian icon, entitled 'Weep Not for Me, Mother', depicting Mary supporting her crucified son, c1900, 13¾ x 11¼in (35 x 28.5cm).
£2,000–2,200 *JAA*

A portrait miniature of Marie de Medici, English School, c1605, 1½in (39mm) high, in a gilt-metal enamelled frame with simulated 'jewels'.
£1,700–1,850 *Bon*

A portrait miniature of a lady, probably Anne of Denmark, Continental School, c1605, 2in (5cm) high.
£13,000–15,000 *Bon*

A pair of portrait miniatures of Napoleon I and Madame Recamier, by Paul Delaroche, on ivory, c1838, 3in (7.5cm) high, in a later double frame.
£520–580 *TMA*

A portrait miniature of Mary Anne Jackson, by Richard Cosway, c1790, 2in (50mm) high, in a gold frame with pearl surround.
£2,700–3,000 *BHa*

A portrait miniature of a lady, by Reginald Easton, c1875, 3in (7.5cm) wide.
£1,600–1,800 *BHa*

A portrait of a young lady, by George Engleheart, c1795, 3in (7.5cm) high, in a gold frame with pearl surround.
£4,400–4,800 *BHa*

A portrait miniature of Marie Caroline, Duchess of Berry, by Jean Baptiste Joseph Duchesne, dated '1822', 3in (7.5cm) high.
£4,200–4,600 *S*

A portrait of a lady, by George Engleheart, c1800, 3in (7.5cm) high, in an ormolu frame and with a fitted leather case.
£3,000–3,300 *S*

A portrait miniature of a naval officer, by Alexander Gallaway, 1812, 4in (10cm) high.
£1,800–2,200 *BHa*

A portrait miniature, by Thomas Hargreaves, c1825, 4in (10cm) high.
£4,500–5,000 *BHa*

A portrait miniature of Lady Rachel Tweeke, by Horace Hone, 1783, 2in (50mm) high.
£4,500–5,000 *BHa*

A portrait miniature of a lady, wearing a lace-trimmed dress and bandeau, signed and dated 'P. Paillou 1796', 3in (7.5cm) high.
£2,500–2,750 *P*

A portrait miniature of a lady, probably by John Wright, c1815, 3¼in (8cm) high.
£800–950 *Bon*

A portrait miniature of a lady, by George Place, c1790, 3in (7.5cm) high.
£1,500–1,700 *BHa*

A Babylonian copper alloy figure of a goddess, 1900–1700 BC, 4¼in (11cm) high.
£10,500–11,500 *S*

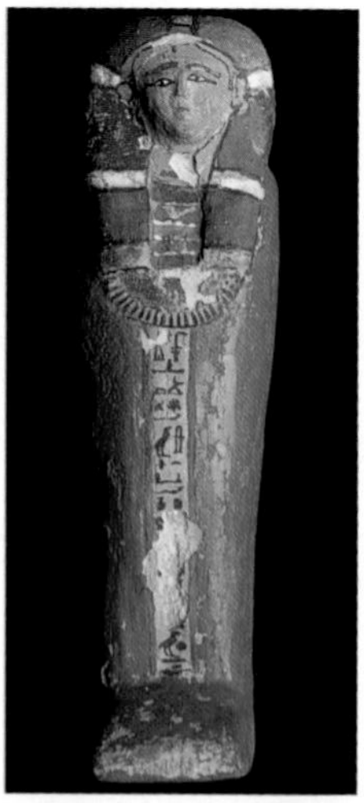

An Egyptian ushabti, 1800–1600 BC, 6in (15cm) high.
£2,400–2,750 *Bon*

An Egyptian bronze model of a cat, with pierced ears, 716–30 BC, 5½in (14cm) high.
£12,500–14,000 *S(NY)*

A Greek alabastron, 6th–5th century BC, 4in (10cm) high.
£4,800–5,300 *S*

A Roman mosaic glass patella cup, set on an applied ring base, restored, 1st century BC/AD, 3½in (9cm) diam.
£4,000–4,500 *Bon*

A Roman glass ribbed bowl, with flattened base, repaired, 1st century AD, 3in (7.5cm) diam.
£6,400–7,000 *S*

A Greek two-handled glass vessel, with applied spiral trail, 600–400 BC, 3½in (9cm) diam.
£4,800–5,500 *Bon*

A Roman marbled glass flask, with an everted rounded rim and marvered trailing, 1st century AD, 4½in (12cm) high.
£9,200–10,000 *S*

A Roman pyxis, the glass blown into a three-part mould, the body with 8 panels with 4 designs repeating twice, lid missing, early 1st century AD, 2in (50mm) diam.
£10,000–11,000 *Bon*

A Roman marble figure of a female, 1st–2nd century BC, 29½in (75cm) high.
£47,000–52,000 *SAnt*

A Romano-British necklace of coloured glass beads, with a silver cruciform pendant, 3rd–4th century AD.
£120–150 *FW&C*

An enamel on copper roundel, late 13thC, 3½in (9cm) diam.
£40,000–45,000 *S(NY)*

A plaque of The Virgin Mary, Limoges, mid-13thC, 3in (7.5cm) high.
£4,500–5,000 *S(NY)*

A Cheyenne hide baby carrier, 40in (102cm) high.
£7,700–8,500 *S(NY)*

An Acoma Olla pottery bowl, c1900, 9½in (24cm) diam.
£1,000–1,100 *YAG*

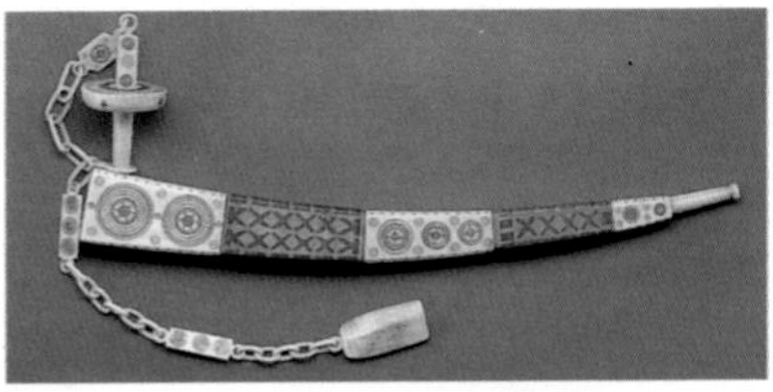

An Inuit lead-inlaid wood and ivory pipe, suspended with chains, 12in (30.5cm) long.
£6,300–7,000 *S(NY)*

A Yombe figurative finial, central African, 7in (18cm) high.
£12,500–15,000 *S(NY)*

A Ekoi headdress, with inset wooden spikes and metal teeth, central African, 12in (30.5cm) high.
£5,000–5,500 *S(NY)*

An Abelam figure, New Guinea, 81in (206cm) high.
£14,000–16,000 *S(NY)*

A Talipun brideprice object, New Guinea, 18½in (47cm) high.
£550–600 *S(A)*

A carved wood stool, in the form of an animal, with coconut scraper, Thailand, 22in (56cm) long.
£380–430 *LHAr*

The user sits astride the stool and uses the animal's tongue to break open coconuts.

A north east Queensland rainforest shield, Australian, 35½in (90cm) high.
£6,000–7,000 *S(A)*

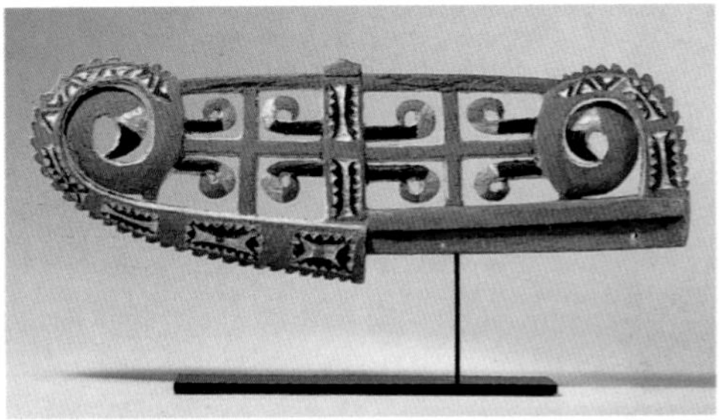

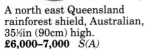

An Admiralty Islands canoe prow ornament, of openwork form, with a section pierced for attachments, with ochre, black and white pigments, 7in (43cm) long.
£1,400–1,800 *S(NY)*

A Fijian whale ivory necklace, largest bead 2in (5cm) long.
£5,000–6,000 *S(NY)*

r. A Maori door lintel, with incised designs, New Zealand, 27¼in (69cm) long.
£3,000–3,300

A French fashion doll, with swivel head, blue eyes, pierced ears and blonde mohair wig, c1890, 12in (30.5cm) high.
£1,300–1,500 *EW*

A bisque doll, with original clothes and wig, c1905, 14½in (37cm) high.
£550–600 *BaN*

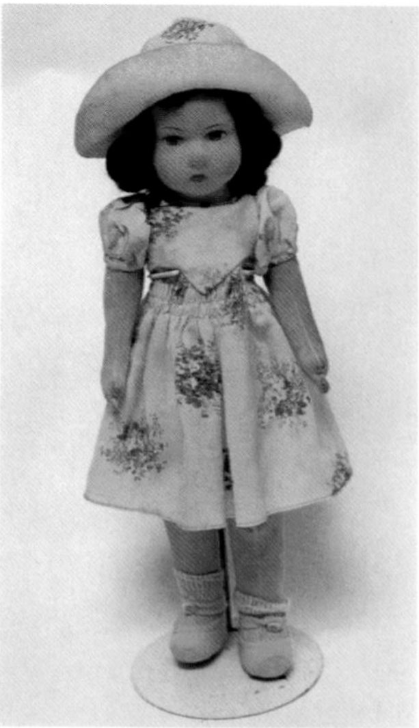

A Chad Valley felt doll, mint condition, 1930s, 17in (43cm) high.
£300–350 *DOL*

A Daniel et Cie bisque-headed *bébé*, with fixed blue eyes, moulded mouth and composition ball-jointed body, stamped, 1900–20, 24½in (62cm) high.
£3,200–3,500 *DN*

A Heinrich Handwerck bisque-headed mulatto doll, incised, c1910, 20½in (52cm) high.
£850–1,000 *YC*

A Jumeau bisque-headed *bébé* doll, c1880, 28in (71cm) high.
£4,500–5,000 *STK*

A Jumeau bisque-headed *bébé* doll, with paperweight eyes, c1885, 25in (63.5cm) high.
£3,500–4,000 *STK*

A Jumeau bisque-headed *bébé* doll, with composition and wood body, c1886, 17in (43cm) high.
£3,800–4,500 *EW*

A J. D. Kestner wooden doll, with sleeping eyes and closed mouth, c1890, 9in (23cm) high.
£600–700 *EW*

A Kestner Bru doll, with jointed ankles, c1899, 19in (48.5cm) high.
£3,500–4,000 *DOL*

A Lenci doll, dressed in Mexican costume, 1920s, 24in (61cm) high.
£800–950 *DOL*

A Lenci felt doll, with painted swivel head, stamped, c1930, 27½in (70cm) high.
£650–720 *S(S)*

An Armand Marseille bisque-headed doll, c1894, 16in (41cm) high.
£400–450 *EW*

A C. Marcoux bisque-headed doll, with fully jointed body, c1890, 13in (33cm) high.
£1,200–1,400 *STK*

An Armand Marseille bisque-headed baby doll, incised mark, c1925, 25½in (65cm) high.
£200–250 *YC*

An Armand Marseille bisque-headed mulatto doll, c1925, 18in (45.5cm) high.
£350–400 *YC*

A Pedigree pot doll, with knitted clothes, 1930s, 17½in (44.5cm) high.
£75–85 *DOL*

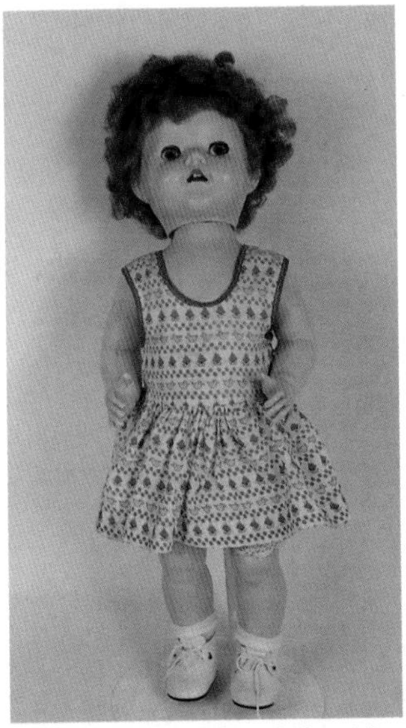

A Pedigree walking doll, with flirty eyes, in original sundress, 1950s, 22in (56cm) high.
£75–85 *CMF*

A Rabery & Delphieu bisque-headed *bébé* doll, with brown paperweight eyes, 1880s, 14in (35.5cm) high.
£2,200–2,500 *STK*

A Märklin gauge one horsedrawn furniture transport wagon on trailer, hand-painted in yellow and red, on a grey painted bogie trailer, with horse harness, c1904.
£5,750–6,500 *S*

A Märklin tinplate clockwork train set, with engine, tender, 3 carriages and rails, c1907, 3in (7.5cm) high, in original box.
£1,650–2,000 *DD*

A Hornby 0 gauge snow plough, the sage green carriage with revolving red fan, c1927, 7in (18cm) long, with original box.
£130–150 *WaH*

A Leeds Model Company 0 gauge 6–8V electric GNR Atlantic locomotive, green with black and white lining, restored, c1926, 10in (25.5cm) long.
£675–750 *WaH*

A Hornby No. 2 Special Tender, mint condition, c1937, 14in (35.5cm) long, in original box, with a LMS No. 2 engine.
£130–150 *HOB*

A Lionel 0 gauge locomotive, tender and 3 Pullman coaches, c1950.
£120–150 *RAR*

Two Trix 00 gauge Diesel Flier carriages, c1951, with original box, 9½in (24cm) wide.
£100–120 *RAR*

Three Exley 0 gauge coaches, red/cream BR MKI and BR brake, and brown/cream GWR 3rd corridor, 1935–40.
£500–550 *AH*

l. A Bassett-Lowke 'Flying Scotsman' LNER 4-6-2 gauge one three-rail locomotive, with 20 volt mechanism, and tender, mint condition, c1936, 11in (28cm) long.
£3,000–3,500 *BKS*

This is one of a limited number made in 1936.

A Märklin clockwork limousine, with adjustable front wheels, hand-painted and lined in light blue and gold, with a grey interior, c1914, 14¼in (36cm) long.
£9,500–10,500 *Bon(C)*

A Ferdinand-Strauss Corporation clockwork Bus-de-Luxe, No. 105, c1925, 13¾in (35cm) long.
£500–550 *BKS*

A Fontaine Fox lithographed tinplate Toonerville Trolley, c1922, 5½in (14cm) wide.
£700–780 *AWT*

A Marx Toys tinplate clockwork jalopy, c1935, 7in (18cm) long.
£240–260 *YAN*

A Dinky Toys Mersey Tunnel Police Van, 1950s, 3in (7.5cm) long.
£65–80 *NTM*

A Charbon's Express Dairy milk float set, roof-board missing, c1935, 7in (18cm) long.
£65–75 *AAC*

A Dinky Supertoys Leyland Comet lorry, No. 531, 1949–54, 5½in (14cm) wide, with original box.
£75–85 *WaH*

A Dinky Supertoys Foden flat truck, No. 902, 1954–60, 7½in (19cm) wide, with original box.
£65–75 *WaH*

A Dinky Toys Big Bedford Heinz 57 Varieties lorry, c1958, 5¾in (14.5cm) wide.
£300–330 *WaH*

A CIJ Renault SNCF Correspondence van, 1950s, 4in (10cm) long.
£20–25 *RAR*

A Corgi Aston Martin DB4, good condition, 1964, 3¾in (9.5cm) long, unboxed.
£22–26 *WaH*

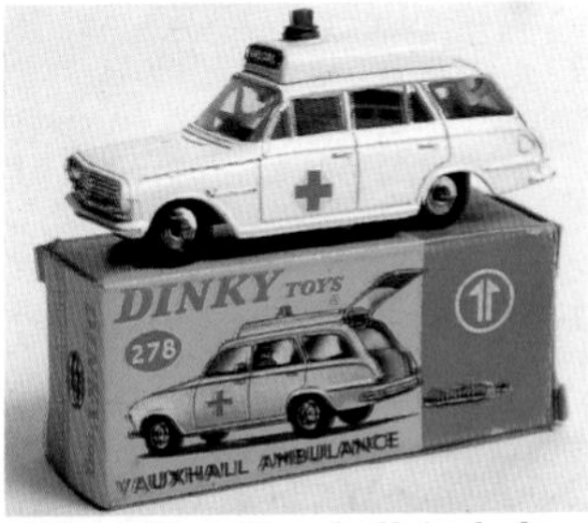

A Dinky Toys Vauxhall Ambulance, No. 278, 1960s, 3¾in (9.5cm) long, with original box.
£65–75 *NTM*

A Roullet & Descamps automaton, with Jumeau head, with 3 movements, c1895, 16½in (42cm) high.
£2,200–2,500 *YC*

A painted wooden Noah's Ark and animals, Erzgebirge, Germany, mid-19thC, 21in (53.5cm) long.
£7,000–8,000 *S*

A German wooden dolls' house, with applied beams, original wallpapers and flooring, later wiring for lighting, some damage, late 19thC, 30in (76cm) high, and some furniture.
£550–600 *S(S)*

A wooden Noah's Ark, with figures of Noah, his wife and children, together with 250 carved and painted animals mostly in pairs, 19thC, 20in (51cm) long.
£2,600–2,850 *DN*

A painted Noah's Ark and various animals, the sloping roof decorated with a dove, late 19thC, 17¼in (44cm) wide.
£600–675 *CGC*

A Lines Brothers rocking horse, late 19thC, 42in (106.5cm) long.
£1,200–1,800 *SPU*

A set of 15 painted lead Robinson Crusoe figures, with trees, marked 'Lama', No. 4, 1860s, figures 2in (5cm) high, with original box.
£200–220 *DD*

A rocking horse, on a sprung metal stand, early 20thC, 69in (175.5cm) long.
£1,200–1,400 *DN*

A Marx Toys tinplate Popeye Express, 1930, 8in (20.5cm) high.
£950–1,100 *YAN*

A Tipp & Co Mickey and Minnie Mouse motorcycle, with engine detailing and Dunlop tyres, c1930, 10in (26cm) long.
£18,000–20,000 *P(Ba)*

A Unique Art Mfg Co, Newark, clockwork Rodeo Joe Crazy Car, American, c1940, 9in (23cm) high.
£270–300 *YAN*

A Chad Valley mohair bear, c1950, 14¼in (36cm) high.
£100–120 *TED*

A Chiltern teddy bear, 1930s, 20in (51cm) high.
£270–300 *CMF*

A teddy bear, probably by Cramer, 18in (45.5cm) high.
£1,200–1,500 *STK*

A Knickerbocker mohair teddy bear, with moulded tin nose, c1930, 19¾in (50cm) high.
£150–200 *TED*

A straw-filled teddy bear glove, 1930s, 8in (20.5cm) high.
£75–85 *CMF*

A Clemens teddy bear, with shaped snout, c1950, 18in (45.5cm) high.
£350–400 *STK*

A straw-filled plush teddy bear on wheels, c1880, 20½in (52cm) long.
£270–300 *AWT*

Beano 32, featuring Big Eggo, Lord Snooty and Pals, slight damage, c1939.
£165–180 *CBP*

Rover, published by D. C. Thompson, a half-yearly volume of 26 comics, 1940.
£400–450 *CBP*

The Dandy Monster Comic, 1947.
£110–120 *CBP*

Lois Lane 1, with taped spine, 1958.
£155–170 *CBP*

W. D. & H. O. Wills, Butterflies & Moths, set of 40 cigarette cards, 1938.
£30–35 *LCC*

John Player & Sons, Tennis, set of 50 cigarette cards, 1936.
£35–45 *LCC*

A poster, *Chamonix,* by F. Tamagno, c1900, 40 x 28in (101.5 x 71cm).
£2,400–2,600 *GSP*

A toy shop advertising poster, *A La Place Clichy*, signed 'E. Vavasseur', c1900, 36 x 59in (92 x 150cm).
£860–950 *S(S)*

Two 'Hold to the Light' Christmas postcards, early 1900.
£10–14 each *MRW*

A poster, *Royal Netherlands Steamship Company,* 1937.
£170–200 *VSP*

Les Sports d'Hiver Au Mont-Revard, by Roger Broders, c1930, 34 x 27in (86.5 x 68.5cm).
£1,000–1,100 *GSP*

A set of 4 Drury Lane pantomime posters, by John Hassall, one slightly damaged, 1920s, 20 x 30in (51 x 76cm).
£160–200 *DN*

An advertising poster, by Jean Cocteau, 1959, 25 x 16in (63.5 x 40.6cm).
£1,100–1,200 *S*

A poster, by Jules Chéret, 1896, 22¼ x 15¼in (56.6 x 38.5cm).
£580–650 *VSP*

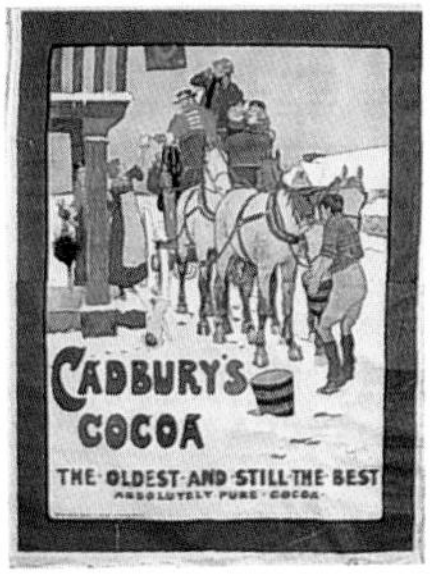

A poster advertising Cadbury's cocoa, by Cecil Aldin, 1899, 78 x 59in (200 x 150cm).
£1,600–1,750 *ONS*

A WWI recruiting poster, by Lucy Kemp-Welch, 1915, 59½ x 39in (151 x 99cm).
£700–800 *ONS*

A poster advertising New York Central Building, by Chesley Bonestell, 1929, 41 x 27in (104 x 68.5cm).
£1,300–1,500 *VSP*

An Imperial Airways poster, c1935, 30 x 20in (76 x 51cm).
£700–800 *ONS*

A poster advertising Air France, 1948, 39½ x 24½in (100 x 62cm).
£350–400 *VSP*

A poster, by Marc Chagall, 1962, 38¾ x 24½in (98.5 x 62cm).
£370–400 *VSP*

A poster advertising Walt Disney's *Lady and the Tramp*, 1955, 30 x 40in (76 x 101.5cm).
£480–550 *S*

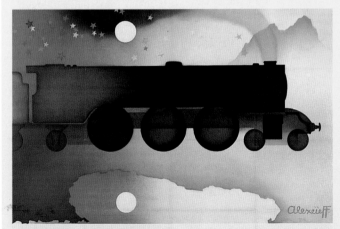

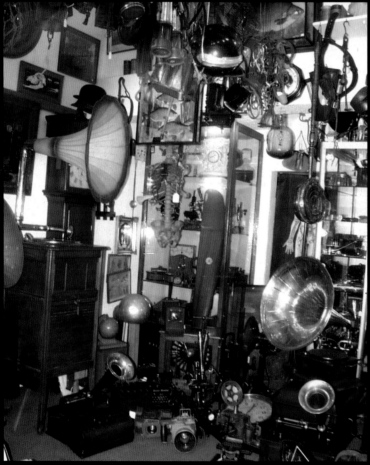

A brass calculator, by George Thorsted, New York, c1855, 9¾in (25cm) diam.
£5,200–5,800 *S*

A French single latitude sundial and compass in the form of a watch, signed 'Rousseau', c1770, 4¼in (10.5cm) diam.
£8,000–9,000 *S*

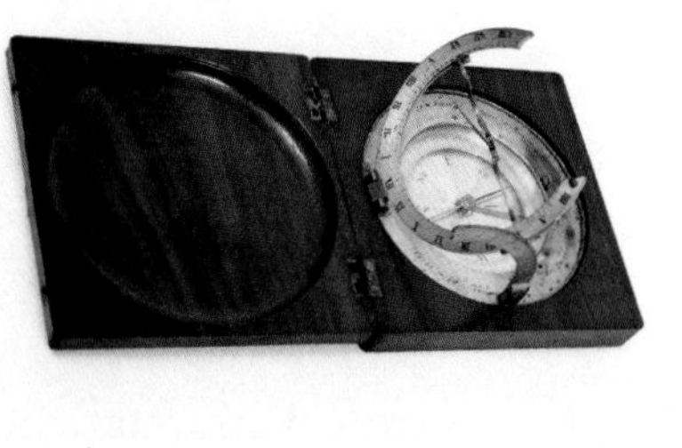

A French travelling sundial with compass, in a mahogany case, c1820, 4in (10cm) wide.
£250–300 *TOM*

A celestial globe, by Richard Cushee, 1731, 15in (38cm) diam.
£4,000–4,500 *S*

A brassed-steel timetable, with paper scales, by Thomas Dunn, 1818, 9in (23cm) diam.
£500–600 *TOM*

A pair of French table globes, signed 'Delamarche', c1800, 17in (43cm) diam.
£7,800–8,500 *S(NY)*

A celestial globe, by Malby, 1831, 16in (40.5cm) diam.
£4,700–5,200 *P(EA)*

A pair of terrestrial and celestial library globes, by James Wylde, on mahogany tripod stands with compass stretchers, c1840, 35in (89cm) high.
£8,000–9,000 *S*

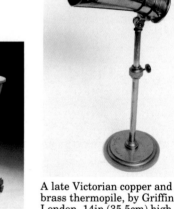

A late Victorian copper and brass thermopile, by Griffin, London, 14in (35.5cm) high.
£140–160 *ET*

A set of brass and mahogany apothecary's scales, with original weights, c1880, 10in (25.5cm) wide.
£250–280 *STK*

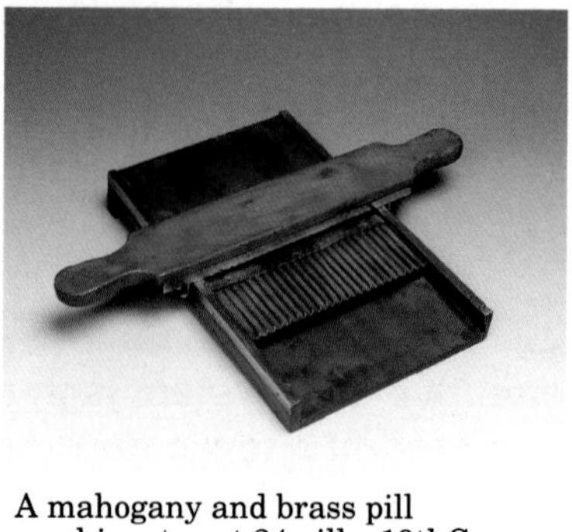

A mahogany and brass pill machine, to cut 24 pills, 19thC, 13½in (34.5cm) wide.
£180–200 *TMA*

An optometer, by Chambers, Inskeep & Co, Chicago, late 19thC, 23in (58.5cm) wide.
£600–700 *ET*

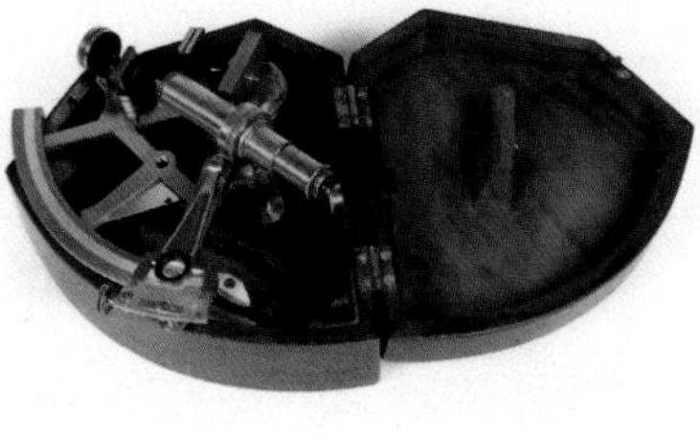

A miniature sextant, by Troughton & Simms, c1835, 7in (18cm) wide.
£2,000–2,200 *DHo*

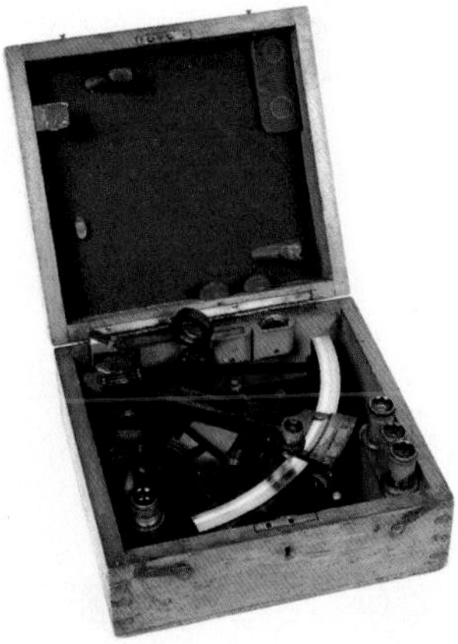

A lattice frame vernier sextant, late 19thC, 11in (28cm) wide.
£500–600 *NC*

A German WWII chronometer, 7in (18cm) square.
£3,500–4,000 *MJa*

A pair of German WWII 7 x 50 Marine Artillery observation binoculars, by Huet, Paris, 10¼in (26cm) high, with original case.
£200–250 *MJa*

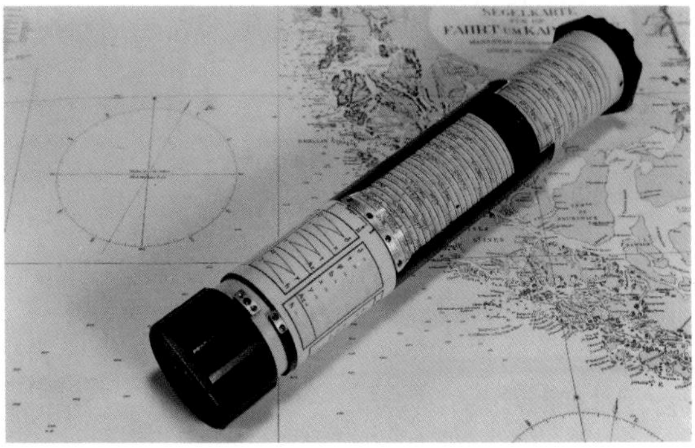

A German WWII naval issue MHR-1 navigator's slide, by Dennert & Pape, Hamburg-Altona, 11¼in (28.5cm) long.
£120–150 *MJa*

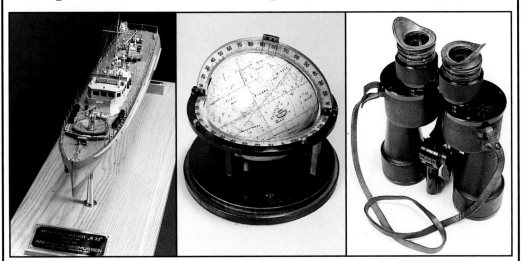

A half model of a Grimsby trawler, mounted on a wooden plaque, c1900, 34in (86.5cm) wide.
£325–375 *Tem*

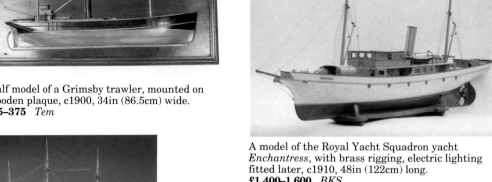

A model of the Royal Yacht Squadron yacht *Enchantress*, with brass rigging, electric lighting fitted later, c1910, 48in (122cm) long.
£1,400–1,600 *BKS*

A fruitwood model of a merchant ship, with 24 hinged gun ports, the deck with figures, 3 boats with oars and accessories, late 18thC, 41in (104cm) long.
£33,000–38,000 *S*

A pair of carved wood dioramas, in parquetry-inlaid walnut frames, each arched top with a stained wood ship, mid-19thC, 26¾in (68cm) wide.
£4,800–5,300 *S(S)*

A French bone model of a 40-gun ship, made by a prisoner-of-war, c1800, 18in (45.5cm) long.
£11,500–13,000 *S*

A painted and varnished wood model of a rigged clipper, on a mahogany stand, late 19thC, 28¼in (72cm) long.
£340–400 *Bea(E)*

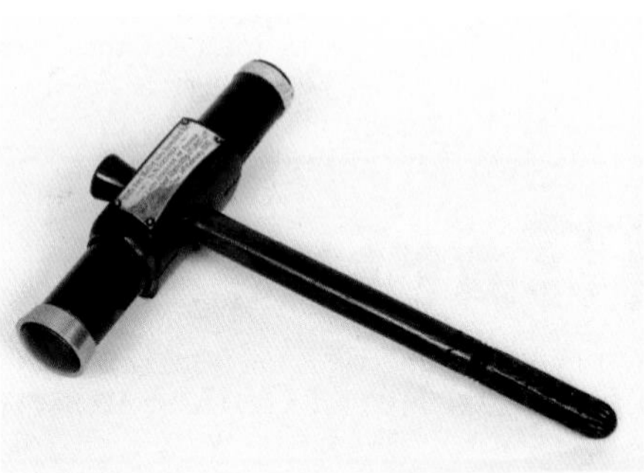

A mahogany launching mallet, with inscribed silver plaque, from the SS *Redsea*, 1930, 11in (28cm) long.
£270–300 *NC*

A turtle shell, painted with a brig within a rope surround, mid-19thC, 23in (58.5cm) wide.
£1,300–1,500 *S*

A carved and painted wood female figurehead, arms missing, late 19thC, 52in (132cm) high.
£10,500–12,500 *S*

Two ship's cannons, signed 'J. J. Wolfe, Southampton', with moulded bands and ball terminals, mounted on oak stepped four-wheeled carriages with brass furniture and iron rings, c1840, 26in (66cm) long.
£9,500–10,500 *DN(H)*

A naval officer's leather-covered oak travelling trunk, the lid mounted with an oil on canvas depicting a clipper, the brass key surround cast 'J. Gieve & Sons', mid-19thC, 42in (106.5cm) wide.
£8,000–9,000 *S*

A composite field armour, with German form close helmet, gorget of 3 lames, mid-16thC, 64in (162.5cm) high.
£18,000–20,000 *WSA*

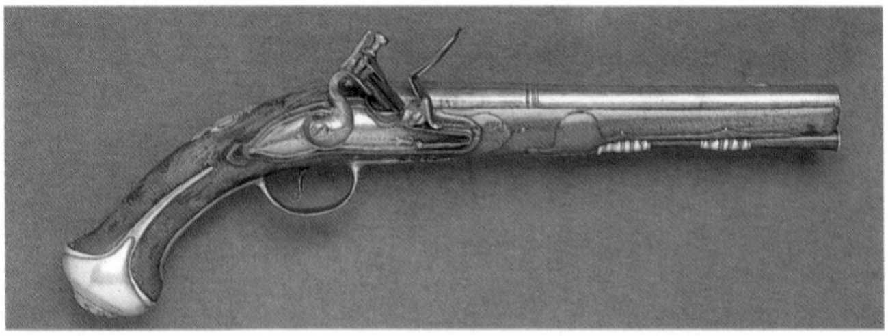

A silver-mounted flintlock pistol, by Le Maire, the 10in (25.5cm) two-stage barrel in .64 calibre smoothbore, London proof mark, c1700.
£1,750–2,000 *B&B*

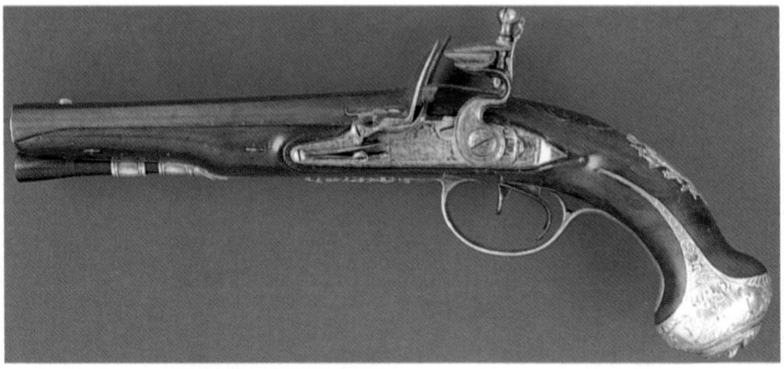

A double-barrelled silver-mounted flintlock carriage pistol, by Henry Hadley, London silver hallmarks for 1765, maker's mark of John King, 24½in (62cm) long.
£3,200–3,500 *Bon*

A pair of flintlock holster pistols, by Smurthwaite, the 11in (28cm) two-stage barrels with swamped muzzles and rings at the breech, Birmingham proof marks, c1715.
£4,750–5,250 *WSA*

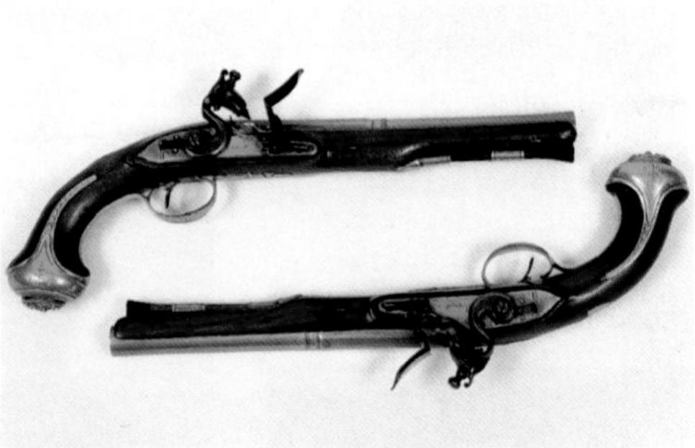

A pair of flintlock holster pistols, by Bennett, London, with walnut full stocks, c1771, brass barrels 8¾in (22cm) long.
£3,400–3,800 *GV*

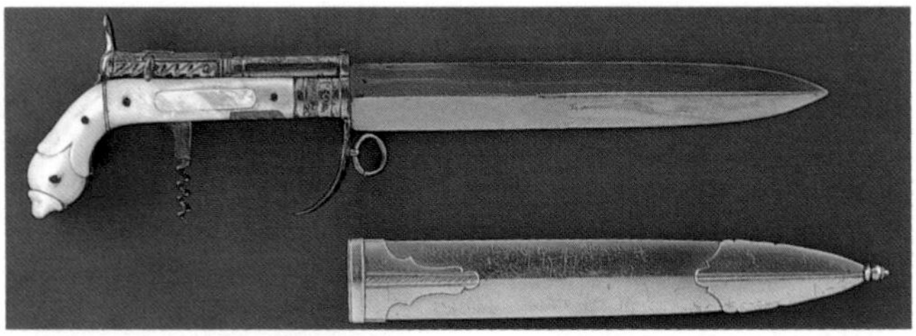

A European combination knife pistol, with a pull-down trigger in the form of a corkscrew, late 19thC, double-edged blade 9in (23cm) long.
£4,500–5,000 *Bon*

A Royal Paisley Volunteers gorget, c1800, 4in (10cm) wide.
£620–750 *BOS*

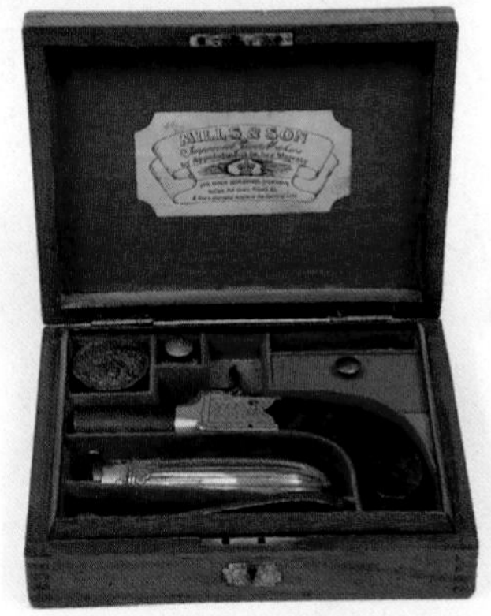

A percussion manstopper pistol, by Mills & Son, c1835, 7in (18cm) long.
£850–1,000 *GV*

A Georgian officer's short coatee of the Hereford Local Militia Archenfield Battalion.
£500–550 *WAL*

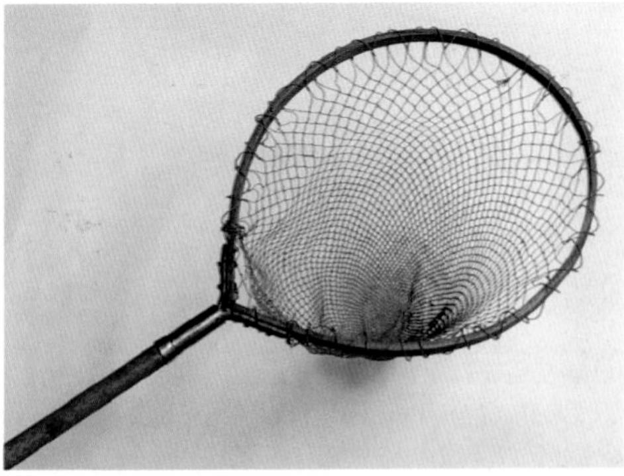

A Hardy fishing net, the wooden hoop with brass fittings, c1890, 60in (152.5cm) long.
£180–200 *RTh*

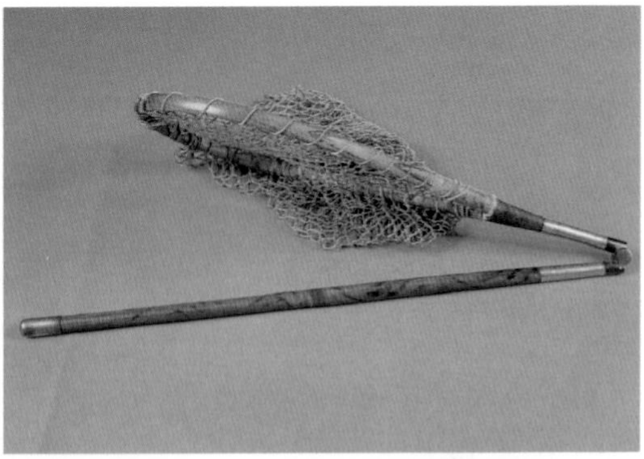

An ash-headed trout landing net, with folding handle, c1910, 42in (106.5cm) extended.
£80–120 *OTB*

A Hardy Perfect 4¼in brass-faced salmon fly reel, c1900.
£500–600 *OTB*

A Hardy leather fly wallet, c1910, 7 x 5in (18 x 12.5cm), with a selection of flies.
£350–400 *RTh*

An Allcock Coxon Aerial reel, with wood backplate, c1910, 4in (10cm) diam.
£500–600 *OTB*

A Hardy Eureka 3⅜in trotting reel, with alloy drum, c1940.
£280–350 *OTB*

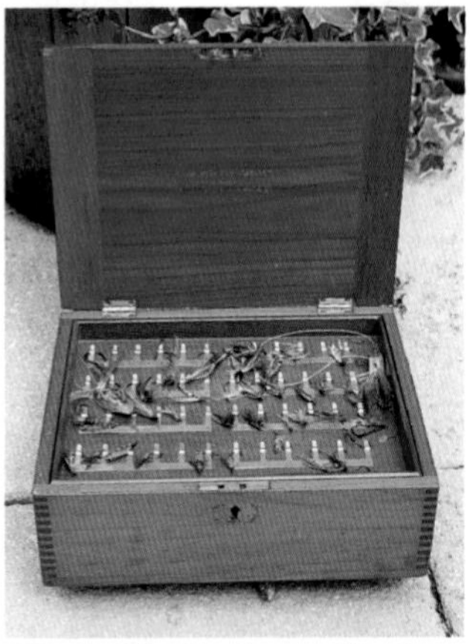

A Hardy 'The Roxborough' salmon fly box, c1914, 10in (25.5cm) wide.
£2,400–2,750 *MUL*

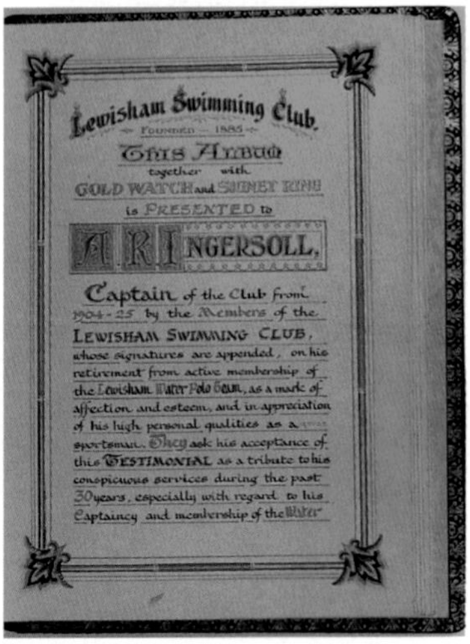

A presentation album, with a framed print and swimming vest, c1908.
£150–200 *WaR*

A silver-plated inkstand, surmounted by a fisherman, on a mahogany base, c1900, 12½in (32cm) wide.
£350–400 *CHe*

An England rugby cap, with tassel, worn by G. Hubbard, 1925.
£180–200 *WaR*

A mahogany billiard table, by E. J. Riley, 1928, 84in (213.5cm) long.
£2,500–2,800 *CBC*

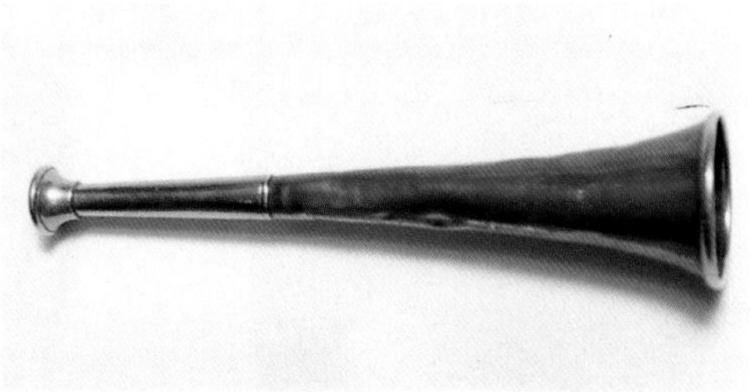

A silver and copper hunting horn, c1910, 9in (23cm) long.
£80–90 *RTh*

A bisque figure, by Salvetti, 1897, 16in (41cm) high.
£1,600–1,800 *MUL*

A Victorian mahogany billiard ball box, by Burroughes & Watts, 12in (30.5cm) wide.
£250–300 *CBC*

An oak cue stand, by George Wright, c1870, 52in (132cm) high.
£1,600–1,800 *CBC*

An Irish red walnut kneehole desk, c1750, 36½in (92.5cm) wide.
£4,500–5,200 *MEG*

An Irish flame mahogany serpentine tea table, c1790, 37in (94cm) wide.
£5,000–5,500 *CHA*

A pair of George III mirrors, 18in (45.5cm) wide.
£16,000–18,000 *S(NY)*

A Killarney marquetry-inlaid table, with scalloped edge, c1870, 3½in (9cm) diam.
£7,500–8,250 *ORE*

An oak bench/table, carved by Killarney students for Princess May, 1893, 36in (91.5cm) diam.
£4,500–5,000 *ORE*

A Belleek earthenware bowl, 1891–1926, 5in (12.5cm) diam.
£600–650 *MLa*

A Belleek Aberdeen jug, 1926–46, 9½in (24cm) high.
£675–750 *MLa*

A Belleek earthenware jug, transfer-printed and hand-painted, 1863–90, 8in (20cm) high.
£700–800 *MLa*

A Irish panelled pine coffer, with original painted finish, c1790, 46in (117cm) wide.
£450–500 *TPC*

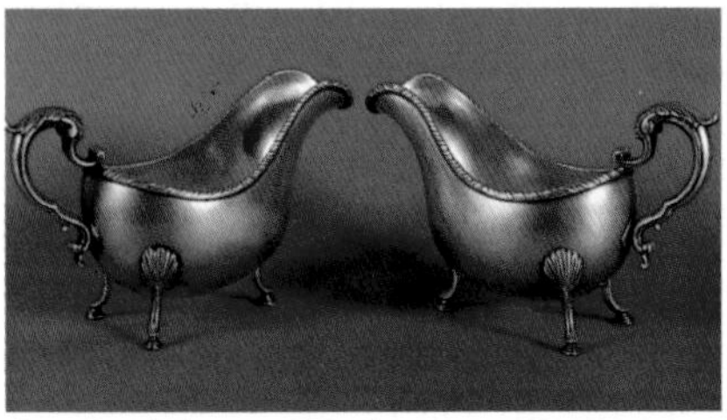

A pair of George III silver sauceboats, with gadrooned rims, by Thomas Jones, Dublin 1778, 26½oz.
£2,800–3,200 *JAd*

A Belleek Tridacna pink coffee pot, with gilding, 1926–46, 7½in (19cm) high.
£270–300 *MLa*

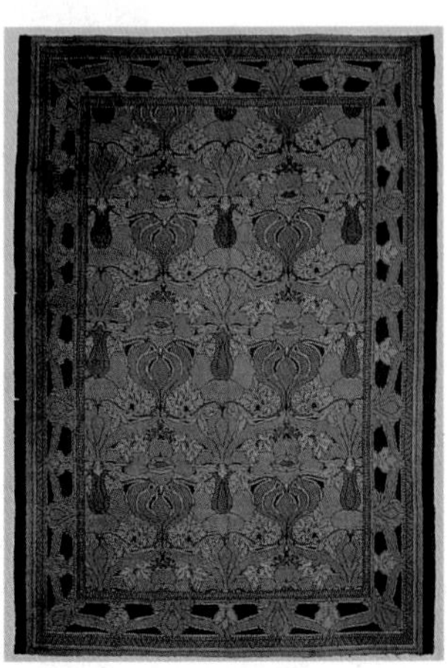

A Donegal wool carpet, made for Liberty & Co, c1900, 224 x 157½in (570 x 400cm).
£18,000–20,000 *P*

CAMERAS

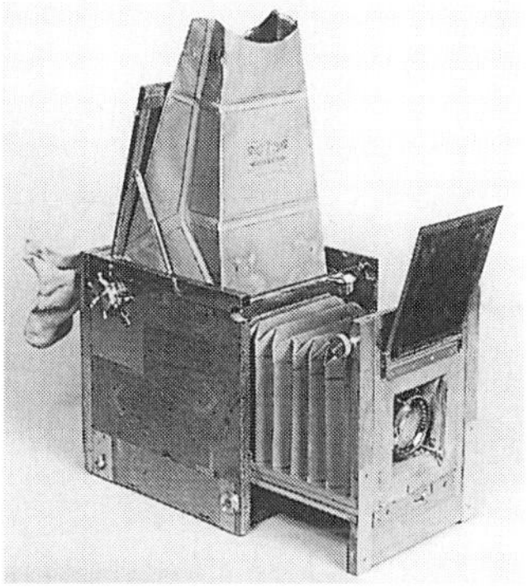

An Adams & Co Minex tropical plate camera, with teak body and lacquered brass fittings, with a Ross 8½in (21.5cm) pres 1:4.5 lens No. 104745, in maker's case, 1910.
£2,750–3,000 *P(Ba)*

An Agfa Colourflex camera, c1963.
£80–100 *VCL*

An Agfa Movexoom 10 sound camera, c1970.
£80–100 *VCL*

A mahogany and brass half-plate field camera, by William Butcher & Sons, London, 1920.
£120–150 *TOM*

A Canon FTb camera, c1971.
£80–100 *VCL*

A Corfield Periflex camera, with a Lumax f/1.9 45mm inter-changeable lens, c1955.
£200–220 *CaH*

l. A Contax IIIA camera, c1957.
£350–400 *VCL*

r. An Eastman Kodak 3A folding Hawk-eye model 4 camera, with Bausch & Lomb rapid rectilinear lens, c1902.
£70–80 *CaH*

l. A Kodak Retina Reflex S Type 034 camera, with a Schneider Retina-Xenar lens 2.8 50mm, c1959.
£100–120 *CaH*

Cameras

Unlike many other collectables, a camera's age is not necessarily reflected in its value. The rarity and quality of a particular model are often far more important than when it was made.

Japanese cameras, which have enjoyed an upsurge in popularity recently, were mass produced in the aftermath of WWII. Their quality became widely appreciated as a result of photojournalists covering the Korean War recognising the superior quality of Japanese lenses. Today, rare and limited edition models by companies such as Nikon or Canon can fetch very high prices.

A Goerz camera, with Dogmar 4.5 12.5cm lens, c1921.
£80–90 *CaH*

A Houghton Ensign Selfix Autorange 16–20 camera, c1955.
£180–200 *VCL*

A Leica model M-3 single stroke conversion camera, with 5cm 1.5 summarit lens, serial No. 748091, 1954–6.
£850–950 *JAA*

A Minolta SR-1 camera, 1959.
£80–100 *VCL*

A Houghton Ensign Midget camera, c1936.
£60–70 *VCL*

A Leica II No. 192857 camera, with a Leitz Elmar 1:3.5 lens, No. 340374, 1926–31.
£260–300 *P(Ba)*

A Leitz Leicina Super camera, with a Vario f/1.9 8-64mm lens, c1971.
£280–320 *CaH*

A Microflex MPP camera, c1959.
£100–120 *VCL*

l. An MPP Mark VIII field camera, c1965.
£350–400 *VCL*

r. A Nikon f2 camera, with photomic body.
£270–300 *VCL*

A Houghton Ensign Selfix 820 fixed lens camera, with a Ross Xpres 3.8 105mm lens, c1950.
£60–80 *CaH*

A Leica black and nickel camera, c1936.
£450–500 *VCL*

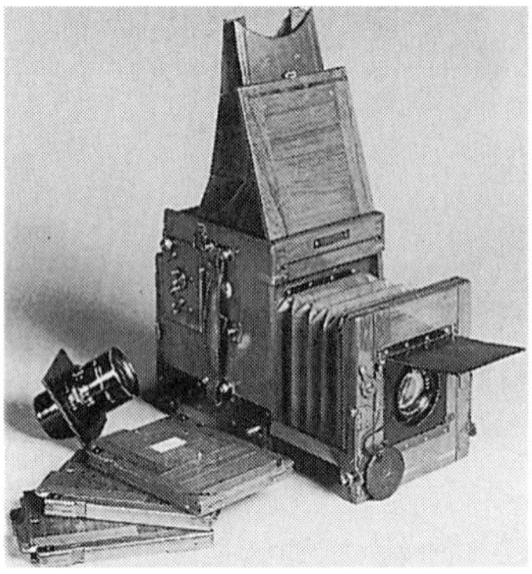

A Marion & Co Ltd Soho Tropical reflex camera, with a Carl Zeiss Tessar 1:4.5 f/18cm lens No. 215682, a Ross of London Telecentric 1:6.8 f=13in lens No. 75611, with fitted case and Gandolfi tripod, 1900–20.
£2,300–2,600 *P(Ba)*

A Minolta SR-7 camera, c1962.
£70–80 *VCL*

A Nikon FM2 camera No. 7133784, with a Nikon Nikkor 50mm 1:1.8 lens No. 3197915, together with a Jessop power-winder Model N-27R, 1970s.
£230–260 *P(Ba)*

A Sanger, Shepherd & Co mahogany half-plate tailboard camera, with bellows and Ross 7in Goerz patent aluminium lens in Koilos shutter, together with accessories, late 19thC.
£230–250 *Bon*

A Voigtländer Superb camera, 1933.
£220–250 *VCL*

r. A Voigtländer Bessa RF with yellow filter, Helomar f/3.5 10.5cm lens, c1936.
£280–320 *CaH*

A Pathe Baby with Camo Motor 9.5 cine camera, with Hermagis f/3.5 20mm lens, 1926–27.
£100–120 *CaH*

A Stirn No. 1 vest camera, the body engraved 'J. Robinson & Sons, Patentees Agents', contained in original retailer's box with a quantity of unused glass plates, German 1886–92.
£1,000–1,200 *S*

A Voigtländer Perkeo II camera, with Color-Skopar f/3.5 80mm lens, c1952.
£130–160 *CaH*

l. A W. Watson & Son stereoscopic binocular camera, with Krauss Tessar lenses, in maker's leather carrying case, 1897.
£1,000–1,200 *P(Ba)*

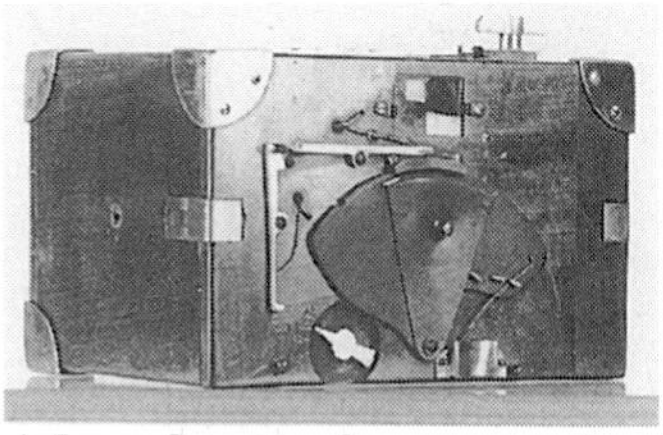

A Luzo detective box camera, by H. J. Redding & Gyles, London, for rollfilm with f/8 lens and sector shutter, with leather case, 1896–99.
£600–700 *Bon*

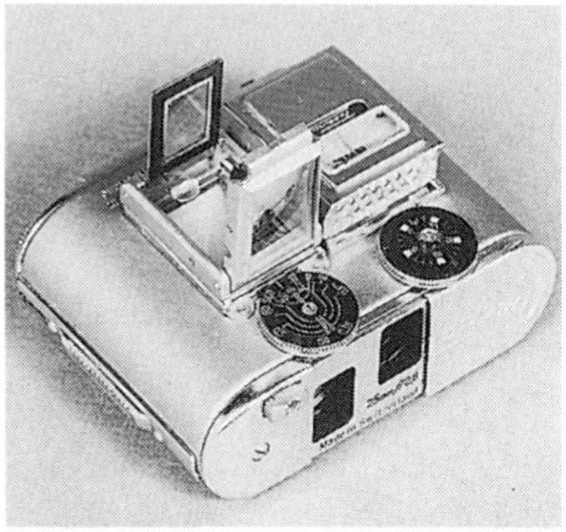

A Tessina 35mm automatic camera No. 464178, with a gold-coloured and chrome metal body, waist level finder and a f/2.8 25mm lens, in Tessina fitted case, together with a Tessina film winder, 1930s.
£700–800 *P(Ba)*

A Voigtländer Bergheil camera, 1933.
£180–200 *VCL*

A Voigtländer Stereflektoskop camera, with triple Heliar 1:4.5 f=75mm lenses No. 804163, No. 808333, No. 804614, with hinged lens cap, plate changing mechanism, 1930s.
£300–330 *P(Ba)*

A Wunsche Reicka camera, with Ross London Zeiss Tessar f/6.3 136mm lens, 1906.
£50–70 *CaH*

A Zeiss Contax II interchangeable lens camera, with a Zeiss Sonnar lens f/2 50mm, c1936.
£280–320 *CaH*

A Zeiss Ikon baby box camera, c1935.
£80–90 *VCL*

A Zeiss Contax camera, c1936.
£70–80 *VCL*

Prices

The price ranges quoted in this book reflect the average price a purchaser would expect to **pay** for a similar item. When selling expect to receive a lower figure. The price will fluctuate according to the condition, rarity, size, colour, provenance and restoration of the item and must be taken into account when assessing values.

A Zeiss Ikon Super Ikonta camera, c1939.
£280–300 *VCL*

A Zeiss Ikon Super Ikonta camera, 1940.
£350–400 *VCL*

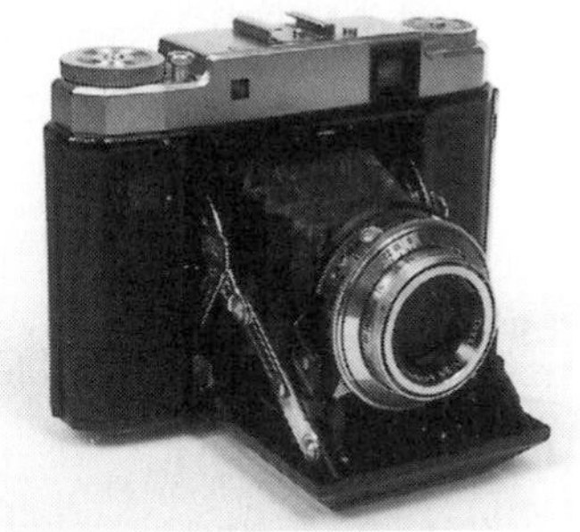

A Zeiss Ikon Super Ikonta camera, c1958.
£220–250 *VCL*

Miscellaneous

A wet plate sliding box form camera, screen and dark slide missing, 1860–70.
£320–400 *HEG*

A mahogany sliding box camera, for 3¾ x 2½in (9.5 x 6.4cm) exposures, with screw clamp adjustment and sliding plate holder, and 3 lenses, mid-19thC.
£160–200 *Bon*

A Salex Junior dark room enlarger, by City Sale and Exchange Ltd, London, c1920.
£90–120 *ET*

ARMS & ARMOUR

Armour

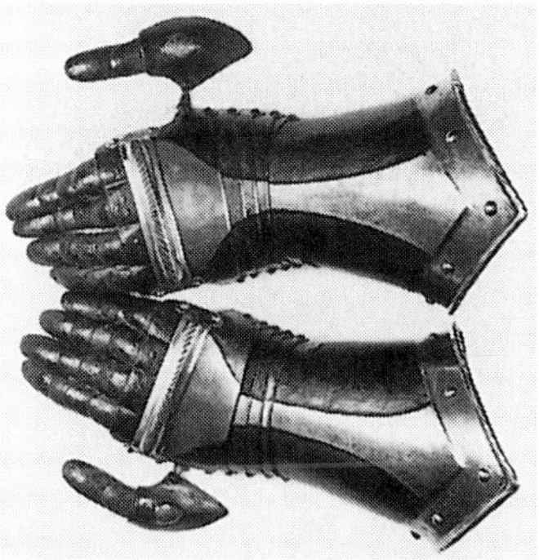

A pair of articulated gauntlets, composed of 6 lames with additional thumb plates and fully articulated fingers, mid-16thC, 12in (30.5cm) long.
£600–700 *ASB*

A Turkish turban helmet, with 2 bands of damascened calligraphy and motifs, extensive old repair, 16thC.
£5,500–6,000 *GSP*

An Italian close helmet, with one-piece skull, visor with damaged peak, pistol proofed pointed upper bevor, late 16thC.
£2,400–2,800 *GSP*

A burgonet, with two-piece skull, decorated with radiating bands and borders formed with pairs of incised lines, English or Flemish, c1630.
£2,800–3,200 *S(S)*

Cromwellian Armour

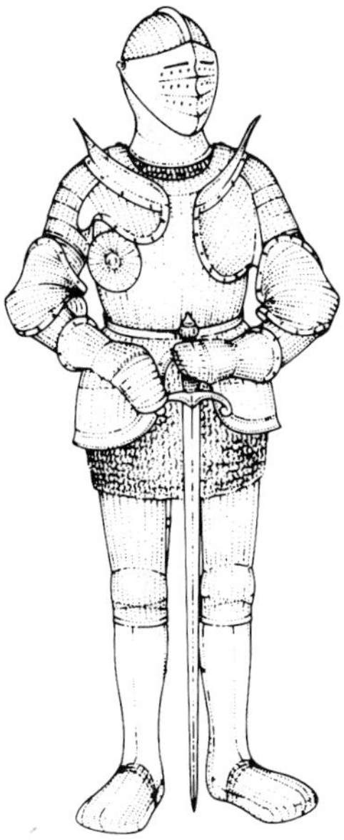

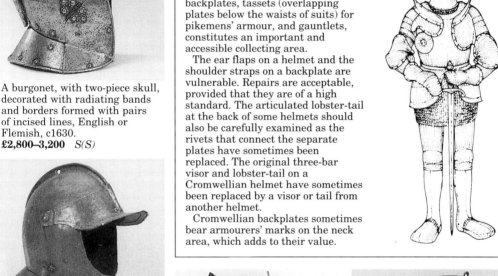

Cromwellian armour, including 'lobster-tailed' helmets, pikemens' pots (simple helmets), breast and backplates, tassets (overlapping plates below the waists of suits) for pikemens' armour, and gauntlets, constitutes an important and accessible collecting area.

The ear flaps on a helmet and the shoulder straps on a backplate are vulnerable. Repairs are acceptable, provided that they are of a high standard. The articulated lobster-tail at the back of some helmets should also be carefully examined as the rivets that connect the separate plates have sometimes been replaced. The original three-bar visor and lobster-tail on a Cromwellian helmet have sometimes been replaced by a visor or tail from another helmet.

Cromwellian backplates sometimes bear armourers' marks on the neck area, which adds to their value.

A Dutch harquebusier's close helmet, the two-piece skull decorated with pairs of incised lines, c1630, 12in (30.5cm) high.
£1,200–1,300 *S(S)*

A Civil War period Cavalry breastplate, damaged, c1640.
£400–450 *Bon*

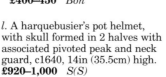

l. A harquebusier's pot helmet, with skull formed in 2 halves with associated pivoted peak and neck guard, c1640, 14in (35.5cm) high.
£920–1,000 *S(S)*

A Continental Cavalry trooper's helmet, the one-piece skull embossed with 4 radial ribs and adjustable nasal bar, the ear flaps pierced and with cut-outs to increase lateral vision, c1630.
£850–950 *WAL*

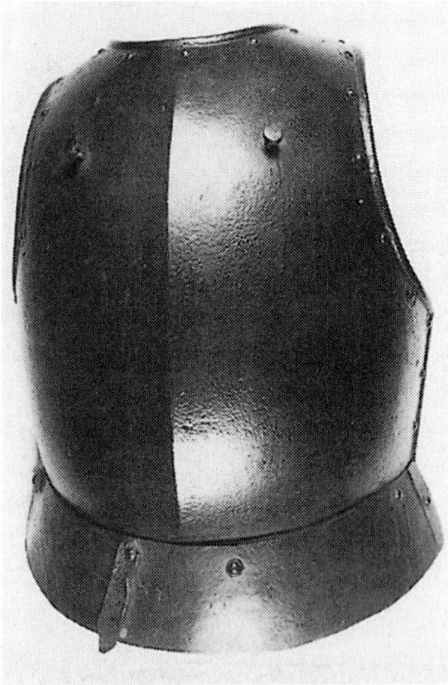

A pikeman's breastplate, with separate skirt for the attachment of tassets, the front with 2 projecting knobs for securing strap from the backplate, mid-17thC, 18in (45.5cm) high.
£600–650 *ASB*

A Cromwellian lobster-tail pot helmet, the pointed brim with turned rim and mounting retaining the sliding nasal, mid-17thC.
£630–700 *B&B*

A central/eastern European lobster-tail pot helmet, with one-piece fluted skull, the nose guard replaced, late 17thC.
£3,200–3,500 *GSP*

A lobster-tail pot helmet, with original ear pieces, late 17thC.
£800–900 *Bon*

An Indo-Persian chainmail shirt, made of small riveted rings, long sleeves with butted brass rings to cuffs, short collar, open front with split skirt, 18thC, 36in (91.5cm) long.
£700–800 *WAL*

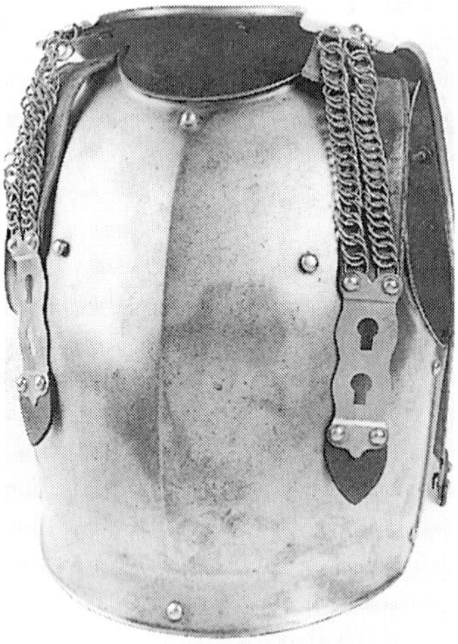

A French curassier's breast- and back-plate, complete with original brass and leather straps, interior of the backplate dated 'May 1828'.
£450–500 *Bon*

Cannons

A model 24PDR bronze cannon and iron-mounted mahogany garrison carriage, built for Colonel Williams's 'New Invention', engraved on the chase and with the arms of the Dukes of Newcastle, dated '1782', 16in (41cm) long.
£1,750–2,000 *S(S)*

A Spanish bronze howitzer, the short barrel in 4 stages with simple astragals adapted with grooves both for sighting and for fitting a vent patch (not present), dated '1788', barrel 33½in (85.5cm) long.
£2,700–3,000 *S(S)*

Two bronze saluting cannons, by Lang, London, each engraved with owner's initial 'N' and Order of the Garter with ducal coronet above, dated '1828', and '1839', barrels 20½in (52cm) long.
£5,300–5,800 *S(S)*

r. A pair of iron cannons, the 59¾in (152cm) barrels mounted on old wooden carriages with iron fittings, 62¼in (158cm) overall.
£1,600–1,800 *P(WM)*

Why send it for auction... when you can have CASH TODAY and no commision to pay

We buy from many of the major UK auction houses and will view collections anywhere in the UK. Before you sell, make sure you call us. We will be happy to give advice without obligation.

Send TODAY for our fully illustrated catalogue (cost, £5 including P&P) which offers the largest selection of antique weapons available by mail order in the UK.

With over 800 expertly described and photographed items, it is an invaluable publication for the collector of antique arms & armour.

We pay top prices for good quality antique weapons, pistols, long arms, swords etc

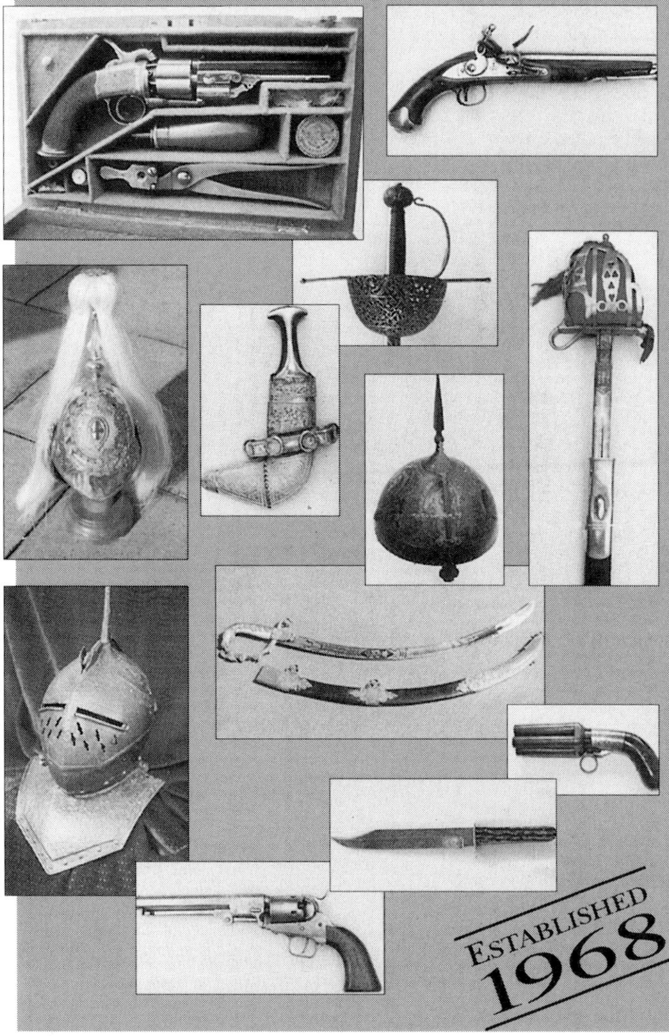

Please telephone or write to:

ANDREW SPENCER BOTTOMLEY

The Coach House, Thongsbridge, Holmfirth,
West Yorkshire HD7 2TT, ENGLAND
Tel: 01484 685234 Fax: 01484 681551 Mobile: 0860 620933

CALLERS BY APPOINTMENT ONLY PLEASE

Email 101661.2007@compuserve.com

Axes & Halberds

l. An executioner's axe, the 12½in (32cm) cutting edge stamped with 2 armourer's marks. *r.* A large doloire fighting axe, with 17in (43cm) cutting edge, armourer's marks and eyebrow stamping, 16thC.
£950–1,100 each *GV*

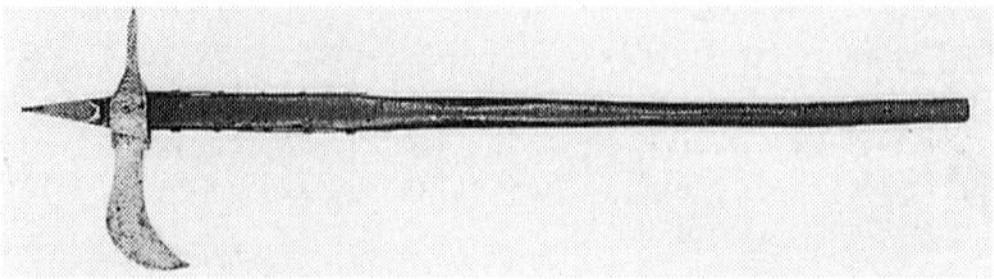

A horseman's poleaxe, the two-piece head on a wooden haft, possibly Swiss, c1700, head 9in (23cm) long.
£2,000–2,200 *S(S)*

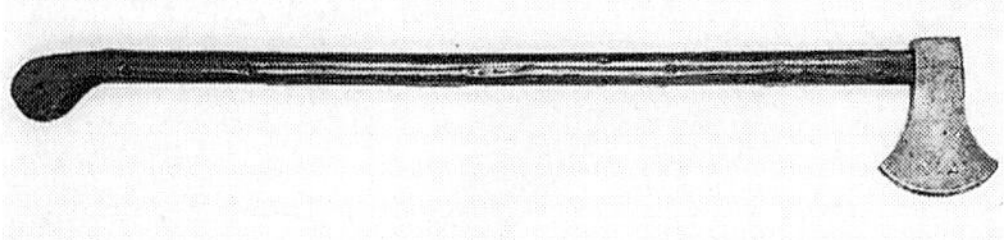

A Polish horseman's fighting axe, the original fruitwood haft formed with a swelling pommel, pierced for a thong, c1700, head 5in (12.5cm) long.
£700–800 *S(S)*

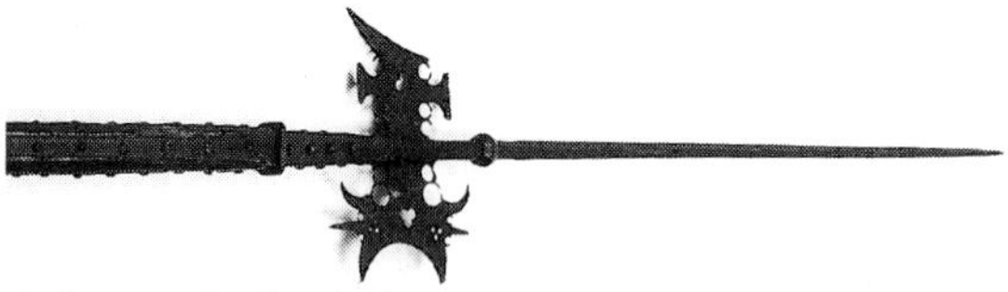

A German halberd, the 39½in (100cm) head with a 31½in (80cm) spike and iron straps, late 16thC.
£700–800 *GV*

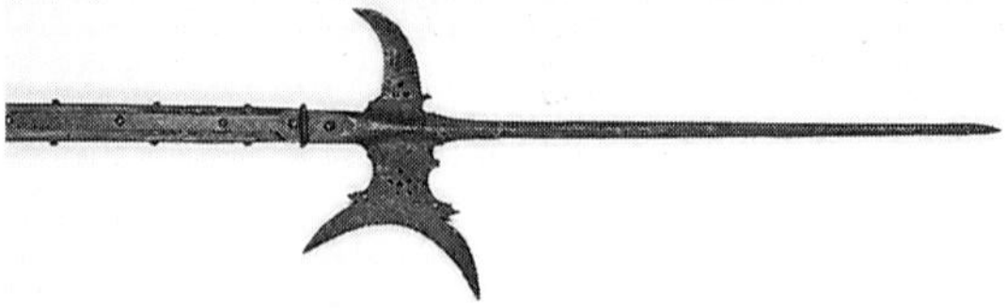

A halberd, the crescentic axe-blade with concave edge and curved beak-shaped fluke, on wooden staff covered with red fabric studded with brass-headed nails, late 16thC, head 28in (71cm) long.
£450–500 *Bon*

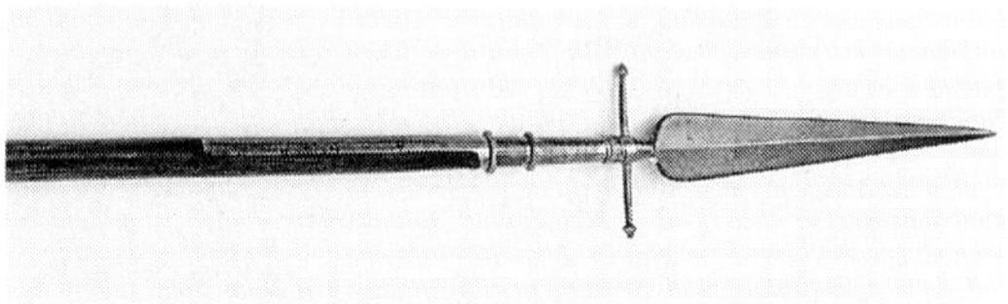

A Napoleonic War British military spontoon, the steel head engraved 'Blackman', on an ash wood shaft, the head can be unscrewed into 3 sections, 80in (203cm) long.
£800–900 *BOS*

A spontoon is a type of halberd often carried by junior infantry officers and senior non- commissioned officers.

Daggers

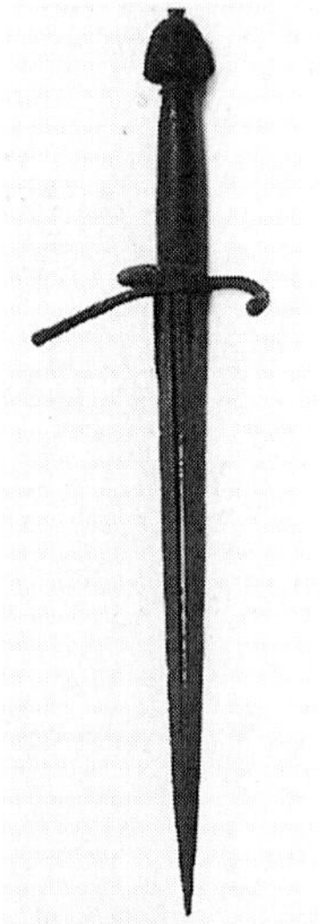

A German left-hand dagger, the lozenge section short blade with deep central pierced fullers, excavated condition, late 16thC, 14½in (37cm) long.
£400–450 *GSP*

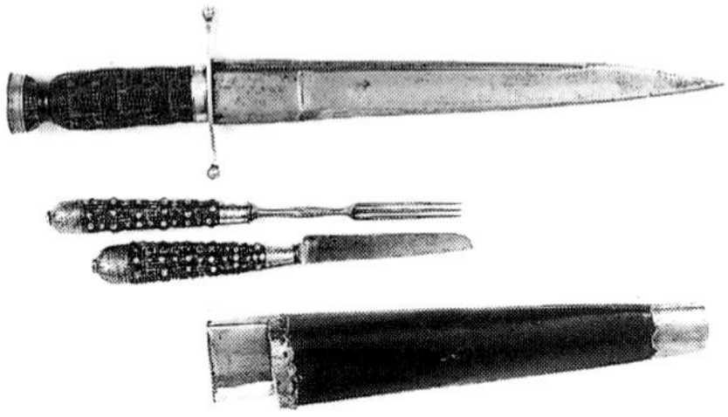

l. A Scottish silver-mounted dirk, c1780, 15in (38cm) long.
£700–800 *BWA*

German Daggers

The Nazis introduced dagger fetishism into 1930s Germany. The most common daggers of the period are those of the German army, navy and airforce, but there were many more patterns such as those of the Nazi Red Cross, Diplomatic Service, Hitler Youth, Railway Protection, Land Customs and so on.

r. A Nazi Radman's dagger, with horn grip, the shaped steel blade fitting into a black metal scabbard with silver-plated mounts, 1930s, 15½in (39.5cm) long.
£270–300 *DD*

An Indian kattar, the armour piercing blade with gold *koftgari* decoration to grip and guard, early 19thC, blade 6½in (16.5cm) long.
£220–260 *Bon*

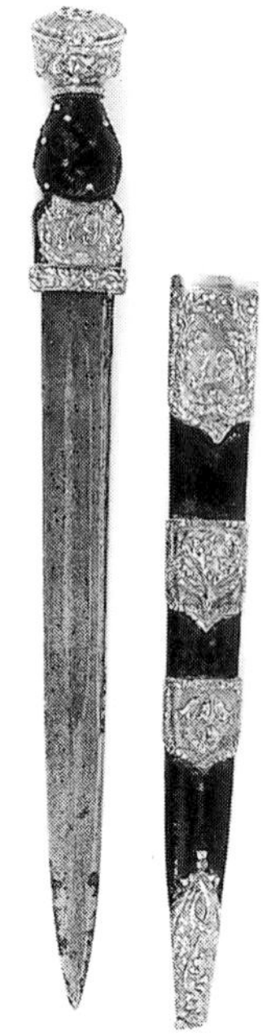

A Cameron Highlanders silver-plated dirk, c1860, 18in (45.5cm) long.
£600–700 *BWA*

Firearms

Blunderbusses

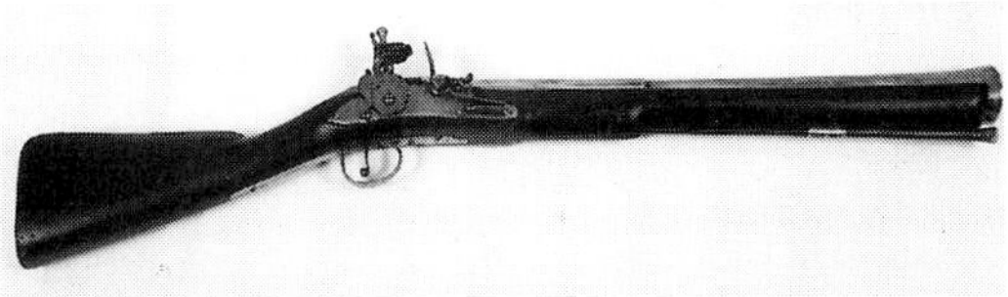

A doglock blunderbuss, the 22½in (57cm) brass three-stage barrel with strawberry leaf engraving and London proofs, the lockplate engraved and signed 'Annelly', the elm fullstock painted black with brass furniture, c1685.
£2,800–3,250 *WSA*

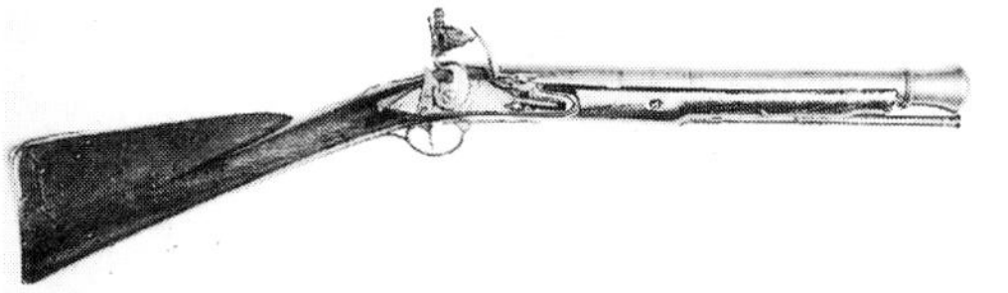

A flintlock blunderbuss, by Michael Memory, Southwark, with three-stage brass barrel signed at the breech, walnut fullstock, engraved brass mounts and early form of acorn finial and pierced side-plate, later iron saddle-bar, and ramrod, London proof marks, mid-18thC, 32in (81.5cm) long.
£600–700 *Bon*

Carbines

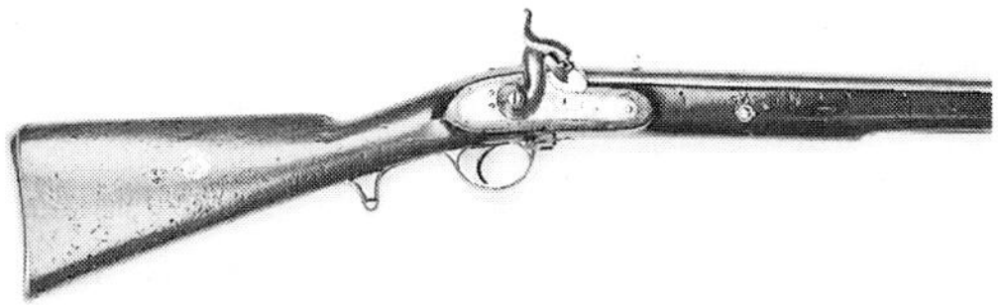

A Yeomanry percussion carbine, the sighted barrel with walnut full stock and regulation brass mounts, with iron saddle-bar, ring and stirrup ramrod, dated '1844', barrel 20in (51cm) long.
£450–500 *Bon*

Proof Marks

Most English firearms from the 18thC onwards bear the viewing mark (of the checker) and the proof mark on the barrel, guaranteeing that it was safe to fire at the time of examination. Many pistols imported into England from Europe during the 19thC bear the Belgian Liège proof mark. Some Continental guns can be found with English proof marks.

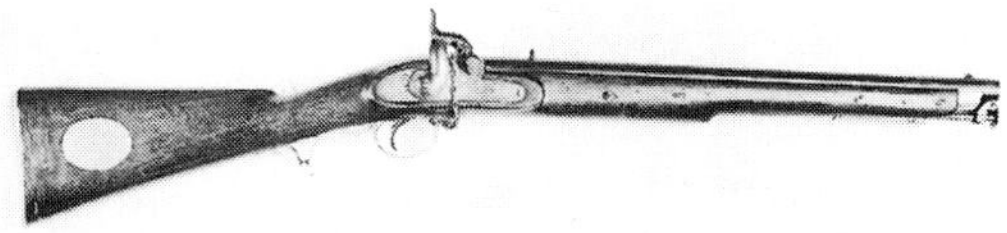

A Victorian percussion Cavalry carbine, associated with the 13th Light Dragoons Charge of the Light Brigade, the 19¾in (50cm) sighted barrel with figured walnut stock butt and regulation brass mounts, the iron saddle-bar with ordnance view and proof marks, dated '1847', 35¾in (91cm) long overall.
£2,000–2,200 *Bon*

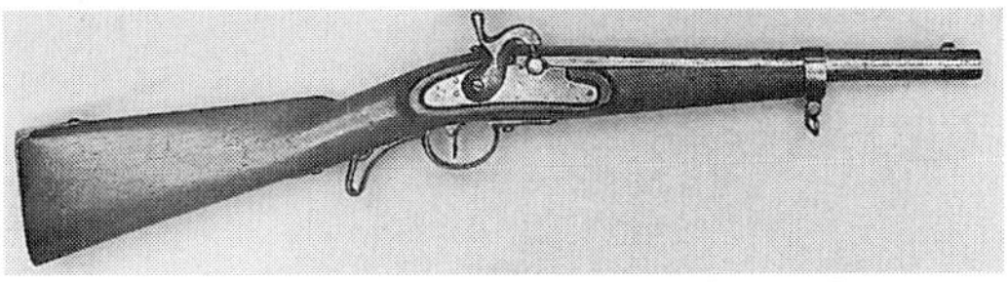

An Austrian 12 bore percussion Cavalry carbine, with Birmingham proofs, converted from flintlock with breech drum, the lock stamped with crown and 'Tower 1865', walnut three-quarter stock with steel mounts, 1865, 30in (76cm) overall.
£280–320 *WAL*

Blunderbusses

Blunderbusses have a flared barrel to enable different sizes of shot to be loaded. Although some have a bayonet or bayonet fitting they were not necessarily intended for army use. Brass was commonly used for blunderbuss barrels as it weathers the elements far better than steel.

An Italian flintlock blunderbuss, with folding butt, signed 'M. Guratti', the iron barrel inlaid with partly engraved brass foliage, engraved tang, signed lock, moulded highly figured walnut three-quarter stock sparsely inlaid with silver wire scrollwork, shaped iron mounts, mid-18thC, barrel 19¾in (50cm) long.
£650–750 *Bon*

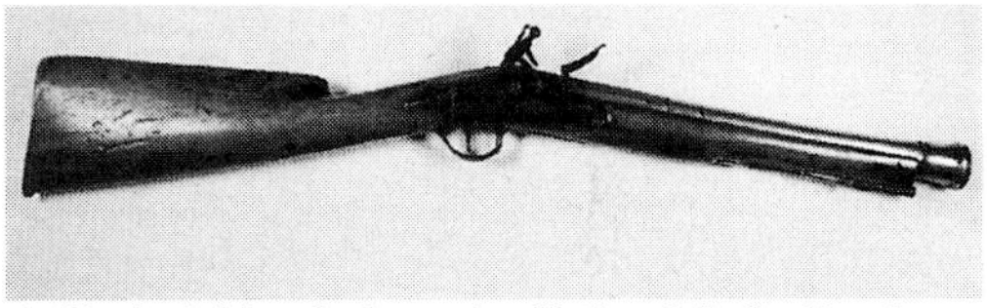

A flintlock blunderbuss, by Ketland & Co, London, the brass barrel with breech section bearing the crowned crossed sceptres proof marks reserved for private arms by the board of ordnance, the walnut stock with straight hand wrist, and brass furniture, c1800, barrel 15¼in (38.5cm) long.
£1,000–1,150 *ASB*

Pistols

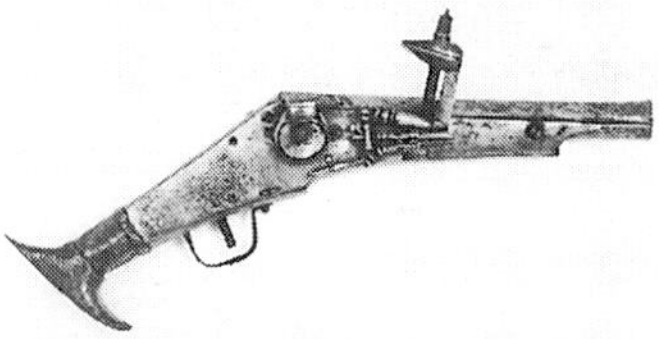

A German wheel-lock pistol, the 15½in (39.5cm) steel body struck with Nuremberg town marks and control and gunsmith's stamp, with fish tail butt, lacks ram rod, late 16thC.
£3,600–4,000 *GSP*

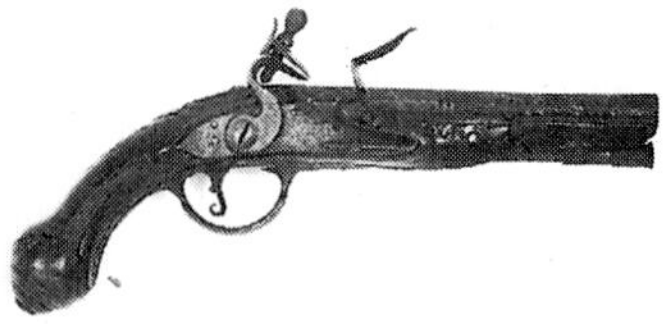

A Spanish flintlock pocket pistol, the 5½in (14cm) two-stage barrel with Castille stamp and 10 fleur-de-lys stamps, in distressed carved walnut stock with chiselled mounts, early 18thC.
£200–220 *GSP*

A Queen Anne flintlock belt pistol, by James Freeman, the 5¼in (13.5cm) cannon barrel with London proofs and maker's mark 'IF' on faceted breech, the walnut butt with silver mounts including side plate, butt cap and escutcheon, c1720.
£1,400–1,600 *WSA*

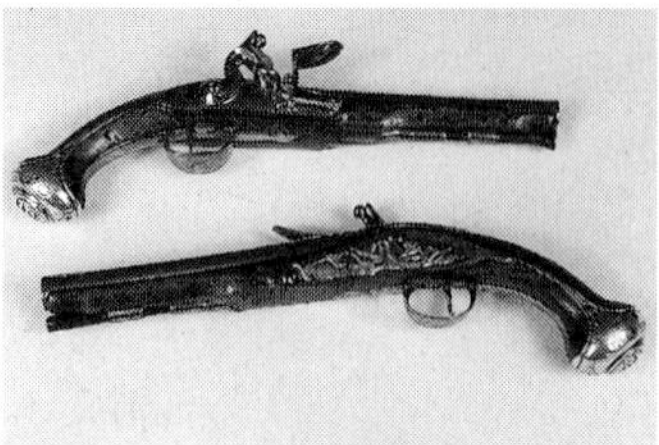

A pair of flintlock holster pistols, the engraved 7½in (19cm) three-stage barrels with London proofs and maker's mark 'RW', signed 'London', the walnut fullstocks with silver long spur butt caps, escutcheons and side plates, mid-18thC.
£4,500–5,000 *WSA*

The escutcheons are engraved 'These pistols were carried by Sir P. Ainslie at the Battle of Dettingen, 1743'.

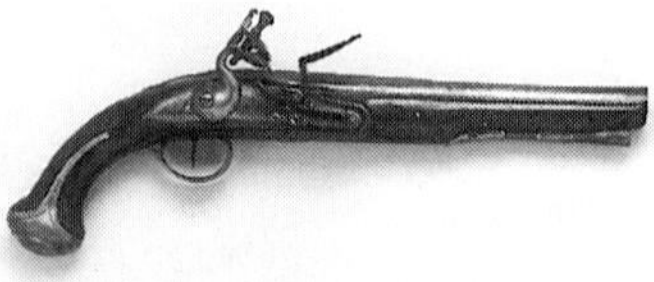

A pair of flintlock pistols, by Clarkson, the 9in (23cm) .65 calibre barrels with slightly swamped muzzle, the breech sections marked 'London', London proofs, engraved brass furniture and full walnut stocks, c1760, 15¼in (38.5cm) long.
£1,600–1,800 *B&B*

Handling Firearms

Never assume a gun is unloaded – a 100 year-old powder charge inside a barrel can still ignite. If in doubt, treat the gun as loaded and seek expert advice.

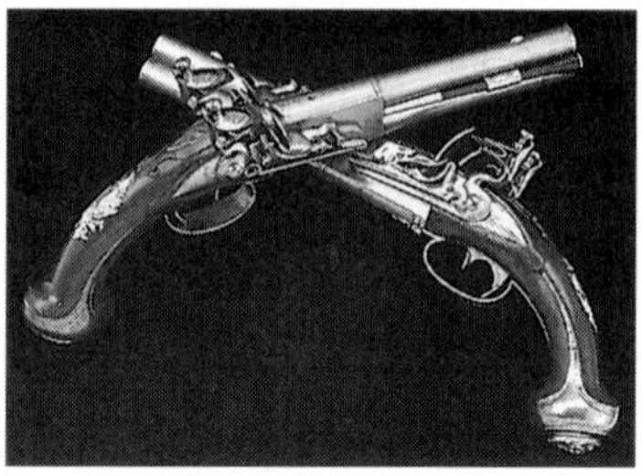

A pair of flintlock over-and-under holster pistols, by James Barbar, London, with engraved breeches, one signed and one inscribed 'London', fitted with external mainsprings and large steel-springs, the moulded figured walnut butts each carved with a shell, silver trophy-of-arms escutcheons engraved with a crest, original iron-mounted whalebone ramrods, c1765, 14¼in (36cm) long.
£7,000–8,000 *S(S)*

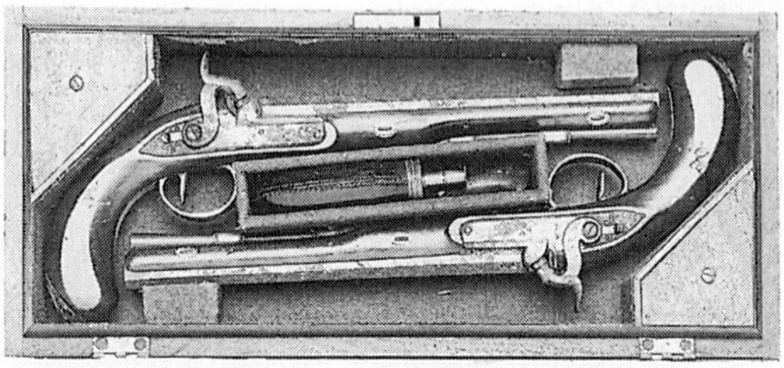

A pair of percussion duelling pistols, with 10in (25.5cm) sighted octagonal barrels signed in gold 'Wogdon, London', full stocked with silver mounts, the butts with oval silver escutcheons engraved with owner's crest and initials, complete with wood ramrods, hallmarked London 1779 and mark of John King, in baize-lined mahogany case.
£4,200–4,600 *Gle*

An officer's brass-barrelled pistol, by Ketland & Adams, London, c1790, 15in (38cm) long.
£750–850 *GV*

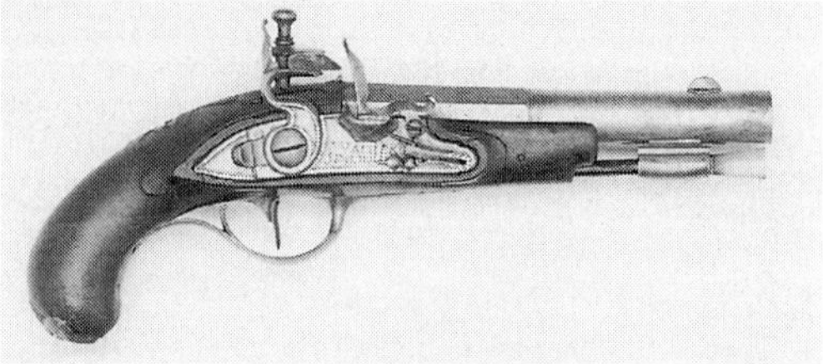

A pair of Swedish flintlock pistols, by Wahlberg, the two-stage barrels lightly swamped towards the muzzles, the walnut half-stocks carved with a flower in low relief behind the barrel tangs, horn-tipped wooden ramrods, original condition, late 18thC, 9½in (24.5cm) long.
£1,600–1,800 *S(S)*

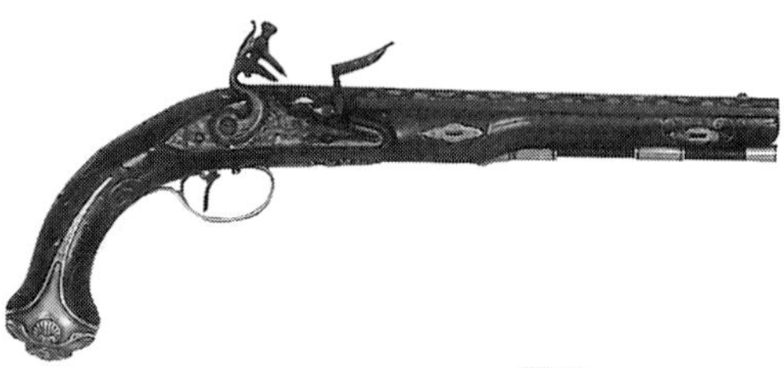

An Indian silver-mounted flintlock 24 bore pistol, by Master Claude Martin, for Lucknow Arsenal, the 10in (25.5cm) barrel chiselled with foliate meanders on a gilt ground, groove sight and gold-lined vent, the ornate silver trigger guard with vase of flowers terminal, late 18thC.
£5,500–6,000 *GSP*

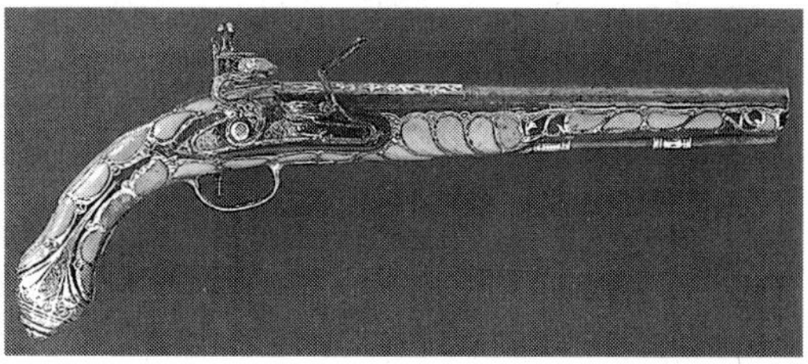

r. A north African silver and coral-mounted flintlock holster pistol, c1900, 18in (45.5cm) long.
£4,200–4,600 *Bon*

A pair of percussion pistols, the side plates and damascus barrels, foliate engraved, incribed 'H. W. Mortimer, London', with steel furniture and walnut butts, the unmarked silver cartouches inscribed 'V. S.', early 19thC, barrels 5½in (14cm) long, in a lined mahogany case, with various accessories.
£1,250–1,400 *WW*

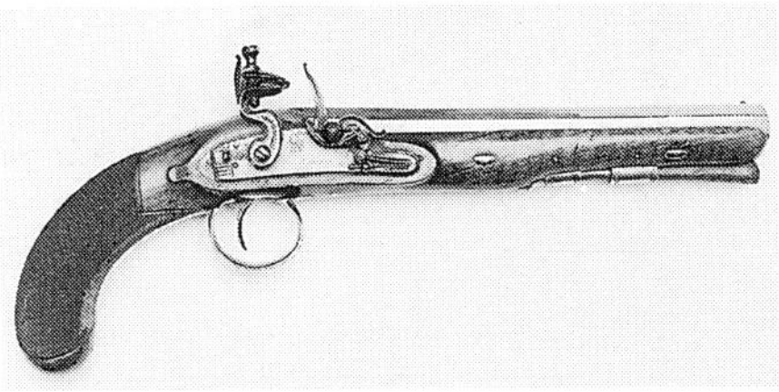

l. A pair of brass-barrelled flintlock pistols, signed 'Rawson, Norwich', the octagonal sighted barrels with engraved tangs, figured walnut full stocks and wooden ramrods, early 19thC.
£1,800–2,000 *Bon*

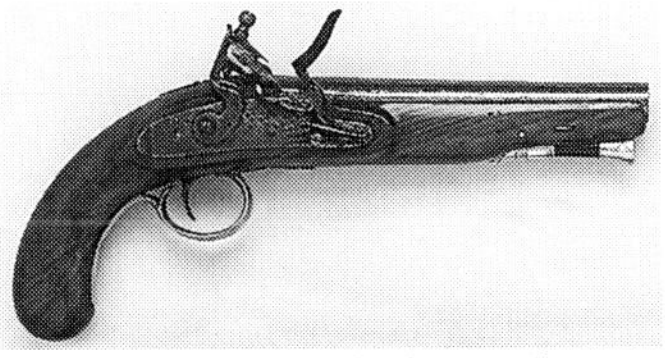

An American flintlock pistol, the 7½in (19cm) round barrel in .56 calibre smoothbore, with walnut fullstock, early 19thC, 12in (30.5cm) long.
£500–550 *B&B*

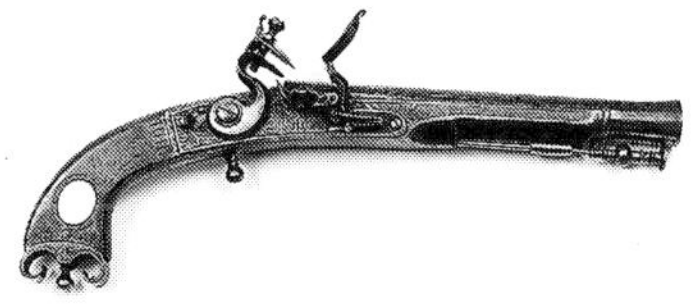

A Scottish steel flintlock pistol, by Ross of Edinburgh, the 7¼in (18.5cm) barrel with steel ramrod and belt hook, the ram's horn butt with pricker and silver escutcheons, c1815.
£1,300–1,600 *GV*

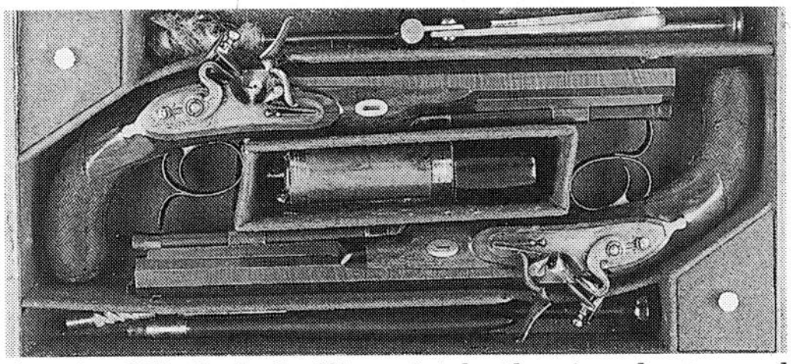

A pair of flintlock duelling pistols, the signed octagonal damascus barrels with platinum-lined breeches, stamped 'Joseph Manton, London', half-stocked with horn fore-end caps, chequered butts with silver escutcheons, complete with horn-tipped wood ramrods, with accessories, c1830, barrels 9¾in (25cm) long.
£8,000–9,000 *Gle*

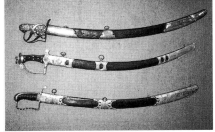

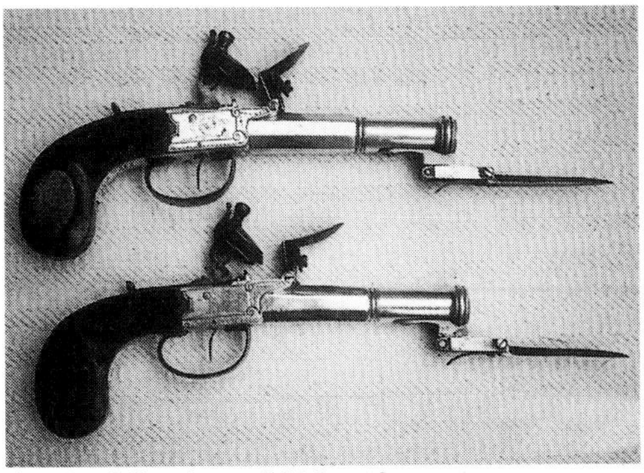

A pair of Continental 50 bore brass cannon barrelled boxlock flintlock travelling pistols, the barrels fitted with spring bayonets, the square-sided frames engraved with flowers and foliage, the walnut grips with silver wire-inlaid decoration, c1820, barrels 3½in (9cm) long.
£1,600–1,800 *ASB*

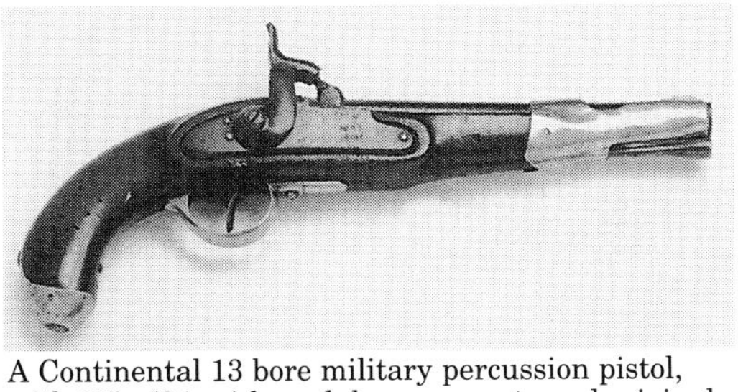

A Continental 13 bore military percussion pistol, with 9½in (24cm) barrel, brass mounts and original ramrod, mid-19thC.
£200–220 *BOS*

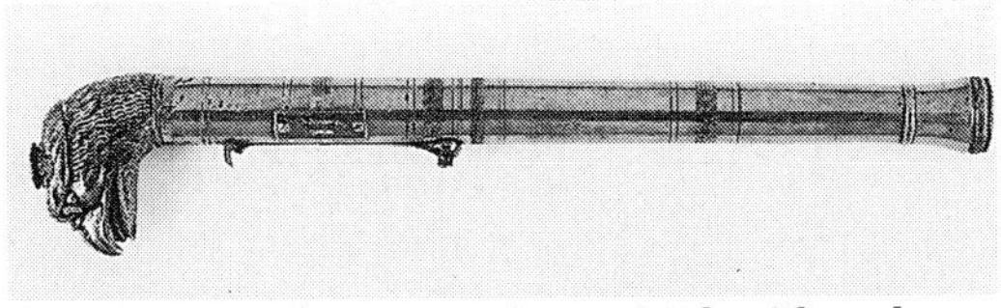

A Day's patent brass truncheon pistol, with under hammer percussion mechanism, the 8½in (21.5cm) barrel with bell mouth muzzle, the grip in the form of a bird's head, with screw cap to cavity, c1860, 15¾in (40cm) long.
£1,300–1,500 *Bon*

Revolvers

A six-shot percussion pepperbox revolver, the 2⅝in (6.5cm) barrel with Birmingham proofs, with engraved German silver frame and chequered walnut grips, c1845.
£550–600 *WSA*

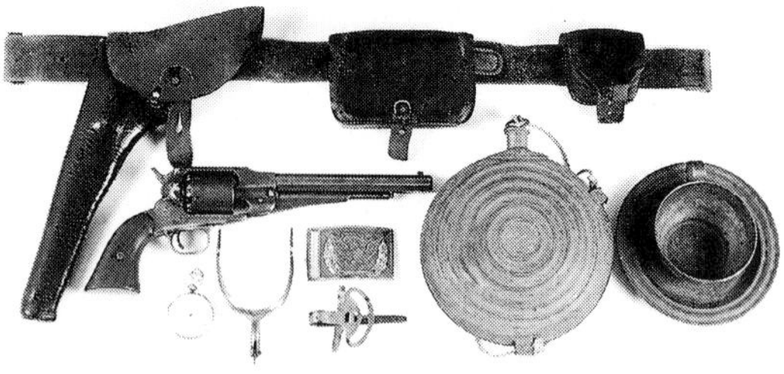

A collection of American Civil War items, belonging to Arthur Manning Rowe, Company B, 2nd New York Cavalry (1847–1917) including .44 calibre 1858 Remington new model revolver, with US issued Eagle belt plate with one-piece silver wreath, and other associated items.
£3,000–3,500 *JAA*

A cased 50 bore Deane-Adams five-shot self-cocking percussion revolver, No. 1000.2, with octagonal sighted barrel and foliate scroll-engraved frame, trigger-guard and pommel, c1850, 14¼in (36cm) long.
£500–550 *Bon*

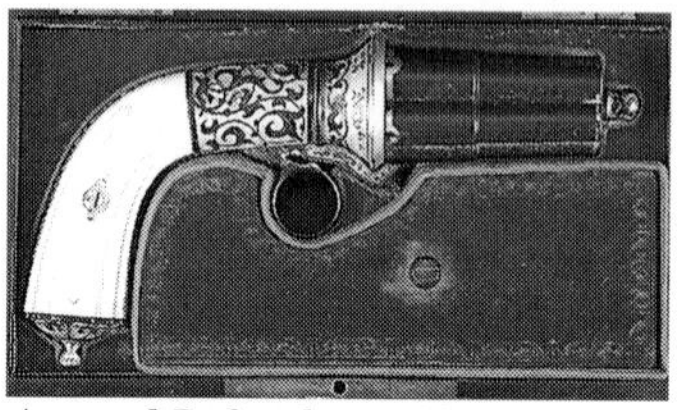

A cased Lefaucheux 10mm pinfire self-cocking pepperbox revolver, serial No. 536, the five-shot tapered 3in (7.5cm) barrel cluster with gold leaf to muzzles, cast action body with integral grip straps, the base with screw-in rod, the whole with polished foliage over stippled gold leaf covered ground, in an oak and burr walnut box, c1850.
£3,000–3,500 *Bon*

A six-shot percussion pepperbox revolver, the 2¾in (7cm) fluted cylinder with bar hammer, scroll engraved rounded nickel silver frame, with two-piece chequered grips, mid-19thC.
£270–300 *EP*

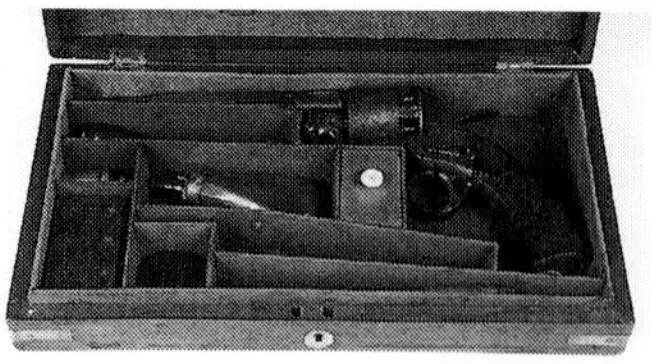

A Webley 3rd Model Longspur 48 bore revolver, No. 1080, the 6in (15cm) octagonal barrel engraved 'H. Egg, 1 Piccadilly, London', with Kerr's pattern ramrod, the 5 shot cylinder with Birmingham proofs, frame engraved, chequered walnut grips, in original brass-bound mahogany case, with accessories, c1855.
£2,200–2,500 *WSA*

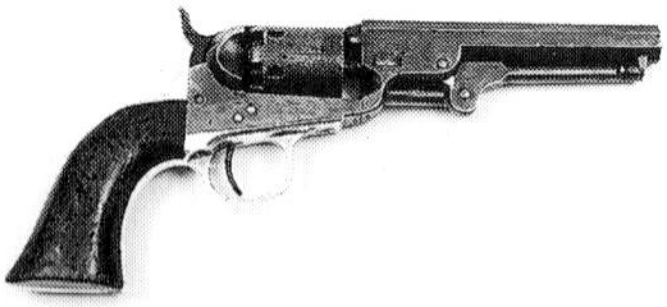

A Colt .31 calibre 6in (15cm) pocket revolver, c1860.
£500–550 *GV*

An Allen's patent pepperbox cast steel six-shot revolver, with revolving barrel, c1857, 8in (20.5cm) long.
£400–450 *GV*

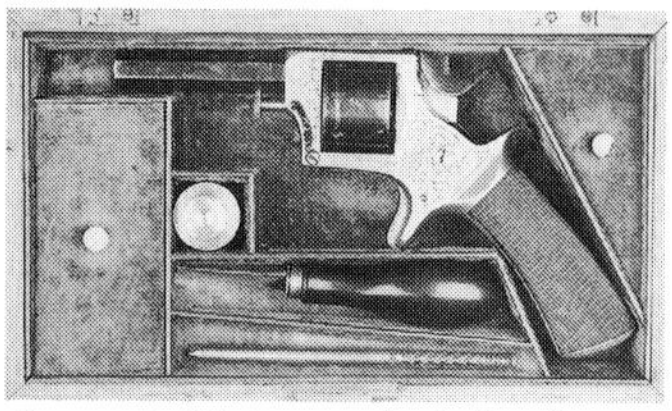

A cased .31 seven-shot rim-fire revolver of Tranter type, with octagonal sighted barrel, scroll-engraved brass frame and grip, Birmingham proof marks, in original case, with accessories, late 19thC, 7¼in (18.5cm) long.
£550–600 *Bon*

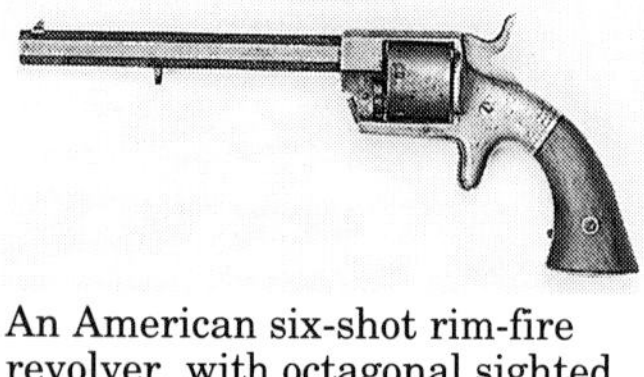

An American six-shot rim-fire revolver, with octagonal sighted barrel, stamped 'Bacon MFG. Co Norwich Con', the swing-out cylinder frame engraved with foliage and walnut grip-scales, some damage, c1860, 13in (33cm) long, in a leather holster.
£250–300 *Bon*

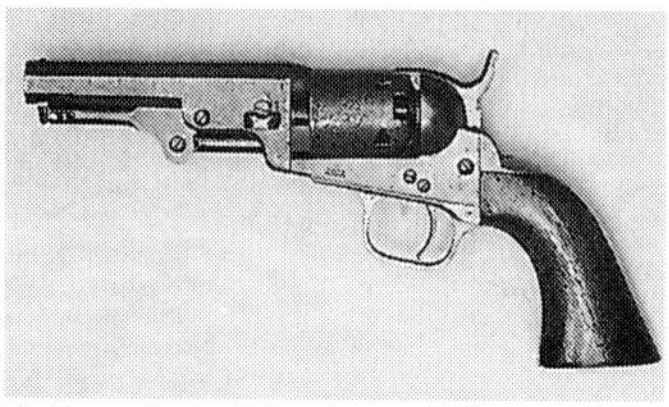

A five-shot .31 colt model 1849 SA pocket percussion revolver, the 4in (10cm) barrel with New York City address, No. 160235 on all parts, stagecoach scene on cylinder, c1849, 9in (23cm) overall.
£500–600 *WAL*

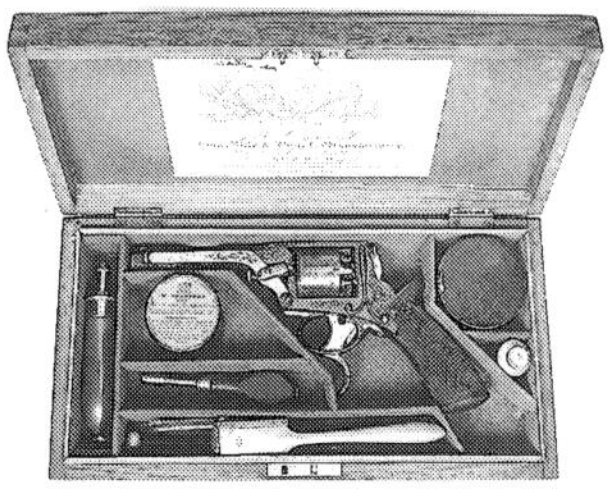

A five-shot 80 bore double trigger Tranter's patent percussion revolver, No. 15549, the 4½in (11.5cm) barrel with engraved frame, London proved, in fitted oak case with accessories, c1860, 9½in (24cm) long.
£1,850–2,000 *WAL*

l. A six-shot bar hammer percussion pepperbox revolver, the 3¾in (9.5cm) barrels with foliate-engraved muzzles, scroll-engraved German silver frame, 2 figured walnut grips, 1830–70.
£850–950 *Gle*

Rifles

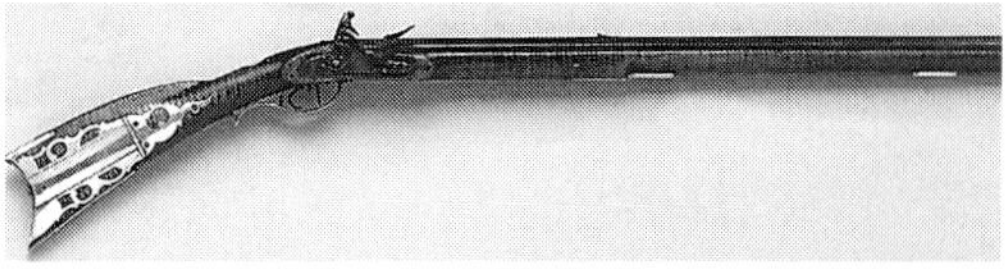

An American fullstocked flintlock rifle, by John Dreisbach, Jr, the 39in (99cm) octagonal barrel with seven-groove rifling in .50 calibre, c1820, 55in (139.5cm) long.
£2,800–3,200 *B&B*

An Enfield three-band rifle, c1857, 56in (142cm) long.
£750–850 *GV*

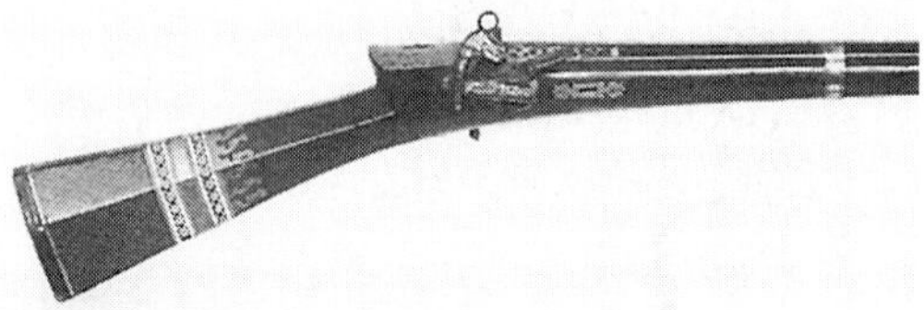

A Turkish 20 bore miquelet-lock rifle, with damascened lock, the 28¾in (72cm) barrel with scrolls to muzzle and breech, the stock with engraved brass, ivory and stained ivory decoration, 19thC.
£1,400–1,600 *GSP*

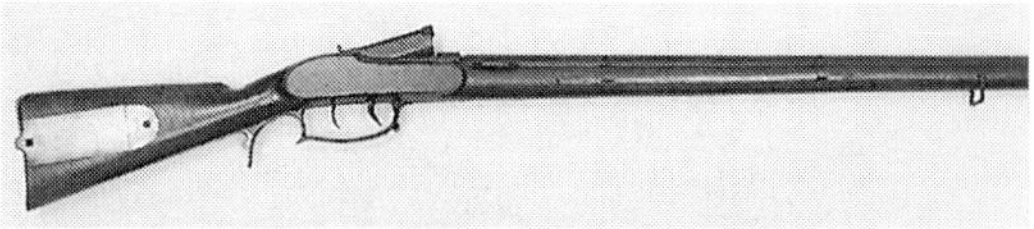

A Melville and Callow's patent breech loading needle fire military rifle, fullstocked with brass mounts, some rust, c1850, 53½in (136cm) barrel.
£850–950 *WAL*

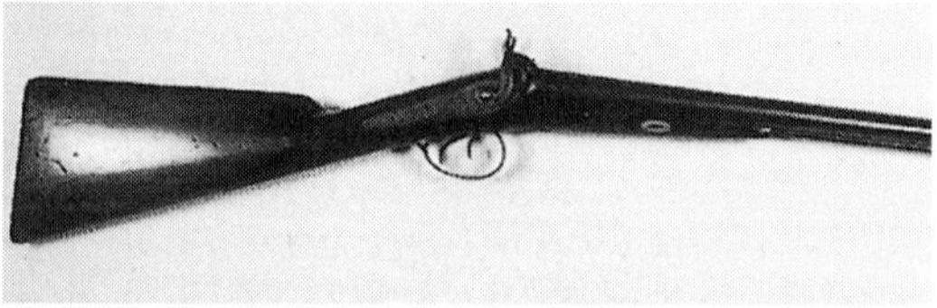

A 17 bore double-barrelled percussion shotgun, with round damascus twist barrels and concave central rib, scroll engraved back action locks, signed 'Pryor Baldock', straight hand walnut stock iron furniture, some wear, c1860, barrels 30in (76cm) long.
£350–400 *ASB*

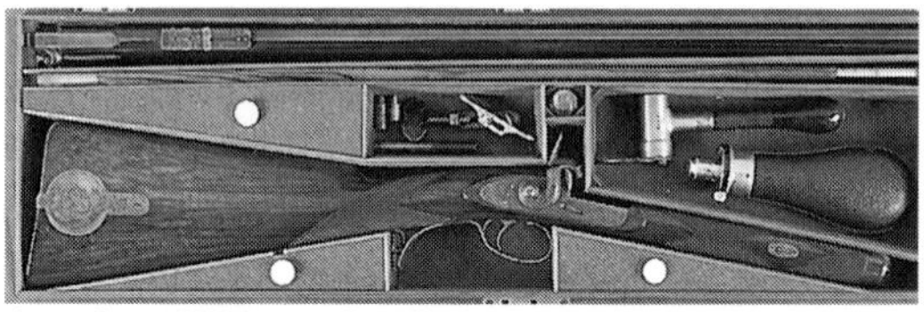

A 52 bore Whitworth rifled percussion single barrelled rifle, by the Whitworth Rifle Company, the half stock chequered at forearm and wrist with horn tip, in original mahogany baize lined box with accessories, c1860, 46in (117cm) long.
£6,500–7,000 *Bon*

Swords

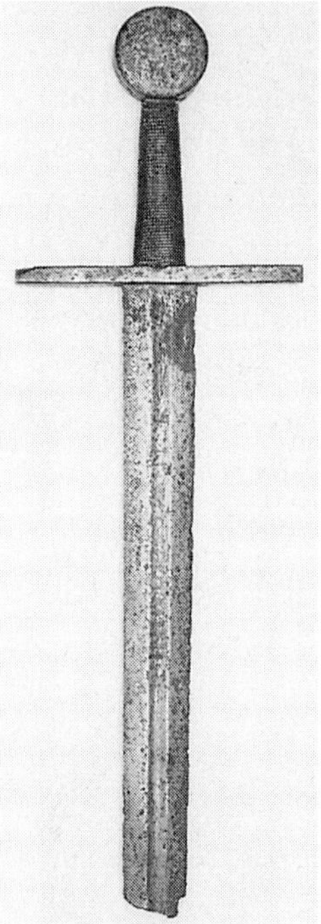

A medieval sword, the remaining portion of the double-edged blade with a narrow fuller on both sides, inscribed 'Inimoi-Homini', inlaid in soft iron, robust guard, the tang with later cord-bound grip, 13thC, blade 14¾in (37.5cm).
£2,800–3,200 *S(S)*

r. A European broadsword, c1700, 36in (91.5cm) long.
£280–350 *BWA*

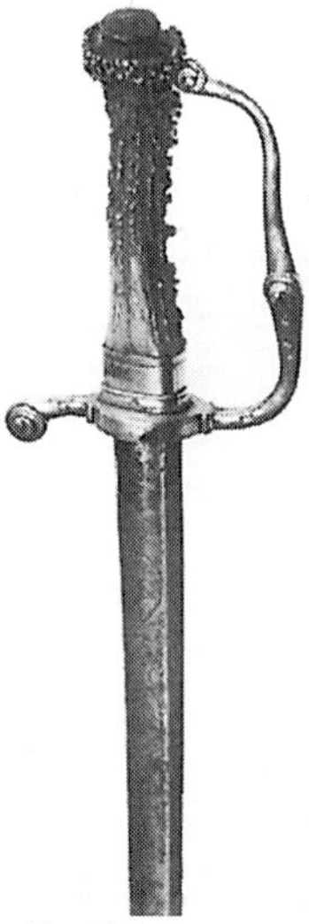

An English hanger, the silver-gilt knuckle guard with central ammonite scroll, terminal and quillon, with staghorn grip, the gently curved single-edged blade with wide fullers etched with floral scrolls, London maker's mark 'WB', late 17thC, 27in (68.5cm) long.
£800–900 *GSP*

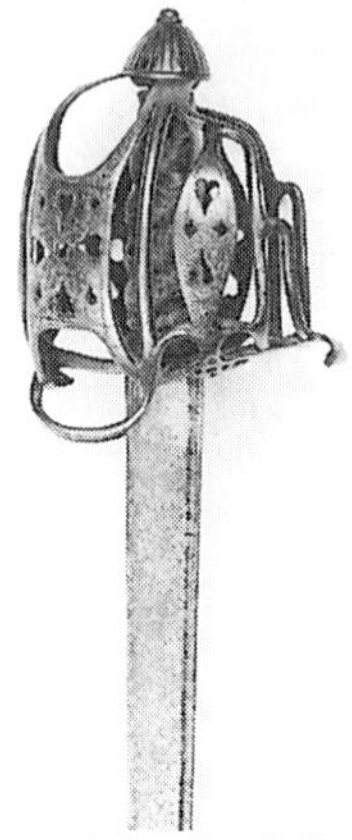

A Scottish basket-hilted backsword, the single-edged blade stamped 'Andria Farara' within the single fuller on both sides, the iron hilt of bars framing engraved and pierced panels, with shagreen-covered wooden grip, parts missing, mid-18thC, blade 32½in (83cm) long.
£1,600–1,800 *Bon*

l. A Dragoon officer's broadsword, with double-edged repointed blade, the basket hilt with loop for reins, saltire cross on side guard, with leather-covered wooden grip, original leather scabbard and iron mounts, c1750, 36½in (92.5cm) long.
£1,250–1,400 *WSA*

Garth Vincent
Antique Arms and Armour
LAPADA MEMBER
THE GUN TRADE ASSOCIATION
THE GUILD OF MASTER CRAFTSMEN
I have customers worldwide and I am interested in purchasing single items or complete collections, advice freely given
Dealer in antique and reproduction arms and armour for the collector, investor and interior decorator
Commission buying at auction
Access & Visa accepted
Brochure available
The Old Manor House,
Allington, Nr Grantham,
Lincolnshire NG32 2DH
Telephone: 01400 281358
Fax: 01400 282658
Mobile: 0385 352151
Email: garthvincent@compuserve.com

A Scottish Dragoon officer's broadsword, by Bland & Foster, the double-edged blade with gilding including a thistle, the basket hilt with fishskin grip, red silk liner, the leather scabbard with iron mounts, c1780, 39¼in (99.5cm) long.
£2,400–2,700 *WSA*

An American Infantry officer's sword, the stirrup type brass hilt with eagle head pommel and reeded black horn grip, the straight single-edged blade with spear point and fuller, the forte engraved with a martial trophy, the American eagle and the retailer's name 'G. Dyer Warranted', c1795, blade 32in (81.5cm) long.
£700–800 *ASB*

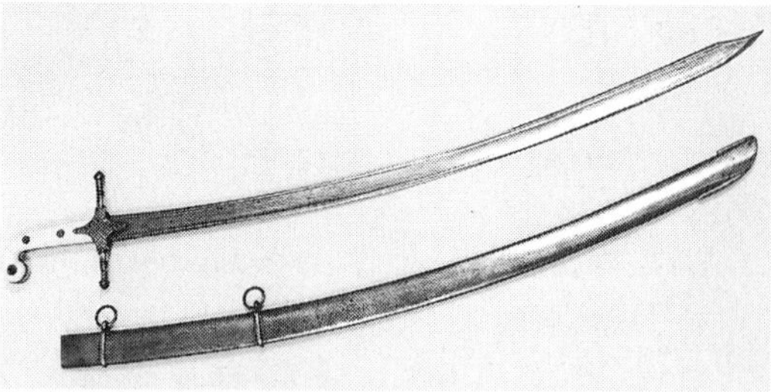

A Georgian officer's mameluke sabre, incribed 'R. Johnston, late Bland & Foster, sword cutler and belt maker to His Majesty, 6 St James's London', 79cm hatchet pointed blade, the gilded brass quillon block with a chevron pattern, the hilt with slab ivory grips, 31¼in (79.5cm) long, in a steel scabbard.
£1,100–1,250 *GV*

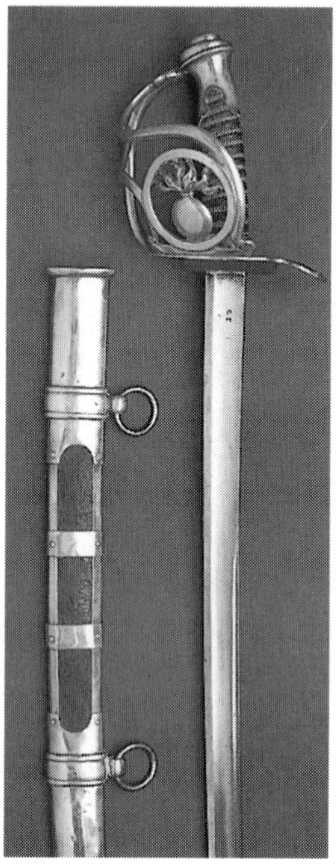

A Model 1802 Grenadier à Cheval de la Garde other rank's sabre, in original wood-lined brass scabbard with original leather panels to cut-outs, blade inscribed at forte 'Manufacture Imperiale du Klingenthal 1811', the hilt with openwork grenade design, blade 38¼in (97cm) long.
£3,200–3,500 *Bon*

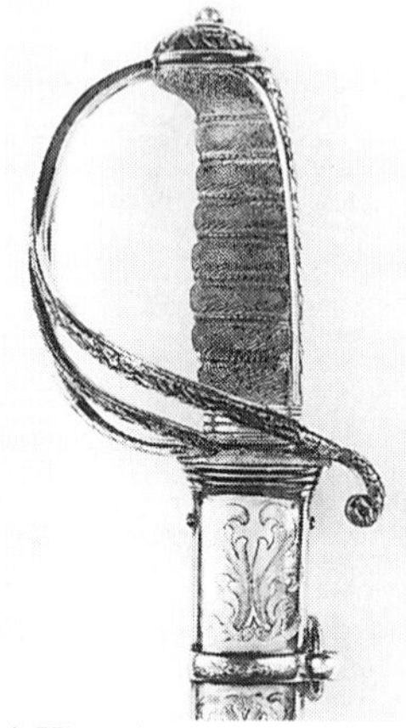

A Victorian presentation sword, etched with scrolling foliage, with VR cypher, arms and inscription, the silver-plated hilt embossed with acorns and oak leaves, with wire-bound fishskin covered grip, the plated steel scabbard engraved with foliate scrolls, dated '1863', blade 35in (89cm) long, in a mahogany case.
£800–900 *Gle*

Miller's is a price GUIDE not a price LIST

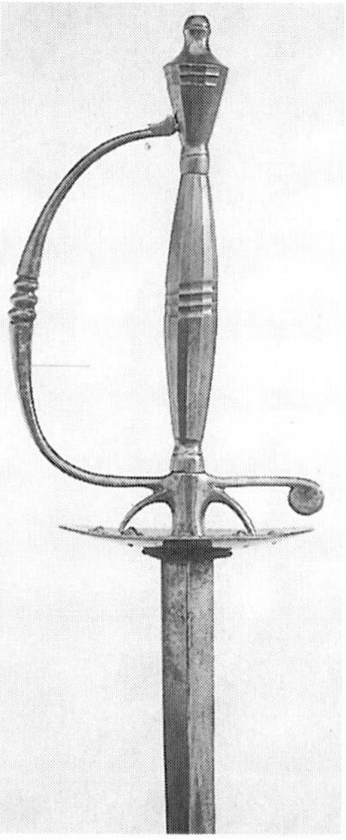

l. An American cut steel-hilted smallsword, by Wells & Company, the blade with hollow triangular section and cut steel hilt, c1800, blade 32½in (82.5cm) long.
£650–750 *B&B*

Identifying Swords and Bayonets

Letters and numbers on edged weapons may provide a clue to the regiment or unit to which they were issued, for example, A 16L stands for A squadron 16th Lancers.

If a military sword bears the British Royal Arms, look in the second quarter of the shield for a fleur-de-lys; if this is present, it is pre-1801. In 1801 Britain relinquished her ancient claim to France and the arms of Scotland replaced the fleur-de-lys. Many British military swords of the latter half of the 18thC have German blades, indicated by Solingen on the back of the blade. Military swords of the 19thC sometimes have officers' initials and/or the name of the regiment engraved on them. Be wary of swords engraved with famous names, especially if offered without provenance.

r. A Nazi Luftwaffe officer's sword, by E. & F. Horster, with wirebound navy blue leather-covered grip, engraved beneath quillons 'Lehrstaffel See', blade 25in (63.5cm) long.
£280–320 *WAL*

MILITARIA
Costume

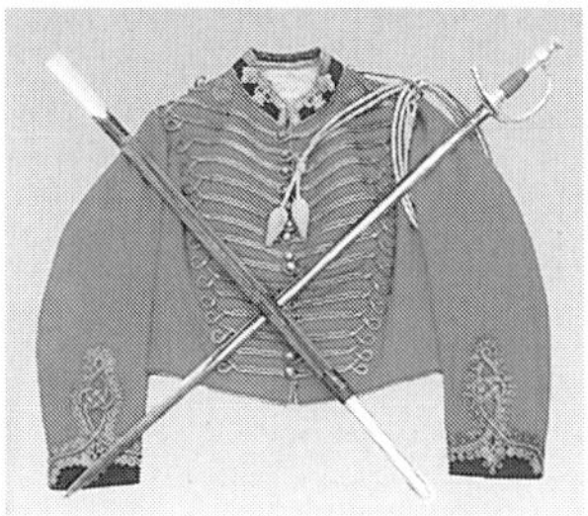

A Hussar pattern scarlet dress tunic, a pair of associated trousers, a Life Guards officer's full dress sword and scabbard by Hamburger, Rogers & Co, a pair of spurs and other items, from Lieutenant Colonel Garratt, 1st Royal Devon Yeomanry, mid-19thC.
£1,000–1,100 *Bea(E)*

Lt Col Garratt's helmet is shown on page 730.

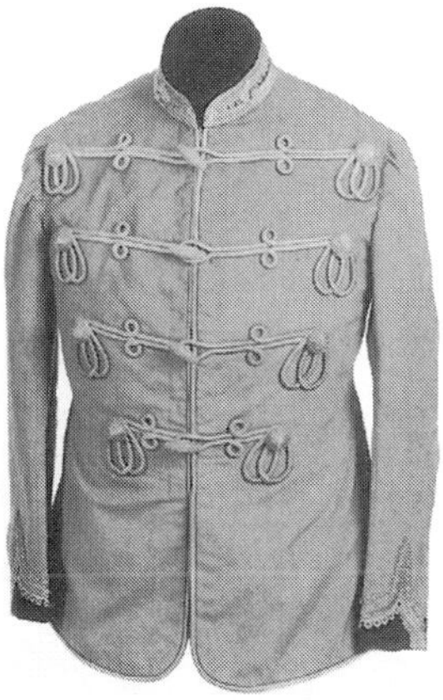

An adjutant-general's or quartermaster-general's tunic, the scarlet melton cloth with blue facings to the collar and cuffs, the collar with 2 rows of gold lace and central scrolling band, mounted with single staff indicating the field rank of major, c1855.
£400–450 *BOS*

r. A first class civil uniform, the full dress coatee with 2 pairs of breeches and one pair of under-drawers, an ostrich-trimmed bicorn hat, gloves and court sword, a levee dress coatee and trousers, and a civilian cloth coatee and breeches, contained in a contemporary tin trunk bearing an identity plate engraved with the owner's name, c1900.
£260–300 *DN*

A Royal Army Medical Corps officer's khaki tunic, with regimental pattern buttons, each cuff with rank lace denoting the rank of lieutenant colonel, the collar with RAMC pattern staff officer's gorgets, breast medal ribbons of Queen's South Africa medal and Africa General Service Medal, with accompanying breeches, 1902.
£320–360 *BOS*

r. A 16th Indian Lancers lieutenant's mess dress uniform, the dark blue melton cloth jacket edged with flat silver bullion lace of regimental pattern and plaited shoulder cords each with bullion rank stars, tailor's label of Rankin of Calcutta and faint ink name, the waistcoat of French grey with ornate silver bullion lace decoration, and blue wool overalls, 1910.
£320–350 *BOS*

A WWI leather naval flying coat, 40in (101.5cm) long.
£700–800 *ET*

A WWII US Marine Corps uniform and equipment, comprising: a steel M1 helmet, herringbone stitched jacket, matching trousers, combat service boots, webbing belt, leather pistol holster and ammunition pouches.
£175–200 *BOS*

A German WWI artillery officer's field grey dress tunic, the black velvet collar and cuffs with scarlet piping dress epaulettes of the 237th Artillery Regiment, with iron cross first class and copy wound badge in brass.
£400–450 *WAL*

Helmets

A Napoleonic foul weather shako of the 5th Grenadiers, covered with light oilcloth, silk ties to left-hand side, the painted grenade badge with '5' on the ball, leather liner, early 19thC.
£675–750 *WAL*

Authenticity

Collectors need not worry unduly about the authenticity of headdress. The wrong badge, plume or chin-chain may be fitted, but the complexity involved in making helmets means that they are unlikely to be faked.

A Leicestershire Yeomanry Cavalry officer's helmet, the black jacked leather skull mounted to the front with a regimental device, with a silver-plated band and spike, and a white horsehair plume, mid-19thC.
£1,000–1,100 *BOS*

This pattern of helmet was introduced to the regiment c1853, and was replaced by the busby in 1873.

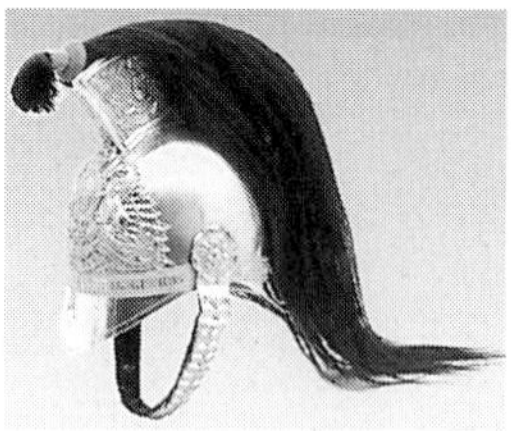

An 1843–47 pattern Heavy Cavalry officer's helmet of the 3rd or Prince of Wales Dragoon Guards, with black horsehair mane and leather lining, in original japanned metal case.
£11,000–12,000 *Bea(E)*

This helmet is in virtually mint condition and was purchased from a house sale at the home of the original owner, Lieutenant Colonel Garratt, in the 1950s.

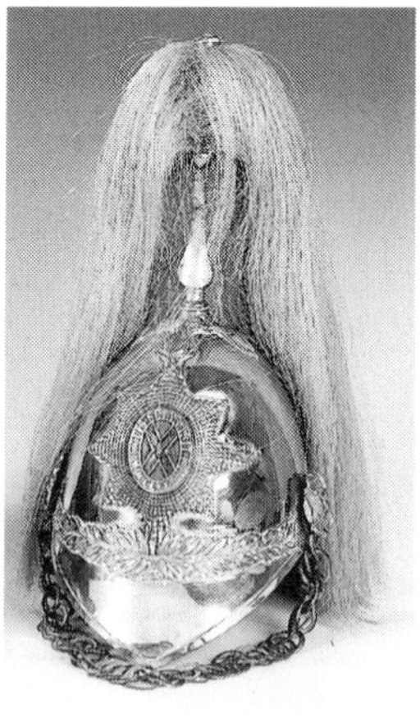

An 1871 pattern 4th Dragoon Guards helmet, with white horsehair plume, badge damaged, numeral '4' missing, 16in (40.5cm) high.
£650–700 *RBB*

A Cardigan Artillery officer's Home Service pattern blue cloth helmet, ball top and rose bosses supporting a velvet-backed chinchain, the Royal Arms in gilt, pre-1901.
£750–850 *BOS*

A Victorian Household Cavalry officer's helmet, the silvered enamelled and gilded helmet plate with gilded chinchain and plume-holder, one rosette missing, enamel chipped.
£1,000–1,100 *S(S)*

An other ranks black patent leather lance cap of the 16th (The Queens) Lancers, with cloth sides to top, yellow and red silk band, yellow braid, brass mounts, leather-backed chinchain and lion's head ear bosses, with hair plume, War Department stamp for 1906.
£270–300 *WAL*

An Edward VII officer's cap of the 16th Lancers, the brass mounts with partly silvered helmet plate, with plume of dark feathers, in japanned metal tin.
£3,000–3,500 *Bon*

A Prussian pickelhaube helmet, with eagle badge and chinstrap, early 20thC.
£500–550 *DN(H)*

A Prussian other ranks reservist pickelhaube, with helmet cover numbered R242 in green baize on khaki canvas, c1914.
£370–400 *Bon*

A Danish Cavalry officer's shako, the blue cloth body with single gold band around crown, leather front peak and red silk quilted lining, the gilt star shako plate containing shield of Royal Danish coat-of-arms, with gold wire pompon to top front edge, c1870.
£340–380 *ASB*

A ERII other ranks white metal helmet of the Life Guards, with brass mounts, leather-backed chinchain, and large ear rosettes with 4 rows of petals, with white hair plume, c1960.
£1,000–1,100 *WAL*

Medals

Medals

Military General Service medals were issued with a bar for battles fought by regiments during the Napoleonic period. They are rare, as they were not issued until 1849 (and therefore bear Queen Victoria's head). Recipients had to be still living to claim them.

A pair awarded to Lieutenant Colonel C. Campbell, Major of Brigade, 3rd Division and 94th Foot, Military General Service 1793–1814, 10 bars, and an Army of India medal, 1799–1826, 3 bars.
£8,000–9,000 *Gle*

A Military General Service medal, 1793–1814, one clasp, awarded to S. McKay, Captain Canadian Militia.
£2,400–2,650 *DNW*

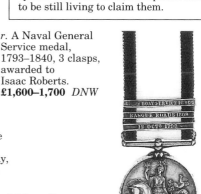

r. A Naval General Service medal, 1793–1840, 3 clasps, awarded to Isaac Roberts.
£1,600–1,700 *DNW*

An Army Gold Cross, for the Peninsula War and the War of 1812, 2 bars, awarded to Major J. Carncross, Royal Artillery.
£11,000–13,000 *RMC*

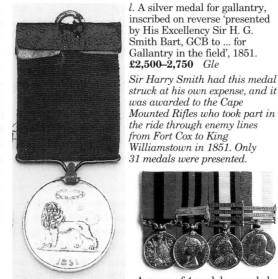

l. A silver medal for gallantry, inscribed on reverse 'presented by His Excellency Sir H. G. Smith Bart, GCB to ... for Gallantry in the field', 1851.
£2,500–2,750 *Gle*

Sir Harry Smith had this medal struck at his own expense, and it was awarded to the Cape Mounted Rifles who took part in the ride through enemy lines from Fort Cox to King Williamstown in 1851. Only 31 medals were presented.

A group of 4 medals awarded to Sergeant Major W. Smith, King's Own Scottish Borderers, comprising: Distinguished Conduct Medal (Victorian), Indian General Service Medal, bar Chin Lushai, 1889–90, Queen's South Africa Medal, King's South Africa Medal.
£850–1,100 *RMC*

A British South African Company medal, with Mashonaland bar and miniature, presented to Chaplain Surridge of the F. H. Pioneers, issued 1927.
£1,300–1,500 *SWO*

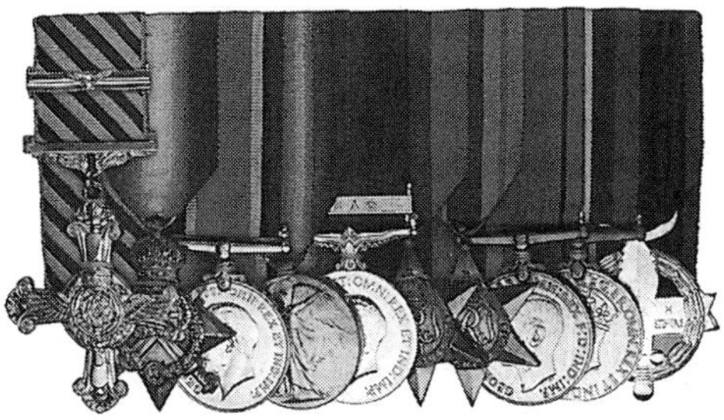

A group of 12 medals awarded to Air Vice-Marshal C. B. S. Spackman, Royal Air Force, late Norfolk Regiment, including CB, CBE, DFC and bar.
£2,700–3,000 *DNW*

A group of 6 medals, comprising: George VI Distinguished Conduct Medal, 1939–45 Star, Africa Star, Italy Star, Defence and War, awarded to WO2 (CSM) J. King, DCM, 6th Btn, Seaforth Highlanders.
£1,700–1,900 *RMC*

l. A group of 6 medals, George VI Air Force Cross, 1939–45 Star, Atlantic Star, Defence Medal, War Medal with Mentioned in Despatches emblem, Air Efficiency Award George VI to Flight Lieutenant P. J. Darke, Royal Air Force.
£800–950 *RMC*

Powder Flasks & Horns

A Continental wheel lock cowhorn powder flask, incised with flowering branches and a fleur-de-lys, with brass fittings, the conical spout with spring-mounted stopper, dated '1610', 10½in (26.5cm) long.
£550–600 *B&B*

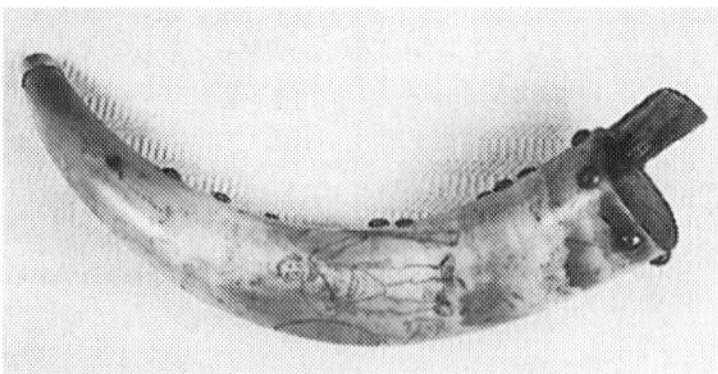

A British or American powder horn, with brass ferrule and leather-covered wooden stopper, decorated with a coat-of-arms, a North American Indian and a Light Infantryman, c1750, 13¼in (33.5cm) long.
£1,600–1,800 *ASB*

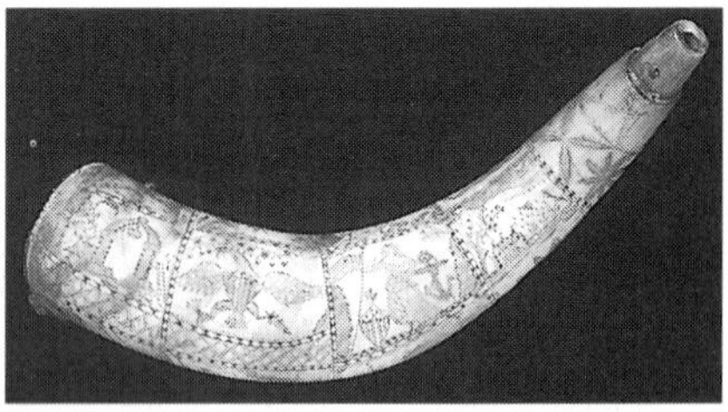

An American wooden powder horn, decorated with engraved, shaded and pricked designs, including Masonic devices, martial trophies, French and American warships, flowerheads, and the national flag, c1790, 13½in (34.5cm) long.
£5,000–5,500 *S(S)*

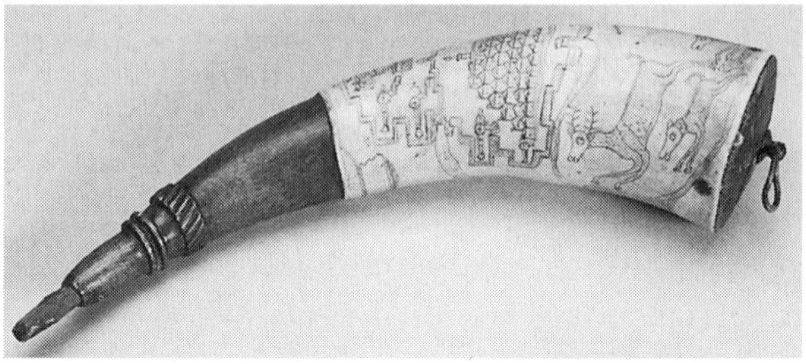

r. An American powder horn, engraved with a map of a fort and roads leading to it, and a stag-hunting scene, 18thC, 10½in (26.5cm) long.
£1,700–1,850 *SK(B)*

Miscellaneous

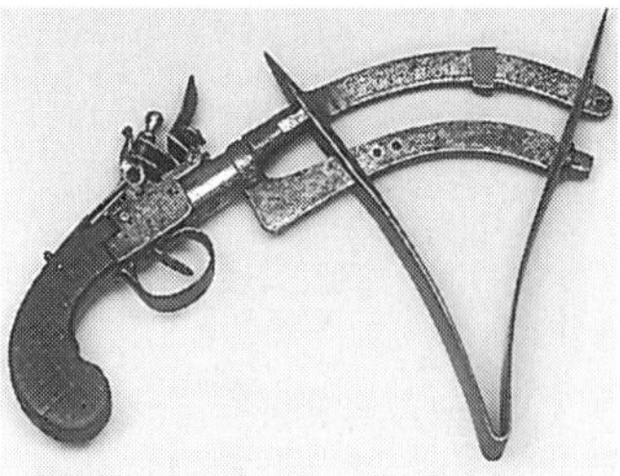

A flintlock powder tester, the brass boxlock frame engraved with panoplies of arms, early 19thC, 12in (30.5cm) long.
£500–550 *B&B*

A box containing 12 cartons, each containing 6 brass boxes for the Princess Mary's Christmas Fund, the lids embossed with a bust of Queen Mary, each box containing a Christmas message from the Queen and a pencil in the form of a bullet, with original string and lead seals, untouched since date of issue, 1914, 13in (33cm) wide.
£3,800–4,200 *BAL*

Her Royal Highness the Princess Mary's Sailors' and Soldiers' Christmas Fund was inaugurated on 14 October 1914, when Princess Mary issued an appeal to the public for funds, so that everyone who was wearing the King's uniform on Christmas Day 1914 should receive a gift.

The standard gift was tobacco, cigarettes, a pipe, a tinder lighter, a Christmas card and a signed photo of Princess Mary, while non-smokers received a packet of acid tablets, stationery and a pencil. Gifts for Indian troops of various religions included confectionery and spices.

A pair of army chaplain's epaulettes, c1840, in associated case.
£100–120 *Bon*

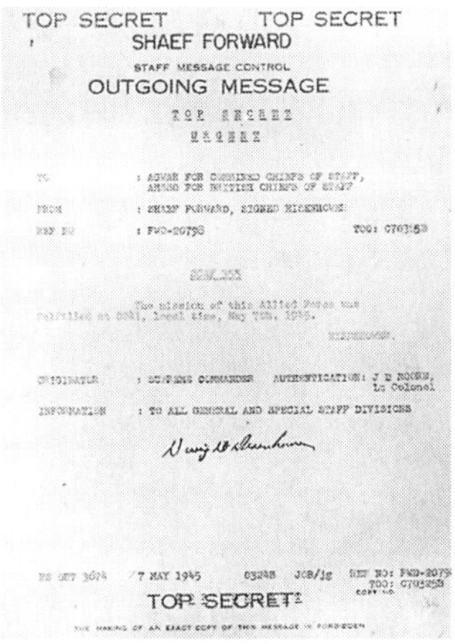

TOP SECRET TOP SECRET
SHAEF FORWARD
STAFF MESSAGE CONTROL
OUTGOING MESSAGE
TOP SECRET

TOP SECRET

A mimeographed document, signed by Dwight D. Eisenhower as Supreme Allied Commander, copy No. 34 of his cable to the Combined Chiefs of Staff and British Chiefs of Staff announcing the end of the war in Europe, 7 May 1945, 10½ x 7½in (26.5 x 19cm), and 4 further mimeographed cables, bound in maroon calf gilt.
£30,000–35,000 *S(NY)*

General Eisenhower signed a very few copies of this historic document as souvenirs for their recipients. This is the 6th copy to be sold at auction since WWII.

A 17th Light Dragoons officer's lance cap plate, mounted with silver Royal Arms with Hanoverian escutcheon, silver skull and crossed bones below, c1828.
£1,000–1,200 *BOS*

The Hanoverian escutcheon was dropped from the Royal Arms in 1837 on Queen Victoria's accession to the throne.

l. A Royal North Devon Mounted Rifles kettledrum banner, scarlet with silver bullion embroidered 'VR' cypher, edged with silver twist wire tassels, c1837, 16 x 35in (40.5 x 89cm).
£350–420 *BOS*

SPORT
Billiards

A late Victorian mahogany billiard table, by R. Stevens & Sons, London, c1880, 144 x 72in (366 x 183cm).
£2,500–3,000 *M&K*

A burr walnut billiard table, by Burroughes & Watts, with steel cushions, carved mouldings and reeded legs, c1890, 144 x 72in (366 x 183cm).
£20,000–25,000 *WBB*

A mahogany billiard table, by Thurston, with reeded legs, c1890, 144 x 72in (366 x 183cm).
£6,500–8,000 *WBB*

An oak refectory dining/billiard table, by E. J. Riley & Co, c1930, 72 x 36in (188 x 91.5cm).
£2,200–2,500 *CBC*

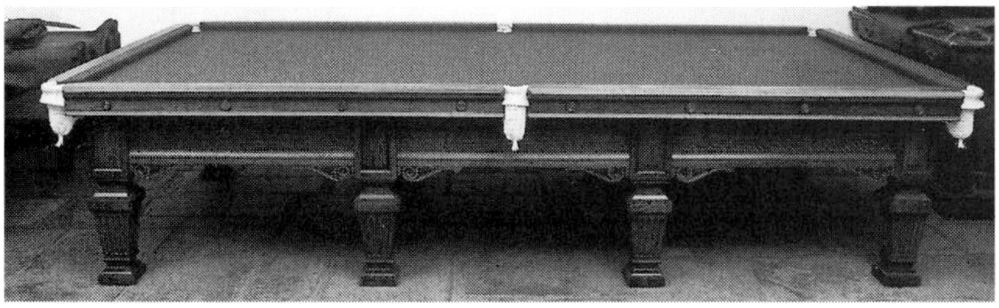

l. An oak billiard table, by Thurston, with matching roller scoreboard on base cabinet, c1870, 144 x 72in (366 x 183cm).
£10,000–12,000 *CBC*

Boxing

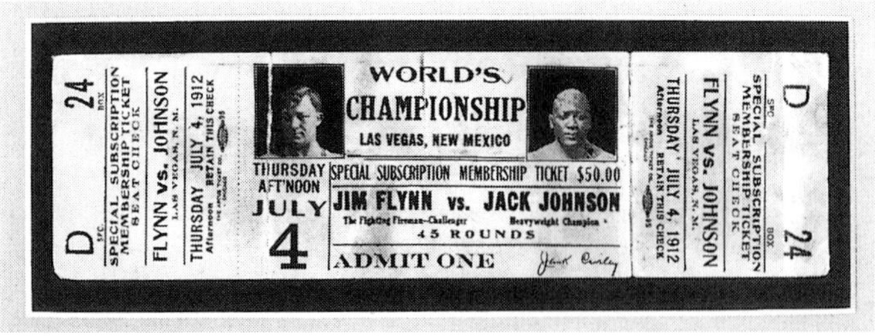

An unusued ticket for the World Championship fight v. Jim Flynn and Jack Johnson, July 4th, 1912.
£270–300 *HALL*

A metal figural lamp, depicting Joe Louis, the back listing Louis' fight record, c1949, 12in (30.5cm) high.
£400–450 *HALL*

A Staffordshire silver lustre jug, painted in sepia with the boxers Molyneux and Cribb, and a verse, with applied handle, slight chips, c1811, 5in (12.5cm) high.
£630–700 *Bon*

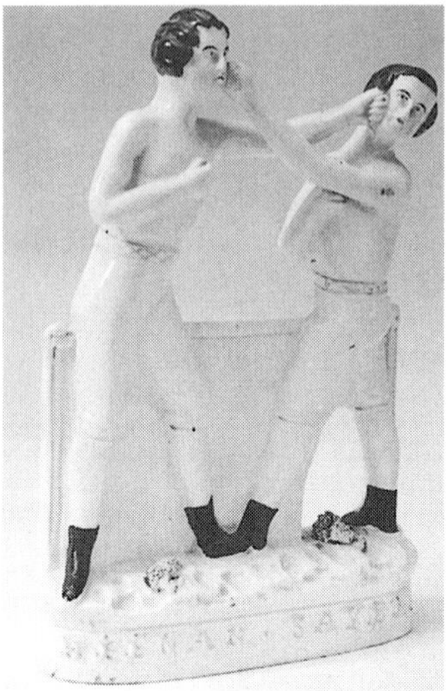

A Staffordshire group of the boxers Heenan and Sayers, 19thC, 8¾in (22cm) high.
£450–550 *P(C)*

Miller's is a price GUIDE not a price LIST

Cricket

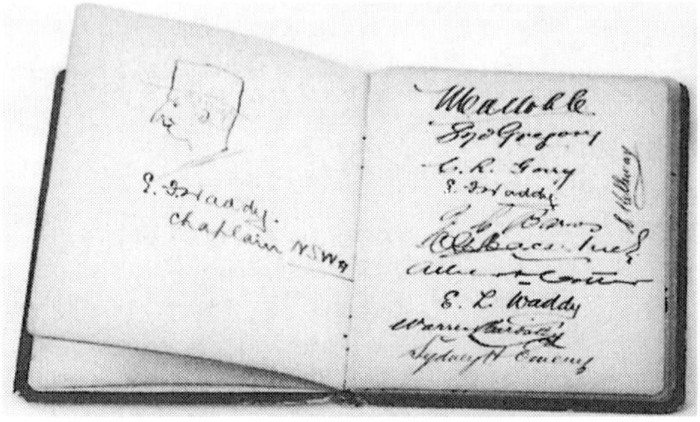

A signed autograph book of the New South Wales, Victoria and South Australia teams, c1908, 15 x 11½in (38 x 29cm).
£400–450 *P(M)*

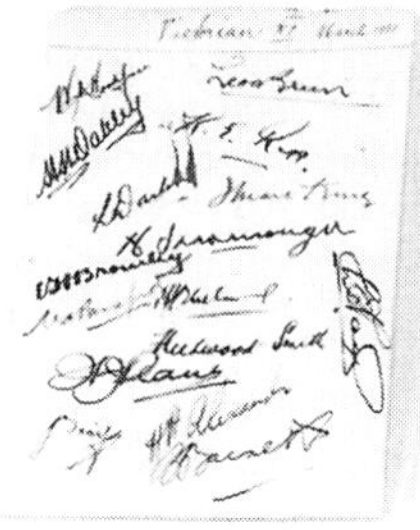

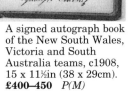

Two autograph book pages, with 17 ink signatures of the Victorian XI team, March 1933, 6 x 4in (15 x 10cm).
£140–160 *P(M)*

r. A cricket ball, mounted on a turned wood stand with a silver plaque inscribed 'Wisden Ball', 1932.
£2,300–2,500 *P(M)*

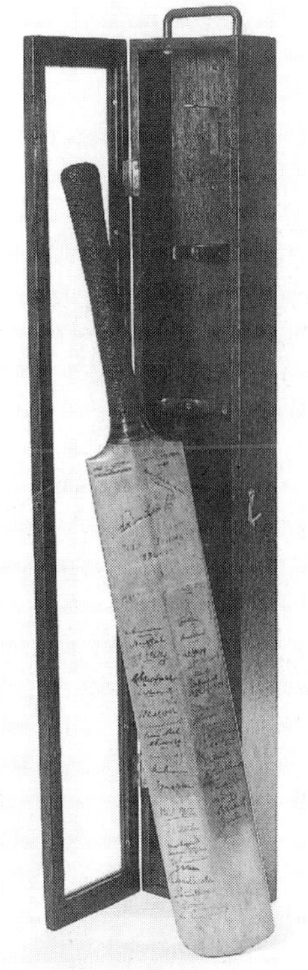

l. A cricket bat, by William Sykes Ltd, used by Don Bradman in the 5th test at Melbourne 1936–37, signed on the reverse in ink by the Australian and England teams, below a further signature of Don Bradman, and above 9 autographs of the Melbourne Cricket Club 1962 team, the face signed in ink by the MCC 1958–59 team, within a glazed wood case, 1936–37.
£7,700–8,500 *P(M)*

A Victorian ceramic bowl, with 2 hand-painted designs of a 17thC game of cricket, 5½in (14cm) diam.
£360–400 *VS*

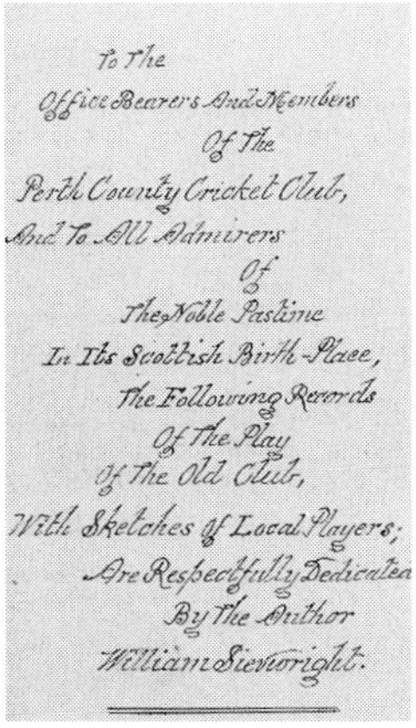

To The
Office Bearers And Members
Of The
Perth County Cricket Club,
And To All Admirers
Of
The Noble Pastime
In Its Scottish Birth-Place,
The Following Records
Of The Play
Of The Old Club,
With Sketches of Local Players;
Are Respectfully Dedicated
By The Author
William Sievwright.

An Historical Sketch of the Perth Cricket Club, by William Sievwright, published by James Barlas, Perth, signed by the author, with a 2nd volume, an updated version entitled *History of Cricket in Perth 1812–1894*, dated '1896', with part of the book in print and part in hand-written manuscript form, bound in leather.
£300–350 *S*

An earthenware ginger beer bottle, for the Rhyl Miner Water Co Ltd, showing stumps, bail, ball and bat, all within a shield, early 20thC, 6½in (16.5cm) high.
£70–80 *VS*

A late Victorian Staffordshire cricketing mug, 6in (15cm) high.
£150–180 *VS*

l. A Doulton Lambeth ceramic lemonade jug, with 3 embossed raised figures of a bowler, a batsman and a wicket-keeper, with floral design, c1900, 7½in (19cm) high.
£800–950 *VS*

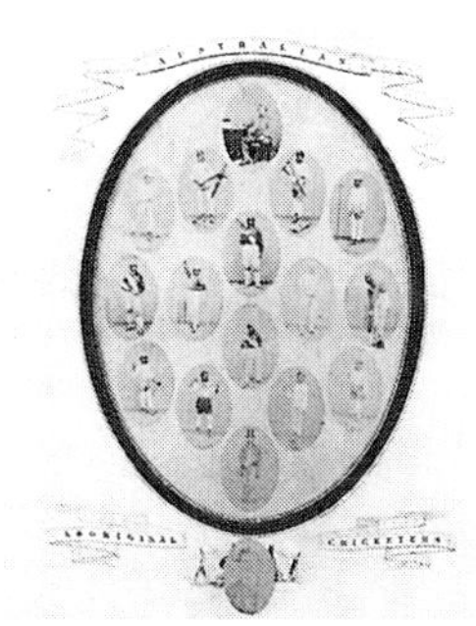

A photograph of an Aboriginal team, by Patrick Dawson, taken in Hamilton, Victoria, incorporating 16 portraits of the team which toured England in 1868, 22 x 18in (56 x 46cm).
£1,200–1,300 *P(M)*

A photograph of Leo O'Brien, 'The Richmond representative of Test Team Season 1932–33, Australia v. England', with a letter to him from the Victorian Cricket Association granting him permission to play for the Richmond Cricket Club, photograph 14¼ x 11½in (36 x 29cm).
£230–260 *P(M)*

l. A signed photograph of the MCC touring team to Australia, 1928–29, 16¼ x 19¾in (41 x 50cm), framed and glazed.
£300–350 *P(M)*

Equestrian

A pewter hunting sandwich box, with leather case, c1905, 6in (15cm) wide.
£120–140 *RTh*

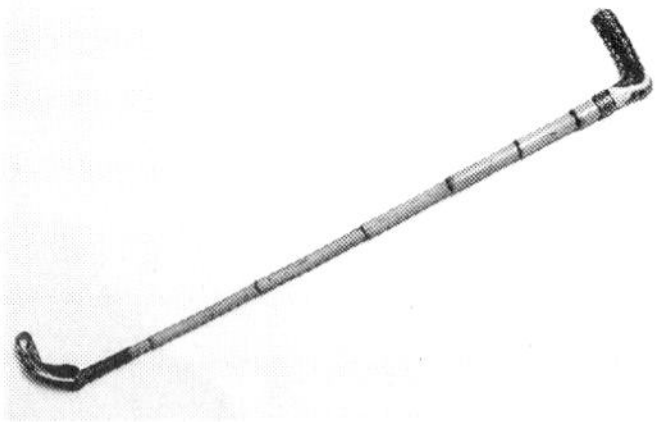

A silver banded hunting crop, by Swaine, Adeney & Brigg, London, 1895, 28in (71cm) long.
£100–120 *RTh*

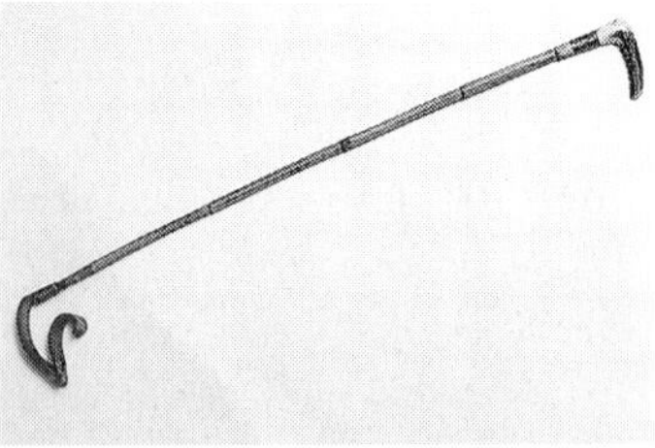

A riding crop, with solid silver band and horn handle, initialled 'W. S.', probably by William Summers, London, 1908, 28in (71cm) long.
£120–140 *RTh*

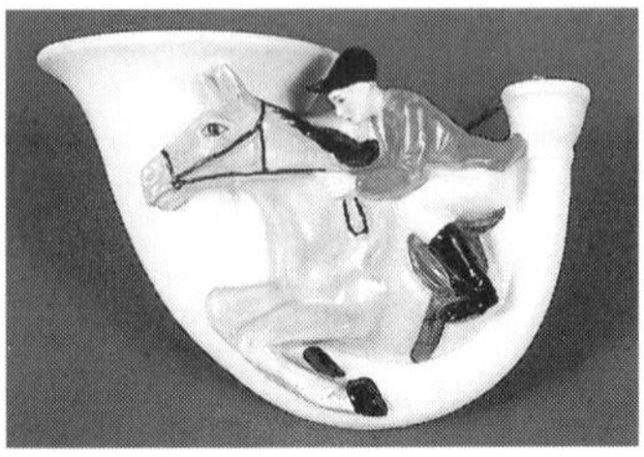

A Goebel wall plaque, in the form of a hunting horn and horseman, 1940s, 6in (15cm) wide.
£55–65 *HEI*

A ceramic octagonal pottery plate, with a portrait of Fred Archer to centre and Classic racing winning details to edge, late 19thC, 9½in (24cm) wide.
£200–250 *VS*

A set of Avery jockey scales, the upholstered seat on mahogany stand, with brass scale at the side and adjustable brass weight, c1880, 25in (63.5cm) wide.
£2,100–2,500 *S(NY)*

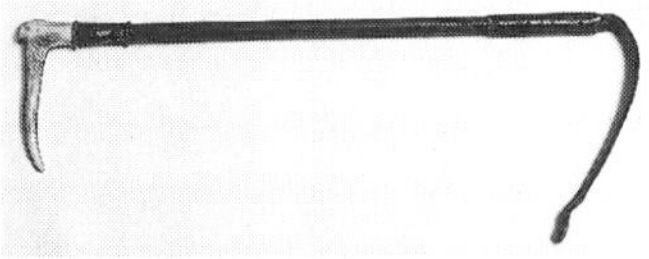

l. A leather riding whip, with bone handle and silver band, hallmarked 1910, 27in (68.5cm) long.
£110–130 *RTh*

Fishing

An Aerial 4in centrepin reel, with perforated drum flange and twin xylenite handles, option check and brass foot, 1920s.
£600–650 *EP*

An Allcock & Co 3½in mahogany trout reel, with brass mounts and slide button, foot stamped, early 20thC.
£45–50 *WW*

A brass plate wind 3¾in salmon reel, by Carter & Co, London, c1900.
£100–125 *OTB*

An Allcock Aerial 5in casting reel, the backplate with optional check, stamped '28', c1925.
£1,200–1,350 *EP*

A Coxon Aerial 4in centrepin reel, c1908, in a wooden box.
£800–900 *EP*

A Hardy Silex No. 2 4in casting reel, with twin ivorine handles, ivorine brake handle, central locking nut, bridged rim tension screw and brass foot, c1911.
£200–220 *EP*

A Hardy 2⅝in all-brass Transitional Perfect trout fly reel, with open ball race and brass bearings, c1894–5.
£2,000–2,200 *Bon(C)*

A Hardy 2¾in brass-faced Perfect trout fly reel, c1900.
£500–600 *Bon(C)*

A Hardy 3⅜in Uniqua trout fly reel, with horseshoe latch, c1903.
£550–600 *EP*

A Hardy 4in alloy combined fly and spinning reel, c1900.
£330–360 *Bon(C)*

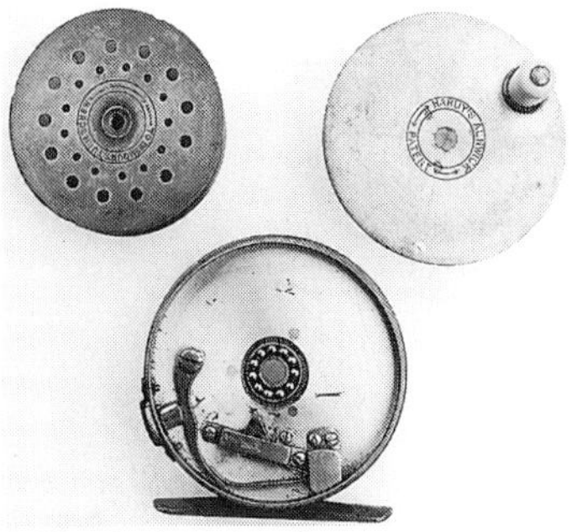

A Hardy 2¾in Perfect narrow drum alloy trout fly reel, with compensating check, 1912.
£900–1,000 *Bon*

A Hardy 3⅜in St George trout fly reel, with ribbed brass foot, 3 screw drum latch and curved Hardy logo, c1930.
£180–200 *OTB*

A brass 4½in trolling winch, by Jones, London, c1850.
£650–800 *OTB*

l. A Malloch 2½in alloy sidecaster reel, with rim control for optional check, brass foot and line guard, c1920.
£110–120 *EP*

A brass, ebonite and nickel silver London style 4½in salmon reel, by G. Little & Co, London, c1870.
£400–500 *OTB*

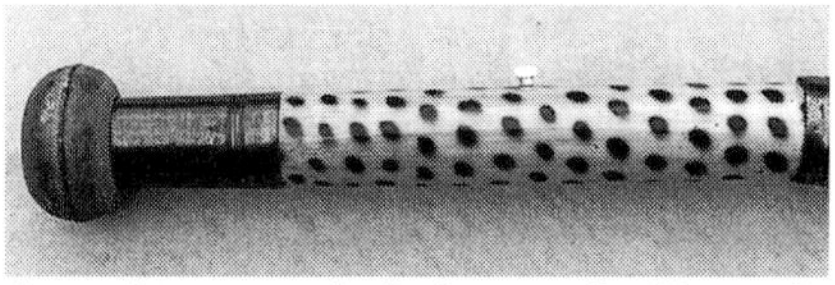

A sand-patterned whole cane, by Eaton & Dellar, with 2 greenheart tips, ivory hook keep to butt and bronzed brass furniture, c1830, 177in (449.5cm) long.
£260–300 *MUL*

A D. Slater 5in salmon reel, with double ivory handles, early 20thC.
£220–240 *WW*

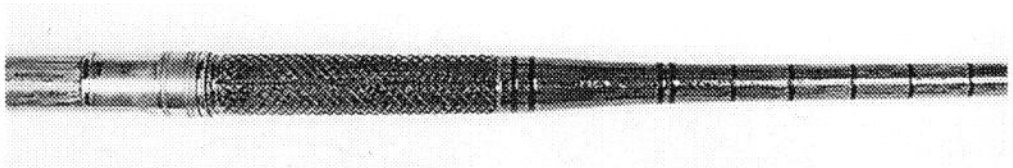

A four-piece fly rod, inscribed 'Alfred – maker – Moorgate St, London' and 'P.Y.G. Exhibition 1851' to butt, with knurled wood grip, 147in (373.5cm) long.
£100–120 *Bon*

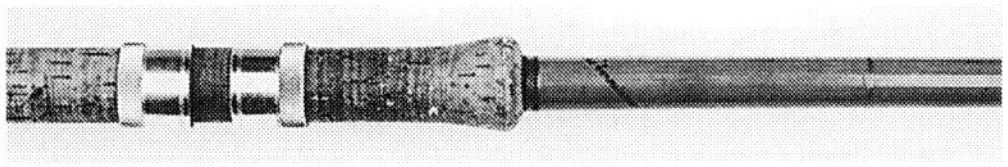

A Hardy's The Connoisseur three-piece coarse fishing rod, with whole cane butt and mid-sections, and built cane tip, 1939, 144in (366cm) long.
£200–220 *Bon(C)*

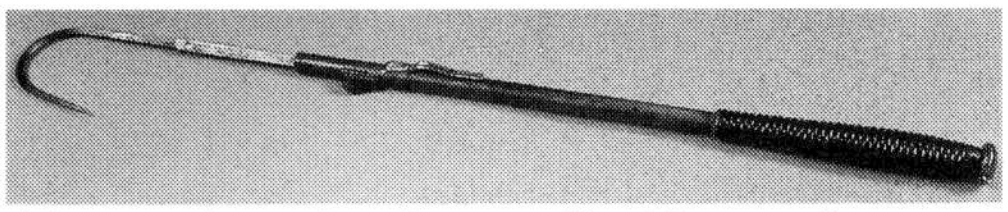

A brass telescopic salmon gaff, with turned rosewood handle, by Ogden & Scotford of London, c1885, 54in (137cm) extended.
£200–250 *OTB*

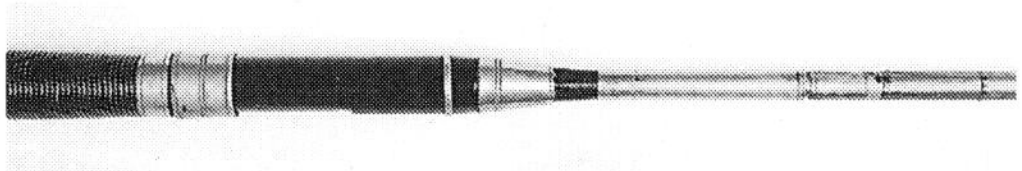

A built cane trout fly rod, by Abbey & Imbrie of New York, the lined tube type tip and butt guides with two-ring eyelets as intermediates, nickel fittings and dowelled ferrules, early 20thC, 98in (249cm) long.
£80–100 *Bon*

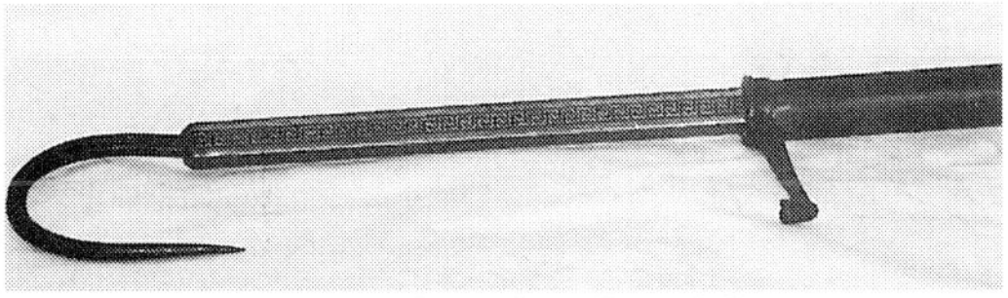

A two-draw brass and steel gaff, with brass pattern boxed section, brass point protector and turned wooden handle with lanyard ring, c1900, 20in (51cm) long closed.
£150–180 *MUL*

l. A Hardy angler's knife No. 3, c1930, 4in (10cm) long.
£450–500 *RTh*

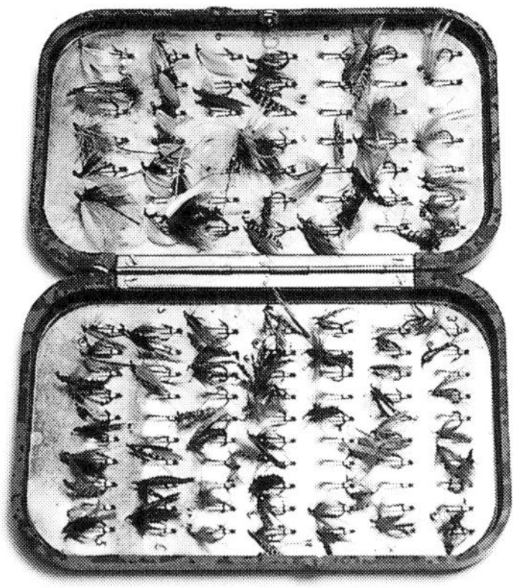

r. A Hardy Neroda trout fly box, with a tortoiseshell finish interior, containing a selection of flies, c1940, 6 x 4in (15 x 10cm).
£220–245 *RTh*

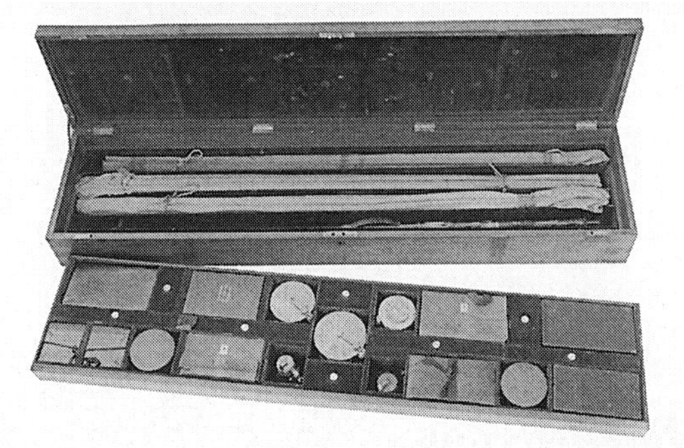

A fisherman's brass-bound mahogany tackle case, by J. Jones, the lift-out tray with velvet-lined compartments containing a selection of reels, rods and other accessories, c1850, case 52½in (133.5cm) long.
£10,500–12,000 *S(S)*

A bowfronted glazed case, containing 8 roach and 2 chub, mounted swimming in different directions in a setting of reeds and grasses, with card inscribed 'caught by J. Ambley on the River Thames at Bray Lock, Oct 6th 1908. Total weight 17lbs 6oz', 50½in (127cm) wide.
£2,600–3,000 *Bon(C)*

Football

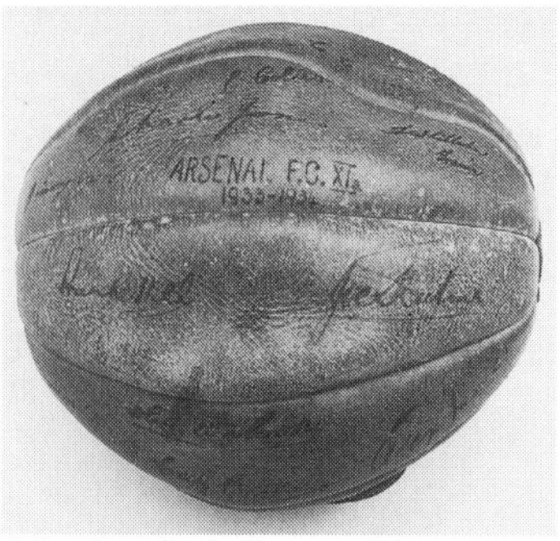

A leather football, signed by 25 players in ink and inscribed 'Arsenal F.C. XIs 1933–34', 1930s.
£550–600 *WW*

A Scottish International football jersey, by Umbro, navy blue with a white V-neck, with embroidered Scottish Football Association badge, No. 4 to back, early 1960.
£160–200 *P(C)*

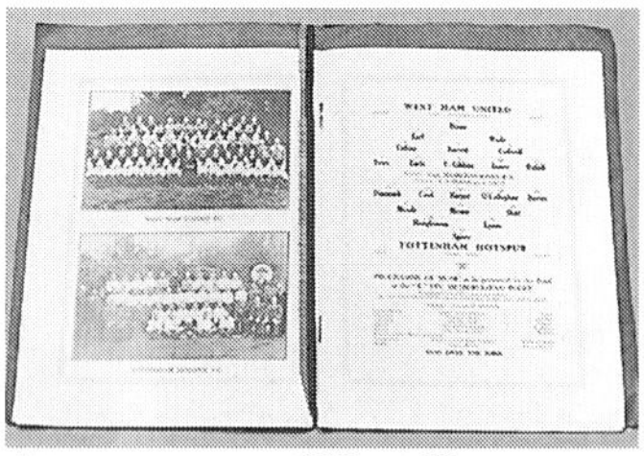

A programme of West Ham United v. Tottenham Hotspur match, 8 December 1930.
£140–160 *P(C)*

A photograph album, containing 49 sepia photographs of Sheffield United FC during the 1898/99 season, when they won the FA cup, 7½ x 6¼in (19 x 16cm).
£5,500–6,000 *P(C)*

A World Cup Final programme of Italy v. Hungary match, in Paris, 1938, 8½ x 10½in (22 x 27cm).
£6,000–6,500 *MUL*

A programme of the Germany v. France match, 16 October 1954, with a signed dinner menu autographed by all players and officials.
£220–250 *MUL*

A ceramic mug, decorated with a coloured vignette of a goal-keeper and 3 footballers, with a gilded background, 1900–14, 3in (7.5cm) high.
£100–120 *VS*

A French plaster figure of a footballer, by Gavvazi of Amiens, c1910, 21in (54cm) high.
£200–250 *MUL*

A spelter figure of a footballer, 1910, 7½in (19cm) high.
£75–100 *WaR*

r. A spelter figure of a footballer, signed 'T. S. Chudin', possibly French, 1930s, 9¾in (25cm) high.
£150–200 *WaR*

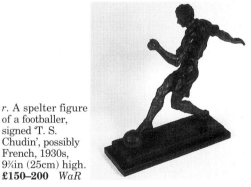

r. A spelter figure of a footballer, on a marble base with an engraved brass plaque reading 'Lev Yashin World Cup 1958 Sweden', 12in (30.5cm) wide.
£1,700–1,850 *MUL*

Golf

A feather-filled golf ball, probably by J. & W. Gourlay, c1850, 1¾in (4.5cm) diam.
£1,850–2,000 *S*

A box of 12 golf balls, in original wrappers and box, c1914.
£500–600 *P(M)*

A Chambers patent golf ball marker, patent No. 18712–10, c1910.
£350–420 *S*

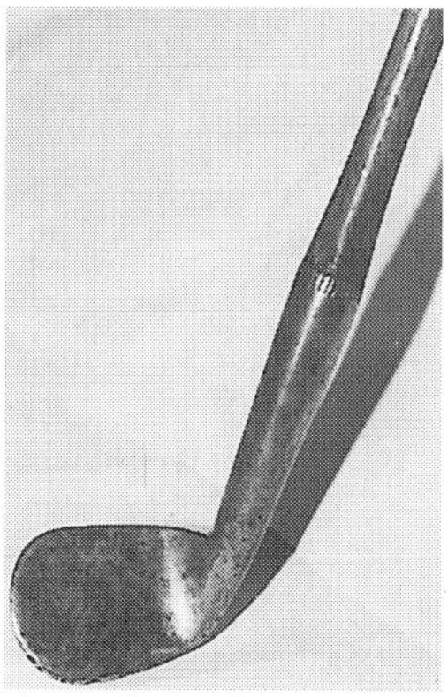

An early track iron, with 5in (12.5cm) thick hozel and 2¼in wide face, with sheepskin grip, c1880.
£450–550 *MUL*

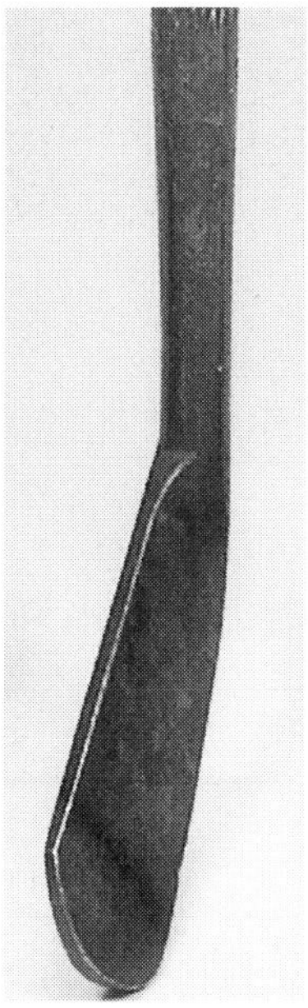

l. A John Gray Prestwick iron, c1865.
£1,250–1,500 *S*

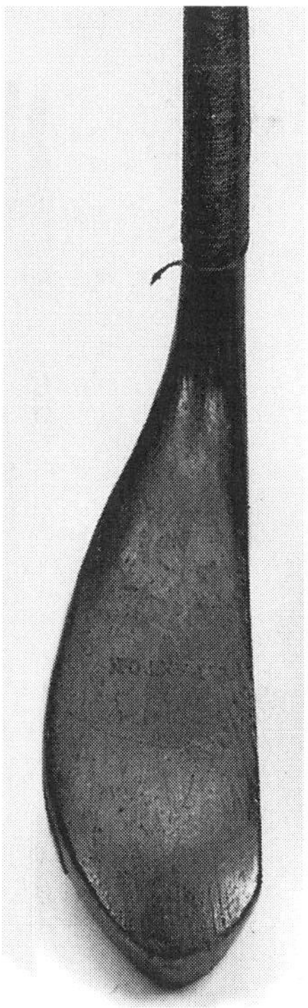

r. A driving putter, by Peter Paxton, Worcestershire, with beech head and greenheart shaft, c1885.
£900–1,100 *S*

A silver-headed putter, inscribed 'Captain's Putter', c1930.
£1,100–1,200 *MUL*

A Copeland Spode jug, with golfing scenes, relief-moulded in white on a blue ground, repaired, c1900, 6in (15cm) high.
£260–300 *VS*

A Copeland Spode teapot, relief-moulded in white with golfing scenes on a blue ground, registered No. 345322, c1899, 6in (15cm) high.
£420–460 *DD*

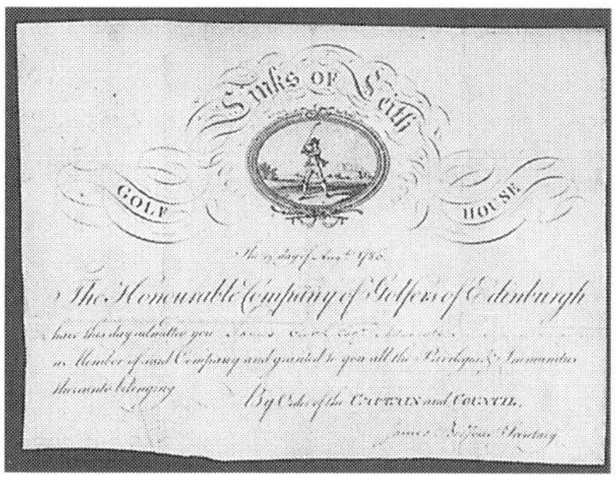

r. An Honourable Company of Edinburgh Golfers' membership certificate on vellum to James Clark Esq advocate, dated '19th August, 1786'.
£3,500–4,200 *S*

Churchman's Cigarettes 'Sporting Celebrities' cigarette card, No. 33, depicting Walter Hagen, 1931.
£40–45 *HALL*

Rugby

A Harlequin cap, worn by G. Hubbard, 1925–26.
£150–200 *WaR*

r. A yellow and black school colours cap, from the Pre-Grammar School of King James, Almondbury 1924–25.
£40–50 *VS*

r. An Australian International Rugby League jersey, in green and gold with embroidered sewn-on badge, dated '1950', 'No. 16' to the back.
£160–175 *P(C)*

A green wool blazer, with gold braiding to sleeves and pockets, the breast pocket with the Australian crest, and 'Rugby Australian League 1950' beneath, worn by Doug McRitchie.
£420–500 *P(M)*

A Copeland Spode three-handled mug, relief-moulded in white with rugby scenes on a blue ground, c1900, 7in (18cm) high.
£450–550 *S*

A watercolour by J. A. Kean, entitled 'The Beginnings of Rugby', depicting young men playing in the grounds at Rugby School, c1900, 17½ x 23in (44 x 58cm).
£4,800–5,200 *S*

Shooting

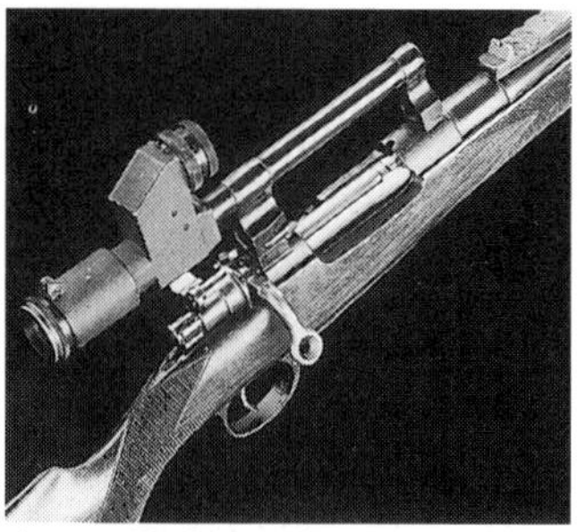

A .350 Rigby rimless magnum bolt action sporting rifle, by Thomas Bland & Sons, No. 17594, mounted with Carl Zeiss GZ 111 2465 prismatic telescopic sight, 1912, barrel 22in (56cm) long.
£2,000–2,200 *S(S)*

Thomas Bland & Sons confirm that the rifle was built in 1912. Gunmakers' catalogues of this period illustrate the new Zeiss patent prismatic telescopic sight and claim that brightness is greater than with any other known prism telescope.

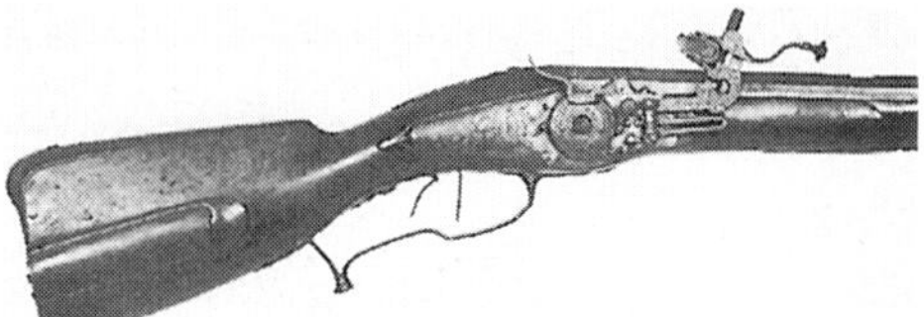

l. A German wheel-lock sporting rifle, the lock signed 'Hans Henrich Dilles, Frankfurt', 17thC, barrel 28in (71cm) long.
£2,800–3,200 *GSP*

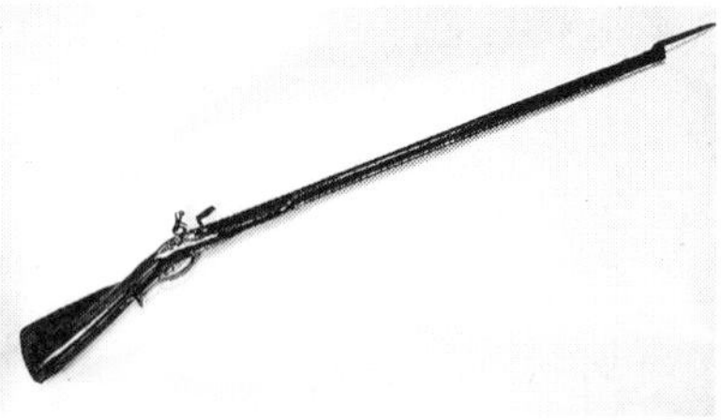

A flintlock sporting gun, by Fiamar, fully stocked in walnut, barrel octagonal going to round, the 7in (18cm) socketed knife bayonet in a compartment in the butt plate, c1750, 59in (150cm) long.
£2,500–3,000 *GV*

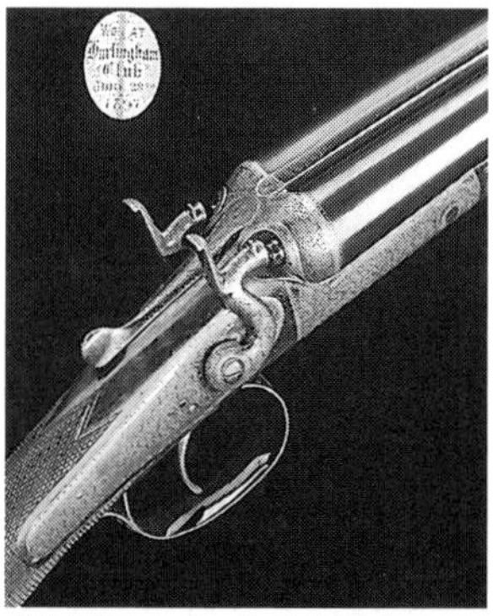

A 12-bore single-trigger hammer pigeon gun, by Stephen Grant & Sons, No. 7055, the escutcheon inscribed 'Won at Hurlingham Club, June 28th 1897', Whitworth barrels 30in (76cm) long.
£8,700–9,500 *S(S)*

The Hurlingham Club was renowned for pigeon shooting competitions held at the turn of the century.

r. A .500 3in (7.5cm) 'C Quality' boxlock non-ejector rifle, by Purdey & Sons, No. 12992, 1890, barrel 28in (71cm) long.
£3,200–3,500 *S*

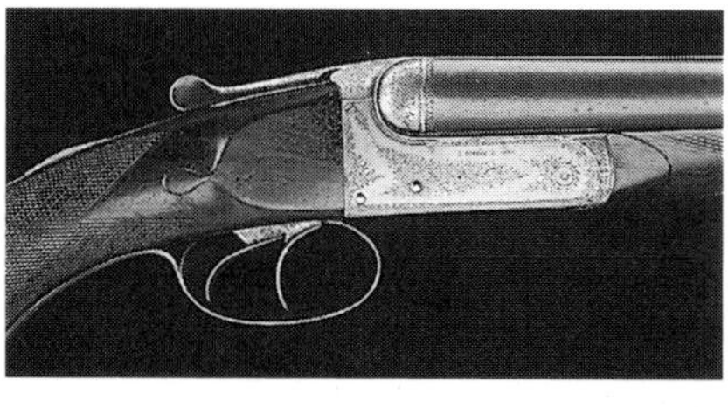

A 'Lorenzoni' flintlock repeating sporting gun, by Wilson, the barrel with flared muzzle, octagonal at breech with London proofs, the breech mechanism profusely engraved, with a walnut butt, c1770, barrel 34½in (87.5cm) long.
£4,500–5,000 *WSA*

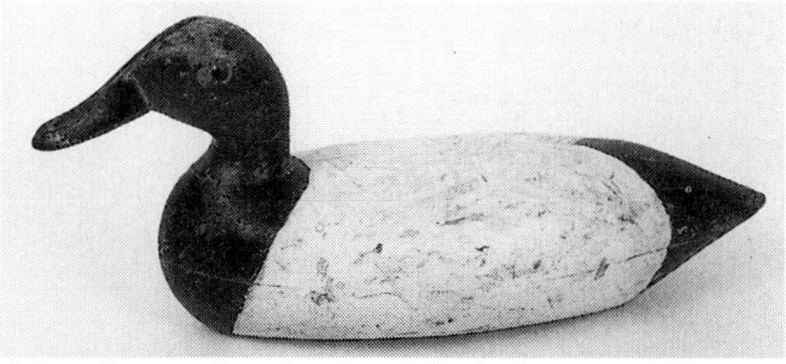

A hand-carved and painted duck decoy, c1875, 15in (38cm) long.
£300–350 *RYA*

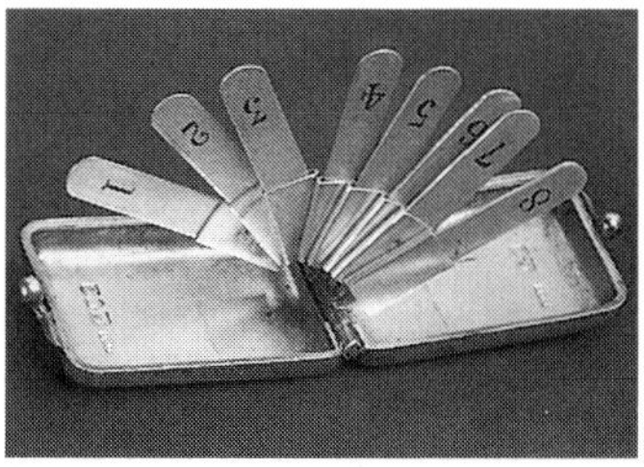

l. A silver place marker, with hinged lid, containing 8 numbered silver pegs, hallmarked, c1920, 2½in (6.5cm) high.
£1,700–1,850 *Bon*

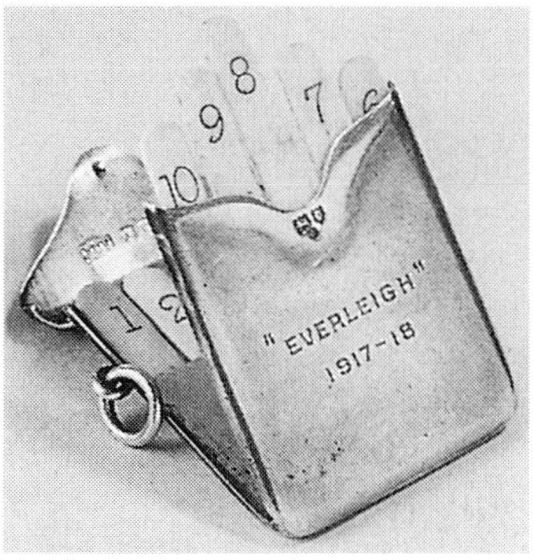

A silver place marker, by J. C. Vickery, the hinged and sprung case opening to reveal 10 ivory numbered markers, London 1912, 2½in (6.5cm) high.
£1,600–1,800 *S(S)*

This device was used to determine in a gentlemanly fashion where each member of the shooting party was to stand. The markers were placed in the case with the numbers pointing downwards, and then each person selected one, in the manner of drawing straws.

A wooden green plover decoy, c1910, 10in (25.5cm) long.
£340–375 *RTh*

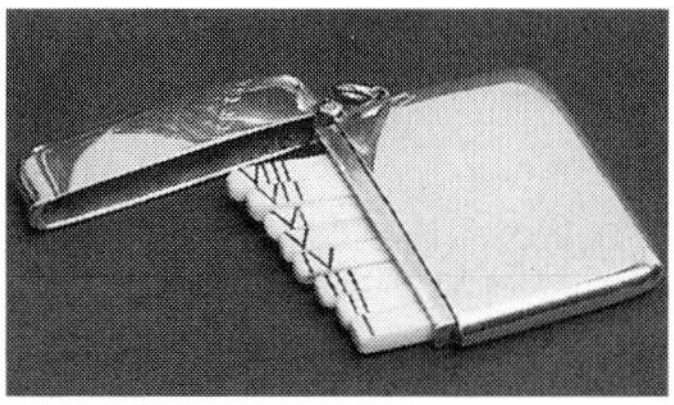

A gold place marker, with hinged lid, containing 8 numbered bone pegs, hallmarked, 1930, 1½in (4cm) high.
£3,000–3,300 *Bon*

Tennis

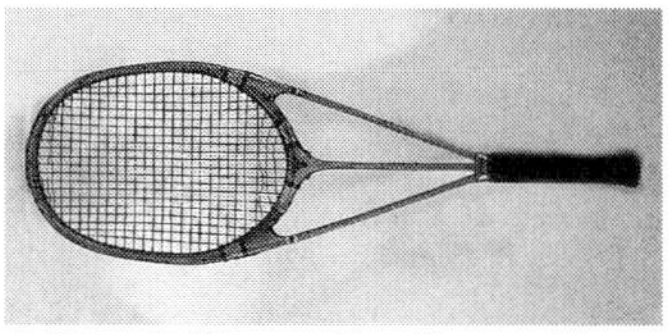

A Hazell Streamline Green Star tennis racket, 1930s, 27in (68.5cm) long.
£175–225 *WaR*

A Clapshaw & Cleave College Tail tennis racket, c1910, 25½in (65cm) long.
£75–85 *WaR*

A collection of *Lawn Tennis & Badminton* magazines, vol. 5, No. 9, April 4th 1912 to No. 23 July 11th, 1912.
£200–250 *MUL*

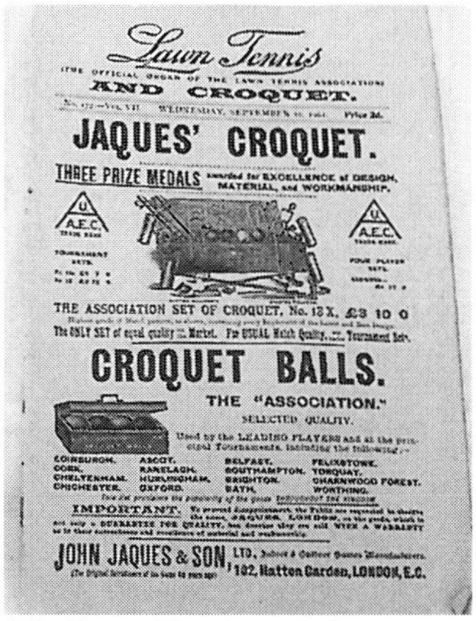

The Lawn Tennis and Croquet magazine, vol. 7, 10th September 1902, with dust wrapper.
£35–40 *MUL*

A silvered spelter tennis trophy, 1920s, 11in (28cm) high.
£150–200 *WaR*

l. The Lawn Tennis and Badminton magazine, vol. 10, Wednesday April 19th, 1905, with original dust wrapper, and vol. 10 index dated '1906'.
£30–35 *MUL*

THE SALE OF THE COLLECTION OF THE DUKE & DUCHESS OF WINDSOR

The nine-day sale of the collection of the Duke and Duchess of Windsor, the longest sale in American history, was held in New York and was the subject of intense interest worldwide. The pre-sale view attracted well over 30,000 people, attesting to the general public's enduring fascination with the story of the man who gave up the throne of the United Kingdom for the woman he loved. Many of the pieces on offer were poignant mementos of the Duke's former life, and included the desk at which, as Edward VIII, he signed the abdication on December 10th, 1936, and a wall-hanging bearing the arms of the Prince of Wales, which hung above the couple's bed in their Paris home.

Among the more personal items sold were a large number of lots relating to pugs (the Windsors' favourite dog), a christening mug given to the Duke by his great-grandmother, Queen Victoria, and the tablecloth used as an altar cloth at the couple's wedding ceremony. The sale totalled over $23 million (£14 million) and the proceeds were donated to charity.

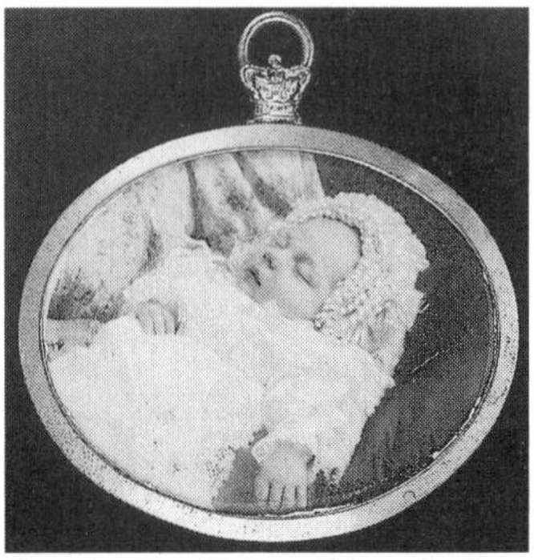

A portrait of Prince Edward of York, wearing his christening robes, by W. & D. Downey, hand-coloured albumen print, the crimson velvet back with a label in Queen Mary's hand 'Pce. Edward of York 1894', in a gilt-metal frame, 2½in (6.5cm) wide.
£17,000–18,500 *S(NY)*

An oil painting of HRH The Prince of Wales on Forest Witch, by Sir Alfred Munnings, PRA, RWS, signed and dated '1921', 54½ x 73¼in (138.5 x 186cm).
£1,500,000+ *S(NY)*

This painting realised nearly 3 times its high estimate, and was the highest price ever paid for a work by Munnings.

The red leather dispatch box of King Edward VIII, by Jon Peck & Son, London, the lid stamped in gilt 'The King', c1936, 16in (40.5cm) long.
£40,000–45,000 *S(NY)*

A Victorian child's silver mug, by Holland, Aldwinckle & Slater, the bell-shaped body decorated with applied foliate strapwork in early 18thC style, engraved with the cyphers of Prince Edward of York, further engraved with inscription 'From VRI 23 June 1895', London 1893, 3½in (9cm) high, on an ebonised wood plinth.
£7,700–8,500 *S(NY)*

This mug was given to Prince Edward of York on his first birthday, June 23, 1895, by his great-grandmother, Queen Victoria.

A Cartier blue lacquer table dressing set, inlaid in gold with the combined monograms of Mrs Wallis Simpson and Edward, Prince of Wales, with original blue morocco case and canvas cover, both initialled 'WWS', c1935, cologne bottles 5in (12.5cm) high.
£4,000–4,500 *S(NY)*

A portrait of Queen Victoria and Prince Edward of York, by Hughes & Mullins, signed in ink in the margin by Queen Victoria, 'Gangan & Little David 1896', albumen print, mounted on card with printed credit 'Hughes & Mullins, Ryde I.W., Photographers to HM the Queen', 4¼ x 6¼in (11 x 16cm).
£5,000–5,500 *S(NY)*

This photograph was probably taken at Osborne House, Isle of Wight. 'Gangan', a childish interpretation of 'great-grandmama', was the royal children's pet name for Queen Victoria.

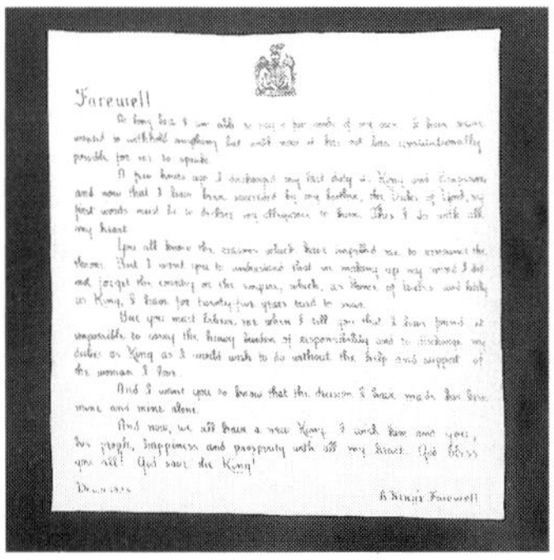

A printed ivory silk commemorative handkerchief, with a navy border, the central ground printed with facsimile script of the abdication speech of King Edward VIII, entitled 'A King's Farewell', and dated 'Dec 11, 1936', 19¼in (49cm) square.
£15,500–17,000 *S(NY)*

A George III mahogany library desk, the green leather-inset top with a gadrooned border, 3 frieze drawers opposing a long dummy drawer, the short sides each with one small and one dummy drawer, c1755, 54in (137cm) wide.
£255,000–300,000 *S(NY)*

This desk was used for the signing of the abdication.

l. A morning suit, comprising a black cashmere herringbone weave tailcoat, matching backless waistcoat, a pair of black and grey striped worsted trousers with American-style waist, with a blue and white pin-striped shirt and white collar, with embroidered cypher 'W' below a coronet, and a blue and white silk tie, 1937.
£17,000–18,500 *S(NY)*

This suit was worn by the Duke of Windsor on the day of his marriage to Wallis Simpson in June 1937. The Duke decided to wear a grey waistcoat for his wedding rather than the matching waistcoat.

A fine lawn tablecloth, appliquéd and embroidered with ivy leaves and berries, with wave shaped appliquéd golden lamé border, together with 12 matching napkins, the corners appliquéd with single vine leaves and tendrils, c1937, 61 x 155in (155 x 394cm).
£15,000–16,500 *S(NY)*

This was used as an altar cloth on the occasion of the marriage of the Duke and Duchess of Windsor at the Château de Candé.

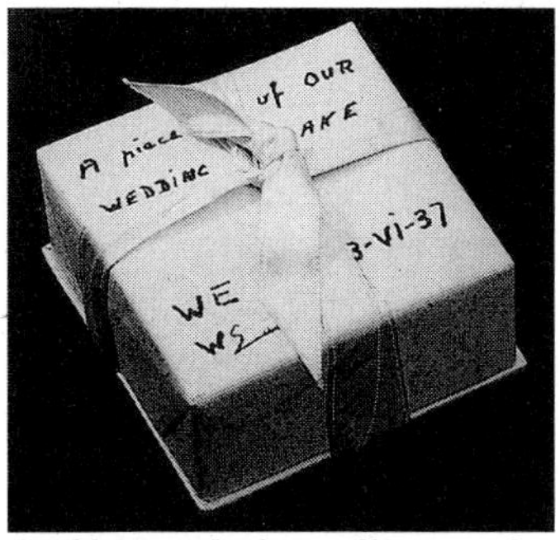

A ribbon-tied white silk-covered cardboard box, containing a piece of the Duke and Duchess of Windsor's wedding cake, inscribed in ink by the Duke and Duchess of Windsor, 'A piece of our wedding cake, WE WE 3-VI-37', 1937, 2¾in (7cm) square.
£18,250–20,000 *S(NY)*

An appliquéd wall hanging, with blue, gold, grey and scarlet wools forming the arms of the Prince of Wales, and the Fort Belvedere bed, with similarly coloured detailing, c1920, hanging 88 x 68½in (223.5 x 174cm).
Wall hanging £55,000–60,000
Bed £6,700–8,000 *S(NY)*

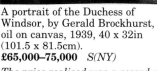

A portrait of the Duchess of Windsor, by Gerald Brockhurst, oil on canvas, 1939, 40 x 32in (101.5 x 81.5cm).
£65,000–75,000 *S(NY)*

The price realised was a record at auction for the artist Gerald Leslie Brockhurst, RA, who painted this portrait of the Duchess in 1939 at the Windsors' Paris home at 24 Boulevard Souchet where they first lived after the abdication.

A simulated aquamarine, green stone, and diamond necklace and matching earclips, by Kenneth Jay Lane, 1965, 17in (43cm) long, with a new fitted red case bearing the cypher 'WE' beneath a crown in gold.
£2,800–3,200 *S(NY)*

r. A Continental porcelain figure of a seated pug, covered in a thick peacock-blue glaze with black-delineated facial details, and wearing an iron-red and gilt collar affixed with gilt-heightened bells, restored, incised mark, late 19thC, 6½in (16cm) high.
£4,000–4,500 *S(NY)*

The Windsor collection featured a large number of pugs, as these were their favourite dogs.

FOCUS ON IRELAND

Traditionally, when the subject of Irish furniture came up in conversation, it was that of 18th century cabriole leg furniture and was of interest mainly to American buyers. Nowadays, Irish furniture is universally appreciated and is increasing in value.

Prior to 1800 not all cabinet makers' names are known due to poor record keeping and sparsity of labels, with the exception of gilt objects such as mirrors and picture frames, which quite often are labelled. From the 19th century makers such as Mack, Williams & Gibton (later Williams & Gibton), Gillington's, Strahan's and Jones stamped or labelled a fair percentage of their output. The firm of Mack, Williams & Gibton used the letters A, B, C or D, followed by a four- or five-digit number to indicate their manufacture. Gillington's, Strahan's and Jones used a stamped number of different sizes and often printed labels were used.

Over the years we have learned to identify with some degree of accuracy the area from which particular furniture originated. Furniture manufactured in Belfast, Cork and Limerick can be identified by their shape; for instance in Belfast a washstand or dressing table has a shaped top on a straight two-drawer or three-drawer kneehole base and sideboards are usually of a running serpentine shape, and do not break with a flat above the legs. In Cork the same dressing table would have a concave shape to both the top and the carcass and usually has stretchers. In Limerick, one finds a provincial version of what could be expected of Cork.

A revival of 18th century design took place after 1850 both in England and Ireland and large quantities of all types of earlier furniture designs were produced. The firm of M. Butler was one of these 'copy' furniture makers whose works were of great quality. They made very good cabriole leg chairs in large sets, following the style of an armchair that is in Malahide Castle. A vast number of carved and gilded mirrors in Chippendale style continued to be manufactured up until the 1920s.

A large amount of satinwood furniture was produced by Butler and Hicks but is commonly rather stiff and not quite as stylish as the older version. However, on the Irish market it is very sought after and often fetches nearly as much as period pieces.

Frequently, the legs of early Irish dining and wing chairs are dovetailed into the seat rails rather than tenoned to the legs. When chairs, chests and cabinets were originally made the underneath was often covered with a red size glue which, over the years, has departed leaving a patchy surface which should show the bare wood, and should look old. It has been said that stains were applied 'to hide something', so look very carefully for signs of alterations with heavily stained areas.

Mark Kenyon

Furniture

l. A set of Irish mahogany open bookshelves, with 2 small drawers on top, standing on hairy paw feet, c1825, 36in (91.5cm) wide.
£3,300–3,600 *GKe*

A Regency Irish mahogany breakfront bookcase, the doors glazed in Gothic style, the base with velvet-covered panels, 66in (167.5cm) wide.
£5,500–6,250 *GKe*

A George III style Irish mahogany secretaire bookcase, late 19thC, 40in (101.5cm) wide.
£2,600–2,850 *SK(B)*

A George III Irish mahogany and brass-bound peat bucket, with swing handle, 15¾in (40cm) diam.
£700–800 *P(G)*

l. An Irish inlaid walnut bureau-cabinet, the shaped panelled doors and fall-front enclosing pigeonholes and shelves, above 2 short and 2 long drawers, on bracket feet, c1720, 38in (96.5cm) wide.
£28,000–32,000 *S*

r. A Georgian Irish bureau top, the dentil moulded cornice with a swan neck pediment, above 2 cushion panelled doors enclosing adjustable shelves and pigeonholes, with candle slides below, 35in (89cm) wide.
£3,600–4,000 *MEA*

A George I Irish walnut document cabinet, crossbanded and herringbone strung, the front with a tall single door simulating 6 drawers with brass drop handles, with fitted interior and 4 secret drawers, on bracket feet, 21in (53.5cm) wide.
£10,500–11,500 *HAM*

An Irish oak step-back Windsor chair, c1725.
£180–200 *EON*

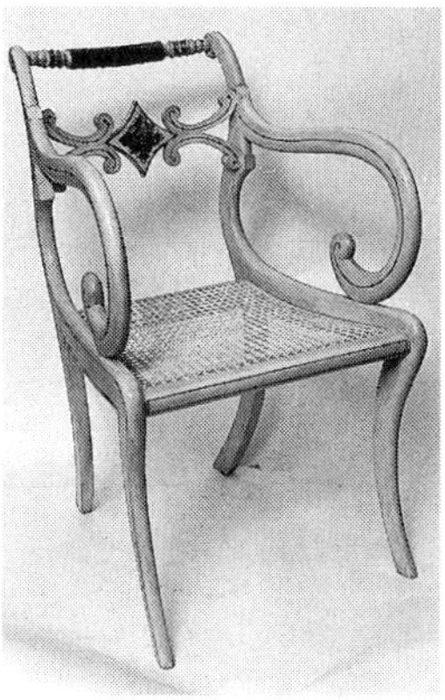

A pair of Irish open armchairs, with cane seats, painted decoration and brass mounts, on sabre legs, c1810.
£2,250–2,750 *GKe*

A set of 12 Irish mahogany dining chairs, including 2 armchairs, with drop-in seats, on turned and reeded front legs, c1825.
£8,500–10,000 *GKe*

A set of 12 Irish mahogany dining chairs, with shaped upholstered backs, on turned and fluted front legs, stamped 'Strahan & Co, Dublin', c1860.
£8,500–10,000 *GKe*

An Irish carved, stripped and waxed linden wood mirror, with dodo birds at the upper corners, c1760, 19½in (49.5cm) wide.
£2,300–2,500 *NOA*

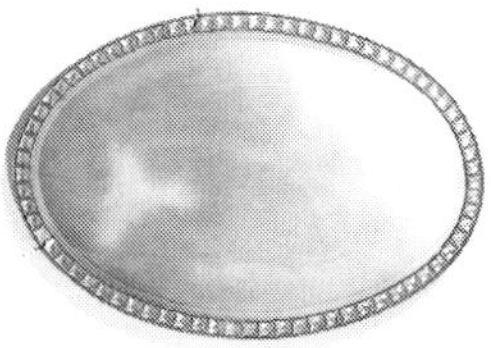

An Irish wall mirror, the frame of clear glass faceted studs, 19thC, 29½in (75cm) wide.
£1,600–1,750 *AH*

l. A pair of Irish dining chairs, with inlaid top-rails, c1830.
£600–700 *STA*

An Irish mahogany sideboard, with cellaret drawer and cupboard, on hairy paw feet, c1830, 78½in (199.5cm) wide.
£2,800–3,200 *STA*

l. A George II Irish mahogany fold-over card table, with baize lining and counter recesses, shell and rosette decorated frieze, concertina action, on carved cabriole legs with paw feet, 37½in (95.5cm) wide.
£11,000–12,000 *P(O)*

An Irish mahogany sideboard, with concave front and bowed ends, on Nelson twist legs with hairy paw feet, c1825, 84in (213.5cm) wide.
£2,800–3,200 *GKe*

This type of spiral reeding is known as Nelson twist, named after the ropes on Admiral Nelson's ship.

An Irish mahogany hunt table, with demi-lune flaps, on 6 square tapering legs, stamped 'Butler of Dublin', 19thC, 64in (162.5cm) long.
£2,000-2,200 *MEA*

An Irish yew wood and marquetry games table, on a waisted pillar platform base, with ebonised carved claw feet, c1850, 31in (78.5cm) wide.
£2,500–2,800 *S(S)*

r. An Irish mahogany bowed breakfront serving table, with acanthus carved cabriole front legs headed with rosettes, on paw feet with casters, c1830, 97in (246.5cm) wide.
£4,000–4,500 *P*

A pair of Irish demi-lune satinwood and tulipwood crossbanded side tables, on slender turned leg supports, c1790, 33in (84cm) wide.
£20,000–22,000 *GKe*

An Irish mahogany three-section serving table, with an arched galleried back and cushion-moulded frieze, on lobed tapering legs with scroll carved spandrels, mid-19thC, 115in (292cm) wide.
£2,000–2,200 *Bon*

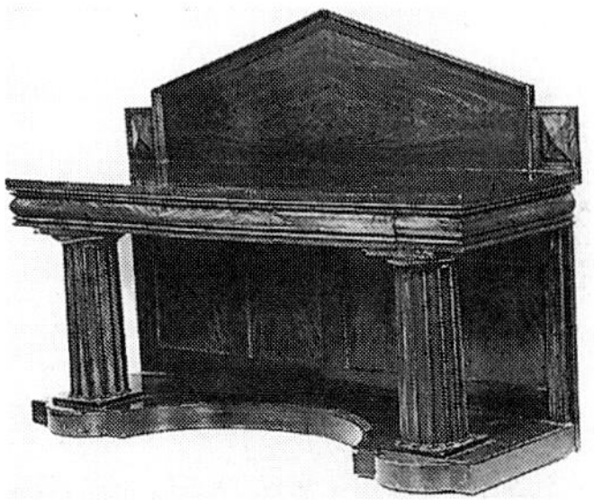

r. A Victorian Irish mahogany side table, attributed to Strahan of Dublin, with 3 moulded frieze drawers, on fluted columns and concave platform, 89in (226cm) wide.
£1,400–1,600 *MEA*

Pine Furniture

An Irish pine butcher's block, c1880, 48in (122cm) wide.
£470–530 *DFA*

An Irish pine country chair, c1850.
£120–140 *ByI*

An Irish pine four-door cupboard, with 2 drawers, c1860, 49in (124.5cm) wide.
£800–900 *ByI*

An Irish pine chicken coop dresser, c1860, 60in (152.5cm) wide.
£1,200–1,500 *ByI*

A set of 4 Irish oak and elm side chairs, c1810.
£380–420 *EON*

An Irish pine dove-tailed chest, bound with wrought iron, c1720, 25½in (65cm) wide.
£180–200 *EON*

An Irish pine cupboard, with breakfront top, panelled doors, and central spice drawer, c1840, 58in (147.5cm) wide.
£1,600–1,800 *HON*

An Irish pine dresser, the top carved with motifs, the base with 2 drawers and central spice drawer, on bracket feet, restored and altered, c1840, 55in (139.5cm) wide.
£700–775 *DFA*

An Irish pine commode chair, c1820.
£220–240 *EON*

An Irish painted pine architectural cupboard, with reeded columns, requires restoration, c1820, 75in (190.5cm) wide.
£2,400–2,700 *HON*

An Irish pine and elm side chair, with original paint, c1840.
£30–40 *TAN*

An Irish pine dressing chest, c1875, 42in (106.5cm) wide.
£280–320 *ByI*

An Irish pine dresser, the base with 2 drawers and 2 cupboard doors, c1890, 59in (150cm) wide.
£750–850 *TAN*

An Irish pine settle, opening to form a bed, c1860, 73in (185.5cm) wide.
£450–500 *DFA*

An Irish pine stool, c1880, 18in (45.5cm) wide.
£25–30 *SA*

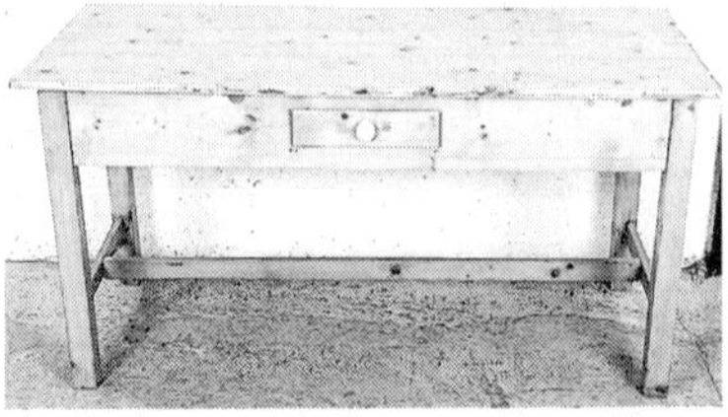

An Irish pine farmhouse table, with a single drawer, c1870, 59in (150cm) long.
£300–335 *ByI*

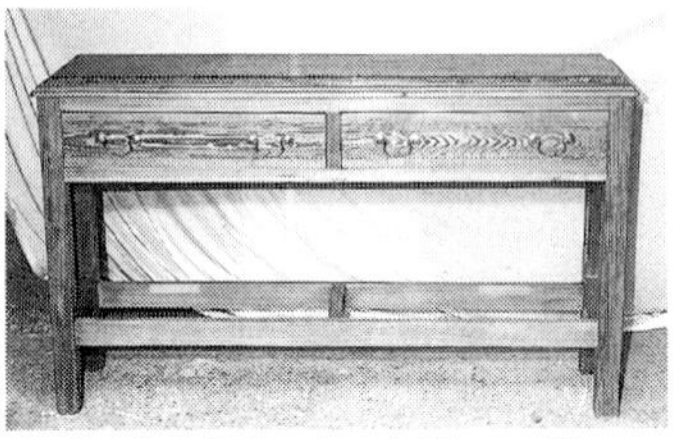

An Irish pitch pine table, with inset marble top, 2 drawers with brass handles, the straight legs joined by stretchers, c1880, 63in (160cm) long.
£330–360 *DFA*

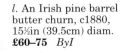

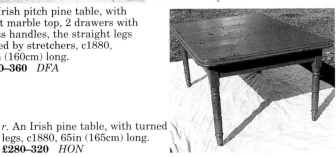

An Irish pitch pine library table, with turned tapering legs, requires restoration, c1880, 132in (335.5cm) long.
£500–600 *HON*

r. An Irish pine table, with turned legs, c1880, 65in (165cm) long.
£280–320 *HON*

Kitchenware

An Irish oak tub, c1870, 17in (43cm) diam.
£80–90 *ByI*

An Irish painted pine butter churn, c1800, 36in (91.5cm) high.
£160–180 *HON*

l. An Irish pine barrel butter churn, c1880, 15½in (39.5cm) diam.
£60–75 *ByI*

An Irish wooden butter stamp, moulded with Tree of Life design, mid-19thC, 5in (12.5cm) diam.
£35–40 *EON*

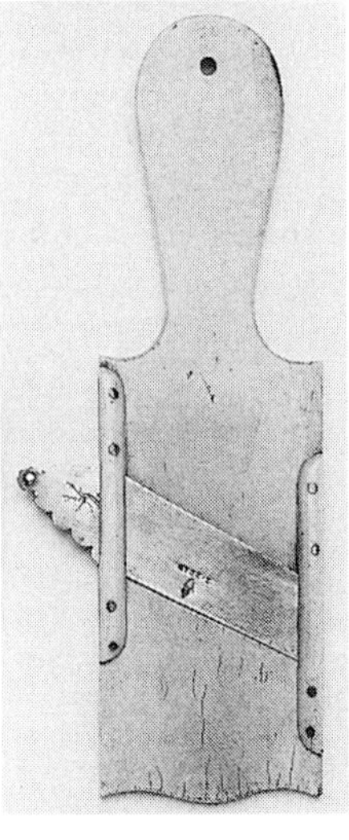

l. An Irish cucumber slice, with ivory frame, the steel blade engraved with a stag's head crest, stamped 'I. Read' below a crowned harp, Dublin, c1800, 9in (23cm) long.
£1,000–1,100 *P*

An Irish stone bottle, stamped 'The Enniskillen Bonded Store Ltd, Market Street, Enniskillen', late 19thC, 15½in (39.5cm) high.
£160–180 *EON*

An Irish copper and brass kettle, 18thC, 11½in (29cm) high.
£130–150 *EON*

Ceramics

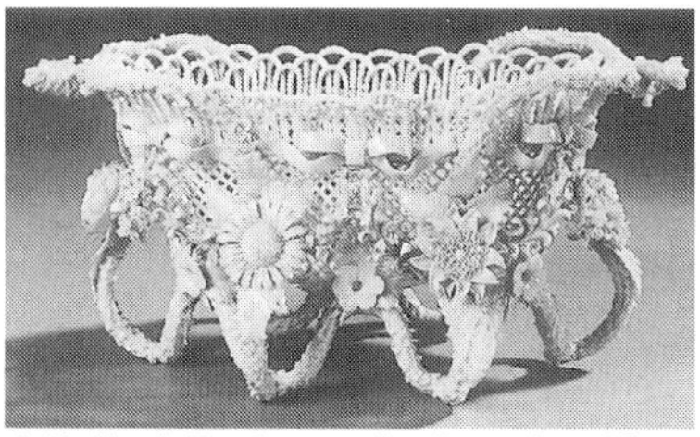

A Belleek Rathmore basket, the sides applied with swags of forget-me-nots and tied with ribbons, the three-strand base on twig supports, the feet applied with blooms, all heightened in lustre, damaged, impressed mark, c1865, 11in (28cm) wide.
£1,600–1,750 *P*

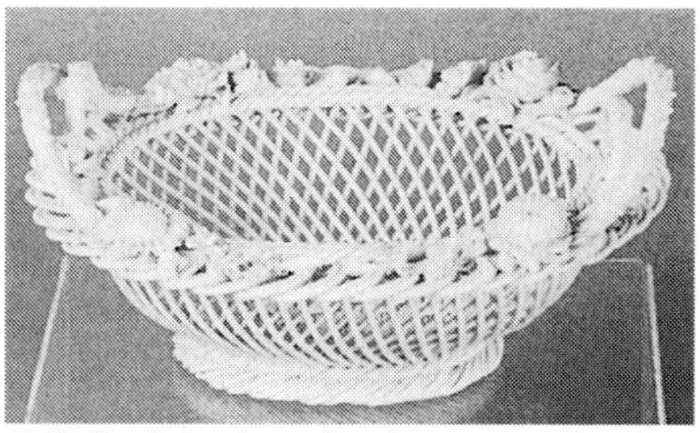

A Belleek basket, the three-strand centre with a rope-twist border, the looped rim applied with flowers and foliage, with a pair of briar stem handles, impressed mark, c1863, 8¼in (21cm) wide.
£370–400 *HYD*

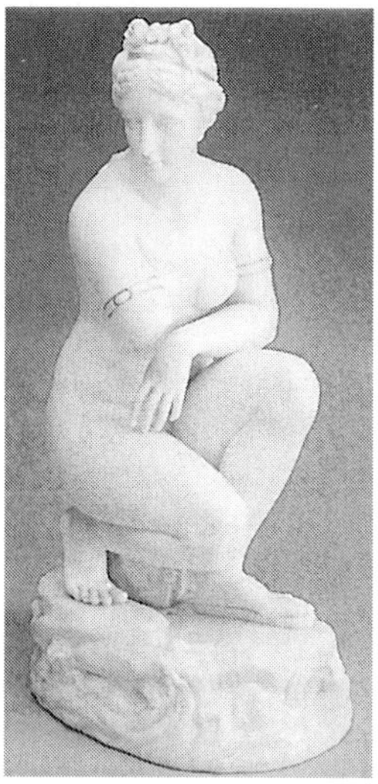

r. A Belleek Parian figure, picked out in gilt, on a wave scroll moulded oval mound base, printed mark in black, c1870, 18½in (47cm) high.
£1,200–1,350 *DN(H)*

A Belleek earthenware jug, c1863, 12¼in (31cm) high.
£480–530 *DeA*

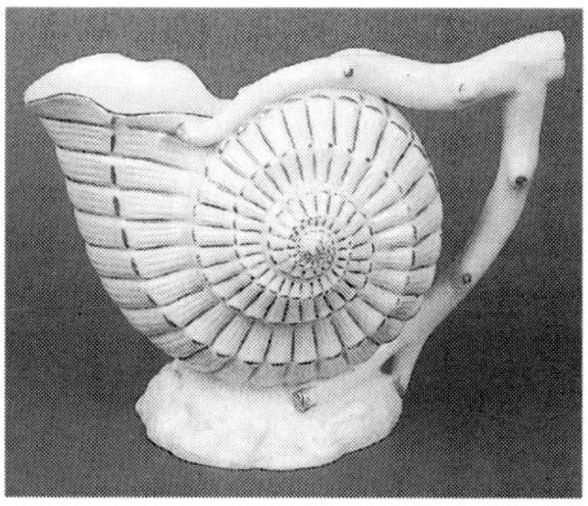

A Belleek cream jug, in the form of a shell, with gilt decoration, c1863, 5½in (14cm) high.
£350–400 *MLa*

The gilding on this piece is unusual, as they were usually left white or have a pink finish to the handle.

A Belleek floral-encrusted 'handbag' vase, c1858, 6in (15cm) wide.
£320–350 *DeA*

A Herbert Cooper porcelain mask jug, marked, c1870, 4in (10cm) high.
£200–220 *STA*

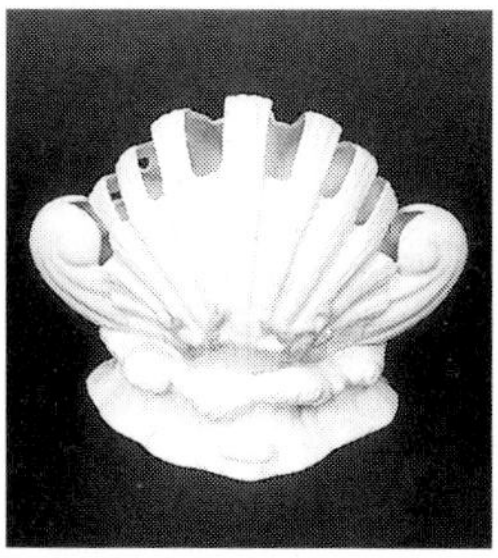

A Belleek violet vase, decorated in pink, c1863, 5½in (14cm) wide.
£375–400 *MLa*

l. A Donovan blue and white tureen, impressed mark, c1820, 7¼in (18.5cm) wide.
£240–270 *STA*

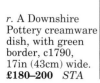

r. A Downshire Pottery creamware dish, with green border, c1790, 17in (43cm) wide.
£180–200 *STA*

Silver

A silver penal pyx, by Thomas Sutton, Dublin 1730, 2in (5cm) diam.
£1,400–1,600 *WELD*

This was used by Roman Catholic priests to carry the host (bread) when the penal laws forbade the practise of Catholicism in Ireland.

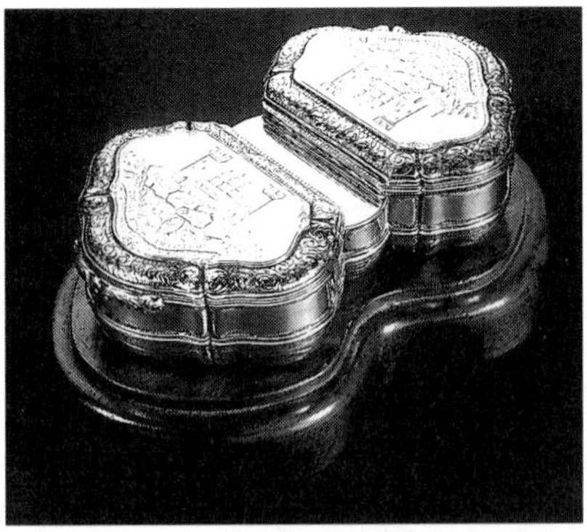

An Irish silver double snuff box, by John Townsend, each of cartouche form, with applied moulded body bands, the covers with leaf-carved thumbpieces and chased borders, the centres engraved with motto, City Arms of Cork, and 'Royal Cork Artillery', Dublin 1855, on a walnut plinth, 7in (17.5cm) wide, 13oz.
£6,000–7,000 *HAM*

This was originally made for the officers of the Royal Cork Artillery and would have been mounted on a large table centrepiece, probably incorporating the horns of a ram's head and forming part of a typical officers' mess snuff mull.

A pair of Irish silver candlesticks, by Gustavus Byrne, Dublin 1793, 10½in (26.5cm) high, 48oz.
£6,000–6,700 *WELD*

l. An Irish silver-gilt cup and cover, by Thomas Sutton, engraved with contemporary arms on a foliate mantle, the cover engraved with a crest, Dublin 1724, 12¾in (32.5cm) high, 52½oz.
£2,300–2,600 *S(NY)*

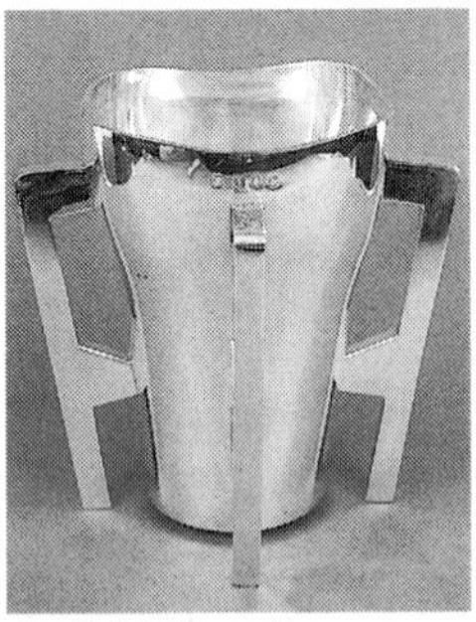

An Irish flared cylindrical four-handled silver cup, with square rim and angular handle supports, Dublin 1907, 7½in (19cm) high.
£675–750 *WeH*

An Irish silver Celtic dish ring, by Wakely & Wheeler, Dublin 1911, 7in (18cm) diam.
£2,200–2,500 *SIL*

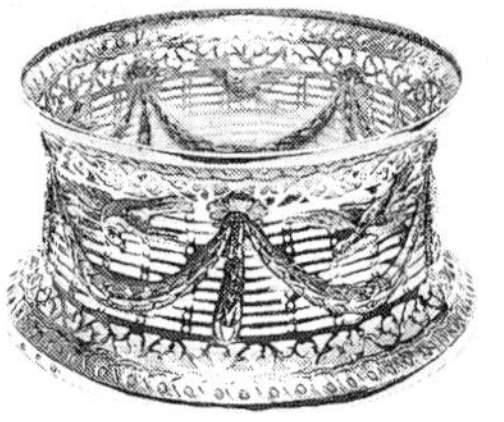

An Irish silver dish ring, by Jos. Jackson, Dublin, c1775, 7½in (19cm) diam.
£7,500–8,500 *WELD*

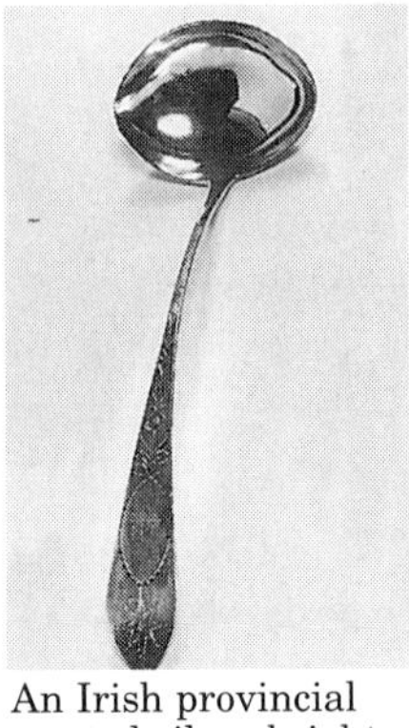

An Irish provincial crested silver bright-cut soup ladle, by Carden Terry and Jane Williams, Cork, c1805, 12in (30.5cm) long, 6½oz.
£800–900 *MEA*

An Irish silver pumpkin-shaped cream or milk jug, by Jas. Fray, Dublin, c1830, 5in (12.5cm) wide, 19oz.
£430–470 *MEA*

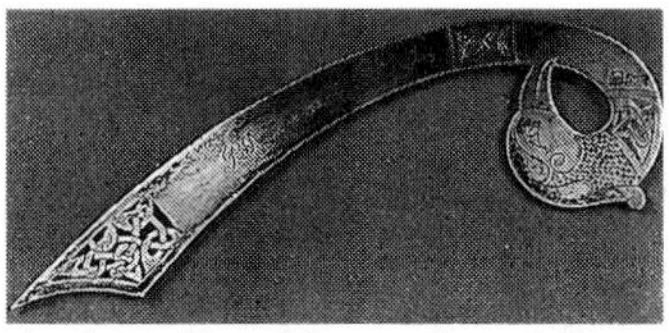

An Irish Republican silver letter opener, by William Egan, in the form of a Celtic bird, with intertwined engraved and pierced decoration, inscribed and dated '1923', Cork 1922, 7in (18cm) long, 2oz.
£800–900 *JAd*

A set of 4 Irish silver salts, by W. Nowlan, Dublin 1825, 4¼in (11cm) diam.
£1,800–2,000 *SIL*

An Irish silver salver, by James Le Bass, engraved with an armorial on 4 shell and scroll chased feet, Dublin 1812, 17in (43cm) diam, 76oz.
£2,000–2,200 *DN*

An Irish silver coffee pot, with armorial engraving, rococo chased with flowers, scrolls and bearded masks, wood scroll handle, possibly by William Williamson, Dublin, c1735, 9¼in (23.5cm) high, 34¾oz.
£1,600–1,800 *S*

An Irish provincial silver tea caddy, by Samuel Reily, Cork, with hinged cover and fitted lock, bright-cut decoration, engraved with a crest, later flower finial, c1800, 4¼in (11cm) diam.
£3,200–3,600 *JAd*

An Irish silver coffee pot, the acanthus leaf-capped spout decorated with concave fluting, the cover applied with a pine cone finial, ivory scroll handle, engraved with a coat-of-arms, maker's mark for Andrew Goodwin, Dublin, c1750, 9¾in (25cm) high, 32oz.
£3,000–3,300 *P*

Irish Marks

Dublin Hibernia

In Ireland, from 1637, silver was marked with an assay mark depicting a crowned harp. This stamp was also used as a Dublin town mark from 1637–1807. After 1807 a stamp showing the seated figure of Hibernia was used as Dublin's town mark.

An Irish embossed silver teapot, by Jas. Fray, Dublin 1828, 12in (30.5cm) wide.
£1,100–1,250 *SIL*

l. An Irish silver baluster-shaped coffee pot, by John Morton, embossed with shells, flowers and leaves, engraved with a crest, on pierced and chased shell and foliate feet, Dublin 1843, 9¾in (25cm) high, 31oz.
£620–680 *DN(H)*

An Irish silver four-piece tea service, applied with chased Celtic open paterae, banding and prunts, maker's mark 'TW', Dublin 1930, 69½oz.
£800–1,000 *WW*

Glass

An Irish glass bowl, with turnover rim, knopped stem and square lemon squeezer foot, c1790, 13in (33cm) diam.
£1,600–1,750 *CB*

An Irish glass canoe-shaped bowl, on a petal-moulded spreading foot, c1790, 12½in (32cm) wide.
£1,500–1,650 *CB*

An Irish glass water jug, cut with flutes, a band of vesica decoration, flutes and prisms, with a notched rim and strap handle, c1810, 6¾in (17cm) high.
£350–400 *Som*

Vesica decoration – a band of plain incised ovals – is particularly associated with Irish table glass.

An Irish wine glass, engraved with swags and stars, on a faceted stem, late 18thC, 4½in (11.5cm) high.
£50–60 *FD*

l. An Irish glass pickle jar, with cut diamond decoration, the domed cut cover with a mushroom finial, on a lemon squeezer foot, c1800, 7¼in (18.5cm) high.
£400–450 *Som*

Clocks & Watches

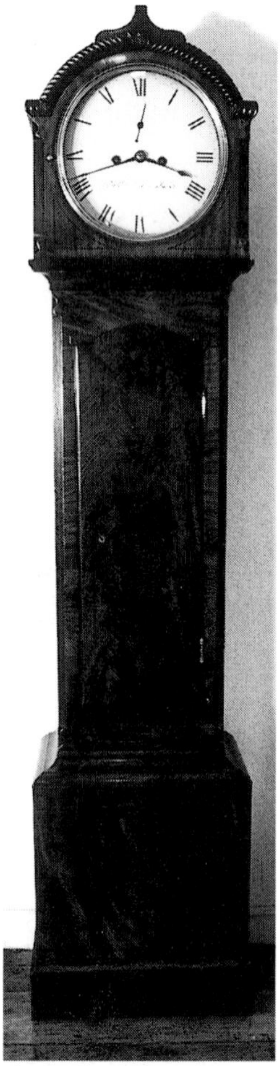

An Irish mahogany 8-day longcase clock, by Buchannan, with enamel painted dial, striking on a bell, early 19thC, 80in (203cm) high.
£2,800–3,000 *TIM*

The crest features a tribute to Admiral Lord Nelson in the form of marine rope carving.

An Irish inlaid mahogany 8-day bracket clock, painted and gilt arch dial signed 'Geo Hauley, Dublin', c1790, 15½in (39.5cm) high.
£4,500–5,500 *BEE*

An Irish silver pair-cased Debaufre pocket watch, signed Warner, Dublin, c1790, 2¼in (58mm) diam.
£550–600 *PT*

This rare escapement, also known as a chaff-cutter, Ormskirk or club-footed verge, was the first frictional rest escapement invented by Debaufre in 1704.

Rugs & Carpets

A Donegal carpet, designed by Gavin Moreton, the Prussian blue field with 5 coral palmettes on saffron vines, with lavender palmettes and flowering branches, the cream border with similar motifs, c1890, 147 x 134in (373.5 x 340.5cm).
£11,000–13,000 *LRG*

A Donegal carpet, in shades of green, cream and coral, c1900, 192 x 151in (488 x 383cm).
£14,000–16,000 *S(NY)*

A Donegal Savonnerie style carpet, woven in cotton and wool with floral medallion and borders, c1940, 158 x 120in (403 x 305cm).
£4,300–4,700 *LIN*

Textiles

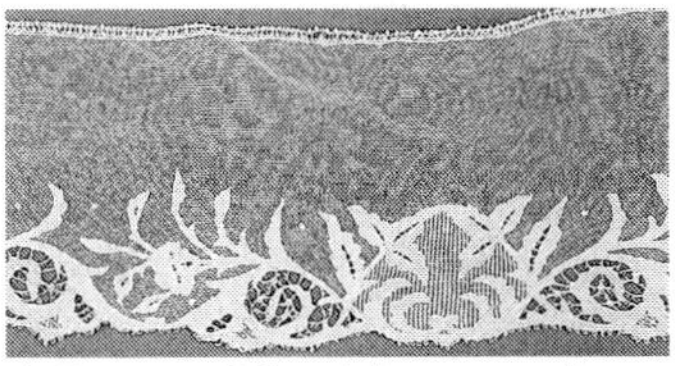

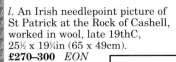

A flounce of Carrickmacross lace, c1900, 120in (305cm) long.
£80–100 *LB*

l. An Irish needlepoint picture of St Patrick at the Rock of Cashell, worked in wool, late 19thC, 25½ x 19¼in (65 x 49cm).
£270–300 *EON*

A Victorian Irish cream lace bodice.
£1,000–1,100 *JVa*

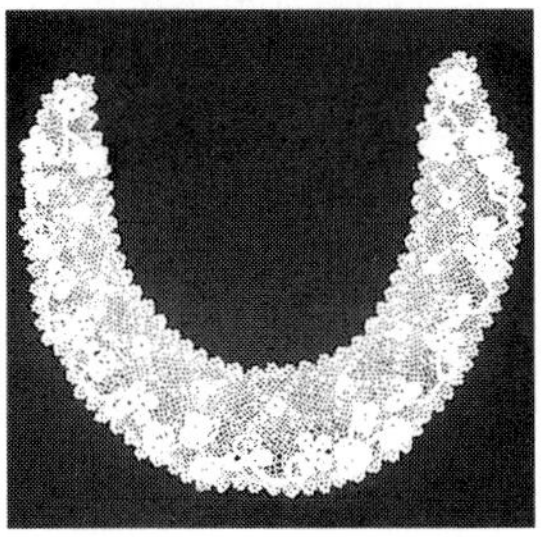

An Irish cream lace collar, c1880, 14in (35.5cm) long.
£50–60 *AIL*

An Irish lace child's dress, from Limerick, late 19thC, 24in (61cm) long.
£80–90 *EON*

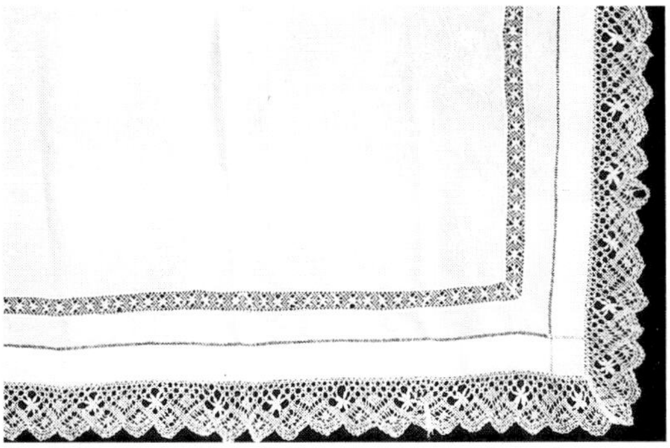

An Irish linen tablecloth, with drawn thread work and hand embroidery, c1900, 54in (137cm) square.
£80–100 *AIL*

Jewellery

A Connemara marble brooch, with silver mounts, c1860, 3in (7.5cm) diam.
£250–300 *BWA*

A Celtic revival silver and copper belt, by Hopkins & Hopkins, the design from the Ardagh chalice links from the Book of Kells, Dublin 1909, 24in (61cm) long.
£630–700 *SIL*

Don't Forget!
If in doubt please refer to the 'How to Use' page at the beginning of this book.

A 9ct gold Claddagh ring, Dublin 1918.
£110–135 *HofB*

Claddagh rings are often in the form of 2 hands clasping a heart, and are given as a token of eternal love.

Boxes

A Killarney box, with floral marquetry inlay, c1860, 6in (15cm) wide.
£200–220 *STA*

A yew wood and mahogany Killarney work fitted sewing box, with marquetry picture of Mucross Abbey on the lid, c1870, 10in (25.5cm) square.
£180–200 *GKe*

Cross Reference
Colour Review

A bog oak box, decorated with shamrocks, 19thC, 2in (50mm) diam.
£60–70 *STA*

Bog oak is a jet substitute, made of peat-preserved wood.

Miniatures

An enamel portrait miniature of Mary Delaney, by Rupert Barber, c1750, 2in (50mm) high.
£1,600–1,800 *SIL*

A portrait miniature of a young boy, by Gustavus Hamilton, on ivory, signed and dated '1766', 1¼in (32mm) high.
£1,250–1,400 *SIL*

A portrait miniature, on ivory, signed and dated 'S. Lover 1822', 5¼ x 4½in (13.5 x 11.5cm).
£1,200–1,350 *SIL*

A portrait miniature of John Ormsby Vandeleur, Colonel 10th Hussars, Irish School, on ivory, 19thC, 3in (7.5cm) high.
£650–720 *MEA*

Books

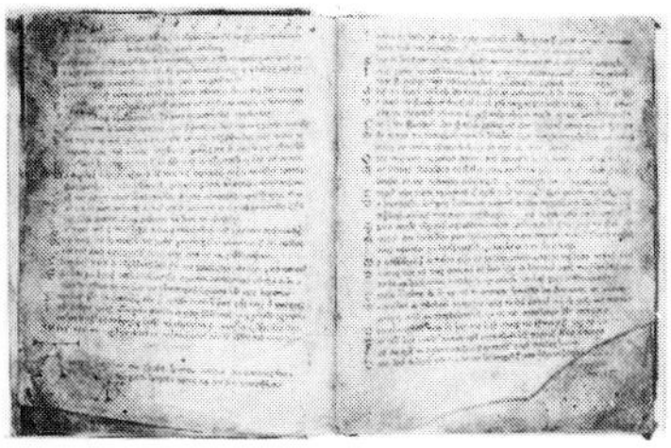

The Nugent Manuscript of Irish Bardic Poetry, *An Duanaire Nuinseannach*, with 49 poems in Gaelic dating from 13th to 16thC, now comprising 48 leaves, (an early set of foliation extended to 55), on vellum, 4°, c1577, with modern vellum gilt boards.
£155,000+ *S*

This is one of the rarest manuscripts to appear for sale in modern times, and the first early Irish manuscript to be auctioned since 1831. It is thought unlikely that any of these will ever change hands again.

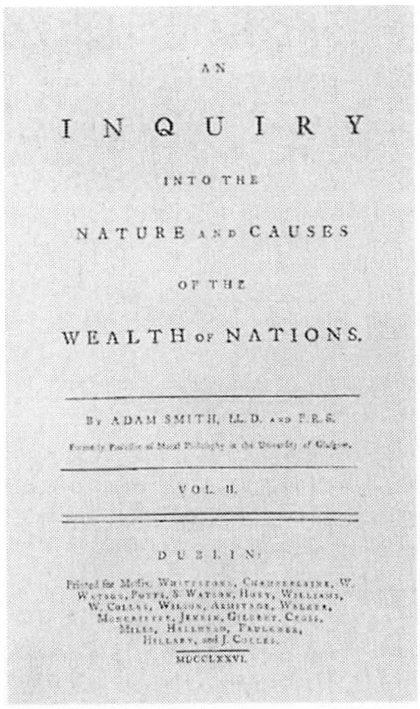

AN
INQUIRY
INTO THE
NATURE AND CAUSES
OF THE
WEALTH OF NATIONS.

BY ADAM SMITH, LL. D. AND F.R.S.

VOL. II.

DUBLIN:

MDCCLXXVI.

Adam Smith, *An Inquiry into the Nature and Causes of the Wealth of Nations*, first Dublin edition, 3 vols, contemporary calf, spines gilt, 8°, 1776.
£2,200–2,500 *BBA*

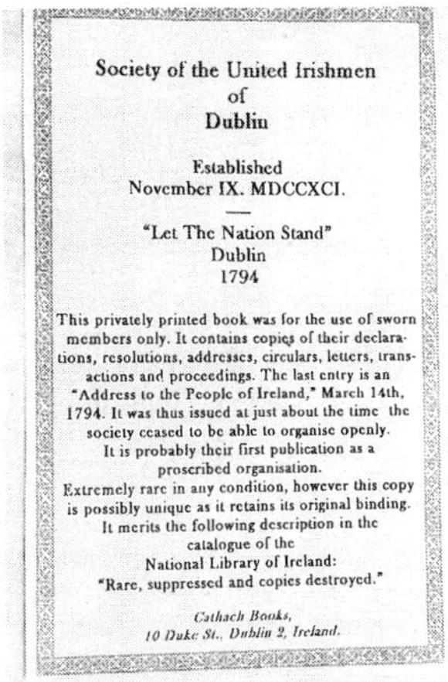

Society of the United Irishmen
of
Dublin

Established
November IX. MDCCXCI.

"Let The Nation Stand"
Dublin
1794

This privately printed book was for the use of sworn members only. It contains copies of their declarations, resolutions, addresses, circulars, letters, transactions and proceedings. The last entry is an "Address to the People of Ireland," March 14th, 1794. It was thus issued at just about the time the society ceased to be able to organise openly. It is probably their first publication as a proscribed organisation.
Extremely rare in any condition, however this copy is possibly unique as it retains its original binding. It merits the following description in the catalogue of the National Library of Ireland:
"Rare, suppressed and copies destroyed."

Cathach Books,
10 Duke St., Dublin 2, Ireland.

Let The Nation Stand, by the Society of the United Irishmen of Dublin, original binding, 1794, 6 x 4in (15 x 10cm).
£2,800–3,200 *CATH*

This copy is possibly unique as it retains its original binding. A copy sold at auction in 1926 realised £22.

Firearms

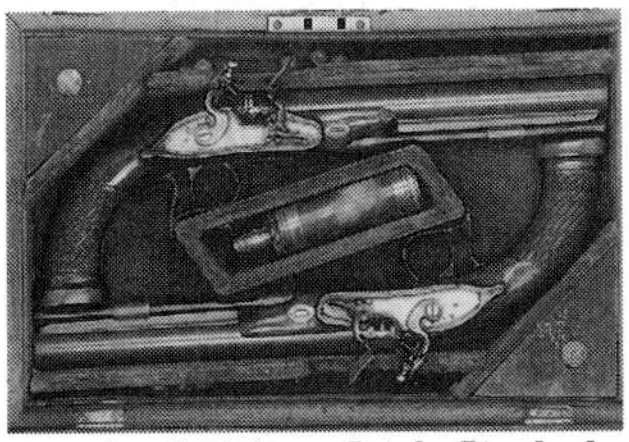

A pair of 20 bore Irish flintlock officer's pistols, signed 'Turner, Dublin', reconverted from flintlock, each with rebrowned twist barrel, walnut half-stock, horn fore-end, horn-tipped wooden ramrod, early 19thC, barrels 9¼in (23.5cm) long, in associated mahogany case with copper flask.
£1,500–1,650 *S(S)*

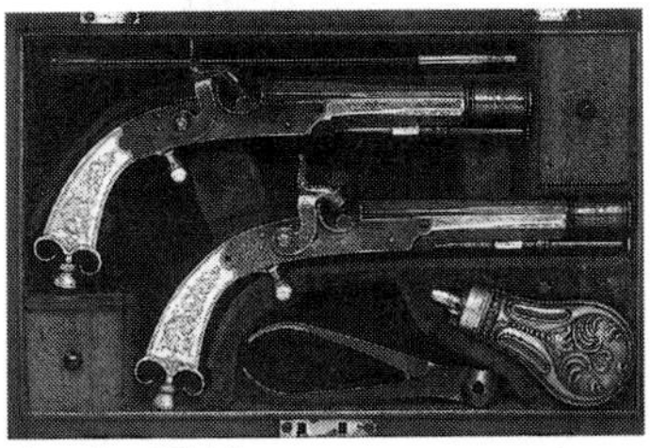

A pair of Irish percussion pistols, in the Highland manner, by Henry Allport, Cork, each with a .54 calibre three-stage barrel, mid-19thC, barrels 6⅝in (16.5cm) long, with brass-bound case and accessories.
£5,600–6,000 *B&B*

An over-and-under back action percussion pistol, by Kavanagh, Dublin, c1860, 8¾in (22cm) long.
£700–800 *Bon*

Miscellaneous

An Irish rustic carved wood walking stick, the knop in the form of a man in period dress, early 19thC, 39in (99cm) long.
£200–250 *P*

l. A violin, by Perry & Wilkinson, Dublin, with original neck and baroque fingerboards, c1803, 14in (35.5cm) long.
£800–900 *CRV*

GLOSSARY

We have defined here some of the terms that you will come across in this book. If there are any terms or technicalities you would like explained or you feel should be included in future, please let us know.

abrash: Tone differences within the colour of a rug, normally due to variations in the dyes.
acid engraving: Technique of decorating glass by coating it in resin, incising a design and exposing the revealed areas to hydrochloric acid fumes.
acid-gilding: 19thC technique for decorating pottery whereby the surface is etched with hydrofluoric acid and the low-relief pattern gilded.
agate ware: 18thC pottery, veined or marbled to resemble the mineral agate.
air-twist: Helical decoration in the stem of wine glasses, developed 1740–70, in which an air bubble in the glass is drawn out and twisted to form complex spirals.
alabastron: Ancient vessel of cylindrical shape with a rounded bottom and lug handles, originally made of alabaster, but later of glass or pottery, used for storing perfumes, unguents etc.
albarello: Pottery vessel used for storing pharmaceutical ingredients.
amboyna: Yellowish-brown burred wood imported from the West Indies and used as a veneer.
American Victorian: Period from 1830–1900 that incorporates several styles of furniture; Victorian, Gothic, Victorian rococo, Victorian renaissance and Eastlake.
anchor escapement: Said to have been invented c1670 by Robert Hooke or William Clement. A type of clock escape mechanism shaped like an anchor, which engages at precise intervals with the toothed escape wheel. The anchor permits the use of a pendulum (either long or short), and gives greater accuracy than was possible with the verge escapement (qv).
arabesque: Scrolling foliate decoration.
Arita: Name of a district in Hizen province on the island of Kyushu in south-west Japan, famous for its porcelain manufacture. Generic term for blue and white or polychrome porcelain produced for the Japanese home market.
armoire: Large French cupboard or wardrobe, usually of monumental character.
associated: Term used in antiques, in which one part of an item is of the same design but not originally made for it. *See marriage.*
Aubusson: French town, centre of production of tapestries and tapestry-weave carpets since 17thC, although formal workshops were not established until c1743.
automaton: Any moving toy or decorative object, usually powered by a clockwork mechanism.
ball-jointed doll: One with ball-jointed limbs, able to swivel in all directions, as opposed to stiff jointed.
barley-twist: Form of turning, popular in the late 17thC, which resembles a spiral of traditional barley sugar.
basalt(es): Black stoneware with a smooth, stone-like finish; perfected by Josiah Wedgwood.
Bauhaus: An influential art school established in Germany in 1919. The name is now synonymous with design style.
bébé: French dolls made by Bru and others in the latter half 19thC, modelled on idealised children of 8–12 years of age.
bezel: Ring, usually brass, surrounding the dial of a clock, and securing the glass dial cover.
bisque: French term for biscuit ware, or unglazed porcelain.
bluejohn: Blue or purple variety of fluorspar mined in Derbyshire, used for vases, tazzas, small ornaments etc.
bombé: Outswelling, curving or bulging. Term used to describe a chest with a bulging front. In fashion from Louis XV period.
bonheur du jour: Small French writing table with a raised back comprising a cabinet or shelves.
boteh: Stylised floral bush found on rugs, similar to a Paisley design.
bowfront: Outwardly curving front.
bracket clock: Originally a 17thC clock which had to be set high up on a bracket because of the length of the weights; now sometimes applied to any mantel or table clock.
bureau bookcase: Bureau with a glazed-fronted bookcase fitted above it.
bureau cabinet: Bureau with a solid-doored or mirrored cabinet fitted above it, often containing further fitted cupboards and drawers.
bureau de dame: Writing desk of delicate appearance and designed for use by ladies. Usually raised on slender cabriole legs and with one or two external drawers.
bureau-plat: French writing table with a flat top and drawers in the frieze.
cabaret set: Tea set on a tray for three or more people.
caddy: Container for tea, usually silver but also ceramic, wood or enamel. Wooden caddies are usually fitted with two compartments and contain a spoon and glass bowl for blending tea.
calamander: Hardwood, imported from Sri Lanka (of the same family as ebony), used in the Regency period for making small articles of furniture, as a veneer and for crossbanding.
camaieu: Porcelain decoration using different tones of a single colour.
cameo glass: Two or more layers of coloured glass in which the top layer/s are then cut or etched away to create a multi-coloured design in relief. An ancient technique popular with Art Nouveau glassmakers in the early 20thC.
candle slide: Small wooden slide designed to carry a candlestick.
Carlton House desk: Distinct type of writing desk which has a raised back with drawers which extend forward at the sides to create an 'enclosed' central writing area. Named after the Prince Regent's London home.
cartouche: Ornate tablet or shield surrounded by scrollwork and foliage, often bearing an inscription, monogram or coat-of-arms.
caryatid: Strictly a female figure used as a support in place of a column, but frequently used to describe a figure of either sex. *See term.*
cased glass: One layer of glass, often coloured, sandwiched between two plain glass layers or vice versa, the outer layer engraved to create a decorative effect. An ancient technique revived in the 19thC. *See cameo glass and overlay.*
Castelli: Maiolica from the Abruzzi region of Italy, noted for delicate landscapes painted by members of the Grue family.
celadon: Chinese stonewares with an opaque grey-green glaze, first made in the Sung dynasty and still made today, principally in Korea.
cellaret: Lidded container on legs designed to hold wine. The interior is often divided into sections for individual bottles.

centrepiece: Ornament, usually decorative rather than functional, designed to occupy the centre of a dining table.
champlevé: Enamelling on copper or bronze, similar to cloisonné, in which a glass paste is applied to the hollowed-out design, fired and ground smooth.
chapter ring: Circular ring on a clock dial on which the hours and minutes are engraved, attached or painted.
character doll: One with a naturalistic face, especially laughing, crying, pouting, etc.
character jug: 20thC earthenware jugs and sometimes mugs, depicting a popular character, such as a politician, general, jockey or actor. Developed from the Toby jug of the 19thC.
chesterfield: Type of large, overstuffed, button-backed sofa introduced in the late 19thC.
chiffonier: Generally a twin door cupboard with one or two drawers above and surmounted by shelves.
chilong: Chinese mythical dragon type lizard.
Chinese export porcelain: 16th–18thC wares made in China specifically for export and often to European designs.
Chinese Imari: Chinese imitations of Japanese blue, red and gold painted Imari wares, made from the early 18thC.
chinoiserie: The fashion, prevailing in the late 18thC, for Chinese style ornamentation on porcelain, wallpapers and fabrics, furniture and garden architecture.
chip carving: Type of simple carved decoration, where the surface has been lightly cut or chipped away.
chryselephantine: Originally a combination of gold and ivory, but now a term used for Art Deco statues made of ivory and a metal, usually bronze.
chuval: Turkic word meaning bag.
cistern tube: Mercury tube fitted into stick barometers, the lower end of which is sealed into a boxwood cistern.
cleat: Strip of wood attached to the edge of a flat surface across the grain for neatness and extra strength.
clock garniture: Matching group of clock and vases or candelabra made for the mantel shelf. Often highly ornate.
cloisonné: Enamelling on metal with divisions in the design separated by lines of fine metal wire. A speciality of the Limoges region of France in the Middle Ages, and of Chinese craftsmen to the present day.
coffer: Strictly a travelling trunk which is banded with metalwork and covered with leather or other material. However, the word tends to be used quite freely to describe various kinds of chests without drawers.
coiffeuse: French term for a dressing table.
Colonial: American object made in the style of the period when the country consisted of 13 Colonies, usually of the 17thC or 18thC.
Commedia dell'Arte: Figures from traditional Italian theatre (Harlequin, Columbine, Scaramouche, Pantaloon) often depicted in 18thC porcelain groups.
coromandel: Imported wood from the Coromandel coast of India, of similar blackish appearance to calamander. Used from c1780 for banding and for small pieces of furniture.
country furniture: General term for furniture made by provincial craftsmen; cottage furniture and especially that made of pine, oak, elm and the fruitwoods.
countwheel: Wheel with segments cut out of the edge or with pins fitted to one face, which controls the striking of a clock. Also known as a locking plate.
credenza: Used today to describe a type of side cabinet which is highly decorated and shaped. Originally it was an Italian sideboard used as a serving table.
crested china: Porcelain decorated with colourful heraldic crests, first made by Goss but, by 1900, being produced in quantity by manufacturers throughout the UK and in Germany.
cup and cover: Carved decoration found on the bulbous turned legs of some Elizabethan furniture.
cut glass: Glass carved with revolving wheels and abrasive to create sharp-edged facets that reflect and refract light so as to sparkle and achieve a prismatic (rainbow) effect. Revived in Bohemia in the 17thC, and common until superseded by pressed glass for utilitarian objects.
Cymric: Trade name used by Liberty & Co for a mass produced range of silverware inspired by Celtic art, introduced in 1899 and often incorporating enamelled pictorial plaques.
deadbeat escapement: Type of anchor escapement (qv) possibly invented by George Graham and used in precision pendulum clocks.
Delft: Dutch tin glazed earthenwares named after the town of Delft, the principal production centre, from the 16thC onwards. Similar pottery made in England from the late 16thC is also termed 'delft' or 'delftware'.
Della Robbia: Florentine Renaissance sculptor who invented technique of applying vitreous glaze to terracotta; English art pottery made at Birkenhead, late 19thC, in imitation of his work.
deng: Chinese ceremonial drinking vessel.
deutsche Blumen: Naturalistically painted flowers used as a popular decorative motif on 18thC pottery and porcelain.
diaper: Surface decoration composed of repeated diamonds or squares, often carved in low relief.
die-stamping: Method of mass-producing a design on metal by machine which passes sheet metal between a steel die and a drop hammer. Used for forming toys as well as stamping cutlery etc.
diorama: Miniature three-dimensional scene.
écuelle: 17th and 18thC vessel, usually of silver, but also of ceramic, for serving soup. Has a shallow, circular bowl, two handles and a domed cover. It often comes complete with a stand.
electroplate: Process of using electrical current to coat a base metal or alloy with silver, invented 1830s and gradually superseding Sheffield plate.
enamel: Coloured glass, applied to metal, ceramic or glass in paste form and then fired for decorative effect.
entablature: Part of a structure which surmounts a column and rests on the capital; the cornice, frieze and architrave.
EPNS: Electroplated nickel silver; i.e. nickel alloy covered with a layer of silver using the electroplate process.
escapement: Means or device which regulates the release of the power of a timepiece to its pendulum or balance.
famille jaune: 'Yellow family'; Chinese porcelain vessels in which yellow is the predominant ground colour.
famille noire: 'Black family'; Chinese porcelain in which black is the predominant ground colour.
famille rose: 'Pink family'; Chinese porcelain decoration with prominent enamel of pink to purple tones.
famille verte: 'Green family'; Chinese porcelain with a green enamel overglaze, laid over yellows, blues, purples and iron red.
fauteuil: French open-armed drawing room chair.
fiddleback: Descriptive of a particular grain of mahogany veneer which resembles the back of a violin.

fielded panel: Panel with bevelled or chamferred edges.
filigree: Lacy openwork of silver or gold thread, produced in large quantities since end 19thC.
flatware (1): Collective name for flat pottery, such as plates, dishes and saucers, as opposed to cups, vases and bowls.
flatware (2): Cutlery.
flow blue: Process used principally after 1840, in which flowing powder is added to the dye used in blue and white transferware so that the blue flows beyond the edges of the transfer, making the pattern less sharply defined. Items using this process were made primarily for the American market.
fluted: Border that resembles a scalloped edge, used as a decoration on furniture, glass, silver and porcelain items.
frosted glass: Glass with a surface pattern made to resemble frost patterns or snow-crystals; common on pressed glass vessels for serving cold confections.
fusee: 18thC clockwork invention; a cone shaped drum, linked to the spring barrel by a length of gut or chain. The shape compensates for the declining strength of the mainspring thus ensuring constant timekeeping.
gadroon: Border or ornament comprising radiating lobes of either curved or straight form. Used from the late Elizabethan period.
gilding: Process of applying thin gold foil to a surface. There are two methods. Oil gilding involves the use of linseed oil and is applied directly onto the woodwork. Water gilding requires the wood to be painted with gesso. The term is also used in ceramics, glass etc.
girandole: Carved and gilt candle sconce incorporating a mirror.
Glasgow School: Term used to describe the style developed in the late 19thC by Charles Rennie Mackintosh and his followers, a simplified linear form of Art Nouveau highly influential on Continental work of the period.
goncalo alves: Brazilian timber sometimes mistaken for rosewood.
grisaille: Monochrome decoration, usually grey, used on ceramics and furniture during the 18th and 19thC.
guéridon: Small circular table designed to carry some form of lighting.
gul: From the Persian word for flower – usually used to describe a geometric flowerhead on a rug.
halberd: Spear fitted with a double axe.
hand pressed: Any glass object made in a hand operated press instead of a machine press.
hard paste: True porcelain made of china stone (petuntse) and kaolin; the formula was long known to, and kept secret by, Chinese potters but only discovered in the 1720s in Meissen, Germany, from where it spread to the rest of Europe and the Americas. Recognised by its hard, glossy feel.
hardwood: One of two basic categories of timber. The hardwoods are from broad-leaved deciduous trees. *See also softwood.*
harewood: Sycamore which has been stained a greenish colour. It is used mainly as an inlay and was known as silverwood in the 18thC.
Hausmaler: German term for an independent painter or workshop specialising in the decoration of faïence, porcelain or glass blanks.
herati: Overall repeating design of a flowerhead within a lozenge issuing small leaves. Used in descriptions of rugs.
Hirado: Japanese porcelain with figure and landscape painting in blue on a white body, often depicting boys at play, made exclusively for the Lords of Hirado, near Arita, mid-18th to mid-19thC.
hiramakie: Japanese term for sponged gold applied level with the surface.
hirame: Japanese lacquer decorated with gold and silver leaf.
Imari: Export Japanese porcelain of predominantly red, blue and gold decoration which, although made in Arita, is called Imari after the port from which it was shipped.
indianische Blumen: Indian flowers; painting on porcelain in the Oriental style, especially on mid-18thC Meissen.
inro: Japanese multi-compartmental medicine or seal container, suspended from the sash of a kimono.
intaglio: Incised gem-stone, often set in a ring, used in antiquity and during the Renaissance as a seal. Any incised decoration; the opposite of carving in relief.
ironstone: Stoneware, patented 1813 by Charles James Mason, containing ground glassy slag, a by-product of iron smelting, for extra strength.
Jacobite glass: Wine glasses engraved with symbols of the Jacobites (supporters of James and Charles Stuart's claims to the English throne). Genuine examples date from 1746 to 1788. Countless later copies and forgeries exist.
jadeite: Type of jade, normally the best and most desirable.
Jugendstil: German Art Nouveau style.
Kakiemon: Family of 17thC Japanese porcelain decorators who produced wares decorated with flowers and figures on a white ground in distinctive colours: azure, yellow, turquoise and soft red. Widely imitated in Europe.
kiku mon: Japanese stylised chrysanthemum.
kilim: Flat woven rugs lacking a pile.
Kirin: Chinese mythical beast with a lion's tail, cloven hooves and the scales of a dragon.
knop: Knob, protuberance or swelling in the stem of a wine glass, of various forms which can be used as an aid to dating and provenance.
koro: Japanese incense burner.
kovsh: Russian vessel used for measuring drink, often highly decorated for ornamental purposes from the late 18thC.
kraak porselein: Dutch term for porcelain raided from Portuguese ships, used to describe the earliest Chinese export porcelain.
krater: Ancient Greek vessel for mixing water and wine in which the mouth is always the widest part.
Kufic: Arabic angular script, used in rugs to refer to stylised geometric calligraphy.
lacca povera: Process whereby prints are cut out, adhered to a painted ground and then varnished.
lambing chair: Sturdy chair with a low seat frequently over a drawer or cupboard, traditionally used by shepherds at lambing time. It has tall enclosed sides for protection against draughts.
Laub und Bandelwerk: German term for a late Baroque framing motif consisting of foliage and strapwork.
linenfold: Carved decoration which resembles folded linen.
loaded: In silverware, a hollow part of a vessel, usually a candlestick, filled with pitch or sand for weight and stability.
made up: Piece of furniture that has been put together from parts of other pieces of furniture. *See marriage.*
maiolica: Tin-glazed earthenware produced in Italy from the 15thC to the present day.
majolica: Heavily-potted, moulded ware covered in transparent glazes in distinctive, often sombre colours, developed by the Minton factory in the mid-19thC.
marriage: Joining together of two unrelated parts to form one piece of furniture. *See associated and made up.*

marvering: Ancient technique where hot threads of softened glass are rolled over a flat surface to smooth and fuse the glass, and to fix trailed decoration.

Meiping: Chinese for cherry blossom, used to describe a tall vase with high shoulders, small neck and narrow mouth.

mihrab: Prayer niche with a pointed arch; the motif which distinguishes a prayer rug from other types.

millefiori: Multi-coloured, or mosaic, glass, made since antiquity by fusing a number of coloured glass rods into a cane, and cutting off thin sections; much used to ornament paperweights.

netsuke: Japanese carved toggles made to secure sagemono ('hanging things') to the obi (waist belt) from a cord; usually of ivory, lacquer, silver or wood, from the 16thC.

niello: Black metal alloy or enamel used for filling in engraved designs on silverware.

nulling (knulling): Decorative carving in the form of irregular fluting which is usually found on early oak furniture.

oinochoe: In ancient times, a small jug with handles.

ojime: Japanese word meaning bead.

okimono: Small, finely carved Japanese ornament.

ormolu: Strictly, gilded bronze but sometimes used loosely for any yellow metal. Originally used for furniture handles and mounts but, from the 18thC, for ink stands, candlesticks etc.

overlay: In cased glass, the top layer, usually engraved to reveal a different coloured layer beneath.

overmantel: Area above a mantelpiece, often consisting of a mirror in an ornate frame, or some architectural feature in wood or stone.

overstuffed: Descriptive of upholstered furniture where the covering extends over the frame of the seat.

ovolo (1): Moulding of convex quarter-circle section, sometimes found around the edges of drawers to form a small overlap onto the carcase.

ovolo (2): Small oval convex moulding chiefly used in repetition.

palmette: In rugs, a cross-section through a stylised flowerhead or fruit.

papier mâché: Moulded paper pulp, suitable for japanning and polishing, used for small articles such as trays, boxes, tea caddies, and coasters.

Parisienne doll: French bisque head fashion doll with a stuffed kid leather body, made by various manufacturers between 1860 and 1890.

pate: Crown of a doll's head to which the wig or hair is attached, usually of cork in better quality dolls.

pâte-sur-pâte: 19thC Sèvres porcelain technique, much copied, of applying coloured clay decoration to the body before firing.

percussion lock: Early 19thC firearm, one of the first to be fired by the impact of a sharp-nosed hammer on the cartridge cap.

pewter: Alloy of tin and lead; the higher the tin content the higher the quality; sometimes with small quantities of antimony added to make it hard with a highly polished surface.

pier glass: Mirror designed to be fixed to the pier, or wall, between two tall windows, often with a matching pier table. Made from mid-17thC.

pietra paesina: Type of limestone which when polished reveals a natural pattern resembling mountain ranges.

plate: Old fashioned term, still occasionally used, to describe gold and silver vessels; not to be confused with 'Sheffield plate', or plated vessels generally, in which silver is fused to a base metal alloy.

pole screen: Small adjustable screen mounted on a pole and designed to stand in front of an open fire to shield a lady's face from the heat.

portrait doll: One modelled on a well known figure.

pot: An inexpensive form of bisque used in the making of dolls before the introduction of plastic.

poupard: Doll without legs, often mounted on a stick; popular in 19thC.

poured wax doll: One made by pouring molten wax into a mould.

powder flask: Device for measuring out a precise quantity of priming powder and made to be suspended from a musketeer's belt or bandolier and often ornately decorated. Sporting flasks are often made of antler and carved with hunting scenes.

powder horn: Cow horn hollowed out, blocked at the wide end with a wooden plug and fitted with a measuring device at the narrow end, used by musketeers for dispensing a precise quantity of priming powder.

pressed glass: Early 19thC invention, exploited rapidly in America, whereby mechanical pressure was used to form glassware in a mould.

puzzle jug: Type of jug made from the 17thC, especially in delft ware, with a syphon system and several spouts, none of which will pour unless the others are blocked.

quarter clock: Clock which strikes the quarter and half hours as well as the full hours.

quarter-veneered: Four consecutively cut identical pieces of veneer laid at opposite ends to each other to give a mirrored effect.

register plate: Scale of a barometer against which the mercury level is read.

regulator: Clock of great accuracy, sometimes used for controlling or checking other timepieces.

rocaille: Shell and rock motifs found in rococo work.

roemer: Originally 16th/17thC German wide bowled wine glass on a thick stem, decorated with prunts, on a base of concentric glass coils, often in green glass (Waldglas). Widely copied throughout Europe in many forms.

rosette: Circular floral ornament.
sabre leg: Elegant curving leg from the end of the 18thC, popular in the Regency period. Also known as Trafalgar leg.
satinwood: Moderately hard, yellow or light brown wood, with a very close grain, found in central and southern India, Coromandel, Sri Lanka and the West Indies.
seal bottle: Wine bottle with an applied glass medallion or seal personalised with the owner's name, initials, coat-of-arms or a date. Produced from the early 17th to the mid-19thC when bottles were relatively expensive.
SFBJ: Société de Fabrication de Bébés et Jouets; association of doll makers founded 1899 by the merger of Jumeau, Bru and others.
shagreen: Skin of shark or ray fish, often used on sword grips and scabbards.
Sheraton revival: Descriptive of furniture produced in the style of Sheraton when interest in his designs was revived during the late Victorian and Edwardian period.
***shou* symbol**: Formal, artistic version of the Chinese character *shou,* meaning long life.
siphon tube: U-shaped tube fitted into wheel barometers where the level of mercury in the short arm is used to record air pressure.
six-hour dial: One with only six divisions instead of twelve, often with the hours 1–6 in Roman numerals and 7–12 superimposed in Arabic numerals.
soft paste: Artificial porcelain made with the addition of ground glass, bone-ash or soapstone. Used by most European porcelain manufacturers during the 18thC, recognised by its soft, soapy feel.
softwood: One of two basic categories of timber. Softwoods are evergreen conifers. *See hardwood.*
spandrel: Decoration in the corner of the field.
spelter: Zinc treated to look like bronze and much used as an inexpensive substitute in Art Nouveau appliqué ornament and Art Deco figures.
standish: Term for a pre-18thC silver inkstand.
stirrup cup: Silver cup, without handles, so-called because it was served, containing a suitable beverage, to huntsmen in the saddle, prior to their moving off. Often made in the shape of an animal's head.
strapwork: Repeated carved decoration suggesting plaited straps.
sympiesometer: Instrument that uses a gas and coloured oil to record air pressure.
table ambulante: Small table which can be easily moved.
table clock: Early type of domestic clock, some say the predecessor of the watch, in which the dial is set horizontally: often of drum shape.
takamakie: Technique used in Japanese lacquerware in which the design is built up and modelled in a mixture of lacquer and charcoal or clay dust, and then often gilded.
tallboy: American term for a chest-on-chest.
tazza: Wide but shallow bowl on a stem with a foot; ceramic and metal tazzas were made in antiquity and the form was revived by Venetian glassmakers in 15thC. Also made in silver from 16thC.
tea kettle: Silver, or other metal, vessel intended for boiling water at the table. Designed to sit over a spirit lamp, it sometimes had a rounded base instead of flat.
teapoy: Piece of furniture in the form of a tea caddy on legs, with a hinged lid opening to reveal caddies, mixing bowl and other tea drinking accessories.
tear: Tear-drop shaped air bubble in the stem of an early 18thC wine glass, from which the air-twist evolved.
term: Pillar or pedestal terminating in a human head or torso, usually armless. *See caryatid.*
tester: Wooden canopy over a bedstead supported on either two or four posts. It may extend fully over the bed, known as a full tester, or only over the bedhead half, known as a half tester.
tête à tête: Tea set for two people.
thuyawood: Reddish-brown wood with distinctive small 'bird's eye' markings, imported from Africa and used as a veneer.
tin glaze: Glassy opaque white glaze of tin oxide; re-introduced to Europe in 14thC by Moorish potters; the characteristic glaze of delftware, faïence and maiolica.
touch: Maker's mark stamped on much, but not all, early English pewter. Their use was strictly controlled by the Pewterer's Company of London: early examples consist of initials, later ones are more elaborate and pictorial, sometimes including the maker's address.
transfer-printed: Ceramic decoration technique perfected mid-18thC and used widely thereafter for mass produced wares. An engraved design is transferred onto a slab of glue or gelatin (a bat), which was then laid over the body of the vessel, leaving an outline. This was sometimes coloured in by hand.
trefoil: Three-cusped figure which resembles a symmetrical three-lobed leaf or flower.
tsuba: Guard of a Japanese sword, usually consisting of an ornamented plate.
Tudric: Range of Celtic-inspired Art Nouveau pewter of high quality, designed for mass-production by Archibald Knox and others, and retailed through Liberty & Co.
tulipwood: Yellow-brown wood with reddish stripe imported from Central and South America and used as a veneer and for inlay and crossbanding.
tyg: Mug with three or more handles.
vargueño: Spanish cabinet with a fall front enclosing drawers.
Venetian glass: Fine soda glass and coloured glass blown and pinched into highly ornamented vessels of intricate form, made in Venice, and widely copied from 15thC.
verge escapement: Oldest form of escapement, found on clocks as early as 1300 and still in use in 1900. Consisting of a bar (the verge) with two flag-shaped pallets that rock in and out of the teeth of the crown or escape wheel to regulate the movement.
vernier scale: Short scale added to the traditional 3in (7.5cm) scale on stick barometers to give more precise readings than had previously been possible.
verre églomisé: Painting on glass. Often the reverse side of the glass is covered in gold or silver leaf through which a pattern is engraved and then painted black.
vesta case: Ornate flat case of silver or other metal for carrying vestas, an early form of match. From mid-19thC.
vitrine: French display cabinet which is often of bombé or serpentine outline and ornately decorated with marquetry and ormolu.
wan: Swastika mark, representing the short writing of the Chinese character *wan,* meaning myriad or ten thousand. Used to represent abundance.
WMF: Short for the German Württembergische Metallwarenfabrik, one of the principal producers of Art Nouveau silver and silver-plated objects, early 20thC.
wrythen: Twisted or plaited.
zitan: Rarest and most expensive Oriental hardwood.

DIRECTORY OF SPECIALISTS

If you wish to be included in next year's directory, or if you have a change of address or telephone number, please advise Miller's Advertising Department by April 1999. We would advise readers to make contact by telephone before visiting a dealer, therefore avoiding a wasted journey.

Antique Dealers' Associations

Oxfordshire

Thames Valley Antique Dealers Association, The Old College, Queen St, Dorchester-on-Thames, Oxon OX10 7HL
Tel & Fax: 01865 341639

Republic of Ireland

Alexander Antiques, 16 Molesworth St, Dublin 2
Tel: 00 353 1 679 1548
Fax: 00 353 1 679 6667

Anthony Antiques Ltd, 7, 8 & 9 Molesworth Street, Dublin 2
Tel: 00 353 1 677 7222

Antique Brass & Electric Light Co, 78 Francis Street, Dublin 2
Tel: 00 353 1454 1178
Mobile: 087 406841

Antique Prints, 16 South Anne Street, Dublin 2
Tel: 00 353 1 671 9523

Athena Fine Art, 54 Orpen Green, Stillorgan Grove, Blackrock, Co. Dublin
Tel: 00 353 1 288 7414

Beaufield Mews Antiques, Woodlands Avenue, Stillorgan, Co. Dublin
Tel: 00 353 1 288 0375
Fax: 288 6945

David Cahill Antiques, Eglinton House, Eglinton Park, Dun Laoghaire, Co. Dublin
Tel: 00 353 1 280 4034
By appointment only

Caxton Prints, 63 Patrick Street, Dublin 8
Tel: 00 353 1 453 0060/ 087 429799

Courtville Antiques, Powerscourt Townhouse Centre, Dublin 2
Tel: 00 353 1 679 4042

H. Danker, 10 South Anne St, Dublin 2
Tel: 00 353 1 677 4009
Fax: 00 353 1 677 4544

De Burca Rare Books, Cloogashel, 27 Priory Drive, Blackrock, Co. Dublin
Tel: 00 353 1 288 2159
Fax: 00 353 1 283 4080

L. & W. Duvallier, Powerscourt Townhouse Centre, South William St, Dublin 2
Tel: 00 353 1 088 535313

Edward Butler, 14 Bachelor's Walk, Dublin 1
Tel & Fax: 00 353 1 873 0296

John Farrington Antiques, 32 Drury Street, Dublin 2
Tel: 00 353 1 679 1899

Fleury Antiques, 57 Francis Street, Dublin 8
Tel: 00 353 1 473 0878
Fax: 00 353 1 473 0371

William Flynn Antiques, Fernside, 135 Templeogue Road, Dublin 6
Tel: 00 353 1 490 0183
Mobile: 088 550080
By appointment

Forsyth's, 89 Francis Street, Dublin 8
Tel: 00 353 1 288 3687

Gorry Gallery, 20 Molesworth Street, Dublin 2
Tel & Fax: 00 353 1 679 5319

Irene Fine Arts, 33a Clarendon St, Dublin 2
Tel: 00 353 1 671 4932
By appointment

Jennifer Jeffers, Co. Dublin
Tel: 00 353 1 284 4253
By appointment only

The Jewel Casket, 17 South Anne St, Dublin 2
Tel: 00 353 1 671 1262

Johnston Antiques, 14 Longford Terrace, Monkstown, Co. Dublin
Tel: 00 353 1 284 4962
Fax: 00 353 1 284 2090
By appointment

Kevin Jones Antiques, 65-66 Francis Street, Dublin 8
Tel: 00 353 1 454 6626

Jorgensen Fine Art, 29 Molesworth Street, Dublin 2
Tel: 00 353 1 661 9758
Fax: 00 353 1 661 9760

Gerald Kenyon Antiques, 10 Lr Ormond Quay, Dublin 1
Tel: 00 353 1 873 0625/0488
Fax: 00 353 1 873 0882

Peter Linden, Georges Avenue, Blackrock, Co. Dublin
Tel: 00 353 1 288 5875
Fax: 00 353 1 283 5616

Lorcan Brereton, 29 South Anne Street, Dublin 2
Tel: 00 353 1 677 1462
Fax: 00 353 1 677 1125

McGahan, Sean, 88 Francis Street, Dublin 2
Tel: 00 353 1 087 581233

Roxane Moorhead Antiques, at Jones Antiques, 65-66 Francis Street, Dublin 8
Tel: 00 353 1 453 3962
Mobile: 086 8147451

Neptune Gallery, 41 South William Street, Dublin 2
Tel & Fax: 00 353 1 671 5021

Gordon Nichol Antiques, 67-68 Francis Street, Dublin 8
Tel: 00 353 1 454 3322

Cynthia O'Connors & Co Ltd, By appointment only
Tel: 00 353 1 840 5045
Fax: 00 353 1 840 1220

O'Sullivan Antiques, 43/44 Francis St, Dublin 8
Tel: 00 353 1 454 1143
Fax: 00 353 1 454 1156

Oman Galleries, 114-116 Capel St, Dublin 1
Tel: 00 353 1 872 4477
Fax: 00 353 1 872 4520

Rembrandt Antiques, c/o 55 Glasthule Road, Sandycove, Co. Dublin
Tel: 00 353 1 280 5956

Sandycove Fine Arts, 55 Glasthule Road, Sandycove, Co. Dublin
Tel: 00 353 1 280 5956

Esther Sexton Antiques, 51 Francis Street, Dublin 8
Tel: 00 353 1 473 0909

The Silver Shop, 23b Powerscourt Townhouse Centre, Dublin 2
Tel & Fax: 00 353 1 679 4147

Timepiece, 57-58 Patrick St, Dublin 8
Tel & Fax: 00 353 1 454 0774

Upper Court Manor Antiques, Hanover Square, 54 Francis Street, Dublin 8
Tel: 00 353 1 473 0037

J. & M. Weldon, 18 South Anne St, Dublin 2
Tel: 00 353 1 677 2742

J. W. Weldon, 55 Clarendon St, Dublin 2
Tel & Fax: 00 353 1 677 1638

Mike McGlynn Antiques, Bunratty, Co. Clare
Tel: 00 353 061 364294

Fortlands Antiques, Fortlands, Charleville, Co. Cork
Tel: 00 353 063 81295

Linda's Antiques, Main Street, Kinsale, Co. Cork
Tel: 00 353 021 774754
Mobile 087 665765

Mona's Antiques, Savoy Centre, Patrick Street, Cork
Tel: 00 353 021 278171

Diana O'Mahony, 8 Winthrop Street, Cork
Tel: 00 353 021 276599

Donal O'Regan, 3 Pauls Lane, Off Paul St, Cork
Tel: 00 353 021 272902

Linda Walsh Antiques, 1st Floor, 151 West End, Mallow, Co. Cork
Tel: 00 353 022 43048

Arcadia Antiques & Gallery, Castle Street, Galway City and Prince of Wales Hotel, Athlone, Co. Galway
Tel: 00 353 091 561861/ 090 274671

Upper Court Manor Antiques, Upper Court Manor, Freshford, Co. Kilkenny
Tel: 00 353 056 32174
Fax: 00 353 056 32325

George Stacpoole, President, Irish Antique Dealers Association, Main Street, Adare, Co. Limerick
Tel: 00 353 61 396 409
Fax: 00 353 61 396 733

Carol's Antiques, Adare, Co. Limerick
Tel: 00 353 061 396977
Fax: 00 353 061 396991

O'Toole Antiques & Decorative Galleries, Upper William St, Limerick
Tel: 00 353 061 414490
Fax: 00 353 061 411378

Greene's Antiques Galleries, The Mall, Drogheda, Co. Louth
Tel: 00 353 041 38286/36212
Fax: 00 353 041 38286

Jonathan Beech, Westport, Co. Mayo
Tel: 00 353 98 28688

Satch Kiely, Westport Quay, Co. Mayo
Tel: 00 353 098 25775

Westport House Antique Shop, Westport, Co. Mayo
Tel: 00 353 098 25430/25404

George Williams Antiques, The Annexe, Newcastle House, Kilmainhamwood, Kells, Co. Meath
Tel: 00 353 046 52740
Mobile: 088 529959
By appointment only

Ivy Hall Antiques, Carrig, Birr, Co. Offaly
Tel: 00 353 0509 20148
By appointment only

Fleury Antiques, Cahir, Co. Tipperary
Tel: 00 353 052 41226
Fax: 00 353 052 41819

Clancy Chandaliers, Villanova, Ballywaltrim, Bray, Co. Wicklow
Tel: 00 353 286 3460
Strictly by appointment

Murtagh Antiques, Delgany, Co. Wicklow
Tel: 00 353 287 6925
Strictly by appointment

Northern Ireland

Brian R. Bolt, 88 Ballaghmore Road, Portballintrae, Bushmills, Co. Antrim BT57 8RL
Tel & Fax: 012657 31129

Robert Christie Antiques, 20 Calhame Road, Straid, Ballyclare, Co. Antrim BT39 9NA
Tel: 01960 341149
Mobile: 0802 968846

Paul Cranny Antiques, Bank Square Gallery, 63 Maghera Street, Kilrea, Co. Derry,
Tel: 012665 40279
Mobile: 0374 166675
Fax: 012665 40279

Lambe Antiques,
41 Shore Road,
Belfast BT15 3PG
Tel: 01232 370761

Marion Langham,
Clanranagh, Tempo,
Co. Fermanagh
Tel: 01365 541247
Fax: 01365 541690

Mac Henry Antiques,
Caragh Lodge, Glen Road,
Jordanstown, Newtownabbey,
Co. Antrim, BT
Tel: 01232 862036
Mobile: 0831 135226
Fax: 01232 853281

Old Cross Antiques,
54 Killysorrell Road,
Ashfield, Dromore, Co. Down
Tel: 01846 692670
By appointment only

P. & B. Rowan,
Carlton House, 92 Malone
Rd, Belfast BT9 5HP
Tel: 01232 666448
Fax: 01232 663725
By appointment only

Parvis & Meriel Sigaroudinia,
Mountain View House,
40 Sandy Lane, Ballyskeagh,
Lisburn, Belfast BT27 5TL
Tel: 01232 621824
By appointment only

Time & Tide Antiques,
Rock Angus House,
2 Ferry Street, Portaferry,
Co. Down, BT22 1PB
Tel & Fax: 012477 28935
Mobile: 0802 418289

Antiquities

Dorset

Ancient & Gothic,
PO Box 356,
Christchurch BH23 1XQ
Tel: 01202 478592

Architectural Antiques

Cheshire

Nostalgia,
61 Shaw Heath,
Stockport SK3 8BH
Tel: 0161 477 7706

Devon

Ashburton Marbles,
Grate Hall, North Street,
Ashburton TQ13 7DU
Tel & Fax: 01364 653189

Dorset

Dorset Reclamation,
Cow Drove, Bere Regis,
Wareham, BH20 7JZ
Tel: 01929 472200
Fax: 01929 472292

Gloucestershire

The Original Reclamation
Trading Company,
22 Elliot Road, Love Lane
Estate, Cirencester GL7 1YS
Tel: 01285 653532
Fax: 01285 644383

Lincolnshire

Britannia Brass Fittings,
Hemswell Antiques Centre,
Caenby Corner Estate,
Hemswell Cliff,
Gainsborough DN21 5TJ
Tel: 01482 227300

Surrey

Drummonds of Bramley,
Birtley Farm, Horsham Rd,
Bramley, Guildford GU5 0LA
Tel: 01483 898766
Fax: 01483 894393

Arms & Militaria

Lincolnshire

Garth Vincent,
The Old Manor House,
Allington,
Grantham NG32 2DH
Tel: 01400 281358
Fax: 01400 282658

Surrey

West Street Antiques,
63 West Street,
Dorking RH4 1BS
Tel & Fax: 01306 883487

Sussex

Wallis & Wallis,
West St Auction Galleries,
Lewes BN7 2NJ
Tel: 01273 480208
Fax: 01273 476562

West Midlands

Weller & Dufty Ltd,
141 Bromsgrove Street,
Birmingham B5 6RQ
Tel: 0121 692 1414
Fax: 0121 622 5605

Yorkshire

Andrew Spencer Bottomley,
The Coach House,
Thongs Bridge,
Holmfirth HD7 2TT
Tel: 01484 685234
Fax: 01484 681551

Barographs

Somerset

Richard Twort,
Tel & Fax: 01934 641900

Barometers

Berkshire

Alan Walker,
Halfway Manor, Halfway,
Nr Newbury RG20 8NR
Tel: 01488 657670
Fax: 01488 657670

West Yorkshire

Kym S. Walker,
Foster Clough,
Hebden Bridge HX7 5QZ
Tel: 01422 882808/886961
Fax: 01422 882808

Beds

Wales

Seventh Heaven,
Chirk Mill, Chirk,
Wrexham,
County Borough,
LL14 5BU
Tel: 01691 777622/773563
Fax: 01691 777313

Worcestershire

S. W. Antiques,
Abbey Showrooms,
Newlands, Pershore,
WR10 1BP
Tel: 01386 555580
Fax: 01386 556205

Billiard Tables

Berkshire

William Bentley Billiards,
Standen Manor Farm,
Hungerford RG17 0RB
Tel: 0181 940 1152/01488
681711/01672 871214
Fax: 01488 685197

Lincolnshire

Cheshire Billiards Co,
Springwood Lodge,
Ermine Street,
Appleby DN15 0DD
Tel: 01724 852359/848775

Surrey

Academy Billiard Co,
5 Camp Hill Industrial
Estate, Camphill Road,
West Byfleet KT14 6EW
Tel: 01932 352067
Fax: 01932 353904

Books

Middlesex

John Ives,
5 Normanhurst Drive,
Twickenham TW1 1NA
Tel: 0181 892 6265
Fax: 0181 744 3944
Reference books.

West Midlands

David Hill, PO Box 3,
Brierly Hill DY5 4YU
Tel & Fax: 01384 70523
Reference books on antiques, art and collectables.

Wiltshire

Dominic Winter Book
Auctions, The Old School,
Maxwell Street,
Swindon SN1 5DR
Tel: 01793 611340
Fax: 01793 491727

Boxes & Treen

Berkshire

Mostly Boxes,
93 High Street,
Eton SL4 6AF
Tel: 01753 858470

London

Coromandel,
PO Box 9772, SW19 3ZG
Tel: 0181 543 9115
Fax: 0181 543 6255

Gerald Mathias,
R5/6 Antiquarius,
135 King's Road,
Chelsea SW3 4PW
Tel & Fax: 0171 351 0484

Somerset

Alan Stacey,
Boxwood Antique Restorers,
By appointment only
Tel & Fax: 01963 33988
Fax: 01963 32555
Cabinet making, polishing, carving and specialists in tortoiseshell, ivory and mother-of-pearl on boxes, caddies and furniture. See our main advertisement in Boxes (Colour) section.

British Antique Furniture Restorers' Association

Cambridgeshire

Ludovic Potts,
Unit 1 & 1A,
Haddenham Business Park,
Station Road, Ely CB6 3XD
Tel: 01353 741537
Fax: 01353 741822
Cane and rushwork, gilding.

Derbyshire

Anthony Allen,
Antique Restorers &
Conservators,
The Old Wharf Workshop,
Redmoor Lane, New Mills,
High Peak SK22 3JS
Tel: 01663 745274
Boulle, marquetry, walnut, oak, veneering, upholstery. Clocks & clock cases, gold frames & pictures.

Dorset

Michael Barrington,
The Old Rectory,
Warmwell,
Dorchester DT2 8HQ
Tel & Fax: 01305 852104
18th & 19thC furniture, gilding, upholstery, antique metalwork. Organ case work & pipe decoration, mechanical models, automata and toys.

Essex

Clive Beardall,
104B High Street,
Maldon CM9 5ET
Tel: 01621 857890

Dick Patterson,
Forge Studio Workshop,
Stour Street,
Manningtree CO11 1BE
Tel: 01206 396222

Gloucestershire

Stephen Hill,
Brewery Antiques,
5 Cirencester Workshops,
Brewery Court,
Cirencester GL7 1JH
Tel: 01285 658817
Mobile: 0976 722028
Fax: 01285 644060

Kent

Timothy Akers,
The Forge, 39 Chancery
Lane, Beckenham BR3 6NR
Tel: 0181 650 9179
Longcase and bracket clocks, cabinet making, French polishing.

London

Marie Louise Crawley,
39 Wood Vale,
SE23 3DS
Tel & Fax: 0181 516 0002
Painted furniture, papier mâché, tôle ware, lacquer and gilding.

Clifford J. Tracy Ltd
6-40 Durnford Street,
Seven Sisters Rd,
N15 5NQ
Tel: 0181 800 4773
Restoration of fine antique furniture.

Norfolk

Michael Dolling,
Church Farm Barns,
Glandford,
Holt NR25 7JR
Tel: 01263 741115

Roderick Nigel Larwood,
The Oaks,
Station Road,
Larling, Norwich NR16 2QS
Tel: 01953 717937
Restorers of fine antique furniture and traditional finishers.

Oxfordshire

Alistair Frayling-Cork,
2 Mill Lane,
Wallingford OX10 0DH
Tel: 01491 826221
Antique furniture restoration, also stringed instruments, clock cases and brass fittings repaired.

Scotland

William Trist,
135 St Leonard's Street,
Edinburgh EH8 9RB
Tel: 0131 667 7775
Fax: 0131 667 4333
Furniture, clocks, barometers, cane & rush seating.

Somerset

Robert P Tandy,
Unit 5, Manor Workshops,
West End, Nailsea,
Bristol BS48 4DD
Tel: 01275 856378
Traditional antique furniture restoration & repairs.

Surrey

Timothy Morris,
Unit 4A, 19 St Peter's St,
South Croydon CR2 7DG
Tel: 0181 681 2992
Furniture & marquetry.

Timothy Naylor,
The Workshop,
2 Chertsey Road, Chobham,
Woking GU24 8NB
Tel: 01276 855122

Wiltshire

William Cook,
High Trees House,
Savernake Forest,
Nr Marlborough SN8 4NE
Tel: 01672 513017
Fax: 01672 514455

CAMERAS

Kent

Stuart Heggie,
14 The Borough,
Northgate,
Canterbury CT1 2DR
Tel & Fax: 01227 470422

London

Jonathan Harris,
18 Ivory House,
Plantation Wharf,
Battersea SW11 3TN
Tel: 0171 738 2881
Fax: 0171 738 2889

Yorkshire

The Camera House,
Oakworth Hall,
Colne Road, Oakworth,
Keighley BD22 7HZ
Tel & Fax: 01535 642333
Cameras & photographic equipment for the user & collector from 1850. Purchases / sales / part exchanges. Repairs–cine / slide video transfers. Valuations for probate & insurance.
Open Wednesday–Friday 10–5, Saturday 10–3, or by appointment
Prop. C. Cox.

CLOCKS

Bedfordshire

House of Clocks,
102-106 Dunstable Street,
Ampthill MK45 2JP
Tel: 01525 403136
Fax: 01525 402680

Cheshire

Coppelia Antiques,
Holford Lodge,
Plumley Moor Road,
Plumley WA16 9RS
Tel: 01565 722197
Fax: 01565 722744

Derbyshire

Dragon Antiques,
1 Tamworth St, Duffield,
Nr Derby DE56 4ER
Tel: 01332 842332

Devon

Musgrave Bickford Antiques,
15 East Street,
Crediton EX17 3AT
Tel: 01363 775042

Essex

It's About Time,
863 London Road,
Westcliff on Sea SS0 9SZ
Tel & Fax: 01702 472574

Gloucestershire

Gerard Campbell,
Maple House, Market
Place, Lechlade GL7 3AB
Tel: 01367 252267

Jeffrey Formby,
Orchard Cottage,
East Street,
Moreton-in-Marsh
GL56 0LQ
Tel & Fax: 01608 650558

Grandfather Clock Shop,
Styles of Stow,
The Little House, Sheep
Street, Stow-on-the-Wold,
GL54 1JS
Tel & Fax: 01451 830455

Hampshire

Bryan Clisby,
Antique Clocks,
at Andwells Antiques,
High Street,
Hartley Wintney
RG27 8NY
Tel: 01252 716436

Clock Workshop,
6A Parchment Street,
Winchester SO23 8AT
Tel: 01962 842331

Humberside

Time & Motion,
1 Beckside,
Beverley, HU17 0PB
Tel: 01482 881574

Kent

Gem Antiques,
28 London Road,
Sevenoaks TN13 1AP
Tel: 01732 743540

Gem Antiques,
21 High Street,
Headcorn TN27 9NH
Tel: 01622 890386

Gaby Gunst,
140 High Street,
Tenterden TN30 6HT
Tel: 01580 765818

Old Clock Shop,
63 High Street,
West Malling ME19 6NA
Tel: 01732 843246

Derek Roberts,
24-25 Shipbourne Road,
Tonbridge TN10 3DN
Tel: 01732 358986
Fax: 01732 771842

Lincolnshire

Pinfold Antiques,
3-5 Pinfold Lane,
Ruskington, CN13 OBB
Tel: 01526 832057
Fax: 01526 834550

London

Chelsea Clocks & Antiques,
Stand H3-4,
Antiquarius,
135 Kings Road,
SW3 4PW
Tel: 0171 352 8646
Fax: 0171 376 4591

The Clock Clinic Ltd,
85 Lower Richmond Road,
SW15 1EU
Tel: 0181 788 1407

Jillings Antiques,
Tel: 0171 235 8600
Fax: 0171 235 9898

Pendulum,
King House,
51 Maddox Street,
W1R 9LA
Tel: 0171 629 6606
Fax: 0171 629 6616

Roderick Antique Clocks,
23 Vicarage Gate,
W8 4AA
Tel: 0171 937 8517

Norfolk

Keith Lawson, LBHI,
Scratby Garden Centre,
Beach Road, Scratby,
Great Yarmouth NR29 3AJ
Tel: 01493 730950

Oxfordshire

Craig Barfoot,
Tudor House,
East Hagbourne OX11 9LR
Tel & Fax: 01235 818968

Republic of Ireland

Jonathan Beech,
Westport, Co. Mayo
Tel: 00 353 98 28688

Scotland

John Mann,
Antique Clocks,
The Clock Showroom,
Canonbie, Near Carlisle,
Galloway DG14 OSY
Tel: 013873 71337/71827
Fax: 013873 71337
Website:
http: / /www.yell.co.uk / sites / mann-antiques /

Shropshire

The Curiosity Shop,
127 Old Street,
Ludlow SY8 1NU
Tel: 01584 875927

Somerset

K&D Antique Clocks,
Bartlett St Antiques Centre,
Bath BA1 2QZ
Tel & Fax: 0117 956 5281

Staffordshire

Essence of Time,
Tudor of Lichfield Antique
Centre, Bore Street,
Lichfield WS13 6LL
Tel: 01543 263951/
01902 764900

Surrey

The Clock Shop,
64 Church Street,
Weybridge KT13 8DL
Tel: 01932 840407/855503

Horological Workshops,
204 Worplesdon Road,
Guildford GU2 6UY
Tel: 01483 576496

Sussex

Churchill Clocks,
Rumbolds Hill,
(Main Street),
Midhurst GU29 9BZ
Tel: 01730 813891
Fax: 01730 813891

Sam Orr,
Antique Clocks,
36 High Street,
Hurstpierpoint,
Nr Brighton BN6 9RG
Tel: 01273 832081

Wiltshire

P. A. Oxley,
The Old Rectory, Cherhill,
Nr Calne SN11 8UX
Tel: 01249 816227
Fax: 01249 821285

Allan Smith Clocks,
Amity Cottage,
162 Beechcroft Road,
Upper Stratton,
Swindon, SN2 6QE
Tel & Fax: 01793 822977

Yorkshire

Brian Loomes,
Calf Haugh Farm,
Pateley Bridge HG3 5HW
Tel: 01423 711163

COMICS

London

Comic Book Postal
Auctions Ltd,
40-42 Osnaburgh Street,
NW1 3ND
Tel: 0171 424 0007
Fax: 0171 424 0008

DECORATIVE ARTS

Greater Manchester

A. S. Antiques
26 Broad Street,
Pendleton,
Salford M6 5BY
Tel: 0161 737 5938
Fax: 0161 737 6626

Hampshire

Bona Art Deco Store,
The Hart Shopping Centre,
Fleet GU13 8AZ
Tel: 01252 616666

Kent

Delf Stream Gallery,
14 New Street,
Sandwich CT13 9AB
Tel: 01304 617684
Fax: 01304 615479

Lincolnshire

Art Nouveau Originals,
Stamford Antiques Centre,
The Exchange Hall,
Broad Street,
Stamford PE1 9PX
Tel: 01780 762605

London

Art Furniture,
158 Camden St,
NW1 9PA
Tel: 0171 267 4324
Fax: 0171 267 5199

Art Nouveau Originals c1900,
4/5 Pierrepont Row Arcade,
Camden Passage, N1 8EF
Tel: 0171 359 4127

Artemis Decorative Arts Ltd,
36 Kensington Church St,
W8 4BX
Tel: 0171 376 0377/
937 9900
Fax: 0171 376 0377

Arts & Crafts Furniture Co,
49 Sheen Lane, SW14 8AB
Tel: 0181 876 6544
Decorative Arts.

Cameo Gallery,
38 Kensington Church
Street, W8 4BX
Tel: 0171 938 4114
Fax: 0171 938 4112

The Collector,
9 Church Street,
Marylebone NW8 8EE
Tel: 0171 706 4586
Fax: 0171 706 2948

Galerie Moderne,
10 Halkin Arcade,
Motcomb Street,
Belgravia SW1X 8JT
Tel: 0171 245 6907
Fax: 0171 245 6341

Pieter Oosthuizen,
1st Floor Georgian Village,
Camden Passage N1 8EF
Tel: 0171 359 3322
Fax: 0171 376 3852

Phillips,
101 New Bond St, W1Y 0AS
Tel: 0171 629 6602

Rumours Decorative Arts,
10 The Mall, Upper Street,
Camden Passage,
Islington N1 0PD
Tel: 01582 873561/0836 277274/0831 103748

Shapiro & Co,
Stand 380, Gray's Antique Market, 58 Davies Street,
W1Y 1LB
Tel: 0171 491 2710

Merseyside

Circa 1900,
11-13 Holts Arcade, India Buildings, Water Street,
Liverpool L2 0RR
Tel: 0151 236 1282
Fax: 07070 603981

Surrey

Gooday Gallery,
20 Richmond Hill,
Richmond TW10 6QX
Tel: 0181 940 8652
Mobile 0410 124540
Art Deco, Art Nouveau, Tribal Art.

Sussex

Art Deco Etc,
73 Upper Gloucester Road,
Brighton BN1 3LQ
Tel & Fax: 01273 329268
Decorative Arts Ceramics.

Wales

Paul Gibbs Antiques,
25 Castle Street, Conwy,
Gwynedd LL32 8AY
Tel: 01492 593429
Fax: 01492 593429

Worcestershire

Rich Designs,
Unit 1, Grove Farm,
Bromyard Road,
Worcester WR2 5UG
Tel: 01905 748214
Fax: 01905 427875

Ephemera

Nottinghamshire

T. Vennett-Smith,
11 Nottingham Road,
Gotham NG11 0HE
Tel: 0115 983 0541
Fax: 0115 983 0114

Republic of Ireland

Whyte's Auctioneers,
30 Marlborough St,
Dublin 1
Tel: 00 353 1874 6161
Fax: 00 353 1874 6020

Exhibition & Fair Organisers

Surrey

Cultural Exhibitions Ltd,
8 Meadrow,
Godalming GU7 3HN
Tel: 01483 422562
Fax: 01483 426077

Exporters

Devon

McBains of Exeter,
Exeter Airport, Clyst,
Honiton, Exeter EX5 2BA
Tel: 01392 366261
Fax: 01392 365572

Essex

F. G. Bruschweiler (Antiques) Ltd,
41-67 Lower Lambricks,
Rayleigh SS6 7EN
Tel: 01268 773761
Fax: 01268 773318

Somerset

MGR Exports,
Station Rd, Bruton BA10 0EH
Tel: 01749 812460
Fax: 01749 812882

Sussex

International Furniture Exporters,
The Old Cement Works,
South Heighton,
Newhaven BN9 0HS
Tel: 01273 611251
Fax: 01273 611574

Lloyd Williams Antiques,
Anglo Am Warehouse,
2A Beach Road,
Eastbourne BN22 7EX
Tel: 01323 648661
Fax: 01323 648658

The Old Mint House,
High St, Pevensey BN24 5LF
Tel & Fax: 01323 762337

Wales

Perpetual Antiques,
Marianne Prysau, Caerwys,
Nr Mold, Clwyd CH7 5BQ
Tel & Fax: 01352 721036

Fishing

Hampshire

Evans & Partridge,
Agriculture House,
High Street,
Stockbridge SO20 6HF
Tel: 01264 810702
Fax: 01264 810944

Kent

The Old Lead Weight,
PO Box 22,
Swanley BR8 8ZX
Tel & Fax: 01322 669554

Old Tackle Box,
PO Box 55,
Cranbrook TN17 3ZU
Tel & Fax: 01580 713979

London

Angling Auctions,
P O Box 2095, W12 8RU
Tel: 0181 749 4175
Fax: 0181 743 4855

The Reel Thing,
17 Royal Opera Arcade,
Pall Mall, SW1Y 4UY
Tel & Fax: 0171 976 1830
Fishing Tackle, Sporting.

Scotland

Timeless Tackle,
1 Blackwood Crescent,
Edinburgh EH9 1QZ
Tel: 0131 667 1407
Fax: 0131 662 4215

Furniture

Berkshire

Hill Farm Antiques,
Hill Farm, Shop Lane,
Leckhampstead,
Nr Newbury RG16 8QG
Tel: 01488 638541/638361
Fax: 01488 638541

Cumbria

Anthemion,
Bridge Street, Cartmel,
Grange-over-Sands
LA11 7SH
Tel: 015395 36295

Anvil Antiques,
Cartmel, Grange-over-Sands
LA11 6QA
Tel: 015395 36362
Oak and country.

Derbyshire

Spurrier-Smith Antiques,
28, 30, 39 & 41 Church St,
Ashbourne DE6 1AJ
Tel: 01335 343669/342198
Fax: 01335 342198

Devon

John Charles Antiques,
Tale Manor,
Tale EX14 0HJ
Tel: 01884 277229
Furniture and fine art.

Dorset

Antiques For All,
Higher Shaftesbury Road,
Blandford Forum
DT11 7TA
Tel: 01258 458011

Essex

Napier House Antiques,
Head Street,
Halstead CO9 2BT
Tel: 01787 477346
Fax: 01787 478757

France

Antiquites du Roy,
Z. A. de Bellevue,
35235 Thorigne Fouillard,
Tel: 00 33 2 99 04 59 81
Fax: 00 33 2 99 04 59 47

Gloucestershire

Berry Antiques,
3 High Street,
Moreton-in-Marsh
GL56 0AH
Tel: 01608 652929

Hampshire

French Antique Shop Ltd,
33B Marmion Road,
Southsea PO5 2AT
Tel: 01705 363385
Mobile 0385 346549
Fax: 01705 346808

Hertfordshire

Bushwood Antiques,
Stags End Equestrian Centre, Gaddesden Lane,
Hemel Hempstead HP2 6HN
Tel: 01582 794700
Fax: 01582 792299

Collins Antiques,
Corner House,
Wheathampstead
AL4 8AP
Tel: 01582 833111

Kent

Douglas Bryan Antiques
The Old Bakery,
St David's Bridge,
Cranbrook TN17 3HN
Tel: 01580 713103
Fax: 01580 712407
Oak & Country.

Flower House Antiques,
90 High Street,
Tenterden TN30 6JB
Tel: 01580 763764

Heirlooms Antiques,
68 High Street,
Tenterden TN30 6AU
Tel: 01580 765535

Pantiles Spa Antiques,
4, 5, 6 Union House,
The Pantiles,
Tunbridge Wells TN4 8HE
Tel: 01892 541377
Fax: 01435 865660

Gillian Shepherd,
Old Corner House Antiques,
6 Poplar Road, Wittersham,
Tenterden TN30 7PG
Tel: 01797 270236

Sparks Antiques,
4 Manor Row,
High Street,
Tenterden TN30 6HP
Tel: 01580 766696

Lincolnshire

Mitchell Simmons Ltd,
Hopton Ironworks,
The Wong,
Horncastle LN9 6EB
Tel: 01507 523854
Fax: 01507 523855

Seaview Antiques,
Stanhope Road,
Horncastle LN9 5DG
Tel: 01507 524524
Fax: 01507 526946

London

Adams Rooms Antiques & Interiors,
18-20 The Ridgeway,
Wimbledon Village
SW19 4QN
Tel: 0181 946 7047/4733
Fax: 0181 946 4588

Butchoff Antiques,
229 & 233 Westbourne Grove, W11 2SE
Tel: 0171 221 8174
Fax: 0171 792 8923

Oola Boola,
166 Tower Bridge Road,
SE1 3LS
Tel: 0171 403 0794/ 0181 693 5050
Fax: 0171 403 8405

Paragon Furniture,
Unit G2 Workshops,
Channel Sea Business Centre, Canning Road,
Stratford E15 3ND
Tel: 0181 503 0199
Fax: 0181 503 0300

Robert Young Antiques,
68 Battersea Bridge Road,
SW11 3AG
Tel: 0171 228 7847
Fax: 0171 585 0489

Middlesex

Phelps Ltd,
133-135 St Margaret's Rd,
East Twickenham TW1 1RG
Tel: 0181 892 1778/7129
Fax: 0181 892 3661

North Yorkshire

Sturman's Antiques,
Main Street, Hawes DL8 3QW
Tel: 01969 667742

Northamptonshire

Paul Hopwell,
30 High Street,
West Haddon NN6 7AP
Tel: 01788 510636
Fax: 01788 510044
Oak & Country.

Oxfordshire

Rupert Hitchcox Antiques,
The Garth,
Warpsgrove, Chalgrove,
Oxford, OX44 7RW
Tel & Fax: 01865 890241

Scotland

Old Style Furniture,
Unit 6, Phoenix Industrial Estate, Baldridgeburn,
Dumfermline, Fife
KY12 9EB
Tel & Fax: 01383 739101

Somerset

Granary Galleries,
Court House, Ash Priors,
Nr Bishops Lydeard,
Taunton TA4 3NQ
Tel: 01823 432402/432816

Suffolk

Hubbard Antiques,
16 St Margaret's Green,
Ipswich IP4 2BS
Tel: 01473 233034
Fax: 01473 212726

Napier House Antiques,
Church St, Sudbury CO10 6BJ
Tel: 01787 375280

Oswald Simpson,
Hall Street,
Long Melford CO1O 9JL
Tel: 01787 377523
Oak & Country.

Wrentham Antiques,
40-44 High Street, Wrentham,
Nr Beccles NR34 7HB
Tel: 01502 675583/675731
Fax: 01502 675707

Surrey

The Chair Set,
82-84 Hill Rise,
Richmond TW10 6UB
Tel: 0181 332 6454
Mobile: 0411 625477
Chairs.

Dorking Desk Shop,
41 West Street,
Dorking RH4 1BU
Tel: 01306 883327/880535

J. Hartley Antiques Ltd,
186 High Street,
Ripley GU23 6BB
Tel: 01483 224318

The Refectory,
38 West Street,
Dorking RH4 1BU
Tel: 01306 742111
Oak & Country – refectory table specialist.

Richmond Antiques,
John Hobson, 28 Hill Rise,
Richmond TW10 6UA
Tel: 0181 948 4638
Furniture – chests of drawers Weekends only. Open Sat 10.30–5.30 Sun 2.00–5.30

Ripley Antiques,
67 High Street,
Ripley GU23 6AN
Tel: 01483 224981
Fax: 01483 224333

Anthony Welling,
Broadway Barn,
High Street, Ripley,
Woking GU23 6AQ
Tel & Fax: 01483 225384
Oak and country.

Sussex

British Antique Replicas,
School Close,
Queen Elizabeth Avenue,
Burgess Hill RH15 9RX
Tel: 01444 245577

Dycheling Antiques,
34 High Street, Ditchling,
Hassocks BN6 8TA
Tel: 01273 842929
Chairs.

Monarch Antiques,
6, 7, 9 &19 Grand Parade,
St Leonard's, TN38 0DD
Tel: 01424 445841
Fax: 01424 716763

Red Lion Antiques,
New St, Petworth GU28 0AS
Tel: 01798 344485
Fax: 01798 342367

Stable Antiques,
Adrian Hoyle,
98a High Street,
Lindfield RH16 2HP
Tel & Fax: 01444 483662

John Yorke Antiques,
Filsham Farm House,
Harley Shute Road,
St Leonard's-on-Sea,
TN38 8BY
Tel: 01424 433109
Fax: 01424 461061

Wales

Country Antiques (Wales),
Castle Mill, Kidwelly,
Carms SA17 4UU
Tel: 01554 890534

Warwickshire

Apollo Antiques Ltd,
The Saltisford, Birmingham
Road, Warwick CV34 4TD
Tel: 01926 494746
Fax: 01926 401477

Coleshill Antiques & Interiors,
12-14 High Street,
Coleshill B46 1AZ
Tel: 01675 462931
Fax: 01675 467416
Furniture and porcelain.

Don Spencer Antiques,
36A Market Place,
Warwick CV34 4SH
Tel: 01926 407989/499857
Fax: 01564 775470
Desks.

West Midlands

L. P. Furniture,
(The Old Brewery), Short
Acre St, Walsall WS2 8HW
Tel: 01922 746764
Fax: 01922 611316

Martin Taylor Antiques,
140B Tettenhall Road,
Wolverhampton WV6 0BQ
Tel: 01902 751166
Fax: 01902 746502

Wiltshire

Cross Hayes Antiques,
19 Bristol Street,
Malmesbury SN16 0AY
Tel: 01666 824260/822062
Fax: 01666 823020

Yorkshire

French Depot,
Halifax Antiques Centre,
Queens Road/Gibbet Street,
Halifax HX1 4LR
Tel: 01422 366657
Fax: 01422 369293

Glass

London

Christine Bridge,
78 Castelnau, SW13 9EX
Tel: 07000 445277
Fax: 07000 329452

Somerset

Somervale Antiques,
6 Radstock Road, Midsomer
Norton, Bath BA3 2AJ
Tel: 01761 412686

Keys

Buckinghamshire

Paul Alan Prescott MBLI,
20 Cambridge Crescent,
High Wycombe HP13 7ND
Tel: 01494 436307
Keys made for Bramah, and most other makes of English patent locks. Postal service only.

Kitchenware

Lincolnshire

Janie Smithson,
Tel & Fax: 01754 810265/
Mobile: 0831 399180
Dairy bygones, enamel wares, laundry items & advertising.

Lighting

Kent

Chislehurst Antiques,
7 Royal Parade,
Chislehurst BR7 6NR
Tel: 0181 467 1530

Marine

Devon

Bond's Nautical Antiques,
34A Lower Street,
Dartmouth TQ6 9AN
Tel & Fax: 01803 835092

Markets & Centres

Berkshire

Stables Antiques Centre,
1a Merchant Place
(off Friar Street),
Reading RG1 1DT
Tel: 0118 959 0290

Buckinghamshire

Marlow Antique Centre,
35 Station Road,
Marlow SL7 1NW
Tel: 01628 473223

Derbyshire

Alfreton Antique Centre,
11 King Street,
Alfreton DE55 7AF
Tel: 01773 520781
40 dealers on 2 floors. Antiques, collectables, furniture, books, postcards, etc Open Mon–Sat 10.00–4.30, Sundays, Bank Holidays 11.00–3.00.

Bakewell Antique &
Collectors' Centre,
King St,
Bakewell DE45 1DZ
Tel: 01629 812496
Fax: 01629 814531
30 established dealers of quality antiques and collectables. Tea and coffee house. Open Mon–Sat 10.00–5.00. Sun 11.00–5.00. Closed Christmas, Boxing Day & New Year's Day.

Gloucestershire

Cirencester Arcade
& Ann's Pantry,
25 Market Place,
Cirencester GL7 2PY
Tel: 01285 644214
Fax: 01285 651267
Antiques, gifts, furnishings etc. Restaurant / tea rooms – private room for hire. Over 60 traders.

Dale House Antiques,
High St,
Moreton-in-Marsh
GL56 0AD
Tel: 01608 650763
Fax: 01608 652424

Hampshire

Dolphin Quay Antique
Centre, Queen Street,
Emsworth PO10 7BU
Tel: 01243 379994
Open 7 days a week (including Bank Holidays) Mon–Sat 10.00–5.00 Sunday 10.00–4.00 Marine / naval antiques, paintings / watercolours / prints, antique clocks, Decorative Arts, furniture, sporting apparel / luggage, specialist period lighting, conservatory / garden antiques, antique pine furniture.

Herefordshire

Ross-on-Wye Antiques
Centre, Gloucester Road,
Ross-on-Wye, HR9 5BU
Tel: 01989 762290
Fax: 01989 762291

Kent

Copperfields Antique
& Craft Centre,
3/4 Copperfields,
Spital Street,
Dartford DA9 2DE
Tel: 01322 281445
Open Mon–Sat 10.00–5.00. Antiques, bygones, collectables, stamps, Wade, SylvaC, Beswick, Royal Doulton, clocks, Victoriana, 1930s–60s, Art Deco, craft, hand-made toys, dolls houses & miniatures, jewellery, glass, china, furniture, Kevin Francis character jugs, silk, lace and lots more.

Lancashire

GB Antiques Centre,
Lancaster Leisure Park,
(the former Hornsea
Pottery), Wyresdale Road,
Lancaster LA1 3LA
Tel: 01524 844734
Fax: 01524 844735
Over 140 dealers in 40,000 sq ft of space. Showing porcelain, pottery, Art Deco, glass, books and linen. Also a large selection of mahogany, oak and pine furniture. Open 7 days a week 10.00–5.00.

Lancashire

Heskin Hall Antiques,
Wood Lane, Nr Eccleston,
Chorley PR7 5PA
Tel: 01257 452044
Fax: 01257 450690

Kings Mill Antiques Centre,
Kings Mill, Queen Street,
Harle Syke, Burnley
BB10 2AD
Tel & Fax: 01282 431953
Open 7 days 10.00–5.00. 6,500sq ft. Trade welcome.

Lincolnshire

Hemswell Antique Centre,
Caenby Corner Estate,
Hemswell Cliff,
Gainsborough DN21 5TJ
Tel: 01427 668389
Fax: 01427 668935

London

Atlantic Antiques Centres,
Chenil House,
181-183 Kings Road,
SW3 5EB
Tel: 0171 351 5353

Bond Street Antiques Centre,
124 New Bond St, W1Y 9AE
Tel: 0171 351 5353

Bourbon-Hanby Antiques
Centre, 151 Sydney Street,
Chelsea SW3 6NT
Tel: 0171 352 2106
Fax: 0171 565 0003

Norfolk

Thetford Antiques &
Collectables, 6 Market
Place, Thetford IP24 2AJ
Tel: 01842 755511

Oxfordshire

Chipping Norton Antiques Centre,
Ivy House, 1 Middle Row,
Chipping Norton OX7 5NH
Tel: 01608 644212

Lamb Arcade Antiques Centre,
83 High Street,
Wallingford OX10 0BS
Tel: 01491 835166
10.00–5.00 daily, Sat till 5.30. Bank Hols 11.00–5.00. Furniture, silver, porcelain, glass, books, boxes, crafts, rugs, jewellery, brass bedsteads and linens, pictures, antique stringed instruments, sports and fishing items, decorative and ornamental items. Coffee shop and wine bar.

Shropshire

Bridgnorth Antique Centre,
High Town,
Whitburn St,
Bridgnorth SY7 9DZ
Tel: 01746 768055
Open 7 days a week 10.00–5.30.

Sussex

Churchill Antiques Centre,
6 Station Street,
Lewes BN7 2DA
Tel: 01273 474842

Queens Road Antique & Flea Market,
197-198 Queens Road,
Hastings TN34 1RG
Tel: 01424 422955/429754
Open 6 days a week 10.00–5.00.

Wales

Offa's Dyke Antique Centre,
4 High Street,
Knighton,
Powys LD7 1AT
Tel: 01547 528635/528940

Warwickshire

Barn Antiques Centre,
Station Road,
Long Marston, Stratford-upon-Avon CV37 8RB
Tel: 01789 721399
Open 7 days 10.00–5.00. Large selection of antique furniture, antique pine, linen and lace, old fireplaces and surrounds, collectables, pictures, prints, silver, china, ceramics and objets d'art, antique style reproduction furniture, clocks, including longcase, country kitchens.

Yorkshire

The Court House,2-6 Town End Road, Ecclesfield,
Sheffield S35 9YY
Tel: 0114 257 0641

Sheffield Antiques Emporium & The Chapel,
15-19 Clyde Road,
(off Broadfield Road),
Heeley, Sheffield S8 0YD
Tel: Chapel: 0114 258 8288
Emporium: 0114 258 4863
Over 70 dealers. We have a centre with a warm and friendly atmosphere, selling a wide range of items including collectables, furniture, pictures, books, militaria, linen, kitchenalia, china, Art Deco, clocks, silver and silver plate etc. An excellent Coffee Shop.
Open 7 days a week Mon–Sat 10.00–5.00 Sundays and Bank Holidays 11.00–5.00.

Miniatures

Gloucestershire

Judy & Brian Harden Antiques
Tel & Fax: 01451 810684
Portrait miniatures.

Musical Instruments

Gloucestershire

Piano-Export,
Bridge Road, Kingswood,
Bristol BS15 4PW
Tel: 0117 956 8300

Kent

Period Piano Company,
Park Farm Oast,
Hareplain Road,
Biddenden,
Ashford TN27 8LJ
Tel & Fax: 01580 291393
Specialist dealer and restorer of period pianos.

Nottinghamshire

Turner Violins,
1-5 Lily Grove,
Beeston NG9 1QL
Tel: 0115 943 0333
Fax: 0115 943 0444

Sussex

Sound Instruments,
Worth Farm, Little Horsted,
Uckfield TN22 5TT
Tel: 01825 750567
Fax: 01825 750566

Oriental

Cambridgeshire

J.W.A. (UK) Ltd, PO Box 6,
Peterborough PE1 5AH
Tel & Fax: 01733 348344
Chinese snuff bottles.

London

Geoffrey Waters Ltd,
F1 to F6 Antiquarius Antiques Centre,
135-141 King's Road,
SW3 4PW
Tel & Fax: 0171 376 5467
Oriental ceramics.

USA

J.W.A. International Inc,
1717 North Bayshore Drive,
Suite 128, Miami,
Florida 33132
Tel: (305) 373 4701
Fax: (305) 373 2415

Packers & Shippers

Dorset

Alan Transport Franklin,
26 Blackmoor Road,
Ebblake Industrial Estate,
Verwood BH31 6BB
Tel: 01202 826539
Fax: 01202 827337

Gloucestershire

A. J. Williams (Shipping),
607 Sixth Avenue,
Central Business Park,
Petherton Road, Hengrove,
Bristol BS14 9BZ
Tel: 01275 892166
Fax: 01275 891333

London

Featherston Shipping Ltd,
7 Ingate Place,
SW8 3NS
Tel: 0171 720 0422/8041
Fax: 0171 720 6330

Stephen Morris Shipping,
Barpart House,
Kings Cross Freight Depot,
York Way,
N1 0UZ
Tel: 0171 713 0080
Fax: 0171 713 0151

Sussex

British Antique Replicas,
School Close,
Queen Elizabeth Avenue,
Burgess Hill RH15 9RX
Tel: 01444 245577

Paperweights

Cheshire

Sweetbriar Gallery,
Robin Hood Lane,
Helsby WA6 9NH
Tel: 01928 723851
Fax: 01928 724153

Pine

Cheshire

Richmond Galleries,
Watergate Building, New Crane St, Chester CH1 4JE
Tel: 01244 317602
Pine, country and Spanish furniture.

Cleveland

European Pine Imports
Tel: 01642 584351
Mobile: 0802 226240
Fax: 01642 645208

Cumbria

Ben Eggleston Antiques,
The Dovecote,
Long Marton,
Appleby CA16 6BJ
Tel & Fax: 01768 361849
Trade only.

Devon

Fine Pine,
Woodland Rd, Habertonford,
Totnes TQ9 7SK
Tel: 01803 732465
Fax: 01803 732771
Antique pine, country furniture, decorative antiques.

Hampshire

Pine Cellars,
39 Jewry St,
Winchester SO23 8RY
Tel: 01962 777546

Pine Cellars,
7 Upper Brook Street,
Winchester
Tel: 01962 870102

Kent

Glassenbury Antique Pine,
Iden Green,
Goudhurst,
Cranbrook TN17 2PA
Tel: 01580 212022

The Old Mill,
High Street,
Lamberhurst TN3 8EQ
Tel: 01892 891196
Fax: 01892 890769

Up Country,
The Old Corn Stores,
68 St John's Road,
Tunbridge Wells TN4 9PE
Tel: 01892 523341
Fax: 01892 530382

Lancashire

Enloc Antiques,
96 Keighley Rd,
Colne BB8 RPH
Tel: 01282 867101
Fax: 01282 867601

London

Antique Warehouse,
9-14 Deptford Broadway,
SE8 4PA
Tel: 0181 691 3062

Netherlands

Jacques Van Der Tol,
Antiek & Curiosa,
Antennestraat 34
1322 A E Almere-Stad
Tel: 00 313 653 62050
Fax: 00 313 653 61993

Nottinghamshire

Harlequin Antiques,
79-81 Mansfield Road,
Daybrook,
Nottingham NG5 6BH
Tel: 0115 967 4590

Republic of Ireland

Delvin Farm Galleries,
Gormonston, Co Meath
Tel: 00 353 1 841 2285
Fax: 00 353 1 841 3730

Old Court Pine
(Alain & Alicia Chawner),
Old Court, Collon,
Co Louth
Tel: 00 353 41 26270
Mobile: 00 353 86 2310084
Fax: 00 353 41 26455

Somerset

East Street Antiques,
42 East Street,
Crewkerne TA18 7AG
Tel: 01460 78060

Gilbert & Dale,
The Old Chapel,
Church Street, Ilchester,
Nr Yeovil BA22 8ZA
Tel: 01935 840464
Fax: 01935 841599
Painted pine.

Westville House Antiques,
Littleton,
Somerton TA11 6NP
Tel & Fax: 01458 273376

Staffordshire

Johnson's,
120 Mill Street,
Leek ST13 8HA
Tel & Fax: 01538 386745
Specialists in English & French, pine & fruitwood, country furniture. Unique objects & decorative accessories. Most items 18thC & 19thC. Open 9.00–5.00 Mon–Sat. Export trade welcome.

Surrey

Grayshott Pine,
Crossways Road, Grayshott,
Hindhead GU26 6HF
Tel: 01428 607478

Sussex

Bob Hoare Antiques,
Unit Q, Phoenix Place,
North St, Lewes BN7 2DQ
Tel: 01273 480557
Fax: 01273 471298

Ann Lingard,
Ropewalk Antiques,
Ropewalk, Rye TN31 7NA
Tel: 01797 223486
Fax: 01797 224700

Graham Price,
Unit 4,
Chaucer Trading Estate,
Dittons Road,
Polegate BN26 6JD
Tel: 01323 487167
Fax: 01323 483904

Wales

Heritage Restorations,
Maes Y Glydfa,
Llanfair Caereinion,
Welshpool,
Powys SY21 0HD
Tel: 01938 810384
Fax: 01938 810900

Pot Board,
30 King Street,
Carmarthen SA31 1BS
Tel: 01834 842699/
01267 236623
Fax: 01834 842788

Wiltshire

North Wilts Exporters,
Farm Hill House,
Brinkworth SN15 5AJ
Tel: 01666 510876/824133

Sambourne House Antiques,
Minety,
Malmesbury
SN16 9RQ
Tel & Fax: 01666 860288

PORCELAIN

Hampshire

Goss & Crested China Ltd,
62 Murray Road,
Horndean, PO8 9JL
Tel: 01705 597440
Fax: 01705 591975
Goss & Crested china.

London

Marion Langham,
Tel: 0171 730 1002
Fax: 0171 259 9266
Belleek.

Republic of Ireland

Delphi Antiques,
Powerscourt Townhouse
Centre,
South William St,
Dublin 2
Tel: 00 353 1 679 0331
Specialists in fine 19thC Irish, English and Continental porcelain, estate jewellery and silver.

Shropshire

Teme Valley Antiques,
1 The Bull Ring,
Ludlow SY8 1AD
Tel: 01584 874686

Warwickshire

Coleshill Antiques & Interiors,
12-14 High Street,
Coleshill B46 1AZ
Tel: 01675 462931
Fax: 01675 467416
Furniture and porcelain.

Yorkshire

Crested China Co,
The Station House,
Driffield YO25 7PY
Tel: 01377 257042
Goss & Crested china.

POSTERS

London

Onslow's, The Depot,
2 Michael Road, SW6 2AD
Tel: 0171 371 0505
Mobile: 0831 473 400
Fax: 0171 384 2682

POTTERY

Berkshire

Special Auction Services,
The Coach House,
Midgham Park,
Reading RG7 5UG
Tel: 0118 971 2949
Fax: 0118 971 2420

Buckinghamshire

Gillian Neale Antiques,
PO Box 247,
Aylesbury HP20 1JZ
Tel: 01296 423754
Fax: 01296 334601

Gloucestershire

Styles of Stow,
The Little House,
Sheep Street,
Stow-on-the-Wold GL54 1JS
Tel & Fax: 01451 830455
Staffordshire figures.

Hampshire

Millers Antiques Ltd,
Netherbrook House,
86 Christchurch Road,
Ringwood BH24 1DR
Tel: 01425 472062
Fax: 01425 472727

Kent

Serendipity,
168 High Street,
Deal CT14 6BQ
Tel: 01304 369165
Staffordshire pottery.

Gillian Shepherd,
Old Corner House Antiques,
6 Poplar Road, Wittersham,
Tenterden TN30 7PG
Tel: 01797 270236
Blue & white transferware.

London

Jonathan Horne,
66b&c Kensington Church St,
W8 4BY
Tel: 0171 221 5658
Fax: 0171 792 3090

Jacqueline Oosthuizen,
23 Cale Street,
Chelsea SW3 3QR
Tel: 0171 352 6071
Fax: 0171 376 3852
Staffordshire pottery.

Rogers de Rin,
76 Royal Hospital Road,
SW3 4HN
Tel & Fax: 0171 352 9007
Wemyss.

Tyne & Wear

Ian Sharp Antiques,
23 Front Street,
Tynemouth NE30 4DX
Tel & Fax: 0191 296 0656

Wales

Islwyn Watkins,
1 High Street, Knighton,
Powys LD7 1AT
Tel: 01547 520145

PUBLICATIONS

London

Antiques Trade Gazette,
17 Whitcomb St, WC2H 7PL
Tel: 0171 930 9958

West Midlands

Antiques Bulletin,
H. P. Publishing,
2 Hampton Court Road,
Harborne,
Birmingham B17 9AE
Tel: 0121 681 8000
Fax: 0121 681 8005

RESTORATION

Essex

Ardley's,
5 East Street,
Coggleshall CO6 1SH
Tel: 01376 563154
Clock restoration.

London

Heritage Restorations,
96 Webber Street,
SE1 0QN
Tel: 0171 928 3624
18th & 19thC furniture specialist.

Surrey

E. Hollander,
1 Bennetts Castle,
89 The Street, Capel,
Dorking RH5 5JX
Tel: 01306 713377
Clock restoration.

ROCK & POP

Cheshire

Collector's Corner,
PO Box 8,
Congleton CW12 4GD
Tel: 01260 270429
Fax: 01260 298996

ROCKING HORSES

Essex

Haddon Rocking Horses Ltd
5 Telford Road,
Clacton on Sea CO15 4LP
Tel: 01255 424745

SCIENTIFIC INSTRUMENTS

Cheshire

Charles Tomlinson,
Chester
Tel & Fax: 01244 318395
Email:Charles.Tomlinson@lineone.net

Gloucestershire

Mark Jarrold,
The Grey House,
Tetbury Street,
Minchinhampton
GL6 9JH
Tel & Fax: 01453 887074
Marine instruments.

Scotland

Early Technology,
84 West Bow,
Edinburgh
EH1 2HH
Tel: 0131 226 1132
Fax: 0131 665 2839

SERVICES

Hampshire

Securikey Ltd,
PO Box 18,
Aldershot
GU12 4SL
Tel: 01252 311888/9
Fax: 01252 343950
Underfloor safes.

London

Air Improvement Centre Ltd,
23 Denbigh St,
SW1V 2HF
Tel: 0171 834 2834
Fax: 0171 630 8485
Specialist suppliers of hygrometers, humidifiers & dehumidifiers.

West Midlands

Retro Products,
The Yard,
Star Street, Lye,
Nr Stourbridge
DY9 8TU
Tel: 01384 894042/373332
Fax: 01384 442065
Fittings and accessories.

SILVER

Gloucestershire

Corner House Antiques,
High Street,
Letchlade GL7 3AE
Tel: 01367 252007

London

The Silver Fund Ltd,
40 Bury Street,
St James's, W1Y 6AU
Tel: 0171 839 7664
Fax: 0171 839 8935

Shropshire

Teme Valley Antiques,
1 The Bull Ring,
Ludlow SY8 1AD
Tel: 01584 874686

TEDDY BEARS

Oxfordshire

Teddy Bears of Witney,
99 High Street,
Witney OX8 6LY
Tel: 01993 702616/706616
Fax: 01993 702344

TEXTILES

Republic of Ireland

Jenny Vander,
20-22 Market Arcade,
George Street,
Dublin 2
Tel: 00 353 1 677 0406
Antique textiles, vintage clothing and antique jewellery.

TOYS

Sussex

Wallis & Wallis,
West St Auction Galleries,
Lewes BN7 2NJ
Tel: 01273 480208
Fax: 01273 476562

Yorkshire

John & Simon Haley,
89 Northgate,
Halifax HX6 4NG
Tel: 01422 822148

TUNBRIDGE WARE

Kent

Bracketts,
Auction Hall,
The Pantiles,
Tunbridge Wells
TN1 1UU
Tel: 01892 544500
Fax: 01892 515191

WATCHES

London

Frank Lord,
4 Royal Arcade,
28 Old Bond Street,
W1X 3HD
Tel: 0171 495 4882

Pieces of Time,
26 South Molton Lane,
W1Y2LP
Tel: 0171 629 2422
Fax: 0171 409 1625

WINE ANTIQUES

Buckinghamshire

Christopher Sykes,
The Old Parsonage,
Woburn, Milton Keynes
MK17 9QM
Tel: 01525 290259
Fax: 01525 290061

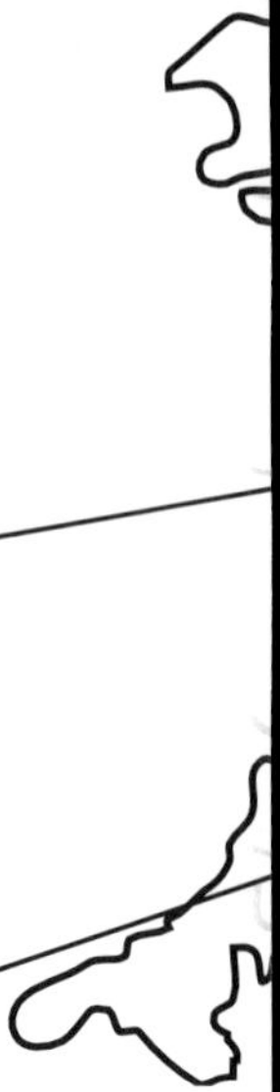

Chancellors AUCTIONS

SALES EVERY THURSDAY
Antique Furniture, Works of Art, Silver, Jewellery, Pictures and Ceramics
ONCE A MONTH
General Furniture and Household Effects
THREE TIMES A MONTH

74 London Road, Kingston-upon-Thames, Surrey KT2 6PX
0181-541 4139

Lawrences Auctioneers

Regular Auction Sales to include
Carpets, Textiles, Miscellaneous Collectables, Ceramics, Silver, Metals, Paintings and Antique Furniture

Valuations for Probate, Insurance and Current Day

Norfolk House, 80 High Street, Bletchingley
Surrey RH1 4PA Telephone: 01883 743323

IBBETT MOSELY Auctioneers

Chattel Auctions and Valuations

A Regular Programme of Sales
of Antique, Victorian and Edwardian Furniture, Works of Art, Silver, Glass, Watches, China, Musical Instruments, Jewellery, etc. etc.

Held in our Saleroom at Sevenoaks.

Also valuations carried out for Probate, Insurance and Family Division.

Complete house clearances undertaken with personal supervision.

Storage facilities available for short periods pending sale.

125 High Street, Sevenoaks, Kent TN13 1UT
Tel: 01732 456731 Fax: 01732 740910

John Bellman

AUCTIONEERS

NEW POUND, WISBOROUGH GREEN,
BILLINGSHURST, WEST SUSSEX RH14 0AZ
TEL: 01403 700858 FAX: 01403 700059

SPECIALISED ANTIQUE AND COLLECTORS AUCTIONS MONTHLY
of approx. 2,000 lots

ANTIQUARIAN AND MODERN BOOK SALES INCLUDING POSTCARDS, CIGARETTE CARDS AND STAMPS

SETTLEMENT: 10 WORKING DAYS AFTER SALE

FREE PRE-SALE VALUATIONS

For further details please contact:
Fiona Milligan

Email: jbellman@compuserve.com
Website: http://www.auctions-on-line.com/jbellman

SIMMONS & SONS

CHARTERED SURVEYORS · INDEPENDENT SINCE 1802

32 Bell Street, Henley-on-Thames, Oxfordshire
Telephone: 01491 571111
Fax: 01491 579833

AUCTIONEERS & VALUERS OF
ANTIQUES, FINE ART & CHATTELS

WORTHING AUCTION GALLERIES
FINE ARTS & CHATTELS

Regular general sales including Victorian, Edwardian & modern furniture and effects

Bi-Monthly Selective Antique Sales

At: Fleet House, Teville Gate,
Worthing, Sussex BN11 1UA
Tel: 01903 205565

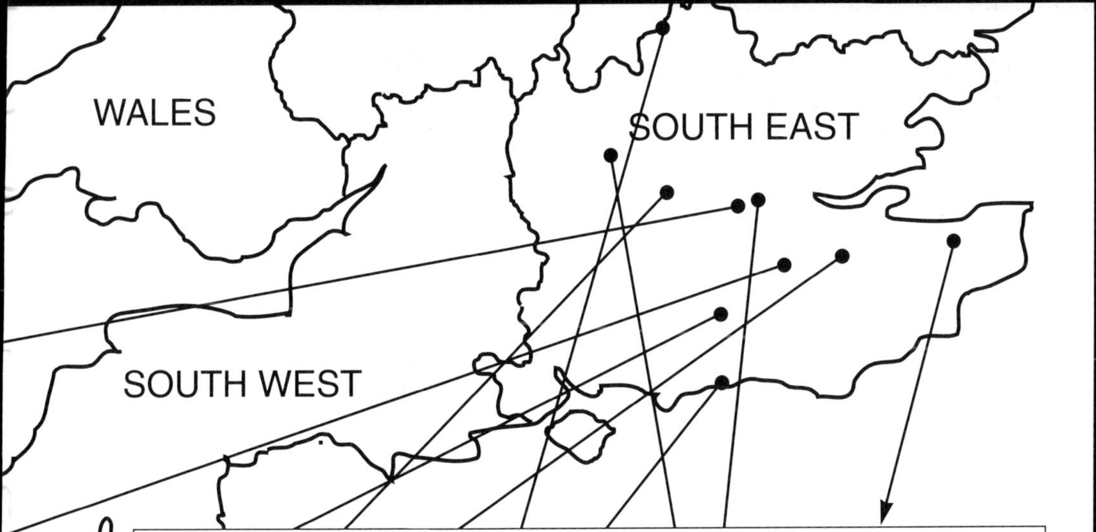

Auctioneers & Valuers of Fine Art, Antiques & Collectors' Items

The CANTERBURY AUCTION Galleries

KENT'S leading Independent Auctioneers and Valuers offer a fully professional yet personal service throughout the South East for the sale of Fine Art, Antiques and Collectors' Items. Detailed Valuations for Insurance, Probate, Family Division and Sale by

Member of the society SOFAA *of Fine Art Auctioneers*

40 STATION ROAD WEST, CANTERBURY, KENT CT2 8AN
TELEPHONE: 01227 763337 FAX: 01227 456770

Wilson Peacock

Auction Centre, 26 Newnham St, Bedford
Telephone 01234 266366

Robert Room
The first Friday of each month
Auction sale of Antique Furniture and Collectors' items.
Catalogues available

General Auction
Over 2,000 lots sold every Saturday

Valuations Undertaken
Auction Advice, Probate, Family Division
Insurance and Accountancy Purposes

Conducting Auction Sales in Bedford for over 80 years

SOAMES
County Auctioneers

AUCTIONEERS & VALUERS OF ANTIQUES & GENERAL CHATTELS

Monthly Sunday Antique Auctions at Gosford Hill School, Kidlington, Oxford & Monthly General Auctions At Various Venues Throughout Oxfordshire.

We Offer A First Class, Friendly Service From Initial Inspection, Appraisal & Valuation Through To Marketing And Auction Sale.

FOR FURTHER ASSISTANCE PLEASE CONTACT MR GARY M. SOAME OR MRS DIANNE TAYLOR
TEL: 01865 300626 FAX: 01865 300432

RICHMOND & SURREY AUCTIONS
AUCTIONEERS, VALUERS & CONSULTANTS

Kew Road, Richmond-upon-Thames, Surrey TW9 2NA
(rear of Richmond Station, opp. Orange Tree Public House)

Telephone 0181-948 6677 Fax 0181-948 2021

✻ EVENING AUCTIONS ✻

Sales every Thursday evening at 6pm

Antiques & later furniture & effects, usual selection of good paintings, jewellery, silver, china & objets d'art

"London's most interesting auction"

Valuations, Probate, On Site Sales by Appointment

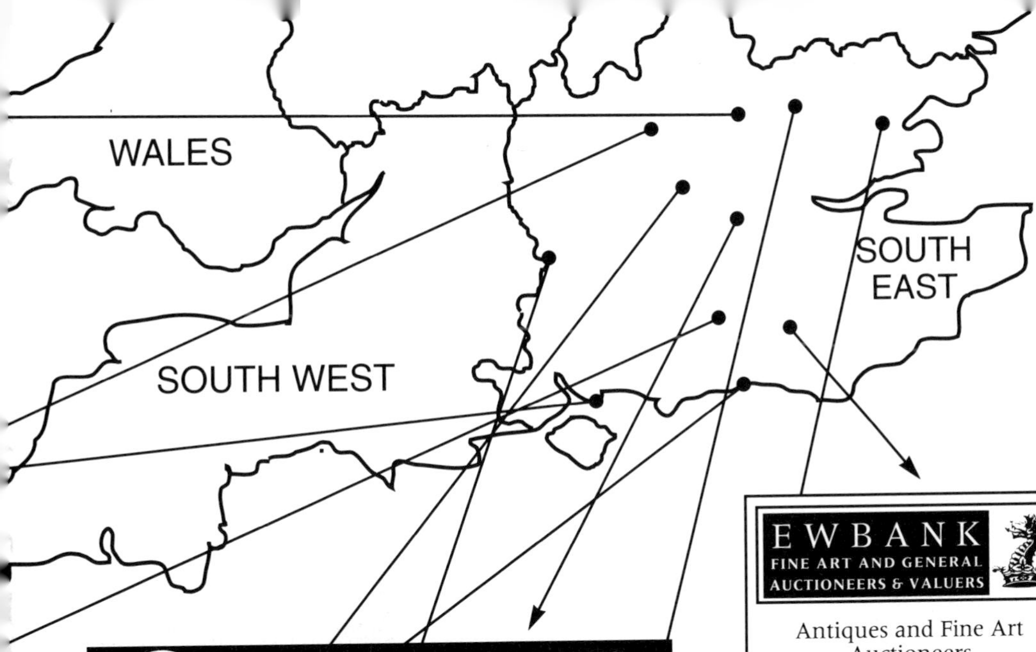
WALES
SOUTH WEST
SOUTH EAST

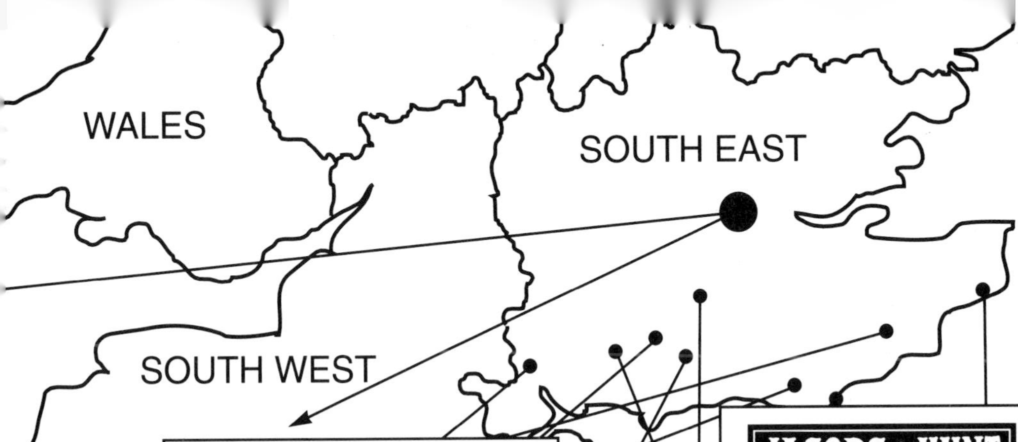
WALES
SOUTH EAST
SOUTH WEST

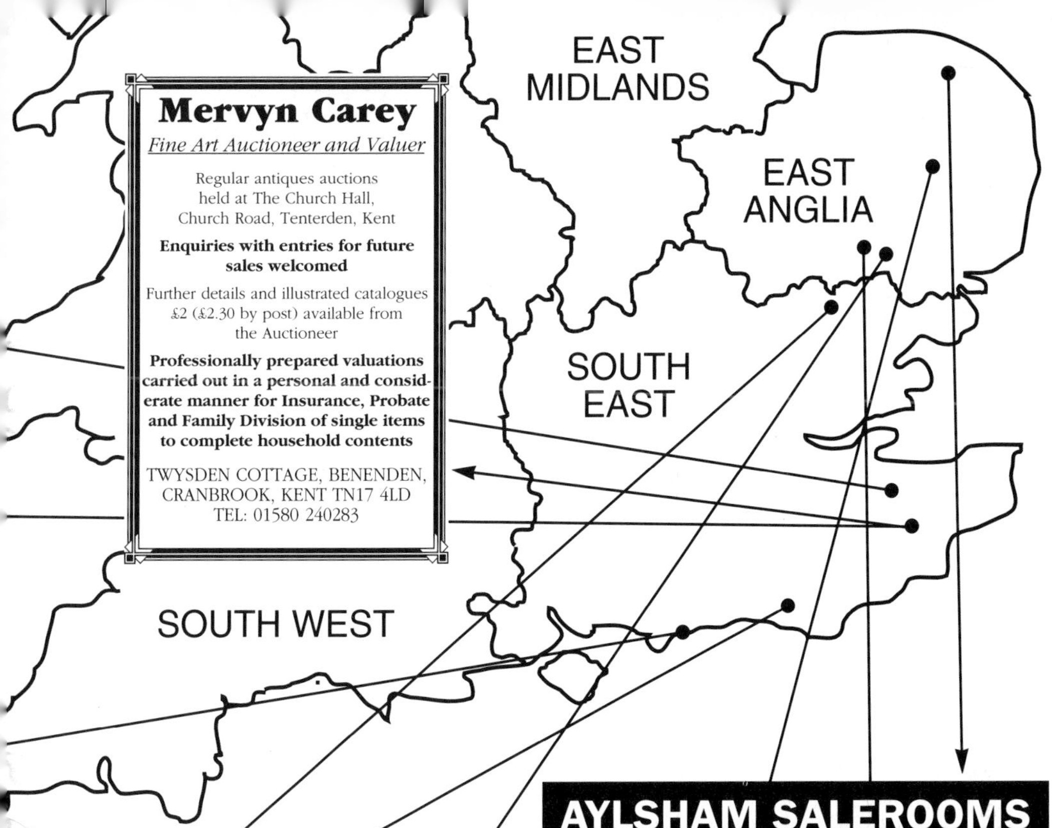
EAST
MIDLANDS
EAST
ANGLIA
SOUTH
EAST
SOUTH WEST

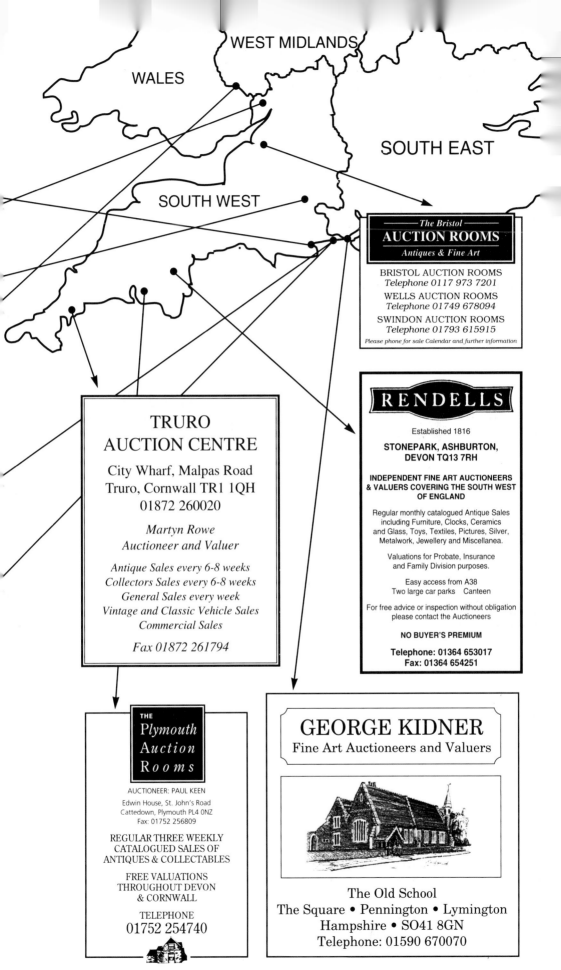

WEST MIDLANDS
WALES
SOUTH EAST
SOUTH WEST

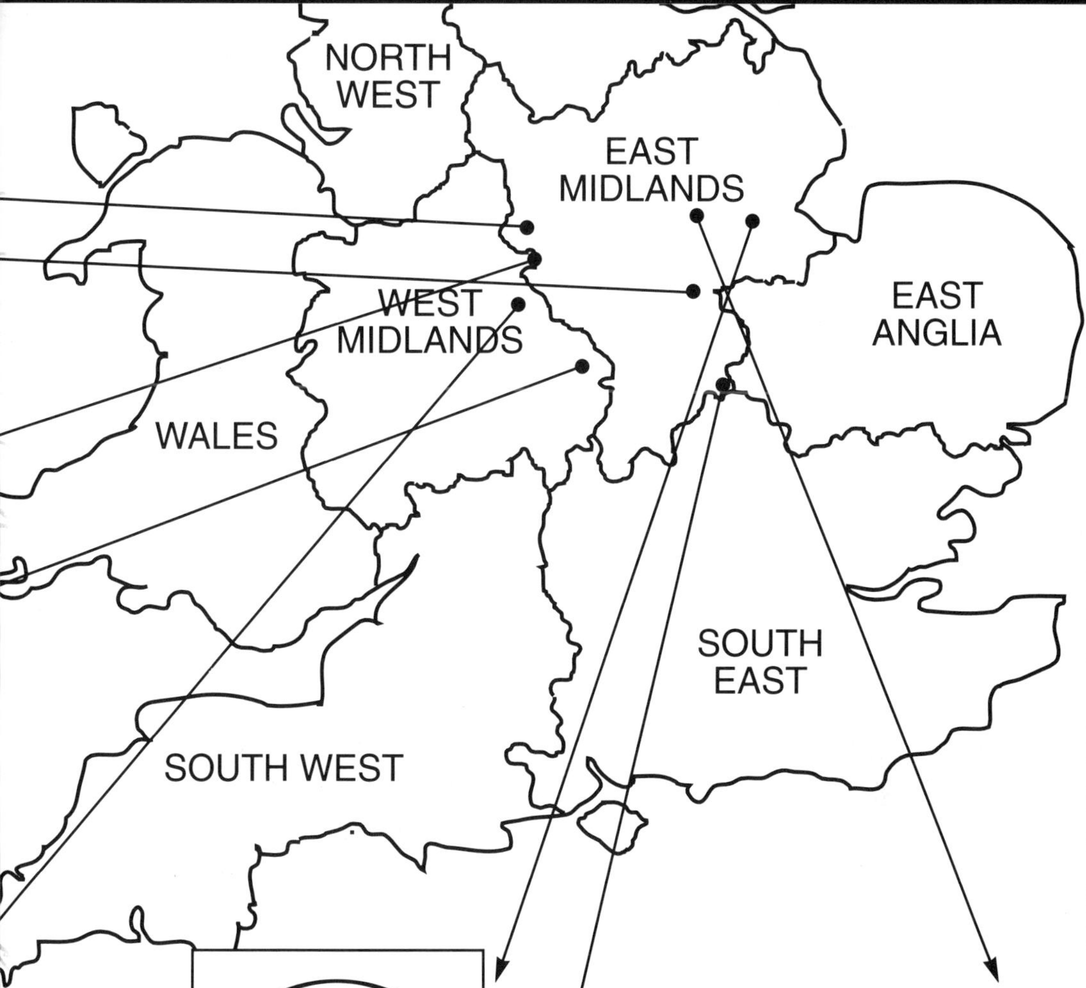

MARILYN SWAIN

THE OLD BARRACKS,
SANDON ROAD, GRANTHAM,
LINCOLNSHIRE NG31 9AS

TEL: 01476 568861 FAX: 01476 576100

Chartered Surveyors of Fine Art and Chattels
Member of the Society of Fine Art Auctioneers

MERRY'S
AUCTIONS

A trading division of Northamptonshire Auctions plc

Chartered Surveyors Auctioneers & Valuers
Estate Agents

MONTHLY CATALOGUED SALES
of
ANTIQUE and LATER
FURNITURE and EFFECTS
including
Jewellery, Silver, Ceramics, Glass
Pictures, Clocks, Books
Collectables and Bygones
FULL HOUSE CLEARANCE SERVICE
For Catalogues and Enquiries
contact Auctioneers Offices:-

**Northampton Auction & Sales Centre,
Liliput Road, Brackmills, Northampton NN4 7BY
Tel: 01604 769990 Fax: 01604 763155**

EST **NEALES** 1840
LEADING INDEPENDENT FINE ART AUCTIONEERS

The Real Alternative
to London for the
Sale of your
Antiques and Works of Art

A telephone call is all that is necessary to obtain helpful specialist advice and valuation

0115 9624141

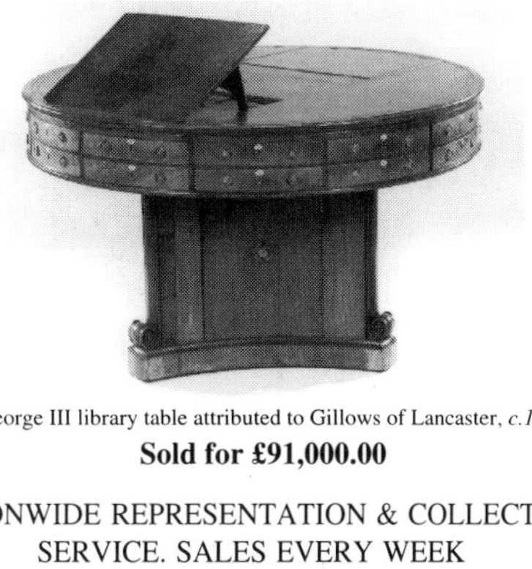

A George III library table attributed to Gillows of Lancaster, *c.1800*
Sold for £91,000.00

NATIONWIDE REPRESENTATION & COLLECTION SERVICE. SALES EVERY WEEK

**Neales, 192 Mansfield Road
Nottingham NG1 3HU**

Cundalls

ANTIQUE AND FINE ART SALES AT THE MILTON ROOMS, MALTON
REGULAR SALES OF RAILWAYANA AND COLLECTORS ITEMS
VALUATIONS FOR INSURANCE, PROBATE AND ALL OTHER PURPOSES

Further details from CUNDALLS, 15 Market Place
Malton, North Yorkshire

Tel: 01653 697820 **Fax: 01653 698305**

SMYTHES

EST 1920

FINE ART, CHATTEL & PROPERTY AUCTIONEERS & VALUERS

THE LOCAL FAMILY FIRM SPANNING THREE GENERATIONS SELLING AND VALUING FOR BANKS, BUILDING SOCIETIES, COUNTY COURTS, LEADING LAW FIRMS AND PRIVATE VENDORS.

SALES BY AUCTION EVERY OTHER TUESDAY AT 10AM
BI-MONTHLY SALES OF ANTIQUE FURNITURE, FINE ART, VETERAN VEHICLES WITH RELATED MEMORABILIA

ESTATE OFFICE AND AUCTION GALLERIES
174 VICTORIA ROAD WEST,
CLEVELEYS, LANCS

TEL: 01253 852184 FAX: 01253 854084

PF&K

Penrith Farmers' & Kidd's plc
Skirsgill Salerooms,
Penrith, Cumbria

Monthly Sales of Antiques, weekly Sales of Household Furnishings.

Telephones:-
Saleroom: 01768 890781
Fax: 01768 895058

DEE · ATKINSON & HARRISON

• Chartered Surveyors • Estate Agents •
Property & Planning Consultants
• Valuers & Auctioneers • Fine Art Salerooms •

REGULAR FINE ART SALES

Fortnightly Collective Sales of
19TH CENTURY AND MODERN FURNITURE AND EFFECTS

Valuations for Probate and Insurance

FREE ADVICE

Fine Art Catalogue Subscriptions
£30 per annum

THE EXCHANGE, DRIFFIELD,
EAST YORKSHIRE 01377 253151
FAX: 01377 241041

BEESTON CASTLE SALEROOMS

WRIGHT MANLEY FINE ART

Internationally Promoted Quarterly Fine Art & Furniture Sales

FORTNIGHTLY COLLECTIVE SALES OF 800 LOTS
ANTIQUE AND HOUSEHOLD FURNISHINGS

Enquiries William Witter ARICS.
Tel. 01829 260318 Fax. 01829 261208
Beeston Castle Salerooms, Taporley, Cheshire CW6 9NJ
(Just off the A49)

CATO CRANE

& COMPANY

ANTIQUES & FINE ART AUCTIONEERS

REGULAR ANTIQUE, GENERAL & COLLECTORS AUCTIONS

Free Pre-sale advice

Also our popular
Antiques and Collectors Seminars

0151 709 5559

6 Stanhope Street, Liverpool
Near Albert Dock, opposite Liverpool Marina
Free adjacent parking

McTEAR'S

Since 1842

Registered in Scotland No. 94987

McTEAR'S

Auctioneers and Valuers
(Established 1842)
CLYDEWAY BUSINESS CENTRE,
8 ELLIOT PLACE,
GLASGOW G3 8EP

Auction Sales of Antique and Reproduction Furniture Jewellery Silver and E.P. Paintings Porcelain and Objects every FRIDAY commencing at 10.30 a.m.
Viewing Day Prior to Sale

IMPORTANT CATALOGUE SALES
held each month

Enquiries regarding our Sales, together with our Valuation, Removal Services, should be made by telephoning

ROBT. McTEAR & CO. (AUCTIONEERS) LTD
TEL: 0141-221 4456 FAX: 0141-204 5035

Offices at:
Greenock, Helensburgh and Oban

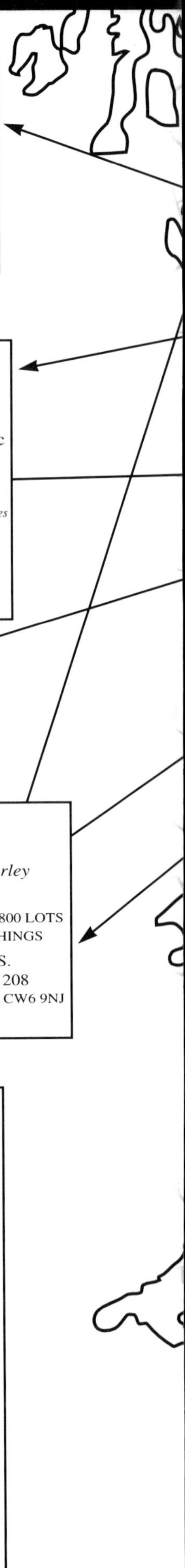

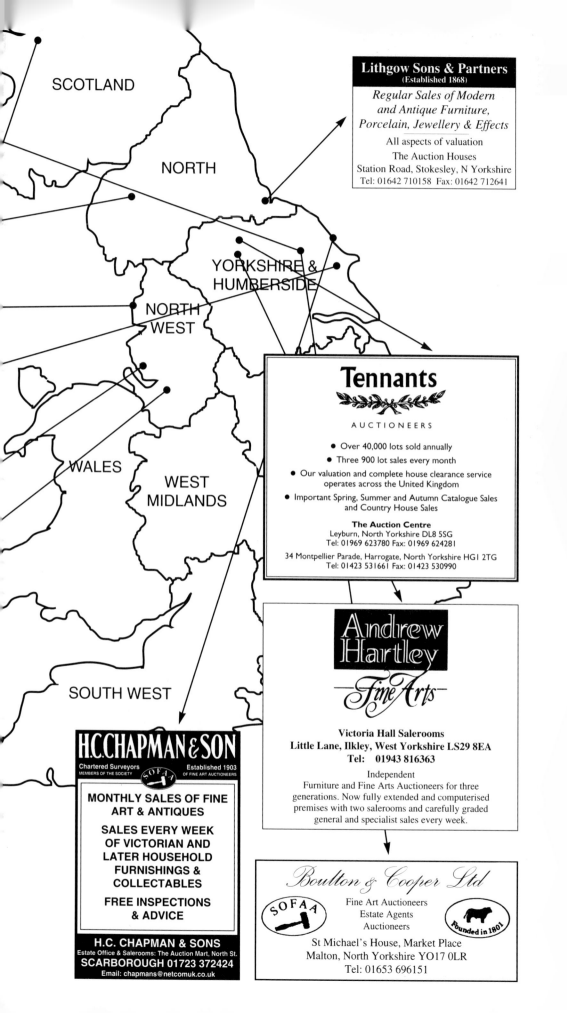

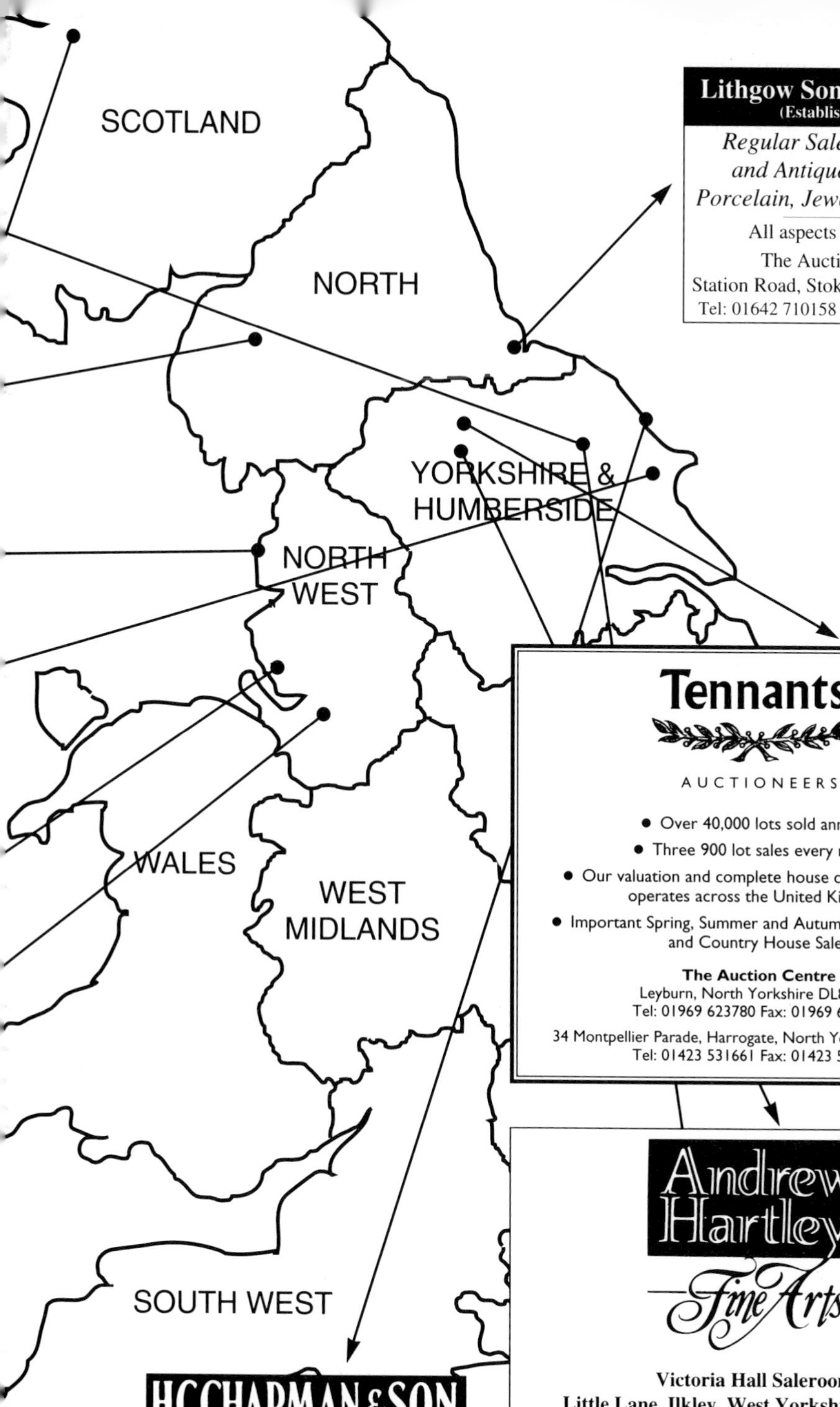
SCOTLAND
NORTH
YORKSHIRE &
HUMBERSIDE
NORTH
WEST
WALES
WEST
MIDLANDS
SOUTH WEST

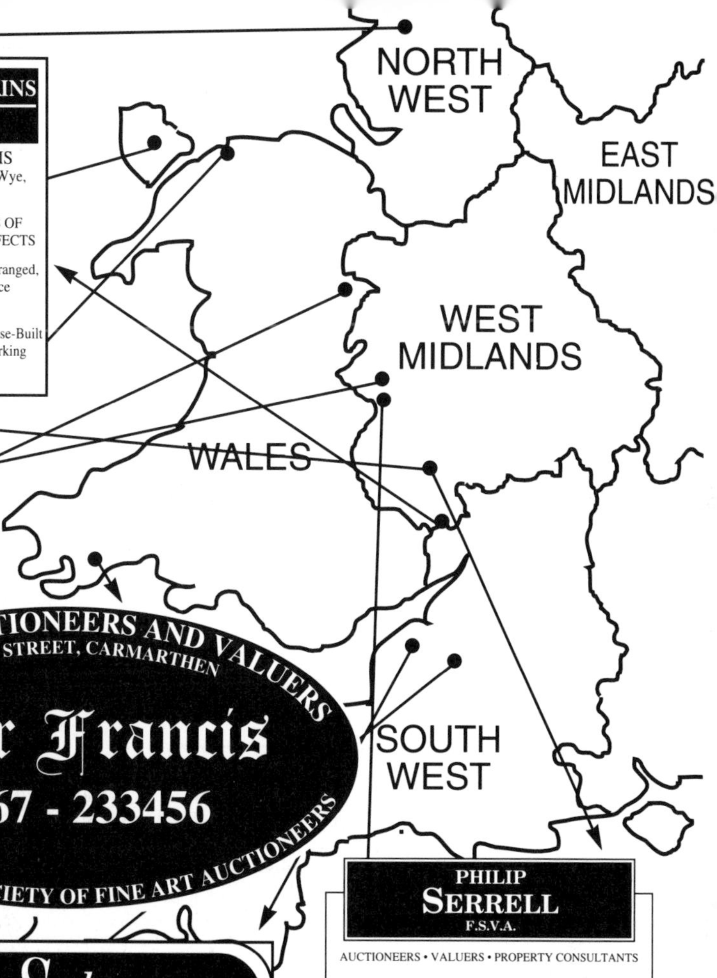

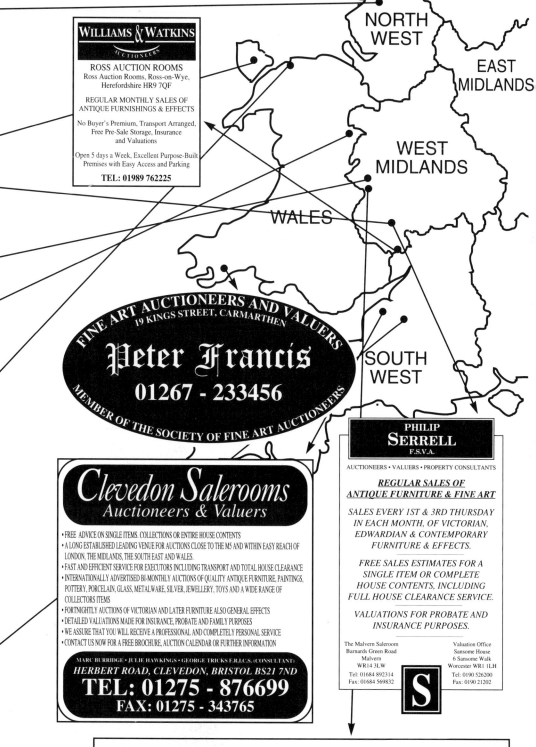

NORTH WEST
EAST MIDLANDS
WEST MIDLANDS
WALES
SOUTH WEST

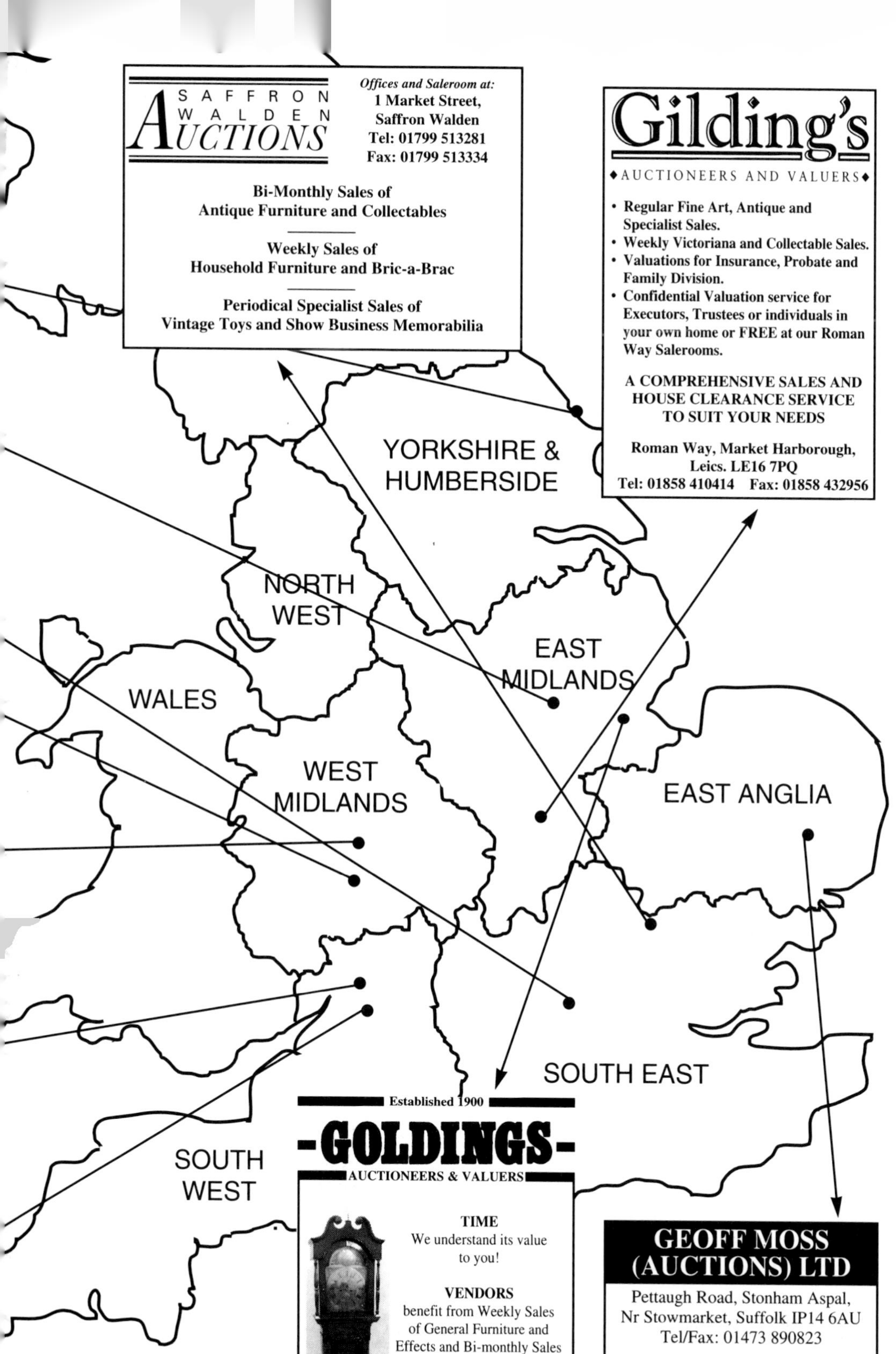

SAFFRON WALDEN AUCTIONS

Offices and Saleroom at:
1 Market Street,
Saffron Walden
Tel: 01799 513281
Fax: 01799 513334

Bi-Monthly Sales of
Antique Furniture and Collectables

Weekly Sales of
Household Furniture and Bric-a-Brac

Periodical Specialist Sales of
Vintage Toys and Show Business Memorabilia

Gilding's

◆AUCTIONEERS AND VALUERS◆

- **Regular Fine Art, Antique and Specialist Sales.**
- **Weekly Victoriana and Collectable Sales.**
- **Valuations for Insurance, Probate and Family Division.**
- **Confidential Valuation service for Executors, Trustees or individuals in your own home or FREE at our Roman Way Salerooms.**

A COMPREHENSIVE SALES AND HOUSE CLEARANCE SERVICE TO SUIT YOUR NEEDS

Roman Way, Market Harborough,
Leics. LE16 7PQ
Tel: 01858 410414 Fax: 01858 432956

Established 1900

-GOLDINGS-

AUCTIONEERS & VALUERS

Sold for £2,000

TIME
We understand its value to you!

VENDORS
benefit from Weekly Sales of General Furniture and Effects and Bi-monthly Sales of Antiques & Fine Art. With payment of proceeds within days of the sale we ensure a quick turnover.

BUYERS
benefit from an excellent supply of fresh-to-the-market goods from property clearances.

Golding Young & Co.
Old Wharf Road, Grantham
Lincolnshire, NG31 7AA
01476 - 565118

GEOFF MOSS (AUCTIONS) LTD

Pettaugh Road, Stonham Aspal,
Nr Stowmarket, Suffolk IP14 6AU
Tel/Fax: 01473 890823

SALE EVERY SATURDAY
1000+ LOTS FROM 10am

Antique furniture, china, silver, pictures, collectables plus general domestic household clearance

SELL AT AUCTION
AT EAST ANGLIA'S FASTEST
GROWING SALE

NO COMMISSION CHARGED
FREE ADVICE & VALUATIONS

DIRECTORY OF AUCTIONEERS

Auctioneers who hold frequent sales should contact us for inclusion in the next edition. Entries must be received by April 1999 and will be repeated in subsequent editions unless we are requested otherwise.

London

Academy Auctioneers
& Valuers,
Northcote House,
Northcote Avenue,
Ealing W5 3UR
Tel: 0181 579 7466

Angling Auctions,
PO Box 2095,
W12 8RU
Tel: 0181 749 4175

Bloomsbury Book Auctions,
3/4 Hardwick Street,
off Rosebery Avenue,
EC1R 4RY
Tel: 0171 833 2636

Bonhams,
Montpelier Street,
Knightsbridge
SW7 1HH
Tel: 0171 393 3994

Bonhams,
65-69 Lots Road,
Chelsea SW10 0RN
Tel: 0171 393 3900

Brooks (Auctioneers) Ltd,
81 Westside,
SW4 9AY
Tel: 0171 228 8000

Christie's,
8 King Street,
St James's
SW1Y 6QT
Tel: 0171 839 9060

Christie's South
Kensington Ltd,
85 Old Brompton Road,
SW7 3LD
Tel: 0171 581 7611

Comic Book Postal
Auctions Ltd,
40-42 Osnaburgh Street,
NW1 3ND
Tel: 0171 424 0007

Criterion Salerooms,
53 Essex Road,
Islington N1 2BN
Tel: 0171 359 5707

Dix-Noonan-Webb,
1 Old Bond Street,
W1X 3TD
Tel: 0171 499 5022

Forrest & Co,
17-31 Gibbins Road,
Stratford E15 2HU
Tel: 0181 534 2931

Glendinings & Co,
101 New Bond Street,
W1Y 9LG
Tel: 0171 493 2445

Harmers of London,
91 New Bond Street,
W1Y 9LA
Tel: 0171 629 0218

Hornsey Auctions Ltd,
54/56 High Street,
Hornsey N8 7NX
Tel: 0181 340 5334

Lloyds International
Auction Galleries,
118 Putney Bridge Road,
SW15 2NQ
Tel: 0181 788 7777

Lots Road Galleries,
71-73 Lots Road
Chelsea SW10 0RN
Tel: 0171 351 7771

MacGregor Nash & Co,
Lodge House,
9-17 Lodge Lane,
North Finchley N12 8JH
Tel: 0181 445 9000

Thomas Moore,
217-219 Greenwich High Rd,
SE10 8NB
Tel: 0181 858 7848

Onslow's,
The Depot, 2 Michael Road,
SW6 2AD
Tel: 0171 371 0505
Mobile 0831 473 400

Phillips,
101 New Bond Street,
W1Y 0AS
Tel: 0171 629 6602

Phillips Bayswater,
10 Salem Road,
W2 4DL
Tel: 0171 229 9090

Proud Oriental Auctions,
Proud Galleries
5 Buckingham St,
WC2N 6BP
Tel: 0171 839 4942

Rippon Boswell & Co,
The Arcade,
South Kensington Station,
SW7 2NA
Tel: 0171 589 4242

Rosebery's Fine Art Ltd,
Old Railway Booking Hall,
Crystal Palace Station Road,
SE19 2AZ
Tel: 0181 778 4024

Sotheby's,
34-35 New Bond Street,
W1A 2AA
Tel: 0171 293 5000

Southgate Auction Rooms,
55 High Street,
Southgate N14 6LD
Tel: 0181 886 7888

Spink & Son Ltd,
5 Kings Street,
St James's SW1Y 6QS
Tel: 0171 930 7888

Town & Country House
Auctions,
42A Nightingale Grove,
SE13 6DY
Tel: 0181 852 3145/
0181 462 1735

Bedfordshire

Wilson Peacock Auction
Centre,
26 Newnham Street,
Bedford MK40 3JR
Tel: 01234 266366

Berkshire

Chancellors,
32 High Street,
Ascot SL5 7HG
Tel: 01344 872588

Dreweatt Neate,
Donnington Priory,
Donnington,
Newbury RG13 2JE
Tel: 01635 31234

Martin & Pole,
12 Milton Road,
Wokingham RG40 1DB
Tel: 0118 979 0460

Padworth Auctions,
30 The Broadway,
Thatcham RG19 3HX
Tel: 01734 713772

Shiplake Fine Art,
31 Great Knollys Street,
Reading RG1 7HU
Tel: 01734 594748

Special Auction Services,
The Coach House,
Midgham Park,
Reading RG7 5UG
Tel: 0118 971 2949

Buckinghamshire

Amersham Auction Rooms,
125 Station Road,
Amersham HP7 0AH
Tel: 01494 729292

Bosley's,
42 West Street,
Marlow SL7 2NB
Tel: 01628 488188

Bourne End Auction Rooms,
Station Approach,
Bourne End SL8 5QH
Tel: 01628 531500

Hamptons,
10 Burkes Parade,
Beaconsfield HP9 1PD
Tel: 01494 672969

Wigley's,
Winslow Sale Room,
Market Square,
Winslow MK18 3AP
Tel: 01296 713011

Cambridgeshire

Cheffins Grain & Comins,
2 Clifton Road,
Cambridge CB2 4BW
Tel: 01223 358721/213343

Goldsmiths,
15 Market Place,
Oundle PE8 4BA
Tel: 01832 272349

Grounds & Co,
2 Nene Quay,
Wisbech PE13 1AG
Tel: 01945 585041

Maxey & Son,
1-3 South Brink,
Wisbech PE13 1RD
Tel: 01945 584609

Cheshire

F. W. Allen & Son,
15/15a Station Road,
Cheadle Hulme SK8 5AF
Tel: 0161 485 6069

Dockrees,
Cheadle Hulme Bus. Centre,
Clemence House,
Mellor Road,
Cheadle Hulme SK7 1BD
Tel: 0161 485 1258

Highams Auctions,
Waterloo House,
Waterloo Road,
Staly Bridge SK15 2AU
Tel: 0161 303 2924/
338 8698

Andrew Hilditch & Son,
Hanover House,
1A The Square,
Sandbach CW11 0AP
Tel: 01270 762048/767246

Frank R. Marshall & Co,
Marshall House,
Church Hill,
Knutsford WA16 6DH
Tel: 01565 653284

John Maxwell of Wilmslow,
133A Woodford Road,
Woodford SK7 1QD
Tel: 0161 439 5182

Phillips North West,
New House,
150 Christleton Road,
Chester CH3 5TD
Tel: 01244 313936

Peter Wilson,
Victoria Gallery,
Market Street,
Nantwich CW5 5DG
Tel: 01270 623878

Wright Manley,
Beeston Castle Salerooms,
Tarporley CW6 0DR
Tel: 01829 260318

County Durham

Denis Edkins,
Auckland Auction Room,
58 Kingsway,
Bishop Auckland
DL14 7JF
Tel: 01388 603095

Thomas Watson & Son,
Northumberland Street,
Darlington DL3 7HJ
Tel: 01325 462559/463485

Cornwall

Jeffery's,
5 Fore Street,
Lostwithiel PL22 0BP
Tel: 01208 872245

Lambrays incorporating
R. J. Hamm ASVA,
Polmorla Walk,
The Platt,
Wadebridge PL27 7AE
Tel: 0120 881 3593

W. H. Lane & Son,
65 Morrab Road,
Penzance TR18 2QT
Tel: 01736 361447

David Lay, ASVA,
Auction House,
Alverton,
Penzance TR18 4RE
Tel: 01736 361414

Pooley & Rogers,
Regent Auction Rooms,
Abbey Street,
Penzance TR18 4AR
Tel: 01736 68814

Martyn Rowe,
Truro Auction Centre,
City Wharf, Malpas Road,
Truro TR1 1QH
Tel: 01872 260020

Cumbria

Cumbria Auction Rooms,
12 Lowther Street,
Carlisle CA3 8DA
Tel: 01228 25259

Hackney & Leigh,
The Auction Centre,
Main Street,
Grange-over-Sands
LE11 6AB
Tel: 015395 33316/33466

Mitchells,
Fairfield House,
Station Road,
Cockermouth CA13 9PY
Tel: 01900 827800

Alfred Mossops & Co,
8 Victoria St,
Winderemere LA23 1AB
Tel: 015394 88222

Penrith Farmers' & Kidd's plc,
Skirsgill Salerooms,
Penrith CA11 0DN
Tel: 01768 890781

Phillips Carlisle,
48 Cecil Street,
Carlisle CA1 1NT
Tel: 01228 42422

James Thompson,
64 Main Street,
Kirkby Lonsdale
LA6 2AJ
Tel: 015242 71555

Thomson, Roddick & Laurie,
24 Lowther Street,
Carlisle CA3 8DA
Tel: 01228 28939/39636

Derbyshire

Neales,
The Derby Saleroom,
Becket Street,
Derby DE1 1HW
Tel: 01332 343286

Richardson & Linnell Ltd,
The Auction Office,
Cattle Market,
Chequers Road,
Derby DE21 6EP
Tel: 01332 296369

Noel Wheatcroft,
Matlock Auction Gallery,
The Old Picture Palace,
Dale Road,
Matlock DE4 3LT
Tel: 01629 584591

Devon

Bearnes,
Avenue Road,
Torquay TQ2 5TG
Tel: 01803 296277

Bearnes,
St Edmund's Court,
Okehampton Street,
Exeter EX4 1DU
Tel: 01392 422800

Bonhams West Country,
Devon Fine Art Auction House, Dowell Street,
Honiton EX14 8LX
Tel: 01404 41872

Michael J. Bowman,
6 Haccombe House,
Netherton,
Newton Abbot TQ12 4SJ
Tel: 01626 872890

Eric Distin,
Chartered Surveyors,
2 Bretonside,
Plymouth PL4 0BY
Tel: 01752 663046/664841

Eldreds Auctioneers & Valuers,
13-15 Ridge Park Road,
Plympton,
Plymouth PL7 2BS
Tel: 01752 340066

Robin A. Fenner & Co,
Fine Art & Antique Auctioneers,
The Stannary Gallery,
Drake Road,
Tavistock PL19 OAX
Tel: 01822 617799/617800

Kingsbridge Auction Sales,
113 Fore Street,
Kingsbridge TQ7 1BG
Tel: 01548 856829

Phillips,
Alphin Brook Road,
Alphington,
Exeter EX2 8TH
Tel: 01392 439025

Plymouth Auction Rooms,
Edwin House,
St John's Rd, Cattedown,
Plymouth PL4 0NZ
Tel: 01752 254740

Potbury's,
High Street,
Sidmouth EX10 8LN
Tel: 01395 515555

Rendells,
Stone Park,
Ashburton TQ13 7RH
Tel: 01364 653017

G. S. Shobrook & Co,
20 Western Approach,
Plymouth PL1 1TG
Tel: 01752 663341

John Smale & Co,
11 High Street,
Barnstaple EX31 1BG
Tel: 01271 42000/42916

Southwest Auctions,
South Street, Newport,
Barnstaple EX32 9DT
Tel: 01837 810756

Martin Spencer-Thomas,
Bicton Street,
Exmouth EX8 2SN
Tel: 01395 267403

Taylors,
Honiton Galleries,
205 High Street,
Honiton EX14 8LF
Tel: 01404 42404

Ward & Chowen,
Tavistock Auction Rooms,
Market Road,
Tavistock PL19 0BW
Tel: 01822 612603

Whitton & Laing,
32 Okehampton Street,
Exeter EX4 1DY
Tel: 01392 52621

Dorset

Chapman, Moore & Mugford,
9 High Street,
Shaftesbury SP7 8JB
Tel: 01747 852400

Cottees of Wareham,
The Market, East Street,
Wareham BH20 4NR
Tel: 01929 552826

Dalkeith Auctions,
Dalkeith Steps, Rear of 81 Old Christchurch Road,
Bournemouth BH1 1EW
Tel: 01202 292905

Hy Duke & Son,
Fine Art Salerooms,
Dorchester DT1 1QS
Tel: 01305 265080

House & Son,
Lansdowne House,
Christchurch Road,
Bournemouth BH1 3JW
Tel: 01202 298044

William Morey & Sons,
The Saleroom,
St Michael's Lane,
Bridport DT6 3RB
Tel: 01308 422078

Phillips Sherborne,
Long Street Salerooms,
Sherborne DT9 3BS
Tel: 01935 815271

Riddetts of Bournemouth,
26 Richmond Hill,
The Square,
Bournemouth BH2 6EJ
Tel: 01202 555686

Semley Auctioneers,
Station Road,
Semley,
Shaftesbury SP7 9AN
Tel: 01747 855122

Southern Counties Auctioneers,
Shaftesbury Livestock Market, Christy's Lane,
Shaftesbury SP7 8PH
Tel: 01747 851735

William Stainer Ltd,
St Andrew's Hall,
Wolverton Road,
Boscombe,
Bournemouth BH7 6HT
Tel: 01202 309999

Essex

Baytree Auctions,
23 Broomhills Ind. Estate,
Braintree CM7 7RW
Tel: 01376 328228

Black Horse Agencies,
Ambrose,
149 High Road,
Loughton IG10 4LZ
Tel: 0181 502 3951

William H. Brown,
Paskell's Rooms,
11-14 East Hill,
Colchester CO1 2QX
Tel: 01206 868070

Cooper Hirst Auctions,
The Granary Saleroom,
Victoria Road,
Chelmsford CM2 6LH
Tel: 01245 260535

Grays Auction Rooms,
Ye Old Bake House,
Alfred Street,
Grays RM17 6DZ
Tel: 01375 381181

Leigh Auction Rooms,
John Stacey & Sons,
88-90 Pall Mall,
Leigh-on-Sea SS9 1RG
Tel: 01702 77051

Saffron Walden Auctions,
1 Market Street,
Saffron Walden CB10 1JB
Tel: 01799 513281

G. E. Sworder & Sons,
14 Cambridge Road,
Stansted Mountfitchet
CM24 8BZ
Tel: 01279 817778

Trembath Welch,
The Old Town Hall,
Great Dunmow CM6 1AU
Tel: 01371 873014

Gloucestershire

Auction Centres Bristol,
Prewett Street, Redcliffe,
Bristol BS1 6TB
Tel: 0117 926 5996

Bristol Auction Rooms,
St John's Place,
Apsley Road,
Clifton, Bristol BS8 2ST
Tel: 0117 973 7201

Bruton, Knowles & Co,
111 Eastgate Street,
Gloucester GL1 1PZ
Tel: 01452 521267

Fraser Glennie & Partners,
The Old Rectory,
Siddington,
Nr Cirencester GL7 6HL
Tel: 01285 659677

Hobbs & Chambers,
Market Place,
Cirencester GL7 1QQ
Tel: 01285 642420

Hobbs & Chambers,
Chapel Walk Saleroom,
Chapel Walk,
Cheltenham GL50 3DS
Tel: 01242 256363

Mallams,
26 Grosvenor Street,
Cheltenham GL52 2SG
Tel: 01242 235712

Moore, Allen & Innocent,
33 Castle Street,
Cirencester GL7 1QD
Tel: 01285 651831

Specialised Postcard Auctions,
25 Gloucester Street,
Cirencester GL7 2DJ
Tel: 01285 659057

Wotton Auction Rooms,
Tabernacle Road,
Wotton-under-Edge
GL12 7EB
Tel: 01453 844733

Hampshire

Andover Saleroom,
41A London Street,
Andover SP10 2NY
Tel: 01264 364820

Basingstoke Auction Rooms,
82-84 Sarum Hill,
Basingstoke RG21 1ST
Tel: 01256 840707

Evans & Partridge,
Agriculture House,
High Street,
Stockbridge SO20 6HF
Tel: 01264 810702

Farnham Auctions Ltd,
169 Fleet Road,
Fleet GU13 8PD
Tel: 01252 810844

Fox & Sons,
5 & 7 Salisbury Street,
Fordingbridge SP6 1AD
Tel: 01425 652121

Jacobs & Hunt,
26 Lavant Street,
Petersfield GU32 3EF
Tel: 01730 233933

George Kidner,
The Old School,
The Square, Pennington,
Lymington SO41 8GN
Tel: 01590 670070

May & Son,
18 Bridge Street,
Andover SP10 1BH
Tel: 01264 323417

D. M. Nesbit & Co,
7 Clarendon Road,
Southsea PO5 2ED
Tel: 01705 864321

Odiham Auction Sales,
The Eagle Works,
Rear of Hartley Wintney Garages, High Street,
Hartley Wintney
RG27 8PU
Tel: 01252 844410

Phillips Fine Art Auctioneers,
54 Southampton Road,
Ringwood BH24 1JD
Tel: 01425 473333

Phillips of Winchester,
The Red House,
Hyde Street,
Winchester SO23 7DX
Tel: 01962 862515

Quay Auctions,
Fletchwood House,
Quayside Road,
Bitterne Manor,
Southampton SO18 1DP
Tel: 01703 211122

Romsey Auction Rooms,
86 The Hundred,
Romsey SO51 8BX
Tel: 01794 513331

Herefordshire

Morris Bricknell,
Stuart House,
18 Gloucester Road,
Ross-on-Wye HR9 5BU
Tel: 01989 768320

Russell, Baldwin & Bright,
Ryelands Road,
Leominster HR6 8NZ
Tel: 01568 611122

Nigel Ward & Co,
Border Property Centre,
Pontrilas HR2 0EH
Tel: 01981 240140

Williams & Watkins,
Ross Auction Centre,
Overross,
Ross-on-Wye HR9 7QF
Tel: 01989 762225

Hertfordshire

Brown & Merry
Tring Market Auctions,
Brook St, Tring HP23 5EF
Tel: 01442 826446

Andrew Pickford,
The Hertford Saleroom,
42 St Andrew Street,
Hertford SG14 1JA
Tel: 01992 583508

Humberside

Gilbert Baitson, FSVA,
The Edwardian Auction
Galleries, Wiltshire Road,
Hull HU4 6PG
Tel: 01482 500500

Dickinson Davy & Markham,
Wrawby Street,
Brigg DN20 8JJ
Tel: 01652 653666

H. Evans & Sons,
1 St James's Street,
Hessle Road,
Hull HU3 3DH
Tel: 01482 23033

Isle of Wight

Watson Bull & Porter,
Isle of Wight Auction
Rooms, 79 Regent Street,
Shanklin PO37 7AP
Tel: 01983 863441

Ways Auction House,
Garfield Road,
Ryde PO33 2PT
Tel: 01983 562255

Kent

Bracketts,
27-29 High Street,
Tunbridge Wells
TN1 1UU
Tel: 01892 533733

Mervyn Carey,
Twysden Cottage,
Benenden,
Cranbrook TN17 4LD
Tel: 01580 240283

Halifax Property Services,
Fine Art Department,
53 High Street,
Tenterden TN30 6BG
Tel: 01580 763200

Halifax Property Services,
15 Cattle Market,
Sandwich CT13 9AW
Tel: 01304 614369

Edwin Hall,
Valley Antiques, Lyminge,
Folkestone CT18 8EJ
Tel: 01303 862134

Hobbs Parker,
Romney House, Ashford
Market, Elwick Road,
Ashford TN23 1PG
Tel: 01233 622222

Hogben Auctioneers,
St John's Street,
Folkestone CT20 1JB
Tel: 01303 240808

Ibbett Mosely,
125 High Street,
Sevenoaks TN13 1UT
Tel: 01732 452246

Lambert & Foster,
77 Commercial Road,
Paddock Wood TN12 6DR
Tel: 01892 832325

Lambert & Foster,
102 High Street,
Tenterden TN30 6HT
Tel: 01580 762083/763233

B. J. Norris,
The Quest, West Street,
Harrietsham,
Maidstone ME17 1JD
Tel: 01622 859515

Phillips,
49 London Road,
Sevenoaks TN13 1AR
Tel: 01732 740310

Phillips Folkestone,
11 Bayle Parade,
Folkestone CT20 1SG
Tel: 01303 245555

Canterbury Auction Galleries,
40 Station Road West,
Canterbury CT2 8AN
Tel: 01227 763337

Town & Country House
Auctions,
North House, Oakley Road,
Bromley Common BR2 8HG
Tel: 0181 462 1735

Walter & Randall,
7-13 New Road,
Chatham ME4 4QL
Tel: 01634 841233

Wealden Auction Galleries,
Desmond Judd,
23 Hendly Drive,
Cranbrook TN17 3DY
Tel: 01580 714522

Peter S. Williams, FSVA,
Orchard End,
Sutton Valence,
Maidstone ME17 3LS
Tel: 01622 842350

Lancashire

Entwistle Green,
Kingsway Ansdell,
Lytham St Annes FY8 1AB
Tel: 01253 735442

Robert Fairhurst & Son,
39 Mawdsley Street,
Bolton BL1 1LR
Tel: 01204 528452/528453

Mills & Radcliffe Inc,
D Murgatroyd & Son,
101 Union Street,
Oldham 0L1 1QH
Tel: 0161 624 1072

David Palamountain,
1-3 Osborne Grove,
Morecambe LA4 4LP
Tel: 01524 423941

Smythe's Son & Walker,
174 Victoria Road West,
Thornton Cleveleys
FY5 3NE
Tel: 01253 852184

Tony & Sons,
4-8 Lynwood Road,
Blackburn BB2 6HP
Tel: 01254 691748

Warren & Wignall Ltd,
The Mill, Earnshaw Bridge,
Leyland Lane,
Leyland PR5 3PH
Tel: 01772 453252/451430

Leicestershire

William H. Brown,
Warner Auction Rooms,
16-18 Halford Street,
Leicester LE1 6AS
Tel: 0116 255 9900

Churchgate Auctions,
The Churchgate Saleroom,
66 Churchgate,
Leicester LE1 4AL
Tel: 0116 262 1416

Gildings,
64 Roman Way, Market
Harborough LE16 7PQ
Tel: 01858 410414

Heathcote Ball & Co,
Castle Auction Rooms,
78 St Nicholas Circle,
Leicester LE1 5NW
Tel: 0116 253 6789

David Stanley Auctions,
Stordon Grange,
Osgathorpe,
Loughborough LE12 9SR
Tel: 01530 222320

Lincolnshire

A. E. Dowse & Son,
Foresters Galleries,
Falkland Way,
Barton-upon-Humber
DN18 5RL
Tel: 01652 632335

Escritt & Barrell,
24 St Peter's Hill,
Grantham NG31 6QF
Tel: 01476 65371

Goldings,
The Grantham Auction
Rooms, Old Wharf Road,
Grantham NG31 7AA
Tel: 01476 565118

Thomas Mawer & Son,
The Lincoln Saleroom,
63 Monks Road,
Lincoln LN2 5HP
Tel: 01522 524984

Richardsons
Bourne Auction Rooms,
Spalding Road,
Bourne PE10 9LE
Tel: 01778 422686

Henry Spencer & Sons
(Phillips),
42 Silver Street,
Lincoln LN2 1TA
Tel: 01522 536666

Marilyn Swain Auctions,
The Old Barracks,
Sandon Road,
Grantham NG31 9AS
Tel: 01476 568861

John Taylor,
Cornmarket Chambers,
Louth LN11 9PY
Tel: 01507 603648

Walter's,
No 1 Mint Lane,
Lincoln LN1 1UD
Tel: 01522 525454

Merseyside

Cato Crane & Co,
Liverpool Auction Rooms,
6 Stanhope Street,
Liverpool L8 5RF
Tel: 0151 709 5559

Hartley & Co,
12 & 14 Moss Street,
Liverpool L6 1HF
Tel: 0151 263 6472/1865

Kingsley & Co,
3-5 The Quadrant, Hoylake,
Wirral L47 2EE
Tel: 0151 632 5821

Outhwaite & Litherland,
Kingsway Galleries,
Fontenoy Street,
Liverpool L3 2BE
Tel: 0151 236 6561

Worralls,
13-15 Seel Street,
Liverpool L1 4AU
Tel: 0151 709 2950

Norfolk

Ewings,
Market Place, Reepham,
Norwich NR10 4JJ
Tel: 01603 870473

Thomas Wm. Gaze & Son,
Diss Auction Rooms,
Roydon Road,
Diss IP22 3LN
Tel: 01379 650306

Nigel F. Hedge,
28B Market Place,
North Walsham NR28 9BS
Tel: 01692 402881

G. A. Key,
Aylsham Salerooms,
8 Market Place,
Aylsham NR11 6EH
Tel: 01263 733195

Northamptonshire

Corby & Co,
30-32 Brook Street,
Raunds NN9 6LR
Tel: 01933 623722

Lowery's,
24 Bridge Street,
Northampton NN1 1NT
Tel: 01604 21561

Merry's Auctioneers,
Northampton Auction
& Sales Centre,
Liliput Rd, Brackmills,
Northampton NN4 7BY
Tel: 01604 769990

Nationwide Surveyors,
28 High Street,
Daventry NN11 4HU
Tel: 01327 312022

Southam & Sons,
Corn Exchange,
Thrapston,
Kettering NN14 4JJ
Tel: 01832 734486

H. Wilford Ltd,
Midland Road,
Wellingborough NN8 1NB
Tel: 01933 222760

Northumberland

Louis Johnson Auctioneers,
63 Bridge Street,
Morpeth NE61 1PQ
Tel: 01670 513025

Nottinghamshire

Bonhams,
57 Mansfield Road,
Nottingham NG1 3PL
Tel: 0115 947 4414

Arthur Johnson & Sons Ltd,
Nottingham Auction Centre,
Meadow Lane,
Nottingham NG2 3GY
Tel: 0115 986 9128

Mellors & Kirk,
The Auction House,
Gregory Street, Lenton
Lane, Nottingham NG7 2NL
Tel: 0115 979 0000

Neales,
192-194 Mansfield Road,
Nottingham NG1 3HU
Tel: 0115 962 4141

C. B. Sheppard & Son,
The Auction Galleries,
Chatsworth Street,
Sutton-in-Ashfield
NG17 4GG
Tel: 01773 872419

Henry Spencer & Sons
(Phillips), 20 The Square,
Retford DN22 6XE
Tel: 01777 708633

T. Vennett-Smith,
11 Nottingham Road,
Gotham NG11 0HE
Tel: 0115 983 0541

Oxfordshire

Dreweatt Neate Holloways,
49 Parsons Street,
Banbury OX16 8PF
Tel: 01295 253197

Green & Co,
33 Market Place,
Wantage OX12 8AH
Tel: 01235 763561/2

Mallams,
24 St Michael's Street,
Oxford 0X1 2EB
Tel: 01865 241358

Phillips,
39 Park End Street,
Oxford OX1 1JD
Tel: 01865 723524

Simmons & Sons,
32 Bell Street,
Henley-on-Thames,
RG9 2BH
Tel: 01491 571111

Soames County Auctions,
Pinnocks Farm Estates,
Northmoor OX8 1AY
Tel: 01865 300626

Shropshire

Halls Fine Art Auctions,
Welsh Bridge,
Shrewsbury SY3 8LA
Tel: 01743 231212

Ludlow Antique Auctions,
29 Corve Street,
Ludlow SY8 1DA
Tel: 01584 875157

McCartneys,
Ox Pasture, Overture Road,
Ludlow SY8 4AA
Tel: 01584 872251

Nock Deighton,
Livestock & Auction Centre,
Tasley, Bridgnorth
WV16 4QR
Tel: 01746 762666

Somerset

Aldridges,
130-132 Walcot Street,
Bath BA1 5BG
Tel: 01225 462830

Black Horse Agencies,
Alder King,
25 Market Place,
Wells BA5 2RG
Tel: 01749 673002

Clevedon Salerooms,
Herbert Road,
Clevedon BS21 7ND
Tel: 01275 876699

Cooper & Tanner,
Frome Auction Rooms,
Frome Market,
Standerwick,
Nr Frome BA11 2PY
Tel: 01373 831010

Dores & Rees,
The Auction Mart,
Vicarage Street,
Frome BA11 1PU
Tel: 01373 462257

John Fleming,
4 & 8 Fore Street,
Dulverton TA22 9EX
Tel: 01398 23597

Gardiner Houlgate,
The Old Malthouse,
Comfortable Place,
Upper Bristol Road,
Bath BA1 3AJ
Tel: 01225 447933

Gribble Booth & Taylor,
13 The Parade,
Minehead TA24 5NL
Tel: 01643 702281

Lawrence Fine Art
Auctioneers,
South Street,
Crewkerne TA18 8AB
Tel: 01460 73041

Phillips,
1 Old King Street,
Bath BA1 2JT
Tel: 01225 310609

Richards,
The Town Hall,
The Square,
Axbridge BS26 2AR
Tel: 01934 732969

Wellington Salerooms,
Mantle Street,
Wellington TA21 8AR
Tel: 01823 664815

Wells Auction Rooms,
66/68 Southover,
Wells BA5 1UH
Tel: 01749 678094

Woodspring Auction Rooms,
Churchill Road,
Weston-super-Mare
BS23 3HD
Tel: 01934 628419

Staffordshire

Hall & Lloyd,
South Street Auction
Rooms,
Stafford ST16 2DZ
Tel: 01785 258176

Louis Taylor Auctioneers
& Valuers,
Britannia House,
10 Town Road, Hanley,
Stoke-on-Trent ST1 2QG
Tel: 01782 214111

Wintertons Ltd,
Lichfield Auction Centre,
Wood End Lane, Fradley,
Lichfield WS13 8NF
Tel: 01543 263256

Suffolk

Abbotts Auction Rooms,
Campsea Ashe,
Woodbridge IP13 0PS
Tel: 01728 746323

Boardman Fine Art
Auctioneers,
Station Road Corner,
Haverhill CB9 0EY
Tel: 01440 730414

William H. Brown,
Ashford House,
Saxmundham IP17 1AB
Tel: 01728 603232

Diamond Mills & Co,
117 Hamilton Road,
Felixstowe IP11 7BL
Tel: 01394 282281

Dyson & Son,
Half Moon House,
High Street,
Clare CO10 8NY
Tel: 01787 277993

Lacy Scott,
Fine Art Department,
10 Risbygate Street,
Bury St Edmunds IP33 3AA
Tel: 01284 763531

Geoff Moss (Auctions) Ltd,
The Stables,
Pettaugh Road,
Stonham Aspal,
Stowmarket IP14 6AU
Tel: 01473 890823

Neal Sons & Fletcher,
26 Church Street,
Woodbridge IP12 1DP
Tel: 01394 382263

Olivers,
Olivers Rooms,
Burkitts Lane,
Sudbury CO10 6HB
Tel: 01787 880305

Phillips,
32 Boss Hall Road,
Ipswich IP1 59J
Tel: 01473 740494

Surrey

Barbers Ltd,
Mayford Centre,
Smarts Heath Road,
Woking GU22 0PP
Tel: 01483 728939

Chancellors,
74 London Road,
Kingston-upon-Thames
KT2 6PX
Tel: 0181 541 4139

Clarke Gammon,
The Guildford Auction
Rooms, Bedford Road,
Guildford GU1 4SJ
Tel: 01483 566458

Crows Auction Gallery,
Rear of Dorking Halls,
Reigate Road,
Dorking RH4 1SG
Tel: 01306 740382

Ewbanks,
Burnt Common
Auction Room
London Road, Send,
Woking GU23 7LN
Tel: 01483 223101

Hamptons Antique & Fine
Art Auctioneers,
Baverstock House,
93 High Street,
Godalming GU7 1AL
Tel: 01483 423567

Lawrences Auctioneers,
Norfolk House,
80 High Street,
Bletchingley RH1 4PA
Tel: 01883 743323

John Nicholson,
The Auction Rooms,
Longfield, Midhurst Road,
Fernhurst GU27 3HA
Tel: 01428 653727

Parkins,
18 Malden Road,
Cheam SM3 8SD
Tel: 0181 644 6633 & 6127

Phillips,
Millmead,
Guildford GU2 5BE
Tel: 01483 504030

Richmond & Surrey
Auctions,
Richmond Station,
Old Railway Parcels Depot,
Kew Road,
Richmond TW9 2NA
Tel: 0181 948 6677

Wentworth Auction Galleries,
21 Station Approach,
Virginia Water GU25 4DW
Tel: 01344 843711

P. F. Windibank,
Dorking Halls, Reigate Rd,
Dorking RH4 1SG
Tel: 01306 884556/876280

Sussex

Ascent Auction Galleries,
11-12 East Ascent,
St Leonards-on-Sea
TN38 0DS
Tel: 01424 420275

John Bellman Auctioneers,
New Pound Business Park,
Wisborough Green,
Billingshurst RH14 0AZ
Tel: 01403 700858

Burstow & Hewett,
Abbey Auction Galleries
& Granary Salerooms,
Lower Lake,
Battle TN33 0AT
Tel: 01424 772374

Peter Cheney,
Western Road Auction
Rooms, Western Road,
Littlehampton BN17 5NP
Tel: 01903 722264/713418

Clifford Dann Auction
Galleries,
20-21 High Street,
Lewes BN7 2LN
Tel: 01273 480111

Denham's,
Horsham Auction Galleries,
Warnham,
Horsham RH12 3RZ
Tel: 01403 255699/253837

Eastbourne Auction Rooms,
182-184 Seaside,
Eastbourne BN22 7QR
Tel: 01323 431444

R. H. Ellis & Sons,
44-46 High Street,
Worthing BN11 1LL
Tel: 01903 238999

Gorringes Auction
Galleries,
Terminus Road,
Bexhill-on-Sea TN39 3LR
Tel: 01424 212994

Gorringes Auction
Galleries,
15 North Street,
Lewes BN7 2PD
Tel: 01273 472503

Graves, Son & Pilcher,
Hove Auction Rooms,
Hove Street,
Hove BN3 2GL
Tel: 01273 735266

Edgar Horn,
Fine Art Auctioneers,
46-50 South Street,
Eastbourne BN21 4XB
Tel: 01323 410419

Raymond P. Inman,
The Auction Galleries,
35 & 40 Temple Street,
Brighton BN1 3BH
Tel: 01273 774777

Lewes Auction Rooms
(Julian Dawson),
56 High Street,
Lewes BN7 1XE
Tel: 01273 478221

Nationwide, Midhurst
Auction Rooms, West St,
Midhurst GU29 9NG
Tel: 01730 812456

Phillips Chichester,
Baffins Hall, Baffins Lane,
Chichester PO19 1UA
Tel: 01243 787548

Rupert Toovey & Co Ltd,
Star Road, Partridge Green
RH13 8RJ
Tel: 01403 711744

Rye Auction Galleries,
Rock Channel,
Rye TN31 7HL
Tel: 01797 222124

Sotheby's Sussex,
Summers Place,
Billingshurst RH14 9AD
Tel: 01403 833500

Stride & Son,
Southdown House,
St John's Street,
Chichester PO19 1XQ
Tel: 01243 780207

Sussex Auction Galleries,
59 Perrymount Road,
Haywards Heath RH16 3DR
Tel: 01444 414935

Wallis & Wallis,
West St Auction Galleries,
Lewes BN7 2NJ
Tel: 01273 480208

Watsons,
Heathfield Furniture
Salerooms, Burwash Road,
Heathfield TN21 8RA
Tel: 01435 862132

Worthing Auction Galleries
Fleet House, Teville Gate,
Worthing BN11 1UA
Tel: 01903 205565/203425

Tyne & Wear

Anderson & Garland,
Marlborough House,
Marlborough Crescent,
Newcastle-on-Tyne NE1 4EE
Tel: 0191 232 6278

Boldon Auction Galleries,
24a Front Street,
East Boldon NE36 0SJ
Tel: 0191 537 2630

Phillips North East,
St Mary's, Oakwellgate,
Gateshead NE8 2AX
Tel: 0191 477 6688

Sneddons,
Sunderland Auction Rooms,
30 Villiers Street,
Sunderland SR1 1EJ
Tel: 0191 514 5931

Warwickshire

Bigwood Auctioneers Ltd,
The Old School, Tiddington,
Stratford-upon-Avon
CV37 7AW
Tel: 01789 269415

Locke & England,
Black Horse Agencies,
18 Guy Street,
Leamington Spa CV32 4RT
Tel: 01926 889100

West Midlands

Biddle and Webb Ltd,
Ladywood Middleway,
Birmingham B16 0PP
Tel: 0121 455 8042

Ronald E. Clare,
Clare's Auction Rooms,
70 Park Street,
Birmingham B5 5HZ
Tel: 0121 643 0226

Frank H. Fellows & Sons,
Augusta House,
19 Augusta St, Hockley,
Birmingham B18 6JA
Tel: 0121 212 2131

Phillips,
The Old House,
Station Road, Knowle,
Solihull B93 0HT
Tel: 01564 776151

K. Stuart Swash FSVA,
Stamford House,
2 Waterloo Road,
Wolverhampton WV1 4DJ
Tel: 01902 710626

Walker, Barnett & Hill,
Waterloo Road Salerooms,
Clarence Street,
Wolverhampton WV1 4JE
Tel: 01902 773531

Weller & Dufty Ltd,
141 Bromsgrove Street,
Birmingham B5 6RQ
Tel: 0121 692 1414

Wiltshire

Henry Aldridge & Son,
Devizes Auction Rooms,
1 Wine Street,
Devizes SN10 1AP
Tel: 01380 729199

Finan, Watkins & Co,
The Square,
Mere BA12 6DJ
Tel: 01747 861411

Hamptons,
20 High Street,
Marlborough SN8 1AA
Tel: 01672 516161

Kidson Trigg,
Friars Farm,
Sevenhampton, Highworth,
Swindon SN6 7PZ
Tel: 01793 861000/861072

Swindon Auction Rooms,
The Planks (off The
Square), Old Town,
Swindon SN3 1QP
Tel: 01793 615915

Dominic Winter Book
Auctions,
The Old School,
Maxwell Street,
Swindon SN1 5DR
Tel: 01793 611340

Woolley & Wallis,
Salisbury Salerooms,
51-61 Castle Street,
Salisbury SP1 3SU
Tel: 01722 424500

Worcestershire

Andrew Grant,
St Mark's House,
St Mark's Close,
Worcester WR5 3DJ
Tel: 01905 357547

Griffiths & Co,
57 Foregate Street,
Worcester WR1 1DZ
Tel: 01905 26464

Philip Laney,
Malvern Auction Centre,
Portland Road,
Malvern WR14 2TA
Tel: 01684 893933

Phipps & Pritchard,
Bank Buildings,
Kidderminster
DY10 1BU
Tel: 01562 822244/6

Philip Serrell,
The Malvern Saleroom,
Barnards Green Road,
Malvern WR14 3LW
Tel: 01684 892314

Village Auctions,
Sychampton Community
Centre,
Ombersley WR2 4BH
Tel: 01905 421007

Richard Williams,
2 High Street,
Pershore WR10 1BG
Tel: 01386 554031

Yorkshire

Audsley's Auctions
11 Morris Lane, Kirkstall,
Leeds LS5 3JT
Tel: 0113 275 8787

Bairstow Eves,
West End Saleroom,
The Paddock,
Whitby YO21 3AX
Tel: 01947 603433

BBR,
Elsecar Heritage Centre,
Wath Road, Elsecar,
Barnsley S74 8HJ
Tel: 01226 745156

Boulton & Cooper,
St Michaels House,
Market Place,
Malton YO17 0LR
Tel: 01653 696151

H. C. Chapman & Son,
The Auction Mart,
North Street,
Scarborough YO11 1DL
Tel: 01723 372424

Cundalls,
15 Market Place,
Malton YO17 0LP
Tel: 01653 697820

M. W. Darwin & Sons,
The Dales Furniture Hall,
Bedale DL8 2AH
Tel: 01677 422846

De Rome,
12 New John Street,
Westgate,
Bradford BD1 2QY
Tel: 01274 734116

Dee, Atkinson & Harrison,
The Exchange Saleroom,
Driffield YO25 7LJ
Tel: 01377 253151

David Duggleby,
The Vine St Salerooms,
Scarborough YO11 1XN
Tel: 01723 507111

Eadon Lockwood & Riddle,
411 Petre Street,
Sheffield S4 8LJ
Tel: 0114 261 8000

Eddisons,
Auction Rooms,
4-6 High Street,
Huddersfield HD1 2LS
Tel: 01484 533151

Andrew Hartley,
Victoria Hall Salerooms,
Little Lane,
Ilkley LS29 8EA
Tel: 01943 816363

Hutchinson Scott,
The Grange,
Marton-le-Moor,
Ripon HG4 5AT
Tel: 01423 324264

Lithgow Sons & Partners,
The Antique House,
Station Road, Stokesley,
Middlesbrough TS9 7AB
Tel: 01642 710158/710326

Malcolms No1 Auctioneers
& Valuers,
The Chestnuts,
16 Park Avenue,
Sherburn-in-Elmet,
Nr Leeds LS25 6EF
Tel: 01977 684971

Christopher Matthews,
23 Mount Street,
Harrogate HG2 8DQ
Tel: 01423 871756

Morphets of Harrogate,
6 Albert Street,
Harrogate HG1 1JL
Tel: 01423 530030

Nationwide Fine Arts
& Furniture,
27 Flowergate,
Whitby YO21 3BB
Tel: 01947 603433

Phillips Leeds,
17a East Parade,
Leeds LS1 2BH
Tel: 0113 2448011

John H. Raby & Son,
The Sale Rooms,
21 St Mary's Road,
Bradford BD8 7QL
Tel: 01274 491121

Henry Spencer & Sons Ltd
(Phillips),
1 St James' Row,
Sheffield S1 1WZ
Tel: 0114 272 8728

Geoffrey Summersgill,
8 Front Street, Acomb,
York YO2 3BZ
Tel: 01904 791131

Tennants,
Auction Centre, Harmby
Road, Leyburn DL8 5SG
Tel: 01969 623780

Tennants,
34 Montpellier Parade,
Harrogate HG1 2TG
Tel: 01423 531661

Thompson's Auctioneers,
Dales Saleroom, The Dale
Hall, Hampsthwaite,
Harrogate HG3 2EG
Tel: 01423 770741

Tudor Auction Rooms,
28 High Street, Carcroft,
Doncaster DN6 8DW
Tel: 01302 725029

Ward Price,
Royal Auction Rooms,
Queen Street,
Scarborough YO11 1HA
Tel: 01723 353581

Wilby's,
6a Eastgate,
Barnsley S70 2EP
Tel: 01226 299221

Wilkinson & Beighton
Auctioneers, Woodhouse
Green, Thurcroft,
Rotherham SY3 8LA
Tel: 01709 700005

Windle & Co,
The Four Ashes,
541 Great Horton Road,
Bradford BD7 4EG
Tel: 01274 57299

Northern Ireland

Anderson's Auctions,
28 Linenhall Street,
Belfast BT2 8BG
Tel: 01232 321401

Temple Auctions Ltd,
133 Carryduff Road,
Temple, Lisburn,
Co Antrim BT27 6YL
Tel: 01846 638777

Morgans Auctions Ltd,
Duncrue Crescent,
Duncrue Road,
Belfast BT3 9BW
Tel: 01232 771552

Rep. of Ireland

James Adam & Sons,
26 St Stephen's Green,
Dublin 2
Tel: 00 3531 676 0261

Denis Drum Ltd,
New Street, Malahide,
Co Dublin
Tel: 00 3531 845 4371

Mealy's,
Chatsworth Street,
Castle Comer,
Co Kilkenny
Tel: 00 353 56 41229

O'Regans of Cork,
21 Lavitts Quay,
Cork
Tel: 00 353 21 271550

Whyte's Auctioneers,
30 Marlborough St,
Dublin 1
Tel: 00 353 1874 6161

Scotland

Lindsay Burns & Co Ltd,
6 King Street,
Perth PH2 8JA
Tel: 01738 633888

Frasers Auctioneers,
8A Harbour Road,
Inverness IV1 1SY
Tel: 01463 232395

William Hardie, Ltd,
15a Blythswood Square,
Glasgow G2 4EW
Tel: 0141 221 6780

J. & J. Howe,
24 Commercial Street,
Alyth, Perthshire PH12 8UA
Tel: 01828 632594

Loves Auction Rooms,
The Auction Galleries,
52-54 Canal Street,
Perth PH2 8LF
Tel: 01738 633337

Robert McTear & Co,
Clydeway Business Centre,
8 Elliot Place,
Glasgow G3 8EP
Tel: 0141 221 4456

John Milne,
9 North Silver Street,
Aberdeen AB1 1RJ
Tel: 01224 639336

Robert Paterson & Son,
8 Orchard Street, Paisley,
Renfrewshire PA1 1UZ
Tel: 0141 889 2435

Phillips Scotland,
65 George Street,
Edinburgh EH2 2JL
Tel: 0131 225 2266

Phillips Scotland,
207 Bath Street,
Glasgow G2 4HD
Tel: 0141 221 8377

Sotheby's,
112 George Street,
Edinburgh EH2 4LH
Tel: 0131 226 7201

Thomson, Roddick & Laurie,
60 Whitesands,
Dumfries DG1 2RS
Tel: 01387 255366

Whytock & Reid,
Sunbury House, Belford
Mews, Edinburgh EH4 3DN
Tel: 0131 226 4911

Wales

E. H. Evans & Co,
Market Place, Kilgetty,
Dyfed SA68 0UG
Tel: 01834 812793/811151

Peter Francis,
The Curiosity Saleroom,
19 King Street,
Carmarthen SA31 1BH
Tel: 01267 233456

Rogers Jones & Co,
33 Abergele Road,
Colwyn Bay LL29 7RU
Tel: 01492 532176

Morgan Evans & Co Ltd,
28-30 Church Street,
Llangefni, Anglesey,
Gwynedd LL77 7DU
Tel: 01248 723303/421582

Morris Marshall & Poole,
10 Broad Street, Newtown,
Powys SY16 2LZ
Tel: 01686 625900

Phillips,
9-10 Westgate Street,
Cardiff, Glam CF1 1DA
Tel: 01222 396453

Players Auction Mart,
Players Ind Est, Clydach,
Swansea SA6 5BQ
Tel: 01792 846241

Rennies,
87 Monnow Street,
Monmouth NP5 3EW
Tel: 01600 712916

Wingetts Auction Gallery,
29 Holt St,
Wrexham LL13 8DH
Tel: 01978 353553

Australia

Phillips,
Level 1, 1111 High Street,
Armadale 3143,
Melbourne, Victoria
Tel: 00 613 9823 1949

Sotheby's,
Queen's Ct, Level 1,
118-122 Queen Street,
Woollahra, NSW 2025
Tel: 61 3 9509 2900

Austria

Dorotheum,
Palais Dorotheum,
A-1010 Wien,
Dorotheergasse 17
Tel: 0043 1 515 600

Canada

Ritchie Inc,
288 King Street East,
Toronto, Ontario M5A 1K4
Tel: 416 364 1864

Waddingtons,
189 Queen Street East,
Toronto, Ontario M5A 1SZ
Tel: 416 362 1678

Holland

Sotheby's Amsterdam,
Rokin 102,
Amsterdam 1012 KZ
Tel: 31 20 550 2200

Van Sabben Poster Auctions,
Oosteinde 30,
1678 HS Oostwoud
Tel: 31 0 229 202589

Hong Kong

Sotheby's,
Li Po Chun Chambers,
18th Floor 189 des Vouex Rd,
Central
Tel: 852 524 8121

Monaco

Sotheby's Monaco,
Le Sporting d'Hiver,
Place du Casino,
98001 Cedex
Tel: 377 (93) 30 8880

Switzerland

Phillips,
27 Ramistrasse, 8001 Zurich
Tel: 411 25 26962

Phillips Geneva,
9 rue Ami-Levrier,
CH-1201 Geneva
Tel: 00 41 22 738 0707

Sotheby's,
13 Quai du Mont Blanc,
Geneva CH-1201
Tel: 41 22 732 8585

Sotheby's Zurich,
Bleicherweg 20,
Zurich CH-8022
Tel: 41 1 202 0011

USA

Butterfield & Butterfield,
220 San Bruno Avenue,
San Francisco CA 94103
Tel: 415 861 7500

William Doyle Galleries,
175 East 87th Street,
New York NY 10128
Tel: 212 427 2730

Dunning's,
325 West Huron St,
Chicago IL 60610
Tel: 312 664 8400

Jackson's Auctioneers,
2229 Lincoln Street,
Cedar Falls IA 50613
Tel: 319 277 2256

Phillips New York,
406 East 79th Street,
New York NY10021
Tel: 00 1 212 570 4830

Selkirk's,
7447 Forsyth Boulevard,
St Louis MO 63105
Tel: 314 726 5515

Skinner Inc,
357 Main Street,
Bolton MA 01740
Tel: 0101 508 779 6241

Skinner Inc,
The Heritage on the
Garden, 63 Park Plaza,
Boston MA 02116
Tel: 001 617 350 5400

Sloan's,
C. G. Sloan & Company Inc,
4920 Wyaconda Road,
North Bethesda MD 20852
Tel: 0101 301 468 4911

Sloan's Auctioneers
& Appraisers,
Miami Gallery,
8861 NW 18th Terrace,
Suite 100, Miami,
Florida 33172
Tel: 305 592 2575

Sotheby's,
1334 York Avenue,
New York NY 10021
Tel: 212 606 7000

Sotheby's,
9665 Wilshire Boulevard,
Beverly Hills,
California 90212
Tel: 310 274 0340

Sotheby's,
215 West Ohio Street,
Chicago, Illinois 60610
Tel: 312 670 0010

INDEX TO DISPLAY ADVERTISEMENTS

INDEX

Italic page numbers denote colour pages; **bold** numbers refer to information and pointer boxes

D